PERSPECTIVES

ON THE WORLD CHRISTIAN MOVEMENT

A Reader

Third Edition

Contributing Editors

David J. Hesselgrave
Professor Emeritus, School of World Mission and Evangelism
Trinity Evangelical Divinity School

Paul G. Hiebert
Professor of Mission and Anthropology, School of World Mission and Evangelism
Trinity Evangelical Divinity School

Stephen T. Hoke
Vice-President of Staff Development and Training, Church Resource Ministries
Adjunct Professor, School of World Mission and Institute of Church Growth
Fuller Theological Seminary

J. Herbert Kane
Professor Emeritus, School of World Mission and Evangelism
Trinity Evangelical Divinity School

Lloyd E. Kwast
Chairman, Department of Missions
Talbot Theological Seminary

Donald A. McGavran
Dean Emeritus, School of World Mission and Institute of Church Growth
Fuller Theological Seminary

Kenneth B. Mulholland
Dean and Professor of Missions
Columbia Biblical Seminary and School of Missions

PERSPECTIVES

ON THE WORLD CHRISTIAN MOVEMENT

A Reader

Third Edition

Editors:

Ralph D. Winter
Founder
U.S. Center for World Mission

Steven C. Hawthorne
Curriculum Development
Institute of International Studies

Associate Editors:

Darrell R. Dorr
D. Bruce Graham
Bruce A. Koch

William Carey Library
P.O. Box 40129
Pasadena, California 91114

paternoster
publishing

European Distributor
Paternoster Press
Carlisle, United Kingdom

Because most of the material in this reader is used by permission, William Carey Library is unable to grant translation, reprint or reproduction permission on all articles. Please note the source as shown on the first page of each article and write the original publisher. If you do not have the address, you may write:

Rights and Permissions
William Carey Library
P.O. Box 40129
Pasadena, California 91114

Published by
William Carey Library
1705 N. Sierra Bonita Ave.
Pasadena, California 91104
Phone (626) 798-0819
ISBN 0-87808-289-1

European distribution by
Paternoster Press
P.O. Box 300
Kingstown Broadway
Carlisle, Cumbria, UK CA3 0QS
E-mail: postmaster@paternoster-publishing.com
ISBN 0-85364-999-5

Cover Design: Chad M. Upham
Cover photos courtesy of Caleb Project

Library of Congress Cataloging-in-Publication Data
Main entry under title:
Perspectives on the world Christian movement : reader / edited by
Ralph D. Winter, Steven C. Hawthorne. – 3rd ed.
    p. cm.
Includes index.
ISBN 0-87808-289-1 (alk. paper)
1. Missions. 2. Evangelistic works. I. Winter, Ralph D. II. Hawthorne, Steven C., 1953-
BV2070.P46 1999   98-51494
266--dc21   CIP
ISBN 0-85364-999-5 (UK)

---

11 10 9 8 7 6 5 4 3 2   Third Edition, Second Printing - July 99
08 07 06 05 04 03 02 01 00 99

Printed in the United States of America

Contents

Foreword xi

Introduction xiii

Acknowledgments xvii

The Biblical Perspective

1. The Living God is a Missionary God
   John R. W. Stott 3
2. Israel's Missionary Call
   Walter C. Kaiser, Jr. 10
3. Everyone's Question: What is God Trying to Do?
   Stanley A. Ellisen 17
4. The Bible in World Evangelization
   John R. W. Stott 21
5. The Biblical Foundation for the Worldwide Mission Mandate
   Johannes Verkuyl 27
6. The Story of His Glory
   Steven C. Hawthorne 34
7. Let the Nations Be Glad!
   John Piper 49
8. On Mission With God
   Henry T. Blackaby and Avery T. Willis, Jr. 55
9. Witness to the World
   David J. Bosch 59
   Two Forces
   Jonathan Lewis 60
10. The Gospel of the Kingdom
    George Eldon Ladd 64
    D-Day before V-E Day
    Ken Blue 72
11. God at War
    Gregory A. Boyd 78
12. Beyond Duty
    Tim Dearborn 90
13. Jesus and the Gentiles
    H. Cornell Goerner 94
14. The Master's Plan
    Robert E. Coleman 100
15. A Man for All Peoples
    Don Richardson 104
    A Violent Reaction to Mercy
    Patrick Johnstone 106

16. Mandate on the Mountain
    Steven C. Hawthorne 108
17. Discipling All The Peoples
    John Piper 113
18. The Turning Point: Setting the Gospel Free
    M.R. Thomas 118
19. Acts of Obedience
    Steven C. Hawthorne 121
20. The Apostle Paul and the Missionary Task
    Arthur F. Glasser 127
21. A Church for All Peoples
    Kenneth B. Mulholland 135
22. The Church in God's Plan
    Howard A. Snyder 137
23. Prayer: Rebelling Against the Status Quo
    David Wells 142
24. Strategic Prayer
    John D. Robb 145
25. Prayer Evangelism
    Ed Silvoso 152
26. Lost
    Robertson McQuilkin 156
27. The Uniqueness of Christ
    Charles Van Engen 162
28. The Supremacy of Christ
    Ajith Fernando 169
29. If I Perish
    Brother Andrew 179
30. Suffering and Martyrdom: God's Strategy in the World
    Josef Tson 181
31. Apostolic Passion
    Floyd McClung 185
32. The Hope of a Coming World Revival
    Robert E. Coleman 188

The Historical Perspective

The Expansion of the World Christian Movement

33. The Kingdom Strikes Back: Ten Epochs of Redemptive History
    Ralph D. Winter 195
34. The Church is Bigger Than You Think
    Patrick Johnstone 214
35. The Two Structures of God's Redemptive Mission
    Ralph D. Winter 220
36. Missionary Societies and the Fortunate Subversion of the Church
    Andrew F. Walls 231
37. The History of Mission Strategy
    R. Pierce Beaver 241
38. Four Men, Three Eras, Two Transitions: Modern Missions
    Ralph D. Winter 253
39. A History of Transformation
    Paul Pierson 262

40. Women In Mission
    Marguerite Kraft and Meg Crossman 269
41. Europe's Moravians: A Pioneer Missionary Church
    Colin A. Grant 274
42. Student Power in World Missions
    David M. Howard 277
43. A Historical Survey of African Americans in World Missions
    David Cornelius 287

Pioneers of the World Christian Movement

44. An Enquiry into the Obligation of Christians to Use Means for the
    Conversion of the Heathens
    William Carey 293
45. The Call to Service
    J. Hudson Taylor 300
46. China's Spiritual Need and Claims
    J. Hudson Taylor 305
47. Tribes, Tongues and Translators
    Wm. Cameron Townsend 309
48. The Glory of the Impossible
    Samuel Zwemer 311
49. The Responsibility of the Young People for the Evangelization of the World
    John R. Mott 317
50. The Bridges of God
    Donald A. McGavran 323

The Status and Future of the World Christian Movement

51. The New Macedonia: A Revolutionary New Era in Mission Begins
    Ralph D. Winter 339
52. World Mission Survey
    Ralph D. Winter and David A. Fraser 354
53. Are We Ready for Tomorrow's Kingdom?
    Ralph D. Winter 369

The Cultural Perspective

Culture and Communication

54. Cultural Differences and the Communication of the Gospel
    Paul G. Hiebert 373
55. Culture, Worldview and Contextualization
    Charles H. Kraft 384
56. The Role of Culture in Communication
    David J. Hesselgrave 392
57. Redemptive Analogy
    Don Richardson 397
58. Why Communicate the Gospel Through Stories?
    Tom A. Steffen 404
59. Three Encounters in Christian Witness
    Charles H. Kraft 408
60. The Flaw of the Excluded Middle
    Paul G. Hiebert 414

61. Social Structure and Church Growth
    Paul G. Hiebert 422
62. Communication and Social Structure
    Eugene A. Nida 429
63. The Viable Missionary: Learner, Trader, Story Teller
    Donald N. Larson 438
64. The Difference Bonding Makes
    E. Thomas and Elizabeth S. Brewster 444
65. Identification in the Missionary Task
    William D. Reyburn 449
66. God's Messenger
    Phil Parshall 456

Gospel and Culture

67. Do Missionaries Destroy Cultures?
    Don Richardson 460
68. Toward a Cross-Cultural Definition of Sin
    T. Wayne Dye 469
69. Cultural Implications of an Indigenous Church
    William A. Smalley 474
70. The Missionary's Role in Culture Change
    Dale W. Kietzman and William A. Smalley 480
71. The Willowbank Report
    The Lausanne Committee for World Evangelization 483

The Strategic Perspective

Strategy for World Evangelization

72. Finishing the Task: The Unreached Peoples Challenge
    Ralph D. Winter and Bruce A. Koch 509
73. Who (Really) Was William Carey?
    Vishal and Ruth Mangalwadi 525
74. The Mission of the Kingdom
    Ralph D. Winter 529
75. On the Cutting Edge of Mission Strategy
    C. Peter Wagner 531
76. Covering the Globe
    Patrick Johnstone 541
77. The Challenge of the Cities
    Roger S. Greenway 553
78. From Every Language
    Barbara F. Grimes 559
79. How Many People Groups are There?
    Larry Walker 562
80. Healing the Wounds of the World
    John Dawson 564

Strategies for Development

81. State of World Need
    World Relief Corporation 569
82. Evangelism: The Leading Partner
    Samuel Hugh Moffett 575

83. What is Poverty Anyway?
   Bryant Myers 578
84. The Urban Poor: Who Are We?
   Viv Grigg 581
85. Transformational Development:
   God at Work Changing People and Their Communities
   Samuel J. Voorhies 586

Strategies for Church Planting

86. Dependency
   Glenn Schwartz 592
87. The Spontaneous Multiplication of Churches
   George Patterson 595
88. His Glory Made Visible: Saturation Church Planting
   Jim Montgomery 606
   The Shopping Window of God
   Wolfgang Simson 608
89. Evangelization of Whole Families
   Chua Wee Hian 613
90. A Church in Every People: Plain Talk About a Difficult Subject
   Donald A. McGavran 617
91. The Evangelization of Animists
   Alan R. Tippett 623
92. Christian Witness to Hindus
   The Lausanne Committee for World Evangelization 632
93. Christian Witness to the Chinese People
   Thomas Wang and Sharon Chan 639
94. Reaching Muslim People with the Gospel
   Ishak Ibrahim 646
95. On Turning Muslim Stumbling Blocks into Stepping Stones
   Warren Chastain 650
96. Going Too Far?
   Phil Parshall 655
   The C1 to C6 Spectrum
   John Travis 658
97. Must all Muslims Leave "Islam" to Follow Jesus?
   John Travis 660
98. Context is Critical: A Response to Phil Parshall's "Going Too Far"
   Dean S. Gilliland 664
99. Going Far Enough: Taking Some Tips From The Historical Record
   Ralph D. Winter 666

Case Studies of Pioneer Church Planting

100. A Pioneer Team in Zambia, Africa
   Phillip Elkins 668
101. A Work of God Among the Hakka of Taiwan
   Ernest Boehr 673
102. The Impact of Missionary Radio on Church Planting
   William Mial 675
103. Pigs, Ponds and the Gospel
   James W. Gustafson 677

104. South Asia: Vegetables, Fish and Messianic Mosques
    Shah Ali with J. Dudley Woodberry 680
105. Reaching the Baranada People of Barunda
    Paul Pearlman 683
106. God Wanted the Matigsalogs Reached
    Jun Balayo 686
107. Sarabia: An Indigenous Arab Church
    Greg Livingstone 688
108. An Upper Class People Movement
    Clyde W. Taylor 690
109. Ann Croft and the Fulani
    Fatima Mahoumet 693
110. Distant Thunder: Mongols Follow the Khan of Khans
    Brian Hogan 694
111. A Movement of Christ Worshipers in India
    Dean Hubbard 698

World Christian Discipleship

112. What it Means to Be a World Christian
    David Bryant 702
113. Reconsecration to a Wartime, Not a Peacetime, Lifestyle
    Ralph D. Winter 705
114. Senders
    Steven C. Hawthorne 708
115. Charting Your Journey to the Nations: Ten Steps to Help Get You There
    Steve Hoke and Bill Taylor 714
116. Join the World Christian Movement
    Ralph D. Winter 718
117. The Power of Integrated Vision
    Bill and Amy Stearns 724
118. The Awesome Potential for Mission Found in Local Churches
    George Miley 729
119. Tentmakers Needed for World Evangelization
    Ruth E. Siemens 733
120. The World at Your Door
    Tom Phillips and Bob Norsworthy 742

World Christian Partnership

121. A Global Harvest Force
    Larry Keyes 744
122. Lessons of Partnership
    Bill Taylor 748
123. The Power of Partnership
    Phillip Butler 753
124. The Lausanne Covenant
   759

Scripture Index, Index, About the Editors

Scripture Index 764
Index 772
About the Editors 781

Foreword

God is raising up a new army of Kingdom volunteers in our day.

Across every continent are emerging "World Christians"—young women and men with world horizons, committed to "Exodus" lifestyles, possessed by the goal of discipling the nations to Jesus Christ the Lord.

At the close of a recent conference in Korea, a hundred thousand Korean youth pledged to spend a year overseas spreading the good seed of the gospel!

In Europe the periodic Lausanne Mission Conferences are now drawing over 10,000 young people.

And in North America the Urbana Conventions of InterVarsity, as well as, the training programs of Campus Crusade, the Navigators, InterVarsity, Youth With A Mission, and many groups and denominations, are part of this stirring.

Like a great eagle, God is hovering over his people's nest, stirring the young birds to spread their wings and carry the eternal gospel to every nation.

At the dedication of the Billy Graham Center at Wheaton College, the Student Body President gave a most moving call for us to be World Christians—dedicated to reaching the lost and feeding the hungry peoples of the world.

At some secular campuses, the Christian student groups are seemingly outstripping some of their Christian-college counterparts with their zeal for evangelism, discipleship and missions!

At the secular university which my son and daughter have attended, the Christian movement has grown from seven to seven hundred in less than a decade! Many of them are eager for their lives to count for more than merely secular success.

We may be on the verge of a movement comparable to the great waves of student volunteers at the beginning of the century.

If so, *Perspectives on the World Christian Movement* can be a key tool. The editors have given to us an impressive (if not exhaustive) collection of readings. I know of nothing quite like it. (Incidentally, the editorial partnership of Dr. Ralph Winter with Steven Hawthorne and friends is in itself a splendid example of the possibilities of partnership between senior missionary experience and younger missionary vision).

I commend this volume because it sets world evangelization in its proper priority.

What beats centrally in the heart of our missionary God, as revealed in the Scriptures, must always be central in the agenda of his missionary people.

Then also, world evangelization appears here as a *possibility*. No sub-Christian pessimism arising from false guilt rules here. Nor is the "vision glorious" intimidated by false Messiahs. Jesus said, "This Gospel of the Kingdom will be preached in all the world as a testimony, then will the end come (Matt. 24:14)." Without apology, arrogance, or timidity, the viewpoint represented in this volume believes that what He has said will be done *will* be done, and wants to be part of it.

Then, as the title says, this volume gives to world evangelization *perspectives*. Today's aspiring missionaries need to understand first the biblical mandate, but also history and culture and strategy. Understanding of the history of missions and the challenge of cross-cultural communication may help to save us from fear on the one hand, and unnecessary mistakes on the other. When Billy Graham was a college president in the late forties his school adopted the slogan, "Knowledge on Fire." This book is based on a belief that missionaries have a calling to *think* as well as to *love* and *give* and *speak*! As John Wesley once said to a critic who was downplaying his education, "God may not need my education, but he doesn't need your ignorance either."

In addition, *Perspectives on the World Christian Movement* can help eager hearted disciples to see world evangelization also in terms of *passion*, *power*, and *participation*. Before evangelism is a program it is a passion. Always, the key to missionary enterprise can be summed up: "Jesus, priceless treasure." Only a new wave of missionaries in love with Jesus, and captured by His boundless promise of the Spirit will truly be His witnesses "to the uttermost parts."

God had one Son and he made him a missionary. My prayer is that the Father would use this book to help equip and send a great host of sons and daughters from every nation to every nation until His name is known and praised by every people.

Leighton Ford, Chairman
Lausanne Committee for
World Evangelization
North Carolina
October, 1981

Introduction

Books of this size don't appear out of nowhere. We'll tell you about that phenomenon in a minute. First, pause for a moment to evaluate the result which you have in your hands.

No one person could ever go to all the places the 105 globally active authors of these pages have been, nor lived through all of their experiences (roughly 3,600 years of alert, dedicated service). However, by drawing together the key thinking of all these marvelous people a given person can peruse these pages and leapfrog over a lot of wandering and blind alleys, avoiding or shortening the crucial process of groping for sound perspective.

BIG book! Can you take the time to mine its wisdom? All of us are rattled and distracted almost every moment of every day. More people pressing in upon us. Less fresh air. Less space. More knowledge. Our young people are the most traveled of any previous generation. We are rafting the white waters of a turbulent world.

So much has changed since the first edition of 1981!

1. Then we were impressed that *The Task Remaining* was too big. Now we are impressed by how relatively small it is.
2. Then the helpers available were mainly Western and the problems were non-Western. Now the helpers are mainly from Africa, Latin America and Asia, and the problems loom larger in the West. The whole world is now intermingling with the West.
3. The number of sincere Bible-reading believers in the world has almost tripled since then, and is racing "out of control" today—with fascinating consequences.

Let's stop for a moment. What is the human being? No other form of life seriously ponders things you can't see with the naked eye—the galactic clusters and the atoms—or knows so much about them. Yet, we are still like children within a largely mysterious universe, whether we try to fathom the galaxies or the mitochondria. We are as oblivious to most of reality as we are about the hundreds of thousands of tiny spiders, called dust mites, which are found in the average pillow. Okay. We can give up and live an animal existence, like a cow munching the grass within eyesight. We can try to push reality out of view. But for those attracted to a book like this the world confronts us forcefully with all the same problems of past centuries. Except they are bigger now—bigger wars, more resistant bacteria, bloated cities, rampant evil and danger—as well as unprecedented problems mixed with unforeseen and incredible gains.

Most older people, looking back on many useless detours, regret that they did not do more reflection earlier. Can you avoid that tragic surprise? Can this book help? It can't be read at one sitting. It won't help if left on the shelf.

Enough musing. Let's get to work. You may have some pressing questions:

- **The book itself.** If this book is a sequel to the second edition (1992), what is different? And what produced it?
- **The course of study.** What is the easiest way for your life to be enriched with the insights here?
- **The perspective.** What is startlingly unusual about this view of the world?
- **The urgency.** Why is all of this so impelling and crucial?

The Book Itself

Well over half the 124 chapters are brand new or extensively revised. Why? The 1981 book was like a vase of rose buds. Now we have a vase of blossomed flowers plus some more buds.

Also, unlike the never-ending film credits naming every person who lifted a finger in the production, this edition drops all that out. Suffice it to say that Steve Hawthorne assembled a brilliant, hard-working team which pulled all this together in an intense sprint of six months (plus 17 years of additional thinking).

Meanwhile, at least five other versions of this course exist.

First, Jonathan Lewis created a much shorter version in Spanish, combining both this *Reader* and the coordinating *Study Guide*—and then translated that back into English! His version, *World Mission*, is now being widely used in both languages.

Next, Bob Hall in New Zealand generated his own use of this *Reader*, providing an alternate guide to go with it. And New Zealand breaks all records for numbers of Perspectives students (per capita).

Then, our own team produced a Sunday School version, *Vision for the Nations*, employing videos and its own study guide (*Participants Reader*) in a 13-week, 45 minute format.

Meg Crossman and her team in Phoenix, Arizona, taking a tip from Jonathan Lewis and Bob Hall, produced an attractive, lighter version which combines both the *Reader* and the *Study Guide* in one three-hole punched, 8.5 by 11 loose-leaf book called *Worldwide Perspectives*.

A similar combination of *Reader* and *Study Guide* is the new loose-leaf *Perspectives Notebook* produced by Steve Hawthorne, the other editor of this book.

Not all versions are slimmed down. Our own team has labored intensively for six arduous years to generate a 32-semester-hour expansion, which already has been adopted as an off-campus degree curriculum by several fully accredited colleges and universities. (See below)

All of these versions, with the exception of Bob Hall's and the various other-language versions, are available from the same publisher—and enthusiastically recommended.

All of these versions are what we call "foundational" education—important for every serious believer. "Vocational" training must follow for specific involvements as, say, missionary on the field or mobilizer at home.

As the senior editor, my time-involvement has decreased while the interest of all of us has increased. That's not entirely new. The very first edition was produced in the main by younger activists who were themselves the product of the course. This is a course!

The Course

Humanly speaking, the extensive readings you have in your hands cannot be easily digested through sheer, individual will-power. Going through this together with others is not just more enjoyable—you can't learn and retain unless you can listen and talk.

Over 600 trained "Coordinators" working directly under our supervision sponsor annually at least 80 15-week classes in the U.S.A. alone. Four week intensives are held in January, June/July here in Pasadena.

But this is just the tip of the iceberg. Many others have their own network of classes using either this *Reader* or other materials mentioned above. And while our own classes have by now included over 30,000 students and church leaders, we know—because we produce the books—that more than an additional 100,000 copies of this volume have been employed in other ways in 100 Christian colleges and seminaries. I understand the Southern Baptist seminaries are cooperating in generating their own reader. That's great. Anyone and everyone is welcome to join the *movement* in any way they feel led. We are all mere spectators of the surprising work of God in our time. Whether or not an individual anywhere can meet with a class, we do recommend a disciplined weekly pattern involving meeting a human being at the end of the week's study—that is, a mentor. In any case, you can, if you wish, get college credit, graduate or undergraduate—even if you use the materials on an individual-study basis. Write to us about the latter. Hundreds are studying by themselves. These are people who do not live near a formal class. Others meet one night a week for fifteen weeks, with different, live professors each week.

Most of these courses follow roughly the following lesson structure of our *Study Guide*:

(Anyone wanting to develop their own study guide for this *Reader* might do well to follow at least these titles—especially if their materials are to be used for some students along with others who are using some of the other materials, which follow basically this outline designed for fifteen sessions.)

Biblical
1. The Living God is a Missionary God
2. The Story of His Glory
3. Your Kingdom Come
4. Mandate For the Nations
5. Unleashing the Gospel

History
6. The Expansion of the Christian Movement
7. Eras of Mission History
8. Pioneers of the World Christian Movement
9. The Task Remaining

Culture
10. How Shall They Hear?
11. Building Bridges of Love

Strategy
12. Christian Development
13. The Spontaneous Multiplication of Churches
14. Pioneer Church Planting
15. World Christian Partnership

(Professors can ask for a guide to the questions in these lessons.)

As already mentioned, not all versions of this course are slimmed down. You can actually earn a B.A. degree (if you already have two years of college) or an M.A. (if you already have a B.A.) using a vastly expanded version of this course. Each college or university has its own name for this larger version we have generated as "Global Civilization," the secular title, or "World Christian Foundations" the religious title. It is a 48 (B.A.) or 32 (M.A.) semester-unit program.

This extensive curriculum employs 120 textbooks, which constitute a marvelous basic library, plus additional "Readers," which encompass over 1,000 additional chapters and articles from other books and journals. All of this is orchestrated in 320 carefully engineered, four-hour study sessions and is designed for part-time, individual study over a period of two years. On the M.A. level this curriculum can be the foundation for a Ph.D. but is more likely going to be a platform for

serious Christian service, full or part time, combining as it does the content of a seminary degree as well as much more than that in the complex picture of global Christian mission. For more information write to the Institute of International Studies, 1605 Elizabeth Street, Pasadena, CA, 91104.

The Perspective

The content of this book and its *Study Guide* has come as a shock to most students. Why? For one thing it is full of so much verifiable optimism!

One major reason for this optimistic perspective is found in the fact that this course traces the Great Commission back to Abraham and presents the historical period of human history as a single unfolding story. It is not common for people to recognize that the commission to Abraham in Genesis 12:1-3 has the basic functional elements of the Great Commission in Matthew 28:18-20. But they are there. It is quite a wrench of conventional Christian perspective to speak of the 2,000-year impact on global history of the believing community of the Jewish people before Christ, and to recognize that God was faithfully unfolding His purpose and expanding His kingdom from Abraham on. Kaiser (Chapter 2) defends us in this.

It is just as uncommon for the average believer today, in a secularized world, to perceive the unbroken thread throughout the next 2,000 years. Is it a single story on a global level? We believe so. This is an unusual perspective.

Briefly, as we said in our earlier preface, we understand that the kingdom of God, which is relentlessly pressing back the darkness of the world today is, nevertheless, "not of this world." We seek not the subjugation of all nations (not "countries") to ourselves nor to any of the many nations in our own country. Thus, while God is calling to Himself a new creation, a new people, we do not believe He is doing away with the nations. All nations must become equidistant to the grace and the blessings of our living Lord and reflect His glory in national praise.

However, it is virtually impossible today to get any very detailed or comprehensive grasp of the World Christian movement. Is this because those actively engaged in the cause are too few in number? Hardly. There may be 500,000 people working full-time in Christian mission efforts far from their home and kindred.

Is it because the cause is too small or has failed? Hardly. You cannot account for a single nation of Africa or Asia represented in the United Nations that is not there for reasons significantly related to the Christian mission. Indeed, the formation of the United Nations itself has some amazing relationships to key people produced by the missionary movement.

Is it because missions are in the decline and are virtually out of date? America's overseas mission force is larger today in personnel and in money than ever in history, and you will soon see that this cause is *not* out of date. The *least* likely reason is that the cause of missions is too new to get into the curriculum. On the contrary, it is in fact the largest and longest-standing concerted effort in the annals of human history, and certainly the most influential.

Why, then, can you search the libraries of the nation, scan college and university catalogs, or peruse the curricula of public schools or even private Christian schools and fail to find a single, substantive course on the nature, the purpose, the achievements, the present deployment, and the unfinished task of the Christian world mission?

The Urgency

As implied earlier, things have changed momentously since the first appearance of this book. The world has never known a more significant transition than we see in the period between the 1974 bombshell of the International Congress on World Evangelization held in Lausanne, Switzerland and the end of the century. That same year the urgent reason for what we call the *Perspectives Study Program* was constituted by the unexpectedly large number of students who awakened to global challenge at the previous December's Urbana Missionary Conference—some 5,000. That same summer the precursor to this course was launched for their benefit on the campus at Wheaton College under the title *Institute of International Studies*. What is Chapter 51 in this book was the senior editor's contribution to one of the plenary sessions at that huge conference at Lausanne which drew more people from more countries than any previous human gathering. Just two years later, in 1976, we published a reader entitled *Crucial Dimensions in World Evangelization*.

But by a quarter of a century later, explosive new, totally unexpected developments have cast a much more optimistic light on things, as well as revealed new obstacles to be surmounted.

For example, there may well be a larger number of sincere Bible-reading followers of Jesus in Africa, India and China than there are, in those countries, sincere Bible-reading followers of Jesus in groups that do call themselves Christian. Hmm! This kind of Biblical faith now "out of control" is pregnant with significance and even danger. Few of these groups have adequate access to the Bible itself, although the Bible is the source of their surprising energy.

Welcome to a rich and disturbing and urgent exploration!

Ralph D. Winter
Pasadena, California
January 1999

Acknowledgments

Acknowledgements for First Edition

The following mission leaders were among those who offered significant suggestions and critique. Much of the strength of the *Reader* is the direct fruit of this help. Any weakness or inadequacy should only be attributed to the editors.

Mr. Dan Bacon, Overseas Missionary Fellowship; Mr. John Bennett, The Association of Church Missions Committees; Dr. Ron Blue, Dallas Theological Seminary; Dr. E. Thomas and Elizabeth S. Brewster, Fuller School of World Mission; Mr. David Bryant, InterVarsity Missions; Mr. Wade Coggins, EFMA; Dr. Harvie Conn, Westminster Theological Seminary; Dr. Ralph Covell, Denver Conservative Baptist Theological Seminary; Dr. Edward R. Dayton, Missions Advanced Research and Communication Center; Dr. Richard DeRidder, Calvin Theological Seminary; Mr. Bob Douglas, Mission Training and Resource Center; Mr. Phil Elkins, Mission Training and Resource Center; Dr. Arthur Glasser, Fuller School of World Mission; Dr. Martin Goldsmith, All Nations Christian College; Dr. John A. Gration, Wheaton College; David Howard, Evangelism Explosion International; Dr. Terry Hulbert, Columbia Bible College; Dr. Arthur P. Johnston, Trinity Evangelical Divinity School; Dr. Walter C. Kaiser Jr., Trinity Evangelical Divinity School; Dr. Dale Kietzman, Christian Resource Management; Dr. Charles Kraft, Fuller School of World Mission; Dr. John Kyle, InterVarsity Mission; Dr. Donald N. Larson, Toronto Institute of Linguistics; Greg Livingstone, North Africa Mission; Lois McKinney, Committee to Assist Ministry Education Overseas; Dr. J.R. McQuilkin, Columbia Bible College; Dr. Charles Mellis, Missionary Internship; Dr. Ken Mulholland, Columbia Bible College; Mr. Michael Pocock, The Evangelical Alliance Mission; Dr. Roger Randall, Campus Crusade for Christ; Mr. Don Richardson, Institute of Tribal Studies; Mr. Waldron Scott, American Leprosy Mission; Dr. Charles R. Tabor, Milligan College; Dr. C. Peter Wagner, Fuller School of World Mission; Dr. Ted Ward, Michigan State University; Dr. Warren Webster, Conservative Baptist Foreign Mission Society; Dr. Sam Wilson, Missions Advanced Research and Communication Center.

Those enjoying the relatively low cost of this collection of readings are in a sense indebted to the dozens of workers who volunteered their time and talent to produce this book. We list the principal workers trusting that none have been omitted.

Susie Adams, Gordon Aeschliman, Sherrie Aeschliman, Patty Aker, Ralph Alpha, Kevin Berasley, Gertrude Bergman, Tim Brenda, Robby Butler, Randy Chan, Karen Clewis, John Cochran, Brad Cronbaugh, Dave Delozier, Lisa Delozier, Linda Dorr, Jan Elder, Jim Fox, Jane Foxwell, Jay Gary, Olgy Gary, Brad Gill, Beth Gill, Christy Graham, Kathy Gunderson, Gene Keller, Lyn Haugh, Barbara Hawthorne, Nancy Hawthorne, Carol Hill, Jerry Hogshead, Marilyn Hogshead, Kitty Holloway, Steve Holloway, Mark Jeffery, Jan Jensen, Jan Josephson, Noelle Lamborn, Shirley Lawson, Helen Lingerfelt, Annette Matsuda, Koleen Matsuda, Jane Mees, Barb Overgaard, Grace Patton, Jack Price, Mary Fran Redding, Cheryl Rose, Joe Ryan, Debbie Sanders, Bob Sjogren, Claudia Smith, Suzanne Smith, Kris Storey, Jodie Van Loon, Tina Warath, Ginny Williamson, Roberta Winter, H.L. Wyatt, Carol Yuke. Graphics by: Carol Hill, Gene Keller and Kris Storey.

Acknowledgements for Third Edition

Thanks to each member and friend of the entire U.S. Center for World Mission. The *Perspectives* program is an expression of their heart and zeal. The editors gratefully acknowledge the contributions of many friends and colleagues who have helped in significant ways. This list no doubt overlooks some who contributed in valuable ways. Thanks to all.

Dwight Baker, Shane Bennett, Laurie Berry-Clifford, John Bibee, Ron Binder, Bryan Bishop, Jeff Borowicki, Michael Boyland, Bruce Bradshaw, Harold Britton, Robby & Jackie Butler, Bob Carlton, Alice Choi, Elise Christol, Keri Comer, Meg Crossman, Premkumar Dharmaraj, Harold Dollar, Ian Downs, Kyle Duncan, William Dyrness, Nathan Fisher, Patty Fraats, Sue Garges, Debbie Greenawalt, Stan Guthrie, Grace Haah, Steve & Sandy Halley, Barbara Hawthorne, Mark & Chiu-Hea Hills, Song Ho, Stephen Hoke, Don Hoke, Jeanette Hui, Brian Humbles, Wendell Hyde, Fawn Imboden, Dr. Todd Johnson, Patrick Johnstone, Ron Kernahan, Linda Koch, Warren Lawrence, Kent & Melissa Lawson, Charles Logston, Jason Mandryk, Jane Mees, Karen Michener, Heather Miller, Dick Moon, Art Moore, Loren Muehlius, Greg Parsons, Fran Patt, Kitty Purgason, Scott Perone, Tony Perone, Kathy Reed, Dr. Ben & Lisa Sells, Kathy & Russ Shubin, Ryan Smith, Phil Sorce, Peggy Sorden, Tom Steller, Mary Upham, Evelyn Varney, Roberta Winter, Dr. Chuck White, Scott White, Stan Williamson, Ron Wilson, Yvonne Wood.

Several groups helped us in special ways:

The editors are most eager to honor the on-going labors of scores of dedicated *Perspectives coordinators*. Many of them made significant contributions to the revision. Their insights have proven exceptionally valuable because of their regular service among the students who are taking the *Perspectives* course.

The Editorial Review group: Corinne Armstrong, Bob Blincoe, Steve Burris, Bob Garrett, Bob Gordon, Judy Lingenfelter, Rick Love, Ken Mulholland, Fran Patt, Bob Stevens and Yvonne Wood.

Scores of *mission leaders and professors of mission* offered vital critique and ideas are far too many to list. We are grateful to all those who have helped evaluate and select. Accept our thanks as an invitation to help us further with your suggestions and critique.

Several *organizations* offered outstanding help: Caleb Project, Global Mapping International, The International Mission Board of the Southern Baptist Convention, The Processors, Wycliffe Bible Translators, and many more who offered help in numerous ways.

The Perspectives revision team has labored with uncommon dedication to Christ and with a delightful camaraderie to serve the World Christian Movement. Abundant thanks to you all: Keith Hall, Linda Jaramillo, Bruce Koch, Lee Purgason, Erin Rosendall, Chad Upham and Jim Zlogar.

Photo and Illustration Credits

The photos on pages 361, 407, 490, 557, 579, 652, and 657 as well as all of the photos used on the cover are courtesy of Caleb Project, Littleton, Colorado. www.calebproject.org

The photo on page 441 is courtesy of Jim Clark.

The photos on pages 453 and 746 are courtesy of Phil Elkins, Altadena, California.

The photos on pages 637 and 647 are courtesy of Bruce Graham, Bremerton, Washington.

The photos on pages 93, 505, 583, 620, and 629 are courtesy of the International Mission Board, Richmond, Virginia. www.imb.org

The photo on page 572 is courtesy of Eric Mooneyham, Duarte, California.

The photo on page 537 is courtesy of Open Doors with Brother Andrew, Santa Ana, California

The photo on page 401 is courtesy of Don Richardson, Woodland Hills, California.

The photos on pages 615 and 642 are courtesy of John Shindeldecker.

The photo on page 676 is courtesy of Trans World Radio, Cary, North Carolina.

The photos on pages 462 and 610 are courtesy of Donald Upham, Arcadia, California.

The photos on pages 148, 356, and 359 are courtesy of World Vision International, Monrovia, California.

The photos on pages 270; 367, 374 (Dick Loving); 363, 447, 477 (Paul Smith); and 272 (Ralph McIntosh) are courtesy of Wycliffe Bible Translators, Huntington Beach, California. www.wycliffe.org

The photo on page 407 is courtesy of the Zwemer Institute, Fort Wayne, Indiana.

The illustrations on pages 125, 256, 439, 599, 603, and 604 are courtesy of Erik Blanton, Riverside, California.

THE
BIBLICAL
PERSPECTIVE

The Living God is a Missionary God

John R. W. Stott

Millions of people in today's world are extremely hostile to the Christian missionary enterprise. They regard it as politically disruptive (because it loosens the cement which binds the national culture) and religiously narrowminded (because it makes exclusive claims for Jesus), while those who are involved in it are thought to suffer from an arrogant imperialism. And the attempt to convert people to Christ is rejected as an unpardonable interference in their private lives. "My religion is my own affair," they say. "Mind your own business, and leave me alone to mind mine."

It is essential, therefore, for Christians to understand the grounds on which the Christian mission rests. Only then shall we be able to persevere in the missionary task, with courage and humility, in spite of the world's misunderstanding and opposition. More precisely, biblical Christians need biblical incentives. For we believe the Bible to be the revelation of God and of his will. So we ask: Has he revealed in Scripture that "mission" is his will for his people? Only then shall we be satisfied. For then it becomes a matter of obeying God, whatever others may think or say. Here we shall focus on the Old Testament, though the entire Bible is rich in evidence for the missionary purpose of God.

The Call of Abraham

Our story begins about four thousand years ago with a man called Abraham, or more accurately, Abram, as he was called at that time. Here is the account of God's call to Abraham.

> Now the LORD said to Abram, "Go from your country and kindred and your father's house to the land that I will show you. And I will make of you a great nation, and I will bless you, and make your name great, so that you will be a blessing. I will bless those who bless you, and him who curses you I will curse; and by you all the families of the earth shall bless themselves." So Abram went, as the LORD had told him; and Lot went with him. Abram was seventy-five years old when he departed from Haran (Gen 12:1-4).

God made a promise (a composite promise, as we shall see) to Abraham. And an understanding of that promise is indispensable to an understanding of the Bible and of the Christian mission. These are perhaps the most unifying verses in the Bible; the whole of God's purpose is encapsulated here.

By way of introduction we shall need to consider the setting of God's promise, the context in which it came to be

John R.W. Stott is Rector Emeritus of All Souls Church in London, President of the London Institute for Contemporary Christianity, and an Extra Chaplain to the Queen. For 25 years (1952-1977) he led university missions on five continents. He has addressed five Urbana Student Missions Conventions. This article was first presented as the opening Bible lecture at Urbana 1976.

Taken from *You Can Tell the World*, edited by James E. Berney. Copyright 1979 by InterVarsity Christian Fellowship/USA. Used by permission of InterVarsity Press, P.O. Box 1400, Downers Grove, IL 60515.

given. Then we shall divide the rest of our study into two. First, *the promise* (exactly what it was that God said he would do) and second—at greater length—*its fulfillment* (how God has kept and will keep his promise). We start, however, with the setting.

Genesis 12 begins: "Now the LORD said to Abram." It sounds abrupt for an opening of a new chapter. We are prompted to ask: "Who is this 'Lord' who spoke to Abraham?" and "Who is this 'Abraham' to whom he spoke?" They are not introduced into the text out of the blue. A great deal lies behind these words. They are a key which opens up the whole of Scripture. The previous eleven chapters lead up to them; the rest of the Bible follows and fulfills them.

What, then, is the background to this text? It is this. "The Lord" who chose and called Abraham is the same Lord who, in the beginning, created the heavens and the earth and who climaxed his creative work by making man and woman unique creatures in his own likeness. In other words, we should never allow ourselves to forget that the Bible begins with the universe, not with the planet earth; then with the earth, not with Palestine; then with Adam the father of the human race, not with Abraham the father of the chosen race. Since, then, God is the Creator of the universe, the earth and all mankind, we must never demote him to the status of a tribal deity or petty godling like Chemosh the god of the Moabites, or Milcom (or Molech) the god of the Ammonites, or Baal the male deity, or Ashtoreth the female deity, of the Canaanites. Nor must we suppose that God chose Abraham and his descendants because he had lost interest in other peoples or given them up. Election is not a synonym for elitism. On the contrary, as we shall soon see, God chose one man and his family in order, through them, to bless all the families of the earth.

We are bound, therefore, to be deeply offended when Christianity is relegated to one chapter in a book on the world's religions as if it were one option among many, or when people speak of "the Christian God" as if there were others! No, there is only one living and true God, who has revealed himself fully and finally in his only Son Jesus Christ.

Monotheism lies at the basis of mission. As Paul wrote to Timothy, "There is one God, and there is one mediator between God and men, the man Christ Jesus" (1 Tim 2:5).

The Genesis record moves on from the creation of all things by the one God and of human beings in his likeness, to our rebellion against our own Creator and to God's judgment upon his rebel creatures—a judgment which is relieved, however, by his first gospel promise that one day the woman's seed would "bruise," indeed "crush," the serpent's head (3:15).

The following eight chapters (Genesis 4-11) describe the devastating results of the Fall in terms of the progressive alienation of human beings from God and from our fellow human beings. This was the setting in which God's call and promise came to Abraham. All around was moral deterioration, darkness and dispersal. Society was steadily disintegrating. Yet God the Creator did not abandon the human beings he had made in his own likeness (Gen 9:6). Out of the prevailing godlessness he called one man and his family, and promised to bless not only them but through them the whole world. The scattering would not proceed unchecked; a grand process of ingathering would now begin.

The Promise

What then was the promise which God made to Abraham? It was a composite promise consisting of several parts.

First, it was the promise of a *posterity*. He was to go from his kindred and his father's house, and in exchange for the loss of his family God would make of him "a great nation." Later in order to indicate this, God changed his name from "Abram" ("exalted father") to "Abraham" ("father of a multitude") because, he said to him, "I have made you the father of a multitude of nations" (17:5).

Second, it was the promise of a *land*. God's call seems to have come to him in two stages, first in Ur of the Chaldees while his father was still alive (11:31; 15:7) and then in Haran after his father had died (11:32; 12:1). At all events he was to leave his own land and, in return, God would show him another country.

Third, it was the promise of a *blessing*. Five times the words *bless* and *blessing* occur in

12:2-3. The blessing God promised Abraham would spill over upon all mankind.

A posterity, a land and a blessing. Each of these promises is elaborated in the chapters that follow Abraham's call.

First, *the land*. After Abraham had generously allowed his nephew Lot to choose where he wanted to settle (he selected the fertile Jordan valley), God said to Abraham: "Lift up your eyes, and look from the place where you are, northward and southward and eastward and westward; for all the land which you see I will give to you and to your descendants forever" (13:14-15).

Second, *the posterity*. Sometime later God gave Abraham another visual aid, telling him to look now not to the earth but to the sky. On a clear, dark night he took him outside his tent and said to him, "Look toward heaven and number the stars." What a ludicrous command! Perhaps Abraham started, "1,2,3,5,10,20,30…," but he must soon have given up. It was an impossible task. Then God said to him: "So shall your descendants be. "And we read: "He believed the Lord." Although he was probably by now in his eighties, and although he and Sarah were still childless, he yet believed God's promise and God "reckoned it to him as righteousness." That is, because he trusted God, God accepted him as righteousness in his sight (15:5-6).

> God chose one man and his family in order, through them, to bless all the families of the earth.

Third, the *blessing*. "I will bless you." Already God has accepted Abraham as righteous or (to borrow the New Testament expression) has "justified him by faith." Now greater blessing is conceivable. It is the foundation blessing of the covenant of grace, which a few years later God went on to elaborate to Abraham: "I will establish my covenant between me and you and your descendants after you…for an everlasting covenant, to be God to you and to your descendants after you and I will be their God" (17:7-8). And he gave them circumcision as the outward and visible sign of his gracious covenant or pledge to be

their God. It is the first time in Scripture that we hear the covenant formula which is repeated many times later: "I will be their God and they shall be my people."

A land, a posterity, a blessing—But what has all that to do with mission? For that, let us turn now from the promise to the fulfillment.

The Fulfillment

The whole question of the fulfillment of Old Testament prophecy is a difficult one in which there is often misunderstanding and much disagreement. Of particular importance is the principle, with which I think all of us will agree, that the New Testament writers themselves understood Old Testament prophecy to have not a *single* but usually a *triple* fulfillment—past, present and future. The past fulfillment was an immediate or historical fulfillment in the life of the nation of Israel. The present is an intermediate or gospel fulfillment in Christ and his Church. The future will be an ultimate or eschatological fulfillment in the the new heaven and the new earth.

God's promise to Abraham received an immediate historical fulfillment in his physical descendants, the people of Israel.

God's promise to Abraham of a numerous, indeed of an innumerable, posterity was confirmed to his son, Isaac (26:4, "as the stars of heaven"), and his grandson, Jacob (32:12, "as the sand of the sea"). Gradually the promise began to come literally true. Perhaps we could pick out some of the stages in this development.

The first stage concerns the years of slavery in Egypt, of which it is written, "The descendants of Israel were fruitful and increased greatly; they multiplied and grew exceedingly strong; so that the land was filled with them" (Ex 1:7; cf. Acts 7:17). The next stage I will mention came several hundred years later when King Solomon called Israel "a great people that cannot be numbered or counted for multitude" (1 Ki 3:8). A third stage was some three hundred fifty years after Solomon; Jeremiah warned Israel of impending judgment and captivity, and then added this divine promise of restoration: "As the host of heaven cannot be numbered and the sands of the sea cannot be measured so I will multiply the descendants of David my servant" (Jer 33:22).

So much for Abraham's posterity; what about the land? Again we note with worship and gratitude God's faithfulness to his promise. For it was in remembrance of his promise to Abraham, Isaac and Jacob that he first rescued his people from their Egyptian slavery and gave them the territory which came on that account to be called "the promised land" (Ex 2:24; 3:6; 32:13), and then restored them to it some seven hundred years later after their captivity in Babylon. Nevertheless, neither Abraham nor his physical descendants fully inherited the land. As Hebrews 11 puts it, they "died in faith *not* having received what was promised." Instead, as "strangers and exiles on the earth" they "looked forward to the city which has foundations, whose builder and maker is God" (Heb 11:8-16, 39-40).

God kept his promises about the posterity and the land, at least in part. Now what about the blessing? Well, at Sinai God confirmed and clarified his covenant with Abraham, and pledged himself to be Israel's God (e.g., Ex 19:3-6). And throughout the rest of the Old Testament God continued to bless the obedient while the disobedient fell under his judgment.

Perhaps the most dramatic example comes at the beginning of Hosea's prophecy, in which Hosea is told to give his three children names which describe God's awful and progressive judgment on Israel. His firstborn (a boy) he called "Jezreel," meaning "God will scatter." Next came a daughter "Lo-ruhamah," meaning "not pitied," for God said he would no longer pity or forgive his people. Lastly he had another son "Lo-ammi," meaning "not my people," for God said they were not now his people. What terrible names for the chosen people of God! They sound like a devastating contradiction of God's eternal promise to Abraham.

But God does not stop there. For beyond the coming judgment there would be a restoration, which is described in words which once more echo the promise to Abraham: "Yet the number of the people of Israel shall be like the sand of the sea, which can be nei-

ther measured nor numbered" (Hos 1:10). And then the judgments implicit in the names of Hosea's children would be reversed. There would be a gathering instead of a scattering ("Jezreel" is ambiguous and can imply either), "not pitied" would be pitied, and "not my people" would become "sons of the living God" (1:10-2:1).

The wonderful thing is that the apostles Paul and Peter both quote these verses from Hosea. They see their fulfillment not just in a further multiplication of Israel but in the inclusion of the Gentiles in the community of Jesus: "Once you were no people but now you are God's people; once you had not received mercy but now you have received mercy" (1 Pet 2:9-10; cf. Rom 9:25-26).

This New Testament perspective is essential as we read the Old Testament prophecies. For what we miss in the Old Testament is any clear explanation of just how God's promised blessing would overflow from Abraham and his descendants to "all families of the earth." Although Israel is described as "a light to lighten the nations," and has a mission to "bring forth justice to the nations" (Isa 42:1-4, 6; 49:6), we do not actually see this happening. It is only in the Lord Jesus himself that these prophecies are fulfilled, for only in his day are the nations actually included in the redeemed community. To this we now turn.

God's promise to Abraham receives an intermediate or gospel fulfillment in Christ and his Church.

Almost the first word of the whole New Testament is the word Abraham. For Matthew's Gospel begins, "The book of the genealogy of Jesus Christ, the son of David, the son of Abraham. Abraham was the father of Isaac...." So it is right back to Abraham that Matthew traces the beginning not just of the genealogy but of the gospel of Jesus Christ. He knows that what he is recording is the fulfillment of God's ancient promises to Abraham made some two thousand years previously. (See also Luke 1:45-55, 67-75.)

Yet from the start Matthew recognizes that it isn't just *physical* descent from Abraham which qualifies people to inherit the promises, but a kind of *spiritual* descent, namely, repentance and faith in the coming Messiah.

This was John the Baptist's message to crowds who flocked to hear him: "Do not presume to say to yourselves, 'We have Abraham as our father,' for I tell you God is able from these stones to raise up children to Abraham" (Matt 3:9; Luke 3:8; cf. John 8:33-40). The implications of his words would have shocked his hearers since "it was the current belief that no descendant of Abraham could be lost."[1]

And God has raised up children to Abraham, if not from stones, then from an equally unlikely source, namely, the Gentiles! So Matthew, although the most Jewish of all the four Gospel writers, later records Jesus as having said, "I tell you, many will come from east and west and sit at table with Abraham, Isaac, and Jacob in the kingdom of heaven, while the sons of the kingdom will be thrown into the outer darkness" (8:11-12; cf. Luke 13:28-29).

It is hard for us to grasp how shocking, how completely topsy-turvy, these words would have sounded to the Jewish hearers of John the Baptist and Jesus. *They* were the descendants of Abraham; so *they* had a title to the promises which God made to Abraham. Who then were these outsiders who were to share in the promises, even apparently usurp them, while they themselves would be disqualified? They were indignant. They had quite forgotten that part of God's covenant with Abraham promised an overspill of blessing to *all* the nations of the earth. Now the Jews had to learn that it was in relation to Jesus the Messiah, who was himself Seed of Abraham, that all the nations would be blessed.

The Apostle Peter seems at least to have begun to grasp this in his second sermon, just after Pentecost. In it he addressed a Jewish crowd with the words: "You are the sons…of the covenant which God gave to your fathers, saying to Abraham, 'And in your posterity shall all the families of the earth be blessed.' God, having raised up his servant [Jesus], sent him to you first, to bless you in turning every one of you from your wickedness" (Acts 3:25-26). It *is* a very notable statement because he interprets the blessing in the moral terms of repentance and righteousness and because, if Jesus was sent "first" to the Jews, he was presumably sent next to the Gentiles, whose "families of the earth" had

been "far off" (cf. Acts 2:39) but were now to share in the blessing.

It was given to the apostle Paul, however, to bring this wonderful theme to its full development. For he was called and appointed to be the apostle to the Gentiles, and to him was revealed God's eternal but hitherto secret purpose to make Jews and Gentiles "fellow heirs, members of the same body, and partakers of the promise in Christ Jesus through the gospel" (Eph 3:6).

Negatively, Paul declares with great boldness, "Not all who are descended from Israel belong to Israel, and not all are children of Abraham because they are his descendants" (Rom 9:6-7).

Who then are the true descendants of Abraham, the true beneficiaries of God's promises to him? Paul does not leave us in any doubt. They are believers in Christ of whatever race. In Romans 4 he points out that Abraham not only received justification by faith but also received this blessing *before he had been circumcised*. Therefore Abraham is the father of all those who, whether circumcised or uncircumcised (that is, Jews or Gentiles), "follow the example of [his] faith" (Rom 4:9-12). If we "share the faith of Abraham," then "he is the father of us all, as it is written, 'I have made you the father of many nations'" (vv. 16-17). Thus neither physical descent from Abraham nor physical circumcision as a Jew makes a person a true child of Abraham, but rather faith. Abraham's real descendants are believers in Jesus Christ, whether racially they happen to be Jews or Gentiles.

What then is the "land" which Abraham's descendants inherit? The letter to the Hebrews refers to a "rest" which God's people enter now by faith (Heb 4:3). And in a most remarkable expression Paul refers to "the promise to Abraham and his descendants, that they should *inherit the world*" (Rom 4:13). One can only assume he means the same thing as when to the Corinthians he writes that in Christ "all things are yours, whether Paul or Apollos or Cephas or the world or life or death or the present or the future, all are yours" (1 Cor 3:21-23). Christians, by God's wonderful grace, are joint heirs with Christ of the universe.

Somewhat similar teaching, both about the nature of the promised blessing and about its beneficiaries, is given by Paul in Galatians 3. He first repeats how Abraham was justified by faith, and then continues: "So you see that it is men of faith who are the sons of Abraham" and who therefore "are blessed with Abraham who had faith" (vv. 6-9). What then is the blessing with which all the nations were to be blessed (v. 8)? In a word, it is the blessing of salvation. We were under the curse of the law, but Christ has redeemed us from it by becoming a curse in our place, in order "that in Christ Jesus the blessing of Abraham might come upon the Gentiles, that we might receive the promise of the Spirit through faith" (vv. 10-14). Christ bore our curse that we might inherit Abraham's blessing, the blessing of justification (v. 8) and of the indwelling Holy Spirit (v. 14). Paul sums it up in the last verse of the chapter (v. 29): "If you are Christ's, then you are Abraham's offspring, heirs according to promise."

But we have not quite finished yet. There is a third stage of fulfillment still to come.

God's promise to Abraham will receive an ultimate or eschatological fulfillment in the final destiny of all the redeemed.

In the book of Revelation there is one more reference to God's promise to Abraham (7:9ff.). John sees in a vision "a great multitude which no man could number." It is an international throng, drawn "from every nation, from all tribes and peoples and tongues." And they are "standing before the throne," the symbol of God's kingly reign. That is, his kingdom has finally come, and they are enjoying all the blessings of his gracious rule. He shelters them with his presence. Their wilderness days of hunger, thirst and scorching heat are over. They have entered the promised land at last, described now not as "a land flowing with milk and honey" but as a land irrigated from "springs of living water"

which never dry up. But how did they come to inherit these blessings? Partly because they have "come out of great tribulation," but mostly because "they have washed their robes and made them white in the blood of the Lamb," that is, they have been cleansed from sin and clothed with righteousness through the merits of the death of Jesus Christ alone. "*Therefore* are they before the throne of God."

Speaking personally, I find it extremely moving to glimpse this final fulfillment in a future eternity of that ancient promise of God to Abraham. All the essential elements of the promise may be detected. For here are the spiritual descendants of Abraham, a "great multitude which no man could number," as countless as the sand on the seashore and as the stars in the night sky. Here too are "all the families of the earth" being blessed, for the numberless multitude is composed of people from every nation. Here also is the promised land, namely, all the rich blessings which flow from God's gracious rule. And here above all is Jesus Christ, the Seed of Abraham, who shed his blood for our redemption and who bestows his blessings on all those who call on him to be saved.

> Now we are Abraham's seed by faith, and the earth's families will be blessed only if we go to them with the gospel.

Conclusion

Let me try to summarize what we learn about God from his promise to Abraham and its fulfillment.

First, he is the God of history.

History is not a random flow of events. For God is working out in time a plan which he conceived in a past eternity and will consummate in a future eternity. In this historical process Jesus Christ, as the Seed of Abraham is the key figure. Let's rejoice that if we are Christ's disciples we are Abraham's descendants. We belong to his spiritual lineage. If we have received the blessings of justification by faith, acceptance with God, and of the indwelling Spirit, then we are beneficiaries today of a promises made to Abraham four thousand years ago.

Second, he is the God of the covenant.

That is, God is gracious enough to make promises, and he always keeps the promise he makes. He is a God of steadfast love and faithfulness. Not that he always fulfills his promises immediately. Abraham and Sarah "died in faith *not* having received what was promised, but having seen it and greeted it from afar" (Heb 11:13). That is, although Isaac was born to them in fulfillment of the promise, their seed was not yet numerous, nor was the land given to them, nor were the nations blessed. All God's promises come true, but they are inherited "through faith *and patience*" (Heb 6:12). We have to be content to wait for God's time.

Third, he is the God of blessing.

"I will bless you," he said to Abraham (Gen 12:2). "God...sent him [Jesus] to you first, to bless you," echoed Peter (Acts 3:26). God's attitude to his people is positive, constructive, enriching. Judgment is his "strange work" (Isa 28:21). His principal and characteristic work is to bless people with salvation.

Fourth, he is the God of mercy.

I have always derived much comfort from the statement of Revelation 7:9 that the company of the redeemed in heaven will be "a great multitude which no man could number." I do not profess to know how this can be, since Christians have always seemed to be a rather small minority. But Scripture states it for our comfort. Although no biblical Christian can be a universalist (believing that all mankind will ultimately be saved), since

Scripture teaches the awful reality and eternity of hell, yet a biblical Christian can—even must—assert that the redeemed will somehow be an international throng so immense as to be countless. For God's promise is going to be fulfilled, and Abraham's seed is going to be as innumerable as the dust of the earth, the stars of the sky and the sand on the seashore.

Fifth, he is the God of mission.

The nations are not gathered in automatically. If God has promised to bless "all the families of the earth," he has promised to do so "through Abraham's seed" (Gen 12:3; 22:18). Now we are Abraham's seed by faith, and the earth's families will be blessed only if we go to them with the gospel. That is God's plain purpose.

I pray that these words, "all the families of the earth," may be written on our hearts. It is this expression more than any other which reveals the living God of the Bible to be a missionary God. It is this expression too which condemns all our petty parochialism and narrow nationalism, our racial pride (whether white or black), our condescending paternalism and arrogant imperialism. How dare we adopt a hostile or scornful or even indifferent attitude to any person of another color or culture if our God is the God of "all the families of the earth?" We need to become global Christians with a global vision, for we have a global God.

So may God help us never to forget his four-thousand-year-old promise to Abraham: "By you and your descendants *all* the nations of the earth shall be blessed."

End Note

1. J. Jeremias, *Jesus' Promise to the Nations*, SCM Press, 1958, p. 48.

Study Questions

1. Why is it important that the Biblical record begins with the Creator God instead of opening with stories about Abraham's God?

2. Describe what Stott means by God's promise having "triple fulfillment"? How was the promise of a land, a posterity, and a blessing fulfilled in the past? How is the promise receiving fulfillment in the present? How will God's promise to Abraham receive its final fulfillment in the future?

Israel's Missionary Call

Walter C. Kaiser, Jr.

T here is a rumor abroad that the Old Testament does not have a missionary message or vision. It is, so goes the popular adage, a book and a message dedicated solely to the Jews and their own nationalistic fortunes. But that rumor and view will not square with the claims that the Old Testament itself makes. Even if we limit our investigation to three key Old Testament texts, we will observe immediately that these three texts present three of the most powerful statements of a missionary call that can be given anywhere.

We would have been more hesitant in our suspecting that the Old Testament has no missionary challenge had we paid close attention to how the Old Testament begins. Certainly the message and scope of the earliest chapters in Genesis, namely Genesis 1-11, are universal in their appeal and international in their audience. Did God not deal with "all the families of the earth" when He moved in saving grace at three specific junctures in Genesis 1-11? To be specific, was it not true that after the Fall of Man, the Flood of the Earth, and the Failure of the Tower of Babel, God gave the grand messages of salvation in Genesis 3:15, 9:27 and 12:1-3?

And should we doubt that the word to Abraham in Genesis 12:1-3 was international and universal in its offer, scope and intention, then let us quickly remind ourselves that it was painted against the backdrop of the Table of the Seventy Nations of all the world in Genesis 10. The same "families of the earth" appear there and in Genesis 12:3.

Old Testament Gentiles Came to Faith

The phenomenon of Gentiles coming to faith in the coming "seed" or "Man of Promise" was not unknown or without constant reminders in the Old Testament. Consider Melchizedek (in Gen 14), a priest-king over Salem (Jerusalem). This Gentile openly confessed his faith in Jehovah (Yahweh). Jethro, a Midianite and Moses' father-in-law, demonstrated his commitment to the same Lord espoused by Moses and Aaron by sitting down with them around a fellowship sacrificial meal in Exodus 18. No one could accuse Balaam of being pro-Jewish or chauvinistic in his attitude, for he badly wanted to oblige the king of Moab and curse the nation of Israel. Yet he was God's oracle of truth, even though he had a very rough start in which his donkey showed keener spiritual insight than he did. Nevertheless, Balaam gave us two fantastic chapters, including the

Walter C. Kaiser, Jr. is the Colman M. Mockler distinguished Professor of Old Testament and President of Gordon-Conwell Theological Seminary in South Hamilton, Massachusetts. He previously taught at Trinity Evangelical Divinity School and Wheaton College and has served as a pastor. Among his numerous writings is the widely read *Toward an Old Testament Theology*.

Adapted from an address given to the students of Trinity Evangelical Divinity School, Deerfield, Illinois, May 14, 1981.

great (and only) star prophecy of the Messiah, in Numbers 23-24.

Time fails me to remind us of whole cities that at times repented at the preaching of one Jewish prophet—for example, Jonah and the Ninevites. Even though God's servant was more than reluctant and became very "down-in-the-mouth" and had a "whale-of-an-experience" (literally) before he finally preached to dirty Gentiles who massacred Jews, the city came to know the Lord in grand proportions because Jonah *did* preach. Even then, he hoped this was one sermon in which no one would come forward.

But some may still doubt that the Old Testament explicitly enjoined believers and messengers in the Old Testament to *go* to the *Gentiles*. Did God, they ask, ever *send* an Israelite or the whole nation with the Great Commission?

Three Basic Texts

There are three basic texts that make it clear that God did do just that. These texts are: Genesis 12:1-3, Exodus 19:4-6, and Psalm 67. These three texts are so basic to our understanding of the missionary mandate that God had designed for the whole nation of Israel that it is impossible to view the Old Testament fairly without treating these texts in their missionary context. Israel had always, in the plan and purpose of God, been responsible for communicating the message of God's grace to the nations. Israel was meant to be a communicating nation.

Lest we think that these three Old Testament texts have no relevance to those of us who live in the Christian era and that their message is a B.C.-dated injunction, let it be plainly declared that they are also God's call to us. Put in outline form, their message is God's call to us:

I. To Proclaim His Plan to Bless the Nations (Gen 12:3)
II. To Participate in His Priesthood as Agents of That Blessing (Ex 19:4-6) and
III. To Prove His Purpose to Bless all the Nations (Ps 67)

Genesis 1-11

No one can say that the Old Testament begins in a chauvinistic way or that the God of that testament was so pro-Jewish that missionary outreach did not occur until the Time of the Gentiles arrived. Genesis 1-11, as we have stated, clearly argues for the reverse. The scope of that text is worldwide in its offer of salvation for all who would believe. The counter theme in those same chapters is the nations questing for a "name" for themselves. Both in Genesis 6:4 and Genesis 11:4, the sole object of mankind was to make a "name" for themselves and to advance their own reputation—but at the expense of the "name" of God.

Thus the "sons of God" (whom I believe to be tyrannical and polygamous despots in the context of Gen 6) took to themselves this divine title along with its presumed prerogatives, and distorted the very instrument of the state that God had set up for justice and abused it for their own desires and lusts. This constituted the second great failure of the pre-patriarchal era of Genesis 1-11. It had been preceded by the Fall of Man in Genesis 3 and it climaxed in the third failure of the Tower of Babel in Genesis 11.

Genesis 12:1-3: Proclaim His Plan

Nevertheless, for each of these three failures, our Lord had a saving word of grace: Genesis 3:15; 9:27; and 12:1-3. It is this third gracious word that concerns us here, for it emphasizes God's word of grace over against the failures of men and their idolatrous questing for a "name" or reputation. Five times God said, "I will bless you," "I will bless you," "I will bless you," "I will bless those blessing you," and "In your seed all the nations of the earth shall be blessed."

No doubt the key word here is *bless* or *blessing*. That same word had characterized this whole section, beginning with the word to Adam and Eve: "He blessed them saying, 'Be fruitful and multiply,'" just as He had also graciously promised to bless the animals.

And yet man continued to seek meaning on his own terms by questing for a "name." Over against the vacuum of that day (and ours), the vacuum of looking for human status, reputation and achievement devoid of God, Genesis 12:2 suddenly announces that God would give Abraham a "name" as a blessing from above, rather than as an achievement of works which left God out of the picture.

The significance of this grandest of all missionary texts cannot be fully appreciated un-

til we begin to realize that there are actually three promises of blessing in Genesis 12:2-3 in which God promises:
1.   "I will make you a great nation,"
2.   "I will bless you," and
3.   "I will make your name great…"

But this is immediately followed by a purpose clause. It is "*so that* you may be a blessing." Not one of these three promises of blessing were to be for Abraham's self-aggrandizement. Indeed, he and his nation were to be blessed so that they might be a blessing. But to whom? How? For the answers to these questions, we must go on with two more promises.

There were to be two whole classes of people: the blessers of Abraham and the cursers of Abraham. The two additional promises were:
4.   "I will bless those blessing you," and
5.   "Those who curse you, I will curse."

Again, however, the writer of Genesis adds a purpose clause, while shifting the tense of the verb, so that a fuller statement of his purpose can be given. Now it was "*so that* in you all the families of the earth might be blessed."

That, then, explains why there was so much blessing. This man and his descendants were to be missionaries and channels of the truth from the very beginning. It is exceedingly important that we recognize that the Hebrew verb in this case must be translated as a passive verb ("be blessed") and not reflexively ("bless themselves"), since all the earlier Hebrew grammars, versions, and New Testament understandings insist on it. It is a matter of grace, not of works or copy-catting!

The nations were to be blessed in this man's "*seed*." Indeed, the "seed" the woman (Gen 3:15), the "seed" of Shem in whose tents God would come to "tabernacle" or "dwell" (Gen 9:27), and the "seed" of Abraham formed one collective whole which was epitomized through its succession of representatives who acted as downpayments and earnests until Christ himself should come in that same line and as a part of that succession and corporate entity.

The recipients of this blessing initially were listed as none other than the 70 nations listed as all "the families" of the earth in Genesis 10. This chapter topically precedes man's

third failure at Babel, which in turn leads in Genesis into the inbursting word of God's purpose and plan to bring all the nations of the world to Himself. The word to Abraham was meant to have a great impact on all the families on the face of the earth. This is indeed high and lofty missionary teaching.

Some may remain somewhat skeptical, saying that they cannot see any gospel or good news in Genesis 12:2-3. Our answer is for those unconvinced doubters to observe that Paul named Abraham in Romans 4:13 the heir of the whole world. That inheritance obviously must be spiritual in its nature. Moreover, Paul plainly stated in Galatians 3:8 that Abraham had the gospel preached to him ahead of time when he received Genesis 12:3: "in you shall all the nations be blessed." That was and still is the Good News of the gospel.

> **Israel was to be God's missionary to the world—and so are we by virtue of the same verses! The mission has not changed in our own day.**

And if we today believe, then we are part of Abraham's "seed" (Gal 3:29). The object of faith and trust is still the same; the focal point for Israel and the nations of the earth is that Man of Promise who was to come in Abraham and David's "seed" and is now come in Jesus Christ.

The message and its content, in fact the whole purpose of God, was that He would make a nation, give them a "name," bless them *so that* they might be light to the nations and thereby be a blessing to all the nations. To shrink back would be evil on Israel's part. Israel was to be God's missionary to the world—and so are we by virtue of the same verses! The mission has not changed in our own day. Abraham and Israel were not intended to be passive transmitters of the "seed" any more than we are to be passive. They were to be a blessing so that they actually could communicate God's gift to the world.

The nations were viewed differently, but the way God dealt with them was always directly related to how they reacted to this Man of Promise who was to come through the nation God had made great, and to which He had given this calling to bless and be a blessing. Israel's calling was not the occasion or basis for rejecting any of the nations of the world, but instead the very means of blessing them all. The quest for a "name," for fame, for reputation still goes on today, when God would give His own "name." He will still give His special "name" to those who will believe in that same "seed." It is the only means by which they and all their kindred upon the face of the earth will be blessed and made part of the family of God.

Some may agree that the object of faith was indeed to be the coming seed from Abraham's stock, but they may not agree that God thereby expected or demanded of Abraham and his successors anything like our missionary mandate. Perhaps they were meant to be entirely passive while God was the whole actor in the Old Testament.

Exodus 19:4-6:
Participate in His Priesthood

Exodus 19:4-6, the second Old Testament text for our consideration, will not allow that interpretation. In Moses' famous "Eagle's Wings Speech," God reviews with Israel how he bore them along from Egypt like an eagle would transport her young learning how to fly. Since they were the recipients of this gift of deliverance, the text pointedly says, "Now therefore...." It implies a natural consequence ought to be forthcoming from God's miraculous aid in their escape from Egypt.

To begin reading Exodus 19:5 without the "now therefore," and to stress the "iffy-ness" of the words that follow, is to miss the emphasis of the text. This text, like Exodus 20:1, must begin in the environment of grace. "I am the Lord your God who brought you up from out of the land of Egypt." The "now therefore..." follows because of the previous blessing of God.

Exodus 19:5-6 goes on to say: "...if you will obey my voice and keep my covenant, you shall be my *special possession* among all peoples; for all the earth is mine, and you shall be my *kingdom of priests* and *a holy nation*

(italics mine)." These are the three ministries God specifies for Abraham's descendants.

In the first place, they were to be God's *special possession*, or as the older translations have it, "my peculiar people." The old English word "peculiar" came from the Latin word which meant valuables or any kind of movable goods which were not, in contrast to real estate, attached to the land, such as jewels, stocks, or bonds. The fact was that Israel was to be God's son, His people, His firstborn (Ex 4:22), and now His special treasure. The emphasis here is on the *portability* of that message and the fact that God has placed such high value on *people*. This is exactly as Malachi 3:17 describes us: "jewels."

Another role Israel was to perform was that of being kings and priests for God. The genitive or construct form, "kingdom of priests," is better translated (based on six occurrences in prose texts) "kings and priests," "kingly priests," or "royal priests." It is here that Israel's missionary role became explicit, if any doubt had remained. The whole nation was to function on behalf of the kingdom of God in a mediatorial role in relation to the nations.

In fact, it was this passage that became the basis for our famous New Testament doctrine of the priesthood of believers (see 1 Pet 2:9; Rev 1:6- 5:10). Unfortunately for Israel, they rejected this priesthood of all believers and urged Moses to go up to the mountain of Sinai on their behalf and as their representative. Nevertheless, even though God's original plan was for the moment frustrated and delayed until New Testament times, it was not defeated, substituted, or scrapped. It remained God's plan for believers. They were to have a mediatorial role!

Israel was to have a third function: a holy nation. Holiness in the Bible is not just a form of ether that invades audiences on Sunday mornings and makes them somewhat listless and passive, but holiness is wholeness. To be "holy" is to be "wholly" the Lord's.

It is a shame that we had to divide the English word into two words: the one religious (holy) and the other secular (wholly), but the root was the same in Anglo-Saxon history. The same is true for the Hebrew root. Israel was to be given wholly over to the Lord as a nation. They were to be set apart not only in their lives, but also in their service. Their calling and election of God was for service and that service had been defined as early as the days of their ancestor Abraham.

As priests were to represent God and mediate his word to the nations, so Israel as a holy nation was to assume two relations: one side towards God, their King, and the other side towards the nations. They were to be a nation for all the times and for all the people—set apart. But instead, Israel began to act for herself, as we also often do, as a club of the pious, rather than remembering her call to be sharers of the blessings, truth, gifts and the "Seed" to the nations. In a sense, they carried a portfolio which read "Ambassadors of the Coming Man of Promise."

Now I have not forgotten the distinction between Israel and the Church. It is possible to distinguish between these two institutions, just as one can distinguish between male and female. Yet that middle wall of partition which demanded death for any Gentile that transgressed and passed its boundaries in the temple complex has now been knocked down by Christ's death. Maleness, femaleness, Jewishness, Gentileness, slave status or whatever no longer matter. All who believe are one "people of God." Indeed, that had been the continuity term to identify all who had belonged to the Savior in all ages. And Peter makes it explicit by calling the Gentile believers of his day "a chosen race, a royal priesthood, a holy nation, God's own people" (1 Pet 2:9). The use of Exodus 19 is very obvious and transparent. The point is, do we recognize the continuity in the purpose and plan of God?

Peter went on to make his point clear. God had called His people by these four titles "so that (they) might declare the wonderful deeds of Him who called (them) out of darkness into His marvelous light" (1 Pet 2:9). The reason why Israel, and now Gentile believers have been named a royal priesthood, a holy nation, the people of God, His chosen race, His special, movable possession, is that we might announce, declare and be His missionaries and witnesses.

None of these gifts were meant to be consumed on ourselves. They were not meant to be mere badges. They were for the purpose of declaring His wonderful deeds and calling people to His marvelous light. Once, says Peter in that same context (borrowing from Hosea's symbolic names for his children), we were: "no people" (Lo-Ammi), "without mercy" (Lo-Ruhamah). But now we are the people of God and now we have received God's mercy and grace.

Peter is trying to show us that the people of God in all ages have been one. Even though we can identify within the one people of God several aspects, such as Israel and Church, and even though we can list several aspects to the single plan and purpose of God that all the nations of the earth might be blessed, nevertheless the unity of all believers and the continuity of that program between Old and New Testaments is a certainty. And in both testaments we were all intended by God to participate in that priesthood who would be agents of blessing to all the nations of the earth. Exodus 19 has shown us that this was God's plan.

Psalm 67: Prove His Purpose

Our third and final text comes from Psalm 67. We have seen how God calls us all: 1) to *proclaim His plan* to the nations in Genesis 12, 2) to *participate in His priesthood* as agents of blessing to all the nations in Exodus 19, and now 3) to *prove His purpose* to bless all the nations in Psalm 67. This Psalm is derived from the Aaronic benediction found in Numbers 6:24-26:

> "Now may the Lord bless you and keep you;
>
> May the Lord make his face shine upon you, and be gracious to you;
>
> May the Lord lift up his countenance upon you, and give you peace."

This word is often heard at the close of most Christian services today.

But look what the Psalmist does here. Rather than saying Yahweh (LORD), Israel's covenantal and personal name for God, he substitutes Elohim (God), the name used when God's relationship to all men, nations and creation is needed. The Psalmist prayed: "May God be gracious to us and bless us." Once more he changed the wording ever so slightly, using the words "among us" (literally) instead of "upon us"..."And may he cause His face to shine among us."

It is significant that this missionary Psalm has applied what God gave through Aaron and the priests to all the peoples. The purpose for this enlarged blessing is given immediately in verse 2: "so that your way may be known upon the earth, your salvation among all the nations (or Gentiles)." That is why God had been gracious and blessed Israel and all who believed. This agrees, then, with Genesis 12:3.

The sentiment was: May God bless us, fellow Israelites. May He be pleased to benefit us. May our crops increase and may our flocks produce abundantly. May our families grow large and may we prosper spiritually, so that the nations may look at us and say that what Aaron prayed for, by way of God's blessing, has indeed happened. The very bounty of God demonstrates that God has blessed us. Therefore, may the rest of His purpose come to pass also, that in blessing Israel all the nations of the earth might come to know Him as well.

This Psalm has been called the Old Testament *Pater Noster* ("Our Father"), or the Old Testament Lord's Prayer. It has three stanzas:

vv. 1-3

(ending with: "Let the people praise thee, O Lord, let all the people praise thee")

vv. 4-5

(ending with the same refrain)

vv. 6-7

This Psalm was probably sung at the Feast of Pentecost. It is all the more remarkable that that is the event where God was to pour out his Spirit on all the nations and an unusual ingathering was to take place—greater than at any previous feast. Deliberately, the Psalmist refers to the ingathering of the harvest as an earnest, a down-payment, and a symbol of the spiritual harvest from every tribe, tongue and nation. So

may the Lord indeed be gracious (full of grace) to us and bless us.

Three times this Psalm refers to the blessing from God: verse one, verse six and verse seven. The structure is almost an exact replica of Genesis 12:2-3. Bless us, bless us, bless us...*so that* all the nations might know the Lord.

The Psalmist calls us to prove and test God's purposes for three reasons. The reasons fit the structure we have already observed. The first is because God has been gracious to us (vv. 1-3). We have experienced the grace of God in His ways and manner of dealing with Israel. We have experienced that grace in the knowledge that His salvation has been extended to all nations. If only all the peoples of all the nations would personally come to know that same grace for themselves!

A second reason is because God rules and guides all nations (vv. 4-5). He is not a judge in a judicial, condemning or punishing sense in this context; instead, He is a royal ruler who judiciously rules in righteousness, as in Isaiah 11:3ff. He is a guide for the nations as the Great Shepherd of Psalm 23:3. Thus the refrain sounds again: Come on, all you peoples of the earth, let's hear it! It's about time you began praising the Lord.

Finally, a third reason is given: the very goodness of God (vv. 6-7). We ought to prove the purpose of God in blessing the nations because He has been so good to us. The land has yielded an abundant increase and our barns, grain bins, and silos are full to overflowing. Was this not an evidence that God answered the prayer of Aaron and the priests in Numbers 6:24-26? The power of God is evident in the very abundance of the harvest.

Now that same power and presence of God which brought the material increase is available for a spiritual increase. If this power were more evident in our lives and preaching, then the spiritual results abroad among the nations and in our own nation would be witnessed by everyone. The point is that the Psalmist did not mouth empty words and forms, but he gave the Psalm so that Israel

> Israel was to be "a light to the nations," just as Abraham had been told, the writer of Exodus had exhorted, and Psalmist had sung.

and we might experience a real change in our lives. The blessing of God comes so that all the ends of the earth might receive spiritual benefit. What has happened materially was only to be an earnest of a blessing with much longer dimensions.

Yes, "God has blessed us; let all the ends of the earth fear Him" (v. 7). The word "fear" here does not mean terror or fright. There are two different usages of the word "fear." Exodus 20:20 urges us: "Fear not, but rather, fear the Lord." Don't be scared, but rather trust and put your whole soul's commitment on Him.

Hence, the fear of the Lord is the beginning of everything: of understanding, of living, of personal holiness, as well as of a vital personal relationship to Him. Fear is one of the Old Testament words for trust and belief. The goodness of God to Israel was meant to be one of God's ways of bringing all the nations on planet earth to fear Him, i.e., to believe the coming Man of Promise, our Lord Jesus Christ. Israel was to be a witnessing, proclaiming, and evangelizing nation. The Gentiles had to be brought to the light.

This purpose for Israel is seen even more clearly in a passage which is not part of this discussion; namely, the "Servant of the Lord" passages of Isaiah 42 and 49. Israel is that servant of the Lord even though the Messiah is the final representative of the whole group par excellence. As such, Israel was to be "a light to the nations," just as Abraham had been told, the writer of Exodus had exhorted, and Psalmist had sung.

The Psalmist longed and deeply desired that God, the King of Israel, might be acknowledged as Lord and Savior of all the families of the earth. Should we do less? Does God call us to anything less than also proving, along with Israel, His purpose in this passage of Psalm 67? God's challenge to Israel is also ours: we are to have a mediatorial role in proclaiming His name among the nations. That is still God's purpose. Is it happening in your life?

May the flame of the gospel, encapsulated in Genesis 12:2-3, and the call to be a holy nation and a royal priesthood fire us for proclaiming the gospel in the days that lie ahead. May we announce, not only to North America but to every single nation on the face of the earth, that Jesus is Lord to the glory of God the Father.

Study Questions

1. Kaiser asserts that God gave a missionary mandate to the people of Israel in the Old Testament by stating a promise of purpose for Israel. How can a promise have mandate force according to Kaiser?

2. Why is it crucial to see that the phenomenon of blessing was not intended to be passive?

3. What is the function of a priesthood according to Kaiser? What does this function have to do with a missionary mandate?

Everyone's Question:
What is God Trying to Do?

Stanley A. Ellisen

The Bible describes God as an eternal King: "The Lord is King forever" (Ps 10:16). It also declares that He is sovereign over all things (Ps 103:19). Being infinite, He is everywhere. So, at every time and place, in all the vast reaches of His universe, God has been in full control. He has never compromised this supreme prerogative of His Godhood. To do so would make Him less than God. It is essential to recognize His undiminished sovereignty if we are to have a proper view of His kingdom. His work of creation, with all the apparent risks involved, was the work of His sovereignty.

Primeval Rebellion

In the operation of His kingdom, God rules by the principle of delegated authority. He organized the angels as a hierarchy, assigning levels of responsibility and spheres of service. To act as His supreme lieutenant in directing this kingdom, God endowed one specific archangel with striking beauty, wisdom, and power (Ezek 28:12-17; Jude 9). He named him Lucifer and gave him a throne from which to rule (Isa 14:12-14). This angel ruled as God's prime minister par excellence.

How long this harmonious arrangement continued in the distant past is not recorded. Endowed with freedom of choice, the crucial test of any creature was allegiance to the will of God. That crucial test came for Lucifer when he shifted his gaze to himself and his God-given features of splendor. Dazzled by his own greatness, he asserted independence and presumed himself to be "like the Most High" (Isa 14:14). In that moment of decision he thrust himself outside the stabilizing axis of God's will and began the swirling catapult into the oblivion of a godless being. His decision was final and never repented of.

Lucifer, however, was not alone in this choice. He evidently had a following of one-third of the angels of heaven (Rev 12:4-7), which also suggests the great allurement of his leadership. With this crowd of rebels he formed a kingdom of his own, a counterfeit kingdom of darkness. His name was changed to Satan (adversary), in keeping with his behavior. If God is sovereign, why didn't He immediately destroy this arch rebel? Why didn't He have a mass execution for the whole horde of disobedient angels? Or at least, why didn't He lock them up forever in the abyss of hell?

The answer is that God does have such a plan, but He is temporarily using these rebels to accomplish another pur-

Stanley A. Ellisen was Professor of Biblical Literature and Chairman of the Division of Biblical Studies at Western Conservative Baptist Seminary in Portland, Oregon. The author of eight books and numerous articles, Ellisen also pastored and planted churches the Pacific Northwest and Southwest. He passed away in 1997.

Reprinted by permission from *Biography of a Great Planet*, Chapter 2, copyright 1975, Tyndale House Publishers, Inc., Wheaton, Illinois.

pose. In the outworking of His program, God was not locked in to a one-track plan, but was able to flex with the punches, so to speak. So deep is His sovereignty that He is able to make the wrath of men to praise Him and all His enemies to serve Him (Ps 76:10). The devastating irony of it for His enemies is that they end up serving Him in spite of themselves. Some of the fallen angels He chained until judgment; others He has allowed a limited liberty until His further purpose is accomplished.

The central fact to observe is that God did allow the formation of a kingdom of darkness. This kingdom formed through voluntary forces led by Satan, not through God's creation, as such. It thus became an opposite pole to God's kingdom of light and an alluring option for all moral creatures in their exercise of moral freedom. It is a counterfeit kingdom running concurrently with the true kingdom of righteousness. Very often it seems to be dominant, not only coercing men and women but winning them. This is partly because of its modus operandi. Contrary to many naive opinions, the devil is not a red monster with a pitchfork, but often a do-gooder. His goal in life is to counterfeit the works of God. This has been his prized ambition ever since he went into business for himself. His first recorded intention ended with the words, "I will be like the Most High" (Isa 14:14). This counterfeiting effort is his most effective ploy, for the more closely he can imitate God's work, the less likely will men be inclined to seek God or pursue His will.

God's Earthly Kingdom Inaugurated

After the fall of Satan, God began another creation: man. He likewise endowed this being with freedom of choice, dangerous though this second venture appears. Freedom of choice was essential to human personality, if man and woman were to be made in the image of God. God's grand design is to reproduce Himself in human personalities, especially His traits of love and holiness. And these divine characteristics can grow only in the soil of moral freedom. Fellowship involves moral choice.

By this freedom, God sought to establish man and woman in a wholesome relation-

ship to His sovereignty. He sought to relate to them by love, not coercion. The bond of love is infinitely stronger than that of muscle. With this in mind He made Adam and Eve partners in His rule. As an initial test they were forbidden to eat of the "tree of the knowledge of good and evil" (Gen 2:17). They were given a choice of compliance or disobedience, clear and simple. The tree was not put there as a teaser or trap, but as an inevitable test. It gave the couple a choice as to whether they would be loyal to God or submit to enticing alternatives presented by the serpent. Had they turned from his evil suggestion to firm commitment to God, they might have eaten of the "tree of life" and been eternally confirmed in righteousness (Gen 3:24; Rev 22:2). But they each disobeyed the direct command of God, and the fall of the human race took place.

By this deliberate action, they declared their independence from the will of God and their affiliation with Satan's kingdom of darkness. The cause of this disaster was not the tree; nor was it the serpent or the devil behind the serpent (Rev 12:9). These provided only an occasion for two individuals to express their freedom of choice with respect to the will of God. The cause of disaster was in their decision. In this test of allegiance they failed and fell, along with the previously fallen host of angels.

To all outward appearance, this second fall of God's creation seemed to dash God's high hopes of extending His kingdom in moral agents. Man was given cosmic responsibilities to have dominion over the earth—but he could not be trusted with a piece of fruit. Was the divine gift of free choice too risky? Would this endowment be the suicidal undoing of the whole race? It certainly seemed to be counterproductive to God's purpose, for sin appeared to be coming up the victor.

The Two Problems Summarized

The dilemma at this point may be summarized as two problems which God acquired in the creative process. One was the fact that His trusted lieutenant, Lucifer, defected and started a counterkingdom, stealing also the allegiance of a large contingent of the angels. The second was that man, made in God's image, also defected and fell into a state of sin and personal disintegration. Thus, God's kingdom was dissected and partially usurped.

The question is often raised as to why God bothered with a salvage operation.

> ## God would ultimately reclaim His total kingdom by destroying Satan and Satan's kingdom, and would redeem believing men in the process by the death of Christ.

Why not destroy everything and start over? Of course this was not within His sovereign plan, nor would it have been a real solution to the deep challenge the double rebellion posed. God not only rose to the insidious challenge of sin, but His great heart of grace initiated an operation that would marvelously redeem sinners. In this plan He addressed Himself to two problems: 1) how to reclaim His usurped kingdom, and 2) how to provide redemption for mankind. The solution God sought could not deal with both problems separately; he thus devised a plan whereby the victory over the counterfeit kingdom would provide salvation for mankind. It could not be achieved by a mere display of divine muscle; the answer was not to crack the whip. Cataclysmic and inclusive judgment would be postponed. It would require action with the depth and power of His greatest attribute: love.

God's Kingdom and Redemptive Programs

When Adam and Eve first sinned, God began His judgment with the serpent (Gen 3:14, 15). In this judgment He also gave the proto-evangel, announcing His redemptive purpose for men. To the serpent He said, "And I will put enmity between you and the woman, and between your seed and her seed; he shall bruise you on the head, and you shall bruise Him on the heel." This message was obviously for man as well as Satan, perhaps more so. In it God prophesied that, following a two-way enmity, two bruisings or crushings would take place. The serpent's head would be crushed by the woman's seed, and the heel of the woman's seed

would be crushed by the serpent. The two figures in this conflict are later declared to be Christ, who was the seed born of a woman (Gal 4:4), and Satan, called "the serpent of old" (Rev 20:2).

By analyzing these two crushings, we get a thumbnail sketch of God's program with respect to Satan and man. The first statement, "He shall bruise you on the head," was a prophecy that Christ would destroy the devil. Christ Himself spoke of His binding Satan, the "strong man" of this world system, and casting him out (Matt 12:29; John 12:31). Christ's death on the cross provided the ground for Satan's final destruction, for "he who builds the scaffold finally hangs thereon." And with his final judgment, the counterfeit kingdom of his making will also be destroyed. This whole process by which God reclaims His authority in all realms and forever stops all rebellion can be though of as God's "kingdom program."

The second crushing announced in Genesis 3:15 is the heel-crushing of the seed of the woman by the serpent. This devilish assault was fulfilled on the cross, where Satan was the driving force behind the crucifixion of Christ. The heel-crushing suggests the temporary nature of Christ's death in contrast to the head-crushing of the serpent. Christ's death on the cross then became the ground for God's redemptive program, the program by which He provided salvation for men.

Thus in this proto-evangel in Eden, God introduced in outline form His twofold program for His kingdom and man's redemption. He would ultimately reclaim His total kingdom by destroying Satan and Satan's kingdom, and would redeem believing men in the process by the death of Christ.

God's Twofold Program Unfolds

The rest of the Old Testament pictures the progressive development of this twofold purpose of God in the earth. The Lord chose two men of faith through whom He inaugurated these programs and set them in motion. The first was Abraham, who lived about 2000 BC. God made a covenant with him, promising among other things a seed that would bless all nations. Paul identified this seed as Christ, and the blessing which was to come through Him he identified as redemption or justification (Gal 3:6-16). Abraham's seed would bring redemption to men, fulfilling the redemptive program.

To fulfill His kingdom purpose, God chose David out of the same lineage about 1000 BC and made a covenant about a kingdom and a royal seed (2 Sam 7:12-16). This seed of David eventually would rule over the house of Israel forever. Besides ruling over Israel, it was later revealed that this anointed One would extend His rule over the whole world (Amos 9:12; Zech 14:9). Through the seed of David, God would fulfill His kingdom program by destroying the rebels and governing the world in righteousness.

Two typical sons
It is interesting to note also that each of these two men was given a son who typified the seed he was promised. Abraham's son, Isaac, typified Christ in His redemptive function, being offered on Mount Moriah as a living sacrifice. David's son, Solomon, typified Christ in His royalty, being a king of glory and splendor. These two sons strikingly typified that seed of Abraham and of David who was looked for with such anticipation throughout the rest of the Old Testament period. In this light, it is no wonder that the Spirit of God begins the New Testament by introducing its central figure as "the son of David, the son of Abraham" (Matt 1:1).

Two typical animals
The Old Testament also portrays the redemptive and kingdom functions of Christ by two symbolic animals. The sacrificial lamb typified Him in His redemptive work as the "Lamb of God who takes away the sin of the world" (John 1:29). It portrayed Him as the Lord's servant who was led "like a lamb…to slaughter" (Isa 53:7).

The other animal typifying Christ in the Old Testament is the lion (Gen 49:9,10). John, in Revelation 5:5, refers to this Old Testament metaphor when he describes Christ as the "Lion…from the tribe of Judah." As the king of the beasts, the lion represents kingly authority. The point is that out of the tribe of Judah would come a Ruler who would rule Israel and the world.

One Glorious Messiah
Though the kingdom purpose is broader, extending to the whole spiritual realm, it could not be accomplished without the redemptive program for man. Notice how John relates the two in his prophetic vision of Revelation 5. After seeing Christ as the Lion and Lamb, he hears the angelic throng loudly acclaim: "Worthy is the Lamb that was slain to receive power and riches and wisdom and might and honor and glory and blessing" (Rev 5:12). He will have shown not only His right but His worthiness to rule as God's Lion, having been slain as God's Lamb.

Christ will finally present this reclaimed kingdom back to the Father (1 Cor 15:24). That presentation will constitute the fulfillment of His commission from the Father in His role as the seed of the woman. And, of supreme importance, the process by which He will have reclaimed that kingdom will be through His redemptive love, not His coercive might. This redemptive grace is the genius of His twofold program, and it will also constitute the basis of His eternal fellowship with men. That divine-human fellowship will not be based on fear or force, but on love.

Study Questions

1. How did God respond to the two rebellions of Satan, and of Adam and Eve? Describe the value of distinguishing God's responses to Satan and to people.

2. How does God's response to the counterfeit kingdom of Satan, give us insight into God's missionary purpose?

3. How is "The Lion" still crushing Satan today? How is "The Lamb" still redeeming people today?

The Bible in World Evangelization

John R. W. Stott

Without the Bible world evangelization would be not only impossible but actually inconceivable. It is the Bible that lays upon us the responsibility to evangelize the world, gives us a gospel to proclaim, tells us to how to proclaim it, and promises us that it is God's power for salvation to every believer.

It is, moreover, an observable fact of history, both past and contemporary, that the degree of the Church's commitment to world evangelization is commensurate with the degree of its conviction about the authority of the Bible. Whenever Christians lose their confidence in the Bible, they also lose their zeal for evangelism. Conversely, whenever they are convinced about the Bible, then they are determined about evangelism.

Let me develop four reasons why the Bible is indispensable to world evangelization.

Mandate for World Evangelization

First, the Bible gives us the *mandate* for world evangelization. We certainly need one. Two phenomena are everywhere on the increase. One is religious fanaticism, and the other, religious pluralism. The fanatic displays the kind of irrational zeal which (if it could) would use force to compel belief and eradicate disbelief. Religious pluralism encourages the opposite tendency.

Whenever the spirit of religious fanaticism or of its opposite, religious indifferentism, prevails, world evangelization is bitterly resented. Fanatics refuse to countenance the rival evangelism represents, and pluralists its exclusive claims. The Christian evangelist is regarded as making an unwarrantable intrusion into other people's private affairs.

In the face of this opposition we need to be clear about the mandate the Bible gives us. It is not just the Great Commission (important as that is) but the entire biblical revelation. Let me rehearse it briefly.

There is but one living and true God, the Creator of the universe, the Lord of the nations and the God of the spirits of all flesh. Some 4,000 years ago he called Abraham and made a covenant with him, promising not only to bless him but also through his posterity to bless all the families of the earth (Gen 12:1-4). This biblical text is one of the foundation stones of the Christian mission. For Abraham's descendants (through whom all nations are being blessed) are Christ and the people of Christ. If by faith we belong to Christ, we are Abraham's spiritual children and have a responsibility to all

John R.W. Stott is Rector Emeritus of All Souls Church in London, President of the London Institute for Contemporary Christianity. Stott has played a key role in articulating biblical foundations for world evangelization. With others, he helped frame the Lausanne Covenant which has become a touchstone for faithfulness in world evangelization for thousands of mission and church leaders.

Adapted from an address delivered in a plenary session of the Consultation on World Evangelization at Pattaya, Thailand, in June 1980. Used by permission.

mankind. So, too, the Old Testament prophets foretold how God would make his Christ the heir and the light of the nations (Ps 2:8; Isa 42:6, 49:6).

When Jesus came, he endorsed these promises. True, during his own earthly ministry he was restricted "to the lost sheep of the house of Israel" (Matt 10:6, 15:24), but he prophesied that many would "come from east and west, and from north and south," and would "sit at table with Abraham, Isaac, and Jacob in the kingdom of heaven" (Matt 8:11, Luke 13:29). Further, after his resurrection and in anticipation of his ascension he made the tremendous claim that "all authority in heaven and on earth" had been given to him (Matt 28:18). It was in consequence of his universal authority that he commanded his followers to make all nations his disciples, baptizing them into his new community and teaching them all his teaching (Matt 28:19).

And this, when the Holy Spirit of truth and power had come upon them, the early Christians proceeded to do. They became the witnesses of Jesus, even to the ends of the earth (Acts 1:8). Moreover, they did it "for the sake of his name" (Rom 1:5; 3 John 7). They knew that God had superexalted Jesus, enthroning him at his right hand and bestowing upon him the highest rank, in order that every tongue should confess his lordship. They longed that Jesus should receive the honor due to his name. Besides, one day he would return in glory, to save, to judge, and to reign. So what was to fill the gap between his two comings? The worldwide mission of the Church! Not till the gospel had reached the ends of the world, he said, would the end of history come (cf. Matt 24:14, 28:20; Acts 1:8). The two ends would coincide.

Our mandate for world evangelization, therefore, is the whole Bible. It is to be found in the creation of God (because of which all human beings are responsible to him), in the character of God (as outgoing, loving, compassionate, not willing that any should perish, desiring that all should come to repentance), in the promises of God (that all nations will be blessed through Abraham's seed and will become the Messiah's inheritance), in the Christ of God (now exalted with universal authority, to receive universal ac-

claim), in the Spirit of God (who convicts of sin, witnesses to Christ, and impels the church to evangelize) and in the Church of God (which is a multinational, missionary community, under orders to evangelize until Christ returns).

This global dimension of the Christian mission is irresistible. Individual Christians and local churches not committed to world evangelization are contradicting (either through blindness or through disobedience) an essential part of their God-given identity. The biblical mandate for world evangelization cannot be escaped.

Message for World Evangelization

Secondly, the Bible gives us the *message* for world evangelization. The Lausanne Covenant defined evangelism in terms of the evangel. Paragraph four begins: "to evangelize is to spread the good news that Jesus Christ died for our sins and was raised from the dead according to the Scriptures, and that as the reigning Lord he now offers the forgiveness of sins and the liberating gift of the Spirit to all who repent and believe."

Our message comes out of the Bible. As we turn to the Bible for our message, however, we are immediately confronted with a dilemma. On the one hand the message is given to us. We are not left to invent it; it has been entrusted to us as a precious "deposit," which we, like faithful stewards, are both to guard and to dispense to God's household (1 Tim 6:20; 2 Tim 1:12-14; 2 Cor 4:1-2). On the other hand, it has not been given to us as a single, neat, mathematical formula, but rather in a rich diversity of formulations, in which different images or metaphors are used.

So there is only one gospel, on which all the apostles agreed (1 Cor 15:11), and Paul could call down the curse of God upon anybody—including himself—who preached a "different" gospel from the original apostolic gospel of God's grace (Gal 1:6-8). Yet the apostles expressed this one gospel in various ways—now sacrificial (the shedding and sprinkling of Christ's blood), now messianic (the breaking in of God's promised rule), now legal (the Judge pronouncing the unrighteous righteous), now personal (the Father reconciling his wayward children), now salvific (the heavenly Liberator coming to rescue the helpless), now cosmic (the universal Lord claiming universal dominion); and this is only a selection.

The gospel is thus seen to be one, yet diverse. It is "given," yet culturally adapted to its audience. Once we grasp this, we shall be saved from making two opposite mistakes. The first I will call "total fluidity." I recently heard an English church leader declare that there is no such thing as the gospel until we enter the situation in which we are to witness. We take nothing with us into the situation, he said; we discover the gospel only when we have arrived there. Now I am in full agreement with the need to be sensitive to each situation, but if this was the point which the leader in question was wanting to make, he grossly overstated it. There is such a thing as a revealed or given gospel, which we have no liberty to falsify.

The opposite mistake I will call "total rigidity." In this case the evangelist behaves as if God had given a series of precise formulas that we have to repeat more or less word for word, and certain images that we must invariably employ. This leads to bondage to either words or images or both. Some evangelists lapse into the use of stale jargon, while others feel obliged on every occasion to mention "the blood of Christ" or "justification by faith" or "the kingdom of God" or some other image.

> In order to reveal himself, he both emptied and humbled himself. That is the model of evangelism which the Bible supplies.

Between these two extremes there is a third and better way. It combines commitment to the fact of revelation with commitment to the task of contextualization. It accepts that only the biblical formulations of the gospel are permanently normative, and that every attempt to proclaim the gospel in modern idiom must justify itself as an authentic expression of the biblical gospel.

But if it refuses to jettison the biblical formulations, it also refuses to recite them in a wooden and unimaginative way. On the contrary, we have to engage in the continuous struggle (by prayer, study, and discussion) to relate the given gospel to the given situation. Since it comes from God we must guard it; since it is intended for modern men and women we must interpret it. We have to combine fidelity (constantly studying the biblical text) with sensitivity (constantly studying the contemporary scene). Only then can we hope with faithfulness and relevance to relate the Word to the world, the gospel to the context, Scripture to culture.

Model for World Evangelization

Thirdly, the Bible gives us the *model* for world evangelization. In addition to a message (what we are to say) we need a model (how we are to say it). The Bible supplies this too: for the Bible does not just *contain* the gospel; it *is* the gospel. Through the Bible God is himself actually evangelizing, that is, communicating the good news to the world. You will recall Paul's statement about Genesis 12:3 that "the Scripture…preached the gospel beforehand to Abraham" (Gal 3:8; RSV). All Scripture preaches the gospel; God evangelizes through it.

If, then, Scripture is itself divine evangelization, it stands to reason that we can learn how to preach the gospel by considering how God has done it. He has given us in the process of biblical inspiration a beautiful evangelistic model.

What strikes us immediately is the greatness of God's condescension. He had sublime truth to reveal about himself and his Christ, his mercy and his justice, and his full salvation. And he chose to make this disclosure through the vocabulary and grammar of human language, through human beings, human images, and human cultures.

Yet through this lowly medium of human words and images, God was speaking of his own Word. Our evangelical doctrine of the inspiration of Scripture emphasizes its double authorship. Men spoke and God spoke. Men spoke from God (2 Pet 1:21) and God spoke through men (Heb 1:1). The words spoken and written were equally his and theirs. He decided what he wanted to say, yet did not smother their human personalities. They used their faculties freely, yet did not distort the divine message. Christians want to assert something similar about the Incarnation, the climax of the self-communicating God. "The Word became flesh" (John 1:14). That is, God's eternal Word, who from eternity was with God and was God, the agent through whom the universe was created, became a human being, with all the particularity of a first-century Palestinian Jew. He became little, weak, poor, and vulnerable. He experienced pain and hunger, and exposed himself to temptation. All this was included in the "flesh," the human being he became. Yet when he became one of us, he did not cease to be himself. He remained forever the eternal Word or Son of God.

Essentially the same principle is illustrated in both the inspiration of the Scripture and the incarnation of the Son. The Word became flesh. The divine was communicated through the human. He identified with us, though without surrendering his own identity. And this principle of "identification without loss of identity" is the model for all evangelism, especially cross-cultural evangelism.

Some of us refuse to identify with the people we claim to be serving. We remain ourselves, and do not become like them. We stay aloof. We hold on desperately to our own cultural inheritance in the mistaken notion that it is an indispensable part of our identity. We are unwilling to let it go. Not only do we maintain our own cultural practices with fierce tenacity, but we treat the cultural inheritance of the land of our adoption without the respect it deserves. We thus practice a double kind of cultural imperialism, imposing our own culture on others and despising theirs. But this was not the way of Christ, who emptied himself of his glory and humbled himself to serve.

Other cross-cultural messengers of the gospel make the opposite mistake. So determined are they to identify with the people to whom they go that they surrender even their Christian standards and values. But again this was not Christ's way, since in becoming human he remained truly divine. The Lausanne Covenant expressed the principle in these words: "Christ's evangelists must humbly seek to empty themselves of all but their personal authenticity, in order to become the servants of others" (paragraph 10).

We have to wrestle with the reasons why people reject the gospel, and in particular give due weight to the cultural factors. Some people reject the gospel not because they perceive it to be false, but because they perceive it to be alien.

Dr. René Padilla was criticized at Lausanne [*the 1974 Congress on World Evangelization—ed.*] for saying that the gospel some European and North American missionaries have exported was a "culture-Christianity," a Christian message that is distorted by the materialistic, consumer culture of the West. It was hurtful to us to hear him say this, but of course he was quite right. All of us need to subject our gospel to more critical scrutiny, and in a cross-cultural situation, visiting evangelists need humbly to seek the help of local Christians in order to discern the cultural distortions of their message.

Others reject the gospel because they perceive it to be a threat to their own culture. Of course Christ challenges every culture. Whenever we present the gospel to Hindus or Buddhists, Jews or Muslims, secularists or Marxists, Jesus Christ confronts them with his demand to dislodge whatever has thus far secured their allegiance and replace it with himself. He is Lord of every person and every culture. That threat, that confrontation, cannot be avoided. But does the gospel we proclaim present people with other threats that are unnecessary, because it calls for the abolition of harmless customs or appears destructive of national art, architecture, music, and festivals, or because we who share it are culture-proud and culture-blind?

To sum up, when God spoke to us in Scripture he used human language, and when he spoke to us in Christ he assumed human flesh. In order to reveal himself, he both emptied and humbled himself. That is the model of evangelism which the Bible supplies. There is self-emptying and self-humbling in all authentic evangelism; without it we contradict the gospel and misrepresent the Christ we proclaim.

Power for World Evangelization

Fourthly, the Bible gives us the *power* for world evangelization. It is hardly necessary for me to emphasize our need for power, for we know how feeble our human resources are in comparison with the magnitude of the task. We also know how armor-plated are the defenses of the human heart. Worse still, we know the personal reality, malevolence and might of the Devil, and of the demonic forces at his command.

Sophisticated people may ridicule our belief, and caricature it, too, in order to make their ridicule more plausible. But we evangelical Christians are naive enough to believe what Jesus and his apostles taught. To us it is a fact of great solemnity that, in John's expression, "the whole world is in the power of the evil one" (1 John 5:19). For until they are liberated by Jesus Christ and transferred into his kingdom, all men and women are the slaves of Satan. Moreover, we see his power in the contemporary world—in the darkness of idolatry and of the fear of spirits, in superstition and fatalism, in devotion to gods which are no gods, in the selfish materialism of the West, in the spread of atheistic communism, in the proliferation of irrational cults, in violence and aggression, and in the widespread declension from absolute standards of goodness and truth. These things are the work of him who is called in Scripture a liar, a deceiver, a slanderer, and a murderer.

So Christian conversion and regeneration remain miracles of God's grace. They are the culmination of a power struggle between Christ and Satan or (in vivid apocalyptic imagery) between the Lamb and the Dragon. The plundering of the strong man's palace is possible only because he has been bound by the One who is stronger still, and who by his death and resurrection disarmed and discarded the principalities and powers of evil (Matt 12:27-29; Luke 11:20-22; Col 2:15).

How then shall we enter into Christ's victory and overthrow the Devil's power? Let Luther answer our question: *ein wörtlein will ihn fällen* ("one little word will knock him down"). There is power in the Word of God and in the preaching of the gospel. Perhaps the most dramatic expression of this in the New Testament is to be found in 2 Corinthians 4. Paul portrays "the god of this world" as having "blinded the minds of the unbelievers, to keep them from seeing the light of the gospel of the glory of Christ..." (v. 4).

If human minds are blinded, how then can they ever see? Only by the creative Word of God. For it is the God who said "let light shine out of darkness" who has shone in our hearts to "give the light of the knowledge of the glory of God in the face of Christ" (v. 6). The apostle thus likens the unregenerate heart to the dark primeval chaos and attributes regeneration to the divine fiat, "Let there be light."

If then Satan blinds people's minds, and God shines into people's hearts, what can we hope to contribute to this encounter? Would it not be more modest for us to retire from the field of conflict and leave them to fight it out? No, this is not the conclusion Paul reaches.

On the contrary, in between verses 4 and 6, which describe the activities of God and Satan, verse 5 describes the work of the evangelist: "We preach...Jesus Christ as Lord." Since the light which the Devil wants to prevent people seeing and which God shines into them is the gospel, we had better preach it! Preaching the gospel, far from being unnecessary, is indispensable. It is the God-appointed means by which the prince of darkness is defeated and the light comes streaming into people's hearts. There is power in God's gospel—his power for salvation (Rom 1:16).

We may be very weak. I sometimes wish we were weaker. Faced with the forces of evil, we are often tempted to put on a show of Christian strength and engage in a little evangelical saber rattling. But it is in our weakness that Christ's strength is made perfect and it is words of human weakness that the Spirit endorses with his power. So it is when we are weak that we are strong (1 Cor 2:1-5; 2 Cor 12:9-10).

> The Word of God will prove its divine origin by its divine power. Let's let it loose in the world!

Let It Loose in the World!

Let us not consume all our energies arguing about the Word of God; let's start using it. It will prove its divine origin by its divine power. Let's let it loose in the world! If only every Christian missionary and evangelist proclaimed the biblical gospel with faithfulness and sensitivity, and every Christian preacher were a faithful expositor of God's Word! Then God would display his saving power.

Without the Bible world evangelization is impossible. For without the Bible we have no gospel to take to the nations, no warrant to take it to them, no idea of how to set about the task, and no hope of any success. It is the Bible that gives us the mandate, the message, the model, and the power we need for world evangelization. So let's seek to repossess it by diligent study and meditation. Let's heed its summons, grasp its message, follow its directions, and trust its power. Let's lift up our voices and make it known.

Study Questions

1. How does Stott support his idea that the whole Bible is the mandate for world evangelization?

2. In the section, referring to "the Message" of world evangelization, Stott clarifies his point by identifying a range of mistakes: "total fluidity" and "total rigidity." Compare these extremes with the similar description of mistakes of identification in the section referring to "The Model."

3. What is the connection between the power of God and the weakness of God's human servants in overcoming evil?

The Biblical Foundation for the Worldwide Mission Mandate

Johannes Verkuyl

The 20th Century has produced a steady stream of literature which regards the Old Testament as an indispensable and irreplaceable base for the Church's missionary task among the nations and peoples of this world. As one who has made frequent use of the literature, I wish to look at four motifs in the Old Testament which form the indispensable basis for the New Testament call to the Church to engage in worldwide mission work: the universal motif, the motif of rescue and saving, the missionary motif, and the antagonistic motif.

The Universal Motif

The God who in the Old Testament identifies himself as the God of Abraham, Isaac and Jacob, and who discloses to Moses his personal name, Yahweh, is the God of the whole world. The experience of a few patriarchs and later the one nation of Israel with this God expands to include the horizon of the entire world. We shall cite only a few of the Old Testament passages to illustrate this universal motif.

The Table of Nations in Genesis 10

Genesis 10, with its passage listing the table of nations, is important for understanding the universal motif of the Old Testament. Gerhard von Rad described it as the conclusion to the history of the Creation. All of the nations issue forth from the creative hand of God and stand under his watchful eye of patience and judgment. The nations are not mere decorations incidental to the real drama between God and man; rather, the nations—that is, mankind as a whole—are part of the drama itself. God's work and activity are directed at the whole of humanity.

This is one of the fundamental truths of Genesis 1-11, the record of history's beginning; it is also found in the moving account of history's end, the book of John's Revelation. The very God who revealed himself to Israel and dwelt among us in Jesus Christ identifies himself as the Alpha and Omega, the beginning and the ending. He does not lay down his work until "every tongue and nation" and "a multitude without number" have been gathered round his throne (Rev 5:9-10 and 7:9-17). God is cutting a path

Johannes Verkuyl was formerly Professor and Head of the Department of Missiology and Evangelism at the Free University of Amsterdam. In 1940 he went to Indonesia as a missionary and spent three years in a Japanese concentration camp. The author of over 250 books and articles, he is now retired.

Excerpted from *Contemporary Missiology: An Introduction*, 1978. Used by permission of Wm B. Eerdmans Publishing Co.

directly through the weary and plodding activities of men in history in order to achieve his goals among the nations.

God's Election of Israel with His Eye on the Nations

After the Bible finishes its account of God's judgment of the nations, so graphically described in the Genesis passage about the Tower of Babel, in chapter 12 it shifts to God's call to Abraham to leave Ur of the Chaldees. The "God of the whole earth" seems at first glance to narrow his interests to the private history of one family and tribe only, but in actuality nothing could be farther from the truth. In de Groot's words, "Israel is the opening word in God's proclaiming salvation, not the Amen."[1] For a time Israel, the "people of Abraham," is separated from the other nations (Ex 19:3ff.; Deut 7:14ff.), but only so that through Israel God can pave the way toward achieving his world-embracing goals. In choosing Israel as a segment of all humanity, God never took his eye off the other nations; Israel was a minority called to serve the majority.[2]

God's election of Abraham and Israel concerns the whole world. He deals so intensely with Israel precisely because he is maintaining his personal claim on the whole world. To speak to this world in the fullness of time, he needed a people. Countless recent studies are emphasizing this very point: God chose Israel in preparation for the complete unwrapping and disclosure of his universal intentions.

Whenever Israel forgot that God chose her with a view to speaking to the other nations and turned away from them in introverted pride, prophets like Amos, Jeremiah and Isaiah lashed out at the people's ethnocentric pretension and charged them with subverting God's actual intentions (see especially Amos 9:9-10).

The Breakthrough of the Universal Motif in the Exile

Israel's experiences during the seventh and sixth centuries B.C. opened her eyes to God's universal intentions. As Israel passed through her catastrophic experience of being trounced by the Babylonians and carted off into exile, the prophets came to see how closely the ca-

reer of Israel was tied in with the history of the nations. Out of the judgment which Israel was feeling there blossomed the eager hope of a new covenant, a new exodus, another Son of David. Jeremiah, Ezekiel and Isaiah all saw the horizon expanding and bore witness that all nations now fall within the spotlight of God's promises. The apocalyptic vision of Daniel predicts the coming of the Son of Man whose kingdom shall put an end to the brutish kingdoms of the world and whose domain shall include all peoples (Dan 7:1-29).

The Motif of Rescue and Liberation

Yahweh, the Redeemer of Israel

The soteriological theme of the Bible, that is, God's work of rescuing and saving both Israel and the other nations, is tied closely to the theme of universalism. Yahweh, the God of all the earth, displayed his love and kept his word to Israel by freeing her from the bonds of slavery with his strong and outstretched arm (see Deut 9:26; 13:5; 15:15; 24:18). This was a basic part of Israel's credo and crucial to understanding the first commandment. This God—the one who saves and frees—alone is God. "You shall have no other gods before me" (Ex 20). This credo transformed Israel from being merely one nation among others into the chosen community which owes its very existence to God's act of deliverance and returns its praises to him in psalms and prayers of thanksgiving.

Yahweh, the Redeemer of the Nations

The prophets of Israel grew increasingly aware that not only Israel would share in God's acts of redemption. God would break in to restore his liberating Lordship over the entire world of the nations.

In their studies, Sundkler and Blauw point out that the prophets develop this theme centripetally; that is, after their rescue the other nations make their pilgrimage back to Zion, the mountain of the Lord. The prophets picture the people of the other nations as returning to Jerusalem, where the God of Israel shall appear as the God of all the peoples (see Isa 2:1-4; Mic 4:1-4; Jer 3:17; Isa 25:6-9; Isa 60; Zech 8:20ff).

Several psalms chant this theme, too. Psalm 87 proclaims Jerusalem as the ecumenical city whose citizens shall some day include inhabitants of the various nations, even from those nations who once most ardently opposed the God of Israel. They shall join in celebrating God's restored fellowship with the peoples.

God's Method of Achieving Liberation

The Bible also describes the means God is using to bring salvation to Israel and the nations. No other Old Testament passage probes more deeply into this matter than the so-called "Servant" songs of Isaiah 40-55. These Servant songs make unmistakable reference to the spread of salvation through the whole world. The Servant shall carry it to the ends of the earth (Isa 49:6), and he will not stop until righteousness prevails throughout the earth. The coastlands are awaiting his instruction (Isa 42:4).

The fourth Servant song in chapter 53 uncovers the secret of *how* the Servant of the Lord shall discharge his mission. This deeply moving passage depicts the Servant becoming a victim of the most savage human butchery.

Every kind of mistreatment human minds can devise shall be done to him. However, the Servant also at that point shall be acting as a substitute who is incurring the judgment of God which was properly due not only to Israel but to all peoples and nations. Moreover, this passage describes the nations as Yahweh's gifts to the Servant in return for his willing obedience to suffer death. He achieved the right to bring salvation and healing to all people.

The Missionary Motif

Connected with the other two Old Testament motifs mentioned previously is the missionary motif. The prophets never tire of reminding Israel that her election is not a privilege which she may selfishly keep for herself; election is a call to service. It involves a duty to witness among the nations. Israel must be a sign to the other nations that Yahweh is both Creator and Liberator. One Servant song (Isa 49:6) refers to Israel's mandate to become a light to the nations.

Virtually every author who attempts to explain this call to Israel comes up with the concept of presence. Chosen by God to become the special recipients of his mercy and justice, Israel now has the corresponding duty to live as the people of God among the other nations in order to show them his grace, mercy, justice, and liberating power. Time and time again the prophets recorded their deep disappointment over Israel's continual sabotage of her divine calling. But however hot their righteous anger burned against Israel's disobedience, the prophets kept on reminding Israel to the very end of her mandate to be present among the people as distinct people and a royal priesthood.

It is worth noting that since the Second World War, a number of missiologists have urged Christian presence as one of the leading methods of engaging in today's mission work. For a variety of reasons and in a variety of manners, they claim that the most suitable form of witness lies in simply being a specific kind of people while living among other people. This is not the place to develop this idea further but only to point out that the idea that presence is witness has deep roots in the Old Testament. The prophets continually claimed that by her very act of living out her divine appointment to serve, Israel becomes a sign and bridge for the other nations.

However, I do not believe it is correct to view the missionary motif only in terms of the concept of presence. I simply do not understand why various writers make such a point of avowing that the Old Testament makes absolutely no mention of a missionary mandate.

In his book *Mission in the New Testament*, Hahn says, for example, that the Old Testament bears a "completely passive character." In my opinion this is an exaggeration. Bachli's book *Israel and die Volker* is closer to the truth by noting that the Exodus account and the Deuteronomic tradition distinguish between *am* ("people") and *qahat* ("the religious community") and expressly mention that already in the desert many individuals had joined the *qahat* who had not been original members of the *am*. The heathen people too who had come along with Israel and dwelt as strangers among God's people, participated in Israel's worship. They heard of God's mighty deeds and joined Israel in songs of praise.

Then there is that striking number of individuals who left their heathen origins and by word-and-deed witness were won over to trust and serve the living God who had shown them mercy. The stories of Melchizedek, Ruth,

Job, the people of Nineveh described in the book of Jonah, and many others in the Old Testament are windows, as it were, through which we may look out on the vast expanse of people outside the nation of Israel and hear the faint strains of the missionary call to all people already sounding forth.

The wisdom literature of the Old Testament is similar in both form and content to both Greek and Egyptian cultures. Without doubt, her own literature served Israel as a means of communicating her beliefs to the other nations.

Moreover, there is no other way of explaining the powerful missionary impact of Judaism during the Diaspora than to affirm that those dispersed Jews *from their earliest days* had heard and understood their call to witness directly as well as by their presence.

The Motif of Antagonism

The above list of Old Testament missionary motifs is incomplete. Intricately connected with each of those mentioned above is the antagonistic motif, that is, Yahweh's powerful wrestling against those powers and forces which oppose his liberating and gracious authority.

The whole Old Testament (and the New Testament as well) is filled with descriptions of how Yahweh-Adonai, the covenant God of Israel, is waging war against those forces which try to thwart and subvert his plans for his creation. He battles against those false gods which human beings have fashioned from the created world, idolized, and used for their own purposes. Think, for example, of the Baals and the Ashtaroth, whose worshipers elevated nature, the tribe, the state and the nation to a divine status. God fights against magic and astrology which, according to Deuteronomy, bend the line between God and his creation. He contends against every form of social injustice and pulls off every cloak under which it seeks to hide (see Amos and Jeremiah, for example).

The whole of the Old Testament burns with a feverish desire to defeat these opposing powers. There are grand visions of that coming kingdom where every relationship is properly restored and when the whole of creation—people, animals, plants, and every other creature—will be in perfect accord with God's intentions for it (see Isa 2, Mic 4, and

Isa 65). The Old Testament longs for this kingdom's final revealing and categorically states its promise that Yahweh shall indeed finally overcome. This too is a highly significant theme for missionary participation. To participate in mission is quite impossible unless one also wages war against every form of opposition to God's intentions wherever it be found, whether in churches, the world of the nations, or one's own life.

The Old Testament ties the antagonistic motif closely with the doxological theme: the glory of Yahweh-Adonai shall be revealed among all peoples. Then every human being shall come to know him as he really is, the "gracious and merciful God, slow to get angry, full of kindness, and always willing to turn back from meting out disaster" (Jonah 4:1-2).

The Book of Jonah

The book of Jonah is so significant for understanding the biblical basis of mission because it treats God's mandate to his people regarding the Gentile peoples and thus serves as the preparatory step to the missionary mandate of the New Testament. But it is also important for catching a glimpse of the deep resistance this mandate encounters from the very servant Yahweh has chosen to discharge his worldwide work.

Today there is much talk and writing about "educating the congregation" and "educating personnel" for mission. Jonah is a lesson in educating a person to be a missionary: it reveals the need for a radical conversion of one's natural tendencies and a complete restructuring of his life to make it serviceable for mission.

Background of the Book

The title of the book is the personal name of the unwilling prophet, Jonah, and harks back to the days of King Jeroboam II (787-746 B.C.) when a prophet named Jonah ben Amittai was living. It is obvious, however, that this *midrash* is intended for reasons quite other than detailing the events of this prophet's life. The author uses this personal name to portray for his readers a missionary who has no heart for the Gentiles and who, like the later Pharisees, cannot tolerate a God who shows them mercy. In the words of the Dutch author Miskotte, "the writer intends to picture a person who is the exact opposite of an apostle." The author of Jonah warns his readers against this intolerant attitude and sets before each of them the question of whether he or she is willing to be transformed into a servant who works to accomplish the mandates of God.

As the author sees it, Israel has become so preoccupied with herself that she no longer directs her eyes toward the world of the nations. Israel, the recipient of all God's revelation, refuses to set foot in alien territory to tell the other peoples God's message of judgment and liberation. But the message of the book also is addressed to the New Testament congregation which tries various ways of evading her Lord's command to speak his message to the world.

Jonah's crafty evasion efforts represent a lazy and unfaithful Church which does not heed its Lord's command. God has to wrestle against Israel's narrow ethnocentrism which tries to restrict his activity to the boundaries of Israel alone and against the Church's ecclesiocentric refusal to go out into the world to proclaim God's message and do his work. The writer is bent on convincing his readers that the radius of God's liberating activity is wide enough to cover both Israel and the Gentiles.

It is a miracle that Jonah, with its strong warning against ethnocentrism, ever made its way into the canon of Scripture. It squarely sets forth man's attempt to sabotage God's worldwide plans so that its readers—Israel, the New Testament church, and us—can hear what the Holy Spirit through the medium of this little book is trying to tell them.

A Short Review of the Book's Eight Scenes

The first scene opens with Jonah receiving the command to go to Nineveh. While the Old Testament usually appeals to the other nations to *come* to Zion, the mountain of God, Jonah, like the disciples of the New Testament (cf. Matt 28:18-20), is told to *go*! The Septuagint translation of Jonah uses the word *poreuomai* in 1:2-3 and again in 3:2-3, the very same verb used by Jesus in his Great Commission recorded in Matthew 28. Where must Jonah go? To Nineveh, of all places. Nineveh, a very center of totalitarianism, brutality, and warlike attitudes. To Nineveh, notorious for the shameful hounding, vicious torture, and

imperialist brazenness it reserved for those who chose to oppose its policies. God wants his servant to warn Nineveh of impending judgment and to call her to repentance. He wants to save *Nineveh*!

But Jonah refuses. He prepares himself, to be sure, but only to *flee* from the face of God who is Lord over all.

In the second, scene God responds to Jonah's flight by sending a mighty storm (1:4-16). The wind obeys Yahweh's commands, but the disobedient Jonah sleeps in the bottom of the boat, oblivious of the fact that the storm is directed at him. At times the Church, too, sleeps right through the storm of God's judgment passing over the world, assuring herself that the wind outside has nothing to do with her. While the crew vainly searches for the storm's cause, Jonah confesses that he worships and fears the God who made both the sea and the dry land, the one God who is above all nations. This God, he claims, is bringing a charge against him, and the only way to quiet the waters is to throw him into the sea. In this scene the crew represents the Gentiles, a people for whom Jonah is totally unconcerned, and yet who themselves are interested in sparing his life. After a second order from Jonah, they throw him overboard and the storm ceases. Scarcely able to believe their eyes, the sailors break forth in praise to the God of Jonah. Their obedience surpasses that of the saboteur Jonah: they are more open to God than the very prophet himself.

The third scene (1:17) describes a large fish which, at Yahweh's instructions, opens its mouth to swallow Jonah and spew him onto the shore at the appropriate time. Jonah simply cannot escape God's missionary mandate. The God who whipped up the stormy winds and directed the sailors to accomplish his purposes now guides a fish as part of his plan to save Nineveh. Yahweh continues his work of reforming and preparing his missionary to be a fit instrument in his plans.

In the fourth scene (2:1-10), Jonah implores God to rescue him from the belly of the fish. He who had no mercy on the Gentiles and refused to acknowledge that God's promises extended to them now appeals for divine mercy, and by quoting lines from various psalms, pants after those promises claimed by worshipers in God's temple.

Yahweh reacts. He speaks to the brute beast and Jonah lands on shore safe and sound. By his very rescue, Jonah was unwittingly a witness of God's saving mercy. Though covered with seaweed, Jonah was nonetheless a testimony that God takes no delight in the death of sinners and saboteurs but rather rejoices in their conversion.

In the fifth scene (3:1-4), God repeats his order to the man whose very life affirms the truth of what he confessed in the belly of the fish: "Salvation is from Yahweh." The Septuagint uses the term *kerygma* in 3:1-2ff. That single word summarizes Jonah's mission: he must *proclaim* that Nineveh, however godless she may be, is still the object of God's concern, and unless she repents, she will be destroyed. His message must be one of threat as well as promise, of judgment as well as gospel.

In the sixth scene (3:5-10), Nineveh responds to Jonah's appeal to repent. The proud, despotic king steps down from his royal throne, exchanges his robes for dust and ashes, and enjoins every man and animal to follow his example. What Israel continually refused to do the heathen Gentiles did do: the cruel king of Nineveh stands as antitype to the disobedient kings of Judah.

The people join the king in repenting. They cease all their devilish work and the terrifying and coercing engines of political injustice come to a halt. In deep penitence they turn away from idols to serve the God who is Lord of every nation and all creation. All this becomes possible because Yahweh is God. The world of the heathen is a potentially productive mission field for no other reason than this: He alone is God.

The curtain closes on this scene with these amazing words: "God saw what they did, and how they abandoned their wicked ways, and he repented and did not bring upon them the disaster he had threatened." Yahweh is faithful to his promises. Still today his will for Moscow and Peking, for London and Amsterdam, is no less "gracious and full of mercy" than it was for Nineveh. To borrow from Luther, who loved to preach from the book of Jonah, the left hand of God's wrath is replaced by his right hand of blessing and freedom.

The seventh scene (4:1-4) recounts the fact that the greatest hurdle to overcome in discharging the missionary mandate was not the sailors, nor the fish, nor Nineveh's king and citizenry, but rather Jonah himself—the recalcitrant and narrow-minded Church. Chapter 4 describes Jonah, who has long since departed the city to find shelter east of the borders. The forty-day period of repentance has passed, but since God has changed his mind about destroying it, the city continues to be nourished by Yahweh's grace and mercy. Jonah is furious that God has extended his mercy beyond the borders of Israel to the Gentiles. He wanted a God cut according to his own pattern: a cold, hard, cruel-natured god with an unbending will set against the heathen. He cannot stand to think of the Gentiles as part of salvation history

This is Jonah's sin, the sin of a missionary whose heart is not in it. He who once pleaded with God for mercy from the desolate isolation of a fish's belly now is angry that this God shows mercy to the nations. He vents his fury in the form of a prayer found in 4:2, the key text of the whole book: "And he prayed to the Lord, 'This, O Lord, is what I feared when I was in my own country, and to forestall it I tried to escape to Tarshish: I knew that thou art a gracious and compassionate God, long-suffering and ever constant, and always willing to repent of the disaster.'" Part of the text comes from an ancient Israelite liturgy which every Israelite knew by heart and could rattle off in worship at the temple or synagogue while half- asleep (cf. Ex 34:6; Ps 86:15: 103:8, 145:8, Neh 9:17). But Jonah cannot stand to think that this liturgy is true not only for Jerusalem, the location of God's temple, but for other places as well—Nineveh, Sao Paulo, Nairobi, New York and Paris.

Why is Jonah really so angry? For no other reason than that God is treating those outside his covenant the same as he is those within. But Jonah's anger in effect is putting himself outside the covenant, for he obstinately refuses to acknowledge the covenant's purpose—to bring salvation to the heathen. He had not yet learned that Israel could not presume upon some special favors from God. Both Israel and the Gentiles alike live by the grace which the Creator gives to all of his creatures. So God comes to his prophet, but no longer as a covenant partner; he comes as the Creator and asks his creature: "Do you have a right to be so angry?"

In the eighth and last scene (4:5-11), one can see God still working to teach his thick-skulled missionary his lessons. He did not catch the point of the storm, the sailors, the fish, and Nineveh's conversion because he did not want to. Now Yahweh tries one more approach—the miraculous tree. A climbing gourd springs up quickly, offers Jonah protection against the beating sun, but as quickly withers and dies, the victim of an attacking worm. Jonah is peeved.

At that point God again turns to his missionary-student, using the tree as his object lesson. The very God who directs the whole course of history, rules the wind and waves and turned Nineveh's millions to repentance now asks tenderly: "Are you so angry over the gourd? You are sorry about the gourd, though you had nothing to do with growing it, a plant which came up in a night and withered in a night. And should not I be sorry for the great city of Nineveh, with its 120,000 who cannot tell their right hand from their left, and cattle without number?"

God spares and rescues. Jerusalem's God is Nineveh's as well. Unlike Jonah, he has no "Gentile complex." And while he never forces any one of us, he tenderly asks us to put our whole heart and soul into the work of mission. God is still interested in transforming obstinate, irritable, depressive, peevish Jonahs into heralds of the Good News which brings freedom.

The book ends with an unsettling question which is never answered: "God reached his goal with Nineveh, but what about Jonah?" No one knows. The question of Israel and the Church and their obedience is still an open one.

The question is one which every generation of Christians must answer for itself. Jacques Ellul closes his book *The Judgment of Jonah* with these words: "The Book of Jonah has no conclusion, and the final question of the book has no answer, except from the one who realizes the fullness of the mercy of God and who factually and not just mythically accomplishes the salvation of the world." [3]

The New Testament church must pay close heed to the message of Jonah's book. Jesus Christ is "One greater than Jonah" (Matt 12:39-41, Luke 11:29-32). His death on the cross with its awful cry of God-forsakenness and his resurrection with its jubilant shout of victory are signs of Jonah for us, pointing to the profound meaning of his whole life and clearly attesting that God loved the whole world so much. If a person draws his lifeblood from the one greater than Jonah and yet declines to spread the Good News among others, he in effect is sabotaging the aims of God himself. Jonah is father to all those Christians who desire the benefits and blessings of election but refuse its responsibility. Thomas Carlisle's poem "You Jonah" closes with these lines:

> And Jonah stalked
> to his shaded seat
> and waited for God
> to come around
> to his way of thinking.
> And God is still waiting for a host of Jonahs
> in their comfortable houses
> to come around
> to his way of loving.

End Notes

1. A. de Groot, *De Bijbel over het Heil der Volken* (Roermond: Romens, 1964).
2. See J. Verkuyl, *Break Down the Walls*, trans. and ed. Lewis B. Smedes (Grand Rapids: Eerdmans, 1973), p. 40.
3. Jacques Ellul, *The Judgment of Jonah* (Grand Rapids: Eerdmans, 1971), p. 103.

Study Questions

1. Why does Verkuyl disagree with various writers who claim the Old Testament makes no mention of a missionary mandate?

2. Jonah is a lesson in the need for a radical conversion of one's natural tendencies and a complete restructuring of one's life to make it serviceable for mission. What were the natural tendencies and restructuring that had to be done in Jonah's life? How was this same need typified in the nation of Israel?

The Story of His Glory

Steven C. Hawthorne

T he Bible is basically a story about God. When we turn to the Bible as a self-help book, we end up bored or frustrated with what seems to be a rambling collection of stories. What if the Bible is more about God than it is about us? How thrilling to discover that every element of scripture—the reports of events, the verses of distilled wisdom, the lyrical prophecies—converge in one central saga of one worthy Person.

We're used to the idea that the Bible is a true story. It's so true that the story is still unfolding to this minute. We are used to hearing that the Bible is a love story. But we tend to see only one side of the love: how God loves people. If the main point of the Bible is that God is to be loved with heart, soul, mind and strength, perhaps it would be wise to read the entire story from God's point of view. When we look at it all from God's viewpoint, the grand love story finally makes sense: God is not just loving people. He is transforming them to become people who can fully love Him. God is drawing people as worshipers to offer freely to Him their love-inspired glory.

God can be loved only when He is known. That's why the story of the Bible is the story of God revealing Himself in order to draw to Himself obedient worship, or glory, from the nations. With God's passionate love at the core, the Bible is truly the story of His glory.

BASIC CONCEPTS OF GLORY

To trace the story of God as the Bible presents it, we need a grasp of three related ideas which define the story at every juncture: glory, the name of God and worship.

Glory

Don't be thrown off by the religious-sounding word "glory." Glory is the relational beauty that every person's heart yearns to behold and even to enter. The word "glory" in scripture refers to the essential worth, beauty and value of people, created things and, of course, the Creator Himself. The Hebrew word for glory is a word meaning weight, substance, and at the same time, brilliance or radiant beauty. To glorify someone is to recognize their intrinsic worth and beauty, and to speak of that feature in a public way. To glorify God is to praise or to speak of Him openly and truth-

Steven C. Hawthorne is the Founder and Director of WayMakers in Austin, Texas. After co-editing the course and book called *Perspectives on the World Christian Movement* in 1981, he launched "Joshua Project" a series of research expeditions among unreached peoples in world class cities. He co-authored (with Graham Kendrick) *Prayerwalking: Praying On Site with Insight,* and has written numerous articles.

fully. Glory is at the heart of true worship throughout the Scriptures:

> All nations whom You have made shall come and worship before You, O Lord; and they shall glorify Your name (Ps 86:9).

> We…worship in the Spirit of God and glory in Christ Jesus…(Phil 3:3).

The idea of "glory" also describes honor that can be given or awarded. When someone is exalted or made great, they are, to some extent, in a biblical sense, glorified. God is so rich in glory that He bestows extravagant honors upon His human servants without compromising His own majesty in the slightest. Jesus exposed our habit of seeking "glory from one another," and yet failing to "seek the glory that is from the one and only God" (John 5:44).

The Name of God

Throughout the larger story, the biblical authors use the idea of the "name of God" as a key idea. To distinguish the functions of reference, revelation and reputation, it may help to sort out the usages with three easy-to-remember categories: *name-tag*, *window* and *fame name*.

Name-tag names

First, there are the names themselves used to designate God in the Bible. God is never anonymous in His story. He uses many names for Himself. Because the function is *reference*, we can call these names, for our purposes, the "name-tag" names of God since a name-tag distinguishes and identifies someone. It is just as true to refer to the God of scripture as "Lord of hosts" as it is to refer to Him as "God Almighty," or "Judge of all the earth" or "King of glory." Each of these names is truly God's name. [1]

Window name

Second, God is pleased to disclose Himself accurately by any of the Biblical names. The function is *revelation*. For example, anyone who spends a few minutes pondering the biblical name "The Lord is my Shepherd" will have a better understanding of the nurturing kindness of God.

Fame name

The third usage of the phrase "the name of God" is the most abundant in the Bible, even though it is little recognized. "God's name" most often refers to the idea of His public renown. I call it God's "fame name." The function is God's *reputation*. God's name is His global namesake. It is the open memory, based on historical incidents, which establishes a reputation worthy of future trust. God's name is the body of truth about Himself which He has displayed and declared in the long-unfolding story of the Bible. The Hebrew people were not only to treasure this story, but they were also to tell it. Unlike the way of many religions, God's revelation was never to be a secret affair for a few people. Isaiah calls Israel to "make known His deeds among the peoples," so that the nations are steadily reminded that "His name is exalted" (Isa 12:4). As we shall see, much of the story of the Bible recounts what God has done to make His name great among the nations.

> God *reveals* glory *to* all nations in order that He might *receive* glory *from* people through worship.

Worship

Why does God want to be known with such precision? God wants to be more than globally famous—He yearns to be truly worshiped.

God Reveals Glory to Receive Glory

God's glory flows in two directions. The first direction of His glory is toward the world. He shows His glory to people throughout the earth. He reveals who He is and what He has done in order to bring about the second direction of glory—that people might give Him glory in loving worship. God *reveals* glory *to* all nations in order that He might *receive* glory *from* people through worship.

Psalm 96 shows these two directions of glory. God mandates a declaration of His glory *to* the nations in verses 2 and 3:

Proclaim good tidings of His salvation
from day to day.
Tell of His glory among the nations,
His wonderful deeds among all the
peoples.

What an eloquent portrayal of the evangelization of the world! But the Psalmist goes on to tell the purpose for world evangelization by describing the second aspect of God's glory: a response of glory *from* the nations toward God in verses 7 to 9:

Give to the LORD, O families of the
peoples,
Give to the LORD glory and strength.
Give to the LORD the glory of His name;
Bring an offering, and come into His
courts.[2]
Worship the LORD in the splendor of
holiness;
Tremble before Him, all the earth."

The heart of mission flows in this amazing economy of glory: God *reveals* His glory *to* all nations in order to *receive* glory *from* all creation.

A Purpose Beyond Salvation

People are indeed saved by the global declaration of God's salvation, but the ultimate value of their salvation is not to be seen in what they are saved *from*, it is what they are saved *for* that really matters. People are saved to serve God in worship. In this respect, we can say that world evangelization is for God. However accustomed we may be to seeing people as being of paramount importance, the Bible is clear: The rationale for mission is the colossal worthiness of God. Examine the logic of Psalm 96:2-4:

Proclaim good tidings of His
salvation....Tell of His glory...among all
peoples. For great is the LORD, and
greatly to be praised; He is to be feared
above all gods.

A Rationale Greater than Supremacy

The rationale for mission seems simple enough: Since God is supreme, every creature should bow down in subjection. But can this really be the logic at the center of the universe? Our hearts won't buy it. There is something more. The Scriptures are loud about the truth that God is love. God calls people to love Him with all that they are. Where is God's love, and ours, in response?

A God who demands worship just because He's supreme doesn't seem like a very loving God. In fact, such a God might not seem like He is worthy to even be admired. God's penchant for praise might make Him appear to be struggling with a low self-image problem. It's foolish to speak of God's jealousy for worship as if He were a petulant tribal deity threatened by rival gods. God is not threatened; rather He is immeasurably saddened by false worship. When people worship anyone or anything besides Him, they become like it. God has better intentions for people.

What is true worship anyway? Worship takes place when people recognize who God is and offer public acknowledgment and freely approach God, personally offering face-to-face gratitude and day-to-day allegiance. Worship is genuine relational interaction with God. That's why God always welcomes us to worship with a gift. He never needs the worship gifts. But the gift brings the giver. That is why the nations are urged to come bringing a gift, offering God tokens of their finest worth (Ps 96:8 and many others). By their sacrifices and gifts, they offer themselves.

Fully Bestowing His Love

Why is God so desirous of worship? Two reasons: He is delighted by the sincere love that comes to Him in true worship. But there is more: By wooing people into true worship, God is able to fully bestow His love upon them. You can see it in Psalm 96:6.

Splendor and majesty are before Him,
Strength and beauty are in His sanctuary.

"Splendor and majesty" do not refer to God's self-experience. Rather, along with "strength and beauty" (the parallel passage says "joy" in 1 Chr 16:27), they are features of God's presence that are to be the experience of people who approach Him in true worship. There can be nothing more splendid or majestic for humans than to be elevated and placed in the gorgeous, heart-stopping grandeur of God's regal presence.

Worship is the way that people glorify God. When looked at from God's point of view, we can see that worship is also God's way of glorifying people—in all the best sense of bringing people into their highest honor. Worship fulfills God's love. He loves people so vastly that He wills to exalt them to something better than greatness; He wants to bring them into an honored nearness to Him. Stretch your mind and your heart as far as you can, but you'll never perceive the extent of what God has prepared for those who love Him (1 Cor 2:9).

Perhaps John got a glimpse of the "splendor and majesty" of those courts in Revelation 5:1-14. He heard all of heaven's myriads raise their voices acclaiming the marvel that God Himself has purchased people from every tribe and tongue. Why has God bought such ignoble humans at the extravagant cost of the blood of His Son? Furthermore, why has He purchased some from every single ethnicity? Of what value are these ones? Their precious value is this: They will be His priests. Some from every people will gladly offer to God the distinctive honors and redeemed glories of their people. Each of the peoples has eternal worth because of Christ's blood. Each of the peoples has an appointed place before Him. God has set His mighty heart to bring them there. It must come forth. The passion of this unrequited love of God for each of the peoples is the very soul of any true missionary enterprise.

> Worship fulfills God's love. He loves people so vastly that He wills to exalt them to something better than greatness; He wants to bring them into an honored nearness to Him.

The psalmist reflects God's zeal for the people groups of earth. God beckons every one of the "families of the peoples," people linked by blood and marriage with generational depth. Each of these extended families has a history and a destiny before God. In formal language they are each invited into His regal presence (Ps 96:7-9). They are not to come empty-handed, but they are to extend to God a sampling of the unique glory and strength of their people. The peoples are to voice praise gifts to God in their many languages, but no people is to offer speculative guesses about what constitutes rightful praise. Only the truth God has revealed about Himself—"the glory of His name"—is the substance and true measure of worthy praise (verse 8).

THE BIBLE AS GOD'S STORY

The Bible is the astounding drama of God's love drawing the worship of the nations. Remember the basic thesis: God *reveals* his glory *to* all peoples so that he may *receive* glory *from* all creation. This double dimension of glory can help make sense out of an apparent jumble of ancient stories.

Abraham

When Abraham arrived in the land of promise, he did not excel as a brilliant missionary, however we might define that role. He's certainly not on record as a great evangelist. He was actually thrown out of Egypt in disgrace (Gen 12:10-20). Abraham's neighbors frightened him into lying about his family. Abraham's rationale for falsely presenting his wife does not reveal an evangelist's confidence that lives might change: "Surely there is no fear of God in this place" (Gen 20:11). But for all his failings, he did the most missionary thing he could have done when he first arrived in the new land: His first act was to establish ongoing public worship of God. "He built an altar to the LORD and called upon the name of the LORD" (Gen 12:7-8). His household may have been the only worshipers at that altar, but God was explicitly worshiped by name and in a public way.

Blessed to Be a Blessing to Be a Blessing
At one point Abraham rescued some of his powerful neighbors from an alliance of marauding nations (Gen 14). After the miraculous victory, Abraham refused to accept the windfall of reward from the king of Sodom. If he accepted the largess, he knew that from that point, he and his family would always be viewed as living under the patronage of that city. Instead he chose to keep himself positioned before the nations as one specifically blessed by God.[3]

With the nations watching, Abraham resolutely named God as the one who would reward and bless him. His bold words (Gen 14:21-24) were substantiated by the gift of goods Abraham offered God. Abraham offered to God the wealth of Sodom as well as that of other nations. He helped foreign nations present a tithe to God, a recognized formal act of worship (Gen 14:18-20). With Melchizedek as presiding priest, Abraham functioned, as a priest, by offering worship gifts on behalf of other nations.

Abraham was blessed in order to be a blessing to the nations (Gen 12:1-3). But the purpose goes beyond the blessing of nations. God Himself is blessed! Melchizedek openly recognized that Abraham was blessed by God. By God's power, Abraham had been a blessing to his neighbors by rescuing enslaved families and their goods. But the grand result was that God Himself would be blessed in praise! Listen to Melchizedek: "Blessed be Abram of God Most High…And blessed be God Most High…" (Gen 14:18-20).

What do we learn from the entire series of events? Abraham made God's name known by his ongoing worship. God made His name great by dramatic redemptive power through His people. The outcome was a multi-national gathering of grateful honor in which God was explicitly worshiped in truth.

Global Purpose Confirmed by Obedience in Worship

The crucial, proving moment of Abraham's life was a worship event (Gen 22). God told Abraham to bring His son Isaac to offer him in an act of worship. It was a test to prove what Abraham and his family would be. Would God find in Abraham an obedient, priestly passion for God (literally, "a fearer of God," Gen 22:12)? Would Abraham prove to be zealous to offer the worship God desired? If so, God would find him to have the kind of faith that God wanted multiplied among the nations. You know the story. At the very moment that Abraham obeyed in worship, God spoke from heaven with solemn oath, declaring forcefully His global purpose to bless the peoples of the earth through Abraham's family (22:18).

The Exodus

God did more for His name than to gain early worship from Abraham. God went global in a big way at the Exodus. At first glance, the story of the Exodus doesn't look like a great missionary event. Thousands of Egyptians died. Grief covered every Egyptian home. What was God doing?

The key passage is Exodus 9:13-16 in which Moses gives an ultimatum to Pharaoh, with a bold word about His purposes:

Thus says the Lord, the God of the Hebrews,

Let My people go, that they may serve Me. For this time I will send all My plagues on you and your servants and your people, *so that you may know that there is no one like me in all the earth*. For if by now I had put forth My hand and struck you and your people with pestilence, you would then have been cut off from the earth. But indeed, for this cause I have allowed you to remain, in order to show you My power, and in *order to proclaim My name through all the earth*'(my italics).

Take note that God never said, "Let My people go!" That's just half the sentence, without the purpose. Take care to hear the entire cry of salvation: "Let my people go, *that they may worship Me!*" (Ex 8:1, 20, 9:1, 13, 10:3) [4]

Pharaoh well understood the entire demand of Moses that the people be released to worship. Pharaoh probably thought that the appeal for a worship vacation was a ploy to disguise plans for escape. Perhaps many of the Hebrews made the same mistake. How many of them may have thought that the plans to worship God in the wilderness were but a ruse to dupe the authorities? Is it any wonder then that many of them remained fixated on matters of comfort, diet, safety and entertainment? They were slow to comprehend that in their escape, God had a purpose for Himself in the sight of the nations. They had turned salvation inside-out: They seriously thought that their rescue was the predominate concern of God. Instead, God was orchestrating a powerful plan to draw the attention of the nations to Himself.

God Brings Global Attention to His Name

God was singling Himself out from all the gods of earth. He was making an "everlasting name" for Himself at the Exodus (Isa 63:11-14 and Neh 9:9-10). He wanted everyone in Egypt and beyond to know that there was absolutely no god like the only living God. He wanted the world to watch a mob of slaves marching in procession to worship Him. God established His reputation as one greater and absolutely different (truly holy, not just holier) than every other deity ever dreamed up by man—an exquisite, almighty, resplendent God. The Exodus was to be a reference point for all subsequent revelation to the world of his character, His holiness, and His power. How did chaos in Egypt reveal the ever-living God?

Judging the Gods of Egypt

Some scholars have noted that every one of the plagues of Egypt was either aimed against the false gods of Egypt or the oppressive power structures that were revered with fanatical zeal.[5] Some Egyptian deities, such as the Nile River, or the great sun god, were embarrassed directly by the plagues of blood and darkness. Other deities were indirectly shamed by exposing their complete inability to do what they were supposed to do.

> **The Exodus events revealed His glory by establishing His name in a global way.**

There were gods who were revered as being able to deal with infestations of insects or to protect cattle from disease. The powerful religious elite was shamed. The deeply revered military was summarily annihilated. Why was God wrecking Egypt before the watching world?

God was executing judgments "against all the gods of Egypt" (Ex 12:12). He was not aiming at destroying people, but devastating one of the most highly regarded collection of false gods in all the earth. If He wanted to destroy the people of Egypt He could have done it quickly. "For if by now I had put forth My hand and struck you..., you would then have been cut off from the earth. But indeed, for this cause I have allowed you to remain...to proclaim My name through all the earth" (Ex 9:15-16).

The Nations Take Notice

Did it work? Did the world take notice of God making His name great? The devastation recorded in the book of Exodus didn't make headlines in Egyptian hieroglyphics, but we should understand that events which put Egypt in a bad light never were chipped into stone.

The Bible reports that the waves of the Red Sea hadn't quite calmed down before Moses led the people in singing, "The LORD is His name....Who is like You among the gods, O LORD? Who is like You, majestic in holiness?" Then they began to list some of the surrounding nations, stating clearly that: "The peoples have heard, and they tremble..." (Ex 15:3,7,15).

Jethro had married into Moses' family, but was still very much a Gentile. He had certainly heard about the God of the Hebrews for years from Moses. Perhaps many peoples and cities had heard something of this great God without trusting or worshiping Him. But listen to Jethro after the plagues of Egypt. "Now I know that the LORD is greater than all the gods; indeed, it was proven when they dealt proudly against the people" (Ex 18:11). Jethro was a leading priest of a foreign people, well-qualified to evaluate religious matters (Ex 18:1).

As we read the story of Moses confronting Egypt today, it might appear that Egypt was just another harsh empire that abused slaves. In Moses' day it was open knowledge that Egypt was a complex of religious, economic, and military powers inextricably enmeshed with spiritual powers. God unraveled the system to show it for what it was at the core— horrid, spiritual evil, dedicated to diverting worshipers from coming to Him. God had blessed Egypt, but Egypt had made itself an enemy of God. God's "judgments" of the plagues and the awesome Red Sea affair (Ex 12:12) are not to be understood as mere punishment for bad deeds. God's intervention put down oppressive evil in order to liberate people. Why were they freed? "Let my people go, *that they may worship Me.*" God had orchestrated the Exodus events so that He revealed His glory by establishing His name in a global way. Then, with the world watching, He drew the people to Himself to establish a way of worship that all other nations could enter.

The Conquest

The conquest of Canaan should be seen in the same light of God winning to Himself a single, holy people of worship. To that people, and by their witness, He will draw every other people to revere and know Him.

Just Recompense

At first glance to modern readers, the conquest may seem like a genocidal land grab rather than an act of a good and loving God. But a close look at the pertinent passages of Scripture shows that God ordained the conquest of Canaan with a double purpose. First, God was bringing just recompense for the "wickedness" of the peoples of the land (Deut 9:5). Long before this God had told Abraham that "the iniquity of the Amorites (was) not yet complete" (Gen 15:16). God had allowed sin to run its full course. We might wonder how the Canaanites felt about God's wrath. The one statement about the conquest recorded from a Canaanite came from a king who acknowledged the righteous execution of God's justice: "As I have done, so God has repaid me" (Judg 1:7).

Demolishing False Worship

The second, and primary reason for the thorough ferocity of the Hebrew conquest was this: God was demolishing systems of false worship in order to preserve the singular devotion of His people and the holiness of His name. Almost every passage describing the rationale behind ousting the peoples living in the land offers this reason: Canaanite worship would swiftly turn the Hebrews "away from following Me to serve other gods." (Deut 4:15-24, 6:13-15, 7:1-8, et al.).

Joshua and Moses both voiced the same God-given rationale for the violence of the conquest: it was, at the core, an annihilation of false worship. God had mandated the destruction so that Israel would never "mention the name of their gods,...or serve them, or bow down to them" (Josh 23:7). While there are difficulties in fully understanding this part of the story of God's people, one thing is clear about the conquest: the point was pure worship. God's objective was not that Israel would be the only people that worshiped Him. His point was to insure that He was the only God that they worshiped.

Idolatry Would Profane the Name

Idolatry doesn't seem to threaten most believers today. The first four commands of the Ten Commandments can mystify or even bore us. Why was God so ferociously passionate about idolatry? Without grasping His global purposes for glory, it may seem that God is over-wrought about a nasty, primitive habit.

But look at idolatry from God's point of view. God had distinguished His name far above any other. Any kind of idolatry would, in effect, profane (that is, bring down as common) God's name, the very name God had just singled out and sounded forth to the world.

Look again at the conquest. The point of the invasion was not that Israel deserved someone else's homeland. God told Israel clearly that they weren't special or favored because of their intrinsic righteousness or their great nobility (Deut 7:6-7). Israel was told repeatedly that God would destroy them just as swiftly if they turned away from His worship to other gods.

The record is clear that the Hebrew people were at several points precariously close to being destroyed. Why? Hadn't God specially loved and saved them? For all the special love God had promised the descendants of Abraham, God was resolute in working for His glory. God was not averse to taking a delay and dealing with another generation. The issue at every juncture was the worship of the people to God and their testimony to His glory.

One instance makes this constant purpose of God clear: the rebellion at Kadesh-Barnea. Israel had followed God through a divinely opened way, and stood on the threshold of fulfilling God's purposes. Spies were sent to check out the land and the people. Ten of the spies spooked the entire people, touching off a hysterical rebellion for self-preservation (Num 13:17-14:10). God was ready to destroy the entire people and start over with Moses, making out of him another people "greater and mightier" than the Hebrews. The point is not that the people had done something so bad that God had become fatally angry. God simply required for His purposes a nation who would at least believe in Him.

Moses actually argues with God, bringing up, as he had in a previous instance (Ex 32:1-14), that the nations were watching. They had heard something of God's name which could be falsified by what God was about to do. "Now if You slay this people as one man, then the nations who have heard of Your fame (literally "name") will say, 'Because the Lord could not bring this people into the land....'" Moses challenges God, telling Him that the nations will conclude that the Hebrew God is weak—all beginnings, but no finish (Num 14:15-16).

Then Moses asks God to magnify Himself according to how God Himself had summarized His name: "The Lord is slow to anger and abundant in lovingkindness, forgiving iniquity and transgression...."[6] A long pause from heaven, and then God said that He had pardoned Israel according to the prayer of Moses. Then God raised His voice, I think, using some of the strongest expressions possible: "But indeed, as I live, all the earth will be filled with the glory of the Lord!" (Num 14:17-21).

What was God saying? That He would continue to use the nation, but wait for another generation. Even though He was taking a delay, He remained everlastingly resolute to bring forth His purpose on earth: to fill the earth with "the glory of the Lord." To fulfill that purpose required an obedient, worshiping, witnessing people.

The Temple

Perhaps the first clear mention of the temple is made on the plains of Moab prior to Joshua leading the people into the land. Moses issues God's directives to destroy "all the places where the nations...serve their gods." Instead of remodeling any of the former places of worship, the shrines were to be completely ruined in order to "obliterate their name from that place." God's name is never to be equivocated with the name of any other deity. Instead, a new and special place would be built, "to establish His name there for His dwelling" (Deut 12:2-14, especially verse 5).

Consider God's declaration of purpose for the temple: "to establish His name there for His dwelling." God wanted to do two things in this special place. First, He wanted to reveal Himself by "His name." It would be a place of revelation as worshipers continually exalt His character and voice the stories and songs about His working. Second, God desired a place of encounter, of relationship, of dwelling. From the earliest mention of a tabernacle God intimated His desire to enjoy an exalted nearness amidst His people, "that I may dwell among them" (Ex 25:8). To "dwell" is a relational affair. It is consummated worship. God coming near His people as they come near to Him. Solomon knew that the temple was not God's domicile. As he dedicated the fabulous structure, he prayed: "But will God indeed dwell with mankind on the earth? Behold, heaven and highest heaven cannot contain You; how much less this house which I have built" (2 Chr 6:18).[7]

David had designed the temple as a place of approaching God with praise. Solomon installed the choirs and priestly musicians that his father had planned. These choirs were to continually "praise and glorify the Lord" using some of the Davidic songs, and no doubt using David's dedicatory hymn found in 1 Chronicles 16:23-33 (another rendition of Ps 96, discussed above), which explicitly beckons "all the families of the peoples" to worship God (v. 28).

According to Solomon's dedication, the house of the Lord is to be a place where God would see, hear and answer His people. But the house was not just for Israel. Solomon makes special mention of "the peoples." He knew that God's purpose for the temple was to welcome all nations to worship.

Solomon knew the story up to that point. God had made Himself vastly famous. People of other nations would seek to know the God of Israel personally. Listen to Solomon's astounding prayer:

"Also concerning the foreigner who is not of your people Israel, when he comes from a far country for your name's sake (for they will hear of Your great name and Your mighty hand, and of Your outstretched arm); when He comes and prays toward this house, hear in heaven Your dwelling place, and do according to all for which the foreigner calls to you, in order that all the peoples of the earth may know Your name, to fear You as do Your people Israel..."(1 Ki 8:41-43).

Solomon did not pray for a few of the individuals to come, but for many from every one of the peoples. Solomon prayed that the nations would meet God as they came to the house to pray and to worship. He did not ask that Gentiles know God in their own Gentile way, but rather that they would know God just as Israel did. Solomon envisioned all peoples joining Israel in the same kind of humble, joyous, worshipful walk with God that Israel enjoyed—"the fear of the Lord."

The Nations Begin To Come

Did the report of God's name go out to the world? Did foreigners ever come to the house of the Lord and learn of the fear of the Lord? Did God answer Solomon's prayer? The best answer to these questions is "Yes" as well as "No."

The record shows that soon after the temple was complete (1 Ki 9:25), the Queen of Sheba "heard about the fame of Solomon *concerning the name of the Lord*"(10:1, my emphasis). She came to learn, she listened to Solomon's wisdom (v. 8), and came away with understanding of the covenant-keeping God who "loved Israel forever." As only a royal potentate might see, she realized that God Himself had established the power of Solomon, and the hope that through God's rulership, there might be "justice and righteousness" (v. 9).

Was this an isolated instance? Apparently not. A few verses later it says that, "All the earth was seeking the presence of Solomon, to hear his wisdom which God had put in his heart" (v. 24). The world didn't honor Solomon for being brainy or clever with court cases. The world recognized that God himself had put wisdom in this man's heart. And what was the first lesson in wisdom that Solomon put forth to the world? "The fear of the Lord is the beginning of wisdom" (Prov 1:7, 9:10). Solomon was introducing the world to the worship of God as well as the life of wisdom under God.

God's purposes were apparently being fulfilled. His name was great. Israel was making it known so that the nations were coming to know God personally. What could have possibly slowed God's unfolding plan to draw the nations to Himself? Only one thing. It was the issue about which God most stringently warned His people: idolatry.

And of all the possible horrors, probably the worst thing happened—Solomon himself led the way into grotesque idolatry. It was one of history's most bitter ironies. Imagine the brilliant hopes with the riches and the desires of the nations turning to Israel. Solomon had consecrated the temple in a spectacle of unimaginable glory. He had closed that event with a blessing of purpose on the building and nation, "so that all the peoples of the earth may know that the LORD is God; there is no one else" (1 Ki 8:60).

And then just three chapters after this climactic opening of doors to the nations to know and fear the only God by name, Solomon's heart was turned "away after other gods." He actually constructed shrines within sight of the holy mountain of God (1 Ki 11:1-8). Can any believing reader of these verses not feel disappointment to the point of nausea? It's hard not to speculate about what might have happened if worship had been pure and steady for at least another generation.

The Persistence of God

God's plan was simple: God would make His name great and then Israel could make His name known. He has always purposed to single out His name from all other gods, and then to welcome the nations to worship Him personally in the light of that revealed name through the witness of the people of Israel.

The story from this point becomes a prolonged up-and-down struggle with idolatry. Various episodes revive fidelity to God's worship, but are followed by stunning new lows of profaning God's name. The uppermost issue throughout the generations is God's glory by Israel's worship. At times the people disregarded the worship of God so greatly that generations would pass without the slightest attention to the simple regimens by which God had invited Israel to meet with Him (the ordinances for worship in the books of Moses). The words of some of the prophets show that even when worship patterns were followed, they were often performed superficially. The prophets exposed perfunctory worship, showing that it perversely lacked the justice and the kindness which was supposed to have thrived behind every offering and prayer to God (Isa 1:11-15, Amos 5:21-24, Mic 6:6-8). Although God delayed the great shaking of Israel and Judah, He finally separated the people from the land which was to showcase the blessing of God. They were exiled to distant lands. And then the utmost tragedy: The house of God was burned and broken to rubble.

Near the end of the time of exile, Daniel cried out for God to enact His promise to restore the temple and His people. Daniel was intensely aware of the entire saga, how God had brought His people out of the land of Egypt with a mighty hand... "(to) make a name for yourself, as it is this day" (Dan 9:15). Daniel's over-riding concern was that the ruins of intended glory on the temple mountain in Jerusalem was a continuing reproach to God's glory to "all those around us." He prayed that God would restore the people and the city so that the glory of His name would be restored. Daniel did not base his request on the supposed greatness of Israel, but "for your own sake, O my God, do not delay, because your city and your people are called by your name" (Dan 9:16-19).

Ezekiel, a near contemporary to Daniel, breathed the same themes. God had restrained His wrath at several junctures from destroying Israel, but God's restraint had been for the sake of His name (Ezek 20:5-22). The dealings of God with Israel were not because of sickly favoritism, but solely for His glory among the nations:

> Thus says the Lord God, 'It is not for your sake, O house of Israel, that I am about to act, but for my holy name, which you have profaned among the nations where you went. And I will vindicate the holiness of my great name which has been profaned among the nations, which you have profaned in their midst. Then the nations will know that I am the Lord.' (Ezek 36:22-23)

The Destiny of Israel: Glory From All Nations

Daniel and Ezekiel weren't the only prophets who saw the ongoing story of Israel as focusing on God's name and glory. Other prophets and psalmists spoke of the history and the destiny of Israel in terms of the nations being drawn to God by name, and worshiping Him with diverse, lavish glory.

> Shout joyfully to God, all the earth. Sing the glory of his name; make his praise glorious. Say to God, 'How awesome are your works!' Because of the greatness of your power your enemies will give feigned obedience to you. All the earth will worship you. And will sing praises to you; they will sing praises to your name (Ps 66:1-4).

> All the kings of the earth will give thanks to You, O Lord, when they have heard the words of Your mouth. And they will sing of the ways of the Lord. For great is the glory of the Lord (Ps 138:4-5).

> For the earth will be filled with the knowledge of the glory of the Lord, as the waters cover the sea (Hab 2:14).

> For then I will give to the peoples purified lips, that all of them may call on the name of the Lord, to serve him shoulder to shoulder. From beyond the rivers of Ethiopia my worshipers, my dispersed ones will bring my offerings (Zeph 3:9-10).

> For from the rising of the sun, even to its setting, my name will be great among the nations, and in every place incense is going to be offered to my name, and a grain offering that is pure; for my name will be great among the nations (Mal 1:11).

These are but a sampling of the scores of prophetic words which tethered Israel's identity to the culmination of God's purposes: the glory of God on earth drawing the worship of all peoples. When the people of God were finally brought back to the land, building the temple was to be top priority. Haggai made it clear that the temple was for God's glory, and for a for a greater glory than had ever come before. "And I will shake all the nations; and the desired of the nations will come; and I will fill this house with glory" (Haggai 1:8, 2:7 KJV). From the exile onward, Israel avoided idolatry. But the lesser national glory they desired never came. They were waiting for a messianic deliverer to free them from oppression. They almost missed the Messiah when He came because Jesus' vision of redemption was for God's kingdom to be enacted among all peoples.

The Glory of God in Christ

Christ is the crescendo of the story of God's glory. At the end of all things, He will have bought and brought people from every tribe and tongue to honor the Father. It's no surprise then, to see how His every move was part of pressing the story of God's glory toward its culmination for all nations.

Jesus summed up His ministry in terms of bringing global glory to His Father:

> "I glorified You on the earth, having accomplished the work which You have given Me to do." And what was the work? "I manifested Your name to the men You gave Me out of the world" (John 17:4,6).

Sanctify Your Name

The prayer Jesus taught His disciples to pray can be easily misunderstood because of the antiquated English translation, "Hallowed be Thy name." This prayer is not a statement of praise. It is explicitly a request in the original language: "Father...sanctify your name!" To paraphrase, "Father lift up, single out, exalt, manifest, and reveal Your name to the people of earth. Become famous for who You really are. Cause the people of earth to know and adore You!" The prayer can be prayed most thoroughly in the global dimension that Jesus taught: "on earth as it is in heaven." There is no question of the primacy of this prayer for all believers. The prayer has to be understood. There can be little doubt that Jesus is teaching the Church to pray for the fulfillment of ancient purposes revealed in the Law, the stories, the songs and the prophecies of Israel for the glory of God.

Christ is the crescendo of the story of God's glory. He will have bought and brought people from every tribe and tongue to honor the Father.

In one telling encounter with the non-Jewish Samaritan woman, Jesus declared God's future for her and other Gentile nations: "An hour is coming, and now is, when the true worshipers shall worship the Father in spirit and truth; for such people the Father seeks to be His worshipers" (John 4:23).

A House of Worship from All Peoples

In His most public hour and most passionate moment, Jesus made an issue of the worship of the peoples. He cleansed the temple of the religious commercialism which formed a blockade prohibiting the nations from approaching God. He quoted Isaiah 56:7, "My house shall be called a house of prayer for all peoples." The religious leaders listening to Him immediately recalled the rest of the passage that Jesus was quoting from Isaiah 56:6-7. Jesus intended for them to hear it fully:

> Also the foreigners who join themselves to the Lord, to minister to Him, and to love the name of the Lord,...even those I will bring to My holy mountain, and make them joyful in My house of prayer. Their burnt offerings and their sacrifices will be acceptable on My altar. *For My house will be called a house of prayer for all the peoples.*

Just before going to His death, He displayed His life purpose, and the purpose of His soon-coming death (John 12:24-32). He openly considered the option of asking the Father to rescue Him from death: "What shall I say, Father, save Me from this hour?" But instead of asking to escape, He said, "But for this purpose I came to this hour." What purpose was this? The purpose bursts forth from His heart in His next statement. It becomes the prayer of His death and His life: "Father! Glorify Your name!" And then, to the bewildered amazement of those standing near Him, God the Father Himself answered Jesus from heaven: "I have both glorified it (My name), and will glorify it again." God's answer from heaven still thunders, if you can hear it. It is God's answer to anyone who yields their life to the Father for the greater glory of His name. Jesus said that the answer didn't come for Him, but for His followers who would come to similar moments of choosing to follow Him (12:30) in accordance with God's ancient purpose. How would Jesus' death glorify God's name? "If I be lifted up, I will draw all people to Myself" (12:32).

Ministry of Surpassing Glory with Paul

Paul saw his life as continuing the ancient purpose toward a huge global outpouring of obedient worship from all nations. His most precise statement of mission purpose was to "bring about the obedience of faith among all the nations *for His name's sake*" (Rom 1:5, emphasis mine). Paul saw the entire world as divided into two categories: where Christ was "named" and where Christ was not yet named. Paul resolutely prioritized his efforts so as to labor where Christ was not named (Rom 15:20).[8]

We can see the double direction of God's glory in Paul's ministry. On the one hand he labored to glorify God by revealing Christ *to* the nations—getting Christ "named." But his highest zeal, the very boast of his being, was in that which was to come back to God *from* the nations. "Because of the grace that was given to me from God, to be a minister of Christ Jesus to the nations, [priesting] the gospel,[9] that my offering of the nations might become pleasing, sanctified by the Holy Spirit. Therefore in Christ Jesus I have found reason for boasting in things pertaining to God"[10] (Rom 15:15-17).

Paul's passionate ambition to "preach the gospel" was based on the far more fundamental commission (or in his language, a "grace that was given") which he had received from God to "priest the gospel." There's no mistaking the imagery. Paul sees himself before God, serving the nations as if he were a priest, instructing and ushering them near to God, helping them bring the glory of their nation to God for His pleasure. Paul's job was not to change the societies and cultures. The Spirit of God was at work transforming and sanctifying the finest possible display of glory from the peoples.

Paul labored at great cost with a brilliant vision before him. It was something he knew was worth working and waiting for. "With one voice" many diverse streams of believers, Jew and Gentile, weak and strong, will together "glorify the God and Father of our Lord Jesus Christ" (Rom 15:6).

A Rehearsal for Eternal Glory

At the end of history, we will marvel at how abundantly God's love has been fulfilled. His love will have triumphed by winning passionate devotion from all peoples. Jesus will have thoroughly fulfilled the promise He uttered to His Father, "I have made Your name known to them, and I will make it known; that the love wherewith You loved Me may be in them…" (John 17:26).

Beyond history, we will have found that all of the worshipful service of the many nations throughout the generations will have been a rehearsal for greater affairs of love and glory, still involving the beautified glory from every people.

Heaven will fill earth: "Behold, the tabernacle of God is among men, and He shall dwell among them, and they shall be His peoples,[11] and God Himself shall be among them" (Rev 21:3).

The peoples will endure everlastingly. The city which is heaven on earth will be adorned by kings of the peoples continually bringing the treasure and fruit of the peoples to God's throne (Rev 21:22-26). We will serve Him, awed and honored by having His very name on our faces. And gazing into His face, we shall serve Him as beloved priests (Rev 22:1-5).

What is an Evangelized World For?

Until now we have cried, "Let the earth hear His voice!" Let us never cease voicing His Word to every creature. But soon comes the day when, by most reckonings, the earth will have heard. What then?

There is another cry, far more ancient. It is a shout for earth's destiny. It is to be lifted today more than ever: "Let all the peoples praise You!" (Ps 67:3-5). We hear even now growing praise from the nations. Now let us focus our deepest affections and boldest plans on the splendor of every people loving God with the sanctified best of their society. What a magnificent hope!

CHANGES IN PRACTICE

This emphasis on the glory of God is far more than a decorative flower on the Great Commission. More than ever we must work together with a shared passion that Christ be named and that Christ is praised in every people. A "doxological" (having to do with glory) vision of world evangelization offers practical wisdom essential for the finishing of the remaining task. Stepping into the story of His glory will help us in three practical ways:

1. Deepen Our Motive Base to a Love for God's Glory

World evangelization is for God. It is common to work out of a concern for the predicament of people—either to see them saved from hell, or to see them served to communal wholeness, or both. Such compassion is biblical and necessary. However, our love for people takes on balance and power when our overriding passion is for God to be honored by the kindness extended in His name; and even more, for God to be thanked personally by the people transformed by the power of the gospel.

Jesus was moved with an abounding compassion as He saw the multitudes as abandoned sheep, but He did not respond to the naked need. He deliberately recast His vision of the same lost crowds with a different metaphor. Instead of beleaguered sheep, He saw the people as carrying great value to God: "His harvest." Who can comprehend God's delight in the fullness of the fruit He receives from people's lives? Jesus began to do just that. From that vision He implored the Lord of the harvest to send out laborers to bring God His harvest (Matt 9:35-38). Jesus knew that in God's ways, volunteering is of little value. Anything of lasting power comes from an authentic "sending" of God. Compassion flows like rivers from one who is truly sent.

Mission efforts which draw their motivation from compassionate response to human predicament will only go so far. Guilt-based appeals to care for hurting or lost people continue to soften our hearts a little. In practice, however, they weary and harden believers to a minimal token obedience. Costly and difficult work needs to be done. Such labor cannot be sustained by the fleeting, momentary zeal generated by appeals for desperate, perishing souls. God's global purpose is an ancient affair, far more than an urgent need. Now more than ever believers need to be nurtured into a

far-reaching jealousy for God's glory. With confident certainty that God will fulfill His promise, we can be deeply moved by needs while acting boldly for God's purpose.

2. Define the Task as Increasing God's Glory

Never has there been a day when Christians are taking so much care to reach all of the world's peoples. Considering people groups and their cultures helps to devise effective gospel communication to specific cultures. The people group approach appears to be useful for evaluating progress and apportioning different assignments for effective collaboration.

Even so, the people group approach has been a contentious issue. For years, some have decried the entire approach as disintegrating the unity of churches or as a cover for stubborn attitudes of colonial domination by Westerners. Recently, others have quietly abandoned the people group approach for other paradigms which seem more workable. Even as nation-states disintegrate overnight into the competing peoples that comprise them, country-by-country approaches to evangelization are still proving attractive. Other geographical approaches range from marking urban centers, to drawing windows of longitude and latitude, to mapping spiritual forces arrayed against the gospel. Of course, the peoples of the earth are geographical, urbanized, nationalized entities. We need to take note of these dimensions as important factors in fashioning useful approaches to any people. But our goal must not be reduced to approaching peoples merely to "impact" them as "targets." We must aim beyond the gospel encounter. We must aim to see obedient worship result for God which may be distinctive to that particular people.

I submit that it is not the people group *approach* which is important, but the people group *result*. What is the result of the gospel? Surely something more than every person having a chance to pass verdict on the message. God has promised to get obedient glory for Himself from every tribe and tongue. He yearns for the unique outpouring of love, righteousness, wisdom and worship that can come from every people. This would be the best rationale for planting indigenous churches. Such a vantage point elevates the distinctive wonder of each people group, and at the same time, enhances the value of extending the gospel breakthrough to every place. Geography matters all the more. Every city and place takes on greater significance as the venue of a unique display of God's Kingdom.

3. Integrate Efforts For God's Glory

The obviously false dichotomy of evangelism and social action can be set aside with a doxological approach. Arguments have swirled around which part of man is more important: Is it more important to save a soul or to heal a community? The question is equally repugnant to all. The most common response has been vague generalizations suggesting that we treat the issue as a "both/and" matter instead of an "either/or" question. We may be able to do better. What if the same issues were resolutely examined and embraced for what comes to God?

Glory comes to God from gospel declaration or a kind deed done in His name. Greater glory resounds when whole communities see Christ's hand transforming their lives.

Some have needlessly proposed a double mandate to fashion a point of balance. The so-called cultural mandate to fill the earth is balanced by the evangelistic mandate to evangelize the world. Is there not a singular purpose of God being served by all the peoples and in all places of the earth? The service of the nations must be a total life obedience of justice and righteousness. The worship offerings now to be brought to God through Christ are words as well as works.

Within the vision for God's glory lies the substance of true unity between churches. With a jealousy for unique glory to come to God from every people, we can easily set aside demands for uniformity of worship and conduct. We can delight in the variety of styles of righteousness, peace, and joy, while increasing in jealousy for the commonly confessed singular truth in the person of Christ.

End Notes

1. What about the name "Yahweh," or, as some translations render it, "Jehovah?" It is no doubt an important name. But we must be careful not to regard the living God as actually having a single, legal "real" name, as if He had a birth certificate on file somewhere. The Bible is consistent in urging us to know Him as He aspires to be globally known. The question of Exodus 3:13 was probably not a reference issue (Which god are you representing, Moses?). It was a reputation concern (What kind of track record has this God built for Himself that would move us to commit such a suicidal act of insurrection against Pharaoh? What is the basis of the trustworthiness of God?). It's possible to understand the tetragrammaton (YHWH) in a verbal sense of "I will cause to be what shall be," which is perfectly in keeping with a God who is both Creator and promise keeper. The larger context brings emphasis on God's final answer to the people's question: "Thus you shall say to the sons of Israel, 'The LORD, the God of your fathers, the God of Abraham, the God of Isaac, and the God of Jacob, has sent me to you.' This is My name forever, and this is My memorial-name to all generations" (Ex 3:15).
2. The Hebrew word often translated "ascribe" is a simple word meaning "give." I use the most literal translation "give" because "ascribe" could make it appear to be an entirely cognitive affair. The context describes this worship as an affair involving gifts from people to God which far surpass mere mental ascriptions.
3. Abram recognized that by God's promise to bless him and his family, God was virtually constituting a new family. The biblical concept of blessing was loaded with overtones of family honor and heritage. A biblical blessing was often a statement of power which bestowed a destiny. A family blessing often became the most valued feature of an inheritance. Many present-day societies restrict the idea of inheritance to shuffling unspent assets after the death of an ancestor. Biblical inheritance was not considered to be the leftovers from one generation trickling down to be consumed by the next. A blessing was known to be a special heritage for future generations of a family, multiplying with increased abundance. The most astounding feature of the blessing promised to Abram (Gen 12:1-3) was that God was entrusting to him an endowment that was destined to impart something substantial to every single family on the planet, far beyond one extended family.

4. See as well the other variations of the appeal to release the Hebrews which reflect that the general Hebrew word translated "serve" is very much in the context of service of worship (Ex 3:12, 4:23, 5:1, 7:16, 8:27, 29, 10:9). See especially Exodus 10:26 which makes it clear that to "serve" was to offer sacrificial gifts to God.

5. See *Moses and the Gods of Egypt*, by John Davis, (Grand Rapids: Baker Book House, 1971)

6. God had given this extensive summary of His dealings as His name at Sinai (Ex 33:19, 34:6-8). It is good news in a capsule about how God does things with people. It is a very significant statement, and was recognized by later generations of Israel as a summary of what was to be proclaimed among the nations (Ps 86:9-15, 145:1-2, 8-12,21). Jonah himself recognized this package of truth as something that he knew, that he had withheld from the Ninevites (Jonah 3:9-4:2).

7. Don't take Solomon's question about God dwelling with people on earth as a word of despair of God ever dwelling with people. His prayer is not intended as a definitive map of the cosmos. It rather fits the self-effacing approach to the Most High. He follows with a profoundly humble appeal, in a most formal framework of courtly language, that the king of all the earth deign to turn his eyes toward a place of encounter and hold audience as he had promised (2 Chr 6:19-21). Compare 2 Chronicles 6:1-2 in which Solomon acknowledges the cloud of God's glory so filling the temple that no priest could endure the dreadful brilliance (2 Chr 5:13-14).

8. A close look at the context shows what Paul means by Christ being "named." It was not a matter of the message of Christ being preached once by a missionary, but rather a "foundation" being laid (Rom 15:20). Paul has just been speaking of specific regions in which the gospel is "fulfilled" or brought to a substantial closure (Rom 15:19). Translations such as "fully preached" or "fully proclaimed" stress the cognitive transfer of gospel information far too steeply, especially in light of the full menu of gospel activities just reviewed in 15:18-19. In light of how Paul uses the idea of "foundation" elsewhere (particularly 1 Cor 3:8-15), I conclude that "Christ is named" when there is a growing movement of obedience to Christ established which has proven potential to articulate and demonstrate the life of Christ to its entire community. This is what many would consider a church.

9. Paul uses the idea of a priest and activates it as a verb so that he effectively says that he is "priesting" the gospel. The image is that of a Hebrew priest whose primary task was to help the people present their worship gifts to God.

10. The idea is "toward the face of God" as if in a temple.

11. Some variant manuscripts with good attestation keep the word "peoples" plural in this passage.

Study Questions

1. How does prayer, which asks God to sanctify His name work, toward fulfilling an ancient purpose of God?

2. Explain how the fulfillment of the Great Commission will result in worship "from every people."

3. Explain how worship both reveals God's glory, and allows God to fully accomplish His love for people.

4. Hawthorne says that the story of the Bible is directed toward God being known and worshiped. Critique his thesis. Is there a coherent story throughout the Bible? Is God's glory the paramount theme? What other options are there?

Let the Nations Be Glad!

John Piper

Missions is not the ultimate goal of the Church. Worship is. Missions exists because worship doesn't. Worship is ultimate, not missions, because God is ultimate, not man. When this age is over, and the countless millions of the redeemed fall on their faces before the throne of God, missions will be no more. It is a temporary necessity. But worship abides for ever.

Worship, therefore, is the fuel and goal of missions. It's the goal of missions because in missions we simply aim to bring the nations into the white hot enjoyment of God's glory. The goal of missions is the gladness of the peoples in the greatness of God. "The Lord reigns; let the earth rejoice; let the many coastlands be glad!" (Ps 97:1). "Let the peoples praise thee, O God; let all the peoples praise thee! Let the nations be glad and sing for joy!" (Ps 67:3-4).

But worship is also the fuel of missions. Passion for God in worship precedes the offer of God in preaching. You can't commend what you don't cherish. Missionaries will never call out, "Let the nations be glad!" who cannot say from the heart, "I rejoice in the Lord…I will be glad and exult in thee, I will sing praise to thy name, O Most High" (Ps 104:34; 9:2). Missions begins and ends in worship.

If the pursuit of God's glory is not ordered above the pursuit of man's good in the affections of the heart and the priorities of the church, man will not be well served and God will not be duly honored. I am not pleading for a diminishing of missions but for a magnifying of God. When the flame of worship burns with the heat of God's true worth, the light of missions will shine to the darkest peoples on earth. And I long for that day to come!

Where passion for God is weak, zeal for missions will be weak. Churches that are not centered on the exaltation of the majesty and beauty of God will scarcely kindle a fervent desire to "declare his glory among the nations" (Ps 96:3).

The Second Greatest Activity in the World

The most crucial issue in missions is the centrality of God in the life of the Church. Where people are not stunned by the greatness of God, how can they be sent with the ringing message, "Great is the Lord and greatly to be praised; he is to be feared above all gods!"? (Ps 96:4). Missions is not first and ultimate: God is. And these are not just words. This truth is the life blood of missionary inspiration and endurance. William

John Piper has been the Senior Pastor at Bethlehem Baptist Church in Minneapolis, Minnesota since 1980. Prior to that he taught Biblical Studies at Bethel College in St. Paul, Minnesota. Among his many books are *Desiring God, The Pleasures of God, A Hunger for God* and *Let the Nations Be Glad*.

From *Let the Nations Be Glad*, by John Piper, Copyright 1993, Baker Book House, Grand Rapids, MI. Used by permission.

Carey, the father of modern missions, who set sail for India from England in 1793, expressed the connection:

> When I left England, my hope of India's conversion was very strong; but amongst so many obstacles, it would die, unless upheld by God. Well, I have God, and His Word is true. Though the superstitions of the heathen were a thousand times stronger than they are, and the example of the Europeans a thousand times worse; though I were deserted by all and persecuted by all, yet my faith, fixed on the sure Word, would rise above all obstructions and overcome every trial. God's cause will triumph. [1]

Carey and thousands like him have been moved and carried by the vision of a great and triumphant God. That vision must come first. Savoring it in worship precedes spreading it in missions. All of history is moving toward one great goal, the white hot worship of God and his Son among all the peoples of the earth. Missions is not that goal. It is the means. And for that reason it is the second greatest human activity in the world.

God's Passion for God—the Foundation for Ours

One of the things God uses to make this truth take hold of a person and a church is the stunning realization that it is also true for God himself. Missions is not God's ultimate goal, worship is. And when this sinks into a person's heart, everything changes. The world is often turned on its head. And everything looks different—including the missionary enterprise.

The ultimate foundation for our passion to see God glorified is his own passion to be glorified. God is central and supreme in his own affections. There are no rivals for the supremacy of God's glory in his own heart. God is not an idolater. He does not disobey the first and great commandment. With all his heart and soul and strength and mind he delights in the glory of his manifold perfections. [2] The most passionate heart for God in all the universe is God's heart.

This truth, more than any other I know, seals the conviction that worship is the fuel and goal of missions. The deepest reason why our passion for God should fuel missions is that God's passion for God fuels mis-

sions. Missions is the overflow of our delight in God because missions is the overflow of God's delight in being God. And the deepest reason why worship is the goal in missions is that worship is God's goal. We are confirmed in this goal by the biblical record [3] of God's relentless pursuit of praise among the nations. "Praise the Lord, all nations! Extol him all peoples!" (Ps 117:1). If it is God's goal it must be our goal.

The Power of Missions is Worship

God's supremacy in his own heart is not unloving. It is in fact the fountain of love. God's full delight in his own perfections overflows in his merciful will to share that delight with the nations. We may reaffirm then the earlier truth that worship is the fuel and goal that drives us in missions, because it is the fuel and goal that drives God in missions. Missions flows from the fullness of God's passion for God and it aims at the participation of the nations in the very passion that he has for himself (cf. John 15:11; 17:13,26; Matt 25:21,23). The power of the missionary enterprise is to be caught up into God's fuel and God's goal. And that means being caught up in worship.

Only One God Works for People Who Wait for Him

This remarkable vision of God as one who "exalts himself to show mercy" (Isa 30:18) impels world missions in more ways than one. One way we have not pondered is the sheer uniqueness of this God among all the gods of the nations. Isaiah realizes this and says, "From of old no one has heard or perceived by the ear, no eye has seen a God besides thee, who works for those who wait for him" (Isa 64:4). In other words Isaiah is stunned that the greatness of God has the paradoxical effect that he does not need people to work for him, but rather magnifies himself by working for them, if they will renounce self-reliance and "wait for him."

Isaiah anticipated the words of Paul in Acts 17:25, "God is not served by human hands as though he needed anything, since he himself gives to all men life and breath and everything." The uniqueness at the heart of Christianity is the glory of God manifest in the freedom of grace. God is glorious because he does not need the nations to work for him. He is free to work for them. "The Son of man came not to be served but to serve and to give his life a ransom for many" (Mark 10:45). Missions is not a recruitment project for God's labor force. It is a liberation project from the heavy burdens and hard yokes of other gods (Matt 11:28-30).

Isaiah says that such a God has not been seen or heard anywhere in the world. "From of old no one has heard or perceived by the ear, no eye has seen a God besides thee." What Isaiah sees everywhere he looks are gods who have to be served rather than serve. For example, the Babylonian gods Bel and Nebo:

> Bel bows down, Nebo stoops, their idols are on beasts and cattle; these things you carry are loaded as burdens on weary beasts. They stoop, they bow down together, they cannot save the burden, but themselves go into captivity. "Hearken to me, O house of Jacob, all the remnant of the house of Israel, who have been borne by me from your birth, carried from the womb; even to your old age I am He, and to gray hairs I will carry you. I have made, and I will bear; I will carry and will save" (Isa 46:1-4; cf. Jer 10:5).

The difference between the true God and the gods of the nations is that the true God carries and the other gods must be carried. God serves, they must be served. God glorifies his might by showing mercy. They glorify theirs by gathering slaves. So the vision of God as one whose passion for his glory moves him to mercy impels missions because he is utterly unique among all the gods.

The Most Shareable Message In the World

There is yet another way that such a God motivates the missionary enterprise. The gospel demand that flows from such a God to the nations is an eminently shareable, doable demand, namely to rejoice and be glad in God. "The Lord reigns; let the earth rejoice; let the many coastlands be glad!" (Ps 97:1). "Let the peoples praise thee, O God; let all the peoples praise thee! Let the nations be glad and sing for joy!" (Ps 67:3-4). "Let the oppressed see it and be glad; you who seek God, let your

hearts revive" (Ps 69:32). "Let all who seek thee rejoice and be glad in thee! May those who love thy salvation say evermore, God is great!" (Ps 70:4). What message would missionaries rather take than the message: Be glad in God! Rejoice in God! Sing for joy in God! For God is most glorified in you when you are most satisfied in him! God loves to exalt himself by showing mercy to sinners.

The liberating fact is that the message we take to the frontiers is that people everywhere should seek their own best interest. We are summoning people to God. And those who come say, "In your presence is fullness of joy and at your right hand are pleasures for evermore" (Ps 16:11). God glorifies himself among the nations with the command, "Delight yourself in the Lord!" (Ps 37:4). His first and great requirement of all men everywhere is that they repent from seeking their joy in other things and begin to seek it only in him. A God who cannot be served [4] is a God who can only be enjoyed. The great sin of the world is not that the human race has failed to work for God so as to increase his glory, but that we have failed to delight in God so as to reflect his glory. For God's glory is most reflected in us when we are most delighted in him.

The most exhilarating thought in the world is that God's inexorable purpose to display his glory in the mission of the Church is virtually the same as his purpose to give his people infinite delight. God is committed to the holy joy of the redeemed, gathered from every tribe and tongue and people and nation, with the same zeal that moves him to seek his own glory in all that he does. The supremacy of God in the heart of God is the driving force of his mercy and the missionary movement of his Church.

Biblical Expressions of the Supremacy of God in Missions

Against the background we have developed so far we may now be able to feel the full force of those biblical texts that emphasize the supremacy of God in the missionary impulse of the Church. The motives we see will confirm the centrality of God in the missionary vision of the Bible.

We have seen some of the Old Testament texts which make the glory of God the centerpiece of missionary proclamation: "Declare his glory among the nations, his marvelous works among all the peoples!" (Ps 96:3). "Proclaim that his name is exalted!" (Isa 12:4). There are many others. But we have not yet seen the straightforward statements of Jesus and Paul and John that say the same thing.

Leaving Family and Possessions for the Sake of the Name

When Jesus turned the rich young ruler away because he was not willing to leave his wealth to follow Jesus, the Lord said, "It will be hard for a rich man to enter the kingdom of heaven" (Matt 19:23). The apostles were amazed and said, "Who then can be saved?" (v. 25). Jesus answered, "With men this is impossible, but with God all things are possible" (v. 26). Then Peter, speaking as a kind of missionary who had left his home and business to follow Jesus, said, "Lo, we have left everything and followed you. What shall we have?" (v. 27). Jesus answered with a mild rebuke of Peter's sense of sacrifice: "Everyone who has left houses or brothers or sisters or father or mother or children or lands, for my name's sake, will receive a hundredfold and inherit eternal life" (v. 29).

The one point of focus for us here is the phrase, "for my name's sake." The motive that Jesus virtually takes for granted when a missionary leaves home and family and possessions is that it is for the sake of the name of Jesus. That means for the sake of Jesus' reputation. God's goal is that his Son's name be exalted and honored among all the peoples of the world. For when the Son is honored, the Father is honored (Mark 9:37). When every knee bows at the name of Jesus, it will be "to the glory of God the Father" (Phil 2:10-11). Therefore God-centered missions exists for the sake of the name of Jesus.

A Missionary Prayer for God's Name to be Hallowed

The first two petitions of the Lord's Prayer are perhaps the clearest statement of all in the teachings of Jesus that missions is driven by the passion of God to be glorified among the nations. "Hallowed be thy name. Thy kingdom come" (Matt 6:9-10). Here Jesus teaches us to ask God to hallow his name

and to make his kingdom come. This is a missionary prayer. Its aim is to engage the passion of God for his name among those who forget or revile the name of God (Ps 9:17; 74:18). To hallow God's name means to put it in a class by itself and to cherish and honor it above every claim to our allegiance or affection. Jesus' primary concern—the very first petition of the prayer he teaches—is that more and more people, and more and more peoples, come to hallow God's name. This is the reason the universe exists. Missions exists because this hallowing doesn't.

> Missions is not the ultimate goal of the Church. Worship is.

How Much He Must Suffer for the Name

When Paul was converted on the Damascus road, Jesus Christ became the supreme treasure and joy of his life. "I count everything as loss because of the surpassing worth of knowing Christ Jesus my Lord" (Phil 3:8). It was a costly allegiance. What Paul learned there in Damascus was not only the joy of sins forgiven and fellowship with the King of the universe, but also how much he would have to suffer. Jesus sent Ananias to him with this message: "I will show him how much he must suffer for the sake of my name" (Acts 9:16). Paul's missionary sufferings were "for the sake of the name." When he came near the end of his life and was warned not to go to Jerusalem, he answered, "What are you doing, weeping and breaking my heart? For I am ready not only to be imprisoned but even to die at Jerusalem for the name of the Lord Jesus" Acts 21:13). For Paul the glory of the name of Jesus and his reputation in the world was more important than life.

"For the Sake of His Name among All the Nations"

Paul makes crystal clear in Romans 1:5 that his mission and calling are for the name of Christ among all the nations: "We have received grace and apostleship to bring about the obedience of faith for the sake of his name among all the nations."

The apostle John described the motive of early Christian missionaries in the same way. He wrote to tell one of his churches that they should send out Christian brothers in a manner "worthy of God." And the reason he gives is that "they have gone out for the sake of the name, taking nothing from the Gentiles" (3 Jn 6-7).

John Stott comments on these two texts (Rom 1:5; 3 Jn 7): "They knew that God had superexalted Jesus, enthroning him at his right hand and bestowing upon him the highest rank, in order that every tongue should confess his lordship. They longed that Jesus should receive the honor due to his name." [5] This longing is not a dream but a certainty. At the bottom of all our hope, when everything else has given way, we stand on this great reality: the everlasting, all-sufficient God is infinitely, unwaveringly, and eternally committed to the glory of his great and holy name. For the sake of his fame among the nations he will act. His name will not be profaned for ever. The mission of the church will be victorious. He will vindicate his people and his cause in all the earth.

The Power of Missions When Love for the Lost is Weak

Compassion for the lost is a high and beautiful motive for missionary labor. Without it we lose the sweet humility of sharing a treasure we have freely received. But we have seen that compassion for people must not be detached from passion for the glory of God. John Dawson, a leader in Youth With a Mission, gives an additional reason why this is so. He points out that a strong feeling of love for "the lost" or "the world" is a very difficult experience to sustain and is not always recognizable when it comes.

> Have you ever wondered what it feels like to have a love for the lost? This is a term we use as part of our Christian jargon. Many believers search their hearts in condemnation, looking for the arrival of some feeling of benevolence that will propel them into bold evangelism. It will never happen. It is impossible to love "the lost." You can't feel deeply for an abstraction or a concept. You would find it impossible to love deeply an unfamiliar individual portrayed in a pho-

tograph, let alone a nation or a race or something as vague as "all lost people."

> Don't wait for a feeling of love in order to share Christ with a stranger. You already love your heavenly Father, and you know that this stranger is created by Him, but separated from Him, so take those first steps in evangelism because you love God. It is not primarily out of a compassion for humanity that we share our faith or pray for the lost; it is first of all, love for God. The Bible says in Ephesians 6:7-8: "With good will doing service, as to the Lord, and not to men, knowing that whatever good anyone does, he will receive the same from the Lord, whether he is a slave or free."

> Humanity does not deserve the love of God any more than you or I do. We should never be Christian humanists, taking Jesus to poor sinful people, reducing Jesus to some kind of product that will better their lot. People deserve to be damned, but Jesus, the suffering Lamb of God, deserves the reward of his suffering. [6]

The Miracle of Love That Weeps

Dawson's words are a wise and encouraging warning not to limit our mission engagement to the level of compassion we feel for people we do not know. However, I don't want to minimize what the Lord is able to do in giving people a supernatural burden of love for distant peoples. For example, Wesley Duewel of OMS International tells the story of his mother's remarkable burden for China and India:

> My mother for years carried a hunger for the people of China and India. For many years practically every day as she prayed during family prayer for these two nations she would break down and weep before she finished praying. Her love was deep and constant, and she will be rewarded eternally for her years of love-burden for those lands. This is the love of Jesus reaching out and mediated through Christians by the Holy Spirit. [7]

I emphasize again that the motive of compassion and the motive of zeal for the glory of God are not separate. God-centered compassion (which is the only kind that cares for people eternally) weeps over the the misery of people who reject God's glory and drink the cup of his wrath. But this weeping is not because of the loss of Christian joy. If that were true unbelievers could blackmail the saints and hold their happiness hostage for eternity. No, the weeping of the saints at the loss of precious souls is, paradoxically, the weeping of joy in God. And the reason joy can weep is because it longs to be extended and expanded into the lives of others who are perishing. Therefore the weeping of compassion is the weeping of joy impeded in the extension of itself to another.

The Call of God

God is calling us above all else to be the kind of people whose theme and passion is the supremacy of God in all of life. No one will be able to rise to the magnificence of the missionary cause who does not feel the magnificence of Christ. There will be no big world vision without a big God. There will be no passion to draw others into our worship where there is no passion for worship.

God is pursuing with omnipotent passion a worldwide purpose of gathering joyful worshipers for himself from every tribe and tongue and people and nation. He has an inexhaustible enthusiasm for the supremacy of his name among the nations. Therefore let us bring our affections into line with his, and, for the sake of his name, let us renounce the quest for worldly comforts, and join his global purpose. If we do this, God's omnipotent commitment to his name will be over us like a banner, and we will not lose, in spite of many tribulations (Acts 9:16; Rom 8:35-39). Missions is not the ultimate goal of the church. Worship is. Missions exists because worship doesn't. The Great Commission is first to delight yourself in the Lord (Ps 37:4). And then to declare, "Let the nations be glad and sing for joy!" (Ps 67:4). In this way God will be glorified from beginning to end and worship will empower the missionary enterprise till the coming of the Lord.

"Great and wonderful are your deeds,
O Lord God the Almighty!
Just and true are your ways,
O King of the ages!
Who shall not fear and glorify your name,
O Lord?
For you alone are holy.
All nations shall come and worship you,
for your judgments have been revealed"
(Rev 15:3-4).

End Notes

1. Quoted in Iain Murray, *The Puritan Hope* (Edinburgh: The Banner of Truth Trust, 1971), p. 140.
2. I have tried to unfold this wonderful truth of the Father's delight in himself, that is, his Son in *The Pleasures of God: Meditations on God's Delight in Being God* (Portland: Multnomah Press, 1991), Chapter One, "The Pleasure of God in His Son."
3. See especially "Appendix One: The Goal of God in Redemptive History," in *Desiring God: Meditations of a Christian Hedonist* (Portland: Multnomah Press, original 1986, 2nd edition 1996), pp. 227-238; and the entirety of *The Pleasures of God*.
4. I am aware that the Bible is replete with pictures of God's people serving him. I have dealt in some detail with the way service can be conceived biblically so as not to put God in the category of an employer who depends on wage earners. See *Desiring God: Meditations of a Christian Hedonist*, pp. 138-143.
5. John Stott, "The Bible in World Evangelization," in Ralph D. Winter and Steven C. Hawthorne, eds., *Perspectives on the World Christian Movement* (Pasadena: William Carey Library, 1981), Chap. 4, this volume.
6. John Dawson, *Taking Our Cities for God* (Lake Mary, Florida: Creation House, 1989), pp. 208-209.
7. Wesley Duewel, *Ablaze for God* (Grand Rapids: Francis Asbury Press of Zondervan Publishing House, 1989), pp. 115-116.

Study Questions

1. Explain the sentence "Missions exists because worship doesn't?"

2. Piper speaks of passion for God's glory in the same breath as saying God is supreme and requires worship. How can we authentically desire what God has required? How does this intentional passion motivate missions?

On Mission With God

Henry T. Blackaby and Avery T. Willis, Jr.

Henry T. Blackaby serves the North American Mission Board of the Southern Baptist Convention, as Special Assistant to the President. He also advises the International Mission Board and LifeWay Christian Resources in the area of prayer and spiritual awakening for global revival. Blackaby is the primary author of *Experiencing God*.

Avery T. Willis Jr. is the Senior Vice President for Overseas Operations at the International Mission Board of the Southern Baptist Convention Board in Richmond, Virginia. In the past, he spent 14 years as a missionary in Indonesia.

God is on mission. He has been on mission throughout history to accomplish His purpose throughout the earth. Each time we see God in the Bible, He is acting in accordance with His purpose: to reveal Himself in order that His name would be glorified, that His Kingdom would be established and that some from every people would be reconciled to Himself.

God Reveals Himself to Reconcile the World To Himself

God has chosen to reveal Himself, His purpose and His ways, involving His people with Him as He invites all the world's peoples to know and worship Him.

- Through Abraham, God revealed Himself as the LORD, the Almighty and the Provider, who wants to bless all the peoples of the world through His people.
- Through Moses, God revealed Himself as the I AM THAT I AM, whose plan is to show His glory to the world through His people, who are to be a kingdom of priests to all peoples.
- Through David, God revealed that His Seed would rule all nations and His Kingdom would be for all peoples.
- Through Jesus, God revealed His love and His purpose to reconcile the world to Himself through Christ's incarnation, crucifixion, resurrection and ascension.
- Through Paul, God revealed that the mystery of the ages is that He includes all peoples in His redemption.
- Through John, God revealed that some from every nation, tribe, tongue and people will worship Him forever.

He is at work all the time, to the very end of time, bringing about this revelation, for all peoples' reconciliation. When this mission is fulfilled, it will not only be the fullest expression of earth's praise, it will be the fullest revelation of God's love.

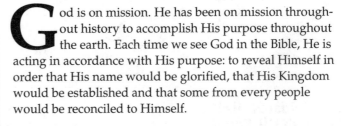

God on Mission

Throughout History in order that...

- *God's Name is Glorified*
- *God's Kingdom is Established*
- *the World is Reconciled to Himself*

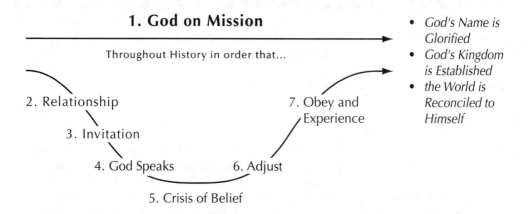

1. God on Mission

→ *Throughout History in order that...*

- *God's Name is Glorified*
- *God's Kingdom is Established*
- *the World is Reconciled to Himself*

2. Relationship

3. Invitation

4. God Speaks

5. Crisis of Belief

6. Adjust

7. Obey and Experience

God Initiates His Work Through His People

God has initiated every part of His work throughout history. Instead of carrying out His mission on His own, God chooses to accomplish His mission in a very personal way. He chooses to involve His people with Him, working through them to accomplish His purposes. When He is about to take a further step to advance His mission, He comes to one or more of His servants. He lets them know what He is about to do. He invites them to join Him, bidding them to adjust their lives to Him so that He can accomplish every aspect of His mission through them. The prophet Amos indicated that, "The Sovereign Lord does nothing without revealing his plan to his servants the prophets" (Amos 3:7).

When God was ready to judge the world, He came to Noah. He intended to glorify Himself by preserving righteousness on the earth. He was going to do it through Noah. When God was ready to set apart a people for Himself, He came to Abraham. God was going to accomplish His will through Abraham. When God heard the cry of the children of Israel and decided to deliver them, He appeared to Moses. God came to Moses because of His purpose. He planned to deliver Israel through Moses and reveal His purpose for them. As He worked through Moses and Israel, God revealed Himself to the entire world.

Moses' experience is a good illustration of how God deals with His people. The diagram above shows seven realities that

Moses learned, that are true for all of God's people. This process can help you understand how God is welcoming you to be part of His mission.

Throughout the Old and New Testaments, God worked in the same way as He did with Moses, inviting His people to be on mission with Him. His ways are the same today. God reveals Himself to us so we can know Him personally. God initiates a relationship with us, and invites us to join Him. As God reveals Himself to us we often experience a crisis of belief that calls for major adjustments in our lives so that we can relate to Him and His mission. As we make the adjustments and obey Him, He moves us into the middle of His activity, in order to experience Him and to enjoy the astounding significance of being on mission with God.

Jesus: On Mission With His Father

God wants us to be like Jesus, who always obeyed Him. Jesus indicated through His life that He was joining the Father in His mission. He announced that He had come not to do His own will, but the will of the Father who had sent Him (Matt 26:42; John 4:34; 5:30; 6:38; 8:29; 17:4). To know the Father's will, Jesus said He watched to see what the Father was doing. Then Jesus joined Him in that work: "I tell you the truth, the Son can do nothing by himself; he can do only what he sees his Father doing, because whatever the Father does the Son also does." (John 5:17,19). Jesus listened to the Father and whatever He heard the Father say, these are the things that He would say (John 14:10-11).

Jesus did not take the initiative but depended on the Father to reveal Himself and what He was doing (John 17:6-8) and He bore witness to the Father, and the Father worked through Him (John 14:10).

The Father loved the Son, and took the initiative to come to Him and reveal what He (the Father) was doing, or was about to do. Jesus kept on looking for the Father's activity around Him, so that He could unite His life with His Father's mission.

Knowing and Working in God's Ways

Even a casual reader of the Bible can see that God's ways and plans are so different from the ways that people accomplish their goals. God said, "My thoughts are not your thoughts, neither are your ways my ways" (Isa 55:8). On their own, people achieve goals by their efficiency and ingenuity. With God on His mission, you must follow Kingdom principles to accomplish Kingdom purposes.

Our ways may seem good to us. We may succeed in moderate accomplishments. When we try to do the work of God in our own ways, however, we will never see the mighty power of God in what we do, and the world will not see God revealing Himself to them. It is only by God's power that people come to know and worship God. When God accomplishes His purposes in His ways through us, people will come to know God. They will recognize that what has happened can only be explained by God. He will receive the glory!

Learning to follow God's ways may be more important than making sincere attempts to do His will. God is eager to reveal His ways to us because they are the only way to accomplish His purposes. God wants to complete His work through you. He can only do that as you adjust your life to Him and to His ways. Start looking for how God welcomes you to join Him and to experience Him. He has involved His people on mission with Him in the same ways all through history:

1. God is always at work around you to accomplish His mission.	*Expect God to encounter you* to reveal what He is doing near you or among distant peoples to reconcile a lost world to Himself.
2. God pursues a continuing love relationship with you that is real and personal.	*Respond to God as He invites you into a covenant relationship of promise and obedience.* God wants to deepen His love relationship with you far more than He wants merely to utilize you for a task.
3. God invites you to become involved in His work when He reveals Himself and His work to you.	*Respond when God calls* you to Himself to be on mission with Him.
4. God speaks to you by the Holy Spirit through the Bible, prayer, circumstances and the church, to reveal Himself, His purposes and His ways.	*Respond as God prepares you* for His mission as you learn His ways with others.
5. God's invitation for you to work with Him always leads you to a crisis of belief that requires faith and action.	*Obey as God sends you* where He can best work through you to accomplish His mission.
6. You must make major adjustments in your life to join God in what He is doing.	*Expect God to empower you* as you make the life changes that open you to co-labor with God according to His ways.
7. You come to know God by experience as you obey Him and He accomplishes His work through you.	*Expect God to guide you* on His mission to reveal Himself and to reconcile a lost world to Himself.

Knowing and Doing God's Will

How can you know God's will? Since all true mission is really God on His mission, there is not a different mission for you, for me, for the people who lived a thousand years ago, or for believers on the other side of the world. He has never been willing that any should perish. God's mission is to glorify His name, to establish His kingdom and to reconcile the world to Himself.

Within this immense global purpose, God does not leave you to guess His will. Since He is pursuing a love relationship with you, you cannot know His will without knowing Him better. As you come to know Him better, He reveals His will in a clearer way. And you are changed as well. You will find that you want to do His will more and more (Phil 2:13).

On mission with God, you will experience that God is love. His will is always best. He pursues a love relationship with you so you can join Him in His mission.

On mission with God, you will experience that God is all-knowing. His directions are always right. He reveals them when you are obedient to Him.

On mission with God, you will experience that God is all-powerful. He enables you to accomplish His will when you are totally dependent on Him.

Let God orient you to Himself and then you will be oriented to His will. The servant does not tell the Master what kind of assignment he needs. The servant waits on his Master for the assignment. As you obey Him, God will prepare you for the assignment that is just right for you.

On Mission With Jesus

Christians are Kingdom people and Christ Himself is the eternal King over His kingdom. He "has made us to be a kingdom and priests to serve his God and Father" (Rev. 1:6). You are called into a partnership with Christ the King. In this partnership, you will become involved in His mission to reconcile a lost world to God. To be related to Christ is to be on mission with Him. You cannot be in relationship with Jesus and not be on mission. Jesus said, "As the Father has sent me, I am sending you" (John 20:21).

Jesus was on mission with the Father, and He calls every one of His followers to join Him in that relationship of love, power and purpose. Never get over how amazing this really is. Nothing could be more precious than to follow God on mission in the same way that Jesus did.

Study Questions

1. "You must make major adjustments in your life to join God in What He is doing." What adjustments did each of these biblical servants have to make to obey God's call: Noah (Gen 6-7), Moses (Ex 3-4) and Paul (Acts 13:1-3; 16:6-10)?

2. What adjustments would you have to make in your life if God were to call you now into a different ministry or to live in a different place?

3. Do you agree that every Christian is being sent "on mission" by Jesus (John 20:21)? If you agree, discuss how every Christian can be taught and trained to be ready for mission.

Witness to the World

David J. Bosch

A careful reading of both Old and New Testaments reveals that God himself is the subject of mission. We have here to do with *Missio Dei*, God's mission. The *martyr*, the witness by word and deed, has its ultimate origin not in the witness himself, but in God. To this we must hasten to add, however that the witness himself is in no way excluded here. He is part of God's mission. But God remains the author.

One of the ways in which the Old Testament in particular has given expression to this conviction, is by laying much emphasis on what God rather than man does, almost to the extent of suggesting that man is inactive. That this is not the intention will hopefully become clear.

The "Servant of the Lord"

It has for a long time been customary to refer to the "Servant of the Lord" in Isaiah 40-55 as the missionary par excellence. This interpretation flows from the centrality of the concept "witness" in those chapters.[1] The "servant" is, however, not an active missionary sent out to the nations. The verb *"yôṣî"* in Isaiah 42:1 is not to be translated as "carry out," "bring to," but rather as "cause to become visible." The NEB translation of this verse is therefore preferable: "…my servant…will *make justice shine* on the nations." It is not the servant's own activities which are emphasized, but the fact that God works in and through him. He is, we are told, brought into the courtroom to witness in the case between God and the nations. He is, however, a very remarkable and, according to our standards, useless witness, for he can neither see nor speak (Isa 42:18-20; 43:8-13). The purpose of this metaphor is, once again, not to say that the witness is indeed blind and deaf, but that, in the final analysis, Yahweh himself is the Witness.

The "servant" of the Lord in Isaiah 40-55 is a paradigm of Israel. Israel's election and existence has no goal in itself. Through Israel God is busy with the nations. Her election is a prolepsis, an anticipation. In and through her God stretches his hand out to the world. His salvific activities in Israel are a sign and signal to the nations. She is called to be "a light to all peoples" (Isa 42:6). God intends doing more than merely restoring the tribes of Judah and bringing back the descendants of Israel: "I will make you a light to the nations, that my salvation may reach to earth's farthest bounds" (Isa 49:6).

David J. Bosch served as a missionary to Transkei from 1957 until 1971 when he joined the faculty of the University of South Africa. He went on to serve as the Dean of Theology and is best known for his books, *A Spirituality of the Road, Witness to the World* and *Transforming Mission*. He passed away in 1992.

Chapter 9   **59**

For many years it has been customary to argue that the Old Testament views mission centripetally—the nations coming towards Israel—whereas the New Testament understanding of mission is centrifugal—from the center, Israel or the Church, missionaries move outward, into the world. It is undoubtedly true that the Old Testament views mission predominantly in centripetal categories. This is however not exclusively so. The metaphor of light in Isaiah 42:6, 49:6 and elsewhere, is particularly appropriate to give expression to both a centripetal and a centrifugal movement. A light shining in the darkness draws people towards it, centripetally, yet at the same time it goes outward, crossing frontiers, allowing, in the words of Isaiah 49:6, God's salvation to reach "to earth's farthest bounds."

In the Old Testament Israel's missionary significance lies, however, predominantly within the framework of centripetal categories. This explains the centrality of Jerusalem or Zion in the Old Testament's universalistic passages. The centripetal category is employed to give expression to the conviction that God, not Israel, is the author of mission.

Zechariah 8 gives classical expression to this. It is Yahweh who, after the exile, gathers his scattered people from the nations (vv. 7-8) and instructs them (vv. 9-19). The nations observe this and spontaneously express the desire also to go to Jerusalem. As many as ten men "from nations of every language" will pluck the robe of a Jew and say: "We will go with you because we have heard that God is with you" (v. 23). It is not Israel's faith, example and witness that act as a magnet here; it is God's faithfulness to Israel that causes the nations to come. And yet, not for a single moment does this suggest that Israel's faith, example and witness are dispensable. Far from it. Once again, therefore, Israel herself is fully involved in God's mission to the nations. She was a pagan whom God elected to salvation; but she retains her new and special position as "non-pagan" only in so far as she accepts and lives up to her responsibility in the world. Primarily this means remaining true to Yahweh; but then this implies remain-

Two Forces   *Jonathan Lewis*

In the fulfillment of Israel's obligation, two forces were at work. The first of these was an *attractive force*, symbolized first by the tabernacle and then by the temple in Jerusalem. These buildings were the places where God's name dwelt. They were holy places, the heart of Israel's religious ceremony and practice. Yet they were not intended just to serve Israel. When Solomon dedicated the temple, it was clear to him that the temple had a wider purpose.

The Bible records several other foreigners who were attracted to Israel because of the evidence of God's blessing, including Ruth, a Moabite woman, and Naaman the Syrian. Hundreds of other unrecorded accounts are evidenced by the fact that on the day of Pentecost there were devout men from "every nation under heaven" (Acts 2:5) staying in Jerusalem. God's plan to reach the nations, however, include much more than a passive attraction.

A second force in operation was an active, *expansive force* which operated to send God's message beyond the borders of Israel. Some examples of Israelites who were used to proclaim God's message to other nations include captives such as Joseph and exiles such a Daniel and Esther. Or consider the prophet Jonah, who was commanded to preach repentance to Nineveh. Jeremiah was appointed as a "prophet to the nations," and it is speculated that he or other messengers may have traveled widely in delivering his many oracles. Nor did God use only the great in this role of bearing His message. It was a little Israelite slave girl who announced His healing

Jonathan Lewis (Ph.D.) is Director of the Intercultural Ministry Centre (AIMC) of the Associated Canadian Theological Schools (ACTS). He also serves as Associate Director of the WEF Missions Commission and edits *Training for Cross-Cultural Ministries*. Born in Argentina, he has worked in the establishment of missionary training centers in Latin America. He is the editor of two published missions courses available in several languages. From *World Mission*, Second Edition, edited by Jonathan Lewis, 1994. Used by permission of William Carey Library, Pasadena, CA.

ing true to the world, in letting her light shine forth, in being an example to the world, indeed, in witnessing by word and deed.

God and Man as Competitors?

It would, however, be wrong to find the real difference between Old and New Testaments in the centripetal—centrifugal distinction. At least three observations can be made to establish that that distinction is a relative one.

First, the centripetal missionary dimension is by no means confined to the Old Testament but characteristic of the New Testament also. Astrologers came from the East to Jerusalem to look for the Savior of the world (Matt 2). Simeon refers to the deliverance which God has prepared "in full view of all the nations: a light that will be a revelation to the heathen…" (Luke 2:31-32). Quoting Isaiah 56:7, Jesus referred to the temple as "a house of prayer for all the nations" (Mark 11:17). The cleansing of the temple moreover suggests that the restoration of Israel should precede the pilgrimage of the nations to Jerusalem. The Roman army officer coming to Jesus

(Matt 8:5) and the Greeks traveling to Jerusalem to see Jesus (John 12:20) give expression to the same idea: Salvation is to be found in Israel and the nations who wish to partake of it, should go there. After all, "it is from the Jews that salvation comes" (John 4:22). The world's salvation can be consummated at one place only—in Jerusalem; this explains the prominence of this city in all four gospels, especially that of Luke (the non-Jew!).

Secondly, we have to point out that the centripetal-centrifugal distinction may easily lead to "true" mission being understood as only centrifugal, as this suggests the crossing of geographical boundaries and proclamation to pagans by word of mouth. We have, however, argued both that the crossing of geographical boundaries constitutes one element only of what the Bible understands by "mission," and also that mission is more than oral preaching to pagans.

Thirdly, there is a tendency to understand mission in the Old Testament as entirely and exclusively "God's work." This implies that New Testament centrifugal mission, in

power to Naaman, the mighty but leprous captain of the Syrian army.

Some might argue that these cases are exceptions and would point out that many of these people were captives or otherwise ministered against their wills. However, volunteerism has never been the deciding factor in furthering God's mission. God will use His people to spread His message, whether they are willing agents or not. Israel's tragic history would have been considerably different if she had been a willing instrument of God's redemptive plan. She was not. God used captivity and exile both to judge Israel's disobedience and to extend her witness beyond her borders.

These two dynamic forces are also present today. On a global scale, many are attracted to "Christian" nations because of the evidence of God's blessing through material wealth and stability. In communities, congregations where God's power and grace are evident also draw people. On a personal level, godly character attracts those who want to possess those same

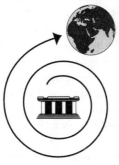

qualities. Yet the gospel will not be spread to all nations simply through passive attraction. There are too many social, cultural, and geographic barriers that need to be crossed for this to happen. God's people must be willing to go to the nations with the good news if they hope to fulfill their covenant obligations.

An Attractive Force
"Come to the Blessing"

An Expansive Force
"Go to the Nations"

which man is ostensibly more actively in-volved, might then be labeled "man's work." With this, however, we enter a very slippery area where God's activity excludes man's and vice versa. Then God and man become competitors.

Some of Jesus' contemporaries indeed be-lieved that God's work, by definition, ex-cluded any human involvement.

We want to put it, categorically, however, that this is a false conception that cannot but be detrimental to the Church. The Bible speaks with a disarming candor here. The disciples are seed (Matt 13:38) and at the same time la-borers bringing in the harvest (Matt 9:37-38); they are members of the flock (Matt 10:16; Luke 12:32; John 10:1-16) but also shepherds (Matt 10:6; John 21:15-7); they are in need of absolution (Matt 18:23-27) but can also give absolution to others (Matt 16:19; 18:18; John 20:23). God has revealed to them the "secrets of the Kingdom" (Matt 13:11), yet they have to seek the Kingdom (Matt 5:20; 6:33; Luke 13:24). They are God's children (Matt 17:26), yet have to become that by loving their en-emies (Matt 5:44-45). They have received eter-nal life (John 3:16-17; 11:25-26) yet still have to go through the gate that leads to life (Matt 7:14). Because they have done what Jesus ex-pected of the rich young ruler, they are "per-fect" (Matt 19:21; cf. Mark 10:28), yet have to keep watch and pray so that they will not fall into temptation (Matt 26:41). The believers must work out their own salvation in fear and trembling, for(!) it is God who works in them (Phil 2:12-13). Therefore Paul can, quite un-selfconsciously, call them "God's fellow-work-ers" (1 Cor 3:9). The key to these apparently complete paradoxes lies in the New Testament expression "in Christ:" "By God's grace I am what I am, nor has his grace been given to me in vain; on the contrary, in my labors I have outdone them all—not I, indeed, but the grace of God working with me" (1 Cor 15:10).

If, however, we regard God and man as competitors and put God's work over against man's, we soon land ourselves in one of two untenable positions. If we emphasize only the one side, our faith adopts the blind, un-bending characteristics of fate; if we empha-size only the other side, we become fanatics and arrogant Zealots.

There is, as the examples quoted from Scripture indicate, a creative tension between God's work and man's, and any attempt to explain it by means of a balanced formula or to codify it precisely in a dogma, risks de-stroying its tender mystery. To recognize this is of the utmost importance for the biblical foundation of mission.

In Christ

Many scholars have underlined the remark-able fact that the so-called "Great Commis-sion" (Matt 28:18-20 and parallels) seems to play no role in the New Testament Church herself, because it is never repeated nor re-ferred to. Two reasons may perhaps be sug-gested to explain this silence. First, the Great Commission is not a commission in the ordi-nary sense of the word. It is, rather, a creative statement in the manner of Genesis 1:3 and elsewhere: "Let there be...." Or, as Newbigin puts it, with reference to Acts 1:8: "The word, 'You shall be my witnesses,' is not a com-mand to be obeyed but a promise to be trusted."[2] It was a promise, however, that could only be perceived in the act of obeying, as Peter discovered when he visited Cornelius and said in amazement: "I now see how true it is that God has no favorites..." (Acts 10:34). Paul referred to it as a "mys-tery," a "secret" only now revealed to him in the act of preaching the gospel to all people, "that through the gospel the Gentiles are joint heirs with the Jews, part of the same body, sharers together in the promise made in Christ Jesus" (Eph 3:6).

A second reason for the silence about the Great Commission in the early church lies in the fact that a mission to the Gentiles was never at issue in the early church—despite the views of scholars such as Ferdinand Hahn, Ernst Käsemann, and others. Heinrich Kasting has convincingly refuted their arguments and shown that the Gentile mission was never a point of controversy in the early church. Opin-ions differed only on the way in which Gen-tiles were to be brought into the church, espe-cially on the question of circumcision.[3] In these circumstances a reference to a "missionary command" would have been irrelevant.

Both these considerations demonstrate that mission in the New Testament is more than a matter of obeying a command. It is, rather, the result of an encounter with Christ. To meet Christ, means to become caught up in a mission to the world.

Mission is a privilege in which to participate. Thus Paul introduces himself to the church in Rome as somebody who, through Christ, has "received the *privilege* of a commission in his name to lead to faith and obedience men in all nations" (Rom 1:5). Mission, for Paul, is the logical consequence of his encounter with the risen Christ on the Damascus road.

Similarly, in the so-called "christological hymn" (Phil 2:6-11), there is no reference to a missionary command. And yet, the worldwide mission falls clearly within the purview of the hymn: "...that at the name of Jesus every knee should bow...and every tongue confess, 'Jesus is Lord'" (vv. 10-11). Mission is therefore, according to the New Testament, a predicate of Christology. This is how it appears in another early Christian hymn: "He who was manifested in the body, vindicated in the spirit, seen by angels; who was proclaimed among the nations, believed in throughout the world, glorified in high heaven" (1 Tim 3:16). Similarly, in 2 Corinthians 5:18-20 and Ephesians 2:14-18 mission is christologically founded as the message of the reconciliation of the world with God; the "service of reconciliation," entrusted to the Church, proceeds from the fact that Jesus, with regard to Jews and Gentiles, has broken down, "in his own body of flesh, the enmity which stood like a dividing wall between them," thus creating "out of the two a single new humanity in himself."

The Church, therefore, is involved in mission because Jesus was given a name above all names (Phil 2:9), and declared Son of God by a mighty act in that he rose from the dead (Rom 1:4); because God was in Christ reconciling the world to himself (2 Cor 5:19) and Jews and Gentiles to one another in a single body to himself through the cross (Eph 2:16). If the Church is "in Christ," she is involved in mission. Her whole existence then has a missionary character. Her conduct as well as her words will convince the unbelievers (1 Pet 2:12) and put their ignorance and stupidity to silence (1 Pet 2:15). "God's scattered people," to whom 1 Peter is addressed (cf. 1:1), are a chosen race, a royal priesthood, a dedicated nation, and a people claimed by God for his own. This new status in Christ has a clear purpose: to proclaim the triumphs of him who has called them out of darkness into his marvelous light (cf. 1 Pet 2:9). Because of this new life in Christ, mission "happens," so to speak, for we read about unbelievers calling upon the Christians for an explanation of the hope that is in them (1 Pet 3:15). This hope was so conspicuous, that the unbelievers became both curious and jealous. To put it in Pauline language: this was the way in which God spread abroad the fragrance of the knowledge of himself (2 Cor 2:14). Wherever the apostle lived, spoke and acted as "Christ fragrance," something happened to the surrounding people.

End Notes

1. See also Allison A. Trites, *The New Testament Concept of Witness* (Cambridge University Press, Cambridge, 1977), pp. 35-47.
2. L. Newbigin, "The Church as Witness", *Reformed Review*, vol. 35, no. 1 (March 1978), p.9.
3. See H. Kasting, *Die Anfänge der urchristlichen Mission* (Chr. Kaiser, Munich, 1969), pp.109-23. Kasting shows that it were Judaistic elements in the early church, not the 'official' early church herself, which tended to limit salvation to Israel. At a later stage, especially after the first century, the 'unofficial', Judaistic position increasingly became the accepted one in Jewish Christianity. That attitude would ultimately become one of the factors leading to the end of Jewish Christianity.

Study Questions

1. What are some examples of centripetal witness in the Bible? In the modern world?

2. Do your best to describe what Bosch calls a "tender mystery," the co-working of God and man in mission. What are some biblical truths which describe the paradox that mission is God's work as well as man's work?

The Gospel of the Kingdom

George Eldon Ladd

George Eldon Ladd was Professor Emeritus of New Testament Exegesis and Theology at Fuller Theological Seminary. Ladd was involved in the Student Volunteer Movement in the early part of this century. He died in 1982 at the age of 71.

Taken from *The Gospel of the Kingdom*, Wm. B. Eerdmans Publishing Company, Grand Rapids, Michigan, 1959. Used by permission.

In a day like this, wonderful yet fearful, men are asking questions. What does it all mean? Where are we going? What is the meaning and the goal of human history? Does mankind have a destiny? Or do we jerk across the stage of time like wooden puppets, only to have the stage, the actors, and the theatre itself destroyed by fire, leaving only a pile of ashes and the smell of smoke?

In ancient times, poets and seers longed for an ideal society. Hesiod dreamed of a lost Golden Age in the distant past but saw no brightness in the present, constant care for the morrow, and no hope for the future. Plato pictured an ideal state organized on philosophical principles, but he himself realized that his plan was too idealistic to be realized. Virgil sang of one who would deliver the world from its sufferings and by whom "the great line of the ages begins anew."

The Hebrew-Christian faith expresses its hope in terms of the Kingdom of God. This biblical hope is not in the same category as the dreams of the Greek poets but is at the very heart of revealed religion. The biblical idea of the Kingdom of God is deeply rooted in the Old Testament and is grounded in the confidence that there is one eternal, living God who has revealed Himself to men and who has a purpose for the human race which He has chosen to accomplish through Israel.

Thus the prophets announced a day when men will live together in peace. God shall then "judge between the nations, and shall decide for many peoples; and they shall beat their swords into plowshares, and their spears into pruning hooks; nation shall not lift up sword against nation, neither shall they learn war any more" (Isa 2:4). Not only shall the problems of human society be solved, but the evils of man's physical environment shall be no more. "The wolf shall dwell with the lamb, and the leopard shall lie down with the kid, and the calf and the young lion and the fatling together, and a little child shall lead them" (Isa 11:6). Peace, safety, security—all this was promised for the happy future.

Then came Jesus of Nazareth with the announcement, "Repent, for the Kingdom of heaven is at hand" (Matt 4:17). This theme of the coming of the Kingdom of God was central in His mission. His teaching was designed to show men how they might enter the Kingdom of God (Matt 5:20; 7:21). His mighty works were intended to prove that the Kingdom of God had come upon them (Matt 12:28). His parables illustrated to His disciples the truth about the Kingdom of God

(Matt 13:11). And when He taught His followers to pray, at the heart of their petition were the words, "Thy Kingdom come, Thy will be done on earth as it is in heaven" (Matt 6:10). On the eve of His death, He assured His disciples that He would yet share with them the happiness and the fellowship of the Kingdom (Luke 22:22-30). And He promised that He would appear again on the earth in glory to bring the blessedness of the Kingdom to those for whom it was prepared (Matt 25:31, 34).

The Meaning of "Kingdom"

We must ask the most fundamental question: What is the meaning of "kingdom"? The modern answer to this question loses the key of meaning to this ancient biblical truth. In our western idiom, a kingdom is primarily a realm over which a king exercises his authority. Not many kingdoms remain in our modern world with its democratic interests; but we think of the United Kingdom of Great Britain and Northern Ireland as the original group of countries which recognize the Queen as their sovereign. The dictionary follows this line of thought by giving as its first modern definition, "A state or monarchy, the head of which is a king; dominion; realm."

The second meaning of a kingdom is the people belonging to a given realm. The kingdom of Great Britain may be thought of as the citizens over whom the Queen exercises her rule, the subjects of her kingdom.

We must set aside our modern idiom if we are to understand biblical terminology. At this point Webster's dictionary provides us with a clue when it gives as its archaic definition: "The rank, quality, state, or attributes of a king; royal authority; dominion; monarchy; kingship. *Archaic*." From the viewpoint of modern linguistic usage, this definition may be archaic; but it is precisely this archaism which is necessary to understand the ancient biblical teaching. The *primary* meaning of both the Hebrew word *malkuth* in the Old Testament and of the Greek word *basileia* in the New Testament is the rank, authority and sovereignty exercised by a king. A *basileia* may indeed be a realm over which a sovereign exercises his authority; and it may be the people who belong to that realm and over whom authority is exercised; but these are secondary and derived meanings.

First of all, a kingdom is the authority to rule, the sovereignty of the king.

This primary meaning of the word "kingdom" may be seen in its Old Testament use to describe a king's rule. Ezra 8:1 speaks of the return from Babylon "in the kingdom" of Artaxerxes, i.e., his reign. 2 Chronicles 12:1 speaks of the establishment of Rehoboam's kingdom or rule. This usage of "kingdom" as a human reign may also be found in such passages as Jeremiah 49:34; 2 Chronicles 11:17, 36:20; Daniel 8:23, Ezra 4:5; Nehemiah 12:22, etc.

The Meaning of "the Kingdom of God"

When the word refers to God's Kingdom, it always refers to His reign, His rule, His sovereignty, and not to the realm in which it is exercised. Psalm 103:19, "The Lord has established His throne in the heavens, and His Kingdom rules over all." God's Kingdom, His *malkuth*, is His universal rule, His sovereignty over all the earth. Psalm 145:11, "They shall speak of the glory of Thy Kingdom, and tell of Thy power." In the parallelism of Hebrew poetry, the two lines express the same truth. God's Kingdom is His power. Psalm 145:13, "Thy Kingdom is an everlasting Kingdom, and Thy dominion endures throughout all generations." The *realm* of God's rule is the heaven and earth, but this verse has no reference to the permanence of this realm. It is God's rule which is everlasting. Daniel 2:37, "You, O king, the king of kings, to whom the God of heaven has given the kingdom, the power, and the might, and the glory." Notice the synonyms for Kingdom: power, might, glory—all expressions of authority. These terms identify the Kingdom as the "rule" which God has given to the king.

One reference in our Gospels makes this meaning very clear. We read in Luke 19:11-12, "As they heard these things, he proceeded to tell a parable, because he was near to Jerusalem, and because they supposed that the Kingdom of God was to appear immediately. He said therefore, 'A nobleman went into a far country to receive a *basileia* and then return.'" The nobleman did not go away to get a realm, an area over which to rule. The realm over which he wanted to reign was at hand. The territory over which he was to rule was this place he left. The problem was that he was no king. He needed authority, the right to rule. He went off to get a "kingdom," i.e., kingship, authority. The Revised Standard Version has therefore translated the word "kingly power."

The Kingdom of God is His kingship, His rule, His authority. When this is once realized, we can go through the New Testament and find passage after passage where this meaning is evident, where the Kingdom is not a realm or a people but God's reign. Jesus said that we must "receive the Kingdom of God" as little children (Mark 10:15). What is received? The Church? Heaven? What is received is God's rule. In order to enter the future realm of the Kingdom, one must submit himself in perfect trust to God's rule here and now.

When we pray, "Thy Kingdom come," (Matt 6:10) are we praying for heaven to come to earth? In a sense we are praying for this, but heaven is an object of desire only because the reign of God is to be more perfectly realized than it is now. Apart from the reign of God, heaven is meaningless. Therefore, what we pray for is, "Thy Kingdom come; *thy will be done* on earth as it is in heaven." This prayer is a petition for God to reign, to manifest His kingly sovereignty and power, to put to flight every enemy of righteousness and of His divine rule that God alone may be King over all the world.

The Mystery of the Kingdom

The fourth chapter of Mark and the thirteenth chapter of Matthew contain a group of parables which set forth the "mystery of the Kingdom of God" (Mark 4:11). A parable is a story drawn from the everyday experience of the people which is designed to illustrate the central truth of our Lord's message. This central truth is called "the mystery" of the Kingdom.

We must first establish the meaning of the term "mystery." A mystery in the biblical sense is not something mysterious, nor deep, dark, profound and difficult. In modern English, the word may bear such connotations, but we cannot interpret the Bible by modern English. In Scripture, "mystery" is often a technical concept whose meaning is set forth in Romans 16:25-26. Paul writes, "Now to

Him who is able to strengthen you according to my gospel and the preaching of Jesus Christ, according to the revelation of the mystery which was kept secret for long ages but is now disclosed and through the prophetic writings is made known to all nations." Here is the biblical idea of mystery: something which has been kept secret through times eternal but is now disclosed. It is a divine purpose which God has designed from eternity but has kept hidden from men. At last, however, in the course of His redemptive plan, God reveals this purpose, and by the Scriptures of the prophets makes it known to all men. A mystery is a divine purpose, hidden in the counsels of God for long ages but finally disclosed in a new revelation of God's redemptive work.

The parables set forth the mystery of the Kingdom—a new truth about the Kingdom of God which was not revealed in the Old Testament but which is at last disclosed in the earthly ministry of our Lord. What is this mystery?

Old Testament perspective of the Kingdom

To answer this question, we must go back into the Old Testament and look at a typical prophecy of the coming of God's Kingdom. In the second chapter of Daniel, King Nebuchadnezzar was given a vision of a great image which had a head of gold, a chest of silver, thighs of bronze, legs of iron, and feet of iron and clay. Then he saw a stone, cut out without hands, which smote the image on the feet and ground it to powder. This dust was swept away by the wind "so that not a trace of them could be found." Then the stone which destroyed the image became a great mountain which filled the whole earth (Dan 2:31-35).

The interpretation is given to us in verses 44 and 45. The image represents the successive nations which were to dominate the course of world history. The meaning of the stone is given in these words: "And in the days of those kings the God of heaven will set up a Kingdom which shall never be destroyed, nor shall its sovereignty be left to another people. It shall break in pieces all these Kingdoms and bring them to an end, and it shall stand forever; just as you saw that a stone was cut from a mountain by no human hand, and that it broke in pieces the iron, the bronze, the clay, the silver, and the gold. A great God has made known to the king what shall be hereafter."

Here is the Old Testament perspective of the prophetic future. The Prophets look forward to a glorious day when God's Kingdom will come, when God will set up His reign on the earth. You will remember that we have discovered that the basic meaning of the Kingdom of God is God's reign. In that day when God sets up *His* reign it will displace all other reigns, all other kingdoms and authorities. It will break the proud sovereignty of man manifested in the rule of the nations which have dominated the scene of earthly history. God's reign, God's Kingdom, God's rule will sweep away every opposing rule. God alone will be King in those days.

The Vision of the Kingdom

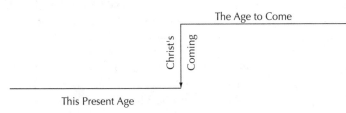

The Messiah brings God's Day of Peace and Power

In the Old Testament perspective, the coming of God's Kingdom is viewed as a single great event: a mighty manifestation of God's power which would sweep away the wicked kingdoms of human sovereignty and would fill all the earth with righteousness.

A new revelation of the Kingdom

We must now turn back to the Gospel of Matthew and relate this truth to our previous study. John the Baptist had announced the coming of the Kingdom of God (Matt 3:2) by which he understood the coming of the Kingdom foretold in the Old Testament. The Coming One would bring a twofold baptism: some would be baptized with the Holy Spirit and experience the Messianic salvation of the Kingdom of God, while others would be baptized with the fires of the final judgment (Matt 3:11). That this is John's meaning is clear from the next verse. Messiah's work will be one of sifting and the separation of men. As the farmer threshes and winnows

his harvest, preserving the good grain and discarding the chaff, Messiah will cleanse His threshing floor, gathering the grain into His barn (salvation for the righteous) but sending the wicked into the fiery judgment (v. 12). The phrase " unquenchable fire" shows that this refers to no ordinary human experience but to the eschatological judgment.

From his prison, John sent messengers to Jesus to ask if He really was the Coming One, or if they were to look for another. John's doubt has often been interpreted as a loss of confidence in his own mission and divine call because of his imprisonment. However, Jesus' praise of John makes this unlikely. John was no reed shaken by the wind (Matt 11:7).

John's problem was created by the fact that Jesus was not acting like the Messiah whom John had announced. Where was the baptism of the Spirit? Where was the judgment of the wicked?

Jesus replied that He was indeed the Bearer of the Kingdom, that the signs of the Messianic Age of prophecy were being manifested. And yet Jesus said, "Blessed is he who takes no offense at me" (Matt 11:6). "Lord, are you He who is to come, or shall we look for another?" (v. 3) Why did John ask that question? Because the prophecy of Daniel did not seem to be in process of fulfillment. Herod Antipas ruled in Galilee. Roman legions marched through Jerusalem. Authority rested in the hands of a pagan Roman, Pilate. Idolatrous, polytheistic, immoral Rome ruled the world with an iron hand. Although Rome exercised great wisdom and restraint in governing her subjects, granting concessions to the Jews because of religious scruples, yet only God possessed the right to rule His people. Sovereignty belongs to God alone. Here was John's problem, and it was the problem of every devout Jew, including Jesus' closest disciples, in their effort to understand and interpret Jesus' person and ministry. How could He be the Bearer of the Kingdom while sin and sinful institutions remained unpunished?

Jesus answered, "Blessed is he who takes no offense at me." What Jesus meant is this. "Yes, the Kingdom of God is here. But there is a mystery—a new revelation about the Kingdom. The Kingdom of God is here, but instead of destroying human sovereignty, it has attacked the sovereignty of Satan. The Kingdom of God is here, but instead of making changes in the external, political order of things, it is making changes in the spiritual order and in the lives of men and women."

The Mystery of the Kingdom

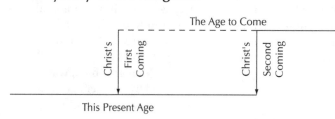

The Messiah Comes Twice

This is the mystery of the Kingdom, the truth which God now discloses for the first time in redemptive history. God's Kingdom is to work among men in two different stages. The Kingdom *is* yet to come in the form prophesied by Daniel when every human sovereignty will be displaced by God's sovereignty. The world will yet behold the coming of God's Kingdom with power. But the mystery, the new revelation, is that this very Kingdom of God has now come to work among men but in an utterly unexpected way. It is not now destroying human rule; it is not now abolishing sin from the earth; it is not now bringing the baptism of fire that John had announced. It has come quietly, unobtrusively, secretly. It can work among men and never be recognized by the crowds. In the spiritual realm, the Kingdom now offers to men the blessings of God's rule, delivering them from the power of Satan and sin. The Kingdom of God is an offer, a gift which may be accepted or rejected. The Kingdom is now here with persuasion rather than with power.

Each of the parables in Matthew 13 illustrates this mystery of the Kingdom; that the Kingdom of God which is yet to come in power and great glory is actually present among men in advance in an unexpected

form to bring to men in the present evil Age the blessings of The Age to Come.

This is the mystery of the Kingdom: before the day of harvest, before the end of the age, God has entered into history in the person of Christ to work among men, to bring to them the life and blessings of His Kingdom. It comes humbly, unobtrusively. It comes to men as a Galilean carpenter went throughout the cities of Palestine preaching the gospel of the Kingdom, delivering men from their bondage to the devil. It comes to men as His disciples went throughout Galilean villages with the same message. It comes to men today as disciples of Jesus still take the gospel of the Kingdom into all the world. It comes quietly, humbly, without fire from heaven, without a blaze of glory, without a rending of the mountains or a cleaving of the skies. It comes like seed sown in the earth. It can be rejected by hard hearts, it can be choked out, its life may sometimes seem to wither and die. But it *is* the Kingdom of God. It brings the miracle of the divine life among men. It introduces them into the blessings of the divine rule. It is to them the supernatural work of God's grace. And this same Kingdom, this same supernatural power of God will yet manifest itself at the end of the age, this time not quietly within the lives of those who receive it, but in power and great glory purging all sin and evil from the earth. Such is the gospel of the Kingdom.

When Will the Kingdom Come?

If we have entered into the enjoyment of the blessings of God's Kingdom, our final question is, what are we to do as a result of these blessings? Are we passively to enjoy the life of the Kingdom while waiting for the consummation at the return of the Lord? Yes, we are to wait, but not passively. Perhaps the most important single verse in the Word of God for God's people today is the text for this study: Matthew 24:14.

This verse refers to the manifestation of God's Kingdom in power and glory when the Lord Jesus returns. There is wide interest among God's people as to the time of Christ's return. Will it be soon, or late? Many prophetic Bible conferences offer messages which search the Bible and scan the newspapers to understand the prophecies and the signs of the times to try to determine how near to the end we may be. Our text is the clearest statement in God's Word about the time of our Lord's coming. There is no verse which speaks as concisely and distinctly as this verse about the time when the Kingdom will come.

The chapter is introduced by questions of the disciples to the Lord as they looked at the temple whose destruction Jesus had just announced. "Tell us, when will this be and what shall be the sign of your coming, and of the close of the age?" (Matt 24:3). The disciples expected This Age to end with the return of Christ in glory. The Kingdom will come with the inauguration of The Age to Come. Here is their question: "When will This Age end? When will You come again and bring the Kingdom?"

Jesus answered their question in some detail. He described first of all the course of This Age down to the time of the end. This evil Age is to last until His return. It will forever be hostile to the gospel and to God's people. Evil will prevail. Subtle, deceitful influences will seek to turn men away from Christ. False religions, deceptive messiahs will lead many astray. Wars will continue; there will be famines and earthquakes. Persecution and martyrdom will plague the Church. Believers will suffer hatred so long as This Age lasts. Men will stumble and deliver up one another. False prophets will arise, iniquity abound, the love of many will grow cold (vv. 4-12).

This is a dark picture, but this is what is to be expected of an age under the world rulers of this darkness (Eph 6:12). However, the picture is not one of unrelieved darkness and evil. God has not abandoned This Age to darkness. Jewish apocalyptic writings of New Testament times conceived of an age completely under the control of evil. God had withdrawn from active participation in the affairs of man; salvation belonged only to the future when God's Kingdom would come in glory. The present would witness only sorrow and suffering.

Some Christians have reflected a similar pessimistic attitude: Satan is the "god of This Age"; therefore God's people can expect nothing but evil and defeat in This Age. The Church is to become thoroughly apostate; civilization is to be utterly corrupted. Christians must fight a losing battle until Christ comes.

The Word of God does indeed teach that there will be an intensification of evil at the end of the Age, for Satan remains the god of This Age. But we must strongly emphasize that God has not abandoned This Age to the Evil one. In fact, the Kingdom of God has entered into This Evil Age; Satan has been defeated. The Kingdom of God, in Christ, has created the Church, and the Kingdom of God works in the world through the Church to accomplish the divine purposes of extending His Kingdom in the world. We are caught up in a great struggle—the conflict of the ages. God's Kingdom works in this world through the power of the gospel. "And this gospel of the Kingdom will be preached throughout the whole world, as a testimony to all nations; and then the end will come" (Matt 24:14).

In this text I find three things. There is a message, there is a mission, there is a motive.

The Message of the Kingdom

The *message* is the gospel of the Kingdom, this Good News about the Kingdom of God.

Some Bible teachers say that the gospel of the Kingdom is not the gospel of salvation. It is rather a gospel announcing the return of Christ which will be preached in the tribulation by a Jewish remnant after the Church is gone. We cannot deal at length with that problem, but we can discover that the gospel of the Kingdom is the gospel which was proclaimed by the apostles in the early Church.

We must first, however, notice a close connection between this verse and the Great Commission. At His Ascension, the Lord commissioned His disciples: "Go therefore and make disciples of all nations, baptizing them in the name of the Father and of the Son and of the Holy Spirit, teaching them to observe all that I have commanded you; and lo, I am with you always, to the close of the age" (Matt 28:19-20). When one compares these verses, they speak for themselves. "What shall be the sign of Your coming, and of the close of the age?" "This gospel of the Kingdom will be preached throughout the whole world, as a testimony to all nations; and then the end will come." "Go therefore and make disciples of all nations... and lo, I am with you always, to the close of the age." Both verses speak about the same mission: worldwide evangelization until the end of the Age. This fact ties together Matthew 28:19 and Matthew 24:14.

The book of Acts relates that the apostles set out upon the fulfillment of this mission. In Acts 8:12, Philip went down to Samaria and preached the gospel. The Revised Standard Version accurately describes his mission in these words: "he preached good news about the Kingdom of God." Literally translated, the words are, "Gospeling concerning the Kingdom of God." New Testament Greek has the same root for the noun, "gospel," and the verb, "to gospel" or "to preach the gospel." It is unfortunate for our understanding of this truth that we do not have the same idiom in English.

> In the face of the power of the Kingdom of God in Christ, death was helpless. This is the Gospel of the Kingdom.

Matthew 24:14 speaks of the "gospel of the Kingdom," and Acts 8:12 speaks of "gospeling about the Kingdom." This gospel of the Kingdom must be preached in all the world. Philip went into Samaria, *gospeling* concerning the Kingdom of God, i.e., preaching the gospel of the Kingdom. We have in Acts 8:12 the same phrases as that in Matthew 24:14, except that we have a verb instead of the noun with the preposition "about" inserted in the phrase.

When Paul came to Rome he gathered together the Jews, for he always preached the gospel "to the Jew first." What was his message? "When they had appointed a day for him, they came to him at his lodging in great numbers. And he expounded the matter, from morning till evening, testifying to the Kingdom of God and trying to convince them about Jesus" (Acts 28:23). The testimony about the Kingdom of God, the gospel of the Kingdom, was the message Paul proclaimed to the Jews at Rome.

However, Paul met the same reaction as had our Lord when he appeared in Israel announcing the Kingdom of God (Matt 4:17). Some believed, but the majority of the Jews rejected his message. Paul then announced the divine purpose for the Gentiles in the face of Israel's unbelief: "Let it be known to you then that this salvation of God has been sent to the Gentiles; they will listen" (Acts 28:28). Paul preached to the Jews the Kingdom of God; they rejected it. Therefore, "this salvation of God" was then offered to the Gentiles. The fact that the gospel of the Kingdom of God is the same as the message of salvation is further proven by the following verses. "And he lived there two whole years at his own expense, and welcomed all who came to him, preaching the Kingdom of God and teaching about the Lord Jesus Christ" (vv. 30-31). The Kingdom was preached to the Jews, and when they rejected it the same Kingdom was proclaimed to the Gentiles. The Good News about the Kingdom of God was Paul's message for both Jews and Gentiles.

Victory over death

We now turn again to the Scripture which most clearly and simply describes what this gospel of the Kingdom is. In 1 Corinthians 15:24-26, Paul outlines the stages of our Lord's redemptive work. He describes the victorious issue of Christ's Messianic reign with the words, "Then comes the end, when He delivers the Kingdom to God the Father after destroying every rule and every authority and power. For He must reign"—He must reign as King, He must reign in His Kingdom—"until He has put all His enemies under his feet. The last enemy to be destroyed is death."

Here is the biblical description of the meaning of the reign of Christ by which His Kingdom shall attain its end. It is the reign of God in the person of His Son, Jesus Christ, for the purpose of putting His enemies under His feet. "The last enemy to be abolished is death." The abolition of death is the mission of God's Kingdom. God's Kingdom must also destroy every other enemy, including sin and Satan; for death is the wages of sin (Rom 6:23) and it is Satan who has the power over death (Heb 2:14). Only when death, sin, and Satan are destroyed will redeemed men know the perfect blessings of God's reign.

The gospel of the Kingdom is the announcement of Christ's conquest over death. We have discovered that, while the consummation of this victory is future when death is finally cast into the lake of fire (Rev 20:14), Christ has nevertheless already defeated death. Speaking of God's grace, Paul says that it has now been "manifested through the appearing of our Saviour Christ Jesus, who abolished death and brought life and immortality to light through the gospel" (2 Tim 1:10). The word here translated "abolish" does not mean to do away with, but to defeat, to break the power, to put out of action. The same Greek word is used in 1 Corinthians 15:26, "The last enemy to be *destroyed* is death." This word appears also in 1 Corinthians 15:24, "Then comes the end, when He delivers the Kingdom to God the Father after *destroying* every rule and every authority and power."

There are therefore two stages in the destruction—the abolition—the defeat of death. Its final destruction awaits the Second Coming of Christ; but by His death and resurrection, Christ has already destroyed death. He has broken its power. Death is still an enemy, but it is a defeated enemy. We are certain of the future victory because of the victory which has already been accomplished. We have an accomplished victory to proclaim.

This is good news about the Kingdom of God. How men need this gospel! Everywhere one goes he finds the gaping grave swallowing up the dying. Tears of loss, of separation, of final departure stain every face. Every table sooner or later has an empty chair, every fireside its vacant place. Death is the great leveller. Wealth or poverty, fame or oblivion, power or futility, success or failure, race, creed, or culture—all our human distinctions mean nothing before the ultimate irresistible sweep of the scythe of death which cuts us all down. And whether the mausoleum is a fabulous Taj Mahal, a massive pyramid, an unmarked forgotten spot of ragged grass, or the unplotted depths of the sea, one fact stands: death reigns.

Apart from the gospel of the Kingdom, death is the mighty conqueror before whom we are all helpless. We can only beat our fists in utter futility against the unyielding and unresponding tomb. But the Good News is this: death has been defeated; our conqueror has been conquered. In the face of the power of the Kingdom of God in Christ, death was helpless. It could not hold Him, death has been defeated; life and immortality have been brought to light. An empty tomb in Jerusalem is proof of it. This is the gospel of the Kingdom.

Victory over Satan

The enemy of God's Kingdom is Satan; Christ must rule until He has put Satan under His feet. This victory also awaits the Coming of Christ. During the Millennium, Satan is to be bound in a bottomless pit. Only at the end of the Millennium is he to be cast into the lake of fire.

But we have discovered that Christ has already defeated Satan. The victory of God's Kingdom is not only future, but a great initial victory has taken place. Christ partook of flesh and blood—He became incarnate—"that through death he might destroy him who has the power of death, that is, the devil, and deliver all those who through fear of death were subject to lifelong bondage" (Heb 2:14-15). The word translated "destroy" is the same word found in 1 Corinthians 15:24 and 26; 2 Timothy 1:10. Christ has nullified the power of death; He has also nullified the power of Satan. Satan still goes about like a roaring lion bringing persecution upon God's people (1 Pet 5:8); he insinuates himself like an angel of light into religious circles (2 Cor 11:14). But he is a defeated enemy. His power, his domination has been broken. His doom is sure. A decisive, *the* decisive, victory has been won. Christ cast out demons, delivering men from satanic bondage, proving that God's Kingdom delivers men from their enslavement to Satan. It brings them out of darkness into the saving and healing light of the gospel. This is the Good News about the Kingdom of God. Satan is defeated, and we may be released from demonic fear and from satanic evil and know the glorious liberty of the sons of God.

Victory over sin

Sin is an enemy of God's Kingdom. Has Christ done anything about sin, or has He merely promised a future deliverance when

He brings the Kingdom in glory? We must admit that sin, like death, is abroad in the world. Every newspaper bears an eloquent testimony of the working of sin. Yet sin, like death and Satan, has been defeated. Christ has already appeared to put away sin by the sacrifice of Himself (Heb 9:26). The power of sin has been broken. "We know this, that our old self was crucified with him so that the body of sin might be destroyed, and we might no longer be enslaved to sin" (Rom 6:6). Here a third time is the word "to destroy" or "abolish." Christ's reign as King has the objective of "abolishing" every enemy (1 Cor 15:24-26). This work is indeed future, but it is also past. What our Lord will finish at His Second Coming He has already begun by His death and resurrection. "Death" has been abolished, destroyed (2 Tim 1:10); Satan has been destroyed (Heb 2:14); and in Romans 6:6, the "body of sin" has been abolished, destroyed. The same word of victory, of the destruction of Christ's enemies, is used three times of this threefold victory: over Satan, over death, over sin.

Therefore, we are to be no longer in bondage to sin (Rom 6:6). The day of slavery to sin is past. Sin is in the world, but its power is not the same. Men are no longer helpless before it, for its dominion has been broken. The power of the Kingdom of God has invaded This Age, a power which can set men free from their bondage to sin.

The gospel of the Kingdom is the announcement of what God has done and will do. It is His victory over His enemies. It is the

D-Day before V-E Day   *Ken Blue*

Through His authentic life, perfect sacrifice and victorious resurrection, Jesus effected a transfer of sovereignty from Satan's pseudokingdom to God's kingdom. Now Jesus claims to possess all authority in heaven and earth (Matt 28:18). God always had this authority, but through the Incarnation it is established in history. And the implications of Jesus' "all authority" are now manifest through the Church in history.

Satan is bound and his pseudo-kingdom is breaking up, yet God has left him room to maneuver. What power and freedom he still possesses and precisely when he is able to exercise these is not entirely clear from Scripture. What is clear from Scripture and increasingly confirmed in our experience is that the kingdom of God has already absorbed the full wrath of Satan's might and survived it. The kingdom of God has already gone through its darkest night. The most dismal evil in all history found its absolute limits at Calvary. After evil had choked on its own venom, it became forever subject to Christ and to us in His name. There is no absolute dualism between God and Satan. The victor at the end of the battle is already crowned. Yet there are still many sick and some demonized people among us who are subjected to the unsanctioned and illegal power of Satan. How are we to understand this ambiguity?

A helpful illustration of how a war already won could continue to be fought comes from the history of World War II. On "D-Day" the allied troops landed successfully at Normandy beach in order to establish a secure beachhead on the European mainland. It was understood by military experts at the time that this operation secured ultimate victory for the allies. There would be, however, many more bloody battles fought before the day on which ultimate victory would be realized: "V-E Day" (Victory in Europe Day).

In God's war with evil, "D-Day" occurred with the death and resurrection of Christ. Ultimate victory is now assured; yet the fight rages on till "V-E Day," the glorious return of Christ. Between these times, the Church presses the battle against the evil which remains in the world. Blood is still shed in these battles, and some of the blood will be ours, but we are assured that the ultimate victory of the past will be fully realized in the future.

Ken Blue is the Pastor of Foothills Church, which he planted in the San Diego area. He has served 30 years in public ministry as a pastor, church planter and a missionary to Eastern Europe. Taken from *Authority to Heal* by Ken Blue. Copyright 1979 by Ken Blue. Used by permission of InterVarsity Press, P.O. Box 1400, Downers Grove, IL 60515.

Good News that Christ is coming again to destroy forever His enemies. It is a gospel of hope. It is also the Good News of what God has already done. He has already broken the power of death, defeated Satan, and overthrown the rule of sin. The gospel is one of promise but also of experience, and the promise is grounded in experience. What Christ has done guarantees what He will do. This is the gospel which we must take into all the world.

The Mission of the Kingdom

In the second place, we find in Matthew 24:14 a *mission* as well as a message. This gospel of the Kingdom, this Good News of Christ's victory over God's enemies, must be preached in all the world for a witness to all nations. This is our mission. This verse is one of the most important in all the Word of God to ascertain the meaning and the purpose of human history.

The meaning of history

The meaning of history is a problem which is today confounding the minds of thinking men. We do not need to be reminded that our generation faces potential destruction of such total proportions that few of us try to envisage the awful reality. In the face of such threatening catastrophe, men are asking as they have never asked before, what is history all about? Why is man on this earth? Where is he going? Is there a thread of meaning, of purpose, of destiny, that will bring mankind to some goal?

In a former generation, the philosophy of progress was widely accepted. Some thinkers charted the meaning of history by a single straight line which traced a gradual but steady incline from primitive savage beginnings upward to a high level of culture and civilization. The philosophy of progress taught that mankind, because of its intrinsic character, is destined to improve until it one day attains a perfect society, free from all evil, war, poverty, and conflict. This view has been shattered upon the anvil of history. Current events have made the concept of inevitable progress intolerable and unrealistic.

Another view interprets history as a series of cycles like a great spiral. There is movement both up and down. There are high points and low points on the spiral. But each ascent is a little higher than the last and each descent is not as low as the preceding. Even though we have our "ups and downs," the movement of the spiral as a whole is upward. This is a modification of the doctrine of progress.

Other interpretations have been utterly pessimistic. Someone has suggested that the most accurate chart of the meaning of history is the set of tracks made by a drunken fly with feet wet with ink, staggering across a piece of white paper. They lead nowhere and reflect no pattern of meaning.

It is the author's conviction that the ultimate meaning of history must be found in the action of God in history as recorded and interpreted in inspired Scripture. Here, Christian faith must speak. If there is no God, man is lost in a labyrinthine maze of bewildering experiences with no thread of meaning to guide him. If God has not acted in history, the ebb and flow of the tides of the centuries wash back and forth aimlessly between the sands of eternity. But the basic fact in the Word of God is that God has spoken, God has been redemptively at work in history, and the divine action will yet bring history to a divinely destined goal.

One travels throughout the Near East and gazes with wonder upon the ruins which bear silent witness to once mighty civilizations. Massive columns still reach to the heavens, while elsewhere only huge mounds scar barren plains marking the accumulated debris of dead civilizations. The Sphinx, the pyramids of Gizeh, the pillars of Persepolis and the towers of Thebes, still bear eloquent testimony to the glory that was Egypt and Persia. One may still climb the Acropolis in Athens or tread the Forum in Rome and feel something of the splendour and glory of first-century civilizations which in some respects have never been surpassed. But today they are ruins, toppled pillars, prostrate statues—dead civilizations.

What is the meaning of it all? Why do nations rise and fall? Is there any purpose? Or will the earth some day become a dead star, lifeless as the moon?

The divine purpose and the chosen people

The Bible has an answer. The central theme of the entire Bible is God's redemptive work in history. Long ago, God chose a small, despised people, Israel. God was not interested in this people for their own sake; God's purpose included all mankind. God in His sovereign design selected this one insignificant people so that through them He might work out His redemptive purpose which eventually would include the entire human race. The ultimate meaning of Egypt, of the Assyrians, of the Chaldeans and of the other nations of the ancient Near East is found in their relationship to this one tiny nation—Israel. God set up rulers and cast them down that He might bring forth Israel. He raised up this people and preserved them. He had a plan, and He was working out this plan in history.

Then came the day when "in the fullness of time" appeared on earth the Lord Jesus Christ, a Jew, a son of Abraham after the flesh. God's purpose with Israel was then brought to a great fulfillment. This does not mean that God is done with Israel. But it does mean that when Christ appeared, God's redemptive purpose through Israel attained its initial objective. Up until that time, the clue to the meaning of the divine purpose in history was identified with Israel as a nation. When Christ had accomplished His redemptive work of death and resurrection, the divine purpose in history moved from Israel, who rejected the gospel, to the Church—the fellowship of both Jews and Gentiles who accepted the gospel. This is proven by our Lord's saying in Matthew 21:43 which is addressed to the nation Israel: "The Kingdom of God will be taken away from you and given to a nation producing the fruits of it." The Church is "a chosen race, a royal priesthood, a holy nation" (1 Pet 2:9); and it is in the present mission of the Church, as it carries the Good News of the Kingdom of God unto all the world, that the redemptive purpose of God in history is being worked out.

The ultimate meaning of history between the Ascension of our Lord and His return in glory is found in the extension and working of the gospel in the world. "This gospel of the Kingdom will be preached throughout the whole world, as a testimony to all nations; and then the end will come." The divine purpose in the nineteen hundred years since our Lord lived on earth is found in the history of

the gospel of the Kingdom. The thread of meaning is woven into the missionary program of the Church. Some day when we go into the archives of heaven to find a book which expounds the meaning of human history as God sees it, we will not draw out a book depicting "The History of the West" or "The Progress of Civilization" or "The Glory of the British Empire" or "The Growth and Expansion of America." That book will be entitled, *The Preparation for and the Extension of the Gospel among the Nations*. For only here is God's *redemptive* purpose carried forward.

This is a staggering fact. God has entrusted to people like us, redeemed sinners, the responsibility of carrying out the divine purpose in history. Why has God done it in this way? Is He not taking a great risk that His purpose will fail? It is now over nineteen hundred years, and the goal is not yet achieved. Why did God not do it Himself? Why did He not send hosts of angels whom He could trust to complete the task at once? Why has He committed it to us? We do not try to answer the question except to say that such is God's will. Here are the facts: God has entrusted this mission to us, and unless we do it, it will not get done.

Let Matthew 24:14 burn in our hearts. God has said this about no other group of people. This Good News of the Kingdom of God must be preached, if you please, by the Church in all the world for a witness to all nations. This is *God's* program. This means that for the ultimate meaning of modern civilization and the destiny of human history, you and I are more important than the United Nations. From the perspective of eternity, the mission of the Church is more important than the march of armies or the actions of the world's capitals, because it is in the accomplishment of this mission that the divine purpose for human history is accomplished.

The Motive of the Kingdom

Finally, our text contains a mighty *motive:* "Then the end will come." The subject of this section is, when will the Kingdom come? I am not setting any dates. I do not know when the end will come. And yet I do know this: When the Church has finished its task of evangelizing the world, Christ will come again. The Word of God says it. Why did He not come in

AD 500? Because the Church had not evangelized the world. Why did He not return in AD 1000? Because the Church had not finished its task of worldwide evangelization. Is He coming soon? He is—if we, God's people, are obedient to the command of the Lord to take the gospel into all the world.

What a sobering realization this is! It is so staggering that some people say, "I cannot believe it! It simply cannot be true that God has committed such responsibility to men." When William Carey wanted to go to India to take the gospel to that country a century and a half ago, he was told, "Sit down, young man; when God wants to evangelize the heathen, He will do it without your help." But Carey had the vision and the knowledge of God's Word not to sit down. He rose up and went to India. He initiated the modern day of worldwide missions.

Our responsibility: to complete the task

God has entrusted to us the continuation and the consummation of that task. Here is the thing that thrills me. We have come far closer to the finishing of this mission than any previous generation. We have done more in the last century and a half in worldwide evangelization than all the preceding centuries since the apostolic age. Our modern technology has provided printing, automobiles, aeroplanes, radios and many other methods of expediting our task of carrying the gospel into all the world. Previously unknown languages are being reduced to writing. The Word of God has now been rendered, in part at least, into over 1,700 languages or dialects, and the number is growing yearly. Here is the challenging fact. If God's people in the English-speaking world alone took this text seriously and responded to its challenge, we could finish the task of worldwide evangelization in our own generation and witness the Lord's return.

Someone will say, "This is impossible. Many lands today are not open to the gospel. We cannot get into China; the doors into India are closing. If the Lord's return awaits the evangelization of the world by the Church, then Christ cannot possibly return in our lifetime, for so many lands are today closed to the gospel that it is impossible to finish the task today."

Such an attitude fails to reckon with God. It is true that many doors are closed at the moment, but God is able to open closed doors overnight, and God is able to work behind closed doors. My concern is not with closed doors; my concern is with the doors that are open which we do not enter. If God's people were really faithful and were doing everything possible to finish the task, God would see to it that the doors were opened. Our responsibility is the many doors standing wide open which we are not entering. We are a disobedient people. We argue about the definition of worldwide evangelization and we debate the details of eschatology, while we neglect the command of the Word of God to evangelize the world.

Someone else will say, "How are we to know when the mission is completed? How close are we to the accomplishment of the task? Which countries have been evangelized and which have not? How close are we to the end? Does this not lead to date-setting?"

I answer, "I do not know." God alone knows the definition of terms. I cannot precisely define who "all the nations" are. Only God knows the exact meaning of "evangelize." He alone, who has told us that this gospel of the Kingdom shall be preached in the whole world for a testimony unto all the nations, will know when that objective has been accomplished. But I do not need to know. I know only one thing: Christ has not yet returned; therefore the task is not yet done. When it is done, Christ will come. Our responsibility is not to insist on defining the terms of our task; our responsibility is to complete it. So long as Christ does not return, our work is undone. Let us get busy and complete our mission.

Becoming biblical realists

Our responsibility is not to save the world. We are not required to transform This Age. The very paragraph of which this verse is the conclusion tells us that there will be wars and troubles, persecutions, and martyrdoms until the very end. I am glad these words are in the Bible. They give me stability. They provide sanity. They keep me from an unrealistic optimism. We are not to be discouraged when evil times come.

However, we have a message of power to take to the world. It is the gospel of the Kingdom. Throughout the course of This Age, two forces are at work: the power of evil, and the Kingdom of God. The world is the scene of a conflict. The forces of the Evil One are assaulting the people of God, but the gospel of the Kingdom is assaulting the kingdom of Satan. This conflict will last to the end of The Age. Final victory will be achieved only by the return of Christ. There is no room for an unqualified optimism. Our Lord's Olivet Discourse indicates that until the very end, evil will characterize This Age. False prophets and false messiahs will arise and lead many astray. Iniquity, evil, are so to abound that the love of many will grow cold. God's people will be called upon to endure hardship. "In the world you have tribulation" (John 16:33). "Through many tribulations we must enter the Kingdom of God" (Acts 14:22). We must always be ready to endure the tribulation as well as the Kingdom and patience which are in Jesus (Rev 1:9). In fact, our Lord Himself said, "He who endures to the end will be saved" (Matt 24:13). He who endures tribulation and persecution to the uttermost, even to the laying down of his life, will not perish but will find salvation. "Some of you they will put to death…But not a hair of your head will perish" (Luke 21:16,18). The Church must always in its essential character be a martyr church. As we carry the gospel into all the world, we are not to expect unqualified success. We are to be prepared for opposition, resistance, even persecution and martyrdom. This Age remains evil, hostile to the gospel of the Kingdom.

There is, however, no room for an unrelieved pessimism. In some prophetic studies, we receive the impression that the end of the Age, the last days, are to be characterized by *total* evil. Undue emphasis is sometimes laid upon the perilous character of the last days (2 Tim 3:1). The visible Church, we are told, is to be *completely* leavened by evil doctrine. Apostasy is so to pervade the Church that only a small remnant will be found faithful to God's Word. The closing days of This Age will be the Laodicean period when the entire professing Church will be nauseatingly indifferent to eternal issues. In such a portrayal of the last days, God's people can expect only defeat and frustration. Evil is to reign. The Church age will end with an unparalleled victory of evil.

Sometimes so much stress is laid upon the evil character of the last days that we receive the impression (unintended, to be sure) that the faster the world deteriorates the better, for the sooner the Lord will come.

It cannot be denied that the Scriptures emphasize the evil character of the last days. In fact, we have already made this emphasis. The evil which characterizes This Age will find a fearful intensification at the very end in its opposition to and hatred of the Kingdom of God. This does not mean, however, that we are to lapse into pessimism and abandon This Age and the world to evil and Satan. The fact is, the gospel of the Kingdom is to be proclaimed throughout the world. The Kingdom of God has invaded This present evil Age. The powers of The Age to Come have attacked This Age. The last days will indeed be evil days, but *"in these last days* (God) has spoken to us by a Son" (Heb 1:2). God has given us a gospel of salvation for the last days, a gospel embodied in One who is Son of God. Furthermore, *"in the last days* it shall be," God declares, "that I will pour out my Spirit upon all flesh" (Acts 2:17). God has spoken for the last days; God has poured out His Spirit in the last days to give power to proclaim the divine Word. The last days will be evil, but not unrelieved evil. God has given us a gospel for the last days, and He has given a power to take that gospel into all the world for a testimony unto all the nations; then shall the end come.

This must be the spirit of our mission in This evil Age. We are not rosy optimists, expecting the gospel to conquer the world and establish the Kingdom of God. Neither are we despairing pessimists who feel that our task is hopeless in the face of the evil of This Age. We are realists, biblical realists, who recognize the terrible power of evil and yet who go forth in a mission of worldwide evangelization to win victories for God's Kingdom until Christ returns in glory to accomplish the last and greatest victory.

Here is the motive of our mission: the final victory awaits the completion of our task. "And then the end will come." There is no other verse in the Word of God which says, "And then the end will come." When will This Age end? When the world has been evangelized. "What will be the sign of your coming and of the close of the age?" (Matt 24:3). "This gospel of the Kingdom will be preached throughout the whole world as a testimony to all nations; and then, AND THEN, the end will come." When? *Then*; when the Church has fulfilled its divinely appointed mission.

"Go Ye Therefore"

Do you love the Lord's appearing? Then you will bend every effort to take the gospel into all the world. It troubles me in the light of the clear teaching of God's Word, in the light of our Lord's explicit definition of our task in the Great Commission (Matt 28:18-20) that we take it so lightly. "All authority in heaven and on earth has been given to me." This is the Good News of the Kingdom. Christ has wrested authority from Satan. The Kingdom of God has attacked the kingdom of Satan; This evil Age has been assaulted by The Age to Come in the person of Christ. All authority is now His. He will not display this authority in its final glorious victory until He comes again, but the authority is now His. Satan is defeated and bound; death is conquered; sin is broken. All authority is His. "Go ye therefore." Wherefore? Because all authority, all power is His, and because He is waiting until we have finished our task. His is the Kingdom; He reigns in heaven, and He manifests His reign on earth in and through His church. When we have accomplished our mission, He will return and establish His Kingdom in glory. To us it is given not only to wait for but also to hasten the coming of the day of God (2 Pet 3:12). This is the mission of the gospel of the Kingdom, and this is our mission.

Study Questions

1. What relationship exists between the mission of the Church and the coming of the Kingdom? According to Ladd, is it possible for Christians to affect the coming of the Kingdom?

2. Describe the significance of the time between the two appearances of the Messiah in terms of Kingdom victory.

3. Explain, specifically and concisely, the message of the Gospel of the Kingdom as victory over evil.

4. Explain, specifically and concisely, the message of the Gospel of the Kingdom as salvation of people.

5. How does Matthew 24:14 supercharge history with meaning for believers?

God at War

Gregory A. Boyd

Gregory A. Boyd (Ph.D., Princeton Theological Seminary) is Professor of Theology at Bethel College and preaching pastor at Woodland Hills Church, both in St. Paul, Minnesota. His books include *Cynic, Sage or Son of God? Recovering the Real Jesus in an Age of Revisionist Replies* and *God at War*.

The Old Testament clearly assumes that something profoundly sinister has entered God's good creation and now perpetually threatens the world. Not all is well in creation, whether it is portrayed as Leviathan, Rahab, Yamm, Behemoth, hostile waters or a wayward rebellious god (e.g., "prince of Persia," Chemosh, *satan*); or portrayed as a battle that took place before the creation of this world or as something taking place in the present. At a fundamental level, the Old Testament presents something askew in creation and, to this extent, its worldview overlaps with the general Near Eastern worldview. But the cosmic warfare dimension of the Old Testament worldview is radically unique among Near Eastern peoples in the way it is played out. This uniqueness has center stage throughout the Old Testament.

Unlike all other warfare worldviews, the Old Testament repeatedly stresses the absolute supremacy of one God over all others and maintains, unequivocally, that this one God is never threatened by His enemies. This emphasis is a solid foundation for everything else the Lord subsequently reveals to humankind. Biblical authors never abandon this foundational monotheistic conviction, but its relation to the warfare motif changes significantly as we move into the New Testament. Here the reality of warfare shares center stage with the supremacy of God. Almost everything that Jesus and the early church are about is colored by the central conviction that the world is caught in the crossfire of a cosmic battle between the Lord and His angelic army and Satan and his demonic army.

Transformation During the Intertestamental Period

The period between the Old and New Testaments significantly transformed the Jewish worldview. From the time of the exodus, the Jews had closely associated the truthfulness of their belief in Yahweh's supremacy with their political successes. His lordship over Israel and over the entire world was, for them, most clearly evidenced by the fact that they had won, and preserved, independent status as a nation. It caused a crisis of faith for them when they were taken into captivity and oppressed by heathen kings. This seemed to imply that Yahweh was not, in fact, the sovereign Lord over the whole earth.

There was, however, another way to explain it. As long as there was hope that Israel someday would regain its independence, their national misfortunes could be interpreted as the result of their own temporary infidelity to Yahweh. In this way, their misfortunes were not an indictment of Yahweh's supremacy, but rather an indictment of themselves. The people believed that when they, as a nation, repented of their sin and turned back to the Lord, He would prove faithful and give them back the Promised Land.[1]

This chastisement theology began to wear thin, however, after several hundred years of painful oppression under pagan authorities. And when the oppression turned into overt bloody persecution under Antiochus IV, many Jews abandoned this theology. Increasingly, Jews in the second and third centuries B.C. began to believe that what was happening to them could not be all their own fault. It followed then that it could not all be due to Yahweh's disciplining will. But if it was not God's will that brought about the disasters they were experiencing, whose will was it? To answer this question, some Jews of this period turned with fresh urgency to the warfare motifs found throughout their Scriptures.

If ever there was a time when it seemed that the raging seas, Leviathan, Satan and demons were having their way with Israel, and with the entire world, this was it. It is not surprising to find, in this oppressive, painful environment, an intensification of the warfare themes of the Hebrew Bible. The conviction that the cosmos is populated with good and evil spiritual beings—and that the earth is caught in the crossfire of their conflict—became centrally important for many Jews. So, too, the apocalyptic hope that Yahweh would soon vanquish Leviathan (or some parallel cosmic figure) and all its cohorts grew in intensity during this intertestamental period.

This intensification of Old Testament themes—this expansion and centralization of the Old Testament ideas about the lesser gods and Yahweh's conflicts with them—constitutes what has come to be called the apocalyptic worldview. If we are to understand the New Testament properly, we must read it against the backdrop of this worldview. The apocalyptic authors intensified the relatively minor Old Testament concept of Yahweh engaging in battle against opposing forces to preserve order in the world. Yahweh must now do battle against these same forces to actually rescue the world. In other words, if Old Testament authors saw Leviathan as threatening the earth, these authors saw the cosmic beast as having already devoured it. In their view, what was needed now was not so much protection from Leviathan, but deliverance out of the belly of the beast itself.

Writing from their own intense experience of evil, the Jews came to the remarkable conclusion that, in a significant sense, the battle between Yahweh and opposing hostile forces for the world had been lost, at least temporarily, by Yahweh. Yet they were certain that Yahweh would ultimately (and soon) reclaim His cosmos, vanquish His foes and reinstate Himself on His rightful throne. In this ultimate eschatological sense, Yahweh could yet be considered Lord over the whole creation. But in this "present age," their conviction was that, as James Kallas describes it, "Satan had stolen the world," and the creation had gone "berserk."[2]

In this "modified dualism," as William F. Albright appropriately labels it,[3] the highest mediating agent of Yahweh has gone bad, abused his incredible God-given authority, taken the entire world hostage, and set himself up as the illegitimate god of the present age. This spells disaster for the cosmos.[4] Fundamentally, it means that the mediating angelic authority structure—one that Yahweh set up at creation—has gone bad at the very top. Because of this, everything underneath this highest authority, both in the heavens and on earth, has been adversely affected. Vast multitudes of powerful angels—having been given authority over various aspects of creation or over lesser angels—can now use this authority to wage war against God and against His people.

It wasn't that all the angels had fallen, but in the minds of these writers, a great many of them had. Demons—sometimes portrayed as mutant offspring of the Nephilim, but other times portrayed as fallen angels themselves—could now freely infest this satanically governed world and work all manner of evil within it. What was to have been a godly council of heaven and a godly army for the Lord had turned itself into a fierce rebel battalion which fought against God, in large part by terrorizing the earth and holding its inhabitants captive. For these apocalypticists, it was no wonder that Yahweh's lordship was not manifested in Israel's political fortune. Nor was it any great mystery why God's people now were undergoing such vicious persecution. Indeed, to these writers, it was no surprise that the entire creation looked like a diabolical war zone. In their view, this is precisely what it was.

Jesus' View of the Satanic Army

Most contemporary New Testament scholars believe it is primarily against this apocalyptic background that we are to understand the ministry of Jesus and the early church.[5] Jesus' teaching, His exorcisms, His healings and other miracles, as well as His work on the cross, all remain, to some extent, incoherent and unrelated to one another until we interpret them within this apocalyptic context—until we interpret them as acts of war. When this hermeneutical step is made, the ministry of Jesus forms a coherent whole.

Satan's rule

As in apocalyptic thought, the assumption that Satan has illegitimately seized the world and thus now exercises a controlling influence over it, undergirds Jesus' entire ministry. Three times the Jesus of John's Gospel refers to Satan as "the prince of this world" (John 12:31, 14:30, and 16:11). Here He uses the word *archōn* which customarily was used to denote "the highest official in a city or a region in the Greco-Roman world."[6] Jesus is saying that, concerning powers that rule over the cosmos, this evil ruler is the highest.

When Satan claims that he can give all "authority" and "glory" of "all the kingdoms of the world" to whomever he wants because it all belongs to him, Jesus does not dispute him (Luke 4:5-6). Instead, He assumes that much to be true. Jesus concurs with the apocalyptic worldview of His day—in agreement with John, Paul and the rest of the New Testament—and believes the entire world is "under the power of the evil one" (1 Jn 5:19) and Satan is "the god of this world" (2 Cor 4:4) and "the ruler of the power of the air" (Eph 2:2). Jesus, therefore, concedes Satan's rulership of the earth. He will not, however,

get back this worldwide kingdom by giving in to Satan's temptation and worshipping this illegitimate tyrant (Luke 4:7-8).[7]

In keeping with the apocalyptic thought of His day, Jesus sees the evil tyrant as mediating and expanding his authority over the world through multitudes of demons that form a vast army under him. Indeed, compared to the apocalyptic views of His day, Jesus somewhat intensifies this conviction. When He is accused of casting out demons by the power of Beelzebul (another name for Satan), He responds by telling His hostile audience, "If a kingdom is divided against itself, that kingdom cannot stand" (Mark 3:24).[8] This builds upon their shared assumption that the demonic kingdom is unified under one "prince" (*archōn*) who is Satan (Mark 3:22; Matt 9:34, 12:24; Luke 11:15). He makes the point that this kingdom of evil, like any kingdom, cannot survive by working at cross-purposes with itself.

Jesus adds that one cannot make significant headway in taking back the "property" of this "kingdom" unless one first "ties up the strong man" who oversees the whole operation (Mark 3:27). This, Luke adds, can be done only when "one stronger than he attacks him and overpowers him" and thus "takes away his armor in which he trusted" and then "divides his plunder" (Luke 11:22). This is what Jesus came to do. His whole ministry was about overpowering the "fully armed" strong man who guarded "his property" (Luke 11:21), namely, God's people and ultimately the entire earth. Far from illustrating how Satan's kingdom works against itself, Jesus' success in casting out demons reveals that His whole ministry was about "tying up the strong man."[9] This entire episode illustrates Jesus' assumption that Satan and demons form a unified kingdom. They are, as John Newport puts it, a "tight-knit lethal organization" that has a singular focus under a single general, Satan.[10]

It is because of this assumption that Jesus refers to the "devil and his angels," implying that fallen angels belong to Satan (Matt 25:41). And for the same reason, Jesus sees demonic activity as, by extension, the activity of Satan himself (e.g., Luke 13:11-16; cf. Acts 10:38; 2 Cor 12:7) and judges everything done against demons as also done against Satan himself.[11] When His seventy disciples return to Him after a successful ministry of driving out demons, Jesus proclaims that He sees "Satan fall from heaven like a flash of lightning" (Luke 10:17-18).[12] The "strong man" and his household clearly stand or fall together. They together form a single, relatively organized army, unified in its singular purpose of hindering God's work and bringing evil and misery to His people. The head of this army, and thus the ultimate principle of all evil, is Satan.[13]

The pervasive influence of Satan's army

As the Gospels portray it, this demonic alien army is vast in number and global in influence.[14] The sheer number of possessions recorded in the Gospels, the large number of multiple possessions, and the many allusions to vast numbers of people who were possessed, reveal the belief that "the number of evil spirits [was] indefinitely large.[15] The world is understood to be saturated with demons whose destructive influence is all-pervasive. Everything about Jesus' ministry tells us that He judged everything not in keeping with the Creator's all-good design as, directly or indirectly, the result of this invading presence. Jesus never once appeals to a mysterious divine will to explain why a person is sick, maimed or deceased.[16] In every instance, He comes against such things as the by-products of a creation that has gone berserk through the evil influence of a satanic army. Many times, he attributes sicknesses to direct demonic involvement.[17]

Jesus diagnoses a woman "with a spirit that had crippled her for eighteen years" as one whom "Satan bound" (Luke 13:11,16). Far from trying to discern some secret, sovereign, divine blueprint behind her grotesque deformity, He treats her as a casualty of war. The one ultimately responsible for her affliction, Jesus claims, was the captain of the opposing battalion himself. In sharp contrast to our typical modern Western approach, James Kallas poignantly expresses Jesus' approach to such matters. "We see polio or crippling and we piously shake our heads and cluck all the trite absurdities of a non-thinking people by saying 'it is the will of God...hard to understand...providence writes a long sentence, we have to wait to get to heaven to read the answer'...Jesus looked at this and in crystal clear terms called it the work of the devil, and not the will of God."[18]

As difficult as Kallas' assessment may be to accept, from a strictly scriptural perspective he is surely correct. In the minds of the disciples, such things as back deformities and diseases were, as Raymond Brown argues, "directly inflicted by Satan." So for them, to be "saved" was not simply about "spiritual regeneration" but also about being delivered from the evil grasp of sickness, from the dominion of Satan.[19]

Further, as Brown and others also make clear, Jesus and the Gospel authors sometimes referred to the diseases people had as "scourgings" or "whippings" (*mastix*, Mark 3:10; 5:29,34; Luke 7:21).[20] The only other times ancient authors used this term to describe physical maladies were to refer to afflictions sent by God upon people.[21] In these particular instances, God was punishing people with a scourging. But this clearly cannot be its meaning here, since Jesus sets people free from this scourging.

For example, after the woman who had been bleeding for twelve years touched his cloak, Jesus says to her, "Daughter, your faith has healed you. Go in peace and be freed from your scourging [*mastix*]" (Mark 5:34).[22] Jesus was certainly not freeing this woman from a God-intended twelve-year whipping. But whose whipping is Jesus freeing her from? In the total context of Jesus' ministry, the only other possibility is that he understood himself to be setting this woman (and all like her) free from the whippings of "the strong man," Satan.

Although Jesus never endorses the apocalyptic tendency to speculate about the names, ranks and functions of various fallen angels, He does go as far as rebuking a deaf and mute spirit (Mark 9:25). Luke describes another exorcism as the driving out of "a demon that was mute" (Luke 11:14).[23] Apparently, there are various kinds of demons within Satan's army with differing functions in afflicting people.

Jesus and the Kingdom of God

It is crucial for us to recognize that Jesus' view about the rule of Satan and the pervasive influence of his army is not simply a marginal piece of first-century apocalyptic thought that He happened to embrace. Rather, it is the driving force behind everything Jesus says and does. In fact, Jesus' concept of "the kingdom of God" is centered on these views. For Jesus, the kingdom of God means abolishing the kingdom of Satan.

Kallas argues that "this world [in Jesus' view] was a demon-infested world in need of liberation, and the advance of God's sovereignty was in direct proportion to the rout of the demons…Exorcism of demons was the central thrust of the message and activity of Jesus."[24] Gustaf Wingren writes that "when Jesus heals the sick and drives out evil spirits, Satan's dominion is departing and God's kingdom is coming (Matt 12:22-29). All Christ's activity is therefore a conflict with the Devil (Acts 10:38). God's Son took flesh and became man that He might overthrow the power of the devil, and bring his works to nought (Heb 2:14f; 1 Jn 3:8)."[25]

As Jesus uses the term, the "kingdom of God" refers to nothing other than His ministry, and the ministry He gave to His disciples, of setting up God's rule where Satan's rule previously had been. If the "kingdom of God" is the central concept of Jesus' ministry and teaching, as all scholars recognize, then the "kingdom of Satan" is, as a corollary concept, central as well.[26]

The Kingdom as a warfare concept

While no orthodox first-century Jew or Christian ever doubted that there existed only one Creator—or that this Creator would reign supreme in the eschaton—the New Testament authors also never doubted that the Creator's will was not the only will being carried out in this present world. Both human and angelic wills oppose God, and He must fight against them. The kingdom of God, therefore, is something that the New Testament authors pray for, not something they consider already accomplished (Matt 6:10; Luke 11:2).[27] They understand that the only way the kingdom of God will be brought about is by overthrowing the illegitimate

kingdom now in place. In this sense, one might say that the New Testament authors, like the apocalyptic authors of their day, held to a "limited dualism."[28]

If the terms the kingdom of God and the kingdom of Satan are correlative concepts in the New Testament, the former can be understood to be expanding only as the latter is diminishing. This is precisely the reason healings and exorcisms played such a central role in Jesus' ministry. "If it is by the finger of God that I cast out the demons," Jesus says, "then the kingdom of God has come to you" (Luke 11:20). To accomplish the one was to accomplish the other. Susan Garrett correctly summarizes this point when she says, "every healing, exorcism, or raising of the dead is a loss for Satan and a gain for God."[29] James Kallas writes that "the arrival of the Kingdom is simultaneous with, dependent upon, and manifested in the routing of demons."[30] For Jesus, healings and exorcisms clearly did not merely *symbolize* the kingdom of God, they *were* the kingdom of God.[31] Warring against Satan and building the kingdom of God are, for Jesus, one and the same activity.[32]

> The "kingdom of God" refers to nothing other than His ministry, and the ministry He gave to His disciples, of setting up God's rule where Satan's rule previously had been.

The Gospels' correlation of Jesus' pronouncements about the Kingdom and His demonstrations of the Kingdom is one of the many ways that Jesus' warfare conception of the kingdom of God is illustrated. Some examples of this recurring phenomenon pertain to the thematic beginnings of Jesus' ministry in Mark and Luke and make the point clear. In the opening of Mark's Gospel, Jesus begins His ministry by announcing that "the kingdom of God has come near; repent, and believe in the good news" (Mark 1:15). This is the complete content of what Mark tells us about Jesus' preaching. But everything that follows informs us, by illustration, what this kingdom preaching means.

After calling His disciples (vv. 16-20), Jesus amazes the people with the authority of His teaching (vv. 21-22). Immediately a man demonized by an unclean spirit cries out, "What have you to do with *us*, Jesus of Nazareth? Have you come to destroy us?" The first-person plural here perhaps indicates that the demon is speaking on behalf of the entire army of which he is a part. But he continues in the singular, "I know who you are, the Holy One of God" (vv. 23-24). In contrast to all earthly players in Mark's narrative, those in the demonic kingdom know who Jesus is and have suspicions about what it is He has come to earth to do (vv. 34; 3:11).[33]

Jesus has come to "destroy the works of the devil" (1 Jn 3:8), and the demons know this means their destruction. He rebukes the demon, telling him to "be silent" (Mark 1:25), literally, "be strangled" (*phimoō*). After Jesus strangles the demon with His divine authority, the demon throws the man to the ground and leaves him with a shriek (v. 26). Mark then notes that the people were again "amazed" at this "new teaching" and new "authority" (v. 27). The two, we see, go hand in hand.[34]

Mark follows this with a record of Jesus' healing of Peter's mother-in-law's fever (vv. 30-31). Jesus assumes this to be demonically induced in a Lukan parallel (Luke 4:38-39). That very evening, "the whole city" brought "all who were sick or possessed with demons" and Jesus "cured many" and "cast out many demons" (Mark 1:32-34). The kingdom of God was indeed near.

Next in Mark's account, Jesus tells his disciples that he wants to go into other villages and "proclaim the message there also" (v. 38). This he proceeds to do, and Mark summarizes his activity by noting, "He went throughout Galilee, proclaiming the message in their synagogues and casting out demons" (v. 39). Jesus then heals a man of leprosy (vv. 40-45), followed immediately by an account of Jesus healing a paralytic on the sabbath (2:1-12). After a brief interlude, we find Jesus again healing people, setting crowds of people free from the "scourges" of the enemy (3:10) and driving out evil spirits (3:11-12).[35] Several verses later

we have Mark's account of the Beelzebul controversy, in which Jesus presents himself as the one who has come to tie up " the strong man" by the power of God (3:20-30). And we are not yet out of Mark's third chapter!

This is what the kingdom of God means. The point is hard to miss. Whatever else the rule of God is about, it is about vanquishing the rule of Satan, and thus about setting people free from demons and from the ungodly infirmities they inflict on people.

Both Matthew's and Luke's accounts of Jesus' ministry begin, quite appropriately, with Jesus confronting the devil in the desert. The cosmic war that has raged throughout the ages is now centered on one person— Jesus.[36] Jesus withstands each temptation, including Satan's offer of all the kingdoms of the world, and defeated, the devil finally leaves Him (Luke 4:1-13). Unlike all other humans, Jesus did not become "a slave to sin" (John 8:34) and thus come under Satan's power. He declares in John that "the ruler of this world has no power over Me; but I do as the Father has commanded Me" (14:30-31; cf. 8:29). One stronger than "the strong man" has finally arrived. It is Jesus who has gotten hold of the devil. And having now defeated him in His own life, Jesus can set out to defeat him on behalf of the entire cosmos.

Jesus launches His mission in Luke from His own hometown. As in Mark, but in a somewhat expanded manner, He begins by announcing that the kingdom of God has arrived in His own person. He stands up in the synagogue and reads from Isaiah that "the Spirit of the Lord is upon Me, because He has anointed Me to bring good news to the poor. He has sent Me to proclaim release to the captives and recovery of sight to the blind, to let the oppressed go free, to proclaim the year of the Lord's favor" (Luke 4:18-19). After a moment of awkward silence, Jesus adds, "Today this scripture has been fulfilled in your hearing" (v. 21). When He is driven out of town (vv. 22-30), we begin to see concretely what this proclamation of the kingdom means. As in Mark, Jesus immediately confronts a demon-possessed man in a Capernaum synagogue. The man cries out, "What have you to do with us, Jesus of Nazareth?" (v. 34) and Jesus strangles the demon, setting the "prisoner" of Satan free (v. 35). With this exorcism, Jesus shows His application of the Isaiah passage to Himself and clearly demonstrates the freedom that was prophesied.

Jesus then proceeds to "rebuke" a demonic fever (v. 39), heal multitudes of sick people (v. 40) and cast out multitudes of shrieking demons (v. 41). Shortly thereafter He heals a man of leprosy (5:12-16), a paralytic (5:17-26) and a man with a withered hand (6:1-10). As Clinton Arnold argues, the point is that the prisoners who are to be set free are "trapped in the bondage and oppression of Satan's kingdom."[37] What the kingdom of God means, therefore, is that the hostile alien kingdom of demonic captivity, oppression, poverty and blindness (physical and spiritual) is coming to an end through the ministry of Jesus. He is the bringer of the kingdom of God, for He is the vanquisher of the kingdom of Satan.

The Work of the Church

In the light of Jesus' view of the kingdom of God, it seems highly peculiar that many New Testament scholars over the past several hundred years have concluded that the historical Jesus was, in one way or another, simply a moral teacher. This testifies to how thoroughly one's naturalistic presuppositions can filter one's reading of the evidence.[38] But it is hardly less puzzling how so many believing Christians today can read these same Gospels, commit themselves to following this Jesus, and yet never seriously consider treating sickness and disease (to say nothing of demonized people) the way Jesus treated them. Far from considering these evils as scourges of the devil the way Jesus did, we modern Christians most often attribute them to God's "mysterious providence." Rather than revolting against them as scourges of the enemy, we are more likely to ask God's help in accepting such difficulties "as from a father's hand."

This testifies to the strength of the post-Augustinian classical-philosophical theistic tradition as well as to Western Enlightenment presuppositions that, until recently, have

> Jesus gives to all who in faith receive it His authority to break down the gates of hell and take back for the Father what the enemy has stolen.

dominated Western thinking, believer and nonbeliever alike. And it goes a long way toward explaining why our "problem of evil" is not the same problem of evil that Jesus and His disciples confronted. If one believes that a good and wise divine purpose ultimately lies behind the sickness, disease and atrocity that make the world a nightmarish place, then one subtly shifts the problem of evil from something one has to war against to something one has to think through. Rather than a problem of overcoming the evil deeds of the devil and his army, the problem of evil becomes a problem of explaining intellectually how an all-good and all-powerful God could will what certainly are evil deeds of the devil.

Perhaps most tragically, when we trade problems in this fashion, we have surrendered a spiritual conflict we are commissioned to fight and ultimately win, for an intellectual puzzle we can never resolve. Whether considered on philosophical, biblical or practical grounds, it is an exceedingly poor trade. If instead we followed the example of our Savior, our basic stance toward evil in the world would be characterized by revolt, holy rage, social activism and aggressive warfare—not pious resignation.

The New Testament proclaims unequivocally that Jesus was victorious over the enemy in His ministry, death and resurrection (Col 2:14-15), but Jesus and the New Testament authors see the ultimate realization of this kingdom victory in the future. This constitutes the well-known "inaugurated eschatology" or the "already-but-not-yet" paradoxical dynamism of New Testament thought.[39] The Kingdom has already come, but it has not yet been fully manifested in world history. Jesus' miracles over nature, as well as His healings, exorcisms and especially His resurrection, were definite acts of war that accomplished and demonstrated His victory over Satan. These acts routed demonic forces and thereby established the kingdom of God both in the lives of people and in nature. Their primary long-term significance, however, was

eschatological. People still are being demonized; people still get sick and die; storms still
rage and destroy lives; famines still prevail
and thousands starve. But the ministry of
Jesus, most especially His death and resurrection, tied up "the strong man" in principle
and established the kingdom of God, the restoration of a new humanity in the midst of a
war zone. In doing this, Jesus set in motion
the forces that will eventually overthrow the
whole of Satan's fatally damaged assault
upon God's earth and upon humanity.[40]

Gustaf Wingren writes about "already/not
yet" dynamic when he speaks of Christ's resurrection and says that:

> the war of the Lord is finished and the great
> blow is struck. Never again can Satan tempt
> Christ, as in the desert. Jesus is now Lord,
> Conqueror. But a war is not finished, a con-
> flict does not cease with the striking of the
> decisive blow. The enemy remains with the
> scattered remnants of his army, and in pock-
> ets here and there a strong resistance may
> continue.[41]

Jesus' miraculous ministry was not simply
symbolic of the *eschaton*. In principle, it
achieved the *eschaton*. In principle, He won
the war, struck the decisive deathblow, vanquished Satan, restored humanity and established the kingdom. Yet some battles must
still be fought before the ultimate victory is
fully manifested. Because of this, Jesus did
not just carry out His warfare ministry; He
commissioned, equipped and empowered
His disciples, and later the whole of the
church, to do the same. He set in motion the
creation of a new humanity by giving us His
power and authority to proclaim and demonstrate the Kingdom just the way He did (e.g.,
2 Cor 5:17-21; Matt 16:15-19; Luke 19:17-20; cf
John 14:12; 20:21).

Jesus gives to all who in faith receive it His
authority to break down the gates of hell and
take back for the Father what the enemy has
stolen, just as he himself has done (Matt
16:18). Now that the strong man is bound,
this is a task we can and must carry out. In
doing so, we, the church, expand the kingdom of God against the kingdom of Satan
and lay the basis for the Lord's return, when
the full manifestation of Christ's victory, and
of Satan's defeat, will occur. In the time between the "already" of Christ's work and the
"not yet" of the *eschaton*, the Church is to be
about what Jesus was about. In a real sense, it
is His "body" here on earth. As such, the
Church is an extension of the ministry Jesus
carried out in His incarnate body while on
earth (2 Cor 5:18-19).

The Church is called to manifest the
truth that God's kingdom has come and
Satan's kingdom is defeated. Under the victorious authority of Christ, the Church is
called to engage and overthrow evil powers
just as Jesus has done. Indeed, when the
Church does this through the Spirit, it is
still Jesus Himself who is doing it. And although His followers can express an exu-
berant confidence in the accomplished
work of the cross, we should not find that
the warfare worldview of Jesus is lessened
among them one iota.

Study Questions

1. How did Jesus' life, teachings and ministry clarify the spiritual battle he was engaged in for the es-
    tablishment of the kingdom of God?
2. How can the church today "manifest the truth of that God's Kingdom has come and Satan's King-
    dom is defeated?"
3. Describe the ramifications of Boyd's view that Jesus was not explaining evil but overcoming evil.
4. In light of Boyd's exposition of Christ's authority and triumph over evil, explain the significance of
    Matthew 28:18 in understanding Matthew 28:19-20.

End Notes

1. On the covenantal theology that lies behind this conception, see G.W. Buchanan, *The Consequences of the Covenant,* NovTSup 20 (Leiden: Brill, 1970), pp. 123-31; as well as D. R. Hillers, *Covenant: The History of a Biblical Idea* (Baltimore: Johns Hopkins University Press, 1969), pp. 120-42.

2. Kallas, James G. *The Significance of the Synoptic Miracles,* Greenwhich, Conn: Seabury Press, 1961), p.54.

3. W.F. Albright, *From the Stone Age to Christianity: Monotheism and the History Process,* 2d ed. (Baltimore: John Hopkins University Press, 1957), p.362.

4. The identification of this "highest mediating agent" differs between (and even within) apocalyptic texts. For example, *1 Enoch* identifies Azazel and Semjaza as leaders of the rebel angels but also speaks of a group of fallen angels called *satans* (adversaries) headed up by Satan. *Jubilees* speaks of Mastema but also speaks of the fallen angels being under Satan. Tobit speaks of Asmodeus (who purportedly was in love with a young woman and killed all prospective husbands, 3:8; 6:13-14), a name that also appears in the rabbinic literature. *Second Enoch* speaks of Satanail, whereas the *Martyrdom of Isaiah* refers to Sammael along with Beliar and Satan. On this, see esp. Barton, "Origin of the Names," as well as Ling, *Significance of Satan, p.* 9; Ferguson, *Demonology, pp.* 76-78; Langton, *Essentials, pp.* 119-38; H. Gaylord, "How Satanel Lost His 'El,'" *JJS 33* (1982): 303-9; W. Foerster, "The Later Jewish View of Satan," in "διάβολος," *TDNT 2:75-79*; J. Russell, *Devil, pp.* 188-89; S. V. McCasland, "The Black One," in *Early Christian Origins. Studies in Honor of Harold R. Willoughby,* ed. A. Wikgren (Chicago: Quadrangle, 1961), pp. 77-80; C. Molenberg, "A Study of the Roles of Shemihaza and Asael in 1 *Enoch* 6-11," *JJS 35* (1984): 136-46.

5. Though the members of the infamous Jesus Seminar claim that one of the seven "pillars of scholarly wisdom" is the view that the historical Jesus' thought world was noneschatological (see R. W. Funk, R. W. Hover and the Jesus Seminar, *The Five Gospels: The Search for the Authentic Words of Jesus* [New York: Macmillan, 1993], p. 4), J. H. Charlesworth is certainly correct in affirming that "one of the strongest consensuses in New Testament research" involves the conviction that Jesus' teaching was fundamentally apocalyptic. See his "Jesus Research Expands with Chaotic Creativity," in *Images of Jesus Today,* ed. J. H. Charlesworth and W. P. Weaver (Valley Forge, Penn.: Trinity, 1994), p. 10. For a critique of the post-Bultmannian view of Jesus as noneschatological, see my *Cynic, Sage or Son of God? Recovering the Real Jesus in an Age of Revisionist Replies* (Wheaton, Ill.: Bridgepoint, 1995), pp. 55-56, 145-50; as well as P. R. Eddy, "Jesus as Diogenes? Reflections of the Cynic Jesus Thesis," *JBL* 115 (1996):449-69; and L. Johnson, *The Misguided Quest for the Historical Jesus and the Truth of the Traditional Gospels* (San Francisco: HarperSanFrancisco, 1995). For several good arguments for an apocalyptic Jesus, see B. F. Meyer, *Christus Faber: The Master-Builder and the House of God* (Allison Park, Penn.: Pickwick, 1992), pp. 41-80; E. P. Sanders, *Jesus and Judaism* (Philadelphia: Fortress, 1985), pp. 222-41, 319-40; B. Witherington, *Jesus, Paul and the End of the World. A Comparative Study in New Testament Eschatology* (Downers Grove, Ill.: InterVarsity Press, 1992), pp. 59-74, 170-80.

6. Arnold *Powers of Darkness,: Principalities and Powers in Paul's Letters* ,(Downers Grove Ill.: InterVarsity Press, 1992), p. 81. The phrase is used of *Beliar* in *Martyrdom of Isaiah* 2:4 (an early first-century apocalyptic work). See J. H. Charlesworth, "A Critical Comparison of the Dualism in IQS 3:13-4:26 and the 'Dualism' Contained in the Gospel of John," in *John and the Dead Sea Scrolls,* ed. Charlesworth (New York: Crossroad, 1990), pp. 76-106. Charlesworth's attempt to demonstrate that John represents a move away from a "hypostatic" personal view of the devil strikes me as forced.

7. The frequent apocalyptic notion that a particular angel was given charge over all creation may be behind the Synoptics' concept of the world being "given" to Satan. See Daniélou, *Jewish Christianity, pp.* 188-89; Gokey, *Terminology, p.* 50. Many in the early postapostolic church held this view. See Daniélou, *Angels and Their Mission,* pp. 45-46. In this case, Satan must be seen as telling the truth when he says that all the kingdoms of the world were given to him. In other words, he did not steal the world, as Kallas maintains *(Synoptic Miracles, p.* 54), and in this sense his power over the world cannot in and of itself be said to be "illegitimate," as I claimed above. Nevertheless, Satan's evil tyranny over the world can be seen as illegitimate even if his God-given authority itself is not.

8. Beelzebul (and its forms Beezebul, Beelzebub) was a frequent name for the ruler of the demonic kingdom in the Talmud, as well as in the *Testament of Solomon.* There has been much discussion and little agreement as to the etymology of this term and its forms. For several summary discussions with various suggested solutions, see T. J. Lewis, "Beelzebul," *ABD,* 1:638-40; W. E. M. Aitken, "Beelzebul," *JBL* 31 (1912): 34-53; W. Foerster, "βεελζεβούλ,"*TDNT* 1:605-06; L. Gaston, "Beelzebul," *TZ* 18 (1962): 247-55; P. L. Day, *An Adversary in Heaven: Satan in the Hebrew Bible,* HSM 43 (Atlanta: Scholars Press, 1988), pp. 151-59; E. C. B. MacLaurin "Beelzebul," *NovT* 20 (April 1978): 156-60; S. J. Wright, "Satan, Beelzebul, Devil, Exorcism," NIDNTT, 3:468-76. For a superb argument that this Q pericope essentially goes back to the historical Jesus, see J. D. G. Dunn, "Matthew 12:28/Luke 11:20—A Word of Jesus?" in *Eschatology and the New Testament: Essays in Honor of George Raymond Beasley-Murray,* ed. W. H. Gloer (Peabody, Mass.: Hendrickson, 1988), pp. 29-49. The accusation that Jesus was possessed by Satan or a demon is repeated in John 7:20; 8:48, 52; and 10:20. It should be noted that the response to the charge in 10:21, "Can a demon open the eyes of the blind?" recalls Mark 3:24 and is predicated on the assumption that blindness is itself a demonic work.

9. Arnold sees this verse as the key to understanding Christ's ministry. "Christ has come to engage this 'strong man' and plunder his house: that is, to release the captives in Satan's kingdom" *(Powers of Darkness,* p. 79). See also J. Ramsey Michaels, "Jesus and the Unclean Spirits," in *Demon Possession,* ed. J. W. Montgomery (Minneapolis: Bethany, 1976), p. 53. E. Ferguson sums up well the picture of the world and of Jesus' ministry assumed in this passage when he notes that this world is "enemy-occupied territory; Satan as its ruler has a fortress to protect his ill-gotten possessions. But there comes one stronger than he. The conqueror liberates the fortress, takes away Satan's power, and takes over his possessions for his own use" *(Demonology of the Early Christian World, pp.* 22-23). See also E. Pagels, *The Origin of Satan* (New York: Random House, 1995), p. 20.

10. Newport J., response to Michaels, J. Ramsey in *Demon Possession A. Medical, Historical, Anthropological, and Theological Symposium,* ed., J.W. Montgomery (Minneapolis: Bethany 1976), p. 90. Forsyth argues that demons are portrayed in the Gos-

pels as "a sort of loosely organized army under their general, Satan" (*Old Enemy, p.* 293; cf. p. 295). See also J. Russell, *Devil, P.* 237; Gokey, *Terminology,* p. 50; Kallas, *Synoptic Miracles,* pp. 67-68. Ling argues that the Gospels differ from previous apocalyptic literature precisely in the intensity with which they affirm that the kingdom of evil is a unified kingdom and focus most of their attention on the head of this kingdom, Satan *(Significance of Satan, pp .* 12-22). Roy Yates also sees this as one of the main contributions of the Gospels. For Jesus, "exorcisms are no longer to be seen as isolated victories over a series of autonomous demons…Jesus does not have an atomistic view of the world of evil, but sees it as a unity under Satan, whose power is beginning to crumble" ("The Powers of Evil in the New Testament," *EvQ* 52, no.2 [1980]: 99).

11. Ferguson, Everett. *Demonology of the Early Christian World,* (New York: Mellen, 1984), p. 12.

12. The passage likely means that the success of the disciples' exorcism ministry was evidence that Satan's kingdom was on its way down. So argues G. E. Ladd, *Jesus and the Kingdom* (New York: Harper & Row, 1964), pp. 145 ff.; and Forsyth, Old *Enemy, pp.* 294-95. Ling argues that Jesus was here drawing the disciples' attention away from their ability to cast out individual demons to "the fact that the kingdom of evil in its entirety was being conquered in the exercise of the authority which was theirs in his name" *(Significance of Satan, p.* 18). Julian Hills, however, argues in the opposite direction. Jesus was, in effect, saying that the disciples were successful in their exorcisms because the demons saw that their leader was already being dethroned by Jesus' exorcist ministry. See J. V. Hills, "Luke 10:18-Who Saw Satan Fall?" *JSNT 46* (1992): 25-40. This verse, incidentally, is the only reference to the fall of Satan in the Gospels, and it is clearly not about his original fall. This absence of speculation sets the Gospels apart from the apocalyptic literature of their time. That Satan was a fallen angel, however, seems to be taken for granted by the Gospel authors and is made more explicit in other New Testament literature (1 Tim 3:6;4 Jude 6, 8-10; 2 Pet 2:4; Eph 2:2; 2 Cor 11:13-14).

13. So Ferguson correctly notes in commenting on this passage, "Evil may have varied manifestations, but ultimately there is only one principle of evil. Instead of a world dominated by many warring demons (a pagan and polytheistic conception), Jesus saw one kingdom of Satan…. Jesus saw his work as demonstrating that the whole dominion of evil was being conquered. The demons functioned as part of a larger whole, the dominion of the devil" *(Demonology, p.* 20).

14. Later rabbinical tradition had it that demons "surround us like the ridge round a field…every one among us has 1,000 on his left hand and 10,000 on his right hand." Moreover, all manner of evil is attributed to them, everything from weakening in the knees to clothes wearing out to sore feet. See Babylonian Talmud *Berakot* 6a, cited in Ferguson, *Demonology, p.* 89. It is unlikely that something of this tradition does not extend back to the first century.

15. Langton, Edward. *The Essentials of Demonology: A Study of Jewish and Christian Doctrine, Its Origin and Development.* (London: Epworth, 1949), p. 147.

16. Some take John 9:1-5 to be an exception to this. I argue against this interpretation in chapter seven. But even if this passage does presuppose a divine purpose for this particular person's blindness, this only slightly qualifies the point being made here.

17. For several informative discussions on the connection between sickness and Satanic/demonic activity in the New Testament, see R. Brown, "The Gospel Miracles," in his *New Testament Essays* (Garden City, N.Y.: Doubleday, 1968), pp. 222-28; E. Yamauchi, "Magic or Miracle? Diseases, Demons and Exorcisms," in *The Miracles of Jesus,* ed. D. Wenham and C. Blomberg, GP 6 (Sheffield: JSOT Press, 1986), pp. 92-93; D. S. Russell, *From Early Judaism to Early Church* (Philadelphia. Fortress, 1986), pp. 90-93; and esp. P. H. Davids, "Sickness and Suffering in the New Testament," in *Wrestling with Dark Angels: Toward a Deeper Understanding of the Supernatural Forces in Spiritual Warfare,* ed. C. P. Wagner and F. D. Pennoyer (Ventura, Calif.: Regal, 1990), pp. 215-37. There is now strong evidence that first-century Jews (hence perhaps Jesus himself) were assisted in their inclination to think of sickness and diseased as demonically induced by the "Solomon/Son of David as exorcist and healer" tradition. J.H. Charlesworth has noted: "We possess traditions that may well derive from the first century C.E. in which Solomon is hailed as an exorcist who controls demons and the sickness, including blindness, the cause" ("The Son of David" Solomon and Jesus [Mark 10:47]," unpublished paper presented to the Jesus Seminar, Rutgers University, New Brunswick, N.J., Oct. 1992, p.12). See also D.C. Duling, "Solomon, Exorcism and the Son of David," *HTR* 68 (1975): 235-52. Thus it may be that Jesus' title as the "Son of David" is linked with his reputation as healer/exorcist. See L Fisher, "Can This Be the Son of David?" in *Jesus and the Historian: Written in Honor of Ernest Cadman Colwell,* ed. F.T. Trotter (Philadelphia: Westminster, 1968), pp. 82-87. For evidence of the prevalence within rabbinic Judaism of the view that much sickness was the result of demonic activity, see H.L. Strack and P. Billerbeck, *Kommentar zum Neuen Testament aus Talmud und Midrasch,* 5 vols. (Munich: Bick, 1922-61), 4:510-35.

18. Kallas, *Synoptic Miracles,* p.63.

19. "Gospel Miracles," p.224.

20. Ibid. Cf. Kallas, *Synoptic Miracles,* p. 79.

21. For references, see BAGD, p 495.

22. My translation. The NIV translates *mastix* as "flogging" in Acts 22:24 and Hebrews 11:36, and the verbs *Mastizō* and *mastigoō* as "to flog" in Matthew 10:17; 20:19; 23:34; Mark 10:34; 15:15; Luke 18:32; John 19:1; Acts 22:24-25; and as "to punish" in Hebrews 12:6. But it translates *mastix* as "suffering," "disease" and "sicknesses" in the Gospels (Mark 3:10; 5:29, 34; Luke 7:21). Such a translation loses the unique forces of this rather unusual usage of this word.

23. See also Mark 9:29 (parallel Matt 17:21), where Jesus assumes there are different "kinds" of demons.

24. Kallas, *Synoptic Miracles,* p. 66.

25. Wingren, Gustaf. *The Living Word: A Theological Study of Preaching and the Church.* (London: Epworth, 1949), p.53; cf. p. 167.

26. The centrality of Satan and the cosmic/spiritual warfare motif in the New Testament received an unprecedented amount of attention just prior to, during and after World War II. The classic statement of this position is Gustaf Aulen's *Christus Victor,* trans. A Hebert (New York: Macmillan, 1961). See also from this period R. Leivestad, *Christ the Conqueror: Ideas of Conflict and Victory in the New Testament* (London: SPCK, 1954); J.S. Stewart, "On a Neglected Emphasis in New Testament Theology," *SJT 4*

(1951): 292-301; E Fascher, *Jesus und der Satan*, Hallische Monographien 11 (Halle: Max Niemeyer, 1949); Schlier, *Principalities and Powers*; Wingren, *Living Word*. This view has received increasing attention in recent scholarship. For strong contemporary representative statements or arguments on the centrality of Satan and of the warfare motif in general for the New Testament, see R. Hiers, "Satan, Demons, and the Kingdom of God," *SJT 27* (1974): 35-47; R. Yates, "Jesus and the Demonic in the Synoptic Gospels," *Irish Theological Quarterly* 44 (1977): 39-57; J. D. G. Dunn and G. H. Twelftree, "Demon-Possession and Exorcism in the New Testament," *Churchman* 94, no. 3 (1980): 211-15; S. R. Garrett, *The Demise of the Devil: Magic and the Demonic in Luke's Writings* (Minneapolis: Fortress, 1989); H. Kruse, "Das Reich Satans," *Bib* 58 (1977): 29-61; Ling, *Significance of Satan*; P. W. Hollenbach, "Help for Interpreting Jesus' Exorcism," *SBLSP*, 1993, ed. E. H. Lovering Jr. (Atlanta, Ga.: Scholars Press, 1993), pp. 124-26; M. Kelsey, *Encounter with God. A Theology of Christian Experience* (Minneapolis: Bethany Fellowship, 1972), pp. 242-45; J. Russell, *Devil*, pp. 222, 227, 234-39; Forsyth, *Old Enemy*, pp. 249, 286, 295-96; Langton, *Essentials*, p. 156; Yamauchi, "Magic or Miracle?" pp. 124-25; Kallas, *Jesus and the Power of Satan*; idem, *Synoptic Miracles*; idem, *The Satanward View* (Philadelphia: Westminster, 1966); W. Kirchschläger, *Jesu exorzistisches Wirken aus der Sicht des Lukas: Ein Beitrag zur lukanischen Redaktion*, Österreichische Biblische Studien 3 (Klosterneuburg: Österreichisches Katholisches Bibelwerk, 1981); W. G. Kümmel, "Liberation from the Spiritual Powers," in his *Theology of the New Testament*, trans. J. E. Steely (Nashville: Abingdon, 1973), pp. 186ff.; J. J. Rousseau, "Jesus, an Exorcist of a Kind," in SBLSP, 1993, pp. 129-53; Bocher, *Christus Exorcista*.

27. See J. Jeremias's observation in "The Lord's Prayer in the Light of Recent Research," in his *Prayers of Jesus* trans. J. Bowden et al., SBT 2/6 (Naperville, Ill.: Allenson, 1967), p. 99. G. E. Ladd *(A Theology of the New Testament* [Grand Rapids: Eerdmans, 1974], pp. 45-56) also draws a strong connection between the coming of the future kingdom and the vanquishing of the evil forces that presently control the world.

28. In the light of the fact that "the satanic and demonic is a dominant theme of the New Testament," Newport argues, we must see the New Testament as constituting "at least a limited dualism" ("Satan and Demons: A Theological Perspective," in *Demon Possession, p.* 331). Similarly, Kvanvig distinguishes this type of Jewish dualism from the cosmic dualism of Zoroastrianism by casting it as a temporary, eschatological and moral dualism rather than a metaphysical dualism. See *Roots of Apocalyptic*, pp. 610-11. See also C. S. Lewis's strong case for a form of biblical dualism in "God and Evil," in *God in the Dock: Essays in Theology and Ethics*, ed. W. Hooper (Grand Rapids, Mich.: Eerdmans, 1970), pp. 21-24. For an argument along similar lines but cast in relationship to Greek philosophical forms of dualism, see A. H. Armstrong, "Dualism: Platonic, Gnostic and Christian," in *Neoplatonism and Gnosticism*, ed. R. T. Wallis and J. Bregman (Albany: SUNY Press, 1992), pp. 33-54. For similar assessments of the apocalyptic or New Testament dualism, see J. G. Gammie, "Spatial and Ethical Dualism in Jewish Wisdom and Apocalyptic Literature," *JBL* 93 (1974): 356-59; J. H. Charlesworth, "A Critical Comparison of the Dualism in 1QS 3:13—4:26 and the 'Dualism' in the Gospel of John," NTS 15 (1968-69): 389-418; Aulen's classic Christus Victor, pp. 4-5, 10-11, 76, 89, 108, 148-49.

29. Garrett, Susan R. *The Demise of the Devil: Majic and the Demonic in Luke's Writings.* (Mineeapolis: Fortress, 1989) p. 55.

30. Kallas, *Synoptic Miracles, p.* 78. See also pp. 55, 66. See E. Stauffer: "The Kingdom of God is present where the dominion of the adversary has been overthrown" *(New Testament Theology* 5th ed., trans. J. Marsh [New York: Macmillan, 1955], p. 124). Similarly, Elaine Pagels notes that for the Gospel authors, "Jesus has come to heal the world and reclaim it for God; in order to accomplish this, he must overcome the evil powers who have usurped authority over the world, and who now oppress human beings" *(Origin of Satan, p. 36).* See also J. Robinson, "The Exorcism Narratives," in *The Problem of History in Mark, and Other Essays* (Philadelphia: Fortress, 1982), pp. 83ff.; Arnold, *Powers of Darkness, p.* 80; Dunn and Twelftree, "Demon-Possession and Exorcism," pp. 219-23; Rousseau, "Jesus, an Exorcist," pp. 150-51. In his recent superb study, Graham Twelftree concludes that "Jesus was the first to make the connection between exorcism and eschatology. For him, his exorcisms were the first or preliminary binding of Satan who would finally be destroyed in the eschaton" *(Jesus the Exorcist*, pp. 217-24).

31. So Brown writes, "The miracle was not primarily an external guarantee of the coming of the kingdom; it was one of the means by which the kingdom came. In particular, Jesus' miracles were the weapons He used to overcome Satan" ("Gospel Miracles," p. 222). See also Yates, "Powers of Evil," pp. 106-7.

32. Against this, Robert Guelich has argued: "We find no hint of any cosmic or ethical dualism in Jesus' ministry as portrayed in the Synoptics. The Kingdom of God is never juxtaposed to a 'kingdom of Satan'" ("Spiritual Warfare: Jesus, Paul and Peretti," *Pneuma* 13, no. 1 [1991]: 41). He thus regards Scripture's warfare motif as strictly metaphorical (p. 34). Interestingly enough, however, Guelich does seem to accept that the coming of the kingdom of God is (literally?) simultaneous with the binding of the strong man and the plundering of his house (pp. 38-39). One of the main reasons Guelich argues against the centrality of the warfare motif in the Gospels' portrayal of Jesus' ministry concerns what he regards as the absence of any struggle or theme of conquest against Satan in this portrayal (pp. 40-42). "In every case," he writes, "Jesus is clearly in control of the situation. There is simply no contest" (p. 40). Against this four points can briefly be made: (1) That Jesus (like Yahweh in the Old Testament) at least had to rebuke Satan and demons shows that they are genuine foes who must be conquered. God is (through Jesus) in control, to be sure, but this control has genuine opposition, and it must therefore be established by "a rebuke." (2) If the Gospel accounts of Jesus' temptation don't represent a genuine struggle with Satan, what would? The meaning of Guelich's observation that "Jesus was vulnerable to Satan's 'temptation' but not to Satan personally" is not clear to me (p. 40). (3) It is, we shall see, possible that in at least one Gospel account Jesus' exorcistic command did not issue in an immediate exorcism (Mark 5:6-10; see Boyd, *God at War*, 1997, chapter seven), and it is certain that the disciples' exorcisms were not always immediate (Matt 9:17-18). Indeed, one of Jesus' healings was not instantaneous (Matt 8:24), and Mark implies that on at least one occasion Jesus could not do certain miracles because of people's lack of faith (Mark 6:5). Hence it seems fair to characterize the ministry of both Jesus and certainly his disciples as a struggle against the enemy. (4) It is clear from the Epistles that followers of Jesus understood themselves to be part of an ongoing cosmic battle and thus to be under constant attack from the enemy (see Boyd, *God at War*, 1997, chapters seven to ten).

33. Ferguson speculates that "the use of these titles of Jesus was an effort by the demon to claim power over him," since knowing someone's name and office was seen as a form of power *(Demonology, p.* 7). Hence Jesus sometimes inquires into the name of the demon(s) he is confronting (Luke 8:30).

34. Forsyth captures the theme well: "the teaching is somehow presented by the event [viz., the exorcism] the people have witnessed—a new teaching: power over the spirits" (*Old Enemy,* p. 286).

35. If Pagels is correct, even the interlude discussion about sabbath propriety is not irrelevant to Mark's warfare perspective, for here (Mark 2:23-26) "Jesus dares claim as precedent for his disciples' apparently casual action [of picking corn] on the Sabbath, the prerogative of King David himself, who, with his men, broke the sacred food laws during a wartime emergency" *(Origin of Satan, p.* 18).

36. Forsyth notes that this is the same apocalyptic cosmic battle motif, but "the battle scheme has now shifted to Christ's life" (*Old Enemy,* p. 289). See also Longman and Reid, *God Is a Warrior,* pp. 91-118. For a fascinating study that draws the literary connections between this portrayal of Satan and Old Testament and apocalyptic warfare motifs, see H. A. Kelly, "The Devil in the Desert," *CBQ* 26 (1964): 190-220. Adrio König sees in the temptation narratives a reversal of Adam's succumbing to temptation, and hence the beginning of a new creation in Jesus' ministry *(New and Greater Things: Re-evaluating the Biblical Message on Creation* [Pretoria: University of South Africa, 1988], pp. 106-7). E. Best goes so far as to argue that Mark locates the central confrontation between Jesus and the devil in the temptation narrative *(The Temptation and the Passion: The Markan Soteriology,* 2d ed., SNTSMS 2 [Cambridge: Cambridge University Press, 1990]).

37. Arnold, *Powers of Darkness,* p. 78.

38. As noted earlier, this is not to say that those critical scholars today who acknowledge that Jesus was perceived to be an exorcist or a healer have necessarily dissociated themselves from an antisupernatural worldview. Many times they have simply expanded a naturalistic worldview and thus account for the supposed exorcisms and healings by psychosomatic and sociological explanations. See, e.g., R. Funk, "Demon: Identity and Worldview," *The Fourth R* 5, no. 3 (1992): 15; Hollenbach, "Jesus, Demoniacs," p. 567; Crossan, *Historical Jesus,* pp. 310-32; Davies, *Jesus the Healer.*

39. Ibid. Cf. Kallas, *Synoptic Miracles,* p. 79.

40. For references, see BAGD, p. 495.

41. Wingren, *Living Word,* p. 62 Cf. p. 164. It is perhaps worth noting here that Scripture does not generally envisage the eschatological kingdom as "above" the earth so much as it envisages it as "on" the earth. All who overcome will "reign *on earth*" (Rev 5:10). Just as our bodies will be transformed but will still be our bodies (1 Cor 15:35-54), so too the earth will be transformed, but it will nevertheless be our earth (see 2 Pet 3:13; Rev 20:8, 21:1, 24)

Beyond Duty

Tim Dearborn

We often focus on the question: "What must we do to obey the Great Commission, make disciples of all nations and hasten the return of our Lord?" This is the wrong beginning point, for it locks us in a human centered perspective. If we begin with the human centered orientation, we continually feel constrained by insufficient resources—and the tasks are far greater than we can possibly fulfill.

Biblical priorities reflected again and again in Scripture ask us to begin instead with these questions:

- Who is the triune God?
- What is God doing in the world?
- How are we to participate with God in his redemptive purposes?

Mission is ultimately not a human response to human need. The Church's involvement in mission is its privileged participation in the actions of the triune God.

A Singular Passion

Lack of interest in mission is not fundamentally caused by an absence of compassion or commitment, nor by lack of information or exhortation. And lack of interest in mission is not remedied by more shocking statistics, more gruesome stories or more emotionally manipulative commands to obedience. It is best remedied by intensifying peoples' passion for Christ, so that the passions of his heart become the passions that propel our hearts.

Mission must never have first place in the Church's life. The Church is to have but one Lord—one passion—the One in whom all the fullness of God dwells, who has reconciled all things to himself (Col 1:19-20). If the church today is in need of a conversion, it is always and only to Jesus Christ. We must say an emphatic "No!" to lesser gods who clamor for our allegiance, and a living and joyous "Yes!" to the One in whom all creation is summed up.

It is insufficient to proclaim that the Church of God has a mission in the world. Rather, *the God of mission has a Church in the world.* Grasp this inversion of subject and object, and participation in God's mission will become a joyous, life-giving privilege. Miss it, and mission involvement will eventually degenerate into a wearisome, overwhelming duty.

If the Church is faithful to the gospel, its focus, passion and delight is always and only Jesus Christ. Once our hearts

Tim Dearborn is the Director of the Institute for Global Engagement for World Vision in Federal Way, Washington. He also serves as Adjunct Professor at Fuller Theological Seminary, Regent College and Seattle Pacific University.

beat in time with that of our Lord, we can experience a joyously passionate engagement in mission.

Mission's Integrating Theme

So many conflicting and competing missions cry for our attention. We're so easily drawn and quartered by the pull of divergent needs and calls. Without a central understanding of the biblical emphasis on the kingdom of God, our terminology becomes one of "I bring you bad news of sad problems."

Efforts to provoke interest in mission are often based on bad news—natural catastrophes, complex humanitarian disasters, unreached people groups, oppressed and exploited minorities, urban or suburban problems and civil wars.

These things are important, but the gospel begins with "I bring you good news of great joy!"

Woven into the fabric of our Christian faith is good news! And yet we've made mission the discussion of bad news and unmet needs. Do any of these sound familiar?

- Thousands of people every day are slipping into Christless eternities.
- 34,000 children die every day from malnutrition and preventable illnesses.
- There are thousands of unreached people groups without a church.
- More Christians have been killed for their faith in this century than in all others combined.
- Genocide, ethnic cleansing, illiteracy, homelessness, poverty, oppression. The list goes on and on.

Sad News of Unsolvable Problems

I must confess I once challenged and provoked people into mission using statistics similar to those mentioned above. I'm not at all suggesting that these are not real needs. The point is this: How shall we respond to these needs?

Good-hearted people always want to respond with compassion and kindness. We worked ourselves into exhaustion with exhortations to give more, do more, be more, care more, serve more, love more, sacrifice more. As fruitful as this could be, something always seemed to be missing.

My church members—including myself—often seemed exhausted. Missionaries we sent seemed overwhelmed by the arduous duty and responsibility on their shoulders.

Materials written to motivate the church in mission are filled with descriptions of tasks we must perform, responsibilities to be carried out, our Lord's commandment and commission to the church; and the desperate needs of the unreached, undernourished and oppressed. And so the Church moves out in mission from a sense of duty, obligation and responsibility to attempt these tasks.

Not surprisingly, this commitment to the missionary enterprise of the Church produces exhausted servants. The tasks are so great and our resources appear to be so small. Yes, we must confront huge problems and fundamental issues—but in the context of a coming kingdom, not in the context of ever-deepening chaos. Missions is not ultimately our response to great need.

No wonder the Church and many organizations' supporters are increasingly disinterested in mission! People cannot handle relentless exposure to catastrophes and crises. This is not the gospel. The gospel is good news of great joy!

The Kingdom of God is Good News of Great Hope

We are witnesses to great hope, not merely grievous hurt. This should be deeply woven into our psyche as Christians. Scripture tells us, "since we are receiving a kingdom which cannot be shaken, let us give thanks" (Heb 12:28).

Frankly, we have not set our hearts toward hope. We look at the world and it seems to us that everything is being shaken. Everything seems to be teetering on the brink of disaster—and yet the undergirding news in Scripture is that we have a kingdom that cannot be shaken. The author of Hebrews affirms this, saying "…we who have taken refuge might be strongly encouraged to seize the hope set before us. We have this hope, a sure and steadfast anchor of the soul" (Heb 6:18-19).

Christ's Great Victory

If we have this utterly reliable anchor, this certain and steadfast hope, then it is actually blasphemous to focus our missionary communication on descriptions of the great void of unmet needs in the world. P.T. Forsyth makes the statement that *"the weakness of much current mission work is that [we] betray the sense that what is yet to be done is greater than what [Christ] has already done. The world's gravest need is less than Christ's great victory."* If we understand biblical faith, we will understand that what Christ has already accomplished is far more determinative, significant, complete and important than anything yet to be done.

In my work with World Vision and discussions with its leaders, we have begun to recognize that sometimes we've inadequately represented mission in our well intentioned promotional and fund raising activities. We've perfected the art of portraying truly heart rending stories, and providing people with pictures and descriptions of real crises, needs and disasters. God has used our best efforts, though flawed, and his people have responded from compassionate hearts. However, if Forsyth is right—and the Bible is emphatic in its documentation of the truth of his statement—then we must change how we communicate mission opportunities. Instead of relying entirely on presentations of need, we must begin inviting people to participate in God's work by making known to all people the "mighty acts of him who called you out of darkness into his marvelous light" (1 Pet 2:9).

Privileged Participation— Not Exhausted Action

Without this news of great hope and full confidence in a completely sovereign God, we will have the sense of mission as an exhausting human enterprise. We'll feel as though we've been handed a mandate, a commission and a duty, and that the job is completely up to us. This inevitably leads to burnout. Mission was never intended to be an exhausting human enterprise. Mission is our privileged participation in the lifegiving action of the triune God.

Seeking First the Kingdom

Jesus invites us to participate in what God is doing in bringing his kingdom. But what does that look like? We all know Matthew 6:33: "Strive first for the kingdom of God." If the kingdom was so central to Jesus' life and ministry, then we cannot afford to be fuzzy about its meaning and significance.

Look at what Jesus said about the kingdom of God:

- The kingdom of God was the subject of Jesus' first message when he told the people that the kingdom of God is at hand (Mark 1:14, Luke 4:18).
- The kingdom was also the subject of his last message (Acts 1:1-8).
- Jesus himself said the kingdom was the goal, the intention and the purpose of all his teaching (Luke 8:10).
- Even Jesus' miracles were called "signs of the kingdom."
- We all know the Lord's Prayer: "Thy kingdom come, thy will be done."
- Jesus even goes so far as to say that the end of this age will not come until the gospel of the kingdom has been proclaimed to all ethnic groups (Matt 24:14).

Signs of the Kingdom

Without this integrating vision of the kingdom of God, mission involvement can degenerate into competition among our own programs, ambitions and desires. When the kingdom of God is the goal of all we do, then competing calls and opposing ambitions fade under the sound of the King's marching orders. To engage in mission is to participate in the King's business.

God Himself brings his kingdom to fruition. He establishes it—not us. God chooses to let us share in his work. We are not told in Scripture that we bring, cause or create the kingdom. We are called by the Spirit of God to participate with him in building God's kingdom, but the responsibility is his. This is not merely a semantic issue. These terms mean the difference between something that is life-giving, or something that can be death-dealing. We have a pivotal role in the coming kingdom of God. The Spirit of God is sent to manifest signs of the kingdom through us. But the work remains God's.

Signs of Kingdom Life

Jesus' miracles were signs of kingdom life. Because he chose to limit himself to time and space, he could cast out only a few demons, and feed only a few people miraculously. In comparison to the population of the world at the time, relatively few were privileged to see Jesus in action. Only those living in Palestine and specifically around Galilee had the opportunity to experience a part of what the kingdom was about. But Jesus' reputation began to spread, so that when he came to a new town, people brought the afflicted to him for healing. Every act of healing illustrated the message, "The kingdom of God has come near...to you" (Luke 10:9). All of God's fullness is on the way. Whole towns and regions were transformed by the hope of the kingdom.

In a similar way, the late Mother Teresa, for example, cared for only a couple of hundred thousand people in Calcutta, but all 18 million people in that city knew that life could be different because of her example. In fact, her good works have come to be known in the global village and have impacted the world.

God desires that we be living signs of the kingdom, to provide visual aids of what life will look like one day when the kingdom is here fully. We will not bring the kingdom or build the kingdom, but our privilege is to live out previews of "coming attractions," revealing what this kingdom will look like.

Both Hands of the Gospel

The King seeks to restore the well-being and wholeness of his creation. The Church is not to be an underground railway to heaven, hiding people on earth until they can escape to glory. Nor is the Church to be another philanthropic organization, kindly doing good works and dispensing aid to those in need. Rather, the Church is the Body of Christ, consciously and explicitly participating in the establishment of his reign on earth. The Church

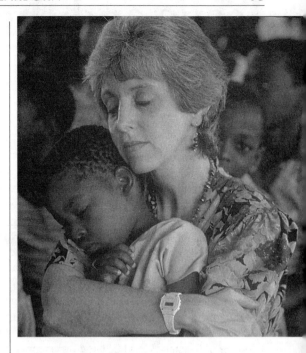

is to be consciously and explicitly Christ's, regardless of the activity.

Therefore, we extend both hands of the gospel: the hand inviting people to repentance, faith and eternal reconciliation with God through Christ Jesus, and the hand manifesting deeds of mercy and compassion, extending the goodness of God's kingdom on earth. One is not a means to the other. Both are equally significant to life in the eternal kingdom as described by Scripture.

No Longer a Somber Duty

To engage in mission is to participate in the coming of the kingdom of God. When the King and his kingdom are the unifying, controlling source and goal of all we do, then competing calls and opposing ambitions fade under the sound of the King's marching orders. Participation in God's mission is no longer a somber duty. It becomes a joyous privilege and an adventure of passion and hope.

Study Questions

1. In the long run, can it be counterproductive to provoke interest in mission by moving people to be concerned with human need?

2. What does Dearborn mean by "signs of the kingdom?"

3. How can missions become a joyous passion instead of a duty?

Jesus and the Gentiles

H. Cornell Goerner

After teaching missions and comparative religion at Southern Baptist Seminary for more than 20 years, in 1957 H. Cornell Goerner became Secretary for Africa, Europe, and the Near East for the Foreign Mission Board of the Southern Baptist Convention. He retired in 1976 from the Foreign Mission Board, and pastored a church near Richmond, Virginia.

We have tried to read our Bible as Jesus read his. This took us quickly through the Old Testament, the only Scriptures Jesus had. In all three sections of the Hebrew Bible, the books of Moses, the Prophets, and the Psalms, we found God's concern for all the nations and peoples of the earth, and his plan for dealing with them through the Messiah. We believe that Jesus mentally "underscored" these passages in his Bible, and planned deliberately to fulfill them by his life, his death, and his resurrection.

Turning now to the New Testament, we find in the Gospels that the words and actions of Jesus confirm this all-inclusive concept of his ministry. The New Testament flows right out of the Old, with unbroken continuity. In the distinctive title he chose for himself, in the strategy of his ministry, and in his clear teachings, it is obvious that Jesus undertook a mission for all mankind.

Malachi and Matthew

As one closes the Old Testament and opens the New, it is as though just a few days intervened. Matthew begins right where Malachi ended. And no one was more conscious of that than Jesus was. He knew that he had come to fulfill what Malachi had predicted.

The four short chapters of Malachi are an unrelieved denunciation of the nation of Israel. It warns of an imminent day of judgment to be announced by a forerunner and then instituted by "the messenger of the covenant." This messenger would come suddenly to the temple and inaugurate a new era, not only for the people of Israel, but for the whole world.

The coming judgment was called "the Day of the Lord." It would be "a great and terrible day" of testing, when the righteous would be separated from the wicked as gold is refined in a smelter, as dirt is removed from clothing by caustic lye soap, as chaff is separated from wheat at the threshing floor and as an unfruitful tree is chopped down and consumed in a furnace (Mal 3:2; 4:1,5).

The judgment would be particularly severe on Israel and its leaders because of specific sins which are denounced: sham and hypocrisy in worship services (1:7-14); social injustice (2:10); pagan religious practices (2:11); divorce (2:16); withholding the tithe (3:8-10). But above all, the prophet declares, God's patience is coming to an end because the people who were supposed to exalt Yahweh and cause him to be reverenced and worshiped among the nations of the world have failed to do so. Instead, they have profaned his name and caused him to be dishonored (1:5-14). But God's purpose will not be defeated, for from east to west, all over the world, his name is to be exalted among the nations, and in every place prayers and worship are to be offered to him (1:11).

The keynote is sounded in Malachi 1:10:

"Oh that there were one among you who would shut the gates, that you might not uselessly kindle fire on My altar! I am not pleased with you," says the Lord of hosts, "nor will I accept an offering from you." "For from the rising of the sun, even to its setting, My name will be great among the nations, and in every place incense is going to be offered to My name, and a grain offering that is pure; for My name will be great among the nations," says the Lord of hosts.

Because God is so concerned that he be exalted among the nations, he is about to act, Malachi warns. He will first send a messenger to prepare the way for him (Mal 3:1). Then he will come himself, as the messenger of the covenant, who will inaugurate the time of judgment (Mal 3:2-3). The forerunner will be an "Elijah," a fiery prophet of doom (Mal 4:5). If he is not heeded, then fierce judgment and destruction will be certain.

All of these elements of Malachi are reflected in the third chapter of Matthew's Gospel. John the Baptist came preaching, "Repent, for the kingdom of heaven is at hand" (Matt 3:2). This is the equivalent of "the Day of the Lord" in Malachi. The time of God's judgment is fast approaching! This is "the wrath to come" (Matt 3:7). John uses the same figures of speech which are found in Malachi; the wheat and chaff are to be separated. To emphasize that the judgment is to be upon the Israelites, and not just the Gentiles, as some of the Jews believed, John declared in effect: "Don't think that you will escape because you are 'sons of Abraham.' I tell you, God is not dependent upon you. He can raise up 'sons of Abraham' from these stones, if he wishes. He will use others, if you are not worthy. You will be judged and punished, regardless of your Hebrew heritage" (Matt 3:9, author's paraphrase).

Jesus picked up this message of warning to the nation of Israel. Immediately after his baptism we are told: From that time Jesus began to preach and say: "Repent, before it is too late. The time is short. The day of God's judgment is at hand."

Jesus identified John the Baptist as the Elijah whom Malachi had promised. Just after John's imprisonment, Jesus declared: "For all the prophets and the Law prophesied until John; and if you are willing to accept it, he is Elijah who is to come. He who has ears to hear, let him hear" (Matt 11:13-15, *RSV*).

Jesus was warning that a turning point in history was at hand. The last of the prophets had been sent to give a final warning before judgment came upon the nation of Israel. Some months later, after the death of John the Baptist, he again identified John as the Elijah foretold by Malachi:

"But I say to you, that Elijah already came, and they did not recognize him, but did to him whatever they wished. So also the Son of Man is going to suffer at their hands." Then the disciples understood that He had spoken to them about John the Baptist (Matt 17:12-13).

During his last week in Jerusalem as he taught in the temple, Jesus was consciously fulfilling what is written in Malachi 3:1- 2:

"Behold, I am going to send My messenger, and He will clear the way before Me. And the Lord, whom you seek, will suddenly come to His temple, and the messenger of the covenant, in whom you delight, behold He is coming," says the Lord of hosts. "But who can endure the day of His coming? And who can stand when He appears? For He is like a refiner's fire and like fullers' soap."

John the Baptist had been sent as a messenger to prepare the way. He had done his work. Now the Lord himself had come to announce a new covenant to replace the Old Covenant that had been broken. ("The Lord whom you seek" is not Yahweh, but the expected Messiah, indicated by *Adon* in the Hebrew. The Lord of hosts who is announcing the coming of the Lord [*Adon*] is Yahweh. Jesus with his knowledge of Hebrew understood this distinction.) The people had been seeking the coming of the Messiah, they thought, but actually they were not ready for his coming and the judgment which it brought. Only those who were spiritually prepared could endure his coming.

This is what it means to close the Old Testament and open the New Testament. Jesus knew that the covenant made at Sinai had been broken again and again by a disobedient people, and after a long line of prophets sent to win them back had failed, God's patience was approaching an end. A new covenant was to be sealed with a faithful remnant of Israel, who would then call the Gentile nations to repentance in the name of the Messiah, the judge of the living and the dead.

Judgment must begin with the house of Israel. It then must be proclaimed to all the nations. This was the note of urgency with which Jesus began his ministry. Matthew fulfills Malachi!

Son of Man

Nothing is more revealing than the personal title which Jesus chose for himself. We have seen that he did not like the term, "Son of David," the popular designation of the Messiah. He realized that he was indeed "the Son of God" referred to in Psalm 2:7, and during his trial before the Sanhedrin, he acknowledged this. But the title which he used throughout his ministry was, "Son of Man." More than forty times in the Gospels the term is used, always by Jesus referring to himself. The disciples never used the term, but called him "Lord," "Master," or "Teacher." For Jesus, the words were almost a substitute for the personal pronoun "I." Again and again he said it: "The Son of Man has nowhere to lay His head" (Matt 8:20). "The Son of Man has authority on earth to forgive sins" (Matt 9:6). "The Son of Man is Lord of the Sabbath" (Matt 12:8). "Then they shall see the Son of Man coming in clouds with great power and glory" (Mark 13:26).

Jesus derived this term from two principal sources: the books of Ezekiel and Daniel. "Son of Man" is the distinctive title applied to the prophet Ezekiel by God, and occurs eighty-seven times. The Hebrew is *ben Adam*, literally, "Son of Adam," or "son of mankind." Originally it meant only "man," as opposed to God, and reminded Ezekiel of his humble status. But by the time of Jesus, the term had become an honorific title of the Messiah, and many passages in Ezekiel were idealized and interpreted messianically. As he read the book, Jesus must have heard God speaking directly to him: "Son of man, I am sending you to the sons of Israel, to a rebellious people" (Ezek 2:3). "Son of man, I have appointed you a watchman to the house of Israel; whenever you hear a word from My mouth, warn them from Me" (3:17).

Especially significant for Jesus were the passages concerning a remnant to be spared (6:8); the new heart and spirit (11:19; 36:26-27); the new everlasting covenant (37:26); and the promise that the Gentile nations would come to know the Lord, God of Israel (37:28; 38:23; 39:7). All these were to be fulfilled by him, as Son of Man.

> **Jesus claimed the title Son of Man for himself, thus identifying with the whole human race, with all the families of mankind.**

There can be no doubt that Daniel 7:13-14 was in the mind of Jesus when he used the title, "Son of Man." There it was an Aramaic term, *bar enash*, instead of *ben Adam*. But the meaning is similar, *enash* being the word for mankind in general, as against an individual male person. In rabbinical commentary and popular thought, the term had already been highly spiritualized, indicating the ideal man, almost divine in nature. The Book of Enoch, an apocalyptic discourse widely circulated during the first century, exalted the figure even beyond Daniel's vision.[1] But it is not necessary to assume that Jesus was influenced by Enoch. The words of Daniel are clear enough:

> I kept looking in the night visions,
> And behold, with the clouds of heaven
> One like a Son of Man was coming,
> And He came up to the Ancient of Days
> And was presented before Him.
> And to Him was given dominion,
> Glory and a kingdom,
> That all the peoples, nations, and

men of every language
Might serve him.
His dominion is an everlasting dominion
Which will not pass away;
And His kingdom is one
Which will not be destroyed (7:13-14).

Jesus knew that this would take place only after his suffering and glorification. He claimed the title for himself, thus identifying himself, not with the Hebrew people or the Jewish nation in any exclusive way, but with the whole human race, with all the families of mankind. He knew that he was the Son of Man and the Suffering Servant.[2]

From the Beginning

As we have already seen, the vision of a universal kingdom was integral to the plan of Jesus from the very beginning of his ministry. The fact that one of the wilderness temptations involved "all the kingdoms of the world and their glory" (Matt 4:8) is conclusive. Jesus *did* aspire to world dominion. His ambition to rule over the nations was not wrong. The temptation was to take a short cut to that noble goal: to adopt the methods of the devil. In rejecting Satan's methods, Jesus did not give up his aim of worldwide authority. Rather, he chose the path of suffering and redemption which he found outlined in the Scriptures.

The first sermon at Nazareth demonstrates that his life purpose extended far beyond the nation of Israel. He was not surprised that his own people did not receive his message. "That's the way it has always been," he said. "The prophets have always found greater faith among foreigners than among their own people" (Luke 4:24, author's paraphrase). He then gave an example: "There were many widows in Israel in the days of Elijah…and yet [he] was sent to none of them, but only to Zarephath, in the land of Sidon, to a woman who was a widow" (Luke 4:25-26). His hearers knew the rest of the story told in 1 Kings 17. Received into a Gentile home, Elijah performed the remarkable miracle of replenishing the flour and oil, then later restored the widow's son to life—not a Jewish widow, but a Gentile!

Jesus did not stop with Elijah. He rubbed salt into the wounded feelings of his audience with the story of Elisha. For Naaman, the Syrian, was not only a Gentile, but a military leader—captain of the Syrian army which at that very time was at war with Israel and had almost eradicated the hapless little nation (2 Kings 5:1-14). Yet, although there were many lepers in Israel, "none of them was cleansed, but only Naaman the Syrian" (Luke 4:27). No more dramatic illustration could have been given that the grace of God was not limited to the people of Israel and that Gentiles often displayed greater faith than those who were considered "children of the kingdom." Small wonder that the proud citizens of Nazareth were infuriated at this brash young man, who insulted their nation and called in question their privileged status as God's "Chosen People"! But for his miraculous power, they would have hurled him to his death on the jagged rocks at the foot of a cliff (Luke 4:28-30).

To the Jews First

Jesus did have a deep conviction of a special mission to the Jewish nation. He expressed this so strongly that some have concluded that he envisioned no mission beyond Israel. But careful consideration of all his words and actions reveals that it was a question of strategy: As Paul later expressed it, his mission was "to the Jew first, and also to the Greek" (Rom 1:16; 2:10).

Jesus' concern for Israel was shown in the instructions to the twelve disciples as he sent them out on their first preaching mission. "Do not go in the way of the Gentiles," he said, "and do not enter any city of the Samaritans; but rather go to the lost sheep of the house of Israel" (Matt 10:5-6). The reason is obvious. The time was short, and doom was coming to the nation, if there was not speedy repentance. The need was urgent, more so for Israel than for the Gentile nations, whose time of judgment would come later. Indeed, in the very same context is the prediction that the preaching ministry of the disciples would be extended to the Gentiles; "You shall even be brought before governors and kings for My sake, as a testimony to the Gentiles" (v. 18). But they must concentrate upon the Jewish cities first, because their time of opportunity was short (v. 23).

Luke tells of a later preaching mission in which seventy others were sent out two by two (Luke 10:1). Just as the twelve apostles symbolically represent the twelve tribes of Israel, the seventy symbolize the Gentile nations. In Genesis 10, the descendants of Noah are listed, seventy in number.

> Jesus moved resolutely toward the cross, fully aware that he was to establish a new interracial, international people, the New Israel.

Rabbinical tradition assumed that this was the total number of nations scattered over the earth after the Tower of Babel, and repeatedly referred to the seventy Gentile peoples. Jesus may have used this means of symbolizing his long-range purpose. The twelve were sent to warn the tribes of Israel of impending judgment. The seventy were sent later on a training mission in preparation for their ultimate mission to the whole world.[3]

Contacts with Gentiles

Most of the public ministry of Jesus was conducted in Jewish territory. Under the circumstances, the number of personal contacts with Gentiles recorded in the Gospels is surprising. He healed a Gadarene demoniac (Matt 8:28-34). Among ten lepers healed, one was a Samaritan, and Jesus remarked upon the fact that only the foreigner returned to thank him (Luke 17:12-19).

A Samaritan woman was the sole audience for one of Jesus' greatest sermons. She received the assurance that the time was near when God would be worshiped, not just in Jerusalem or at Mt. Gerizim, but all over the world, "in spirit and in truth" (John 4:5-42).

A Canaanite woman's faith was rewarded when her daughter was healed. Much has been made of Jesus' puzzling remark at the beginning of the encounter: "I was sent only to the lost sheep of the house of Israel" (Matt 15:24). This may have been a deliberate rebuke of his disciples, who wanted to send her away with her request unanswered, and who shared the racial prejudice which was common at the time. The significant point is that Jesus *did* minister to this Gentile woman, and praised her faith in the presence of his disciples and the Jewish onlookers (v. 28).

The centurion whose servant was healed was almost certainly a Roman. Commander of a band of one hundred foreign soldiers quartered at Capernaum to keep the peace, he was despised by the Jews who resented this "army of occupation." Conscious of his own authority as a military man, he humbly assured Jesus that it would not be necessary for him to go to his house to heal the servant (and thus perhaps render himself unclean by entering a Gentile home). "Just say the word and my servant will be healed," he declared with genuine faith (Matt 8:8). Jesus turned and announced to the Jewish crowd which was following him: "I tell you the truth: I have not found a single Hebrew who showed as much faith as this Gentile military leader" (Matt 8:10, author's paraphrase). He did not stop there, but continued with this solemn prediction: "I tell you, many such foreigners shall come from the east and the west to join Abraham, Isaac, and Jacob in the kingdom of heaven. But many others who thought they were 'sons of the kingdom' (the Chosen People of Israel) shall be shut out" (v. 11-12, author's paraphrase).

The coming of a group of Greeks precipitated the final crisis in the inner life of Jesus: his decision to move on to the cross. It is clear that these were not merely Hellenized Jews, but aliens, either inquirers or proselytes, who had accepted Judaism and thus were qualified to worship in the temple area, at least in the court of the Gentiles. Their request for an audience caused Jesus to declare: "The hour has come for the Son of Man to be glorified" (John 12:23). The deep interest of the Greeks was evidence that the world was ready for his redemptive mission to be culminated by his atoning death: "And I, if I be lifted up from the earth, will draw all men to Myself." "All men"—Greeks as well as Jews; Gentiles and Hebrews alike—this is the clear implication of these profound words recorded by John (12:32).

The Final Week

The events of that last week in Jerusalem bear eloquent testimony to the fact that Jesus, refusing to be a nationalistic Jewish Messiah, moved resolutely toward the cross, fully aware that he was to establish a new interracial, international people, the new Israel, destined to become worldwide in its scope as a spiritual kingdom. He entered the city on a donkey, in order to fulfill Zechariah's prediction of a king who would speak peace to the nations, and whose dominion would be from sea to sea (Zech 9:9-10). He cleansed the court of the Gentiles, declaring sternly, "My house shall be called a house of prayer for all the nations" (Mark 11:17). Standing in the temple, he denounced the chief priests and Pharisees, the official leaders of the Jewish nation, for having failed to be good stewards of the truths of the Kingdom which had been entrusted to the Chosen People, and solemnly declared, "Therefore, I say unto you, the kingdom of God will be taken away from you, and given to a nation producing the fruit of it" (Matt 21:43). He predicted the fall of Jerusalem and the destruction of the temple within that generation (Matt 24:34; Mark 13:30; Luke 21:32); but when asked concerning the end of the age, he said, in effect: "Don't be misled. It will not be as soon as some think. For this gospel of the Kingdom shall be preached in the whole world for a witness to all nations, and after that the end shall come" (Matt 24:4-14, author's paraphrase). Concerning his return in glory, he was purposely vague, declaring, "Of that day and hour no one knows, not even the angels of heaven, nor the Son, but the Father alone" (Matt 24:36). But when he does come, he promised, "*all nations* will be gathered before Him, and He will separate them from one another, as the shepherd separates the sheep from the goats" (25:32, author's italics).

Just before the Passover, at a house in Bethany, an adoring woman anointed his body with costly ointment. When she was criticized for her extravagance, Jesus stoutly defended her with these words: "She did it to prepare Me for burial. Truly I say unto you, wherever this gospel is preached in the whole world, what this woman has done shall also be spoken of in memory of her" (26:13).

The next evening in the upper room with his disciples, he sealed the New Covenant with them, in anticipation of his death. He declared as he passed the cup, "This is My blood of the covenant, which is to be shed on behalf of many for forgiveness of sins" (v. 28). Only the eleven were present, and all were Jews. But Jesus knew that the small nucleus of a new Chosen People, the remnant of Israel, was soon to be enlarged, as the many for whom he died heard the good news and accepted him as Lord and Savior.

End Notes

1. William Manson, *Jesus the Messiah* (London: Hodder and Stoughton, 1943), pp. 102 f.
2. Alfred Edersheim, *The Life and Times of Jesus the Messiah* (Grand Rapids, MI: Eerdmans, 1950), p.173.
3. *The Broadman Bible Commentary* (Nashville: Broadman Press, 1971), p. 149.

Study Questions

1. What events and statements could give the impression that Jesus came just for the nation of Israel?

2. Why does Goerner claim that Jesus' emphasis upon "the lost sheep of the house of Israel" was a strategic emphasis?

3. Describe some connections between the Old and New Testaments that give continuity to the Bible.

The Master's Plan

Robert E. Coleman

T he plan of this study has been to trace the steps of Christ as portrayed in the Gospels to discern a motivating reason for the way He went about His mission. His tactics have been analyzed from the standpoint of His ministry as a whole, hoping thereby to see the larger meaning of His methods with men.

His Objective Was Clear

The days of His flesh were but the unfolding in time of the plan of God from the beginning. It was always before His mind. He intended to save out of the world a people for Himself and to build a church of the Spirit which would never perish. He had His sights on the day His Kingdom would come in glory and in power. This world was His by creation, but He did not seek to make it His permanent abiding place.

No one was excluded from His gracious purpose. His love was universal. Make no mistake about it. He was the "Savior of the world" (John 4:42). God wanted all men to be saved and to come to a knowledge of the truth. To that end Jesus gave Himself to provide a salvation from all sin for all men. In that He died for one, He died for all. Contrary to our superficial thinking, there never was a distinction in His mind between home and foreign missions. To Jesus it was all world evangelism.

He Planned to Win

His life was ordered by His objective. Everything He did and said was a part of the whole pattern. It had significance because it contributed to the ultimate purpose of His life in redeeming the world for God. This was the motivating vision governing His behavior. His steps were ordered by it. Mark it well. Not for one moment did Jesus lose sight of His goal.

That is why it is so important to observe the way Jesus maneuvered to achieve His objective. The Master disclosed God's strategy of world conquest. He had confidence in the future precisely because He lived according to that plan in the present. There was nothing haphazard about His life—no wasted energy, not an idle word. He was on business for God (Luke 2:49). He lived, He died, and He rose again according to schedule. Like a general plotting his course of battle, the Son of God calculated to win. He could not afford to take a chance. Weighing every alternative and variable factor in human experience, He conceived a plan that would not fail.

Robert E. Coleman is Director of the School of World Missions and Evangelism and Professor of Evangelism at Trinity Evangelical Divinity School in Deerfield, Illinois. He serves as Director of the Billy Graham Institute of Evangelism at Wheaton, Illinois. He is a founding member of the Lausanne Committee for World Evangelization. Coleman is the author of 20 books, including *The Master Plan of Evangelism*, which has sold over two million copies.

Excerpts from *The Master Plan of Evangelism* by Robert E. Coleman. Copyright 1972, 1993 by Fleming H. Revell Company. Used by permission.

Men Were His Method

It all started by Jesus calling a few men to follow Him. This revealed immediately the direction His evangelistic strategy would take. His concern was not with programs to reach the multitudes, but with men whom the multitudes would follow. Remarkable as it may seem, Jesus started to gather these men before He ever organized an evangelistic campaign or even preached a sermon in public. Men were to be His method of winning the world to God.

> Jesus was not trying to impress the crowd, but to usher in a kingdom. This meant that He needed men who could lead the multitudes.

The initial objective of Jesus' plan was to enlist men who could bear witness to His life and carry on His work after He returned to the Father. Having called His men, Jesus made it a practice to be with them. This was the essence of His training program—just letting His disciples follow Him.

Jesus expected the men He was with to obey Him. They were not required to be smart, but they had to be loyal. This became the distinguishing mark by which they were known. They were called His "disciples" meaning that they were "learners" or "pupils" of the Master. It was not until much later that they started to be called "Christians" (Acts 11:26), although it was inevitable, for in time obedient followers invariably take on the character of their leader.

Jesus was always building up in His ministry to the time when His disciples would have to take over His work, and go out into the world with the redeeming gospel. This plan was progressively made clear as they followed Him.

His Strategy

Why? Why did Jesus deliberately concentrate His life upon comparatively so few people? Had he not come to save the world? With the glowing announcement of John the Baptist ringing in the ears of multitudes, the Master easily could have had an immediate following of thousands if He wanted them. Why did He not then capitalize upon His opportunities to enlist a mighty army of believers to take the world by storm? Surely the Son of God could have adopted a more enticing program of mass recruitment. Is it not rather disappointing that one with all the powers of the universe at His command would live and die to save the world, yet in the end have only a few ragged disciples to show for His labors?

The answer to this question focuses at once the real purpose of His plan for evangelism. Jesus was not trying to impress the crowd, but to usher in a kingdom. This meant that He needed men who could lead the multitudes. What good would it have been for His ultimate objective to arouse the masses to follow Him if these people had no subsequent supervision nor instruction in the Way? It had been demonstrated on numerous occasions that the crowd was an easy prey to false gods when left without proper care. The masses were like helpless sheep wandering aimlessly without a shepherd (Matt 9:36; 14:14; Mark 6:34). They were willing to follow almost anyone that came along with some promise for their welfare, be it friend or foe. That was the tragedy of the hour—the noble aspirations of the people were easily excited by Jesus, but just as quickly thwarted by the deceitful religious authorities who controlled them. The spiritually blind leaders of Israel (cf., Matt 23:1-39; John 8:44; 9:39-41; 12:40), though comparatively few in number, completely dominated the affairs of the people. For this reason, unless Jesus' converts were given competent men of God to lead them on and protect them in the truth, they would soon fall into confusion and despair, and the last state would be worse than the first. Thus, before the world could ever be permanently helped, men would have to be raised up who could lead the multitudes in the things of God.

Jesus was a realist. He fully realized the fickleness of depraved human nature as well as the satanic forces of this world amassed against humanity, and in this knowledge He based His evangelism on a plan that would meet the need. The multitudes of discordant and bewildered souls were potentially ready to follow Him, but Jesus individually could not possibly give them the personal care they needed. His only hope was to get men imbued with His life who would do it for Him. Hence, He concentrated Himself upon those who were to be the beginning of this leadership. Though He did what He could to help the multitudes, He had to devote Himself primarily to a few men, rather than to the masses, in order that the masses could at last be saved. This was the genius of His strategy.

It all comes back to His disciples. They were the vanguard of His enveloping movement. "Through their word" He expected others to believe on Him (John 17:20), and these in turn to pass the word along to others, until in time the world might know who He was and what He came to do (John 17:21,23). His whole evangelistic strategy—indeed, the fulfillment of His very purpose in coming into the world, dying on the cross, and rising from the grave—depended upon the faithfulness of His chosen disciples to this task. It did not matter how small the group was to start with so long as they reproduced and taught their disciples to reproduce. This was the way His Church was to win—through the dedicated lives of those who knew the Saviour so well that His Spirit and method constrained them to tell others.

Jesus intended for the disciples to produce His likeness in and through the Church being gathered out of the world. Thus His ministry in the Spirit would be duplicated many fold by His ministry in the lives of His disciples. Through them and others like them it would continue to expand in an ever enlarging circumference until the multitudes might know in some similar way the opportunity which they had known with the Master. By this strategy the conquest of the world was only a matter of time and their faithfulness to His plan.

Jesus had built into His disciples the structure of a church that would challenge and triumph over all the powers of death and hell. It had started small like a grain of mustard seed, but it would grow in size and strength until it became a tree "greater than all the herbs" (Matt 13:32; cf. Mark 4:32; Luke 13:18,19). Jesus did not expect that everyone would be saved (He recognized realistically the rebellion of men in spite of grace), but He did foresee the day when the Gospel of salvation in His Name would be proclaimed convincingly to every creature. Through that testimony His Church militant would someday be the Church universal even as it would become the Church triumphant.

It was not going to be an easy conquest. Many would suffer persecution and martyrdom in the battle. Yet no matter how great the trials through which His people would pass, and how many temporal skirmishes were lost in the struggle, the ultimate victory was certain. His Church would win in the end. Nothing could permanently prevail against it "or be strong to its detriment, or hold out against it" (Matt 16:18, *Amplified New Testament*).

The principle of giving evangelistic work assignments to His disciples was conclusively demonstrated just before He returned to heaven after His crucifixion and resurrection. On at least four occasions as He met with His disciples He told them to go out and do His work. It was first mentioned to the disciples, with the exception of Thomas, on the first Easter evening as they were assembled in the Upper Room. After Jesus had showed the astonished disciples His nail-scarred hands and feet (Luke 24:38-40), and had partaken of the meal with them (41-43), He then said, "Peace be unto you: as the Father hath sent Me, even so I send you" (John 20:21). Whereupon Jesus assured them again of the promise and authority of the Holy Spirit to do the work.

A little later as Jesus had breakfast with His disciples by the Sea of Tiberias, He told Peter three times to feed His sheep (John 21:15,16,17). This admonition was interpreted to the fisherman as the proof of his love to the Master.

On a mountain in Galilee He gave His Great Commission to, not only the eleven disciples (Matt 28:16), but also to the whole church, numbering then about 500 brethren (1 Cor 15:6). It was a clear proclamation of His strategy of world conquest. "All authority hath been given unto Me in heaven and in earth. Go ye therefore, and make disciples of all the nations, baptizing them into the name of the Father and of the Son and of the Holy

Ghost, teaching them to observe all things whatsoever I commanded you: and lo, I am with you always, even unto the end of the world" (Matt 28:18-20; cf., Mark 16:15-18).

Finally, before He ascended back to the Father, Jesus went over the whole thing again with His disciples for the last time, showing them how things had to be fulfilled while He was with them (Luke 24:44-45). His suffering and death, as well as His resurrection on the third day, was all according to schedule (v. 46). Jesus went on to show His disciples "that repentance and remission of sins should be preached in His name unto all nations, beginning from Jerusalem" (v. 47). And for the fulfillment of this divine purpose, the disciples were no less a part than their Master. They were to be the human instruments announcing the good tidings, and the Holy Spirit was to be God's personal empowerment for their mission. "Ye shall receive power, when the Holy Ghost is come upon you: and ye shall be my witnesses both in Jerusalem, and in all Judea and Samaria, and unto the uttermost part of the earth" (Acts 1:8; cf. Luke 24:48,49).

Clearly Jesus did not leave the work of evangelism subject to human impression or convenience. To His disciples it was a definite command, perceived by impulse at the beginning of their discipleship, but progressively clarified in their thinking as they followed Him, and finally spelled out in no uncertain terms. No one who followed Jesus very far could escape this conclusion. It was so then; it is so today.

Christian disciples are sent men and women—sent out in the same work of world evangelism to which the Lord was sent, and for which He gave His life. Evangelism is not an optional accessory to our life. It is the heartbeat of all that we are called to be and do. It is the commission of the Church which gives meaning to all else that is undertaken in the name of Christ. With this purpose clearly in focus, everything which is done and said has the glorious fulfillment in God's redemptive purpose.

Study Questions

1. Why did Jesus not use His reputation, power, and influence to enlist a mighty army of believers to take the world by storm?

2. What was the genius of Jesus' strategy? Do you think this should be followed today? Why or why not?

3. How do evangelistic strategies today compare with Jesus' strategy?

A Man for All Peoples

Don Richardson

Millions of Christians know, of course, that Jesus, at the end of His ministry, commanded His disciples to "go and make disciples of all [peoples]" (Matt 28:19). We respectfully honor this last and most incredible command He gave with an august title—the Great Commission. And yet millions of us deep down in our hearts secretly believe, if our deeds are an accurate barometer of our beliefs (and Scripture says they are), that Jesus really uttered that awesome command without giving His disciples ample warning.

Read cursorily through the four Gospels and the Great Commission looks like a sort of afterthought paper-clipped onto the end of the main body of Jesus' teachings. It is almost as if our Lord, after divulging everything that was really close to His heart, snapped His fingers and said, "Oh yes, by the way, men, there's one more thing. I want you all to proclaim this message to everyone in the world, regardless of his language and culture. That is, of course, if you have the time and feel disposed."

Did Jesus hit His disciples with the Great Commission cold turkey? Did He just spring it on them at the last minute without fair warning and then slip away to heaven before they had a chance to interact with Him about its feasibility? Did He fail to provide reasonable demonstration on ways to fulfill it?

How often we Christians read the four Gospels without discerning the abundant evidence God has provided for an entirely opposite conclusion! Consider, for example, how compassionately Jesus exploited the following encounters with Gentiles and Samaritans to help His disciples think in cross cultural terms.

A Roman Centurion

On one occasion (Matt 8:5-13), a Roman centurion, a Gentile, approached Jesus with a request on behalf of his paralyzed servant. Jews, on this occasion, urged Jesus to comply. "This man deserves to have you do this, because he loves our nation and has built our synagogue," they explained (Luke 7:4-5).

In fact, walls and pillars of a synagogue built probably by that very centurion still stand two thousand years later near the north shore of the Sea of Galilee! But notice the implication of the Jews' reasoning. They were saying, in effect, that if the centurion had not thus helped them, neither should Jesus help the centurion or his pitifully paralyzed servant! How clannish of them! Little wonder Jesus could not help sighing occasionally,

Don Richardson pioneered work for Regions Beyond Missionary Union (RBMU) among the Sawi tribe of Irian Jaya in 1962. Author of *Peace Child*, *Lords of the Earth*, and *Eternity in Their Hearts*, Richardson is now Minister-at-Large for WORLD TEAM (formerly RBMU). He speaks frequently at missions conferences and Perspectives Study Program classes.

"O unbelieving and perverse generation…how long shall I stay with you? How long shall I put up with you?" (Matt 17:17).

Jesus responded to the centurion, "I will go and heal him." At that moment the centurion said something quite unexpected: "'Lord, I do not deserve to have you come under my roof. But just say the word, and my servant will be healed. For I myself am a man under authority, with soldiers under me….' When Jesus heard this, he was astonished," wrote Matthew. What was so astonishing? Simply this—the centurion's military experience had taught him something about authority. As water always flows downhill, so also authority always flows down an echelon (a chain of command). Whoever submits to authority from a higher level of an echelon is privileged also to wield authority over lower levels. Jesus, the centurion noticed, walked in perfect submission to God: therefore Jesus must have perfect authority over everything below Him on the greatest echelon of all—the cosmos! Ergo! Jesus must possess an infallible ability to command the mere matter of the sick servant's body to adapt itself to a state of health!

"I tell you the truth," Jesus exclaimed, "I have not found anyone in Israel with such great faith!" As in many other discourses, Jesus exploited the occasion to teach His disciples that Gentiles have just as great a potential for faith as Jews! And they make just as valid objects for the grace of God too!

Determined to maximize the point, Jesus went on to say: "I say to you that many will come from the east and the west [Luke, a Gentile writer, adds in his parallel account: 'and from the north and the south'] and will take their places at the feast with Abraham, Isaac and Jacob in the kingdom of heaven. But the subjects of the kingdom [this could only mean the Jews as God's chosen people] will be thrown outside, into the darkness, where there will be weeping and gnashing of teeth" (Matt 8:7-12; Luke 13:28,29).

Feasts are usually called to celebrate. What would you guess that future feast attended by Abraham and a host of Gentile guests will celebrate?

Intimations of the Great Commission to follow could hardly have been clearer! Wait, there is still much more!

A Canaanite Woman

Still later, a Canaanite woman from the region of Tyre and Sidon begged Jesus' mercy on behalf of her demon-possessed daughter. Jesus at first feigned indifference. His disciples, glad no doubt to see their Messiah turn a cold shoulder to a bothersome Gentile, concurred at once with what they thought were His true feelings. "Send her away," they argued, "for she keeps crying out after us" (Matt 15:21-28).

Little did they know that Jesus was setting them up. "I was sent only to the lost sheep of Israel," He said to the woman. Having already manifested an apparent insensitivity toward the woman, Jesus now manifests an apparent inconsistency also. He has already healed many Gentiles. On what basis does He now reject this one's plea? One can imagine the disciples nodding grimly. Still they did not suspect. Undissuaded, the Canaanite woman actually knelt at Jesus' feet, pleading, "Lord, help me!"

"It is not right to take the children's bread." Then He added the crusher—"and toss it to their dogs!" "Dogs" was a standard epithet Jews reserved for Gentiles, especially Gentiles who tried to intrude upon Jewish religious privacy and privilege. In other words, Jesus now complements His earlier "insensitivity" and "inconsistency" with even worse "cruelty."

Was this really the Savior of the world talking? No doubt His disciples thought His reference quite appropriate for the occasion. But just when their chests were swollen to the full with pride of race, the Canaanite woman must have caught a twinkle in Jesus' eye and realized the truth!

"Yes, Lord," she replied ever so humbly, not to mention subtly, "but even the dogs eat the crumbs that fall from their master's table!" (see also Mark 7:26-30).

"Woman, you have great faith!" Jesus glowed. "Your request is granted!" No, He was not being fickle! This was what He intended to do all along. Immediately preceding this event, Jesus had taught His disciples about the difference between real versus figurative uncleanness. This was His way of driving the point home.

"And her daughter was healed from that very hour," Matthew records (v. 28).

A Samaritan Village

When on a later occasion Jesus and His band approached a certain Samaritan village, the Samaritans refused to welcome Him. James and John, two disciples whom Jesus nicknamed "sons of thunder" for their fiery tempers, were incensed. "Lord," they exclaimed indignantly (stamping their feet), "do you want us to call fire down from heaven to destroy them?"

Jesus turned and rebuked James and John. Some ancient manuscripts add that He said, "You do not know what kind of spirit you are of, for the Son of Man did not come to destroy men's lives, but to save them" (Luke 9:51-56, including disputed portion).

With those words, Jesus identified Himself as a Savior for Samaritans!

Greeks at Jerusalem

Later on, some Greeks came to a feast at Jerusalem and sought audience with Jesus. Philip and Andrew, two of Jesus' disciples, relayed the request to Jesus who, as usual, exploited the occasion to get another wedge in for the "all-peoples perspective": "But I, when I am lifted up from the earth, will draw all men to myself" (John 12:32). This prophecy foreshadowed the manner of Jesus' death—crucifixion! But it also foretold the effect! All men—not merely in spite of Jesus' humiliation, but because of it—would be drawn to Him as God's anointed deliverer. On the surface this statement could be interpreted to mean that everyone in the world will become a Christian. Since we know that this is quite unlikely, the

A Violent Reaction to Mercy   *Patrick Johnstone*

Jesus' teaching struck at the core of the erroneous world-view of the Jews and the disciples. Luke even shows the opening of the public ministry of Jesus to be a dramatic enunciation of his global vision which then provoked a violent reaction from the Jews.

Luke 4:16-30 records that Jesus stood to read from Isaiah 61 with startling results. In our English translation we find rapt attention in verse 20, then open admiration in verse 22, but by verse 28, a short while later, they are so violently opposed to him that they are tying to murder him by throwing him over a cliff. What went so badly wrong? Maybe our English translations have missed the point—because the missiological nature of Jesus' announcement was not understood by the translators. The RSV rendering of Luke 4:22:

> And all spoke well of him and wondered at the gracious words which proceeded out of his mouth….

The underlined words could be translated literally from Greek as *"all bore witness to him,"* which is ambiguous and could also have a negative meaning *"and all condemned him."* A novel and illuminating translation and paraphrase goes as follows:

> They protested with one voice and were furious because he only spoke about (God's year of) mercy (and omitted the words about the Messianic vengeance).

The Jews knew the passage well, and expected Jesus to go on to read the words in the second phrase of Isaiah 61:2, but he ended the reading in mid-sentence and omitted these words:

> …and the day of vengeance of our God.

The astonishment of the Jews quickly turned to anger because the expected vengeance on the Gentiles was not expressed. Jesus made it worse by reminding the protesters of the ministry of Elijah to a leprous Syrian general and to a Sidonian widow. He amply demonstrated that he had deliberately omitted that phrase and that his intended ministry was not to wreak vengeance on the Gentiles, but to save them—even passing over the most needy people of Jewish society, the lepers and widows. This the Jews could not accept and provoked the extreme response of an attempted murder.

statement probably means instead that some of all kinds of men will be drawn to Jesus when they learn that His death atoned for their sins. And that is exactly what the Abrahamic Covenant promised—not that all people would be blessed, but that all peoples would be represented in the blessing. Jesus' disciples thus gained still another fair warning of the Great Commission soon to follow!

On the Road to Emmaus

Just as the disciples still did not believe Jesus' intimations of Gentile evangelism, so also they never really believed Him when He said He would rise from the dead. But He surprised them on both counts! Three days after His entombment He resurrected! And one of His first encounters after resurrection began in incognito fashion with two of His disciples on a road leading to Emmaus (Luke 24:13-49). During the opening exchange the two disciples, still not recognizing Jesus, complained: "We had hoped that [Jesus] was the one who was going to redeem Israel" (v. 21); they did not add, "and make Israel a blessing to all peoples." A blind spot in their hearts still effectively obscured that part of the Abrahamic Covenant.

"How foolish you are," Jesus responded, "and how slow of heart to believe all that the prophets have spoken! Did not the Christ have to suffer these things and then enter his glory?" (vv. 25,26).

Then, beginning with the five "books of Moses and all the prophets, he explained to them what was said in all the Scriptures concerning himself." He had covered much of that ground before, but He went over it again—patiently (v. 27). And this time, the two disciples' hearts burned within them as He opened the Scriptures (v. 32). Was a wider perspective at last winning its way into their hearts?

Later they recognized Jesus, but at the same moment He vanished from their sight! They retraced their steps at once to Jerusalem, found the eleven (as the disciples were called for a while after Judas' defection) and recounted their experience. But before they finished talking, Jesus Himself appeared among them, and the eleven experienced the end of the story for themselves!

As unerringly as a swallow returning to its nest, Jesus returned to the Scriptures and their central theme: "Then he opened their minds so they could understand the Scriptures. He told them, 'This is what is written: the Christ will suffer and rise from the dead on the third day, and repentance and forgiveness of sins will be preached in his name to all nations [i.e., *ethne*—peoples], beginning at Jerusalem. You are witnesses of these things'" (Luke 24:45-48).

Go and Make Disciples

Notice, however, that He still did not command them to go. That would come a few days later, on a mountain in Galilee where—as far as the disciples were concerned—it all started. And here is the working of the command which the Abrahamic Covenant had already foreshadowed for 2,000 years, and which Jesus for three long years had been preparing His disciples to receive: "All authority in heaven and earth has been given to me. Therefore go and make disciples of all nations, baptizing them in the name of the Father and of the Son and of the Holy Spirit, and teaching them to obey [note the limitation that follows] everything I have commanded you. And surely I will be with you always, to the very end of the age" (Matt 28:18-20).

It was not an unfair command. The Old Testament foreshadowed it. Jesus' daily teaching anticipated it. His frequent prejudice-free ministry among both Samaritans and Gentiles had given the disciples a real-life demonstration of how to carry it out. Now He added the promise of His own authority bequeathed and His own presence in company—if they obeyed!

Still later, moments before He ascended back into heaven from the Mount of Olives (near Bethany), He added a further promise: "You will receive power when the Holy Spirit comes on you; and you will be my witnesses...." Then followed Jesus' famous formula for the exocentric progression of the gospel: "...in Jerusalem, and in all Judea and Samaria, and to the ends of the earth" (Acts 1:8).

It was Jesus' last command. Without another word, and without waiting for any discussion of the proposal, He ascended into heaven to await His followers' complete obedience to it!

Mandate on the Mountain

Steven C. Hawthorne

"And the angel answered and said to the women, "…Go quickly and tell His disciples that…'He is going before you into Galilee, there you will see Him.'"—Matthew 28:5-7

"Go and take word to My brethren to leave for Galilee, and there they shall see Me."—Matthew 28:10

"But the eleven disciples proceeded to Galilee, to the mountain which Jesus had designated. And when they saw Him, they worshiped Him; but some were doubtful."—Matthew 28:16-17

They waited on the mountain, one of the highest hills overlooking the Sea of Galilee. There wasn't any question of being in the right place. They had met with Jesus there before. Jesus had sometimes prayed there.[1] In fact, James, John and Peter took them to the very spot where they said Jesus had appeared in blazing white glory.

They stared at the lake below, breaking the silence to remember out loud some of the things that happened around the lake. There were only eleven of them now. To a man, each of them wondered privately what would happen when Jesus came. Expectations ran high and wild. Time passed slowly. They waited and wondered.

He had never been predictable, even in the early Galilee days. What would happen now that He had died? Or was He alive? Each of them had already seen Him again, or what seemed to be Him. None of the encounters had been routine. He had walked through locked doors. Or He had managed to walk for miles at the side of close friends while remaining incognito, then vanishing when they recognized Him. Or He had appeared to be a gardener doing morning routines. Or just another guy on the beach. You could be staring at Him and not know it was Him, and then look again and nearly die of shock when you suddenly recognized Him. Ever since His death, and what certainly looked like His resurrection, He had met them unannounced, by surprise, apparently at random moments. But now there was an appointed place to meet Him. What would He say? It's hard to imagine how Jesus could have arranged an encounter that would have gotten their attention any more than He did.

Even though they were each looking out for Him, when He finally appeared, He startled them all as He slowly

Steven C. Hawthorne is the Founder and Director of WayMakers in Austin, Texas. After co-editing the course and book called *Perspectives on the World Christian Movement* in 1981, he launched a series of research expeditions among unreached peoples in world class cities called "Joshua Project." He co-authored (with Graham Kendrick) *Prayerwalking: Praying On Site with Insight*, and has written numerous articles.

walked toward them from a distance. Who was this person? Was He really alive? Or was He a ghost? Some doubted, but every single one of them bowed down and worshipped Him. That must have surprised them too. This was the first time they had worshiped Him in full-blown honor of who He was.[2] They would never forget it. And they would not forget what He said.

When He spoke, His voice wasn't loud, but the words were so direct that it felt like He was speaking right through them. As if there were a crowd of people behind them. Later they would realize that He had been speaking to everyone that would ever follow Him.

Four times in His statement, Jesus used the word "all" to declare the destiny of all of history. Looking at each of the four "alls" may be the simplest way for us to understand what He said: all authority, all peoples, all that He commanded, and all the days.

All Authority

There was something different about Jesus as they watched Him stride closer to them. Yes, He was alive from the dead. That was enough to addle their minds; but there was something else about Him, as if He was supercharged with an awesome power. He exerted confident authority as long as they had known him. He had always been open about His authority: He had simply done whatever His Father had given Him to do with heaven-bestowed authority. But He was greater now. He was not wearing a crown or swinging a scepter. He was their friend Jesus, with the same deep smile and patient grace. But He was somehow immense before them. He was regal and global and dangerous. He was king of all the earth. They knew it before He even said a word.

"All authority has been given to me in heaven and on earth." It didn't surprise them at all that Jesus spoke about Himself. It made sense as He spoke. God Almighty, the Ancient of Days, had bestowed upon Jesus unsurpassed authority. They would ponder it for years and never fathom the depths of it all, but it made sense: Christ had triumphed over evil at the cross. Because of that victory the Father had exalted and honored His Son as the head of all humankind. He now held dominion over angelic entities that inhabit unseen heavenly realms. He now had power to push history in any direction that suited Him. He had been given kingdom authority to bring forth the fullness of the Kingdom of God.

I think John, one of the eleven who was there on the mountain, much later in his life was shown this very transfer of authority from Father to the Son from heaven's time-altered viewpoint (Rev 5:1-14). John was shown God Almighty, seated on His throne, holding a seven-sealed scroll in His hand. All of heaven yearned to see what was in this document, virtually the deed of earth's destiny. God's answer to every injustice and grief appeared to be bound in it, ready for implementation. The scroll contained the fates and glories of the final generation of every nation. The highest hopes ever imagined are all surpassed in it: every evil vanquished; every worthy person honored. It was the missing final chapter to the human story, a wondrous finale' under the headship of a Messiah.

Why did John weep when he saw hope in written form? Without a worthy person, God's purposes would be left unfulfilled. There was no executor. Could it be that there was no one with authority to carry out His will? "Stop weeping" John is told. A worthy one was found: "behold, the Lion that is from the tribe of Judah, the Root of David, has overcome so as to open the book and its seven seals" (Rev 5:5). The person of God's choice is fully human, from the lineage of David, but He is altogether divine, the Lamb that comes from the very center of the throne. The Father grants this glorious man Christ Jesus the ultimate authority to carry out all of His will.

The Ancient of Days has awarded all things to the Son of Man. Who will ever withstand His wisdom? Who can daunt His determination to heal the nations? What demonic power might ever intimidate Him in the slightest way? Who can deflect His desire to gather all peoples to Himself? Never has there been such power in the hands of any person. He will never be surpassed. He will never abdicate His Kingship. He will never stop until He has finished the fullness of the Father's purpose.

All the Peoples

This glorious man now stood before them. He paused after speaking of His authority, letting purpose virtually crackle in the air. He could authorize anything. What would He call for?

"Therefore… go and disciple all the peoples."

They understood then what later readers of translations may miss, that the primary action word was "disciple." The other action words, "go…baptizing…and teaching" were all commanded actions, but they each filled out part of what Jesus meant by the pivotal command: "Disciple all the peoples."

A Goal, Not a Process

Jesus spoke as if they could see every single nation from the hill on which He stood. To disciple each one of the nations meant that there would be a once-for-all change among every one of the tribes, languages, and peoples.

In the syntax of His sentence, the Greek word translated "make disciples" required an object for the discipling action.[3] The scope of that object (in this case "all the peoples") would define the extent of the discipling action. The mandate should never be abbreviated as merely "make disciples," as if Jesus simply wanted the process of disciple-making to happen. The expression must stand as a whole: "disciple all the peoples." Jesus was setting out a super-goal. A discipling movement was in the destiny of every people on earth. He was giving them the task of starting the movements.

Jesus did not emphasize the process of communicating the gospel. In fact, He said nothing about the gospel itself. They were not mandated merely to expose people to the gospel. They were commissioned to bring about a result, a response, a global following of Jesus from every people. It was a task to be accomplished. And it would be completed. No doubts crossed their minds about that. Jesus always finished everything He set out to do.

The Peoples

Most translations today read "all nations." When modern ears hear the word "nation" we immediately think of the idea of a "country" or a "nation state." But the Greek word is *ethne* from which we get our word "ethnic." Although the term sometimes was used to refer to all non-Jews or to all non-Christians, when it is used with the Greek word meaning

"all," it should be given its most common meaning: an ethnic or cultural people group.

For clarity we use the term "people group." Today, as it was in the days of those disciples, people still group together in enduring ethnic identities. There are several facets to the way people groups are identified: Linguistic, cultural, social, economic, geographic, religious, and political factors can each be part of what gives formation to the peoples of the earth. From the viewpoint of evangelization, a "people group" is the largest possible group within which the gospel can spread as a discipling, or church planting movement without encountering barriers of understanding or acceptance.

The disciples would not have for a moment mistaken the mandate to refer to the political nation-states of the world. Each of the eleven were from a region called "Galilee of the Gentiles" (the Greek word translated "Gentiles" in Matt 4:15 is the identical word ethne which means "peoples" or "nations" in Matt 24:14 and 28:20). Galilee in that day was known for a multiplicity of diverse peoples living with different languages and customs (John 12:20-21, Matt 8:28 and others).

They knew the Scriptures spoke of peoples. They knew themselves as descendants of Abraham, destined to bless the clans and extended "families" of the world (Gen 12:3, 22:18, 28:14). They knew of the Messianic Son of Man, whose kingdom reign would extend over "all peoples, nations, and people of every language" (Dan 7:14).

Going to the nations

Christ told them to be ready to change locations in order to do this task. The "going" was not an incidental matter, as if He was saying, "whenever you happen to go on a trip, try to make a few disciples wherever you are." For years they had traveled with Him, watching and helping as He systematically covered entire regions (Mark 1:38, Matt 4:23-25). He had sent them more than once to specific peoples and places, always directing them to enter into significant relationships in order to stimulate lasting movements of hope in Christ's kingdom. The gospel was not to be announced without actually going to the places where people lived (Matt 10:5-6, 11-13, Luke 10:1-3, 6-9). Now He was sending them to distant lands to do more of the same in order to leave behind household-based movements of discipleship and prayer.

All that I Commanded

Jesus gave them two simple specifics about discipling the peoples: baptizing and teaching. Before we interpose our much later understanding of what baptism was all about, or what makes for ideal topics for teaching, consider what those first followers of Jesus must have heard.

A People For His Name

Jesus phrased the directive, "baptizing them into the name of the Father and the Son and the Holy Spirit." They had met Jesus while John was baptizing people. That baptism marked a repentance from former life, a cleansing and a participation in the people of God ready for the fullness of the kingdom of God.

The disciples had begun to baptize people too, eventually baptizing even more than John the Baptizer (John 4:1-2). By that baptism people had declared their repentance and readiness to follow the soon-to-come Messiah. It marked a loyalty change. The baptized person was virtually pledging themselves to live under the governance of the Messiah when He arrived.

Now Jesus was again sending them to baptize. They could not have fully comprehended at that moment, but they would later see what Jesus meant by the result: A new community would be formed by this baptism. The three-fold name was not a formula to chant emptily while performing the ritual. Those they baptized were to be introduced to God personally as He had fully revealed Himself. They were no longer waiting for a mystery Messiah. Every baptized disciple could relationally encounter the Father who had given His Son, and who would bestow on them the Holy Spirit of God.

World-over, by this baptism, God would gain for Himself a people who would know personally what God wanted declared globally. The baptized people would wear His name publicly in every people group. They would later recognize that God was forming, from all the peoples, "a people for His name" (Acts 15:14).

Living Under His Lordship

When Jesus said "teaching" they would not have had the slightest impression that they were to transfer mere knowledge to newcomers.

They heard Him say, "teaching them to obey." They were not sent to round up students for classes in Hebrew ways and thought. They were supposed to train people to know and follow Jesus in the fullest way that He could be known. Their evangelism was to be primarily a matter of life-obedience rather than pressing for conformity of beliefs. It was all about faith, but aimed, as Paul described it later, for "the obedience of faith among all the peoples." (Rom 1:5).

Obeying Jesus had never been a vague, subjective affair, with every devotee of Jesus fabricating His own sense of discipline. Jesus had taught them very few and very clear commands. None of these commands had anything to do with the legalistic merit-making of religious systems. The primary command is a simple and universal command, addressed to all of His followers: "Love one another." It's impossible to love "one another" on one's own. It takes two or more to fulfill this reciprocal command in a conscious way. Jesus was forming a community of life-giving joy under His Lordship.

They were amazed by the rightness of it all. How fitting, how proper, how calmly urgent it was to summon people to follow Him from every nation. Jesus wasn't expressing runaway ambitions. The Ancient of Days had exalted Him as the only redeemer and the final judge of every man, woman, and child who had ever lived. Only He could fulfill the destiny of every clan and tribe of earth's peoples.

All the Days

"And lo, I am with you…" The final command was actually "Behold!" which meant "Watch for me. Keep utterly focused on me. Lean and look to me."[4] He had just commissioned them to go the most distant places of the planet. But He was not sending them away from Him. He was actually beckoning them to come nearer to Him than they ever had been. He was not merely passing on some of His power. That might have been the case if He was announcing His departure. Instead, He declared that He was on the planet to stay, wielding every ounce of His authority until the end of days. He Himself would be with them every single day until the end of the age.[5]

Not long after, from another mountain near Jerusalem, they would watch Him as He was lifted into the sky (Acts 1:9-12). From that city "they went out and preached everywhere." As they went, they were convinced that Jesus had not just disappeared. He had been enthroned in heaven. But they remembered what He had said about being with them.[6] And He was! As the Gospel of Mark records it, at the same time that Jesus sat "at the right hand of God," He also "worked with them" as they departed to the four corners of the planet to evangelize distant lands (Mark 16:19-20).

The age of which Jesus spoke has not yet ended. Every day since that meeting, Jesus has been "with" those who are fulfilling His mandate.

As you read this, today is also one of those days. Jesus knew this very day would come when He spoke on the mountain. He knew about you. And He knew about the peoples that would follow Him during the days of your life. Can you imagine yourself on the mountain, knees to the ground, eleven men at your side, hushed to hear Him say these words? You have every right to imagine yourself being there, because Jesus actually spoke these words. And when He spoke these words, He spoke with deliberate clarity to every person who would ever follow Him. That includes me and you. What shall we do in response to Him? He has given all of His people a mandate to labor with all of his authority to bring about obedience to all He commanded among all the peoples. How can we do other than give Him all that we are?

End Notes

1. Angels had directed them to Galilee "He is going before you into Galilee, there you will see Him" (Matt 28:7) and to a mountain "to the mountain which Jesus had designated" (Matt 28:16). It was probably the same mountain near the Sea of Galilee (Mark 9:9,14,30) where Jesus had appeared in glory, hearing the Father's voice with Peter, James, and John present (Mark 9:1-9 = Matt 17:1-8 = Luke 9:28-36). This event is sometimes referred to as "The Transfiguration."

2. After Jesus had been seen walking on water, Matthew 14:33 mentions that those who were in the boat worshiped him. Mark says that they were merely astonished with hardened hearts. Matthew 28:17 may be describing a similar occasion of bewildered fear, but in my view, Matthew 28 is the beginning point of sustained worship of Jesus for all that they knew him to be.

3. The verb *"mathetuesate"* in this form is transitive, which means that it requires a direct object to make sense. The entire phrase must be taken together, *"mathetuesate panta ta ethne"* as an integral verbal idea.

4. Some English versions translate the word for "Behold" as an interjection instead of an imperative with the word "Surely" or "Lo."

5. The Greek expression translated "every day" uses the same Greek word translated as "all" three times earlier in the passage.

6. Regarding the expression "I am with you," compare Genesis 26:3, 24; 28:14-21; Exodus 3:12; Deuteronomy 31:8, 23; Joshua 1:5; Judges 6:16. When God speaks to Isaac, Jacob, Moses, Joshua and Gideon, saying "I am with you" it is in the context of a nearly impossible mission. Temple builders Solomon, and later, those working with Haggai, were told to look for God being with them (1 Ki 11:38, and Hag 1:13, 2:4). Since God announces that He Himself will be the primary power as each of these accomplished their respective missions, it is almost as if God was really saying to them, "You will be with me." In these passages, and most likely in Matthew 28:20, the point is not reassurance or comfort in solitude, but rather God's empowering leadership.

Study Questions

1. What are the four "alls" in Matthew 28:18-20?

2. Why is Christ's authority essential for this particular mandate?

3. Why does Hawthorne assert that the mandate is greater than the process of making disciples?

Discipling All The Peoples

John Piper

> "And Jesus came and said to them, "All authority in heaven and on earth has been given to me. Go therefore and make disciples of all nations, baptizing them in the name of the Father and of the Son and of the Holy Spirit, teaching them to observe all that I have commanded you; and lo, I am with you always, to the close of the age." (Matt 28:19-20)

The words of our Lord are crucial for understanding the missionary task of the Church. Specifically, the words "make disciples of all nations" must be closely examined. They contain the very important phrase "all nations" which is often referred to in the Greek form *panta ta ethne (panta = all, ta = the, ethne = nations)*. The reason this is such an important phrase is that *ethne*, when translated as "nations," sounds like a political or geographic grouping. That is its most common English usage. But we will see that this is not what the Greek means. Nor does the English always mean this. For example, we say the Cherokee Nation or the Sioux Nation. This means something like: people with a unifying ethnic identity. In fact, the word "ethnic" comes from the Greek word *ethnos* (singular of *ethne*). Our inclination then might be to take *panta ta ethne* as a reference to "all the ethnic groups." "Go and disciple all the ethnic groups."

But this is precisely what needs to be tested by a careful investigation of the wider biblical context.

The Singular Use of *Ethnos* in the New Testament

In the New Testament, the singular *ethnos* never refers to Gentile individuals. [1] This is a striking fact. Every time the singular *ethnos* does occur, it refers to a people group or "nation"— often the *Jew*ish nation, even though in the plural it is usually translated "Gentiles" in distinction from the Jewish people. [2]

Here are some examples to illustrate the corporate meaning of the singular use of *ethnos*.

> Nation (*ethnos*) *will* rise against nation (*ethnos*) and kingdom against kingdom, and there will be famines and earthquakes in various places. (Matt 24:7)

> Now there were dwelling in Jerusalem devout men from every nation (*ethnous*) under heaven. (Acts 2:5)

> By your blood you ransomed men for God from every tribe and tongue and people and nation (*ethnous*). (Rev 5:9)

John Piper has been the Senior Pastor at Bethlehem Baptist Church in Minneapolis, Minnesota since 1980. Prior to that he taught Biblical Studies at Bethel College in St. Paul, Minnesota. Among his many books are *Desiring God, The Pleasures of God, A Hunger for God* and *Let the Nations Be Glad*.

What this survey of the singular establishes is that the word *ethnos* very naturally and normally carried a corporate meaning in reference to people groups with a certain ethnic identity. In fact the reference in Acts 2:5 to "every nation" is very close in form to "all the nations" in Matthew 28:19. And in Acts 2:5 it must refer to people groups of some kind.

The Plural Use of *ethnos* in the New Testament

Unlike the singular, the plural of *ethnos* does not always refer to "people groups. " It sometimes simply refers to Gentile individuals.[3] Many instances are ambiguous. What is important to see is that in the plural, the word can refer either to an ethnic group or simply to Gentile individuals who may not make up an ethnic group. For example, to illustrate the meaning of Gentile individuals consider the following texts:

Acts 13:48—When Paul turns to the Gentiles in Antioch after being rejected by the Jews, Luke says, "And when the Gentiles heard this, they were glad and glorified the word of God." This is a reference not to nations but to the group of Gentile individuals at the synagogue who heard Paul.

1 Corinthians 12:2—"You know that when you were Gentiles, you were led astray to dumb idols." In this verse "you" refers to the individual Gentile converts at Corinth. It would not make sense to say, "When you were nations...."

These are perhaps sufficient to show that the plural of *ethnos* does not *have to* mean nation or "people group." On the other hand the plural, like the singular, certainly can, and often does, refer to "people groups." For example:

Acts 13:19—Referring to the taking of the promised land by Israel, Paul says, "And when he had destroyed seven nations (*ethne*) in the land of Canaan, he gave them their land as an inheritance."

Revelation 11:9—"For three and a half days men from the peoples, tribes, tongues and nations (*ethnon*) gaze at their dead bodies." In this sequence it is clear that "nations" refers to some kind of ethnic grouping, not just to Gentile individuals.

It can be seen then that in the plural *ethne* can mean Gentile individuals who may not be part of a single people group, or it can mean (as it always does in the singular) a people group with ethnic identity. This means that we cannot yet be certain which meaning is intended in Matthew 28:19. We cannot yet answer the question whether the task of missions is merely reaching as many individuals as possible or reaching all the people groups of the world.

The Use of *panta ta ethne* in the New Testament

Our immediate concern is with the meaning of *panta ta ethne* in Matthew 28:19, "Go and make disciples of *all nations.*"

Out of the 18 uses of *panta ta ethne* (or its variant) only the one in Matthew 25:32 would seem to demand the meaning "Gentile individuals." (See the comments above on that verse.) Three others demand the people group meaning on the basis of the context (Acts 2:5; 10:35; 17:26). Six others require the people group meaning on the basis of the Old Testament connection (Mark 11:17; Luke 21:24; Acts 15:17; Galatians 3:8; Revelation 12:5; 15:4). The remaining eight uses (Matt 24:9; 24:14; 28:19; Luke 12:30; 24:47; Acts 14:16; 2 Tim 4:17; Rom 1:5) could go either way.

What can we conclude so far concerning the meaning of *panta ta ethne* in Matthew 28:19 and its wider missionary significance?

The singular use of *ethnos* in the New Testament always refers to a people group. The plural use of *ethnos* sometimes must be a people group and sometimes must refer to Gentile individuals, but usually can go either way. The phrase *panta ta ethne* must refer to Gentile individuals only once, but must refer to people groups nine times. The remaining eight uses may refer to people groups. The combination of these results suggests that the meaning of *panta ta ethne* leans heavily in the direction of "all the nations (people groups)."

The Old Testament Hope

The Old Testament is replete with promises and expectations that God would one day be worshiped by people from all the nations of the world. We will see that these promises form the explicit foundation of New Testament missionary vision.

The phrase *panta ta ethne* occurs in the Greek Old Testament some 100 times and virtually never carries the meaning of Gentile individuals but always carries the meaning "all the nations" in the sense of people groups outside Israel. [4]

All the Families of the Earth Will Be Blessed

Foundational for the missionary vision of the New Testament was the promise which God made to Abram in Genesis 12:1-3.

> [1] Now the Lord said to Abram, "Go from your country and your kindred and your father's house to the land that I will show you. [2] And I will make of you a great nation and I will bless you and make your name great, so that you will be a blessing. [3] I will bless those who bless you, and him who curses you I will curse; and by you *all the families of* the earth shall be blessed."

This promise for universal blessing to the "families" of the earth is essentially repeated in Genesis 18:18; 22:18; 26:4; 28:14.

In 12:3 and 28:14 the Hebrew phrase for "all the families" (*kol mishpahot*) is rendered in the Greek Old Testament by *pasai hai phulai*. The word *phulai* means "tribes" in most contexts. But *mishpaha* can be, and usually is, smaller than a tribe.[5] For example when Achan sinned, Israel is examined in decreasing order of size: first by tribe, then by *mishpaha* (family), then by household (Josh 7:14).

So the blessing of Abraham is intended by God to reach to fairly small groupings of people. We need not define these groups with precision in order to feel the impact of this promise. The other three repetitions of this Abrahamic promise in Genesis use the phrase "all the nations" (Hebrew: *kol goyey*) which the Septuagint translates with the familiar *panta ta ethne* in each case (18:18; 22:18; 26:4). This again suggests strongly that the term *panta ta ethne* in missionary contexts has the ring of people groups rather than Gentile individuals.

The New Testament explicitly cites this particular Abrahamic promise twice. In Acts 3:25 Peter says to the Jewish crowd, "You are the sons of the prophets and of the covenant which God gave to your fathers, saying to Abraham, 'And in your posterity shall *all the families* of the earth be blessed.'"

The other New Testament quotation of the Abrahamic promise is in Galatians 3:6-8.

> [6] Thus Abraham "believed God, and it was reckoned to him as righteousness." [7] So you see that it is men of faith who are the sons of Abraham. [8] And scripture, foreseeing that God would justify the Gentiles *(ta ethne)* by faith, preached the gospel beforehand to Abraham, saying, "In you shall all the nations *(panta ta ethne)* be blessed."

What we may conclude from the wording of Genesis 12:3 and its use in the New Testament is that God's purpose for the world is that the blessing of Abraham, namely, the salvation achieved through Jesus Christ, the seed of Abraham, would reach to all the ethnic people groups of the world. This would happen as people in each group put their faith in Christ and thus become "sons of Abraham" (Gal 3:7) and heirs of the promise (Gal 3:29). This event of individual salvation as persons trust Christ will happen among "all the nations."

The Great Commission: It Was Written!

Luke's record of the Lord's words in Luke 24:45-57, when examined with their likely Old Testament context, shows further evidence for Christ's desire for all the peoples.

"Then He opened their minds to understand the Scriptures, and said to them, 'Thus it is written, that the Christ should suffer and on the third day rise from the dead, and that repentance and forgiveness of sins should be preached in His name to *all nations (panta ta ethne),* beginning from Jerusalem.'"

The context here is crucial for our purposes. First, Jesus "opens their minds to understand the *Scriptures.*" Then he says "Thus *it is written*" (in the Old Testament), followed (in the original Greek) by three coordinate infinitive clauses which make explicit what is written in the Old Testament: first, that the Christ is *to suffer,* second, that he is *to rise* on the third day, and third, that repentance and forgiveness of sins are to *be preached* in his name to "all nations."

So Jesus is saying that his commission to take the message of repentance and forgiveness to *all nations* "is written" in the Old Testament "Scriptures." This is one of the things he opened their minds to understand. But what is the Old Testament conception of the worldwide purpose of God (which we saw above)? It is just what Paul saw that it was—a purpose to bless all the families of the earth and win a worshiping people from "all nations."[6]

Therefore we have strong evidence that the *panta ta ethne* in Luke 24:47 was understood by Jesus not merely in terms of Gentile individuals, but as an array of world peoples who must hear the message of repentance for the forgiveness of sin.

A House of Prayer for All Nations

Another pointer to the way Jesus thought about the worldwide missionary purposes of God comes from Mark 11: 17. When Jesus cleanses the temple he quotes Isaiah 56:7:

Is it not written, "My house shall be called a house of prayer for all the nations (*pasin tois ethnesin*)?"

The reason this is important for us is that it shows Jesus reaching back to the Old Testament (just like he does in Luke 24:45-47) to interpret the worldwide purposes of God. He quotes Isaiah 56:7 which in the Hebrew explicitly says, "My house shall be called a house of prayer for all peoples (*kol ha'ammim*)."

The people group meaning is unmistakable. Isaiah's point is not that every individual Gentile will have a right to dwell in the presence of God, but that there will be converts from "all peoples" who will enter the temple to worship. That Jesus was familiar with this Old Testament hope, and that he based his worldwide expectations on references to it (Mark 11:17; Luke 24:45-47), suggests that we should interpret his "Great Commission" along this line.

Back to the "Great Commission" in Matthew

We come back now to our earlier effort to understand what Jesus meant in Matthew 28:19 when he said, "Go and make disciples of *panta ta ethne*." This command has its corresponding promise of success in Matthew 24:14, "And this gospel of the kingdom will be preached throughout the whole world, as a testimony to all nations (*pasin tois ethnesin*); and then the end will come." The scope of the command and the scope of the promise hang on the meaning of *panta ta ethne*.

My conclusion from what we have seen in this chapter is that one would have to go entirely against the flow of the evidence to interpret the phrase *panta ta ethne* as "all Gentile individuals" (or "all countries"). Rather, the focus of the command is the discipling of all the people groups of the world. This conclusion comes from the following summary of our biblical investigation:

1. In the New Testament the singular use of *ethnos* never means Gentile individuals, but always means people group or nation.
2. The plural *ethne* can mean either Gentile individuals or people groups. Sometimes context demands that it mean one or the other. But in most instances it could carry either meaning.
3. The phrase *panta ta ethne* occurs 18 times in the New Testament. Only once must it mean Gentile individuals. Nine times it must mean people groups. The other 8 times are ambiguous.
4. Virtually all of the 100 or so uses of *panta ta ethne* in the Greek Old Testament refer to nations in distinction from the nation of Israel.
5. The promise made to Abraham that in him "all the families of the earth" would be blessed and that he would be "the father of many nations" is taken up in the New Testament and gives the mission of the Church a people group focus because of this Old Testament emphasis.
6. The Old Testament context of Jesus' missionary commission in Luke 24:46-47 shows that *panta ta ethne* would most naturally have the meaning of "all the peoples or nations."
7. Mark 11: 17 shows that Jesus probably thinks in terms of people groups when he envisions the worldwide purpose of God.

Therefore in all likelihood Jesus did not send his apostles out with a general mission merely to win as many individuals as they could, but rather to reach all the peoples of the world and thus to gather the "sons of God" which are scattered (John 11:52), and to call all the "ransomed from every tongue and tribe and people and nation" (Rev 5:9), until redeemed persons from "all the peoples praise him" (Rom 15:11).

Thus when Jesus says in Matthew 24:14 that "the gospel must first be preached to all *nations (panta ta ethne),"* there is no good reason for construing this to mean anything other than that the gospel must reach *all the peoples* of the world before the end comes. And when Jesus says, "go and make disciples of *all the nations (panta ta ethne),"* there is no good reason for construing this to mean anything other than that the missionary task of the church is to press on to all the unreached peoples until the Lord comes. Jesus commands it and he assures us that it will be done before he comes again. He can make that promise because he himself is building his Church from all the peoples. All authority in heaven and on earth have been given to him for this very thing (Matt 28:18).

End Notes

1. Galatians 2:14 appears to be an exception in the English text ("If you, though a Jew, live like a *Gentile* and not like a Jew, how can you compel the Gentiles to live like Jews?"). But the Greek word here is not *ethnos,* but the adverb *ethnikos,* which means to have the life patterns of Gentiles.

2. Following are all the singular uses in the New Testament. Matthew 21:43; 24:7 (= Mark 13:8 = Luke 21:10); Luke 7:5; 23:2 (both references to the Jewish nation); Acts 2:5 ("Jews from every nation"); 7:7; 8:9; 10:22 ("whole nation of the Jews"), 35; 17:26; 24:2, 10, 17; 26:4; 28:19 (the last five references are to the Jewish nation); John 11:48, 50, 51, 52; 18:35 (all in reference to the Jewish nation); Revelation 5:9; 13:7; 14:6; 1 Peter 2:9. Paul never uses the singular.

3. For example, Matthew 6:32; 10:5; 12:21; 20:25; Luke 2:32; 21:24; Acts 9:15; 13:46, 47; 15:7,14,23; 18:6; 21:11; 22:21; Romans 3:29; 9:24; 15:9,10,11,12,16; 16:26; Galatians 2:9; 3:14; 2 Timothy 4:17; Revelation 14:18; 16:19; 19:15-20:8; 21:24. When I use the term "Gentile individuals" in this chapter I do not mean to focus undue attention on specific persons. Rather, I mean to speak of non-Jews in a comprehensive way without reference to their ethnic groupings.

4. My survey was done searching for all case variants of *panta ta ethne* in the plural. The following texts are references to Greek Old Testament (LXX) verse and chapter divisions which occasionally do not correspond to the Hebrew and English versions. Genesis 18:18; 22:18; 26:4; Exodus 19:5; 23:22; 23:27; 33:16; Leviticus 20:24, 26; Deuteronomy 2:25; 4:6,19,27; 7:6,7,14; 10:15; 11:23; 14:2; 26:19; 28:1,10,37,64; 29:23-30:1,3; Joshua 4:24; 23:3, 4, 17, 18; 1 Samuel 8:20; 1 Chronicles 14:17; 18:11; 2 Chronicles 7:20; 32:23; 33:9; Nehemiah 6:16; Esther 3:8; Psalm 9:8; 46:2; 48:2; 58:6,9; 71:11,17; 8 81:8; 85:9; 112:4; 116:1; 117:10; Isaiah 2:2; 14:12, 26; 25:7; 29:8; 34:2; 36:20; 40:15, 17; 43:9; 52:10; 56:7; 61:11; 66:18,20; Jeremiah 3:17; 9:25; 25:9; 32:13,15; 33:6; 35:11,14; 43:2; 51:8; Ezra 25:8; 38:16; 39:21, 23; Daniel 3:2, 7; 7:14; Joel 4:2, 11, 12; Amos 9:12; Obadiah 1: 15, 16; Habakkuk 2:5; Haggai 2:7; Zechariah 7:14; 12:3, 9; 14:2, 16, 18, 19; Malachi 2:9; 3:12.

5. Karl Ludwig Schmidt argues that the *mishpahot are* "smaller clan-like societies within the main group or nation." *(Theological Dictionary of the New Testament, Vol.* 2, ed. Gerhard Kittel, trans. by Geoffrey Bromiley [Grand Rapids: Wm. B. Eerdmans Publishing Co., 1964], p. 365.)

6. From all the uses of *panta ta ethne* in the Old Testament that Jesus may be alluding to, at least these relate to the missionary vision of the people of God: Genesis 18:18; 22:18; 26:4; Psalm 48:2; 71:11,17; 81:8; 85:9; 116:1; Isaiah 2:2; 25:7; 52:10; 56:7; 61:11; 66:18-20 (all references are to the LXX verse and chapter divisions).

Study Questions

1. Piper states that sometimes the word *ethnos* refers to Gentile people rather than people groups. On what grounds does he assert that Matthew 28:19 refers to people groups?

2. How does Piper make a connection between the language of Genesis 12:3 and the New Testament words for people groups?

3. What difference does it make for missions work if *panta ta ethne* refers to people groups?

The Turning Point:
Setting the Gospel Free

M.R. Thomas

The greatest crisis the New Testament church ever faced was actually a culture clash, although some believed the issues were doctrinal. They could not imagine life without Moses and the Law. Over the centuries, the laws of Moses had become more than religion. They had become deeply ingrained traditions which gave the Jews their identity as a people. Yet God showed Paul that the Gentiles could not live with the Jewish traditions. Paul came to understand that the Gentiles should not be forced to accept a gospel that was mired in confusion over what was grace and what was simply Jewish tradition.

When new believers are required to take on a new set of customs to be part of "God's family," they quickly confuse grace, which is received by faith, with works. And if they adopt a new human culture, they become outsiders to their own people. This, in turn, results in a gospel that is immobilized. To require people to embrace anything beyond what is found in scripture puts a yoke on them that they should not bear. Anything more than scripture is too much. This may seem obvious, but it is something we often ignore. It is a confusion that has created recurring tension throughout the history of missions. And it creates tension still today when we can't resist including a few amendments to the gospel of grace.

Jesus' Earthly Ministry

When the Lord Jesus commissioned His followers to make disciples of all nations, they were to be His witnesses in Jerusalem, in all Judea and Samaria, and to the ends of the earth. During His time with His disciples, Jesus revealed Himself as the Son of God and trained them for the task ahead. "As the Father has sent me, I am sending you," He told them (John 20:21). And He promised the Holy Spirit to empower and to guide them. There was a spectacular beginning to the work of missions on the day of Pentecost. The Holy Spirit came as promised and the gospel was preached to an audience of "God-fearing Jews from every nation under the sun" (Acts 2:5). A tremendous response followed and thousands believed. Acts 1-12 describes the growth of the gospel from Jerusalem to Antioch, over a period of about 14 years.

Gospel to the Jews

This was a unique time; the movement of the gospel was almost entirely within the Jewish community. God had prepared

M.R. Thomas is from India. His insights emerge from decades of discipling Hindu people.

Used by permission.

the Jewish community over a period of 2,000 years for its Messiah. They had His Word in the writings of Moses and the prophets and in the Psalms. They knew the stories and had embraced the promises of a Messiah to come. The early disciples understood the gospel as the actual fulfillment of the messianic prophecies. They believed Jesus was the promised Messiah.

This truth about Jesus and their experiences as "witnesses" to Christ's death and resurrection compelled the Jewish Christians to take the gospel to the whole Jewish world. And the gospel fit well into their existing Jewish religious practices. As always, their activities centered around the Temple. They continued to observe the Jewish traditions, customs and feasts. They held to all that was familiar, except that in Jesus, they now had their Messiah. In their minds, Judaism had been validated; the ancient scriptures had been fulfilled. Most Jewish Christians were not aware that they were, in fact, a part of a new global work by God Himself.

Gospel to the Gentiles

A few had more insight into the changes Christianity would bring. Stephen must have understood that it was impossible for the gospel message to remain within the boundaries of Judaism. He must have recognized that the Temple, with its rituals and institutions, was a thing of the past. His defense, when he was arrested, reveals his understanding of God's purposes. He was brought before the Sanhedrin under the charge that he spoke "against this holy place and against the law," that he had said, "Jesus of Nazareth will destroy this place and change the customs of Moses handed down to us" (Acts 6:13-14). When Stephen answered by referring to Isaiah 66:1-2, he reflected the same radical change Jesus communicated to the Samaritan woman at the well—that the time "has now come when the true worshipers will worship the Father in spirit and in truth" (John 4:23).

Stephen was stoned to death. With the outbreak of persecution, many Jewish Christians were forced to flee Jerusalem. For these people, the Temple now ceased to be the focal point of their worship; the gospel was extended geographically. "Now those who had been scattered by the persecution in connec-

tion with Stephen traveled as far as Phoenicia, Cyprus and Antioch, telling the message *only to the Jews*" (Acts 11:19). These Christians still believed that Jesus was exclusive Jewish property. From their perspective, they were the "heirs" of the gospel. But some of them *"began to speak to the Greeks also"* (Acts 11:20). This was of greatest significance.

This indeed was a turning point! God blessed their efforts and "the Lord's hand was with them and a great number of people believed" (Acts 11:21). This fact triggered the movement of the gospel into the Gentile world as the apostolic teams of Paul, Barnabas and others set out from Antioch. Acts 13–28 records the spread of the gospel into the Gentile world. It was not without tension and conflict, but through them, God's eternal purposes were clarified and understood.

Insight into the chasm between the world of the Jewish believers, and that of the Gentiles, helps us understand and learn from the tensions the early disciples worked through. There was one exceptional case, before Antioch and Paul's mission to the Gentiles, in which the gospel spilled over from its Jewish mold into a Gentile's home. This was the apostle Peter's visit to the home of Cornelius, a Roman military officer who was "devout and God-fearing and prayed to God regularly" (Acts 10:2). Peter visited Cornelius under coercion by the Holy Spirit. He even told his Gentile host, "You are well aware that it is against our law for a Jew to associate with a Gentile or visit him" (Acts 10:28). But God had put Peter through a special preparation which helped him add, "but God has shown me that I should not call any man impure or unclean." Peter overcame a major mental block and when he heard Cornelius' story, he received fresh insight that caused him to exclaim, "I now realize how true it is that God accepts men from every nation who fear Him" (Acts 10:34-35).

With this realization Peter began to explain the gospel to all who had gathered at Cornelius' house. Even before he finished, God ratified his message by sending the Holy Spirit! The Jewish believers "were astonished that the gift of the Holy Spirit had been poured out even on the Gentiles" (Acts 10:45). But Peter found himself in trouble when he returned to Jerusalem. The Jewish believers there "criticized him and said, 'You went into the house of uncircumcised men and ate with them'" (Acts 11:2-3). Peter explained all that had happened. With this, his critics concluded, "So then, God has even granted the Gentiles repentance unto life" (Acts 11:18).

This early episode gives us a glimpse of the struggles that the early disciples experienced in understanding God's work and the unfolding of the gospel. But the real tensions were yet to come. God had chosen Paul to take the gospel to the Gentiles. It probably took several years for Paul to grasp God's purposes for the Jews and all peoples. He came to understand that the gospel of Christ was distinct from the Jewish law and tradition, that salvation was by faith in Jesus Christ apart from the law. He grew to realize that the gospel of grace was for all peoples and that there is no difference between Jew and Gentile. This understanding was not his own invention; it was revealed to him. It was the message he preached on his first missionary journey with Barnabas when God "opened the door of faith to the Gentiles" (Acts 14:27). Many Gentiles turned to Christ at this time, and the gospel was sown into the Gentile soil.

Some Jewish Christians, probably from Jerusalem and Judea, did not agree with Paul's message. They said, "Unless you are circumcised, according to the custom taught by Moses, you cannot be saved" (Acts 15:1). These people went about "correcting" the gospel Paul preached believing he had left out the need for circumcision. He had not told the Gentiles to observe Jewish customs, nor had he instructed them to keep the Jewish special days and feasts. When Paul heard about this, he was furious.

At the Jerusalem Council, some of the Jewish Christians maintained vehemently that "The Gentiles must be circumcised and required to obey the law of Moses" (Acts 15:5). It is important to notice the process and the basis on which conclusions were drawn as the apostles and elders considered the issue. After much dis-

cussion and debate, Peter recalled the Cornelius episode and the lessons that came from the experience. He said, "God showed that He accepted them by giving the Holy Spirit to them, just as He did to us; He purified their hearts by faith" (Acts 15:8-9). Then Peter put his finger on the core issue by saying, "Why do you try to test God by putting on the necks of the (Gentile) disciples a yoke that neither we nor our fathers have been able to bear?" (Acts 15:10) Paul and Barnabas spoke next, and "the whole assembly became silent as they listened" to what "God had done among the Gentiles" (Acts 15:12). Finally, James spoke up, quoting from Amos. Echoing Peter's observation, he said, "We should not make it difficult for the Gentiles who are turning to God" (Acts 15:19).

The Gospel Today

The purity and mobility of the gospel was at stake on that day. The essence of the gospel was distinguished from its Judaic cultural background. How far would the good news have gone if Paul had lost this debate? The entire movement of Christ-followers called "The Way," would have ended up like one of the hundreds of splinter sects of Judaism which are now defunct. Instead God orchestrated a dramatic change: to follow Christ, Gentiles would no longer have to become Jewish in cultural ways. God had opened the door of faith to the nations.

The first century disciples had to sort out the universal glory of Jesus from the cultural patterns of Judaism before they could obey the Great Commission and take the gospel to all nations. This is our challenge today as well. We, too, must sort out Jesus from our religious traditions, from "our" Christianity. We, too, must free the gospel from the amendments we've made to the grace of Jesus Christ. We, too, must be ready to celebrate the ways that Christ is obeyed fully, but differently, amidst the diverse cultures of the nations. Only then will the gospel continue to go forward "unhindered" (Acts 28:31).

Study Question

1. What cultural rules have modern Christians added to biblical expectations for those of faith?

2. What process should a group of missionaries go through to determine which if any natural practices are to be tolerated or opposed for new believers?

Acts of Obedience

Steven C. Hawthorne

W ere the apostles quick to obey the Great Commission? A better question would be to ask if they were obedient to Jesus. If obedience to the Great Commission means they should have packed up and moved to Siberia within a month or two of hearing Jesus' mandate to disciple the nations—as Matthew records it—then perhaps they were slow. But the way Luke describes Christ's mandate and their subsequent obedience, I hope to be as obedient as they were.

It might appear from a blended reading of Matthew and Acts that the apostles were foot-dragging slow in getting on with launching the global mission of Matthew 28. But Luke's account in itself is powerfully instructive for us. Let's be sure to understand Luke's point before we conclude that the apostles failed to fulfill something that Matthew wrote.

It's worth a close look at Luke's story.

I see three ways that the apostolic leaders in Acts were obedient—persistence in big-picture vision, boldness in public witness, and faithfulness to help peoples to follow Christ unhindered by cultural non-essentials.

Persistence with Big-Picture Vision

Before Jesus left, He had "by the Holy Spirit given orders to the apostles" (Acts 1:2). How did Jesus give orders by the Spirit?

On the day of His rising, Jesus met two of His followers on the road to Emmaus (Luke 24:13-35). They were of the inner circle of believers, but not part of the twelve apostles. They were probably heading toward a safe place away from Jerusalem. The enemies of Jesus had murdered Him even with crowds of adoring people in the city. Hostile authorities would have little difficulty tracking down and annihilating the remaining leaders of the entire movement. For all they knew, they were being hunted at that very hour.

They could only listen in amazement as an apparent stranger (actually Jesus) spoke to them in what may have seemed to be a very rude fashion: "O foolish men and slow of heart to believe in all that the prophets have spoken!" He went on to say, "Was it not necessary for the Christ to suffer these things and to enter into His glory?" And with that basic outline—sufferings followed by glory—He walked through the entire story of scripture (24:26-27). The story made sense with a Messiah at the center of it all and at the end of it all. Everything culminated in God's appointed

Steven C. Hawthorne is the Founder and Director of WayMakers in Austin, Texas. After co-editing the course and book called *Perspectives on the World Christian Movement* in 1981, he launched a series of research expeditions among unreached peoples in world class cities called "Joshua Project." He co-authored (with Graham Kendrick) *Prayerwalking: Praying On Site with Insight*, and has written numerous articles.

Messiah entering "His glory." This expression "His glory" was a vision of the Messiah entering a time of lasting honor and peace for all the nations.[2] The story of scripture had a coherence and a culmination in the Messiah.

With such ferocious hope freshly kindled (they said, "Were not our hearts burning within us?" 24:32) they hurried back into the danger zone of Jerusalem, re-entering the barricaded room where the grieving apostles were hiding (John 20:19, Luke 24:33). Suddenly, Jesus Himself was in the room. He repeated the same unfolding saga of scripture. Jesus gave even more detail to how He would enter His glory: His name would be honored world over as as forgiveness of sins was declared to all peoples. Then He added a significant item for their strategic obedience: The global expansion of His glory would all be launched "from Jerusalem" (Luke 24:45-47).

As Luke goes on to tell it in Acts, during the next 39 days Jesus went over the story of the kingdom of God many times. During one of these encounters, Jesus gave them firm orders "not to leave Jerusalem" (Acts 1:4). Telling people not to leave town may seem like a strange way to launch a missionary movement. But one fact, often overlooked, will help: Jerusalem was not their home! These men were from Galilee. Message-bearing angels, who certainly knew their geography well, addressed them as "Men of Galilee" (Acts 1:11).[3] The Jerusalem elite could pick out their Galilean accents in the dark (Matt 26:73, Luke 22:59).

Jerusalem was the most dangerous place on the planet for them. Avowed enemies, with power great enough to murder with impunity, had sought to arrest them in the garden days before (Mark 14:50-52, John 18:8-9), and would likely try again. No wonder Luke records that He told them to stay in Jerusalem. If He hadn't, they might have drifted back into the comfort zone of their homes in Galilee.

But, these men and women followed Jesus' orders explicitly. They stayed in the city. You have to admire their courage. They stayed and they prayed in an upper room. When the promised outpouring of power came upon them, they immediately went public. From that point they remained in the public eye, perhaps risking their lives to do so.

When persecution arose, the apostles did not scatter. Their witness in Jerusalem was not yet complete. They remained where it was most strategic—and yet most dangerous. They were arrested, shamed, censured and beaten more than once (Acts 4:1-21, 5:17-41). Still they continued. Eventually, James was killed (12:2). Even then, they remained in Jerusalem, refusing to flee. Any of the opposing powers could have found them. And that's exactly what happened. Peter was arrested. It took an angelic deliverance to eventually convince him to seek a safer place out of town (12:17). There is no indication that any of the rest of the twelve went with him. These were stubbornly obedient people. It seemed that no amount of threat could intimidate them.

The lesson for obedience today

As He did on the Emmaus road, we should look for Christ Himself to come alongside of us, even in our foolish and self-absorbed moments, and remind us of the "big picture" of all that God has been doing throughout history. We can expect that Christ is well able to give us orders today "by the Holy Spirit." Specific guidance will mesh with the big-picture vision of Christ's glory. Their willingness to obey may have been tenuous and confused, but it was enough for the Father to fill them with resolve and steadfast obedience to meet the specific moment in history.

Boldness in Costly Public Witness

Were they faithful to the mandate Christ had given them? As Luke records it, they were to take a public stand as witnesses (Luke 24:48, Acts 1:8). To act as a "witness" in Luke's way of speaking had very little to do with personal one-on-one communication of the gospel to friends and family. Only in recent times has the term "witness" been equated with general gospel communication. Reading Luke's use of the term "witness" reveals that almost every time someone acted as a witness, they did so in a public setting.[4]

Why was a public declaration in courts or in the streets so important? God wanted something more significant than a widespread awareness of Christ's resurrection. God was establishing an unshakable church. A witness not only asserted the facts of Jesus, but by their readiness to suffer, they also established the profound value of following Jesus.

The ordeal of public trial served to distinguish the movement of Christ followers, placing the entire church in public view. Ordinary men and women went on public display, along with their Christ-like character. Even their enemies recognized "them as having been with Jesus" (Acts 4:13). Their lives became an expression of the highest ideals of their people (5:13). The function of witnessing could not be reduced to a brief communicative action—it was a process. Their obedience as witnesses transpired over weeks or months or longer.

Witnessing has to do with the paradox of shame and glory. After one courtroom appearance, Peter and his fellow witnesses rejoiced that they had been considered worthy to suffer shame for His name (5:41). Jesus relays word to Paul by Ananias that he was a chosen instrument "to bear My name before the Gentiles and kings and the sons of Israel." It sounds like a regal duty, but the cost is severe—a testimony comprised of suffering. The very next phrase the Lord gives Paul is this: "for I will show him how much he must suffer for My name's sake" (9:15-16). Their shame brought Christ's glory.

The lesson for obedience today

Witnessing is not so much personal sharing of the gospel as it is the public establishing of the church. It will take more than slick communication to plant churches where there are none. The drama of Acts may be a portrait of the way any new church is planted. There may be exceptions, but for the most part, the record shows that thriving movements for Jesus must emerge into the public view. Secret movements grow weak and often disappear entirely. Movements that endure bear Christ's name boldly and at the same time display much that is recognized as the finest ideals of their people. How does this happen? By men and women (usually ordinary local people rather than missionaries), who are falsely accused and are brought into a setting of open testimony. At that moment, the value of following Christ is established.

Faithfulness to Accelerate Gospel Breakthrough

Even while in Jerusalem, the apostles acted in ways that showed they were consciously serving the advance of the Word of God (Acts 6:4). But they did not stay camped in Jerusalem. They watched the expansion of the gospel with vigilant eagerness. When they heard of the gospel advancing, they moved immediately to validate, bless, and support it (8:14-25; 11:22). When it became clear that churches had multiplied throughout Judea, Galilee, and Samaria, Peter himself toured the entire region, "traveling through all those parts" helping the church to increase (9:31-32).

It was during that same venture that Peter received further orders by the Holy Spirit Himself: "the Spirit said to him, 'Behold, three men are looking for you. But arise, go downstairs, and accompany them without misgivings; for I have sent them Myself'" (10:19-20).

Peter has been characterized as a racist on the doorstep of Cornelius, as if he growled something like, "I shouldn't even be here. What do you want anyway?" Read his words to Cornelius for yourself. To me, they sound more like the words of someone apologizing for former attitudes. They certainly reflect a quickness to obey. "You yourselves know how unlawful it is for a man who is a Jew to associate with a foreigner or to visit him; and yet God has shown me that I should not call any man unholy or unclean. That is why I came without even raising any objection when I was sent for."

> Today we must do all that we can to welcome people to Christ through that door of faith, helping them follow Christ without carrying a "greater burden."

Within hours of hearing the Holy Spirit give directions to go to the Gentiles with the gospel, Peter went. He went through the doors of Cornelius' house that the Holy Spirit had dramatically opened. But another door opened that day. And Peter, and the other apostles were the ones who God used to keep it open. It was not a door for missionaries to go to people. It was rather the door of faith for all the nations to follow Jesus without divorcing themselves from their culture.

Because the apostles had been faithful to remain in Jerusalem, they were in position to hold open the door that God had opened for the nations. The "beginning from Jerusalem" (Luke 24:47) was to be the launching of a global movement. God drew the apostles together in body, heart and mind for one of the most important moments of history—the Jerusalem council recorded in Acts 15. At that point the gospel was precariously close to becoming just another splinter group in the Judaic tradition. Instead, the gathered apostles were able to affirm that God "had opened a door of faith to the peoples" (Acts 14:27).

It was thought by some of the early Christians that God wanted all the Gentiles who were to be saved to join all the cultural and religious traditions of the people of Israel. Some were insisting that Gentile believers become circumcised, essentially becoming proselytes of the Jewish religious culture rather than simply following Jesus. This would mean that Gentiles would, in effect, leave their own people in order to know God. But God made it clear during the events of the book of Acts that although Gentiles were to enjoy *spiritual* unity with Israel, a Gentile did not need to become a *cultural* Jew, leaving his family, culture, roots and name in order to become a disciple of Christ.

Peter reminded the apostles that they had earlier recognized that God wanted the message of life to go to the nations. They had "glorified God, saying, 'Well then, God has granted to the Gentiles also the repentance that leads to life'" (Acts 11:18). In order to convince everyone, Peter recounted his story; Paul told what God was doing in the present hour; and James declared that the promises of God in scripture were now being fulfilled. The decision was to present no hindrance, no blockade in the open door that God had thrown open for the nations (Acts 15:1-31). No works of the law ("law" meaning religious, cultural traditions) were required for salvation.[5] Men and women of any people were to be saved by faith and to follow Christ in what Paul would later call "the obedience of faith" (Rom 1:5).

As large-scale movements can be observed, it's rare that people have been as swift or as faithful to follow a course of action that so thoroughly transcended the religious prejudices of their day. Few movements in history have been as swift or as decisive to enable other peoples to follow God in ways that were culturally different from their own. They saw God open the door of faith for the Gentile peoples. They were determined to allow no hindrance to arise that would block the way of any people following Christ in simple freedom of faith.

The lesson for obedience today

We have not been so bold to hold open the door of faith in our day. Thousands of people groups are now hindered from following Christ. Millions of people today are being turned away from the gospel, not by Christ, or by the repentance that He calls for. They are turning away because well-meaning zealots for Christian traditions have demanded adherence to so-called "Christian" cultural traditions. Superficial matters such as diet, dress, music, family names or any number of other peripheral matters are not what the gospel is all about. If we insist that these kinds of things are essential, we may have to recognize that we are pressing for a "Christian circumcision" that God has not really required. God has opened the door of faith. We could not have done it ourselves. The courageous obedience of the Acts 15 council is ours to continue. Today, we must do all that we can to welcome people to Christ through that door of faith, helping them follow Christ without carrying a "greater burden" (15:28) of other biblically-founded traditions which are not the essentials of obeying Christ in faith. Only then will the gospel be declared and the nations be able to follow Christ "unhindered" (Acts 28:31).

The Wall and The Canyon

There are two parts to the missionary task. The first is to see that the gospel is understood in such a way that Christ and His salvation is revealed. The second is to see that the gospel is received in such a way that Christ is openly followed. We have often seen communication as the larger task because the wall looms before the missionary. Actually, the far greater task is to serve people so that they can follow Christ in a way that is in keeping with their culture.

The Wall of Communication
- Barrier of understanding
- Challenge faced by missionary
- To communicate the gospel
- Miracle of revelation
- Seen on the "E-scale"

The Canyon of Conversion
- Barrier of acceptance
- Challenge faced by respondent people
- To follow Christ
- Miracle of repentance
- Seen on the "P-scale"

Over the Wall:
Cross-cultural Communication

We are to work to make the good news understood by every people in its own language and culture. Communication is our work: to minimize the difficulty any people has in understanding God's message. We must clearly communicate the gospel so that God's intended miracle of revelation of Christ in the gospel is unhindered. Every creative device should be examined. No mother tongue should be left unlearned or untranslated if it will mean that God's Word will fail to gain a heart-hearing.

Across the Canyon:
Facilitating a Following of Christ

We are to work to see that the good news is received by every people. The gospel will not be received by every person. But no people should reject Christ because of a false impression that He is calling them to commit cultural suicide by abandoning and divorcing themselves from their own people. On the other hand, no "cheap grace" should be broadcast such as an easy, quick conversion. Certainly, God calls all people to heartfelt repentance, but repentance is not to salute Western lifestyle or churchly traditions.

The vegetarian Hindu must not fear becoming Christian because Christians supposedly must eat meat and drink blood. The Chinese may be reluctant to follow Jesus because of a misunderstanding that conversion means complete repudiation of their ancestral past. The nomad ought not believe that all Christians must live in cities and speak English. Such misimpressions may seem trivial, but to men and women in unreached people groups, they present very real barriers of the magnitude of something like a sex change would be in America. Christ did not die for Muslims to eat pork or for aborigines to wear shoes.

It is not enough for someone to hear the gospel. It is not enough to understand it. People must be able to see the gospel lived out in all of its radical freshness and heavenly power. That kind of reality can only be seen in the fellowship and worship of a church in that culture. The word must be made flesh once again, as it were, in that culture.

End Notes

1. What we have of Mark's account says that they were powerfully obedient with no mention of being slow at all (Mark 16:20). Matthew mentions nothing beyond the commission. John only prophetically tells of Peter's final act of obedience (John 21:18).

2. The phrase "His glory" does not refer to Christ's exaltation alone into the heavenly realms. The fullness of the Messiah's glory, as reflected in the Scriptures Jesus was recounting, has to do with being obeyed within history (Isa 2:2-4; Eze 37:24-28; Ps 2, 22, 89, 110, and many others).

3. The fact that Jerusalem was NOT their home exposes the wrongness of interpreting Acts 1:8 as it is commonly understood: as a progressive succession of evangelism from home to distant lands. This common view likens anyone's hometown to the singular city of Jerusalem with the phrase "our own Jerusalem." This breathtakingly ethnocentric notion serves to detach present-day evangelism efforts from the very historic unfolding that Jesus was trying to emphasize. The reality is that there was only one beginning of the gospel. In God's history there will never be another subsequent Pentecost point. Every later initiative is a down-line fruition of that outpouring and obedience. We are now in "the uttermost parts," not repeating the scenario reaching of "our-own-Jerusalem." Acts 1:8 is a geographical reference as much as it is a historic one. Every place in America is farther from Jerusalem than anywhere in Asia or Africa.

4. References to witnesses or witnessing in Acts are all in a public arena (1:8,1:22, 2:32, 3:15, 4:33, 5:32, 10:39, 10:41, 10:43, 13:31, 14:3, 15:8, 16:2, 20:26, 22:15, 22:18, 22:20, 23:11, 26:16, 26:22).

5. They determined that there would be no requirement except what God had given to all of humankind to Noah. The forbidding of idolatry and eating food strangled in blood has clear connection with Noahic prohibitions (Gen 9:1-17). Is the fornication mentioned in Acts (15: 20, 29, 21:25) alluded to in Genesis? The Hebrew idea of the cause of the flood is surely linked to the illicit unions of Genesis 6:1-6. It does not matter whether the participants were human or angelic. This is the first clear occurrence of sexual sin with God's disfavor.

Study Questions

1. What indicators do you see in Luke's writings that the apostles were obedient to what they were told and given? What indicators are there that they were slow to obey?

2. What does it mean to "witness?" Hawthorne distinguishes a modern, person-to-person understanding from an ancient public, courtroom understanding. Of what value was the public witness in Acts? How long did it take to do this witnessing?

3. Place yourself in the role of an individual in an unreached people group. From this position, explain the two barriers of the wall and the canyon.

The Apostle Paul and the Missionary Task

Arthur F. Glasser

> By the power of the Holy Spirit…I have fully preached the gospel of Christ…not where Christ has already been named, lest I build on another man's foundation, but as it is written, "They shall see who have never been told of him, and they shall understand who have never heard of him." (Rom 15:19-21)

I n this chapter we shall trace the Apostle Paul's approach to the task of evangelizing the nations. We will begin with a brief review of the calling of God that made Paul an apostle and set him apart "for the gospel of God…to bring about the obedience of faith for the sake of his name among all the nations" (Rom 1:1,5). Only a few years earlier our Lord had been crucified, followed by his resurrection on the third day. Then began those glorious forty days during which the disciples became fully assured that he had truly conquered death and that their task would be to "make disciples of all nations" (Matt 28:19). He then ascended to heaven and the disciples began to prepare themselves for the baptism of the Holy Spirit (Acts 1:12-14). After ten days, on the morning of the Jewish Day of Pentecost, the Lord sent the Holy Spirit upon the community he had gathered and empowered to become a missionary movement. When this took place the members of that small company (only 120) "began to speak" under his unction (Acts 2:4). Spirit and speech—by these the Church emerged as a witnessing community. From that time forward the Church knew that it was of her very essence to bear witness to their resurrected and glorified Christ. Out of this witness all her other activities would arise.

The story following Pentecost is well known. The Church, a living organism, soon demonstrated its capacity as a life-communicating presence. On that first day its numbers increased by 3,000. The flame of its worship and devotion went from heart to heart. In the weeks and months that followed, this living Church demonstrated its capacity to reach outward in a spontaneous fashion with the good news of Jesus Christ. In Acts 2–12 we trace the exciting possibilities of what has been termed "near neighbor evangelism." In Jerusalem, all Judea, Samaria and Galilee—among the people of Palestine—those devoted believers reaped the harvest where Jesus and his disciples had earlier sowed the good seed of the Word of God (Luke 8:11). During this period, and scholars believe it lasted a few years, many things happened. Messianic Jewish congregations grew in size and number. Their members faced

Dean Emeritus and former Senior Professor of Theology, Mission and East Asian Studies at the School of World Mission at Fuller Theological Seminary, Arthur F. Glasser served as a missionary in western China with the China Inland Mission (now Overseas Missionary Fellowship) and was also OMF's Home Secretary for North America for twelve years. He was editor of *Missiology* from 1976 to 1982.

Adapted from *Crucial Dimensions in World Evangelization*, by Arthur F. Glasser, et al., 1976. Used by permission of William Carey Library, Pasadena, CA.

courageously the persecution of their countrymen. Many priests were converted. Stephen, a prominent believer, was stoned to death. Revival broke out in Samaria, and Peter took the gospel to Cornelius and his household, the first Gentile converts. But of central interest to us, about five years after Pentecost, God singled out a rabid persecutor of this new faith and began to transform him into the greatest missionary of all time—the Apostle Paul (Acts 9). We now begin his story.

Called to Be an Apostle

The first century of the Christian era was marked by intense missionary activity on the part of Jewish believers. Saul the Pharisee, who later became Paul the Apostle, was among those ardent Jews whose life was dedicated to God, and to bringing the blessings of the Jewish law to his contemporaries. Perhaps he was referring to this when he wrote: "I advanced in Judaism beyond many of my own age among my people, so extremely zealous was I for the traditions of my fathers" (Gal 1:14). Incidentally, we should remember that although he had been born in Tarsus, a largely Gentile city in Cilicia, Asia Minor, Saul had been "brought up in Jerusalem at the feet of Gamaliel, and educated according to the strict manner of the law" (Acts 22:3). This means he was no typical Jew of the Diaspora (the Jews scattered throughout the Mediterranean world). As a youth his direct contact with Gentiles had been minimal; some scholars feel he moved to Jerusalem with his parents shortly after his sixth birthday.

At any event, when he first appears in the New Testament, Saul is a young man, approving the stoning of Stephen (Acts 8:1) and opposing violently this growing Jewish Messianic movement, even trying to destroy it (Gal 1:13). It was while traveling to Damascus in the midst of this violent career that Saul was suddenly overtaken by Jesus Christ (Phil 3:12). In those moments of initial encounter—of repentance, surrender and dawning faith—Saul received his Call to missionary service. He later wrote: "It pleased God to reveal his Son to me, in order that I might preach him among the Gentiles" (Gal 1:16).

It was within the context of his encounter with the risen Lord on the road to Damascus

that he learned how he was to preach the gospel to them. He was given the following evangelistic methodology: "I send you to *open* their eyes, that they may *turn* from darkness to light and from the power (lit. *authority*) of Satan to God, that they may *receive* the forgiveness of sins and a *place* among those who are sanctified by faith in me" (Acts 26:18). In other words, the sequence was to begin with making people conscious of personal need, then to alert them to the Lord who is sufficient to meet every need. But to receive his salvation and the life of the Spirit, they must deliberately repent of their sin and reject the authority of Satan over their lives by receiving Jesus as their Lord. Only then will they be able to receive the forgiveness of their sins and access into the life and worship of a local congregation. Paul gladly embraced this evangelistic method (actually, Jesus had followed this method in his own earthly ministry). Where previously he had sought to destroy the followers of Jesus, he now sought to proclaim that Jesus was the Messiah of the Jewish People and the Savior of the World. From that time on Paul remained faithful to every aspect of this "heavenly vision" of the glorified Christ (26:19-20).

Prepared for Missionary Service

The seven or perhaps nine years following Paul's conversion and missionary calling were his "hidden years." During this period he apparently received little continuous help from mature believers. Even so, the Lord led him through a succession of experiences that often characterize the initial training of many faithful servants of Jesus Christ. Initially, Paul enjoyed fellowship with Jewish believers (Damascus), then began to witness with them in Jewish synagogues. A brief period of persecution followed. God then wisely intervened, and for three years his life was characterized by personal withdrawal, spiritual communion and divine instruction (Arabia). This was necessary so that Paul could find in God himself the sole source of life and blessing. Even so, a brief visit with key believers was then necessary to assure him that his understanding of the redemptive gospel was correct (Jerusalem). Following this, Paul was sent back to his original home environment (Tarsus, Syria, the province of Cilicia) to serve, before being thrust out into ministry further afield. Finally, God deliberately called this man, destined for future leadership in his Church, to work under human authority for a time before giving him an independent ministry (Antioch).

What seems amazing is that God spent such a long period training one who already knew the Hebrew Scriptures so well. This suggests that it is unwise to push young believers too soon into active service, or into places of personal responsibility and demanding leadership. Paul later wrote: "Do not be hasty in the laying on of hands." (i.e., setting people apart to bear responsibilities in a local congregation—1 Tim 5:22). Perhaps he was putting into words his recognition that God had been deliberately slow in sending him forth as a missionary to the Gentiles.

The Significance of the Apostolic Band

We have mentioned that Acts 2–13 describes the evangelistic possibilities for "near neighbor outreach" latent within local congregations. We have referred to the manner in which the Christian movement expanded from Jerusalem to Judea to Samaria, and from there to the edges of Jewish Palestine. Chapter 11 brings this story to a climax by showing how a largely Gentile church was planted in Antioch, the fourth largest city in the Mediterranean world, and how God destined it to become the key to the evangelization of the western Mediterranean. Its cluster of small congregations ("house churches") was so dynamic that Barnabas, who was sent from Jerusalem to supervise and aid in its ministry, became convinced that a more vigorous and able man was needed to prepare the new converts for incorporation into the life of the emerging congregations. He thought of Paul and set forth to Cilicia to seek him. Eventually he found him, and the two men combined their strength to lead the church "for an entire year." It is impossible to speak of this church without using superlatives. It was noteworthy as a true cosmopolitan, most evangelistic, well taught, and outstandingly generous company of the Lord's people. And yet, in Acts 13:1-5 the church is described as burdened, and on its knees "worshiping the Lord and fasting."

What was the problem? The fact that the leaders of the Antioch church were fasting conveys the impression that they were seeking guidance as to the church's responsibility to take the gospel beyond Antioch to the diverse peoples of the Mediterranean world. Antioch's Christians had no doubt as to the suitability of the gospel for all people. What they lacked was a method for sharing the gospel with them. The earlier method of "near neighbor, spontaneous outreach" would only work within a homogeneous culture. What was now needed was a structured way of extending the knowledge of Christ, one that would surmount all the barriers, whether geographic, linguistic, cultural, ethnic, sociological, or economic. So they prayed and fasted. They were truly earnest!

In response, the Holy Spirit led them to take a decisive step for which there was no earlier precedent. The account twice refers to this, perhaps to underscore that the decision was in response to the Holy Spirit's presence and direction. They "organized what in later times would have been called a foreign mission."[1] When Barnabas and Saul were designated as its charter members, the church merely "let them go" (vs. 3) because it was essentially the Holy Spirit whose authority and designation were behind "sending them forth" (vs. 4).

From this we cannot but conclude that both the congregational parish structure and the mobile missionary band structure are equally valid in God's sight. Neither has more right to the name "church" since both are expressions of the life of the people of God. Indeed, this record clearly challenges the widely held notion that "the local assembly is the mediating and authoritative sending body of the New Testament missionary."[2] Furthermore, there is no warrant for the view that Paul,

> for all his apostolic authority, was sent forth by the church (God's people in local, visible congregational life and in associational relationship with other congregations) and, equally important, felt himself answerable to the church.[3]

This mobile team was very much on its own. It was economically self-sufficient, although not unwilling to receive funds from local congregations. It recruited, trained, and on occasion disciplined its members. The Holy Spirit provided for its direction: like Israel in the wilderness, it had both leaders and followers.

The band was apostolic in the sense that its members regarded themselves as the envoys of God to the unbelieving world. They lived "under the continual constraint of crossing the border between belief and unbelief in order to claim the realms of unbelief for Christ."[4] Only when there are no more frontiers to be crossed—only when Jesus Christ has returned and subdued all peoples under his authority—will it be possible to say that the need for such missionary bands has finally come to an end.

From this time on, the Apostle Paul's missionary methodology was an expression of the activities of the apostolic band. It should be noted that this sodality structure (Roman Catholic Church "a society with religious or charitable objectives") is not biologically self-perpetuating, as the local congregation would be. One joins the band (or mission) by commitment to the Lord for active participation in its efforts to extend the Christian movement. Acts 14:21-23 describes the sequence of its activities as: preaching the gospel; making disciples; bringing converts to a sense of their corporateness as members of Christ and of one another and as custodians of the gospel of the kingdom; and finally, organizing them into local congregations in which individual members commit themselves to one another and to the order and discipline of the Spirit of God.

After their first missionary journey was completed, the members "sailed to Antioch" and "gathered the church together and declared all that God had done with them, and how he had opened a door of faith to the Gentiles" (Acts 14:27).

The Strategy of the Apostolic Band

But what plan did the band follow in its missionary outreach? It seems to have had two general objectives. First, in those early years the band sought to visit all the Jewish synagogues scattered throughout the Roman Empire, beginning in Asia Minor. Since the gospel was "to the Jew first" (Rom 1:16), this was natural. Indeed, Paul was deeply committed to this. In those days almost every Jewish synagogue had its Gentile proselytes and "God-fearers"— Gentile men and women who had already broken with pagan idolatry and were attracted to the ethical monotheism of the Jewish people, but who had stopped

short of full membership. Paul knew that at these synagogues he would contact evidence of God's prior work among Gentiles. Only in synagogues could he contact both Jews and Gentiles. Should the Jewish synagogue community in any one place largely reject his message, he would then turn his attention to the Jews and Gentiles in its midst who had responded. We recall his words in Pisidian Antioch to the resistant Jews:

> It was necessary that the word of God should be spoken first to you. Since you thrust it from you, and judge yourselves unworthy of eternal life, behold we turn to the Gentiles. For so the Lord has commanded us, saying, "I have set you to be a light for the Gentiles, that you may bring salvation to the uttermost parts of the earth" (Acts 13:46-47).

It should be noted that this initial outreach to Jews and Gentiles was not "mission" in the modern sense of the term. Mission implies reaching those without faith in God. In contrast, the Jews already possessed "the sonship, the glory, the covenants, the giving of the law, the worship, and the promises." To them "belonged the patriarchs, and of their race, according to the flesh, is the Christ" (Rom 9:4-5). Hence, the Apostle Paul shared the good news of the coming of their Messiah, and the significance of his cross and resurrection. Henceforth, whenever Jews rejected this gospel, he sought to "make them jealous" through proclaiming what God was doing among the Gentiles who were responding (Rom 11:11,14). God had unfinished business to complete with his ancient people. And this particular responsibility is still a priority task for the Church in our day. The gospel is "to the Jew first."

The second general objective that underlay Paul's missionary strategy was to plant Messianic synagogues wherever he found Jewish people responsive to the gospel and Gentile congregations wherever the majority of believers were Gentiles. We must keep in mind that the first century of the Christian Era was *par excellence* the great century of Jewish missionary activity (Matt 23:15). Furthermore, circling virtually every synagogue in those days was a ring of Gentiles, mostly Greek "God-fearers," who had been drawn by the witness of Jews to the worship of the true God and to a quality of life far surpassing anything practiced in the Roman world. Although attracted by Jewish moral strength, intellectual vigor, disciplined living, and wholesome family life, most of these Gentiles stopped short of receiving circumcision and becoming Jews. Inevitably Paul was determined to win these spiritually hungry Gentiles to faith in Jesus and make them the nuclei of Greek-speaking congregations of the emerging Christian movement.

When Luke wrote that "all the residents of Asia heard the word of the Lord, both Jews and Greeks (Acts 19:10), he probably meant that the band's outreach extended throughout Asia, the southwestern portion of present day Turkey, and that the new congregations of fulfilled Jews and redeemed Greeks were together involved in preaching the new faith. Inevitably, those Jews who remained deep within rabbinic Judaism were "made jealous." So it is today—the missionary obedience of the churches and the results they achieve cannot but stir Jewish people to reflect on why Jews appear to be unwilling to share with the nations their knowledge of the one God, the Creator of all peoples.

Spiritual Gifts and the Ministry

In his letters to newly founded congregations, Paul frequently stressed the wonderful fact that God through the Holy Spirit "gave gifts" to his people and thereby fully provided for their growth in grace and their participation in evangelistic witness. This subject has many aspects and is worthy of careful study. When he said that there were "varieties of service (ministry)" (1 Cor 12:5), Paul was underscoring the diversity of roles which characterize the service of Christians within the fellowship of local congregations and among the peoples of the world. To Paul the word "ministry" embraced the total range of Christian duties (Eph 4:8,12). All disciples of Christ are called to this service and are given various gifts (1 Pet 4:10). These gifts represent acts of divine grace (Rom 12:6) and are to be distinguished from "the fruit of the Spirit" (Gal 5:22-23). Ideally, when every part of the Body of Christ is "working properly," it grows in size, in spiritual depth and vigor (Rom 12:4-8). But before we underscore the unique missionary significance of

"spiritual gifts" we need to keep in mind their basic internal and external functions.

Internal "service" embraces the local congregation's ministry to the Lord in worship (by prayer, praise, sacrament and the hearing of the Word of God), the ministry of its members to one another for "their common good" (1 Cor 12:7; 2 Cor 8:4), and the ministry of teaching by which the believing congregation is inculcated with the norms of the apostolic tradition (Acts 6:4; Rom 12:7). Worship, sharing, and instruction are essential to the vitality of any local congregation's inner life—the "*koinonia*" or joint participation of the people of God in the life, leadership and service of the Lord among them.

> By his example and through his teaching, Paul reminded the churches of their apostolic calling. They had been sent by God into the world to reach beyond their local neighborhoods with the gospel.

External "service" likewise has three components. They are frequently described as the "mission" of the Church since they embrace all that Christians have been sent into the world to accomplish. There is the specific calling to minister to those in special need such as "the poor, the widow, the orphan, the prisoner, the homeless and the stranger within the gate." Paul clearly taught that God has equipped certain men and women for such works of mercy and relief (Rom 12:8; Gal 6:10a). In addition, there is the ministry of reconciliation whereby Christians work for concord between people and for social justice within society. Since Paul preached a gospel which proclaimed that sinners could be reconciled to God through Christ's redemptive cross, he was not indifferent to the obligation to work for the reconciliation of estranged individuals and hostile groups within society (2 Cor 5:18-21). Finally, there is the ministry of evangelism whereby Christians confront men and women with the good news of redemptive salvation through Christ's death, burial, and resurrection. Christians are to serve their unsaved contemporaries because they are the followers of the Great Servant. And their supreme service is to bring non-Christians to the Servant himself.

So then, we can conclude that through Paul's pointed instruction that all "born again" Christians have been given "the manifestation of the Spirit for the common good" (1 Cor 12:7), he did not overlook the mandate of Christ for world evangelization.

None of Paul's exhortations was more pointed than the challenge he pressed on Corinthian believers at the end of a lengthy discussion of spiritual gifts. He urged them to "covet earnestly the higher gifts" (12:31). Even though all Christians have been sovereignly granted a particular spiritual gift which they are responsible to uncover and exercise (through active participation in the course of seeking to be useful in meeting unmet needs within the local community), Paul would have them give particular attention to what he called "higher gifts." Apparently, by this he was referring to gifts directly related to the oral ministry of the Word of God. Furthermore, he was calling his fellow believers to reach out in their service and seek opportunities to minister the Word of God, by counseling, teaching or in evangelistic outreach. By prayer they should covet with intense desire this "apostolic gift" and seek to become God's envoys, his evangelists, his church planters in the unbelieving world. By prayer, they should seek the Lord's anointing with the prophetic gift to become his spokespersons, or his revivalists, to the professing Church. Or they should covet the pastoral gift and become his teachers, his shepherds to local congregations. As D. L. Moody used to say: "Covet usefulness! Make your plans big, because God is your Partner."

Church and Mission

"I was appointed a preacher and apostle (I am telling the truth, I am not lying), a teacher of the Gentiles in faith and truth" (1 Tim 2:7). Paul was determined to see the Church grow. Indeed, he regarded it her chief and irreplaceable task: to preach the gospel to all mankind and to incorporate all those who believed into her communal life. He felt that

only through the deliberate multiplication of vast numbers of new congregations would it be possible to evangelize his generation. As an apostle, a member of an apostolic band, he saw himself laboring on the fringes of gospel advance, doing this priority work.

This inevitably meant that Paul made crucial the relation between his band and the new congregations they were bringing into existence through the blessing of God. Indeed, we cannot understand his preoccupation with gathering funds from the Gentile churches to bring relief to the Jewish churches (e.g. Rom 15:25-27) unless this was somehow related to his deliberate efforts to fulfill his Lord's desire that the churches express their essential oneness "that the world may believe" (John 17:21).

Furthermore, Paul also struggled to achieve and maintain a symbiotic relationship between his apostolic band and the churches it had planted. True, some of the churches promptly forgot him and displayed little interest in his evangelistic and missionary endeavors. Other churches opposed Paul and showed a surprising vulnerability to syncretistic thinking, false teaching, and gross carnality. Still other churches remained so weak that he had to care for them as a nurse cares for little children. But there were vital churches, such as the one in Philippi, which loved him and expressed that love with sacrificial gifts.

In turn, by his personal example and through his teaching, Paul constantly reminded the churches of their apostolic calling. They had been sent by God into the world to reach beyond their local neighborhoods with the gospel. Their task was to bring into God's kingdom the nations for which Christ died and which had yet to acknowledge him as their king.

The most striking illustration of Paul's desire to establish this symbiotic relationship between local church and mobile mission is found in his epistle to the church in Rome. When he wrote this letter, he was midway through his great missionary career and the outreach of his apostolic team in the Eastern Mediterranean had just been completed. Indeed, he could state that "from Jerusalem and as far around as Illyricum" (present day Yugoslavia) "the gospel of Christ" had been "fully preached" (Rom 15:19). In contrast, the

Western Mediterranean represented unrelieved darkness, with but one point of light: the scattered Jewish and Gentile believers in Rome. Apparently, this believing community had been on Paul's mind for some years as he agonized in prayer and deliberated about his future ministry (15:22).

So, he took pen in hand and wrote this tremendous epistle. As a "task theologian" he carefully selected certain themes and developed them to prepare the Roman Christians for his missionary strategy. They had to realize anew the abounding sin of man, with all the world guilty before God (1:18-3:20). Then they had to be convinced of the abounding grace of God to sinners, and his offer of justification to the believing because of Christ's redemptive work (3:21-5). What followed was their need to be reminded that God promised abounding grace to Christians for holiness of life and fruitfulness in service through the Holy Spirit's indwelling presence and power (6:1–8:39). He then wrote of God's abounding grace to the nations, for although Israel had failed through unbelief, God was nonetheless determined to evangelize the Gentile world through the Church and restore Israel at his return (9:1–11:26). An intensely practical person, Paul had to mention various practical matters such as the recognition and exercise of spiritual gifts (12:1-21), the relation of church to political authorities (13:1-7), and the essentiality of love to enable the diversity within the believers in Rome to put united heart and conscience into the task of reaching the nations (13:8–15:6).

Only after this extensive review (15:15) does Paul reveal his strategy for the believers at Rome: that they were to constitute themselves a second Antioch, the new base of operations for the mission of his apostolic band to Spain and the Western Mediterranean (15:22-24). As such, they would have a significant role to fill, providing Paul and his team with experienced men and—most important of all—undertaking for their financial and prayer support. In other words, this epistle was written to give a strong cluster of house churches in a great pagan city a sense of their missionary responsibility for peoples beyond their borders. Through its participation in the missionary obedience of Paul's apostolic band, these believers in Rome would attain a new sense of their identity as the "sent" and "sending people" of God (1:11-15). Church and Mission—the fixed congregation and the mobile team—so that the "gospel of the kingdom will be preached throughout the whole world, as a testimony to all nations; and then the end will come" (Matt 24:14).

The Strategy of Suffering

One final element remains. We cannot trace the Apostle Paul's missionary career without being impressed again and again with the fact that his whole life was marked by suffering. When the Lord Jesus called him to the apostolate he said: "I will show him how much he must suffer for the sake of my name" (Acts 9:16). Although set free by the Lord Jesus, Paul knew that this freedom was only granted that he might take God's love to all. According to New Testament usage the word "Lord" means an owner of slaves. Whereas in our day we tend to think of ourselves as the "servants" of the Lord, in Paul's day Christians saw themselves differently. Paul knew that if he was to be a co-laborer with the Lord, he knew that he was no less than "the slave of all" (1 Cor 9:19-23).

This brings us to the deepest level of Christian experience and service, down to the reality where life is lived in tension with one's times and in spiritual encounter with the forces that seek to hinder the efforts of the people of God to liberate others with the gospel. Indeed, one cannot enter into the fabric of Paul's thought and experience without becoming aware that all his letters (with the possible exception of Philemon) make reference to Satan, who constantly sought to thwart his plans (e.g., 1 Th 2:18). Paul writes of the "mystery of lawlessness," the "elemental spirits of the world," the "god of this age," "principalities and authorities"—and reveals in his writings that he was fully aware of their varied strategies against the gospel. Indeed, references to these "world powers" penetrated every dimension of his mission strategy. Although they still sought to posture themselves as his all-powerful adversaries, Paul knew they had been wonderfully vanquished by Christ at the Cross (Col 2:8-15). He knew these spiritual powers could be overcome by faith and love, by prayer and obedience—and by suffering. In this connection, he wrote: "We are appointed unto afflictions"

(1 Th 3:3). This points up a cardinal principle: the gospel cannot be preached and the people of God cannot be gathered into congregations within the nations (John 11:52) without individuals here and there "completing what is lacking in Christ's afflictions" in order to accomplish this task (Col 1:24).

By "Christ's afflictions" Paul was not referring to his atoning sufferings on the Cross. Those sufferings he alone was capable of enduring, and when he completed that awesome task he cried out: "It is finished!" His redemptive work was over "once and for all" (Heb 9:26).

In contrast, his incomplete afflictions are related to all that he encountered physically, emotionally, and spiritually that he might give himself fully to all the demands of his public ministry. He experienced bodily weariness, much hostility ("he came to his own home, and his own people did not receive him"—John 1:11), and spiritual opposition. Such afflictions confront all who deliberately involve themselves in active service for Christ, especially when they seek to bear public witness to the gospel. They are "incomplete" in the sense that each successive generation of the people of God must willingly embrace sufferings if the world-wide missionary task is to be completed. Only then will this privilege be forever ended. Today,

however, it is automatically extended to all who "covet earnestly the higher gifts." One cannot serve Christ effectively without paying this price!

Face the full implications of what this means. The spirit world is always present, and the demons are never friendly—especially to those who are determined to serve the Lord. This was Paul's experience. And he suffered in order to overcome them, using the weapons provided by his victorious Lord.

Were he among us today, he would call for our active resistance to all that hinders the ongoing missionary purpose of God—the powers in religious structures, in intellectual structures ('ologies and 'isms), in moral structures (codes and customs) and in political structures (the tyrant, the market, the school, the courts, race, and nation).[5] The good news our generation needs to hear includes the breaking in of the Kingdom of God by the One who renders all opposing forces inoperative. But those who serve in his name will suffer. The cross is still the cross. It is not without reason that Paul exhorted fellow Christians to "put on the whole armor of God" that they might "be able to stand against the wiles of the devil" (Eph 6:10-18). Putting on armor is the language of warfare. Let us never forget that the service of Christ involves spiritual conflict, and suffering!

Endnotes

1. Neill, Stephen, *The Church and Christian Union*. (London: Oxford University Press), 1968, p. 80.
2. Peters, George W., *A Biblical Tehology of Missions*, (Chicago: Moody Press), 1972, p. 219.
3. Cook, Harold R., 1975, "Who Really Sent the First Missionaries?" *Evangelical Missions Quarterly*, October 1975:234.
4. Bocking, Ronald, 1961 *Has the Day of the Missionary Passed?* Essays on Mission, No. 5. London, London Missionary Society, p. 24.
5. Yoder, John Howard, *The Politics of Jesus*. (Grand Rapids: William B. Eerdmans Publishing Co.), 1972, p. 465.

Study Questions

1. What were the crucial elements in the initial period of training in Paul's life prior to his being sent forth into missionary service? What crucial elements do we stress in the preparation of missionaries today?

2. Glasser says churches have "apostolic calling" and yet it is necessary for the formation of "apostolic bands." Is there a conflict? How does the letter to Rome speak to this?

3. Why does Glasser use the term "strategy of suffering?" Was Paul's suffering intentional? How was it strategic?

A Church for All Peoples

Kenneth B. Mulholland

Although intensely personal, the Christian faith is not individualistic. Jesus came not only to save sinners, but also to build His church (Matt 16:18). He came to establish communities of His followers among every people group on the face of the earth—communities that would reach out to others cross-culturally to share the good news of salvation.

When Peter ended his Pentecost message, he appealed not just for individual conversion, but also for a public identification with other believers (Acts 2:38). When people came to Christ, they were incorporated into a new and caring community which is both universal and local by the very fact that it includes all God's people in all places and in all times. Yet, while it transcends both space and time, it is also a community which expresses itself visibly and locally through groups of believers gathered into congregations.

In his masterful commentary on the book of Acts, John R. W. Stott describes the marks of the first Spirit-filled community that emerged following the Day of Pentecost:

> First, they were related to the apostles (in submission). They were eager to receive the apostles' instructions. A Spirit-filled church is an apostolic church, a New Testament church, anxious to believe and obey what Jesus and His apostles taught. Secondly, they were related to each other (in love). They persevered in the fellowship, supporting each other and relieving the needs of the poor. A Spirit-filled church is a loving, caring, sharing church. Thirdly, they were related to God (in worship). They worshiped Him in the temple and in the home, in the Lord's supper and in the prayers, with joy and with reverence. A Spirit-filled church is a worshiping church. Fourthly, they were related to the world (in outreach). No self-centered, self-contained church (absorbed in its own parochial affairs) can claim to be filled with the Spirit. The Holy Spirit is a missionary Spirit. So a Spirit-filled church is a missionary church.[1]

The New Testament letters, which are replete with references to "one another," bear witness to the mutual interdependence meant to characterize the life of these early Christian communities. In fact, these letters, most of which are addressed to Christian churches located in the principal cities of the Roman Empire, deal with matters of Christian faith and practice related to the nurture and development of congregational life.

Kenneth B. Mulholland is Dean of Columbia Biblical Seminary & Graduate School of Missions. He also serves as Professor of Missions and Ministry Studies. For 15 years, he and his family were missionaries in Central America.

From *World Mission: An Analysis of the World Christian Movement*, Second Edition, Part 1, The Biblical/Historical Foundation, edited by Jonathan Lewis, 1994. Used by permission of William Carey Library, Pasadena, CA.

A variety of metaphors illumine not only the relationship between God and His people, but also the mutual interdependence that characterizes God's people. Christians are branches of the same vine, living stones in the same building, sheep in the same flock, children in the same family, organs in the same body.

These congregations are meant to be kingdom communities. Jesus taught His disciples to pray that God's will be done on earth as it is in heaven. The Church is a colony of heaven. It is a segment of humanity in which the ground rules are defined by God's will. In a sense, the Church is meant to be a pilot project of the kingdom of God, a kingdom outpost, an anticipation of Christ's reign on earth. Thus, the Church glorifies God, that is, makes God "look good," by continuing in the world the works of the kingdom which Jesus began. Although the Church cannot avoid entirely the organizational and institutional forms of the culture in which it exists, essentially the Church is the community of the King.

This means that the goal of Christian missions is not limited to mere physical presence among unbelievers nor to the verbal proclamation of the gospel among those who have never heard it. It is not limited to establishing a network of mission stations across a defined geographical area. Neither is it confined to dotting the countryside of a given nation with a series of preaching points or developing Bible study groups in scattered urban neighborhoods. Nor is it restricted to the conversion of individual persons. The goal of missions is to establish within every people group in the world, within every piece of the human mosaic, indigenous church movements which are capable of so multiplying congregations that the entire people group is both evangelized and incorporated into the fellowship of the church.

However, the goal of planting new congregations which are capable of paying their own bills, making their own decisions, and evangelizing their own kind of people is not sufficient. For many years, missionaries believed that when these objectives had been accomplished, the missionary task was complete. Behind this conviction lay the assumption that only affluent, well-educated Christians were capable of establishing church movements in new cultural and linguistic spheres. The newly established churches in Africa, Asia, and Latin America were too deprived economically and educationally to engage in cross-cultural mission. We now realize that for mission to go full circle, it is necessary for the churches established by missionaries to become sending churches in order to gather the momentum necessary to penetrate each of the world's remaining unreached people groups. Thus, today's existing mission societies relate increasingly not just to the churches which they have brought into being, but to the mission structures which have emerged and are emerging from those churches.

Where there are no churches, there shall be churches. The Apostle Paul captured this central thrust of biblical missions when he testified to the Christians living in Rome: "And I have so made it my aim to preach the gospel, not where Christ was named, lest I should build on another man's foundation" (Rom 15:20). Cultural boundaries must be crossed. Social barriers must be penetrated. Linguistic obstacles must be bridged. Religious resistance must be overcome. A church movement must be brought into being within each people group. Churches that feel a responsibility themselves to work cross-culturally must be planted. That is the purpose of missions.

End Notes

1. Stott, J. R. W. (1990). The Spirit, the Church and the World: The Message of Acts (p. 87). Downers Grove, IL: InterVarsity Press.

Study Questions

1. What are the important features of the congregations that need to be planted among all peoples?

2. How is it possible for mission "to go full circle?"

The Church in God's Plan

Howard A. Snyder

God has a cosmic plan, a master plan of redemption. He intends to bring about far more than filling heaven with saved souls. The Bible speaks of a divine plan for the whole creation, and the Church has a central role in that plan. The Bible shows what the Church is, and defines its mission.

Master of a Great Household

God's cosmic plan is stated most concisely in the first three chapters of Ephesians. Paul speaks of "the will of God" (1:1), "his pleasure and will" (1:5), "the mystery of his will according to his good pleasure, which he purposed in Christ" (1:9). Paul repeatedly says God "chose," "appointed" and "destined" us according to his will.

Note especially Ephesians 1:10. The word sometimes translated "plan" is *oikonomia*, which comes from the word for "house" or "household." It refers to the oversight of a household, or to the plan or arrangement for household management. The idea "is that of a great household of which God is the Master and which has a certain system of management wisely ordered by Him."[1]

Paul here sees God's plan as a cosmic strategy having to do with all creation. God's plan is "to unite all things in him, things in heaven and things on earth" (1:10 RSV). Five times in Ephesians Paul speaks of "the heavenly realms." God is the "Father of all who is over all and through all and in all," and Christ has "ascended higher than all the heavens, in order to fill the whole universe" (4:6,10).

Reconciliation: Not Just "Plan B"

But what is God's master plan? Simply this: *that God may glorify himself by uniting all things under Christ.* "God's plan is to unite and reconcile all things in Christ so that people can again serve their maker."[2]

God's plan is for the restoration of his creation, for overcoming the damage done to persons and nature through the Fall. God's design to reconcile all things may seem merely to fulfill his original intention at creation. But this is to speak humanly, from our underside view of reality; we must not suppose that God's cosmic plan for reconciliation is "Plan B," a second-best, back-up plan that God thought up because he failed at creation. For God's eternal plan predates both the Fall and the creation; it

Howard A. Snyder serves as Professor of the History and Theology of Mission at Asbury Theological Seminary in Wilmore, Kentucky. He has served as a pastor and seminary professor in São Paulo, Brazil. He has written a number of books, among them, *The Problem of Wineskins.*

Excerpts from *Community of The King*, copyright 1977, by InterVarsity Christian Fellowship of the USA. Used by permission.

existed in the mind of God "before the creation of the world" (Eph 1:4).[3]

This plan includes not only the reconciliation of people to God, but the reconciliation of "all things in heaven and on earth" (Eph 1:10). Or, as Paul puts it in Colossians 1:20, it is God's intention through Christ "to reconcile to himself all things, whether things on earth or things in heaven, by making peace through his blood, shed on the cross." Central to this plan is the reconciliation of persons to God through the blood of Jesus Christ. But the reconciliation won by Christ reaches to all the alienations that resulted from sin—alienation from ourselves, between people, and between humanity and the physical environment. As mind-boggling as the thought is, Scripture teaches that this reconciliation even includes the redemption of the physical universe from the effects of sin as everything is brought under its proper headship in Jesus Christ (Rom 8:19-21). Or as the New International Version suggests in translating Ephesians 1:10, God's purpose is "to bring all things in heaven and on earth together under one head, even Christ."[4] The implication is stunning: under Christ's Lordship everything is to be brought to a greater fullness than it experienced before the Fall.

Paul places our personal salvation in cosmic perspective. We are permitted no either/or here. No spiritual tunnel vision. The redemption of persons is the *center* of God's plan, but it is not the *circumference* of that plan.

The Church in God's Cosmic Plan

A remarkable phrase occurs in Ephesians 3:10. God's cosmic plan, Paul says, is that "through the church, the manifold wisdom of God should be made known to the rulers and authorities in the heavenly realms."[5]

Let us look closely at this passage:

In reading this, then, you will be able to understand my insight into the mystery of Christ, which was not made known to men in other generations as it has now been revealed by the Spirit to God's holy apostles and prophets. This mystery is that through the gospel the Gentiles are heirs together with Israel, members together of one body, and sharers together in the promise in Christ Jesus (3:4-6).

The mystery, now made known, is that Gentiles as well as Jews may share in God's promised redemption. In fact Jew and Gentile are brought together into "one body." Through Jesus Christ, as Paul had explained already, God has "made the two one and has destroyed the barrier, the dividing wall of hostility." So all Christians are one body, "one new man." This was "through the cross, by which he put to death their hostility" (Eph 2:14-16).

Note the two dimensions here. Jewish and Gentile believers are reconciled both to God and to each other. They have joined in a reconciling relationship to Jesus that transcends and destroys their old hostility toward each other. No longer enemies, they are now brothers and sisters.

What then is the mystery of God's plan? It is that in Christ, God acts so powerfully that He can overcome hatreds and heal hostilities. Jew and Gentile are "reconciled to God in one body." The mystery is not merely that the gospel is preached to Gentiles; it is that through this preaching Gentile believers are now "heirs together" and "members of one body."

God's plan for the Church extends to the fullest extent of the cosmos:

His intent was that now, through the church, the manifold wisdom of God should be made known to the rulers and authorities in the heavenly realms, according to his eternal purpose which he accomplished in Christ Jesus our Lord (10-11).

By God's "manifold wisdom" the Church displays an early fullness of what Christ will accomplish at the conclusion of all the ages. The spectacle is to reach beyond the range of humanity, even to angelic realms. The Church is to be God's display of Christ's reconciling love, bringing Jew and Gentile together as brothers and sisters in the community of God's people. But Jew and Gentile only? Was the miracle of the gospel exhausted by the reconciliation of Jew and Gentile in the first century A.D.? Certainly not! There is more to the mystery of God's plan. The initial, historic reconciliation shows us that God reconciles all alienated persons and peoples to Himself through the blood of the cross. It started with the reconciliation of Jew and Gentile and extends to free and slave, man and woman, black and white, rich and poor (Col 3:10-11; Gal 3:28). It will ultimately extend to "every family on heaven and earth" (Eph 3:15).

The Biblical Vision of the Church

The Bible says the Church is nothing less than the Body of Christ. It is the Bride of Christ (Rev 21:9), the flock of God (1 Pet 5:2), the living temple of the Holy Spirit (Eph 2:21-22). Virtually all biblical figures for the Church emphasize an essential, living, love relationship between Christ and the Church. This underscores the key role of the Church in God's plan and reminds us

> The people of God must have a visible, local expression, and at the local level the Church is the community of the Holy Spirit.

that "Christ loved the church and gave himself up for her" (Eph 5:25). If the Church is the body of Christ—the means of the head's action in the world—then the Church is an indispensable part of the gospel, and ecclesiology is inseparable from soteriology. Therefore, to adopt what might be called an "anti-church stance" would be to dilute the very gospel itself and at the same time to demonstrate a misunderstanding of what the Bible means by "the Church."

The Bible shows the Church in the midst of culture, struggling to be faithful but sometimes adulterated by unnatural alliances with paganism and Jewish legalism. In Scripture the earthly and heavenly sides of the Church fit together in one whole and do not leave us with two incompatible churches or with a split-level view of the Church. The Church is one; it is the one Body of Christ that now exists both on earth and "in the heavenly realms" (Eph 1:3; 2:6; 3:10). This view of the Church is sharply relevant for the modern age for reasons which are basic to the biblical view of the Church.[6]

First, *the Bible sees the Church in cosmic/historical perspective.* The Church is the people of God which God has been forming and through which he has been acting down through history. In this sense the Church has roots that go back into the Old Testament, back even to the Fall. Its mission stretches forward into all remaining history and into eternity. This horizontal line is the historical dimension.

The cosmic dimension reminds us that our space-time world is really part of a larger, spiritual universe in which God reigns. The Church is the body given to Christ, the conquering Savior. God has chosen to place the Church with Christ at the very center of His plan to reconcile the world to himself (Eph 1:20-23).

The Church's mission, therefore, is to glorify God by continuing in the world the works of the Kingdom which Jesus began (Matt 5:16). This both justifies and demands the Church's broader ministry "to preach good news to the poor...to proclaim freedom for the prisoners and recovery of sight for the blind, to release the oppressed, to proclaim the year of the Lord's favor" (Luke 4:18-19).

Second, *the Bible sees the Church in charismatic, rather than in institutional, terms.* While the Church is, in a broad sense, an institution, it is more fundamentally a charismatic community. That is, it exists by the grace (*charis*) of God and is built up by the gifts of grace (charismata) bestowed by the Spirit. As seen biblically, it is not structured the same way a business corporation or university is, but is structured like the human body—on the basis of life. At its most basic level it is a community, not a hierarchy; an organism, not an organization (1 Cor 12; Rom 12:5-8; Eph 4:1-16; Matt 18:20, 1 Pet. 4:10-11).

Third, *the Bible sees the Church as the community of God's people.* Here the cosmic and the charismatic are united, and we see the Church as both within the world and as transcending the world.

Since the Church is the people of God, it includes all God's people in all times and in all places, as well as those who have now crossed the space-time boundary and live in the immediate presence of God. But the people of God must have a visible, local expression, and at the local level the Church is the community of the Holy Spirit. As Samuel Escobar has said, "God calls those who become His people to be part of a community. So the new humanity that Christ is creating becomes visible in communities that have a quality of life that reflects Christ's example."[7]

The Church finds its identity in this unified, complementary rhythm of being a people and a community, both within a city or culture and within the larger worldwide context.

The biblical figures of body of Christ, bride of Christ, household, temple or vineyard of God, and so forth, give us the basic idea of the Church. Any contemporary definition must be in harmony with these figures or models. But these are metaphors and not definitions. I believe the most biblical definition is to say the Church is *the community of God's people*. The two key elements here are the Church as a people, a new race or humanity, and the Church as a community or fellowship—the *koinonia* of the Holy Spirit.[8]

The Community of God's People

These twin concepts emphasize that the Church is, in the first place, people—not an institutional structure. They emphasize further that the Church is no mere collection of isolated individuals, but that it has a corporate or communal nature which is absolutely essential to its true being. And finally, these truths show that being a community and a people is a gift from God through the work of Jesus Christ and the indwelling of the Holy Spirit. It is not produced by human techniques or plans. The Church is constituted the people of God by the action of Jesus Christ, and this reality opens the door to the possibility of true and deep community. Here the figure of the body takes on added meaning, including both the fact of community and the fact of peoplehood.

This concept of peoplehood is firmly rooted in the Old Testament and underlines the objective fact of God's acting throughout history to call and prepare "a chosen people, a royal priesthood, a holy nation, a people belonging to God" (1 Pet 2:9; compare Ex 19:5-6). The Greek word for "people" is *laos*, from which comes the English "laity." This reminds us that the *whole* Church is a laity, a people. Here the emphasis is on the *universality* of the Church—God's people scattered throughout the world in hundreds of specific denominations, movements and other structures. It is the inclusive, worldwide, corporate reality of the multitude of men and women who throughout history, have been reconciled to God through Jesus Christ. This fact celebrates the moving of God in history to constitute a pilgrim people and is especially related to the concept of the covenant. *Seen in cosmic/historical perspective, the Church is the people of God.*

On the other hand, the Church is a community or fellowship, a *koinonia*. This emphasis is found more clearly in the New Testament and grows directly out of the experience of Pentecost. If peoplehood underlines the continuity of God's plan from Old to New Testament, community calls attention to the "new covenant," the "new wine," the "new thing" God did in the resurrection of Jesus Christ and the Spirit's baptism at Pentecost. The emphasis here is on the *locality* of the Church in its intense, interactive common life. *Seen as a charismatic organism, the Church is the community of the Holy Spirit.*

The Church as community emphasizes the local, temporal life of the Church in a given cultural context. Here we come down from the ethereal heights to the nitty-gritty business of Christians living together, sharing a common life. Here also we discover the basic fact that true community is essential for effective witness. And here too, as a result, we face the problem of wineskins— the necessity of dealing with practical structures in order to permit and encourage true community.

It is critically important—especially in a worldwide, multicultural situation such as the Church faces today—to be clear that the essence of the Church is people, not organization; that it is a community, not an institution. The great divide in contemporary thinking about the Church is located precisely here. Biblically, the Church is the community of God's people, and this is a spiritual reality which is valid in every culture. But all ecclesiastical institutions—whether seminaries, denominational structures, mission boards, publishing houses or what have you—are not the Church. Rather, they are supportive institutions created to serve the Church in its life and mission.

They are culturally bound and can be sociologically understood and evaluated. But they are not themselves the Church. And when such institutions are confused with the Church, or seen as part of its essence, all kinds of unfortunate misunderstandings result, and the Church is bound to a particular, present cultural expression.

The Church is the Body of Christ, the community of the Holy Spirit, the people of God. It is the community of the King and the agent in the world of God's plan for the reconciliation of all things. God's agent of the Kingdom must not be considered just one means among many. For from the cross to eternity it remains true that "Christ loved the Church and gave himself up for her to make her holy...and to present her to himself as a radiant Church, without stain or wrinkle or any other blemish" (Eph 5:25-27).

End Notes

1. W. Robertson Nicoll, ed., *The Expositor's Greek Testament* (Grand Rapids: Eerdmans, 1961), 3:259. Thus our word *economic*. Note also the word *oikonomia*, and its various translations in Ephesians 3:2; Colossians 1:25; 1 Timothy 1:4; Luke 16:2-4.
2. Bernard Zylstra, quoted in *Perspective* (newsletter of the Association for the Advancement of Christian Scholarship), 7, no. 2 (March/April, 1973), p. 141.
3. Note the recurrence of this significant phrase in Matthew 13:35; 25:34; John 17:24; Ephesians 1:4; Hebrews 4:3; 1 Peter 1:20; Revelation 13:8; 17:8. These passages make it clear that Christ was appointed as Savior from eternity and that God's kingdom plan is eternal.
4. See Gerhard Kittel and Gerhard Friedrick, eds., *Theological Dictionary of the New Testament* (Grand Rapids: Eerdmans, 1964-74), 2:681-8.
5. The phrase *through the church* is ambiguously translated "by the church" in the AV, thus making the force of the fact that the Church is the *agent* of God's plan.
6. The three points which follow summarize Chap. 13 of Howard A. Snyder's *Radical Renewal: The Problem of Wineskins Today* (Houston, TX: Torch Publications, 1996).
7. Samuel Escobar, "Evangelism and Man's Search for Freedom, Justice, and Fulfillment" in *Let the Earth Hear His Voice*, compendium of the International Congress on World Evangelization, Lausanne, 1974, ed. by J. D. Douglas (Lausanne: World Wide Publications, 1975), p. 312.
8. Hans Kung similarly describes the Church as "the People of God...the community of the faithful"; the Church is "the community of the new people of God called out and called together." *Structures of the Church*, trans. Salvator Attanasio (London: Burns and Oates. 1964), pp. x, 11.

Study Questions

1. God's plan is described in terms of reconciliation and at the same time, a subjugation under Christ's headship. Are these contradictory ideas? How are they integrated in Ephesians?

2. Is the church the result of reconciliation; or is it the agent of reconciliation?

3. Why does Snyder define the Church as a community? What other options are there? Why is this an important understanding for advancing the gospel?

Prayer:
Rebelling Against the Status Quo

David Wells

David Wells is the Academic Dean, Gordon-Conwell Theological Seminary-Charlotte, and the Andrew Mutch Distinguished Professor of Historical and Systematic Theology at Gordon-Conwell Theological Seminary, South Hamilton, Massachusetts.

Adapted from "Prayer: Rebelling Against the Status Quo," *Christianity Today*, Vol. XVII (17), No. 6, November 2, 1979. Used by permission.

You will be appalled by the story I am about to relate to you. Appalled, that is, if you have any kind of social conscience.

A poor black, living on Chicago's South Side, sought to have her apartment properly heated during the frigid winter months. Despite city law on the matter, her unscrupulous landlord refused. The woman was a widow, desperately poor, and ignorant of the legal system; but she took the case to court on her own behalf. Justice, she declared, ought to be done. It was her ill fortune, however, to appear repeatedly before the same judge who, as it turned out, was an atheist and a bigot. The only principle by which he abode was, as he put it, that "blacks should be kept in their place." The possibilities of a ruling favorable to the widow were, therefore, bleak. They became even bleaker as she realized she lacked the indispensable ingredient necessary for favorable rulings in cases like these—namely, a satisfactory bribe. Nevertheless, she persisted.

At first, the judge did not so much as even look up from reading the novel on his lap before dismissing her. But then he began to notice her. Just another black, he thought, stupid enough to think she could get justice. Then her persistence made him self-conscious. This turned to guilt and anger. Finally, raging and embarrassed, he granted her petition and enforced the law. Here was a massive victory over "the system"—at least as it functioned in his corrupted courtroom.

In putting the matter like this I have not, of course, been quite honest. For this never really happened in Chicago (as far as I know), nor is it even my "story." It is a parable told by Jesus (Luke 18:1-8) to illustrate the nature of petitionary prayer.

The parallel Jesus drew was obviously not between God and the corrupt judge, but between the widow and the petitioner. This parallel has two aspects. First, the widow refused to accept her unjust situation, just as the Christian should refuse to resign himself or herself to the world in its fallenness. Second, despite discouragements, the widow persisted with her case as should the Christian with his or hers. The first aspect has to do with prayer's *nature* and the second with its *practice*.

I want to argue that our feeble and irregular prayer, especially in its petitionary aspect, is too frequently addressed in the wrong way. When confronting this failing, we are inclined to flagellate ourselves for our weak wills, our insipid desires, our ineffective technique and our wandering minds. We keep thinking that somehow our *practice* is awry and we rack our brains to see if we can discover where. I suggest that the problem lies in a misunderstanding of prayer's nature and our practice will never have that widow's persistence until our outlook has her clarity.

What, then, is the nature of petitionary prayer? It is, in essence, rebellion—rebellion against the world in its fallenness, the absolute and undying refusal to accept as normal what is pervasively abnormal. It is, in this its negative aspect, the refusal of every agenda, every scheme, every interpretation that is at odds with the norm as originally established by God. As such, it is itself an expression of the unbridgeable chasm that separates Good from Evil, the declaration that Evil is not a variation on Good but its antithesis.

Or, to put it the other way around, to come to an acceptance of life "as it is," to accept it on its own terms—which means acknowledging the *inevitability* of the way it works—is to surrender a Christian view of God. This resignation to what is abnormal has within it the hidden and unrecognized assumption that the power of God to change the world, to overcome Evil by Good, will not be actualized.

Nothing destroys petitionary prayer (and with it, a Christian view of God) as quickly as resignation. "At all times," Jesus declared, "we should pray" and not "lose heart," thereby acquiescing to what is (Luke 18:1).

The dissipation of petitionary prayer in the presence of resignation has an interesting historical pedigree. Those religions that stress quietistic acquiescence always disparage petitionary prayer. This was true of the Stoics who claimed that such prayer showed that one was unwilling to accept the existent world as an expression of God's will. One was trying to escape from it by having it modified. That, they said, was bad. A similar argument is found in Buddhism. And the same result, although arrived at by a different process of reasoning, is commonly encountered in our secular culture.

Secularism is that attitude that sees life as an end in itself. Life, it is thought, is severed from any relationship to God. Consequently the only norm or "given" in life, whether for meaning or for morals, is the world as it is. With this, it is argued, we must come to terms; to seek some other referent around which to structure our lives is futile and "escapist." It is not only that God, the object of petitionary prayer, has often become indistinct, but that his relationship to the world is seen in a new way. And it is a way that does not violate secular assumption. God may be "present" and "active" in the world, but it is not a presence and an activity that changes anything.

Against all of this, it must be asserted that petitionary prayer only flourishes where there is a twofold belief: first, that God's name is hallowed too irregularly, his kingdom has come too little, and his will is done too infrequently; second, that God himself can change this situation. Petitionary prayer, therefore, is the expression of the hope that life as we meet it, on the one hand, *can* be otherwise and, on the other hand, that it *ought* to be otherwise. It is therefore impossible to seek to live in God's world on his terms, doing his work in a way that is consistent with who he is, without engaging in regular prayer.

That, I believe, is the real significance of petitionary prayer in our Lord's life. Much of his prayer life is left unexplained by the Gospel writers (e.g., Mark 1:35; Luke 5:16; 9:18; 11:1), but a pattern in the circumstances that elicited prayer is discernible.

First, petitionary prayer preceded great decisions in his life, such as the choosing of the disciples (Luke 6:12); indeed, the only possible explanation of his choice of that ragtag bunch of nonentities, boastful, ignorant and uncomprehending as they were, was that he had prayed before choosing them. Second, he prayed when pressed beyond measure, when his day was unusually busy with many competing claims upon his energies and attention (e.g., Matt 14:23). Third, he prayed in the great crises and turning points of his life, such as his baptism, the Transfiguration, and the Cross (Luke 3:21; 9:28-29). Finally, he prayed before and during unusual temptation, the most vivid occasion being Gethsemane (Matt 26:36-45). As the "hour" of evil descended, the contrast between the way Jesus met it and the way his disciples met it is explained only by the fact that he persevered in prayer and they slept in faintness of heart. Each of these events presented our Lord with the possibility of adopting an agenda, accepting a perspective, or pursuing a course that was other than God's. His rejection of the alternative was each time signaled by his petitionary prayer. It was his means of refusing to live in this world or to do his Father's business on any other terms than his Father's. As such, it was rebellion against the world in its perverse and fallen abnormality.

To pray declares that God and his world are at cross-purposes; to "sleep," or "faint," or "lose heart" is to act as if they are not. Why, then, do we pray so little for our local church? Is it really that our technique is bad, our wills weak, or our imaginations listless? I don't believe so. There is plenty of strong-willed and lively discussion—which in part or in whole may be justified—about the mediocrity of the preaching, the emptiness of the worship, the superficiality of the fellowship, and the ineffectiveness of the evangelism. So, why, then, don't we pray as persistently as we talk? The answer, quite simply, is that we don't believe it will make any difference. We accept, however despairingly, that the situation is unchangeable, that what is will always be. This is not a problem about the practice of prayer, but rather about its *nature*. Or, more precisely, it is about the nature of God and his relationship to this world.

Unlike the widow in the parable, we find it is easy to come to terms with the unjust and fallen world around us—even when it intrudes into Christian institutions. It is not always that we are unaware of what is happening, but simply that we feel completely impotent to change anything. That impotence leads us, however unwillingly, to strike a truce with what is wrong.

In other words, we have lost our anger, both at the level of social witness and before God in prayer. Fortunately, he has not lost his; for the wrath of God is his opposition to what is wrong, the means by which truth is put forever on the throne and error forever on the scaffold. Without God's wrath, there would be no reason to live morally in the world and every reason not to. So the wrath

of God, in this sense, is intimately connected with petitionary prayer that also seeks the ascendancy of truth in all instances and the corresponding banishment of evil.

The framework Jesus gave us for thinking about this was the Kingdom of God. The Kingdom is that sphere where the king's sovereignty is recognized. And, because of the nature of our king, that sovereignty is exercised supernaturally. In Jesus, the long-awaited "age to come" arrived; in him and through him, the Messianic incursion into the world has happened. Being a Christian, then, is not a matter of simply having had the right religious experience but rather of starting to live in that sphere which is authentically divine. Evangelism is not successful because our technique is "right," but because this "age" breaks into the lives of sinful people. And this "age to come," which is already dawning, is not the possession of any one people or culture. God's "age," the "age" of his crucified Son, is dawning in the whole world. Our praying, therefore, should look beyond the concerns of our private lives to include the wide horizon of all human life in which God is concerned. If the Gospel is universal, prayer cannot restrict itself to being local.

It is not beside the point, therefore, to see the world as a courtroom in which a "case" can still be made against what is wrong and for what is right. Our feebleness in prayer happens because we have lost sight of this, and until we regain it we will not persist in our role as litigants. But there is every reason why we should regain our vision and utilize our opportunity, for the Judge before whom we appear is neither an atheist nor corrupt, but the glorious God and Father of our Lord Jesus Christ. Do you really think, then, that he will fail to "bring about justice for his chosen ones who cry to him night and day? Will he keep putting them off?" "I tell you," our Lord declares, "he will see that they get justice, and quickly" (Luke 18:7-8).

Study Questions

1. What relationship exists between petitionary prayer and the mission of the church?

2. Wells states that we have two problem areas with petitionary prayer: its practice and its nature. Can you restate these problems? Which is the most important? Why?

3. Take note of Wells' interpretation of the "Lord's Prayer." How is this a "mission" prayer?

Strategic Prayer

John D. Robb

John D. Robb is Unreached Peoples Program Director with MARC, the Missions Advanced Research and Communications Center of World Vision International. He served as a missionary to Malaysia with Overseas Missionary Fellowship. He has traveled extensively in approximately 100 countries presenting unreached people group seminars and facilitating strategic prayer initiatives.

Reprinted by permission from *World Vision*, February-March, 1997.

A giant tree stood on the banks of the Awash River in an arid valley about two hour drive from Addis Ababa, Ethiopia. It had been there for generations and seemed eternal. Unable to bring the water in the river to the higher level of the land, the people who lived in the surrounding district had suffered through famines over the years. In their suffering, the people looked to the tree for help. They worshiped the towering giant, believing a spirit had given it divine powers. Adults would kiss its great trunk as they passed by. They spoke of the tree in hushed, reverential tones and the children said, "This tree saved us."

When World Vision began a development project in 1989, including an irrigation system to make the valley's parched earth bloom for the first time, the great tree stood like a forbidding sentinel of an old order. It presided over the community of people, enslaving them through fear. The people were convinced that the spirits must be propitiated with animal sacrifices and the strict observance of taboos. The World Vision workers saw how the villagers worshiped the tree and recognized that it was an idolatrous barrier to the entrance of Christ's kingdom and the transformation of the entire community.

One morning as the World Vision staff prayed together, one of Jesus' promises struck them as particularly relevant. It said, "If you have faith, you can say to this tree, 'Be taken up and removed' and it will obey you" (Matt 21:21). With this reminder, they began to pray in faith that God would bring down the menacing Goliath. Soon, the whole community knew that the Christians were praying about the tree. Six months later, the tree began to dry up. Its leafy foliage disappeared, and finally it collapsed like a stricken giant into the river. The people were astonished. "Your God has done this!" they said. "Your God has dried up the tree!" Within a few weeks, about a hundred villagers received Jesus Christ because they had seen His power displayed in the spectacular answer to the Christians' prayers.

The Spiritual Nature of Social Problems

Christians have been divided for years over the most effective means of transforming our world. Is it through verbal proclamation of the gospel or with social action? In truth, the two cannot be separated. Without both, there simply is no good news. One thing ties them together—prayer. When prayer to our God of temporal justice and eternal salvation is emphasized, evangelism and social action are linked in the most essential way. The God who inspires prayer for the world stirs the hearts of His people both to share His good news and to dispense love and mercy. When we see people coming to Christ, health improving, economic opportunity increasing, and kingdom values growing, we find that believers have been praying. Because of the nature of evil in the world, prayer is essential.

As we seek to help the poor and to stand against injustice, Christians sometimes forget that we are also fighting against principalities and powers. Since the Garden of Eden, human beings have gained control over other individuals and whole societies by cooperating with Satan and his evil spirits. This has led to wide-scale famine, disease, poverty, slavery, injustice and suffering. Whenever we try to help the victims of these tragedies, we enter a fray that involves the great socio-spiritual forces that rule the world's massive institutions, social structures and systems. Both Satan and his powers are dedicated to destroying the human beings who are made in the image of God. Satan is the master deceiver, the author of idolatry, who seeks to dominate the world by undermining faith in God, twisting values and promoting false ideologies. He infiltrates institutions, governments, communications media, educational systems and religious bodies, using them to seduce humankind over to the worship of money, fame, success, power, pleasure, science, art, politics and religious idols.

Socio-spiritual forces of evil clench societies in a dark, destructive grip in two related ways. The first is by openly idolatrous and cultic covenants and the second through false patterns of thinking which blind people to the reality of God and the hope He brings.

The Devastation of Idolatry

Throughout much of the Old Testament, Satan induced Israel to drift from their allegiance to God and dally with the false gods of the Egyptians, Amorites, Canaanites and Edomites. The Israelites suffered the consequences God had assured them would come about if they did so—oppression, slavery, for-eign invasion and poverty (Judg 6:6; 10:16; Deut 28). The same sin, and its consequences, afflict the world today.

Northern India is one of the world's darkest regions. Indians estimate there may be more than three hundred million gods in that region. Kali, the goddess of destruction, is a regional deity worshipped in Calcutta, West Bengal. Anyone who has been to Calcutta knows the devastating impact she and her worship have had on the people of that city. Elsewhere in the world, the occult is behind some of the most brutal injustices of the century. In Cambodia, the Khmer Rouge—who killed as many as two million people in the 1970s—were based in two occult strongholds. Shiva, the Hindu god of destruction and regeneration, and Naga, the serpent god, are worshipped in these northern locations. During Liberia's civil war, SIM missionaries reported that many of the combatants practiced *juju*, a kind of African magic or witchcraft, to gain power. They wore fetishes, called spirits to come into them, got drunk and murdered whole villages of innocent people.

The Despair of Strongholds

When Satan is not influencing people through open idolatry or fear of spirits, we still find that people are controlled by false ways of thinking which lock them in spiritual darkness. The Apostle Paul mentions this kind of bondage in 2 Corinthians 10:4. He talks about "arguments and every pretension that sets itself up against the knowledge of God." George Otis, Jr., writes that, from the context of this passage,

> "these strongholds are not demons or geographical locations, but psychic habitats. The word *argument*, often translated *imagination*, is an interesting one, taken from the Greek word *logismos*; it is defined more precisely as calculative reasonings over time (as opposed to random, occasional thoughts). This definition makes these arguments or imaginations look more like what they almost certainly are—religious or philosophical systems."[1]

In the above passage, Paul uses the Greek word *hupsoma* which is translated as "pretension" or "high thing." It was an astrological term meaning "the sphere in which astrological powers hold sway." [2] This indicates that Paul considered the patterns of thinking of those who opposed the gospel to be influenced by such powers.

Francis Frangipane also identifies these strongholds as within the mind, "the spiritual fortresses wherein Satan and his legions hide and are protected." He says that "these fortresses exist in the thought-patterns and ideas that govern individuals and churches as well as communities and nations." [3]

For example, the idea of fate in Hinduism imprisons millions of people in spiritual and economic poverty. This insurmountable force of fate supposedly determines the caste you were born into, and if you were born into a poor caste, there is little chance you can better your life by becoming an attorney or an accountant. This thinking is a satanic stronghold, a deception that keeps people in bondage to poverty. Development efforts among people who are imprisoned by fatalistic world views are limited in their impact because these people are convinced that nothing will ever change.

Besides hindering people from achieving their God-given potential, strongholds in the mind can be used by the evil one to unleash horrific destruction. When Hutu extremists took over the government of Rwanda in 1994, they used dehumanizing ethnic stereotypes by speaking of the Tutsi people as "cockroaches" that needed to be exterminated. In only three months, up to a million Tutsis, along with moderate Hutus who refused to take up arms against their Tutsi neighbors, were murdered by bands of roving killers.

What shall we do in the face of socio-spiritual evil? Undoubtedly, we must share the truth of God's word to offset such deception, but we must also be aggressive in prayer.

Dealing with Supernatural Evil Forcefully

Evil spirits cannot be reformed or negotiated with. They can only be expelled in a forceful way that has to be considered an act of spiritual violence. We think of Jesus as the standard for a peace-loving, non-violent approach to one's enemies, but he taught it was to *human* enemies only that we are to turn the

other cheek, not to demonic foes. He never allowed Satan and the demons to have their way. Instead he took a forceful, authoritative, even violent posture, at every turn rebuking, resisting and casting out these evil forces.

He also spoke of the violent struggle and counterattack that would attend the coming of the kingdom. He said, "The kingdom of heaven suffers violence and the violent take it by force" (Matt 11:12). Many biblical scholars agree this means that the kingdom has been under attack from violent foes. Human beings and their institutions captured and killed John the Baptist. Religious leaders in league with the Roman authorities opposed Jesus and had him executed. Behind these human forces, however, Jesus saw the one He often called the "prince of this world." He speaks of Satan in Mark 3:27 and says this strong man must be bound if his captives are to be liberated. Binding a strong man involves violent combat, yet it is a battle the Church can win through the power of God. Jesus Himself promised that "the gates of hell will not prevail against my Church."

The Apostle Paul, too, emphasized that "our struggle is not against flesh and blood, but against the rulers, against the authorities, against the powers of this dark world and against the spiritual forces of evil in the heavenly realms" (Eph 6:12). Prayer is the decisive weapon in this struggle—and is often aggressive and violent. The structures and forces of injustice, oppression and war are so overwhelming that all our efforts to help will fail unless we first invite God into the fray. Until we have achieved victory in prayer, it is hopeless to engage the outer world in combat.

I am not saying that prayer is all that is necessary to change the world. Many evangelical Christians have used prayer for too long as a substitute for action—dumping back on God the responsibility for doing what He has already commanded us to do throughout Scripture. Yet neither is social action a substitute for prayer. There is still a profound air of mystery surrounding prayer and how God uses our praying to transform the world. Theologian Walter Wink writes that

"prayer is not magic; it does not always work; it is not something we do, but a response to what God is already doing within us and the world. Our prayers are the necessary opening that allows God to act without violating our freedom. Prayer is the ultimate act of partnership with God."[4]

Paradoxically, the most aggressive and powerful spiritual warfare must be waged out of great personal brokenness and weakness. Jesus' triumph over the forces of darkness through the utter humiliation and powerlessness of the cross is the primary example. Similarly, we are strongest against evil when we come to the cross with Jesus—confessing and renouncing our own complicity with the powers of darkness.

Lessons in Prayer

In 1994 a group of Cambodian Christian leaders told me about the intensity of their spiritual battle and requested support from a team of outside prayer leaders. The following March, I took a team to assist sixty Cambo-

dian pastors and evangelists in prayer for their nation. We quickly encountered the influence of the spirit of murder, exemplified in the worship of Shiva, god of destruction, and Naga, the serpent god who was said to be the guiding spirit of the Cambodian people. On the second day of the conference, the Spirit of God spoke through one of the members of the team saying, "Some of you have blood on your hands." In the room, were former Khmer Rouge killers who had executed hundreds, perhaps thousands, of people. Great weeping followed, with confession of heinous acts in the killing fields.

This self-humbling and open confession led to a time in which the Cambodian Christians renounced the ancient covenants that were made by the Cambodian kings with the powers of darkness in the temples at Angkor, in the northern part of the country. This deep outpouring of emotion and confession of sin began a process of reconciliation that led, in turn, to the formation of a national Christian fellowship. At this writing, the number of churches has grown from about 100 to over 500. In addition, the Khmer Rouge have been badly weakened, if not destroyed, as a terrorist movement.

There were several features of this prayer initiative which can be a valuable lesson for other prayer efforts:

1. *There was much prayer preceding and accompanying this effort.* Our team and the Cambodian Christians were not praying alone. We were supported by thousands of people who interceded for us around the world. United prayer—joining the prayers of God's people around the world in a special focus for particular places and people—is a powerful combination.

2. *Local leadership carried out the dramatic acts of identificational repentance.* Our team sought to be servants and catalysts, recognizing that God had given the local leaders the primary authority to break the pacts of spiritual darkness.

3. *Humility and brokenness were essential for all who took part.* There was no smug triumphalism on the part of either our team members or the Cambodian Christians.

4. *We depended on God's leading at every point.* Everyone involved in our prayer effort sought to be led by God's Spirit. We prepared ourselves with objective information about the present situation in the country, as well as its history, then waited for the subjective direction of the Holy Spirit.

5. *We prayed in a holistic manner.* We prayed for the government, the various people groups—many still unreached—and the social needs of the nation, as well as for the unity and vitality of the church. We prayed for God's *shalom* to come upon Cambodia with a lasting spiritual and social transformation.

6. *Effective prayer is persistent prayer.* Long after our team's visit to Cambodia, those who took part continued to pray. Recent disunity and outright conflict among different factions in the government have made it clear that intercessors must never let down their guard. They must watch over their nation like sentinels upon the wall; otherwise, the evil one will come in the back door, creating division and destruction when least expected.

Can anything good come out of Cali?

In answer to the prayers of intercessors, God's *shalom* and transformation has also been at work in Cali, Colombia.[5] Until recently, this Latin American city was in the grip of the infamous Cali drug cartel. It has been called the largest, richest and best organized criminal group in history—controlling most forms of government and huge amounts of money and perpetrating the most obscene violence. Anyone who opposed them was simply liquidated. In sheer desperation, the pastors of Cali agreed to meet every week to pray for the city, beginning in January 1995.

In May of that year, the pastors' association hosted an all-night prayer vigil at the civic auditorium which seats about 27,000. They had hoped a few thousand people would turn out and fill the bottom section. Instead, 30,000 showed up to pray throughout the night! In the words of one organizer, "The primary purpose of the vigil was to take a stand against the cartels and their unseen spiritual masters. Both have been ruling our city and nation for too long. After humbling ourselves before God and one another, we symbolically extended Christ's scepter of authority over Cali—including its bondage over cocaine, violence and corruption."

The first result of the prayer meeting was that immediately after it the city went an entire day without murder. This was a newsworthy event in that the average had been multiple homicides per day. (There were fifteen thousand murders in Colombia during the first six months of 1993—giving it the highest homicide rate in the world, eight times that of the United States.) During the next four months, 900 cartel-linked officers were fired from the police force. Then, several intercessors reported dreams in which they saw angels apprehending the leaders of the drug cartel. Within six weeks of these visions, the Colombian government declared all-out war on the drug cartel bosses. By August of that year—only three months after God's revelation to the intercessors—Colombian authorities had captured all seven cartel leaders.

The believers in Cali decided to hold a second all-night prayer rally. In preparation, they surveyed the political, social and spiritual needs in 22 administrative sections of the city. Then they prayed in specific terms about what they had learned. Again, dramatic changes followed. Colombian authorities launched an anti-corruption investigation—not only within the city government of Cali, but even up to the office of the nation's president.

Since that time, the city of Cali has grown economically with more than 25 percent improvement. Upon seeing the impact of the believers' prayers, the mayor of Cali announced, "This city needs Jesus Christ to bring peace." The city authorities have provided sound systems and platforms for 22 concurrent evangelism crusades with 40 national and international evangelists. Crime statistics have dropped. And the incidence of AIDS, which had been the highest in the Latin American continent, has been lowered.

The churches in Cali have grown tremendously in a "spiritual explosion." According to church growth specialist, Peter Wagner, Cali has become a cutting edge city, since its spiritual awakening is spreading to other cities. But a price for this has been paid in spiritual backlash. In the past two years, over 200 pastors in Colombia have been killed by guerrillas or paramilitary forces.

Reaching Unreached Peoples

Aggressive, strategic prayer is an essential component in reaching unreached people groups for two reasons. First, unreached peoples are, by definition "churchless" peoples. However they may be delineated by ethnic, linguistic, or social features, unreached peoples are those which do not yet have a flourishing church planting movement announcing and demonstrating the gospel of the Kingdom. God intends for churches to be an open display of obedience to Christ. Satan works to deny that obedience by trapping a people in society-wide presumptions about reality. We're not sure how these strongholds get their start; probably by trapping people in their own highminded speculations as they pursue self-sufficiency. But we can see that in settings in which Christ is not obeyed—where there is no church—such strongholds go unchallenged, sometimes for centuries, gaining strength with every passing generation. Bold, determined spiritual warfare is required to weaken and dislodge these fortresses of presumption which are blockading "the knowledge of God" and denying "the obedience of Christ" (2 Cor 10:3-5). No amount of human persuasion can liberate an entire people from such darkness. Prayer is utterly essential. Only God can move by His mercy to open such society-wide blindness to the light of Christ.

The second reason prayer is paramount for unreached peoples is for God to send laborers. Usually unreached peoples have been neglected or resistant so there are few, if any, missionaries working to reach them. Christ ordered His first followers to examine the places where the harvest was great but the laborers were few and then to boldly entreat the Lord of the harvest to do what only God can do: Raise up and send effective laborers. It is thrilling to see wonderful breakthroughs among unreached people groups. In every case, we can find sustained strategic prayer on behalf of the people group preceding the breakthroughs. Mission history is replete with astounding stories of God summoning laborers from all over the world, opening doors of access, thwarting the threats of enemies, and demonstrating the gospel in power with precise timing. As we act in coordinated, strategic, united prayer, we are more able than ever to see that such moves of God are matched by prayers that have asked God to do these things. We can only conclude that the Lord of the harvest intends to send laborers among each of the peoples of the world.

In our day we see immense cooperative efforts to pray for unreached peoples. The "Pray Through The Window" efforts of 1993-1999 linked the prayers of tens of millions for specific unreached people groups. Hundreds of teams traveled to prayerwalk among these peoples, like the aforementioned venture to Cambodia. Such prayer journeys simply help people pray in the very places they expect God to bring forth His answers. If God is the true initiator of prayer, and we see people praying in such abundant ways, we should not be surprised to see some of the greatest moves of His hand—reaching nations and transforming societies—in the near future.

God Listens and the World Changes

In the Book of Revelation, the Apostle John describes a God-given vision of humankind's history. It is filled with images of God and celestial beings interacting with one another and with our world. In these verses, the Lamb of God opens seven seals—each affecting the history of this planet. By the end of chapter seven, all of heaven is singing and worshiping God, wondering what will happen next in human history. However, at the beginning of chapter eight, all fall silent. Seven angels with seven trumpets stand before God ready to announce the unfolding fate of the world, but they must wait until the eighth angel offers God incense which includes all the prayers of the saints—prayers for justice and victory. Nothing can happen until the fragrance of these prayers rises before God.

Prayer is the most powerful form of social action because God responds directly to prayer. Prayer is the most powerful part of mission to unreached peoples, because God does what only He can do. Even in the most hopeless of situations, He breaks through the false dominion of the enemy, bringing spiri-

tual light and breathing life for lasting social transformation.

God uses the act of praying both to change us and to change the future. As Walter Wink puts it,

> History belongs to the intercessors who believe the future into being...Even a small number of people totally committed to the new inevitability in which they affix their imaginations can decisively affect the shape the future takes. These shapers of the future are the intercessors who call out the future, the longed-for new present; they believe the future into being.[6]

End Notes

1. Otis Jr., George, *The Twilight Labyrinth* (Grand Rapids, MI: Chosen Books, 1997), p. 281.
2. Friedrich, Gerhard, ed., *Theological Dictionary of the New Testament* (Grand Rapids, MI: Erdmans Publishing Co., 1972), p. 614.
3. Francis Frangipane, *The Three Battlegrounds* (Marion, IA: River of Life Ministries, 1989), pp.14-15.
4. Wink, Walter, *Engaging the Powers: Discernment and Resistance in a World of Domination* (Minneapolis, MN: Fortress Press, 1992), p. 312.
5. Otis, pp. 298-303.
6. Wink, p. 299.

Study Questions

1. Robb asserts that prayer is essential for social action because of the nature of spiritual darkness which holds people back from significant change. How does prayer help?

2. Explain how the two structures of spiritual darkness—idolatry and strongholds—inhibit evangelization and social transformation?

3. Robb mentions two reasons why prayer is crucial when dealing with unreached peoples. What are these two reasons? Are these points unique to unreached peoples?

Prayer Evangelism

Ed Silvoso

The Great Commission began with a city: Jerusalem. "But you shall receive power when the Holy Spirit has come upon you; and you shall be My witnesses both in Jerusalem, and in all Judea and Samaria, and even to the remotest part of the earth" (Acts 1:8). At a time when the vast majority of the world population resided in rural areas, Jesus chose a city as the starting point of His disciples' mission. Just as the Great Commission began with a city, it will most likely end when the last city in the remotest part of the earth is evangelized.

Cities are important to God. He feels strongly about cities, and their demise saddens Him. In the Old Testament, God dispatched prophets to plead with city dwellers for repentance, and He greatly rejoiced when cities like Nineveh repented, in spite of Jonah's frustration. Jesus Himself wept openly over Jerusalem.

Jesus commanded his disciples not to leave Jerusalem until they had been endued with power from on high. Acts 1:8 implies that once power descended on them, they were not to proceed on to Judea and Samaria until Jerusalem had been evangelized. As Jesus spelled out this strategy—first Jerusalem and from there, fanning out in ever-growing circles all the way to the ends of the earth—I can imagine Peter fighting the urge to suggest a change of venue. "Lord," he might have said, "what about beginning in the uttermost parts of the earth and slowly working our way back to Jerusalem? By then things will have cooled considerably around here."

Definitely there would have been some logic to Peter's suggestion. Jerusalem was the most difficult city in which to start. Jesus had been publicly crucified as a criminal. Among many of the populace it had been a popular verdict. The prevailing religion was irretrievably intertwined with the state. The council of elders had powerful connections with the occupying Roman army, which had shown nothing but contempt for Jesus.

Peter, Jesus' most enthusiastic follower, had denied Him in public. Judas, His administrator, had betrayed Him for a few pieces of silver. The rest of His disciples were confused and in hiding, fearful of being wiped out by the powers that had murdered Jesus.

The disciples' most convincing argument to support their witness—Jesus' resurrection—had been successfully portrayed as a farce. The Jewish elders and the Roman soldiers had cunningly conspired to implant in the people's minds

Ed Silvoso, a native of Argentina, is the founder of Harvest Evangelism, Inc. This interdenominational missionary organization is dedicated to reaching cities for Christ by providing models and training in strategic prayer evangelism.

From *That None Should Perish*, by Ed Silvoso, Copyright 1994, Regal Books, Ventura, CA, 93003. Used by permission.

the notion that Jesus did not rise from the dead. Instead, they said, His disciples had stolen and hidden His body.

Finally, the group of disciples who received the Great Commission with specific instructions to begin in Jerusalem had no political, social or economic clout. Similarly, they were despised by the establishment as ignorant and unlearned in a city that prided itself in intellectualism. To add insult to injury, social prejudice was effectively used to discredit this band of Galileans. "Can anything good come out of Galilee?" was perhaps one of the most popular contemporary put-downs see (John 1:45-46). Humanly speaking, the disciples' chances of success were absolutely nonexistent.

However, Jesus clearly commanded them to begin in Jerusalem with the implication not to leave the city until they had succeeded there. If there was ever a difficult assignment, this was it.

From the Upper Room to Every Living Room

Within weeks of Jesus' departure, however, the disciples were accused by the religious experts in Jerusalem of having fulfilled the Great Commission in that city. Speaking on behalf of the council of elders, the high priest told them, "You [the disciples] have filled Jerusalem with [His] teaching" (Acts 5:28). There is only one way to "fill a city" and that is by doing it house by house. When their sworn enemies spontaneously concede like this, it is safe to assume that the disciples had succeeded in a big way.

How much time elapsed between Acts 1:8 and Acts 5:28? Just a few weeks! In a matter of weeks, the church went from the Upper Room to every living room in the city.

Furthermore, the spiritual avalanche did not stop in the outskirts of Jerusalem. It rumbled from one city to the next, fueled by religious persecution. It passed through the city of Samaria, where it faced and defeated the challenge of counterfeit religion, and multitudes rejoiced. It rolled into Antioch, overcoming the challenge of racism and cultural prejudice.

Some time later, Barnabas and Paul were sent to take the gospel to cities in the remote parts of earth. One of those cities was Ephesus. During Paul's visits, he baptized a total of 12 men and introduced them to the Holy Spirit. It appears that these 12 men, along with a cluster of God-fearing Jews from the local synagogue, became the charter members of the church in Ephesus.

The parallel with the disciples in Jerusalem in Acts 1:8 is strikingly similar. A small band of 12 men and their friends, facing one of the most thriving metropolises. The local cult of Artemis permeated every aspect of the city. The political and economic powers were deeply intertwined with this thriving religious enterprise. To make things worse, Paul and his fledgling band of new converts were forced out of the synagogue to move into a nonreligious building (Acts 19:9). So a quasi-comical picture developed: the proponents of a new religion meeting in a rented hall facing the temple of Artemis, whose sumptuous shrine gave identity to the city and the entire region. Humanly speaking, there was never a more uneven fight.

However, two years later, the entire city of Ephesus had heard the gospel, and one of the most dramatic power encounters registered in the entire Bible had taken place, resulting in multitudes of converts (Acts 19:11-20).

It happened again! A small struggling church had reached an entire city, and from there it had spread to the region beyond.

The Beginning of Prayer Evangelism

The statement made in Acts 19:10 clearly indicates that the Great Commission was indeed fulfilled in Ephesus and in Asia Minor. By this I mean that the Early Church publicly testified to everybody living there that Jesus is God, that He died for the sins of mankind, that He rose from the dead and was ready to come into their lives in a tangible way. All of this was validated by God through the signs that followed the preaching as first outlined in Mark 16:20, "Then the disciples went out and preached everywhere, and the Lord worked with them and confirmed His word by the signs that accompanied it."

How did the Early Church manage to take the gospel from the confining environment of the Upper Room to cities all over Asia Minor?

The Bible does not spell out a specific method. However, right after Pentecost, in the book of Acts, we have a description of the lifestyle of the Early Church. Acts 2:42 probably sums it up well: "And they were continually devoting themselves to the apostles' teaching and to fellowship, to the breaking of bread and to prayer." The lifestyle consisted of four elements: (1) the study of the doctrine of the apostles; (2) fellowship; (3) the breaking of bread; and (4) prayer. This particular verse makes it very clear that the new believers did this "continually."

It is interesting to note that only one of these four elements reaches beyond the group: prayer. Studying the doctrine, fellowshipping and breaking bread were ministries to the group. In home meetings all over Jerusalem, clusters of believers enjoyed each other in unity. They joyfully celebrated the Lord's Supper while they assimilated what the Holy Spirit taught through the apostles, all in an atmosphere of intense dialogue with God through prayer.

When we pray for felt needs and God answers, their eyes are opened to the reality and power of God, and this in turn leads them to recognize their need for salvation.

Can you imagine the beauty and the effectiveness of those prayers? They were directed by the sound teaching of the apostles, fueled by a desire to see the Lord's return as highlighted during the breaking of bread and empowered by the spiritual unity reflected in the fellowship they had with each other. Undoubtedly, those were very effective prayers! Could it be that prayer was the primary vehicle used to reach entire cities for Christ?

I suggest that prayer—this kind of prayer—is the key to the successful fulfillment of the Great Commission, then and now.

If this is so, where else in the sacred record can we go to gain further insight? Since Paul was the most effective church-planter in the New Testament, and Timothy was one of his closest associates, I suggest

we look at 1 Timothy 2:1-8. In this passage, Paul gives Timothy instructions regarding prayer and evangelism:

> First of all, then, I urge that entreaties and prayers, petitions and thanksgivings, be made on behalf of all men, for kings and all who are in authority, in order that we may lead a tranquil and quiet life in all godliness and dignity. This is good and acceptable in the sight of God our Savior, who desires all men to be saved and to come to the knowledge of the truth. For there is one God, and one mediator also between God and men, the man Christ Jesus, who gave Himself as a ransom for all, the testimony borne at the proper time.... Therefore I want the men in every place to pray, lifting up holy hands, without wrath and dissension (1 Tim 2:1-6,8).

To capture the full impact of this passage, it is necessary to clarify a point that has been distorted by our cultural bias. Paul was not writing to the senior pastor of a local church as we know it today. Nor was he outlining the format for a midweek prayer meeting. Quite the contrary. Paul was addressing Christians who did not own church buildings or have midweek prayer meetings the way we do. This passage has to do as much with public prayer meetings as with private ones. Rather than suggesting the order of service for a church meeting, Paul here presents a citywide prayer strategy since the Greek of 1 Timothy 2:8 literally says, "I want men to pray in every place!" I believe this passage embodies the essence of evangelism as practiced by the Early Church—the essence of what I call "prayer evangelism." Let's take a closer took.

"First of all, then, I urge that entreaties and prayers, petitions and thanksgivings, be made on behalf of all men" (v. 1). Paul is telling Timothy to organize the church so that prayers are said everywhere on behalf of all men in particular cities. As you know, in this passage the word "men" is used in the generic sense. It means men and women. The first assignment, then, was to make sure that everybody in town was prayed for.

When we hear the expression "a tranquil and quiet life," we usually visualize a self-serving scenario. Practically speaking, we may take this to mean that city hall will approve the user's permit for our new youth facility, that the county planning commission will vote favorably on the expansion of our conference center, that the state board of education will leave us alone and not interfere with our Christian school curriculum. In essence, we take it to mean "leave us alone" so we may enjoy a quiet and tranquil life! However, this is not the main thrust of this passage.

Paul says that the outcome of the prayer thrust should be to live in *all* godliness and honesty. There is only one way for Christians to live in an environment characterized by *all* godliness and honesty: it is for many unbelievers to become Christians, and those who don't, to become aware of the existence of God *and begin to fear Him*. Then, and only then, all godliness and honesty will permeate the city where the church exists.

The objective of Paul's instructions to Timothy is very simple and extremely clear: pray that everybody in your city, and especially those in authority, *will become Christians!* To this end, Jesus has already made provision by "[giving] Himself as a ransom for all" (1 Tim 2:6). The will of God has been clearly stated: God wants all men to be saved (v. 4). What is it that is still lacking? That the Church begin to pray for *all* people (vv. 1,2).

What shall we pray for all people? We must become aware of the difference between the most important need a person has and what the person feels is his most important need—what is known as a "felt need." Usually these two are not one and the same. Lost people are unable to clearly see their most important need, their salvation, because "the god of this world has blinded the minds of the unbelieving" to the gospel (2 Cor 4:4). When we pray for felt needs and God answers, their eyes are opened to the reality and power of God, and this in turn leads them to recognize their need for salvation. That is what Paul may have had in mind when he said that the Lord sent him "to open their eyes so that they may turn from darkness to light and from the dominion of Satan to God" (Acts 26:18). We usually limit ourselves to asking God in private that people will come to Jesus. This is important. We must go beyond this first step. We must discern what it is that they consider important and pray for that need to be met by God. When this happens, it acts as an eye-opener as far as the gospel is concerned.

In 2 Peter 3:9 we read that God is patient toward us (the believers), not willing that any (of the unbelievers) should perish, but that all should come to repentance. This passage, along with 1 Timothy 2:4-6 states in unequivocal terms that God's will is for all people to be saved. Of course, this does not necessarily mean that all people will be saved. That issue is a very complex one, but for the purpose of knowing how to pray according to the will of God, it should suffice that God's will is known: He wishes all people to be saved and for none to perish. This is His will, and we must frame our prayers accordingly.

Study Questions

1. How can prayer for felt needs result in someone's eyes being opened to God?

2. Describe how Silvoso traces the process of prayer moving from the upper room to every living room. How does this prayer result in entire cities being evangelized according to Silvoso?

3. Define "prayer evangelism."

Lost

Robertson McQuilkin

> Salvation is found in no one else, for there is no other name under heaven given to men, by which we must be saved (Acts 4:12).

Have you ever experienced the terror of being lost—in some trackless mountain wilderness, perhaps, or in the labyrinth of a great, strange city? Hope of finding your way out fades and fear begins to seep in. You have likely seen that fear of lostness on the tear-streaked face of a child frantically screaming or quietly sobbing because he is separated from his parent in a huge shopping center. Lost. Alone.

Equally terrifying and more common is the feeling of being hopelessly entangled or trapped in a frustrating personal condition or circumstance: alcoholism, cancer, divorce. Incredibly alone! Lost.

The Bible uses the word "lost" to describe an even more terrible condition. Those who are away from the Father's house and haven't found the way back to Him are "lost." Jesus saw the crowds of people surging about Him as sheep without a shepherd, helpless and hopeless, and He was deeply moved.

Worse than being trapped and not knowing the way out is to be lost and not even know it, for then one does not look for salvation, recognize it when it comes, nor accept it when it is offered. That's being lost.

How many are lost in our world? We are told there are 200 million evangelicals. Some of these are no doubt lost, but at least that many people believe Jesus is the only way of salvation and that through faith in Him one is forgiven and made a member of God's family. Surely some who are not evangelical have saving faith. So let us double the number to a hypothetical 400 million. Those who remain number more than four billion people or nine of every ten on earth. These are the lost—longing for salvation but not finding it, or trusting some other way to find meaning and hope.

The tragedy of this century of exploding population is that three of four people have never heard with understanding the way to life in Christ, and even more tragic, half the people of the world cannot hear because there is no one near enough to tell them. As we approach the end of the second millennium A.D., one of every two on planet Earth lives in a tribe or culture or language group that has no evangelizing church at all. If someone does not go in

Robertson McQuilkin is President Emeritus of Columbia International University. For 22 years he served as President of Columbia International University and prior to that was a missionary to Japan for 12 years.

From *The Great Omission*, by Robertson McQuilkin, Copyright 1984, Baker Book House, Grand Rapids, MI. Used by permission.

from the outside they have no way of knowing about Jesus.

But are these people in the "dark half of the world" really lost? What of those who have never had a chance, who have never heard— are any of them lost? Are all of them lost?

Throughout Church history there have been those who teach that none will finally be lost. The old universalism taught that all ultimately will be saved because God is good. Not much was heard of this position from the days of Origen in the third century until the nineteenth century when it was revived, especially by the Universalist Church. Simultaneously with the founding of the Universalist Church, which was honest enough to be up front and call itself by that name, this teaching began to spread in many mainline denominations.

There are problems with this position. Philosophically, such a teaching undermines belief in the atoning death of Christ. For if all sin will ultimately be overlooked by a gracious deity, Christ never should have died. It was not only unnecessary, it was surely the greatest error in history, if not actually criminal on the part of God for allowing it to happen. Universalism, therefore, philosophically demands a view of the death of Christ as having some purpose other than as an atonement for sin.

Another problem the Universalists face is that Scripture consistently teaches a division after death between those who are acceptable to God and those who are not. This teaching, and that concerning the atonement, are so strong in the Bible that Universalists did not accept the authority of Scripture. Thus the marriage between the Universalist Church and the Unitarian Church was quite natural.

A New Universalism arose in the twentieth century which took the Bible more seriously. It was Trinitarian. Christ did die for sinners, and *all* will ultimately be saved on the basis of Christ's provision.

Karl Barth and many of his neo-orthodox disciples took such a position. All will be saved because God is all-powerful. His purposes will be accomplished. And He purposes redemption.

There were philosophical and biblical problems with this position also. Philosophically, if all will be saved eventually, for whatever reason, preaching the gospel is not really necessary. Why did Christ make this the primary mission of the church if all will ultimately find acceptance with God with or without the gospel? The more serious problem is biblical: Christ clearly taught of an eternal hell, of a great gulf between the saved and the lost (Luke 16:19-31). In fact, He clearly taught that the majority are on the broad road that leads to destruction (Matt 7:13-14).

Because Universalism cannot be reconciled with biblical data, there were those who promoted what was called a "Wider Hope." Not all will be saved, but many who have not heard of Christ will be saved because God is just and will not condemn the sincere seeker after truth. The problem is that if sincerity saves in religion, it is the only realm in which it saves. For example, it does not save in engineering. The architect who designed the magnificent John Hancock building in Boston was sincere. The builder was sincere. The glassmaker was sincere. The owner, especially, was sincere. But when the giant sheets of glass began to fall on the streets below, sincerity did not atone for error. Neither does sincerity save in chemistry. We do not say, "If you drink arsenic, sincerely believing it to be Coca-Cola, according to your faith be it unto you." Sincerity does not alter reality. We shall consider the question of God's justice later.

The 19th century doctrine of the Wider Hope has been superseded by what I call the "New Wider Hope." According to this teaching, those who live by the light they have may be saved on the merits of Christ's death through general revelation. Or, at least, they will be given a chance at death or after death. This is a more conservative version of the New Universalism. Richard Quebedeaux identifies this position as held by some "younger evangelicals," the New Left. A practical problem is that preaching the gospel seems almost criminal, for it brings with it greater condemnation for those who reject it, whereas they conceivably could have been saved through general revelation had they not heard the gospel. It certainly seems less urgent to proclaim the way of salvation to those who may well be saved without that knowledge. A mutation of this view is the idea that only those who reject the gospel will be lost. This viewpoint is not widespread because it makes bad news of the Good News! If people are lost only if they hear and reject, it is far better not to hear and be saved. According to this view, it would be better to destroy the message than to proclaim it!

For one committed to the authority of Scripture, our debate concerning the reasonableness of each position must yield to the authority of Scripture. What does Scripture teach concerning the eternal spiritual condition of those who have not heard the gospel?

> "For God so loved the world that He gave His one and only Son, that whoever believes in Him shall not perish but have eternal life. For God did not send His Son into the world to condemn the world, but to save the world through Him. Whoever believes in him is not condemned, but whoever does not believe stands condemned already because he has not believed in the name of God's one and only Son."

> "Whoever believes in the Son has eternal life, but whoever rejects the Son will not see life, for God's wrath remains on him" (John 3:16-18, 36).

Scripture teaches clearly that there are those who perish and those who do not. Notice that it is those who believe *on Christ*— not simply those who, through their encounter with creation and their own innate moral judgment, believe in a righteous Creator— who receive eternal life. God's intent is to "save the world through Him [Christ]" (3:17). The word "through" speaks of agency: it is by means of Jesus Christ that a person gains eternal life.

The passage does not deny other agencies, however. The Japanese proverb assures us that many roads lead up famed Mount Fuji but they all reach the top. This is the Japanese way of expressing the viewpoint that all religions will have a good outcome. But Jesus Christ Himself said, "No one comes to the Father except through me" (John 14:6). In other words, Jesus Christ is the *only* agency of salvation.

The New Wider Hope would affirm this. Salvation is by Jesus Christ alone. But, it would hold, that does not mean Jesus Christ must be known by a person for that person to be saved.

Jesus assures us that people will be judged because they have not believed on the *name* (John 3:18). Peter is even more explicit in telling us that there is no salvation in any other *name* given among men (Acts 4:12). Surely it is no accident that the name is so prominent in the Bible, especially in teaching on saving faith. Peter did not say, "in no other person." When a person is named, the identity is settled and ambiguity is done away with. Peter does not make room for us to call on the Ground of Being or the great "all." You will be saved, he tells us, if you call on and believe in the name of Jesus of Nazareth, the Messiah. John, Jesus and Peter are not the only ones with this emphasis. Paul also speaks to the issue:

> ..."Everyone who calls on the name of the Lord will be saved." How, then, can they call on the one they have not believed in? And how can they believe in the one of whom they have not heard? And how can they hear without someone preaching to them? And how can they preach unless they are sent? As it is written, "How beautiful are the feet of those who bring good news!" (Rom 10:13-15).

The ones who call on *the name* are the ones who will be saved. But what of those who have not heard so they cannot call? Paul does not assure us that those who have not heard may simply believe on whatever they have heard. Rather, "faith comes from hearing the message, and the message is heard through the word of Christ" (Rom 10:17).

Scripture is very clear that there are two kinds of people, both in life and in death: the saved and the lost. It is also very clear on the way of salvation. But still, for those who truly care, questions may remain: Is God loving, powerful, fair, just?

Is God loving? Yes, God is good and that is why men are lost. In love He created a being in His own image, not a robot programmed to respond as the Maker designed. In creating such a being to freely love and be loved, God risked the possibility of such a being rejecting His love in favor of independence or even self-love. Humankind did, in fact, choose this option. Still true to His character, God provided a way back even though the cost was terrible. But the way back must not violate the image of God in man and must not force an obedient response. Rather, the God of love chooses to wait lovingly for the response of love. Those who wish to reject Him may do so.

But is it fair and just for God to condemn those who have not had an opportunity to respond to His offer of grace? The Bible does not teach that God will judge a person for rejecting Christ if he has not heard of Christ. In fact, the Bible teaches clearly that God's judgment is based on a person's response to the truth he has received.

"That servant who knows his master's will and does not get ready or does not do what his master wants will be beaten with many blows. But the one who does not know and does things deserving punishment will be beaten with few blows. From everyone who has been given much, much will be demanded; and from the one who has been entrusted with much, much more will be asked" (Luke 12:47-48).

"When you enter a town and are welcomed, eat what is set before you. Heal the sick who are there and tell them, ' The kingdom of God is near you.' But when you enter a town and are not welcomed, go into its streets and say, 'Even the dust of your town that sticks to our feet we wipe off against you. Yet be sure of this: The kingdom of God is near.' I tell you, it will be more bearable on that day for Sodom than for that town. Woe to you, Korazin! Woe to you, Bethsaida! For if the miracles that were performed in you had been performed in Tyre and Sidon, they would have repented long ago, sitting in sackcloth and ashes. But it will be more bearable for Tyre and Sidon at the judgment than for you. And you, Capernaum, will you be lifted up to the skies? No, you will go down to the depths. He who listens to you listens to me; he who rejects you rejects me; but he who rejects me rejects him who sent me" (Luke 10:8-16).

Judgment is against a person in proportion to his rejection of moral light. All have sinned; no one is innocent. Therefore, all stand condemned. But not all have the same measure of condemnation, for not all have sinned against equal amounts of light. God does not condemn a person who has not heard of Christ for rejecting Him, but rather for rejecting the light he does have.

Not all respond to the light they have by seeking to follow that light. But God's response to those who seek to obey the truth they have is the provision of more truth. To him who responds, more light will be given:

The disciples came to him and asked, "Why do you speak to the people in parables?"

He replied, "The knowledge of the secrets of the kingdom of heaven has been given to you, but not to them. Whoever has will be given more, and he will have an abundance. Whoever does not have, even what he has will be taken from him. This is why I speak to them in parables:

"Though seeing, they do not see; though hearing, they do not hear or understand."

In them is fulfilled the prophecy of Isaiah:

"You will be ever hearing but never understanding; you will be ever seeing but never perceiving. For this people's heart has become calloused; they hardly hear with their ears, and they have closed their eyes. Otherwise they might see with their eyes, hear with their ears, understand with their hearts and turn, and I would heal them."

But blessed are your eyes because they see, and your ears because they hear" (Matt 13:10-16).

He said to them, "Do you bring in a lamp to put it under a bowl or a bed? Instead, don't you put it on its stand? For whatever is hidden is meant to be disclosed, and whatever is concealed is meant to be brought out into the open. If anyone has ears to hear, let him hear."

"Consider carefully what you hear," he continued. "With the measure you use, it will be measured to you—and even more. Whoever has will be given more; whoever does not have, even what he has will be taken from him" (Mark 4:21-25).

This repeated promise of additional light to those who obey the light they have is a basic and very important biblical truth concerning God's justice and judgment. Cornelius, the Roman officer, responded to the light he had with prayer and good deeds. God did not leave him in ignorance and simply accept him on the basis of his response to the initial light he had received. God sent Peter to him with additional truth (Acts 10). To him who had, more was given. Since this is revealed as God's way of dealing with men, we can be very sure that every person has received adequate light to which he may respond. God's existence and His power are made clearly evident to all people through creation (Rom 1:18-21) and through each person's innate moral judgment or conscience (Rom 2:14,15). To the one who responds obediently, God will send additional light.

Of course, His method for sending this light is a human messenger. Paul makes clear in his letter to the church at Rome (10:14,15) that the solution to the terrible lost condition of men is the preacher who is sent, the "beautiful feet" of him who goes. Ultimately, then, the problem is not with God's righteousness, but with ours.

But suppose no one goes? Will God send some angel or some other special revelation? Scripture is silent On this, and, I believe, for good reason. Even if God did have such an alternative plan, were He to reveal that to us, we who have proved so irresponsible and disobedient would no doubt cease altogether obedience to the Great Commission.

But the question will not go away. How does one respond in a Japanese village when a new convert inquires, "What about my ancestors?" My response is simple: I am not the judge. "Will not the judge of all the earth do right?" (Gen 18:25). Abraham pleaded with God for the salvation of innocent people who did not deserve to be condemned and destroyed along with the guilty. He was appealing to God's justice, and God responded with grace more than Abraham dared ask. This crucial question recorded in the first book of the Bible is answered in the last: "Yes, Lord God Almighty, true and just are your judgments" (Rev 16:7). We are not called as judge—either of God, whose ways we do not fully know, nor of man, whose destiny we are not called upon to settle. Rather, we are commissioned as His representatives to find the lost, declare amnesty to the captive, release the prisoner.

We may not be able to prove from Scripture with absolute certainty that no soul since Pentecost has ever been saved by extraordinary means without the knowledge of Christ. But neither can we prove from Scripture that a single soul has been so saved. If there is an alternative, God has not told us of it. If God in His revelation felt it mandatory not to proffer such a hope, how much more should we refrain from such theorizing. It may or may not be morally right for me to think there may be another way and to hope there is some other escape. But for me to propose it to other believers, to discuss it as a possibility, is certainly dangerous, if not immoral. It is almost as wrong as writing out such a hope so that those who are under the judgment of God may read it, take hope, and die. As long as the truth revealed to us identifies only one way of escape, this is what we must live by and proclaim.

Consider the analogy of a security guard charged with the safety of residents on the 10th floor of a nursing home. He knows the floor plan posted in a prominent place, and it is his responsibility in case of fire to get the residents to the fire escape which has been clearly marked. Should a fire break out and lives be put in jeopardy, it would be his responsibility to get those people to the fire escape. If he discusses with the patients or with a colleague the possibility of some other unmarked fire escape or recalls to them the news report he read of someone who had jumped from the 10th floor of a building and survived, he could surely be charged with criminal negligence. He must live and labor in obedience to the facts that are certain and not delay to act. He must not lead people astray on the basis of conjecture or logical deduction from limited information.

When all has been said that can be said on this issue, the greatest remaining mystery is not the character of God nor the destiny of lost people. The greatest mystery is why those who are charged with rescuing the lost have spent two thousand years doing other

> In creating such a being to freely love and be loved, God risked the possibility of such a being rejecting His love in favor of independence or even self-love.

things, good things, perhaps, but have failed to send and be sent until all have heard the liberating word of life in Christ Jesus. The lost condition of human beings breaks the Father's heart. What does it do to ours?

In a dream I found myself on an island—Sheep Island. Across the island sheep were scattered and lost. Soon I learned that a forest fire was sweeping across from the opposite side. All were doomed to destruction unless there were some way of escape. Although there were many unofficial maps, I had a copy of the official map and there discovered that indeed there was a bridge to the mainland, a narrow bridge, built, it was said, at incredible cost.

My job, I was told, would be to get the sheep across that bridge. I discovered many shepherds herding the sheep which were found and seeking to corral those which were within easy access to the bridge. But most of the sheep were far off and the shepherds seeking them few. The sheep near the fire knew they were in trouble and were frightened; those at a distance were peacefully grazing, enjoying life.

I noticed two shepherds near the bridge whispering to one another and laughing. I moved near them to hear the cause of joy in such a dismal setting. "Perhaps the chasm is narrow somewhere, and at least the strong sheep have opportunity to save themselves," said one. "Maybe the current is gentle and the stream shallow. Then at least the courageous can make it across." The other responded, "That may well be. In fact,

wouldn't it be great if this proves to be no island at all? Perhaps it is just a peninsula and great multitudes of sheep are already safe. Surely the owner would have provided some alternative route." And so they relaxed and went about other business.

In my mind I began to ponder their theories: Why would the owner have gone to such great expense to build a bridge, especially since it is a narrow bridge, and many of the sheep refuse to cross it even when they find it? In fact, if there is a better way by which many will be saved more easily, building the bridge is a terrible blunder. And if this isn't an island, after all, what is to keep the fire from sweeping across into the mainland and destroying everything? As I pondered these things I heard a quiet voice behind me saying, "There is a better reason than the logic of it, my friend. Logic alone could lead you either way. Look at your map."

There on the map, by the bridge, I saw a quotation from the first undershepherd, Peter: "For neither is there salvation in any other, for there is no other way from the island to the mainland whereby a sheep may be saved." And then I discerned, carved on the old rugged bridge itself, "I am the bridge. No sheep escapes to safety but by me."

In a world in which nine of every ten people are lost, three of four have never heard the way out, and one of every two cannot hear, the Church sleeps on. "Why?" Could it be we think there must be some other way? Or perhaps we don't really care that much.

Study Questions

1. State and briefly describe the four different views of salvation reviewed in the article, as well as McQuilkin's own.

2. What scriptural support does McQuilkin give to his view?

The Uniqueness of Christ

Charles Van Engen

We live at the dawn of the most exciting missionary era ever. Never before could we say that there are Christians in every nation on earth. With about 1.5 billion Christians circling the globe, the Christian faith now has the potential of evangelizing the other 4.5 billion people in a way never before possible. The global reawakening of interest in spirituality, in the spirit world and in religious phenomena provides an unprecedented opportunity for calling people to faith in Jesus Christ. In today's world, our assertion that Christ is unique, is heard as an assessment that other religions are to be disregarded. Chapman pointed out that "to speak of 'other religions' is ultimately to refer to two-thirds of the human race. The world's other religions present a challenge to Christians not only because they have worldviews that conflict at many points with our own, but also because their influence is growing....We must do more...than simply reassert the uniqueness of Christ in old categories, more than just produce strategies for reaching people of other faiths. We must first do some hard thinking about religions."[1]

Three Broad Categories

In recent times, the attitudes of Christians toward other religions generally are classified in three broad categories: pluralist, inclusivist and exclusivist.[2] Notice that two of these words sound essentially positive. "Pluralist" is positive in terms of the multicultural and multireligious world in which we live. "Inclusivist" is positive in terms of opening our arms to receive all those who are loved by God. But "exclusivist" sounds like a negative word. Pluralists and inclusivists feel quite negative about the content of the so-called exclusivist position. In fact, few of us would like to be accused of being individually, institutionally, culturally, economically, politically or socially exclusive.

Consider the basis on which these positions are compared. If the basis is tolerance, the pluralist and inclusivist would seem to espouse tolerance, the exclusivist intolerance. What if the basis for comparison is love? The pluralist loves everyone, as does the inclusivist, for they both refuse, as Clark Pinnock says, "to limit the grace of God to the confines of the Church."[3] It is the so-called exclusivist who "restricts hope" and therefore relegates people of other religions to "zones of darkness," refusing to love all peoples enough to

Charles Van Engen is the Arthur F. Glasser Professor of Biblical Theology of Mission at the School of World Mission at Fuller Theological Seminary. He is the author or editor of numerous books including *God So Loves the City: Seeking a Theology for Urban Mission* and *Mission on the Way*.

Adapted from *Mission on the Way* by Charles Van Engen. Copyright 1996. Published by Baker Book House. Used by permission.

offer them a "wider hope."[4] If the basis of comparison is global openness versus parochialism, the exclusivist position looks ancient and out-of-date, narrow and parochial. If the basis of comparison is optimism versus pessimism, the inclusivist position is, in Pinnock's words, "optimistic of salvation"[5] while the so-called exclusivists demonstrate a "negative attitude toward the rest of the world,"[6] and a "pessimism of salvation, or darkly negative thinking about people's spiritual journeys."[7]

I'm not sure I want to be an exclusivist. I'm even less inclined to be an exclusivist when I hear what the open, accepting, loving and tolerant pluralists say about me! John Hick argues that the exclusivist's...

> entirely negative attitude to other faiths is strongly correlated with ignorance of them....Today, however, the extreme evangelical Protestant who believes that all Muslims go to hell is probably not so much ignorant as blinded by dark dogmatic spectacles through which he can see no good in religious devotion outside his own group....

> If all human beings must, in order to attain the eternal happiness for which they have been created, accept Jesus Christ as their Lord and Savior before they die, then the great majority of humanity is doomed to eternal frustration and misery....To say that such an appalling situation is divinely ordained is to deny the Christian understanding of God as gracious and holy love.[8]

Apparently exclusivists are not nice people! Of course I'm speaking tongue-in-cheek, but can we not do better? At the very least, it seems that we need to continue our search for better conceptualization and articulation of what a so-called exclusivist position involves. Perhaps we even need a new word. Let me suggest a fourth perspective: the "evangelist" paradigm. I have chosen this name because I want to present a paradigm whose starting point and center is the evangel—the confession by the disciples that "Jesus Christ is Lord."

An Important Distinction: Faith Does Not Equal Culture

Before we look at the missiological implications of this fourth paradigm of "evangelist,"

however, let's examine two presuppositions. The first deals with the relationship of faith and culture. Paul Hiebert says:

> The gospel must be distinguished from all human cultures. It is divine revelation, not human speculation. Since it belongs to no one culture, it can be adequately expressed in all of them. The failure to differentiate between the gospel and human cultures has been one of the great weaknesses of modern Christian missions. Missionaries too often have equated the good news with their own cultural background. This has led them to condemn most native customs and to impose their own customs on converts. Consequently, the gospel has been seen as foreign in general and Western in particular. People have rejected it not because they reject the lordship of Christ, but because conversion often has meant a denial of their cultural heritage and social ties.[9]

The difference between faith and culture is supported not only anthropologically, but also historically and biblically. Historically, a review of the history of the Church demonstrates that the gospel of faith in the lordship of Jesus Christ has always tended to break out of the cultural molds that would imprison it. Originally the gospel was not Western at all—it was Middle Eastern. It began among Aramaic-speaking Jews. Then it took shape in all the cultures surrounding Jerusalem that are referred to in Acts 2—in Greek, Roman, North African, Ethiopian, Indian, Near Eastern and Arabic cultures. It expanded to the Franks, Scandinavia, the British Isles, and on and on. To closely associate any culture with biblical faith, one must ignore the historical expansion of the Church.

Even more profoundly, the distinction between faith and culture is biblically essential. This issue is at the heart of Acts and Romans.[10] The issue here is precisely how a single faith in Christ's lordship can take shape in a variety of cultures. The difference between faith and culture is also essential for an understanding of Galatians, Ephesians and Colossians. Paul speaks of the mystery "that through the gospel the Gentiles (the *ethnē*, comprising a multiplicity of cultures) are heirs together with Israel, members together of one body, and sharers together in the promise in Christ Jesus"

(Eph 3:6). 1 Peter and Revelation also would be difficult to understand were there no distinction between faith and culture.

The nature of the world in which we now live has made the equation of faith and culture more dangerous than ever. Christians and non-Christians alike share this in common. All are radically impacted by the largest redistribution of people the globe has ever seen. In this new reality, all of us are called upon to find ways of affirming cultural relativity: tolerance, understanding, justice, equality and co-existence within the new multiculturalism. If one views faith and culture as nearly synonymous and also begins to be open to *cultural* relativism, the next step is some form of *religious* pluralism.[11] If one goes all the way with this process, one arrives at the pluralist position. If one cannot go that far—feeling strongly constrained to hold tightly to the uniqueness of the cosmic Christ-event—one arrives at the inclusivist position. If one refuses to accept cultural relativism, but holds faith and culture to be synonymous, one arrives at an exclusivist position reminiscent of the cultural Protestantism of the nineteenth century.

> The only truly unique and distinctive aspect of Christian faith is a personal relationship of the Christian with the resurrected and ascended Jesus Christ of history.

A Crucial Starting Point: Good People Damned or Condemned People Saved?

The second presupposition deals with the form of the question of salvation asked by each of the four paradigms. We must be conscious of the radical difference between the pluralist/inclusivist stance on the one hand and the exclusivist/evangelist stance on the other. The bottom-line theology of salvation of the pluralist and inclusivist positions asks, "Given the fact that humanity is basically good, and God is a God of love, how is it possible that God could condemn so much of humanity to eternal punishment?" The exclusivists and evangelists ask the question differently: "Given the fact of the fall, and that 'all have sinned and fall short of the glory of God' (Rom 3:23), how is it possible that so much of humanity can be saved?"

A Foundational Conviction: Knowing the Historic Jesus

Now before developing the major missiological implications of the "evangelist" paradigm, I want to clarify a foundational commitment from which all else derives. I am making a conscious choice to highlight the Christian's personal relationship with the historic Jesus Christ who was born, lived in Palestine during a specific historical time, ministered, died, rose, ascended and is coming again. The absolutely radical claim of the canonical text of the Bible is that this Jesus lives today and that He is the one with whom the Christian disciple relates personally by faith.

Even John Hick recognized the implications of this position: "If Jesus was literally God incarnate, the second Person of the holy Trinity, living a human life, so that the Christian religion was founded by God-on-earth in person, it is then very hard to escape from the traditional view that all mankind must be converted to the Christian faith."[12] But he opted to understand the narrative about Jesus Christ as a "metaphorical" rather than a literal description of a verifiable historical fact.[13] This decision was coupled with his prior conclusion that "any viable Christian theodicy must affirm the ultimate salvation of all God's creatures.[14] The combination of these two factors leads logically to a pluralist position.

The Fourth Position: Evangelist

In developing the missiological implications of the evangelist paradigm, I will try to present a trinitarian and kingdom-oriented perspective that may help us listen to the other three paradigms and critique them as well. In so doing, we need to be able to move past the pessimism about mission, faith and the Church that is exhibited by pluralists and inclusivists alike. At the same time, we must be more open than traditional exclusivists have been to a modern global village of interreligious encounter and multicultural diversity. In our new global society, we can no longer afford to create, protect and preserve our own seemingly safe sanctuaries of religious exclusivity.

Our study of the implications of the evangelist paradigm will be limited to three basic categories. This paradigm of approaching other religions is a way that is: (1) faith-particularist, (2) culturally pluralist, and (3) ecclesiologically inclusivist.

Faith-Particularist

The first element of this new paradigm is personal. It deals not with religious systems or theoretical religions as such, but with people and personal faith.[15] It has to do with personal faith in, and allegiance to, Jesus who lived and ministered in Palestine at a specific time in history.[16] The only truly unique and distinctive aspect of Christian faith (the term "particularist" refers to that which is unique and distinctive instead of general and universal) is a personal relationship of the Christian with the resurrected and ascended Jesus Christ of history.[17] In the evangelist paradigm, confession of Jesus as Lord involves a personal relationship that breaks the bonds of all religious systems. It means that we are not so much adherents of Christianity. We are simply disciples of Christ. Following Christ is a vital relationship rather than subscribing to a religious formula. It is not neat, logical or coherent. It is not exclusive, nor arrogant, nor triumphalistic. Rather, it is humble confession, repentance and obedience. Thus the major question is not if one is a member within a particular religious system, even if it is a Christian tradition. Rather, the crucial issue is whether or not one relationally belongs to the person of Jesus Christ. The ultimate question is the question of discipleship—of one's proximity to, or distance from, Jesus the Lord.

The evangelist paradigm calls into question the institutional structures of all churches, and especially of Christianity as a religious system, for the churches now are viewed as the fellowship of disciples whose allegiance is to Jesus more than to a particular institution. The evangelist paradigm also calls into question the inclusivist perspective that the cosmic Christ-event effectively saves for all persons regardless of their personal relationship with Jesus Christ. And it brings into question the pluralists' relativistic reduction of the confession "Jesus Christ is Lord" to Jesus being only "a christ" among many.

On the other hand, the confession of Jesus as Lord also highlights all that cannot be called "lord" by the Christian. The confession calls for stripping away the layers of the artichoke[18] of cultural accretions that Christians have added to the basic confession. As Paul declares in Romans, and we see modeled in Acts, our faith requires us to confess with our mouths and believe in our hearts that Jesus is Lord. That's all there is. Nothing else really matters. All else is to be held lightly. Everything else is negotiable. Thus, when we call people of other cultures and faiths to confess "Jesus is Lord," it is not *our* Jesus (exclusivist), nor is it *a* Jesus (pluralist), nor is it the cosmic amorphous idea of Jesus Christ (inclusivist). Rather, it is Jesus *the Lord* who calls for conversion and transformation of all who confess His name. Because of this, it is only in humility, in personal repentance and in prayer—with the expectation of a great diversity in cultural forms—that we may invite others to join us in confessing *Jesus* as Lord.

Culturally Pluralist

Along with the historicity and relationality of Jesus Christ, we must also affirm the universality of Christ's messianic lordship. Jesus the Christ is the Creator and Sustainer of all the universe, as the first chapters of John, Ephesians and Colossians all state. All of us are concerned about the whole of humanity and the care of God's creation. We wonder how humans can live together in

The Missiological Implications of the Evangelist Paradigm

Faith-Particularist	Culturally Pluralist	Ecclesiologically Inclusivist
"**Jesus** Christ is Lord"	"Jesus **Christ** is Lord"	"Jesus Christ is **Lord**"
(God the Son)	(God the Father)	(God the Holy Spirit)

The Elements of Pluralism—
A Creation Paradigm

1. Starting point: creation and the fact of religious pluralism
2. Concern about peoples of various faiths coexisting together
3. Bible regarded as only the Christian's book (one of many holy books)

4. Jesus Christ regarded as equal to the leaders of other religions
5. No conversion, no transformation

6. No concern for personal relationship with Jesus Christ

7. Mission regarded as irrelevant, unnecessary, demeaning, disrespectful

The Elements of Inclusivism—
A Paradigm of Universal Salvation

1. Starting point: the unique Christ event as ontologically affecting all people
2. Concern about peoples of various faiths coexisting together
3. Bible regarded as God's inspired revelation for all

4. Strong concern about the uniqueness of Christ
5. Conversion regarded as good, but not necessary; transformation de-emphasized
6. Personal relationship to Jesus Christ regarded as desirable, not normative

7. Mission defined as telling people they are already saved in Jesus Christ

---

peace and justice, especially in the midst of increasingly difficult clashes between conflicting religious allegiances. Given our universal concerns, we need a trinitarian missiology that is kingdom-oriented.[19] We must also remember that Christ's lordship is not only over the Church, but also over all the world. The pluralist and inclusivist perspectives, however, confuse the manner, scope and nature of Christ's kingly rule over the Church (willing subjects) and over all humanity (unwilling subjects).[20]

The lordship of Christ brings into question the exclusivist position on other cultures and religions as well. It opens up a much greater breadth for contextualized encounter between Christians and the many cultures of our world. Not all so-called non-Christian culture is sinful, but neither is everything in culture relative. Rather, we are called to "test the spirits" (1 John 4:1-3). This broad, all-encompassing Christology means that we must listen carefully to the new Christologies that are arising in Asia, Africa and Latin America. Everything that does not contradict the biblical revelation concerning the historical Jesus Christ our Lord is open for consideration. As Hendrikus Berkhof says: "That Christ is *the* truth does not mean that there are no truths to be found anywhere outside of Him, but it does mean that all such truths are fragmentary and broken unless they become integrated in Him as the center."[21]

Ecclesiologically Inclusivist

This third missiological implication of the evangelist paradigm has to do with the kingdom of God and the Church (The term "ecclesiological" derives from the Greek word for church, *ekklesia*). The Kingdom leads us to the Church, to the disciples of Jesus Christ the Lord. The Church is not only a gathering of individuals, it is much more because it includes Jesus Christ who is not only Lord of creation; He is also head of the Church. Thus Jesus sent His Spirit at Pentecost to establish the Church. The Church belongs to no human person, and church growth must be growth in the numbers of disciples of Jesus, not proselytism to expand someone's little churchly kingdom. The evangelist paradigm seeks to correct the triumphalism and arrogance of which the exclusivists have sometimes been accused.[22]

Because Jesus Christ the Lord is the head of the Church, the Church's mission is to participate in the mission of Jesus the Christ. In Acts 13 Paul says that Christ's disciples, the Church, are commanded to be a "light to the nations." It is the Church's responsibility,

The Elements of Exclusivism—
A *Church-centered Paradigm*

1. Starting point: the Church as the ark of salvation
2. Concern that all non-Christians become Christians in the Church
3. Bible regarded as God's inspired revelation proclaimed through the Church

4. Strong concern about uniqueness of Christ

5. Strong emphasis on conversion and transformation in and through Jesus Christ (and the Church)
6. Personal relationship with Jesus a necessity
7. Mission defined as rescuing people out of sinful cultures into the Church

The Elements of Evangelism—
A *Fourth Paradigm*

1. Starting point: the confession "Jesus Christ is Lord" [24]
2. Concern about human coexistence amidst multiple cultures and religions
3. Bible regarded as God's inspired revelation for all humanity—it has new things to say to each new culture where the gospel takes root
4. Strong emphasis on confessing anew in word and life, "Jesus is Lord"
5. Strong emphasis on conversion and sometimes on transformation

6. Personal relationship with Jesus Christ a necessity
7. Mission defined as calling people in multiple cultures to conversion, confession, and new allegiance, personally and corporately, to Jesus Christ as Lord

---

therefore, to focus on the whole of humanity. It is the Church, not some cosmic idea, that gathers disciples. And the Church—of which Christ is head—is called to proclaim that Jesus is the Lord of all humanity, not simply "a christ" for the Christian.

An Outward Movement to the Nations

This world-encountering Church is as broad as all humanity (pluralist), as accepting as Christ's cosmic lordship (inclusivist), and as incorporating and gathering as Christ's disciples (exclusivist). Clearly, the scandal associated with this Church is that it is filled with fallible human beings; yet it is still the Church of Jesus Christ. Just as clearly, the shape of this Church needs to be reconsidered in today's world of multiple religions and cultures.

> The Church cannot escape the fact that to confess Jesus as Lord moves it profoundly toward its own universality—a movement outward to the nations. This is climactically presented to us in the Great Commission of Matthew 28:18-20: "*Full* authority in heaven and on earth has been committed to me. Go forth therefore and make all nations my disciples."…Thus the mission of Jesus becomes inescapable and utterly

binding for all of his disciples. They cannot confess Jesus is Lord without at the same time proclaiming His lordship over all people….So Jesus Christ, the Lord of all people, all creation, and Lord of the Church, sends His people to a radical encounter with the world.[23]

Ultimately any new paradigm of the Christian's response to other cultures involves only a restatement of the mystery of the gospel for all people, a mystery that "for ages past was kept hidden in God, who created all things. His intent was that now, through the Church, the manifold wisdom of God should be made known…according to His eternal purpose which He accomplished in Christ Jesus our Lord. In him and through faith in Him we may approach God with freedom and confidence" (Eph 3:9-12). If Paul and the early church could so emphatically state such a conviction in the midst of their amazing cultural and religious diversity, we, too, can feel confident in doing so. Although our subject is incredibly complex, the heart of it is really quite simple. "Jesus Christ is Lord." In the midst of many cultures and people of many faiths, we must be bold. We must learn more profoundly how to be evangelists who are faith-particularist, culturally pluralist, and ecclesiologically inclusivist.

End Notes

1   Chapman's article in *Christianity Today* developed some of the themes of his address delivered at Lausanne II (Manila, 1989). Robert Coote 1990, p.15, reported that "only Colin Chapman...dared to broaden the examination of what the gospel means for those who have never heard of Jesus Christ."

2   The use of these particular terms seems to be a rather recent phenomenon. In *No Other Name?* (1985) Paul Knitter spoke of "models" of Christian attitudes to other religions: the conservative evangelical, the mainline Protestant, the Catholic and the theocentric. In doing so, he downplayed the pluralist, inclusivist and exclusivist typology. In *God Has Many Names* (1982) John Hick referred to the three major types of approaches, but the words themselves as typological categories are not strongly emphasized (Netland 1994). On the evangelical side Mark Heim in *Is Christ the Only Way?* (1985) and Ajith Fernando in *The Christian's Attitude toward World Religions* (1987) did not structure their work around these three perspectives. In a good reader on *Christianity and Other Religions* (1980) John Hick and Brian Hebblethwaite mentioned "religious pluralism" and "Christian absolutism," but did not use the three-part typology. Among the earliest uses of this three-part typology were Paul Knitter's and Francis Clooney's articles in *Religious Studies Review* 15.3 (July 1989): pp.197–209, surveying significant new books in the field. Carl Braaten seemed to accept the threefold typology in 1987, mentioning Gavin D'Costa and Alan Race as utilizing it, but he did not indicate where it came from (1987, p. 17).

3.   Pinnock, Clark H. 1992. *A Wideness in God's Mercy: The Finality of Jesus Christ in a World of Religions.* Grand Rapids: Zondervan. p. 15.

4.   Ibid. p. 14.

5.   Ibid. p. 153.

6.   Ibid. p. 13.

7.   Ibid. p. 182.

8.   Hick, John. 1982. *God Has Many Names.* Philadelphia: Westminster. pp. 29-31.

9.   Hiebert, Paul G. 1985. *Anthropological Insights for Missionaries.* Grand Rapids: Baker. p. 531.

10. See Van Engen for an outline of the faith-culture dynamic in Romans, as seen from a missiological point of view. 1996. *Mission on The Way: Issues in Mission Theology.* Grand Rapids: Baker, pp . 165–67

11. W. A. Visser't Hooft emphasized the importance of the distinction between faith and culture already in 1963 (p. 85): "To transform the struggle between the religions concerning the ultimate truth of God into an intercultural debate concerning values is to leave out the central issue at stake...the central affirmation of the faith, that God revealed Himself once for all in Jesus Christ."

12. Hick, John. 1982. *God Has Many Names.* Philadelphia: Westminster. p. 19.

13. Ibid. p. 19.

14. Ibid. p. 17.

15. Taber, Charles R., and Betty J. Taber. 1992. "A Christian Understanding of 'Religion' and 'Religions'" *Missiology* v. 20.1 (January): pp. 69-78.

16. Hiebert, Paul G. 1979. "Sets and Structures: A Study of Church Patterns." In *New Horizons in World Mission,* edited by David J. Hesselgrave, Grand Rapids: Baker, pp. 217-27.
     —1983. "The Category Christian in the Mission Task." *International Review of Mission 72,* no. 287 (July): p. 427.
     —1994. *Anthropological Reflections on Missiological Issues.* Grand Rapids: Baker. pp. 125-130.

17. Gnanakan, Ken R. 1989. *Kingdom Concerns: A Biblical Exploration towards a Theology of Mission.* Bangalore: Theological Book Trust.

18. At one time I used the onion as a metaphor. But onions have no center—artichokes do.

19. Verkuyl, Johannes. 1993. "The Biblical Notion of Kingdom: Test of Validity for Theology of Religion." In *The Good News of the Kingdom,* edited by Charles Van Engen et al., pp. 71-81. Maryknoll, N.Y.: Orbis.

20. See Van Engen. 1981. *The Growth of the True Church.* Amsterdam: Rodopi. 277–305;——1991. *God's Missionary People: Rethinking the Purpose of the Local Church..* Grand Rapids: Baker, pp. 108–17.

21. Berkhof, Hendrikus. 1979. *Christian Faith: An Introduction to the Study of the Faith.* Grand Rapids: Eerdmans. p. 185.

22. Gnanakan, Ken R. 1992. *The Pluralist Predicament.* Bangalore: Theological Book Trust. p. 154.

23. Van Engen, Charles. 1991. pp. 93-94.

24. For some discussion of this most essential kerygmatic confession by the early church and some of its missiological implications, see Van Engen, 1991, pp. 92–94.

The Supremacy of Christ

Ajith Fernando

Ajith Fernando is the National Director of Youth for Christ in Sri Lanka. He presently leads the Youth for Christ evangelistic outreach to English speaking youth in Colombo. He helped translate the NIV style Sinhala Bible, and has authored nine books in Sinhala and/or English including *The Christian's Attitude Toward World Religions*. He has presented Bible expositions at Urbana Missions Conventions in 1987, 1990 and 1993. He holds honorary doctorates from Asbury Seminary, Gordon-Conwell Seminary and Trinity Evangelical Divinity School.

This article is a short excerpt adapted from the full length book called *The Supremacy of Christ* by Ajith Fernando, Copyright 1995. Used by permission of Crossway Books, a division of Good News Publishers, Wheaton, Illinois 60187.

Pluralism has become a dominant philosophy today. Eastern religions have adopted a strong missionary stance, New Age thinking is making huge inroads into different spheres of Western society, and the evangelical movement, especially in the West, seems to have lost its cutting edge commitment to the radical truth of the gospel. The shift from thinking of Christianity in absolute terms is evidenced by a great deal of skepticism about the possibility of knowing truth. A poll by George Barna yielded the statistic that 67 percent of the North American people believe there is no such thing as absolute truth. What is more surprising is that 53 percent of those claiming to be Bible-believing conservative Christians said there is no such thing as absolute truth.[1] With such major shifts occurring in the minds of many within the Church, pluralism and relativism have become keys to understanding religious truth in many circles.

The philosophy of *pluralism* lies at the heart of the thinking of the New Age movement and also of some so-called Christian theologies. It fits in well with Buddhist and Hindu thought too. We are not talking here of the pluralism that allows for the existence of political, ethnic and cultural differences in a society or a church. Rather, we are referring to "a philosophical stance" that recognizes more than one ultimate principle and claims, therefore, that it is not possible for us to recognize any one system of thought as absolute truth. Religious pluralism espouses a new idea of revelation. Over the years, Christians have understood revelation as God's disclosure of truth to humanity. They believe He did this generally in ways accessible to all people, through nature and conscience, specifically in the Scriptures, and supremely in Jesus Christ. According to religious pluralism, truth is not *disclosed* to us but *discovered* by us through our experience. The writings of the different religions are thought to be different discoveries—through human experience—of the one God. And since the different religions are taken to be different expressions of the Absolute, each is believed to contain facets of the truth.

Most careful students of religion, however, recognize that different religions move on different axes. In truth, the similarities between Christianity and other religions are in peripheral things, not in the essentials of the faith. It is simply not correct to say that they teach essentially the same thing. Those who promote pluralism today must reckon with the fact that this attitude is completely opposite to that of the New Testament church. New Testament preachers and writers responded to the pluralism of their day with strong affirmations of the exclusiveness and supremacy of Christ. Paul's ministry in Athens (Acts 17:16-34) and the Epistles to Colosse and Ephesus are good examples of this. While a view of Christ that denies His supremacy gains followers all over the world, the life and work of Jesus Himself show there are reasonable grounds for believing that Jesus is indeed supreme.

JESUS AS ABSOLUTE TRUTH

In light of the developments in contemporary thinking, it is not surprising that many Christians are asking whether Christian claims to a unique and absolute revelation still hold in this era. Into this environment of uncertainty about truth, biblical Christians come with the assertion that we can know absolute truth. We claim that we have found it in Jesus, that Jesus is the Truth. He says, "I am the way, the truth and the life" (John 14:6). When Jesus said He is the truth He means He is the personification, the embodiment, of truth. Jesus says not only, "What I say is true"—meaning "I am true"—but "I am the truth," the ultimate reality. This revelation is not something discovered primarily by experience. The pluralist says that Christian revelation is actually the record of the religious experiences of a given people. We say it is ultimate truth disclosed by God and not primarily discovered by humankind.

Jesus substantiates His claim to be the Truth in the verses that follow John 14:6. He first expands on this by explaining what it means to claim that He is the truth: it means He is equal with God. Verse 7 says, "If you really knew me, you would know my Father as well. From now on, you do know him and have seen him." To know Jesus is to know the Father. Leon Morris points out that when Jesus says we can know God, He "goes beyond anything that the holy people of old normally claimed....Jesus brings to those who believe something new and outstanding in religious experience, the real knowledge of God."[2]

Jesus makes one more strong point in John 14:7. He says, "From now on, you do know

him and have seen him." Jesus is saying that the disciples have seen God the Father. William Barclay comments that "it may well be that to the ancient world this was the most staggering thing that Jesus ever said. To the Greeks, God was characteristically *The Invisible.* The Jews would count it as an article of faith that no man has seen God at any time."[3] Yet Jesus claims to be equal with God and says that when we see Jesus, we see God the Father.

From the teaching of Jesus in John 14:6-7, we conclude that *absolute truth can be known because the Absolute has become concrete in history in the person of Jesus* (see also John 1:14, 18). Herein is the argument for our belief in absolute truth. We say Jesus is God, therefore, to know Jesus is to know the Absolute. Our belief in the absoluteness of the Christian gospel is an extension of our belief that Jesus is God incarnate. It is interesting that John Hick, who is perhaps this generation's most prominent pluralist, rejects the Christian doctrine of incarnation. [4]

A Personal Response to the Truth

Now we come to the question of how and in what sense we know absolute truth. If truth is a Person, then we will know the truth in the way we know persons—through facts about them and through relationship. We know the Absolute through a relationship because that is the way He has chosen to communicate truth. He did it personally. Therefore, to enter into the knowledge of the Absolute, we need to get to know God. John's Gospel has a lot to say about belief as the way to know God. The word *belief* appears 98 times in John. It essentially means "to trust." J. Carl Laney says, "'Believing' in Christ does not merely refer to intellectual assent to a proposition about Christ. Rather, the biblical concept of 'belief' involves a personal response and commitment to Christ's Person."[5] This opens the way to a knowledge of absolute truth.

E. Stanley Jones tells the story about an unbelieving doctor who lay dying. A Christian doctor sat beside him and urged him to surrender, to have faith in Christ. The dying doctor listened in amazement. Light dawned. And he joyously said, "All my life I have been bothered with what to believe, and now I see it is *whom* to trust."[6] Belief is entrusting ourselves to Jesus. We love Him as our friend and follow Him as our Lord. This is the reason the basic call of Christ is not "Follow my teaching" but "Follow me."

Because we know the Absolute personally, we can say that we know absolute truth. But this knowledge is not only something subjective. At the heart of the Christian gospel are some objective facts. The gospel of Jesus is about certain things that happened in history, including certain claims Jesus made. There are propositions in revelation about which there can be no compromise; and the truth about Jesus' relationship with God is one of them. For example, in John 14:11, He commands His disciples, "Believe me when I say that I am in the Father and the Father is in me."

The Words of Jesus Affirm His Absoluteness

In John 14:10b Jesus explains how we can believe His claim to be equal with God and therefore absolute truth: "The words I say to you are not just my own. Rather, it is the Father, living in me, who is doing His work." When Jesus speaks, it is the Father who is working through Him. We would have expected Jesus to say, "the Father speaks through me." Instead He says, "the Father who dwells in me does His works." This is because, as Archbishop William Temple put it, "The *words* of Jesus are the *works* of God."[7]

What Jesus is saying here is that we must take His words seriously because when He speaks, God speaks. His words affirm His claims to deity. The authenticating value of the words of Jesus lies in two areas. First, their relevance and penetrating insight suggest that this is no ordinary person who is speaking and that in His words lie God's answer to life's problems. Second, His claims about Himself leave us with the inescapable conclusion that Jesus views Himself as equal to God.

In the 20 centuries since Jesus lived, many people have come to the conclusion that Jesus' claims for Himself are true simply by reading the Gospels. I heard a story about a young non-Christian man who was studying English and was using one of the Gospels for reading. He suddenly got up in the middle of a lesson, paced up and down the room, and said, "These are not the words of a man, these are the words of God!" Jesus says that His words themselves ought to convince people.

Ten Qualities of Jesus' Words

1. *His teaching is profound, yet simple.* Bishop Stephen Neill says, "The quality of ordinariness runs through much of the teaching of Jesus. It is this perhaps which has given to His words their extraordinary power to move the hearts of men and women through almost 20 centuries."[8] The temple guards who were sent to arrest Jesus returned without Him. And when they were asked, "Why didn't you bring him in?" they responded, "No one ever spoke the way this man does" (John 7:46).

2. *He speaks with great authority.* Shortly before His ascension, Jesus tells His disciples: "All authority in heaven and on earth has been given to me" (Matt 28:18). The way He speaks befits one who can make such a claim. About His teaching He says, "Heaven and earth will pass away, but my words will never pass away" (Matt 24:35). After the Sermon on the Mount, "the crowds were amazed at his teaching, because he taught as one who had authority, and not as their teachers of the law" (Matt 7:28-29). R. T. France says, "Any other Jewish teacher made sure that his teaching was documented with extensive quotations from Scripture and with the names of his teachers added to give weight to his opinion; his authority must always be second-hand. But not Jesus. He simply laid down the law."[9]

3. *He claims to have the authority to forgive sin.* When He forgives the sins of a paralytic and the people question His right to do this, He proves it by performing a miracle. He says He is doing it "that [they] may know that the Son of Man has authority on earth to forgive sins" (Mark 2:10).

4. *He not only tells people to "Follow my teaching," He says, "Follow me" and demands total allegiance.* He says, "Anyone who loves his father or mother more than me is not worthy of me; anyone who loves his son or daughter more than me is not worthy of me; and anyone who

does not take his cross and follow me is not worthy of me" (Matt 10:37-38).

5. **He takes on titles that are given to God in the Old Testament.** Psalm 27:1 says, "The Lord is my light and my salvation." Jesus says, "I am the light of the world" (John 8:12). Psalm 23:1 says, "The Lord is my shepherd." Jesus says, "I am the good shepherd" (John 10:11).

6. **He considers Himself worthy of receiving the honor that is due to God.** Isaiah 42:8 says, "I am the Lord; that is my name! I will not give my glory to another or my praise to idols." He says, "Moreover, the Father judges no one, but has entrusted all judgment to the Son, that all may honor the Son just as they honor the Father" (John 5:22-23).

7. **He claims to have a unique Father-Son relationship with God.** He calls Himself God's Son and He calls God "my Father." "My Father" is not the way Jews usually referred to God. They did speak of "our Father" and while they might use "my Father" in prayer, they usually qualified it with something like "in heaven" "to remove the suggestion of familiarity."[10] The various references in the Gospels show that Jesus intends to convey that He has a relationship no other human being can have with God.

8. **He claims to be the judge of humankind.** He says of Himself in John 5:27, "And [the Father] has given him authority to judge because he is the Son of Man" (John 5:27). Leon Morris points out that "if Jesus was anything less than God [this] is a claim entirely without foundation....No creature can determine the eternal destiny of His fellow creatures."[11]

9. **He says that He will give us things that only God can give.** In John 5:21, He says, "For just as the Father raises the dead and gives them life, even so the Son gives life to whom he is pleased to give it." He said He gives "water welling up to eternal life" (John 4:14). He speaks of giving "my peace" (John 14:27) and "my joy" (John 15:11).

10. **His opponents, the Jewish leaders, understood the implication of His claims.** In a discussion about the Sabbath, Jesus makes the statement, "My Father is always at his work to this very day, and I, too, am working." The next verse says, "For this reason the Jews tried all the harder to kill him; not only was he breaking the Sabbath, but he was even calling God his own Father, making himself equal with God" (John 5:17-18). Someone said of the words of Christ, "If it is not superhuman authority that speaks to us here, it is surely superhuman arrogance."[12]

The Works of Jesus Authenticate His Words

Jesus, however, knew that some people would not accept the startling claims He made for Himself. So he said in John 14:11, "Believe me when I say that I am in the Father and the Father is in me; or at least believe on the evidence of the miracles [lit. works] themselves." He meant that if we consider His works, we would be challenged to take His words seriously. The first way to look at His works is through His spotless life. Even those who do not accept some of His claims generally agree that Jesus lived an exemplary life. If He was a good man, then should we not take seriously what He consistently kept saying about Himself?

A second way of looking at the works of Jesus is through His miracles. In the Gospels the miracles are often presented as evidence to support the claims of Christ. When the people murmur about Jesus' statement to the paralytic that his sins are forgiven, He heals the man so "that you may know that the Son of Man has authority on earth to forgive sins" (Mark 2:8-11). When the Jews accuse Him of blasphemy saying, "You, a mere man, claim to be God" (John 10:33), Jesus says in His response, "Do not believe me unless I do what my Father does. But if I do it, even though you do not believe me, believe the miracles, that you may learn and understand that the Father is in me, and I in the Father" (John 10:37-38).

If a person is to really consider the works of Christ, that person must come to grips with His claims of absolute supremacy because His works authenticate His words. I have a friend in Sri Lanka who was a devout Buddhist and a voracious reader. One day he went to his city's public library and checked out a book on the life of Christ. After reading it he realized that Jesus' life was unparalleled in human history. He knew he had to do something about the claims Jesus made. He went in search of someone who could tell him more about Christ.

This contact with Christians led to his becoming a fervent follower of Jesus Christ.

> When we come to Jesus, when we enter into a relationship with the Truth, we realize that we are in touch with the Absolute.

If we believe that the Gospels give an objective account of the life of Christ, then we cannot take the view of the modern-day pluralist. The absolute lordship of Christ does not emerge from a few proof texts in some isolated passages in the Gospels. It shines through all of it. If we take out those passages that contain teaching about the absolute lordship of Christ, we are left with no life of Christ at all. The same material that gives evidence to His being a good man also gives evidence that He is Absolute Lord. It is impossible to say that Jesus was good but not absolute. The view of the pluralist on this matter is untenable.

Of course, pluralists may reject the historicity of the gospel records and thus dismiss the claims made for Christ in the Gospels. Many pluralists say that these statements were not made by Jesus himself but were invented by the Gospel writers based on their subjective experiences and their ideas about Christ. It is beyond the scope of this article to respond to this view. But let me state here that there is a strong case for the historical reliability of the gospel records which has been amply demonstrated in several recent books. [13]

A Comprehensive Case for Absoluteness

Different people are attracted to different aspects of the comprehensive case for Christ's absoluteness. Once they open their hearts to one aspect, the others soon fall into place. But the final appeal of the gospel is the cumulative effect of all these points. Others have taught the things that Jesus taught. Recently a leading Sri Lankan lawyer presented what many considered to be a convincing case against the uniqueness of Christianity by showing that the ethical teachings of Jesus are also found in the other religions. That is true to a certain extent. But the teachings of Jesus are not the sum of the gospel. Those ethical teachings are inextricably linked with His claims to absoluteness.

The feature of the gospel that makes it exclusive is its completeness. Jesus was the perfect example of a holy and loving human being. He taught sublime truths, claimed to be equal with God, and performed miracles to substantiate those claims. Most importantly, He sacrificed His life, claiming He must die to save the world. God gave proof of the validity of this scheme of salvation by raising Jesus from the dead. This last point is the clincher. The most unique thing about the gospel of Jesus is His death and resurrection for the salvation of the whole world. This ultimately separates the gospel from the rest of the religions of the world.

The Joy of Truth

There is an intense joy over truth to be had in this era of the New Covenant. When we come to Jesus, when we enter into a relationship with the Truth, we realize that we are in touch with the Absolute. This is firm ground. This is what people are thirsting for in this confusing age. What a joy the discovery of such truth is! It gives an eternal foundation on which to build one's life. This, in turn, brings a great security that is a springboard to lasting joy.

Jesus succinctly described this experience when He said, "You will know the truth, and the truth will set you free" (John 8:32). As we experience the truth, we find freedom from dependence on this unstable world for fulfillment, freedom from the dehumanizing power of sin, freedom to dwell in the sphere of eternity where there are springs of eternal joy (Ps 16.11) that will satisfy our deepest aspirations. Realizing that Jesus is the Truth is an experience unmatched by other faiths. It is an experience of the eternal God, and only the eternal God can give us eternal joy.

JESUS AS THE WAY

If Christianity is Christ, then His cross is the greatest key to understanding Him. The space given to the last week before the crucifixion is evidence of how important the disciples considered His death to be. It occupies about 30 percent of Matthew, 37 percent of Mark, 25 percent of Luke, and 41 percent of John.[14] The English theologian P. T. Forsyth says, "Christ is to us just what His cross is. All that Christ was in heaven or on earth was put into what He did there....You do not understand Christ till you understand His cross."[15] When Jesus says in John 14:6 that He is the way, He means that He will become the way through His death, as the context of this verse (John 13:33-14:5) reveals.

What the Cross of Christ achieved is so vast and so deep that numerous interpretations of it have appeared in the history of the Church.[16] Here we will describe what it achieved by looking at six concepts found in the New Testament.

1. *Substitution.* Perhaps the most basic feature about Jesus' death is that He took our place and bore the punishment for our sins. He was our substitute. Peter, who first revolted against the idea of Jesus' being crucified, later wrote two significant statements about this: "He himself bore our sins in his body on the tree, so that we might die to sins and live for righteousness; by his wounds you have been healed" (1 Pet 2:24) and "For Christ died for sins once for all, the righteous for the unrighteous, to bring you to God" (1 Pet 3:18).

2. *Forgiveness.* The immediate result of our appropriating the benefits of the death of Christ is the forgiveness of sins. His death was necessary for the forgiveness to be granted, as Hebrews 9:22 explains: "In fact, the law requires that nearly everything be cleansed with blood, and without the shedding of blood there is no forgiveness." The message of forgiveness is one of the most revolutionary aspects of the Christian gospel and is missing in most other religious systems.

3. *Propitiation.* This word is related to the rituals of the temple where sacrifices were given to turn away God's wrath against sin. The meaning is well expressed in the rendering of 1 John 2:2 in *The Living Bible:* "He is the one who took God's wrath against our sins upon himself, and brought us into fellowship with God." Propitiation focuses on the seriousness of sin and God's wrath against it, which is borne by Jesus. Perhaps the reason we find this difficult to accept is that the doctrine of God's wrath has been neglected by the Church. Today we are surprised to read descriptions of God like the following: "Your eyes are too pure to look on evil; you cannot tolerate wrong" (Hab 1:13). We have lost the abhorrence for sin that is found in the Bible. Yet in both the Old and New Testaments, wrath is considered part of the essential nature of God.

4. *Redemption.* This comes from the marketplace where, in those days, slaves were purchased for a price. It speaks of the purchase of our salvation through the payment of a price for our sins. Ephesians 1:7 says, "In him we have redemption through his blood, the forgiveness of sins, in accordance with the riches of God's grace." The focus is on the freedom we receive from the captivity of sin through the price paid by Christ.

5. *Justification.* This word comes from the law courts and means "to pronounce, accept and treat as just." This figure comes from the law court, and it denotes "a judicial act of administering the law—in this case by declaring a verdict of acquittal, and so excluding all possibility of condemnation."[17] Romans 4:25 says, "He was delivered over to death for our sins and was raised to life for our justification." Romans 5:16-18 describes what happened in our justification: "The judgment followed one sin and brought condemnation, but the gift followed many trespasses and brought justification.... Consequently, just as the result of one trespass was condemnation for all men, so also the result of one act of righteousness was justification that brings life for all men."

6. *Reconciliation.* This comes from family life and friendship. Paul says, "God was reconciling the world to himself in Christ, not counting men's sins against them" (2 Cor 5:19). Reconciliation is necessary

because sin is rebellion against God and results in enmity between God and humankind. Romans 5:10 says, "when we were God's enemies, we were reconciled to him through the death of his Son." The result is "peace with God" (Rom 5:1) and adoption into His family (John 1:12).

The Challenge of the Cross

Jesus is the way to salvation; He came to the world in order to bring this salvation to humanity. Implied in this is the fact that we cannot save ourselves and there is no other way to salvation except through Jesus. Christianity, then, is a religion of grace, of God's acting in Christ to save us. Many who are confronted with the Christian belief in grace ask, "Should we not save ourselves? Why should another die for us?" Most people would like to save themselves. Stephen Neill has said, "The last thing that modern individuals want is that anyone should do anything for them."[18] The message of the cross cuts at the heart of human pride, which is the essence of sin. Adam and Eve's sin was that they wanted to save themselves, independent of God. They did not want to be dependent on a supreme God for salvation or for anything else. The same thing happens today. People like to think that they are saving themselves. It makes them feel good and helps to temporarily still the voice of insecurity and emptiness that is theirs because they are separated from their Maker. This may account for the fact that religions like Buddhism, Hinduism and New Age, which offer people ways to save themselves through several lives (reincarnation), are growing even in the West.

Also distant from the biblical idea that we are guilty before God and in need of salvation is the belief of Hinduism and the New Age movements that we are all part of the divine. A statement from Swami Muktananda, who had a great influence on Werner Erhard, founder of EST and FORUM, expresses well the mood of many people today: "Kneel to your own self. Honor and worship your own being. God dwells within you as You."[19] New Age analyst Theodore Roszak says that our goal is "to awaken the god who sleeps at the root of the human being."[20] Fallen humanity, in its natural state of rebellion against God, would prefer this approach to salvation.

When someone asks me the question, "Should we not pay for our sins?" I usually respond in the following way: the principle of paying for one's sins is found in every religion. The Bible also says, "Do not be deceived: God cannot be mocked. A man reaps what he sows" (Gal 6:7). Buddhists and Hindus call this the law of *karma*. But the effects of a principle or law can be overcome by a more powerful force. Take the law of gravity. According to this law, if I hold a book up and let go of it, it will fall. But I can use another more powerful force and overcome the force that operates through the law of gravity. By catching the falling book and raising my arm, I can overcome the force of gravity and make the book reverse its direction. When I do that I do not break the law of gravity. I use a force that overcomes its effects.

God did something like this with us. He created us to live with Himself. But we chose to live independent of Him. By doing this we heaped a terrible load of guilt upon ourselves. Those who try to offset this by their own efforts soon find that they don't have the strength to do so. However much they try, they are not able to tilt the scales of their lives in the direction of their innocence. The Christian gospel says that, seeing our helpless condition, our Creator did not abandon us. He brought into operation the law of love. And He let that save us. But He did so without breaking the law of justice or canceling its demands. What He did in love was to satisfy its demands. The demands of justice were not ignored or canceled. They were fully satisfied. And the only way that God could do that was by having His spotless Son take the punishment that was due to us. What we see here is an amazing love. He did for us what we could not do for ourselves. We call this grace, the result of which is salvation. I know of many Hindus and Buddhists who, when despairing of their efforts to save themselves, have found this message of salvation through the grace of Christ to be very good news.

JESUS AS THE LIFE

The way in which Jesus is the life (John 14:6) is another important aspect of the supremacy of Christ. Eternal life is the primary result of Christ's saving work (John 3:16; 5:24). Jesus often says that this life has to do with a relationship we have with Him. In John 17:3 He says, "Now this is eternal life: that they may know you, the only true God, and Jesus Christ, whom you have sent."

In John 10:11 Jesus teaches that the relationship we have with Him is based on His commitment to us: "I am the good shepherd. The good shepherd lays down his life for the sheep." Then Jesus immediately goes on to refer to selfish people who fail us, people who do not have such a commitment to us. They desert us in our time of need rather than care for us as Jesus does. He says, "The hired hand is not the shepherd who owns the sheep. So when he sees the wolf coming, he abandons the sheep and runs away. Then the wolf attacks the flock and scatters it. The man runs away because he is a hired hand and cares nothing for the sheep" (John 10:12-13). Jesus knows that this world is full of relationships that fail. In fact, the deep wounds that have been caused by people who have disappointed us have a very strong place in our emotional lives. The fact that His loving commitment to us heals us from the wounds we have received in life is an important aspect of the uniqueness of Christ.

> **Jesus as He is portrayed in the Bible is not only unique but also supreme. He is our message to the world.**

In John 10:10 Jesus described the life he gives by saying, "I have come that they may have life, and have it to the full." It is a completely fulfilling life with the fulfillment of a love-relationship with God. Therefore this fulfillment is not an impersonal pleasure or "kick" that He gives us through specific experiences. All other ways of life fall short of the fullness of life that only the One who created us can give. This is what Francis of Assisi (1182-1226) found out. He was the son of a wealthy cloth merchant. After Francis' spiritual awakening in his twenties, his father was convinced that he was insane and denounced him. Francis took on a lifestyle of poverty. But he did not miss the riches he gave up. He said, "To

him who tastes God, all the sweetness of the world will be but bitterness." Jesus explained this same kind of fulfillment saying, "I am the bread of life. He who comes to me will never go hungry, and he who believes in me will never be thirsty" (John 6:35). After we come to Him, healthy ambition and restlessness is not lost. That would make life boring. In fact, we have a new thirst for God, for His glory and for His ways. But the world's hunger that takes away our joy and peace is gone for good.

God created us for relationship with Him. Without that we are as good as dead. As John said, "He who has the Son has life; he who does not have the Son of God does not have life" (1 Jn 5:12). When people who are created for life do not have it, they are restless. St. Augustine (354–430) said, "You have made us for yourself, and our hearts are restless until they find rest in you." The noted French inventor and mathematician Blaise Pascal (1623–62) referred to this restlessness as the God-shaped vacuum found in every human being. The work of Christ in us takes away that restlessness and gives us the fulfillment that we seek from life. This is the subjective aspect of the uniqueness of Christ, and in a world that places so much emphasis on subjective experience it may be one of the most attractive features of Christianity to those outside the faith.

His Work Forms a New Humanity

God has also formed us for relationship with each other, and the gospel meets this need too in a unique way through what we may call the new humanity. One of the great effects of the work of Christ is the forming of this new humanity, which Paul called the Body of Christ. Jesus talks about this new humanity in His discussion about His death in John 10. He says, "I have other sheep that are not of this sheep pen. I must bring them also. They too will listen to my voice, and there shall be one flock and one shepherd" (John 10:16).

Some people use this reference to the "other sheep" to claim that there will also be salvation for those who remain outside the Church. They say that the work of Christ has won salvation for all, both inside and outside the Church. But it is most unlikely that the book that talks so much of the necessity of believing in Jesus for salvation should teach that it is possible for people to be saved without such belief. The verb *pisteuo*, "to believe," appears 98 times in John.[21] In fact, Jesus says here, "they too will listen to my voice." The implication is that they will respond to the gospel. When Jesus refers to "this sheep pen," He seems to be referring to the Jews. That makes the "other sheep" non-Jews. Jesus is saying that His death is going to bring non-Jews into the flock also. This is a theme that appears elsewhere in John (11:52; 12:20-21). It is implied in the statements that present Jesus as the Savior of the whole world (John 1:29; 3:16-17). The result of bringing the sheep into the fold is a new humanity "in Christ." Paul contrasts the new humanity with the old in Romans 5:10-20 and 1 Corinthians 15:20-22. These passages say that those who are in Adam experience the consequence of Adam's sin, whereas those who are in Christ experience the consequence of Jesus' saving act.

While John 10:16 teaches that the death of Christ makes it possible for other sheep to come into Christ's flock, the way this will happen today is through the Church's going out and bringing them in. John 10:16, then, is a missionary verse. William Barclay, commenting on this verse, says, "The dream of Christ depends on us; it is we who can help him make the world one flock with him as its shepherd."[22] It is fitting that description of the death of Jesus in John 10:11-15 climaxes with the missionary challenge in verse 16. The great Scottish theologian James Denney (1856–1917), speaking at a missionary convention, to the surprise of all there spent most of his talk describing the meaning of propitiation. But this gave him the background to drive home his main point at the conclusion. He said that if propitiation is true, then taking its message to the world (missions) should be our priority.

In the last part of John 10:16, Jesus mentions the result of having these other sheep come in: "and there shall be one flock and one shepherd." What we have here is an initial statement about the universal Church

that Paul is later going to teach about in some detail. He will use the figure of the Body of Christ to refer to the Church[23] and views those who are "in Christ" by faith as belonging to it. Here Jesus is saying that the Gentiles will come in, and they will belong to the same flock as the Jews. If the Jews who were listening understood what Jesus meant by this statement, it would have been a very revolutionary thought for them. They always thought that they were separate and superior to other races because they were the chosen people of God. "Only by becoming a full citizen could a non-Jew find entry into Jewish religious groups."[24] Jesus is implying here that His death would make such a step unnecessary. A significant feature of the biblical description of the work of Christ is its emphasis on how the Cross and Resurrection broke earthly distinctions between people. This is a theme the Church has often failed to preach and practice, but it is certainly a unique feature that the gospel has to offer to a world torn by communal prejudice and strife.

The Resurrection is Proof

Christianity makes claims about the uniqueness and exclusiveness of its founder that no other religion makes. How do we know these claims are true? While we have given several reason above, the clincher is the Resurrection of Jesus. At the conclusion of his message to the inquiring Athenians, Paul says, "[God] has given proof of this to all men by raising him [Christ] from the dead" (Acts 17:31). Despite all of Jesus' teaching about His mission, even His disciples are bewildered by His death. On Easter Sunday, when the women share the news of the Resurrection as reported by the angels, Luke 24:11 says, "But they did not believe the women, because their words seemed to them like nonsense." Once the disciples know, however, that Jesus indeed is risen, they cannot be stopped. They go straight to the hostile people in Jerusalem and proclaim that Jesus is the Messiah [Christ]. Peter declares that the Resurrection of Jesus demonstrates that "God has made this Jesus, whom you crucified, both Lord and Christ [Messiah]" (Acts 2:36). The New Testament, then, insists that the Resurrection was God's authentication of the supremacy of Jesus.

The Creator of the world has indeed presented the complete solution to the human predicament. As such it is supreme; it is unique; and it is absolute. So we have the audacity in this pluralistic age to say that Jesus as He is portrayed in the Bible is not only unique but also supreme. He is our message to the world. A Hindu once asked Dr. E. Stanley Jones, "What has Christianity to offer that our religion has not?" He replied, "Jesus Christ."

End Notes

1. George Barna, *What Americans Believe* (Ventura, Calif.: Regal, 1991), quoted in Charles Colson, *The Body* (Dallas: Word, 1992), pp. 171, 184.

2. Leon Morris, *Reflections on the Gospel of John*, vol. 3 (Grand Rapids, Mich.: Baker, 1988), p. 495.

3. William Barclay, *The Gospel of John*, vol. 2 in The Daily Bible Study, rev. ed. (Philadelphia: Westminster, 1975), p. 159.

4. See John Hick, "Jesus and the World Religions," in *The Myth of God Incarnate*, ed. John Hick (London: SCM Press, 1977), pp. 167-85.

5. J. Carl Laney, *Moody Gospel Commentary: John* (Chicago: Moody Press, 1992), p. 20.

6. From E. Stanley Jones, "The Christ of the Indian Road" (1925), in *Selections from E. Stanley Jones* (Nashville: Abingdon, 1972), p. 224.

7. William Temple, *Readings in John's Gospel* (1939, 1940; reprint, Wilton: Moorhouse Barlow, 1985), p. 225 (italics his).

8. Stephen Neill, *The Supremacy of Jesus* (London: Hodder and Stoughton, 1984), p. 67.

9. R.T. France, *Jesus the Radical* (Leicester: InterVarsity Press, 1989), p. 204.

10. Leon Morris, "The Gospel According to St. John," in *The New International Commentary on the New Testament* (Grand Rapids, Mich.: Eerdmans, 1971), p. 313.

11. Leon Morris, *The Lord from Heaven* (Liecester and Downers Grove, Ill.: InterVarsity Press, 1974), p. 36.

12. Quoted in W. Griffith Thomas, *Christianity Is Christ* (1948; reprint, New Canaan, Conn: Keats Publishing, 1981), p. 26.

13 See especially Craig Blomberg, *The Historical Reliability of the Gospels* (Leicester and Downers Grove, Ill.: InterVarsity Press, 1987).

14. Calculated from figures provided in Griffith Thomas, *Christianity Is Christ*, p. 34.

15. P.T. Forsyth, *The Cruciality of the Cross* (London: Hodder and Stoughton, 1909, pp. 44-45 quoted in John Stott, *The Cross of Christ* (Liecester and Downers Grove, Ill.: InterVarsity Press, 1986), p. 43.

16. For a comprehensive description of the different views that have emerged in history, see, H. D. McDonald, *The Atonement of the Death of Christ* (Grand Rapids, Mich.: Baker, 1985).

17. J. I. Packer, "Justification," in *The Evangelical Dictionary of Theology*, ed. Walter A. Elwell (Grand Rapids, Mich.: Baker, 1984), p. 593.

18. Stephen Neill, *The Supremacy of Jesus* (London: Hodder and Stoughton, 1984), pp. 147-48.

19. Quoted in Douglas R. Groothuis, *Unmasking the New Age* (Downers Grove, IL: InterVarsity Press, 1986), p. 21.

20. Theodore Roszak, *Unfinished Animals* (New York: Harper and Row, 1977), p. 225, quoted in Groothuis, *Unmasking*, p. 21.

21. It is surprising that the noun *pistis* does not appear at all in John.

22. William Barclay, *Gospel of John*, vol. 2, p. 66.

23. See 1 Cor 12:27; Rom 12:5; Eph 1:22-23; 4:12, 15; Col 1:18.

24. Robert Banks, *Paul's Idea of Community* (Grand Rapids, Mich.: Eerdmans; 1988), p. 116.

Study Questions

1. How does Fernando argue that the uniqueness of Christ points to "the supremacy of Christ?"

2. Explain how Christ's death, as decribed in John 10:11-16, provides hope for a "new humanity."

3. Why is it essential to affirm Christ's uniqueness in an atmosphere of pluralism?

If I Perish

Brother Andrew

My last meeting with Iranian pastor Haik Hovsepian-Mehr was especially memorable. For many years he had served as a shepherd for the churches in Iran, always declaring the gospel wisely but openly. As we parted we shook hands and he said to me, "Brother Andrew, when they kill me it will be for speaking and not for being silent." He said "when." He did not say "if." He knew he would be killed. The next month he was murdered.

He had suffered for his faith for years. He was killed for his faithfulness to declare it. He was a rare and precious man, but he was not alone. There are millions of beleaguered Christians living in areas where their faith costs them greatly. It cost them most when they proclaim their faith.

As they suffer with Christ, they become the message by saying, "I am willing to die for Him and I'm willing to die for you because that is what He did!"

I'm convinced that we are living in what appears to be the the most cruel period of history. More people suffer for Christ's name than in any other generation. As Christians who are not under such persecution, we must find any way that we can to help our persecuted brothers and sisters. They need us more than ever—our presence, our encouragement, our support, our teaching, our fellowship, and perhaps more than anything else, our prayers.

Our prayers are crucial because our best praying will move us into our best action. I'm reminded of another man who prayed for God's suffering people from the land which is now Iran. This man was Nehemiah. Nehemiah belonged to a small Jewish minority group in what is now Iran. He was a man of good standing and high position, with relatives living in extremely difficult circumstances. Receiving news of the desperate situation in Jerusalem, he sat down and wept for many days. Hearing the need, he took it as a call to act.

He spoke up for God's people in high government circles, as we need to do. He was bold with sustained service for a beleaguered people, as we need to be. His prayer shows us a way to pray with passion and we need to pray now more than ever.

The plight of God's people in Jerusalem in that day is similar to the suffering that Christians endure in many lands today. Nehemiah heard of the temple in ruins and of God's name being defiled. There are lands where God's household has suf-

Brother Andrew is the founder and Director of Open Doors International. This ministry began in 1955 and now has over two hundred full-time workers with offices in 20 countries. His well-known book, *God's Smuggler* has sold ten million copies in 30 languages.

fered so severely for so many generations that the church no longer exists there. I have sometimes referred to this suffering church as "the vanished church." And there are other places where there has never been a church. When new churches are planted in these places, they are sure to suffer. How will we respond to the report of God's people being broken, imprisoned, enslaved, beaten, cold and hungry?

Nehemiah's response was amazing: Even though he was a man of action, and a well-trained administrator, he fasted and prayed before the God of heaven.

The passion of his prayer is even more important than his petition. Three aspects of his passion in prayer worth noting are:

- *his zeal for the glory of God*
- *love for his people*
- *counting his own life as nothing.*

Nehemiah reminded God of His promise to gather His people from all over the world to worship His name openly (Neh 1:8-9). Zeal for the glory and name of Jesus should also be our motivation. For how many of us is this true? Do we pray for the glory of God's name, or do we pray only for ourselves?

Nehemiah identified with his people. He had a fairly comfortable position. The problems weren't of his own doing. But he identified so greatly with the whole family of God's people that he prayed on their behalf as if he had been responsible for their predicament. That sense of responsibility spurred him into action. Do we put on sackcloth like Nehemiah, for the sins of our people, our church? Or do we wash our hands in innocence and pass the blame to politicians and church leaders?

Nehemiah's compassion moved him to action because he owned the suffering people as if they were his own family. He also identified himself as a servant of God. He knew that to serve God you must serve people. He didn't shirk from being in touch with people and having compassion for them.

After an appeal for the glory of God and acknowledgment of his own guilt and that of his family and people, he at last gets around to the request: "Oh, Lord, let me find favor with the king." Nehemiah was laying his life on the line by pleading with this heathen king for Jerusalem and the Jewish people.

What was Nehemiah afraid of? What are Christians in Iran, Iraq, Egypt and Pakistan afraid of? They fear the leader of their country, who by definition is of a different faith, and who can suppress the Christian minority with impunity. We learn from Nehemiah that in such countries, we should pray for favor in the eyes of that leader.

Let's pray that Christian leaders in Iran—and all the other countries—will find favor with the man in power. We can ask that boldly, because every leader in power is accountable to God, whether in a Muslim country, communist China, or in a so-called Christian country.

When we ask for favor with the leaders of regimes hostile to the gospel, we position ourselves well to express God's favor upon them. The Bible clearly teaches that the only solution is forgiveness and reconciliation. When I visited a Christian town totally destroyed in one night by a wild Muslim mob, leaving between ten and twenty thousand Christians homeless, having seen all their possessions destroyed, we had a big gathering of Christians and Muslims and we spoke about forgiveness and reconciliation.

We should pray for favor boldly, but not presumptuously. In many cases God allows an even greater witness for His glory in which God displays His own favor, as He did in the case of Stephen, whose last words repeated Christ's last words of forgiveness (Luke 23:34, Acts 7:60). The story of Nehemiah is not simple. Even with the leader expressing favor, Nehemiah endured years of opposition. We should not expect something easy. We should pursue what is worthy, whatever the cost.

We can only pray like Nehemiah if we have the attitude of Nehemiah: First, zeal for the glory of God, then, a deep compassion desiring the well-being of the people. And then with Esther's attitude (Est 4:16), we leave the rest up to God: "If I perish, I perish."

Study Questions

1. Why should Christians pray for favor with leaders who may be hostile to the gospel?

2. How do the three passions in Nehemiah's prayer (glory, love, life not counted) work together?

Suffering and Martyrdom:
God's Strategy in the World

Josef Tson

J esus Christ as King of kings and Lord of lords, calls people to Himself and demands from them total allegiance to Himself. Nothing of this world, not father or mother, husband or wife, son or daughter, or material goods, ought to stand between Him and His children. Jesus expects them to learn from Him and to become like Him. Then Jesus sends them into the world as His Father sent Him into the world, to spread His message and to be His witnesses. He knows that the world will hate His witnesses and will turn against them with merciless violence. Nonetheless, He expects them to meet that hatred with love, and to face that violence with glad acceptance, following His example by suffering and dying for the lost world. Their suffering and martyrdom are prompted by their allegiance to His own Person and are endured for the purpose of spreading His gospel. Christ's disciples do not seek these things for their own sake, and they do not inflict these on themselves. Their goal is not to suffer and to die; on the contrary, their goal is Christ's Person and Christ's cause in the world, the spreading of His gospel.

Suffering for Christ is not only the suffering of persecution. It begins when one leaves close relatives for the service of Christ. For some, it means selling their possessions and giving them to the poor, which often means giving them for the propagation of the gospel. For others, suffering for Christ may mean agonizing in prayer for the cause of Christ, or agonizing and toiling for the building up of the body of Christ and the perfecting of the saints. Again, to clarify this concept, suffering for Christ is not a self-inflicted suffering. The disciple of Christ seeks to do the will of Christ and to promote the cause of Christ. However, suffering for Christ does mean that the disciple will voluntarily involve himself in suffering and in sacrificial living for Christ and His gospel.

Furthermore, a disciple of Christ thinks as a slave of Christ: he is totally at the disposition of the Master. It is the Master who decides what kind of service this particular disciple should perform. The first duty of the disciple is, therefore, to discover the will of his Master and to do it with joy and passion. If and only if the disciple does his duty, can he be certain that his Master is always with him, living in and through him to accomplish His own purposes.

Martyrdom is the function God gives to some of His elect to literally die for the sake of Christ and His gospel. From

Josef Tson is the President of the Romanian Missionary Society in Wheaton, Illinois, and the former President of Emmanuel Bible Institute in Oradea, Romania.

Taken from *Suffering, Martyrdom and Rewards in Heaven*, Josef Tson, Copyright 1997, University Press of America. Used by permission.

what the Scriptures intimate, it is apparent that there is a fixed number of God's children who have been predestined by God for this supreme sacrifice. For some, martyrdom might be a quick event, like being shot or beheaded, but for others it could also be preceded by torture. God may have in His plan a long martyrdom of toiling in a labor camp or the misery and pain of a long imprisonment. In such a situation, even if the Christian is released after some time and the actual death occurs at home because of his health having been shattered by the long detention and suffering, I believe that God still reckons the death as a martyrdom. In our more sophisticated age, martyrdom might also take the shape of an imprisonment in a psychiatric hospital—a modern form of torture that is possibly the most cruel form of martyrdom where one's mental health and even one's personality are utterly ruined by means of drugs and other psychological torture.

God does everything with a purpose. If He chooses to call His children to suffering and self-sacrifice, He must have very important purposes to achieve through them. Hence, it is the duty of the children to obey their Father even if they do not understand the purpose or rationale behind the Father's command. But the Father wants His children to understand Him because He wants them to develop a mind like His. Therefore, He has revealed His mind, His purposes, and His methods to His children in His written Word and in His Incarnate Word.

God entered into history by sending His Incarnate Son as a suffering slave who would end His own earthly life enduring torture and martyrdom. In this event, God revealed to us that suffering and self-sacrifice are His specific methods for tackling the problems of rebellion, of evil, and of the sin of mankind. Self-sacrifice is the only method consistent with His own nature. For instance, God cannot respond to hate with hate, because if He did, he would borrow not only the method but also the nature of the one who is the originator of hate, the evil one. God can only respond with love, because He is love, and by suffering and sacrificing Himself for the ones who hate Him, He expresses the essence of His own nature.

Now, the ones who are born of God have become partakers of the nature of God (2 Pet 1:4). Therefore, the children of God are called to tackle the problems of this world with the same *agape* love which is the nature of God (1 John 4:4-21). More than this, Christ united Himself with His brethren in a union that is comparable to His union with the Father (John 17:21-26). Christ lives in them and continues His work in the world through them. But He has not changed the strategy He used when He was in the world. His method is still the method of the cross. With this in mind, Christ told His disciples that He would send them into the world just as His Father had sent Him into the world, in other words, He sent them to be in the same position and to conquer by the same method namely, the method of the cross. For precisely this reason, Jesus asked them to take up their own crosses and to follow His example by going into all the world to preach the gospel (to witness), to serve others, and to die for others. Their crosses represent their voluntary sacrificial involvement in the fulfillment of their Father's purposes with mankind.

Three basic things are achieved by the deaths of the martyrs:
1. The triumph of God's truth
2. The defeat of Satan
3. The glory of God

Martyrdom and the Triumph of God's Truth

The unredeemed world lives in spiritual darkness. The eyes of unbelievers have been darkened by Satan, resulting in their hatred of the light of truth. For people who have lived a long time in darkness, a bright light that suddenly shines upon them produces pain. They cannot stand the light. They hate the light, and they do their best to put it out. Jesus explained the world's reaction to His own coming into the world in these terms (John 3:19-20), and He told His disciples to expect exactly the same kind of treatment.

Speaking in modern terms, each group of people on this planet considers its own religion to be one of its most precious treasures. Thus telling them that their faith is wrong or untrue becomes an unforgivable offense and insult against them. The attempt to change their religion is perceived as an attack on their "national identity." This is why Christian missionaries are met with hostility and violence in every place to which they carry the gospel. For his part, the missionary must be convinced that the population to which he takes the Word lives in the lie of Satan and is damned to hell as a result of it. If the missionary is not convinced of this, he will not risk his life to kindle the light in their midst.

> When the ambassador of Christ speaks the truth in love, and meets death with joy, a strange, miracle occurs: the eyes of unbelievers are opened, they are enabled to see the truth of God.

However, when the ambassador of Christ speaks the truth in love, and meets death with joy, a strange, miracle occurs: the eyes of unbelievers are opened, they are enabled to see the truth of God, and this leads them to believe in the gospel. Ever since the centurion's eyes were opened at Calvary, ever since he believed that Jesus was the Son of God *because* he had seen *the manner of His death* (Mark 15:39), thousands and thousands of Christian martyrdoms over the centuries have produced the same results. Moreover, this was precisely what Tertullian had in mind when he wrote that the blood of the martyrs is the seed out of which new Christians are born. Many, many groups of people on this planet have testified that the darkness which had been over them was dissipated only when a missionary was killed there. However, countless areas and peoples of the world today so experience a darkness that will be vanquished only when enough Christians have given up their lives in martyrdom.

Martyrdom and the Defeat of Satan

Jesus saw His own coming into this world as an invasion of the strong man's house in order to spoil his goods (Matt 12:29). He saw the Prince of this world being cast out at His own death (John 12:31-33), and as a result of the ministry of His own disciples (Luke 10:17-19). Jesus taught them not to be afraid of the ones who can kill only the body, and He charged them to bravely lose their lives in order to gain the victory (Matt 10:26-39).

Hence, John was simply following the teaching of his Lord when he depicted the casting out of Satan and his defeat through the deaths of the martyrs in Revelation 12:9-11.

Satan has two instruments with which he keeps humans in bondage and slavery. His first instrument is sin. The sins of people are Satan's "certificate of ownership." But this document was nailed to the cross of Calvary and was canceled by the death of Christ (Col 2:14-15). Satan's second instrument is the fear of dying (Heb 2:14-15). Again, by His own death, Jesus liberated His own from the fear of death. When the martyrs meet their death without fear, Satan's last instrument is rendered powerless, and he is crushed and defeated.

As the deceiver of the nations, Satan maintains their enslavement by keeping them in the darkness of his deception. When the martyrs cause the truth of God to shine brightly among the nations, those who were formerly in the bondage of darkness respond by turning back to God. The death of the martyrs opens the eyes of unbelievers, and when they see the light, Satan's power over them is gone. We have further proof of this reality in the Book of Revelation, where we see the knowledge of God coming to all the nations as a result of the deaths of the martyrs (Rev 11:1-19; 14:1-12; 15:2-4). The martyrs are shown to defeat Satan by bringing all the nations to God through their witness and death.

The story of Job shows us another aspect of Satan's defeat by the faithfulness in suffering of God's people. Job's refusal to curse God demonstrated to the whole population of heaven that God had genuine worshipers on the earth, thus proving Satan wrong. The suffering of Job was watched by the hosts of heaven as an extraordinary spectacle. It appears that Paul had the experience of Job in mind when, speaking of the suffering of the apostles, he said that they "have become a spectacle to the world, both to angels and to men" (1 Cor 4:9).

Writing from prison about his own ministry, Paul told the Ephesians that "the rulers and the authorities in the heavenly places" now have the opportunity of knowing God's "manifold wisdom" as it is being manifested in the Church (Eph 3:10). Paul was talking about the same wisdom of God that he had earlier described in 1 Corinthians 1: 17-31. This is the wisdom of God which the world considers utter foolishness: that He sent His only Son to die on the cross. However, the manifestation of God's wisdom in this world did not end with Jesus on the cross; it is continued in His children when they obey God's commission to go into the world and to sacrifice themselves for the cause of Christ. As they conquer by dying, God's children demonstrate His wisdom to the whole cosmos. Moreover, by their witness and death, Satan is discredited and defeated.

Martyrdom and the Glory of God

Jesus described the outcome of His crucifixion as both His own glorification and as the glorification of God (John 12:27-32; 13:31-32). Yet death by crucifixion was one of the most shameful and barbaric modes of execution; how could that be considered an act glorifying to God? The answer becomes clear when one sees what that act has revealed to the world. In Christ's voluntary suffering for the salvation of mankind, the true nature of God was revealed. His essence was shown to be perfect love, utterly and unconditionally giving itself to others, even enduring pain and death for them. The glory of God shines through the beauty and splendor of self-sacrifice as nowhere else, and most importantly, this glory of God, the glory of His self-sacrificing love, shines out in each martyrdom. For this reason, John referred to the martyrdom of Peter as "the kind of death by which Peter would glorify God" (John 21:19, NIV). It was also the reason why Paul was so determined to glorify Christ by his own dying (Phil 1:20, NASB).

Martyrdom has the power of revealing the love of God to those in darkness. Herein lies its power to convince and to persuade: people see the love of God in the death of the martyr and are compelled to believe in God's love and sacrifice for them. Paul expressed the same idea in the concept of reflecting the image of Christ or the glory of God to other people through our suffering and our loving self-sacrifice for others (2 Cor 3:18; 4:1-15). As the knowledge of Christ and the grace of God is spread to more and more people through the sacrifice of the children of God, there is more and more thanksgiving, praise, and glory given to God.

Study Questions

1. How does Tson limit his definition of martyrdom? Does any kind of suffering end up being suffering for Christ?

2. How does Tson think that dying for Christ's works for the defeat of Satan?

3. Explain how martyrdom can glorify God.

Apostolic Passion

Floyd McClung

What is apostolic passion?
The term "passion" is used to describe everything from romance to hunger pangs. I don't know what it means to you, but for me passion means whatever a person is willing to suffer for. In fact, that's the root meaning of the word. It comes from the Latin *paserre*, to suffer. It is what you hunger for so intensely that you will sacrifice anything to have it. The word "apostle" means a sent one, a messenger. "Apostolic passion," therefore, is a deliberate, intentional choice to live for the worship of Jesus in the nations. It has to do with being committed to the point of death to spreading His glory. It's the quality of those who are on fire for Jesus, who dream of the whole earth being covered with the Glory of the Lord.

I know when apostolic passion has died in my heart. It happens when I don't spend my quiet time dreaming of the time when Jesus will be worshiped in languages that aren't yet heard in heaven. I know it's missing from my life when I sing about heaven, but live as if earth is my home. Apostolic passion is dead in my heart when I dream more about sports, toys, places to go and people to see, than I do about the nations worshiping Jesus.

I have lost it, too, when I make decisions based on the danger involved, not the glory God will get. Those who have apostolic passion are planning to go, but willing to stay. You know you have it when you are deeply disappointed that God has not called you to leave your home and get out among those who have never heard His name. If you will not suffer and sacrifice for something, you are not passionate about it. If you say you will do anything for Jesus, but you don't suffer for Him—then you aren't really passionate about Him and His purposes on earth.

If you don't have it, how do you go about getting this thing called apostolic passion? Is it like ordering pizza—at the door in 30 minutes or less, guaranteed? Is there an 800 number to call? Or better yet, just send us your special gift of $15 or more, and we'll rush you some passion, express delivery, overnight mail. If you're like me, you need help figuring out how to grow this thing called passion. I am motivated by reading how the apostle Paul got it. He chose it.

Paul says in Romans 15 that it is his ambition—his passion, if you will—to make Christ known. It began for him with a revelation of Jesus that he nurtured all his adult life.

Floyd McClung is the founder and Director of All Nations Institute in Trinidad, Colorado. For years he served as International Director of Youth With A Mission. He began his international ministry in Afghanistan. One of his new books, *Living on the Devil's Doorstep* tells the story of the ministry he pioneered in Amsterdam, Holland.

Paul not only encountered Christ on the road to Damascus, he kept on meeting Jesus every day. This revelation of Jesus, and his study of God's purposes, gave birth to Paul's apostolic passion. Knowing Jesus and making Him known consumed the rest of Paul's life. He "gloried in Christ Jesus in his service to God" (Rom 15:17). By comparison, everything else was dung, garbage, stinking refuse. Paul's ambition was born from his understanding that God longed for His Son to be glorified in the nations. It was focused so that the "Gentiles might become an offering acceptable to God, sanctified by the Holy Spirit" (Rom 15:16).

Human enthusiasm cannot sustain apostolic passion. When God invests His own passion in you—the desire to see His name glorified among all people—you must build and develop what God has given you. Four things will help:

1. Apostolic Abandonment

Too many people want the fruit of Paul's ministry without paying the price that Paul paid. He died. He died to everything. He died daily. He was crucified with Christ. This strong-willed, opinionated man knew that he must die to self. He knew that in his flesh, he couldn't generate the revelation of Jesus; he couldn't sustain the heart of Christ. So he died. He abandoned his life. He abandoned himself.

We live in a world of competing passions. If we do not die to self and fill our lives with the consuming passion of the worship of God in the nations, we will end up with other passions. It's possible to deceive ourselves into thinking we have biblical passions when, in reality, all we have done is to baptize the values of our culture and give them Christian names. We will have chosen apostolic passion only when our hearts are filled with God's desire for His Son to be worshiped in the nations.

May I encourage you, dear friend, to give up your life? I challenge you to pray this prayer: "Lord, be ruthless with me in revealing my selfish ambition and my lack of willingness to die to myself."I guarantee that He will answer your prayer—and quickly.

2. Apostolic Focus

The greatest enemy of the ambition to see Jesus worshiped in the nations is lack of focus. You can run around expending energy on all sorts of good ministries, and not get one step closer to the nations. I don't have anything against all the projects and ministries out there—God's people do them, and I don't question their obedience to God. But the Church has an apostolic calling, an apostolic mission. God has called us to the nations. We must focus, or we won't obey.

Focus on what? I believe God wants a people for Himself. Activity without a desire that God have a people for Himself is just activity—not missions. You can have evangelism without missions. Short-term ministries are great, as long as they focus on raising up workers to plant churches. You might say, "I'm not called to plant churches." Yes, you are! It's always the will of God to have a people who worship His Son in the nations. You'll never have to worry about making God mad if you try to plant a church. It seems crazy to me that people are under the delusion they need a special calling to save souls, to disciple them, and to get them together to love Jesus. Whatever ministry you are with, you must understand one thing: church planting is not for us, it's for God. We do it so God will have a people to worship Him!

3. Apostolic Praying

A young man in Bible school offered to help David Wilkerson years ago when he was ministering on the streets of New York City. Wilkerson asked him how much time he spent in prayer. The young student estimated about 20 minutes a day. Wilkerson told him, "Go back, young man. Go back for a month and pray two hours a day, every day for 30 days. When you've done that, come back. Come back, and I might consider turning you loose on the streets where there is murder, rape, violence and danger…If I sent you out now on 20 minutes a day, I'd be sending a soldier into battle without any weapons, and you would get killed."

You can get into heaven, my friend, without a lot of prayer. You can have a one-minute quiet time every day and God will still love you. But you won't hear a "well done, good and faithful servant" on one-minute conversations with God. And you certainly can't make it on that kind of prayer life in the hard places where Jesus is not known or worshiped. Here's a challenge for you: Read everything Paul says about prayer, then ask yourself, "Am I willing to pray like that?" Paul said that he prayed "night and day... with tears... without ceasing... with thankfulness... in the Spirit... constantly... boldly... for godly sorrow... against the evil one."

4. Apostolic Decision-Making

If you live without a vision of the glory of God filling the whole earth, you are in danger of serving your own dreams of greatness, as you wait to do "the next thing" God tells you. There are too many over-fed, under-motivated Christians hiding behind the excuse that God has not spoken to them. They are waiting to hear voices or see dreams—all the while living to make money, to provide for their future, to dress well and have fun.

The Apostle Paul was guided by his passions. Acts 20 and 21 tell of his determination to go to Jerusalem despite his own personal anticipation of suffering, the warnings of true prophets, and the intense disapproval of his friends. Why would Paul go against his own intuition—let alone the urgings of prophets and weeping entreaties of close friends? He had a revelation of greater priority, of greater motivation: the glory of God.

Apostolic decision-making starts with a passion for God's glory in the nations, then asks: "Where shall I serve you?" Most people do the opposite. They ask the where-and-when questions without a revelation of His glory in the nations. Is it any wonder they never hear God say "go!" They have not cultivated a passion for the passions of God. All kinds of lesser desires can be holding them captive. They might never realize it.

Present your gifts, vocations and talents to the Lord. Press into God. Stay there until you long to go out in His name. Remain there and nurture the longing to see the earth bathed with His praise. Only then will you be able to trust your heart if you hear God say, "stay." Only those who long to broadcast His glory to the nations have the right to stay.

If you have apostolic passion, you are one of the most dangerous people on the planet. The world no longer rules your heart. You are no longer seduced by getting and gaining but devoted to spreading and proclaiming the glory of God in the nations. You live as a pilgrim, unattached to the cares of this world. You are not afraid of loss. You even dare to believe you may be given the privilege of dying to spread His fame on the earth. The Father's passions have become your passions. You find your satisfaction and significance in Him. You believe He is with you always, to the end of life itself. You are sold out to God, and you live for the Lamb. Satan fears you, and the angels applaud you.

Your greatest dream is that His name will be praised in languages never before heard in heaven. Your reward is the look of pure delight you anticipate seeing in His eyes when you lay at His feet and the just reward of His suffering: the worship of the redeemed.

You have apostolic passion!

Study Questions

1 McClung implies that passion has more to do with values that emotions. How is this different from the way the word "passion" is commonly used?

2. McClung suggests that everyone is called to see that churches are planted among all peoples. Is he saying that everyone must make an effort to go as a missionary? Or is he saying that God's desire for glory summons every believer to do all they can for His glory?

3. What relationship is there between passion and willingness to suffer?

The Hope of a Coming World Revival

Robert E. Coleman

W e go forth in the confidence that someday the harvest will be gathered from the ends of the earth. This promise certainly accentuates the possibility of a mighty cosmic revival before the end of the age. Is this hope realistic? If so, it gives us reason to walk on tiptoes.

An Exciting Prophecy

Considering the convulsive struggles of our civilization, any discussion of last things seems relevant today. The growing concern for the world's unreached billions, and how the church will reach them, makes the subject even more pertinent.

Scripture does point to some kind of a climactic spiritual conflagration, though the time and extent of its coming can be variously understood. Most of the references to this coming world revival are bound up with other historical situations, such as the return of the Jews from captivity and the restoration of their nation. How one understands the millennium, tribulation, and rapture must also be taken into account. Obviously those who see Christ returning to take away his Church before his millennial reign will look at the awakening from a different perspective than those who view it as an aspect of the millennium. Notwithstanding the differences, nothing in the varying positions necessarily precludes a coming world revival.

Let us admit that the complexity of the biblical prophecies makes any conclusion tentative. Yet, recognizing that we now only see through the glass darkly, it is possible to discern an outline of a future movement of revival that will make anything seen thus far pale by comparison.

A Universal Outpouring of the Holy Spirit

The day is envisioned when the church in all parts of the world will know the overflow of God's presence. No one will be excluded, as Joel prophesied, "And it shall come to pass afterward, that I will pour out my spirit upon all flesh; and your sons and your daughters shall prophesy, your old men shall dream dreams, your young men shall see visions: and also upon the servants and upon the handmaids in those days will I pour out my spirit" (Joel 2:28 29), a statement clearly indicating that all classes of people from around the world will feel the impact of this spiritual rejuvenation. Peter associated this promise with the coming of the Holy Spirit at Pentecost (Acts 2:16,17). Yet the universal dimension of the prophecy of Joel

Robert E. Coleman is Director of the School of World Missions and Evangelism and Professor of Evangelism at Trinity Evangelical Divinity School in Deerfield, Illinois. He serves as Director of the Billy Graham Institute of Evangelism at Wheaton, Illinois. He is a founding member of the Lausanne Committee for World Evangelization and President of the Christian Outreach Foundation. Coleman is the author of 20 books.

Excerpted from *The Spark that Ignites*, 1989, Worldwide Publications, Minneapolis, MN. Used by permission of the author.

was not experienced fully, in that the Spirit did not then come upon God's people from all over the world. Of course, potentially the first Pentecostal visitation reached to "all flesh," even to them that "are far off" (Acts 2:39). This was typified by the Spirit-filled disciples' witness to the people present that day from "every nation under heaven" (Acts 2:5). But in actual extent that outpouring was confined to the city. As the Church gradually moved out in the strength of the Holy Spirit, the flame spread to Judea, to Samaria, and finally to many distant places of the civilized world. The message is still going out. But complete fulfillment of the prophecy awaits a glorious day to come.

Certainly a spiritual awakening around the world would be in keeping with the all-embracing love of God (John 3:16). In a dramatic way, it would give notice of the gospel mandate to reach "the uttermost part of the earth" (Acts 1:8; cf. Matt 28:19; Mark 16:15; John 20:21), fulfilling at last the promise to Abraham that in him all peoples on the earth shall be blessed (Gen 12:3; 22:18). The worship of God by all the families of the nations, so long foretold, would then be a reality (see Ps 22:27; 86:9; Isa 49:6; Dan 7:14; Rev 15:4), and God's name would be great among the Gentiles, "from the rising of the sun even unto the going down of the same" (Mal 1:11).

According to this reasoning, the church age began and will end in a mighty spiritual baptism. What happened at the first Pentecost may be seen as the "early" display of the refreshing rain from heaven, while the closing epic is the "latter rain" (Joel 2:23; Hosea 6:3; Zech 10:1; Jas 5:7). Water or rain, it will be remembered, is often symbolic of the Holy Spirit (John 7:37-39).

Strange Demonstrations of Power

In describing the Spirit's outpouring, Joel foretells "wonders in the heavens and in the earth, blood, and fire, and pillars of smoke. The sun shall be turned into darkness, and the moon into blood, before the great and the terrible day of the Lord comes" (Joel 2:30, 31; cf. Acts 2:19, 20). Yet these phenomena are not mentioned as happening in the account of the first Pentecost, so apparently they are yet to occur.

Jesus spoke of days immediately "after the tribulation" in similar terms, adding that "the stars shall fall from heaven, and the powers of the heavens shall be shaken" (Matt 24:29; cf. Rev 6:12,13). It seems that God will summon the forces of nature to bear witness to what is happening on the earth.

Adding to the spectacle, some persons will have the power to perform wondrous deeds, such as turning water to blood (Rev 11:6; cf. Gal 3:5). Naturally Satan will do what he can to counterfeit that which he knows is real. We are warned of "false Christs" and "false prophets" of this time who will show "great signs and wonders to deceive the elect" (Matt 24:24; cf. Ex 7:10-12; Matt 7:15-20; 2 Th 2:9,10). The sensory appeal is always fraught with danger, which is all the more reason why we are exhorted to try the spirits. If they are not Christ-exalting, then they are not of God (1 Jn 4:1-3).

Unprecedented Trouble

Those fearful conditions of the last days described in Matthew 24 and intermittently in Revelation 6 to 17 also seem to characterize this period. And things will get worse as the end approaches (cf. 2 Tim 3:12; 2 Th 2:1-3).

Famines, pestilence and earthquakes of staggering proportions will occur. Wars and intrigue will fill the earth. Hate will bind the hearts of men. No one will feel secure. As moral integrity breaks down, apostasy in the Church will increase. Those who do not conform to the spirit of the age will be hard pressed, and many will be martyred. Clearly, the cost of discipleship will be high.

Yet amid this terrible adversity, Scripture indicates that revival will sweep across the earth. When God's "judgments are in the earth, the inhabitants of the world will learn righteousness" (Isa 26:9). Dreadful calamities will mingle with awesome displays of salvation—the terrors will actually create an environment for earnest heart searching. Not everyone will turn to God, of course. Some persons will remain unrepentant and become even more brazen in their sin. But the world will be made to confront, as never before, the cross of Jesus Christ.

How it will all end is not clear. Possibly the revival will close and there will be "a falling away" before the Lord returns (2 Th 2:3). Some Bible students believe that the worst tribulation will come after the church is caught up. Others think that Christians will be taken out of the world midway through this dreadful period.

However viewed, Scripture gives us no reason to think that the last great revival will avert the coming catastrophe. The line of no return will have already been passed. Judgment is certain. Revival may delay, but it will not prevent, the final day of reckoning.

Cleansing of the Church

Through the purging of revival, God's people will be brought to the true beauty of holiness. Our Lord expects to present his bride unto himself "a radiant church, without stain or wrinkle or any other blemish, but holy and blameless" (Eph 5:27, cf. 1 Jn 3:2,3; 2 Cor 7:1; 1 Pet 1:13-16; 3:4). The trials of the last days will serve as fires to refine the gold of Christian character. Out of them the bride of Christ, "arrayed in fine linen, clean and white," will emerge ready for the marriage supper of the Lamb (Rev 19:7-9; cf. Dan 12:10). To this end, the "latter rain" of the Spirit is intended to bring "the precious fruit" of the church to maturity in preparation for the Lord's return (Jas 5:7; cf. SS 2:10-13).

The Church should not fear affliction, though it cause anguish and even death. Suffering may be necessary to convince us that we do not live by bread alone. When received as an expression of God's trust, our suffering can be a means of helping us comprehend more of the love of Christ, who "suffered for us, leaving us an example, that ye should follow his steps" (1 Pet 2:21; cf. Heb. 2:10; 5:8). Without hardship, probably few of us would learn much about the deeper life of grace.

> As we anticipate the coming world revival, prayer is our greatest resource.

A purified church will be able to receive unhindered the power of the outpoured Spirit, and thereby more boldly enter into the mission of Christ. It is also reasonable to believe that this greater concurrence with God's program will multiply the manifestation of ministry gifts in the Body (Eph 3:7-15; cf. Rom 12:6-8; 1 Cor 12:4-11; 1 Pet 4:10-11). This

would further call attention to the momentous awakening on earth.

Tremendous Ingathering of Souls

The coming world revival will naturally result in multitudes calling upon the name of the LORD for salvation (Joel 2:32; Acts 2:21; cf. Rom 10:13). And the same revival will also prepare workers for that great harvest of souls. People who are full of the Holy Spirit are committed to God's work. They want to be where laborers are needed most, and there is no more pressing need than bringing the gospel to hell-bound men and women.

Significantly, Jesus said that the fulfillment of his preaching mission would precede His return. "This gospel of the kingdom will be preached in the whole world as a testimony to all nations, and then the end will come" (Matt 24:14, cf. Luke 12:36,37; 14:15-23). Doubtless the passion to get out the message while there is yet time will increase with the revival, even as the witnesses multiply. That the gospel will eventually penetrate "every nation, tribe, people and language" is clear from the description of the innumerable multitude of the white-robed saints gathered around the throne of God in heaven (Rev 7:9, cf. 5:9). The Great Commission will finally be fulfilled.

Many believe that Jews will be among the lost who turn to Christ at that time. At least, there are prophecies which speak of their general repentance and acceptance of the Messiah (see Ezek 20:43, 44: Jer 31:34; Rom 11:24), and of God's pardon and blessing (see Jer 31:27-34; 32:37; 33:26; Ezek 16:60-63; 37:1-28; Hos 6:1,2; Amos 9:11-15; Rev 7:1-8). The world revival seems a logical time for this to happen. Pretribulationists might put the Jewish awakening after the rapture of the church, making a great deal of Romans 11:25-26, which speaks of Israel's being saved when the fulness of the Gentiles is come. This passage, however, could serve equally well to support the idea of revival before Christ comes again.

Whatever position one might hold, there can be little question that the greatest day of evangelism is before us. The harvesting may be short in duration, and may require enormous sacrifice, but it will be the most far-reaching acceptance of the gospel this world has ever seen.

Preparing for Christ's Return

The massive turning to Christ by people from the four corners of the earth will prepare the way for the coming of the King. Our Lord's return may be waiting now on this spiritual revolution. "Behold, the husbandman waiteth for the precious fruit of the earth, and hath long patience for it, until he receive the early and latter rain. Be ye also patient; stablish your hearts: for the coming of the Lord draweth nigh" (Jas 5:7, 8).

The fact that our Lord has not already returned to establish his kingdom is evidence of his desire to see the church perfected and the gospel presented to every person for whom he died. God is "longsuffering toward us, not willing that any should perish, but that all should come to repentance" (2 Pet 3:9). But we dare not presume upon his patience. None of us can be so sure of our understanding of prophecy as to preclude his return at any moment. Every day we should be ready to meet the Lord, the more so as we see the night approaching.

Anticipation of our Lord's return is a summons to action. We must cast off anything that blocks the flow of the Holy Spirit and commit ourselves to being about the Father's business. World evangelization now is the responsibility around which our lives should be centered. Whatever our gifts, we are all needed in the witness of the gospel.

Uniting in Prayer

As we anticipate the coming world revival prayer is our greatest resource. The prophet reminds us, "Ask ye of the Lord rain in the time of the latter rain" (Zech 10:1). "When the tongue faileth for thirst," God says, "I will open rivers in high places, and fountains in the midst of the valleys" (Isa 41:18; cf. 44:3). Surely it is time to "seek the LORD, till he come and rain righteousness" upon us (Hos 10:12; cf. Joel 2:17; Acts 1:14). There is no other way to bring life to the Church and hope to the barren fields of the world.

As the first Great Awakening was sweeping America in 1748, Jonathan Edwards, responding to a proposal from church leaders in Scotland, published, "A Humble Attempt to Promote Explicit Agreement and Visible Union of God's People in Extraordinary Prayer, for the Revival of Religion and the Advancement of Christ's Kingdom on Earth, Pursuant to Scripture Promises and Prophecies Concerning the Last Time." It was an appeal for the Church to unite in earnest intercession for world revival, based on the text of Zechariah 8:20-22:

> It shall yet come to pass, that there shall come people, and the inhabitants of many cities: And the inhabitants of one city shall go to another, saying, "Let us go speedily to pray before the Lord, and to seek the Lord of hosts: I will go also." Yea, many people and strong nations shall come to seek the Lord of hosts.

About this passage Edwards said:

> From the representation made in this prophecy, it appears…that it will be fulfilled something after this manner; first, that there shall be given much of a spirit of prayer to God's people in many places, disposing them to come into an express agreement, unitedly to pray to God in an extraordinary manner, that he would appear for the help of his church, and in mercy to mankind, and to pour out his Spirit, revive his work, and advance his spiritual kingdom in the world as he has promised; and that this disposition to such prayer, and union in it, will spread more and more, and increase in greater degrees; with which at length will gradually be introduced a revival of religion, and a disposition to greater eagerness in the worship and service of God, amongst his professing people; that this being observed, will be the means of awakening others, making them sensible of the wants of their souls, and exciting in them a great concern for their spiritual and everlasting good, and putting them upon earnest crying to God for spiritual mercies, and disposing them to join with God's people…and that in this manner religion shall be propagated, until the awakening reaches these that are in the highest stations, and until whole nations be awakened, and there be at length an accession of many of the chief nations of the world to the Church of God…And thus that shall be fulfilled "O thou that hearest prayer, unto thee shall all flesh come" (Psalm 65:2).[1]

Edwards's plea for God's people to come together in fervent and constant prayer for revival still speaks with urgency. Not only does it call us to our most essential ministry of intercession, but it also reminds us of the way God has ordained to quicken his Church and to disseminate her witness until finally the nations of the earth shall come and worship before the LORD.

Living in Expectancy

Billy Graham in his last message at the Lausanne Congress in 1974 expressed succinctly both the realism and the hope we have in awaiting "the climactic movement and the total fulfillment of what was done on the Cross." Then, reflecting upon the future, he added:

I believe there are two strains in prophetic scripture. One leads us to understand that as we approach the latter days and the second coming of Christ, things will become worse and worse. Joel speaks of "multitudes, multitudes in the valley of decision!" The day of the Lord is near in the valley of decision. He is speaking of judgment.

But I believe as we approach the latter days and the coming of the Lord, it could be a time also of great revival. We cannot forget the possibility and the promise of revival, the refreshing of the latter days of the outpouring of the Spirit promised in Joel 2:28 and repeated in Acts 2:17. That will happen right up to the advent of the Lord Jesus Christ.

Evil will grow worse, but God will be mightily at work at the same time. I am praying that we will see in the next months and years the "latter rains," a rain of blessings, showers falling from heaven upon all the continents before the coming of the Lord. [2]

All of us should join in this prayer, even as we look expectantly to what lies ahead. Something great is on the horizon. You can almost feel it in the air. Though forces of evil are becoming more sinister and aggressive, there is a corresponding cry for spiritual awakening. Across the world never has there been more yearning by more people for spiritual reality, nor has the church ever had the means it now has to take the glad tidings of salvation to the lost, unreached peoples of the earth. What a day to be alive!

Certainly this is not a time for despair. The King's coming is certain. And in preparation for his return we may be the very generation that will see the greatest movement of revival since the beginning of time.

End Notes

1. Jonathan Edwards, A Humble Attempt..., *The Works of President Edwards,* Vol. 3 (New York: Leavitt, Trow and Co., 1818), pp. 432, 433. The full discourse, encompassing pages 423-508, lifts up the promise of world revival, and the need to pray unitedly for it, more than any other writing in the English language. The appeal for concerts of prayer also comes out in George Whitefield's ministry during this same period, and, indeed, continued in revival efforts through the nineteenth century. In recent years it has been picked up again by such international voices as the Lausanne Committee for World Evangelization. For a contemporary exposition of the movement, and practical direction in how you can become involved, see David Bryant's *With Concerts of Prayer* (Ventura: Regal Books, 1984); or his more recent, *Operation: Prayer* (Madison: Inter-Varsity Christian Fellowship, 1987); historical background is given by J. Edwin Orr in *The Eager Feet: Evangelical Awakenings,* 1790-1830 (Chicago: Moody Press, 1975).

2. Billy Graham, "The King is Coming," in *Let the Earth Hear His Voice, Official Reference Volume for the International Congress on World Evangelization, Lausanne, Switzerland,* ed. J. D. Douglas (Minneapolis: World Wide Publications, 1975), p. 1466.

Study Questions

1. Explain how Coleman can be so confident that Christ's coming again will be preceded by a global revival.

2. Coleman expects great problems to "fill the earth." Will these difficulties help or hinder the harvest? Or does it matter?

3. Will the Great Commission be fulfilled before Christ's second coming? What is Coleman's view on this?

4. What will characterize the global revival?

THE
HISTORICAL
PERSPECTIVE

The Kingdom Strikes Back:
Ten Epochs of Redemptive History

Ralph D. Winter

After serving ten years as a missionary among Mayan Indians in the highlands of Guatemala, Ralph D. Winter was called to be a Professor of Missions at the School of World Mission at Fuller Theological Seminary. Ten year later, he and his wife, Roberta, founded a mission society called the Frontier Mission Fellowship (FMF) in Pasadena, California. This in turn spawned the U.S. Center for World Mission and the William Carey International University, both of which serve other missions working at the frontiers of mission. He is the General Director of the Frontier Mission Fellowship. See expanded biographical sketch at the end of the book.

Man has virtually erased his own story. Human beings as far back as we have any paleological record have been fighting each other so much that they have destroyed well over 90 percent of their own handiwork. Their libraries, their literature, their cities, their works of art are mostly gone. Even the little that remains from the distant past is riddled with evidences of a strange and pervasive evil that has grotesquely distorted man's potential.

This is strange because apparently no other species treats its own with such deadly hatred. The oldest skulls bear mute witness that they were bashed in and roasted to deliver their contents as food for other human beings. An incredible array of disease germs also cuts down population growth.

World population in Abraham's day is estimated at 27 million—less than the population of California in AD 2000. But, the small slow-growing population of Abraham's day is mute, and ominous evidence exists of the devastating combination of war and pestilence, both the relentless impact of the Evil One. World population growth back then was one-sixteenth of today's global rate. As hatred and disease are conquered, world population instantly picks up speed. If today's relatively slow global growth rate to have happened in Abraham's day, our present world population (of 6 billion) would have been reached back then in just 321 years! Thus, in those days, evil must have been much more rampant than now.

We are not surprised, then, to find that the explanation for this strange evil comes up in the oldest detailed written records—surviving documents that are respected by Jewish, Christian and Muslim traditions whose adherents make up more than half of the world's population. These documents called "the Torah," by Jews, the "Books of the Law" by Christians, and "the Taurat" by Muslims not only explain the strange source of evil but also describe a counter-campaign and then follow the progress of that campaign through many centuries.

To be specific, the first eleven chapters of Genesis constitute a scary "introduction" to the entire problem, indeed, to the plot of the entire Bible. Those few pages describe three things: 1) a glorious and "good" original creation; 2) the entrance of a rebellious and destructive evil—superhuman, demonic person—resulting in 3) a humanity caught up in that rebellion and brought under the power of that evil person.

Don't ever think that the whole remainder of the Bible is simply a bundle of divergent, unrelated stories as taught in Sunday School. Rather, the Bible consists of a single drama: the entrance of the Kingdom, the power and the glory of the living God in this enemy-occupied territory. From Genesis 12 to the end of the Bible, and indeed until the end of time, there unfolds the single, coherent drama of "the Kingdom strikes back." This would make a good title for the Bible itself were it to be printed in modern dress (with Gen 1-11 as the introduction to the whole Bible). In this unfolding drama we see the gradual but irresistible power of God reconquering and redeeming His fallen creation through the giving of His own Son at the very center of the 4000-year period ending in 2000 BC. This is tersely summed up: "The Son of God appeared for this purpose, that He might destroy the works of the devil" (1 Jn 3:6).

One stirs up hate, distorts even DNA sequences, perhaps authors suffering and all destruction of God's good creation. Satan's devices may very well include devising virulent germs in order to tear down confidence in God's loving character.

Therefore this "blessing" is a key concept. The English word *blessing* is not an ideal translation. We see the word in use where Isaac confers his "blessing" on Jacob and not on Esau. It was not "blessings" but "a blessing," the conferral of a family name, responsibility, obligation, as well as privilege. It is not something you can receive or get like a box of chocolates you can run off with and eat by yourself in a cave, or a new personal power you can show off like rippling muscles. It is something you *become* in a permanent *relationship and fellowship* with your Father in Heaven. It returns "families," that is, *nations* to His household, to the Kingdom of God, so that the nations "will declare His glory." Preventing the nations from declaring His glory are any evidences of God's inability to cope with evil. If the Son of

> The Bible consists of a single drama: the entrance of the Kingdom, the power and the glory of the living God in this enemy-occupied territory.

This counterattack against the Evil One clearly does not await the appearance of the good Person in the center of the story. Indeed, there would seem to be five identifiable epochs of advance *prior* to the appearance of Christ as well as five after that event. The purpose of this chapter is mainly to describe the five epochs *after* Christ. However, in order for those later epochs to be seen as part of a single ten-epoch 4,000-year unfolding story, we will note a few clues about the first five epochs.

The theme that links all ten epochs is the grace of God intervening in a "world which lies in the power of the Evil One" (1 Jn 5:19), contesting an enemy who temporarily is "the god of this world" (2 Cor 4:4) so that the nations will praise God's name. His plan for doing this is to reach all peoples by conferring an unusual "blessing" on Abraham and Abraham's seed (Abraham's children-by-faith), even as we pray "Thy Kingdom come." By contrast, the Evil One's plan is to bring reproach on the Name of God. The Evil

God appeared to destroy the works of the Devil, then what are the Son of God's followers and "joint heirs" supposed to do to bring honor to His Name?

This "blessing" of God is in effect conditioned upon its being shared with other nations, since those who yield to and receive God's blessing are, like Abraham, those of faith who subject themselves to God's will, become part of His Kingdom, and represent the extension of His rule, His power, His authority within all other peoples.

The First Half of the 4,000-Year Story

The story of the "strike back" as we see it in Genesis 12 begins in about 2000 BC. During roughly the next 400 years, Abraham was chosen, and moved to the geographic center of the Afro-Asian land mass. The time of Abraham, Isaac, Jacob and Joseph (often called the Period of the Patriarchs) displays relatively small breakthroughs of witness to the surrounding nations even though the

Ten Epochs of Redemptive History: *The First Half 2000 – 0 BC*

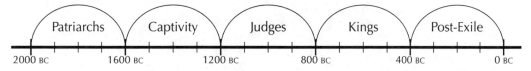

| Patriarchs | Captivity | Judges | Kings | Post-Exile |

2000 BC   1600 BC   1200 BC   800 BC   400 BC   0 BC

central mandate to restore God's control over all nations (Gen 12:1-3) is repeated twice again to Abraham (18:18, 22:18), and once to both Isaac (26:4) and Jacob (28:14,15).

Joseph observed to his brothers, "You sold me, but God sent me." He was obviously a great blessing to the nation of Egypt. Even Pharaoh recognized that Joseph was filled with the Spirit of God (Gen 41:38, *TLB*). But this was not the *intentional* missionary obedience God wanted. Joseph's brothers, for example, had not taken up an offering and sent him to Egypt as a missionary! God was in the missions business whether they were or not.

The next four periods, roughly 400 years each, are: 2) the Captivity, 3) the Judges, 4) the Kings and 5) that of the Babylonian Exile and dispersion (*diaspora*). During this rough and tumble, the promised *blessing* and the expected *mission* (to extend God's rule to all the nations of the world) all but disappear from sight. As a result, where possible, God accomplished His will through the *voluntary* obedience of His people, but where necessary, He accomplished His will through *involuntary* means. Joseph, Jonah, the nation as a whole when taken captive represent the category of *involuntary* missionary outreach intended by God to force the extension of the blessing. The little girl carried away captive to the house of Naaman the Syrian was able to share her faith. Naomi, who "went" a distance away, shared her faith with her children and their non-Jewish wives. On the other hand, Ruth, her daughter-in-law, Naaman the Syrian, and the Queen of Sheba all "came" *voluntarily*, attracted by God's blessing-relationship with Israel.

Note, then, the four different "mission mechanisms" at work to bless other peoples: 1) going voluntarily, 2) involuntarily going without missionary intent, 3) coming voluntarily, and 4) coming involuntarily (as with Gentiles forcibly settled in Israel—2 Kings 17).

Thus, we see in every epoch the active concern of God to forward His mission, with or without the full cooperation of His chosen nation. When Jesus appears, it is an incriminating "visitation." He comes to His own, and "His own receive Him not" (John 1:11). He is well received in Nazareth until He refers to God's desire to bless the Gentiles. At that precise moment (Luke 4:28) an explosion of homicidal fury betrays the fact that this chosen nation—chosen to receive *and to mediate* the blessing (Ex 19:5, 6; Ps 67; Isa 49:6)—has grossly fallen short. There was indeed a sprinkling of fanatical "Bible students" who "traversed land and sea to make a single proselyte" (Matt 23:15). But such outreach was not so much to be a blessing to the other nations as it was to sustain and protect Israel. They were not always making sure that their converts were "circumcised in heart" (Deut 10:16, 30:6, Jer 9:24-26, Rom 2:29).

In effect, and under these circumstances, Jesus did not come to *give* the Great Commission but to *take it away*. The natural branches were broken off while other "unnatural" branches were grafted in (Rom 11:13-24). But, despite the general reluctance of the chosen missionary nation—typical of other nations later—many people groups were in fact touched due to the faithfulness and righteousness of some. These groups come to mind: Canaanites, Egyptians, Philistines (of the ancient Minoan culture), Hittites, Moabites, Phoenicians (of Tyre and Sidon), Assyrians, Sabeans (of the land of Sheba), Babylonians, Persians, Parthians, Medes, Elamites and Romans.

The Second Half of the Story

The next 2,000-year period is one in which God, on the basis of the intervention of His Son, makes sure that the other nations are both blessed and *similarly called* "to be a blessing to all the families of the earth." In each case, "Unto whomsoever much is given, of him (of that people) shall much be re-

Ten Epochs of Redemptive History: *The Second Half 0 – 2000* AD

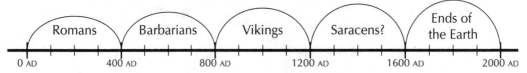

| Romans | Barbarians | Vikings | Saracens? | Ends of the Earth |

0 AD   400 AD   800 AD   1200 AD   1600 AD   2000 AD

quired." Now we see the Kingdom striking back in the realms of the Armenians, the Romans, the Celts, the Franks, the Angles, the Saxons, the Germans, and eventually even those ruthless pagan pirates further north called the Vikings. All these people-basins will be invaded, tamed and subjugated by the power of the gospel, and in turn expected to share that blessing with still other peoples (instead of raiding them).

But in one sense the next five epochs are not all that different from the first five epochs. Those nations that are blessed do not seem terribly eager to share that unique blessing and extend that new kingdom. The Celts are the most active nation in the first millennium to give an outstanding missionary response. As we will see—just as in the Old Testament—the conferral of this unique blessing will bring sober responsibility, dangerous if unfulfilled. And we will see repeated again and again God's use of the full range of His four missionary mechanisms.

The "visitation" of the Christ was dramatic, full of portent and strikingly "in due time." Jesus was born a member of a subjugated people. Yet in spite of her bloody imperialism, Rome was truly an instrument in God's hands to prepare the world for His coming. Rome controlled one of the largest empires the world has ever known, forcing the Roman peace (the "Pax Romana") upon all sorts of disparate and barbaric peoples. For centuries Roman emperors had been building an extensive communication system, both in the 250,000 miles of marvelous roads which stretched throughout the empire, and in the rapid transmission of messages and documents somewhat like the Pony Express on the American frontier. In its conquests, Rome enveloped at least one civilization far more advanced than her own— Greece. Highly-educated artisans and teachers were taken as slaves to every major city of the empire where they taught the Greek

language. Greek was thus understood from England to Palestine.

Equally important to our thesis is the less known but empire-wide substratum of obedience and righteousness—the massive and marvelous presence of diaspora Jews, more respected in their dispersion than in their home land! Scholars agree that their numbers had grown to 10 percent of the Roman population. The virile element within this Jewish presence—those "circumcised in heart"— played a large part in attracting many Gentiles to the fringes of the synagogues. Many of these Gentiles, like those of Cornelius' household, became earnest Bible readers and worshipers—people the New Testament calls "devout persons" or "God-fearers." This way the faith jumped the ethnic borders! Such *God-fearers* became the steel rails on which the Christian movement expanded. This movement was basically the Jewish faith in Gentile clothing, something—take note— which was understandably hard for earnest Jews to conceive.

How else could a few Gospels and a few letters from St. Paul have had such a widespread impact within so many different ethnic groups in such a short period of time?

Stop and ponder: Jesus came, lived for 33 years on earth, confronted His own unenthusiastic missionary nation, was rejected by many, was crucified and buried, rose again, and underscored the same longstanding commission to all who would respond, before ascending to the Father. Today even the most agnostic historian stands amazed that what began in a humble stable in Bethlehem of Palestine, a backwater of the Roman Empire, in less than 300 years was given control of the emperors' palace in Rome. How did it happen? It is a truly incredible story.

No Saints in the Middle?

It is wise to interrupt the story here. If you haven't heard this story before you may confront a psychological problem. In church circles today we have fled, feared or forgotten these middle centuries. Hopefully, fewer and fewer of us will continue to think in

> **Perhaps the most spectacular triumph of Christianity in history was its conquest of the Roman Empire in roughly twenty decades.**

terms of what may be called a fairly extreme form of the "BOBO" theory—that the Christian faith somehow "Blinked Out" after the Apostles and "Blinked On" again in our time, or whenever our modern "prophets" arose, be they Luther, Calvin, Wesley, Joseph Smith, Ellen White or John Wimber. The result of this kind of BOBO approach is that you have "early" saints and "latter-day" saints, but *no saints in the middle.*

Thus, many Evangelicals are not much interested in what happened prior to the Protestant Reformation. They have the vague impression that the Church was apostate before Luther and Calvin, and whatever there was of real Christianity consisted of a few persecuted individuals here and there. For example, in the multi-volume *Twenty Centuries of Great Preaching*, only half of the first volume is devoted to the first 15 centuries! In evangelical Sunday Schools, children are busy as beavers with the story of God's work from Genesis to Revelation, from Adam to the Apostles—and their Sunday School publishers may even boast about their "all-Bible curriculum." But this only really means that these children do not get exposed to all the incredible things God did with that Bible between the times of the Apostles and the Reformers, a period which is staggering proof of the unique power of the Bible! To many people, it is as if there were "no saints in the middle."

In the space available, however, it is only possible to outline the Western part of the story of the kingdom striking back—and only outline. It will be very helpful to recognize the various cultural basins in which

that invasion has taken place. Kenneth Scott Latourette's *History of Christianity* gives the fascinating details, a book extending the story beyond the Bible. (A book more valuable than any other, apart from the Bible!)

Note the pattern in the chart on page 211. Latourette's "resurgences" correspond to our "renaissances."

In Period I, Rome was won but did not reach out with the gospel to the barbaric Celts and Goths. Almost as a penalty, the Goths invaded Rome and the whole western (Latin) part of the empire caved in.

In Period II, the Goths were added in, and they and others briefly achieved a new "Holy" Roman Empire. But this new sphere did not effectively reach further north with the gospel.

In Period III, again almost as a penalty, the Vikings invaded these Christianized Celtic and Gothic barbarians. In the resulting agony, the Vikings, too, became Christians.

In Period IV, Europe now united for the first time by Christian faith, reached out in a sort of pseudo-mission to the Saracens in the great abortion known as the Crusades.

In Period V, Europe now reached out to the very ends of the earth, but still done with highly mixed motives; intermingled commercial and spiritual interests was both a blight and a blessing. Yet, during this period, the entire non-Western world was suddenly stirred into development as the colonial powers greatly reduced war and disease. Never before had so few affected so many, even though never before had so great a gap existed between two halves of the world. What will happen in the next few years?

Will the immeasurably strengthened non-Western world invade Europe and America just as the Goths invaded Rome and the Vikings overran Europe? Will the "Third World" turn on us in a new series of "Barbarian" invasions? Will the OPEC nations gradually buy us out and take us over? Clearly we face the reaction of an awakened non-Western world that is suddenly beyond our control. What will be the role of the gospel? Can we gain any insight from these previous cycles of outreach?

Period I: Winning the Romans, A.D. 0–400

Perhaps the most spectacular triumph of Christianity in history was its conquest of the Roman Empire in roughly 20 decades. There is a lot more we would like to know about this period. Our lack of knowledge makes much of it a mystery, and the growth of Christianity sounds impossible, almost unbelievable—especially if we do not take into account the Jewish substratum. Only the early part of the story starts out emblazoned in the floodlight of the New Testament epistles themselves. Let's take a glance at that.

There we see a Jew named Paul brought up in a Greek city, committed to leadership in the Jewish tradition of his time. Suddenly he is transformed by Christ and gradually comes to see that the essence of the faith of the Jews as fulfilled in Christ could operate without Jewish garments. He realized that an inner circumcision of the heart could be clothed in Greek language and customs as well as Semitic! It should have become crystal clear to everyone that anyone can become a Christian and be transformed in the inner man by the living Christ, whether Jew, Greek, Barbarian, Scythian, slave, free, male or female. The Greeks didn't have to become Jews—undergo physical circumcision, take over the Jewish calendar of festivals or holy days nor even observe Jewish dietary customs—any more than a woman had to be made into a man to be acceptable to God. What *was* necessary was the "obedience of faith" (Rom 1:5, 16:26).

Paul based his work on the radical biblical principle (unaccepted by many Jews to this day) that it is circumcision of the *heart* that counts (Jer 9), and that the new believers of a new culture did not have to speak the language, wear the clothes, or follow all the customs of the sending church. This meant that for Greeks the cultural details of the Jewish law were no longer to be considered mandatory. Therefore, to the Jews, Paul continued as one "under the law of Moses," but to those unfamiliar with the Mosaic law, he preached the "law of Christ" in such a way that it could be fulfilled dynamically and authentically in the new circumstances. While to some he appeared to be "without law," he maintained that he was not without law toward God. Indeed, as far as the basic purpose of the Mosaic Law is concerned, the Greek believers immediately developed the functional equivalent to it in their own cultural terms while most of them held on as well to what is often called the Old Testament. After all, it was "the Bible of the early church" (as well as of the Jews), that had led them to belief in the first place.

We may get the impression that mission activity in this period benefitted very little from deliberately organized effort. That may well be only because its structure was transparent: Paul apparently worked within a well-known "missionary team" structure used by the Pharisees—even by Paul himself when he was a Pharisee! Paul's sending congregation in Antioch certainly undertook some responsibility. But, basically, they "sent him off" more than they "sent him out." His traveling team had all of the authority of any local church. He did not look for orders from Antioch.

There is good reason to suppose that the Christian faith spread in many areas by the "involuntary-go" mechanism, because Christians were often dispersed as the result of persecutions. We know that fleeing Arian Christians had a lot to do with the conversion of the Goths. We have the stories of Ulfilas and Patrick whose missionary efforts were in each case initiated by the accident of their being taken captive.

Furthermore, it is reasonable to suppose that Christianity followed the trade routes of the Roman Empire. We know that there was a close relationship and correspondence between Christians in Gaul and Asia Minor. Yet we must face the fact that the early Christians of the Roman Empire (and Christians today!) were only rarely willing and able to take conscious practical steps to fulfill the Great Commission. In view of the amazing results in those early decades, however, we are all the more impressed by the innate power of the gospel itself.

One intriguing possibility of the natural transfer of the gospel within a given social unit is the case of the Celts. Historical studies clarify for us that the province of Galatia in Asia Minor was called so because it was settled by *Galatoi* from Western Europe (who as late as the fourth century still spoke both their original Celtic tongue and also the Greek of that part of the Roman Empire). Whether or not Paul's Galatians were merely Jewish traders living in the province of Galatia, or were from the beginning Celtic *Galatoi* who were attracted to synagogues as "God fearers," we note in any case that Paul's letter to the Galatians is especially wary of anyone pushing over on his readers the mere *outward customs* of the Jewish culture and confusing such customs with *essential biblical faith* which he preached to both Jew and Greek (Rom 1:16). A matter of high missionary interest is the fact that Paul's preaching had tapped into a cultural vein of Celtic humanity that may soon have included friends, relatives and trade contacts reaching a great distance to the west. Thus Paul's efforts in Galatia may give us one clue to the surprisingly early penetration of the gospel into the main Celtic areas of Europe, comprising a belt running across southern Europe clear over into Galicia in Spain, Brittany in France and up into the western and northern parts of the British Isles.

There came a time when not only hundreds of thousands of Greek and Roman citizens had become Christians, but Celtic-speaking peoples and Gothic tribal peoples as well had believed within their own forms for various versions of biblical faith, both within and beyond the borders of the Roman Empire. It is probable that the missionary work behind this came about mainly through unplanned processes involving Christians from the eastern part of the Roman Empire. In any case this achievement certainly cannot readily be credited to the planned missionary initiative of *Latin-speaking* Romans in the West. This is the point we are trying to make.

One piece of evidence is the fact that the earliest Irish mission compounds (distinguished from the Latin-Roman type by a central chapel) followed a ground plan derived from Christian centers in *Egypt*. And *Greek*, not Latin, was the language of the early churches in Gaul. Even the first organized mission efforts of John Cassian and Martin of Tours, for example, *came from the East* by means of commune structures begun in Syria and Egypt. Fortunately, these organized efforts carried with them a strong emphasis on literacy and the studying and copying of biblical manuscripts and ancient Greek classics.

As amazed pagan leaders looked on, the cumulative impact of this new, much more acceptable clothing of biblical faith grew to prominent proportions by AD 300. We don't know with any confidence what personal reasons Constantine had in AD 312 for declaring himself a Christian. We know that his mother in Asia Minor was a Christian, and that his father, as a co-regent in Gaul and Britain, did not enforce in his area the Diocletian edicts commanding persecution of Christians. However, by this time in history the inescapable factor is that there were enough Christians in the Roman Empire to make an official reversal of policy toward Christianity not only feasible but politically wise. I well recall a lecture by the late Professor Lynn White, Jr. of U.C.L.A., one of the great medieval historians, in which he said that even if Constantine had not become a Christian, the empire could not have held out against Christianity more than another decade or two! The long development of the Roman Empire had ended the local autonomy of the city-state and created a widespread need for a sense of belonging—he called it a crisis of identity. At that time Christianity was the one religion that had no nationalism at its root, partly because it was rejected by the Jews! It was not the folk religion of any one tribe. In White's words, it had developed "an unbeatable combination." However, this virtue became a mixed blessing once it became aligned with the Empire.

Thus, it is the very power of the movement which helps to explain why the momentous imperial decision to *tolerate* Christianity almost inevitably led to its becoming (roughly 50 years later) the *official* religion of the Empire. Not long after the curtain rises on Christianity as an officially *tolerated* religion, the head of the Christian community in Rome turns out astonishingly to be the strongest and most trusted man around. That's why Constantine, when he moved the seat of government to Constantinople, left his palace (the famous Lateran Palace) to the people of the Christian community as their "White House" in Rome. In any case, it is simply a matter of record that by AD 375,

Christianity had become the official religion of Rome. If it had merely been an ethnic cult, it could not have been even a candidate as an official religion of the Empire.

Ironically, however, once Christianity became locked into a specific cultural tradition and political loyalty, it tended automatically to alienate all who were anti-Roman. Even being *tolerated* instantly created suspicion and then soon widespread slaughter of "Christians" in Arabia and what is now Iran. This persecution stopped for three years, when a Roman emperor (Julian the Apostate) *opposed* Christianity and tried to roll things back to the pagan gods! Meanwhile, even in the case of anti-Roman populations within the Empire's boundaries, as in North Africa, the foundation was laid for people to turn to Islam as an alternative. This in one sense was a cultural breakaway from Christianity just as Christianity had been a breakaway from the Jewish form of the biblical faith. Similarly "Black Muslims" today deliberately reject the "white man's religion."

Thus, the political triumph of what eventually came to be known as *Christianity* was in fact a mixed blessing. The biblical faith could wear other than Jewish clothes; it was now dressed in Roman clothes; but if these new clothes were normative, it would not be expected to spread far beyond the political boundaries of the Roman Empire. It didn't, except in the West. Why was that?

No one questions that when Christianity became the official religion of the Roman Empire, it became ill-equipped by its very form to complete the Great Commission with any populace that was anti-Roman. As we might expect, only Christianity of a heretical variety was accepted by the Germanic tribes while Rome was still strong militarily. But once the tribal peoples discovered it possible to invade and conquer the western half of the Roman Empire, the Catholic and Orthodox forms of the faith became less threatening because the Goths and others could now try to acquire the prestige of the Roman language and culture without being dominated by the Roman legions.

Note, however, the domino results of partially Christianized Gothic barbarians threatening Rome: the Romans in defense pulled their legions out of Britain. As a result, four centuries of Roman literacy in southern Britain were soon extinguished by a new form of invading barbarians—Angles, Saxons and Frisians who, compared to the Goths, were total pagans, cruel and destructive. What would happen now? Thus began the "First" of the two Dark Ages.

Period II: Winning the Barbarians, A.D. 400–800

It is a fact that when the earlier (Gothic) tribal peoples became Christianized into an antagonistic Arian form of the faith, they became a greater and greater military threat to Rome. All it took for this threat to become a true menace was for the feared Huns to punch into Europe from Central Asia. This pushed the panicked Visigoths (and then the Ostrogoths and then the Vandals) inside the Empire. In the turmoil and confusion these tribal incursions somewhat unintentionally wrecked the entire network of civil government in the West (in today's Italy, Spain and North Africa). Later they tried seriously to rebuild it.

(Was all this something like the post-colonial chaos in Africa after the Second World War?) In fact, the only reason the city of Rome itself was not physically devastated by the invasions, which arrived finally at the gates of Rome in 410, was that these Gothic Barbarians were, all things considered, really very respectful of life and property, especially that of the churches! It was a huge benefit to citizens of Rome that earlier informal missionary effort—for which Latin Roman Christians could claim little credit—had brought these peoples into at least a superficial Christian faith. Even secular Romans observed how lucky they were that the invaders held high certain standards of Christian morality. Not so the Angles and Saxons who invaded Britain.

We are tantalized by the reflection that this much was accomplished by informal and almost unconscious sharing of the gospel—e.g. the news and authority of the *blessing* being extended to all Gentile nations. How much better might it have been if the Romans—during that brief hundred years of official flourishing of Christianity (310-410) prior to the first Gothic invasion of the city of Rome—had been devoted to energetic and intentional missionary effort. Even a little heretical Christianity prevented the Barbarians from that total disregard of civilization which was to be shown by the Vikings in the third period. Perhaps a little more missionary work might have prevented the complete collapse of the governmental structure of the Roman Empire in the West. Today, for example, the ability of the new African states to maintain a stable government is to a great extent dependent upon their degree of Christianization (that is, both in knowledge and morality).

In any case, we confront the ominous phenomenon of partially Christianized barbarian hordes being emboldened and enabled to pour in upon a complacent, officially Christian empire that had failed effectively to reach out to them. The tribal peoples were quick to acquire Roman military skills, often serving as mercenaries in the Roman legions.

[These events may remind us of our relation to the present-day colossus of China. The country of China, like the Barbarians north of Rome, has been crucially affected by Christianity even though bitterly opposed to its alien connections. And they have gained nuclear power. Can you imagine why they vigorously opposed the Pope's appointment of a Cardinal within their midst? After the Second World War they adopted "Chinese communism" extensively and profoundly, which was a kind of superficial "faith" embodying a number of distinctively Christian ingredients—despite the often grave distortion of those Christian elements. Just as a modicum of Christian faith in some ways strengthened the hand of the Barbarians against the Romans, so the country of China today is awesomely more dangerous due to the cleansing, integrating and galvanizing effect of the Communist philosophy and cell (structure which is clearly derived from the West, and indirectly from the Christian tradition itself). You can imagine the Barbarians criticizing the softness and degeneracy of the Roman Christians just as

the country of China denounced both the Russians for failing to live up to Communist standards and the West for its pornography and crime.]

Whether or not the Romans had it coming (for failing to reach out), and whether or not the Barbarians were both encouraged and tempered in their conquest by their initial Christian awareness, the indisputable fact is that while the Romans lost the western half of their empire, the Barbarian world, in a very dramatic sense, gained a Christian faith.

The immediate result: right within the city of Rome appeared two "denominations," the one Arian and the other Athanasian. Also in the picture was the Celtic "church," which was more a series of missionary compounds than it was a denomination made up of local churches. Still less like a church was an organization called the Benedictines, which came along later to compete with the Celts in establishing missionary compounds all over Europe. By the time the Vikings appeared on the horizon there had spread up through Europe over 1,000 such mission compounds.

Mission compounds? Protestants, and perhaps even modern Catholics, must pause at this phenomenon. Our problem in understanding these strange (and much misunderstood) instruments of evangelization is not so much our ignorance of what these people did as our prejudice which developed because of decadent monks who lived almost a thousand years later. It is wholly unfair for us to judge the work of a traveling evangelist like Columban or Boniface by the stagnation of the wealthy Augustinians in Luther's day—although we must certainly pardon Luther for thinking such thoughts.

It is indisputable that the chief characteristic of these "Jesus People" in this second period, whether they were Celtic *peregrini* (wandering evangelists) or their parallel in Benedictine communes, was the fact that they held the Bible in awe. They sang their way

> **Benedictine communes held the Bible in awe...and they primarily enabled the Kingdom and the power and the glory to be shared with the barbaric Anglo-Saxons and Goths.**

through the whole book of Psalms each week as a routine discipline. It was primarily they who enabled the Kingdom and the power and the glory to be shared with the barbaric Anglo-Saxons and Goths.

It is true that many strange, even bizarre and pagan customs were mixed up as secondary elements in the various forms of Christianity that were active during the period of the Christianization of Europe. The headlong collision and ongoing competition between Western Roman and Celtic (mainly of Eastern origin) forms of Christianity undoubtedly resulted in an enhancement of common biblical elements in their faith. But we must remember the relative chaos introduced by the invasions, and therefore not necessarily expect to see the usual parish churches that once were familiar in rural America dotting the landscape.

Enter: The Orders

Under the particular circumstances of that time, similar to many chaotic corners of the world today, the most durable structure around was the *order*—a fellowship much more highly disciplined and tightly-knit than the usual American Protestant congregation today. Its "houses" came to dot the landscape of Europe. We must admit, furthermore, that these novel Christian communities not only were the source of spirituality and scholarship during the Middle Ages, but they also preserved the technologies of the Roman industrial world—tanning, dyeing, weaving, metalworking, masonry skills, bridge building, etc. Their civil, charitable and even scientific contribution is, in general, grossly underestimated—especially by Protestants who have developed unfriendly stereotypes about "monks." Probably the greatest accomplishment of these disciplined Christian communities is seen in the simple fact that almost all our knowledge of the Roman world is derived from their libraries, whose silent testimony reveals the appreciation they had, even as Christians, for the "pagan" authors of ancient times.

Thus, in our secular age it is embarrassing to recognize that had it not been for these highly literate "mission field" Christians who preserved and copied manuscripts (not only of the Bible but of ancient Christian and non-Christian classics as well), we would know no more about the Roman Empire today than we do of the Mayan or Incan empires, or many other empires that have long since almost vanished from sight.

Many Evangelicals might be jolted by the Wheaton professor who wrote an appreciative chapter about these disciplined *order* structures entitled, "The Monastic Rescue of the Church." One sentence stands out:

> The rise of monasticism was, after Christ's commission to his disciples, the most important—and in many ways the most beneficial—institutional event in the history of Christianity (p. 84).[1]

Curiously, our phrase *Third World* comes from those days when Greek and Latin were the first two worlds and the barbarians to the north were the *Third World*. Using this phrase, Barbarian Europe was won more by the witness and labors of Celtic and Anglo-Saxon converts of the Celts—"Third World missionaries"—than by the efforts of missionaries deriving from Italy or Gaul. This fact was to bear decisively upon the apparently permanent shift of power in Western Europe from the Mediterranean to northern Europe. Even as late as AD 596, when Rome's first missionary headed north (with serious faintheartedness), he incidentally crossed the path of the much more daring and widely-traveled Irish missionary, Columban, one of the scholarly Celtic *peregrini* who had worked his way practically to Rome's doorstep and who was already further from his birthplace than Augustine was planning to go from his.

We are not surprised that Constantinople was considered the "Second Rome" by those living in the East, nor that both Aachen (in Charlemagne's France) and Moscow were later to compete for recognition as new Romes by the descendants of the newly Christianized Franks and Slavs, respectively. Neither the original Rome as a city nor the Italian peninsula as a region were ever again to be politically as significant as the chief cities of the new nations—Spain, France, Germany, and England.

Enter Charlemagne

Toward the end of the second period, as with the end of each of these periods, there was a great flourishing of Christianity within the new cultural basin. The rise of a strong man like Charlemagne facilitated communication throughout Western Europe to a degree unknown for 300 years. Under his sponsorship a whole range of issues—social, theological, political—were soberly restudied in the light of the Bible and the writings of earlier Christian leaders in the Roman period. Charlemagne was a second Constantine in certain respects, and his influence was unmatched in Western Europe during a half a millennium.

But Charlemagne was much more of a Christian than Constantine and as such industriously sponsored far more Christian activity. Like Constantine, his official espousal of Christianity produced many Christians who were Christians in name only. There is little doubt that the great missionary Boniface was slain by the Saxons because his patron, Charlemagne (with whose military policies he did not at all agree) had brutally suppressed the Saxons on many occasions. Then, as in our own recent past, the political force of a colonial power did not so much pave the way for Christianity, as turn people against the faith. Of interest to missionaries is the fact that the great centers of learning established by Charlemagne were copies and expansions of newly established mission compounds deep in German territory, themselves outposts that were the work of British and Celtic missionaries from sending centers as far away to the west as Britain's Iona and Lindisfarne.

Indeed, the first serious attempt at anything like public education was initiated by this great tribal chieftain, Charlemagne, on the advice and impulse of Anglo-Celtic missionaries and scholars from Britain, such as Alcuin, whose projects eventually required the help of thousands of literate Christians from Britain and Ireland to man schools founded on the Continent. It is hard to believe, but formerly "barbarian" Irish teachers of Latin (never a native tongue in Ireland) were eventually needed to teach Latin in Rome. This indicates extensively how the tribal invasions of other barbarians had broken down the civilization of the Roman Empire. This reality underlies Thomas Cahill's book, *How the Irish Saved Civilization*.

The Celtic Christians and their Anglo-Saxon and Continental converts especially treasured the Bible. Mute testimony to the Bible as their chief source of inspiration is that the highest works of art during these "dark" centuries were marvelously "illuminated" biblical manuscripts and devoutly ornamented church buildings. Manuscripts of non-Christian classical authors, though preserved and copied, were not illuminated. Through the long night of the progressive breakdown of the Western part of the Roman Empire, when the tribal migrations reduced almost all of life in the West to the level of the tribesmen themselves, the two great regenerating ideals were the hope of building anew the glory that was once Rome, and the hope of making everything subject to the Lord of Glory. The one really high point, when these twin objectives were most nearly achieved, was during Charlemagne's long, vigorous career centered around the year 800. As one recent scholar put it,

> In the long sweep of European history, from the decline of the Roman Empire to the flowering of the Renaissance nearly a thousand years later, his [Charlemagne's] is the sole commanding presence.

No wonder recent scholars call Charlemagne's period the Carolingian Renaissance, and thus replace the concept of a single lengthy "dark ages" for a more precise perspective of a First Dark Ages early in this period, and a Second Dark Ages early in the next period, with a "Carolingian Renaissance" in between.

Unfortunately, the rebuilt empire (later to be called the Holy Roman Empire) was unable to find the ingredients of a Charlemagne in his successor; even more ominously, a new threat now posed itself externally. Charlemagne had been eager for his own peoples to be made Christian—the Germanic tribes. He offered wise, even spiritual leadership in many affairs, but did not throw his weight behind any kind of bold mission outreach to the Scandinavian peoples to the north. What missionary work was begun under his son was too little and too late. This fact contributed greatly to the undoing of the his empire.

Period III: Winning the Vikings, A.D. 800–1200

No sooner had the consolidation in Western Europe been accomplished under Charlemagne than a new menace appeared to peace and prosperity. This new menace—the Vikings—would create a second period of at least semi-darkness to last 250 years. These savages further north had not yet been effectively evangelized. While the tribal invaders of Rome, who created the First Dark Ages, were rough forest people, they were, for the most part, nominally Arian Christians. The Vikings, by contrast, were neither civilized nor even lightly Christian. There was another difference: the Vikings were men of the sea. This meant that key island sanctuaries for missionary training, like Iona, or like the offshore promontory of Lindisfarne (connected to the land only at low tide), were as vulnerable to attacking seafarers as they had been invulnerable to attackers from the land. In this new period both of these mission centers were sacked more than a dozen times, their occupants slaughtered or sold off as slaves. It seems unquestionable that the Christians of Charlemagne's empire would have fared far better had the Vikings had at least the appreciation of the Christian faith that the earlier barbarians had when they overran Rome. The very opposite of the Visigoths and Vandals who spared the churches, the Vikings seemed attracted like magnets to the monastic centers of scholarship and Christian devotion. They took a special delight in burning churches, in putting human life to the sword right in the churches, and in selling monks into slavery. These depraved people even sold into North African slavery the raided daughters of nearby antagonistic Vikings. A contemporary's words give us a graphic impression of their carnage in "Christian" Europe:

> The Northmen cease not to slay and carry into captivity the Christian people, to destroy the churches and to burn the towns. Everywhere, there is nothing but dead bodies—clergy and laymen, nobles and common people, women and children. There is no road or place where the ground is not covered with corpses. We live in distress and anguish before this spectacle of the destruction of the Christian people.[2]

No wonder the Anglican prayer book contains the prayer, "From the fury of the Northmen, O Lord, deliver us." Once more, when Christians did not reach out to them, pagan peoples came after what the Christians possessed. And once more, the phenomenal power of Christianity manifested itself: the conquerors became conquered by the faith of their captives. Usually it was the monks sold as slaves or Christian girls forced to be their wives and mistresses who eventually won these savages of the north. In God's providence their redemption became more important than the harrowing tragedy of this new invasion of barbarian violence and evil which fell upon God's own people whom He loved. After all, He spared not His own Son in order to redeem us! Thus, again, what Satan intended for evil, God used for good.

And once more, the phenomenal power of Christianity manifested itself: the conquerors became conquered by the faith of their captives.

In the previous hundred years, Charlemagne's scholars had carefully collected the manuscripts of the ancient world. Now the majority were to be burned by the Vikings. Only because so many copies had been made and scattered so widely did the fruits of the Charlemagnic literary revival survive at all. Once scholars and missionaries had streamed in peace from Ireland across England and onto the continent, and even out beyond the frontiers of Charlemagne's empire. Under the brunt of these new violent invasions from the north, the Irish volcano which had poured forth a passionate fire of evangelism for three centuries cooled almost to extinction. Viking warriors, newly based in Ireland, followed the paths of the earlier Irish peregrini across England and onto the continent, but this time ploughing waste and destruction rather than new life and hope.

There were some blessings in this horrifying disguise. Alfred the Great, a tribal chieftain ("king") of Wessex, successfully headed up guerrilla resistance and was equally concerned about spiritual as well as physical losses. As a measure of emergency, he gave up the ideal of maintaining the Latin tongue as a general pattern for worship and began a Christian library in the vernacular—the Anglo-Saxon. This was a decision of monumental importance which might have been delayed several centuries had the tragedy of the Vikings not provided the necessity which was the mother of this invention.

In any case, as Christopher Dawson puts it, the unparalleled devastation of England and the Continent was "not a victory for paganism." The Northmen who landed on the Continent under Rollo became the Christianized Normans, and the Danish who took over a huge section of middle England (along with invaders from Norway who planted their own kind in many other parts of England and Ireland) also were soon to become Christians. The gospel was too powerful. One result was that a new Christian culture spread back into Scandinavia. This stemmed largely from England from which came the first monastic communities and early missionary bishops. What England lost, Scandinavia gained.

It must also be admitted that the Vikings would not have been attracted either to the churches or to the monasteries had not those centers of Christian piety to a great extent succumbed to luxury. The switch from the Irish to the Benedictine pattern of monasticism was an improvement in many respects, but apparently allowed greater possibilities for the development of an unchristian opulence and glitter which attracted the greedy eyes of the Norsemen. Thus, another side-benefit of the new invasions was their indirect cleansing and refinement of the Christian movement. Even before the Vikings appeared, Benedict of Aniane inspired a rustle of reform here and there. By 910, at Cluny, a novel and significant step forward was begun. Among other changes, the authority over a monastic center was shifted away from local politics, and for the first time beyond anything previous whole networks of "daughter" houses arose which were related to a single, strongly spiritual "mother" house. The Cluny revival, moreover, produced a new reforming attitude toward society as a whole.

The greatest bishop in Rome in the first millennium, Gregory I, was the product of a Benedictine community. So also, early in the second millennium, Hildebrand was a product of the Cluny reform. His successors in reform were bolstered greatly by the Cistercian revival which went even further. Working behind the scenes for many years for wholesale reform across the entire church, he finally became Pope Gregory VII for a relatively brief period. But his reforming zeal set the stage for Pope Innocent III, who wielded greater power (and all things considered, greater power for good) than any other Pope before or since. Gregory VII had made a decisive step toward wresting control of the church from secular power—this was the question of "lay investiture." It was he who allowed Henry IV to wait for three days out in the snow at Canossa. Innocent III not only carried forward Gregory's reforms, but had the distinction of being the Pope who authorized the first of a whole new series of mobile mission orders—the Friars.

Our First Period ended with a barely Christian Roman Empire and a somewhat Christian emperor—Constantine. Our second period ended with a reconstitution of that empire under a Christianized barbarian, Charlemagne, who was devoutly and vigorously Christian. Can you imagine an emperor who wore a monk's habit? Our third period ends with a pope, Innocent III, as the strongest man in Europe, made strong by the Cluny, Cistercian and allied spiritual movements which together are called the Gregorian Reform. The scene was now an enlarged Europe in which no secular ruler could survive without at least tipping his hat to the leaders in the Christian movement. It was a period in which European Christians had not reached out in missions, but they had at least with phenomenal speed grafted in the entire northern area, and had also deepened the foundations of Christian scholarship and devotion passed on from the Europe of Charlemagne.

The next period would unfold some happy and unhappy surprises. Would Europe now take the initiative in reaching out with the Gospel? Would it sink in self-satisfaction? In some respects it would do both.

Period IV: Winning the Saracens? A.D.1200–1600

The fourth period began with a spectacular, new evangelistic instrument—the Friars— and after the disaster of the prolonged plague would end with the greatest, the most vital, and most disruptive reformation of all. However, the Christian movement had already been involved for a hundred years in the most massive and tragic misconstrual of Christian mission in all of history. Ironically, part of the "flourishing" of the faith toward the end of the previous period led to disaster: never before had any nation or group of nations in the name of Christ launched as energetic and sustained a campaign into foreign territory as did Europe in the tragic debacle of the Crusades. This was in part the carry-over of the Viking spirit into the Christian Church. All of the major Crusades were led by Viking descendants.

While the Crusades had many political overtones (they were often a unifying device for faltering rulers), they would not have happened without the vigorous but misguided sponsorship of Christian leaders. They were not only an unprecedented blood-letting to the Europeans themselves and a savage wound in the side of the Muslim peoples (a wound which is not healed to this day), but they were a fatal blow even to the cause of Greek/Latin Christian unity and to the cultural unity of eastern Europe. In the long run, though Western Christians held Jerusalem for a hundred years, the Crusaders by default eventually gave the Eastern Christians over to the Ottoman sultans. Far worse, they established a permanent image of brutal, militant Christianity that alienates a large proportion of mankind, tearing down the value of the very word *Christian* in missions to this day.

Ironically, the mission of the Crusaders would not have been so appallingly negative had it not involved so high a component of abject Christian commitment. The great lesson of the Crusades is that goodwill, even sacrificial obedience to God, is no substitute for a clear understanding of His will. Significant in

this sorry movement was an authentically devout man, Bernard of Clairvaux, to whom are attributed the words of the hymn *Jesus the Very Thought of Thee*. He preached the first crusade. Two Franciscans, Francis of Assisi and Raymond Lull, stand out as the only ones in this period whose insight into God's will led them to substitute for warfare and violence the gentle words of the evangel as the proper means of extending the blessing God conferred on Abraham and had always intended for all of Abraham's children-of-faith.

At this point we must pause to reflect on this curious period. We may not succeed, but let us try to see things from God's point of view, treading with caution and tentativeness. We know, for example, that at the end of the First Period after three centuries of hardship and persecution, just when things were apparently going great, invaders appeared and chaos and catastrophe ensued. Why? That followed the period we have called the "Classical Renaissance." It was both good and not so good. Just when Christians were translating the Bible into Latin and waxing eloquent in theological debate, when Eusebius, as the government's official historian, was editing a massive collection of previous Christian writings, when heretics were thrown out of the empire (and became, however reluctantly, the only missionaries to the Goths), when Rome finally became officially Christian... then suddenly the curtain came down. Now, out of chaos God would bring a new cluster of people groups to be included in the "blessing," that is, to be confronted with the claims, privileges, and obligations of the expanding Kingdom of God.

Similarly, at the end of the Second Period, after three centuries of chaos during which the rampaging Gothic hordes were eventually Christianized, tamed and civilized, Bibles and biblical knowledge proliferated as never before. Major biblical-missionary centers were established by the Celtic Christians and their Anglo-Saxon pupils. In this Charlemagnic (actually "Carolingian") renaissance, thousands of public schools led by Christians attempted mass biblical and general literacy. Charlemagne dared even to attack the endemic use of alcohol. Great theologians tussled with theological/political issues, The Venerable Bede became the Eusebius of this period (indeed, when both Charlemagne and Bede were much more Christian than Constantine and Eusebius). And, once again, invaders appeared and chaos and catastrophe ensued. Why?

Strangely similar, then, is the third period. In its early part it only took two and a half centuries for the Vikings to capitulate to the "counterattack of the Gospel." The "renaissance" ensuing toward the end of this period was longer than a century and far more extensive than ever before. The Crusades, the cathedrals, the so-called Scholastic theologians, the universities, most importantly the blessed Friars, and even the early part of the Humanistic Renaissance make up this outsized 1050-1350 outburst of a Medieval Renaissance, or the "Twelfth Century Renaissance." But then suddenly a new invader appeared—the Black plague—more virulent than ever, and chaos and catastrophe greater than ever occurred. Why?

Was God dissatisfied with incomplete obedience? Or was Satan striking back each time in greater desperation? Were those with the blessing retaining it and not sufficiently and determinedly sharing it with the other nations of the world? More puzzling, the plague that killed one-third of the inhabitants of Europe killed a much higher proportion of the Franciscans: 120,000 were laid still in Germany alone. Surely God was not trying to judge their missionary fire. Was He trying to judge the Crusaders whose atrocities greatly outweighed the Christian devotional elements in their movement? If so, why did He wait several hundred years to do that? Surely Satan, not God, inflicted Christian leadership in Europe so greatly. Would not Satan rather have that happen than for the Crusaders to die of the plague?

Perhaps it was that Europe did not sufficiently listen to the saintly Friars; that it was not the Friars that went wrong, but the hearers who did not respond. God's judgment upon Europe then might have been to take the Gospel away from them, to take away the Friars and their message. Even though to us it seems like it was a judgment upon the messengers rather than upon the resistant hearers, is this not one impression that could be received from the New Testament as well?

Jesus Himself came unto His own, and His own received Him not, yet Jesus rather than the resisting people went to the cross. Perhaps Satan's evil intent—of removing the messenger—God employed as a judgment against those who chose not to hear.

In any case, the invasion of the Bubonic plague, first in 1346 and every so often during the next decade, brought a greater setback than the Gothic, the Anglo-Saxon or the Viking invasions. It first devastated parts of Italy and Spain, then spread west and north to France, England, Holland, Germany and Scandinavia. By the time it had run its course 40 years later, one third to one half of the population of Europe was dead. Especially stricken were the Friars and the truly spiritual leaders. They were the ones who stayed behind to tend the sick and to bury the dead. Europe was absolutely in ruins. The result? There were three rival Popes at one point, the humanist elements turned menacingly humanistic, peasant turmoil (often based in justice and even justified by the Bible itself) turned into orgies and excesses of violence. "The god of this world" must have been glad, but out of all that death, poverty, confusion and lengthy travail, God birthed a new reform greater than anything before it.

Once more, at the end of one of our periods, a great flourishing took place. Printing came to the fore, Europeans finally escaped from their geographical cul de sac and sent ships for commerce, subjugation and spiritual blessing to the very ends of the earth. And as a part of the reform, the Protestant Reformation now loomed on the horizon: that great, seemingly permanent, cultural decentralization of Europe.

Protestants often think of the Reformation as a legitimate reaction against the evils of a monstrous Christian bureaucracy sunken in decadence and corruption. But it must be admitted that this re-formation was much more than that. This great decentralization of Christendom was in many respects the result of an increasing vitality which—although this is unknown to most Protestants—was just as evident in Italy, Spain and France as in Moravia, Germany and England. Everywhere we see a return to a study of the Bible and the appearance of new life and evangelical preaching. The Gospel encouraged believers to be German, not merely permitted Germans to be Roman Christians. Nevertheless, that marvelous insight was one of the products of a renewal already in progress. (Luther produced not the *first* but the *fourteenth* translation of the Bible into German.) Unfortunately, the marvelous emphasis on justification by faith—which was preached as much in Italy and Spain as in Germany at the time Luther loomed into view—became identified and ensnarled with German nationalistic (separatist) hopes and was thus, understandably, suppressed as a dangerous doctrine by political powers in Southern Europe.

It is merely a typical Protestant misunderstanding that there was not as much a revival of deeper life, Bible study and prayer in Southern Europe as in Northern Europe at the time of the Reformation. The issue may have appeared to the Protestants as faith vs. law, or to the Romans as unity vs. division, but such popular scales are askew because it was much more a case of over reaching Latin uniformity vs. national and indigenous diversity. The vernacular had to eventually conquer.

While Paul had not demanded that the Greeks become Jews, nevertheless the Germans had been obliged to become Roman. The Anglo-Saxons and the Scandinavians had at least been allowed their vernacular to an extent unknown in Christian Germany. Germany was where the revolt then reasonably took place. Italy, France, and Spain, which were formerly part of the Roman Empire and extensively assimilated culturally in that direction, had no equivalent nationalistic steam behind their reforming movements and thus became almost irrelevant in the political polarity of the scuffle that ensued.

However—here we go again—despite the fact that the Protestants won on the political front, and to a great extent gained the power to formulate anew their own Christian tradition and certainly thought they took the Bible seriously, they did not even talk of mission outreach. Rather, the period ended with *Roman* Europe expanding both politically and religiously on the seven seas. Thus, entirely unshared by Protestants for at least two centuries, the Catholic variety of Christianity actively promoted and accompanied a world-wide movement of scope unprecedented in the annals of mankind, one in which there was greater Christian missionary awareness than ever before. But, having lost non-Roman Europe by insisting on its Mediterranean culture, the Catholic tradition would now try to win the rest of the world without fully understanding what had just happened.

But why did the Protestants not even try to reach out? Catholic missionaries for two hundred years preceded Protestant missionaries. Some scholars point to the fact that the Protestants did not have a global network of colonial outreach. Well, the Dutch Protestants did. And, their ships, unlike those from Catholic countries, carried no missionaries. This is why the Japanese—once they began to fear the Christian movement Catholic missionaries planted—would allow only Dutch ships into their ports. Indeed, the Dutch even cheered and assisted the Japanese in the slaughter of the budding Christian (Catholic) community.

Period V: To the Ends of the Earth, A.D. 1600–2000

The period from 1600 to 2000 began with European footholds in the rest of the world. Apart from taking over what was relatively an empty continent by toppling the Aztec and Inca empires in the Western hemisphere, Europeans had only tiny enclaves of power in the heavily populated portions of the rest of the non-Western world. By 1945, Europeans had achieved virtual control over 99.5% of the non-Western world. This would not last. The peoples inhabiting the colonial empires had grown significantly in knowledge and initiative, just as the Goths had grown strong outside the bounds of the Roman empire. The Second World War mightily distracted the Western nations from their colonial hold on the rest of the world. That did it. Nationalism exploded.

Twenty-five years later, the Western nations had lost control over all but 5% of the non-Western population of the world. This 1945-1969 period of the sudden collapse of Western control, coupled with the unexpected upsurge of significance of the Christian movement in the non-Western world, I have elsewhere called "the twenty-five unbelievable years." If we compare this period to the collapse of the

Pulses in Western Civilization

As the faith moved in to each new cultural basin it struggled before gaining acceptance in a flourishing period which scholars have called a "Renaissance."

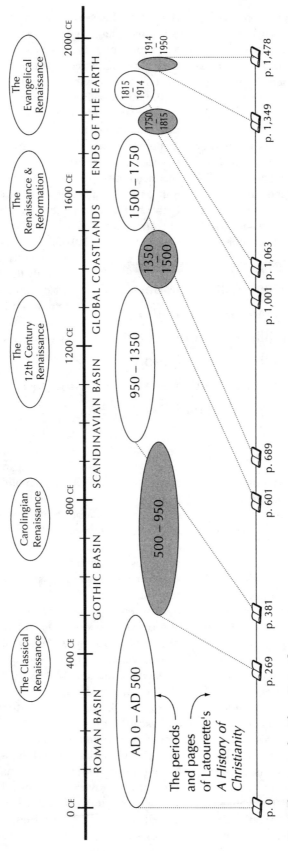

Renaissance in Five Epochs

The dark-lined upper grid of 400-year "epochs" is designed to be easy to remember not to determine the reality of history. However, the most significant expansions of the Christian faith are reflected at least roughly in this way. More importantly, the existence of five "renaissances" is also highlighted.

The lower line represents the pages Latourette devotes to the timeline above. The unshaded ovals represent what Latourette calls "Resurgences" of Christianity, while the shaded ovals represent "Recessions."

The most important thing revealed by this comparison is the fact that all four of Latourette's "Resurgences" correspond to the "Renaissances" of the upper timeline. The only significant difference is that he does not honor the Carolingian Renaissance to the extent many other scholars do.

One reason Latourette saw this differently is that he was concerned strictly with what is called "Christianity" (which is not illogical in a book entitled *A History of Christianity*) and thus does not consider the Islamic movement a largely positive expression of the same "Judaic" tradition.

In any case, Islam, although starting later, became an advance far more illustrious than our Western upbringing normally allows us to realize. By the time of the Renaissance in fourth epoch, Islam had become politically, culturally, militarily, and even numerically, superior to "Christianity." In many ways this had been true for more than half of the Christian period. This is not surprising since much of the expansion of Islam built on a Christian substratum, just as Christianity had earlier built on Jewish a substratum.

Western Roman Empire's domination over its conquered provinces of Spain, Gaul and Britain, and to the breakdown of control over non-Frankish Europe under Charlemagne's successors, we might anticipate—at least by the logic of sheer parallelism—that the Western world itself will soon be significantly dominated by non-Westerners.

With some reason, ever since the collapse of Western power became obvious (during "the twenty-five unbelievable years"), there have been many who have decried the thought of any further missionary effort moving from the West to the non-Western world. Perhaps they have confused the inappropriateness of political control with a need to cut ties of faith in any further foreign missions.

The true situation is actually very different. In fact, the absence of political control for the first time in many areas has now begun to allow non-Western populations to yield to the Kingdom of Christ without simultaneously yielding to the political kingdoms of the Western world. Here we see a parallel to the Frankish tribal people accepting the faith of Rome only after Rome had lost its military power. This new openness to Catholic Christianity continued among the Anglo-Saxons, Germans and Scandinavians up until the time when the emergence of strong papal authority, mixed with power politics, became a threat to legitimate national ambitions, and led to a Reformation which allowed nationalized forms of Christianity to break away.

The present spectacle of a Western world flaunting the standards of Christian morality in more obvious ways than ever may dissuade non-Christian nations from embracing the Christian faith; but it may also tend to disassociate the treasure of Christian ideals from a Western world which has, until this age, been their most prominent sponsor. When Asians accuse Western nations of immorality in warfare, they are appealing to Christian values, certainly not the values of any nation's pagan past. In this sense, Christianity has already

> There will be the defeat of Satan's power holding millions of people hostage in thousands of peoples— peoples which have too long "sat in darkness" and who "shall see a great light" (Matt 4:16).

conquered the world. No longer, for example, is the long-standing Chinese tradition of ingenious torture likely to be boasted about in China nor highly respected anywhere else, at least in public circles.

But this worldwide transformation has not come about suddenly. Even the present, minimal attainment of worldwide Christian morality on a tenuous public level has been accomplished only at the cost of a great amount of sacrificial missionary endeavor (during the four centuries of Period Five), missionary labors which have been mightier and more deliberate than at any time in 2,000 years. The first half (1600-1800) of this fifth period was almost exclusively a Roman show. By the year 1800 it was painfully embarrassing to Protestants to hear Roman missionaries writing off the Protestant movement as apostate simply because it was not sending missionaries. But by that same year, Roman missionary effort had been forced into sudden decline due to the curtailment of the Jesuits, and the combined effect of the French Revolution and ensuing chaos which then cut the European economic roots of Catholic missions.

However, the year 1800 marks the awakening of the Protestants from two-and-a-half centuries of inactivity, if not theological slumber, in regard to missionary outreach across the world. The 1800 to 2000 year period is treated in the chapter "The Three Eras of Modern Missions." During this final period, for the first time, Protestants equipped themselves with organizational structures of mission comparable to the Catholic orders and began to make up for lost time. Unheralded, unnoticed, and all but forgotten in our day except for ill-informed criticism, Protestant missionary efforts in this period, more than Catholic missions, led the way in establishing throughout the world the democratic apparatus of government, the schools, the hospitals, the universities and the political foundations of the new nations. Rightly understood, Protestant missionaries, along with their Roman Catholic counterparts, are surely not less than the prime movers of the tremendous energy that is mushrooming in the Third World today. Take China, for example. Two of its greatest modern leaders, Sun Yat-sen and Chiang Kai-shek, were both Christians. Teng Hsiao-P'ing's "Four Modernizations" were principal emphases of the Western mission movement in China. Missions had planted a university in every province of China, etc.

But, if the Western home base is now to falter and to fail as the tide is reversed through the rising power of its partially evangelized periphery (as is the pattern in the earlier periods), we can only refer to Dawson's comment on the devastation wrought by the Vikings—that this will not be a "victory for paganism." The fall of the West will, in that case, be due in part to a decay of spirit. It will also be due to the pagan power in the non-Western world emboldened and strengthened by its first contact with Christian faith. It may come as a most drastic punishment to a Western world that has always spent more on cosmetics than it has on foreign missions—and lately ten times as much.

From a secular or even nationalistic point of view, the next years may be a very dark period for the Western world. The normal hopes and aspirations of Christian people for their own country may find only a very slight basis for optimism. But if the past is any guide at all, even this will have to be darkness before the dawn. The entire Western world in its present political form may be radically altered. We may not even be sure about the survival of our own country. But we have every reason to suppose from past experience that the Christian, biblical faith will clearly survive in one form or another.

We can readily calculate that during the 20th century, Westerners dropped from 18% to 8% of the world population. But we cannot ultimately be pessimistic. Beyond the agony of Rome was the winning of the Barbarians. Beyond the agony of the Barbarians was the winning of the Vikings. Beyond the agony of the Western world we can only pray that there will be the defeat of Satan's power holding millions of people hostage in thousands of peoples—peoples which have too long "sat in darkness" and who "shall see a great light" (Matt 4:16). And we can know that there is no basis in the past or in the present for assuming that things are out of the control of the Living God.

If we in the West insist on keeping our blessing instead of sharing it, then we will, like other nations before us, have to lose our blessing for the remaining nations to receive it. God has not changed His plan in the last 4,000 years. But how much better not to focus on how to retain but to strive intentionally to extend that marvelous "blessing"! That way "in you and in your descendants all of the peoples of the world will be blessed." This is the only way we can continue in God's blessing. The expanding Kingdom is not going to stop with us (although it may leave us behind). "This Gospel of the Kingdom must be preached in the whole world as a testimony to all peoples, and then shall the end come" (Matt 24:14). God can raise up others if we falter. Indeed, the rest of this book indicates that is already happening.

End Notes

1. Mark A. Noll, *Turning Points, Decisive Moments in the History of Christianity* (Grand Rapids: Baker Books, 1997), p. 84.

2. Christopher Dawson, *Religion and the Rise of Western Culture*, (New York: Image Books, 1991), p. 87.

Study Questions

1. Illustrate this thesis: "The conferring of the blessing brings sober responsibility, dangerous if unfulfilled."

2. Explain the cultural and social dynamics behind the Protestant Reformation.

3. Winter contends that history is a "single, coherent drama." What are the outlines of the "plot"? What themes are repeated? What major lessons are to be observed?

The Church is Bigger Than You Think

Patrick Johnstone

Patrick Johnstone is Director of Research at WEC International. While serving many years as a missionary in several different countries in Africa, he began to develop well-researched materials designed to help Christians lift-up informed intercession for world evangelization. The result was his well known book, *Operation World*, which is used around the world as a tool for praying for the unreached.

From *The Church is Bigger than you Think*, Chapters 6-8. Copyright 1998, Christian Focus Publications, Great Britian. Used by permission.

saiah 53 describes the plan of God for the redemption of sinners to be achieved through the Suffering Servant. This had meaning to the Jewish people as a portrayal of the Messiah, but its full meaning could only be seen after the atoning death of the Lord Jesus Christ. It is a spiritual redemption, therefore it follows on that the words in Isaiah 54 also have a spiritual application—more meaningful to the Church of Gentiles and Jews of the new covenant than to the Jews of the old. The language is of physical restoration from Babylon after exile but this was a faint foreshadowing of the greater spiritual truth of a return to God that had global implications and related to the preaching of the gospel. Paul himself applied Isaiah 54:1 to the Church. (Gal 4:27-28) Many great commentators have also applied this prophecy primarily to the Church. James Denney said: "By coming to the Church, Isaiah causes us to understand more deeply the value and efficacy of the Servant's atoning work. The sufferings of the servant were for the Church, His body, not for Himself."[1]

I therefore, unashamedly, make the same application here. The verse itself is extraordinary:

> Sing O barren one, who did not bear;
> Break forth into singing and cry aloud,
> you who have not been in travail!
> For the children of the desolate one will be more
> than the children of her that is married, says the Lord.

The barren woman is no longer grieving over the shame of her childlessness, but suddenly rejoicing over a mighty increase of spiritual progeny rather than over the few physical children expected of a married woman.

There is the note of restoration, new life and resulting joy. It is the language of life, revival and of abundant spiritual growth. God does give times of awakening, times of refreshing and times of restoration. Some have a pessimistic view of the world and of ourselves as the Church in it, "Things will only get worse!" Often this comes from a gloomy perspective of Scripture and understanding of how things will be when Jesus returns, "…when the Son of Man returns, will He find faith on earth?"[2] Many use this verse as a justification for an unbelieving heart. Jesus was challenging us not to be gloomy and give up, but to believe in him when we intercede. In Isaiah 54:1 is a promise for us to expect the present and coming world-wide harvest into the Kingdom.

The Historical Basis for Expecting a Harvest

There are many periods in the history of the Church where there have been times of barrenness and spiritual life was at a low ebb. God then stepped in with outpourings of His Holy Spirit in local, national and even regional revivals.

The first and most remarkable was at the first post-resurrection Pentecost. It was there that the barren Old Testament Church among the Jews was empowered by the Holy Spirit to spread across the known world of that time. This prophecy in Isaiah 54:1 had special meaning for that time and, no doubt, Jesus expounded on this in His resurrection ministry. It was likely to have been in His thinking when He promised that the gates of Hades would not prevail against the Church.[3] However this was certainly not the last, and all through the history of the Church there have been such revivals. These have been meticulously researched and described in Edwin Orr's volumes on the history of revivals.[4] The frequency and impact of these awakenings and revivals has markedly increased in the past two hundred years. Those living in the West long for such again and wonder whether this could ever happen, but maybe do not fully realize what amazing awakenings and revivals have burst out on other continents in recent years.

Many examples of national revivals could be given. Britain has had such century after century—through Wycliffe in the fifteenth century, the Reformation in the sixteenth, the Puritans in the seventeenth, the Wesley-Whitefield revival in the eighteenth and the Evangelical Revival of the mid-nineteenth. Lutheran Finland, Norway and Sweden have had a series of revivals over the past 200 years. The effects of the Welsh and Pentecostal Revivals at the beginning of this century continue to reverberate around the world to this day. Millions in the last 50 years have been revived and sinners added to the Kingdom through such outpourings. A few of the more significant ones were in East Africa in the 1940s and '50s,[5] Korea in the midst of the terrible Korean War[6] in the 1950s and '60s, China (1945-48) and Cambodia (1975)[7] in the lull before the storm of Communism decimated the Church in those lands, Indonesia—especially West Timor[8]—and also many other parts of that largely Muslim nation. Nagaland and Mizoram, remote states in north east India, became the most evangelical states in the world in recent years in which the majority of the population was radically changed by the reviving work of the Holy Spirit. In the 1970s and '80s came the massive turnings to God in China and in Latin America which decisively shifted the centre of gravity of Evangelical Christianity away from the lands that were for centuries its birthplace, haven and prison.

There is much cause for rejoicing. The growth of the Church today is on a scale that is unique in the history of the world. The outpouring of the Spirit at the birth of the Church was world wide in its scope and outworkings, but the numbers involved were not on the scale we have seen in increasing numbers over the past 200 years. We can expect this to happen, for what else would give the convincing proof of the victory of Jesus other than a world wide demonstration of that victory? I would go further; I believe we are now in the time of the final ingathering before the end. During the last 10 years, more were added to the evangelical community, through new-birth conversions and birth into evangelical families, than the population on earth in that Pentecost year.

We are far closer to achieving the basic goals set out for us by the Lord Jesus in His resurrection ministry than many have given credit. We still have an enormous task, but it is a task that can be accomplished. Jesus gave us an achievable goal, and I want to demonstrate that this is so in this section. Jesus told us plainly that the world will become a most unpleasant place and evil will multiply and even apparently triumph,[9] but at the same time His people will multiply and spread across the face of the earth. Everything is heading towards a climax—both evil and good. It will be high tide at midnight. The darkness will increase at that midnight hour, but that will also be the high tide of the Church as she is readied for the Bridegroom.

We have much about which we can rejoice. I delight in sharing with believers the factual basis for such a statement. Speaking about the Kingdom does not always have to be a gloomy affair; it is often one of rejoicing. There are many causes of concern and rightly so, but many preachers dwell too much on the negatives, and this is communicated in their public ministry. I believe that one of the hindrances to vision for mission in past centuries has been a profound pessimism about the world and the future. People respond better to encouragement. They are better able to face the negatives from the strong positive ground of the promised hope of the growth and success of the Kingdom of God. Isaiah does just this, he offers hope of a mighty harvest to the discouraged people of God. This is now my aim. I believe that every preacher and every teacher should be armed with facts of the world wide Kingdom with its challenges and growth and communicate these to their people. This will stimulate vision, intercession and action.

The Spread of the Gospel: Exposure and Response

The diagram below shows three worlds of humankind and their proportions for each century over the last 2,000 years.[10] These worlds are not defined geographically, but rather on the basis of response to the Christian faith.

1. **World C**—all persons who individually are Christians anywhere in the world. This is Christianity in its broadest expression and includes Roman Catholic, Orthodox, Protestant, Anglican, Evangelical and all derived or deviant forms of Christianity. The growth and declines of Christianity over these two millennia as a percentage of the world's population is clearly shown.

2. **World B**—all non-Christians who have heard the gospel, or who live within societies and areas where they were or are likely to hear it during their lifetime. These are evangelized non-Christians.[11] It is a measure of the growing edge of the Kingdom of God which should be much bigger than the visible Church. Only in the early church and in our day has this been true.[12]

3. **World A**—all non-Christians who are unevangelized and likely to remain so without a new effort by Christians to bring the gospel to them.

It is possible that in the space of those first 45-50 years nearly 30% of the world's population at that time had been exposed to the Good News. Those early apostles certainly made up for initial lost time. They truly were turning the world upside down. By the end of the fifth century this had risen to about 40%. Despite the slow start we can certainly admire the extraordinary achievements of Apostolic Christianity.

Then followed a millennium of conflict and decline as Christianity increasingly became a European phenomenon. Notice how from 500 to 1800 the non-Christian proportion of the world was increasing, the Christian population was either static or in decline and the proportion of the world's population even being exposed to the gospel in serious decline. Only in our times has the percentage of the world's evangelized population rapidly increased. This graph shows that the Mark 16:15 command of Jesus that the gospel be preached to every person is at last attainable in our own times. Of course this is not the whole Great Commission. Exposure to the gospel is an inadequate first step, but a necessary precursor to the discipling and church planting ministries which we find in Matthew 28:18-19.

The Spread of Christianity

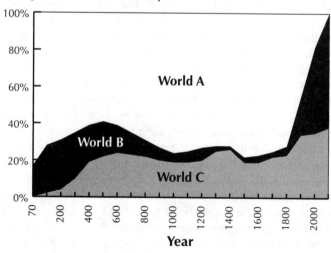

Two Millennia of Evangelizing Peoples

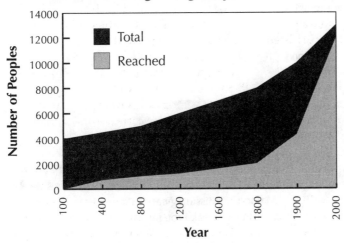

Although many peoples are still unreached, the number is only a fraction of that of 100 years ago. The goal is attainable in our generation—if we mobilize prayer and effort and work together to disciple the remaining least reached peoples.

The diagram on the next page gives a breakdown of the 13,000 peoples in the world by the penetration of the gospel. These are approximated to the nearest 500 for simplicity.

Following Gospel Progress Among the Peoples

We can also follow the progress of discipling the peoples of the world. This is so fundamental to the whole vision for fulfilling the Great Commission that this will be given in some detail. First, the diagram above gives a picture of the progress over the 2,000-year history of the preaching of the gospel.

The two lines in the diagram show first the estimated number of peoples over these two millennia. We have listed in Genesis 11 the 70 peoples that were recorded after the Babel fiasco. No one knows how many ethno-linguistic peoples there were at the time of Christ—this is a reasonable estimate. The number of peoples has considerably increased over the last two centuries for two main reasons, the numerical increase of nation-states dividing peoples into multiple components and the migration of ethnic communities from continent to continent. We reckon that there are now nearly 13,000 distinct ethno-linguistic peoples in the countries of the world.[13]

We can be more sure about the number of peoples that were evangelized at different periods in subsequent history. It is interesting to see how few of the world's peoples had been reached by 1800. The number of peoples reached had considerably increased by 1900, but even then more than half the peoples of the world were still completely unreached. The dramatic change has been in the latter part of this century.

This simplified representation of the state of discipling of the world's peoples gives a measure of the progress. Briefly, here is the meaning of these four columns:

1. **Column 1:** Nearly half the world's peoples today have a majority of their population that would claim to be Christian. This would include all Protestant, Catholic, Orthodox, indigenous and fringe sectarian groups. This is what an individual would perceive his or her religious identity to be, whatever our value judgments as to the validity of that claim. This is the basis of all the statistics used in the *World Christian Encyclopedia*, Barrett's annual Statistics Table on World Mission and in *Operation World*."[14] These are cultures that have been permeated with the gospel and Christian values—even if later generations only retain a notional concept of being a Christian.[15]

2. **Column 2:** Missiological breakthrough is the term coined by Ralph Winter[16] to define that point in the evangelization of a people when the impact of the gospel becomes so significant that there is both a "critical mass" of indigenous believers and where Christianity has become a viable component of the indigenous culture. The 3,000 or so peoples in this category would also include peoples such as the Koreans among whom enormous church growth has taken place this cen-

tury, yet Korean Christians are still under one third of the total population. The same is true for such peoples as the Singaporean Chinese, the Indian Tamil and the Kenyan Turkana.

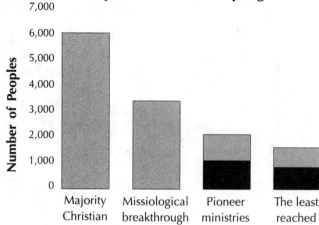

The World's Peoples and Their Discipling

3. **Columns 3 and 4** represent the 3,500 or so peoples in the countries of the world that are still pioneer fields for mission endeavour. The indigenous Church is either non-existent or still too small or culturally marginalized to impact their entire people in this generation without outside help. Of these, probably about 1,200-1,500 peoples have either no indigenous church at all or no residential cross-cultural team of missionaries seeking to reach them.

4. **The darker sections of Columns 3 & 4** represent those peoples listed in the AD2000 Movement Joshua Project List. The criteria for inclusion are: Population over 10,000 and less than 5% Christian or 2% Evangelical.[17]

Never before have we had so clear a picture of the boundaries of the unfinished task in discipling peoples. We dare not underestimate the tough challenges we face in order to accomplish this task, but at last we can see that the achievement of the task is within our grasp.

The Joshua Project of the AD2000 and Beyond Movement is the largest strategic mobilization of Christians in history to disciple the peoples of the world. Support and enthusiasm has come from across a wide spectrum of denominations, agencies and countries. In the latter, the involvement has been predominantly non-Western, but, sadly, with Christians in European countries showing the lowest level of interest. The vision is for a church for every people by the year 2000. That vision may not actually be fully attained by that year, but we are already seeing a significantly increased level of commitment for church planting ministries to the specific peoples without churches. My desire is that by the end of the year 2000 we should have committed teams of cross-cultural workers to every significant ethno-linguistic people in the world. The actual conversion of individuals and the timing of the breakthrough for the gospel is the work of the Holy Spirit in whom we must trust, and not in our grandiose planning or clever techniques.

Study Questions

1. Explain the difference between tracing the progress of the Gospel throughout the total population of earth and following the progress of the Gospel among the earth's people groups. Which assessment is most encouraging to you?

2. What grounds does Johnstone offer here to expect that the entire task of world evangelization can be completed?

Endnotes

1. Denney 1972:360.
2. Luke 18:8.

3. Matthew 16:18-19.
4. Orr 1973. This book recounts the way God used William Carey and others to start the Union of Prayer which began the Second Great Awakening in Britain and then in the USA, providing the impetus for the new mission movement.
5. Roy Hession in his book, *The Calvary Road*, spread the message of that revival round the world. The revival began in the land of Rwanda in the 1930s and spread to much of East and Central Africa. It is tragic how the land of revival of two generation ago became that of ethnic hatred and genocide in the 1990s.
6. Campbell 1957. *The Christ of the Korean Heart*. London, England: Christian Literature Crusade.
7. Burke *Anointed for Burial.*
8. Koch, Kurt. 1970.
9. Matthew 24
10. For these definitions and statistics I am indebted to David Barrett (Barrett 1990:25 et seq.).
11. Barrett 1987b for clear definitions which demonstrate that evangelism and conversion are not the same in biblical teaching, though in many modern books the two are equated.
12. I do not want to imply that mission work is only valid in World A. This is not true. There are many millions in World B and C who have need to hear and understand the whole gospel, and have not had that opportunity. However the individuals in Worlds B and C have the probability of hearing the gospel with existing outreach.
13. The probability is that in the next century the number of spoken languages is likely to go down rapidly as smaller languages die out. Some have said that we may lose 3,000 languages and their associated cultures. The rapid urbanization of the world and the use of mass media are two major contributory factors.
14. Barrett 1998, Johnstone 1993, The January Issue of the *International Bulletin of Missionary Research* over the years 1985 onwards.
15. Brierley 1996. Peter Brierley of the Christian Research association has developed this term **notional Christian** in the various Christian Handbooks to categorize the large numbers of individuals in long-Christianized countries who retain no meaningful link with organized Christianity, nor have any clear understanding of the content of the gospel, but who would still think of themselves as "Christian."
16. Winter, in many issues of *Mission Frontiers Magazine*, USCWM.
17. The Joshua Project list was compiled by researchers using various listings of the world's peoples from 1994 onwards. The 1,700 ethnolinguistic peoples listed are for use in mobilizing prayer and outreach to them from the global Church. The smaller peoples and those with marginally more Christians and ministry to them are not forgotten; these are more the concern of national, regional and more specialized agency/church partnerships for groups of similar peoples.

The Two Structures of God's Redemptive Mission

Ralph D. Winter

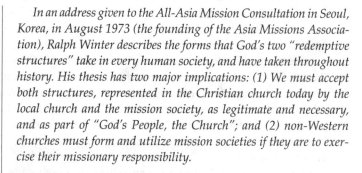

In an address given to the All-Asia Mission Consultation in Seoul, Korea, in August 1973 (the founding of the Asia Missions Association), Ralph Winter describes the forms that God's two "redemptive structures" take in every human society, and have taken throughout history. His thesis has two major implications: (1) We must accept both structures, represented in the Christian church today by the local church and the mission society, as legitimate and necessary, and as part of "God's People, the Church"; and (2) non-Western churches must form and utilize mission societies if they are to exercise their missionary responsibility.

I t is the thesis of this article that whether Christianity takes on Western or Asian form, there will still be two basic kinds of structures that will make up the movement. Most of the emphasis will be placed on pointing out the existence of these two structures as they have continuously appeared across the centuries. This will serve to define, illustrate and compare their nature and importance. The writer will also endeavor to explain why he believes our efforts today in any part of the world will be most effective only if both of these two structures are fully and properly involved and supportive of each other.

Redemptive Structures in New Testament Times

First of all, let us recognize the structure so fondly called "the New Testament Church" as basically a Christian synagogue.[1] Paul's missionary work consisted primarily of going to synagogues scattered across the Roman Empire, beginning in Asia Minor, and making clear to the Jewish and Gentile believers in those synagogues that the Messiah had come in Jesus Christ, the Son of God; that in Christ a final authority even greater than Moses existed; and that this made more understandable than ever the welcoming of the Gentiles without forcing upon them any literal cultural adaptation to the ritual provisions of the Mosaic Law. An outward novelty of Paul's work was the development eventually of wholly new synagogues that were not only Christian but Greek.

Very few Christians, casually reading the New Testament (and with only the New Testament available to them), would surmise the degree to which there had been Jewish evangelists who went before Paul all over the Roman Empire—a movement that began 100 years before Christ. Some of these were the people whom Jesus himself described as "travers-

After serving ten years as a missionary among Mayan Indians in the highlands of Guatemala, Ralph D. Winter was called to be a Professor of Missions at the School of World Mission at Fuller Theological Seminary. Ten years later he and his wife, Roberta, founded a mission society called the Frontier Mission Fellowship (FMF) in Pasadena, California. This in turn spawned the U.S. Center for World Mission and the William Carey International University, both of which serve other missions working at the frontiers of mission. He is the General Director of the Frontier Mission Fellowship. See expanded biographical sketch at the end of the book.

ing land and sea to make a single proselyte." Saul followed their path; Paul built on their efforts and went beyond them with the new gospel he preached, which allowed the Greeks to remain Greeks and not be circumcised and culturally assimilated into the Jewish way of life. Paul had a vast foundation on which to build: Peter declared "Moses is preached in every city (of the Roman Empire)" (Acts 15:21).

Yet not only did Paul apparently go to every existing synagogue of Asia,[2] after which he declared, "…all Asia has heard the gospel," but, when occasion demanded, he established brand new synagogue-type fellowships of believers as the basic unit of his missionary activity. The first structure in the New Testament scene is thus what is often called the *New Testament Church*. It was essentially built along Jewish synagogue lines,[3] embracing the community of the faithful in any given place. The defining characteristic of this structure is that it included old and young, male and female. Note, too, that Paul was willing to build such fellowships out of former Jews as well as non-Jewish Greeks.

There is a second, quite different structure in the New Testament context. While we know very little about the structure of the evangelistic outreach within which pre-Pauline Jewish proselytizers worked, we do know, as already mentioned, that they operated all over the Roman Empire. It would be surprising if Paul didn't follow somewhat the same procedures. And we know a great deal more about the way Paul operated. He was, true enough, sent out by the church in Antioch. But once away from Antioch he seemed very much on his own. The little team he formed was economically self-sufficient when occasion demanded. It was also dependent, from time-to-time, not alone upon the Antioch church, but upon other churches that had risen as a result of evangelistic labors. Paul's team may certainly be considered a structure. While its design and

form is not made concrete for us on the basis of remaining documents, neither, of course, is the structure of a New Testament congregation defined concretely for us in the pages of the New Testament. In both cases, the absence of any such definition implies the pre-existence of a commonly understood pattern of relationship, whether in the case of the congregational structure or the missionary band structure which Paul employed earlier as Saul the Pharisee, and later, at the time the Antioch congregation in Acts 13:2 released Paul and Barnabas for missionary work.

Thus, on the one hand, the structure we call the *New Testament church* is a prototype of all subsequent Christian fellowships where old and young, male and female are gathered together as normal biological families in aggregate. On the other hand, Paul's *missionary band* can be considered a prototype of all subsequent missionary endeavors organized out of committed, experienced workers who affiliated themselves as a second decision beyond membership in the first structure.

Note well the *additional* commitment. Note also that the structure that resulted was something definitely more than the extended outreach of the Antioch church. No matter what we think the structure was, we know that it was not simply the Antioch church operating at a distance from its home base. It was something else, something different. We will consider the missionary band the second of the two redemptive structures in New Testament times.

In conclusion, it is very important to note that neither of these two structures was, as it were, "let down from heaven" in a special way. It may be shocking at first to think that God made use of either a *Jewish* synagogue pattern or a *Jewish* evangelistic pattern. But this must not be more surprising than the fact that God employed the use of the pagan Greek language, the Holy Spirit guiding the biblical writers to lay hold of such terms as *kurios* (originally a pagan term), and pound them

> The harmony between the modality and the sodality achieved by the Roman Church is perhaps the most significant characteristic of this phase of the world Christian movement

into shape to carry the Christian revelation. The New Testament refers to a synagogue dedicated to Satan, but this did not mean that Christians, to avoid such a pattern, could not fellowship together in the synagogue pattern. These considerations prepare us for what comes next in the history of the expansion of the gospel, because we see other patterns chosen by Christians at a later date whose origins are just as clearly "borrowed patterns" as were those in the New Testament period.

In fact, the profound missiological implication of all this is that the New Testament is trying to show us *how to borrow effective patterns;* it is trying to free all future missionaries from the need to follow the precise *forms* of the Jewish synagogue and Jewish missionary band, and yet to allow them to choose comparable indigenous structures in the countless new situations across history and around the world—structures which will correspond faithfully to the *function* of patterns Paul employed, if not their *form!* It is no wonder that a considerable body of literature in the field of missiology today underlies the fact that world Christianity has generally employed the various existing languages and cultures of the world-human community—more so than any other religion—and in so doing, has cast into a shadow all efforts to canonize as universal any kind of mechanically formal extension of the New Testament church— which is "the people of God" however those individuals are organized. As Kraft has said earlier, we seek *dynamic equivalence*, not formal replication.[4]

The Early Development of Christian Structures within Roman Culture

We have seen how the Christian movement built itself upon two different kinds of structures that had pre-existed in the Jewish cultural tradition. It is now our task to see if the *functional* equivalents of these same two structures were to appear in later Christian cultural traditions as the gospel invaded that larger world.

Of course, the original synagogue pattern persisted as a Christian structure for some time. Rivalry between Christians and Jews, however, tended to defeat this as a Christian

pattern, and in some cases to force it out of existence, especially where it was possible for Jewish congregations of the dispersion to arouse public persecution of the apparently deviant Christian synagogues. Unlike the Jews, Christians had no official license for their alternative to the Roman Imperial cult.[5] Thus, whereas each synagogue was considerably independent of the others, the Christian pattern was soon assimilated to the Roman context, and bishops became invested with authority over more than one congregation with a territorial jurisdiction not altogether different from the pattern of Roman civil government. This tendency is well confirmed by the time the official recognition of Christianity had its full impact: the very Latin word for Roman magisterial territories was appropriated—the *diocese*—within which parishes are to be found on the local level.

In any case, while the more "congregational" pattern of the independent synagogue became pervasively replaced by a "connectional" Roman pattern the new Christian parish church still preserved the basic constituency of the synagogue, namely, the combination of old and young, male and female—that is, a biologically perpetuating organism.

Meanwhile, the monastic tradition in various early forms developed as a second structure. This new, widely proliferating structure undoubtedly had no connection at all with the missionary band in which Paul was involved. Indeed, it more substantially drew from Roman military structure than from any other single source. Pachomius, a former military man, gained 3,000 followers and attracted the attention of people like Basil of Caesarea, and then through Basil, John Cassian, who labored in southern Gaul at a later date.[6] These men thus carried forward a disciplined structure, borrowed primarily from the military, which allowed nominal Christians to make a second-level choice—an additional specific commitment.

Perhaps it would be well to pause here for a moment. Any reference to the monasteries gives Protestants culture shock. The Protestant Reformation fought desperately against certain degraded conditions at the very end of the 1000-year Medieval period. We have no desire to deny the fact that conditions in monasteries were not always ideal; what the average Protestant knows about monasteries may be correct for certain situations; but the popular Protestant stereotype surely cannot describe correctly all that happened during the 1000 years! During those centuries there were many different eras and epochs and a wide variety of monastic movements, radically different from each other, as we shall see in a minute; and any generalization about so vast a phenomenon is bound to be simply an unreliable and no doubt prejudiced caricature.

Let me give just one example of how far wrong our Protestant stereotypes can be. We often hear that the monks "fled the world." Compare that idea with this description by a Baptist missionary scholar:

> The Benedictine rule and the many derived from it probably helped to give dignity to labor, including manual labor in the fields. This was in striking contrast with the aristocratic conviction of the servile status of manual work which prevailed in much of ancient society and which was also the attitude of the warriors and non-monastic ecclesiastics who constituted the upper middle classes of the Middle Ages.... To the monasteries...was obviously due much clearing of land and improvement in methods of agriculture. In the midst of barbarism, the monasteries were centres of orderly and settled life and monks were assigned the duty of road-building and road repair. Until the rise of the towns in the eleventh century, they were pioneers in industry and commerce. The shops of the monasteries preserved the industries of Roman times.... The earliest use of marl in improving the soil is attributed to them. The great French monastic orders led in the agricultural colonization of Western Europe. Especially did the Cistercians make their houses centres of agriculture and contribute to improvements in that occupation. With their lay brothers and their hired laborers, they became great landed proprietors. In Hungary and on the German frontier the Cistercians were particularly important in reducing the soil to cultivation and in furthering colonization. In Poland, too, the German monasteries set advanced standards in agriculture and introduced artisans and craftsmen.[7]

For all of us who are interested in missions, the shattering of the "monks fled the world"

stereotype is even more dramatically and decisively reinforced by the magnificent record of the Irish *peregrini*, who were Celtic monks who did more to reach out to convert Anglo-Saxons than did Augustine's later mission from the South, and who contributed more to the evangelization of Western Europe, even Central Europe, than any other force.

From its very inception this second kind of structure was highly significant to the growth and development of the Christian movement. Even though Protestants have an inbuilt prejudice against it for various reasons, as we have seen, there is no denying the fact that apart from this structure it would be hard even to imagine the vital continuity of the Christian tradition across the centuries. Protestants are equally dismayed by the other structure—the parish and diocesan structure. It is, in fact, the relative weakness and nominality of the diocesan structure that makes the monastic structure so significant. Men like Jerome and Augustine, for example, are thought of by Protestants not as monks but as great scholars; and people like John Calvin lean very heavily upon writings produced by such monks. But Protestants do not usually give any credit to the specific structure within which Jerome and Augustine and many other monastic scholars worked, a structure without which Protestant labors would have had very little to build on, not even a Bible.

We must now follow these threads into the next period, where we will see the formal emergence of the major monastic structures. It is sufficient at this point merely to note that there are already by the fourth century two very different kinds of structures—the diocese and the monastery—both of them significant in the transmission and expansion of Christianity. They are each patterns borrowed from the cultural context of their time, just as were the earlier Christian synagogue and missionary band.

It is even more important for our purpose here to note that while these two structures are *formally* different from—and historically unrelated to—the two in New Testament times, they are nevertheless *functionally* the same. In order to speak conveniently about the continuing similarities in function, let us now call the synagogue and diocese *modalities*, and the missionary band and monastery *sodalities*. Elsewhere I have developed these terms in detail, but briefly, a modality is a structured fellowship in which there is no distinction of sex or age, while a sodality is a structured fellowship in which membership involves an adult second decision beyond modality membership, and is limited by either age or sex or marital status. In this use of these terms, both the *denomination* and the *local congregation* are modalities, while a mission agency or a local men's club are sodalities.[8] A secular parallel would be that of a town (modality) compared to a private business (a sodality)—perhaps a chain of stores found in many towns. The sodalities are subject to the authority of the more general structures, usually. They are "regulated" but not "administered" by the modalities. A complete state socialism exists where there are no regulated, decentralized private initiatives. Some denominational traditions, like the Roman and the Anglican, allow for such initiatives. Many Protestant denominations, taking their cue from Luther's rejection of the sodalities of his time, try to govern everything from a denominational office. Some local congregations cannot understand the value or the need for mission structures. Paul was "sent off" not "sent out" by the Antioch congregation. He may have reported back to it but did not take orders from it. His mission band (sodality) had all the autonomy and authority of a "traveling congregation."

In the early period beyond the pages of the Bible, however, there was little relation between modality and sodality, while in Paul's time his missionary band specifically nourished the congregations—a most significant symbiosis. We shall now see how the medieval period essentially recovered the healthy New Testament relationship between modality and sodality.

The Medieval Synthesis of Modality and Sodality

We can say that the Medieval period began when the Roman Empire in the West started to break down. To some extent the diocesan pattern, following as it did the Roman civil-governmental pattern, tended to break down

at the same time. The monastic (or sodality) pattern turned out to be much more durable, and as a result gained greater importance in the early Medieval period than it might have otherwise. The survival of the modality (diocesan Christianity) was further compromised by the fact that the invaders of this early Medieval period generally belonged to a different brand of Christian belief—they were Arians. As a result, in many places there were both "Arian" and "Catholic" Christian churches on opposite corners of a main street—something like today, where we have Methodist and Presbyterian churches across the street from each other.

Again, however, it is not our purpose to downplay the significance of the parish or diocesan form of Christianity, but simply to point out that during this early period of the Medieval epoch the specialized house called the *monastery*, or its equivalent, became ever so much more important in the perpetuation of the Christian movement than was the organized system of parishes, which we often call the church *as if there were no other structure making up the church*.

Perhaps the most outstanding illustration in the early Medieval period of the importance of the relationship between modality and sodality is the collaboration between Gregory the Great and a man later called Augustine of Canterbury. While Gregory, as the bishop of the diocese of Rome, was the head of a modality, both he and Augustine were the products of monastic houses—a fact which reflects the dominance even then of the sodality pattern of Christian structure. In any case, Gregory called upon his friend Augustine to undertake a major mission to England in order to try to plant a diocesan structure there, where Celtic Christianity had been deeply wounded by the invasion of Saxon warriors from the continent.

As strong as Gregory was in his own diocese, he simply had no structure to call upon to reach out in this intended mission other than the sodality, which at this point in history took the form of a *Benedictine* monastery. This is why he ended up asking Augustine and a group of other members of the same monastery to undertake this rather dangerous journey and important mission on his behalf. The purpose of the mission, curiously, was not to extend the Benedictine form of monasticism. The remnant of the Celtic "church" in England was itself a network of sodalities since there were no parish systems in the Celtic area. No, Augustine went to England to establish diocesan Christianity, though he himself was not a diocesan priest. Interestingly enough, the Benedictine "Rule" (way of life) was so attractive that gradually virtually all of the Celtic houses adopted the Benedictine Rule, or *Regula* (in Latin).

This is quite characteristic. During a lengthy period of time, perhaps a thousand years, the building and rebuilding of the modalities was mainly the work of the sodalities. That is to say the monasteries were uniformly the source and the real focal point of new energy and vitality which flowed into the diocesan side of the Christian movement. We think of the momentous Cluny reform, then the Cistercians, then the Friars, and finally the Jesuits—all of them strictly sodalities, but sodalities which contributed massively to the building and the rebuilding of the *Corpus Cristianum*, the network of dioceses, which Protestants often identify as "the" Christian movement.

In failing to exploit the power of the sodality, the Protestants had no mechanism for missions for almost 300 years.

At many points there was rivalry between these two structures, between bishop and abbot, diocese and monastery, modality and sodality, but the great achievement of the Medieval period is the ultimate synthesis, delicately achieved, whereby Catholic orders were able to function along with Catholic parishes and dioceses without the two structures conflicting with each other to the point of a setback to the movement. The harmony between the modality and the sodality achieved by the Roman Church is perhaps the most significant characteristic of this phase of the world Christian movement and continues to be Rome's greatest organizational advantage to this day.

Note, however, that is not our intention to claim that any one organization, whether modality or sodality, was continuously the champion of vitality and vigor throughout the thousands of years of the Medieval epoch. As a matter of fact, there really is no very impressive organizational continuity in the Christian movement, either in the form of modality or sodality. (The list of bishops at Rome is at many points a most shaky construct and unfortunately does not even provide a focus for the entire Christian movement.) On the other hand, it is clear that the sodality, as it was recreated again and again by different leaders, was almost always the structural prime mover, the source of inspiration and renewal which overflowed into the papacy and created the reform movements which blessed diocesan Christianity from time to time. The most significant instance of this is the accession to the papal throne of Hildebrand (Gregory VII), who brought the ideals, commitment and discipline of the monastic movement right into the Vatican itself. In this sense are not then the papacy, the College of Cardinals, the diocese, and the parish structure of the Roman Church in some respects a secondary element, a derivation from the monastic tradition rather than vice versa? In any case it seems appropriate that the priests of the monastic tradition are called *regular priests*, while the priests of the diocese and parish are called *secular priests*. The former are voluntarily bound by a *regula*, while the latter as a group were other than, outside of ("cut off") or somehow less than, the second-decision communities bound by a demanding way of life, a *regula*. Whenever a house or project or parish run by the regular clergy is brought under the domination of the secular clergy, this is a form of the "secularization" of that entity. In the lengthy "Investiture Controversy," the regular clergy finally gained clear authority for at least semi-autonomous operation, and the secularization of the orders was averted.

The same structural danger of *secularization* exists today whenever the special concerns of an elite mission sodality fall under the complete domination (e.g. administration not just regulation) of an ecclesiastical government, since the Christian modalities (congregations)

inevitably represent the much broader and, no doubt, mainly inward concerns of a large body of all kinds of Christians, who, as "first-decision" members, are generally less select. Their democratic majority tends to move away from the high-discipline of the mission structures, and denominational mission budgets tend to get smaller across the decades as the church membership "broadens."

We cannot leave the Medieval period without referring to the many unofficial and often persecuted movements which also mark the era. In all of this, the Bible itself seems always the ultimate prime mover, as we see in the case of Peter Waldo. His work stands as a powerful demonstration of the simple power of a vernacular translation of the Bible where the people were unable to appreciate either Jerome's classical translation or the celebration of the Mass in Latin. A large number of groups referred to as "Anabaptists" are to be found in many parts of Europe. One of the chief characteristics of these renewal movements is that they did not attempt to elicit merely celibate participation, although this was one of their traits on occasion, but often simply developed whole "new communities" of believers and their families, attempting by biological and cultural transmission to preserve a high and enlightened form of Christianity. These groups usually faced such strong opposition and grave limitations that it would be very unfair to judge their virility by their progress. It is important to note, however, that the average Mennonite or Salvation Army community, where whole families are members, typified the desire for a "pure" church, or what is often called a "believers" church, and constitutes a most significant experiment in Christian structure. Such a structure stands, in a certain sense, midway between a modality and a sodality, since it has the constituency of the modality (involving full families) and yet, in its earlier years, may have the vitality and selectivity of a sodality. We will return to this phenomenon in the next section.

We have space here only to point out that in terms of the durability and quality of the Christian faith, the 1000-year Medieval period is virtually impossible to account for apart from the role of the sodalities. What

happened in the city of Rome is merely the tip of the iceberg at best, and represents a rather superficial and political level. It is quite a contrast to the foundational well-springs of Biblical study and radical obedience represented by the various sodalities of this momentous millennium, which almost always arose somewhere else, and were often opposed by the Roman hierarchy.

The Protestant Recovery of the Sodality

The Protestant movement started out by attempting to do without any kind of sodality structure. Martin Luther had been discontented with the apparent polarization between the vitality he eventually discovered in his own order and the very nominal parish life of his time. Being dissatisfied with this contrast, he abandoned the sodality (in which, nevertheless, he was introduced to the Bible, to the Pauline epistles and to teaching on "justification by faith,") and took advantage of the political forces of his time to launch a full-scale renewal movement on the general level of church life. At first, he even tried to do without the characteristically Roman diocesan structure, but eventually the Lutheran movement produced a Lutheran diocesan structure which to a considerable extent represented the readoption of the Roman diocesan tradition. But the Lutheran movement did not in a comparable sense readopt the sodalities, the Catholic orders, that had been so prominent in the Roman tradition.

This omission, in my evaluation, represents the greatest error of the Reformation and the greatest weakness of the resulting Protestant tradition. Had it not been for the so-called Pietist movement, the Protestants would have been totally devoid of any organized renewing structures within their tradition. The Pietist tradition, in every new emergence of its force, was very definitely a sodality, inasmuch as it was a case of adults meeting together and committing themselves to new beginnings and higher goals as Christians without conflicting with the stated meetings of the existing church. This phenomenon of sodality nourishing modality is prominent in the case of the early work of John Wesley. He absolutely prohibited any abandonment of the parish churches. A contemporary example is the widely influential so-called *East African Revival*, which has now involved a million people but has very carefully avoided any clash with the functioning of local churches. The churches that have not fought against this movement have been greatly blessed by it.

However, the Pietist movement, along with the Anabaptist new communities, eventually dropped back to the level of biological growth; it reverted to the ordinary pattern of congregational life. It reverted from the level of the sodality to the level of the modality, and in most cases, rather soon became ineffective either as a mission structure or as a renewing force.

What interests us most is the fact that in failing to exploit the power of the sodality, the Protestants had no mechanism for missions for almost three hundred years, until William Carey's famous book, *An Enquiry*, proposed "the use of means for the conversion of the heathen." His key word *means* refers specifically to the need for a sodality, for the organized but non-ecclesiastical initiative of the warmhearted. Thus, the resulting Baptist Missionary Society is one of the most significant organizational developments in the Protestant tradition. Although not the earliest such society, reinforced as it was by the later stages of the powerful "Evangelical Awakening" and by the printing of Carey's book, it set off a rush to the use of this kind of "means" for the conversion of the heathen, and we find in the next few years a number of societies forming along similar lines—12 societies in 32 years.[9] Once this method of operation was clearly understood by the Protestants, 300 years of latent energies burst forth in what became, in Latourette's phrase, "The Great Century." By helping to tap the immense spiritual energies of the Reformation, Carey's book has probably contributed more to global mission than any other book in history other than the Bible itself!

The 19th Century is thus the first century in which Protestants were actively engaged in missions. For reasons which we have not space here to explain, it was also the century of the lowest ebb of Catholic mission energy. Amazingly, in this one century Protestants,

building on the unprecedented world expansion of the West, caught up with 18 centuries of earlier mission efforts. There is simply no question that what was done in this century moved the Protestant stream from a self-contained, impotent European backwater into a world force in Christianity. Looking back from where we stand today, of course, it is hard to believe how recently the Protestant movement has become prominent.

Organizationally, however, the vehicle that allowed the Protestant movement to become vital was the structural development of the sodality, which harvested the vital "voluntarism" latent in Protestantism, and surfaced in new mission agencies of all kinds, both at home and overseas. Wave after wave of evangelical initiatives transformed the entire map of Christianity, especially in the United States, but also in England, in Scandinavia and on the Continent. By 1840, the phenomenon of mission sodalities was so prominent in the United States that the phrase the "Evangelical Empire" and other equivalent phrases were used to refer to it, and now began a trickle of ecclesiastical opposition to this bright new emergence of the second structure. This brings us to our next point.

The Contemporary Misunderstanding of the Mission Sodality

Almost all mission efforts in the 19th Century, whether sponsored by interdenominational or denominational boards, were substantially the work of initiatives independent of the related ecclesiastical structures. Toward the latter half of the 19th Century, there seemed increasingly to be two separate structural traditions.

On the one hand, there were men like Henry Venn and Rufus Anderson, who were the strategic thinkers at the helm of older societies—the Church Missionary Society (CMS) in England and American Board of Commissioners for Foreign Missions (ABCFM), respectively. These men championed the semi-autonomous mission sodality, and they voiced an attitude which was not at first contradicted by any significant part of the leaders of the ecclesiastical structures. On the other hand, there was the centralizing perspective of denominational leaders, principally the Presbyterians, which gained ground almost without reversal throughout the latter two-thirds of the 19th Century, so that by the early part of the 20th Century the once-independent structures which had been merely *related* to the denominations gradually became *dominated* by the churches, that is *administered*, not merely *regulated*. Partially as a result, toward the end of the 19th Century, there was a new burst of totally separate mission sodalities called the *Faith Missions*, with Hudson Taylor's China Inland Mission (CIM) taking the lead. It is not widely recognized that this pattern was mainly a recrudescence of the pattern established earlier in the century, prior to the trend toward denominational boards.

though centralized church control of mission efforts is the only proper pattern.

As a result, by the Second World War, a very nearly complete transmutation had taken place in the case of almost all mission efforts related to denominational structures. That is, almost all older denominational boards, though once semi-autonomous or very nearly independent, had by this time become part of unified budget provisions. At the same time, and partially as a result, a whole host of new independent mission structures burst forth again, especially after the Second World War. As in the case of the earlier emergence of the Faith Missions, these tended to pay little attention to denominational leaders and their aspirations for church-centered mission. The Anglican church with its CMS, USPG, etc., displays the Medieval synthesis, and so, almost unconsciously, does the American CBA with its associated

> Among Protestants, there continues to be deep confusion about the legitimacy and proper relationship of the two structures that have manifested themselves throughout the history of the Christian movement.

All of these changes took place very gradually. Attitudes at any point are hard to pin down, but it does seem clear that Protestants were always a bit unsure about the legitimacy of the sodality. The Anabaptist tradition consistently emphasized the concept of a pure community of believers and thus was uninterested in a voluntarism involving only part of the believing community. The same is true of Alexander Campbell's "Restoration" tradition and the Plymouth Brethren. The more recent sprinkling of independent "Charismatic Centers," with all their exuberance locally, tend to send out their own missionaries, and have not learned the lesson of the Pentecostal groups before them who employ mission agencies with great effect.

U.S. denominations, lacking tax support as on the Continent, have been generally a more selective and vital fellowship than the European state churches, and, at least in their youthful exuberance, have felt quite capable as denominations of providing all of the necessary initiative for overseas mission. It is for this latter reason that many new denominations of the U.S. have tended to act as

CBFMS (now CBI), CBHMS (now MTTA) structures. Thus, to this day, among Protestants, there continues to be deep confusion about the legitimacy and proper relationship of the two structures that have manifested themselves throughout the history of the Christian movement.

To make matters worse, Protestant blindness about the need for mission sodalities has had a very tragic influence on mission fields. Protestant missions, being modality-minded, have tended to assume that merely modalities, e.g., churches, need to be established. In most cases where mission work is being pursued by essentially semi-autonomous mission sodalities, it is the planting of modalities, not sodalities, that is the only goal. Mission agencies (even those completely independent from denominations back home) have tended in their mission work to set up churches and not to plant, in addition, mission sodalities in the so-called mission lands.[10] The marvelous "Third World Mission" movement has sprung up from these mission field churches, but with embarrassingly little encouragement from the Western mission societies, as sad and surprising as that may seem.

It is astonishing that most Protestant missionaries, working with (mission) structures that did not exist in the Protestant tradition for hundreds of years, and without whose existence there would have been no mission initiative, have nevertheless been blind to the significance of the very structure within which they have worked. In this blindness they have merely planted churches and have not effectively concerned themselves to make sure that the kind of mission structure within which they operate also be set up on the field. Many of the mission agencies founded after World War II, out of extreme deference to existing church movements already established in foreign lands, have not even tried to set up *churches*, and have worked for many years merely as auxiliary agencies in various service capacities helping the churches that were already there.

The question we must ask is how long it will be before the younger churches of the so-called mission territories of the non-Western world come to that epochal conclusion (to which the Protestant movement in Europe only tardily came), namely, that there need to be sodality structures, such as William Carey's "use of means," in order for church people to reach out in vital initiatives in mission, especially cross-cultural mission. There are already some hopeful signs that this tragic delay will not continue. We see, for example, the outstanding work of the Melanesian Brotherhood in the Solomon Islands.

Conclusion

This article has been in no sense an attempt to decry or to criticize the organized church. It has assumed both the necessity and the importance of the parish structure, the diocesan structure, the denominational structure, the ecclesiastical structure. The modality structure in the view of this article is a significant and absolutely essential structure. All that is attempted here is to explore some of the historical patterns which make clear that God, through His Holy Spirit, has clearly and consistently used a structure other than (and sometimes instead of) the modality structure. It is our attempt here to help church leaders and others to understand the legitimacy of *both* structures, and the necessity for both structures not only to exist but to work together harmoniously for the fulfillment of the Great Commission and for the fulfillment of all that God desires for our time.

End Notes

1. One can hardly conceive of more providentially supplied means for the Christian mission to reach the Gentile community. Wherever the community of Christ went, it found at hand the tools needed to reach the nations: a people living under covenant promise and a responsible election, and the Scriptures, God's revelation to all men. The open synagogue was the place where all these things converged. In the synagogue, the Christians were offered an inviting door of access to every Jewish community. It was in the synagogue that the first Gentile converts declared their faith in Jesus. Richard F. DeRidder, *The Dispersion of the People of God* (Netherlands: J.H. Kok, N.V. Kampen, 1971), p. 87.

2. In Paul's day Asia meant what we today call Asia Minor, or present-day Turkey. In those days no one dreamed how far the term would later be extended.

3. That Christians in Jerusalem organized themselves for worship on the synagogue pattern is evident from the appointment of elders and the adoption of the service of prayer. The provision of a daily dole for widows and the needy reflected the current synagogue practice (Acts 2:42, 6:1). It is possible that the epistle of James reflected the prevailing Jerusalem situation: in James 2:2 reference is made to a wealthy man coming "*into your assembly*." The term translated "assembly'"is literally "synagogue," not the more usual word "church." Glenn W. Barker, William L. Lane and J. Ramsey Michaels, *The New Testament Speaks* (New York: Harper and Row Co., 1969), pp. 126-27.

4. "Dynamic Equivalence Churches," *Missiology: An International Review* , 1, no. 1 (1973), p. 39ff.

5. Christians, it said, resorted to formation of "burial clubs," which were legal, as one vehicle of fellowship and worship.

6. Latourette, Kenneth Scott, *A History of Christianity* (New York: Harper & Brothers, 1953), pp. 181, 221-34.

7. Latourette, Kenneth Scott, *A History of the Expansion of Christianity* , vol. 2, *The Thousand Years of Uncertainty* (New York: Harper & Brothers, 1938), pp. 379-80.

8. Winter, Ralph D., "The Warp and the Woof of the Christian Movement," in his and R. Pierce Beaver's, *The Warp and Woof: Organizing for Christian Mission* (South Pasadena, CA.: William Carey Library, 1970), pp. 52-62.

9. The London Missionary Society (LMS) and the Netherlands Missionary Society (NMS) in 1795, the Church Missionary Society (CMS) in 1799, the CFBS in 1804, the American Board of Commissioners for Foreign Mission (ABCFM) in 1810, the American Baptist Missionary Board (ABMB) in 1814, the Glasgow Missionary Society (GMS) in 1815, the Danish Missionary Society (DMS) in 1821, the FEM in 1822, and the Berlin Mission (BM)in 1824.

10. Winter, Ralph D., "The Planting of Younger Missions," in *Church/Mission Tensions Today*, ed. by C. Peter Wagner (Chicago: Moody Press, 1972).

Study Questions

1. Define the terms "modality" and "sodality," and give present-day and historic examples of each.

2. Do you agree with Winter's thesis that sodality structures within the church are both legitimate and necessary? What practical significance does your answer suggest?

3. What does Winter claim was "the greatest error of the Reformation and the greatest weakness of the resulting Protestant tradition"?

Missionary Societies and the Fortunate Subversion of the Church

Andrew F. Walls

Part One

Andrew F. Walls served as a missionary in Sierra Leone and Nigeria. He taught for many years in the University of Aberdeen, Scotland, before becoming Founding Director of the Centre for the Study of Christianity in the Non-Western World at the University of Edinburgh. Retired from the directorship, he now divides the year between Edinburgh Centre, Princeton Theological Seminary (where he is Guest Professor of Ecumenics and Mission) and the Akrofi-Christaller Memorial Centre in Akropong, Ghana.

This first appeared in *The Evangelical Quarterly* (No. 2, 1988): 141-55.

Taken from *The Missionary Movement in Christian History*, 1996. Used by permission of Orbis Books, Maryknoll, New York 10545.

It is surprising how little attention the voluntary society has attracted in studies of the 19th-century Church, considering the immense impact on Western Christianity and the transformation of world Christianity which (through its special form in the missionary society) it helped to effect. The origins of the modern voluntary society lie in the last years of the 17th century. It was put to new uses in the 18th century and in the 19th century developed new ways of influencing, supplementing, and bypassing the life of Church and State alike. Let the American missionary statesman Rufus Anderson describe its progress. Writing in 1837 on "The Time for the World's Conversion Come,"[1] he lists the signs of the times that seem to him to indicate that the time is at hand when the prophecies will be fulfilled and the earth will be filled with the knowledge of God as the waters cover the sea.[2] Some of these signs have to do with technological progress; never before had the logistics of access to the whole world been so easy. "It was not until the present century that the evangelical churches of Christendom were ever really organized with a view to the conversion of the world."[3] Anderson identifies the characteristically Protestant form of organization for this purpose as the voluntary association:

> …what we see in Missionary, Bible, Tract and other kindred societies, not restricted to ecclesiastics, nor to any one profession, but combining all classes, embracing the masses of the people; and all free, open, and responsible…. It is the *contributors of the funds,* who are the real association… the individuals, churches, congregations, who freely act together, *through such agencies* for an object of common interest…. This Protestant form of association—free, open, responsible, embracing all classes, both sexes, all ages, the masses of the people—is peculiar to modern times, and almost to our age.[4]

Anderson here recognizes several important features of the voluntary association: its instrumental character, its relatively recent origin, and its special structure. It differed from all previous structures in that it was open in its membership, that lay people were as much involved as ministers, and that its organization was rooted in a mass membership, who felt responsibility for it and contributed generously to its support. Like the New England Congregationalist he was, he states that such associations could only arise in countries which had an open, responsible form of government, where Protestantism had prepared the way for civil liberty; and that missionary facilities were the beneficiaries of vastly improved land communications and of vastly increased international seaborne commerce. He is right, of course, that a voluntary society could hardly have flourished in contemporary Spain or Naples; and he gives us an early hint that the missionary society as we know it arose from seizing the opportunities offered by a particular phase of Western political, economic, and social development.

Let us return to the instrumental nature of the missionary society. As Anderson puts it, in a voluntary association, individuals, churches, and congregations freely act together for an object of common interest. It is essentially a pragmatic approach, the design of an instrument for a specific purpose. The first of the modern religious societies arose in sober High Church congregations in London at the end of the 17th century. They arose in response to the preaching of men like the German-born Anthony Homeck who called the congregations to a more devout and holy life. Companies of earnest people met to pray and read the scriptures and visit the poor; others to "reform the manners" of the nation by rebuking profanity and seeking to keep prostitutes off the streets.[5] They were seeking a practical response to serious preaching; answering, as it were, the question "What shall we do?" They encountered a good deal of suspicion and hostility—why were certain people meeting together? Why were the meetings necessary? Were the church services not good enough for them? Against the background of the times any sectional meetings took on the appearance of political disaffection or ecclesiastical discontent. Yet societies for mutual support in the Christian life, or for more effective expression of Christian teaching, grew more and more. They were important in John Wesley's spiritual formation, and essential to the development of his work[6] Meanwhile those (relatively few) Churchmen who thought seriously about evangelization outside the normal sphere of the Church realized that nothing could be done without a new structure: hence the foundation of the Society of Providing Christian Knowledge and the Society for the Propagation of the Gospel. These were not voluntary societies in the true sense of the term; they held Parliamentary charters, and care was taken to link their management with the bishops of the Church of England.[7] As a result, the things they could do well were largely things that the Church had always done: that is, ordain and equip clergy. The Societies did enable these equipped clergy to be sent abroad, mostly to the Americas, where they were applied to the rescue of English colonists from Presbyterianism and vice. The visions of a wider missionary sphere caught by some of the founders were not realized until into the 19th century, and even a bishop of London anxious to see such enterprise started by the societies found himself utterly frustrated.[8]

The Church structures could only do what they had always done; a new concept needed a new instrument. The title of William Carey's seminar tract of 1792 is itself eloquent. He calls it *An Enquiry into the Obligations of Christians to Use Means for the Conversion of the Heathens, In Which the Religious State of the Different Nations of the World, the Success of Former Undertakings and the Practicability of Further Undertakings, Are Considered.*[9]

The crucial words are "the obligation to *use means.*" There is theology in Carey's pamphlet, and there is history, and there is demography; but at the heart of it lies the responsibility of Christians for means to seek the appropriate instrument, to accomplish a task which God has laid upon them.

In the final section of the *Enquiry,* having established the obligation of Christians, traced the history of former attempts to fulfill it, indicated its scope in the then contemporary world, and demolished the arguments for deciding fulfillment to be impossible, Carey seeks to identify the appropriate means. The first of these is united prayer. "The most glorious works of grace that ever took place, have been in answer to prayer, and it is in this way, we have the greatest reason to suppose, that the glorious outpouring of the Spirit which we expect at last, will be bestowed."[10] He is writing against the background of a movement for regular prayer which had been sparked off through the reading of Jonathan Edwards' call for a "concert of prayer" more than forty years earlier.[11] Edwards himself had been led to make his call on learning of the groups of young men meeting for prayer following the revival at Cambuslang in the West of Scotland in 1742.[12] Carey goes on to illustrate his argument of united prayer as an efficient means. Since the monthly prayer meetings had started in Carey's own Midland Baptist circle, "unimportunate, and feeble as they have been, it is to be believed that God has heard, and in a measure answered them." The first evidence is that the churches involved have in general grown. There is no thought of distinction between home and overseas mission here— those praying for "the increase of Christ's Kingdom" will be concerned for both.[13]

Other evidence concerns the clarification of issues that had long perplexed and divided the Church, and from opportunities to preach the gospel in unaccustomed places. Even more opportunities could be expected from "the spread of civil and religious liberty, accompanied by a diminution in the spirit of popery." English Dissenters like Carey were not afraid to pray for the spread of civil and religious liberty, and some of them saw in the aspects of the French Revolution the shaking of the power of antichrist. Indeed, one of the objections raised against missions, in the General Assembly of the Church of Scotland and elsewhere, was their association with such people, who were thought to have revolutionary aims under their cloak of "civil and religious liberty." In like vein, Carey rejoices at the first Parliamentary attempt "to abolish the inhuman slave trade," and hopes it may be persevered in; and at the establishment of the free Christian settlement of Sierra Leone.[14]

What, then, can one see from even a modest attempt to bring groups together for a common purpose in prayer? Revival in the churches, clearer theological understanding, new evangelistic openings, the French Revolution, the assault on the Slave Trade, a Christian outpost in West Africa? These, says Carey, "are not to be reckoned small things." He sees no incongruity in grouping together events in his own circle of Baptist churches and events in the great movements of the time. God works in both, and

> if an holy solicitude had prevailed in all the assemblies of Christians in behalf of their Redeemer's kingdom, we might partially have seen before now, not only an *open door* for the gospel, but *many running to and fro,* and knowledge increased; or a diligent use of those means which providence has put in our power, accompanied with a greater blessing than ordinary from heaven.[15]

Prayer, he goes on, may be the only thing which Christians of all denominations can unreservedly do together; but we must not omit to look for the use of means to obtain what we pray for. Then he takes an analogy from the contemporary commercial world. When a trading company has obtained their charter, the promoters will go to the utmost limits to put the enterprise on a proper footing. They select their stock, ships, and crews with care; they seek every scrap of useful information. They undergo danger at sea, brave unfriendly climates and peoples, take risks and pay for it all in anxiety, because their minds are set on success. Their *interest* is involved; and does not the interest of Christians lie in the extension of Messiah's Kingdom?

And so he comes to his proposal:

> Suppose a company of serious Christians, ministers and private persons, were to form themselves into a society, and make a number of rules respecting the regulation of the plan, and the persons who are to be employed as missionaries, the means of defraying the expense, etc., etc. This society must consist of persons whose hearts are in the work, men of serious religion, and possessing a spirit of perseverance; there must be a determination not to admit any person who is not of this description, or to retain him longer than he answers to it.[16]

From the members of this society, a committee might be appointed to gather information—just like the trading company—collect funds, scrutinize possible missionaries, and equip them for their work. All this sounds so trite today, because we are used to the paraphernalia of committees and councils of reference and subscriptions and donations. So it is hard to remember that the average 18th century Christian was not used to such things at all. Most Christians thought in terms only of a parish church, with its appointed minister or, if English Dissenters or Scots Seceders, in terms of a congregation which called its minister. The "instrumental" society, the voluntary association of Christians banding together to achieve a defined object, was still in its infancy. It is significant that Carey—a man of the provinces and of humble station—takes his analogy from commerce; organizing a society is something like floating a company. He is looking for the appropriate means to accomplish a task which cannot be accomplished through the usual machinery of the Church. We could take the other early missionary societies one by one; whether the Church Missionary Society, formed by evangelical supporters of the established Church of England, or the London Missionary Society, enthusiastically maintained by English Dissenters, or the various enterprises in Scotland. They are all equally pragmatic in their origins. The simple fact was that the church as then organized, whether episcopal, or presbyterian, or congregational, could not effectively operate mission overseas. Christians had accordingly to "use means" to do so.

There never was a *theology* of the voluntary society. The voluntary society is one of God's theological jokes, whereby he makes tender mockery of his people when they take themselves too seriously. The men of high theological and ecclesiastical principle were often the enemies of the missionary movement. When (or rather, if) the elder Ryland barked out at Carey, "Young man, sit down; when God wants to convert the heathens, He'll do it without your help or mine" (one of those stories which is probably not true but which *ought* to be true), he was simply expressing a standard form of Protestant doctrine formulated a century earlier as an apologetic against Roman Catholics. When Roman Catholics pointed to their propagation of the faith in the Americas and in Africa and Asia in the 17th century and said to Protestants, "Where are your missionaries?" there

was an accepted theological answer. It began with the well known Protestant argument that the apostolic office was once and for all. Since therefore, the command "Go ye into all the world…" was addressed by the Lord to the apostles, that commission was fulfilled in the days of the apostles. To take it upon oneself to fulfill it now was presumptuous and carnal; it was taking to oneself the office of the apostle, the very error of the Pope himself. Carey has no difficulty in reducing this argument to absurdity. Where, he asks his fellow Baptists, is there then any justification for baptizing—is not that equally an apostolic office?[17] The (Anglican) Church Missionary Society was commenced at the insistence of devout pragmatists such as John Venn and Charles Simeon. They had trouble from some of their more doctrinaire evangelical brethren who feared that the Anglican Prayer Book might not always be adhered to on the mission field; while many Irish Churchmen regarded the Society as a distraction from the "real" work of combating Rome.

Part Two

Untheological development as it may have been, the voluntary society had immense theological implications. It arose because none of the classical patterns of church government, whether episcopal, presbyterian, congregational, or connexional, had any machinery (in their late 18th century form anyway) to do the tasks for which missionary societies came into being. By its very success, the voluntary society subverted all the classical forms of church government, while fitting comfortably into none of them. To appreciate this we have to remember how fixed and immutable these forms appeared to 18 century men. They had been argued out for centuries, each on the basis of scripture and reason—and still all three forms remained, putting Christians into classes, categorizing them unambiguously. People had spent themselves for the sake of the purity of these forms, had shed their blood

> At the heart of Carey's pamphlet lies the responsibility of Christians to seek the appropriate instrument, to accomplish a task which God has laid upon them.

for them, had been on occasion ready to shed the blood of others for them. And then it suddenly became clear that there were things— and not small things, but big things, things like the evangelization of the world—which were beyond the capacities of these splendid systems of gospel truth. The realization removes some of the stiffness from the theological ribs. Here is Carey:

> If there is any reason for me to hope that I shall have any influence upon any of my brethren, and fellow Christians, probably it may be more especially amongst them of my own denomination.... I do not mean by this, in any wise to confine it to one denomination of Christians. I wish with all my heart, that every one who loves our Lord Jesus Christ in sincerity, would in some way or other engage in it. But in the present divided state of Christendom, it would be more likely for good to be done by each denomination engaging separately in the work, than if they were to embark in it conjointly. There is room enough for us all...and if no unfriendly interference took place, each denomination would bear good will to the other, and wish, and pray for its success...but if all were intermingled, it is likely that their private discords might...much retard their public usefulness.[18]

Carey's reasons for basing a mission denominationally are thus entirely pragmatic. He has no *theological* objection to a united mission; indeed he invites all Christians to the work. But to form a society you must begin where you are, with people who already form a nucleus, with people who already have some cohesion, mutual trust, and fellowship. Let suspicion and lack of trust enter, and the society is doomed. It was, of course, possible to start from the same ecumenical theological premise as Carey and reach a different conclusion about the basis for the missionary society. So it was with the founders of The Missionary Society, so-called because it was hoped that it would comprehend all men of good will, whether episcopal, presbyterian, or congregational. As other societies appeared, however, it soon became known as the London Missionary Society. At its inauguration one of the preachers cried "Behold us here assembled with one accord to attend the funeral of *bigotry*.... I could almost add, cursed be the man who shall attempt to raise

her from the grave."[19] In witness to this the founders devised what they designated the "fundamental principle":

> Our design is not to send Presbyterianism, Independency, Episcopacy, or any other form of Church Order and Government (about which there may be difference of opinion among serious Persons), but the Glorious Gospel of the blessed God to the Heathen: and that it shall be left (as it ever ought to be left) to the minds of the Persons whom God may call into the fellowship of His Son from among them to assume for themselves such form of Church Government, as to them shall appear most agreeable to the Word of God.[20]

It would be possible to argue that this fundamental principle was in fact a Congregational principle especially with that parentheses "as it ever ought to be left"; and one might go further to give this as the reason why the LMS became substantially, though never in name or completely, a society supported by Congregationalists. However it is far more important to note that the foundation of the LMS demonstrates at the end of the 18 century something that would have been inconceivable at its beginning: a common ground of action for Episcopalians and Presbyterians, Independents and Methodists. The common ground is a society, a common means for people who start from different bases but have a common aim.

The society becomes the vehicle for catholic spirit. It is not the source of that spirit, but a product of it and a means of expression for it. Carey proposes a denominational society for the most ecumenical reasons; the fathers of the London Missionary Society produce a non-denominational society for very similar reasons. But in these days Churchman and Dissenter might meet at the dinner table or the coffee house and talk, but there was no means whereby they could ever *act* together till it was provided in the voluntary society. But the challenge of the society to the traditional structures went still deeper than this, and it was the missionary societies that presented the challenge most acutely. They were created for the spread of the gospel; which was one of the reasons for which parishes and congregations in principle existed. But they were *not* parishes or congregations, and they worked in a quite different way. They could not be digested by any of the classical systems whereby parishes or congregations were linked—even when the societies were themselves explicitly denominational.

A new type of church government was growing up alongside the old, parasitically attached to forms that had seemed permanent, argued over till there was no more to say.

It is no surprise, then, that throughout the 19th century societies multiplied to deal with specific social abuses or meet special social needs. Nor is it surprising that in the wake of the 1859 Revival a new group of missionary societies arose, many reviving the old hope of a non-denominational structure for all of good will; nor that the same period saw many new societies for aspects of home mission and evangelism in sectors that were not being noticeably covered by the regular church machinery.

Part Three

According to Anderson, part of the special significance of the voluntary society is that it is not restricted to ecclesiastics. This points to another way in which the voluntary society subverted the old church structures: it altered their power base. It was the voluntary society which first made the laymen (except a few who held office or special position in the state) of real significance above parish or congregational level. As the societies developed, people, whether clerical or lay, who had previously been of no particular significance in their churches, came to be of immense significance in the societies. This is well illustrated in the history of the Church Missionary Society. The CMS was begun by a group of clerical nobodies. They were a handful of London ministers, not all of them even beneficed, a Fellow of Cambridge College, a few people from the country—not a bishop, or a dean, or an archdeacon among them. From the point of view of influence, their only strong point was that they had the support of some notable laymen, prominent members of Parliament like William Wilberforce and Henry Thornton, who would make well-sounding Vice-Presidents or competent treasurers. And indeed, when it becomes necessary to speak to the Archbishop of Canterbury about the Society,

the layman Wilberforce has to do it; there is no clergyman in the group with sufficient weight to talk to an archbishop.[21] But in the whole of the 19th century, did any archbishop hold a more extensive or more important *episcope* than Henry Venn? Venn, the Secretary of the CMS for 30 years in the middle of the century, never held more than a small prebend in the church, but no bishop had so wide a diocese. Few can have had more clergy, none had nearly so much direct influence on his clergy.[22] Some of his predecessors and successors were laymen, of whom the best known is Dandeson Coates. As the century proceeded, still more dramatic developments took place. Medical and other specialists personnel in certain societies came to take the executive places once thought the sphere of the minister and the theologian. And then came women, to take place in the leadership and organization of societies, far earlier than they could decently appear in most other walks of life. A mother-in-Israel such as Mrs. Grattan Guinness was not just a patroness, a species of sanctified Baroness Burdett Coutts, but an animator, a motivator, an organizer. The vision of the need which led to the Mission of Lepers (now the Leprosy Mission) came to the missionary Wellesley Bailey, but the organizer and the focus was the redoubtable Miss Pym of Dublin. And so another quiet revolution took place in the church; and just because the society never became properly digested within the systems of the church, no one raised difficulties about the ordination of women, or even about their being silent in the church. If the voluntary society was one of the Lord's theological jokes, the stately structures of church government, hallowed by centuries of doctrinal exposition and smothered in polemical divinity, had by the end of the 19th century become the scene of a hilarious comedy.

Part Four

Anderson speaks also of the voluntary society "embracing the masses of the people." This points to another vital feature of the voluntary society. It depended for its very existence on regular participation; it developed means of gaining that participation at local level. Carey's proposals were implemented on the basis of a small group of Baptists in the English Midlands who already knew each other well. The LMS was a much bigger affair, partly because its sponsors, men like David Bogue and George Burder, were more eminent in their denominational constituency than was Carey in his; even so, for its coherence and dynamic it depended on committed groups of people in certain areas, especially London and Warwickshire. The Church Missionary Society illustrates the point best of all. It began as a result of discussions in a ministers' fraternal, and for a long time it was a congeries of ministers who met in London and corresponded with their evangelical clerical friends round the country. For nearly 15 years it could get hardly any candidates from within Britain. Almost all their employable candidates came from Germany, as a result of correspondence with the Continental missionary societies.[23] From about 1814, the situation slowly changed, and one reason must surely be that the CMS had put into practice a new form of organization already pioneered by the Bible Society: a network of locally organized auxiliary associations. Local Church Missionary Associations could vary from large cities like Bristol, where they might be supported by prominent noble and civil figures, to quite small rural parishes or other natural units (there was, for instance, a Cambridge Ladies Association from 1814, before there was any general association for the city or the university). The CMS was transformed. It ceased to be a committee of clergymen meeting in London; it became the group of people meeting in the parish to learn of the latest news from India or West Africa, and the eager readers of the missionary magazines. Its lynchpin was no longer a distant distinguished secretary, but the collector in the parish who went round collecting—perhaps only a penny a week from some—and promoting the sales of the *Missionary Register*. People of the most modest position and income became donors, supporters of the overseas work, felt themselves to be sharing in it. And the recruiting pattern of the society changed. It began to get offers for missionary service from within the nation. And this at the very point when missionary work was becoming visibly dangerous, when the missionary mortality in certain fields was at its height. The reason must surely be related to the devel-

opment whereby the society was rooted locally among Christians all over the country. The society took a local embodiment, developed a broad spread of participants, gave scope to lay commitment and enthusiasm.

Part Five

The part played by the missionary magazines in this process has not yet received sufficient attention from scholars. The voluntary societies, and the missionary societies in particular, created a new reading public and used it to sensitize public opinion. The roots of the process lie in the slave trade abolition movement, which was, of course, promoted by many people who also actively supported missionary societies. The abolition of the slave trade was perhaps the first victory won by modern propaganda methods, by the use of the media to educate and mobilize public opinion. The missionary societies gradually took over the same role. The year 1812 saw the birth of the first of the great missionary magazines, *Missionary Register*. The *Register* printed news from all over the world and, in the catholic spirit of missionary endeavour, from all agencies. It was eagerly read all over the country. The circulation of such magazines was much wider than that of other prestigious journals like the *Edinburgh Review* and the *Quarterly Review* which went into the libraries of the country houses of the gentry. The missionary magazine went to many people who had never previously been periodical readers at all. The magazines helped to form opinion, they developed images and mental pictures, they built up attitudes. Their effect on popular reference books in the 19th century was considerable. The average reader of the *Missionary Register* or the other missionary magazines knew exactly what he thought the British government should do about the temple tax in Bengal, or about the *sati* of Hindu widows, or the opium trade, or slave running. And a mass readership was produced, a readership concerned and informed about the world outside their own country as perhaps no other group in the nation.

One example must suffice. In the middle of the century the CMS became involved in one of the first modern churches in inland Africa, in the Egba state of Abeokuta in

Yorubaland. When the Egba looked in danger of being overwhelmed by the Kingdom of Dahomey and the interests of the slave trade, the CMS used its influence in government circles to gain moral and a degree of logistical support for the Egba.[24] The mighty Dahomian army withdrew, and Henry Venn noted universal satisfaction in Britain "from the ministers of Her Majesty's government to the humble collector of a penny a week." He was not exaggerating; Her Majesty's ministers had acted because of evidence marshalled by the missionary society, and doubtless countless penny-a-week collectors followed the events in Africa with bated breath, and gave thanks with the missionaries for the deliverance of Abeokuta and its church. But how many people in Britain in the 1850s would have heard of Abeokuta, or been able to distinguish the King of Dahomey from the Queen of Sheba? Most of those that could do so would have gained their knowledge from the window on the world provided by the missionary magazines.

Part Six

The later years of the 19th century saw the development of a multitude of new missionary societies, many of them belonging to the new category of "faith missions" of which the China Inland Mission was the pioneer and prototype. They represent a development of the voluntary society rather than a totally new departure. They embody and take to their logical conclusion principles which were already present in the older societies. To some extent they represented a reform movement, going back to first principles; rather as Cistercians and Carthusians reasserted the Benedictine ideal when they thought that Jeshurun had waxed fat and kicked. They continued the revolutionary effect of the voluntary society on the church, assisting its declericalization, giving new scope for women's energies and gifts, adding an international dimension which hardly any of the churches, growing as they did within a national framework, had any means of expressing. After the age of the voluntary society, the Western Church could never be the same again.

The missionary society was, as Carey indicated, a use of means for a specific purpose. The original purpose was what Carey called "the conversion of the heathens." The purpose of both the older and the newer societies was essentially evangelistic; inasfar as it was formulated, the theory was that when the church was founded the mission would move on. In practice it did not, perhaps could not, happen that way. As new churches appeared, the society remained as a natural channel of communication, through which flowed aid, personnel, money, materials, technical expertise. The societies, as we have seen, developed other roles, as educators of church and public, as a conscience for peoples and governments. All these roles were already established in the missionary societies before 1830, and they are all there still.

> From age to age it becomes necessary to use new means for the proclamation of the gospel beyond the structures which unduly localize it.

But neither the fears of 19th century Churchmen nor the hopes of 19th century missionaries comprehended a situation so soon in which Africans, Asians, and Latin Americans would form the majority of Christians, and that on them would lie so soon the main responsibility for the evangelization of the world. The new chapter of Church history which has begun arises, not from the failure of the missionary movement, but from its success. It may now be appropriate to re-examine the "obligation to use means," and the purpose for which our "means" is directed. Societies established for an evangelistic purpose may produce strictly bilateral connections, so that churches formed as a result of "our" work have relations only with "us." Is this a measure of the fullness of the Body of Christ? And relationships so easily become finance-dominated; it is hard to keep relations on an equal footing when the regular topic of conversation is money, and how much. And the societies were designed for one-way traffic; all the assumptions were that one party would do all the giving and the other all the receiving. Now, our desperate need in the West is to be able to receive, and we have also an "obligation to use means" for the sharing of all the gifts that God has given to all his people.

The voluntary society, and its special form in the missionary society, arose in a particular period of Western social, political, and economic development and was shaped by that period. It was providentially used in God's purpose for the redemption of the world. But as Rufus Anderson noted long ago, it was but the modern, Western form of a movement that has periodically reappeared from an

early period of Christian history. In one sense, monasteries were voluntary societies, and "it was by means of associations such as these that the Gospel was originally propagated among our ancestors, and over Europe."[25] From age to age it becomes necessary to use new means for the proclamation of the gospel beyond the structures which unduly localize it. Some have taken the word "sodality" beyond its special usage in Catholic practice to stand for all such "use of means" by which groups voluntarily constituted labor together for specific gospel purposes. The voluntary societies have been as revolutionary in their effect as ever the monasteries were in their sphere. The sodalities we now need may prove equally disturbing.

End Notes

1. This tract has been published several times since it appeared in the *Religious Magazine,* Boston, 1837-38. It is most recently reprinted in R. Pierce Beaver, ed., *To Advance the Gospel: Selections From the Writings of Rufus Anderson* (Grand Rapids: Eerdmans, 1967), pp. 59-76, and since this is also the most accessible version the references given are to it.

2. *Ibid.,* p. *61.*

3. *Ibid.,* p. *64.*

4. *Ibid.,* p. *65.*

5. On the background see W. K. Lowther Clarke, *Eighteenth Century Piety* (London: SPCK, 1946*);* N. Sykes, Edmund Gibson, Bishop of London 1669-1748: *A Study of Politics and Religion in the Eighteenth Century* (London: Oxford University Press, 1926*).*

6. See, e.g., J. S. Simon, *John Wesley and the Religious Societies* (London: Epworth, 1921), and *John Wesley and the Methodist Societies* (London, 1923).

7. See W. K. Lowther Clarke, A *History of the S.P.C.K.* (London: SPCK, 1959); and H.P. Thompson, *Into All Lands: The History of the Society for the Propagation of the Gospel 1701-1750* (London: SPCK, 1951). It is significant that Thompson's first section after his account of SPG origins deals with "The American Colonies 1701-1783," and the first four sections of "The Years of Awakening, 1783-1851" deal with the home scene and with Canada. The primary tasks of the SPG were with English colonists. Thomas Bray, the moving spirit in its formation, had a much wider vision (cf. Thompson, p. 17); but in practice men like Thomas Thompson (cf. Thompson, pp. 67ff), a chaplain in Maryland who traveled to West Africa in the 1750s to visit the place of origin of the plantation slaves, were rare. The young John Wesley hoped to preach to the Native Americans when he became a missionary in Georgia; in fact he was able to see little of them.

8. Cf. G. D. McKelvie, *The Development of Official Anglican Interest in World Mission 1788-1809, With Special Reference to Bishop Beilby Porteus.* Ph.D. thesis (University of Aberdeen, 1984).

9. Published in Leicester, 1792, and several times reprinted. A facsimile edition with introduction by E. A. Payne was published by the Carey Kingsgate Press (London, 1961).

10. Carey, *An Enquiry,* pp. 78f.

11. *An Humble Attempt to Promote Explicit Agreement and Visible Union of God's People in Extraordinary Prayer for the Revival of Religion and the Advancement of Christ's Kingdom on Earth, Pursuant to Scripture—Promises and Prophecies Concerning the Last Time* (Boston, *1747).*

12. A. Fawcett, *The Cambuslang Revival: The Scottish Evangelical Revival of the Eighteenth Century* (London: Banner of Truth, *1971).*

13. Carey, p. *79.*

14. *Ibid.,* pp. 79-80.
15. *Ibid.,* p. 80.
16. *Ibid.,* pp. *82-83.*
17. *Ibid.,* pp. 8ff.
18. *Ibid.,* pp. 84.
19. David Bogue. The sermon is summarized and quoted in R. Lovett, *The History of the London Missionary Society 1795-1895* (London: Oxford University Press, 1899), *1:55f.*
20. Lovett, *History,* pp. 21f.
21. See Michael Hennell, *John Venn and the Clapham Sect* (London: Lutterworth, 1958), chapt. 5.
22. Cf. W. R. Shenk, *Henry Venn, Missionary Statesman* (Maryknoll, N.Y.: Orbis Books, 1983).
23. On early missionary recruitment, see chapter 12 of this volume, "Missionary Vocation and the Ministry."
24. S. O. Biobaku, *The Egba and Their Neighbors 1842-72* (Oxford: Clarendon Press, *1957); cf.* J. F. Ade Ajayei, *Christian Missions in Nigeria 1841-1891: The Making of a New Elite* (London: Longmans, *1965),* pp. *71-73.*
25. Beaver, p. 64.

Study Questions

1. Explain the title of this article. Why were missionary societies subversive? Why was that subversion a fortunate thing?

2. Using the terms "modality" and "sodality" explain the rise of what Walls calls "missionary societies."

3. Who does Walls refer to as sometimes being "enemies of the missionary movement?" Why?

4. Explain what Walls means by "God's theological jokes."

The History of Mission Strategy

R. Pierce Beaver

Fifteen centuries of missionary action preceded the rise of Protestant world mission. These pages will present a capsule history of mission strategy before the rise of Protestant efforts, briefly trace the course of Protestant strategy, and unfortunately for lack of space, completely omit reference to modern Roman Catholic missions.

Boniface

The first instance of a well-developed mission strategy, in the twentieth century understanding of the term, is that employed in the English mission to the continent of Europe by Boniface in the eighth century. Boniface preached to Germanic pagans in a language so akin to their own that they could understand. He did use aggression: he defied their gods, demolished their shrines, cut down the sacred trees, and built churches on holy sites. But he made converts, and educated and civilized them. He founded monasteries which not only had academic schools but programs which taught people agriculture, grazing, and domestic arts. This made possible a settled society, a well-grounded church, and good Christian nurture. Into a second line of educational and domestic science institutions Boniface brought nuns from England. This is the first time that women were formally and actively enlisted in mission work. Clergy and monks were recruited from the people. All of this activity was supported by the church "back home" in England. Boniface sent reports and requests. He discussed strategy with people back home. The bishops, monks, and sisters in turn sent Boniface personnel, money, and supplies. They also undergirded the mission with intercessory prayer.

Unhappily, such a true sending mission ceased to exist because of the ravages which invaders wreaked on the people of England. Mission on the continent became too much an instrument of imperial expansion, both political and ecclesiastical, for it was employed by the Frankish kings, their German successors, the Byzantine emperor, and the Pope. Consequently, the Scandinavian kings kept out missionaries from the continent and in the evangelization of their countries used English missionaries who were their own subjects or who had no political connections.

The Crusades

The series of European wars against the Muslims, called the Crusades, can hardly be considered a form of true mis-

As a professor at the University of Chicago, R. Pierce Beaver specialized in the history of missions in America, and was for fifteen years a formative director of the Missionary Research Library in New York City. Beaver authored, among other books, *All Loves Excelling*, a description of the initiatives of American women in missions. He died in 1982.

From *Southwestern Journal of Theology*, Volume XII, Spring 1970, No. 2, 1970. Used by permission.

sion. They made mission to Muslims almost impossible down to the present because they left an abiding heritage of hatred in Islamic lands. Yet even before the Crusades had ended, Francis of Assisi had gone in love to preach to the sultan and had created a missionary force which would preach in love and in peace. Ramon Lull, the great Franciscan tertiary, gave up his status as a noble high in the court of Aragon and devoted his life to mission to Muslims as "the Fool of Love." He would convince and convert by reason, using the instrument of debate. To this end he wrote his *Ars Magna*, which was intended to answer convincingly any question or objection which could be put by Muslim or pagan, and devised a kind of intellectual computer into which the various factors could be registered and the right answer would come forth. Lull for many decades before his martyrdom ceaselessly begged popes and kings to establish colleges for the teaching of Arabic and other languages and for the training of missionaries, and urged upon them many schemes for sending missionaries abroad.

Colonial Expansion

It was in the period of the sixteenth to eighteenth centuries that Christianity actually became a worldwide religion in connection with the expansion of the Portuguese, Spanish, and French empires. When the Pope divided the non-Christian lands of the earth already discovered or yet to be discovered between the crowns of Portugal and Spain, he laid upon the monarchs the obligation to evangelize the peoples of those lands, to establish the church, and to maintain it. Mission was thus made a function of government.

The Portuguese built a trade empire, and except in Brazil, held only small territories under direct rule. There they suppressed the ethnic religions, drove out the upper class who resisted, and created a Christian community composed of their mixed-blood descendants and converts from the lower strata of society.

Spain, on the other hand, endeavored to transplant Christianity and civilization, both according to the Spanish model. Ruthless exploitation killed off the Carib Indians and stimulated the heroic struggle for the rights of the remaining Indians by Bartholome de las Casas and other missionaries. Since then, protection of primitive people against exploitation by whites and by colonial governments has been an important function of missions. After that mighty effort abolished slavery and forced baptism, the missionaries were made both the civilizers and protectors of the Indians. A mission would be established on a frontier with a central station about which a town was gathered and Indians brought into permanent residence. There was usually a small garrison of soldiers to protect both missionaries and Christian Indians. Satellite stations and smaller towns were connected with the central one. The Indians were taught by catechists and supervised by priests in the cultic life of the church. They were actively enlisted in participation, serving as acolytes, singers, and musicians. Folk festivals were Christianized, and the Christian feasts and fasts were introduced. Indian civil officers performed a wide range of supervisory functions under the careful oversight of the missionaries. Farms and ranches were developed and the Indians were taught all aspects of grazing and agriculture. Thus the Indians were preserved, civilized, and Christianized, not killed off or displaced as would later be the case in the United States. Unfortunately, when the government decided that the missions had civilized the Indians, the missions were "secularized"; the missionaries replaced by diocesan clergy usually of low quality and too few in number; regular government officers came in as rulers in place of the missionaries and lacking their love for the people; the lands were parceled out among Spanish settlers; and the Indians were gradually reduced to peonage.

French policy in Canada was the opposite of the Spanish. Only a small colony was settled to be a base for trade and a bulwark against the English. The French wanted the furs and other products of the forests and consequently disturbed Indian civilization as little as possible. The missionaries had to develop a strategy consonant with this policy. Therefore, they lived with the Indians in their villages, adapting to conditions as well as they could, preaching, teaching, baptizing individuals, performing the rites of the church, allowing the converts still to be Indians. Some permanent towns with church and school were founded on the borders of French settlements, but most of the inhabitants were transient.

On the other side of the globe in what was to become French Indo-China, now Vietnam, where the region came under French rule only much later, a radical new evangelistic strategy was devised by Alexander de Rhodes. This was necessary because the French missionaries were persecuted and expelled from the region for long periods. Evangelization could only be achieved by native agents. Rhodes created an order of native lay evangelists living under rule who won converts by the thousands. Stimulated by this experience, Rhodes and his associates founded the Foreign Mission Society of Paris dedicated to the policy of recruiting and training a diocesan clergy, who would be the chief agents in the evangelization of the country and the pastoral care of the churches, rather than missionaries. It was a policy marked by outstanding success.

Mission Strategists of the 17th Century

The first modern mission theorists appeared in the 17th century in connection with this great expansion of the faith, including Jose de Acosta, Brancati, and Thomas a Jesu. They wrote manuals of missionary principles and practice, described the qualifications of missionaries, and told them how to work with the people. In 1622 there was created in Rome the Sacred Congregation for the Propagation of the Faith which henceforth gave central direction to Roman Catholic missions and established colleges or institutes for the training of missionaries.

The great and courageous innovators in this period were the Jesuits who went to the Orient through Portuguese channels but defied Portuguese restrictions. They were of many nationalities. These were the modern pioneers in accommodation, acculturation, adaptation, or indigenization—whatever one may wish to call it. The first venture was in Japan where the missionaries adapted to Japanese houses, costume, most customs, and the etiquette of social intercourse. They did not, however, make use of Shinto and Buddhist terms and concepts, forms, or rites in presentation of the gospel and establishing the church. They did make great use of the Japanese language in production of Christian literature printed on the mission press by Japanese converts. The heaviest burden in evangelism and teaching was borne by native deacons and catechists. A few were admitted to the priesthood. A large Christian community soon came into being. When the Shogun, fearing foreign aggression, closed Japan to all outsiders and persecuted Christianity in the 17th century, many thousands suffered martyrdom. Christianity went underground and endured until Japan was opened to western intercourse two centuries later.

> It will help as we pray, study, plan and experiment if we know the past history of mission strategy.

A second experiment at Madurai in South India went much farther. Robert de Nobili believed that the Brahmin caste must be won if Christianity were to succeed in India. Consequently, he became a Christian Brahmin. He dressed like a guru or religious teacher, observed the caste laws and customs, and learned Sanskrit. De Nobili studied the major schools of Hindu philosophy and presented Christian doctrine as much as possible in Hindu terms. He is one of the very few evangelists who won many Brahmin converts.

The most noted attempt at accommodation was in China, where the strategy was set by Matteo Ricci and developed by his successors as head of the mission, Schall and Verbiest. Just as in Japan, the missionaries adopted the national way of life and fundamentals of Chinese civilization, but they went much farther and gradually introduced Christian principles and doctrine through the use of Confucian concepts. They permitted converts to engage in ancestral and state rites, regarding these as social and civil rather than religious in character. The missionaries gained tremendous influence as mathematicians, astronomers, cartographers, and masters of various sciences, thus introducing Western learning to the Chinese, making friendships with influential persons, and finding opportunities personally to present the faith. They served the emperor in many capacities. All of this had one purpose—to open the way for the gospel. Success crowned the strategy, and a large Christian community developed, including influential persons in high places.

Other missionaries, however, were unable to appreciate anything that was not European and were absolutely wedded to traditional Roman Catholic terminology and practices. Motivated by nationalistic and party jealousies, they attacked the Jesuits and laid charges against them in Rome. Ultimately Rome pronounced against the Jesuits' principles, banned their practices, and required that all missionaries going to the Orient take an oath to abide by that ruling. Chinese Christians were forbidden to practice family and state rites. It was henceforth impossible for any Christian to be a genuine Chinese and a Christian simultaneously. The profession of the Christian faith appeared to strike at the root of filial piety, which was the very foundation of Chinese society. Two centuries later, the oath was abolished and modified rites permitted. The Jesuits lost the battle but ultimately won the war. Today, almost all missionaries of all churches acknowledge the necessity of accommodation or indigenization.

New England Puritans: Missions to the American Indians

The participation of Protestants in world mission began early in the 17th century simultaneously with the evangelistic work of the chaplains of the Dutch East Indies Company and the New England missions to the American Indians. Mission was a function of the commercial company, but many of its chaplains were genuine missionaries. They had little influence on later mission strategy, but it was the Puritan missions to the American Indians that would provide the missions of a later day with inspiration and models. The aim of the missionaries was to preach the gospel so effectively that the Indians would be converted, individually receive salvation, and be gathered into churches where they would be nurtured in the faith under strict discipline. The intention was to make

of the Indian a Christian man of the same type and character as the English Puritan member of a gathered Congregationalist church. This involved civilizing the Indian according to the British model.

Evangelism was the first item in the strategy. Preaching was the "grand means," supplemented by teaching. Most missionaries followed John Eliot in beginning with public preaching, although Thomas Mayhew, Jr., was very successful at Martha's Vineyard in beginning with a slow, individual, personal approach. Heavily doctrinal sermons stressing the wrath of God and the pains of hell, just like those given an English congregation, were addressed to the Indians. But David Brainerd, who like the Moravians preached the love of God rather than His wrath, was extremely effective in moving men and women to repentance.

The second point of the strategy was to gather the converts into churches, but the new Christians were at first put through long years of probation before the first churches were organized. On the contrary, when the second phase of the Indian mission opened in the 1730's, this delay was no longer required and the churches were speedily gathered and organized. The converts were being instructed and disciplined in the faith, both before and after the organization of the churches.

A third strategic emphasis was the establishment of Christian towns. John Eliot and his colleagues in the mission believed that segregation and isolation were necessary to the converts' growth in grace. They must be removed from the baneful influence of their pagan brethren and of bad white men. It was thought that in purely Christian towns of "Praying Indians," the new members could live together under the strict discipline and careful nurture of the white missionaries and Indian pastors and teachers. This would insure what Cotton Mather called "a more decent and English way of living." Christianization and civilization would be simultaneous and indistinguishable. Eliot put his towns under a biblical form of government based on Exodus 18, but the General Court of Massachusetts, which gave the land and built the church and school, appointed English commissioners over the towns in 1658. Within the towns the Indians did live together under a covenant between them and the Lord, and both personal and community life were regulated by laws of a biblical flavor.

Most of the towns of the Praying Indians did not survive the devastation of King Philip's War in 1674, but the strategy of the special Christian town was again followed when John Sergeant established the Stockbridge mission in 1734. Stockbridge was not so closed a place as those earlier towns. There was constant movement between town and forest, even to great distances. Stockbridge Christians could, therefore, be evangelistic agents in their natural relationships.

Whatever may have been achieved in the development of Christian character in the early towns, no evangelistic influence could be exerted by the inhabitants, cut off as they were from other Indians. Throughout the 19th and early 20th centuries missionaries to primitive people in Africa and the isles would continue to be enamoured of the idea of guaranteeing the purity of the converts' faith and conduct by segregating them in separate Christian villages or wards. The usual effect was to alienate the Christians from their people, to create a "mongrel" kind of society neither native nor European, and to prevent any evangelistic impact on others. A separated people cannot pass on the contagion of personal faith.

At the center of each town or mission station was a church flanked by a school house. Sermons on Sunday and in prayer meetings, catechization, and general elementary education all tended to nurture the convert in faith and civilization.

John Eliot's *Indian Catechism* was the first book ever to be published in an American Indian language. Both the vernacular and the English language were used. The English would enable the Indian to adjust better to white society, but his own tongue was more effective in imparting an understanding of Christian truth. Eliot produced textbooks in both languages. Reading, writing, and simple arithmetic were taught along with Bible study and religious instruction. Agricultural and domestic crafts were also introduced so that support in a settled and civilized way of life might be possible. In the second century of the mission, strategic considerations led John Sergeant to introduce the boarding school, so that youths could be entirely separated from the old life and brought up in the new. This institution, too, would become a primary strategic resource of the missions in the 19th century.

It is to the credit of the New England Puritans that they never doubted the transforming power of the gospel nor the potential ability of the Indians. They expected that some of them at least could attain the same standard as Englishmen. Therefore, more than the rudimentary schooling of the towns was required. Some promising youths were sent to the Boston Latin Grammar School, and a few were placed in the Indian College at Harvard College. Sergeant's boarding school at Stockbridge and Eleazer Wheelock's school at Lebanon, Connecticut, were better conceived efforts at a higher degree of education.

Worship, spiritual nurture, and education all demanded a vernacular literature of rather broad dimensions. Eliot produced the Massachusetts Bible and a library of other literature, to which a few of his colleagues added.

Absolutely fundamental to the entire plan of New England mission strategy was the recruiting and training of native pastors and teachers. Both the missionaries and their supporters realized that only native agents could effectively evangelize and give pastoral care to their people. In 1700 there were thirty-seven Indian preachers in Massachusetts. Unfortunately, the old Christian Indian towns declined under continuing white pressure and with them the supply of ministers and teachers also declined to the vanishing point.

Perhaps the most lasting effects of the Indian missions of the 17th and 18th centuries were two: first, they inspired numerous missionary vocations in a later day as men read the lives of Eliot and Brainerd; and second, they endowed the great overseas Protestant enterprise with its initial strategic program. This included evangelism through preaching, organization of churches, education aimed at Christian nurture and the attainment of civilization in European terms, Bible translation, literature production, use of the vernacular language, and the recruitment and training of native pastors and teachers.

The Danish-Halle Mission

The American missions to the indigenous population had been supported by missionary societies organized in England and Scotland, but missionaries had not been sent from Britain. The first sending mission from Europe was the Danish-Halle Mission. Beginning in 1705, the King of Denmark sent German Lutheran missionaries to his colony of Tranquebar on the southeast coast of India. The pioneer leader, Bartholomew Ziegenbalg, developed a strategy which was bequeathed to later generations of missionaries, although in some respects he was far ahead of his time. He stressed worship, preaching, catechization, education, translation work, and the production of vernacular literature. He blazed a trail in the study of Hindu philosophy and religion, discerning the great importance of such knowledge for evangelization and church growth, but the authorities in Germany decried such activity. This mission early added medical work to its program. It also pioneered in the use of Tamil lyrics in worship.

The most famous of the Halle missionaries after Ziegenbalg was one of the last, Christian Frederick Schwartz, who spent his life in ministry in the British-controlled portion of south India. He had a remarkable influence with Indians of all religions and with Europeans of several nationalities, both troops and civilians. His strategy was unique and unplanned. Although still a European to all appearances, Schwartz actually became in effect a guru or spiritual teacher, loved and trusted by all. Persons of all religions and castes could gather around him as his disciples regardless of the difference in their status. His ministry was essentially a remarkable kind of adaptation or accommodation to the culture.

Moravian Missions

The most distinctive strategy developed in the 18th century was that of the Moravian Church developed under the direction of Count Zinzendorf and Bishop Spangenberg. The Moravian missionaries, beginning in 1734, were purposely sent to the most despised and neglected people. These missionaries were to be self-supporting. That emphasis led to the creation of industries and business concerns which not only supported the work but brought the missionaries into intimate contact with the people. Such self-support could not be undertaken among the American Indians, however, and consequently communal settlements, such as Bethlehem in Pennsylvania and Salem in North Carolina, were founded with a wide range of crafts and industries, the profits of which supported the mission.

> Moravian missionaries were told not to apply their own standards to other peoples, rather, to be alert to the recognition of the God-given distinctive traits, characteristics and strong points of those people.

Moravian missionaries were told not to apply "the Herrnhut yardstick" (i.e., German home base standards) to other peoples and to be alert to the recognition of the God-given distinctive traits, characteristics and strong points of those people. Furthermore, the missionaries were to regard themselves as assistants to the Holy Spirit. They were to be primarily messengers, evangelists, preachers, who were not to stress heavy theological doctrines but rather tell the simple gospel story of God's loving act of reconciliation of men to Himself in Christ our Savior, who lived and died for all men. In God's providence the time would come when the Holy Spirit would bring converts into the church in large numbers. Meanwhile the missionary messengers would gather the first fruits. If there should be no response, they were to go elsewhere. Actually, the missionaries left only when persecuted and driven out. They were remarkably patient and did not give up readily.

The Great Century of Protestant Missions

Out of all these earlier beginnings there came the great Protestant missionary overseas enterprise of the 19th century. It took initial form in Britain with the founding of the Baptist Missionary Society by William Carey in

1792. Organization had begun in the United States in 1787 and a score of societies came into being, all having a worldwide objective. However, the frontier settlements and the Indians absorbed all their resources. At length a student movement in 1810 broke the deadlock and launched the overseas mission through the formation of the American Board of Commissioners for Foreign Missions. The Triennial Convention of the Baptist Denomination for Foreign Missions was next organized in 1814 followed in 1816 by the United Foreign Missionary Society.

The new societies and boards began their work with the strategic presuppositions and methods inherited from the American Indian missions and the Danish-Halle Mission. For many years, the directors at home thought that they understood fully how the mission was to be carried out and detailed instructions were handed each missionary when he sailed. After half a century or so it was discovered that the experienced missionaries on the field could best formulate strategy and policy, which might then be ratified by the board back home. There was in 1795 a conflict over strategy in the London Missionary Society between two strong personalities. One man wanted well-educated ordained missionaries sent to countries of high civilization and high religions. The other wanted artisan missionaries under an ordained superintendent to be sent to primitive peoples in the South Seas to Christianize and civilize them. Both objectives were accepted.

Even in countries with a high culture, such as India and China, European missionaries stressed the "civilizing" objective as much as their brethren in primitive regions because they regarded the local culture as degenerate and superstitious—a barrier to Christianization. During the early decades there was never debate about the legitimacy of the stress on the civilizing function of missions. Debate was only about priority; which came first, Christianization or civilization? Some held that a certain degree of civilization was first necessary to enable a people to understand and accept the faith. Others argued that one should begin with Christianization since the gospel inevitably produced a hunger for civilization. Most persons believed that the two mutually interacted and should be stressed equally and simultaneously.

India was soon receiving the greatest degree of attention from mission boards and societies, and the strategy and tactics developed there were copied and applied in other regions. The Baptist "Serampore Trio" of Carey, Marshman, and Ward was especially influential in the early period. Although Carey sought individual conversions, he wanted to foster the growth of a church that would be independent, well sustained by a literate and Bible-reading laity, and administered and shepherded by an educated native ministry. This self-educated genius was not content with establishing elementary schools, but founded a college. The King of Denmark (Serampore was a Danish colony) gave him a college charter which permitted the giving of even theological degrees. At Serampore there were schools for Indians and for foreign children. The vast program of Bible translation and printing, ranging beyond the Indian vernaculars even to the Chinese, established the high priority of such work among all Protestants. Other literature was produced for the churches. The Trio also demonstrated the importance of scholarly research for mission strategy and action, producing linguistic materials needed by all, and taking the leadership in the study of Hinduism.

Furthermore, this famous Trio worked for the transformation of society under the impact of the gospel, and they became a mighty force for social reform, bringing pressure on the colonial government and leading Hindus to enlightened views on old wrongs and their elimination. These men were influential in causing the abolition of *suttee* or widow-burning, temple prostitution, and other dehumanizing customs. Carey also introduced modern journalism, publishing both vernacular Bengali and English newspapers and magazines. He stimulated a renaissance of Bengali literature. It was a very comprehensive mission which was based at Serampore.

Much like Robert de Nobili before him, the Scotsman Alexander Duff believed that the Indian populace could be won for Christ only if the Brahmin caste were first brought to our Lord. He sought to win Brahmin youths through a program of higher education in the English language. Where he succeeded in large measure, others failed; but his venture led to tremendous emphasis being put on English language schools and colleges. They produced few converts, but they did give economic advancement which made for the welfare of the churches, and to the pleasure of the colonial establishment, they produced English-speaking staff for the civil service and commercial houses. Such education soon consumed a large part of the resources of all the missions.

At the same time without any strategic planning there developed huge concentrated central mission stations where the converts clustered in economic and social dependence on the missionaries. Unless a convert came to Christianity with an entire social group, he was cast out of his family and lost his livelihood. Simply to keep such persons alive they were given jobs as servants, teachers, and evangelists. The church became over-professionalized, laymen being paid to do what they should have done voluntarily. This bad practice passed on to missions in other regions. In such a main station there were the central church, the schools, the hospital, and often the printing press. A missionary was pastor and ruler of the community. Such a system had little place for a native pastor as William Carey had planned, and there were only preaching points, no organized churches, in the villages for fifty miles and more in the hinterland. Then in 1854-55, Rufus Anderson went on deputation to India and Ceylon. He caused the American Board missionaries to break up the huge central stations, to organize village churches, and to ordain native pastors over them. He decreed that education in the vernacular should be the general rule and education in English the exception.

Mission Strategists of the 19th Century

The two greatest mission theoreticians and strategists of the 19th century were also the executive officers of the largest mission agencies. Henry Venn was general secretary of the Church Missionary Society in London. Rufus Anderson was foreign secretary of the American Board of Commissioners for Foreign Missions. Anderson's mission strategy dominated American mission work for more than a century as did that of Venn in the British scene. The two men arrived independently at practically the same basic principles and in later years mutually influenced each other. Together they established as the recognized strategic aim of Protestant mission the famous "three-self" formula to which British and American missions gave assent from the middle of the 19th century until World War II: the goal of mission is to plant and foster the development of churches which will be self-governing, self-supporting, and self-propagating.

Rufus Anderson was a Congregationalist and Venn an Anglican Episcopalian, but both would build the regional church from the bottom upward. Venn wanted a bishop appointed as the crowning of the process of development when there was an adequate native clergy and a church supported by the people. Anderson protested the great stress on "civilization" and the attempt to reform society overnight, holding that such change would eventually result from the leaven of the gospel in the life of a nation. He based his strategy on that of Paul as he found it recorded in the New Testament.

According to Anderson, the task of the missionary was to preach the gospel and gather the converts into churches. He was always to be an evangelist and never a pastor or ruler. Churches were to be organized at once out of converts who showed a change of life towards Christ without waiting for them to reach the standard expected of American Christians with two thousand years of Christian history behind them. These churches were to be put under their own pastors and were to develop their own local and regional polity. The missionaries would be advisers, elder brothers in the faith to the pastors and people.

Both Anderson and Venn taught that when the churches were functioning well the missionaries should leave and go to "regions beyond" where they would begin the evangelistic process once again. The whole point of church planting was to be evangelism and mission. The churches would engage spontaneously in local evangelism and in a sending mission to other peoples. Mission would beget mission. In Anderson's view education in the vernacular would be for the sole purpose of serving the church, or raising up a laity of high quality and an adequately trained ministry. All ancillary forms of work were to be solely for evangelism and for the edification of the church.

The British missions resisted Anderson's views on vernacular education. American missions adopted his strategy officially and unofficially and in theory held to his system for more than a century. However, after his day they stressed secondary and higher education in English to an ever greater extent. This was partly due to the fact that social Darwinism had converted Americans to the doctrine of inevitable progress. This led to the replacement of the old eschatology with the idea that the Kingdom of God was coming through the influence of Christian institutions such as schools. Also by the end of the 19th century a second great strategic objective had been more or less explicitly added to the three-self formula, that is the leavening and transformation of society through the effect of Christian principles and the Christian spirit of service infused into the common life. High schools and colleges were essential to this aim.

John L. Nevius, Presbyterian missionary in Shantung, devised a strategy which somewhat modified that of Anderson, placing more responsibility on the layman. He advocated leaving the layman in his own craft or business and in his usual place in society. He was to be encouraged to be a voluntary, unpaid evangelist. Nevius advocated also constant Bible study and rigorous stewardship in combination with voluntary service and proposed a simple and flexible church government. His brethren in China did not adopt his system, but the missionaries in Korea did so with amazing success.

A Colonialist Mentality

Despite the avowed continued adherence to the Anderson-Venn formula, there was a great change in missionary mentality and consequently in strategy in the last quarter of the 19th century. Under Venn, British missions in west Africa, for example, had aimed at (1) the creation of an independent church under its own clergy which would evangelize the interior of the continent, and (2) the creation of an African elite, i.e., an intelligentsia and middle class, which would produce the society and economy which could support such a church and its mission. Almost immediately after Venn's termination of leadership, mission executives and field missionaries took the view that the African was of inferior quality and could not provide ministerial leadership, which consequently would be furnished indefinitely by Europeans. The African middle-class businessman and intellectual was despised. This imperialist viewpoint was an ecclesiastical variant of the growing devotion to the theory of "the white man's burden," and it reduced the native church to a colony of the foreign planting church.

A very similar development occurred in India in the 1880's. Americans and others caught this colonialist mentality by contagion from the British. German missions, under the guidance of their leading strategist, Professor Gustav Warneck, were simultaneously aiming at the creation of *Volkskirchen*, national churches, but until their full development had been reached, the churches were kept in bondage to the missionaries. Paternalism thwarted development. Thus all missions were paternalist and colonialist at the turn of the century. This unhappy state of affairs lasted until the studies and surveys made for the World Missionary Conference at Edinburgh in 1910 suddenly destroyed complacency and inertia. They revealed that the native church was really a fact and was restive under paternal domination. Consequently, following the Conference, there was a tremendous drive for "devolution" of authority from the mission organization to the church, and practically all boards and societies gave lip service, at least, to this ideal.

Evangelism, Education, and Medicine

Missionary strategy of the 19th century (down to Edinburgh 1910), in summary, aimed at individual conversions, church planting, and social transformation through three main types of action, which became known as evangelism, education, and medicine. Evangelism included preaching in all its forms, the organizing and fostering of churches, Bible translation, literature production, and the distribution of Bibles and literature.

In the realm of education, industrial schools were stressed in earlier times but generally abandoned because of the desire for an academic education. By the end of the century, a vast educational system was in existence in Asian countries, ranging from kindergarten to college, and including medical and theological schools. Africa, however, was neglected with respect to secondary and collegiate education.

The first doctors sent abroad were sent primarily to take care of the families of other missionaries, but it was soon discovered that medical service to the general populace brought good will and provided an evangelistic opportunity. Thereupon, it was made a major branch of mission work. It was not until the middle of the 20th century that it came to be realized that health services in the name and spirit of the Great Physician are in themselves a dramatic form of the preaching of the gospel. But at a very early date, even the rural evangelistic missionary had taken to carrying a medicine bag with him on his travels.

Female education in the Orient proved to be the most effective force for the liberation and social uplift of women.

It was the same spirit of general helpfulness and cultivation of good will, as well as out of a desire to improve the economic base of the church, that missionaries introduced improved poultry and livestock and better seeds along with new crops. The great orchard industry in Shantung was introduced in this manner.

With regard to the other religions, mission strategy was aggressive, seeking their displacement and total conversion of the peoples. This aggressive spirit declined towards the end of the century, and something of an appreciation of the work of God in the other faiths grew slowly until by 1910 many regarded them as "broken lights" which were to be made whole in Christ and as bridges to the gospel.

The customs of the Oriental peoples made it almost impossible for male missionaries to reach women and with them children in large numbers. Missionary wives endeavored to set up schools for girls and to penetrate the homes, zenanas, and harems, but they did not have enough freedom from home-making and child care and they could not itinerate. Realistic strategy demanded that adequate provision be made for women and children, but the boards and societies were stubbornly resistant to sending single women abroad for such work. Finally in desperation the women in the 1860's began organizing their own societies and sent forth single women. A whole new dimension was thus added to mission strategy: the vast enterprise to reach women and children with the gospel, to educate girls, and to bring adequate medical care to women.

When women came into the church, their children followed them. Female education proved to be the most effective force for the liberation and social uplift of women. The emphasis which the women placed on medical service led the general boards to upgrade the medical work, and greater stress was put on medical education. Out of these two great endeavors of American women, followed by the British and Europeans, there opened to women of the Orient what are today their most prestigious professions, medical service both as physicians and nurses, and teaching.

Comity

One more feature of 19th century missionary strategy must be listed. This was the practice of comity. Southern Baptists were among the founders and practitioners of comity. Good stewardship of men and money held a high priority among boards and societies. Waste was abhorred, and there was a strong desire to stretch resources as far as possible. The practice of comity was intended to make some agency responsible for the evangelism of every last piece of territory and every people. It was further intended to prevent double occupancy of a region (excepting big cities) and overlapping of mission programs, so that competition might be eliminated along with denominational differences which would confuse the inhabitants and thus hamper evangelism. Prior occupation of territory was recognized, the newcoming missions went to unoccupied areas. This custom produced "denominationalism by geography," but the general expectation was that when the missionaries left for the "regions beyond," the nationals would put the several pieces together into a national church which might be different from any of the planting churches.

Missions agreed on recognizing each other as valid branches of the one Church of Christ, on baptism and transfer of membership, on discipline, on salaries, and on transfer of national workers. These agreements led to further cooperation in the establishment of regional and national boards for the arbitration of conflicts between missions and to union Bible translation projects, publication agencies, secondary schools and colleges, teacher training schools, and medical schools. Effective strategy called more and more for doing together all things which could be better achieved through a united effort. City, regional, and national missionary conferences in almost every country provided occasions for common discussion and planning.

Consultations and Conferences

Such cooperation on the mission fields led to increasing home base consultation and planning. The World Missionary Conference at Edinburgh in 1910 inaugurated the series of great conferences: Jerusalem 1928, Madras 1938, Whitby 1947, Willingen 1952, and Ghana 1957-58. In these, the directions of strategy were largely determined, and then applied locally through further study and discussion in national and regional bodies. The International Missionary Council was organized in 1921, bringing together national missionary conferences (such as the Foreign Missions Conference of North America, 1892) and national Christian councils (such as the N.C.C. of China), and thus there was established a universal system at various levels for the voluntary study of problems and planning of strategy in common by a host of sovereign mission boards. In 1961 the I.M.C. became the Division of

World Mission and Evangelism of the World Council of Churches.

From 1910 to World War I, the most notable development of strategy was increasingly putting the national church in the central place, giving it full independence and authority, and developing partnership between the Western churches and the young churches. "The indigenous church" and "partnership in obedience" were watchwords which expressed the thrust of prevailing strategy. The participants in the Jerusalem Conference in 1928 defined the indigenous church, underscoring cultural accommodation. The Madras Conference of 1938 restated the definition, emphasizing witness to Christ in "a direct, clear, and close relationship with the cultural and religious heritage of [the] country." Whitby, 1947, held up the ideal of "partnership in obedience."

Since World War II

A radically different mission strategy, based on Paul, was expounded by Roland Allen in his books *Missionary Methods: St. Paul's or Ours?* and *The Spontaneous Expansion of the Church*, but he gathered no following until after World War II, when the missionaries of the faith missions especially rallied to his standard. In barest essentials this is his strategy: the missionary communicates the gospel and transmits to the new community of converts the simplest statement of the faith, the Bible, the sacraments, and the principle of ministry. He then stands by as a counseling elder brother while the Holy Spirit leads the new church, self-governing and self-supporting, to develop its own forms of polity, ministry, worship, and life. Such a church is spontaneously missionary. Allen's theory applied to new pioneer beginnings. The old boards and societies were dealing with churches already old and set in their ways; they seldom sought untouched fields.

One after another, the mission organizations on the fields were dissolved. Resources were placed at the disposal of the churches and missionary personnel assigned to their direction.

The Western boards and societies initiated very little that was new in the way of strategy, but much to develop new methods:

agricultural missions or rural development, some urban industrial work, mass media communications, more effective literature. This was the final state of a mission which had been in progress for three hundred years. Now the world was no longer divided into Christendom and heathendom. There could no longer be a one-way mission from the West to the remainder of the world. The base for a mission was established in almost every land, because there existed a Christian church and community with an obligation to give the gospel to the whole world. The moment for a new world mission with a radical new strategy had arrived. The revolution which swept the non-western portions of the world during and after World War I unmistakably put an end to the old order of Protestant missions.

A new age of world mission has arrived, one in which other religions are now engaged in world mission also. A new understanding of mission, a new strategy, new organization, new ways, means, and methods are the demand of this hour in the central task of the Church which shall never end until the Kingdom of God has come in all its glory. It will help as we pray, study, plan and experiment if we know the past history of mission strategy.

Study Questions

1. Beaver summarizes some mission strategy debate as differing as far as which came first: "Christianization" or "civilization." Discuss this same issue using the contemporary terms "transformation," "contextualization" and "syncretism."

2. Which strategies depended on colonial power the most? Which strategies were most likely to be advanced with minimal ongoing missionary presence?

Four Men, Three Eras, Two Transitions: Modern Missions

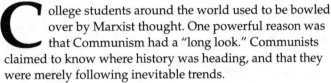

Ralph D. Winter

C ollege students around the world used to be bowled over by Marxist thought. One powerful reason was that Communism had a "long look." Communists claimed to know where history was heading, and that they were merely following inevitable trends.

Recently, evangelicals, too, have thought a lot about trends in history and their relationship to events to come. The massive response a while back to Hal Lindsey's books and films about possible events in the future has shown us that people are responsive to a "where are we going?" approach to life.

In comparison to the Communists, Christians actually have the longest look, backed up by a mass of hard facts and heroic deeds. Yet for some reason, Christians often make little connection between discussion of prophecy and future events, and discussion of missions. They see the Bible as a book of prophecy, both in the past and for the future. Yet, as Bruce Ker has said so well, "The Bible is a missionary book throughout….The main line of argument that binds all of it together is the unfolding and gradual execution of a missionary purpose."

Did I ever hear Ker's thought in Sunday School? Maybe. But only in later years have I come to a new appreciation of the fact that the story of missions begins long before the Great Commission. The Bible is very clear: God told Abraham he was to be blessed and to be a blessing to all the families of the earth (Gen 12:1-3). Peter quoted this on the day he spoke in the temple (Acts 3:25). Paul quoted the same mandate in his letter to the Galatians (3:8).

Yet some Bible commentators imply that only the first part of that verse could have happened right away. They agree that Abraham was to begin to be blessed right away, but somehow they reason that two thousand years would have to pass before either Abraham or his descendants could begin "to be a blessing to all the families on earth." They suggest that Christ needed to come first and institute his Great Commission—that Abraham's lineage needed to wait around for 2,000 years before they would be called upon to go the ends of the earth to be a blessing to all the world's peoples (this could be called "The Theory of the Hibernating Mandate"). Worse still, one scholar, with a lot of followers in later decades, propounded the idea that in the Old Testament the peoples of the world were not expected to receive

After serving ten years as a missionary among Mayan Indians in the highlands of Guatemala, Ralph D. Winter was called to be a Professor of Missions at the School of World Mission at Fuller Theological Seminary. Ten years later he and his wife, Roberta, founded a mission society called the Frontier Mission Fellowship (FMF) in Pasadena, California. This in turn spawned the U.S. Center for World Mission and the William Carey International University, both of which serve other missions working at the frontiers of mission. He is the General Director of the Frontier Mission Fellowship. See expanded biographical sketch at the end of the book.

missionaries but to go to Israel for the light, and that from the the New Testament and thereafter it was the reverse, that is, the peoples to be blessed would not come but those already having received the blessing would go to them. This rather artificial idea gained acceptance partially by the use of the phrase, "centripetal mission in the Old Testament and centrifugal mission in the New Testament." Fact is, there is both in both periods, and it is very confusing to try to employ an essentially "Mickey Mouse" gimmick to explain a shift in strategy that did not happen. The existence of 137 different languages in Los Angeles makes clear that now, in the New Testament-and-after period, nations are still coming to the light.

A more recent and exciting interpretation (see Walter Kaiser's chapter two) observes that Israel, as far back as Abraham, was accountable to share that blessing with other nations. In the same way, since the time of the apostle Paul, every nation which has contained any significant number of "children of Abraham's faith" has been similarly accountable (but both Israel and the other nations have mainly failed to carry out this mandate).

The greatest scandal in the Old Testament is that Israel tried to be blessed without trying very hard to be a blessing. However, let's be careful: *The average citizen of Israel was no more oblivious to the second part of Gen. 12:1-3 than the average Christian today is oblivious to the Great Commission!* How easily our study Bibles overlook the veritable string of key passages in the Old Testament which exist to remind Israel (and us) of the missionary mandate: Gen 12:1-3, 18:18, 22:18, 28:14, Ex 19:4-6, Deut 28:10, 2 Chr 6:33, Ps 67, 96, 105, Isa 40:5, 42:4, 49:6, 56:3, 6-8, Jer 12:14-17, Zech 2:11, Mal 1:11.

Likewise, today nations which have been singularly blessed by God may choose to resist and try to conceal any sense of their obligation to be a blessing to other nations. But that is not God's will. "Unto whomsoever much is given, of him shall much be required" (Luke 12:48).

Thus, how many times in the average church today is the Great Commission mentioned? Even less often than it comes up in the Old Testament! Yet the commission applies. It applied then, and it applies today.

I believe it has been constantly applicable from the very moment when it was first given (Gen 12:1-3). As individual Christians and as a nation we are responsible "to be a blessing to all the families of the earth."

This mandate has been overlooked during most of the centuries since the apostles. Even our Protestant tradition plugged along for over 250 years minding its own business and its own blessings (like Israel of old)—until a young man of great faith and incredible endurance appeared on the scene. In this chapter we are going to focus in on the A.D. 1800-2000 period which his life and witness kicked off. No other one person can be given as much credit for the vibrant new impetus of the last two hundred years. He was one of four such influential men whom God used, all of them with severe handicaps. Three great "eras" of new plunging forward into newly perceived frontiers resulted from their faith and obedience (it took two of them to launch the third and final era). Four stages of mission strategy characterized each of these eras. Two perplexing "transitions" of strategy inevitably appeared as the fourth stage of one era contrasted with the first stage of the next. It is easier to see this in a diagram. Better still, the story.

The First Era

An "under thirty" young man, William Carey, got into trouble when he began to take the Great Commission seriously. When he had the opportunity to address a group of ministers, he challenged them to give a reason why the Great Commission did not apply to them. They rebuked him, saying, "When God chooses to win the heathen, He will do it without your help or ours." He was unable to speak again on the subject, so he patiently wrote out his analysis, "An Enquiry Into the Obligations of Christians to Use Means for the Conversion of the Heathens."

The resulting small book convinced a few of his friends to create a tiny missions agency, the "means" of which he had spoken. The structure was flimsy and weak, providing only the minimal backing he needed to go to India. However, the impact of his example reverberated throughout the English-speaking world, and his little book became the Magna Carta of the Protestant mission movement.

William Carey was not the first Protestant missionary. For years the Moravians had sent people to Greenland, America and Africa. But his little book, in combination with the Evangelical Awakening, quickened vision and changed lives on both sides of the Atlantic. Response was almost instantaneous: a second missionary society was founded in London; two in Scotland; one in Holland; and then still another in England. By then it was apparent to all that Carey was right when he had insisted that organized efforts in the form of missions societies were essential to the success of the missionary endeavor.

In America, five college students, aroused by Carey's book, met to pray for God's direction for their lives. This unobtrusive prayer meeting, later known as the "Haystack Prayer Meeting," resulted in an American "means"—the American Board of Commissioners of Foreign Missions. Even more important, they started a student mission movement which became the example and forerunner of other student movements in missions to this day.

In fact, during the first 25 years after Carey sailed to India, a dozen mission agencies were formed on both sides of the Atlantic, and the First Era in Protestant missions was off to a good start. Realistically speaking, however, missions in this First Era was a pitifully small shoe-string operation, in relation to the major preoccupations of most Europeans and Americans in that day. The idea that we should organize in order to send missionaries did not come easily, but it eventually became an accepted pattern.

Carey's influence led some women in Boston to form women's missionary prayer groups, a trend which led to women becoming the main custodians of mission knowledge and motivation. After some years women began to go to the field as single missionaries. Finally, by 1865, unmarried American women established women's mission boards which, like Roman Catholic women's orders, only sent out single women as missionaries and were run entirely by single women at home.

There are two very bright notes about the First Era. One is the astonishing demonstration of love and sacrifice on the part of those who went out. Africa, especially, was a forbidding continent. All mission outreach to Africa prior to 1775 had totally failed. Of all Catholic efforts, all Moravian efforts, nothing remained. Not one missionary of any kind existed on the continent on the eve of the First Era. The gruesome statistics of almost inevitable sickness and death that haunted, yet did not daunt, the decades of truly valiant missionaries who went out after 1790 in virtually a suicidal stream cannot be matched by any other era or by any other cause. Very few missionaries to Africa in the first 60 years of the First Era survived more than two years.

> During the first 25 years after Carey sailed to India, a dozen mission agencies were formed on both sides of the Atlantic.

As I have reflected on this measure of devotion I have been humbled to tears, for I wonder—if I or my people today could or would match that record. Can you imagine our Urbana students today going out into missionary work if they knew that for decade after decade 19 out of 20 of those before them had died almost on arrival on the field?

A second bright spot in this First Era is the development of high quality insight into mission strategy. The movement had several great missiologists. In regard to home structure, they clearly understood the value of the mission structure being allowed a life of its own. For example, we read that the London Missionary Society experienced unprecedented and unequaled success, "due partly to its freedom from ecclesiastical supervision and partly to its formation from an almost equal number of ministers and laymen." In regard to field structure, we can take a note from Henry Venn who was related to the famous Clapham evangelicals and the son of a founder of the Church Missionary Society. Except for a few outdated terms, one of his most famous paragraphs sounds strangely modern:

> Regarding the ultimate object of a Mission, viewed under its ecclesiastical result, to be

the settlement of a Native Church under Native Pastors upon a self-supporting system, it should be borne in mind that the progress of a Mission mainly depends upon the training up and the location of Native Pastors; and that, as it has been happily expressed, the "euthanasia of a Mission" takes place when a missionary, surrounded by well-trained Native congregations under Native Pastors, is able to resign all pastoral work into their hands, and gradually relax his superintendence over the pastors themselves, 'til it insensibly ceases; and so the Mission passes into a settled Christian community. Then the missionary and all missionary agencies should be transferred to the "regions beyond."

Take note: There was no thought here of the national church launching its own mission outreach to new pioneer fields! Nevertheless, we see here something like *stages of mission activity*, described by Harold Fuller of SIM in the alliterative sequence:

Stage 1: A Pioneer stage—first contact with a people group.

Stage 2: A Paternal stage—expatriates train national leadership.

Stage 3: A Partnership stage—national leaders work as equals with expatriates.

Stage 4: A Participation stage—expatriates are no longer equal partners, but only participate by invitation.

Slow and painstaking though the labors of the First Era were, they did bear fruit, and the familiar series of stages can be observed which goes from no church in the pioneer stage to infant church in the paternal stage and to the more complicated mature church in the partnership and participation stages.

Samuel Hoffman of the Reformed Church in America Board puts it well: "The Christian missionary who was loved as an evangelist and liked as a teacher, may find himself resented as an administrator."

Mission-Church Relations: Four Stages of Development

Stage One: Pioneer
Requires gift of leadership, along with other gifts.
No Believers—missionary must lead and
do much of the work himself.

mission

Stage Two: Parent
Requires gift of teaching.
The young church has a growing child's
relationship to the mission. But the "parent"
must avoid "paternalism."

church   mission

Stage Three: Partner
Requires changes from parent-child
relation to adult-adult relation.
Difficult for both to change, but essential to the
church's becoming a mature "adult."

church   mission

Stage Four: Participant
A fully mature church assumes leadership.
As long as the mission remains, it should use its gifts
to strengthen the church to meet the original objectives
of Matt 28:19-20. Meanwhile the mission should be
involved in Stage One elsewhere.

church   mission

Lucky is the missionary in whose own career this whole sequence of stages takes place. More likely the series represents the work in a specific field with a succession of missionaries, or it may be the experience of an agency which in its early period bursts out in work in a number of places and then after some years finds that most of its fields are mature at about the same time. But rightly or wrongly, this kind of succession is visible in the mission movement globally, as the fever for change and nationalization sweeps the thinking of almost all executives at once and leaps from continent to continent, affecting new fields still in earlier stages as well as old ones in the latter stages.

> Taylor was more concerned for the cause than for a career: At the end of his life he had spent only half of his years of ministry in China.

At any rate, by 1865 there was a strong consensus on both sides of the Atlantic that the missionary should go home when he had worked himself out of a job. Since the First Era focused primarily upon the coastlands of Asia and Africa, we are not surprised that literal withdrawal would come about first in a case where there were no inland territories. Thus, symbolizing the latter stages of the First Era was the withdrawal of all missionaries from the Hawaiian Islands, then a separate country. This was done with legitimate pride and fanfare and fulfilled the highest expectations, then and now, of successful progress through the stages of missionary planting, watering and harvest.

The Second Era

A second symbolic event of 1865 is even more significant, at least for the inauguration of the Second Era. A young man, after a short term and like Carey still under thirty, in the teeth of surrounding counter advice established the first of a whole new breed of missions emphasizing the inland territories. This second young upstart was given little but negative notice, but like William Carey, brooded over statistics, charts and maps. When he suggested that the inland peoples of China

needed to be reached, he was told you could not get there, and he was asked if he wished to carry on his shoulders the blood of the young people he would thus send to their deaths. This accusing question stunned and staggered him. Groping for light, wandering on the beach, it seemed as if God finally spoke to resolve the ghastly thought: "You are not sending young people in the interior of China. I am." The load lifted.

With only trade school medicine, without any university experience much less missiological training, and a checkered past in regard to his own individualistic behavior while he was on the field, he was merely one more of the weak things that God uses to confound the wise. Even his early antichurch-planting missionary strategy was breathtakingly erroneous by today's church-planting standards. Yet God strangely honored him because his gaze was fixed upon the world's least-reached peoples. Hudson Taylor had a divine wind behind him. The Holy Spirit spared him from many pitfalls, and it was his organization, the China Inland Mission—the most cooperative, servant organization yet to appear—that eventually served in one way or another over 6,000 missionaries, predominantly in the interior of China. It took 20 years for other missions to begin to join Taylor in his special emphasis—the unreached, inland frontiers.

One reason the Second Era began slowly is that many people were confused. There were already many missions in existence. Why more? Yet as Taylor pointed out, all existing agencies were confined to the coastlands of Africa and Asia, or islands in the Pacific. People questioned, "Why go to the interior if you haven't finished the job on the coast?"

I am not sure the parallel is true today, but the Second Era apparently needed not only a new vision but a lot of new organizations. Taylor not only started an English frontier mission, he went to Scandinavia and the Continent to challenge people to start new agencies. As a result, directly or indirectly, over 40 new agencies took shape to compose the faith missions that rightly should be called frontier missions as the names of many of them still indicate: China Inland Mission, Sudan Interior Mission, Africa Inland Mission, Heart of Africa Mission, Unevangelized Fields Mission, Regions Beyond Missionary Union. Taylor was more concerned for the cause than for a career: At the end of his life he had spent only half of his years of ministry in China. In countless trips back from China he spent half of his time as a mobilizer on the home front. For Taylor, the cause of Christ, not China, was the ultimate focus of his concern.

As in the early stage of the First Era, when things began to move, God brought forth a student movement. This one was more massive than before—the Student Volunteer Movement for Foreign Missions, history's single most potent mission organization. In the 1880s and 90s there were only 1/37th as many college students as there are today, but the Student Volunteer Movement netted 100,000 volunteers who gave their lives to missions. Twenty-thousand actually went overseas. As we see it now, the other 80,000 had to stay home to rebuild the foundations of the missions endeavor. They began the Laymen's Missionary Movement and strengthened existing women's missionary societies.

However, as the fresh new college students of the Second Era burst on the scene overseas, they did not always fathom how the older missionaries of the First Era could have turned responsibility over to national leadership at the least educated levels of society. First Era missionaries were in the minority now, and the wisdom they had gained from their experience was bypassed by the large number of new college-educated recruits. Thus, in the early stages of the Second Era, the new college-trained missionaries, instead of going to new frontiers, sometimes assumed leadership over existing churches, not reading the record of previous mission thinkers, and often forced First Era missionaries and national leadership (which had been painstakingly developed) into the background. In some cases this caused a huge step backward in mission strategy.

By 1925, however, the largest mission movement in history was in full swing. By then Second Era missionaries had finally learned the basic lessons they had first ignored, and produced an incredible record. They had planted churches in a thousand new places, mainly "inland," and by 1940 the reality of the "younger churches" around the world was widely acclaimed as the "great new fact of our time." The strength of these churches led both national leaders and missionaries to assume that all additional frontiers could simply be mopped up by the ordinary evangelism of the churches scattered throughout the world. More and more people wondered if, in fact, missionaries weren't needed so badly! Once more, as in 1865, it seemed logical to send missionaries home from many areas of the world.

For us today it is highly important to note the overlap of these first two eras. The 45 year period between 1865 and 1910 (compare 1934 to 1980 today) was a transition between the strategy appropriate to the mature stages of Era 1, the Coastlands era, and the strategy appropriate to the pioneering stages of Era 2, the Inland era.

Shortly after the World Missionary Conference in Edinburgh in 1910, there ensued the shattering World Wars and the worldwide collapse of the colonial apparatus. By 1945 many overseas churches were prepared not only for the withdrawal of the colonial powers, but for the absence of the missionary as well. While there was no very widespread outcry, "Missionary Go Home," as some supposed, nevertheless things were different now, as even the people in the pews at home ultimately sensed. Pioneer and paternal were no longer the relevant stages, but partnership and participation.

In 1967, the total number of career missionaries from America began to decline (and it has continued to do so to this day). Why? Christians had been led to believe that all necessary beachheads had been established. By 1967, over 90 percent of all missionaries from North America were working with strong national churches that had been in existence for some time.

The facts, however, were not that simple. Unnoticed by most everyone, another era in missions had begun.

Three Eras of the Modern Missions Movement

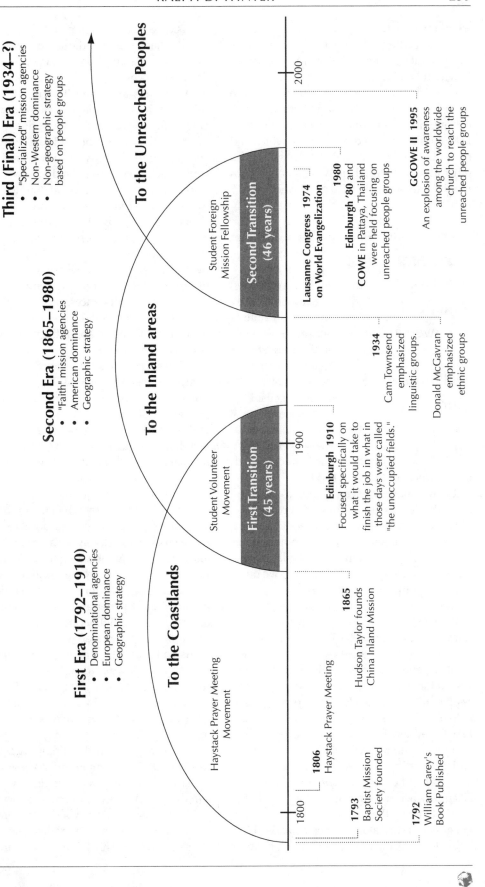

First Era (1792–1910)
- Denominational agencies
- European dominance
- Geographic strategy

Second Era (1865–1980)
- "Faith" mission agencies
- American dominance
- Geographic strategy

Third (Final) Era (1934–?)
- "Specialized" mission agencies
- Non-Western dominance
- Non-geographic strategy based on people groups

To the Coastlands

To the Inland areas

To the Unreached Peoples

First Transition (45 years)

Second Transition (46 years)

Haystack Prayer Meeting Movement

Student Volunteer Movement

Student Foreign Mission Fellowship

1792
William Carey's Book Published

1793
Baptist Mission Society founded

1806
Haystack Prayer Meeting

1865
Hudson Taylor founds China Inland Mission

1800

1900

2000

Edinburgh 1910
Focused specifically on what it would take to finish the job in what in those days were called "the unoccupied fields."

1934
Cam Townsend emphasized linguistic groups.

Donald McGavran emphasized ethnic groups

Lausanne Congress 1974 on World Evangelization

1980
Edinburgh '80 and **COWE** in Pattaya, Thailand were held focusing on unreached people groups

GCOWE II 1995
An explosion of awareness among the worldwide church to reach the unreached people groups

The Third Era

This era was begun by a pair of young men of the Student Volunteer Movement—Cameron Townsend and Donald McGavran. Cameron Townsend was in so much of a hurry to get to the mission field that he didn't bother to finish college. He went to Guatemala as a "Second Era" missionary, building on work which had been done in the past. In that country, as in all other mission fields, there was plenty to do by missionaries working with established national churches.

But Townsend was alert enough to notice that the majority of Guatemala's population did not speak Spanish. As he moved from village to village, trying to distribute scriptures written in the Spanish language, he began to realize that Spanish evangelism would never reach all Guatemala's people. He was further convinced of this when an Indian asked him, "If your God is so smart, why can't he speak our language?" He was befriended by a group of older missionaries who had already concluded the indigenous "Indian" populations needed to be reached in their own languages. He was just 23 when he began to move on the basis of this new perspective.

> The task is not an American one, nor even a Western one. It will involve Christians from every continent of the world.

Surely in our time one person comparable to William Carey and Hudson Taylor is Cameron Townsend. Like Carey and Taylor, Townsend saw that there were still unreached frontiers, and for almost a half century he has waved the flag for the overlooked tribal peoples of the world. He started out hoping to help older boards reach out to tribal people. Like Carey and Taylor, he ended up starting his own mission, Wycliffe Bible Translators, which is dedicated to reaching these new frontiers. At first he thought there must be about 500 unreached tribal groups in the world. (He was judging by the large number of tribal languages in Mexico alone). Later, he revised his figure to 1,000, then 2,000, and now it is closer to 5,000. As his conception of the enormity of the task has increased, the size of his organization has increased. Today it numbers over 4,000 adult workers.

At the very same time Townsend was ruminating in Guatemala, Donald McGavran was beginning to yield to the seriousness, not of linguistic barriers, but of India's amazing social barriers. Townsend "discovered" the tribes; McGavran discovered a more nearly universal category he labeled "homogeneous units," which today are more often called "people groups." Paul Hiebert has employed the terminology of "horizontal segmentation" for the tribes which each occupied their own turf, and "vertical segmentation" for groups distinguished not by geography but by rigid social differences. McGavran's terminology described both kinds even though he was mainly thinking about the more subtle vertical segmentation.

Once such a group is penetrated, diligently taking advantage of that missiological breakthrough along group lines, the strategic "bridge of God" to that people group is established. The corollary of this truth is the fact that *until* such a breakthrough is made, normal evangelism and church planting cannot take place.

McGavran did not found a new mission (Townsend did so only when the existing missions did not properly respond to the tribal challenge). McGavran's active efforts and writings spawned both the church growth movement and the frontier mission movement, the one devoted to expanding within already penetrated groups, and the other devoted to deliberate approaches to the remaining unpenetrated groups.

As with Carey and Taylor before them, for twenty years Townsend and McGavran attracted little attention. But by the 1950s both had wide audiences. By 1980, 46 years from 1934, a 1910-like conference was held, focusing precisely on the forgotten groups these two men emphasized. The Edinburgh-1980 World Consultation on Frontier Missions was the largest mission meeting in history, measured by the number of mission agencies sending delegates. And wonder of wonders, 57 Third World agencies sent delegates. This is the sleeper of the Third Era! Also, a simultaneous youth meeting, the International Student Consultation on Frontier Missions, pointed the way for all future mission meetings to include significant youth participation.

As happened in the early stages of the first two eras, the Third Era has spawned a number of new mission agencies. Some, like the New Tribes Mission, carry in their names reference to this new emphasis. The names of others, such as Gospel Recordings and Mission Aviation Fellowship, refer to the new technologies necessary for the reaching of tribal and other isolated peoples of the world. Some Second Era agencies, like Regions Beyond Missionary Union, have never ceased to stress frontiers, and have merely increased their staff so they can penetrate further—to people groups previously overlooked.

More recently many have begun to realize that tribal peoples are not the only forgotten peoples. Many other groups, some in the middle of partially Christianized areas, have been completely overlooked. These peoples are being called the "Unreached Peoples" and are defined by ethnic or sociological traits to be people so different from the cultural traditions of any existing church that missions (rather than evangelism) strategies are necessary for the planting of indigenous churches within their particular traditions.

If the First Era was characterized by reaching coastland peoples and the Second Era by inland territories, the Third Era must be characterized by the more difficult-to-define, non-geographical category which we have called "Unreached Peoples"—people groups which are socially isolated. Because this concept has been so hard to define, the Third Era has been even slower getting started than the Second Era. Cameron Townsend and Donald McGavran began calling attention to forgotten peoples over 40 years ago, but only recently has any major attention been given to them. More tragic still, we have essentially forgotten the pioneering techniques of the First and Second Eras, so we almost need to reinvent the wheel as we learn again how to approach groups of people completely untouched by the gospel!

We know that there are about 10,000 people groups in the "Unreached Peoples" category, gathered in clusters of similar peoples, these clusters numbering not more than 3,000. Each individual people will require a separate, new missionary beachhead. Is this too much? Can this be done?

Can We Do It?

The task is not as difficult as it may seem, for several surprising reasons. In the first place, the task is not an American one, nor even a Western one. It will involve Christians from every continent of the world.

More significant is the fact that when a beachhead is established within a culture, the normal evangelistic process which God expects every Christian to be involved in replaces the missions strategy, because the mission task of "breaking in" is finished.

Furthermore, "closed countries" are less and less of a problem, because the modern world is becoming more and more interdependent. There are literally no countries today which admit no foreigners. Many of the countries considered "completely closed"—like Saudi Arabia—are in actual fact avidly recruiting thousands of skilled people from other nations. And the truth is, they prefer devout Christians to boozing, womanizing, secular Westerners.

But our work in the Third Era has many other advantages. We have potentially a world-wide network of churches that can be aroused to their central mission. Best of all, nothing can obscure the fact that this could and should be the *final* era. No serious believer today dare overlook the fact that God has not asked us to reach every nation, tribe and tongue without intending it to be done. No generation has less excuse than ours if we do not do as He asks.

Study Questions

1. Describe the emphasis of each of the three eras and explain the tensions inherent in the transition from one era to another.

2. Name the key figure, approximate dates, and student movement associated with each era.

3. Explain the four stages of mission activity.

A History of Transformation

Paul Pierson

T he Church of Jesus Christ, especially its missionary arm, has generally understood the transformation of society to be an essential part of its task. While the focal point of mission has always been to communicate the Good News of Christ, calling people to repent and believe and be baptized into the Church, Christians have always understood their mission to be fulfilled in teaching the nations "to observe all things" that Christ has commanded. Expectation of people obeying Christ has always fueled hope that the culmination of this process of evangelization would bring about transformation of the social situations, the physical conditions, and the spiritual lives of believers. Sometimes changes were remarkable, at other times disappointing. But even when there was great cultural misunderstanding and error, the desire to bring individuals and societies more into conformity with the kingdom of God has remained an integral part of mission.

Often missionaries moved into cultures which were already undergoing change. They helped produce some of that change, often channeling it positively, or working against some of its harsher aspects. Missionaries often envisioned a model of transformed communities that looked suspiciously like those they had known in their own cultures; however, there is no doubt this transforming dimension was an essential aspect of mission, and for the most part, beneficial. [1]

Monasticism: Communities of Preservation and Transformation

Nearly all missionaries during the period from the fourth to the eighteenth centuries were monks. Though most of the monastic movements were expressly missionary, others were not, but nearly all of the monastic movements brought about significant social transformation.

There were dozens of monastic movements, among them were the *Benedictines* and those movements which were born out of them, the *Nestorians,* who moved from Asia Minor into Arabia, India, and across central Asia to China, the *Orthodox,* who went north into the Balkans and Russia, the *Celts,* who arose in Ireland, then moved into Scotland and England, and back to the continent, and later, the *Franciscans, Dominicans,* and *Jesuits.*

Even though the *Benedictines* were not purposely missionary, they and the other groups moved into areas where

Paul Pierson is a Senior Professor of Mission and Latin American Studies at the School of World Mission at Fuller Theological Seminary. He was Dean of the School of World Mission from 1980 to 1993. He also pastored churches and served as a missionary to Brazil and Portugal.

the Christian faith had not yet penetrated, forming communities which modeled and taught the Faith to the "barbarian" tribes moving into central and Western Europe. The original intent of monasticism was to encourage men to develop lives of discipline and prayer, far from the concerns of normal life. But the monasteries and the soon-to-follow women's houses became self-sustaining communities organized around rules for daily life which included both work and worship. Work was both manual and intellectual, in the fields and in the library. This was a revolutionary concept in the ancient world where manual work was seen as fit only for slaves. Monks also became scholars, thus for the first time, the practical and the theoretical were embodied in the same persons. So the monks have been called the first intellectuals to get dirt under their fingernails! This helped create an environment favorable to scientific development and the monasteries became centers of faith, learning, and technical progress.

Monasticisms contribution to learning is well known, but its impact on agricultural development is not as widely recognized. Hannah wrote that in the seventh century "it was the monks who possessed the skill, capital, organization, and faith in the future to undertake large projects of reclamation over fields long desolated by the slave system of village life...and the barbarian hordes.... Immense tracts of barren heath and water-soaked fen were by the monasteries' hands turned into excellent agricultural land."[2]

In the twelfth century the *Cistercians* withdrew from society and cultivated new land in deserted places. They worked out new methods of agricultural administration and became the greatest wool producers in Europe, furnishing the raw material for the textile industry.

The *Nestorians*, who flourished from the fifth to the thirteenth centuries, moved across central Asia into India and China. Christians in the West know little about this remarkable movement because most of the fruit of its labor was lost. Yet as one scholar noted, "Nestorian missionaries introduced letters and learning among people who were previously illiterate, including Turks,

Vigurs, Mongols, and Manchus, all of whom are said to derive their alphabets from Syriac, the language of the Nestorians."[3]

Orthodox monks from the Eastern Church did the same. Ulfilas moved north of the Danube in the fourth century and was the first to reduce a northern European language to writing, doing so, of course, to translate the Scriptures. In the third century the Armenians were the first national group to adopt Christianity, and in ad 406 their language was reduced to writing so that the Scriptures and other Christian literature might be made available. Constantine (later known as Cyril) and his brother Methodius went to the Balkans and devised two alphabets used to translate the Scriptures and establish the Church. The Cyrillic script is still in use in Russia today.

When Patrick returned to Ireland from England he initiated the remarkable *Celtic* missionary movement that would continue for centuries, and which would be a source of missionary zeal and learning. His spiritual descendants moved from Ireland to Scotland, then to England, across the channel to the low countries, and finally into central Germany. They were later instrumental in the con version of Scandinavia. They combined a deep love of learning, spiritual discipline, and missionary zeal. As a result "Ireland became literate for the first time in Patrick's generation." [4] The great monastery at Fulda, founded in the eighth century by St. Boniface from this tradition, became the main center of learning for much of Germany.

During the Carolingian Renaissance under Charlemagne, the monasteries of the Celtic tradition were again the major centers of education and change. Hannah wrote, "On the whole they were able to achieve their destiny as Christian leaven in a rude society, to implant and preserve a Christian culture like a cultivated garden amid a wilderness of disorder."[5]

Forerunners of the Protestant Missionary Movement

For nearly two centuries after the Reformation Protestants engaged in very little missionary activity outside of Europe. But in the late sixteenth century several movements arose, the members of which sought to renew the Church and carry the Reformation further, from doctrine into life. These movements would form the launching pad of Protestant missions, and included *Puritanism, Pietism, Moravianism,* and the *Wesleyan/Evangelical* revivals.

The *Puritans* focused on conversion and a more authentic Christian life. They also developed the first Protestant mission theology. Two of their greatest mission advocates were Richard Baxter, an effective pastor and prolific writer, and John Eliot. Eliot went to New England and became an effective missionary to the Algonquin Native Americans, translating the Bible into their language and forming a number of Christian villages. Rooy wrote of him:

> He traveled on foot and horseback, taxing his strength to the utmost…to bring the gospel to the natives. He brought cases to court to prevent defrauding of Indian land, pleaded clemency for convicted Indian prisoners, fought the selling of Indians into slavery, sought to secure lands and streams for Indian use, established schools for Indian children and adults, translated books, and attempted to show a deep humanitarianism that accompanied their concern for salvation.[6]

Pietism laid the foundation for greater changes, and just in time. In the seventeenth century the Thirty Years War had devastated Germany. Misery abounded, class differences were exaggerated, the level of Christian understanding and life was low, and the Lutheran Church was dominated by the State. The truth of faith was seen in terms of propositions rather than experiential or ethical event or demands. Thus, between the irrelevance of the Church and the widespread despair and atheism brought about by the Thirty Years War, Christianity soon lost its healing and transforming power.[7]

Philip Jacob Spener, influenced by Puritan writers during his theological studies, found the situation of his parishioners deplorable when he became the pastor in Frankfort. He began to invite groups into his home for dis-

cussion of the sermon, Bible study, prayer, and mutual support, thus initiating a movement its opponents called Pietism.

Spener insisted that Christianity consisted not only of knowledge, but must also include the practice of the Faith. Along with his emphasis on the necessity of the new birth and a holy life, he included a great concern for the needy.

A. H. Francke was Spener's successor as leader of the movement. He taught that rebirth should lead to transformed individuals and then to a reformed society and world. For him faith and action were inseparable. He demonstrated this to a remarkable extent in his influence at the University of Halle and his parish at Glaucha. Piety meant genuine concern for the spiritual and physical well being of one's neighbor. So the Pietists fed, clothed, and educated the poor. Francke established schools for poor children, including girls, a novelty at the time. He also founded an orphanage and other institutions to aid the poor. These were supported by faith alone and became the model later for the ministry of George Mueller in Bristol and the China Inland Mission.

The first Protestant missionaries to Asia came from the Pietist movement. Influenced by his Pietist court chaplain, in 1706 Frederick IV of Denmark sent two men from Halle to his colony in Tranquebar, India. Bartholomew Ziegenbalg and Heinrich Plutschau were the first of about 60 Pietists who went to India in the eighteenth century. Ziegenbalg, who remained until his death in 1719, was remarkably holistic in his understanding of the task. He studied the religious beliefs and practices of the Hindus, translated the Scriptures, planted a church, advocated the ordination of Indian pastors, set up a printing press, and established two schools.

The greatest of his successors, C. F. Schwartz, not only built up the church but worked with orphans and became an ambassador of peace between Muslim rulers and the British. Arriving in 1750, he remained un-

> The Pietism Movement was the parent of all those saving agencies which have arisen within Christendom for the healing of religious, moral, and social evils.

til his death in 1798. A great German missiologist wrote that "Pietism was the parent of missions to the heathen...also of all those saving agencies which have arisen within Christendom for the healing of religious, moral, and social evils...a combination which was already typically exemplified in A. H. Francke."[8]

The *Moravians*, with roots both in the Pre-Reformation Hussite movement and Pietism, were one of the most remarkable movements in history. Known for their 24 hour, 100 year prayer watch, they were a highly disciplined, monastic-like community of married men and women devoted to win "souls for the Lamb." During their early years, one of every 14 members became a missionary, often going to the most difficult fields.

The fourth stream leading to the Protestant missionary movement flowed from the *Wesleyan/Evangelical* revival in England, with John Wesley as its best known leader, and the First Great Awakening in North America. Since the awakening in North America was in many respects an outgrowth of Puritanism, we will examine only the movement in England.

Even before their salvation, the Wesleys and the other members of the "Holy Club" at Oxford showed concern for the poor and prisoners. At the same time they pursued the spiritual disciplines which earned them the name, "Methodists."

John Wesley began to preach immediately after his conversion in 1734. While the clear focus was on evangelism and Christian nurture, especially among the neglected poor, he wrote, "Christianity is essentially a social religion, to turn it into a solitary religion is indeed to destroy it." [9] The impact of the movement on social reform in England is well known. Robert Raikes started Sunday schools to teach poor children to read and give them moral and religious instruction on the only day of the week they were not working. Others organized schools among miners and colliers. John Howard tirelessly worked for reform of the appalling conditions in local prisons, then moved Parliament to pass laws for prison reform.

Evangelicals worked to regulate child labor in the emerging factories and promoted the education of the masses. A group of wealthy Anglican evangelicals at Clapham, a suburb of London, spent their time, fortunes, and political influence in a number of religious and social projects, including the long and successful campaign of William Wilberforce and others, to end slavery in the British Empire. The Church Missionary Society, the greatest of the Anglican societies, was established in 1799. Several other societies were established, all motivated by the revival.

The Protestant Missionary Movement

William Carey is rightly called "the Father of Protestant Missions," even though others had engaged in such missions earlier. In 1792 he formed the Baptist Missionary Society; the following year he sailed to India. His writing and example were the catalyst in the creation of similar societies in Europe and in the United States, leading to what has been called "the great century" of missions. His primary goal was to lead people to personal faith in Jesus Christ and eternal salvation; however he saw no conflict between that goal and his other activities in education, agriculture, and botany.

Carey labored widely to withstand social evils and bring change in Asia. He was better known as a horticulturist around the world than as a missionary. He fought valiantly against the practice of infanticide, the burning of widows, the inhuman treatment of lepers (who were often buried or burned alive), and the needless deaths at the great religious pilgrimages of the time. He also founded Serampore College, which was established primarily to train pastors and teachers, but also provided for the education of others in Christian literature and European science.

False Recognition

Many nineteenth century missionary movements labored intentionally for social transformation, most without recognition, except at times in a false and negative light. For example, at Andover Seminary, Samuel Mills and his colleagues from the Haystack Prayer Meeting took the initiative in establishing the American Board of Commissioners for Foreign Missions in 1810. One of the early fields chosen was Hawaii (then known as the Sandwich Islands). Those early missionaries were maligned by James Michner; but the reality was much different from the picture he painted. Their major focus was the conversion of men and women to Christ and the gathering of converts into churches. But they also worked to protect the Hawaiian people from the sexual and economic exploitation of the sailors and traders who came to the islands. The missionaries worked to end infantacide and other destructive practices. After a few decades the islands were dotted not only with churches, but with schools in which Hawaiian children were taught by Hawaiian teachers. Several years later others devised a system of writing the language using Roman characters, translating the Bible and various textbooks. By 1873 they had published 153 different works and 13 magazines, along with an almanac in the local language.

A Striking Comparison

Many lesser known missionaries have demonstrated great concern for the totality of human need. One of them was Willis Banks, an obscure Presbyterian evangelist who worked in a backward area of southern Brazil. He built the areas first brickyard, brought children to live with his family, taught them to read, and then sent them back to teach others. Using a home medical guide, he treated infections, tuberculosis, malaria, worms, and malnutrition.

Banks introduced better methods of agriculture and care of livestock. He build the first sawmill in the area and constructed machinery to cut silage. An anthropologist who visited the area 20 years after Banks' death gave a striking illustration of the resulting community development. He visited two isolated villages, both situated in virtually identical circumstances, with inhabitants of the same racial and cultural backgrounds. The village of Volta Grande was Presbyterian and had benefited from Banks' evangelism and leadership. The people lived in houses of brick and wood, used water filters and in some cases had home produced electricity. They owned canoes and motor launches for travel to a nearby city and cultivated vegetables along with the

traditional rice, beans, corn, manioc, and bananas. They had two herds of dairy cattle and produced and consumed milk, cheese, and butter. They received and read newspapers, had the Bible and other books readily available, and all were literate. The community had pooled its resources to build a school and donated it to the State with the stipulation that a teacher be provided and paid. Consequently there was an excellent primary school there and many of its graduates continued their studies in the city. Religious services were held three times a week even though the pastor could visit only once a month.

The inhabitants of Jipovura, the other village, lived in daub and wattle houses with no furniture. They engaged only in marginal agriculture, and did not boil or filter their water. They had no canoes, used tiny kerosene lamps for light, and were mostly illiterate. A school had been donated to the community by a few Japanese families who had once lived in the area, but the people showed no interest in maintaining it and had ruined the building by stealing its doors and windows. Leisure time was filled by playing cards and drinking the local sugarcane rum. Alcoholism was common.[10]

Virtually all missionary movements in history have been concerned about social transformation in one way or another. It has been seen as part of the ministry of communicating and living out the gospel. Major emphasis has been placed on education, health care, agriculture, and ministries of social uplift for girls, women, and other neglected and oppressed members of society.

Establishing Education

Educational institutions usually had three goals: to prepare leadership for the church, to be an instrument to improve society, and to evangelize non-Christian students.

Degrees of success varied, but include the following examples:

- The tribal groups of Northeast India, which became heavily Christian beginning late in the last century, have the second highest literacy rate in the nation.
- In 1915 illiteracy among nominal Roman Catholics in Brazil was between 60 and

80 percent, while that of Protestants (who normally came from the poor) was one fourth of that figure.[11]

- Most schools in Africa during the colonial period were established by missionaries. Leslie Newbegin pointed out in the 50s that in a 400-page United Nations document on education in Africa, not a single line revealed the fact that 90% of the schools being described were there because of missionaries. [12]

- Many of the outstanding universities in Asia were the result of missions, including Yonsei University and Ehwa Women's University in Seoul.

- Reporting on the educational work of the Basel Mission in the Gold Coast (Ghana), the Phelps-Stokes Commission reported in 1921, "The educational effort of the Basel Mission in the Gold Coast has produced one of the most interesting and effective systems of schools observed in Africa.... First of all their mechanical shops trained and employed a large number of natives as journeymen.... Secondly the commercial activities reached the economic life of the people, influencing their agricultural activities and their expenditures for food and clothing."

- In addition to the primary and secondary mission schools, teacher training institutions were established to expand educational opportunities.

Bringing Medical Care

Early in the movement a limited amount of medical knowledge was often regarded as necessary for evangelistic missionaries. But by the middle of the last century fully trained physicians were being sent to the field. The first was Dr. John Scudder, sent by the American Board to India. His granddaughter, Dr. Ida Scudder, later established perhaps the greatest of all missionary medical centers at Vellore, India. Dr. Peter Parker introduced eye surgery into China. His successor, Dr. John Kerr, published 12 medical works in Chinese, built a large hospital, and was the first in China to open an institution for the mentally ill. Presbyterians in Thailand established 13 hospitals and 12 dispensaries.

Touching the Neglected and Oppressed

Along with educational, medical, and agricultural ministries, others focused on some of the most neglected and depressed members of their societies. Half of the tuberculosis work in India was done by missions, and Christian institutions took the lead both in treatment and the training of workers among those afflicted. Missions also took the lead in working with lepers in several Asian countries, and established orphanages for abandoned children.

A few missionaries went beyond social service and attacked the political and social injustices of colonialism. A celebrated example took place in the Belgian Congo at the turn of the century. Two Presbyterian missionaries from the United States observed the forced labor of the Africans in the rubber industry, and published articles calling the monopolistic economic exploitation "twentieth century slavery." This garnered international attention; the missionaries were sued for libel, with the suit finally dismissed.

> The Christian mission movement has had dramatic positive impact on every continent and continues to do so in even greater ways.

Serving Women

One of the most significant results of Christian missions in many societies came through their role in ministering to and raising the status of women. In many of the cultures women were relegated to a very low status and had almost no rights. Missionaries, usually single women, evangelized them, teaching them to see themselves as children of God. Then girls and women were encouraged to study, develop their gifts, and in some cases, enter professions such as education and medicine.

Focusing first on the evangelization of women in cultures where men could not have contact with most women, the missionaries soon branched out into educational and medical work with women. Soon women were employed as lay evangelists, called 'Bible women,' especially in China and Korea. Even though they were not yet given equal status with men, these faithful workers had a powerful impact not only on the growth of the Church but on the status of other women. When the first Protestant missionaries arrived in Korea in 1884 and 1885, a woman had virtually no status in society except as the daughter of her father, the wife of her husband, or the mother of her oldest son. By the middle of this century the world's largest women's university had been established in Seoul and its President, Dr. Helen Kim, was recognized as one of Korea's greatest educators as well as a leader in evangelization.

Women missionaries from the United States initiated the first medical work for women in India and China, established the first girls' schools, and eventually founded nursing and medical schools for women. This had a powerful impact on the medical care of women, as well as their status in society. As a result medicine is among the most prestigious professions open to women in India, and there are thousands of women physicians in that nation today. Dr. Clara Swain, the first woman medical missionary appointed to a field, arrived in India in 1870. Beaver makes it clear that Swain and others saw no separation between their medical and evangelistic work. Their manifestation of loving concern for their patients as individuals, and their mediation of the love of God in Christ for persons were as important as their scientific knowledge and technical skill. The writings and speeches of the women medical missionaries make it clear that they considered themselves evangelists.[13]

The story goes on. The Christian mission movement has had dramatic positive impact on every continent and continues to do so in even greater ways. Even though the basic aim of many of these mission efforts was to call people to faith in Him, and plant the Church, the effects of those efforts has been seen to eventually extend to every part of the societies in which the church has been planted. There is much to disappoint and admire in the record; but overall, the Christian movement is bringing a measure of fulfillment of God's promise that Abraham's descendents would bring blessing to all the families of the earth.

End Notes

1. Hutchinson, William. *Errand to the World.* Chicago, Univ. of Chicago Press,1987.
2. Hannah, Ian. *Monasticism*, London, Allen and Unwin, 1924. pp. 90,91.
3. Stewart, John. *The Nestorian Missionary Enterprise.* Edinburgh, T and T Clark, 1928. p. 26.
4. Stimson, Edward. *Renewal in Christ.* New York Vantage Press, 1979. p.147.
5. Hannah, Ian. *Monasticism*, London, Allen and Unwin, 1924. p. 86.
6. Rooy, Sidney. *The Theology of Missions in the Puritan Tradition.* Grand Rapids, Eerdmans, 1965.
7. Sattler, Gary. *God's Glory, Neighbor's Good.* Chicago, Covenant Press. 1982. p. 9.
8. Dubose, Francis (ed.) *Classics of Christian Mission.* Nashville, Broadman, 1979. p. 776.
9. Bready, John W. *This Freedom Whence.* New York, American Tract Society, 1942. p. 113.
10. Williams, Emilio. *Followers of the New Faith.* Nashville, Vanderbilt Univ. Press. 1967. pp. 181-185.
11. Pierson, Paul. *A Younger Church in Search of Maturity.* San Antonio, Trinity University Press, 1974. pp. 107,108.
12. As reported by Ralph D. Winter. Winter, p.199.
13. Beaver, R. Pierce. *American Protestant Women in Mission*, Grand Rapids, Eerdmans, 1980. p.135.

Study Questions

1. Was the education, economic and societal transformation which characterized early mission efforts, seen as separate from or integrated with evangelistic work?

2. What unique contribution did the monastic movement bring in the realms of the science of agriculture?

Women In Mission

Marguerite Kraft and Meg Crossman

Marguerite Kraft served as a missionary to the Kamwe people of Northern Nigeria. She is now Professor of Anthropology and Linguistics at the School of Intercultural Studies, Biola University and author of *Worldview and the Communication of the Gospel* and *Understanding Spiritual Power*.

Meg Crossman was the Executive Director of I.C.A.R.E. prison ministries for 10 years. Meg is best known as a mission mobilizer and a coordinator of the Perspectives course in Tempe, Arizona. She edited a version of the Perspectives course called *Worldwide Perspectives*.

From *Worldwide Perspectives*, edited by Meg Crossman, 1996. Used by permission of William Carey Library, Pasadena, CA.

After the last road ended, it was a two-day hike to where the Balangao people lived. The Balangao, a tribe of former headhunters, still sacrificed to powerful and demanding spirits who caused sickness, death and constant turmoil. Two single women missionaries, trained in Bible translation, were on their way to work among them.

When they arrived, they were greeted by men wearing G-strings and women wrapped in cloth from homemade looms. It is hard to say who was more amazed. The Balangao had asked for Americans to come live with them and write their language, but they never dreamed the Americans would be women!

An old man offered to be their father and was faithful in looking after them. Besides the work of translation, these women began giving medical assistance, learning about the spirit world, and answering questions about life and death. One of them, Jo Shetler, stayed for 20 years, winning her way into the hearts and lives of these people and completing the New Testament translation. Because of this dedication, thousands now know Jesus as Lord of the Balangao.[1]

Jo Shetler, a shy farm girl with a dream, has stirred many with her story. However, stories remain unwritten of multitudes of women who likewise obeyed the call of God to serve Him on the far horizons. Many women do not realize how greatly God can use their giftedness and commitment in situations such as this.

From the Earliest Days

The Book of Acts records the account of Priscilla, a woman specifically used of God to touch people in at least three different nations: Rome, Greece, and Asia Minor. Apparently a native of the eastern area of Asia Minor, this woman of Jewish faith lived with her husband, Aquila, in Rome until the Jews were expelled. When they met Paul in Corinth, they may already have become believers. They hosted Paul, led a house church, and were assigned by Paul to disciple the eloquent and committed Egyptian Jew, Apollos, "instructing him in the way of God more perfectly" (Acts 18:26).

Paul recognized and honored their gifts and they moved with him to the work in Ephesus. Since Priscilla's name is almost always listed first, some scholars suggest that "the wife was more prominent and helpful to Church."[2] It is perhaps most interesting to note that her role in cross-cultural service, leadership, and teaching were perceived as so normal they did not require special comment or explanation by the writer of Acts. Her role seems to have been accepted and expected rather than extraordinary.

Many women were martyred for their love for Jesus in the first three centuries of Christianity. Lucia of Sicily, who lived about A.D. 300, was involved in Christian charitable work there. After marrying a wealthy nobleman, she was ordered to stop giving to the poor; she refused and was sent to jail. There she was persecuted and condemned to death. Melania, coming from a wealthy family in Rome with estates all around the Mediterranean, used her resources to give to the poor and to build monasteries and churches for both men and women in Africa and Jerusalem. Her missionary journeys started as she fled from Rome during the invasion by the Goths in A.D. 410. As a refugee, she and many other women played an important role in the great missionary movement. Some women were taken as hostages to Northern Europe where they later married their captors and evangelized them.[3] Clare, who lived and worked in the early thirteenth century, was a reformer where Christianity had forgotten the poor. She founded the Franciscan order of barefoot nuns in Italy.[4] Women who chose to remain single, serve God, and live the cloistered life were given the opportunity through the accepted ecclesiastical framework to proclaim the gospel. In the Catholic tradition, priests, bishops and nuns built churches and hospitals, and founded schools and orphanages in order to establish the faith.

In The Early Missionary Movement

The Protestant Reformation in the Sixteenth Century brought about changes in the role of women in Christianity. The reformers reemphasized that women's role was in the home to be supportive of men. Arthur Glasser writes, "...the reformers also subjected women to the confining perspective that their only recognized vocation was marriage. With the dissolution of the convents, women lost their last chance of churchly service outside the narrow circle of husband, home and children."[5] Within Protestantism, the problem then arose as to whether women had the

right to respond to the promptings of the Holy Spirit to proclaim the word of God.

In the early days of the Protestant mission advance, most women who went to the field were wives of missionaries. Discerning men recognized that contact with women in most non-Western societies was impossible for them, so women had to undertake this responsibility. They received little recognition for the heavy load they carried, managing the home and children as well as developing programs to reach local women and girls.

Initially, single women could only go to the field to care for missionaries' children or serve alongside the missionary family. However, little by little, new opportunities arose. R. Pierce Beaver describes the work of Cynthia Farrar in India, Elizabeth Agnew in Ceylon, and other single women who began to supervise women's schools.[6] Quietly, they helped in zenanas and harems. Doors opened through medical service. Yet their effective work was seldom publicized.

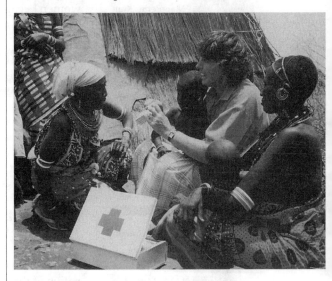

However, leaders like D.L. Moody, A.B. Simpson, and A.J. Gordon believed in encouraging women's gifts for public ministry. Both J. Hudson Taylor, founder of China Inland Mission, and Fredrik Franson, founder of TEAM (the Evangelical Alliance Mission), saw the need to recruit and send women to evangelize cross-culturally. In 1888, Taylor wrote, "We are manning our stations with ladies."[7] Throughout its initial history, his mission expected women, both single and married, to carry out all the missionary duties, including preaching and teaching.

In Jane Hunter's study of correspondence and published articles from women on the field, she discovered the "vast majority of women missionaries were motivated by a deep sense of commitment to God, far more than by any desire to attain personal recognition or power."[8] From such moving reports, women in the churches at home caught a dynamic world vision, volunteering their money, time, energy, organizational ability, and prayer support. Leaders such as Annie Armstrong and Helen Barret Montgomery dedicated themselves to developing missionary prayer groups, raising funds, and mobilizing Christians to support field work of all kinds.[9]

A New Way of Sending

The Civil War in the United States became a catalyst for change in the way women were sent. After the Civil War, so many men died that women were either widowed or unlikely to marry. This forced women into an unusual range of responsibilities. They ran businesses, banks, farms, formed colleges, and for the next 50 years inherited a larger role than men as the major muscle of the mission movement.[10]

Since missionary boards still refused to send women directly to the work, women simply organized their own boards. First was the Women's Union Missionary Society. In the years to follow, many others were created. Their funds were raised above and beyond the regular denominational mission giving, indicating the phenomenal job of missions awareness these boards were achieving on the home front. They built women's colleges, specifically to train women for missionary service. Besides rousing women to go overseas, more than 100,000 women's missionary societies became active in local churches, an unmatched base for prayer and funding.

By 1900, over 40 denominational women's societies existed, with over three million active women raising funds to build hospitals and schools around the world, paying the salaries of indigenous female evangelists, and sending single women as missionary doctors, teachers, and evangelists.[11] By the early decades of the 20th Century, the women's missionary movement had become the largest women's movement in the United States, and women outnumbered men on the mission field by a ratio of more than two to one.[12] Sadly, as these boards were persuaded to combine with the denominational boards in the 1920s and 30s, women gradually lost their opportunity to direct the work.

And Still Today

Overall, probably two-thirds of the missions force has been, and currently is, female. Many mission executives agree that the more difficult and dangerous the work, the more likely women are to volunteer to do it! David Yonggi Cho concludes from his experience that women are the best choice for difficult, pioneering work. "We have found that in these situations, women will never give up. Men are good for building up the work, but women are best for persevering when men get discouraged."[13]

Some fear that because of the unique obstacles of reaching the Muslim world, Western women can play no part. Yet in a nomadic Muslim group in Sub-Saharan Africa, a single woman is effectively training Imams (Islamic teachers) in the gospel. They perceive her to be non-threatening, "just a woman." Building upon a foundation of interpersonal relationship and Bible knowledge, she does not give them answers herself, but directs them to the Word. The Lord has confirmed her teaching, giving dreams and visions to these leaders. As they have been converted, they are now training many others. She is accepted as a loving, caring elder sister, who gives high priority to their welfare.

Jim Reapsome's editorial in *World Pulse* (Oct. 9, 1992) advocating more training and more support for women received an al-

> The pioneer spirit, full of dedication and faithfulness, which women throughout history have shown will set the standard.

most immediate letter of thanks from a missionary to a Muslim group in Southeast Asia. He wrote:

> Interestingly enough, despite the common emphasis on training and using men, here in—, some of the best evangelists are all *women*! In fact, three of our most important co-workers (who are really doing the most cutting-edge ministry) are women. In terms of Americans, we only have one single man who made the sacrifice to come here but four single women, with three more on the way. In the face of chauvinistic Islam, it is good to be reminded that true Christianity is not chauvinistic, but an equally exciting call to new, fulfilling life for women and men.[14]

of their work. With their holistic approach to missions, women were committed to healing. Thus, medical missions were dominated by women for many years. Since women were less involved in denominational activities and more focused on human need, it was easier for them to be ecumenically-minded and risk cooperation for common purposes. Women led in founding ecumenical mission organizations.

In recent years, women have played important roles in mission specialization. Wycliffe Bible Translators found over the years that teams of single women did well on the field—-a far greater number of such teams successfully finish translations than teams of single men. Elizabeth Greene, a woman pilot who served in the Air Force in WWII, was one of the founders of Mission Aviation Fellowship. Gospel Recordings, providing Christian tapes and records in many languages (using native speakers to give the Word rather than waiting for a printed translation) was founded through Joy Ridderhof's vision and effort. Ruth Siemens' creative idea resulted in Global Opportunities, assisting lay persons to find tentmaker positions overseas. Women have been permitted great latitude in Christian ministry, with their work ranging from evangelism and church planting to translating Scripture and teaching in seminaries.

Opportunities In Special Areas

Women in mission have demonstrated a holistic approach with emphasis on both evangelism and meeting human needs. They have shown a deep commitment to and concern for women and children. Education, medical work, and struggles against foot binding, child marriage, female infanticide, and oppressive social, religious, and economic structures were commonly the focus

Christian women today need to know and celebrate their heritage. We can study women of greatness who served in Christ's cause and claim them as our role models. From Mary Slessor, single woman pioneer in Africa, to Ann Judson of Burma and Rosalind Goforth of China, wives who fully served; from Amy Carmichael of India to Mildred Cable in the Gobi Desert; from Gladys Aylward, the little chambermaid determined to get to China, to

Eliza Davis George, black woman missionary to Liberia; from translator Rachel Saint to medical doctor Helen Roseveare; from Isobel Kuhn and Elisabeth Elliot, mobilizing missionary authors, to Lottie Moon, pacesetting mission educator; from simple Filipino housemaids in the Middle East to women executives in denominational offices to unsung Bible women in China, the roll is lengthy and glorious!

The roll is, however, incomplete, expectantly awaiting the contribution of current and future generations. God's women now enjoy freedoms and opportunities their forebearers never anticipated. Most small businesses started in the United States are owned by women. Women now hold highly responsible positions in government, business, law, and medicine. "To whom much is given, much is required." How will women of God today harvest such opportunities for their Father's purposes?

Women, stirred by the task that lies ahead, can mobilize, devoting their skills, their accessibility, their knowledge, their tenderness, their intuitiveness, their own distinctive fervor to the work. The pioneer spirit, full of dedication and faithfulness, which women throughout history have shown will set the standard. The task is too vast to be completed without all God's people!

End Notes

1. Shetler, Joanne, *The Word Came With Power* (Portland, OR: Multnomah Press, 1992).
2. Jamieson, Fausset and Brown, *Commentary on the Whole Bible* (Grand Rapids, MI: Zondervan Publishing House, 1961), p. 1,117, on Acts 18:18
3. Malcolm, Kari Torjesen, *Women at the Crossroads: A Path Beyond Feminism and Traditionalism* (Downers Grove, IL.: InterVarsity Press, 1982), pp. 99-100
4. Ibid., p. 104
5. Glasser, Arthur, "One-half the Church—and Mission," *Women and the Ministries of Christ*, eds., Roberta Hestenes and Lois Curly (Pasadena: Fuller Theological Seminary, 1978) pp. 88-92
6. Beaver, R. Pierce, *American Protestant Women in World Mission* (Grand Rapids, MI: William B. Eerdmans Publishing Company, 1980), pp.59-86
7. Beaver, R. Pierce, *All Loves Excelling* (Grand Rapids, MI: Eerdmans, 1968), p. 116
8. Tucker, Ruth, *Guardians of the Great Commission* (Grand Rapids, MI: Academie Books, 1988), p. 38
9. Ibid., pp. 102-110
10. Winter, Ralph, personal interview, September 1991
11. Robert, Dana L., *American Women in Mission: A Social History of Their Thought and Practice* (Macon, GA.:Mercer University Press, 1996), p. 129
12. Tucker, Ruth, *Guardians of the Great Commission* (Grand Rapids, MI: Academie Books, 1988) p. 10
13. Paul Yonggi Cho at El Shaddai Pastor's Fellowship luncheon in Phoenix, AZ, March 1988
14. Personal letter to Jim Reapsome, October 25, 1992. Used with permission.

Study Questions

1. Why might teams of single women bible translators have a more successful record of completing the translation?

2. How might women missionaries be especially effective in male-dominated cultures?

3. In what times and in what ways did women play a dominant role in missions?

Europe's Moravians:
A Pioneer Missionary Church

Colin A. Grant

Sixty years before Carey set out for India and 150 years before Hudson Taylor first landed in China, two men, Leonard Dober, a potter, and David Nitschmann, a carpenter, landed on the West Indian island of St. Thomas to make known the gospel of Jesus Christ. They had set out in 1732 from a small Christian community in the mountains of Saxony in central Europe as the first missionaries of the Moravian Brethren, who in the next 20 years entered Greenland (1733), North America's Indian territories (1734), Surinam (1735), South Africa (1736), the Samoyedic peoples of the Arctic (1737), Algiers and Ceylon, and Sri Lanka (1740), China (1742), Persia (1747), Abyssynia and Labrador (1752).

This was but a beginning. In the first 150 years of its endeavor, the Moravian community was to send no less than 2,158 of its members overseas! In the words of Stephen Neil, "This small church was seized with a missionary passion which has never left it."

The Unitas Fratum (United Brethren), as they had been called, have left a record without parallel in the post-New Testament era of world evangelization, and we do well to look again at the main characteristics of this movement and learn the lessons God has for us.

Spontaneous Obedience

In the first place, *the missionary obedience of the Moravian Brethren was essentially glad and spontaneous*, "the response of a healthy organism to the law of its life," to use Harry Boer's words. The source of its initial thrust came as a result of a deep movement of God's Spirit that had taken place among a small group of exiled believers. They had fled the persecution of the anti-Reformation reaction in Bohemia and Moravia during the 17th century and had taken shelter on an estate at Berthesdorf at the invitation of Nicolas Zinzendorf, an evangelical Lutheran nobleman.

The first tree for their settlement, which was later to be named Herrnhut ("The Lord's Watch"), was felled by Christian David (himself to go overseas as a missionary at a later stage) in 1722 to the strains of Psalm 84. Five years later, so deeply ran the new tides of the grace and love of God among them that one of their number wrote: "The whole place represented truly a tabernacle of God among men. There was nothing to be seen and heard but joy and gladness."

Colin A. Grant was a missionary in Sri Lanka for twelve years with the British Baptist Missionary Society. He was chairman of the Evangelical Missionary Alliance and Home Secretary of the Evangelical Union of South America. Grant died in 1976.

Used by permission from "Europe's Moravians: A Pioneer Missionary Church," *Evangelical Missions Quarterly*, 12:4, (October 1976), published by EMIS, P.O. Box 794, Wheaton, IL 60189.

This was God's preparation for all that was to follow. Challenged through meeting with Anton, an African slave from St. Thomas during a visit to Denmark for the coronation of King Christian VI, Dober and Nitschmann volunteered to go and were commissioned. To them it was a natural expression of their Christian life and obedience.

Dr. A. C. Thompson, one of the main nineteenth century recorders of the early history of Moravian missions, wrote: "So fully is the duty of evangelizing the heathen lodged in current thought that the fact of anyone entering personally upon that work never creates surprise...It is not regarded as a thing that calls for widespread heralding, as if something marvelous or even unusual were in hand."

What a contrast to the hard worked for interest that characterizes much of the missionary sending scene today! Rev. Ignatius Latrobe, a former secretary of the Moravian missions in the United Kingdom during the last century, wrote: "We think it a great mistake when, after their appointment, missionaries are held up to public notice and admiration and much praise is bestowed upon their devotedness to their Lord, presenting them to the congregations as martyrs and confessors before they have even entered upon their labours. We rather advise them quietly to set out, recommended to the fervent prayers of the congregation..." No clamor, no platform heroics, no publicity, but an ardent, unostentatious desire to make Christ known wherever his name had not been named. This became knit into the ongoing life and liturgy of the Moravian Church, so that, for example, a large proportion of public prayer and subsequent hymnology was occupied with this subject.

Passion for Christ

In the second place, this surging zeal had as its prime motivation a *deep, ongoing passion and love for Christ*, something that found expression in the life of Zinzendorf himself. Born in 1700 into Austrian nobility, he came early under godly family influences and soon came to a saving knowledge of Christ. His early missionary interest was evidenced in his founding, with a friend, in his student days of what he called "The Order of the Grain of Mustard Seed" for the spread of Christ's kingdom in the world.

He became not only host to, but the first leader of the Moravian believers and himself made visits overseas in the interests of the gospel. "I have one passion, and it is Him, only Him," was his central chord and it sounded through the more than 2,000 hymns he wrote.

William Wilberforce, the great evangelical English social reformer, wrote of the Moravians: "They are a body who have perhaps excelled all mankind in solid and unequivocal proofs of the love of Christ and ardent, active zeal in his service. It is a zeal tempered with prudence, softened with meekness and supported by a courage which no danger can intimidate and a quiet certainty no hardship can exhaust." Today, we need a full theological formulation of our motivation in mission and an adequate grasp of what we believe. But if there is no passionate love for Christ at the center of everything, we will only jingle and jangle our way across the world, merely making a noise as we go.

Courage in the Face of Danger

As Wilberforce indicated, a further feature of the Moravians was that *they faced the most incredible of difficulties and dangers with remarkable courage*. They accepted hardships as part of the identification with the people to whom the Lord had sent them. The words of Paul, "I have become all things to all men" (1 Cor 9:22), were spelled out with a practicality almost without parallel in the history of missions.

Most of the early missionaries went out as "tentmakers," working their trade (most of them being artisans and farmers like Dober and Nitschmann) so that the main expenses involved were in the sending of them out. In areas where white domination had bred the façade of white superiority (e.g. Jamaica and South Africa) the way they humbly got down to hard manual work was itself a witness to their faith. For example, a missionary named Monate helped to build a corn mill in the early days of his work in the Eastern Province of South Africa, cutting the two heavy sandstones himself. In so doing, he not only amazed the Kaffirs among whom he was working, but was enabled to "chat" the gospel to them as he worked!

To go to such places as Surinam and the West Indies meant facing disease and possible death; the early years took their inevitable toll. In Guyana, for instance, 75 out of the first 160 missionaries died from tropical fevers, poisoning and such. Men like Andrew Rittmansberger died within six months of landing on the island. The words of a verse from a hymn written by one of the first Greenland missionaries expresses something of the fibre of their attitude: "Lo through ice and snow, one poor lost soul for Christ to gain; Glad, we bear want and distress to set forth the Lamb once slain."

The Moravians resolutely tackled new languages without many of the modern aids, and numbers of them went on to become outstandingly fluent and proficient in them. This was the stuff, then, of which these men were made. We may face a different pattern of demands today, but the need for a like measure of God-given courage remains the same. Is our easy-going, prosperous society producing "softer" men and women?

Tenacity of Purpose

We finally note that *many Moravian missionaries showed a tenacity of purpose that was of a very high order,* although it must immediately be added that there were occasions when there was a too hasty withdrawal in the face of a particularly problematical situation (e.g., early work among the Aborigines in Australia in 1854 was abandoned suddenly because of local conflicts caused by a gold rush).

One of the most famous of Moravian missionaries, known as the "Eliot of the West," was David Zeisberger. From 1735, he labored for 62 years among the Huron and other tribes. On one occasion, after he had preached from Isaiah 64:8, one Sunday morning in August, 1781, the church and compound were invaded by marauding bands of Indians. In the subsequent burnings, Zeisberger lost all his manuscripts of Scripture translations, hymns and extended notes on the grammar of Indian languages. But like Carey, who was to undergo a similar loss through fire in India years later, Zeisberger bowed his head in quiet submission to the overruling providence of God and set his hand and heart to the work again.

Are we becoming short on missionary perseverance today? By all means let us acknowledge the value in short-term missionary assignments and see the divine purpose in many of them. But where are those who are ready to "sink" themselves for God overseas? Let us look at such problems as children's education and changing missionary strategy under the Lord's direction full in the face; but if men are to be won, believers truly nourished, and churches encouraged into the fullness of life in Christ, a great deal of "missionary staying power" of the right sort is going to be needed in some places.

Of course, these Moravians had their weaknesses. They concentrated more on evangelism than on the actual planting of local churches and they were consequently very weak on developing Christian leadership. They centered their approach on "the missionary station," even giving them a whole succession of biblical place names, such as Shiloh, Sarepta, Nazareth, Bethlehem, etc. Since most of the early missionaries went out straight from the "carpenter's bench" because of the spontaneous nature of their obedience, they were short on adequate preparation. In fact, it was not until 1869 that the first missionary training college was founded at Nisky, 20 miles from Herrnhut.

Despite all this, the words of J. R. Weinlick bring home the all-pervading lesson we have to learn from the Moravians today. "The Moravian Church was the first among Protestant churches to treat this work as *a responsibility of the Church* as a whole (emphasis mine), instead of leaving it to societies or specially interested people." True, they were a small, compact and unified community, and therefore it may be said that such a simple missionary structure as they possessed was natural. It is doubtful, however, if this can ever be made an excuse for the low level of missionary concern apparent in many sectors of God's Church today, or for the complex, and often competing, missionary society system we struggle with at the present time. Have we ears to hear and wills to obey?

Study Questions

1. Which of the characteristics of the Moravians is most absent from the Christian Church today? Which is most evident?

2. What is your answer to the question posed at the end of this article? Why?

Student Power in World Missions

David M. Howard

W hy take time to read about the past? Why not get down to business to today's issues and planning for the future?

We learn from the past so that we can live effectively in the present and plan wisely for the future. He who will not learn from history is doomed to repeat her mistakes.

We learn about the Lord's working in past times so that we can understand him better and trust him more fully.

We turn to the Bible for basic information about those mighty deeds. And since the Lord did not cease those glorious workings when he terminated the writing of the Bible, we turn to later sources to learn of his subsequent deeds.

In particular, what has he been doing over the centuries in terms of work among college students in fulfilling the Great Commission?

Earliest Traces

Perhaps the earliest traceable instance in which students had a definite part in promoting a world outreach is found in Germany in the early 17th century. Gustav Warneck, the great historian-theologian of missions, writes of seven young law students from Lubeck, Germany, who, while studying together in Paris, committed themselves to carry the gospel overseas. At least three of them finally sailed for Africa. All trace has been lost of two of these, but the name of Peter Heiling has survived. After a two-year stay in Egypt, he proceeded to Abyssinia in 1634. He spent some 20 years in that land, where he translated the Bible into Amharic and finally died a martyr.

Heiling had no successors, and thus there was no continuation of what he began. But the translation of the Scriptures was a significant contribution that unquestionably made its impact.

The important thing to note here is that his original impetus to leave his own land and carry the gospel to another part of the world came when he banded together with fellow students to pray and work for the extension of the Church overseas.

The Moravians

The name of Count Nicolaus Ludwig von Zinzendorf (1700-1760) stands high in missionary annals as a leader of the Moravian movement—one of the first, most effective and

David M. Howard is President of the Latin America Mission in Miami, Florida, having served as a missionary for 15 years in Columbia and Costa Rica. For 10 years he served as the International Director of the World Evangelical Fellowship. He has served as Missions Director of InterVarsity Christian Fellowship and Director of the IVCF Urbana Conventions in 1973 and 1976.

most enduring of missionary enterprises. Zinzendorf had the good fortune to know personally both Spener and Francke, the great leaders of the Pietists. The emphasis on a personal relationship to Jesus as Lord became the most influential factor in his early life. Before the age of ten he had determined that his lifelong purpose should be to preach the gospel of Jesus Christ throughout the world.

From 1710 to 1716, Zinzendorf studied in the Paedagogium founded by Francke in Halle, Germany. With five other boys he formed the Order of the Grain of Mustard Seed, whose members were bound together in prayer. The purposes were to witness to the power of Jesus Christ, to draw other Christians together in fellowship, to help those who were suffering for their faith, and to carry the gospel of Christ overseas. The same vision was carried over in his university days at Wittenberg and Utrecht. He never lost sight of this purpose.

In April, 1731, Zinzendorf attended the coronation of Christian VI of Denmark in Copenhagen. There he met Anthony Ulrich, from St. Thomas in the West Indies, who shared with the Count his deep desire that his brothers in the West Indies should hear the gospel. So deeply impressed was Zinzendorf that he saw the relationship between this and the commitments he had made as a student. By August, 1732, arrangements had been made for the first two Moravian missionaries to sail for St. Thomas.

Thus, the modern worldwide missionary movement (which traces parts of its roots to the Moravians of 1732) was actually born in the hearts of a group of students who joined together at Halle to pray for world evangelism.

The Wesleys

At the same time God was also moving among students in England, Charles Wesley entered Christ Church College, Oxford, in 1726, from which his brother, John, had just graduated. Because of his desire to know God better he formed a small society of students for the study of the classics and the New Testament. They became known as the "Holy Club" (in derision from their fellow students) and as the "Methodists" (because of their methodical approach to life). John Wesley returned as a teaching fellow to Lincoln College at Oxford and joined his brother in the activities of this group.

In addition to worship and study, the group translated their piety into an outreach to the poor, the hungry and the imprisoned. This facet of the activities became an increasingly important part of their club.

While John Wesley is usually known as an evangelist and theologian and Charles as a hymn writer, they both began their fruitful careers as overseas missionaries. In October, 1735, the two brothers sailed for the colony of Georgia with General Oglethorpe. John Wesley's journal indicated that he was not yet sure of his own salvation at this point and that his sailing for Georgia was partly a quest for knowing God better. At the same time, he had the desire to share what he knew of Christ with the Indians of America.

Shortly after Wesley arrived in Georgia, the English colonists there tried to persuade him to remain in Savannah as their pastor. However, his desire to preach the gospel to the unevangelized Indians caused him to write in his Journal:

> Tuesday, November 23 (1736)—Mr. Oglethorpe sailed for England, leaving Mr. Ingham, Mr. Delamotte, and me at Savannah, but with less prospect of preaching to the Indians than we had the first day we set foot in America. Whenever I mentioned it, it was immediately replied, "You cannot leave Savannah without a minister."

> To this indeed my plain answer was, "I know not that I am under any obligation to the contrary. I never promised to stay here one month. I openly declared both before, at, and ever since, my coming hither that I neither would nor could take charge of the English any longer than till I could go among the Indians."

This desire to share the message of Christianity with the Indians who did not know Jesus Christ was apparently a direct outgrowth of the fellowship of students at Oxford who sought to know God better through their "Holy Club."

Charles Simeon

No summary of the movement of God among students in England would be complete without reference to Charles Simeon. As a student at Cambridge University in 1779, Simeon came to know Christ. Following his graduation in 1782, he was appointed Fellow of King's College, ordained to the ministry and named incumbent of Holy Trinity Church at Cambridge. Thus began a remarkable ministry that was to span fifty-four years.

Students who came under Simeon's influence later became some of the great leaders of the church both in Great Britain and around the world. His informal gatherings of undergraduates in his home for Bible study and prayer were perhaps the most influential part of his work. Scores of students first came to a personal relationship to Jesus Christ. Here they began to understand the Word of God and its implications for their lives. And here they received their first visions of reaching out to others with that Word.

> The modern worldwide missionary movement was actually born in the hearts of a group of students who joined together to pray for world evangelism.

This outreach took very practical forms. In 1827, a group of five students, strongly influenced by Simeon's preaching at Holy Trinity Church, formed the Jesus Lane Sunday School in an attempt to reach the boys and girls of the community. Among those who taught in this Sunday School were men such at Conybeare, Howson, and Westcott, later to be known through the world for biblical scholarship.

Another example of outreach in which Simeon had direct influence was the forming of an auxiliary of the British and Foreign Bible Society at Cambridge in 1811. The purpose of the Society had always been to make available the Word of God throughout the world in the language of the people. The involvement of students in this auxiliary undoubtedly served to broaden their horizons and help them see how they could relate to world evangelization.

Simeon's influence continued long after his death in 1836. The "Simeonites" (as the students who attended his informal gatherings were dubbed) continued their activities in the Jesus Lane Sunday School and elsewhere in an outreach with the gospel. In 1848, the Cambridge Union for Private Prayer was formed and became a vital factor in the spiritual life and witness of many.

In 1857, David Livingstone visited Cambridge and delivered a moving missionary address. Partly as a result of this visit, the Cambridge University Church Missionary Union was established early in 1858 for the purpose of encouraging "a more extended missionary spirit by frequent meetings for prayer and the reading of papers, and for bringing forward an increased number of candidates for missionary employment."

The Inter-Varsity Fellowship of England traces its origins directly to the work begun by Charles Simeon. The Cambridge Inter-Collegiate Christian Union was formed in 1877. From small beginnings, this movement soon spread to other British universities, then to other countries and finally around the world.

The Cambridge Seven

In 1882, the American evangelist, D. L. Moody, visited Cambridge during a tour of Britain. The results of one week of meetings were beyond expectations as great impact was made at the university. Immediately after his visit, there was a rapid increase in the number of students who applied to the Church Missionary Society of the Anglican Church for service overseas.

About the same time there was a mounting interest in a new mission, the China Inland Mission, recently founded by J. Hudson Taylor. In 1883-84, a group of seven outstanding students (six of them from Cambridge) applied to the China Inland Mission. They were all brilliant and talented men with good background and upbringing and a variety of athletic and academic abilities.

Montagu H. P. Beauchamp, son of Sir Thomas and Lady Beauchamp, was a brilliant student. William W. Cassels was son of a businessman. Dixon Edward Hoste was converted under D. L. Moody. He held a commission in the Royal Artillery and was later to become the successor of Hudson Taylor as director of the China Inland Mission. Arthur

Polhill-Turner was the son of a member of Parliament. Outgoing and quick, he played cricket and made friends easily at Cambridge. He, too, was converted under D. L. Moody. Arthur's brother, Cecil Polhill-Turner, was commissioned in the Dragoon Guards. Stanley P. Smith, son of a successful London surgeon, became captain of First Trinity Boat Club and stroke of the Varsity crew at Cambridge. Although he was brought up in a Christian home, he committed his life to Christ under the ministry of D. L. Moody. Charles Thomas Studd was the son of wealthy parents who knew every luxury of life. He was captain of the cricket team at Cambridge and generally considered the outstanding cricketer of his day.

In a variety of ways the Spirit of God began to move upon each of these men concerning going to China. Slowly but relentlessly, the Spirit brought each one to a place of commitment and subsequently to an application for missionary service. Sensing a unity of purpose and outlook, these seven desired to share their vision with fellow students. Following graduation, they traveled extensively throughout England and Scotland, visiting campuses and churches. Their impact for missionary work was far beyond the few months of time they invested in this tour. In February, 1885, the seven sailed for China, to be followed in subsequent years by scores of students who, under their influence, had given themselves to Jesus Christ to reach other parts of the world.

Thus the forward movement of the church continued to be inspired by youth. Whether it was among students at Halle with Zinzendorf, or at Oxford with the Wesleys, or at Cambridge with C. T. Studd and his fellows, the Holy Spirit continued to use students as spearheads in awakening the church to its worldwide responsibilities.

Samuel Mills

On the North American continent, the beginnings of overseas interest on the part of the Church can be traced directly to student influence, and more precisely, to the impact of one student, Samuel J. Mills, Jr. (1783-1818). Born in Connecticut as the son of a Congregational minister, Mills was brought up in a godly home. His mother reportedly said of him, "I have consecrated this child to the service of God as a missionary." This was a remarkable statement since missionary interest was practically unknown in the churches of that day, and no channels (such as mission boards) for overseas service existed in America. Mills was converted at the age of 17 as a part of the Great Awakening that began in 1798 and touched his father's church. His commitment to world evangelism seemed to be an integral part of his conversion experience. From the moment of conversion on through the years of his study and for the rest of his public ministry, he never lost sight of this purpose.

The Haystack Prayer Meeting

In 1806, Mills enrolled in Williams College, Massachusetts. This school had been profoundly affected by the religious awakening of those years, and devout students on campus had a deep concern for the spiritual welfare of their fellow students. Mills joined with them in their desire to help others.

It was Mills' custom to spend Wednesday and Saturday afternoons in prayer with other students on the banks of the Hoosack River or in a valley near the college. In August, 1806, Mills and four others were caught in a thunderstorm while returning from their usual meeting. Seeking refuge under a haystack, they waited out the storm and gave themselves to prayer. Their special focus of prayer that day was for the awakening of foreign missionary interest among students. Mills directed their discussion and prayer to their own missionary obligation. He exhorted his companions with the words that later became a watchword for them, "We can do this if we will."

Bowed in prayer, these first American student volunteers for foreign missions willed that God should have their lives for service wherever he needed them, and in that self-dedication really gave birth to the first student missionary society in America. Kenneth Scott Latourette, the foremost historian of the Church's worldwide expansion, states, "It was from this haystack meeting that the foreign missionary movement of the churches of the United States had an initial impulse."[1]

The exact location of the haystack was unknown for a number of years. Then, in 1854,

Bryan Green, one of those present in 1806, visited Williamstown and located the spot. A monument was erected on the site in 1867. Mark Hopkins, who was then president of the American Board of Commissioners for Foreign Missions, gave the dedicatory address in which he said, "For once in the history of the world, a prayer meeting is commemorated by a monument."

The Society of Brethren

Back at Williams College, students continued to meet for prayer. They were influential in leading a number of other students into a commitment for overseas service. In September, 1808, deciding to organize formally, they founded The Society of the Brethren for the purpose of giving themselves to extend the gospel around the world.

Desiring to extend the influence of this Society to other colleges, one of the members transferred to Middlebury College to found a similar society. In 1809, following his graduation from Williams College, Mills enrolled at Yale with the dual purpose of continuing theological studies and of imparting missionary vision to the students there.

Here he met Henry Obookiah, a Hawaiian, who encouraged him with the need of evangelizing the Hawaiian Islands. Obookiah did much in the next few years to stimulate student interest in evangelizing the Pacific Islands. He died prematurely before he was able to return to his homeland, but Latourette says of him, "The story of his life and missionary purpose was a major stimulus to the sending, in 1819, the year after his death, of the first missionaries of the American Board to Hawaii." (James Michener's caricature of Abner Hale as the first missionary to Hawaii, in his novel *Hawaii*, should not be allowed to obscure the commitment which led Obookiah, Mills and other students to be concerned for the evangelization of those who had never heard of Christ.)

The American Board of Commissioners for Foreign Missions

In June, 1810, the General Association of Congregational Churches met in Bradford, Massachusetts, in annual meeting. Samuel Mills (then studying at Andover Theological Seminary), with several fellow students, including Adoniram Judson, presented a petition requesting the formation of a society which could send them out as foreign missionaries. On June 29, the Association recommended to the assembly "That there be instituted by this General Association a Board of Commissioners for Foreign Missions, for the purpose of devising ways and means, and adopting and prosecuting measures for promoting the spread of the gospel to heathen lands." Although not legally incorporated until 1812, the Board began activities immediately. It was interdenominational in character, enjoying the support of numerous church bodies. Volunteers were recruited and prepared.

On February 19, 1812, Adoniram Judson and Samuel Newell and their wives sailed for India, and five days later Samuel Nott, Gordon Hall and Luther Rice also embarked on another ship for India. These first American missionaries joined hands with the great English pioneer, William Carey, who since 1793 had been evangelizing in India. Judson and Rice subsequently persuaded the Baptists of North America to form their own missionary society, which became the second foreign board in the United States.

Thus, within four years of the haystack prayer meeting, these students had been influential in the formation of the first North American missionary society, and a year and a half later, the first volunteers were on their way to Asia.

The Student Volunteer Movement

In the history of modern missions, probably no single factor has wielded a greater influence in the world wide outreach of the Church than the Student Volunteer Movement (SVM). The names of its great leaders—men of the stature of John R. Mott, Robert C. Wilder, Robert E. Speer, to name a few—stand high in the annals of the foreign missionary movement. Its watchword, "The evangelization of the world in this generation," was so profoundly influential in motivating students for overseas service that John R. Mott could write, "I can truthfully answer that next to the decision to take Christ as the leader and Lord of my life, the watchword has had more influence than all other ideals and objectives combined to widen my horizon and enlarge my conception of the Kingdom of God."

The SVM had its distant roots in the famous Haystack Prayer Meeting held at Williams College in 1806. Out of that meeting grew two very influential developments. First was the Society of Brethren at Andover Theological Seminary. Second was the American Board of Commissioners for Foreign Missions, the first North American foreign mission agency. One of the members of the Society of Brethren in later years was Royal Wilder, who sailed for India under the ABCFM in 1846. Returning to the U.S. for health reasons in 1877, he settled in Princeton, NJ, where his son, Robert, soon formed the "Princeton Foreign Missionary Society." The members of this Society declared themselves "willing and desirous, God permitting, to go to the unevangelized portions of the world." Their prayers and activities bore fruit in the summer of 1886.

At the invitation of D. L. Moody, 251 students gathered at Mt. Hermon, Massachusetts, for a month-long Bible conference in July 1886. A great burden for world evangelization was gripping some of these students. A memorable address given by one of the Bible teachers, Dr. A. T. Pierson, contained the seed form of the SVM watchword, and he is generally credited with having originated it. As a result of Pierson's challenge, plus other motivations, including "The meeting of the Ten Nations" and lengthy prayer meetings, 100 students volunteered for overseas service during the conference.

The foundations of the SVM were laid that summer, and the movement was formally organized in 1888. During the school year 1886-87, Robert G. Wilder and John Forman, both of Princeton, travelled to 167 different schools to share the vision they had received of world evangelization. During that year, they saw 2,106 students volunteer for missionary work. Among these were Samuel Zwemer and Robert E. Speer, whose influence in missions during the next decades is almost incalculable.

The SVM was formally organized in 1888 with John R. Mott as its chairman. A fivefold purpose was developed:

> The fivefold purpose of the Student Volunteer Movement is to lead students to a thorough consideration of the claims of foreign missions upon them personally as a lifework; to foster this purpose by guiding students who become volunteers in their study and activity for missions until they come under the immediate direction of the Mission Boards; to unite all volunteers in a common, organized, aggressive movement; to secure a sufficient number of well-qualified volunteers to meet the demands of the

"The Mount Hermon One Hundred"

various Mission Boards; and to create and maintain an intelligent, sympathetic and active interest in foreign missions on the part of students who are to remain at home in order to ensure the strong backing of the missionary enterprise by their advocacy, their gifts and their prayers.[2]

Taking a cue from the Princeton Foreign Missionary Society with its "pledge," the SVM developed a declaration card. The purpose of the card was to face each student with the challenge of the "evangelization of the world in this generation." The card stated: "It is my purpose, if God permit, to become a foreign missionary." When a student signed this, it was understood as his response to the call of God. Every student was expected to face the issue and either to respond to it in the affirmative or else show that God was clearly leading him elsewhere.

Growth and Outreach

The growth of the SVM in the following three decades was nothing short of phenomenal. In 1891, the first international student missionary convention sponsored by SVM was held in Cleveland, Ohio. It was decided that such a convention should be held every four years in order to reach each student generation. Until the 1940's, this became a pattern, interrupted only by World War I. The first convention at Cleveland was attended by 558 students representing 151 educational institutions, along with 31 foreign missionaries and 32 representatives of missionary societies.[3]

By the time of the Cleveland convention, there were 6,200 Student Volunteers from 352 educational institutions in the United States and Canada. And 321 volunteers had already sailed for overseas service. In addition, 40 colleges and 32 seminaries were involved in financial support of their alumni who had gone overseas as Volunteers.[4] All of this had taken place in just five years since the Mt. Hermon conference. The Movement had also reached out and planted seeds of similar movements in Great Britain, Scandinavia, and South Africa.

An educational program in the schools was initiated and spread rapidly. Mott could later write that "At one time before the war the number in such circles exceeded 40,000 in 2,700 classes in 700 institutions."[5]

These efforts on the local campuses, the quadrennial conventions, plus literature, speaking tours and other activities, resulted in thousands of students volunteering for overseas service. "By 1945, at the most conservative estimate, 20,500 students from so-called Christian lands, who had signed the declaration, reached the field, for the most part under the missionary societies and boards of the churches."[6]

In 1920 (the peak year statistically) 2,783 students signed the SVM decision card, 6,890 attended the quadrennial convention in Des Moines, and in 1921, 637 Volunteers sailed for the field, this being the highest number in any single year. The motivations were genuine, the grounding in biblical principles was solid, and the leadership had a burning vision for world evangelism.

Confusion and Decline

But in 1920, an ominous change began to take place. "The Missionary Review of the World" (a journal founded by Royal Wilder in 1887) analyzed the SVM convention at Des Moines as follows:

> The Des Moines Volunteer Convention... was marked by a revolt against the leadership of the "elder statesman." That convention was large in number but the delegates were lacking in missionary vision and purpose and were only convinced that a change of ideals and of leadership was needed. They rightly believed that selfishness and foolishness had involved the world in terrible war and bloodshed and they expressed their intention to take control of Church and State in an effort to bring about better conditions. The problems of international peace, social justice, racial equality and economic betterment obscured the Christian foundations and ideals of spiritual service.

From the high point of 1920, the SVM experienced a rapid decline, 38 Volunteers sailed for the field in 1934 (as compared with 637 in 1921); 25 Volunteers enrolled in SVM in 1938 (as compared with 2,783 in 1920). In 1940, 465 delegates attended the quadrennial convention in Toronto (as compared with the 6,890 at Des Moines in 1920).

Here was a movement whose influence on students and the world mission of the Church had been incalculable. Yet it could be said of SVM that "by 1940 it had almost ceased to be a decisive factor either in student religious life or in the promotion of the missionary program of the churches."[7]

What had happened to precipitate, or to allow, such a drastic decline?

Dr. William Beahm has highlighted the following factors, while stating that no one reason by itself is an adequate explanation of the steady decline.

1. Many changes of leadership broke the continuity of its life and left the subtle impression of a sinking ship from which they were fleeing.
2. There was increasing difficulty in financing its program. This was closely related to the depression and the loss of Mott's leadership.
3. The program tended to become top-heavy. In 1920 the Executive Committee was expanded from six to thirty members.
4. Its emphasis upon foreign mission seemed to overlook the glaring needs in America, and so the Movement appeared to be specialized rather than comprehensive.
5. When the interest of students veered away from missions, it left the Movement in a dilemma as to which interest to follow—student or missionary.
6. There was a great decline in missionary education. One reason for this was the assumption that discussion of world problems by students was an improvement over the former types of informative procedure. The Conventions came to have this discussional character.
7. Their emphasis shifted away from Bible study, evangelism, lifework decision and foreign mission obligation on which the SVM had originally been built. Instead, they now emphasized new issues such as race relations, economic injustice and imperialism.
8. The rise of indigenous leaders reduced the need for Western personnel.
9. The rise of the social gospel blotted out the sharp distinction between Christian America and the "unevangelized portions of the world."
10. Revivalism had given way to basic uncertainty as to the validity of the Christian faith, especially of its claim to exclusive supremacy. Accordingly, the watchword fell into disuse and the argument for foreign missions lost its force.[8]

By the 1924 convention, attention was turning rapidly from world evangelism to the solution of social and economic problems. "The Missionary Review" stated that in 1924 "they failed to make much impression or to reach any practical conclusions."

Termination of the SVM

After 1940, its activities moved steadily away from an emphasis on overseas missions as SVM became more involved in political and social matters. In 1959, the SVM merged with the United Student Christian Council and the Interseminary Movement to form the National Student Christian Federation (NSCF). This in turn was allied with the Roman Catholic National Newman Student Federation and other groups in 1966 to form the University Christian Movement (UCM). The purpose of the UCM at its inception was threefold: "to provide an ecumenical instrument for allowing the church and university world to speak to each other, to encourage Christian response on campuses to human issues, and to act as an agent through which sponsors could provide resources and services to campus life."[9] It is obvious that these purposes, while legitimate in themselves, show little relationship to the original objectives of the SVM as spelled out at Mt. Hermon and in subsequent developments.

On March 1, 1969, the General Committee of the University Christian Movement at its meeting in Washington, D. C., took action in the form of an affirmative vote (23 for, 1 against, 1 abstention) of the following resolution: "We the General Committee of the UCM, declare that as of June 30, 1969, the UCM ceases to exist as a national organization...."[10]

Thus, the final vestiges of the greatest student missionary movement in the history of the church were quietly laid to rest 83 years after the Spirit of God had moved so unmistakably upon students at Mt. Hermon.

No human movement is perfect, nor can it be expected to endure indefinitely. But the great heritage left by the SVM can still speak to our generation. The reasons for its decline can serve as warning signals. Its principal emphases can redirect our attention to the basic issues of today: emphasis on personal commitment to Jesus Christ on a lifelong basis; acceptance of the authority of the Word of God and emphasis on personal Bible study; sense of responsibility to give the gospel of Christ to the entire world in our generation; reliance on the Holy Spirit; emphasis on student initiative and leadership to carry out these objectives.

Recent Advances

Yet God does not leave himself without a witness. By the mid-1930s, with the decline in missionary interest, with the Great Depression taking its toll, with war clouds rising again in Europe, with the liberal-fundamentalist controversy raging, the Church was deeply discouraged. But once again God moved upon students who would not be deterred from fulfilling God's call, in spite of surrounding circumstances.

In 1936 at Ben Lippen Bible Conference grounds in North Carolina, a group of students shared their concern that SVM seemed to have changed its original purposes. Convinced that they could not sit idly by and watch the Church give up its missionary outreach, they decided to act. The following week, a delegation from Ben Lippen went to Keswick, N.J., to share with a similar student conference the burden God had given to them. After careful consultation with some SVM leaders, and feeling that their purposes were now different, they decided to form a new organization.

Thus, the Student Foreign Missions Fellowship was organized in 1938 and SFMF was formally incorporated under student leadership, and chapters were formed throughout the country. Rapid growth was experienced, and once again the Church was awakened through students who refused to be daunted by the circumstances for their times.

In 1939, Inter-Varsity came to the U.S. from Canada. It was soon evident that one of its purposes, that of fomenting missionary interest among students, overlapped directly with the purposes of SFMF. After several years of prayer and consultation, both groups felt led by God to a merger that was consummated in November, 1945, the SFMF becoming the Missionary Department of IVCF.

In December, 1946, the newly-merged SFMF and IVCF sponsored their first international missionary convention, attended by 575 students, at the University of Toronto. The first convention was held in 1948 at the University of Illinois, Urbana, where it has been held since that time.

Following World War II there was a great upsurge of missionary concern. Veterans who had fought in the Pacific and Europe returned to the campuses deeply desirous to go back and share the gospel with the people who so recently had been their enemies. These veterans had seen the world, life, and death in a way few students before or since had seen it. God used them to lead others into an understanding of mission obligation. From many campuses in the late 1940s and early 1950s, more students went overseas in missionary endeavor than at any other comparable period in history.

However, during the 1950s it seemed as though the human race was begging for a breather. This general lull took its toll in missionary interest as well. Once again there was a decline in the churches and among students.

CONVENTION FOR MISSIONARY ADVANCE
UNIVERSITY OF TORONTO - 1946 - 47

In sharp contrast, the student world of the 1960s was marked by activism, violent upheavals, and negative attitudes. The anti-government, anti-establishment, anti-family, anti-church attitudes were also expressed in anti-missions reactions. Seldom have missions been looked upon with less favor by students than during that decade.

However, early in the next decade a sudden, unexpected change took place. Apparently recognizing that negativism was not going to solve the problems of the world, students began to take a more positive attitude and to work for change from within "the system." Nowhere was this more dramatically seen than at the Urbana student missionary conventions. Inter-Varsity uses world evangelism decision cards at these conventions as a regular part of the process of stimulating student responses to missions. In 1970 seven percent of the students at Urbana signed these cards. Three years later, 28 percent signed the card. The number grew to 50 percent by the 1976 convention. This percentage has remained above 50 percent since then.

> Now, as we turn toward a new millenium, we are still riding the crest of a great wave of student interest and activism in missions.

Now, as we turn toward a new millenium, we are still riding the crest of a great wave of student interest and activism in missions. Summer programs and short-term assignments overseas have increased dramatically in recent years. The Perspectives Study Program of the U.S. Center for World Mission's Training Division, and similar programs of missionary preparation, have been attracting steady streams of candidates.

Today's students have the great privilege of standing on the shoulders of their forebears to view with thanksgiving what God has done in the past and to look ahead to the future with hope.

End Notes

1. Kenneth Scott Latourette, *These Sought a Country* (New York: Harper and Brothers, 1950), p. 46.
2. John R. Mott, *Five Decades and a Forward View* (New York: Harper and Brothers, 1939), p. 8.
3. Robert P. Wilder, *The Student Volunteer Movement: Its Origin and Early History* (New York: The Student Volunteer Movement, 1935), p. 58.
4. Watson A. Omulogoli, *The Student Volunteer Movement: Its History and Contribution* (master's thesis, Wheaton College, 1967), p. 73.
5. Mott, *Op. cit.*, p. 12.
6. Ruth Rouse and Stephen C. Neill, *A History of the Ecumenical Movement,* 1517- 1948 (Philadelphia: Westminster Press, 1967), p. 328.
7. William H. Beahm, *Factors in the Development of the Student Volunteer Movement for Foreign Missions,* unpublished Ph.D. dissertation, University of Chicago, 1941.
8. *Ibid.,* pp. 14-15.
9. Report of Religious News Service, April 1, 1969.
10. *News Notes*, Department of Higher Education, National Council of the Churches of Christ in the U.S.A., New York, XV, No. 3, March, 1969.

Study Questions

1. Trace the roots of the Student Volunteer Movement.

2. If another student missions movement were to arise today, how do you think it would be similar to and different from the SVM in its origin, characteristics, and effects? What factors would promote the development of such a movement? What factors would hinder its development?

3. In your own words, explain the decline of the SVM and the lessons to be learned by contemporary students.

A Historical Survey of African Americans in World Missions

David Cornelius

Although their ability to carry out a concern for world missions has varied throughout the years, a missionary theme endures in African American churches today. African Americans have turned their hearts toward world missions since the time slaves began to accept Christianity. Their involvement can be traced back to the 18th and 19th centuries when African American missionaries went not only to Africa, but to the Caribbean islands as well. God is building on and extending this heritage to bring forth an even greater mission zeal in our day.

For much of the 20th century, North American Christians as a whole have felt that African Americans were not interested in world missions. This opinion is based in part on the fact that few of the North American Christians serving today as long-term missionaries are African Americans. Most churches with predominately African American memberships have chosen to carry out the mandate of The Great Commission at home. International missions[1] have been left, for the most part, in the hands of "white Christians."

While the observations which led to this opinion are accurate, the conclusion is not necessarily true. The fact is that African American Christians *are* interested in international missions. African Americans *do* feel the responsibility to fulfill the overarching mandate of our Lord's command to make disciples of *all* nations. African Americans have a history of costly engagement in missions abroad.

African American Pioneer in International Missions

The historic involvement of African Americans in international missions may be seen as far back as the 18th century. "The foreign mission motif predates home missions in general among black Baptists."[2] From the time slaves began accepting Christianity, it was in their hearts to carry the gospel of Christ not only back to their Fatherland, but also to other parts of the world. According to historical records, African American missionaries not only went to Africa in the 18th and 19th centuries, but to Canada and the Caribbean islands as well. Though the ability to carry out their convictions has varied over the years, this missionary theme has endured throughout the history of the African American church.

David Cornelius is the Director of African American Church Relations and Co-Director of the International Volunteer Fellowship of the International Mission Board, Southern Baptist Convention in Richmond, Virginia. For nine years he served as a missionary in Nigeria.

Pentecostal Pioneers

Though it is the largest African American Pentecostal denomination, the missionary endeavors of the Church of God in Christ (COGIC, founded in 1907) were largely domestic before the end of World War II. In fact, it was only after the Civil Rights period that the COGIC began to emphasize international missions in Africa and the Caribbean.[3]

Methodist Pioneers

Both the African Methodist Episcopal (AME) and African Methodist Episcopal Zion (AMEZ) denominations started missionary work in Africa during the 19th century. The denominations established work in West Africa in the early years, and in South Africa toward the end of the 19th century.

Rev. Daniel Coker, who had been pastor of the Bethel AME Church, Baltimore, Maryland, has the distinction of being the first African American Methodist missionary to serve in Africa. Coker, with help from the American Colonization Society (ACS)[4], sailed to Sierra Leone in 1820, only a few months before Baptist missionary Rev. Lott Carey (sometimes spelled Cary) left Virginia for Liberia. The third major African American Methodist denomination, the Christian Methodist Episcopal (CME), began its formal missionary work in Africa in 1911 as a joint venture with the Methodist Episcopal Church, South. They chose Zaire as their first international mission field and have since sponsored missionary efforts in South Africa, West Africa and the Caribbean.

Baptist Pioneers

Although Methodists are older as a denomination among African Americans, Baptists have a more extensive record in the area of international missions. George Liele and Prince Williams were pioneers.

Rev. George Liele (sometimes spelled "Lisle"), a freed slave and preacher from South Carolina, left the United States for Jamaica in 1783. By 1784, he had founded the First Baptist Church of Kingston, Jamaica. It is interesting to note that just as the spread of the gospel in New Testament times was due, in part, to persecution (Acts 8:1), so Liele left the country of his birth for fear of being persecuted (re-enslaved).

Another freed slave from South Carolina, Rev. Prince Williams, left Saint Augustine, Florida, some time following the Revolutionary War. Around 1790, he organized a Baptist church. In 1801 he secured land and built a small house of worship.[5]

The Vision of Lott Carey

By 1790, David George, Hector Peters and Sampson Calvert all had arrived in Africa and begun preaching on its West Coast. It was not until Lott Carey came on the scene, however, that a more structured approach to world missions began to emerge. Born in 1780, Carey worked as a young man in Richmond's tobacco warehouse district. Through his own savings and with help from sympathetic white people, he raised the money to purchase both his freedom and that of his family. He also learned to read and write by attending a night school conducted by William Crane, a deacon of the First Baptist Church of Richmond.

Carey's grandmother had become a Christian after being taken from Africa as a slave. She longed to see the gospel preached in her homeland and believed her grandson could be used of God as a missionary. Carey became a powerful and well known preacher. In 1815, he led in the organization of the African Baptist Foreign Missionary Society. It was the first organization for world missions founded by African Americans in the United States.[6]

Through the intervention of William Crane and the Richmond Baptist Missionary Society, the General Missionary Convention of the Baptist Denomination in the United States of America for Foreign Missions (known simply as the Triennial Convention because it met every three years), which had been organized in 1814, agreed to support Lott Carey and Colin Teague (a free African American preacher who shared Carey's desire to preach the gospel to the Africans). On Jan. 16, 1821, after several years of working toward fulfilling his dream of preaching the gospel to the Africans, Carey, along with Colin Teague and their families, sailed for Liberia.

The funds for their journey came from several sources, including contributions from their own pockets (some $1,500 from the sale of Carey's farm), the African Baptist Foreign

Missionary Society, some white people who were sympathetic to his cause and the American Colonization Society. Shortly after their arrival in Liberia they established the Providence Baptist Church.[7]

Carey labored and established a colony in which he served as chief political, religious and military leader, and medical officer. In spite of the difficulties faced, he felt that Africa was the best place for him and his family (and any blacks who did not want the hue of their skin to hinder their advancement in the society in which they lived). Because of his stands on various issues, he incurred the disfavor of some of the colonial rulers. Carey died in an explosion in 1828.[8]

Long before The Emancipation Proclamation, African American Christians made efforts to participate in international missions. During the 19th century prior to 1863, African Americans (primarily those who were free) made numerous attempts to establish a national entity that would enable them to carry out their mission work, both domestically and internationally, more effectively. Lack of finances was a major hindrance to success. On occasions, they requested assistance from white Christians and their organizations. In some cases, assistance was given; in others, it was refused. Occasionally there was disagreement as to whether or not to join with white-controlled missionary societies in order to carry out their work. In some cases, the two races did work together; in others, blacks chose to work independently, expressing concern that whites would dominate the relationship and decide what would be done with little or no consideration of what their black partners wanted.

From 1843 to 1845, the long-standing tension between northern and southern Christians over the issue of slavery came to a head. It resulted in separation of both the Methodist and Baptist denominations into basically two groups: pro-slavery and anti-slavery. For the Baptists, it meant the rupture of the fragile alliance between Northerners (who were mostly anti-slavery), and Southerners (who were mostly pro-slavery) in the Triennial Convention. On May 8, 1845, a new convention, the Southern Baptist Convention (SBC), was born from this rupture.

Early on, the young SBC sought to show that in spite of the stand of both individuals and member congregations on the slavery issue, they possessed great interest in the spiritual welfare of blacks and slaves. Before the founding meeting was over, two boards had been established. One, the Board for Domestic Missions, focused on evangelizing inhabitants of the United States (including blacks and Indians). The other, the Foreign Mission Board, was to focus on helping Southern Baptists to evangelize abroad.

By 1846, a year after the founding of its Foreign Mission Board, the new convention had appointed two African Americans as missionaries (John Day and A. L. Jones). Over the next 40 years, the board either appointed or gave support to at least 62 black missionaries.[9] The vast majority of these served in Africa.

Baptists After the Emancipation Proclamation

Soon after the effective date of the Emancipation Proclamation (Jan. 1, 1863), African Americans, who had just been freed from slavery by the Proclamation, began leaving white Baptist churches and organizing their own churches and associations. Driven in part by a desire to become more efficient and effective in evangelizing Africa, black Baptists continued to attempt to organize a national convention. Attempts at forming a national convention were hindered, in part, by regionalism. It would not be until 1895 that black Baptists would succeed in organizing an enduring national convention.

Between 1863 and 1895, African Americans continued seeking to "flesh out" their God-given mandate of sending missionaries to evangelize Africa. A number of outstanding African American missionaries moved these efforts forward. [10] Among them was a Virginia-born preacher named William W. Colley.

The Passion of William W. Colley

Colley is recognized as the only African American Baptist to have served as an appointed missionary of both a white-administered missionary-sending agency and a black-administered missionary-sending agency. William W. Colley was appointed by the Foreign Mission Board, SBC in 1875 to serve in West Africa as the assistant to W. J. David, a white missionary from Mississippi. In November 1879, he returned to the United States with the conviction that more blacks should be involved in international missions, especially in Africa. As he traveled back and forth across the country, he urged black Baptists to take an independent course in mission work and form their own sending agency.[11] Colley's effort is considered the primary force in the founding of the Baptist Foreign Mission Convention (BFMC) on November 24, 1880. The BFMC became one of three conventions that merged in 1895 to form the National Baptist Convention USA, Inc., the first truly national convention of black Baptists in the United States.[12]

Colley was among the first missionaries appointed by the BFMC in 1883. He, along with his wife, Joseph and Hattie Presley, John J. Cole and Henderson McKinney, was sent to West Africa.

It has been said, speaking of missionaries in those days, that Africa was the white man's graveyard (referring to the many white missionaries who died as a result of disease contracted while serving in Africa). It may also be said that Africa was the black man's graveyard. Of the first dozen missionaries sent to Africa by the BFMC, 11 either died on the field or became so ill that they had to return to the United States. The popular notion (held by both whites and blacks) that African Americans could tolerate the conditions in Africa better than could whites was proven to be untrue.

The years during which the BFMC operated (1880-1895) were characterized by waxing and waning of both interest and support. During the early years, there was great excitement over the work being done in Africa. As the years passed and hardship and tragedy struck, causing one missionary after another to leave the field, interest seemed to decline. During the entire existence of the BFMC, those states which had missionaries on the field whom they could claim as their own seemed to give stronger support to the convention. There were other factors in the decreasing support.[13] In the end, it was the founding of such agencies as the Foreign Mission Board of the National Baptist Convention USA, Inc.

and the Lott Carey Baptist Foreign (and Home) Mission Convention that has continued to foster the international missions efforts of black Baptists in the United States.

Always Moving Beyond Hindrances

Historically, there have been factors that have worked against full participation of African Americans in international missions. As a result, throughout much of their history, African Americans have achieved neither their full desire nor their full potential in the international missions arena. Many of those hindering factors have been eliminated, but others remain. Even so, there is a powerful heritage of moving beyond hindrances.

During the years of slavery, many who had the desire to serve as international missionaries were limited in obvious ways. But as soon as African Americans began to shed the chains of slavery, they began to press their way to foreign lands with the gospel. African Americans have worked in partnership with white Christians, and they have formed their own conventions and agencies. There have been periods when white Christians did not want increasing numbers of African Americans serving on international mission fields alongside them.[14] At other times African American participation was discouraged by governmental actions: refusal of visas or unreasonably high fees for visas; some colonial governments even refused to honor lawfully obtained visas for certain African countries when they were in power. Whatever the circumstances, God empowered African Americans as His missionaries.

In the midst of the post-Emancipation activity of African American Christians to evangelize Africa, there was also the struggle to gain fully functional freedom in the United States. It did not take long for Jim Crow laws mandating segregation to spread across the land. It became the calling of the black church to lead in this struggle.

On the home front, there was the aftermath of the Civil War in which segregation and discrimination, fostered by Jim Crow laws, caused the plight of many blacks in the United States to be worse than it was during slavery. This meant that, being the only institution that African Americans had under their control, the black church had to lead in the struggle of her people for full citizenship and human rights in the country of their birth. Somewhere in the struggle, the vision for world evangelization that many of the early black Christian leaders had exhibited became blurred. As a result, large scale neglect of the international missions enterprise was experienced among African Americans. In spite of this, neither the interest in nor the sense of responsibility for a lost, dying world was diminished.

Many of the negatives of the 19th century have passed away. In spite of all that has changed for the good, things are still not what they should be. Various walls of separation still exist in some areas. The color of one's skin is still a hindrance in some arenas. Attempts at segregation are still being made by some. However, in spite of these challenges, tremendous strides are being made in world evangelization because the Body of Christ continues to learn to work together as *one*, learning what *unity* really is!

Onward to Fulfill the Commission

This brief summary shows that African Americans are not newcomers in the area of international missions. With even a cursory look at current events, one is left standing in awe at what God is doing with African Americans in international missions. Where do we go from here?

Numerous organizations established to mobilize African Americans toward more participation in international missions have been born over the past three decades. Mainline white denominations and missionary-sending agencies have begun to actively seek and enlist blacks to serve overseas alongside the white missionaries. African American denominational leaders are being challenged to provide more opportunities for their constituents to participate in international missions in a meaningful way.

God is raising up a new generation of pastors in the African American church: pastors who are being led to seek out opportunities for their own involvement, and that of their congregations, in international missions. International partnerships between black congregations, associations, state conventions and fellowships in the United States and overseas entities are developing at an ever increasing rate. The number of African American Christians participating in short-term international missions opportunities continues to rise. Finally, there is a developing trend toward ever increasing numbers of African Americans giving their lives overseas, serving long-term as Christian missionaries.

The African American church is a sleeping giant in the area of international missions: a giant that is being awakened by her Lord. Only God knows the extent to which His Kingdom will be strengthened as the full potential of this giant in international missions is realized!

End Notes

1. In this article, the term "international missions" is used instead of the more familiar term "foreign missions." While they may be used interchangeably, the author's preference is"international," due primarily to some negative connotations that the word "foreign" has incurred over the years. "Foreign" will be used only to designate proper names of organizations to which the author may refer.
2. Leroy Fitts, *A History of Black Baptists* (Nashville: Broadman Press, 1985), p. 109.
3. C. Eric Lincoln and Lawrence H. Mamiya, *The Black Church in the African American Experience* (Durham: Duke University Press,1990), p. 90.
4. While it is clear that the motives of the ACS were racist and self-serving (they wanted to send freed slaves back to Africa in order that they not be problematic to the white slave owners in the United States) men like Coker, who accepted their help in getting to Africa, were far more interested in spreading the gospel among the Africans. The Society even went so far as to negotiate with African leaders for property to be used for colonization by those returning.
5. Fitts., p. 110.
6. William J. Harvey, III, *Bridges of Faith Across the Seas* (Philadelphia: The Foreign Mission Board of the National Baptist Convention USA, Inc., 1989), p. 16.

7. Along with William Crane and some others, they had organized the Providence Baptist Church in Richmond before they sailed for West Africa. Today, this church continues to have an effective ministry in the city of Monrovia, Liberia.

8. History reports that the explosion was an accident that occurred as he was preparing to defend the colony against an invading tribe. Some, however, believe that Carey's death was an assassination. Proponents of this theory believe that they have evidence to support their belief.

9. A record of these individuals may be found in the archives of the International Mission Board, located in its home office building in Richmond, VA.

10. Others were Solomon Cosby and Harrison N. Bouey. Bouey was appointed by the South Carolina Baptist Educational,Missionary and Sunday School Convention. That convention is now known as the Baptist Educational and Missionary Convention of South Carolina.

11. For a list of possible reasons with explanations, along with a more extensive discussion on W. W. Colley's missionary ministry, see Sandy D. Martin's book, *Black Baptists and African Missions: The origins of a Movement 1880-1915* (Macon, GA.: Mercer University Press, 1989), pp. 49ff.

12. The National Baptist Convention USA, Inc. was organized in Sept., 1895. It resulted from a merger of three smaller conventions: the Baptist Foreign Mission Convention (founded in 1880), the American National Baptist Convention (founded in 1886) and the Baptist National Educational Convention (founded in 1893). The resolution leading to the founding of this convention read, in part, "That there shall be one national organization of American Baptists. Under this, there shall be a Foreign Mission Board, with authority to plan and execute the Foreign Mission work, according to the spirit and purpose set forth by the Foreign Mission Convention of the United States." Stated another way, a major part of the work of the new convention was to be to carry on the foreign mission focus of the Baptist Foreign Mission Convention.

13. As early as 1886, a decline in support for the BFMC could be seen. By 1888, the convention's work was severely impaired. By the early 1890's, the convention's work, for all practical purposes, did not exist. Several factors may have contributed to this declining support. 1. Prior to the founding of the BFMC, a number of states appointed and sent their own missionaries. Even after the founding of the convention, this practice continued. 2. There were those who chose to work with white missionary societies and organizations, believing these groups to be the more "legitimate" channels for Baptists to do missionary work since they had been established for some time. 3. During the late 1880's, the economy was especially bad for African Americans. In addition to the country's economy being in a slump, segregation and discrimination was having a devastating impact on African Americans. 4. Complaints from missionaries on the field that they were not being paid in a timely manner, or that they were not receiving support at all, may have contributed to a decline in Black Baptists' confidence in the convention's governing board. 5. During those periods of time when there were no BFMC missionaries on the field, the support was noticeably less. By 1894, the Convention had no missionaries on the field. No doubt, this had a devastating impact on the support given to the Convention.

14. There have always been those African Americans who were willing, and even anxious, to serve alongside their white brothers and sisters on the international mission field. Even here, there have been hindrances. During the 19th century, African American missionaries serving under appointment of white-administered missionary-sending agencies most often had to have white supervisors available before being sent to the field. It was well past the mid-20th century before most white-administered sending agencies (especially those that are denominationally based) would accept African American candidates. These hindrances no longer exist. Even before the time of Carey, there were black Christians who felt that God had given them as a race the mandate to have primary responsibility for taking the gospel back to Africa. Many of the efforts to start state, regional and national bodies had this mandate as a driving force. The desire was so strong that a number of leaders sought to have black Baptists join with white Baptists in order to expedite this mission (even though the sting of their mistreatment in white churches during and after slavery was still fresh). Some opponents of these suggested alliances argued that white American Christians had ignored Africa and that if blacks did not chart their own course, the missions efforts of the whites would dilute, and even hinder, the efforts being made by blacks to evangelize Africa.

An Enquiry into the Obligation of Christians to Use Means for the Conversion of the Heathens

William Carey

Expect great things from God. Attempt great things for God.

Excerpted from *An Enquiry Into the Obligation of Christians to Use Means for the Conversion of the Heathens*, William Carey, New Facsimile Ed., Carey Kingsgate Press, London, (1792), 1962.

In 1792 an impoverished and youthful English pastor, part-time teacher, and shoemaker undertook the task of setting down his convictions in a small pamphlet, counteracting the prevailing view in his day that the Great Commission no longer applied to Christians. He possessed few literary graces. He avoided the limelight. He even belonged to one of the smaller bodies of dissenting churches of that day. Yet, William Carey's Enquiry *and personal example over the next 40 years resulted in a major revolution in outlook and outreach of the Christian Church, primarily as his emphasis established for Protestants the validity and necessity of mission "order" structures.*

Carey and a colleague, under the newly formed Baptist Missionary Society, sailed for India in 1793, eventually settling in Serampore, a Danish enclave near Calcutta. Carey, Joshua Marshman and William Ward, the "Serampore Trio", translated and printed parts of the Bible into several Asian languages and founded a school for the training of Indian Christians. With little formal education but possessing extraordinary perseverance and conviction, Carey weathered financial crises, natural disasters, family illness, and criticisms from England to make advances in evangelism, philology, the natural sciences, and education. He exhorted others and himself to "expect great things from God; attempt great things for God."

Today, Carey is recognized as the "father of Protestant missions," since historians date the modern era of Protestant missions back to the publishing date of his Enquiry. *Dr. Ernest A. Payne observes, "He who reads the* Enquiry *today is struck, first of all, by its sober matter-of-factness and its modernity. More than a fourth of the pages are taken up with schedules detailing the different countries of the world, their length and breadth, the number of their inhabitants and the religions there represented. Throughout there is a clear division into sections and the points are numbered. The contents are brief, logical, precise, more like a Blue Book or a committee's report than a prophetic call to the Church of Christ. There is here no appeal to eloquence or sentiment, no elaborate building up of proof-texts from the Bible, no involved theological argument, but a careful setting down of facts. The very title is characteristic of the author...." George Smith, writing in 1885, called it "the first and still the greatest missionary treatise in the English language." It has not yet been surpassed in simplicity or cogency.*

What follows is a composition of extracted paragraphs from Carey's original 87-page Enquiry.

As our blessed Lord has required us to pray that his kingdom may come, and his will be done on earth as it is in heaven, it becomes us not only to express our desires of that event by word, but to use every lawful method to spread the knowledge of his name. In order to do this, it is necessary that we should become in some measure acquainted with the religious state of the world; and as this is an object we should be prompted to pursue, not only by the Gospel of our Redeemer, but even by the feelings of humanity, so an inclination to conscientious activity therein would form one of the strongest proofs that we are the subject of grace, and partakers of that spirit of universal benevolence and genuine philanthropy, which appear so eminent in the character of God himself.

Sin was introduced amongst the children of men by the fall of Adam, and has even since been spreading its baneful influence. By changing its appearances to suit the circumstances of the times, it has grown up in ten thousand forms, and constantly counteracted the will and designs of God. One would have supposed that the remembrance of the deluge would have been transmitted from father to son, and have perpetually deterred mankind from transgressing the will of their Maker; but so blinded were they, that in the time of Abraham gross wickedness prevailed wherever colonies were planted, and the iniquity of the Amorites was great, though not yet full. After this, idolatry spread more and more, till the seven devoted nations were cut off with the most signal marks of divine displeasure. Still, however, the progress of evil was not stopped, but the Israelites themselves too often joined with the rest of mankind against the God of Israel.

Yet God repeatedly made known his intention to prevail finally over all the power of the devil, and to destroy all his works, and set up his own kingdom and interest among men, and extend it as universally as Satan had extended his. It was for this purpose that the Messiah came and died, that God might be just, and the justifier of all that should believe in him. When he had laid down his life, and taken it up again, he sent forth his disciples to preach the good tidings to every creature, and to endeavor by all possible methods to bring over a lost world to God. They went forth according to their divine commission, and wonderful success attended their labours; the civilized Greeks and uncivilized barbarians, each yielded to the cross of Christ, and embraced it as the only way of salvation. Since the apostolic age, many other attempts to spread the Gospel have been made, which have been considerably successful, notwithstanding which a very considerable part of mankind is still involved in all the darkness of heathenism. Some attempts are still being made, but they are inconsiderable in comparison to what might be done if the whole Body of Christians entered heartily into the spirit of the divine command on this subject. Some think little about it, others are unacquainted with the state of the world, and others love their wealth better than the souls of their fellow creatures.

In order that the subject may be taken into more serious consideration, I shall enquire, whether the commission given by our Lord to his disciples be not still binding on us— take a short view of former undertakings— give some account of the present state of the world, consider the practicability of doing something more than is done—and the duty of Christians in general in this matter.

An Enquiry Whether the Commission Given by Our Lord to His Disciples Be Not Still Binding On Us

Our Lord Jesus Christ, a little before his departure, commissioned his apostles to *Go, and teach all nations*; or, as another evangelist expresses it, *Go into all the world, and preach the Gospel to every creature.* This commission was as extensive as possible, and laid them under obligation to disperse themselves into every country of the habitable globe, and preach to all the inhabitants, without exception, or limitation. They accordingly went forth in obedience to the command, and the power of God evidently wrought with them. Many attempts of the same kind have been made since their day and which have been attended with various success, but the work has not been taken up or prosecuted of late years (except by a few individuals) with that zeal and perseverance with which the primitive Christians went about it. It seems as if many thought the commission was sufficiently put in execution by what the apostles and others have done; that we have enough to do to attend to the salvation of our own countrymen; and that, if God intends the salvation of the heathen, he will some way or other bring them to the Gospel, or the Gospel to them. It is thus that multitudes sit at ease, and give themselves no concern about the far greater part of their fellow-sinners, who to this day, are lost in ignorance and idolatry. There seems also to be an opinion existing in the minds of some, that because the apostles were extraordinary officers and have no proper successors, and because many things which were right for them to do would be utterly unwarrantable for us, therefore it may not be immediately binding on us to execute the commission, though it was so upon them. To the consideration of such persons I would offer the following observations.

FIRST, If the command of Christ to teach all nations be restricted to the apostles, or those under the immediate inspiration of the Holy Ghost, then that of baptizing should be so, too; and every denomination of Christians, except the Quakers, do wrong in baptizing with water at all.

SECONDLY, If the command of Christ to teach all nations be confined to the apostles, then all such ordinary ministers who have endeavoured to carry the Gospel to the heathens, have acted without a warrant, and run before they were sent. Yea, and though God has promised the most glorious things to the heathen world by sending his Gospel to them, yet whoever goes first, or indeed at all, with that message, unless he have a new and special commission from heaven, must go without any authority for so doing.

THIRDLY, If the command of Christ to teach all nations extend only to the apostles, then, doubtless, the promise of the divine presence in this work must be so limited; but this is worded in such a manner as expressly precludes such an idea. *Lo, I am with you always, to the end of the world....*

It has been objected that there are multitudes in our own nation, and within our immediate spheres of action, who are as ignorant as the South-Sea savages, and that therefore we have work enough at home, without going into other countries. That there are thousands in our own land as far from God as possible, I readily grant, and that this ought to excite us to ten-fold diligence to our work, and in attempts to spread divine knowledge amongst them is a certain fact; but that it ought to supersede all attempts to spread the Gospel in foreign parts seems to want proof. Our own countrymen have the means of grace, and may attend on the word preached if they choose it. They have the means of knowing the truth, and faithful ministers are placed in almost every part of the land, whose spheres of action might be much extended if their congregations were but more hearty and active in the cause; but with them the case is widely different, who have no Bible, no written language (which many of them have not), no ministers, no good civil government, nor any of those advantages which we have. Pity therefore, humanity, and much more Christianity, call loudly for every possible exertion to introduce the Gospel amongst them.

A Short Review of Former Undertakings for the Conversion of the Heathen

...Thus far the history of the acts of the Apostles informs us of the success of the word in the primitive times; and history informs us of its being preached about this time, in many other places. Peter speaks of a church at Babylon; Paul proposed a journey to Spain, and it is generally believed he went there, and likewise came to France and Britain. Andrew preached to the Sythians, north of the Black Sea. John is said to have preached in India, and we know that he was at the Isle of Patmos, in the Archipelago. Philip is reported to have preached in upper Asia, Sythia, and Phrygia; Bartholomew in India, on this side of the Ganges, Phrygia, and Armenia; Matthew in Arabia, or Asiatic Ethiopia, and Parthia; Thomas in India, as far as the coast of Coromandel, and some say in the island of Ceylon; Simon, the Canaanite, in Egypt, Cyrene, Mauritania, Libya, and other parts of Africa, and from thence to have come to Britain; and Jude is said to have been principally engaged in the lesser Asia, and

Greece. Their labours were evidently very extensive, and very successful; so that Pliny, the younger, who lived soon after the death of the apostles, in a letter to the emperor, Trajan, observed that Christianity had spread, not only through towns and cities, but also through whole countries. Indeed before this, in the time of Nero, it was so prevalent that it was thought necessary to oppose it by an Imperial Edict, and accordingly the proconsuls, and other governors, were commissioned to destroy it…

A Survey of the Present State of the World

In this survey I shall consider the world as divided, according to its usual division, into four parts, Europe, Asia, Africa, and America, and take notice of the extent of the several countries, their population, civilization, and religion…The following Tables will exhibit a more comprehensive view of what I propose, than anything I can offer on the subject.

(Editor's note: the following charts are just 4 of 24 charts Carey included in the "Enquiry.")

EUROPE.

Countries.	EXTENT. Length. Miles.	EXTENT. Breadth. Miles.	Number of Inhabitants.	Religion.
Great-Britain . .	680	300	12,000,000	Protestants, of many denominations.
Ireland	285	160	2,000,000	Protestants, and Papists.
France	600	500	24,000,000	Catholics, Deists, and Protestants.
Spain	700	500	9,500,000	Papists.
Portugal . . .	300	100	2,000,000	Papists.
SWEDEN, *including* Sweden proper, Gothland, Shonen, Lapland, Bothnia, and Finland . .	800	500	3,500,000	The Swedes are serious Lutherans, but most of the Laplanders are Pagans, and very superstitious.
Isle of Gothland . .	80	23	5,000	
—— Oesel . . .	45	24	2,500	
—— Oeland . . .	84	9	1,000	
—— Dago	26	23	1,000	

AMERICA.

Countries.	EXTENT. Length. Miles.	EXTENT. Breadth Miles.	Number of Inhabitants.	Religion.
Peru	1800	600	10,000,000	Pagans and Papists.
Country of the Amazons	1200	900	8,000,000	Pagans.
Terra Firma . . .	1400	700	10,000,000	Pagans and Papists.
Guiana	780	480	2,000,000	Ditto.
Terra Magellanica . .	1400	460	9,000,000	Pagans.
Old Mexico . . .	2220	600	13,500,000	Ditto, and Papists.
New Mexico . . .	2000	1000	14,000,000	Ditto.
The States of America	1000	600	3,700,000	Christians, of various denominations.
Terra de Labrador, Nova-Scotia, Louisiana, Canada, and all the country inland from Mexico to Hudson's-Bay .	1680	600	8,000,000	Christians, of various denominations, but most of the North-American Indians are Pagans.

AFRICA.

Countries.	EXTENT. Length. Miles.	EXTENT. Breadth. Miles.	Number of Inhabitants.	Religion.
Biledulgerid .	2500	350	3,500,000	Mahometans, Christians, and Jews.
Zaara, or the Desart .	3400	660	800,000	Ditto.
Abyssinia . . .	900	800	5,800,000	Armenian Christians.
Abex	540	130	1,600,000	Christians and Pagans.
Negroland . . .	2200	840	18,000,000	Pagans.
Loango	410	300	1,500,000	Ditto.
Congo	540	220	2,000,000	Ditto.
Angola	360	250	1,400,000	Ditto.
Benguela . . .	430	180	1,600,000	Ditto.
Mataman . . .	450	240	1,500,000	Ditto.
Ajan	900	300	2,500,000	Ditto.
Zanguebar . . .	1400	350	3,000,000	Ditto.
Monoemugi . . .	900	660	2,000,000	Ditto.

ASIA.

Countries.	EXTENT. Length. Miles.	EXTENT. Breadth Miles.	Number of Inhabitants.	Religion.
Ifle of Ceylon . . .	250	200	2,000,000	Pagans, except the Dutch Chriftians.
—— Maldives . .	1000 *in number.*		100,000	Mahometans.
—— Sumatra . . .	1000	100	2,100,000	Ditto, and Pagans.
—— Java	580	100	2,700,000	Ditto.
—— Timor . . .	2400	54	300,000	Ditto, and a few Chriftians.
—— Borneo . . .	800	700	8,000,000	Ditto.
—— Ceieoes . .	510	240	2,000,000	Ditto.
—— Boutam . . .	75	30	80,000	Mahometans.
—— Carpentyn . .	30	3	2,000	Chriftian Proteftants.
—— Ourature . .	18	6	3,000	Pagans.
—— Pullo Lout . .	60	36	10,000	Ditto.

Befides the little Iflands of Manaar, Aripen, Caradivia, Pengandiva, Analativa, Nainandiva. and Nindundiva, which are inhabited by Chriftian Proteftants.

This, as nearly as I can obtain information, is the state of the world; though in many countries, as Turkey, Arabia, Great Tartary, Africa, and America, except the United States, and most of the Asiatic Island, we have no accounts of the number of inhabitants, that can be relied on. I have therefore only calculated the extent, and counted a certain number on an average upon a square mile; in some countries more, and in others less, according as circumstances determine.... All these things are loud calls to Christians, and especially to ministers, to exert themselves to the utmost in their several spheres of action, and to try to enlarge them as much as possible.

The Practicability of Something Being Done, More Than What is Done, for the Conversion of the Heathen

The impediments in the way of carrying the Gospel among the heathen must arise, I think, from one or other of the following things;—either their distance from us, their barbarous and savage manner of living, the danger of being killed by them, the difficulty of procuring the necessities of life, or the unintelligibleness of their languages.

FIRST, *As to their distance from us*, whatever objections might have been made on that account before the invention of the mariner's compass, nothing can be alleged for it, with any colour of plausibility in the present age. Men can now sail with as much certainty through the Great South Sea as they can through the Mediterranean, or any lesser sea. Yea, and providence seems in a manner to invite us to

the trial, as there are to our knowledge trading companies, whose commerce lies in many of the places where these barbarians dwell....

SECONDLY, *As to their uncivilized and barbarous way of living*, this can be no objection to any, except those whose love of ease renders them unwilling to expose themselves to inconveniences for the good of others.

It was no objection to the apostles and their successors, who went among the barbarous *Germans* and *Gauls*, and still more barbarous *Britons!* They did not wait for the ancient inhabitants of these countries to be civilized before they could be Christianized, but went simply with the doctrine of the cross and Tertullian could boast that "those parts of Britain which were proof against the Roman armies were conquered by the Gospel of Christ." It was no objection to an Eliot, or a Brainerd, in later times. They went forth, and encountered every difficulty of the kind, and found that a cordial reception of the Gospel produced those happy effects which the longest intercourse with Europeans without it could never accomplish. It is no objection to commercial men. It only requires that we should have as much love to the souls of our fellow creatures, and fellow sinners, as they have for the profits arising from a few otter-skins, and all these difficulties would be easily surmounted...

THIRDLY, *In respect to the danger of being killed by them*, it is true that whoever does go must put his life in his hand, and not consult with flesh and blood; but do not the goodness of the cause, the duties incumbent on us as the creatures of God, and Christians, and the perishing state of our fellow men, loudly call upon us to venture all and use every warrantable exertion for their benefit? Paul and Barnabas, who *hazarded their lives for the name of our Lord Jesus Christ*, were not blamed as being rash, but commended for so doing, while John Mark who through timidity of mind deserted them in their perilous undertaking was branded with censure. After all, as has been already observed, I greatly question whether most of the barbarities practiced by the savages upon those who have visited them have not originated in some real or supposed affront, and were therefore, more properly, acts of self-defense than proofs of ferocious dispositions. No wonder if the imprudence of sailors should prompt them to offend the simple savage, and the offense be resented; but Eliot, Brainerd and the Moravian missionaries, have been very seldom molested. Nay, in general the heathen have showed a willingness to hear the Word, and have principally expressed their hatred of Christianity on account of the vices of nominal Christians.

FOURTHLY, *As to the difficulty of procuring the necessaries of life,* this would not be so great as may appear as first sight; for though we could not procure European food, yet we might procure such as the natives of those countries which we visit subsist upon themselves...

It might be necessary, however, for two, at least, to go together, and in general I should think it best that they should be married men, and to prevent their time from being employed in procuring necessaries, two, or more, other persons, with their wives and families, might also accompany them, who should be wholly employed in providing for them. In most countries it would be necessary for them to cultivate a little spot of ground just for their support, which would be a resource to them whenever their supplies failed. Indeed a variety of methods may be thought of, and when once the work is undertaken, many things will suggest themselves to us, of which we at present can form no idea.

> Were the children of light but as wise in their generation as the children of this world they would stretch every nerve to gain so glorious a prize.

FIFTHLY, *As to learning their languages,* the same means would be found necessary here as in trade between different nations. In some cases interpreters might be obtained, who might be employed for a time; and where these were not to be found, the missionaries must have patience, and mingle with the people, till they have learned so much of their language as to be able to communicate their ideas to them in it. It is well known to require no very extraordinary talents to learn, in the space of a year, or two at most, the language of any people upon earth, so much of it at least, as to be able to convey any sentiments we wish to their understandings.

An Enquiry into the Duty of Christians in General, and What Means Ought to be Used, in Order to Promote this Work

If the prophecies concerning the increase of Christ's kingdom be true, and if what has been advanced, concerning the commission given by him to his disciples being obligatory on us, be just, it must be inferred that all Christians ought heartily to concur with God in promoting his glorious designs, for *he that is joined to the Lord is one spirit.*

One of the first, and most important of those duties which are incumbent upon us, is *fervent and united prayer....* I trust our *monthly prayer-meetings* for the success of the Gospel have not been in vain. It is true a want of importunity too generally attends our prayers; yet unimportunate and feeble as they have been, it is to be believed that God has heard, and in a measure answered them.... If an holy solicitude had prevailed in all the assemblies of Christians in behalf of their Redeemer's kingdom, we might probably have seen before now, not only an *open door* for the Gospel, but *many running to and fro, and knowledge increased;* or a diligent use of those means which providence has put in our power, accompanied with a greater blessing than ordinary from heaven.

Many can do nothing but pray, and prayer is perhaps the only thing in which Christians of all denominations can cordially, and unreservedly unite; but in this we may all be one, and in this the strictest unanimity ought to prevail….

We must not be contented however with praying, without *exerting ourselves in the use of means* for the obtaining of those things we pray for. Were *the children of light* but *as wise in their generation as the children of this world* they would stretch every nerve to gain so glorious a prize, nor ever imagine that it was to be obtained in any other way.

When a trading company has obtained their charter they usually go to its utmost limits; and their stocks, their ships, their officers, and men are so chosen, and regulated, as to be likely to answer their purpose; but they do not stop here, for encouraged by the prospect of success, they use every effort, cast their bread upon the waters, cultivate friendship with everyone from whose information they expect the least advantage….

Suppose a company of serious Christians, ministers and private persons, were to form themselves into a society, and make a number of rules respecting the regulation of the plan, and the persons who are to be employed as missionaries, the means of defraying the expense, etc., etc. This society must consist of persons whose hearts are in the work, men of serious religion, and possessing a spirit of perseverance; these must be a determination not to admit any person who is not of this description, or to retain him longer than he answers to it.

From such a society a *committee* might be appointed, whose business it should be to procure all the information they could upon the subject, to receive contributions, to enquire into the characters, tempers, abilities and religious views of the missionaries, and also to provide them with necessaries for their undertakings.

If there is any reason for me to hope that I shall have any influence upon any of my brethren, and fellow Christians, probably it may be more especially amongst them of my own denomination. I would therefore propose that such a society and committee should be formed amongst the *particular Baptist denomination*.

I do not mean by this, in any wise to confine it to one denomination of Christians. I wish with all my heart, that everyone who loves our Lord Jesus Christ in sincerity would in some way or other engage in it. But in the present divided state of Christendom, it would be more likely for good to be done by each denomination engaging separately in the work than if they were to embark in it conjointly.

In respect to *contributions* for defraying the expenses, money will doubtless be wanting…If congregations were to open subscriptions of one penny, or more per week, according to their circumstances, and deposit it as a fund for the propagation of the Gospel, much might be raised in this way.

We are exhorted to *lay up treasure in heaven, where neither moth nor rust doth corrupt, nor thieves break through and steal*. It is also declared that *whatsoever a man soweth, that shall he also reap*. These Scriptures teach us that the enjoyments of the life to come bear a near relation to that which now is a relation similar to that of the harvest, and the seed. It is true all the reward is of mere grace, but it is nevertheless encouraging what a *treasure,* what an *harvest* must await such characters as Paul, and Eliot, and Brainerd, and others, who have given themselves wholly to the work of the Lord. What a heaven will it be to see the many myriads of poor heathens, of Britons amongst the rest, who by their labours have been brought to the knowledge of God. Surely a *crown of rejoicing* like this is worth aspiring to. Surely it is worthwhile to lay ourselves out with all our might in promoting the cause and kingdom of Christ.

Study Questions

1. Note the prominence in Carey's pamphlet of statistics, "…loud calls to Christians, and especially to ministers, to exert themselves to the utmost in their several spheres of action…." Are Christians *today* moved to action by statistics? Why or why not?

2. Carey concludes the pamphlet with a brief description of the "means" he advocates. Summarize his definition of "means."

The Call to Service

J. Hudson Taylor

In study of the Divine Word I saw that the apostolic plan was not to raise ways and means, but *to go and do the work*, trusting in His sure Word.

James Hudson Taylor, founder of the China Inland Mission, was herald of a new era in Protestant missions. "A Retrospect" provides further autobiographical details. In "The Call to Service," Taylor describes his spiritual, academic, and practical preparations for missionary service in China. After seven years in China with the Chinese Evangelization Society, he was compelled by failing health to return home to England in 1860. "A New Agency Needed" details Taylor's growing convictions over the next five years that God was calling him to take personal responsibility for the millions in China's inland provinces by forming a mission agency exclusively focused on them. Carrying the weight of widespread opposition from contemporary mission leaders, but equally haunted by the "accusing map" of China in his study, Taylor came to a decision while wandering the beaches of Brighton on a summer Sunday in 1865.

The Call to Service

The first joys of conversion passed away after a time, and were succeeded by a period of painful deadness of soul, with much conflict. But this also came to an end, leaving a deepened sense of personal weakness and dependence on the Lord as the only Keeper as well as Savior of His people. How sweet to the soul, wearied and disappointed in its struggle with sin, is the calm repose of trust in the Shepherd of Israel.

Not many months after my conversion, having a leisure afternoon, I retired to my own chamber to spend it largely in communion with God. Well do I remember that occasion. How in the gladness of my heart I poured out my soul before God; and again and again confessing my grateful love to Him who had done everything for me—who had saved me when I had given up all hope and even desire for salvation—I besought Him to give me some work to do for Him, as an outlet for love and gratitude; some self-denying service, no matter what it might be, however trying or however trivial; something with which He would be pleased, and that I might do for Him who had done so much for me. Well do I remember, as in unreserved consecration I put myself, my life, my friends, my all, upon the altar, the deep solemnity that came over my soul with the assurance that my offering was accepted. The presence of God became unutterably real and blessed; and though but a child under sixteen, I remember stretching myself on the

"The Call to Service," from *A Retrospect*, Overseas Missionary Fellowship, n.d.

ground, and lying there silent before Him with unspeakable awe and unspeakable joy.

For what service I was accepted I knew not; but a deep consciousness that I was no longer my own took possession of me, which has never since been effaced. It has been a very practical consciousness. Two or three years later, propositions of an unusually favorable nature were made to me with regard to medical study, on the condition of my becoming apprenticed to the medical man who was my friend and teacher. But I felt I dared not accept any binding engagement such as was suggested. I was not my own to give myself away; for I knew not when or how He whose alone I was, and for whose disposal I felt I must ever keep myself free, might call for service.

Within a few months of this time of consecration, the impression was wrought into my soul that it was in China the Lord wanted me. It seemed to me highly probable that the work to which I was thus called might cost my life; for China was not then open as it is now. But few missionary societies had at that time workers in China, and but few books on the subject of China missions were accessible to me. I learned, however, that the Congregational minister of my native town possessed a copy of Medhurst's *China*, and I called upon him to ask a loan of the book. This he kindly granted, asking me why I wished to read it. I told him that God had called me to spend my life in missionary service in that land. "And how do you propose to go there?" he inquired. I answered that I did not at all know; that it seemed to me probable that I should need to do as the Twelve and the Seventy had done in Judea—go without purse or scrip, relying on Him who had called me to supply all my need. Kindly placing his hand upon my shoulder, the minister replied, "Ah, my boy, as you grow older you will get wiser than that. Such an idea would do very well in the days when Christ Himself was on earth, but not now."

I have grown older since then, but not wiser. I am more than ever convinced that if we were to take the direction of our Master and the assurances He gave to His first disciples more fully as our guide, we should find them to be just as suited to our times as to those in which they were originally given.

Medhurst's book on China emphasized the value of medical missions there, and this directed my attention to medical studies as a valuable mode of preparation.

My beloved parents neither discouraged nor encouraged my desire to engage in missionary work. They advised me, with such convictions, to use all the means in my power to develop the resources of body, mind, heart, and soul, and to await prayerfully upon God, quite willing should He show me that I was mistaken, to follow His guidance, or to go forward if in due time He should open the way to missionary service. The importance of this advice I have often since had occasion to prove. I began to take more exercise in the open air to strengthen my physique. My feather bed I had taken away, and sought to dispense with as many other home comforts as I could in order to prepare myself for rougher lines of life. I began also to do what Christian work was in my power, in the way of tract distribution, Sunday-school teaching, and visiting the poor and sick, as opportunity afforded.

After a time of preparatory study at home, I went to Hull for medical and surgical training. There I became assistant to a doctor who was connected with the Hull school of medicine, and was surgeon also to a number of factories, which brought many accident cases to our dispensary, and gave me the opportunity of seeing and practicing the minor operations of surgery.

And here an event took place that I must not omit to mention. Before leaving home my attention was drawn to the subject of setting apart the first fruits of all one's increase and proportionate part of one's possessions to the Lord's service. I thought it well to study the question with my Bible in hand before I went away from home, and was placed in circumstances which might bias my conclusions by the pressure of surrounding wants and cares. I was thus led to the determination to set apart not less than one-tenth of whatever moneys I might earn or become possessed of for the Lord's service. The salary I received as medical assistant in Hull at the time now referred to would have allowed me with ease to do this. But owing to changes in the family of my kind friend and employer, it was necessary for me to reside out of doors. Comfortable quarters were secured with a relative, and in addition to the sum determined on as remuneration for my services I received the exact amount I had to pay for board and lodging.

If the whole resources of the Church of God were well utilized, how much more might be accomplished!

Now arose in my mind the question, Ought not this sum also to be tithed? It was surely a part of my income, and I felt that if it had been a question of Government income tax it certainly would not have been excluded. On the other hand, to take a tithe from the whole would not leave me sufficient for other purposes; and for some little time I was much embarrassed to know what to do. After much thought and prayer I was led to leave the comfortable quarters and happy circle in which I was now residing, and to engage a little lodging in the suburbs—a sitting-room and bedroom in one—undertaking to board myself. In this way I was able without difficulty to tithe the whole of my income; and while I felt the change a good deal, it was attended with no small blessing.

More time was given in my solitude to the study of the Word of God, to visiting the poor, and to evangelistic work on summer evenings than would otherwise have been the case. Brought into contact in this way with many who were in distress, I soon saw the privilege of still further economizing, and found it not difficult to give away much more than the proportion of my income I had at first intended.

About this time a friend drew my attention to the question of the personal and premillennial coming of our Lord Jesus Christ, and gave me a list of passages bearing upon it, without note or comment, advising me to ponder the subject. For a while I gave much time to studying the Scriptures about it, with the result that I was led to see that this same Jesus who left our earth in His resurrection body was so to come again, that His feet were to stand on the Mount of Olives, and that He was to take possession of the temporal throne of His father David which was promised before His birth. I saw, further, that all through the New Testament the coming of the Lord was the great hope of His people, and was always appealed to as the strongest motive for consecration and service, and as the greatest comfort in trial and affliction. I learned, too, that the period of His return for His people was not revealed, and that it was their privilege, from day to day and from hour to hour, to live as men who wait for the Lord; that thus living it was immaterial, so to speak, whether He should or should not come at any particular hour, the important thing being to be so ready for Him as to be able, whenever He might appear, to give an account of one's stewardship with joy, and not with grief.

The effect of this blessed hope was a thoroughly practical one. It led me to look carefully through my little library to see if there were any books there that were not needed or likely to be of further service, and to examine my small wardrobe, to be quite sure that it contained nothing that I should be sorry to give an account of should the Master come at once. The result was that the library was considerably diminished, to the benefit of some poor neighbors, and to the far greater benefit of my own soul, and that I found I had articles of clothing also which might be put to better advantage in other directions.

It has been very helpful to me from time to time through life, as occasion has served, to act again in a similar way; and I have never gone through my house, from basement to attic, with this object in view, without receiving a great accession of spiritual joy and blessing. I believe we are all in danger of accumulating—it may be from thoughtlessness, or from pressure of occupation—things which would be useful to others, while not needed by ourselves, and the retention of which entails loss of blessing. If the whole resources of the Church of God were well utilized, how much more might be accomplished! How many poor might be fed and naked clothed, and to how many of those as yet unreached the Gospel might be carried! Let me advise this line of things as a constant habit of mind, and a profitable course to be practically adopted whenever circumstances permit.

A New Agency Needed

"My thoughts are not your thoughts, neither are your ways My ways, saith the Lord. For as the heavens are higher than the earth, so are My ways higher than your ways, and my thoughts than your thoughts" (Isa 55:8, 9). How true are these words! When the Lord is bringing in great blessing in the best possible way, how oftentimes our unbelieving hearts are feeling, if not saying, like Jacob of old, "All these things are against me." Or we are filled with fear, as were the disciples when the Lord, walking on the waters, drew near to quiet the troubled sea, and to bring them quickly to their desired haven. And yet mere common-sense ought to tell us that He, whose way is perfect, can make no mistakes; that He who has promised to "perfect that which concerneth" us, and whose minute care counts the very hairs of our heads, and forms for us our circumstances, must know better than we the way to forward our truest interests and to glorify His own Name.

"Blind unbelief is sure to err
And scan His work in vain;
God is His own Interpreter,
And He will make it plain."

To me it seemed a great calamity that failure of health compelled my relinquishing work for God in China, just when it was more fruitful than ever before; and to leave the little band of Christians in Ningpo, needing much care and teaching, was a great sorrow. Nor was the sorrow lessened when on reaching England, medical testimony assured me that return to China, at least for years to come, was impossible. Little did I then realize that the long separation from China was a necessary step towards the formation of a work which God would bless as He has blessed the China Inland Mission. While in the field, the pressure of claims immediately around me was so great that I could not think much of the still greater needs of the regions farther inland; and, if they were thought of, could do nothing for them. But while detained for some years in England, daily viewing the whole country on the large map on the wall of my study, I was as near to the vast regions of Inland China as to the smaller districts in which I had labored personally for God; and prayer was often the only resource by which the burdened heart could gain any relief.

As a long absence from China appeared inevitable, the next question was how best to serve China while in England, and this led to my engaging for several years, with the late Rev. F. F. Gough of the C.M.S., in the revision of a version of the New Testament in the colloquial of Ningpo for the British and Foreign Bible Society. In undertaking this work, in my short-sightedness I saw nothing beyond the use that the Book, and the marginal references, would be to the native Christians; but I have often seen since that, without those months of feeding and feasting on the Word of God, I should have been quite unprepared to form, on its present basis, a mission like the China Inland Mission.

In the study of that Divine Word I learned that, to obtain successful laborers, not elaborate appeals for help, but, *first*, earnest *prayer to God* to *thrust forth laborers*, and, second, the deepening of the spiritual life of the Church, *so that men should be able to stay at home*, were what was needed. I saw that the apostolic plan was not to raise ways and means, but to *go and do the work*, trusting in His sure Word who has said, "Seek ye *first* the kingdom of God and His righteousness, and all these things shall be added unto you."

In the meantime the prayer for workers for Chehkiang was being answered. The first, Mr. Meadows, sailed for China with his young wife in January 1862, through the kind cooperation and aid of our friend Mr. Berger. The second left England in 1864, having her passage provided by the Foreign Evangelization Society. The third and fourth reached Ningpo on July 24th, 1865. A fifth soon followed them, reaching Ningpo in September 1865. Thus the prayer for the five workers was fully answered; and we were encouraged to look to God for still greater things.

Months of earnest prayer and not a few abortive efforts had resulted in a deep conviction that *a special agency was essential* for the evangelization of Inland China. At this time I had not only the daily help of prayer and conference with my beloved friend and fellow-worker, the late Rev. F. F. Gough, but also invaluable aid and counsel from Mr. and Mrs. Berger, with whom I and my dear wife (whose judgment and piety were of priceless value at this juncture) spent many days in prayerful deliberation. The grave difficulty of possibly interfering with existing missionary operations at home was foreseen; but it was concluded that, by simple trust in God, suitable agency might be raised up and sustained without interfering injuriously with any existing work. I had also a growing conviction that God would have me to seek from Him the needed workers, and to go forth with them. But for a long time unbelief hindered my taking the first step.

How inconsistent unbelief always is! I had no doubt that, if I prayed for workers, "in the name" of the Lord Jesus Christ, they would be given me. I had no doubt that, in answer to such prayer, the means for our going forth would be provided, and that doors would be opened before us in unreached parts of the Empire. But I had not then learned to trust God for *keeping* power and grace for myself, so no wonder that I could not trust Him to keep others who might be prepared to go with me. I feared that in the midst of the dangers, difficulties, and trials which would necessarily be connected with such a work, some who were comparatively inexperienced Christians might break down, and bitterly reproach me for having encouraged them to undertake an enterprise for which they were unequal.

Yet, what was I to do? The feeling of blood-guiltiness became more and more intense. Simply because I refused to ask for them, the laborers did not come forward— did not go out to China—and every day tens of thousands were passing away to Christless graves! Perishing China so filled my heart and mind that there was no rest by day, and little sleep by night, till health broke down. At the invitation of my beloved and honored friend, Mr. George Pearse (then of the Stock Exchange), I went to spend a few days with him in Brighton.

On Sunday, June 25th, 1865, unable to bear the sight of a congregation of a thousand or more Christian people rejoicing in their own security, while millions were perishing for lack of knowledge, I wandered out on the sands alone, in great spiritual agony; and there the Lord conquered my unbelief, and I surrendered myself to God for this service. I told Him that all the responsibility as to issues and consequences must rest with Him; that as His servant, it was mine to obey and follow Him— His, to direct, to care for, and to guide me and those who might labor with me. Need I say that peace at once flowed into my burdened heart? There and then I asked Him for twenty-four fellow-workers, two for each of eleven inland provinces which were without a missionary, and two for Mongolia; and writing the petition on the margin of the Bible I had with me, I returned home with a heart enjoying rest such as it had been a stranger to for months, and with an assurance that the Lord would bless His own work and that I should share in the blessing. I had previously prayed, and asked prayer, that workers might be raised up for the eleven then unoccupied provinces, and thrust forth and provided for, but had not surrendered myself to be their leader.

About this time, with the help of my dear wife, I wrote the little book, *China's Spiritual Need and Claims*. Every paragraph was steeped in prayer. With the help of Mr. Berger, who had given valued aid in the revision of the manuscript, and who bore the expense of printing an edition of 3000 copies, they were soon put in circulation. I spoke publicly of the proposed work as opportunity permitted, specially at the Perth and Mildmay Conferences of 1865, and continued in prayer for fellow-workers, who were soon raised up, and after due correspondence were invited to my home, then in the East of London. When one house became insufficient, the occupant of the adjoining house removed, and I was able to rent it; and when that in its turn became insufficient, further accommodation was provided close by. Soon there were a number of men and women under preparatory training, and engaging in evangelistic work which tested in some measure their qualifications as soul-winners.

Study Questions

1. Can you see any connection between Taylor's "call to service" and his later conclusion that "a new agency is needed"?

2. In your own words, state the reasons for Taylor's hesitancy to assume responsibility for a new missions agency.

China's Spiritual Needs and Claims

J. Hudson Taylor

Shall not the low wail of helpless, hopeless misery, arising from one-half of the heathen world, pierce our sluggish ear, and rouse us, spirit, soul, and body, to one mighty, continued, unconquerable effort for China's salvation?

Taken from *China's Spiritual Needs and Claims*, by Hudson Taylor, 1895.

As mentioned in the previous article, Taylor wrote China's Spiritual Needs and Claims *in keeping with his crucial decision made at Brighton to recruit workers for the China Inland Mission. Further editions were printed in the succeeding years, and the following excerpts are from one of these later editions. Taylor here concludes with a backward glance at the effects of the first edition of the pamphlet and at the first years of the China Inland Mission. His own life and that of the agency he formed gave testimony to his frequent assertion, "There is a living God. He has spoken His word. He means just what He says, and will do all that He has promised."*

> If thou forbear to deliver them that are drawn unto death,
> And those that are ready to be slain;
> If thou sayest, Behold, we knew it not;
> Doth not He that pondereth the heart consider it?
> And He that keepeth thy soul, doth not He know it?
> And shall not He render to every man according to his works?
> *Proverbs 24: 11, 12.*

It is a solemn and most momentous truth that our every act in this present life—and our every omission too—has a direct and important bearing both on our own future welfare, and on that of others. And as believers, it behoves us to do whatsoever we do in the name of our Lord Jesus Christ. In His name, and with earnest prayer for His blessing, the following pages are written; in His name, and with earnest prayer for His blessing, let them be read. The writer feels deeply that, as a faithful steward he is bound to bring the facts contained in these pages before the hearts and consciences of the Lord's people. He believes, too, that these facts must produce *some* fruit in the heart of each Christian reader. The legitimate fruit will undoubtedly be—not vain words of empty sympathy, but—effectual fervent prayer, and strenuous self-denying effort for the salvation of the benighted Chinese. And if in any instance they fail to produce this fruit, the writer would urge the consideration of the solemn words at the head of this page,— "If thou forbear to deliver them that are drawn unto death, and those that are ready to be slain; if thou sayest, Behold, we knew it not; doth not He that pondereth the heart consider it? and He that keepeth *thy* soul, doth not He know it? and shall not He render to every man according to his works?"

Very early in the course of His ministry, the Lord Jesus taught His people that they were to be *the light*—not of Jerusalem, not of Judea, nor yet of the Jewish nation, but—*of the world*. And He taught them to pray—not as the heathen, who use vain and unmeaning repetitions; nor yet as the worldly-minded, who ask first and principally (if not solely) for their own private benefit and need: "For," said He, "*your* Father knoweth what things *ye have need of before ye ask Him. After this manner therefore pray ye:*"

> Our Father which art in heaven,
> Hallowed be Thy name;
> Thy kingdom come;
> *Thy will be done; as in heaven, so in earth.*

And it was only after these petitions, and quite secondary to them, that any personal petitions were to be offered. Even the very moderate one, "Give us *this day* our daily bread," followed them. Is not this order too often reversed in the present day? Do not Christians often really feel, and also act, as though it was incumbent upon them to *begin* with, "Give us this day our daily bread;" virtually concluding with, "If consistent with this, may Thy name be hallowed too?" And is not Matthew 6:33, "Seek ye *first* the kingdom of God, and His righteousness; and all these things shall be *added* unto you;" practically read, even amongst the professed followers of Christ, seek first all *these things* (food and clothing, health, wealth, and comfort), and then the kingdom of God and His righteousness? Instead of honouring Him with the first fruits of our time and substance, are we not content to offer Him the fragments that remain after our own supposed need is supplied? While we thus refuse to bring the tithes into His storehouse and to prove the Lord therewith, can we wonder that He does not open the windows of heaven, and pour us our the fullness of blessing that we desire?

We have a striking exemplification of the manner in which we should seek first the kingdom of God and His righteousness, in the life and in the death of our Lord Jesus Christ. And when risen from the dead, ere He ascended on high, He commissioned His people to make known everywhere the glad tidings of salvation—full and free—through faith in His finished work. This duty He enjoined on us; enjoined in the most unmistakable form, and to the most definite extent; saying, "*Go* Ye, into *all* the world, and preach the gospel to every creature." Grievously has the Church failed in fulfilling this command. Sad it is to realize that so

near to the close of the nineteenth century of the Christian era, there are immense tracts of our globe either wholly destitute of, or most inadequately provided with, the means of grace and the knowledge of salvation.

In order to enable our readers to realize the vast extent of the outlying districts of the Chinese empire, we would suggest a comparison of them with those countries which are nearer home.

The whole continent of Europe has an area of 3,797,256 square miles; Manchuria, Mongolia, the Northwestern Dependencies, and Thibet, together, have an area of 3,951,130 square miles. These extensive regions contain many millions of our fellow creatures, but except the four missionaries in Newchwang, they have no missionary. They are perishing, and they are left to perish. Among them no missionary resides to make known that wisdom, the merchandise of which "is better than the merchandise of silver, and the gain thereof than fine gold." Throughout this immense territory, larger than the whole continent of Europe, with the exception noted above, there is not a single ambassador for Christ from all the Protestant churches of Europe and America to carry the word of reconciliation, and to pray men in *Christ's* stead, "Be ye reconciled to God." How long shall this state of things be allowed to continue?

Think of the over eighty millions beyond the reach of the Gospel in the seven provinces, where missionaries have longest laboured; think of the over 100 millions in the other eleven provinces of China Proper, beyond the reach of the few missionaries labouring there; think of the over twenty millions who inhabit the vast regions of Manchuria, Mongolia, Thibet, and the Northwestern Dependencies, which exceed in extent the whole of Europe—an aggregate of over 200 millions beyond the reach of all existing agencies—and say, how shall

> God's name be hallowed by them,
> His kingdom come among them, and
> His will be done by them?

His name, His attributes they have never heard. His kingdom is not proclaimed among them. His will is not made known to them!

Do you *believe* that each unit of these millions has a precious soul? And that "there is none other name under heaven given amongst men whereby they must be saved" than that of *Jesus*? Do you *believe* that He *alone* is "the Door of the sheepfold"; is the "Way, the Truth, and the Life"? that *"no man* cometh unto the Father but by Him"? If so, think of the state of these unsaved ones; and solemnly examine yourself in the sight of God, to see whether you are doing *your utmost* to make Him known to them.

We have now presented a brief and cursory view of the state and claims of China. To have entered into them at all in detail would have required for each province more time and space that we have devoted to the consideration of the whole empire. We have shewn how *God* has blest the efforts which have been put forth; and have endeavoured to lay before you the facilities which at present exist for the more extensive evangelization of this country. We have sought to press the great command of our risen Savior, *"Go ye, into all the world,* and preach the gospel to *every creature:"* and would point out that the parable of our Lord, contained in Matthew 25, it was not a *stranger*, but a *servant*; not an *immoral*, but an *unprofitable* one who was to be cast into outer darkness, where there is weeping and gnashing of teeth. "If ye love me," said our Master, "keep my commandments;" and one of these was, "Freely ye have received, freely give." We have shewn that in seven provinces of China Proper after allowing far more than they can possibly accomplish to the Protestant missionaries and their native assistants, there still remains an overwhelming multitude altogether beyond the sound of the Gospel. We have further shewn that there are eleven other provinces in China Proper still more needy,—eleven provinces, the very smallest of which exceeds Burmah in population, and which average each the population of both Scotland and Ireland combined! And what shall we say of the vast regions of Tartary and Thibet—more extensive than the whole continent of Europe—all without any Protestant missionary save the four in Newchwang? The claims of an empire like this should surely be not only admitted, but realized! Shall not the eternal interests of one-fifth of our race stir up the deepest sympathies of our nature, the most strenuous efforts of our blood-bought powers? Shall not the low wail of helpless, hopeless misery, arising from one-half of the heathen world, pierce our sluggish ear, and rouse us, spirit, soul, and body, to one mighty, continued, unconquerable effort for China's salvation? That, strong in God's strength, and in the power of His might, we

Proportion of Missionaries to the Population in the Eighteen Provinces of China Proper.

Province.	Population.*	No. of Missionaries.†	Proportion to Population.	Or, One Missionary to a Population exceeding that of
KWANG-TUNG	17½ millions	100	1 to 170,000	Huddersfield and Halifax (166,957).
FUH-KIEN	10 ,,	61	1 to 163 000	Newcastle (155,117).
CHEH-KIANG	12 ,,	58	1 to 206,000	Hull (191,501).
KIANG-SU	20 ,,	85	1 to 227,000	Bristol (220,915).
SHAN-TUNG	19 ,,	60	1 to 316,000	Sheffield (310,957).
CHIH-LI	20 ,,	68	1 to 294,000	Newcastle and Portsmouth (291,395).
HU-PEH	20½ ,,	43	1 to 476,000	Nottingham and Edinburgh (472,324).
KIANG-SI	15 ,,	12	1 to 1,250,000	New York (1,207,000).
GAN-HWUY	9 ,,	15	1 to 600,000	Liverpool (586,320).
SHAN-SI	9 ,,	30	1 to 300,000	Salford and Huddersfield (299,911).
SHEN-SI	7 ,,	13	1 to 530,000	Glasgow (521,999).
KAN-SUH	3 ,,	9	1 to 333,000	Sheffield (310,957).
SI-CHUEN	20 ,,	17	1 to 1,176,000	Glasgow and Liverpool (1,108,319).
YUN-NAN	5 ,,	10	1 to 500,000	Sheffield and Newcastle (466 074).
KWEI-CHAU	4 ,,	2	1 to 2,000,000	{ Glasgow, Liverpool. Birmingham, Manchester (1.919,595).
KWANG-SI	5 ,,	0	0 to 5 millions	Ireland (no Missionary).
HU-NAN	16 ,,	3 itinerating	0 to 16 ,,	Four times Scotland.
HO-NAN	15 ,,	3	1 to 5 ,,	London.

* The estimate of population is that given in the last edition of "China's Spiritual Need and Claims."
† The number of Missionaries is according to an account corrected to March, 1887.

may snatch the prey from the hand of the mighty, may pluck these brands from the everlasting burnings, and rescue these captives from the thraldom of sin and Satan, to grace the triumphs of our sovereign King, and to shine forever as stars in His diadem!

We cannot but believe that the contemplation of these solemn facts has awakened in many the heartfelt prayer, "Lord, what wilt Thou have me to do, that Thy name may be hallowed, Thy kingdom come, and Thy will be done in China?" It is the prayerful consideration of these facts, and the deepening realization of China's awful destitution of all that can make man truly happy, that constrains the writer to lay its claims as a heavy burden upon hearts of those who have experienced the power of the blood of Christ; and to seek, first from the Lord, and then from His people, the men and the means to carry the gospel into every part of this benighted land. We have to do with Him who is the Lord of all power and might, whose arm is not shortened, whose ear is not heavy; with Him whose unchanging word directs us to ask and receive, that our joy may be full; to open our mouths wide, that He may fill them. And we do well to remember that this gracious God who has condescended to place His almighty power at the command of believing prayer, looks not lightly upon the blood-guiltiness of those who neglect to avail themselves of it for the benefit of the perishing; for He it is who has said, "If thou forbear to deliver them that are drawn unto death, and those that are ready to be slain; if thou sayest, Behold, we knew it not, doth not He that pondereth the heart consider it? and He that keepeth thy soul, doth not He know it? And shall not He render to every man according to his works?"

Such considerations as the foregoing caused the writer in 1865 so to feel the overwhelming necessity for an increase in the number of labourers in China that, as stated in the first edition of this appeal, he did not hesitate to ask the great Lord of the harvest to call forth, to *thrust* forth, twenty-four European, and twenty-four native evangelists, to plant the standard of the cross in all the unevangelized districts of China Proper and of Chinese Tartary.

The same considerations lead us today to cry to God for many more. Those who have never been called to prove the faithfulness of the covenant-keeping God, in supplying, in answer to prayer, the pecuniary need of His servants, might deem it a hazardous experiment to send evangelists to a distant heathen land, with "*only* God to look to." But in one whose privilege it has been for many years past to prove the faithfulness of God, in various circumstances—at home and abroad, by land and by sea, in sickness and in health, in necessities, in dangers, and at the gates of death,—such apprehensions would be wholly inexcusable. The writer has seen God, in answer to prayer, quell the raging of the storm, alter the direction of the wind and give rain in the midst of prolonged drought. He has seen Him, in answer to prayer, stay the angry passions and murderous intentions of violent men, and bring the machinations of His people's foes to nought. He has seen Him, in answer to prayer, raise the dying from the bed of death, when human aid was vain; has seen Him preserve from the pestilence that walketh in darkness, and from the destruction that wasteth at noonday. For more than twenty-seven years he has proved the faithfulness of God in supplying the pecuniary means for his own temporal wants, and for the need of the work he has been engaged in. He has seen God, in answer to prayer, raising up labourers not a few for this vast mission-field, supplying the means requisite for their outfit, passage, and support, and vouchsafing blessing on the efforts of many of them, both among the native Christians and the heathen Chinese in fourteen out of the eighteen provinces referred to.

Study Questions

1. As with Carey, Taylor is deeply moved by the statistics before him. What "fruit" does he insist must result from consideration of the "facts"?

2. What observations does Taylor make about the nature and purpose of prayer?

Tribes, Tongues and Translators

Wm. Cameron Townsend

We realize, that there are still many, many barriers to overcome. However, we have tasted of God's faithfulness and power and are not frightened by the obstacles that face us. We dare to sing again with utmost confidence of the mighty faith that laughs at impossibilities and shouts, "It shall be done!"[1]

William Cameron Townsend founded Wycliffe Bible Translators and its sister agency, the Summer Institute of Linguistics. Starting out as a student to distribute portions of the Bible in Spanish, he was overtaken by the conviction that Spanish Bibles were inadequate for the Indian tribes of Guatemala. He completed a translation of the New Testament into Cakchiquel in 1931 and then turned his attention to other tribes. Others soon joined him. Using linguistics and technological advances, Wycliffe translators have fanned out across the globe in the last 50 years, reducing languages to writing, translating portions of the Bible, and enriching tribal societies as well as facilitating their response to the pressures of majority peoples. "Uncle Cam" has been recognized and appreciated by kings and presidents as well as by the "little people" of the world, and growing numbers of Christians are joining his vision to take the Scriptures to 3,000 further languages that are an essential key to 5,000 tribal groups. He died in 1982 at the age of 85.

Don't be a fool, friends told me fifty years ago when I decided to translate the Word for the Cakchiquel Indians, a large tribe in Central America. "Those Indians aren't worth what it would take to learn their outlandish language and translate the Bible for them. They can't read anyhow. Let the Indians learn Spanish," they said.

My friends used these same arguments fourteen years later, when, after having seen the transformation the Word brought to the Cakchiquels, I dreamed of reaching all other tribes. When I included even the small primitive groups in Amazonia in my plan, my friends added other arguments: "They'll kill you," said one old, experienced missionary. "Those jungle tribes are dying out anyway. They kill each other as well as outsiders with their spears, or bows and arrows. If they don't kill you, malaria will get you, or your canoe will upset in the rapids and you'll be without supplies and a month away from the last jumping-off place. Forget the other tribes, and stay with the Cakchiquels."

But I couldn't forget them. And one day God gave me a verse that settled the matter for me. He said: "The Son of Man is come to save that which was lost. How think ye? If a man have a hundred sheep, and one of them be gone astray, doth he not leave the ninety and nine, and goeth into the mountains and seeketh that which is gone astray?" (Matt 18:11-12)

"Tribes, Tongues and Translators," adapted from *Who Brought the Word,* by permission of Wycliffe Bible Translators, Inc., Huntington Beach, CA 92648, 1963.

That verse guided me; I went after the "one lost sheep," and four thousand young men and women have followed suit.

We call ourselves the "Wycliffe Bible Translators," in memory of John Wycliffe who first gave the whole Bible to the speakers of English. Half our members are dedicated to linguistic and translation work among the tribespeople, bringing them the Word. The other half are support personnel; teachers, secretaries, pilots, mechanics, printers, doctors, nurses, accountants and others who man the supply lines, keeping oatmeal, cooking oil, milk for the babies and other necessities moving toward the front lines. Our tools are linguistics and the Word, administered in love and in the spirit of service to all without discrimination.

The tribes are being reached. Geographical barriers once so formidable are surmounted today by our planes and short-wave radios. The newly-developed science of descriptive linguistics breaks the barriers of strange tongues. Witchcraft, killings, superstition, ignorance, fear and sickness are giving way before the Light of the Word, literacy, medicine and contact with the best in the outside world. Tribesmen formerly lost to the lifestream of their respective nations are being transformed by the Word. And whether the transformation occurs in the mountains of Southern Mexico, the jungles of Amazonia or the desert plains of Australia, it is a spectacular leap out of the old into the new.

Doors into the tribes are rapidly opening to our type of approach. The way the Bible translation program has moved forward during the past fifty years encourages us to expect the completion of the task by the turn of the century. In order to take the Word to 3,000 more Bibleless tribes, many more translators and support personnel are needed. The pace must be accelerated. Each translation may take from five to 25 or more years and involves not only the linguist we send to each tribe but also one or more tribal informants.

Politically, this seems to be the day of neglected countries and neglected tribes. Spiritually this may be their day as well. The man of Luke 14:16 invited many to the great supper he had prepared but they declined. Then he sent messengers into the cities and invited the masses on the streets but still there was room. Finally he sent his messengers to the country trails to bring in guests. They came. Perhaps at long last a special day of opportunity has come for the out-of-the-way tribes who have never had the slightest chance.

> In order to take the Word to 3,000 more Bibleless tribes, many more translators and support personnel are needed.

We know that all of them *must* hear the message of God's love, for they are included in both the Great Commission and in the prophetic vision of the vast throng of the redeemed recorded in Revelation 7:9, "After this I beheld and lo, a great multitude which no man could number of all nations and kindreds and peoples and TONGUES, stood before the throne and before the Lamb, clothed with white robes and palms in their hands." They can get there only if they hear the Word in a language they can understand. How else could they be saved?

May God stir the hearts of many to join us in completing our God-given task of reaching every tribe.

End Notes

1. Steven, Hugh. *Wycliffe in the Making—The Memoirs of W. Cameron Townsend 1920-1933*. Harold Shaw Publishers, Wheaton, Ill., 1995. p. 254

Study Questions

1. What similarities do you observe between Carey, Taylor, and Townsend?

2. Townsend cites three biblical passages as grounds for translation among "Bibleless tribes." Restate the different thrust of each of these passages for missions work among unreached peoples.

The Glory of the Impossible

Samuel Zwemer

Does it really matter how many die or how much money we spend in opening closed doors if we really believe that missions are warfare and that the King's glory is at stake?

When Robert Wilder visited Hope College in 1887 on behalf of the Student Volunteer Movement, Samuel Zwemer was completing his senior year. Responding to Wilder's appeal, Zwemer became a volunteer and soon organized a mission to Arabia with other students. After 23 years with the Arabian Mission in Basrah, Bahrain, Muscat, Kuwait and service as the first candidate secretary of the SVM, Zwemer began a career of speaking and writing that radiated out to the Muslim world from an interdenominational study center in Cairo. A prolific and gifted author, Zwemer wrote books and articles to challenge the church in Muslim evangelism, provided scholarly studies on historical and popular Islam, and produced writings and tracts in Arabic for Muslims and Christians in the Middle East. For 36 years he edited The Muslim World, *an English quarterly review of current events in the Muslim world and a forum for missionary strategy among Muslims, complementing this service with personal evangelism among the students and faculty of Al-Azhar, Cairo's famous training center for Muslim missionaries. Zwemer was an outstanding evangelical leader, an honored speaker in SVM gatherings, and the driving force behind the Cairo 1906 and Lucknow 1911 conferences which inaugurated a less confrontational and more positive approach to Muslims. James Hunt observed of this statesman, "He may be said to have been a man of one idea. While his interests and knowledge were wide, I never talked with him ten minutes that the conversation did not veer to Islam..." "The Glory of the Impossible" is taken from an SVM publication of 1911.*

From *The Unoccupied Mission Fields of Africa and Asia,* Student Volunteer Movement for Foreign Missions, Chapter 8, pp. 215-231, 1911.

The challenge of the unoccupied fields of the world is one to great faith and, therefore, to great sacrifice. Our willingness to sacrifice for an enterprise is always in proportion to our faith in that enterprise. Faith has the genius of transforming the barely possible into actuality. Once men are dominated by the conviction that a thing must be done, they will stop at nothing until it is accomplished. We have our "marching orders," as the Iron Duke [Arthur Wesley, Duke of Wellington] said, and because our Commander-in-Chief is not absent, but with us, the impossible becomes not only practical but imperative. Charles Spurgeon, preaching from the text, "All power is given unto Me...Lo I am with you always," used these words: "You have a factor here that is absolutely infinite, and what does it matter as to what other factors may be. 'I will do as much as I can,' says one. Any fool can do that. He that believes in Christ does what he can not do, attempts the impossible and performs it."[1]

Frequent set-backs and apparent failure never disheartened the real pioneer. Occasional martyrdoms are only a fresh incentive. Opposition is a stimulus to greater activity. Great victory has never been possible without great sacrifice. If the winning of Port Arthur required human bullets,[2] we cannot expect to carry the Port Arthurs and Gibraltars of the non-Christian world without loss of life. Does it really matter how many die or how much money we spend in opening closed doors, and in occupying the different fields, if we really believe that missions are warfare and that the King's glory is at stake? War always means blood and treasure. Our only concern should be to keep the fight aggressive and to win victory regardless of cost or sacrifice. The unoccupied fields of the world must have their Calvary before they can have their Pentecost. Raymond Lull, the first missionary to the Muslim world, expressed the same thought in medieval language when he wrote: "As a hungry man makes dispatch and takes large morsels on account of his great hunger, so Thy servant feels a great desire to die that he may glorify Thee. He hurries day and night to complete his work in order that he may give up his blood and his tears to be shed for Thee."[3]

An Inverted Homesickness

The unoccupied fields of the world await those who are willing to be lonely for the sake of Christ. To the pioneer missionary the words of our Lord Jesus Christ to the apostles when He showed them His hands and His feet, come with special force: "As my Father hath sent Me, even so send I you" (John 20:21). He came into the world, and it was a great unoccupied mission field. "He came unto His own, and His own received Him not" (John 1:11). He came and His welcome was derision, His life, suffering, and His throne, the Cross. As He came, He expects us to go. We must follow in His footprints. The pioneer missionary, in overcoming obstacles and difficulties, has the privilege not only of knowing Christ and the power of His resurrection, but also something of the fellowship of His suffering. For the people of Tibet or Somaliland, Mongolia or Afghanistan, Arabia or Nepal, the Sudan or Abyssinia, he may be called to say with Paul, "Now I rejoice in my sufferings for you and fill to the brim the penury of the afflictions of Christ in my flesh for His body's sake which is the Church" (Greek text, Col 1:24; cf. Mark 12:44 and Luke 21:4). What is it but the glory of the impossible! Who would *naturally* prefer to leave the warmth and comfort of hearth and home and the love of the family circle to go after a lost sheep, whose cry we have faintly heard in the howling of the tempest? Yet such is the glory of the task that neither home-ties nor home needs can hold back those who have caught the vision and the spirit of the Great Shepherd. Because the lost ones are His sheep, and He has made us His shepherds and not His hirelings, we must bring them back.

> Although the road be rough and steep
> I go to the desert to find my sheep.

"There is nothing finer nor more pathetic to me," says Dr. Forsyth, "than the way in which missionaries unlearn the love of the old home, die to their native land, and wed their hearts to the people they have served and won; so that they cannot rest in England, but must return to lay their bones where they spent their hearts for Christ. How vulgar the common patriotisms seem beside this inverted homesickness, this passion of a kingdom which has no frontiers and no favored race, the passion of a homeless Christ!"[4]

James Gilmour in Mongolia, David Livingstone in Central Africa, Grenfell in the Congo, Keith Falconer in Arabia, Dr. Rijnhart and Miss Annie Taylor in Tibet, Chalmers in New Guinea, Morrison in China, Henry Martyn in Persia, and all the others like them had this "inverted homesickness," this passion to call that country their home which was most in need of the Gospel. In this passion all other passions died; before this vision all other visions faded; this call drowned all other voices. They were the pioneers of the Kingdom, the forelopers of God, eager to cross the border-marches and discover new lands or win new empires.

The Pioneer Spirit

These forelopers of God went not with hatchet and brand, but with the sword of the Spirit and with the fire of Truth they went and blazed the way for those that follow after. Their scars were the seal of their apostleship, and they gloried also in tribulation. Like the pioneer Apostle, "always bearing about in the body the dying of the Lord Jesus," and approving themselves "as ministers of God in stripes, in imprisonments, in tumults, in watchings, in fasting."

Thomas Valpy French, Bishop of Lahore, whom Dr. Eugene Stock called "the most distinguished of all Church Missionary Society missionaries," had the real pioneer spirit and knew the glory of the impossible. After forty years of labors abundant and fruitful in India, he resigned his bishopric and planned to reach the interior of Arabia with the Gospel. He was an intellectual and spiritual giant. "To live with him was to drink in an atmosphere that was spiritually bracing. As the air of the Engadine [a favorite tourist ground in Switzerland] is to the body, so was his intimacy to the soul. It was an education to be with him. There was nothing that he thought a man should not yield—home or wife or health if God's call was apparent. But then every one knew that he only asked of them what he himself had done and was always doing." And when Mackay, of Uganda, in his remarkable plea for a mission to the Arabs of Oman called for "half a dozen young men, the pick of the English universities, to make the venture in faith,"[5] this lion-hearted veteran of sixty-six years responded alone. It was the glory of the impossible. Yet from Muscat he wrote shortly before his death:

> If I can get no faithful servant and guide for the journey into the interior, well versed in dealing with Arabs and getting needful common supplies (I want but little), I may try Bahrein, or Hodeidah and Sana, and if that fails, the north of Africa again, in some highland; for without a house of our own the climate would be insufferable for me— at least during the very hot months—and one's work would be at a standstill. But I shall not give up, please God, even temporarily, my plans for the interior, unless, all avenues being closed, it would be sheer madness to attempt to carry them out. [6]

"I shall not give up"—and he did not till he died. Nor will the Church of Christ give up the work for which he and others like him laid down their lives in Oman. It goes on.

The Apostolic Ambition

The unoccupied provinces of Arabia and the Sudan await men with the spirit of Bishop French. For the ambition to reach out from centers already occupied to regions beyond, even when those very centers are undermanned and in need of reinforcement, is not Quixotic or fantastic, but truly apostolic. "Yes, so have I been ambitious," said Paul, "to preach the Gospel not where Christ was already named, lest I should build on another man's foundation; but as it is written, they shall see to whom no tidings of Him came, and they who have not heard shall understand" (Rom 15:20-21). He wrote this when leaving a city as important as Corinth, and goes on to state that this is the reason why he did not yet visit Rome, but that he hopes to do so on his way to Spain! If the uttermost confines of the Roman Empire were part of his program who had already preached Christ from Jerusalem to Illyricum in the first century, we surely, at the beginning of the twentieth century, should have no less ambition to enter every unoccupied field that "they may see to whom no tidings came and that those who have not heard may understand."

> There is no instance of an Apostle being driven abroad under the compulsion of a bald command. Each one went as a lover to his betrothed on his appointed errand. It was all instinctive and natural. They were equally controlled by the common vision, but they had severally personal visions which drew them whither they were needed. In the first days of Christianity, there is an absence of the calculating spirit. Most of the Apostles died outside of Palestine, though human logic would have forbidden them to leave the country until it had been Christianized. The calculating instinct is death to faith, and had the Apostles allowed it to control their motives and actions, they would have said: "The need in Jerusalem is so profound, our responsibilities to people of our own blood so obvious, that we must live up to the principle that charity begins at home. After we have won the people of Jerusalem, of Judea and of the Holy Land in general, then it will be time enough to go abroad; but our problems, political, moral and religious, are so unsolved here in this one spot that it is manifestly absurd to bend our shoulders to a new load."[7]

It was the bigness of the task and its difficulty that thrilled the early Church. Its apparent impossibility was its glory, its worldwide character its grandeur. The same is true today. "I am happy," wrote Neesima of Japan, "in a meditation on the marvelous growth of Christianity in the world, and believe that if it finds any obstacles it will advance still faster and swifter even as the stream runs faster when it finds any hindrances on its course."[8]

Hope and Patience

He that ploweth the virgin soil should plow in hope. God never disappoints His husbandmen. The harvest always follows the seed time. "When we first came to our field," writes missionary Hogberg from Central Asia, "it was impossible to gather even a few people to hear the glad tidings of the Gospel. We could not gather any children for school. We could not spread gospels or tracts. When building the new station, we also had a little chapel built. Then we wondered, Will this room ever be filled up with Muslims listening to the Gospel? Our little chapel has been filled with hearers and still a larger room! Day after day we may preach as much as we have strength to, and the Muslims no longer object to listen to the Gospel truth. 'Before your coming hither no one spoke or thought of Jesus Christ, now everywhere one hears His name,' a Muhammadan said to me. At the beginning of our work they threw away the Gospels or burnt them, or brought them back again——now they buy them, kiss the books, and touching it to the forehead and pressing it to the heart, they show the highest honor that a Muslim can show a book."[9]

But the pioneer husbandman must have long patience. When Judson was lying loaded with chains in a Burmese dungeon, a fellow prisoner asked with a sneer about the prospect for the conversion of the heathen. Judson calmly answered, "The prospects are as bright as are the promises of God."[10] There is scarcely a country today which is not as accessible, or where the difficulties are greater, than was the case in Burma when Judson faced them and overcame.

Challenge of the Closed Door

The prospects for the evangelization of all the unoccupied fields are "as bright as the promises of God." Why should we longer wait to evangelize them? "The evangelization of the world in this generation is no play-word," says Robert E. Speer. "It is no motto to be bandied about carelessly. The evangelization of the world in this generation is the summons of Jesus Christ to every one of the disciples to lay himself upon a cross, himself to walk in the footsteps of Him who, though He was rich, for our sakes became poor, that we through His poverty might be rich, himself to count his life as of no account, that He may spend it as Christ spent His for the redemption of the world."[11] Who will do this for the unoccupied fields?

> Anxiety, sickness, suffering, danger… all these are nothing when compared with the glory which shall hereafter be revealed in and for us.

The student volunteers of today must not rest satisfied until the watchword, peculiarly their own, finds practical application for the most neglected and difficult fields, as well as the countries where the harvest is ripe and the call is for reapers in ever increasing numbers. The plea of destitution is even stronger than that of opportunity. Opportunism is not the last word in missions. The open door beckons; the closed door challenges him who has a right to enter. The unoccupied fields of the world have, therefore, a claim of peculiar weight and urgency. "In this twentieth century of Christian history there should be no unoccupied fields. The Church is bound to remedy the lamentable condition with the least possible delay."[12]

Make a Life, Not a Living

The unoccupied fields, therefore, are a challenge to all whose lives are unoccupied by that which is highest and best; whose lives are occupied only with the weak things or the base things that do not count. There are eyes that have never been illumined by a great vision, minds that have never been gripped by an unselfish thought, hearts that have never thrilled with passion for another's wrong, and hands that have never grown weary or strong in lifting a great burden. To such the knowledge of these Christless millions in lands yet unoccupied should come like a new call from Macedonia, and a startling vision of God's will for them. As Bishop Brent remarks, "We never know what measure of moral capacity is at our disposal until we try to express it in action. An adventure of some proportions is not uncommonly all that a young man needs to determine and fix his manhood's powers."[13] Is there a more heroic test for the powers of manhood than pioneer work in the mission field? Here is opportunity for those who at home may never find elbow-room for their latent capacities, who may never find adequate scope elsewhere for all the powers of their minds and their souls. There are hundreds of Christian college men who expect to spend life in practicing law or in some trade for a livelihood, yet who have strength and talent enough to enter these unoccupied fields. There are young doctors who might gather around them in some new mission station thousands of those who "suffer the horrors of heathenism and Islam," and lift their burden of pain, but who now confine their efforts to some "pent-up Utica" where the healing art is subject to the law of competition and is measured too often merely in terms of a cash-book and ledger. They are making a living; they might be making a life.

Bishop Phillips Brooks once threw down the challenge of a big task in these words: "Do not pray for easy lives; pray to be stronger men. Do not pray for tasks equal to your powers; pray for powers equal to your tasks. Then the doing of your work shall be no miracle, but you shall be a miracle."[14] He could not have chosen words more applicable if he had spoken of the evangelization of the unoccupied fields of the world with

all their baffling difficulties and their glorious impossibilities. God can give us power for the task. He was sufficient for those who went out in the past, and is sufficient for those who go out today.

Face to face with these millions in darkness and degradation, knowing the condition of their lives on the unimpeachable testimony of those who have visited these countries, this great unfinished task, this unattempted task, calls today for those who are willing to endure and suffer in accomplishing it.

No Sacrifice, But a Privilege

When David Livingstone visited Cambridge University, on December 4, 1857, he made an earnest appeal for that continent, which was then almost wholly an unoccupied field. His words, which were in a sense his last will and testament for college men, as regards Africa, may well close this book:

> For my own part, I have never ceased to rejoice that God has appointed me to such an office. People talk of the sacrifice I have made in spending so much of my life in Africa. Can that be called a sacrifice which is simply paid back as a small part of a great debt owing to our God, which we can never repay? Is that a sacrifice which brings its own blest reward in healthful activity, the consciousness of doing good, peace of mind, and a bright hope of a glorious destiny hereafter? Away with the word in such a view, and with such a thought! It is emphatically no sacrifice. Say rather it is a privilege. Anxiety, sickness, suffering, or danger, now and then, with a foregoing of the common conveniences and charities of this life, may make us pause, and cause the spirit to waver, and the soul to sink, but let this only be for a moment. All these are nothing when compared with the glory which shall hereafter be revealed in and for us. I never made a sacrifice.

> I beg to direct your attention to Africa. I know that in a few years I shall be cut off in that country, which is now open; do not let it be shut again! I go back to Africa to try to make an open path for commerce and Christianity; do you carry out the work which I have begun. *I leave it with you.*[15]

End Notes

1. Charles Spurgeon's sermon on "Our Omnipotent Leader," in *The Evangelization of the World* (London, 1887).
2. Tadayoshi Sakurai, *Human Bullets*. The experience of a Japanese officer at Port Arthur and a revelation of Japanese patriotism and obedience.
3. Raymond Lull, "Liber de Contemplations in Deo," in Samuel M. Zwemer's *Raymund Lull: first missionary to the Moslems* (New York and London: Funk and Wagnalls, 1902), p. 132.
4. P.T. Forsyth, *Missions in State and Church: Sermons and Addresses* (New York: A. C. Armstong, 1908), p. 36.
5. Mrs. J. W. Harrison, *Mackay of Uganda*, pp. 417-430.
6. S. M. Zwemer, *Arabia: The Cradle of Islam; studies in one geography people and politics of one peninsula with an account of Islam and mission work...*(New York: F. H. Revell, 1900), p. 350.
7. Charles H. Brent, *Adventure for God* (New York: Longmans, Green, 1905), pp. 11-12.
8. Robert E. Speer, *Missionary Principles and Practice: a discussion of Christian missions and of some criticisms upon them* (New York: F. H. Revell, 1902), p. 541.
9. S. M. Zwemer, Letter to Commission No. 1, World Missionary Conference, Edinburgh, 1910.
10. Arthur Judson Brown, *The Foreign Missionary: an incarnation of a world movement* (New York: Fleming H. Revell, 1932), p. 374.
11. Speer, *op. cit.*, p. 526.
12. Report of World Missionary Conference, Edinburgh, 1910, Vol. 1.
13. Brent, *op. cit.*, p. 135.
14. Phillips Brooks, *Twenty Sermons* (New York: E. P. Dutton & Co., 1903), p. 330.
15. William Garden Blaikie, *Personal Life of David Livingstone...* (New York: Harper & Bros., 1895?), pp. 243-244.

Study Questions

1. What does Zwemer mean by "inverted homesickness?"

2. Are the challenges in this article an inspiration or a disturbance to you? Restate the challenge in this article in your own words.

3. Review the arguments Zwemer offers for people to consider "unoccupied fields." Restate his arguments with today's situation in view. Are there presently "unoccupied fields?"

The Responsibility of the Young People for the Evangelization of the World

John R. Mott

If I could take every one of you on a long journey...that you might see what I have seen, that you might hear what I have heard, that you might feel what I have felt, the last iota of skepticism which may linger as to the need of these people of knowing Christ would vanish.

John R. Mott was a sophomore at Cornell when, tardily entering a lecture room where J. K. Studd was speaking, he heard Studd say as if to him, "Young man, seekest thou great things for thyself? Seek them not! Seek ye first the kingdom of God." Mott's subsequent conversion and commissioning started him down a path that led to attendance at the Mt. Hermon Conference in 1886, where the Student Volunteer movement was born and where he became a volunteer and leader. He served on the SVM's original executive committee and was its chairman over 30 years, simultaneously providing able leadership for what at that time was a highly evangelistic YMCA and World's Student Christian Federation. Latourette comments, "Combining a simple faith issuing from a complete commitment to Christ with a commanding platform presence, world-wide vision, skill in discerning and enlisting young men of ability, and the capacity to win the confidence of men of affairs, and reaching out across ecclesiastical barriers to unite Christians of many traditions in the endeavor to win all mankind to the faith, Mott became one of the outstanding leaders in the entire history of Christianity." To the day he died he classified himself simply as an evangelist. The following address, given in April 1901, but vibrant with relevance today, gives a glimpse of his heart and mind.

It is a most inspiring fact that the young people of this generation do not apologize for world-wide missions. It would seem that that Christian who in these days would apologize for missions is either ignorant or thoughtless, because a man who apologizes for missions apologizes for Christianity, because that is essentially a missionary enterprise. He apologizes for the Bible, because missions constitute its central theme. He apologizes for the prayer of his Lord and for the Apostles' Creed. He apologizes for the fatherhood of God, and in doing so also for the brotherhood of man. If he is a Christian, he apologizes for every whit of spiritual life that is in himself; and, worst of all, he apologizes for Jesus Christ, who is the Propitiation not for our sins only but for the sins of the world. I repeat, he is either ignorant or thoughtless.

Grounds of Belief in World Evangelization

Not only do the students and other young people of our day, however, not apologize for this world-wide enterprise, but they believe in it as has no preceding generation of young people. They are believing in it with a depth of conviction, and manifesting their belief with a practical sympathy and

From *Missionary Issues of the Twentieth Century* (Reprint), 1901.

purpose and action, such as has never been witnessed in any preceding age in the history of the Church. If you ask me tonight to give you the grounds of their belief, and in this way to define their responsibility for the world's evangelization, I would place at the threshold the fundamental reason that they feel their obligation to preach Christ because all people need Christ.

All People Need Christ

The need of the non-Christian world is an extensive need. South of this country we have not less than fifty millions of people in Mexico, the West Indies, Central America, and the South American republics. In the Levant there are tens of millions of others. In the Dark Continent, at the most conservative estimate, there are over one hundred and fifty millions; in the East Indies and the other islands of the Southern seas, fifty millions more; in India, Burma, Ceylon, and Siam, not less than three hundred millions; in the Sunrise Kingdom of Japan, over forty millions; and not less than four hundred millions in China and the states that fringe upon her, Korea, Manchuria, Mongolia, and Tibet.

Over one thousand millions! Can we grasp the number? No, indeed! It is indeed an extensive need. It is not only an extensive need, but it is an intensive one; and the intensive need of the non-Christian world is indescribably great. The Scriptures maintain this much. They show us most vividly the condition of men apart from Jesus Christ. They present today, as every world traveler will tell you, an unexaggerated picture of the moral and spiritual condition of over two-thirds of the human race. Not only the Scriptures but scientific observation proves to be a demonstration that those peoples without Christ have a need which is very deep. Think of them tonight, living in darkness and ignorance, steeped in superstition and idolatry, in degradation and corruption; see them, under what a load of shame and sorrow and sin and pain and suffering, as they live and move on in silence to the tomb; notice the fearful inroads and onslaughts of the forces of evil. And remind yourselves that they do not have those powers of resistance which we have as the result of Christian heredity, Christian environment,

and the domination of Christian ideas and ideals. They fight a losing battle. If I could take every one of you on a long journey of nearly two years, through those great sections of the non-Christian world, that you might see what I have seen, that you might hear what I have heard, that you might feel what I have felt, the last iota of skepticism which may linger in the mind of any one here as to the need of these people of knowing Christ would vanish. Truly their need is indescribably great. It comes back to haunt me in the watches of the night; and if God spares my life and my plans can be properly shaped, I want in a few months hence to put my life once more alongside those young men who are fighting their losing fight.

We are trustees of the gospel, and in no sense sole proprietors.

Unless Christ is borne to these regions, these people are without hope. I used to doubt that when I was studying comparative religion, and when I went as a delegate to the Parliament of Religions in Chicago several years ago. But when I had opportunity to make a scientific study of the problem (and a scientific study takes account of all the facts, and not simply of theories) all my skepticism vanished. As I went up and down densely populated provinces and presidencies and native states, as I conversed with over thirteen hundred missionaries, representing some eighty missionary societies (and I know of no university education that means more to a man than to sit at the feet of missionaries), as I talked with hundreds of civilians and native students and priests, as I visited countless shrines and temples and holy places, as I witnessed the superstitions, the abominations, the cruelties, the injustices, within the immediate confines of these sacred places, so called, the conviction became ever deeper and stronger that these nations without Christ are without hope. Yes, I believe to the core of my being that Christ some day must have sway over this whole world. He is not going to divide the world with Buddhism and Confucianism and Hinduism and Mohammedanism; he is going to have complete sway. It takes no prophet in our time to see that that Church which conquered the Roman Empire, which cast the spell of the matchless Christ over the nations of Western and Northern Europe, which has moved with giant strides among the nations and is shaking them today—that that Church will prevail. He shall reign from sea to sea. When He girds on his conquering sword all the ends of the earth shall see the salvation of our God.

We Owe Christ to All Men

I would note also that this obligation which is felt so deeply by the young people of our day is intensified by a further consideration, not only that all men need Christ, but that we owe Christ to all men. To have a knowledge of Christ is to incur a tremendous responsibility to those that have it not. You and I have received this great heritage, not to appropriate it to our own exclusive use, but to pass it on to others. It concerns all men. We are trustees of the gospel, and in no sense sole proprietors. Every Chinese, every East Indian, every inhabitant of the Southern seas, has the right to know of the mission of Jesus Christ; and you and I violate the eighth commandment if we keep this knowledge from them. You may show me the very best disciple of any one of these religions—and I have seen men living noble lives who are devotees of those religions—I say he has a right to know of the life and death and resurrection of Jesus Christ, and of his mission to mankind. What a colossal crime against two-thirds of the human race to withhold this surpassing knowledge!

The weight of responsibility becomes still greater when we stop to ask ourselves the question: If we do not take this knowledge of Christ to these people, who will? What should move us, fellow young men, and what should move the young women here, and those whom we all represent, to fling ourselves into this enterprise and bear Christ to these people? It would seem that the claims of our common humanity and of universal brotherhood would be sufficient to inspire us to go ourselves or to send substitutes. If that is not sufficient, the golden rule of Jesus Christ, by which I take it every one of us desires to fashion conscientiously his life, would lead us logically and irresistibly to do so. If that does not move us, the example of our Lord in this

practical age ought to stir us to action, because those who say they abide in him ought themselves so to walk even as he walked. If that does not move us, then every thoughtful and reflecting person, it would seem, should be moved by the Great Commission or the marching orders of the Church of God. The last commandment of Christ is operative until it is repealed. We have had no intimation that it has been repealed. It is not optional, as some would assume, but obligatory. It awaits its fulfillment by a generation which shall have the requisite faith and courage, and audacity and the purpose of heart, to do their duty to the whole world. It would seem to me that every Christian who is a Christian of reality ought to be a missionary Christian; for, as Archbishop Whately has said—mark his language, note it well: "If my faith be false, I ought to change it; whereas if it be true, I am bound to propagate it." There is no middle ground; either abandon my religion or be a missionary in spirit.

World Evangelization is Essential to our own Best Life

There is yet a third consideration; and that is, that the young people of our day should seek to evangelize the world because it is essential to their own best life. If all men need Christ, and if we owe a knowledge of Christ to all men, manifestly it is our duty to take that knowledge to them. To know our duty and to do it not is sin. Continuance in the sin of neglect and disobedience necessarily weakens the life and arrests the growth. What loss of spiritual life, what loss of energy and of faith, the Church of Christ has already suffered from a fractional obedience to the last command of our Lord!

The young people's movements of our day, like our own Epworth League, the Baptist Young People's Union, the Young People's Society of Christian Endeavor, the St. Andrew's Brotherhood, the Young Men's and the Young Women's Christian Associations, need nothing so much as some mighty objective to call out the best energies of mind and heart. We find precisely such an objective in the sublime enterprise of filling the earth with a knowledge of the Lord as the waters cover the deep. If we would save our Christian young people's movements from their perils of ease and luxury and selfishness and slothfulness and unreality, we must necessarily take up some great and scriptural object like this, and give ourselves to it with holy abandon.

This point comes to mean more when we remember that the largest manifestation of the presence of Christ is to those that are obedient to his missionary command. Have you ever reflected upon it that the baptism of the Holy Spirit is invariably associated with testimony and witness-bearing? Therefore we can do nothing which will mean so much to the home church as to develop this foreign missionary spirit. If we would have the Holy Spirit working with mighty power in all our communities—and is this not our greatest need?—we shall have this experience as we walk in the pathway of our missionary Leader in obedience to his command.

An Urgent Obligation

The obligation to evangelize the world, which presses in upon the young people of our day, is also a most urgent obligation. The Christians who are now living must preach Christ to the non-Christians who are now alive, if they are ever to hear of Christ. The Christians of a past generation cannot do it; they are dead and gone. The Christians of the next generation cannot do it; by that time the present non-Christians will be dead and gone. Obviously, each generation of Christians must make Christ known to its own generation of non-Christians, if they are to have the knowledge of Christ. But we might just as well get the Christians who come after us to love God for us, or get them to love our neighbors for us, as to be obedient for us. Moreover (and I am now speaking to those of my own generation), we are living in a time of unexampled crisis. It is also a time of marvelous opportunity. The world is better known and more accessible than in any other generation which has ever lived. The need of the world is more articulate and intelligible than it has ever been, and the resources of the Church are far greater today, as well as her ability to enter these open doors, than has been the case in any preceding generation. It would seem that this would impose a great burden of responsibility upon our generation; greater than upon any other generation. You and I cannot excuse ourselves by

doing what our fathers did. The world is smaller today to us than this country was to our fathers. We have the opportunity to do larger things, and we are going to be judged by our talents and the use of them. God forbid that we should lack vision in these days to take advantage of the tide that is rising to sweep multitudes into the all-embracing kingdom of Jesus Christ.

The forces of evil are not putting off their work until the next generation. When I was in Japan I found that militarism and materialism said: "Let us engulf Japan in this generation, and we shall not be so much concerned about subsequent generations." Commerce and avarice and international jealousies say: "Give us China in this generation." In India I discovered that rationalism said: "Let us have the right of way in the Indian universities for this one generation, and we will hold that great continent for several generations." In the Turkish Empire lust and cruelty said: "Let us go unchecked in this generation." Why should not the Church of God rise in her might, and give herself to this task as no preceding generation has done?

Keep Ourselves Informed

How can the young men and young women of our day best discharge their obligation to the world's evangelization? Well, manifestly we must keep ourselves informed concerning the great enterprise of world-wide missions.

The words of Christ, in an entirely different connection, suggest themselves to me now: "Ye do err, not knowing the Scriptures, nor the power of God." If there is any place where the power of God is being manifested today more than elsewhere, it is in the non-Christian world where the arm of God has been made bare and where we are witnessing such marvelous triumphs of the gospel of the Son of God.

We do ourselves an injustice if we do not keep in vivid touch with this wonderful missionary movement. To do the will of God, we must know the needs of man. I fail to see how any young men or young women can be perfectly sure that they are doing what God wants them to do, if they are not carrying on a thorough study of this great world. Every young Christian in the Church ought to have an ambition to know the kingdom of Jesus Christ, its great fields, its marvelous triumphs, its problems, its inspiring opportunities, and its transcendent resources. We can have no better creed than the creed of St. Augustine: "A whole Christ for my salvation, a whole Bible for my staff, a whole Church for my fellowship, and a whole world for my parish." Let us be satisfied with nothing less than the worldwide horizon of Jesus Christ our Lord.

Each band of young people should also be a center for disseminating information concerning the work of God in the world. There is a shocking amount of ignorance and of flimsy excuses and objections concerning world-wide missions, which will be banished only by an educational campaign. Therefore, let me endorse with strong conviction everything that has been said on this platform from this morning until tonight, and which has been so ably stated by the different advocates, on the inestimable importance of educating on missions beginning even with the child at the mother's knee, reaching up through the Sunday school up to the ministrations of the pastor, so that we will have a generation who will have knowledge adequate to meet the opportunity that confronts this generation. There is no subject, unless it be the study of the Life of Christ, the study of which is more broadening, more deepening, more elevating, more inspiring than the subject of world-wide missions. No subject more broadening; it embraces all mankind. No subject more deepening; it takes us down to the very depths of the designs of God. Surely no subject more elevating. I can think of nothing that so lifts a man out of himself. And can anything be more inspiring than that enterprise which commanded the life and death and resurrection of our Lord?

Bands of Intercession and Sacrifice

Each one of our bands of young people, whether it be large or small, should also be a band of intercession. There is an old Jewish proverb that "He prays not at all in whose prayers there is no mention of the kingdom of God." Everything vital to missions hinges upon prayer. This is one of my strongest convictions, but I pass it at this time, as I shall have an opportunity to enlarge upon it fully tomorrow night.

Every one of our organizations of young people should be a school of self-sacrifice. Believe me, there is need in our day of more heroic and self-denying giving. We need to teach young men and young women that they are the stewards, not simply of a tenth, but of all they possess, and that we are responsible, not alone for the good use of our money, whether it be little or great, but for its best possible use. Let every one of us be guided by that scriptural principle which governed the life of Livingstone, that we will place no value upon anything we have or may possess, except in its relation to the kingdom of God. This would revolutionize the habits of giving of the Christian Church.

> Let us be satisfied with nothing else than leaving the deepest mark on our generation.

An Offering of Young People

We need not only more money, but also more of our best young men and young women for this work. We were all impressed by the magnificent offering of $50,000 by the delegates here last night. But there is still needed, in order to make this convention reach its highest climax, a great offering of the most consecrated young men and women of this convention. May we not have many here who, as the result of fighting to the end of self, shall say with glad abandonment of self: "Here am I, send me"? Remember the German proverb: "The good is the enemy of the best." Let us be satisfied with nothing else than leaving the deepest mark on our generation. And remember also that if it is a good thing to go where we are needed, it is more Christlike to go where we are needed the most. Is there anything which reason and conscience can summon which would take issue with that position? God grant that we may step into the footsteps of our Lord, to go to the most destitute fields of our own country and the great open places beyond! May God move the parents here tonight not only not to interfere and hinder, but rather to facilitate the favorable decision of our own sons and daughters to enter upon this exalted service! O, it is a solemn responsibility for any father or mother in these days to do anything by word, or other expression or attitude, to keep a son or daughter who is qualified from entering upon this unutterably important work of preaching Christ where he is not known. Rather, in the spirit of God, who spared not his only Son, but delivered him up for us all, we shall be willing to make this sacrifice for the sake of Christ, who has done so much for us.

Live or Die for the Evangelization of the World

"I must work the works of Him that sent me, while it is day: the night cometh, when no man can work" (John 9:4). Therefore, friends, in view of the awful need of men who tonight are living without Christ; in view of the infinite possibilities of the life related to Christ as mighty Saviour and risen Lord; in view of the magnitude of the task which confronts the Church of this generation; in view of the impending crisis and the urgency of the situation; in view of the conditions which favor a great onward movement within the Church of God in view of the dangers of anything less than a great onward movement; in view of the great cloud of witnesses who gathered around us last night, of those who subdued kingdoms and wrought righteousness—yes, in view of the constraining memories of the Cross of Christ and the love wherewith he hath loved us, let us rise and resolve, at whatever cost of self-denial, that live or die, we shall live or die for the evangelization of the world in our day.

Study Questions

1. What grounds does Mott put forward for placing the responsibility of world evangelization on young people?

2. Identify the statement in this address that you feel might have been the greatest catalyzing force in challenging young people of his day to evangelize the world in their generation.

The Bridges of God

Donald A. McGavran

> It is of the utmost importance that the Church understand how peoples, not merely individuals, become Christian.

Known worldwide as perhaps the foremost missiologist, Donald A. McGavran was born in India of missionary parents and returned there as a third-generation missionary himself in 1923, serving as a director of religious education and translating the Gospels in the Chhattisgarhi dialect of Hindi. He founded the School of World Mission at Fuller Theological Seminary. McGavran died in 1990 at the age of 93. McGavran authored several influential books, including *The Bridges of God*, and *Understanding Church Growth*.

From *The Bridges of God* (Revised Edition) by Donald Anderson McGavran. Published in the United Kingdom by World Dominion Press, 1955. Revised edition 1981. Distributed in the United States by Friendship Press, New York. Used by permission.

The Bridges of God appeared in 1954, and it has since become known as the classic summons for missionaries to utilize the "bridges" of family and kinship ties within each people group thereby prompting "people movements" to Christ. This is contrasted with the "Mission Station Approach," dominant in missionary strategy of the nineteenth century, whereby individual converts are gathered into "colonies" or compounds isolated from the social mainstream. McGavran claims that whereas the latter approach was necessary and useful in the nineteenth and early twentieth centuries, "a new pattern is at hand, which, while new, is as old as the Church itself."

The Crucial Question in Christian Missions

Much study has been devoted to world evangelization. We know the answers to many questions about the propagation of the Gospel. But what is perhaps the most important question of all still awaits an answer. That question is: *How do peoples become Christian?*

This article asks how clans, tribes, castes, in short how *peoples* become Christian. Every nation is made up of various layers of strata of society. In many nations each stratum is clearly separated from every other. The individuals in each stratum intermarry chiefly, if not solely, with each other. Their intimate life is therefore limited to their own society, that is, to their own people. They may work with others, they may buy from and sell to the individuals of other societies, but their intimate life is wrapped up with the individuals of their own people. Individuals of another stratum, possibly close neighbors, may become Christians or Communists without the first stratum being much concerned. But when individuals of their own kind start becoming Christians, that touches their very lives. How do chain reactions in these strata of society begin? *How do peoples become Christian*?

Here is a question to which not speculation but knowledge must urgently be applied. The question is how, in a manner true to the Bible, can a Christian movement be established in some class, caste, tribe or other segment of society which will, over a period of years, so bring groups of its related families to Christian faith that the whole people is Christianized in a few decades? It is of the utmost importance that the Church should understand how peoples, and not merely individuals, become Christian.

The Unfamiliar in People Movements

Individualistic Westerners cannot without special effort grasp how peoples become Christian. The missionary movement is largely staffed by persons from the West or by nationals trained in their ideas, and while evangelization has been carried on with correct enough views on how individuals have become Christian, there have been hazy or even erroneous views on how peoples become Christian.

Western individualism obscures group processes

In the West, Christianization is an extremely individualistic process. This is due to various causes. For one thing, in Western nations there are few exclusive subsocieties. Then too, because freedom of conscience exists, one member of a family can become Christian and live as a Christian without being ostracized by the rest of the family. Furthermore, Christianity is regarded as true, even by many who do not profess it. It is considered a good thing to join the Church. A person is admired for taking a stand for Christ. There have been no serious rivals to the Church. Thus individuals are able to make decisions as individuals without severing social bonds.

Again, with the disruption of clan and family life following upon the industrial revolution, Westerners became accustomed to do what appealed to them as individuals. As larger family groupings were broken up through migration, the movement of rural folk to the cities, and repeated shifts of homes, people came to act for themselves without consulting their neighbors or families. A habit of independent decision was established. In the Christian churches this habit was further strengthened by the practice of revival meetings appealing for individual decisions to the accompaniment of great emotion. Indeed, the theological presupposition was not merely that salvation depended on an individual act of faith in Christ (which is unquestioned), but also that this act was somehow of a higher order if it were done against family opinion (which is dubious). Separate individual accessions to the Church were held by some to be not only a better, but the only valid, way of becoming a Christian.

Had the question arisen as to how peoples became Christian, the answer would have been given that it was by individual after individual becoming soundly converted.

Of the social organism which is a people, or of the desirability of preserving the culture and community life, indeed, of enhancing them through the process of conversion, there tended to be little recognition. Peoples were thought of as aggregates of individuals whose conversion was achieved one by one. The social factor in the conversion of peoples passed unnoticed because peoples were not identified as separate entities.

However, a people is not an aggregation of individuals. In a true people intermarriage and the intimate details of social intercourse take place within the society. In a true people individuals are bound together not merely by common social practices and religious beliefs but by common blood. A true people is a social organism which, by virtue of the fact that its members intermarry very largely within its own confines, becomes a separate race in their minds. Since the human family, except in the individualistic West, is largely made up of such castes, clans and peoples, the Christianization of each nation involves the prior Christianization of its various peoples as peoples.

Because of the intense battle against race prejudice, the concept of separate races of men is discredited in many circles. Missionaries often carry this antipathy to race into their work in tribes and castes who believe themselves to be separate races, marry within their people and have an intense racial consciousness. But to ignore the significance of race hinders Christianization. It makes an enemy of race consciousness, instead of an ally. It does no good to say that tribal peoples ought not to have race prejudice. They do have it and are proud of it. It can be understood and should be made an aid to Christianization.

What to do and what not to do

To Christianize a whole people, the first thing not to do is snatch individuals out of it into a different society. Peoples become Christians where a Christward movement occurs *within that society*. Bishop J. W. Pickett, in his important study *Christ's Way to India's Heart*, says:

The process of extracting individuals from their setting in Hindu or Moslem communities does not build a Church. On the contrary it rouses antagonism against Christianity and builds barriers against the spread of the Gospel. Moreover, that process has produced many unfortunate, and not a few tragic results in the lives of those most deeply concerned. It has deprived the converts of the values represented by their families and friends and made them dependent for social support to the good life and restraint on evil impulses upon men and women, their colleagues in the Christian faith, with whom they have found it difficult to develop fellowship and a complete sense of community. It has sacrificed much of the convert's evangelistic potentialities by separating him from his People. It has produced anaemic Churches that know no true leadership and are held together chiefly by common dependence on the mission or the missionary.

Equally obviously the Christianization of a people requires reborn men and women. A mere change of name accomplishes nothing. While the new convert must remain within his people, he must also experience the new birth. "If ye then be risen with Christ, set your affection on things above, not on things on the earth." The power of any People Movement to Christ depends in great measure on the number of truly converted persons in it. We wish to make this quite clear. The Christianization of peoples is not assisted by slighting or forgetting real personal conversion. There is no substitute for justification by faith in Jesus Christ or for the gift of the Holy Spirit.

Thus a Christward movement within a people can be defeated either by extracting the new Christians from their society (i.e. by allowing them to be squeezed out by their non-Christian relatives) or by the non-Christians so dominating the Christians that their new life in Christ is not apparent. An incipient Christward movement can be destroyed by either danger.

The group mind and group decision

To understand the psychology of the innumerable subsocieties which make up non-Christian nations, it is essential that the leaders of the Churches and missions strive to see life from the point of view of a people, to whom individual action is treachery. Among those who think corporately only a rebel would strike out alone, without consultation and without companions. The individual does not think of himself as a self-sufficient unit, but as part of the group. His business affairs, his children's marriages, his personal problems, or the difficulties he has with his wife are properly settled by group thinking. Peoples become Christian as this group-mind is brought into a lifegiving relationship to Jesus as Lord.

> A change of religion involves a community change. Only as its members move together, does change become healthy and constructive.

It is important to note that the group decision is not the sum of separate individual decisions. The leader makes sure that his followers will follow. The followers make sure that they are not ahead of each other. Husbands sound out wives. Sons pledge their fathers. "Will we as a group move if so-and-so does not come?" is a frequent question. As the group considers becoming Christian, tension mounts and excitement rises. Indeed, a prolonged informal vote-taking is under way. A change of religion involves a community change. Only as its members move together, does change become healthy and constructive.

Groups are usually fissured internally. This has a definite bearing on group decision. If in some town or village there are 76 families of a given people, they may be split into several sub-groups. Often such divisions are formed by rivalries between prominent men. Often they are geographical: the lower section of the village as against the upper section. Often they are economic: the landed as opposed to the landless. Often they depend on education, marriage relationships, or attitudes toward customs. Group thinking usually occurs at its best within these sub-groups. A sub-group will often come to decision before the whole. Indeed, a sub-group often furnishes enough social life for it to act alone.

Peoples become Christian as a wave of decision for Christ sweeps through the group mind, involving many individual decisions but being far more than merely their sum. This may be called a chain reaction. Each decision sets off others and the sum total powerfully affects every individual. When conditions are right, not merely each sub-group, but the entire group concerned decides together.

Terms defined

We call this process a "People Movement." "People" is a more universal word than "tribe", "caste" or "clan." It is more exact than "group." It fits everywhere. Therefore in this article we shall speak of People Movements to Christ.

The Characteristic Pattern of the Great Century

Dr. Latourette has given the name "the Great Century" to the time between 1800 and 1914. He says: "When consideration is given to the difficulties which faced it, in the nineteenth century, Christianity made amazing progress all around the world. It came to the end of the period on a rapidly ascending curve. Its influence on culture was out of all proportions to its numerical strength. It had an outstanding role as a pioneer in new types of education, in movements of the relief and prevention of human suffering and in disseminating ideas."

How did Christianization proceed during the Great Century? This is a most important question because most of our present thinking is coloured by the missionary effort of that century. When we think of missions today, we think of those with which we are familiar, and which prevailed in China, Africa, India and other countries during the Great Century. Since this century produced a radically new and different approach, the older kind of missions which existed for 1,800 years have tended to be forgotten. The missionary and the Churches tend to think that the only kind of missions and the only kind of Christian-ization possible is that used with greater or lesser effect during the past 150 years. The Great Century created a new method to meet a new situation. Both situation and method are worthy of our closest study.

The new situation described: the gulf of separation

Missions were carried on from the ruling, wealthy, literate, modern countries, which were experiencing all the benefits of political and religious freedom, an expanding production, and universal education. In the year 1500, European visitors to India and China described countries which compared favourably with their own. But by the nineteenth century the West had progressed while the East had stood still, so that there was a great gap between them. Western missionaries went to poor, illiterate, medieval and agricultural countries. The gap widened with the passage of the years, for the progress of the West continued to be greater than that of the East. While it is true that missionaries tried to identify themselves with the people, they were never able to rid themselves of the inevitable separateness which the great progress of their home lands had imposed upon them.

This gulf became very clear in the living arrangements which European and American missionaries found necessary. Their standard of living at home was many times higher than that of the average citizen on the mission fields, though it could not compare with that of the few wealthy Chinese, Japanese and Indians. Modern medicine was unknown. Health demanded big bungalows on large sites. Servants were cheap and saved much domestic labour. The people of the land generally walked, but the missionary was accustomed to a conveyance and so he used one. The colour of his skin also set him apart. He could not melt into the generality of the inhabitants of the land as Paul could. He was a white man, a member of the ruling race. To this day in the rural sections of India, seven years after independence, the white missionary is frequently addressed as *Sarkar* (Government). The missionary was an easy victim not only to malaria but to intestinal diseases. He had to be careful about what he ate. The Western style of cooking agreed with him, whereas the Eastern style did not. So in matters of food also there came to be a great gulf between him and the people of the land.

There were practically no bridges across this gulf. There was nothing even remotely similar to the Jewish bridge over which

Christianity marched into the Gentile world. Staggering numbers of people lived on the fertile plains of Asia, but not one of them had any Christian relatives! Even in the port cities there were none. *Més alliances* between white soldiery, rulers or commercial people and the women of the various lands were so resented on the one hand and despised on the other that they served as barriers rather than bridges. The normal flow of the Christian religion simply could not take place. Separated by colour, standard of living, prestige, literacy, mode of travel, place of residence, and many other factors, the missionary was, indeed, isolated from those to whom he brought the message of salvation.

The missionaries did learn the languages of the country and learned them well. They served the people with love, taught their children, visited in their homes, went with them through famines and epidemics, ate with them, bought from them and sold to them, and, more than any other group of white men in the tropics, were at one with them. Thus, it will be said, this emphasis on the separateness of the missionary is exaggerated. To the student of the growth and spread of religions, however, it is apparent that these casual contacts described above are just that— casual contacts. They are not the living contacts, the contacts of tribe and race and blood, which enable the non-Christian to say, as he hears a Christian speak: "This messenger of the Christian religion is one of my own family, my own People, one of us." Casual contacts may win a few individuals to a new faith, but unless these individuals are able to start a living movement within their own society, it does not start at all.

The separateness we describe seemed likely to last a long time. It existed in an unchanging world, where the dominance of the West and the dependence of the East seemed to be permanent. Missionaries thought, "There will be centuries before us, and, in a 400-year relationship like that of Rome to her dependent peoples, we shall gradually bring these peoples also into the Christian faith."

This grave separateness faced Christian missions during the Great Century. When the churches and their missionaries have no relations, no contacts and no bridges over interracial gulfs, what do they do? How do they carry out the command of their Lord? When there is no living approach, how do they go about the Christianization of peoples?

The new method evolved: the exploratory mission-station approach

If there is any aspect that is typical of modern missions, it is the mission station with its gathered colony. Missionaries facing the gulf of separation built mission stations and gathered colonies of Christians.

They acquired a piece of land, often with great difficulty. They built residences suitable for white men. Then they added churches, schools, quarters in which to house helpers, hospitals, leprosy homes, orphanages and printing establishments. The mission station was usually at some center of communication. From it extensive tours were made into the surrounding country-side. It was home to the missionary staff and all the activities of the mission took place around the station.

Together with building the station, the missionaries gathered converts. It was exceedingly difficult for those hearing the Good News for the first time, knowing nothing of Christians, or of Christianity save that it was the religion of the invading white men, to accept the Christian religion. Those who did so were usually forced out of their own homes by fierce ostracism. They came to live at the mission colony, where they were usually employed. Orphans were sheltered. Slaves were bought and freed. Women were rescued. Some healed patients became Christian. Many of these usually came to live at the mission station. They were taught various means of earning a livelihood and directed into various forms of service. They formed the gathered colony.

This kind of mission approach took shape out of the individualistic background typical of much Protestantism in the eighteenth and nineteenth centuries. To be a Christian was to come out and be separate. For converts to leave father and mother invested their decisions with a particular validity. To gather a compound full of Christians out of a non-Christian population seemed a good way to proceed. Frequently it was also the only possible way. The universal suspicion and often the violent hostility with which Christianity was regarded would have forced into the gathered colony pattern even those who consciously sought integration.

This, then, was the pattern which was characteristic of most beginnings in the Great Century. We call it the exploratory mission

> A moderate amount of missionary assistance, at places where the churches feel their need, produces results far beyond that which those accustomed to the mission station tradition would consider possible.

station approach, but from the point of view of the resulting churches, it was the exploratory gathered colony approach.

It was excellent strategy in its day. It was a probe to ascertain which peoples were ready to become Christian. Christianity must be seen to be stable before it will be accepted as a way of salvation. Peoples are not going to commit their destinies to a faith which is here today and gone tomorrow. Men must see over a period of years what the Christian life means and what Christ does to persons and to groups. While the Good News is first being presented and the Christian life demonstrated the mission station and the gathered colony are essential. As we look back over the last hundred years it seems both necessary and desirable for there to have been this approach. With all its limitations, it was the best strategy for the era. This approach has been no mistake. It fitted the age which produced it. It was inevitable.

The road branches according to response

This beginning, adopted by practically all missions, may be considered as a road running along a flat and somewhat desolate plain and then dividing, one branch to continue along the plain, the other to climb the green fertile hills. Whether missions continued on the flat accustomed road (of the gathered church approach) or ascended the high road by means of the People Movement Approach depended on the response given to the Christian message by the population and on the missionaries' understanding of that response.

Where the number of conversions remained small decade after decade, there the mission remained the dominant partner and the Mission Station Approach continued and, indeed, was strengthened. It was strengthened because the gathered colony furnished Christian workers so that the mission could expand mission healing, mission teaching and mission preaching. Where the number of conversions mounted steadily with every passing decade, there the church became the dominant partner and the mission turned up the hill road. It started using the People Movement Approach. Scores of thousands became Christians.

These two roads, these two ways of carrying on mission work, are distinct and different. Clear thinking about missions must make a sharp differentiation between them. Each must be described separately. The People Movements, the hill road, will be described in the next section. The remainder of this section will be devoted to describing the widening road on the plain, the way in which the exploratory phase gradually turned into the permanent Mission Station Approach or gathered colony approach.

Small response was not expected by the early missionaries. The exploratory Mission Station Approach was not launched as an accommodation to a hardhearted and irresponsive population. It was regarded as *a first stage after which great ingathering would occur.* Even after the Basel Mission had lost eight of its first ten missionaries in nine years, the heroic Andreas Riis wrote back from the Gold Coast in Africa, "Let us press on. All Africa must be won for Christ. Though a thousand missionaries die, send more." The exploratory gathered colony approach was adopted with the expectation that the Christian faith would sweep non-Christian lands bringing them untold blessings.

But these expectations were often frustrated by meager response. In the light of the event Professor Latourette can now serenely write:

The advanced cultures and faiths of Asia and North Africa did not yield so readily as did those of the primitive folk, either to Western civilization or to Christianity. This was to be expected. It has usually been characteristic of advanced cultures and their religions that they have been much slower to disintegrate before an invading civilization.

But the meager response was not expected by the early messengers of the Church. It was disappointing.

A factor in the small response, whose importance cannot be overestimated, is that, partly because of the individualistic bias of the missionaries and partly because of the resistance of the hearers, conversions were mainly *out* of the nation. Converts felt that they were joining not merely a new religion, but an entirely foreign way of living—proclaimed by foreigners, led by foreigners and ruled by foreigners. Converts came alone. Often even their wives refused to come with them. Naturally conversions were few. A vicious circle was established: the few becoming Christian one by one set such a pattern that it was difficult for a Christward movement to be started, and by the lack of a movement converts continued to come one by one and in very small numbers. In many parts of the field it was psychologically difficult for a person to become a Christian as it would be for a white man in South Africa to join a Negro church knowing that his children would intermarry with the black children. The person not only became a Christian, but he was generally believed to have "joined another race." When, among peoples which intermarry only amongst themselves, a man becomes a Christian, his old mother is likely to reproach him, saying, "Now whom will your sons marry? They cannot get wives from amongst us any more."

The exploratory approach becomes permanent: terms defined

Where meager response continued, there gathered colony missions gradually accommodated themselves to carrying on mission work among populations which would not obey the call of God. Once this occurred we may say that the mission, which had started its road-building on the plain, with the intention of reaching high fertile land as soon as possible, settled down to road-building on the barren plain as its God-given duty. It found plenty of good work to do. It never admitted, even to itself, that it had really given up hope of reaching the hills; but that is what had actually happened.

The churches born of the mission station approach

The first aim of missions is the establishment of churches. So, as we start to examine the results of the Mission Station Approach we turn to an inspection of the kind of churches which mission stations have fathered. These we shall call Mission Station churches or gathered colony churches.

They have some favorable characteristics. They are composed of greatly transformed individuals. The membership is literate. They come to church with hymn books. They can read their Bibles. Many among them are specially trained beyond the ordinary school. In some stations there are many high school and college graduates on the church rolls. The membership contains a goodly proportion of day laborers and artisans, household helps and casual labourers, as well as teachers, preachers, medical workers, clerks, and other white-collar workers. In some places factory and railway employees form a considerable part of the membership. On the whole the Mission Station Churches are made up of people who are soundly Christian. There is not much superstition among them and not much temptation to revert to the old non-Christian faiths. The membership is proud of being Christian, and feels that it has gained tremendously by belonging to the Christian fellowship. There are, of course, many nominal Christians and some whose conduct brings shame on the church. But even these are likely to send their children to Sunday School and church!

They are organized into strong congregations. They have good permanent church buildings on land indubitably theirs. The pastors and ministers are usually qualified people. The services or worship are held regularly. The elders, deacons and other elected members form church councils and govern the church. The giving would probably compare favorably in regard to percentage of income with that in the Western churches, though often most of it is provided by those in mission employ. In some churches the giving is exemplary and there are many tithers. All told, the impression is that of small, tight, well-knit communities, buttressed by intermarriage and considering themselves to be a part of world Christianity.

On the debit side, these mission station churches are lacking in the qualities needed for growth and multiplication. They are, in truth, gathered churches, made up of individual converts, or "brands snatched from the burning," or famine orphans, or a mixture of all three. The individual converts and rescued persons have usually been disowned by their non-Christian relatives. The famine orphans have no close connection with loving brothers and sisters and uncles and aunts. Furthermore, the lives of these Christians have been so changed, and they find such satisfaction in the fellowship of their own sort (i.e. other mission station Christians) that they feel immeasurably superior to their own unconverted relatives.This is particularly true when they come from the oppressed classes. The second generation of Christians is even farther removed from their non-Christian relatives than the first, while in the third generation, in the very land where they live, the gathered church members know as a rule no non-Christian relatives at all. The precious linkages which each original member had as he came from non-Christian society and which are so needed for reproduction are all gone. A *new people* has been established which intermarries only within itself and thinks of itself as a separate community.

The Christians of the gathered colony approach have a vivid realization of the power of education. It has been education, they feel, that has lifted them out of the depths. They are keen for their children to receive as much education as possible. They skimp and scrape that their boys and girls may go on to school and proceed as far as possible on the road to a B.A. or an M.A. But they do not always have a vivid experience of the power of God. Many would grant that it was Christian education which had lifted them—an education given to them in the name of Jesus Christ. But on such experiences as the power of the Spirit, the forgiveness of sins and the blessedness of faith, many mission station Christians are likely to

have a weak witness. "Become Christians and educate your children," they are likely to say. "It won't do you much good but it will be wonderful for your sons and daughters."

Gathered colony churches usually have a vivid consciousness of the mission as their parent. The churches tend to feel that it is the business of the missionary to head up a wealthy social service agency, designed to serve the Christian community. It sometimes happens that the members of a mission station church, sensing the obvious fact that there is only limited employment in a mission station, look on new converts as a labor union would on immigrants. They draw the easy conclusion that if more people become Christians, the resources of the mission will be spread thinner and there will be less for each of the existing Christians. Cases have occurred where they have actually discouraged possible converts from becoming Christian.

Gathered colony churches are often overstaffed. They are too richly served by foreign missions. Their members acquire a vested interest in the *status quo*. In one typical mission station church of 700 souls we find a missionary in charge of two primary schools and one middle school for day pupils, another in charge of a middle boarding school for girls, a missionary doctor and his nurse wife who run a hospital, and an evangelistic missionary who gives half his time to the Christian community. Then there is a national minister who is a high school graduate with theological training, five high school graduates who teach the older boys and seven high school graduates who teach the older girls, four evangelists, five Bible women and a primary school staff of six. Missionaries, who, with less than half these resources, are shepherding large numbers of Christians who have come to Christ in some People Movement, may gasp with unbelief that such heavy occupation could occur. Yet both the national and the missionary leaders of such mission station churches consider that they really are managing with a minimum degree of foreign aid!

But—the era is drawing to a close

However, as Latourette points out, the era is passing. The days in which the mission stations can exert a major influence on the affairs of Eastern nations are drawing to a close. The sleeping nations are now awake. At the headquarters of the provincial and national governments are whole departments, amply provided with millions of money raised by taxes, whose chief duty it is to plan for the future of the nations. The tens of thousands of students who journey to the West for education, the flood of publications in all the major languages of the land, the advent of the movie, the loudspeaker and programs of social education, the sensitiveness to foreign criticism, the intense desire to prove their own nation the equal of any on earth, and the resentment felt at foreign leadership—all these presage the end of an era in which mission stations in the urban centers exerted an influence out of all proportion to their numbers.

Mission schools in Asia and North Africa no longer have the influence which they once had. In the beginning they were the only schools. But now they form a small percentage of the total, and are being crowded into the background. It is still true that there are a few outstanding Christian schools in most countries, mission schools, convent schools, which are known as the best in the land. Even so, they do not get one percent of the students. There was a day when they had 50 percent of the sons of the leading families. Mission educationists cannot dodge the plain fact that mission schools cannot expect to wield the influence which they did in the days when Western cultures were first arriving in Asia and Africa.

What is true of schools is also true of mission station hospitals. Up till 1945 the Central Provinces of India had not produced a single qualified doctor. Its university had no standard medical school. The only fully qualified doctors were a few immigrants from other provinces and missionary doctors from abroad. But today there are four hundred students in the medical college of its university. As this flood of physicians flows out over the cities and towns and eventually the villages of this province, the present near monopoly of the Christian hospitals is likely to be destroyed. The same sort of thing is taking place in one awakened nation after another.

Non-Christian nations are impatient with foreign tutelage. They believe it is demeaning to their national pride to admit to the need for guidance from any Western nation. The East, particularly India, honestly believes that, except for mechanization and industrialization, the West has little to give to the "spiritual East." The excoriations heaped upon Western nations by their own prophets, crying out against race prejudice, economic injustice and recurrent wars, are taken at their face value by the nations of the East. The West comes to be looked upon as soul-less, materialistic, unjust, money-mad, and moved by none but ulterior motives. The temper of these days in the East is not that of humbly sitting at the feet of missionary tutors.

It would be giving a distorted impression if the last few paragraphs were to imply that Christian missions have no more usefulness as cultural "hands across the sea." In the days ahead when nations are forced into closer and closer co-operation, all friendly efforts to interpret nations to each other will be of value. The continued residence of Westerners in the East will doubtless do good. But the days of great secular influence of foreign mission stations apart from great national Churches are probably about over.

They should be over for a further reason: there is now a use for mission resources which will do more for nation building, more for international peace, and more for the Church than the further penetration of non-Christian faiths and cultures from the vantage point of a mission station.

Salute and farewell

So has run the characteristic pattern of the Great Century. An age of tremendous mission expansion in terms of geography and influence; an age of heroism and devotion and self-sacrifice; an age of the meeting of two cultures separated by a wide gulf which, through the mission stations, outposts of goodwill and faith, has slowly drawn closer to the point where one world is in sight; an age when there is hardly a race or nation in which there is not found the Church.

So has run its pattern. But that age is now over. A new age is upon us. A new pattern is demanded. A new pattern is at hand, which, while new, is as old as the Church itself. It is a

God-designed pattern by which not ones but thousands will acknowledge Christ as Lord, and grow into full discipleship as people after people, clan after clan, tribe after tribe and community after community are claimed for and nurtured in the Christian faith.

The God-given People Movements

While the typical pattern of missionary activity has been that of the Mission Station Approach, occasionally People Movements to Christ have resulted. These have not as a rule been sought by missionaries—though in Oceania, Indonesia and Africa there have been some exceptions. The movements are the outcome of the mysterious movement of the Spirit of God. Their pattern of growth is very different from that described in the last chapter. They have provided over 90 percent of the growth of the newer churches throughout the world. The great bulk of the membership and of the congregations of the younger churches consist of converts and the descendants of converts won in People Movements.

In spite of this, we maintain that People Movements were the exception and that the typical approach of the last century was the Mission Station Approach. The number of mission stations from which Christian movements have started is small compared with the number serving static churches. Mission enterprises are, for the most part, those which serve non-Christians and gathered colony churches. The leadership of many conferences on missions comes largely from those who know and are immersed in the Mission Station Approach. And, as Dr. Hendrik Kraemer writes: "Missionary thinking and planning in this revolutionary period are still overwhelmingly influenced by the Mission Station Approach." The Mission Station Approach must then be taken as the typical outcome of the past years, and the People Movements as the exceptions.

In dividing mission work into these two varieties—that operating through the Mission Station Approach and that operating through the People Movements—it is recognized that some mission work cannot be classified under either head. For example, the translation and printing of the Scriptures. We are not attempting an exhaustive classification, but a practical one into which more than 90 per cent of missionary activity can be placed.

Some people movements described

Adoniram Judson went to Burma as a missionary to the cultured Buddhist Burmese. But he took under his wing a rough character, by name Ko Tha Byu, a Karen by race. The Karens were among the backward tribes of Burma. They were animistic peasants and were supposed by the Burmese to be stupid inferior people. "You can teach a buffalo, but not a Karen," was the common verdict. Judson spent six months trying to teach this former criminal, now his servant, the meaning of the redemptive death of our Lord Jesus Christ, and made such little progress that he was inclined to take the common verdict as true. However, he persisted, and a few months later Ko Tha Byu became a convinced, if not a highly illuminated, Christian.

As Judson toured Burma, speaking to the Burmese of that land, Ko Tha Byu, the camp follower, spoke to the humble Karen in each vicinity. The Karens started becoming Christian. Here a band of ten families, there one or two, and yonder a jungle settlement of five families accepted the Lordship of Christ. We do not have the data to prove that those who came were interrelated, but it is highly probable that connected families were coming in. A chain reaction was occurring. We can reasonably assume that among his close relatives alone, to say nothing of cousins and second cousins, Ko Tha Byu had a host of excellent living contacts. The early converts doubtless came from among these, and their relatives.

Judson, translating the Bible into Burmese, was concerned with more important matters than a Christian movement among a backward tribe. For years he considered the Karen converts a side issue. However, the next generation of missionaries included some who were veritable Pauls, expanding the movement as far along the paths and across the rice paddies as possible. Today there is a mighty Christian Movement among the Karens and their related tribes in Burma, numbering hundreds and thousands of souls. The Christian Karens are the educated Karens and will provide the leadership for the mixed population of Karens, Kachins and other tribes which predominate in parts of Burma. The Christward Movement among the Karens may well be the source of a church numbering millions, and exercising a decisive influence upon the history of all South-East Asia.

By contrast, the Mission Station Approach to the Buddhist Burmese has yielded its ordinary quota of small, static mission station churches with a membership of perhaps 20,000 souls for all Burma.

The Karen Christians are good Christians. In a hundred sections of Burma there are communities of Christian Karens with their own church building, their own pastor, their own tradition of regular worship, their own Sunday school, and a Christian tribal life which augurs well for the permanence of the Christian Churches of Burma. The Karens, discipled through a People Movement, and now in the process of perfecting, are not under the delusion that a nominal Christianity is worth anything to God. The thousands of churches scattered across the country contain a normal proportion of earnest Spirit-filled Christians. They are "reborn Baptists" who will compare favorably with the reborn Baptists of any land.

We stress this because it is a mistake to assume that People Movement Christians, merely because they have come to the Christian faith in chains of families, must inevitably be nominal Christians. Such an assumption is usually based on prejudice, not fact. All Churches face the problem of how to avoid creating nominal Christians. Even Western Churches, made up of only those individual converts who testify to regeneration, soon come to have a second and third generation who easily grow up to be nominal Christians. The policies of the churches vary in their ability to produce Christians vividly

conscious of their own salvation. People Movements in themselves do not encourage the production of nominal Christians.

Up in the north of Pakistan there was a lowly people called Churas. They were the agricultural laborers in a mixed Muslim and Hindu civilization. They formed about 7 per cent of the total population, and were Untouchables. They were oppressed. They skinned dead cattle, cured the skins, collected the bones and sold them. They had been largely overlooked by the missionaries preaching Christ to the respectable members of the Hindu and Muslim communities, and organizing their few hard-won converts into mission station churches. Then a man named Ditt from among the Churas turned to Christ, continued to live among his people, despite their attempts at ostracism, and gradually brought his relatives to the Christian faith. The missionaries were at first dubious about admitting to the Christian fellowship these lowest of the low, lest the upper castes and the Muslims take offense and come to think of the Christian enterprise as an "untouchable" affair. But those who became Christians were pastored and taught and organized into churches. Because the converts came as groups without social dislocation the efforts of the pastors and the missionaries could be given largely to teaching and preaching. Attention did not have to be diverted to providing jobs and wives, houses and land for individual converts. The Mission to whom God had entrusted this Movement was made up of devout men and women and they gave themselves to the task. The outcome was at the end of about eighty years there are no more Churas in that section of India. *They have all become Christians.*

Whereas the Church in mission station areas often numbers no more than one-tenth of 1 per cent of the total population, in the Chura area *the Church numbers 7 per cent of the population.* There are congregations in many of the villages and a Christian witness is maintained, not by foreign missionaries, but by the citizens of Pakistan.

In Indonesia there is a large mission work. In addition to static gathered colonies there have been also a comparatively large number of God-given People Movements. In the

> There is so much that is mysterious and beyond anything we can ask or think, and so much evident working of divine Power, that we must confess that People Movements are gifts of God.

north of Sumatra there is a flourishing Batak People Movement, numbering hundreds of thousands. In 1937, on the island of Nias, off the north-west coast of Sumatra, there were 102,000 Christians: in 1916 there were none. In the northern parts of the Celebes the Minahasa tribes were by 1940 fairly solidly Christian and in the center the growth of People Movements was rapid. There were tribal movements toward Christ in the Moluccas, the Sangi and the Talaud Islands. Around the year 1930 between eight and ten thousand a year were being baptized in Dutch New Guinea. By 1936 the number of Protestant Christians was reported to be 1,610,533. The Roman Church also has increased by numerous People Movements. In 1937 there were 570,974 members of the Roman Catholic Church. After 1950 new large People Movements in Sumatra and after 1960 in Irian and Kalimantan have taken place.

The only instance in the entire world of a hundred thousand Muslims being won to Christ occurs in Indonesia, in the midst of these numerous People Movements. It is also interesting that in Indonesia there is apparently a bridge between the natives and the Chinese immigrants, a bridge over which Christianity can cross. If this were strengthened it might well happen that more Chinese would become Christian indirectly *via* the People Movements of Indonesia than have been won in China itself.

In Africa there have been a large number of People Movements. The day is not far off when most of Africa south of the Sahara will have been discipled.

There is an instructive case of People Movements in the Gold Coast. These have grown into a great Presbyterian Church. For 19 years (1828-47) the Basel Mission of Switzerland battled to establish a foothold in the Gold Coast. Of the 16 missionaries sent out ten died shortly after arrival. The daring expedient had to be adopted of bringing in eight West Indian families to demonstrate that black men could read the white man's Book, and to provide missionaries less susceptible to the ravages of the climate. During this time there had not been a single baptism. The first four baptisms were in 1847 among the Akim

Abuakwa tribe. The following table shows how the Church grew.

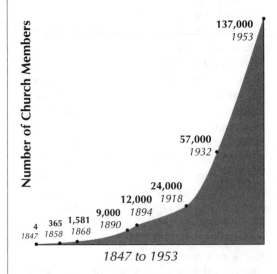

1847 to 1953

Till about 1870 the records show evidence of the exploratory Mission Station Approach. Slaves were purchased, freed, and employed at the mission stations for instruction. Runaway slaves were given shelter. Laborers on mission buildings were settled on mission land. In 1868 there was one missionary for each thirty Christians. The Basel Mission had a gathered colony at each of its nine mission stations. But in the decade 1870 to 1880 outlying chains of families started becoming Christian, and several stations among the Tsui-speaking tribes began to be surrounded by small Christian groups in scattered villages. Schools were established in each and the groups gradually became churches. An important feature of this movement, like many other African People Movements, was that pagan parents frequently sent their children to Christian schools, desiring them to become Christians. The school thus had enormous influence.

Early growth was tribe-wise. Teacher-preachers, the slightly educated first generation Christian workers on whom so much of the discipling of the tribes of Africa has depended, were usually recruited from each tribe in which a Christian movement started. They were then trained and sent back to that tribe to teach others, shepherd the Christians and win others to Christ. Later, as Christian movements arose in practically all the tribes, they became a uniting factor in the life of the nation, and workers were appointed more or less regardless of tribal relationships.

The churches born of people movements

The most obvious result of Christian missions which have been fathering and furthering Christward movements is a tremendous host of Christian churches. It has been calculated that there are well over a hundred thousand congregations of Christians brought to a knowledge of God through recent Christian People Movements. These exist in most of the non-Christian countries.

Let us consider the unexpectedly large number of People Movements. The islands of the Pacific have been largely discipled by People Movements. India has its extensive list of movements from the Malas and Madigas, the Nagas and Garas, the Mahars and Bhils, and many others. Indonesia and Burma total well over a score of People Movements of some power. Africa has numerous tribes in which the churches are growing in tribe-wise fashion. Two new People Movements are being reported in 1980: One in Mindanao and one in Mexico. Our list might be made much larger. Each of these hundreds of People Movements is multiplying Christian congregations as it grows.

These scores of thousands of congregations have many features in common. Many members of the churches are illiterate. In some lands the percentage of illiteracy in the People Movement churches is over 80. The pastors of the churches are usually men with about seven years of schooling plus some seminary training. The church buildings are often temporary adobe or wattle buildings, though there are many well-built churches among the older congregations. In new People Movements, the missionary usually plays an important role—starting, funding, and developing them. The pastoring of the congregations is almost entirely in the hands of the nationals however. In older, larger People Movements to-day national ministers head the Church, while missionaries work as assistants directed by the church council. The services to Christians, so marked in the Mission Station Approach, are very much curtailed. The numbers of children are so great that, aside from small

unsatisfactory primary schools, few children get a chance at education. In the mission station churches it is common practice for every child to be sent, largely at mission expense, through school as far as his intelligence will allow him to go. But in the People Movement churches the bulk of the Christian population has available to it only such educational advantages as the average non-Christian shares. This makes for an illiterate and ignorant church membership.

In some African countries, the school picture is totally different. Government does its education through missions. In such lands the children of the People Movements have excellent educational opportunities and the membership of the churches is growing up largely literate.

Scattered as the congregations are it is difficult to reach them with medical aid. Cholera and small-pox epidemics, sudden death from cerebral malaria, infant maladies which carry off children like flies, and health conditions which are a scandal to the human race, are characteristic of these myriad rural churches.

Yet People Movement Churches are remarkably stable. There are reversions, specially in the early days, but on the whole, once a *people* has become Christian, it stays Christian even in the face of vigorous persecution. In addition to the faith of each individual and the courage which comes from world-wide fellowship, the very bonds of relationship and social cohesion keep weak individuals from denying the faith.

Unvalued pearls

One of the curious facts about People Movements is that they have seldom been sought or desired. Pickett records, in Christian Mass Movements in India, that most People Movements have actually been resisted by the leaders of the church and mission where they started. These leaders often had grave doubts whether it was right to take in groups of individuals, many of whom seemed to have little ascertainable personal faith. Nevertheless, despite a certain degree of repression, movements did occur. One wonders what would have happened had missions from the beginning of the "Great Century" been actively searching and praying for the coming of

Christward marches by the various peoples making up the population of the world.

Those People Movements which did occur were seldom really understood. The way of corporate decision was obscured by the Western preference for individual decision. The processes of perfecting the churches were confused with the process by which a people turns from idols to serve the living God. Even where there has been great growth, as in parts of Africa, faulty understanding of People Movements has resulted in much less than maximum growth and has caused needless damage to tribal life.

Christward movements of peoples are the supreme goal of missionary effort. Many who read this book will not agree with this, and, indeed, it has never been generally accepted. Yet we not only affirm it, but go further and claim that the vast stirrings of the Spirit which occur in People Movements are God-given. We dare not think of People Movements to Christ as merely social phenomena. True, we can account for some of the contributing factors which have brought them about; but there is so much that is mysterious and beyond anything we can ask or think, so much that is a product of religious faith, and so much evident working of divine Power, that we must confess that People Movements are gifts of God. It is as if in the fullness of time God gives to His servants the priceless beginning of a People Movement. If that succeeds, the church is firmly planted. If it fails, the missionary forces are back to the preliminary stages of exploration. Yet the essential recognition that the People Movements to Christ is the supreme goal is not often made by Christian leaders. Gifts of God come and go unrecognized; while man-directed mission work is carried faithfully, doggedly forward.

It is time to recognize that when revival really begins in China, Japan, Africa, the Muslim world, and India, it will probably appear in the form of People Movements to Christ. This is the way in which Evangelical Christianity spread in Roman Catholic Europe at the time of the Reformation. It is the best way for it to spread in any land.

Five Great Advantages

People Movements have five considerable advantages. *First, they have provided the Christian movement with permanent churches rooted in the soil of hundreds of thousands of villages.* For their continued economic life they are quite independent of Western missions. They are accustomed (unfortunately too accustomed) to a low degree of education. Yet their devotion has frequently been tested in the fires of persecution and found to be pure gold. They are here to stay. They are permanent comrades on the pilgrim way.

They have the advantage of being naturally indigenous. In the Mission Station Approach the convert is brought in as an individual to a pattern dominated by the foreigner. The foreigner has set the pace and the style, often to his own dismay. But such denationalization is a very minor affair in true People Movements. In them the new Christians seldom see the missionary. They are immersed in their own cultures. Their style of clothing, of eating and of speaking continues almost unchanged. Their churches are necessarily built like their houses—and are as indigenous as anyone could wish. They cannot sing or learn foreign tunes readily, so local tunes are often used. Thus an indigenous quality, highly sought and rarely found by leaders of the Mission Station Approach churches, is obtained without effort by the People Movement churches. Church headquarters, however, need to make special efforts to keep thoroughly indigenous their training of People Movement youth and leadership.

People Movements have a third major advantage. With them "the spontaneous expansion of the Church" is natural. The phrase "spontaneous expansion" sums up the valuable contribution to missionary thinking made by Roland Allen and World Dominion. It requires that new converts be formed into churches which from the beginning are fully equipped with all spiritual authority to multiply themselves without any necessary reference to the foreign missionaries. These might be helpful as advisers or assistants but should never be necessary to the completeness of the Church or to its power of unlimited expansion. Spontaneous expansion involves a full trust in the Holy Spirit and a recognition that the ecclesiastical traditions of the older churches are not necessarily useful to the younger churches arising out of the missions from the West. New groups of converts are expected to multiply themselves in the same way as did the new groups of converts who were the early churches. Advocates of spontaneous expansion point out that foreign directed movements will in the end lead to sterility and antagonism to their sponsors, and that therefore the methods now being pursued, here called the Mission Station Approach, will never bring us within measurable distance of the evangelization of the world.

> In order to be called a bridge, a connection must be large enough to provide for the baptism of enough groups in a short enough time and a small enough area to create a People Movement in the other community.

Desirable as spontaneous expansion is, it is a difficult ideal for the Mission Station Approach churches to achieve. They might be freed from all bonds to the Western churches, they might be convinced that they had all the spiritual authority needed to multiply themselves, they might be filled with the Holy Spirit and abound in desire to win others to Christ, and yet—just because they form a separate people and have no organic linkages with any other neighboring people—they would find it extremely difficult to form new churches. In People Movement churches, on the contrary, spontaneous expansion is natural. Both the desire to win their "own fold" and the opportunity to bear witness in unaffected intimate conversation are present to a high degree. There is abundant contact through which conviction can transmit itself. True, in People Movements this natural growth can be and, alas, sometimes has been, slowed down by the atmosphere and tech-

niques of the all-pervading gathered colony approach. But once these are recognized and renounced by the leaders of the People Movement churches, it becomes comparatively easy for spontaneous expansion to occur. Missions can then, like Paul, deliberately attempt to use the relatively unplanned expansion of a Christward People Movement to achieve still greater and more significant enlargement. Thus we come to the most marked advantage of these movements.

These movements have enormous possibilities of growth. That these possibilities are to-day largely ignored and unrecognized even by the leader of the churches does not diminish either the truth or the importance of this fact.

The group movements are fringed with exterior growing points among their own peoples. As Paul discovered, the Palestinian movement had growing points in many places outside that country. Just so, every Christward movement has many possibilities of growth on its fringes. For example, the Madigas have become Christians in large numbers. They are the laborers of South India. They have migrated to many places in India and even abroad. One cannot help wondering whether a fervent proclamation by a modern Madiga St. Paul carrying the news that "We Madigas are becoming Christian by tens of thousands each year: we have found the Savior and have as a people come into possession of the unsearchable riches of Christ," might not start Madiga Movements in many parts of the world.

People Movements also have internal growing points; that is, the unconverted pockets left by any such sweeping movement. Here the leaders of the Christian forces must be alert to see to it that strategic doorways are entered while they are open. Doorways remain open for about one generation. Then they close to the ready flow of the Christian religion. Until the discipling of the entire people, there will be both internal and external growing points. Both will yield large returns if cultivated.

Of rarer occurrence are the bridges to other communities, such as that over which St. Paul launched his Gentile movements. In order to be called a bridge, the connection must be large enough to provide not merely for the baptism of individuals, but for the baptism of enough groups in a short enough time and a small enough area to create a People Movement in the other community. More of these bridges would be found if they were assiduously sought. More would be used for the expansion of the Christian faith if leaders could be led to understand them and become skilled in their use.

The possibilities for growth in People Movements are not by any means confined to developing new movements. Leaders of People Movement churches find that after the church has attained power and size the normal process of growth, including the baptism of individual seekers on the fringes of the congregations, often produce more quiet regular in-gatherings year after year than was the case during the period of the greatest exuberance of the movement. One might conclude that once a People Movement church has gained a hundred thousand converts, and has become indigenous to the land and forms a noticeable proportion of the population, it is likely to keep on growing. A moderate amount of missionary assistance, at places where the churches feel their need, produces results far beyond that which those accustomed to the mission station tradition would consider possible.

The fifth advantage is that these movements provide a sound pattern of becoming Christian. Being a Christian is seen to mean not change in standard of living made possible by foreign funds, *but change in inner character made possible by the power of God.* In well-nurtured People Movement churches, it is seen to mean the regular worship of God, the regular hearing of the Bible, the giving to the church, the discipline of the congregation, the spiritual care exercised by the pastor, habits of prayer and personal devotion and the eradication of un-Christian types of behavior. This life, centering in the village church, often built by the Christians themselves, is seen to be the main feature of the Christian religion. There are no impressive institutions to divert attention from the central fact. Christians become "people with churches, who worship God" rather than "people with hospitals who know medicine," or "people with schools who get good jobs." The health of the Christian movement requires that the normal pattern be well known, not merely to the non-Christian peoples, but to the leaders of church and mission and to the rank and file of members. The People Movement supplies the pattern which can be indefinitely reproduced. It is the pattern which with minor variations has obtained throughout history.

Study Questions

1. Briefly define the term "the bridges of God" and explain the significance of these bridges for mission strategy.

2. Are group decisions valid? Why or why not? Explain the strategic importance of encouraging "multi-individual" decisions.

3. At the time McGavran wrote *The Bridges of God*, the term "unreached people group" had not yet been used. What is the significance of the idea of "people movements" for the ministry among "unreached peoples?"

The New Macedonia:

A Revolutionary New Era in Mission Begins

Ralph D. Winter

Donald McGavran commented, "At the International Congress on World Evangelization, Dr. Ralph Winter proved beyond any reasonable doubt that in the world today 2,700,000,000 men and women cannot hear the gospel by 'near neighbor evangelism.' They can hear it only by E-2 and E-3 evangelists who cross cultural, linguistic and geographical barriers, patiently learn that other culture and language, across the decades preach the gospel by word and deed, and multiply reproductive and responsible Christian churches." The following article is the text of this address, given at the July 1974 Lausanne Congress. McGavran added, "Nothing said at Lausanne had more meaning for the expansion of Christianity between now and the year 2000."

After serving ten years as a missionary among Mayan Indians in the highlands of Guatemala, Ralph D. Winter was called to be a Professor of Missions at the School of World Mission at Fuller Theological Seminary. Ten years later he and his wife, Roberta, founded a mission society called the Frontier Mission Fellowship (FMF) in Pasadena, California. This in turn spawned the U.S. Center for World Mission and the William Carey International University, both of which serve other missions working at the frontiers of mission. He is the General Director of the Frontier Mission Fellowship. See expanded biographical sketch at the end of the book.

In recent years, a serious misunderstanding has crept into the thinking of many evangelicals. Curiously, it is based on a number of wonderful facts: the gospel has now gone to the ends of the earth. Christians have now fulfilled the Great Commission in at least a geographical sense. At this moment of history we can acknowledge with great respect and pride those evangelists of every nation who have gone before us and whose sacrificial efforts and heroic accomplishments have made Christianity by far the world's largest and most widespread religion, with a Christian church on every continent and in practically every country. This is no hollow victory. Now more than at any time since Jesus walked the shores of Galilee, we know with complete confidence that the gospel is for all men, that it makes sense in any language and that it is not merely a religion of the Mediterranean or of the West.

This is all true. On the other hand, many Christians as a result have the impression that the job is now nearly done and that to finish it we need only to forge ahead in local evangelism on the part of the now worldwide church reaching out wherever it has already been planted. Many Christian organizations ranging widely from the World Council of Churches to many U.S. denominations, even some evangelical groups, have rushed to the conclusion that we may now abandon traditional missionary strategy and count on local Christians everywhere to finish the job.

This is why *evangelism* is the one great password to evangelical unity today. Not everyone can agree on foreign mission strategies, but more people than ever agree on evangelism because that seems to be the one obvious job that remains to be done. All right! There is nothing wrong with evangelism. Most conversions must inevitably take place as the result of some Christian witnessing to a near neighbor and that is evangelism.

The awesome problem is the additional truth that most non-Christians in the world today are not culturally near neighbors of any Christians and that it will take a special kind of "cross-cultural" evangelism to reach them.

CROSS-CULTURAL EVANGELISM: THE CRUCIAL NEED

Examples of the Need

Let us approach this subject with some graphic illustrations. I am thinking, for example, of the hundreds of thousands of Christians in Pakistan. Almost all of them are people who have never been Muslims and do not have the kind of relationship with the Muslim community that encourages witnessing. Yet they live in a country that is 97 per cent Muslim! The Muslims, on their part, have bad attitudes toward the stratum of society represented by the Christians. One group of Christians has boldly called itself *The Church of Pakistan*. Another group of Christians goes by the name *The Presbyterian Church of Pakistan*. While these are *"national"* churches in the sense that they are part of their countries, they can hardly be called national churches if this phrase implies that they are culturally related to that vast bloc of people who constitute the other 97 per cent of the country, namely, the Muslims. Thus, although the Muslims are geographically near neighbors of these Christians they are not *cultural near-neighbors* and thus *normal evangelism* will not do the job.

Or take the Church of South India, a large church which has brought together the significant missionary efforts of many churches over the last century. But while it is called *The Church of South India*, 95 per cent of its members come from only five out of the more that 100 social classes (castes) in South India. Ordinary evangelism on the part of existing Christians will readily persuade men and women of those same five social classes. However, it would be much more difficult— it is in fact *another kind of evangelism*—for this church to make great gains within the 95 other social classes which make up the vast bulk of the population.

Or take the great Batak church in Northern Sumatra. Here is one of the famous churches of Indonesia. Its members have been doing a great deal of evangelism among fellow Bataks of whom there are still many thousands whom they can reach without learning a foreign language, and among whom they can work with the maximum efficiency of direct contact and understanding. But at the same time, the vast majority of all the people in Indonesia speak other languages and are of other ethnic units. For the Batak Christians of Northern Sumatra to win people to Christ from other parts of Indonesia will be a distinctly different kind of task. It is *another kind of evangelism*.

Or take the great church of Nagaland in Northeast India. Years ago, American missionaries from the plains of Assam reached up into the Naga hills and won some of the Ao Nagas. Then these Ao Nagas won practically their whole tribe to Christ. Next thing, Ao Nagas won members of the nearby Santdam Naga tribe that spoke a sister language. These new Santdam Naga Christians then proceeded to win almost the whole of their tribe. This process went on until the majority of all fourteen Naga tribes became Christian. Now that most of Nagaland is Christian—even the officials of the state government are Christian—there is the desire to witness elsewhere in India. But for these Nagaland Christians to win other people in India is as much a foreign mission task as it is for Englishmen, Koreans or Brazilians to evangelize in India. This is one reason why it is such a new and unprecedented task for the Nagas to evangelize the rest of India. Indian citizenship is one advantage the Naga Christians have as compared to people from other countries, but citizenship does not make it easier for them to learn any of the hundreds of totally foreign languages in the rest of India.

In other words, for Nagas to evangelize other peoples in India, they will need to employ a radically different kind of evangelism. The easiest kind of evangelism, when they used their own language to win their own people, is now mainly in the past. The second kind of evangelism was not a great deal more difficult—where they won people of neighboring Naga tribes, whose languages were sister languages. The third kind of evangelism, needed to win people in far-off parts of India, will be much more difficult.

Different Kinds of Evangelism

Let's give labels to these different kinds of evangelism. Where an Ao Naga won another Ao, let us call that *E-1 evangelism*. Where an Ao went across a tribal language boundary to a sister language and won the *Santdam*, we'll call it *E-2 evangelism*. (the E-2 task is not as easy and requires different techniques.) But then if an Ao Naga goes to another region of India, to a totally strange language, for example, Telegu, Korhu or Bhili, his task will be considerably more difficult than E-l or even E-2 evangelism. We will call it *E-3 evangelism*.

Let us try out this terminology in another country. Take Taiwan. There, also, there are different kinds of people. The majority are Minnans, who were there before a flood of Mandarin-speaking people came across from the mainland. Then there is the huge bloc of Hakka-speaking people who came from the mainland much earlier. Up in the mountains, however, a few hundred thousand aboriginal peoples speak Malayo-Polynesian dialects entirely different from Chinese. Now if a Mainlander Chinese Christian wins others from the mainland, that's E-l evangelism. If he wins a Minnan Taiwanese or a Hakka, that's E-2 evangelism. If he wins someone from the hill tribes, that's E-3 evangelism, and remember, E-3 is a much more complex task, performed at a greater *cultural* distance.

Thus far we have only referred to language differences, but for the purpose of defining evangelistic strategy, any kind of obstacle, any kind of communication barrier affecting evangelism is significant. In Japan for example, practically everybody speaks Japanese, and there aren't radically different dialects of Japanese comparable to the differ-

ent dialects of Chinese. But there are social differences which make it very difficult for people from one group to win others of a different social class. In Japan, as in India, social differences often turn out to be more important in evangelism than language differences. Japanese Christians thus have not only an E-l sphere of contact, but also E-2 spheres that are harder to reach. Missionaries going from Japan to other parts of the world to work with non-Japanese with totally different languages are doing an evangelistic task on the E-3 basis.

Lastly, let me give an example from my own experience. I speak English as a native language. For ten years, I lived and worked in Central America, for most of the time in Guatemala, where Spanish is the official language, but where a majority of the people speak some dialect of the Mayan family of aboriginal languages. I had two languages to learn. Spanish has a 60 per cent overlap in vocabulary with English, so I had no trouble learning that language. Along with the learning of Spanish, I became familiar with the extension of European culture into the New World, and it was not particularly difficult to understand the lifeways of the kind of people who spoke Spanish. However, because Spanish was so easy by comparison, learning the Mayan language in our area was, I found, enormously more difficult. In our daily work, switching from English to Spanish to a Mayan language made me quite aware of the three different "cultural distances." When I spoke of Christ to a Peace Corpsman in English, I was doing E-l evangelism. When I spoke to a Guatemalan in Spanish, it was E-2 evangelism. When I spoke to an Indian in the Mayan language, it was the much more difficult E-3 evangelism.

Now where I live in Southern California, most of my contacts are in the E-1 sphere,

> In Japan, as in India, social differences often turn out to be more important in evangelism than language differences.

but if I evangelize among the million who speak Spanish, I must use E-2 evangelism. Were I to learn the Navajo language and speak of Christ to some of the 30,000 Navajo Indians who live in Los Angeles, I would be doing E-3 evangelism. Reaching Cantonese-speaking refugees from Hong Kong with the Good News of Christ would also be, for me, an E-3 task. Note, however, that what for me is E-3 could be only E-2 for someone else. American-born Chinese, who have significant exposure to the Cantonese-speaking subculture, would find Hong Kong refugees only an E-2 task.

Everyone who is here in this Congress has his own E-1 sphere in which he speaks his own language and builds on all the intuition which derives from his experience within his own culture. Then perhaps for almost all of us there is an E-2 sphere—groups of people who speak languages that are a little different, or who are involved in culture patterns sufficiently in contrast with our own as to make communication more difficult. Such people can be reached with a little extra trouble and with sincere attempts, but it will take us out of our way to reach them. More important, they are people who, once converted, will not feel at home in the church which we attend. In fact, they may grow faster spiritually if they can find Christian fellowship among people of their own kind. More significant to evangelism, it is quite possible that with their own fellowship, they are more likely to win others of their own social grouping. Finally, each of us here in Lausanne has an E-3 sphere: Most languages and cultures of the world are totally strange to us; they are at the maximum cultural distance. If we attempt to evangelize at this E-3 distance, we have a long uphill climb in order to be able to make sense to anyone.

In summary, the master pattern of the expansion of the Christian movement is first for special E-2 and E-3 efforts to cross cultural barriers into new communities and to establish strong, on going, vigorously evangelizing denominations, and then for that national church to carry the work forward on the really high-powered E-1 level. We are thus forced to believe that until every tribe and tongue has a strong, powerfully evangelizing church in it, and thus, an E-1 witness within it,

E-2 and E-3 efforts coming from outside are still essential and highly urgent.

CROSS-CULTURAL EVANGELISM: THE BIBLICAL MANDATE

At this point, let us ask what the Bible says about all this. Are these *cultural* differences something the Bible takes note of? Is this something which ought to occupy our time and attention? Is this matter of cultural distance something which is so important that it fits into a Congress like this? Let us turn to the Bible and see what it has to say.

Acts 1:8: An Emphasis on Cultural Distance

Let us go to that vital passage in the first chapter of Acts, so central to this whole Congress, where Jesus refers his disciples to the worldwide scope of God's concern—"in Jerusalem, in all Judea, and in Samaria and unto the uttermost part of the earth." If it were not for this passage (and all the other passages in the Bible which support it), we would not even be gathered here today. Without this biblical mandate, there could not have been a Congress on World Evangelization. It is precisely this task—the task of discipling all the nations—which includes all of us and unifies all of us in a single, common endeavor. Notice, however, that Jesus does not merely include the whole world. He distinguishes between different parts of that world and does so according to the relative distance of those people from his hearers. On another occasion he simply said, "Go ye into all the world," but in this passage he has divided that task into significant components.

At first glance you might think that he is merely speaking geographically, but with more careful study, it seems clear that he is not talking merely about *geographical* distance, but about cultural distance. The clue is the appearance of the word *Samaria* in this sequence. Fortunately, we have special insight into what Jesus meant by *Samaria*, since the New Testament records in an extended passage the precise nature of the evangelistic problem Jews faced in trying to reach the Samaritans. I speak of the well-known story of Jesus and the woman at the well. Samaria was not far away in the geographical sense. Jesus had to pass there whenever he went from Galilee to Jerusalem. Yet when Jesus spoke to this Samaritan woman, it was immediately obvious that he faced a special cultural obstacle. While she was apparently close enough linguistically for him to be able to understand her speech, her very first reply focused on the significant difference between the Jews and the Samaritans—they worshipped in different places. Jesus did not deny this profound difference, but accepted it and transcended it by pointing out the human cultural limitations of both the Jewish and the Samaritan modes of worship. He spoke to her heart and by passed the cultural differences.

Meanwhile, the disciples looking on were mystified and troubled. Even had they understood that God was interested in Samaritans, they probably would have had difficulty grappling with the cultural differences. Even if they had tried to do so, they might not have been sensitive enough to by pass certain differences and go directly to the heart of the matter—which was the heart of the woman.

Paul acted on the same principle when he sought to evangelize the Greeks, who were at an even greater cultural distance. Just imagine how shocked some of the faithful Jewish Christians were when they heard rumors that Paul by passed circumcision, one of the most important cultural differences to the Jews, even Christian Jews, and went to the heart of the matter. He was reported to them as saying, "Neither circumcision nor uncircumcision is worth anything in comparison to being in Christ, believing in him, being baptized in his name, being filled with his Spirit, belonging to his body."

At this point we must pause long enough to distinguish between cultural distance and *walls of prejudice*. There may have been high walls of prejudice involved where Jews encountered Samaritans, but it is obvious that the Greeks, who did not even worship the same God, were at a far greater *cultural distance* from the Jews than were the Samaritans, who were close cousins by comparison. It is curious to note that sometimes those who are closest to us are hardest to reach. For example, a Jewish Christian trying to

evangelize would understand a Samaritan more easily than he would understand a Greek, but he would be more likely to be hated or detested by a Samaritan than by a Greek. In Belfast today, for example, the problem is not so much cultural distance as prejudice. Suppose a Protestant who has grown up in Belfast were to witness for Christ to a nominal Belfast Catholic and an East Indian. He would more easily understand his Catholic compatriot, but might face less prejudice from the East Indian. Generally speaking, then, cultural distance is more readily traversed than high walls of prejudice are climbed.

But, returning to our central passage, it is clear that Jesus is referring primarily neither to geography nor walls of prejudice when he lists *Judea, Samaria,* and *the ends of the earth.* Had he been talking about prejudice, Samaria would have come last. He would have said, "in Judea, in all the world, and *even in Samaria.*" It seems likely he is taking into account cultural distance as the primary factor. Thus, as we today endeavor to fulfill Jesus' ancient command, we do well to be sensitive to *cultural distance.* His distinctions must underlie our strategic thinking about the evangelization of the whole world.

Evangelism in the Jerusalem and Judea sphere would seem to be what we have called *E-1 evangelism,* where the only barrier his listeners had to cross in their proposed evangelistic efforts was the boundary between the Christian community and the world immediately outside, involving the same language and culture. This is "near neighbor" evangelism. Whoever we are, wherever we live in the world, we all have some near neighbors to whom we can witness without learning any foreign language or taking into account any special cultural differences. This is the kind of evangelism we usually talk about. This is the kind of evangelism most meetings on evangelism talk about. One of the great differences between this Congress and all previous congresses on evangelism is its determined stress on *crossing cultural frontiers where necessary* in order to evangelize the whole earth. The mandate of this Congress does not allow us to focus merely on Jerusalem and Judea.

The second sphere to which Jesus referred is that of the Samaritan. The Bible account shows that although it was relatively easy for Jesus and his disciples to make themselves understood to the Samaritans, the Jew and the Samaritan were divided from each other by a frontier consisting of dialectal distinctions and some other very significant cultural differences. This was *E-2 evangelism*, because it involved crossing a *second* frontier. First, it involved crossing the frontier we have referred to in describing E-1 evangelism, the frontier between the church and the world. Secondly, it involved crossing a frontier constituted by significant (but not monumental) differences of language and culture. Thus we call it E-2 *evangelism*.

E-3 evangelism, as we have used the phrase, involves even greater cultural distance. This is the kind of evangelism that is necessary in the third sphere of Jesus' statement, "to the uttermost part of the earth." The people needing to be reached in this third sphere live, work, talk, and think in languages and cultural patterns utterly different from those native to the evangelist. The average Jewish Christian, for example, would have had no head start at all in dealing with people beyond Samaria. If reaching Samaritans seemed like crossing two frontiers (thus called E-2 evangelism), reaching totally different people must have seemed like crossing three, and it is reasonable to call such a task *E-3 evangelism*.

One Christian's Judea is Another Christian's Samaria

It is very important to understand the full significance of the distinctions Jesus is making. Since he was not talking about geographical, but cultural distance, the general value of what he said has striking strategic application today. Jesus did not mean that all down through history Samaria specifically would be an object of special attention. One Christian's Judea might be another Christian's Samaria. Take Paul, for example. Although he was basically a Jew, he no doubt found it much easier to traverse the cultural

> One Christian's Judea might be another Christian's Samaria.

distance to the Greeks than did Peter, because unlike Peter, Paul was much better acquainted with the Greek world. Using the terminology we have employed, where an E-1 task is near, E-2 is close, and E-3 is far (in cultural, not geographical distance), we can say that reaching Greeks meant working at an E-2 distance for Paul; but for Peter it meant working at an E-3 distance. For Luke, who was himself a Greek, reaching Greeks was to work only at an E-1 distance. Thus, what was distant for Peter was near for Luke. And vice versa: reaching Jews would have been E-1 for Peter, but more likely E-3 for Luke. It may well be that God sent Paul rather than Peter to the Gentiles partially because Paul was closer culturally. By the same token, Paul, working among the Greeks at an E-2 distance, was handicapped by comparison with E-1 "nationals" like Luke, Titus, and Epaphroditus; and, as a matter of evangelistic strategy, he wisely turned things over to "national" workers as soon as he possibly could. Paul himself, being a Jew, often began his work in a new city in the Jewish synagogue where he himself was on an E-1 basis and where, with the maximum power of E-1 communication, he was able to speak forcefully without any non-Jewish accent.

Let us straightforwardly concede right here that, all other things being equal, the national leader always has a communication advantage over the foreigner. When the evangelists went from the plains of Assam up into the Naga hills, it must have been very much harder for them to win Ao Nagas than it was for Ao Naga Christians to do so, once a start had been made. When the first German missionaries preached to the Bataks, they must have had a far greater problem than when the faith, once planted, was transmitted from Batak to Batak. E-1 evangelism—where a person communicates to his own people—is obviously the most potent kind of evangelism. People need to hear the gospel in their own language. Can we believe God intends for them to hear it from people who speak without a trace of accent? The foreign missionary communicator may be good, but he is not good enough. If it is so important for Americans to have thirty translations of the New Testament to choose from, and even a "Living Bible," which allows the Bible to speak in colloquial English, then why must many peoples around the world suffer along with a Bible that was translated for them by a foreigner, and thus almost inevitably speaks to them in halting phrases?

This is why the easiest, most obvious surge forward in evangelism in the world today will come if Christian believers in every part of the world are moved to reach outside their churches and win their cultural near neighbors to Christ. They are better able to do that than any foreign missionary. It is a tragic perversion of Jesus' strategy if we continue to send missionaries to do the job that local Christians can do better. There is no excuse for a missionary in the pulpit when a national can do the job better. There is no excuse for a missionary to be doing evangelism on an E-3 basis, at an E-3 distance from people, when there are local Christians who are effectively winning the same people as part of their E-l sphere.

In view of the profound truth that (other things being equal) E-l evangelism is more powerful than E-2 or E-3 evangelism, it is easy to see how some people have erroneously concluded that E-3 evangelism is therefore out-of-date, due to the wonderful fact that there are now Christians throughout the whole world. It is with this perspective that major denominations in the U.S. have at some points acted on the premise that there is no more need for missionaries of the kind who leave home to go to a foreign country and struggle with a totally strange language and culture. Their premise is that "there are Christians over there already." With the drastic fall-off in the value of the U.S. dollar and the tragic shrinking of U.S. church budgets, some U.S. denominations have had to curtail their missionary activity to an unbelievable extent, and they have in part tried to console themselves by saying that it is time for the national church to take over. In our response to this situation, we must happily agree that wherever there are local Christians effectively evangelizing, there is nothing more potent than E-l evangelism.

However, the truth about the superior power of E-l evangelism must not obscure the obvious fact that E-l evangelism is literally *impossible* where there are no witnesses

within a given language or cultural group. Jesus, as a Jew, would not have had to witness directly to that Samaritan woman had there been a local Samaritan Christian who had already reached her. In the case of the Ethiopian eunuch, we can conjecture that it might have been better for an Ethiopian Christian than for Philip to do the witnessing, but there had to be an initial contact by a non-Ethiopian in order for the E-l process to be set in motion. This kind of initial, multiplying work is the primary task of the missionary when he rightly understands his job. He must decrease and the national leader must increase. Hopefully Jesus' E-2 witness set in motion E-l witnessing in that Samaritan town. Hopefully Philip's E-2 witness to the Ethiopian set in motion E-l witnessing back in Ethiopia. If that Ethiopian was an Ethiopian Jew, the E-l community back in Ethiopia might not have been very large, and might not have effectively reached the non-Jewish Ethiopians. As a matter of fact, scholars believe that the Ethiopian church today is the result of a much later missionary thrust that reached, by E-3 evangelism, clear through to the ethnic Ethiopians.

Thus, in the Bible, as in our earlier illustrations from modern mission history, we arrive at the same summary:

E-1 Powerful, but E-3 Essential

The master pattern of the expansion of the Christian movement is first for special E-2 and E-3 efforts to cross cultural barriers into new communities and to establish strong, on-going, vigorously evangelizing denominations, and then for that national church to carry the work forward on the really high-powered E-1 level. We are thus forced to believe that until every tribe and tongue has a strong, powerfully evangelizing church in it, and thus an E-1 witness within it, E-2 and E-3 efforts coming from outside are still essential and highly urgent. From this perspective, how big is the remaining task?

CROSS-CULTURAL EVANGELISM: THE IMMENSITY OF THE TASK

Unfortunately, most Christians have only a very foggy idea of just how many peoples there are in the world among whom there is no E-l witness. But fortunately, preparatory studies for this Congress have seriously raised this question: Are there any tribal tongues and linguistic units which have not yet been penetrated by the gospel? If so, where? How many? Who can reach them? Even these preliminary studies indicate that cross-cultural evangelism must still be the highest priority. Far from being a task that is now out-of-date, the shattering truth is that at least four out of five non-Christians in the world today are beyond the reach of any Christian's E-l evangelism.

"People Blindness"

Why is this fact not more widely known? I'm afraid that all our exultation about the fact that every *country* of the world has been penetrated has allowed many to suppose that every *culture* has by now been penetrated. This misunderstanding is a malady so widespread that it deserves a special name. Let us call it "people blindness"—that is, blindness to the existence of separate *peoples* within *countries*—a blindness, I might add, which seems more prevalent in the U.S. and among U.S. missionaries than anywhere else. The Bible rightly translated could have made this plain to us. The "nations" to which Jesus often referred were mainly ethnic groups within the single political structure of the Roman government. The various nations represented on the day of Pentecost were for the most part not *countries* but *peoples*. In the Great Commission as it is found in Matthew, the phrase "make disciples of all *ethne* (peoples)" does not let us off the hook once we have a church in every country—God wants a strong church within every people!

"People blindness" is what prevents us from noticing the sub-groups within a country which are significant to development of effective evangelistic strategy. Society will be seen as a complex mosaic, to use McGavran's phrase, once we recover from "people blindness." But until we all recover from this kind of blindness, we may confuse the legitimate desire for church or national unity with the illegitimate goal of uniformity. God apparently loves diversity of certain kinds. But in any case this diversity means evangelists have to work harder. The little ethnic and cul-

tural pieces of the complex mosaic which is human society are the very subdivisions which isolate four out of five non-Christians in the world today from an E-l contact by existing Christians. The immensity of the cross-cultural task is thus seen in the fact that in Africa and Asia alone, one calculation has it that there are 1,993 million people virtually without a witness. The immensity of the task, however, lies not only in its bigness.

Need for E-2 Evangelism in the United States

The problem is more serious than re-translating the Great Commission in such a way that the peoples, not the countries, become the targets for evangelism. The immensity of the task is further underscored by the far greater complexity of the E-2 and E-3 task. Are we in America, for example, prepared for the fact that most non-Christians yet to be won to Christ (even in our country) will not fit readily into the kinds of churches we now have? The bulk of American churches in the North are middle-class, and the blue-collar worker won't go near them. Evangelistic crusades may attract thousands to big auditoriums and win people in their homes through television, but a large proportion of the newly converted, unless already familiar with the church, may drift away simply because there is no church where they will feel at home. Present-day American Christians can wait forever in their cozy, middle-class pews for the world to come to Christ and join them. But unless they adopt E-2 methods and both *go out after these people and help them found their own churches*, evangelism in America will face, and is already facing, steadily diminishing returns. You may say that there are still plenty of people who don't go to church who are of the same cultural background as those in church. This is true. But there are many, many more people of differing cultural bacgrounds who, even if they were to become fervent Christians, would not feel comfortable in existing churches.

If the U.S.—where you can drive 3,000 miles and still speak the same language—is nevertheless a veritable cultural mosaic viewed evangelistically, then surely most other countries face similar problems. Even in the U.S., local radio stations employ more than forty different languages. In addition to these language differences, there are many equally significant social and cultural differences. Language differences are by no means the highest barriers to communication.

The need, in E-2 evangelism, for whole new worshiping groups is underscored by the phenomenon of the Jesus People, who have founded hundreds of new congregations. The vast Jesus People Movement in the U.S. does not speak a different language so much as it involves a very different lifestyle and thus a different style of worship. Many American churches have attempted to employ the guitar music and many of the informal characteristics of the Jesus Movement, but there is a limit to which a single congregation can go with regard to speaking many languages and employing many life-styles. Who knows what has happened to many of the "mods" and "rockers" who were won as a result of Billy Graham's London Crusades? On the one hand, the existing churches were understandably culturally distant from such people, and on the other hand, there may not have been adequate E-2 methods employed so as to form those converts into whole new congregations. It is this aspect of E-2 evangelism which makes the cross-cultural task immensely harder. Yet it is essential. Let us take one more well-known example.

When John Wesley evangelized the miners of England, the results were conserved in whole new worshiping congregations. There probably would never have been a Methodist movement had he not encouraged these

> The phrase "make disciples of all *ethne* (peoples)" does not let us off the hook once we have a church in every country—God wants a strong church within every people!

lower-class people to meet in their own Christian gatherings, sing their own kind of songs, and associate with their own kind of people. Furthermore, apart from this E-2 technique, such people would not have been able to win others and expand the Christian movement in this new level of society at such an astonishing rate of speed. The results rocked and permanently changed England. It rocked the existing churches, too. Not very many people favored Wesley's contact with the miners. Fewer still agreed that miners should have separate churches!

A Clear Procedural Distinction

At this point we may do well to make a clear procedural distinction between E-1 and E-2 evangelism. We have observed that the E-2 sphere begins where the people you have reached are of sufficiently different backgrounds from those of people in existing churches that they need to form their own worshiping congregations in order best to win others of their own kind. John, chapter four, tells us that "many Samaritans from that city believed in him (Jesus) because of the woman's testimony." Jesus evangelized the woman by working with great sensitivity as an E-2 witness; she turned around and reached others in her town by efficient E-1 communication. Suppose Jesus had told her she had to go and worship with the Jews. Even if she had obeyed him and gone to worship with the Jews, she would on that basis have been terribly handicapped in winning others in her city. Jesus may actually have avoided the issue of where to worship and with what distant Christians to associate. That would come up later. Thus the Samaritans who believed the woman's testimony then made the additional step of inviting a Jew to be with them for two days. He still did not try to make them into Jews. He knew he was working at an E-2 distance, and that the fruits could best be conserved (and additional people best be won) if they were allowed to build *their own fellowship of faith*.

A further distinction might be drawn between the kind of cultural differences Jesus was working with in Samaria and the kind of differences resulting from the so-called "generation gap." But it really does not matter, in evangelism, whether the distance is cultural, linguistic, or an age difference. No matter what the reason for the difference or the permanence of the difference, or the perceived rightness or the wrongness of the difference, the procedural dynamics of E-2 evangelism techniques are quite similar. The E-2 sphere begins whenever it is necessary to found a new congregation. In the Philippines we hear of youth founding churches. In Singapore we know of ten recently established youth break-away congregations. Hopefully, eventually, age-focused congregations will draw closer to existing churches, but as long as there is a generation gap of serious proportions, such specialized fellowships are able to win many more alienated youth by being allowed to function considerably on their own. It is a good place to begin.

Whatever we may decide about the kind of E-2 evangelism that allows people to meet separately who are different due to temporary *age differences*, the chief factors in the immensity of the cross-cultural task are the much more profound and possibly permanent *cultural differences*. Here, too, some will always say that true cross-cultural evangelism is going too far. At this point we must risk being misunderstood in order to be absolutely honest. All around the world, special evangelistic efforts continue to be made which often break across culture barriers. People from these other cultures are won, sometimes only one at a time, sometimes in small groups. The problem is not in winning them; it is in the cultural obstacles to proper follow-up. Existing churches may cooperate up to a point with evangelistic campaigns, but they do not contemplate allowing the evangelistic organizations to stay long enough to gather these people together in churches of their own. They mistakenly think that being joined to Christ ought to include joining existing churches. Yet if proper E-2 methods were employed, these few converts, who would merely be considered somewhat odd additions to existing congregations, *could* be infusions of new life into whole new pockets of society where the church does not now exist at all!

The Muslim and Hindu Spheres

A discussion of the best ways to organize for cross-cultural evangelism is beyond the scope of this paper. It would entail a great deal of space to chart the successes and failures of different approaches by churches and by parachurch organizations. It may well be that E-2 and E-3 methods are best launched by specialized agencies and societies working loyally and harmoniously with the churches. Here we must focus on the nature of cross-cultural evangelism and its high priority in the face of the immensity of the task. Aside from the Chinese mainland sector, the two greatest spheres in which there is a tragic paucity of effective cross-cultural evangelism are the Muslim and the Hindu. Our concluding words will center in these two groups, which, in aggregate, number well over one billion people.

As we have earlier mentioned, a converted Muslim will not feel welcome in the usual Presbyterian Church in Pakistan. Centuries-old suspicions on both sides of the Muslim-Hindu fence make it almost impossible for Muslims, even converted Muslims, to be welcomed into the churches of former Hindu peoples. The present Christians of Pakistan (almost all formerly Hindu) have not been at all successful in integrating converted Muslims into their congregations. Furthermore, it is not likely even to occur to them that Muslims can be converted and form their own separate congregations. The enormous tragedy is that this kind of impasse postpones serious evangelism along E-2 lines wherever in the world there are any of the 664 million Muslims. Far to the east of Mecca, in certain parts of Indonesia, enough Muslims have become Christians that they have not been forced one by one to join Christian congregations of another culture. Far to the west of Mecca, in the middle of Africa on some of the islands of Lake Chad, we have reports that a few former Muslims, now Christians, still pray to Christ five times a day and worship in Christian churches on Friday, the Muslim day of worship. These two isolated examples suggest that Muslims can become Christians without necessarily undergoing serious and arbitrary cultural dislocation. There may be a wide, new, open door to the Muslims if we will be as cross-culturally alert as Paul was, who did not require the Greeks to become Jews in order to become acceptable to God.

Vast *new* realms of opportunity may exist in India, too, where local prejudice in many cases may forestall effective "near-neighbor" evangelism. Indians coming from a greater distance might by E-2 or E-3 methods be able to escape the local stigmas and establish churches within the 100 or so social classes as yet untouched. It is folly for evangelists to ignore such factors of prejudices, and their existence greatly increases the immensity of our task. Prejudice of this kind adds to cultural distance such obstacles that E-2 evangelism, where prejudice is deep, is often more difficult than E-3 evangelism. In other words, scholarly, well-educated Christians from Nagaland or Kerala might possibly be more successful in reaching middle-class Hindus in South India with the gospel than Christians from humble classes who have grown up in that area and speak the same language, but are stigmatized in local relationships. But who dares to point this out? It is ironic that national Christians all over the non-Western world are increasingly aware that they do not need to be Westernized to be Christian, yet they may in some cases be slow to sense that the challenge of cross-cultural evangelism requires them to allow other people in their own areas to have the same liberty of self-determination in establishing culturally divergent churches of their own.

In any case, the opportunities are just as immense as the task. If 600 million Muslims await a more enlightened evangelism, there are also 500 million Hindus who today face monumental obstacles to becoming Christians other than the profound spiritual factors inherent in the gospel. One keen observer is convinced that 100 million middle-class Hindus await the opportunity to become Christians—but there are no churches for them to join which respect their dietary habits and customs. Is the kingdom of God meat and drink? To go to the special efforts required by E-2 and E-3 evangelism is not to let down the standards and make the gospel easy—it is to disentangle the irrelevant elements and to make the gospel clear. Perhaps everyone is not able to do this special kind of work. True, many more E-1 evangelists will eventually be necessary to finish the task. But the highest priority in evangelism today is to develop the cross-cultural knowledge and sensitivities involved in E-2 and E-3 evangelism. Where necessary, evangelists from a distance must be called into the task. Nothing must blind us to the immensely important fact that at least *four-fifths* of the non-Christians in the world today will never have any straightforward opportunity to become Christians unless the Christians themselves go more than halfway in the specialized tasks of cross-cultural evangelism. Here is our highest priority.

QUESTIONS ABOUT THE THEOLOGICAL NATURE OF THE TASK

The main theological question, raised more often than any other, is so profound that I feel I must devote my remaining time to it. The question was stated in many ways in your response papers, but is basically this: "Will not our unity in Christ be destroyed if we follow a concept of cross-cultural evangelization which is willing to set up separate churches for different cultural groups within the same geographical area?" It is only with humble dependence upon the Holy Spirit to honor the Word of God above the secular influences to which we all are subject, that I dare to proceed with a perspective which I myself could not understand nor accept until several years ago. I was brought up in the United States, where for many people integration is almost like a civil religion, where such people almost automatically assume that eventually everyone will speak English and really shouldn't speak any other language. To me cultural diversity between countries was a nuisance, but cultural diversity within a country was simply an evil to be overcome. I had no thought of excluding anyone from any church (and I still do not), but I did unconsciously assume that the best thing that could happen to Black, White, Chicano, etc., was that they all would eventually come to the White, Anglo-Saxon, Protestant church and learn to do things the way that I felt was most proper.

Following this kind of American culture-Christianity, many missionaries have assumed that there ought to be just one national church in a country—even if this means none at all for certain sub-groups. Such missionaries, in all earnestness, have assumed that the denominational pluralism in their own home country is simply a sin to be avoided. They have assumed that *Southern* Baptists aren't necessary in *Northern* India, even though, as a matter of fact, in Boston today most of the Anglo churches have been sitting around waiting for the Arabs and the Japanese to come to their churches, and it has taken Southern Baptists to go into Northern United States and plant Arab churches and Japanese churches, and Portuguese churches, and Greek churches, and Polish churches, right under the nose of hundreds of good-willed Anglo churches which have been patiently waiting for these people to assimilate to the Anglo way of life. With one or two fine exceptions, the Anglo churches, with all their evangelistic zeal, simply did not have the insight to do this kind of E-2 and E-3 evangelism.

> Let us glory in the fact that God has allowed different life-styles to exist in different forms, and that this flexibility has been exercised throughout history.

Christian Unity and Christian Liberty

For my own part, after many years of struggling with this question, I am now no less concerned than before about the unity and fellowship of the Christian movement across all ethnic and cultural lines, but I realize now that Christian unity cannot be healthy if it infringes upon Christian liberty. In terms of evangelism, we must ask whether the attempt to extend, for example in Pakistan, an external form into the Muslim culture is more important than making the gospel clear to such peoples within their own culture. Can we not condition our desire for uniformity by an even greater desire for effective preaching of the gospel? I personally have come to believe that unity does not have to require uniformity, and I believe that there must be such

a thing as healthy diversity in human society *and in the Christian world Church*. I see the world Church as the gathering together of a great symphony orchestra where we don't make every new person coming in play a violin in order to fit in with the rest. We invite the people to come in to play the same score—the Word of God—but to play their own instruments, and in this way there will issue forth a heavenly sound that will grow in the splendor and glory of God as each new instrument is added.

The Example of the Apostle Paul

But some of you have said, "OK, if that is what you mean, what about the Apostle Paul? Did he set up separate congregations for masters and slaves?" I really don't know. I don't think so. But that does not mean that didn't happen. In a recent monograph by Paul Minear entitled *The Obedience of Faith*, the author suggests that in Rome there were probably five separate congregations of Christians, who numbered a total 3000, and that Paul's letter to the Romans was written actually to a cluster of churches in the city of Rome. He also suggests that these churches were very different from each other, some being composed almost entirely of Jewish Christians, and others (the majority) almost entirely of Gentile Christians. "Instead of visualizing a single Christian congregation, therefore, we should constantly reckon with the probability that within the urban area were to be found forms of Christian community which were as diverse, and probably also as alien, as the churches of Galatia and those of Judea." But whatever the case in Rome, Paul in his travels was usually dealing with the phenomenon of house churches, where whole households, masters and slaves, quite likely worshiped together. We cannot believe he ever separated people. However, we do know that he was willing to adopt in different places a radically different approach, as he put it, "for those under the law and for those not under the law." When, for example, he established an apparently non-Jewish congregation among the Galatians, it was obviously different, perhaps radically different from that of the Jewish congregations elsewhere. We know this because Jewish Christians followed Paul to the Galatians and tried to make them conform to the Jewish Christian pattern. Galatia is a clear case where it was impossible for Paul to submit simultaneously both to the provisions of the Jewish Christian way of life and at the same time to the patterns of an evidently Greek (or perhaps Celtic) congregation.

Paul's letter to the Galatians, furthermore, shows us how determined he was to allow the Galatian Christians to follow a different Christian life-style. Thus, while we do not have any record of his forcing people to meet separately, we do encounter all of Paul's holy boldness set in opposition to anyone who would try to *preserve a single normative pattern* of Christian life through a cultural imperialism that would *prevent* people from employing their own language and culture as a vehicle for worship and witness. Here, then, is a clear case of a man with cross-cultural evangelistic perspective doing everything within his power to guarantee liberty in Christ to converts who were different from his own social background.

This same thing is seen when Paul opposed Peter in Antioch. Peter was a Galilean Jew who was perhaps to some extent bi-cultural. He could have at least been able to understand the predominantly Greek life-style of the Antioch church. Indeed, he did seem to fit in until the moment other Jewish Christians came to the door. At this point Peter also discovered that in a given situation he had to choose between following Jewish or Greek customs. At this point he wavered. Did he lack the Spirit of God? Did he lack the love of God? Or did he fail to understand the way of God's love? Peter did not question the validity of a Greek congregation. Peter had already acknowledged this before his Jewish compatriots walked in the door. The point was that Peter was pained for others to know him as one who could shift from one community to the other. What this means to us today is quite clear. There were in fact in the New Testament period two significantly different communities of believers. Peter was regarded the apostle to the circumcision and Paul to the uncircumcision. Peter identified more easily with the Jews, and no doubt had a hard time explaining to Jews his experience at Cornelius' household, namely his discovery that Greek congre-

gations were to be considered legitimate. Paul, on the other hand, was able to identify more closely with the Greek congregations. They were perhaps eventually his primary missionary target, even though in a given locality he always began with the Jews.

The Equality of Diversity

One clue for today is the fact that where Paul found some Christians to be overly scrupulous about certain foods, he counseled people in those situations to abide by the stricter sensibilities of the majority. However, it is always difficult to make exact parallels to a modern situation. The New Testament situation would compare more easily to modern India today were it the case that the only Christians in India were Brahmins (and other members of the middle castes) with their highly restrictive diet. Then we would envision Brahmin Christians finding it hard to allow the less restrictive meat-eating groups to become Christian; but the actual situation is very nearly the reverse. In India today it is those who eat meat who are Christians, and the problem is how to apply Paul's missionary strategy to this situation. In regard to food restrictions, it is as though the Brahmins are "under the law," not the present Christians. In this situation can we imagine Paul saying, "To those under the law I will go as under the law if by all means I may win some"? Can we hear him say as an E-2 or E-3 evangelist, "If meat makes my brother offended, I will eat no meat"? Can we hear him defending worshiping groups among the Brahmins against the suggestion *or expectation* that they should change their diet or join congregations of very different life-style in order to be accepted as Christians? Against the accusation that he was dividing the church of Christ, can we hear Paul insist that "in Christ there is neither Jew nor Greek, low caste nor high caste"? Is this not the actual force of his oft repeated statement that these different kinds of people, following their different cultural patterns, are all equally acceptable to God? Was he really announcing a policy of local integration, or was he insisting on the equality of diversity?

Note very carefully that this perspective does not enforce (nor even allow) a policy of segregation, nor any kind of ranking of Christians in first- and second-class categories. It rather guarantees equal acceptability of different traditions. It is a clear-cut apostolic policy against forcing Christians of one life-style to be proselytized to the cultural patterns of another. This is not a peripheral matter in the New Testament. True circumcision is of the heart. True baptism is of the heart. It is a matter of faith, not works, or customs, or rites. In Christ there is freedom and liberty in this regard—people must be free either to retain or abandon their native language and life-style. Paul would not allow anyone to glory either in circumcision or in uncircumcision. He was absolutely impartial. He was also widely misunderstood. Paul's problem ultimately was in gaining acceptance by the Jews, and it was Asian Jews, possibly Christians, who pointed him out in the temple and thus finally caused his martyrdom for his belief in the separate liberty of the Greek Christian tradition. Let no one who seeks to be a missionary in the tradition of the Apostle Paul expect that working between two cultures will be easy to do. But he can take heart in the fact that the hazards of the profession are more than justified by the urgent missionary purposes of the cross-cultural evangelist.

If, for example, a cross-cultural evangelist encourages members of a Brahmin family to begin worship services in their own home, does he insist that they invite people from across town to their very first meeting? On the other hand, any Brahmin who becomes a Christian and who begins to understand the Bible will soon realize, whether it was entirely clear before or not, that he now belongs to a world family within which there are many tribes and tongues—indeed, according to the Book of Revelation (Rev 7:9), this kind of diversity will continue right down to the end of time. When the cross-cultural evangelist allows the development of a Brahmin congregation, he is not thereby proposing Brahmin segregation from the world church. He is not suggesting that the Brahmin Christians shun other Christians, but that Brahmins be included within the world church. He is merely affirming their liberty in Christ to

retain those elements of their life-style that are not inimical to the gospel of Christ. He is not increasing their alienation. He is giving them the Word of God which is the passkey to the ultimate elimination of all manner of prejudices, and is already signing them into a world Christian family which embraces all peoples, tribes and tongues as equals.

Unity and Uniformity

Now, I regret that this subject is so delicate, and I would not embark upon it if it were not so urgently significant for the practical evangelistic strategies which we must have if we are going to win the world for Christ. I would not even bring it up. Yet I must say I believe this issue is the most important single issue in evangelism today.

Many people asked me what I meant by the strategic value of the establishment of youth churches. It is important to realize the youth situation is highly parallel to the situa-

---

Christian unity cannot be healthy if it infringes upon Christian liberty.

---

tion we have just discussed. It is by no means a case where we are suggesting that young people not be allowed in adult services. We are not suggesting segregation of the youth. Youth churches are not ends, but means. We are not abandoning the thought that young people and older people should often be in the same service together. We are merely insisting, with what I pray is apostolic intuition, that young people have the freedom in Christ to meet together by themselves if they choose to, and *especially if this allows them to attract other young people who would likely* not come to Christ in an age-integrated service.

It is a curious fact that the kind of culturally sensitive evangelism I have been talking about has always been acceptable wherever people are geographically isolated. No one minds if Japanese Christians gather by themselves in Tokyo, or Spanish-speaking Christians gather by themselves in Mexico, or Chinese-speaking Christians gather by themselves in Hong Kong. But there is considerable confusion in many people's minds as to whether Japanese, Spanish and Chinese Christians should be allowed or encouraged to gather by themselves in Los Angeles. Very specifically, is it good evangelistic strategy to found separate congregations in Los Angeles in order to attract such people? Do Cantonese-speaking non-Christians need a Cantonese-speaking congregation to attract them to Christian faith and fellowship? If you talk to different people, you will get different answers. In my opinion, this question about evangelistic strategy in the forming of separate congregations must be considered an area of Christian liberty, and is to be decided purely on the basis of whether or not it allows the gospel to be presented effectively to more people—that is, whether it is evangelistically strategic. Some go as far as granting separate *language* congregations, but hesitate when the differences between people are social and non-linguistic. Somehow they feel that people may be excused for meeting separately if their language is different, but that the gospel urges us to ignore all other cultural differences. Many people are literally outraged at the thought that a local congregation would deliberately seek to attract people of a certain social level. And yet, while no one should be excluded from any church under any circumstances, it is a fact that where people can choose their church associations voluntarily, they tend to sort themselves out according to their own way of life pretty consistently. But this absolutely must be their own free choice. We are never suggesting an enforced segregation. Granting that we have this rich diversity, let us foster unity and fellowship between *congregations* just as we now do between *families* rather than to teach everyone to worship like Anglo-Americans. Let us glory in the fact that the *world* Christian family now already includes representatives of more different languages and cultures than any other organization or movement in human history. Americans may be baffled and perplexed by world diversity. God is not. Let us glory in the fact that God has allowed different life-styles to exist in different forms, and that this flexibility has been exercised throughout history. Let us never be content with mere isolation, but let us everlastingly emphasize that the great richness of our Christian tradition can only be realized as these differing life ways maintain creative contact. But let us be cautious about hastening to uniformity. If the whole world church could be gathered into a single congregation, Sunday after Sunday, there would eventually and inevitably be a loss of a great deal of the rich diversity of the present Christian traditions. Does God want this? Do we want this?

Jesus *died* for these people around the world. He did not die to preserve our Western way of life. He did not die to make Muslims stop praying five times a day. He did not die to make Brahmins eat meat. Can't you hear Paul the Evangelist saying we must go to these people within the systems in which they operate? True, this is the cry of a cross-cultural evangelist, not a pastor. We can't make every local church fit the pattern of every other local church. But we must have radically new efforts of cross-cultural evangelism in order to effectively witness to 2387 million people, and we cannot believe that we can continue virtually to ignore this highest priority.

Study Questions

1. Explain the difference between E-l, E-2, and E-3 evangelism. Which of the three does Winter consider most powerful? Why? Which does he consider most urgent? Why?

2. "Christian unity cannot be healthy if it infringes upon Christian liberty." Do you agree? What significance does this issue have for "practical evangelistic strategies"?

World Mission Survey

Ralph D. Winter and David A. Fraser

After serving ten years as a missionary among Mayan Indians in the highlands of Guatemala, Ralph D. Winter was called to be a Professor of Missions at the School of World Mission at Fuller Theological Seminary. Ten years later he and his wife, Roberta, founded a mission society called the Frontier Mission Fellowship (FMF) in Pasadena, California. This in turn spawned the U.S. Center for World Mission and the William Carey International University, both of which serve other missions working at the frontiers of mission. He is the General Director of the Frontier Mission Fellowship. See expanded biographical sketch at the end of the book.

David A. Fraser is currently Associate Professor of Sociology at Eastern College in St. Davids, Pennsylvania. Fraser was formerly a professor at Columbia Bible College in Columbia, South Carolina.

Adapted by permission from *Eternity Magazine,* Copyright Oct.-Dec., 1977; Jan.-May 1978. Alliance of Confessing Evangelicals, Inc., 1716 Spruce Street, Philadelphia, PA 19103.

Is This "Post-Christian" Europe?

For much of the 20th Century, it seemed like Christian Europe may have given its faith to the rest of the world but itself failed to keep the faith. The mission movement sparked by William Carey certainly produced a stupendous spread of God's light. Vast parts of Africa, Asia and the Pacific Islands have lit up as the result of tens of thousands of missionaries mainly from the Western World. Yet the flames of Christendom in the heartlands of Europe and the Soviet Union for 70 long years seemed to flicker and gradually grow dim. The faith of millions seemed to decay like a radioactive element into a powerful secularism. Some people even began speaking of a "post-Christian" Europe in the 1950's. However, there were many evidences of continuing Christian vitality even before the collapse of European Communism.

What was happening during the 20th Century was not so much the snuffing out of Christianity as it was the disestablishment of a Christendom in which certain denominations were official (like the Church of England, the Church of Sweden, etc.). Your membership was formed at birth. In the 20th Century, the rapid decline of vigor of such "state churches" was linked with the rise of secular communism in Eastern Europe and secularism in Western Europe and the United States; it looked like Europe and the entire Western world was becoming "Post Christian." Centralized Christendom could be quelled by central, totalitarian governments. Many of the surface indicators of "establishment Christendom" waned: membership registrations, church weddings, perfunctory attendance all decreased. Formerly hidden nominal Christians became much more evident.

At no time in the 20th Century was the grass-roots Christian movement ever extinguished. By the time the Communist bloc crumbled, there were actually more recognized Christians in the Soviet Union than there had been in total population at the time of the Communist Revolution. Church members outnumbered Communist party members about ten to one.

Now we're seeing the grass-roots movements flourish. Cell-based churches are exploding in many European areas. A phenomenal rise in united prayer has sustained a conviction for evangelism and ignited a veritable conflagration of new Christian movements.

Missions to Europe and Eurasia

During the years that Christianity was pummeled in Eastern Europe and the Soviet Union by political disapproval and ideological warfare, the Church trimmed down and discovered a new inner strength. Restrictions limited outside missions to occasional preaching tours, Bible-smuggling, radio programs and a few quiet missionaries. But from within, renewal and revival generated movements of witness and mission. In fact, startling as it may seem, even before the collapse of communism, there were more devout believers behind the Iron Curtain than in Western Europe!

Western Europe has long been the focus of a growing influx of missionaries from the English-speaking West. Focused largely on converting nominal Christians to active faith in Jesus Christ, these missionaries have peppered Europe with Bible institutes, seminaries, conferences and evangelistic crusades. The dissolution of the USSR has released these energies to be extended eastward. Now the vast ethnic diversity of the former USSR and the dozens of autonomous ethnically-diverse republics within the Russian Federation are open for evangelization. Take for example Romania, where the showing of the Jesus film is widespread—a majority of the population has now seen it. The simpler, more lithe and reproducible church structures are multiplying among specific peoples in previously sealed Albania and Bulgaria.

However, the non-European guest workers such as the Turks in West Germany are only being marginally evangelized. Where evangelism is occurring, it is often being done by "diaspora" missionaries. Hundreds of Korean missionaries have followed the Korean influx to Europe. Filipino, Chinese and Indian pastors are working in Europe among their own kinsmen. But there remain large groups of unreached peoples, e.g., making up Europe's millions of Muslims.

Missions from Europe and Eurasia

While only one in five of the current Protestant mission force in the world comes from greater Europe, the percentage may increase greatly in view of the dramatic changes throughout Europe.

An examination of the work of some of the older European overseas missions, as in America, reveals a pattern of success-stagnation: a great deal of effort is concentrated on strengthening the existing churches that have resulted from past evangelism, not on reaching the large blocs of unreached peoples. And, many of the missions from other traditions are found largely in diaspora situations (Russian Orthodox missionaries have largely followed settlements of Russians).

The picture is nevertheless a bright one. Europe's churches must cope with massive numbers of nominal Christians, but where the church is being reborn there are now no restrictions holding back any surge of new missions. The marvelous "AD 2000 Movement" has gone around the world galvanizing national forces to reach out to the unreached peoples within their own sphere. This movement has, with great vision, included the incredible spiritual resources of the many new Eastern European countries, so long held back by atheistic totalitarian forces.

Latin America—No Longer Slow To Accept the Challenge of Missions

Five miles of pews (or benches) in a single church building! Does that seem too many for the church you attend? Yet this was only the first shipment of wooden benches for the auditorium rising in Sao Paulo, Brazil. If ultimately they were in fact to seat 25,000 in that auditorium, my calculations showed that they would need about two more miles of pews. Churches are multiplying in almost every country of Latin America in phenomenal ways. On just one street in Guatemala, within five kilometers of each other there are four churches with more than 5,000 members each. In Bogota, Columbia there are ten churches with more than 2,000 members, some with many more. One church in El Salvador hires four entire bus companies every Sunday just to transport people to church. There are more new churches (about 3,000) in Brazil each year than in any other country in the world.

The evangelical movement is virile, valiant and growing many places between two and three times the general population growth rate. But it hasn't always been this way. At the beginning of the 20th Century, there were only a small handful of life-giving Bible-reading churches. With the traditional Protestant denominations giving the gospel a new start, the real explosion didn't take place until the 1940's with Pentecostal movements touching masses of poor people.

> There may be more practicing Christians in Latin America than in North America.

A generation later, the neo-Pentecostal movement flourished, centering on huge mega-churches, reaching the middle and upper classes. When this author (Ralph Winter) left Latin America in 1967, Guatemala was 5% evangelical. Now it is more like 30%. There may be more practicing Christians in Latin America than in North America. Conservative estimates indicate that there are 72 million people in Latin America who declare themselves to be evangelical Christians.

Missions from Latin America

Luis Bush, born in Argentina, stepped up to a podium in 1987 to address hundreds of leaders from almost every area of Latin America. Bush declared that "Latin America is no longer a mission field; but instead is a missionary force." The setting was one of the most significant gatherings in the history of Latin America. It was COMIBAM (Iberio-American Missionary Cooperation) in Sao Paulo, Brazil. That gathering spawned a virile ongoing movement. COMIBAM has become an international mission movement with networking churches and mission organizations in 25 Latin American countries. Latin Americans are discovering that they are as able as anyone else to organize mission societies! Indeed, in the inevitable logic of mission strategy on a global level, Latin America is now rapidly transforming itself into a major mission base to reach Asia's millions—Muslims, Hindus and Chinese. Asia is where most of the non-Christians of today's world are.

In the 10 years since COMIBAM was launched, Latin Americans have founded 400 new mission agencies and sent out more than 4,000 new missionaries for trans-cultural mission on five continents. That's a huge escalation in mission obedience in one decade, but they aren't content. One COMIBAM leader challenged his comrades at COMIBAM '97, "If the Korean churches with only 12 million Christians could send out 5,000 missionaries, then we, with far more than 60 million Evangelical Christians, should have sent out more than 20,000!"

Latins have been particularly captured by the vision of evangelizing peoples within the 10/40 Window. Latins feel especially close to the Muslims of the world because Spain was occupied by Muslims for seven centuries and tens of thousands of Spanish words are derived from Arabic. Let's take a closer look at the Muslims.

"Muslims for Jesus" Strategy Explored

Imagine you're a geographer living in a world where continents move several miles a year. Earthquakes weekly thrust up new islands or level mountain ranges. Lakes vanish over-night, their waters gulped by thirsty cracks in the earth. What headaches in trying to draw a map! Every year the atlases and textbooks would have to be rewritten and relearned. A place known to be located at one point this year would have to be repositioned next year because of how much it had moved.

Such is the Muslim world. Not just because of the Gulf War. That brief war merely gives us a clue to what has massively modified the dynamics of the entire Middle East: oil. Titanic changes are affecting everything we thought we once knew about Islam's nearly one billion people. It is no longer the world Samuel Zwemer tried to reach with the good news. What used to be major features of its land-scape are being transformed overnight. New maps must be drawn if the Christian is to dis-cover passable highways to use in carrying the gospel to responsive Muslim peoples.

Muslims are on the move. While there are 42 countries with Muslim majorities, 40 other countries contain significant minorities. Petro-migration is thrusting Muslims out of tradi-tional isolation. Six million reside in Western Europe. The USA boasts a dozen cities with more than 50,000 Muslims (and more than 70 Muslim sects competing for allegiance)! $15 million was spent on a mosque in Chicago. Yet the largest populations of Muslims are not found in oil-rich countries or the West but in Indonesia, Pakistan, Bangladesh, India, the People's Republic of China and Turkey.

More Christians are flooding into the heartlands of Islam around Mecca than ever before. Professionals, technicians, skilled la-borers are being imported from dozens of countries to modernize sheikdoms and help the deserts bloom. 50,000 Arab Christians are employed in Saudi Arabia. 13,000 foreign Christians work in Qatar. Foreigners outnum-ber the citizens in the United Arab Emirates (240,000 to 225,000) and no one has counted how many Christians there are among these Western technicians. Modernization is revolu-tionizing the atmosphere and opportunity for Christian-Muslim relationships.

There is a creeping optimism emerging in Christian circles. The long glacial age that be-gan with the Christian Crusades in the Middle Ages appears to be thawing as traditionally icy attitudes towards Christianity seem to be melting. Not that there aren't places where Muslim conversion is met with death or where there are purgatories of hatred such as Lebanon with Christian and Muslim strug-gling in a death grip. But there are signs of new receptivity to the gospel. Promising de-velopments are appearing on the horizon:

1. The Ancient Christian Churches in Mus-lim lands (17 million members in the Middle East and Northern Africa) are be-ing shown that they can break out of their ethnic and cultural defensiveness and win Muslims to Jesus. The Orthodox Egyptian Coptic Church has been under-going a steady, massive revival for the past 30 years and now it is resulting in 30 to 40 baptisms of Muslim converts a week. But this is still the exception rather than the rule. Centuries of turmoil and battering have made the ancient churches generally ingrown enclaves whose cultural difference from the Is-lamic community is so great that it is al-most impossible for a Muslim convert to join them without betraying his own cul-tural heritage or without remaining a "foreigner" to the Christian community with centuries of cultural divergence.

2. Cross-cultural ministry is finding explo-sive response where greater cultural sen-sitivity is being used in evangelistic ap-proaches. The enrollment in one non-Arab country correspondence course added 3900 Muslims in the first six months. A high percentage continued on to comple-tion and advanced courses. Significant numbers evidenced new-found faith in letters and testimonies. Yet the Church is barely exploiting the tremendous oppor-tunity of the Muslim world. There are about 500 North American Protestant mis-sionaries engaged in Muslim evangeliza-tion, a bare 1% of the missionary force for 25% of the world's unreached population.

3. Secret believers and Christian sympa-thizers have multiplied. Muslim follow-ers of Jesus still hesitate to take any step such as public baptism since it would send all kinds of wrong signals to their own people. Islam has formidable social and economic barriers for anyone leav-

ing its fold. Apostasy is the supreme betrayal. Yet there are thousands, perhaps millions, secretly believing in Jesus who long for some new, creative form of Christian movement that would not appear to be treason to their own people and blasphemy to God.

4. New strategies are being explored to see if a "Muslims for Jesus" movement could not be a viable reality in a manner similar to the "Jews for Jesus" movement. Just as the apostle Paul suggested that he be a Greek to the Greeks and a Jew to the Jews, so such principles might suggest being a Muslim to the Muslims. Some evangelical evangelists to Islam are saying that Muslims might truly become believers in Jesus Christ as Savior and Lord without calling themselves Christian, even as the "Messianic Jews" did. In some situations what may be needed is the encouragement of new Christian congregations with a Muslim cultural orientation, churches centered on Jesus Christ but with Islamic cultural forms, where, in fact, the word "Christian" is not even employed.

5. The old malaise and paralysis characteristic of Christian attitudes toward Muslim evangelization seems to be vanishing. Quiet conferences and consultations are forging new concepts and organizations. Hundreds of turned-on mission candidates ought to reconsider the enormous gap between the opportunity and the actual staffing of culturally sensitive approaches to Muslims. The believing followers of Christ are now at the very edge of what could be the most significant advance in reaching unreached Muslims in history—especially if we don't think we have to make them into "Christians" any more than Paul felt he had to make Greeks into Jews. In several places around the world there are movements running into the thousands which consist of blood-washed followers of Christ, whose Qur'an is now the Christian Bible, but who do not refer to themselves as Christians.

6. Some scholars feel that illuminating parallels can be drawn between the major cultural streams flowing out of the incarnation, death and resurrection of Jesus Christ: Islam being an Arabic movement, but then there are the cultural synergies of Russian Orthodoxy, Greek Orthodoxy, Ethiopian Orthodoxy, Eastern-Rite Roman Catholicism, Latin-Rite Roman Catholicism, German Lutheranism, English Anglicanism, and the variety of American sects. As well thousands of even more strange cultural traditions have evolved among the mission field believers of the world.

In each case, the gospel has put on "native" dress. The pre-Christian English sunrise service honoring the spring goddess of fertility, named Eostre, is now our Easter service (which benefits us only if we keep our minds and hearts on the biblical meaning assigned to it).

The pagan Roman practice of giving and receiving gifts on the 25th of December caught on in Latin-speaking countries but not in the Greek and Russian speaking countries, understandably. But the Christian adaptation of this pagan holiday, although celebrated on the same day of the year, does not say anything about the meaning of Saturn, after which this day in the Roman pagan calendar was named (the Saturnalia).

The Assyrian Church of the East (hundreds of thousands of these Christians live in Iraq) had an interesting custom of praying 7 times a day. Muhammed borrowed this custom for Islam, but he cut it down to 5 times a day so as to avoid awaking believers in the dead of night.

Even the Christian Syriac and Arabic word, "Allah," which Christians had been using for "God" for centuries was adopted by Muhammed for Islam. It is still the word for God in the Christian Bibles in those languages.

Bethlehem's Star Over China

The attics of Western memory are stuffed with an incredible array of pictures of China: weather-beaten junks, pagodas with upturned eaves on mist-enshrouded mounts, Dr. Fu Manchu, firecrackers and gaudy dragons, Kung Fu, Stillwell and Chiang Kai Shek, missionary graves, hordes of fanatics waving little Red Books. China has been one of the great obsessions of the West.

And well she might be! The major tides of history indicate that a major wave of the future may be from China. Across the centuries she has been weak only to have the tide of affairs reverse and carry her back to preeminence as the most advanced, powerful, albeit isolated nation on the face of the earth, a position she has held more often and longer than any other society. Christianity will have to sail that tide if she is to be part of China's future.

> Despite the increased repression following the Tienanmen Square incident, there is nothing so sure, so extensive, so durable, as Christianity in China.

The Church contemplates her more than a billion citizens as the largest single unified bloc of humanity, one which has a very widespread Christian element. At the height of missionary activity in Mainland China, nearly 10,000 Catholic and Protestant missionaries were active. When the Communists took over in 1949, one tangible result of a century and a half of effort was a formal Christian community of 3.2 million Catholics and 1.8 million Protestants, a bare one percent of the whole of China.

The Christian movement under the People's Republic has experienced a radical change and some shrinkage due to the loss of nominal members, some martyrdom, and minor migration. The pressures of successive waves of repression interspersed with brief periods of toleration for many years robbed the church of its more visible organized expressions. "Institutionless" Christianity is what began expanding at an astounding rate. The Communists tried to rid China once and for all of Christians during the dreaded ten-year "Cultural Revolution," but only succeeded in refining and spreading the faith. Due to many factors, the government began to allow certain buildings to reopen as "official" churches where the government could monitor events. Initially, 100 were allowed. They were immediately but unexpectedly packed. Then, a few more, and more, and soon it was over 12,000 "official" churches. No one can hazard a guess at the church's real size, though some have estimated that there may be more than 80 million believers, and more than 20,000 "house" churches. The latter are without full-time clergy, denominational structure, church buildings, budgets, or seminaries. Their meetings are informal and semi-clandestine. Their theologies represent wide diversity, perhaps wild diversity.

Some have held out hope that this scattered church under pressure will repeat the story of the early church, gradually leavening the whole of China. And the church is experi-

encing some growth through healings and exorcism, moving along the lattice work of family relationships with which a Chinese screens himself in a hostile world.

Restrictions continue to be stringent so that open proclamation in late 1998 was forbidden. Millions of Christians go in and out of China each year but not openly as evangelists or Christian witnesses.

Radio waves do reach behind the bamboo curtain. Government presses actually print Bibles—perhaps due to outside pressures and the sheer economic profit from the world's most sought after book. There are reports of greater Christian freedom and activity in South East China and conversions in areas such as Northern Thailand where crossing the border is possible. Despite the increased repression following the Tienanmen Square incident, there is nothing so sure, so extensive, so durable, as Christianity in China.

Outside mainland China the picture is even more hopeful. Overall, five to seven percent of some 40 million profess faith in Christ. Of course there are striking variations. In some cases there is burgeoning growth. Six hundred churches serve the one of eight people in Hong Kong who follow Christ. About 10 percent of the 1.7 million Chinese in the USA are Protestant or Catholic. In other instances the Christian presence has only begun to penetrate Chinese populations. Thailand's 7.3 million Chinese have only a tiny church among them with only 10,000 Protestants. Restaurant workers in Europe, such as those in the 50 Chinese restaurants of Vienna, are virtually without a Christian fellowship.

More importantly, there are indications that the Chinese church is taking major strides as a maturing body. Rapid and soaring increases are reported in many of the 70 countries with significant Chinese minorities. With that growth has come a new awareness of world mission. From Chinese churches and sending agencies there are now over 700 Chinese missionaries throughout the world. The majority of them, however, are not in cross-cultural ministry but are serving Chinese churches.

It may well be that this new movement of God's Spirit will equip the Christians of the diaspora for an as yet unforeseen opportunity to reach into mainland China sometime in near the future, but it may also be that when that day comes, as in the case of the opening of the USSR, it will be a two-way street as the believers whose faith has endured hardship become a blessing to those outside of their former prisons.

If the door to China were to open next year, what would happen? Many American-born Chinese Christians no longer speak any Chinese dialects. To evangelize in traditional fashion would require a relearning of their roots, their languages and cultures. English-speaking Chinese would be in real demand to again enter their homeland and through language teaching be ambassadors for Christ. Other parts of the Chinese diaspora are similar. Seventy percent of Indonesia's 3.6 million Chinese are Indonesian born. They speak Indonesian and live like Indonesians.

It is clear that China now contains one of the world's largest numbers of devout, praying Christians. Probably no people group, unreached or not, is very far removed, culturally, from another Chinese group within which the Gospel is now strong.

Any Hope, India?

Remember "Wrong Way Corrigan?" He took off in a small plane from the New York airport and flew across the Atlantic in the repetition of Lindbergh's feat. He had filed a legal flight pattern to some nearby spot in the U.S. and then calmly flew across the Atlantic, pretending he had gone the wrong way. "They let Lindbergh do it. Why not me?"

God played a trick akin to that with William Carey, that brilliant young rural schoolteacher in England in the late 1700's. Carey had plotted and planned for years to go to those islands in the Pacific newly discovered by Captain Cook. (Those islands today are 75% Christian in at least nominal church membership.) He landed instead in India which is still 97% non-Christian. God had the best idea because East India is the closest thing to a crossroads of the world's great blocs of non-Christians—Chinese, Hindus and Muslims. Caste Hindus alone make up over 600 million in 1998, and are mainly in India, that amazing country.

Why is India so amazing? Although smaller in size than Argentina, it has 25 times the population (more than the whole world in the days of Columbus). Furthermore, it has 1,652 distinct languages and dialects, and the world's largest democracy. It is the largest non-Christian country that is at all open to the gospel.

India is also amazing in that it even exists as a functioning nation. When the British were forced out in 1947, and literally millions were killed in the bloodshed that later separated Pakistan from a reduced India, many despaired that India could ever pull itself together and survive. Yet today India is in many ways doing magnificently. With a literacy rate of 52%, 15% functionally literate, it nevertheless has fifty times as many radios as it did at independence and for many years has boasted of the world's largest motion picture industry. Today it out numbers all other countries in its computer software industry.

What staggers the imagination is the human diversity of India. Most countries are stratified with layers of people ranging from the downtrodden to the aristocracy. But India is not merely vertically stratified by the world's most rigidly defined social system, it is also horizontally cut up due to the linguistic and racial differences that chop India into at least a thousand pieces. Nowhere in the world are cultural differences more difficult to ignore. The most astonishing thing of all is that the Christian church of India has valiantly tried to ignore those distinctions. The church lives outside the caste system but almost entirely on the bottom level of society. Therefore, most Indians who join a Christian church must virtually part ways, downward from all their social and family relationships. Instead of determinedly taking the gospel into the thousands of social compartments of India, the prevailing strategy, insofar as there is one, at the grass roots level is to tear down the social fabric, not just the prejudices embodied therein.

Thus the Church of South India braved all prejudices by sending a lower class

Photo courtesy of Caleb Project

bishop to an upper class segment of their church in Kerala, thereby tweaking the nose of the caste system in India. This is all right for a bishop at his level, but the practical requirements of evangelism at the grass roots level of local churches are something else. This is a very delicate subject since at first glance there seems to be a collision between the demands of Christian unity and the freedoms of Christian liberty.

But do Hindus want to become Christians, if they are not forced to join a different caste? Some estimates indicate that about 100 million Hindus—people who have been in contact with Christians of other castes for many years—would become followers of Christ tomorrow if the number of Bible-believing fellowships made up of their own people were to expand significantly without calling themselves "Christians." This growing sphere, some reports suggest, may already include more than 30 million devout peole.

What, pray tell, are missionaries and Indian Christians doing if they are not trying to penetrate one by one the thousands of subcultures of India? The answer is, they are doing other things. Aren't they evangelizing at all? Wouldn't it be great if the twenty-five million Christians in India would get out there and really evangelize?

Yes, certainly, but two-thirds of the Christians in India need themselves to be evangelized, just as is true in North America today. The real shocker is that according to one study 98% of the evangelism in India is devoted to re-winning nominal Christians rather than to penetrating the frontiers that effectively wall off 750 million people.

One of the great marvels of history is the impact of missions on the course of India. While less than 3% of the population is Christian, over half of all the nurses are Christian (it was once 90%); 600 hospitals are there because of missions; and thousands of schools of all kinds. Hinduism itself has significantly changed. The subtle impact of the missionary movement is a story that may never fully be told. Missionaries introduced not just hospitals and schools, but invented khaki colored clothing (it wouldn't show the village dust) and a special and superior kind of tile roofing used now all over India. They brought an end to the custom of widow burning. And the fact that many states of India even today prohibit all liquor is mute testimony of an impact far larger than church statistics. In South India, where most of the Christians are to be found, their presence is felt strongly. In the states of northeast India where 50 to 70 to 95% of the population of the mountain peoples are Christians, the transformation is even more spectacular— from being headhunters as late as 1934, now to being devout Christians, some with Ph.D's. The stories behind all of these achievements almost defy comparison for sheer excitement.

For many years it was rare when mission agencies sprouted from Indian soil itself. Now there is the India Mission Association which includes over 70 different mission agencies and 12,000 missionaries, although many others also exist to make India the leading country for "Third World" mission societies.

The Indian Missionary Society followed by the National Missionary Society and then the Indian Evangelical Mission and the Friends Missionary Prayer Band (in 1903, 1905, 1965, 1968, respectively) were early examples of the simple fact that Indians who believe the gospel are willing and able to do both home and foreign mission work. Three of these four early societies determinedly refuse to accept any foreign funds (one was offered a million dollars of foreign money), feeling that the development of sacrificial outreach among their people is as important as the outreach itself. India's strict rules against sending currency out of the country may require collaboration with other countries in order for some opportunities to be grasped. But the Friends Missionary Prayer Band sends its missionaries from south India to north India where there are very few Christians. Indeed north India contains by far the largest bloc of reachable non-Christians. Pioneer missionary techniques are by no means out of date where the world's largest presently reachable mission field is still to be found.

Tribes: An Endangered Species

The race is on! Tribes are vanishing faster than we are succeeding in translating Scripture into their languages. Technology is leveling the tropics, immobilizing the nomads, dispossessing the weak, deculturizing the alien, and decimating the primitive. Tribes fall prey to epidemics, economic exploitation, modern weaponry and nationalism. In Brazil alone, an Indian population of at least 3 million in 1500 A.D. at the first European contact was reduced to 200,000 by 1968 and to 80,000 since then.

Yet, in many areas of the world the strongest, most aggressive churches are found among tribal peoples. At present, even excluding Africa, thanks in part to the world's largest mission, the Wycliffe Bible Translators, there are at least 10,000 Protestant missionaries who focus on tribal peoples.

It is virtually impossible to generalize about over 3,000 cultural groups ranging from several million people to minuscule groups of a few dozen individuals. Living in every imaginable habitat, following a mind-boggling array of different customs and expe-

riencing radically different fates, tribal groups vividly express the range and complexity of the unfinished task. But there are several patterns that are apparent from a broad, sweeping overview.

> Missionaries have been in the forefront of those resisting making tribal peoples into jungle slum dwellers. Where whole tribes have become Christian, economic and educational uplift has been enormous.

Receptivity

In general, tribal groups are refugees, living in perpetual fear of aggression from other tribes or more powerful civilizations. Often they are able to survive by finding out how to live where no one else would want the land, in incredibly mountainous areas as in West Cameroon, or South China, or Northeast India, or the precipitous highlands (or gigantic swamps of the coastlands) of the great island of New Guinea, the tiny atolls of the South Pacific, or the swamps and jungles of the upper Amazon.

This is one reason they have been the most highly responsive peoples to modern missions, more so than the more secure peasant peoples which constitute the great world religions of Islam, Buddhism, Hinduism and Confucianism.

Also, tribal peoples, characterized by beliefs called "animism" (each group having its own distinctive religious system and worldview) have found conversion to Jesus Christ and His book easier than those who already have their own religious book and literary tradition. Tremendous successes can be illustrated in Oceania, where 70 to 90 percent are Christian; Burma, where 97 percent of all Burmese Christians are tribal; and northeast India, where among the tribal peoples the Nagas are now 70 percent Christian, the Garos and Khasis, 50 percent, and the Mizos, virtually 99 percent! Though the tribal population is only seven percent of India, it represents 15 percent of all Christians in India.

But it must be admitted that within certain types of tribal peoples the Church has made little impact. Nomadic peoples have almost never been reached until and unless they became settled. Hunters and gatherers, like the Pygmies of Africa, and the pastoral peoples who exploit the enormous arid belt running from Morocco to Manchuria, still are solidly outside the faith. Bedouins, shepherds, reindeer and cattle herders await a new creative strategy to give the gospel mobility and vitality for them.

In North America, there were no forests dense enough or deserts forbidding enough to protect the indigenous peoples from the invading hordes who claimed "manifest destiny" to their ancestral lands. Some native peoples fought back, some fled for refuge, others like the Cherokee accepted the white man's faith and culture, only to be driven out of their towns and schools to desolate "Indian Territories" like Oklahoma. Today, there are still 266 Native American tribes recognized in North America. Nearly 200 of these are considered "unreached." Of those that have established churches, few can be considered truly indigenous because of cultural imperialism, patronizing approaches, and institutionalized dependencies that have accompanied the compassionate hearts of

missionaries who have served them. Healing the wounds of the past will require humility and the reconciliation that can only come as we are united in Christ as equals.

Some have observed that Native Americans are more receptive to Asians and other non-whites who bring the gospel, particularly those who understand the animist worldview. This is consistant with the historic fact that many peoples are often most resistant to messengers from those whose proximity to them in geography and history has provoked a longstanding animosity. God is a global God. Can we doubt that He will fail to send laborers to America's tribes from other continents and cultures?

Privilege

Of course we are not advocating any lessening of commitment to tribal peoples. But who knows what the impact might be and how the numbers of churches might multiply if those other parts of God's vineyard were to receive equal attention and care?

Change

It is impossible to keep tribal peoples isolated and "safe" from modern society. For good and mostly for bad, the tribal groups are being transformed. Where the faith in Jesus Christ has been potent, it has eased the impact of the modern world. Missionaries have been among the most ardent defenders of the rights and dignity of the tribals. Their voices have been heard against multi-national corporations land seizures, local hostilities, and governmental neglect. Missionaries have been in the forefront of those resisting making tribal peoples into jungle slum dwellers. Where whole tribes have become Christian, economic and educational uplift has been enormous. But new problems of survival and finding a place in the modern world system put even greater demands on mission agencies.

Opportunity

Evangelization remains a basic task in many areas. India's 14 million tribals, concentrated in the north central hills, need to be evangelized. Indian Christians in the south and the tribal Christians of the northeast are beginning the task, just as Navajo Christians are sending missionaries to the Laplanders and to Mongolia (where, in the latter case, the people have a number of similar customs!). Reconversion is needed in regions where second and third generation "Christians" are growing up with no vital experience with Christ or where tribes have left their first love for a syncretistic revival of traditional religion. Economic and educational developments cry out with enormous needs, which evangelical missions are now more responsibly meeting.

850 Million Other Asians: Latent or Blooming?

We have already glanced at huge blocs of unreached Chinese, Hindus, and Muslims, most of them in Asia. Beyond them are some 850 million other Asians—most of whom are influenced by Buddhism, but who live in a variety of situations. Let's take five different looks at Asia:

1. "Christianized" Asia. There are those who live in "Christianized" areas such as the Philippines and Oceania. Overall, 80-95% of these regions would nominally claim to be Christians.

    Here the dominant problem is the need to convert "Christians" to Christ. That is quite a different matter from converting peoples with no professed allegiance or knowledge to the Savior. Missionaries tackle the situation in large numbers; although the population of the Christianized areas make up only 15% of the 850 million people, fully 50% of the Protestant missionaries in these countries are seeking to making active believers out of nominal Christians.

2. Dynamic Christian Asia. There are those who live in areas where vigorous, dynamic Christian movements are thriving. This brings us to the first law of these peoples: Where Buddhism has prevailed, the gospel has languished. Dynamic Christian movements are found largely in tribal animists such as the 3 million Karen of Burma and Thailand or among large ethnic groups such as the Koreans where Buddhism is weak. But Korea shows that Buddhists

can grasp the significance of Jesus. About one out of four people in South Korea are Christians. It is said that when the border to North Korea opens, there will be a million "evangelists" flowing northward to share their joy in Christ as at least that many split-up families attempt to reunite. With Billy Graham's visit the beginning of the end of the hermit kingdom of the North draws closer, and sits astride a peninsula with the strongest concentration of active Christians anywhere in Asia. One of the greatest explosions of the gospel is in Nepal. The United Mission to Nepal (dozens of missions and hundreds of missionaries) had done medical, educational and agricultural work for years under a government agreement prohibiting overt evangelization. By 1960, there may have been only a few hundred believers. By late 1998, there were well over 75,000. Stalwart Nepalese leaders are enacting nationwide plans to bring the gospel to every region and people in their country.

3. Christian Minorities—Sizable but Paralyzed. There are those who live in areas with sizable Christian minorities that are currently static or stymied. These are the Roman Catholic showplaces of Sri Lanka (Catholics outnumbered Protestants 7 to 1) and Vietnam (where the ratio is 11 to 1) with nearly 10% of the populace in each country professing some form of Christianity. Sri Lanka sees itself as the haven of "pure" Buddhism. Missions from the outside are limited. The Church is ineffective in reaching the Sinhala Buddhist majority and grows only out of biological necessity. Revival is the only hope at present. Vietnam's evangelical Church was experiencing significant growth especially among the tribal peoples, when the war ended. Little reliable information is known but the few indications coming out of Vietnam reveal the Church is continuing even though activities are greatly restricted. Vietnam's 6 million Catholics are a large and influential group but their numbers are not growing substantially by conversion.

4. Christian Minorities—Small but Stalled. There are those who live in areas where a tiny church is well established, the gospel is regularly proclaimed, but the growth of the Christian movement is negligible. Burma exhibits such a pattern. Three percent profess Christ, but the majority of them are not the ethnic Burmese but tribal animists who have come into the Church in large movements. They are of a different culture and social order than the Burmese Buddhists who will not be easily or readily evangelized by them. Japan is a unique case. The Western Church has sent large numbers of missionaries. Prominent and influential Japanese have followed Christ resulting in major cultural impact upon Japanese life. A government survey indicates Jesus Christ is the most admired religious leader in Japan. Yet a tiny percent of Japan's people is willing to identify with the well established but slow growing church. The one exception is among Japanese who have migrated to other countries. Sixty percent of Brazil's nearly one million Japanese now profess Christ as Roman Catholics. An additional 3% (7,000) attend 80 evangelical congregations.

5. Precarious Beginnings. There are areas and peoples where the Church is at best precarious and where evangelization is either restricted or neglected. The tiny countries of Bhutan and Sikkim perched on the Himalayas have few known Christians. There are only handfuls of small struggling churches along the southern border of Bhutan. Cambodia's tiny church of 5,000 Protestants was exploding with growth when the country fell to the Khmer Rouge. There have been encouraging signs since then, but the struggle goes on. Laos had a much larger missionary presence and church before it too closed to the West. But it was largely a tribal church, and many members fled to Thailand. Mongolia, on the edge of China, was once in this category. It had long been one of the few countries on earth where there was no known church as late as 1990. But by late 1998, it is an almost totally new picture. Thousands of new believers can be found in scores of growing churches.

Phenomenal advances in once gospel-poor regions should move the Church to her knees in hope and in prayer that the Lord of the universe will show his love to these long restricted areas.

God's African Story Filled With Harvest

Someday there will be more Christians in Africa than on any other continent in the world! Africa's missionary story in this century is filled with astounding miracles and sacrifices. Kenya in 1900 had less than 2,000 Christians; today there are more than 25 million. If we could somehow whisk into the present the two Protestant missionaries who opened up the Democratic Republic of the Congo (formerly Zaire) in 1880, they would hardly comprehend that by 1999 nearly 96 percent of the citizens identified with Christian traditions!

Some would call this rapid growth alarming because the Church has hardly been able to keep pace in teaching and caring for those coming to Christ. But that is only part of the picture.

If we were to conceive of Sub-Sahara Africa as a village with a population of 1000, the religious make-up would show 267 Muslims, living in the north. The Christians would claim 573, with 213 Roman Catholics and 360 Protestants, Orthodox, Anglicans and Independents. Not all of them would practice their faith. Many would not be evangelical. Many would still practice elements of traditional African religions.

But they would represent an enormous pool of favorable response to Jesus Christ, and they would have some of the most dynamic revival forces to be found in Christendom. The remainder of the village would be 154 residents who maintain their involvement in traditional African religions.

At first glance it might seem that Muslims and Christians compete in a close race for followers with the Muslims forging ahead.

Oil money is establishing Muslim universities in Black Africa, and in some Muslim places, such as Sudan and Uganda, the Christians have been harried and killed. Even so, since 1950 Islam has made few solid advances below the imaginary "Muslim line," 100 miles south of the Sahara. The Church is growing more rapidly than Islam in most parts of Black Africa where the large group of unevangelized tribes remain.

The law of sowing and reaping has worked well here. The Western church has sent enormous amounts of personnel and money. Schools and hospitals are to be found in all parts of Africa because Christians have cared. The top political and business elite in country after country received training from missionary schools. There are literally hundreds of Bible schools and seminaries. Over 580 languages have the Bible or portions of scriptures.

Even in 1998, the high level of concern of the Western church can be symbolized by the fact that Africa with 10 percent of the world's population contains nearly 23 percent of the Western missionaries. The relatively lavish involvement of the Church with Africa (though even here it has been small in face of need) has resulted in a large harvest.

Does this mean there is no need for missionaries in Africa? Some of the African church leaders have been calling for a halt to foreign church money and missionaries. This would give the growing churches of Africa time to develop their own strength and initiative. But there are over 40 million people speaking some 1200 languages that are still without any portion of scripture in their language. Researchers indicate that there are over 1,000 tribal peoples that still remain largely unevangelized. These neglected groups will only be reached when some agency, national or foreign catches a vision.

It would be difficult to catalog the hundreds of missionaries who proclaim the various gospels of some 6,000 African independent churches which have split off from mission churches to develop a more African form of Christianity. These African Initiated Churches (AICs) include more than 32 million people! Many of these AICs are heretical, but rather than reject them, any opportunity to assist their leaders in understanding the scriptures could lead many toward biblical orthodoxy.

A number of crucial tasks remain before the Church. Millions are streaming into

Africa's crowded cities. The churches have a great responsibility to shepherd the Christians who seek a better life there. In Nairobi, Kenya, 80% claim to be "Christian", but only 12% are actually involved in a local fellowship. Most were reared in rural areas, became Christians in mission schools and then were baptized. Now they drift toward secularism and nominalism. Who will care for their future?

There are titanic transformations taking place all over Africa. Much of the potential of post-colonial Africa has been squandered by decades of tyrants, coupes, and devastating civil and guerrilla wars. Nation building is barely keeping pace with tyranny. In country after country, like a bomb with a delayed-action fuse, events have led to gruesome civil wars and destabilized governments.

Africa provides only two percent of the world's production and faces tremendous problems in economic and social development. Western mission agencies and churches are heavily involved in fostering this transformation. Christianity itself is undergoing Africanization. New worship forms, new approaches to polygamy, new theologies are all being developed in a serious attempt to incorporate Christianity in less Western garb. Africa may be the next Christian continent but there will be hardly anything drab or staid about it.

Study Questions

1. What opportunities for and which obstacles to missions advancement are apparent from each of the areas surveyed in this article?

2. What is the dominant impression left by these articles? guarded optimism? caution? skepticism? enthusiasm?

Are We Ready for Tomorrow's Kingdom?

Ralph D. Winter

A Jewish rabbi in Los Angeles has thrown down the gauntlet to wayward Westernized Jews. He claims that his own Orthodoxy is the only genuine form of the Jewish faith. Conservative and Reformed Jewish congregations have gone the way of "Christianity"!

The idea is that the true faith can only be contained in a certain, specific true culture, the original culture.

Holding on to a "true culture" is not very likely to succeed if only because we can look around and see that Jewish Orthodoxy is a very small piece of the global pie, even of all those who think they are holding on to the true Biblical faith, and even among those who specifically hold on to a Jewish culture of some sort.

OK, so the Roman socialites threw rice at a wedding. Do Jews who live in Rome have to do that? So the Romans had a big party, giving gifts to each other on December 25th. Should Jews take up the practice? Well, not even Greek Christians took up the 25th of December. To this day they are not impressed by what was in Jesus' day the Roman pagan holiday for Saturn—the "Saturnalia."

More ironic still is the plain fact that much of Jewish Orthodoxy today consists of large and small additions over the centuries since the Christians grabbed the faith and ran with it, certainly long after the sacred days of Hebrew culture. And, when was that? In King David's day, in Moses' day, in Abraham's day? Wow! Not even the Jewish Bible portrays a single cultural way of life.

It would seem that God has determinedly been kicking people out of one culture into a new one (Abraham to Canaan, to Egypt, to the dispersion of the Northern tribes, to the booting out of the Judean tribes, on and on). What is going on? It looks as if God wants them to learn how to carry their faith into different cultures, not just preserve a given way of life within a discordant culture. The Bible, as a whole, would seem to sit in judgment upon every human cultural tradition, no matter whether it is Abrahamic, Mosaic, Davidian, first century Jewish, Paul's mixture with Greek elements, Roman-Latin, Germanic, Anglo-Saxon, or you name it.

Now then, is "God's culture" fixed as an evangelical American pop culture with its CDs, DVDs, television, horrifying divorce rate, childcare centers, etc?

Quite honestly, are our missionaries—any of them—now assuming that the ultimate achievement of the

After serving ten years as a missionary among Mayan Indians in the highlands of Guatemala, Ralph D. Winter was called to be a Professor of Missions at the School of World Mission at Fuller Theological Seminary. Ten years later he and his wife, Roberta, founded a mission society called the Frontier Mission Fellowship (FMF) in Pasadena, California. This in turn spawned the U.S. Center for World Mission and the William Carey International University, both of which serve other missions working at the frontiers of mission. He is the General Director of the Frontier Mission Fellowship. See expanded biographical sketch at the end of the book.

Biblical faith is what we have today in evangelical Christianity?

If not, when are we going to seriously contemplate the future form of what we call the Christian faith?

OK, forget the turgid theologies of contextualization. Take a look for just one second at the actual global record. It is not too early to recognize that the largest growing edge of Biblical faith is not Jewish Orthodoxy, not Roman Catholicism, not Eastern Orthodoxy, not German Lutheranism, not Anglicanism, not American "mainline" denominationalism, not Evangelicalism, not Pentecostalism, not the Charismatic renewal, etc.

What is it? It is the often ignored but vast company of those "outside and beyond" what we usually call Christianity. In Africa it is the 32 million "African Initiated Churches." In India it is a phenomenon perhaps the same size which is arising within the 600 million caste sphere, where "Christianity" by that name is virtually absent. In China it is the "house church" movement which, up to this point, we in the West like to call Christian, but at closer look might not fit very well at all.

The fact is that anything Western has its attractions and detractions, and while most cities of the world are superficially Westernized, Western Christianity has really only successfully lapped up minorities around the world, peoples who had nothing to lose by opting for an outside, foreign culture as against an oppressive majority culture. This is most obvious in India. It is perhaps true in China. It is true in much of Africa. The growing edge may more and more be the kind of thing we would call cultic or at least anomalous in this country.

Are we prepared for that? Does our attitude towards "home grown" aberrant forms of basically Biblical faith in this country match what is needed in the rest of the world? Can we trust the Bible eventually to balance out these thousands of new, "out of control" movements? Can we digest the plain fact that the entire Islamic tradition is, like Roman Catholicism, full of "non-Christian" elements which we despise, yet is clearly the product of the impact of the Bible (unlike Hindu culture)? What do we do with such forms of quasi-Biblical faith?

Study Questions

1. Why is it difficult to evaluate our own cultural forms of Christianity?

2. What influence can be expected to correct or balance out errant forms of the Christian faith?

THE
CULTURAL
PERSPECTIVE

Cultural Differences and the Communication of the Gospel

Paul G. Hiebert

Paul G. Hiebert is Chairman of the Department of Mission and Evangelism and Professor of Mission and Anthropology at Trinity Evangelical Divinity School. He previously taught Anthropology and South Asian Studies at Fuller Theological Seminary's School of World Mission. Hiebert served as a missionary in India with the Mennonite Brethren Board. He is the author of *Cultural Anthropology, Anthropological Insights for Missionaries,* and *Case Studies in Mission* with his wife, Frances H. Hiebert.

Adapted from *Crucial Dimensions in World Evangelization*, by Arthur F. Glasser, et al. , 1976. Used by permission of William Carey Library, Pasadena, CA.

You were excited. You were accepted as a missionary. The church held a big farewell in which you were center stage when all your life you had sat only in the pews. There was the thrilling, sorrowful parting at the airport, the flight in the giant 747, and a little uneasiness as you landed in a strange country. But friends were there to meet you. You couldn't read the menu at the restaurant so you pointed knowingly at something you didn't recognize and took your chances. You recognized half the food on the plate. The other half looked inedible—was it roasted insects or goat's entrails? Later you went to the market to buy oranges but the woman couldn't understand a word you said. You pointed to your mouth and rubbed your stomach like a little child. You had to pay her, but all you could do was hold out a handful of the strange coins for her to take what she wanted. You were sure you were cheated. You got on a bus to go across town, and got lost. You imagined yourself spending the next ten years riding the bus trying to get home. You got sick and you were sure the local doctor didn't know how to treat American diseases. Now you are sitting on your bed, wanting to go back where you came from. How did you get yourself into this anyway, and what do you say to your church after a few weeks of 'missions' abroad? "The job is done"? "I can't take it"?

Your reaction is perfectly normal.

Level of Satisfaction

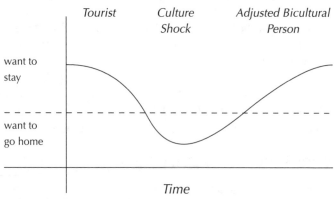

Culture shock is a sense of cultural disorientation in a different society.

It is the culture shock everyone experiences when they enter a new culture. Tourists do not really experience it because they return to their American-style hotels after riding around looking at the native scenery. Culture shock is not a reaction to poverty or to the lack of sanitation. For foreigners coming to the U.S. the experience is same. It is the shock in discovering that all the cultural patterns we have learned are now meaningless. We know less about living here than the children, and we must begin again to learn the elementary things of life—how to speak, greet one another, eat, market, travel, and a thousand other things. Culture shock really sets in when we realize that *this now is going to be our life and home.*

THE CONCEPT OF CULTURE

To understand culture shock and the problems of intercultural communication, we need to first understand the concept of "culture." We will begin with a simple definition that we can modify later, as our understanding of the concept grows. Culture is "the more or less integrated systems of beliefs, feelings and values, and their associated symbols, patterns of behavior and products shared by a group of people." Let us unpack this definition.

Patterns of Behavior and Products

Most people begin learning a culture by observing the behavior of the people and looking for patterns in their behavior. We see two Americans grasp each other's hand and shaking them. In Mexico we see them embrace. In India each puts his hands together and raises them toward his forehead with a slight bow of the head—a gesture of greeting that is efficient, for it permits a person to greet a great many others in a single motion, and clean, for people need not touch each other. The latter is particularly important in a society where the touch of an untouchable defiles a high caste person and forces him to take a purification bath. Among the Siriano of South America, people spit on each other's chests in greeting.

Probably the strangest form of greeting was observed by Jacob Loewen in Panama. Leaving the jungle on a small plane with the local native chief, he noticed the chief go to all his fellow tribesmen and suck their mouths. When Loewen inquired about this custom, the chief explained that they had learned this custom from the white man. They had seen that every time white people went up in planes, they sucked the mouths of their people as magic to insure a safe journey. Americans, in fact, have two types of greeting, shaking hands and sucking mouths, and we must be careful not to use the wrong form with the wrong people.

Not all behavior is culturally shaped. In formal situations, behavior and speech are carefully circumscribed by the culture. Everyday life is usually less formal; we are allowed to choose from a range of permissible behaviors. Our choices reflect the occasion (swimming suits are out of place in the classroom) and our personalities. Our culture is the sets of rules that govern the games of life that we play in our society. Like players in most games, we often try to "bend the rules" a little and get away with it. If we are caught, we are punished; but if not, we gain some advantage or sense of achievement. All cultures have ways to enforce their rules, such as gossip, ostracism and force, but not all violators are punished. A society may ignore some transgressors, particularly those who are important and powerful. Or it may be unable to enforce a specific rule, particularly when a great many people break it. In those cases cultural ordinances may die, and the culture changes accordingly.

Culture also includes material objects—houses, baskets, canoes, masks, carts, computers, and the like. People live in nature and must adapt or mold it for their own purposes. Most traditional societies live in an environment largely formed by nature. In complex industrial societies, much of the human environment is culturally molded. Electricity blurs the distinction between day and night, and planes and phones break the barriers of geographic distance.

Human behavior and material objects are readily observable. Consequently, they are important entry points in our study of a culture.

THE HEART OF CULTURE: BELIEFS, FEELINGS AND VALUES

At the heart of a culture is the shared beliefs, feelings and values of a community of people. Through their experiences, people form mental pictures or maps of their world. For instance, a person living in Chicago has a mental image of the streets around her home, those she uses to go to church and work, and the major arteries she uses to get around town. Obviously, there are a great many streets not on her map and as long as she does not go to these areas, she has no need for knowing them.

Not all our ideas reflect the realities of the external world. Many are the creations of our minds, used to bring order and meaning to our experiences. For example, we see a great many trees in our lifetime, and each is different from all others. But it would be impossible for us to give a separate name for each of them, or to each bush, each house, each car—in short, to every experience we have. In order to think and speak we must reduce this infinite variety of experiences into a manageable number of concepts by generalizations. We call these shades of color "red," those "orange," and the third set "yellow." These categories are the creations of our minds. Other people in other languages lump them together into a single color, or divide them into two or more colors. Do these people see as many colors as we? Certainly. The fact is, we can create as many categories in our minds as we want, and we can organize them into larger systems for describing and explaining human experiences. Culture is a people's mental map of their world. This is not only a map *of* their physical world, but also a map *for* determining action. It provides them with a guide for their decisions and behavior.

Beliefs

Shared beliefs about the nature of reality makes communication and community life possible. They provide people with the categories and logic they use to experience the world. Beliefs also tells people what exists and what does not. For instance, most Westerners believe in atoms, electrons, gravity and DNA, although they have never seen them. South Indian villagers believe in fierce *rakshasas*—spirits with big heads, bulging eyes, fangs and long wild hair, which inhabit trees and rocky places, and jump on unwary travelers at night. Not all Indians believe in *rakshasas*, just as not all Americans believe in God. But all must take into account the categories that exist in their culture.

Feelings

Culture also has to do with the feelings people have—with their notions of beauty, tastes in food and dress, likes and dislikes, and ways of enjoying themselves or expressing sorrow. People in one culture like their food hot, in another, sweet or bland. In some cultures people are encouraged to sing in sharp, piercing voices, in others to sing in deep, mellow tones. Members of some societies learn to express their emotions and may be aggressive and bellicose; in others they learn to be self-controlled and calm. Some religions encourage the use of meditation, mysticism and drugs to achieve inner peace and tranquility. Others stress ecstasy through frenzied songs, dances and self-torture.

The affective dimension of culture is reflected in standards of beauty, and taste in clothes, houses and food. It also plays an important part in human relationships—in our notions of etiquette and fellowship. We communicate love, hate, scorn and a hundred other attitudes, by our facial expressions, tones of voice and gestures.

Values and Allegiances

Culture includes the values by which people judge the experiences of their lives. These values determine what is right and wrong, what is good and what is evil, in the culture. For example, in ancient Japan it was a sin to beat a horse while it is lying on its back, and to sow seed where someone else has already done so. In parts of India, losing one's temper is a greater sin than sexual immorality.

More or Less Integrated

A culture is made up of a great many patterns of behavior, ideas and products. But it is more than the sum of them. These patterns are integrated, more or less, into larger cultural complexes and total cultural systems by a worldview which forms the core of the culture. This worldview is made up by the fundamental cognitive, affective and evaluative assumptions the people make about reality. Because these assumptions are taken for

The Dimensions of Culture

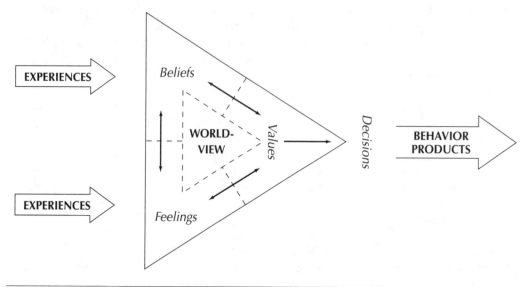

granted, they are generally unexamined and therefore largely implicit. They are what people 'think with,' not what they 'think about.' People believe that the world really is the way they see it. Those who disagree are wrong or crazy.

To see this integration of cultural patterns we need only observe the average American. On entering an auditorium to listen to a musical performance, she looks until he finds a chair—a platform on which to perch himself. If all these platforms are occupied, he leaves because the auditorium is "full." Obviously, there are a great many places on the floor where he can sit, but this is not culturally acceptable, at least not at the performance of a symphony orchestra.

At home Americans have different kinds of platforms for sitting in the living room, at the dining table, at a desk and on the lawn. They have large platforms on which they sleep at night. When they travel abroad, their greatest fear is being caught at night without a platform in a private room, so they make hotel reservations well ahead of time and pay hundreds of dollars for a single night's sleep. People from many parts of the world know that all one needs at night is a blanket to keep clean and warm, and a flat space—and the world is full of flat places. At the airport, at three in the morning, American travelers are draped uncomfortably over chairs because they would rather be dignified than comfortable. Travelers from other parts of the world sleep soundly stretched out on the floor.

Not only do Americans sit and sleep on platforms, they build their houses on them, hang them on their walls, and put fences around them to hold their children. Why this obsession with platforms? Behind all these behavior patterns is a basic worldview assumption that floors are dirty. This explains their obsession for getting off the floor. It also explains why they keep their shoes on when they enter the house, and why the mother scolds the child when it picks a potato chip off the floor and eats it, even though the floor has just been washed.

In Japan the people believe floors are clean. They take their shoes off at the door, and sleep and sit on mats on the floor. When we walk into their home with our shoes on, they feel much like we do when someone walks on our couch with their shoes on.

CULTURAL DIFFERENCES AND THE MESSENGER

So long as we live in our own culture, we are largely unaware of it. When we enter new cultures, however, we become keenly aware of the fact that other people live differently. At first we see the differences in dress, food, language and behavior. Then we learn that there are profound differences in beliefs, feelings and values. Finally, we begin to realize that there are fundamental differences in worldviews. People in different cultures do not live in the same world with different labels attached to it, but in radically different worlds.

Cultural differences are at the center of the missionary task which is to minister to 'others.' How can we communicate the Gospel in other languages, and plant vital churches in cultures which differ markedly from our own?

Misunderstandings

After we get beyond our initial culture shock, we are faced with three lifelong problems. The first has to do with cognitive misunderstandings. Some missionaries in Congo had trouble in building rapport with the people. Finally, one old man explained the people's hesitancy to befriend the missionaries. "When you came, you brought your strange ways," he said. "You brought tins of food. On the outside of one was a picture of corn. When you opened it, inside was corn and you ate it. Outside another was a picture of meat, and inside was meat, and you ate it. And then when you had your baby, you brought in small tins. On the outside was a picture of babies, and you opened it and fed the inside to your child!" To us, the people's confusion sounds foolish, but it is all too logical. In the absence of other information, the people must draw their own conclusions about our actions. We do the same about theirs. We think they have no sense of time when, by our culture, they show up late. We accuse them of lying, when they tell us things to please us rather than as they really are (although we have no trouble saying "Just fine!" when someone asks "How are you?"). The result is cultural misunderstanding, and this leads to poor communication and poor relationships.

Edward Hall points out how different views of time can lead to confusion (1959). When, for example, two Americans agree to meet at ten o'clock, they are "on time" if they show up from five minutes before to five minutes after ten. If one shows up at fifteen after, he is "late" and mumbles an unfinished excuse. He must simply acknowledge that he is late. If he shows up at half past, he should have a good apology, and by eleven he may as well not show up. His offense is unpardonable.

In parts of Arabia, the people have a different concept or map of time. If the meeting time is ten o'clock, only a servant shows up at ten—in obedience to his master. The proper time for others is from ten forty-five to eleven fifteen, just long enough after the set time to show their independence and equality. This arrangement works well, for when two equals agree to meet at ten, each shows up, and expects the other to show up, at about ten forty-five.

The problem arises when an American meets an Arab and arranges a meeting for ten o'clock. The American shows up at ten, the "right time" according to him. The Arab shows up at ten forty-five, the "right time" according to him. The American feels the Arab has no sense of time at all (which is false), and the Arab is tempted to think Americans act like servants (which is also false).

Misunderstandings are based on ignorance of the beliefs, feelings and values of another culture. The solution is to learn how the other culture works. Our first task in entering a new culture is to be a student of its ways. Whenever a culture 'makes no sense' to us, we must assume that the problem is ours, because the people's behavior makes sense to them.

Ethnocentrism

Most Americans shudder when they enter an Indian restaurant and see people eating curry and rice with their fingers. Imagine diving into the mashed potatoes and gravy with your hand at a Thanksgiving dinner. Our response seems natural, to us. Early in life each of us grows up at the center of our own world. In other words, we are egocentric. Only with a great deal of difficulty do we learn to break down the circle we draw between me and You, and learn to look at things from the viewpoint of others in our group. Similarly, when we first encounter other cultures, we find it hard to see the world through other cultural eyes. We are ethnocentric.

The root of ethnocentrism is our human tendency to respond to other people's ways by using our own affective assumptions, and to reinforce these responses with deep feelings of approval or disapproval. When we are confronted by another culture, our own is called into question. Our defense is to avoid the issue by concluding that our culture is better and other people are less civilized.

But ethnocentrism is a two-way street. We feel that people in other cultures are primitive, and they judge us to be uncivilized. Some North Americans were hosting a visiting Indian scholar at a restaurant, when one of them who had never been abroad asked the inevitable question, "Do you really eat with your fingers in India?" Implicit in his question, of course, was his cultural attitude that eating with one's fingers is crude and dirty. North Americans may use fingers for carrot sticks, potato chips, and sandwiches, but never for mashed potatoes and gravy or T-bone steaks. The Indian scholar replied, "You know, in India we look at it differently than you do. I always wash my hands carefully before I eat, and I only use my right hand. And besides, my fingers have not been in anyone else's mouth. When I look at a fork or spoon, I often wonder how many other strangers have already had them in their mouths!"

Ethnocentrism occurs wherever cultural differences are found. North Americans are shocked when they see the poor of other cultures living in the streets. People in those same societies would be just as appalled to observe how we North Americans surrender our aged and sick and the bodies of our departed to strangers for care.

The solution to ethnocentrism is empathy. We need to learn to appreciate other cultures and their ways. But our feelings of superiority and our negative attitudes toward strange customs run deep and are not easily rooted out.

Premature Judgments

We have misunderstandings on the cognitive level and ethnocentrism on the affective level. On the evaluative level we tend to judge another culture too quickly, before we learn to understand and appreciate them. Our initial assessment is often that they are somehow inferior and ignorant.

As people learn to understand and appreciate other cultures, they come to respect these cultures as viable ways of organizing human life. Some are stronger in one area, such as technology, and others in other areas such as family ties. But all "do the job," that is, they all make life possible and more or less meaningful. Out of this recognition of the integrity of all cultures, emerged the concept of cultural relativism: the belief that all cultures are equally good—that no culture has the right to stand in judgment of others.

This position of cultural relativism is very attractive. It shows high respect for other people and their cultures and avoids the errors of ethnocentrism and premature judgments. The price we pay, however, in adopting total cultural relativism is the loss of such things as truth and righteousness. If all explanations of reality are equally valid, we can no longer speak of error, and if all behavior is justified according to its cultural context, we can no longer speak of sin. There is then no need for the gospel and no reason for mission.

What other alternative do we have? How do we avoid the errors of premature and ethnocentric judgments and still affirm truth and righteousness? There is a growing awareness that all human activities are full of judgments. Scientists expect one another to be honest and open in reporting their findings and careful in the topics of their research. Social scientists must respect the rights of their clients and the people they study. Businessmen, government officials, and others also have values by which they live. We cannot avoid making judgments, nor can a society exist without them.

On what basis, then, can we judge other cultures without becoming ethnocentric? We have a right as individuals to make judg-

ments with regard to ourselves, and this includes judging other cultures. But these judgments should be well informed. We need to understand and appreciate other cultures *before* we judge them. Our tendency to make premature judgments is based on ignorance and ethnocentrism.

As Christians, we claim another basis for evaluation, namely, Biblical norms. As divine revelation we stand in judgment of all cultures, affirming the good in human creativity and condemning the evil. To be sure, non-Christians may reject these norms and use their own. We can only present the gospel in a spirit of redemptive love and let it speak for itself. Truth, in the end, does not depend on what we think or say, but on reality itself. When we bear witness to the gospel, we do not claim a superiority for ourselves, but affirm the truth of divine revelation.

> We need to let the gospel work in the lives of new Christians, and recognize that the same Holy Spirit who leads us is at work in them.

But what keeps us from interpreting the Scripture from our own cultural point of view, and so imposing many of our own cultural norms on other people? First, we need to recognize that we bring our cultural biases with us when we interpret the Scriptures. We must be open to recognizing these biases when they are pointed out to us. We also need to let the gospel work in the lives of new Christians and recognize that the same Holy Spirit who leads us, is at work in them. We need to allow them the greatest privilege we allow ourselves, the right to make mistakes and to learn from them.

Second, we need to study both the culture in which we minister and our own in order to compare and evaluate the two. The process of genuinely seeking to understand another culture breaks down our cultural biases, and enables us to appreciate the good in other cultures. It is important, too that Christian leaders in other societies learn our culture to understand us.

The dialogue between us and our national colleagues is important in building bridges of cultural understanding. It is also important in helping us develop a more culture-free understanding of God's truth and moral standards as revealed in the Bible. Our colleagues can detect our cultural blind spots better than we can, just as we often see their cultural prejudgments better than they. Dialogue with Christians from other cultures helps keep us from the legalism of imposing foreign beliefs and norms on a society without taking into account its specific situations. It also helps keep us from a relativism that denies truth and reduces ethics to cultural norms.

Evaluation in the Three Dimensions

As humans, we pass judgments on beliefs to determine whether they are true or false, on feelings to decide likes and dislikes, and on values to differentiate right from wrong. As missionaries we are faced with evaluating other cultures and our own along each of these dimensions.

On the cognitive level, we must deal with different perceptions of reality, including diverse ideas about hunting, farming, building houses, human procreation and diseases. For example, in south India villagers believe illnesses are caused by angry local goddesses. Consequently, sacrifices must be made to them to stop the plague. We must understand the people's beliefs in order to understand their behavior, but we may decide that modern theories of disease are more effective in stopping illnesses. On the other hand, after examining their knowledge of hunting wild game, we may conclude that it is better than our own.

We need to evaluate not only the people's folk sciences, but also their religious beliefs, for these affect their understanding of Scripture. Although they already have concepts such as God, ancestors, sin and salvation, these may or not be adequate for an understanding of the gospel.

Becoming Global Christians

Something happens to us when we learn to live deeply in a new culture: we become global people. Our parochialism, based on our unquestioned feeling that there is really one civilized way to live, and our way is it, is shattered. We must deal with cultural variety—with the fact that people build cultures in different ways, and that they believe their cultures are better than ours. Aside from some curiosity at our foreignness, they are not interested in learning our ways.

But to the extent we identify with people of another culture and become global, we find ourselves alienated from our kinsmen and friends in our homeland. This is not reverse culture shock, although we will experience that when we return home after a long stay abroad. It is a basic difference in how we now look at things. We have moved from a philosophy that assumes uniformity to one that has to cope with variety, and our old friends often don't understand us when we return. In time, we may find our closest associates are other global people.

In one sense, global people never fully adjust to one culture—their own or their adopted one. Within themselves, they are part of both. When Americans are abroad, they dream of America, and need little rituals that reaffirm this part of themselves—a food package from home, a letter, an American visitor from whom they can learn the latest news from "home." When in America, they dream of their adopted country, and need little rituals that reaffirm this part of themselves—a visitor from that country, a meal with its food. Global people seem happiest when they are flying from one country to the other.

CULTURAL DIFFERENCES AND THE MESSAGE

Cultural differences affect the messengers, but they also affect the gospel message. Each society looks at the world in its own way, and that way is encoded in its language and culture. No language is unbiased, no culture theological neutral. Consequently, the translation and communication of the gospel in new cultures is no easy task. If we do not understand this, we are in danger of being ineffective messengers at best, and, at worst, of communicating a gospel that is misunderstood and distorted.

Cultural differences affect the message in several ways. First, the messengers must communicate in the language the people understand. This means learning new languages and translating the Bible into these languages. This involves not only using local words that have similar meanings to the original, but also checking that the meanings of those words in the broader context of that culture do not introduce distortion. Second, new believers must learn how to deal with their old cultural ways. Can they continue to participate in local festivals, sing old songs, cremate the dead, venerate their ancestors and go to the diviner for guidance? Birth rites, weddings, funerals and other rituals must be made indigenous, yet truly Christian. Third, if the church is to function well, church buildings, forms of worship and leadership styles must be adapted to fit the local cultural practices. Fourth, evangelistic methods must be chosen that fit the culture. Methods that work in small tribal societies normally do not work in rural or urban settings. Nor do methods appropriate for the city, work in tribal and rural societies. Finally, the people must develop a theology in which Scripture speaks to them in their particular historical and cultural settings. These are all part of the contextualization of the gospel in new cultural settings.

Contextualization raises difficult questions that must be addressed. We will examine three of them.

Gospel and Culture

What is the relationship between the gospel and culture? We must distinguish between them, for if we do not, we will be in danger of making our culture the message. The gospel then becomes democracy, capitalism, pews and pulpits, Robert's Rules of Order, and suits and ties on Sunday. One of the primary hindrances to communication is the foreignness of the message and, to a great extent, the foreignness of Christianity has been the cultural load we have placed upon it. As Mr. Murthi, an Indian evangelist, put it, "Do not bring us the gospel as a potted plant. Bring us the seed of the gospel and plant it in our soil."

It is not always easy to distinguish between the gospel and human cultures for the gospel, like any message, must be put into cultural forms to be understood and communicated by people. We cannot think without conceptual categories and symbols to express them. But we can be careful to let the biblical message shape not only our beliefs, but also the categories and assumptions of our culture.

A failure to differentiate between the biblical message and other messages leads to confusion between cultural relativism and Biblical absolutes. For example, in many churches where it was once considered sinful for women to cut their hair or wear lipstick, or for people to attend movies, these are now acceptable. Some, therefore, argue that today, premarital sex and adultery are thought to be sinful, but that in time they, too, will be accepted.

It is true that many things we considered sin are now accepted in the church. Are there, therefore, no moral absolutes? We must recognize that each culture defines certain behaviors as "sinful," and that, as the culture changes, its definition of what is sin also changes. There are, on the other hand, moral principles in Scripture that we hold to be absolute. Even here we must be careful, however, for some biblical norms, such as leaving the land fallow every seventh year and not reaping the harvest (Lev 25) or greeting one another with a holy kiss (1 Th 5:26) seem to apply to specific cultural situations.

Contextualization Versus Noncontextualization

Cultures are made up of systems of beliefs and practices that are built upon implicit assumptions that people make about themselves, about the world around them, and about ultimate realities. How can Christians communicate and embody the gospel in terms of these worldviews and the beliefs and practices associated with them, when many of these are unbiblical?

One response has been to reject most of the old beliefs and customs as "pagan." Drums, songs, dramas, dances, body decoration, marriage customs and funeral rites are frequently condemned because they are thought to be directly or indirectly related to traditional religions, hence unacceptable for Christians. This wholesale rejection of old cultural ways creates problems. First, it leaves a cultural vacuum that needs to be filled, and this is often done by importing the customs of the missionary. Drums, cymbals, and other traditional instruments are replaced by organs and pianos. Instead of creating new lyrics that fit native music, Western hymns and melodies are introduced. Pews replace mats on floors, and western style churches are built, although they appear incongruous alongside mud huts and thatch gathering halls. It is no surprise, then, that Christianity is often seen as a foreign religion, and Christian converts as aliens in their own land.

A second problem arises when missionaries attempt to suppress old cultural ways. These simply go underground. New converts come to church for worship, but during the week turn to shamans and magicians for answers to the everyday problems of their lives.

A third problem with the wholesale condemnation of traditional cultures is that it not only turns missionaries and church leaders into police, but keeps converts from growing by denying them the right to make their own decisions. A church only grows spiritually if its members learn to apply the teachings of the gospel to their own lives.

A second response to traditional ways is to see them as basically good, and to accept them uncritically into the church. Few, if any, changes are seen as necessary when people become Christians. Those who advocate this approach have a deep respect for others and their cultures, and recognize the high value people place on their own cultural heritage. They also recognize that the "foreignness" of the gospel has been one of the major barriers to its acceptance in many parts of the world.

This approach has serious weaknesses. It overlooks the fact that there are corporate and cultural sins as well as personal transgressions. Sin is found in cultural beliefs and exhibited as group pride, segregation against others and idolatry. The gospel calls not only individuals, but societies and cultures to change. Contextualization must mean the communication of the gospel not only in ways the people understand, but in ways that also challenge them individually and corporately to turn from their evil ways.

Another weakness in uncritical contextualization is that it opens the doors to syncretisms of all kinds. If Christians continue in beliefs and practices that stand in opposition to the gospel, these in time will mix with their newfound faith and produce various forms of neopaganism.

If both uncritical rejection and uncritical acceptance of old ways undermine the mission task, what should we and Christian converts do with the people's cultural heritage? A third approach is to evaluate it in the light of biblical teachings. The first step is to study the old ways in order to understand them. The missionary and church leaders should help new converts to examine their traditional practices. The next step is to lead the church in a Bible study related to the question under consideration. For example, the leaders can use the occasions of weddings and funerals to teach Christian beliefs about marriage and death. This is a critical step, for if the people do not clearly understand the biblical teachings, they will be unable to deal with their cultural ways. The third step is for the congregation to evaluate critically their own past customs in the light of their new biblical understandings, and to make decisions regarding their use. They will keep many of their old ways, because these do not distort the gospel. They will reject other ways as unchristian. They will reinterpret other ways to convey the Christian message. For example, they will give Christian words to their native lyrics. They will develop new symbols and rituals to communicate the gospel in ways they understand. And out of the process they will create beliefs and practices that are both biblical and contextually appropriate.

Conversion and Unforeseen Side Effects

Since cultural traits are linked together into larger wholes, changes in one or more of them often lead to unforeseen changes in other areas of the culture. For example, in one part of Africa, when the people became Christians, their villages also became dirty. The reason for this was that they were now not afraid of evil spirits which they believed hid in refuse. So they no longer had to clean it up.

Many cultural traits serve important functions in the lives of the people. If we remove these without providing a substitute, the consequences can be tragic. In some places husbands with more than one wife had to give up all but one when they became Christian. But no arrangements were made for the wives who were put way. Many of them ended up in prostitution or slavery.

What implications does an understanding of culture and cultural differences have for us when we minister in another culture? We need to recognize that the effective communication of the gospel is central to our task. There is little point going ten thousand miles to give our lives if we cannot bridge the final five feet. Inter-cultural communication is a complex process. If we do not understand it, we will be unable to communicate the gospel to the people.

As we learn to effectively communicate the gospel interculturally, however, we must never overlook the fact that God is at work through his Spirit in the hearts of the people, preparing them for the Good News. Without this, true conversion and Christian maturity is impossible. God uses the imperfect means of human beings to make his message known to us and through us, to others. And even when we are unskilled in transmitting the message, he often uses it to transform the lives of people. This is not to justify our neglect of understanding intercultural communication, but to say that, in the end, the communication of the gospel depends on the work of God in the hearts of people whom he has prepared. Christian communication must always be accompanied by prayer and obedience to the guidance of the Holy Spirit.

Study Questions

1. What integrates beliefs, values, and feelings within a given culture?

2. Distinguish the errors of ethnocentrism and what Hiebert calls "premature judgments."

3. How is it possible to become what Hiebert calls "global people?"

4. Of what use for cross-cultural communication is identifying beliefs, feelings and values?

Culture, Worldview and Contextualization

Charles H. Kraft

Charles H. Kraft has been Professor of Anthropology and Intercultural Communication at Fuller Theological Seminary, School of World Mission, since 1969. With his wife, Marguerite, he served as a missionary in Nigeria. He teaches and writes in the areas of anthropology, cross-cultural communication, prayer and spiritual warfare. Among his numerous books are, *Christianity in Culture*, *Anthropology for Christian Witness* and *Christianity with Power*.

Written for this volume, 1998. Used by permission of the author.

A key question for Christians who work cross-culturally is, "What is God's view of culture? Is Jewish culture created by God and therefore to be imposed on everyone who follows God? Or is there some indication in scripture that God takes a different position?" I believe we have our answer in 1 Corinthians 9:19–22, where Paul articulates his (and God's) approach to cultural diversity. Paul says, "While working with Jews, I live like a Jew" but "when working with Gentiles, I live like a Gentile." His approach, then, is to "become all things to all men, that I may save some of them by whatever means are possible."

The early Christians were Jewish. It was natural for them to believe that the cultural forms in which the gospel came to them were the only right ones for everyone. So, they believed, everyone who comes to Jesus must also convert to Jewish culture. But God used the apostle Paul, himself a Jew, to teach his generation and ours a different approach. In the above text, he articulates God's approach. Then in Acts 15:2ff, we find him arguing fiercely against the majority position of the early church for the right of Gentiles to follow Jesus *within* their own socio-cultural contexts. God Himself had shown first Peter (Acts 10), then Paul and Barnabas, that this was the right way, by giving the Holy Spirit to Gentiles who had not converted to Jewish culture (Acts 13–14).

But the Church has continually forgotten the lesson of Acts 15. We have continually reverted to the assumption that becoming Christian means becoming like us culturally. When, after New Testament times, the church required everyone to adopt Roman culture, God raised up Luther to prove that God could accept people who spoke German and worshipped in German ways. Then Anglicanism arose to show that God could use English language and custom, and Wesleyanism arose to let the common people of England know that God accepted them in their culture. And so it has been that there are major cultural issues in the development of every new denomination.

But sadly, the problem persists. Communicators of the gospel continue imposing their culture or denomination on new converts. [So we attempt to apply anthropological insight to missions to protect those to whom we go from our inclination to make them like us.] If, then, we take a scriptural approach, we should *adapt ourselves and our presentation of God's message to the culture of the receiving people*, not misrepresent God as some early Jewish Christians did (Acts 15:1) by requiring that converts become like us to be acceptable to God.

Culture and Worldview Defined

The term *culture* is the label anthropologists give to the structured customs and underlying worldview assumptions which people govern their lives. Culture (including worldview) is a peoples' way of life, their design for living, their way of coping with their biological, physical and social environment. It consists of learned, patterned assumptions (worldview), concepts and behavior, plus the resulting artifacts (material culture).

Worldview, the deep level of culture, is the culturally structured set of assumptions (including values and commitments/allegiances) underlying how a people perceive and respond to reality. Worldview is *not separate* from culture. *It is included in culture* as the deepest level presuppositions upon which people base their lives.

A culture may be likened to a river, with a surface level and a deep level. The surface is visible. Most of the river, however, lies beneath the surface, and is largely invisible. But anything that happens on the surface of the river is affected by such deep-level phenomena as the current, the cleanness or dirtiness of the river, other objects in the river and so on. What happens on the surface of a river is both a response to external phenomena and a manifestation of the deep-level characteristics of the river.

So it is with culture. What we see on the surface of a culture is patterned human behavior. But this patterned or structured behavior, though impressive, is the lesser part of the culture. In the depths, are the assumptions we call *worldview,* on the basis of which people govern their surface-level behavior. When something affects the surface of a culture it may change that level. The nature and extent of that change will, however, be influenced by the deep-level worldview structuring within the culture.

Culture (including worldview) is a matter of structure or patterns. Culture does not *do* anything. Culture is like the script an actor follows. The script provides guidelines within which actors ordinarily operate,

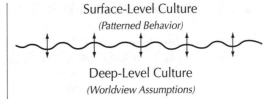

Surface-Level Culture
(Patterned Behavior)

Deep-Level Culture
(Worldview Assumptions)

though they may choose on occasion to modify the script, either because they have forgotten something or because someone else changed things.

There are several levels of culture (including, of course, worldview). The "higher" the level, the more diversity is included in it. For example, we may speak of culture at *multinational* level as "Western culture" (or worldview), or "Asian culture," or "African culture." Such cultural entities include a large number of quite distinct national cultures. For example, within *Western culture* there are varieties called German, French, Italian, British and American. Within *Asian culture* are varieties called Chinese, Japanese and Korean. These national cultures, then, can include many *subcultures*. In America, for example, we have Hispanic Americans, American Indians, Korean Americans and so on. And within these subcultures we can speak of *community cultures, family cultures* and even *individual cultures.*

In addition, the term "culture" can designate types of strategies (or coping mechanisms) used by people of many different societies. Thus, we can speak of entities such as *a culture (or worldview) of poverty, deaf culture, youth culture, culture of factory workers, taxi drivers' culture,* even *culture of women.* Identifying people in this way is often helpful in working out strategies for their evangelization.

People and Culture

Just as in drama we recognize the difference between actors and their scripts, so it is with culture. It has been common for both nonspecialists and specialists to refer to culture as if it was a person. We often hear statements such as "Their culture *makes* them do it," or "Their worldview *determines* their view of reality." Note that the italicized verbs in these statements give the impression that a culture behaves like a person.

As in drama, the patterns are there and the actors ordinarily follow them by habit. But the "power" that keeps people following their cultural script is the power of habit, something inside of people, not any power that culture possesses in itself. *Culture (including worldview) has no power in and of itself.*

People ordinarily follow the patterns of their culture, but not always. People regularly modify old customs and create new ones. Though the habits that result in great conformity are strong, we can change our customs. It is important that cross-cultural witnesses recognize both the possibility of change and the place and power of habit.

The distinction we are making is embodied in the contrast between the words *culture* and *society*. Culture refers to the structure, society refers to the people themselves. When we feel pressure to conform, it is the pressure of people (i.e., social pressure) that we feel, not the pressure of cultural patterning (the script) itself.

The chart below summarizes the distinction between people's behavior and the cultural structuring of that behavior.

Cultures and Worldviews Are to Be Respected

Cultural/worldview structuring functions both outside of us and inside of us. We are totally submerged in it, relating to it much as a fish relates to water. And we are usually as unconscious of it as a fish must be of the water or as we usually are of the air we breathe. Indeed, many of us only notice culture when we go into another cultural territory and observe customs different from our own.

Unfortunately, when we see others living according to cultural patterns and with worldview assumptions different from our own we often feel sorry for them, as if their ways are inferior to ours. If we are able, then, we may seek ways to "rescue" them from their customs. One of the tragedies of American (including missionary) attempts to help other peoples is that we have so often shown little respect for their traditional customs.

The way of Jesus is, however, to honor a people's culture and its incorporated worldview, not to wrest them from it. Just as He entered the cultural life of the Jews to communicate with them, so we are to enter the cultural matrix of the people we seek to win. Following Jesus' example, we note that working from within involves a biblical critique of a people's culture and worldview assumptions as well as acceptance of them as starting points. But if we are to witness effectively, we have to speak and behave in ways that honor the only way of life they have ever known. Likewise, if the Church is to be as meaningful to receiving peoples as Jesus wants it to be, it needs to be as appropriate to their cultural lives (though not uncritical of unbiblical customs and assumptions) as the early Church was to the lives of first century peoples. We call such appropriate churches "dynamic equivalence churches" (Kraft 1979),

People *(Society)*	Culture
Surface-Level Behavior What we do, think, say or feel either consciously or unconsciously, mostly habitually but also creatively	**Surface-Level Structure** The cultural patterns in terms of which we habitually do, think, say or feel
Deep-Level Behavior Assuming, evaluating and committing mostly habitually but also creatively: 1. Concerning choosing, feeling, reasoning, interpreting and valuing. 2. Concerning the assigning of meaning. 3. Concerning explaining, relating to others, committing ourselves, and adapting to or deciding to try to change things that go on around us.	**Deep-Level Structure** *(Worldview)* The patterns in terms of which we carry out the assumptions, evaluations and commitments of deep-level behavior. Patterns of choosing, feeling, reasoning, interpreting, valuing, explaining, relating to others, committing ourselves and adapting to or deciding to try to change things that go on around us.

"contextualized churches" (see below) or "inculturated churches."

CHARACTERISTICS OF CULTURE (INCLUDING WORLDVIEW)

There are a number of characteristics of culture and worldview that may be listed. Space does not allow us to detail these. A fuller discussion of them may be found in my book *Anthropology for Christian Witness* (1996).

CHARACTERISTICS OF CULTURE AND WORLDVIEW

1. Culture/worldview provides a *total design for living,* dealing with every aspect of life and providing people with *a way to regulate their lives.*
2. Culture/worldview is a legacy from the past, *learned as if it were absolute and perfect.*
3. Culture/worldview *makes sense to those within it.*
4. But *no culture/worldview seems to be perfectly adequate* either to the realities of biology and environment or to the answering of all of the questions of a people.
5. Culture/worldview is an *adaptive system,* a *mechanism for coping.* It provides patterns and strategies to enable people to adapt to the physical and social conditions around them.
6. Culture tends to show *more or less tight integration* around its worldview. Worldview assumptions provide the "glue" with which people hold their culture together.
7. Culture/worldview is *complex.* No simple culture/worldview has ever been found.
8. Cultural/worldview practices and assumptions are *based on group or "multipersonal" agreements.* A social group unconsciously agrees to govern themselves according to their cultural patterns.
9. Culture/worldview is *structure.* It doesn't *do* anything. People do things either according to their cultural script or by modifying that script. Any supposed power of culture or worldview lies in the *habits* of people.
10. Though analytically we need to treat people and culture/worldview as separate entities, *in real life people and culture/worldview function together.*

ADDITIONAL CHARACTERISTICS OF WORLDVIEW

1. A worldview consists of the *assumptions (including images)* underlying all cultural values, allegiances and behaviors.
2. Worldview assumptions and images underlie *our perception of reality and responses to it.*
3. There are two realities, REALITY as God sees and perceptual reality as we with human limitations see (1 Cor 13:12). Our worldview provides us with *the lens, model or map* by of which we perceive, interpret, structure and respond to God's REALITY.
4. Worldview assumptions or premises are learned from our elders, *not reasoned out, but assumed to be true without prior proof.* It seldom occurs to us that there may be people of other groups who do not share our assumptions.
5. We organize our lives and experiences according to our worldview and *seldom question it* unless our experience challenges some of its assumptions.
6. In cross-cultural ministry, *the problems that arise from differences in worldview are the most difficult to deal with.*

The Subsystems of Culture

With worldview at the center, influencing all of culture, we can divide surface-level culture into *subsystems.* There are many cultural subsystems, some of which are diagrammed below. These subsystems provide various behavioral expressions of worldview assumptions.

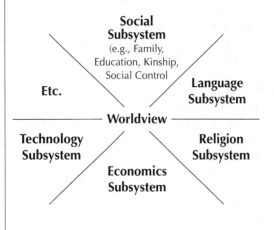

Though it is tempting to present Christianity as the replacement of a traditional religion with the religious forms of Western Christianity, this is the wrong way to witness. Christianity is to be directed at the worldview of a people so that it will influence each of these subsystems from the very core of the culture. Truly converted people (whether in America or overseas) need to manifest biblical Christian attitudes and behavior in all of their cultural life, not just in their religious practices.

If we are to reach people for Christ and to see them gathered into Christ-honoring and culture-affirming churches, we will have to deal with them within their culture and in terms of their worldview. We will do this either wisely or unwisely. It is hoped that by understanding more of what culture and worldview are all about, we can deal with them more wisely than might otherwise have been the case.

Worldview and Culture Change

Significant culture change is always a matter of changes in the worldview. Just as anything that affects the roots of a tree influences its fruit, so anything that affects a people's worldview will affect the whole culture and, of course, the people who operate in terms of that culture.

Jesus knew this. When He wanted to get across important points, He aimed at the worldview level. Someone asked, "Who is my neighbor?" So He told them a story and then asked who was being neighborly (Lk 10:29-37). He was leading them to reconsider and, hopefully, change a basic value down deep in their system.

On another occasion Jesus said, "You have heard that it was said, 'Love your friends, hate your enemies.' But now I tell you: love your enemies and pray for those who persecute you....If anyone slaps you on the right cheek, let him slap your left cheek too" (Matt 5:43,44, 39 GNB). Again the seeds were being planted for change at the deep worldview level.

When there is change at a deep level, however, it frequently throws things off balance. And any imbalance at the worldview center of a culture tends to cause difficulty through the rest of the culture. For example, when we in the U.S. believed at the worldview level that we could not be defeated in war, but then could not win in Vietnam, there was a deep sense of demoralization that rippled throughout the society, contributing greatly to the disequilibrium in our land at this time.

Major worldview problems can be caused when even good changes, introduced by well-meaning people such as missionaries, are applied at the surface level without due attention to the deep-level meanings people attach to them. For example, the almost universal missionary requirement that Africans who have more than one wife divorce the "extras" before they can be baptized has led both Christian and non-Christian Africans to certain undesirable worldview assumptions concerning the Christian God. Among these are: God is against the real leaders of African society, God is not in favor of women having help and companionship around the home, God wants men to be enslaved to a single wife (like whites seem to be), God favors divorce, social irresponsibility and even prostitution. None of these conclusions is irrational or far-fetched from their point of view. Though we believe God intends that each man have only one wife, this change was forced too quickly, unlike God's patient approach in the Old Testament where He took many generations to do away with the custom.

As mentioned, even good changes, if they are introduced in the wrong way can lead to cultural disequilibrium and demoralization. Among the Ibibio people of southern Nigeria the message of God's gracious forgiveness resulted in many people turning to the Christian God because He was seen as much more lenient than their traditional god. But the converts saw no need to be righteous, since they believed God would always forgive them, whatever they did. In aboriginal Australia, among the Yir Yoront people, the introduction by missionaries of steel axes to replace the traditional stone axes had a powerful disruptive effect simply because the axes were given to the women and younger men who traditionally were required to borrow axes from the older men. This change, though providing the people with better technology, challenged their worldview assumptions, leading to the destruction of the authority of the leaders, widespread social disruption and the near extinction of the people. Add to such examples the enormous damage (both cultural and spiritual) among non-Western peoples that has been done through the influence of Western schools (including those run by missions), and you can understand that there are at least a few valid reasons (among the invalid ones) for certain anthropologists to be critical of missionary work.

Contextualized *(Appropriate)* Christianity

The aim of Christian witness is to see people come to Christ and to be formed into groups we call churches that are both biblically and culturally appropriate. The process by means of which the church becomes "inculturated" in the life of a people has been called "indigenization," but now is more frequently referred to as "contextualization."

The contextualization of Christianity is part and parcel of the New Testament record. This is the process that the apostles were involved in as they took the Christian message that had come to them in Aramaic language and culture and communicated it to those who spoke Greek. In order to contextualize Christianity for Greek speakers, the apostles expressed Christian truth in the thought patterns of their receptors. Indigenous words and concepts were used (and transformed in their usage) to deal with such topics as God, church, sin, conversion, repentance, initiation, "word" (*logos*) and most other areas of Christian life and practice.

The early Greek churches were in danger of being dominated by Jewish religious practices because those who led them were Jews. God, however, led the apostle Paul and others to struggle against the Jewish Christians to develop a contextualized Christianity for Greek-speaking Gentiles. In order to do this, Paul had to fight a running battle with many of the Jewish church leaders who felt that it was the job of Christian preachers to simply impose Jewish theological concepts on new converts (see Acts 15). These conservative Jews were the heretics against whom Paul fought for the right for Greek-speaking Christians to have the gospel expressed in their language and culture. We conclude from such passages as Acts 10 and 15 that it is the intent of God that biblical Christianity be "reincarnated" in every language and culture at every point in history.

Biblically, the contextualization of Christianity is not simply to be the passing on of a *product* that has been developed once for all in Europe or America. It is, rather, the imitating of the *process* that the early apostles went through. To return to our tree analogy, Christianity is not supposed to be like a tree that was nourished and grew in one society and then was transplanted to a new cultural environment, with leaves, branches and fruit that mark it indelibly as a product of the sending society. The gospel is to be *planted as a seed* that will sprout within and be nourished by the rain and nutrients in the cultural soil of the receiving peoples. What sprouts from true gospel seed may look quite different above ground from the way it looked in the sending society, but beneath the ground, at the worldview level, the roots are to be the same and the life comes from the same source.

In a truly contextualized church, even though the surface level "tree" may look different, the essential message will be the same and the central doctrines of our faith will be in clear focus, since they are based on the same Bible. But the formulation of that message and the relative prominence of many of the issues addressed will differ from society to society. For cultural reasons, such things as what the Bible says about family relationships, fear and evil spirits, and the advocacy of dance and prescribed rituals will be much more in focus in contextualized African Christianity than they might be in America.

God intends today's Christianity to be dynamically equivalent to New Testament Christianity, perceived by people today as excitingly relevant to the problems they struggle with. Though many non-Western churches today are dominated by Western approaches to doctrine and worship, it is not scriptural that they remain so. There are, of course, similar basic problems (e.g., the problem of sin, the need for a relationship with Christ) that peoples of all societies need to deal with. But the ways those problems manifest themselves differ from people to people and need to be approached in different ways, culturally appropriate ways, for each cultural group.

Contextualizing Christianity is Very Risky

There are great risks involved in attempting to promote a Christianity that is culturally and biblically appropriate.The risk of *syncretism* is always present. Syncretism is the mixing of Christian assumptions with those worldview assumptions that are incompatible with Christianity so that the result is not biblical Christianity.

Syncretism exists whenever people practice Christian rituals because they consider them magic, or use the Bible to cast spells on people or, as in India, consider Jesus just another of many human manifestations of one of their dieties, or as in Latin America, practice pagan divination and witchcraft right in the churches, or insist that people convert to a different culture to become Christians. In America it is syncretistic, unbiblical Christianity that sees "the American way of life" as identical with biblical Christianity or assumes that, by generating enough faith we can pressure God into giving us whatever we want, or that we should out of love and tolerance regard homosexuality and even homosexual "marriage" to go unopposed despite clear biblical condemnations.

But there are at least two paths to syncretism. One is by importing foreign expressions of the faith and allowing the receiving people to attach their own worldview assumptions to these practices with little or no guidance from the missionaries. The result is a kind of "nativistic" Christianity or even, as in Latin America, "Christo-paganism." Roman Catholic missionaries, especially, have fallen into this trap by assuming that when people practice so-called "Christian" rituals and use "Christian" terminology, they mean by them the same thing that European Christians mean.

The other way to syncretism is to so dominate a receiving people's practice of Christianity that both the surface-level practices and the deep-level assumptions are imported. The result is a totally foreign, unadapted kind of Christianity that requires people to worship and practice their faith according to foreign patterns and to develop a special set of worldview assumptions for church situations that are largely ignored in the rest of their lives. Their traditional worldview, then, remains almost untouched by biblical principles. This is the kind of Christianity evangelical Protestants have most often advocated, probably out of a fear of the first kind of syncretism. In many situations, this kind of Christianity is attracting some of those who are westernizing. But the masses of traditional people find little or nothing in Christianity that meets their needs, simply because it is presented and practiced in foreign ways to which they cannot connect.

> We are to always point to the Holy Spirit (not ourselves) as the Guide while participating with them in discovering His leading.

Though we must be cautious concerning syncretism, there is a middle road that involves deep trust in the Holy Spirit's ability to guide people and the receiving people's ability to follow that guidance. We, then, are to always point to the Holy Spirit (not ourselves) as the Guide while participating with them in discovering His leading. We can assure people that the Holy Spirit will always guide them in accordance with the Scriptures. Practicing this approach, missionary Jacob Loewen chose to never answer directly any questions from the new Christians such as, "What should we do?" Instead, he would ask them, "What is the Holy Spirit showing you?" Only after they had struggled with the answer to that question would he participate with them in seeking guidance, and even then his approach was to offer them at least three alternative approaches from which they might choose. In response to this approach they usually developed a fourth alternative that was uniquely their own. If that approach worked they would continue it. If it did not, they felt free to change it in needed ways, since it was their own and did not come with the prestige that often accompanies the suggestions of respected outsiders.

Though the risk of syncretism is always present when Christians attempt to inculturate Christianity, it is a risk that needs to be taken in order that people experience New Testament Christianity. Whether in a pioneer situation or after a foreign brand of our faith has been practiced for years, the quest for a vital, dynamic, biblical, contextualized Christianity will require experimenting with new, culturally and biblically appropriate ways of understanding, presenting and practicing the "faith which once and for all God has given to his people" (Jude 3 GNB). It will especially require attention to what is going on at the worldview level. To this end the insights of anthropologists into culture and worldview can be harnessed to enable us to advocate a Christianity that is truly contextualized, truly relevant and truly meaningful.

Understanding Culture Aids Contextualization

Understandings of culture and worldview such as those presented above have helped us greatly in our attempts to understand what biblical and cultural appropriateness means. Among the understandings that have come from such studies are the following:

1. God loves people as they are culturally. As we see from the Bible, He is willing to work within everyone's culture and language without requiring them to convert to another culture.
2. The cultures and languages of the Bible are not special, God-made cultures and languages. They are normal human, indeed pagan cultures and languages, just like any of the more than 6,000 cultures and languages in our world today. The Bible demonstrates that God can use any pagan culture (even Greek or American) with its language to convey His messages to humans.
3. The Bible shows that God worked with His people in culturally appropriate ways. He took customs already in use and invested them with new meaning, guiding people to use them for His purposes and on the basis of new worldview understandings. Among such customs are circumcision, baptism, worship on mountains, sacrifice, the synagogue, the temple, anointing and praying. God wants churches today to be culturally appropriate, using most of the customs of a people but attaching new meaning to them by using them for God's purposes. In this way, people get changed at the worldview level as well as at the surface.
4. But God's working within culture never leaves that culture unchanged. God changes people first, then through them the cultural structures. Whatever changes are to take place in the structures are to be made by the people themselves on the basis of their understandings of the Scriptures and God's workings in their lives, led and empowered by the Holy Spirit, not pressured by an outsider.
5. Though contextualization within a new culture risks a nativistic kind of syncretism, a Christianity that is dominated by foreign cultural forms with imported meanings is anti-scriptural and just as syncretistic. We are, therefore, to follow scripture and risk the use of receptor-culture forms.

References

Kraft, Charles H. *Anthropology for Christian Witness.* Maryknoll, NY: Orbis, 1996.
Kraft, Charles H. *Christianity in Culture.* Maryknoll, NY: Orbis, 1979.

Study Questions

1. How does worldview affect behavior?

2. Does culture cause any specific actions? Does it influence patterns of thought or action?

3. Why do we seldom question our worldview assumptions?

The Role of Culture in Communication

David J. Hesselgrave

David J. Hesselgrave is Professor Emeritus of Missions at the School of World Mission and Evangelism at Trinity Evangelical Divinity School in Deerfield, IL. He served twelve years in Japan under the Evangelical Free Church. He is the founder and past director of the Evangelical Missiological Society. Among his published works are *Planting Churches Cross-Culturally*, *Communicating Christ Cross-Culturally* and *Scripture and Strategy*.

From *Communicating Christ Cross-Culturally* by David J. Hesselgrave. Used by permission of Zondervan Publishing House.

There was a time in history when the insurmountable barriers between the earth's peoples seemed to be mainly physical. The problem was one of transporting people, messages and material goods across treacherous seas, towering mountains and trackless deserts. Missionaries knew all too well how formidable those challenges were. Today, thanks to jumbo jets, giant ocean vessels and towering antennae, those earlier problems have been largely resolved. We can deliver a man, or a Bible or a sewing machine almost anywhere on the face of the earth within a matter of hours. We can transmit a message electronically within seconds.

There is a very real danger, however, that as our technology advances and enables us to cross geographical and national boundaries with singular ease and increasing frequency, we may forget that it is the cultural barriers which are the most formidable. The gap between our technological advances and our communication skills is one of the most challenging aspects of modern civilization. Western diplomats have come to realize that they need much more than a knowledge of their message and a good interpreter or English-speaking national. Many educators have come to the position that cross-cultural communication is essential for citizenship in this new world. Missionaries now understand that much more than a microphone and increased volume is involved in penetrating cultural barriers.

A Complex Proposition

Unfortunately, intercultural communication is as complex as the sum total of human differences. The word "culture" is a very inclusive term. It takes into account linguistic, political, economic, social, psychological, religious, national, racial and other differences. Louis Luzbetak writes:

> "Culture is a design for living. It is a plan according to which society adapts itself to its physical, social, and ideational environment. A plan for coping with the physical environment would include such matters as food production and all technological knowledge and skill. Political systems, kinships and family organization, and law are examples of social adaptation, a plan according to which one is to interact with his fellows. Man copes with this ideational environment through knowledge, art, magic, science, philosophy, and religion. Cultures are but different answers to essentially the same human problems."[1]

Missionaries must come to an even greater realization of the importance of culture in communicating Christ. In the final analysis, they can effectively communicate to the people of any given culture only to the extent that they understand all aspects of that culture.

Before missionaries go to another country the first time, they often think of the great distance they must travel to get to their field of labor. But once they arrive on the field, the greatest problem to be faced is in the last few feet. What a shock! The missionary has studied for many years. He has traveled thousands of miles to communi-

cate the gospel of Christ. He now stands face-to-face with the people of his respondent culture and he is unable to communicate the most simple message! Ask experienced missionaries about their frustrating experiences on the field and most of them will respond by telling of their problems in communication.

Missionaries should prepare for this frustration. They have been preoccupied with their message. By believing it, they were saved. By studying it, they have been strengthened. Now they want to preach it to those who have not heard it—for that is a great part of what it

A Three-Culture Model of Missionary Communication

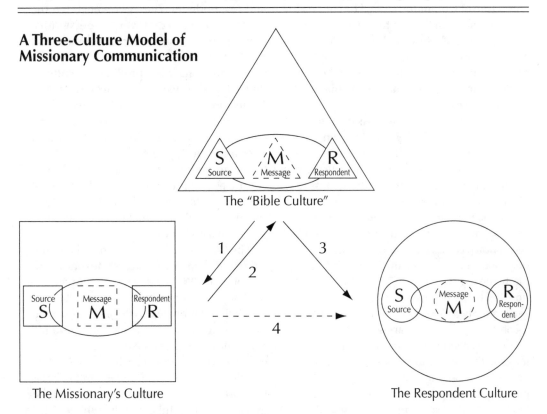

The "Bible Culture"

The Missionary's Culture

The Respondent Culture

1. The Christian message emanates from the "Bible Culture" and comes to the missionary in the language and forms appropriate to the "Missionary's Culture."

2. The first task of the missionary is to go back to the biblical text and interpret in the light of the language and forms of the context in which it was originally given (decoding).

3. The next task of the missionary is to translate and communicate the biblical message, (indeed, the Bible itself) into the language and forms that will make it understandable to the hearers and readers in the "Respondent Culture" (encoding).

4. This latter task should be undertaken with a view to minimizing the incursions from the "Missionary's Culture" as much as possible.

means to be a missionary. But before they can do so effectively, they must study again, not just the language, but also the audience. They must learn, before they can teach. They must listen, before they can speak. They not only need to know the message for the world, but they also need to know the world in which the message must be communicated.

A Three-Culture Model

Eugene Nida of the American Bible Society has made important contributions toward an understanding of the communication problems of the missionary. In his chapter on "Structure of Communication," the discussion and diagram furnish the basis for our consideration of a three-culture model of missionary communication.[2] The reader will greatly benefit by a reading of Nida's original text since modifications have been made here for our purposes.

As a communicator, the missionary must look at two cultures other than his own (see figure). In the first place, he looks to the Scriptures. The message is not really his. He did not originate it. He was not there when it was first given, nor is he a member of the culture in which the message was communicated. He knows that he must be diligent to present himself "approved to God as a workman who does not need to be ashamed, handling accurately the word of truth" (2 Tim. 2:15). In relationship to the biblical message, the missionary is simply a messenger, an ambassador—a secondary, never a primary source.

In the second place, when the missionary looks to the people to whom he or she has been sent. If only they could understand , be persuaded to repent, be instructed in the truths of God's Word, and put their faith in the one Savior and Lord. Looking at the respondent culture, he realizes that he will never be an indigenous source. He will always be limited in his ability to contextualize the biblical message. The respondent culture will always be his adopted culture, never his native culture.

It is this intermediary role, between the culture of the Bible and the missionary's target culture, that constitutes the unusual opportunity of the missionary as an ambassador of Christ. It is a special challenge because

of the comprehensive and demanding nature of the task.

The missionary message is the message of the Bible. It was given by God through the apostles and prophets in the languages and cultural contexts of the Bible. For the sake of simplification, we will say that "Bible Culture" includes all cultural contexts in which the message of the Bible was originally given—whether in Judah at the time of Ezra, Jerusalem at the time of Christ, or Athens at the time of Paul. In those cultural contexts, there were sources (Ezra, our Lord Christ or Paul), messages and respondents. The *sources* encoded the *messages* in forms that were understandable to the *respondents* who were members of those cultures.

The missionary is a product of a culture that is likely very different—whether his home address is in London, Chicago or Seoul. He has been brought up in his own culture and schooled in its language, world view and value system. He has received the Christian message in the context of his own culture as it was communicated by sources who, most likely, were also products of that culture. We will label that culture the "Missionary's Culture."

Then there are the people in still another culture with its own sources, messages and respondents. We will label this third culture the "Respondent Culture" (or "target culture"). In relationship to this respondent culture, the missionary has immediate and ultimate objectives. First, he desires to communicate Christ in such a way that the people will understand, repent and believe the gospel. Second, he wants to commit the message to "faithful men who will be able to teach others" (2 Tim 2:2) in culturally relevant terms that only indigenous leaders can fully command.

The Bible Culture Context

The missionary task now can be seen in clearer perspective. The missionary must traverse cultural boundaries in two directions. The first challange is to properly *decode* the biblical message in accordance with recognized rules of Bible interpretation. He is to study the Scriptures, in the original languages if possible, but always in terms of the "Bible Culture" context. Any sound system of hermeneutics must take into account the cultural context in which the message was originally communicated, the background and syntax and style, the characteristics of the audience, and the special circumstances in which the message was given. This process is essential to Bible exegesis. The Bible interpreter constantly must guard against the tendency to project the meanings of his own cultural background into the exegetical process with the result that the original meaning is missed or perverted. This tendency is heightened by the fact that, for the most part, all of us learn our own culture quite unconsciously and uncritically.

A friend of mine joined a tour group to the Holy Land. While walking under a tree in the Jordan Valley, the guide reached up, picked some fruit, peeled away the husk and ate the fruit. As he did so, he turned to the group and said, "According to the Bible, John the Baptist's diet consisted of this fruit and wild honey. This is the locust." Almost to a person, the members of the group expressed astonishment. They had always assumed that the locusts mentioned in Matthew and Mark were grasshoppers! As a matter of fact, they may have been correct. The point is that they had not thought of this second possibility because in their own culture "grasshopper locusts" are prevalent while "locust fruit" is not.

The Respondent Culture Context

Proper exegesis, however, is but the beginning of missionary responsibility. The missionary must now look in another direction—that of the "Respondent Culture" with its own world view, value system and codes of communication. He must remember that respondents in that culture have imbibed as deeply of their culture's ideas and values as he has of his own. It is likely that they will be more ignorant of the "Bible Culture" than non-Christian members of the "Missionary's Culture" are. And they will exhibit the same tendency to generalize and project their own cultural understandings into the message of the "Bible Culture."

The second challenge for the missionary, therefore, is to *encode* the biblical message in the language and forms that are meaningful to the people of the "Respondent Culture" The goal is to communicate as much as possible of the biblical message, with as *minimal intrusion* of influences from his own culture as possible.

This is not the simple task that many have supposed. Consider what was involved in translating Revelation 3:20 in terms that were meaningful to the Zanaki people in Africa. One could not say to the Zanaki people who live along the winding shores of sprawling Lake Victoria, "Behold, I stand at the door and knock" (Rev 3:20). This would mean that Christ was declaring Himself to be a thief because thieves in Zanaki land made a practice of knocking on the door of a hut that they hoped to burglarize. If they heard any movement inside, they would dash off into the dark. An honest man would come to a house and call the name of the person inside, identifying himself by his voice. Accordingly, in the Zanaki translation it was necessary to say, "Behold, I stand at the door and call." This wording may be slightly strange to us, but the meaning is the same. In each case, Christ is asking people to open the door. He is no thief and He will not force an entrance. When He come to us, "He knocks," but in Zanaki, "He calls." If anything, the Zanaki expression is a little more personal than our own.[3]

There remains yet another important aspect of missionary communication in the context of the "Respondent Culture." We have said that the ultimate goal of the missionary is to raise up effective sources of the Christian message from within the target culture. Missionary communication that does not keep this goal in mind is myopic. The world mission of the Church has been greatly weakened by a lack of vision at this point. It has been all too easy for Western missionaries and teachers to encourage (often unconsciously) national leaders to become Western in their thinking and approach. After a course in cross-cultural communication, an Asian pastor confessed that throughout his years of ministry he had preached "Western sermons" to Asian audiences. After all, he had learned the gospel from North American missionaries and had studied his theology, homiletics and evangelism from English and German textbooks. The great percentage of his Christian training had been in the language and patterns of Western culture. It is no wonder his Christian communication lacked respondent cultural relevance even though, in this case, the respondent culture was his own.

Furthermore, for the most part, missionaries have not communicated Christ's concern for other peoples beyond the "Respondent Culture." As a result, many Christians in Hong Kong have little vision for Indonesia, and many Christians in Venezuela exhibit little concern for unbelievers in Peru. When missionary vision is born (and it has been born in many "mission field" churches), it seldom occurs as a result of the ministry of the "Western" missionary. Though the state of affairs is ironic and deplorable, it is understandable. The missionary's own missionary concern has been expressed in terms of his target culture. Unless he sees the whole world as the object of God's love, and communicates this to national Christians, their vision will tend to be limited by his own!

End Notes

1. Louis J. Luzbetak, *The Church and Cultures* (Techny, IL.: Divine Word, 1963), pp. 60-61.
2. Eugene A. Nida, *Message and Mission: The Communication of the Christian Faith* (New York: Harper and Row, 1960), pp. 33-58.
3. Eugene A. Nida, *God's Word in Man's Language* (New York: Harper and Row, 1952), pp. 45-46.

Study Questions

1. How do we go about learning the culture of another person or another group of people that we might communicate effectively?

2. How can study of the culture related to a Bible passage help us know how to decode the biblical message for a respondent culture?

Redemptive Analogy

Don Richardson

When a missionary enters another culture, he or she is conspicuously foreign. This is to be expected, but often the gospel is labeled as foreign, too. How can it be explained so that it seems culturally right?

The New Testament approach is to communicate by way of *redemptive analogy*.

Consider these examples:

- The Jewish people practiced lamb sacrifice. John the Baptist proclaimed Jesus as the perfect, personal fulfillment of that sacrifice by saying, "Behold the *Lamb of God*, who takes away the sin of the world!" This is *redemptive analogy*.

- When Jesus spoke to Nicodemus, a Jewish teacher, both knew that Moses had lifted up a serpent of brass upon a pole so that Jews, dying of snakebite, could look at it and be healed. Jesus told Nicodemus that "as Moses lifted up the serpent in the wilderness, even so must the Son of Man be lifted up, that whoever believes in Him should not perish, but have everlasting life." This too is *redemptive analogy*.

- A Jewish multitude, recalling that Moses provided miraculous manna on a six-day-a-week basis, hinted that Jesus ought to repeat His miracle of the loaves and fishes on a similar schedule. Jesus replied, "Moses gave you not the *true* bread from heaven. The true bread from heaven is He who comes down from heaven and gives life to the world…I am that Bread of Life!" Once again, *redemptive analogy*.

When some charged that Christianity was destroying Jewish culture, the writer of the Epistle to the Hebrews showed how Christ actually fulfilled all the central elements of Jewish culture—the priesthood, tabernacle, sacrifices, and even the Sabbath rest. We call these redemptive analogies because they facilitate human understanding of redemption. Their God-ordained purpose is to precondition the mind in a culturally significant way to recognize Jesus as Messiah. Outside of scripture, it appears that God's general revelation is the source of redemptive analogies worldwide (see Ps 19:1-4 and John 1:9).

A Powerful Strategy for Today

This strategy of redemptive analogy can be applied by missionaries today as they discern the particular redemptive analogies of each culture. Consider the advantage:

Don Richardson pioneered work for Regions Beyond Missionary Union (RBMU) among the Sawi tribe of Irian Jaya in 1962. Author of *Peace Child*, *Lords of the Earth*, and *Eternity in Their Hearts*, Richardson is now Minister-at-Large for WORLD TEAM (formerly RBMU). He speaks frequently at mission conferences and Perspectives Study Program classes.

Used by permission of Don Richardson.

When conversion is facilitated by redemptive analogy, people are made aware of spiritual meaning dormant within their own culture. In this way, conversion does not deny their cultural background. Instead, they experience heightened insight into both the Scriptures and their own cultural heritage, and thus they are better prepared to share Christ meaningfully with other members of their society.

Finding and Using Redemptive Analogies

The Sawi "Peace Child."

As told in the book *Peace Child*, the Sawi tribe, my wife and I were shocked to learn, honored treachery as a virtue. Accordingly, Judas Iscariot seemed to them to be the hero of the gospel. Within the Sawi culture, however, existed a means of making peace that required a father to entrust one of his own children to an enemy father who would raise the child. This child was called a "peace child." At a crucial juncture of tribal strife, we were able to present Christ as God's "Peace Child." The Sawi soon grasped the redemptive story of God as the greatest Father giving His Son to reconcile alienated people. Today, seventy percent of the Sawi profess faith in Jesus.

The Damal and the Hai.

The Sawi are not the only tribe with a surprising redemptive analogy. Less than a generation ago, the Damal people of Irian Jaya were living in the Stone Age. A subservient tribe, they lived under the shadow of a politically more powerful people called the Dani. The Damal talked of a concept called *hai*. *Hai* was a Damal term for a long anticipated golden age, a Stone Age utopia in which wars would cease, men would no longer oppress one another and sickness would be rare.

Mugumenday, a Damal leader, yearned to see the advent of *hai*. At the end of his life, he called his son Dem to his side and said, "My son, *hai* has not come during my lifetime. Now you must watch for *hai*. Perhaps it will come before you die."

Years later, missionary couples entered the Damal valley where Dem lived. After tackling the Damal language, they began to teach the gospel. The people, including Dem, listened politely. Then one day Dem, now a mature adult, rose to his feet and said, "Oh, my people, how long our forefathers waited for *hai*. How sadly my father died without seeing it. But now, don't you understand, these strangers have brought *hai* to us! We must believe their words, or we will miss the fulfillment of our ancient expectation."

Virtually the entire population welcomed the gospel. Within a few years congregations sprang up in nearly every Damal village. But that was not the end.

The Dani and Nabelan-Kabelan.

The Dani, haughty overlords of the Damal, were intrigued by all the excitement in Damal villages. Curious, they sent Damal-speaking Danis to inquire. Learning that the Damal were rejoicing in the fulfillment of their ancient hope, the Dani were stunned. They too had been awaiting the fulfillment of something they called *nabelan-kabelan*. This was the belief that one day immortality would return to humankind.

Was it possible that the message which was *hai* to the Damal could also be *nabelan-kabelan* to the Dani? By then one of the missionary couples, Gordon and Peggy Larson, had been assigned to work among the Dani. Dani warriors noted that they often mentioned a man named Jesus who not only could raise the dead, but Himself as well. Suddenly, things fell into place for the Dani as they had for the Damal. The word spread. In valley after valley, the once barbarous Dani listened to the words of life. A church was born.

The Asmat and the "New Birth."

The concept of "new birth" relates to Irian Jaya's stone-age Asmat tribe through another redemptive analogy. Nicodemus, a learned Jewish scholar, had difficulty understanding what Jesus meant when He spoke of people being born again. Nicodemus asked, "How can a man be born when he is old? Can he enter into his mother's womb a second time and be born?" Yet the new birth of the gospel can be understood by Irian Jaya's Asmat tribe. They have a way of making peace that requires children from two warring villages to pass through a symbolic birth canal formed by the bodies of a number of men and women from both villages. Those who pass through the canal are considered *reborn* into the kinship system of their enemy's village. Rocked, lullabied, cradled and coddled like newborn infants, they become the focus of a joyful celebration. From then on, they may travel freely back and forth between the two formerly warring villages, serving as living peace bonds. For centuries, this custom has impressed deeply upon the Asmat mind the vital concept: True peace can come only through a new birth experience!

Suppose God called you to communicate the gospel to the Asmat people. What would be your logical starting point? Let us assume you have learned their language and are competent enough to discuss the things that are dear to their hearts. One day you visit a typical Asmat man—let's call him Erypeet—in his longhouse. First you discuss with him the former period of war and the new birth transaction that brought it to an end. Then you say, "Erypeet, I too am very interested in new birth. You see, I was at war with an enemy named God. While I was at war with God, life was grim, as it was for you and your enemies. But one day my enemy God approached me and said, 'I have prepared a new birth whereby I can be born in you and you can be born again in Me, so that we can be at peace....'"

By this time Erypeet is leaning forward on his mat. "You and your people have a new birth too?" he asks. He is amazed to find that you, an alien, are sophisticated enough to even *think* in terms of a new birth, let alone *experience* one!

"Yes," you reply.

"Is it like ours?"

"Well, there are some similarities and there are some differences," you say. "Let me tell you about them...." And Erypeet understands.

Why the difference between Erypeet's and Nicodemus's responses? Erypeet's mind has been pre-conditioned by Asmat redemptive analogy to acknowledge man's need for a new birth. Your task is to convince him that he needs *spiritual* rebirth.

Do redemptive analogies like these occur by mere coincidence? No, because their strategic use is foreshadowed in the New Testament, and because they are so widespread, we can discern the grace of God at work. After all, our God is far too sovereign to be merely lucky.

The Yali and the Osuwa.

Has a culture been found that is lacking concepts that form redemptive analogies? A formidable candidate for this grim distinction was the cannibal Yali culture of Irian Jaya described in *Lords of the Earth*. If ever a tribe needed a Christ-foreshadowing belief that a missionary could appeal to, it was the Yali. By 1966, missionaries of the Regions Beyond Missionary Union (now World Team) had succeeded in winning about twenty Yali to Christ. Priests of the Yali god Kembu promptly martyred two of the twenty. Two years later, they killed missionaries Stan Dale and Phillip Masters, driving about one hundred arrows into each of their bodies. Then the Indonesian government, also threatened by the Yali, stepped in to quell further uprisings. Awed by the power of the government, the Yali decided they would rather have missionaries than soldiers. But the missionaries could find no analogy in Yali culture to make the gospel clear.

Another missionary and I conducted a much belated "culture probe" to learn more about Yali customs and beliefs. One day a young Yali named Erariek shared with us a story from his past. He said, "Long ago my brother Sunahan and a friend named Kahalek were ambushed by enemies from across the river. Kahalek was killed, but Sunahan fled to a circular stone wall nearby. Leaping inside it, he turned, bared his chest at his enemies, and laughed at them. The enemies immediately lowered their weapons and hurried away."

I nearly dropped my pen. "Why didn't they kill him?" I asked.

Erariek smiled. "If they had shed one drop of my brother's blood while he stood within that sacred stone wall—we call it an *osuwa*—their own people would have killed them."

Yali pastors and the missionaries working with them now have a new evangelistic tool.

Christ is the spiritual Osuwa, the perfect place of refuge. Yali culture instinctively echoes the Christian teaching that man needs a place of refuge. Ages earlier they had established a network of *osuwa* in areas where most of their battles took place. Missionaries had noticed the stone walls, but had never discovered their full significance.

Using Indigenous Names for God

Another special category of redemptive analogy relates to usable names for God—aliases for Elohim—found in thousands of languages worldwide. Christians err whenever we too readily assume that pagans know nothing of God. In fact, a startling number of pagan cultures possess amazingly clear concepts about a Supreme God who created all things. Scripture tells us to expect this because of God's general revelation both through creation and conscience. For example:

1. "Since the creation of the world," Paul the Apostle wrote, "God's invisible qualities—His eternal power and divine nature—have been clearly seen, being understood from what has been made, so that men are without excuse" (Rom 1:20). This belief, that men already know something about God even before they hear of either Jewish law or the Christian gospel, was a cornerstone of Paul's theology of evangelism. He expressed it in a Lycaonian town called Lystra, proclaiming that "in the past, He (God) let all nations go their own way; yet He has not left Himself without testimony. He has shown kindness by giving you rain from heaven," etc. (Acts 14:16,17).

2. In his famous letter to Roman Christians, Paul wrote that "when Gentiles do by nature things required by the law they show that the requirements of the law are written on their hearts" (Rom 2:14,15).

3. John the Apostle declared that Jesus Christ is "the true Light that gives light to *every* man" (John 1:9). And King Solomon wrote that God has "set eternity in the hearts of men." He added the cautionary statement that man of himself still "cannot fathom what God has done from beginning to end" (Eccl 3:11). According to the Hebrew scholar Gleason Archer,

Solomon's statement means that humankind has a God-given ability to grasp the concept of eternity, with all its unsettling implications for moral beings.[1]

4. It was Solomon's father, King David, who penned the eloquent appreciation of God's universal testimony to Himself through creation that reads "the heavens declare the glory of God; the skies proclaim the works of His hands. Day after day they pour forth speech; night after night they display knowledge. There is no speech or language where their voice is not heard. Their voice goes out into all the earth, their words to the end of the world" (Ps 19:1-4). David then focuses upon the sun, describing it as a "bridegroom coming forth from his pavilion" and a "champion rejoicing to run his course" (Ps 19:5,6). Perhaps more than any other scripture, this one fittingly introduces King Pachacutec.

Pachacutec's Mini-Reformation

Pachacutec may be history's finest example of what Paul, John, Solomon and David meant in the above quotations. Pachacutec was an Inca who lived between AD1400 and 1448.[2] He was also the entrepreneur who designed and built Macchu Picchu, perhaps the first mountain resort in the New World. After the Spanish invasion of Peru, Macchu Picchu became a last sanctuary for the Inca upper class.

Pachacutec and his people worshipped the sun, which they called Inti. But Pachacutec became suspicious of Intis' credentials. Like King David, King Pachacutec studied the sun. It never did anything, as far as Pachacutec could tell, except rise, shine, cross the zenith and set. The next day, the same thing—rise, shine, cross the zenith, set. Unlike David, who likened the sun to a bridegroom or a champion, Pachacutec said, "Inti seems to be but a laborer who has to perform the same chores daily. And if he is merely a laborer, surely he cannot be God! If Inti were God, Inti would do something original once in a while!"

He thought again and observed, "Mere mist dims the light of Inti. Surely if Inti were God, nothing could dim his light!" Thus did Pachacutec tumble to a crucial realization—he had been worshipping a mere *thing* as creator!

But if Inti wasn't God, to whom could Pachacutec turn? Then he remembered a name his father had once extolled—*Viracocha*! According to his father, Viracocha was none other than a god who created *all things*. All things including Inti! Pachacutec came to a brisk decision. This Inti-as-God nonsense had gone far enough! He called an assembly of the priests of the sun, a pagan equivalent of a Nicene Council. Standing before the assembly, Pachacutec explained his reasoning about the supremacy of Viracocha. Then he commanded that Inti, from that time forward, be addressed as "kinsman" only. Prayer, he said, must be directed to Viracocha, the supreme God.

While generally ignoring Pachacutec, scholars have widely acclaimed Akhenaten, an Egyptian King (1379-1361 B.C.), as a man of rare genius because he attempted to replace the grossly confused idolatry of ancient Egypt with the purer, simpler worship of the sun as sole God.[3] Pachacutec, however, was leagues ahead of Akhenaten in his realization that the sun, which could merely *blind* human eyes, was no match for a God too great even to be seen by human eyes. If Akhenaten's sun worship was a

step above idolatry, Pachacutec's choice of an invisible God was a leap into the stratosphere!

Why have modern scholars, religious as well as secular, virtually ignored this amazing man? Perhaps it was because Pachacutec stopped short of an even greater achievement. One important measure of a man of genius is his ability to communicate his insight to "common" people. Great religious leaders from Moses to Buddha and Paul to Luther have all excelled in this skill. Pachacutec never even tried. Deeming the masses of his people too ignorant to appreciate the worth of an invisible God, he deliberately left them in the dark about Viracocha. Pachacutec's reformation, amazing as it was, became only a mini-reformation, limited to upper classes only. Upper classes are notoriously short-lived social phenomena. Less than a century after Pachacutec's death, ruthless conquistadors obliterated the upper classes of Pachacutec's empire and his reformation ended.

Was Viracocha really the true God, the God of creation? Or was he merely a figment of Pachacutec's imagination, an impostor? If Paul the Apostle had lived in Pachacutec's

day, and if one of his missionary journeys had taken him all the way to Peru, would he have denounced Pachacutec's insight as a delusion? Or would he have agreed that "Yahweh's name in this land is Viracocha." It's not difficult to deduce Paul's attitude toward this question. When he preached the gospel among Greek-speaking peoples, he did not impose a Jewish name for God—Jehovah, Yahweh, Elohim, Adonai or El Shaddai—upon them. Rather he placed his apostolic seal upon a two-hundred-year-old decision of the translators of the Septuagint version of the Old Testament. They had given the God of the Jews a completely Greek name—*Theos*. Paul followed suit.

Interestingly, translators of the Septuagint did not try to equate the Greek god Zeus with Yahweh. Nor did Paul. Although Greeks esteemed Zeus as "king of the gods," he was also viewed as the offspring of two other gods, Cronus and Rhea. Hence the name Zeus could not qualify as a synonym for Yahweh, the uncreated. Later, the Latin cognate of Theos—Deus—was accepted as the equivalent of Yahweh fo Roman Christians!

And when Paul preached the gospel in Athens, he boldly equated Yahweh with an "unknown God" that was associated with a certain altar in the city. Paul said, "What you worship as something unknown I am about to proclaim to you!"

An Opportunity for the Gospel

A principle emerges. Contrary to the belief of Jehovah's Witnesses, there is nothing innately sacred about any particular combination of sounds or letters as a name for the Almighty. He can have ten thousand aliases, if need be, in ten thousand languages. It is impossible to talk about an uncreated Creator without meaning HIM. Anyone capable of protesting that "some of His attributes are missing" is responsible to fill them in! Any theological vacuum surrounding any culture's concept of God is not an obstacle to the gospel—it's an opportunity!

As it has spread around the world, Christianity has continued to confirm, from Paul's time to now, the concept of a Supreme God in a thousand human traditions:

- When Celtic missionaries reached the Anglo-Saxons in northern Europe, they did not impose upon them Jewish or Greek names for Deity. Instead they used Anglo-Saxon words like "Gött," "God" or "Gut."
- In 1828 American Baptist missionaries, George and Sarah Boardman, found the Karen people of southern Burma believing that a great God named Y'wa (shades of Yahweh) had long ago given their forefathers a sacred book! Alas, the forefathers, rascals that they were, had lost it! But according to a persistent Karen tradition, one day a white brother would restore the lost book to the Karen people, bringing them back into fellowship with Y'wa. The tradition predicted that he would appear carrying a black object under his arm. George Boardman, who had a habit of tucking his black, leatherbound Bible under his arm, became the white brother, and a hundred thousand Karen people were baptized as believers within a few decades!
- In 1867 Norwegian Lutheran missionary, Lars Skrefsrud, found thousands of Santal people in India wistfully regretting their forefathers' rejection of Thakur Jiu, the genuine God. Skrefsrud proclaimed that Thakur Jiu's Son had come to earth to reconcile estranged humanity to himself. The result: Within a few decades, over a hundred thousand Santal received Jesus Christ as their Savior!
- Presbyterian pioneers in Korea discovered a Korean name for God—Hananim, the Great One. Rather than sweeping Hananim aside and imposing a foreign name for God, they proclaimed Jesus Christ as the Son of Hananim. Within some eighty years, more than two and a half million Koreans have become followers of Jesus Christ!
- During the 1940's, Albert Brant of the Sudan Interior Mission found thousands of Gedeo tribesmen in Ethiopia believing that Magano, the Creator, would one day send a messenger to camp under a certain sycamore tree. Unsuspectingly, Albert camped under that tree and an awesome response to the gospel began, bringing 250 churches to birth in less than three decades.

These breakthrough narratives can be multiplied by the hundreds from the history of missions. Truly Paul, John, Solomon and David were right! God has not left Himself without the witnesses of general revelation. How tragic that earlier generations were not swifter to obey the Great Commission. What might have happened if gospel messengers had helped Pachacutec to find in Jesus Christ the fulfillment of what he—because eternity was in his heart—knew must be true?

How many other Pachacutecs will die unconfirmed? How many generations of Pachacutecs will rise up in the judgment to join Ninevah and the Queen of Sheba in reproach of indifferent believers (Luke 11:31-32)? Let us strive to be—for our generation—the Boardmans, the Skrefruds, the Brants, who care enough to go and tell!

In our generation, the choice of language to refer to God is a crucial matter. For example, some Christians believe that Islam's Arabic name for God, *Allah*, should not be accepted as a viable synonym for Elohim. Let it be known that millions of Christians in Indonesia use *Allah* for God and *Tuhan Allah* for Lord God. Perhaps because of this, Indonesian Christians have been much more effective in winning Muslims to Christ than any other Christians. Let it also be known that Muslims in some Muslims nations, knowing the access the name "Allah" gives to the Muslim heart, are passing laws to forbid Christians from using it in reference to the gospel of Christ.

Concepts like the Sawi Peace Child, the Damal *hai*, the Dani *nabelan-kabelan*, the Asmat new birth and the Yali *osuwa* are at the heart of the cultures of humankind. When messengers of the gospel ignore, discredit or obliterate distinctives like these, resistance to the gospel may harden into cultural concrete. But as redemptive analogy identifies and confirms the cultural components that result from God's influence through general revelation, the Bible itself, God's special revelation, can be lifted up as the consummate revelation of God, from God and for God. Hundreds of areas remain where the response to the gospel has been slight, or even non-existent. In these areas, sensitive probes of culture may discover wonderful possibilities for the penetration of the gospel through redemptive analogy.

End Notes

1. From a personal interview with Gleason Archer.
2. *Indians of the Americas* (Wash., D.C.: National Geographic Society, 1955), pp. 293-307.
3. *The Horizon Book of Lost Worlds* (New York: American Heritage Publishing, 1962), p. 115.

Study Questions

1. Imagine yourself as a new missionary. How will you apply the strategy of looking for a redemptive analogy among the people you are working with?

2. How does the concept of general revelation affect how a missionary might relate the name (character) of God and biblical truth?

Why Communicate the Gospel Through Stories?

Tom A. Steffen

I thought that I had finally learned enough of the Ifugao language and culture (Philippines) to allow me to do some public evangelism. I developed some Bible lessons that followed the topical outline we received in pre-field training: the Bible, God, Satan, humanity, sin, judgment, and Jesus Christ. I began by introducing my Ifugao listeners to the authority-base (the Bible). Then I quickly moved on to the second part of the outline (God), and so forth, culminating with Jesus Christ. I presented the lessons in a topical, systematic format. My goal was not only to communicate the gospel, but to communicate it in such a way that the Ifugao could effectively articulate it to others.

But as I taught, I soon realized that the Ifugao found it difficult to follow the topical presentations, and found it even harder to explain the content to others. I was astonished and perplexed.

Something needed to change, so I added a number of stories from the Old Testament to illustrate the abstract (theoretical) concepts in the lessons through pictorial (concrete) characters and objects. I told stories about creation, the fall, Cain and Abel, the flood, the escape from Egypt, the giving of the Ten Commandments, the Tabernacle, Elijah and Baal, all of which would provide foundation for Jesus' story. Their response was phenomenal. Not only did the evangelistic sessions come alive, the recipients became instant evangelists, telling the stories to friends enthusiastically and effectively. From then on I integrated stories in all my evangelistic efforts.

Back to the Power of Story

After the Ifugao reintroduced me to the power of story I began to research the topic.[1] I soon discovered that many disciplines, including management, mental and physical health, apologetics, theology, and anthropology rely heavily on telling stories. Communicating through story is much more than a fad.

Sadly, though, storytelling has become a lost art for many Christian workers in relation to evangelism. Few present the gospel using Old Testament stories to lay a solid foundation for understanding the life of Christ, or connect these stories of hope to the target audience's story of hopelessness. Rather, many prefer to outline four or five spiritual laws, and prove the validity of each through finely honed arguments.

A number of hollow myths bias this preference against storytelling in evangelism: (1) stories are for children;

Tom A. Steffan is Associate Professor of Intercultural Studies and Director of the Doctor of Missiology program at the School of Intercultural Studies, Biola Univeristy, La Mirada, California.

From *Passing the Baton*, by Tom A. Steffen, 1993. Used by permission of William Carey Library, Pasadena, CA.

(2) stories are for entertainment; (3) adults prefer sophisticated, objective, propositional thinking; (4) character derives from dogmas, creeds, and theology; (5) storytelling is a waste of time in that it fails to get to the more meaty issues. As a result of these and other related myths, Christian workers have often unwittingly set aside storytelling. To help reconnect God's story to evangelism-discipleship, I will highlight seven reasons why storytelling should become a skill practiced by all Christian workers who communicate the gospel.

1. Storytelling is a universal form of communication. No matter where you travel in this world, you will find that people love to tell and listen to stories. Age doesn't change this desire. Young children, teenagers, and seniors, all love to enter the life experiences of others through stories.

Whatever the topic discussed, stories become an integral part of the dialogue. Stories are used to argue a point, interject humor, illustrate a key insight, comfort a despondent friend, challenge the champion, or simply pass the time of day. Now matter what its use, a story has a unique way of finding its way into a conversation.

Stories are heard anywhere. You can hear stories in churches, court houses, movie theaters, homes, buses, cars, locker rooms, prisons, and walks in the woods. Geographic location does little to deter the flow of stories.

Not only do all people tell stories, they have a need to do so. This leads us to the second reason for storytelling.

2. More than half of the world's population prefer the concrete mode of learning. Illiterate and semi-literate people in the world probably outnumber people who can read.[2] People with such backgrounds tend to express themselves more through concrete forms (story and symbol) than abstract concepts (propositional thinking and philosophy).

A growing number of Americans prefer the concrete mode of communication. This is due, at least in part, to a major shift in communication preference. One of the reasons behind this shift (and the dropping literacy rate) is the television. With the average TV sound bite now around 13 seconds, and the average image length less than three seconds (often without linear logic), it is no wonder

that those under its daily influence have little time or desire for reading which helps develop and reinforce linear thought. Consequently, newspaper businesses continue to dwindle while video production companies proliferate. If Christian workers rely too heavily on abstract, literary foundations for evangelism and teaching, two-thirds of the world may turn their attention elsewhere.[3]

3. Stories connect with our imagination and emotions. Effective communication touches not only the mind, it also reaches the seat of emotions—the heart. Unlike principles, precepts, and propositions, stories take us on an opened-ended journey that touches the whole person.

While stories provide dates, times, places, names, and chronologies, they simultaneously provoke tears, cheers, fear, anger, confidence, defensiveness, conviction, sarcasm, fantasy, despair, and hope. Stories draw listeners into the lives of the characters (people, animals, or objects, real or fictitious). Listeners (participants) not only hear what happened to such characters; through the imagination they vicariously enter the experience. Schneidau eloquently captures this point when he states: "Stories have a way of tapping those feelings that we habitually anesthetize."[4]

People appreciate stories because they mirror their total lives, weaving together fact and feeling. Stories unleash the imagination, making learning an exciting, life-changing experience.

4. Every major religion uses stories to socialize its young, convert potential followers, and indoctrinate members. Buddhism, Islam, Hinduism, Judaism, Christianity—all use stories to expand (and limit) membership, assure ongoing generational conversion, and bring disciples to maturity. Whether Paul was evangelizing Jews or Gentiles, the audience heard relevant stories. Unbelieving Jews heard about cultural heroes, such as Abraham, Moses, and David (Acts 13:13-43). Unbelieving Gentiles heard about the powerful God behind the creation story (Acts 14:8-18; 17:16-34). Maturing believers heard the same stories with a different emphasis.

All major religions use stories to differentiate true members from false, acceptable behavior from unacceptable. Stories create committed communities. Could one of the reasons for this be that stories provide an inoffensive, non-threatening way of challenging one's basic beliefs and behavior?

Major literary styles of the Bible

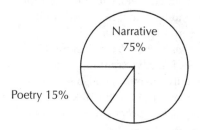

Narrative
75%

Poetry 15%

Thought-organized 10%

5. Approximately 75 percent of the Bible is story. Three basic styles of literature dominate the landscape of the Scriptures—story, poetry, and thought-organized format—but story is predominant (see figure above). Over the centuries, the writers of the Bible documented a host of characters: from kings to slaves, from those who followed God to those who lived for personal gain. Such stories serve as mirrors to reflect our own perspective of life, and more importantly, God's. Koller astutely points out:

> The Bible was not given to reveal the lives of Abraham, Isaac, and Jacob, but to reveal *the hand of God* in the lives of Abraham, Isaac, and Jacob; not as a revelation of Mary and Martha and Lazarus, but as a revelation of *the Savior* of Mary and Martha and Lazarus.[5]

Poetry covers approximately 15 percent of the Bible. Songs, lamentations, and proverbs provide readers and listeners with a variety of avenues to express, and to experience deep inner emotions. These portions of Scripture demonstrate the feeling side of people, and illuminate the feelings of God as well.

The remaining ten percent is composed in a thought-organized format. The apostle Paul's Greek-influenced writings fall under this category, where logical, linear thinking tends to dominate. Many Westerners schooled in the tradition of the Greeks, myself included, prefer to spend the majority of time in the Scripture's smallest literary style. Yet if God communicated the majority of his message to the world through story, what does this suggest to Christian workers?

6. Stories create instant evangelists. People find it easy to repeat a good story. Whether the story centers around juicy gossip or the gospel of Jesus Christ, something within each of us wants to hear and tell such stories. Suppressing a good story is like resisting a jar full of your favorite cookies. Sooner or later, the urge is too strong and the cookie gets eaten, the story gets told. Told stories get retold.

Because my Ifugao friends could relate well to the life-experiences of Bible characters, they not only applied the stories to their lives, they immediately retold them to family and friends, even before they switched faith allegiance to Jesus Christ. Stories create storytellers.

7. Jesus taught theology through stories. Jesus never wrote a book on systematic theology, yet he taught theology wherever he went. As a holistic thinker, Jesus often used parabolic stories to tease audiences into reflecting on new ways of thinking about life.

As Jesus' listeners wrestled with new concepts introduced innocently yet intentionally through parables, they were challenged to examine traditions, form new images of God, and transform their behavior. Stories pushed the people to encounter God and change. It wasn't comfortable to rise to the challenge of Jesus' stories: to step out of the boat, taste new wine, display the golden lampstands, turn from family members, extend mercy to others, search for hidden objects, and donate material goods and wealth to the poor—none of it was inviting. But the stories had thrown open possibilities that made it difficult to remain content with life as it had been. Whichever direction the listeners took, they found no middle ground. They had met God. Jesus' stories, packed with theology, caused reason, imagination, and emotions to collide, demanding a change of allegiance.

Conclusion

The Bible begins with the story of creation and ends with a vision of God's recreation. Peppered generously between *alpha* and *omega* are a host of other stories. While stories dominate the Scripture landscape, they rarely enter the Christian worker's evangelism-discipleship strategies intentionally. Leland Ryken cogently asks:

Photo courtesy of Caleb Project

Why does the Bible contain so many sto-ries? Is it possible that stories reveal some truths and experiences in a way that no other literary form does—and if so, what are they? What is the difference in our pic-ture of God when we read stories in which God acts, as compared with theological statements about the nature of God? What does the Bible communicate through our imagination that it does not communicate through our reason? If the Bible uses the imagination as one way of communicating truth, should we not show an identical con-fidence in the power of the imagination to convey religious truth? If so, would a good starting point be to respect the story qual-ity of the Bible in our exposition of it?[6]

Is it not time for today's Christian workers to revitalize one of the world's oldest, most universal and powerful art forms—storytell-ing? I believe so. I also believe that Christian workers, with training and practice, can ef-fectively communicate the finished story of Jesus Christ, and connect it to the target audience's unfinished story. Presenting an overview of Old and New Testament stories that unveils the history of redemption will highlight for the listeners the Storyline (Jesus Christ) of the sacred Storybook (Bible). Should this happen, the gospel will be much more easily understood, and more frequently communicated to family and friends.

End Notes:

1. For more information on storytelling see Chapter 11 in my *Passing the Baton: Church Planting That Empowers* (1997) that looks at the Chronological Teaching model, and *Reconnecting God's Story for Ministry: Crosscultural Storytelling at Home and Abroad* (1996), both available through the Wil-liam Carey Library.
2. Barrett, David B., 1997, Annual Statistical Table on Global Mission: 1997. *International Bulletin of Missionary Research, 21(1)*:24-25.
3. Klem, Herbert V., 1982, *Oral Communication of the Scripture: Insights From African Oral Art*. Pasa-dena CA: William Carey Library.
4. Schneidau, Herbert N., 1986, Biblical Narrative and Modern Consciousness, Frank McConnel, ed., In *The Bible and the Narrative Tradition*. (New York: Oxford University Press), pp. 136.
5. Koller, Charles W., 1962, *Expository Preaching Without Notes*. Grand Rapids, MI: Baker Book House, p. 32.
6. Ryken, Leland, 1979, The Bible: God's Story-book. *Christianity Today*, 23(23): 38.

Study Questions

1. If God conveyed the majority of the biblical message to the world through story, what does this suggest to Christian workers?

2. Why is storytelling effective to communicate cross-culturally?

Three Encounters in Christian Witness

Charles H. Kraft

W e're hearing more about power encounter these days among non-charismatics. We are more open and less afraid of spiritual power than we used to be. Several missionary training institutions now include courses on power encounter. But there are extremes we want to avoid. My task in this article is to offer an approach to power encounter that is biblically balanced with two other encounters that evangelicals have always emphasized.

The Basic Concept

The term "power encounter" comes from missionary anthropologist Alan Tippett. In his 1971 book, *People Movements in Southern Polynesia*, Tippett observed that in the South Pacific the early acceptance of the gospel usually occurred when there was an "encounter" demonstrating that the power of God is greater than that of the local pagan deity. This was usually accompanied by a desecration of the symbol(s) of the traditional deity by its priest or priestess, who then declared that he or she rejected the deity's power, pledged allegiance to the true God, and vowed to depend on God alone for protection and spiritual power.

At such a moment, the priest or priestess would eat the totem animal (e.g., a sacred turtle) and claim Jesus' protection. Seeing that the priest or priestess suffered no ill effects, the people opened themselves to the gospel.[1] These confrontations, along with those classic biblical power encounters (e.g., Moses vs. Pharaoh, Ex 7-12, and Elijah vs. the prophets of Baal, 1 Ki 18) formed Tippett's view of power encounter.

More recently, the term has been used more broadly to include healings, deliverances, or any other "visible, practical demonstration that Jesus Christ is more powerful than the spirits, powers, or false gods worshiped or feared by the members of a given people group."[2] The concept of "taking territory" from the enemy for God's kingdom is seen as basic to such encounters.

According to this view, Jesus' entire ministry was a massive power confrontation between God and the enemy. The ministry of the apostles and the Church in succeeding generations is seen as the continuing exercise of the "authority and power over all demons and all diseases" given by Jesus to his followers (Luke 9:1). Contemporary stories about such encounters come from China, Argentina, Europe, the Muslim world, and nearly everywhere else where the Church is growing rapidly.

Charles H. Kraft has been Professor of Anthropology and Intercultural Communication at Fuller Theological Seminary, School of World Mission, since 1969. With his wife, Marguerite, he served as a missionary in Nigeria. He teaches and writes in the areas of anthropology, cross-cultural communication, prayer and spiritual warfare. Among his numerous books are, *Christianity in Culture, Anthropology for Christian Witness* and *Christianity with Power*.

Revised from "What Kind of Encounters Do We Need in our Christian Witness?," *Evangelical Missions Quarterly*, 27:3 (July 1991), published by EMIS, P.O. Box 794, Wheaton, IL 60189. Used by permission.

Tippett observed that most of the world's peoples are power-oriented and respond to Christ most readily through power demonstrations.[3] Gospel messages about faith, love, forgiveness, and the other facts of Christianity are not likely to have nearly the impact on such people as the demonstrations of spiritual power. My own experience confirms Tippett's thesis. Therefore, cross-cultural workers ought to learn as much as possible about the place of power encounter in Jesus' ministry and ours.

Additional Encounters

Of course, missionaries face several questions about power encounter. One of the basic ones is how to relate power concerns and approaches to our traditional emphases on truth and salvation. Let me suggest that we need to use a three-pronged approach to our witness.

Jesus battled Satan on a broader front than simply power encounters. If we are to be biblically fair and balanced, we must give two other encounters equal attention—allegiance encounters and truth encounters. We need to focus on the close relationship in the New Testament between these three encounters. Here's an outline that will help:

Jesus Christ Confronts Satan

1. *Jesus confronts Satan concerning power*: This results in power encounters to release people from satanic captivity and bring them into freedom in Jesus Christ.

2. *Jesus confronts Satan concerning allegiance*: This results in allegiance or commitment encounters to rescue people from wrong and bring them into relationship to Jesus Christ.

3. *Jesus confronts Satan concerning truth*: This results in truth encounters to counter ignorance or error and to bring people to correct understandings about Jesus Christ.

Throughout the world many Christians who have committed themselves to Jesus Christ, and who have embraced much Christian truth, have not given up their pre-Christian commitment to and practice of what we call spiritual power. The powers of darkness that they formerly followed have not been confronted and defeated by the power of Jesus. So they live with a "dual allegiance" and a syncretistic understanding of truth.

Therefore, some mistakenly assume that if they confront people with healing and deliverance campaigns to show them Christ's power, they will turn to him in droves. They assume that those who experience God's healing power will automatically commit themselves to the source of that power.

However, I know of several such campaigns that have produced few, if any, lasting conversions. Why not? Because little attention was paid to leading the people from an experience of Jesus' power to a commitment to him. These people are accustomed to accepting power from any source. Therefore, they see no greater compulsion to commit themselves to Jesus than to any of the other sources of power they regularly consult.

I believe Jesus expects power demonstrations to be as crucial to our ministries as they were to his (Luke 9:1,2). However, any approach that advocates power encounter without giving adequate attention to the other two encounters—allegiance and truth—is not biblically balanced. Many people who saw or experienced power events during Jesus' ministry did not turn to him in faith. This should alert us to the inadequacy of power demonstrations alone as a total evangelistic strategy.

A Balance of Encounters

We can see the three kinds of encounters outlined above in Jesus' ministry. Typically, he started by teaching, followed by a power demonstration, then a return to teaching, at least for the disciples (e.g., Luke 4:31ff; 5:1ff, 17ff; 6:6ff, 17ff, etc.). Appeals for allegiance to the Father or to himself appear both implicitly and explicitly throughout his teaching. Jesus seems to have used power demonstrations more when interacting with people who had not yet become his followers, focusing more on the teaching of truth with those already committed to him.

His appeal for allegiance to at least the first five apostles (Peter, Andrew, James, John—Luke 5, and Levi—Luke 5:27-28) occurred after significant power demonstrations. Once his followers had successfully negotiated their allegiance encounter, their subsequent growth was primarily a matter of learning and practicing more truth.

First century Jews, like most people today, were very concerned about spiritual power. Paul said they sought power signs (1 Cor 1:22). Jesus' usual practice of healing and deliverance from demons soon after entering a new area (e.g., Luke 4:33-35,39; 5:13-15; 6:6-10,18-19, etc.) may be seen as his way of approaching them at the point of their concern. When he sent out his followers to the surrounding towns to prepare the way for him, he commanded them to use the same approach (Luke 9:1-6; 10:19).

Jesus' reluctance to do miraculous works merely to satisfy those who wanted him to prove himself (Matt 12:38-42; 16:1-4) would, however, seem to indicate his power demonstrations were intended to point to something beyond the mere demonstration of God's power. I believe that he had at least two more important goals. First, Jesus sought to demonstrate God's nature by showing his love. As he said to Philip, "If you have seen me, you have seen the Father" (John 14:9). He freely healed, delivered, and blessed those who came to him and did not retract what he had given, even if they did not return to thank him (Luke 17:11-19). He used God's power to demonstrate his love.

Second, Jesus sought to lead people into the most important encounter, the allegiance encounter. This is clear from his challenge to the Pharisees when they demanded a miracle, that the people of Nineveh who repented would accuse the people of Jesus' day who did not do likewise (Matt 12:41). Experiencing God's power may be both pleasant and impressive, but only allegiance to God through Christ really saves.

The Nature and Aims of the Encounters

The three encounters—power, allegiance, and truth—are not the same, but they are each intended to initiate a process crucial to the Christian experience aimed at a specific goal.

1. The concern of the truth encounter is understanding. The vehicle of that encounter is teaching.

2. The concern of the allegiance encounter is relationship. The vehicle of that encounter is witness.

3. The concern of the power encounter is freedom. Its vehicle is spiritual warfare.

Truth and understanding have a lot to do with the mind; allegiance and relationship rest primarily in the will; and freedom is largely experienced emotionally.

1. *Truth encounters.* Truth encounters in which the mind is exercised and the will is challenged seem to provide the context within which the other encounters take place and can be interpreted. Jesus constantly taught truth to bring his hearers to ever greater understandings about the person and plan of God. To teach truth, he increased their knowledge. However, in scripture, knowledge is grounded in relationship and experience; it is not simply philosophical and academic. The truth encounter, like the other two, is personal and experiential, not merely a matter of words and head knowledge.

When we focus on knowledge and truth, we enable people to gain enough understanding to be able to accurately interpret the other two encounters. For example, a power demonstration has little, or wrong, significance unless it is related to truth. Knowledge of the source of, and the reason for, the power are essential for proper interpretation of a power event. The need for such knowledge is probably why Jesus used his power demonstrations in the context of teaching his disciples.

Truth Encounters

Start	→	Process	→	Aim
Awareness		Leading to knowledge		Understanding of truth

2. *Allegiance encounters.* Allegiance encounters, involving the exercise of the will in commitment and obedience to the Lord, are the most important of the encounters. For without commitment and obedience to Jesus, there is no spiritual life.

The initial allegiance encounter leads a person into a relationship with God. Through successive encounters between our will and God's, we grow in intimacy with and likeness to him, as we submit to his will and practice intimate association with him. Initial allegiance and the relationship that proceeds from it are tightly linked to truth, both because they are developed within the truth encounter and because a relationship with God is the true reason for human existence.

Implied in the allegiance encounter is the cultivation of the fruits of the Holy Spirit, especially love toward God and man. We are to turn from love of (or, commitment to) the world that is under the control of the evil one (1 Jn 5:19) to God who loved the world and gave himself for it. As we grow in our relationship with him, we become more like him, conforming to the image of Christ (Rom 8:29).

Allegiance Encounters

Start →	Process →	Aim
Commitment to Jesus	Growth in relationship	Character of Jesus Christ

3. *Power encounters.* Power encounters contribute a different dimension to Christian experience. They focus on freedom from the enemy's captivity. Satan is the blinder (2 Cor 4:4), restricter, hinderer, crippler—the enemy who attempts to keep people from allegiance to God and truth. Though he works on all human faculties, the enemy seems particularly interested in crippling people emotionally. If people are to move into commitment to Christ they need emotional freedom.

Power Encounters

Start →	Process →	Aim
Healing, deliverance, etc.	Increasing freedom, etc.	Victory over Satan

For the one who is healed, delivered, blessed, or otherwise freed from the enemy's grip, the major payoff is freedom. However, for an observer, the impact is likely to be quite different. If properly interpreted, the encounter communicates basic truths about God's power and love. The observer sees that God is worthy of his trust because he is willing and able to free people from Satan's destructive hold.

Power Encounters–An Observer's View

Start →	Process →	Aim
Attract attention	Demonstration	Trust God

Although we do not call them power encounters, our demonstrations of love, accep-

tance, forgiveness, and peace in troubled times—plus a number of other Christian virtues—play the same role of attracting attention and leading people to trust God. These all witness to the presence of a loving God willing to give abundant life and bring release from the enemy.

The Encounters Work Together

Our missionary witness needs to use all three encounters together, not separately, as we can see in this three-part circle:

People need freedom from the enemy to (1) open their minds to receive and understand truth (2 Cor 4:4), and (2) to release their wills so they can commit themselves to God. However, they can't understand and apply Christian truth, nor can they exercise power, without a continuing commitment to God. Nor can they maintain the truth and their allegiance without freedom from the enemy won through continual power encounters. We constantly need each of these dimensions in our lives.

The diagram below shows the interworkings of these three aspects of Christian life and witness in more detail.

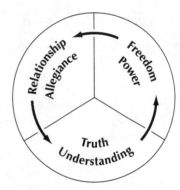

There are three stages in the process, the third of which results in witness to those at the start of Stage 1. At the start (Stage 1), people are under Satanic captivity in ignorance and error and are committed to some non-Christian allegiance. Through power encounters, they gain freedom from that captivity, moving from the blindness and will-weakening of the enemy into openness to the truth. Through truth and allegiance encounters, they receive enough understanding to act on, plus enough challenge to induce them to commit themselves to Christ.

In the second stage, having made their allegiance to Jesus, people need continued spiritual warfare to attain greater freedom from the enemy's continued efforts to harass and cripple them. They also need continued teaching and challenges to greater commitment and obedience. They grow in their relationship to God and his people through continued encounters in all three areas.

In the third stage, this growing relationship results in power encounters through prayer to break the enemy's power to delude, harass, cause illness, demonize, and the like. These encounters are accompanied by truth and allegiance encounters, so that believers are challenged to greater commitment and obedience, especially in witness to those in the first stage.

Beyond our own Christian growth lies our witness. At the end of his ministry, Jesus taught much about his relationship to his followers and theirs to each other (e.g., John 14-16), as well as about the authority and power he would give them (Acts 1:8). He carefully related power and authority to witness (e.g., Matt 28:19, 20; Mark 16:15-18; Acts 1:8).

He told the disciples to wait for spiritual power before they embarked on witness (Luke 24:49; Acts 1:4), just as Jesus himself had waited to be empowered at his own baptism (Luke 3:21,22). We are not fully equipped to witness without the freedom-bringing, truth-revealing power of the Holy Spirit (Acts 1:8).

Some Guidelines for Evangelicals

Because Satan is a master at deceit and counterfeiting, we must encounter or confront him, rather than simply ignore him. And we know as we confront him that greater is he who is in us than he who is in the world (1 Jn 4:4), and we thank God that Jesus has "stripped the spiritual rulers and authorities of their power" (Col 2:15). But we are still at war and we are commanded to put on armor and fight against the "wicked spiritual forces in the heavenly world" (Eph 6:11-12). So, although we know how this war will end, many battles remain and we need to know our enemy and how to fight him.

As we survey the world's mission fields, we find many places where Christians still have dual allegiances. Many believers, including

	START	NEED	PROCESS	RESULT
STAGE I	Satanic captivity	Freedom to understand	Power encounter	
	Ignorance/error	Enough understanding to act on	Truth encounter	Commitment to Jesus Christ
	Non-Christian commitment	Challenge to commit to Christ	Allegiance encounter	
STAGE II	Commitment to Jesus Christ	Spiritual warfare to provide protection, healing, blessing, deliverance	Power encounter	Growing relationship to God and His people
		Teaching	Truth encounter	
		Challenges to greater commitment and obedience	Allegiance encounter	
STAGE III	Growing relationship to God and His people	Authoritative prayer	Power encounter	Witness to those at the beginning of Stage I
		Teaching	Truth encounter	
		Challenges to witness	Allegiance encounter	

pastors, still go to shamans, priests, and other spirit mediums. At the same time, charismatic and Pentecostal churches specializing in power encounter evangelism and witness are growing rapidly in most parts of the world.

Many of us evangelicals grew up with a knowledge-truth brand of Christianity that pays little if any attention to power encounters. But we go out to witness and evangelize among people who have grown up in spirit-oriented societies and often find that solid, lasting conversions to Christ are hard to achieve with our knowledge-truth approach alone.

Satan counterfeits truth, instills damning allegiances, and provides power. He has, as it were, three arrows in his quiver. However, generally, evangelical missionaries have only two, so their work often founders on the rocks of dual allegiance and nominalism.

We encounter allegiance to other gods and spirits with the challenge to commitment to Jesus Christ. But when the people need heal-ing, or seek fertility, or when there isn't enough rain, or there are floods, too often our answer is the hospital, the school, and modern agriculture. We provide secular answers to what to them (and the Bible) are basically spiritual issues.

We have encountered Satan's counterfeit "truths" with the exciting truths of Christianity, but often in such an abstract way that our hearers have seen little verification of that truth in our lives. In most cases, both missionaries and the local Christians are more impressed with scientific truth than with biblical truth.

The missing element for them and for us is the "third arrow," genuine New Testament power, the continual experience of the presence of God, who every day does things the world calls miracles. We must encounter Satan's counterfeit power with God's effective power. Truth and commitment alone won't do. We need all three kinds of biblical encounters if we are to succeed in our world mission.

End Notes

1. Alan Tippett, *People Movements in Southern Polynesia* (Chicago: Moody Press, 1971), p. 206.
2. C. Peter Wagner, *How to Have a Healing Ministry* (Ventura, Calif.: Regal Books, 1988), p. 150. See also John Wimber, *Power Evangelism* (New York: Harper-Row, 1985), pp. 29-32, and Charles Kraft, *Christianity With Power* (Ann Arbor: Servant, 1989).
3. Tippett, op. cit., p. 81.

Study Questions

1. In your experience, which "encounter" has been emphasized most as you've received Christian nurture, truth, commitment, or power? Which has been emphasized the least?

2. Are these encounters independent or interdependent? Does growth in one area affect the others?

The Flaw of the Excluded Middle

Paul G. Hiebert

Paul G. Hiebert is Chairman of the Department of Mission and Evangelism and Professor of Mission and Anthropology at Trinity Evangelical Divinity School. He previously taught Anthropology and South Asian Studies at Fuller Theological Seminary's School of World Mission. Hiebert served as a missionary in India with the Mennonite Brethren Board. He is the author of *Cultural Anthropology, Anthropological Insights for Missionaries,* and *Case Studies in Mission* with his wife, Frances H. Hiebert.

This article first appeared in "The Flaw of the Excluded Middle," *Missiology* 10:35-47, January 1982.

From *Anthropological Reflections on Missiological Issues,* by Paul G. Hiebert, Copyright 1994, Baker Book House, Grand Rapids, MI. Used by permission.

T he disciples of John the Baptist asked Jesus, "Are you he who is to come, or shall we look for another?" (Luke 7:20 RSV). Jesus answered, not with logical proofs, but by a demonstration of power in curing the sick and casting out evil spirits. This much is clear. Yet when I once read the passage from my perspective as a missionary in India and sought to apply it to missions in my day, I felt a sense of uneasiness. As a Westerner, I was used to presenting Christ on the basis of rational arguments, not by evidences of his power in the lives of people who were sick, possessed, and destitute. In particular, the confrontation with spirits that appeared so natural a part of Christ's ministry belonged in my mind to a separate world of the miraculous—far from ordinary everyday experiences.

Another situation, early in my ministry in India, gave me the same uneasiness. One day, while teaching in the Bible school in Shamshabad, I saw Yellayya standing in the door at the back of the class. He looked tired, for he had walked many miles from Muchintala where he was an elder in the church. I assigned the class some reading and went with him to the office. When I asked why he had come, he said that smallpox had come to the village a few weeks earlier and had taken a number of children. Doctors trained in Western medicine had tried to halt the plague, but without success. Finally, in desperation the village elders had sent for a diviner, who told them that Museum, goddess of smallpox, was angry with the village.

To satisfy her and stop the plague, the village would have to perform the water buffalo sacrifice. The village elders went around to each household in the village to raise money to purchase the buffalo. When they came to the Christian homes, the Christians refused to give them anything, saying that it was against their religious beliefs. The leaders were angry, pointing out that the goddess would not be satisfied until every household gave something as a token offering— even one paisa would do.[1] When the Christians refused, the elders forbade them to draw water from the village wells, and the merchants refused to sell them food.

In the end some of the Christians had wanted to stop the harassment by giving the paisa, telling God they did not mean it, but Yellayya had refused to let them do so. Now, said Yellayya, one of the Christian girls was sick with smallpox. He wanted me to pray with him for God's healing. As I knelt, my mind was in turmoil. I had learned to pray as a child, studied prayer in seminary, and preached it as a pastor. But now I was to pray for a sick child as all the village watched to see if the Christian God was able to heal.

Why my uneasiness both in reading the Scriptures and in the Indian village? Was the problem, at least in part, due to my own worldview—to the assumptions I as a Westerner made about the nature of reality and how I viewed the world? But how does one discover these assumptions since they are so taken for granted that we are rarely even aware of them? One way is to look at the worldview of another culture and to contrast it with the way we view the world.

Ills and Remedies in an Indian Village

There are many illnesses in an Indian village. According to the Indian worldview, people become sick with "hot" diseases, such as smallpox, and must be treated with "cold" medicines and foods; or they have "cold" diseases like malaria and need "hot" foods and medicines. Some need treatment for boils, cuts, and broken bones, others for mental illnesses. Women may be cursed with barrenness. Individuals or whole families may be plagued by bad luck, by constantly being robbed or by having their houses burn down. Or they may be seized by bad temper, jealousy, or hatred. They may be possessed by spirits or be injured by planetary forces or black magic.

Like all people, Indian villagers have traditional ways to deal with such diseases. Serious cases, particularly those that are life-threatening or have to do with relationships, they take to the *sadhu* (saint), a person of god who claims to heal by prayer. Because the god knows everything, including the nature and causes of the illness, the saints ask no questions. Moreover, because they are spiritual, they charge no fees, although those healed are expected to give a generous offering to the god by giving it to the saint.

Other cases villagers take to a *mantrakar* or magician, particularly cases in which the villagers suspect some evil human or supernatural cause. The magician cures by knowledge and control of supernatural spirits and forces believed to exist on earth. If, for example, one

were to venture out on an inauspicious day when the evil forces of the planets are particularly strong, he or she might be bitten by a viper. To cure this the magician would have to say the following mantra (magical chant) seven times—once for each stripe across the viper's back: OM NAMO BHAGAVATE. SARVA PEESACHI GRUHAMULU NANU DZUCHI PARADZURU. HREEM, KLEM, SAM PHAT, SVAHA. This combines a powerful formula to counter the evil forces with a series of powerful sounds (hreem, klem, sam, phat, svaha) that further empower the formula. Sometimes the magician uses visual symbols (*yentras*; sample below) or amulets to control spirits and forces in this world. Because they can divine both the nature and the cause of the evil plaguing the patient, they need ask no questions, and, like the saints, they receive the offerings of those who have been helped.

A third type of medical practitioner are the *vaidyudu* (doctors), who cure people by means of scientific knowledge based on the *ayyurvedic* or *unani* systems of medicine. Because of their skills in diagnosis, these, too, ask no questions. Villagers report that these *vaidyudu* feel their wrists, stomachs, and bodies and are able to determine their illnesses. They charge high fees, for this knowledge is powerful, but they give a guarantee: medicines and services are paid for only if the patient is healed.

In addition, there are village quacks who heal people with folk remedies. Their knowledge is limited so they must ask questions about the illness: Where does it hurt and for how long has the pain been felt?

Have they been with someone sick? What have they eaten? For the same reason they charge low fees and give no guarantees. People have to pay for the medicines before receiving them. It should not surprise us that Western doctors are often equated at the beginning with the quacks.

What happens to villagers who become Christians? Most of them take problems they formerly took to the saints to the Christian minister or missionary. Christ replaces Krishna or Siva as the healer of spiritual diseases. Many of them in time turn to Western allopathic medicines for many of the illnesses they had taken to the doctor and quack. But what of the plagues that the magician cured? What about spirit possession or curses or witchcraft or black magic? What is the Christian answer to these?

Often the missionary evangelist or doctor has no answer. These do not really exist, they say. But to people for whom these are very real experiences in their lives, there must be another answer. Therefore, many of them return to the magician for cures.

This survival of magic among Christians is not unique to India. In many parts of the world, the picture is the same. In the West, magic and witchcraft persisted well into the 17th Century, more than a thousand years after the gospel came to these lands.

AN ANALYTICAL FRAMEWORK

In order to understand the biblical texts, the Indian scene, and the failure of Western missionaries to meet the needs met by magicians, we need an analytical framework. To create this framework, we need two dimensions of analysis (see chart below).

The Seen-Unseen Dimension

The first dimension is that of immanence–transcendence. On one end is the empirical world of our senses. All people are aware of this world and develop folk sciences to explain and

Framework for the Analysis of Religious Systems

Organic Analogy
Based on concepts of living beings relating to other living beings. Stresses life, personality, relationships, functions, health, disease, choice, etc. Relationships are essentially moral in character.

Mechanical Analogy
Based on concepts of impersonal objects controlled by forces. Stresses impersonal, mechanistic, and deterministic nature of events. Forces are essentially amoral in character.

Unseen or Supernatural
Beyond immediate sense experience. Above natural explanation. Knowledge of this based on inference or on supernatural experiences.

High Religion Based on Cosmic Beings:
cosmic gods; angels; demons; spirits of other worlds

High Religion Based on Cosmic Forces:
kismet; fate; Brahman and karma; impersonal cosmic forces

Other Worldly
Sees entities and events occurring in other worlds and in other times.

Folk or Low Religion
local gods and goddesses; ancestors and ghosts; spirits; demons and evil spirits; dead saints

Magic and Astrology
mana; astrological forces; charms, amulets and magical rites; evil eye, evil tongue

This Worldly
Sees entities and events as occurring in this world and universe.

Seen or Empirical
Directly observable by the senses. Knowledge based on experimentation and observation.

Folk Social Science
interaction of living beings such as humans, possibly animals and plants.

Folk Natural Science
interaction of natural objects based on natural forces.

control it. They develop theories about the natural world around them—how to build a house, plant a crop, or sail a canoe. They also have theories about human relationships—how to raise a child, treat a spouse, and deal with a relative. When a Naga tribal person attributes the death of the deer to an arrow, or a Karen wife explains the cooking of a meal in terms of the fire under the pot, they are using explanations based upon empirical observations and deductions. Western science, in this sense, is not unique. Western science may be more systematic in the exploration of the empirical world, but all people have folk sciences.

Above this level (more remote from the experience of humans) are beings and forces that cannot be directly perceived but are thought to exist on this earth. These include spirits, ghosts, ancestors, demons, and earthly gods and goddesses who live in trees, rivers, hills, and villages. These live, not in some other world or time, but with humans and animals of this world and time. In medieval Europe these beings included trolls, pixies, gnomes, brownies, and fairies, all of which were believed to be real. This level also includes supernatural forces, such as mana, planetary influences, evil eyes, and the powers of magic, sorcery and witchcraft.

Furthest from the immediate world of human experience are transcendent worlds beyond this one—hells and heavens and other times, such as eternity. In this transcendent realm fit African concepts of a high god, and Hindu ideas of Vishnu and Siva. Here is located the Jewish concept of Jehovah, who stands in stark contrast to the baals and ashtaroth of the Canaanites, who were deities of this world, of the middle zone. To be sure, Jehovah entered into the affairs of this earth, but his abode was above it. On this level, too, are the transcendent cosmic forces such as karma and kismet.

The Organic-Mechanical Continuum

Scholars have widely noted that humans use analogies from everyday experience to provide pictures of the nature and operations of the larger world. Two basic analogies are particularly widespread:

1. organic analogy—sees things as living beings in relationship to each other,

2. mechanical analogy—sees things as inanimate objects that act upon one another like parts in a machine.

In the organic analogy the elements being examined are thought to be alive in some sense, to undergo processes similar to human life and to relate to each other in ways that are analogous to interpersonal relationships. For example, in seeking to describe human civilizations, philosopher Oswald Spengler and historian Arnold Toynbee speak of them in terms of an organic analogy: Civilizations are born, they mature, and they die. Similarly, traditional religionists see many diseases as caused by evil spirits that are alive, that may be angered, and that can be placated through supplication or the offering of a sacrifice. Christians see their relationship to God in organic terms. God is a person and humans relate to him in ways analogous to human relationships.

Organic explanations see the world in terms of living beings in relationship to one another. Like humans and animals, objects may initiate actions and respond to the actions of others. They may be thought to have feelings, thoughts and wills of their own. Often they are seen as social beings who love, marry, have offspring, quarrel, war, sleep, eat, persuade, and coerce one another.

In the mechanical analogy, all things are thought to be inanimate parts of greater mechanical systems. They are controlled by impersonal forces or by impersonal laws of nature. For example, Western sciences see the world as made up of lifeless matter that interacts on the basis of forces. When gravity pulls a rock down to the earth it is not because the earth and rock wish to meet—neither earth nor rock have any thought in the matter. In Western science even living beings often are seen as being caught up in a world ultimately made up of impersonal forces. Just as we have no choice about what happens to us when we fall out of a tree, so it is often thought that we have no control over the forces in early childhood that are believed to have made us what we are today.

Mechanical analogies are essentially deterministic; living beings in a mechanistic system are subject to its impersonal forces. But if they know how these forces operate, they can manipulate or control them for their own advantage. In a sense they exert god-like control over their own destiny.

Mechanistic analogies are basically amoral. Forces are intrinsically neither good nor evil. They can be used for both. Organic analogies, on the other hand, are characterized by ethical considerations. One being's actions always affect other beings.

Many of the similarities among modern science, magic and astrology that have been pointed out by anthropologists are due to the fact that all three use mechanistic analogies. Just as scientists know how to control empirical forces to achieve their goals, the magician and astrologer control supernatural forces of this world by means of chants, charms and rituals to carry out human purposes.

One of the greatest cultural gaps between Western people and many traditional religionists is found along this dimension. The former have bought deeply into a mechanical view of this universe and of the social order.[2] To them the basis of the world is lifeless matter controlled by impersonal forces. Many tribal religionists see the world as alive. Not only humans, but also animals, plants, and even rocks, sand, and water are thought to have personalities, wills, and life forces. Theirs is a relational, not a deterministic, world.

The Excluded Middle

The reasons for my uneasiness with the biblical and Indian worldviews should be clear: I had excluded the middle level of supernatural this-worldly beings and forces from my own worldview. As a scientist I had been trained to deal with the empirical world in naturalistic terms. As a theologian I was taught to answer ultimate questions in theistic terms. For me the middle zone did not really exist. Unlike Indian villagers, I had given little thought to spirits of this world, to local ancestors and ghosts, or to the souls of animals. For me these belonged to the realm of fairies, trolls, and other mythical beings. Consequently, I had no answers to the questions they raised (see chart above next column).

How did this two-tiered worldview emerge in the West? Belief in the middle level began to die in the 17th and 18th Centuries with the growing acceptance of a Platonic

Western Two-Tiered View of Reality

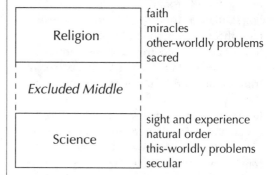

| Religion | faith
miracles
other-worldly problems
sacred |

Excluded Middle

| Science | sight and experience
natural order
this-worldly problems
secular |

dualism and of a science based on materialistic naturalism.[3] The result was the secularization of science and the mystification of religion. Science dealt with the empirical world using mechanistic analogies, leaving religion to handle other-worldly matters, often in terms of organic analogies. Science was based on the certitudes of sense experience, experimentation and proof. Religion was left with faith in visions, dreams and inner feelings. Science sought order in natural laws. Religion was brought in to deal with miracles and exceptions to the natural order, but these decreased as scientific knowledge expanded.

It should be apparent why many missionaries trained in the West had no answers to the problems of the middle level—they often did not even see it. When tribal people spoke of fear of evil spirits, they denied the existence of the spirits rather than claim the power of Christ over them. The result, Lesslie Newbigin has argued, is that Western Christian missions have been one of the greatest secularizing forces in history.[4]

What are the questions of the middle level that Westerners find so hard to answer, and how do they differ from questions raised by science and religion? Science as a system of explanation, whether folk or modern, answers questions about the nature of the world that is directly experienced. All people have social theories about how to raise children and organize social activities. All have ideas about the natural world and how to control it for their own benefit.

Religion as a system of explanation deals with the ultimate questions of the origin, purpose and destiny of an individual, a society, and the universe. In the West the focus is on the individual; in the Old Testament it was on Israel as a society.

What are the questions of the middle level? Here one finds the questions of the uncertainty of the future, the crises of present life, and the unknowns of the past. Despite knowledge of facts such as that seeds once planted will grow and bear fruit, or that travel down this river on a boat will bring one to the neighboring village, the future is not totally predictable. Accidents, misfortunes, the intervention of other persons, and other unknown events can frustrate human planning.

How can one prevent accidents or guarantee success in the future? How can one make sure that a marriage will be fruitful, happy and enduring? How can one avoid getting on a plane that will crash? In the West these questions are left unanswered. They are accidents, luck, or unforeseeable events, and hence unexplainable. But many people are not content to leave so important a set of questions unanswered, and the answers they give are often stated in terms of ancestors, demons, witches and local gods, or in terms of magic and astrology.

Similarly, the crises and misfortunes of present life must be handled: sudden disease and plagues, extended droughts, earthquakes, business failures, and the empirically unexplainable loss of health. What does one do when the doctors have done all they can and a child grows sicker, or when one is gambling and the stakes are high? Again, many seek answers in the middle level.

And there are questions one must answer about the past: Why did my child die in the prime of life? Who stole the gold hidden in the house? Here again trans-empirical explanations often provide an answer when empirical ones fail.

Because the Western world no longer provides explanations for questions on the middle level, many Western missionaries have no answers within their Christian worldview. What is a Christian theology of ancestors, of animals and plants, of local spirits and spirit possession, and of principalities, powers, and rulers of the darkness of this world (Eph 6:12)? What does one say when new tribal converts want to know how the Christian God tells them where and when to hunt, whether they should marry this daughter to that young man, or where they can find the lost money? Given no answer, they return to the diviner who gives definite answers, for these are the problems that loom large in their everyday life.

Implications for Missions

What implications does all of this have for missions? First, it points out the need for

A Holistic Theology

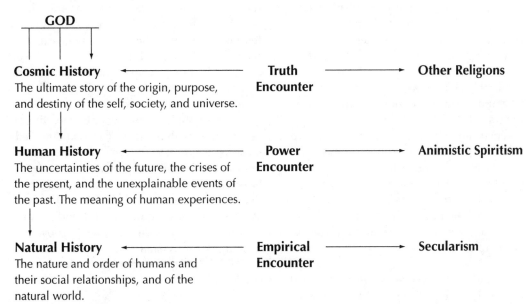

missionaries to develop holistic theologies that deal with all areas of life (see diagram p. 419), that avoid the Platonic dualism of the West, and that take seriously both body and soul.

On the highest level, this includes a theology of God in cosmic history—in the creation, redemption, purpose and destiny of all things. Only as human history is placed within a cosmic framework does it take on meaning, and only when history has meaning does human biography become meaningful.

On the middle level, a holistic theology includes a theology of God in human history—in the affairs of nations, of peoples, and of individuals. This must include a theology of divine guidance, provision and healing; a theology of ancestors, spirits and invisible powers of this world; and a theology of suffering, misfortune and death.

On this level some sections of the Church have turned to doctrines featuring saints as intermediaries between God and humans. Others have turned to doctrines of the Holy Spirit to show God's active involvement in the events of human history. It is no coincidence that many of the most successful missions have provided some form of Christian answer to middle-level questions.

On the bottom level, a holistic theology includes an awareness of God in natural history—in sustaining the natural order of things. So long as the missionary comes with a two-tiered worldview, with God confined to the supernatural and the natural world operating for all practical purposes according to autonomous scientific laws, Christianity will continue to be a secularizing force in the world. Only as God is brought back into the middle of our scientific understanding of nature will we stem the tide of Western secularism.

There are two dangers against which we must guard when we formulate a theology that deals with the questions raised at the middle level. These middle-level questions include the meaning of life and death for the living; well-being and the threats of illness, drought, flood, and failure; and guidance in a world of unknowns. The first danger is secularism. This is to deny the reality of the spiritual realm in the events of human life, and to reduce the reality of this world to purely materialistic explanations. This is the answer offered by modern science.

The second danger is a return to a Christianized form of animism in which spirits and magic are used to explain everything. In spiritism, the spirits dominate reality, and humans must constantly battle or appease them to survive. In magic, humans seek to control supernatural powers through rituals and formulas to achieve their own personal desires. Both spiritism and magic are human and ego-centered; a person can gain what he or she wants by manipulating the spirits and controlling the forces. Both reject a God-centered view of reality, and both reject worship, obedience and submission as the human response to God's will. The early church struggled against the animistic worldviews around it. Today there is a danger of returning to a Christianized animism in reaction to the secularism of the modern worldview.

Scripture offers us a third worldview that is neither secular nor animistic. It takes spiritual realities very seriously. In contrast to secular writings, it is full of references to God, angels, Satan and demons. However, it takes the natural world and humans very seriously. In contrast to the Greek and Roman mythologies, and other great religious texts such as the Avesta and Mahabharata, the Bible does not focus its primary attention on the activities of the spirit world.[5] Rather, it is the history of God and of humans, and their relationship to each other. Humans are held responsible for their actions. They are tempted, but they choose to sin. God calls them to salvation, and they must respond to his call. The Bible also presents creation as an orderly world, operating according to divinely ordained principles.

In saying this, I do not want to deny the need to deal with the spirit world and related subjects. Yet we need to center our theology on God and his acts and not, as modern secularism and animism do, on human beings and their desires. We need to focus on worship and our relationship to God, and not on ways to control God for our own purposes through chants and formulas.

The line between worship and control is subtle, as I learned in the case of Muchintala. A week after our prayer meeting, Yellayya returned to say that the child had died. I felt thoroughly defeated. Who was I to be a missionary if I could not pray for healing and receive a positive answer? A few weeks later he returned with a sense of triumph. "How can you be so happy after the child died?" I asked.

"The village would have acknowledged the power of our God had he healed the child," Yellayya said, "but they knew in the end she would have to die. When they saw in the funeral our hope of resurrection and reunion in heaven, they saw an even greater victory—over death itself—and they have begun to ask about the Christian way."

I began to realize in a new way that true answers to prayer are those that bring the greatest glory to God, not those that satisfy my immediate desires. It is all too easy to make Christianity a new magic in which we as gods can make God do our bidding.

Having formulated a theological response to the problems of the middle zone, it is important that we test the beliefs of the people we serve. Some things such as lightning, smallpox, and failure in business which they may attribute to nature spirits, can better be explained through the order of creation under the superintendence of God. Other things are indeed manifestations of Satan and the other fallen angels. But much of Satan's work lies hidden to the people, and we must discern and oppose it.

In confronting animistic worldviews, our central message should always focus on the greatness, holiness and power of God, and his work in human lives. It is he who delivers us from the power of the evil one and gives us the power to live free, victorious Christian lives.

End Notes

1. The pisa is the smallest coin in India, now worth about .03 of one penny.
2. Peter L. Berger, Brigitte Berger, and Hansfried Kellner, *The Homeless Mind: Modernization and Consciousness* (New York: Random House, 1973).
3. Roger K. Bufford, *The Human Reflex: Behavioral Psychology in Biblical Perspective* (San Francisco: Harper and Row, 1981), p. 30.
4. Lesslie Newbigin, *Honest Religion for Secular Man* (Philadelphia: Westminster, 1966).
5. This is reflected in a simple word count in the Bible. In the *KJV* the word God is used 3,594 times, Jehovah 4 times, Christ 522 times, Jesus 942 times, and Spirit of God 26 times. Many other references to lord and spirit also refer to God. There are 362 references to angels and cherubim, and 158 to Satan, Lucifer, the evil one, and demons. There are 4,324 references to humans.

Study Questions

1. According to Hiebert, why is it necessary for the Western Christian missionary to regain "the excluded middle" to function effectively?

2. What sort of training would best re-infuse Westerners with a more holistic view of "middle-level" spiritual issues?

3. Hiebert warns against two dangers. What are they? He then offers a third worldview centered on God and his acts. What is your answer to Hiebert's question, "What implications does all of this have for missions?"

Social Structure and Church Growth

Paul G. Hiebert

Paul G. Hiebert is Chairman of the Department of Mission and Evangelism and Professor of Mission and Anthropology at Trinity Evangelical Divinity School. He previously taught Anthropology and South Asian Studies at Fuller Theological Seminary's School of World Mission. Hiebert served as a missionary in India with the Mennonite Brethren Board. He is the author of *Cultural Anthropology*, *Anthropological Insights for Missionaries*, and *Case Studies in Mission* with his wife, Frances H. Hiebert.

Adapted from *Crucial Dimensions in World Evangelization*, by Arthur F. Glasser, et al. , 1976. Used by permission of William Carey Library, Pasadena, CA.

P eople are social beings, born, raised, married, and usually buried in the company of their fellow humans. They form groups, institutions and societies. Social structure is the ways in which they organize their relationships with one another and build societies.

Societies can be studied on two levels: that of interpersonal relation and of the society as a whole. A study of missions at each of these levels can help us a great deal in understanding how churches grow.

INTERPERSONAL RELATIONSHIPS: THE BICULTURAL BRIDGE

When a missionary goes overseas and settles down, what does he do? Whatever his specific task, he is involved in interpersonal relationships with a great many people. Many of these are not Christians, but, most likely, he will spend much of his time with Christian converts. He will go to the market, or preach in the village square, but his closest relationships will be with national pastors, evangelists, teachers and other Christians. What are the characteristics of these various relationships?

It is clear that in most cases communication across cultures is multi-stepped. The missionary receives the message in his family, church and school. He communicates it to national Christian leaders who in turn pass it on to local Christians and non-Christians in the cities and villages. With few exceptions, the greatest share of the mission work in a country is done by these unheralded nationals.

Here, in order to see how a structural analysis is used, we will look at one link in this chain of communication—the relationship between the missionary and his national counterpart. This has sometimes been called the bicultural bridge, and is the critical step in which much of the translation of the message into a new culture occurs.

The bicultural bridge is a set of relationships between people from two cultures. But it is more. It is itself a new culture. The missionary can never truly "go native." She will set up housing, institutions and customary ways of doing things that reflect her home culture, in part, and, in part, are adapted from the culture in which she finds herself. Her national counterparts do the same. It is true that they have not moved out of their own culture, but their interaction with the missionary exposes them to a great many foreign influences that can potentially alienate them from their home culture.

A great deal of energy in the bicultural setting is spent on defining just how this new culture should operate. Should the missionary have a car in a society where most of the people do not? If so, should his national counterparts have them too? Where should the missionary send her children to school—to the local schools, to a school for missionary children, or to those in North America? What food should the missionary eat, what dress should he wear and what kind of house should he and the national workers have? These and a thousand more questions arise in the bicultural setting.

Status and Role

The term "status" has a number of common meanings, but anthropologists use it in a specific sense, defining it as the "positions in a social system occupied by individuals." At the level of interpersonal relationships, a social organization is made up of a great many such positions: teachers, priests, doctors, fathers, mothers, friends and so on.

Each status is associated with certain behavioral expectations. For example, we expect a teacher to act in certain ways towards her students. She should show up for class and lead it. She should not sleep in class, or come in a dressing gown. A teacher should also act in certain ways vis-a-vis her administrators, the parents of the students and the public.

All interpersonal relationships can be broken down into complimentary role pairs: teacher-student, pastor-parishioner, husband-wife, etcetera. The nature of the relationship between two individuals is based very much on the statuses they choose.

The Missionary and the Nationals.

"What are you?" This question is repeatedly asked of a person who goes abroad. The people ask because they want to know how to relate to the newcomer.

Missionaries generally answer, "We are missionaries." In stating this they are naming a status with its associated roles, all of which are perfectly clear to themselves. They know who "missionaries" are, and how they

should act. But what about the nationals, particularly the non-Christians who have never met a missionary before? What do they think of these foreigners?

Here we must come back to cultural differences, again. Just as languages differ, so also the roles found in one culture differ from those found in another culture. "Missionary" is an English word, representing a status and roles found in the West. In most other cultures it does not exist. When a missionary shows up in these cultures, the people must observe him and try to deduce from his behavior which of their roles he fits. They then conclude that he is this type of person and expect him to behave accordingly. We, in fact, do the same thing when a foreigner arrives and announces that he is a "sannyasin." From his looks we might conclude he is a hippie, when, in fact, he is a Hindu saint.

> Our example is Christ who, because of His love, became incarnate among us in order to bring us God's Good News.

How have the people perceived the missionaries? In India the missionaries were called *"dora."* The word is used for rich farmers and small-time kings. These petty rulers bought large pieces of land, put up compound walls, built bungalows and had servants. They also erected separate bungalows for their second and third wives. When the missionaries came they bought large pieces of land, put up compound walls, built bungalows, and had servants. They, too, erected separate bungalows, but for the missionary ladies stationed on the same compound.

Missionary wives were called "dorasani." The term is used not for the wife of a dora for she should be kept in isolation away from the public eye, but his mistress whom he often took with him in his cart or car.

The problem here is one of cross-cultural misunderstanding. The missionary thought of himself as a "missionary," not realizing that there is no such thing in the traditional Indian society. In order to relate to him, the ·

people had to find him a role within their own set of roles, and they did so. Unfortunately, the missionaries were not aware of how the people perceived them.

A second role into which the people often put the missionary in the past was "colonial ruler." He was usually white, like the colonial rulers, and he sometimes took advantage of this to get the privileges given the rulers. He could get railroad tickets without waiting in line with the local people, and he could influence the officials. To be sure, he often used these privileges to help the poor or oppressed, but by exercising them, he became identified with the colonial rulers.

The problem is that neither of the roles, rich landlord or colonial ruler, permitted the close personal communication or friendship that would have been most effective in sharing the gospel. Their roles often kept the missionaries distant from the people.

But what roles could the missionaries have taken? There is no simple answer to this, for the roles must be chosen in each case from the roles in the culture to which she goes. At the outset she can go as a "student," and request that the people teach her their ways. As she learns the roles of their society, she can choose one that allows her to communicate the gospel to them effectively. But when she chooses a role, she must remember that the people will judge her according to how well she fulfills their expectations of that role.

The Missionary and National Christians.

The relationship between a missionary and national Christians is different from that between him and non-Christians. The former, after all, are his "spiritual children" and he, their "spiritual father."

This parent-child relationship is vertical and authoritarian. The missionary is automatically in charge. He is the example that the people must imitate, and their source of knowledge. But people soon become tired of being children, particularly when they are older and in many ways wiser than their parents. If not permitted to be responsible for themselves, they will never mature, or they will rebel and leave home.

The missionary is also imprisoned by this parental role. Not only is it difficult for him to form close relations with the people, with them as his equals, but also he feels he can admit to no wrong. If he were to confess personal sins and weaknesses to the people, he fears that they will lose their faith in Christ. But he is also their model for leadership roles, and they soon come to believe that no leader should admit to sin or failure. Obviously the missionary and the national leaders do sin, and because of their roles, they have ways of confessing sin and experiencing the forgiveness of the Christian community without destroying their ministry.

Another role into which missionaries can slip, often unawares, is that of "empire builders." Each of us needs to feel that we are part of an important task. From this it is only a small step to seeing ourselves as the center of this task and indispensable. We gain personal followers and build large churches, schools, hospitals and other institutions that prove our worth.

However, this role, like the first, is not the best for effective communication. From a structural perspective, it is a vertical role in which communication proceeds from the top down. There is little feedback from the bottom up. People below comply with the orders from above, but often do not internalize the message and make it their own. From a Christian perspective, this role does not fit the example of Christ. On the contrary, it can lead to an exploitation of others for our own personal gain.

What roles can the missionary take? Here, because the missionary and the nationals are Christians, we can turn to a Biblical model—that of siblings and servanthood. As members of one body we must stress our equality with our national brothers and sisters. There is no separation into two kinds of people, "we" and "they." We trust the nationals just as we trust our fellow missionaries, and we are willing to accept them as colleagues and as administrators over us. Assignments of leadership within the church are not based on culture, race or even financial power. They are made according to God-given gifts and abilities.

There is leadership in the Church, just as there must be in any human institution if it is to function. But the Biblical concept of leadership is servanthood. The leader is one who seeks the welfare of the others and not himself (Matt 20:26-28). He is dispensable, and in this sense the missionary is most dispensable of all, for his task is to plant the church and to move on when his presence begins to hinder its growth.

Identification

Good relationships involve more than choosing suitable roles. Within a role the individual expresses different attitudes that show her deep feelings toward the other person.

If we feel that somehow we are a different kind of people from those with whom we work, this will be communicated to them in a number of subtle ways. We may live apart from them, allow them only into our living rooms which are public space and not permit our children to play with theirs. Or we may allow no nationals on mission committees.

When we identify with the people, we will do so in formal ways—at an annual feast given to the staff of the school or hospital, in their homes, but only on formal invitation and on the committees by allowing a few to participate. We may even wear the native dress on certain occasions. But formal identification is identification at arm's length. It stresses the basic difference between people, even as it demonstrates their superficial oneness.

The real test of identification is not what we do in formal, structured situations. It is how we handle our informal time, and our most precious belongings. When the committee meeting is over, do we go aside with fellow Americans to discuss cameras, thereby excluding our national colleagues by our use of space and the topic of discussion? Do we frown on our children playing with the local children?

But is it possible for a missionary ever to "go native?" Obviously not. It takes immigrants from Northern Europe three or four generations to assimilate into American culture, and where the cultural differences are greater, it takes even longer.

The basic issue in identification is not formal equivalence—living in the same houses, eating the same food and wearing the same dress. We can do so and still communicate to people the mental distinction we make between them and us. The issue is one of mental maps and basic feelings. If we indeed, see and feel ourselves to be one of them, this message will come through, even if we have different life styles. A national gives us his best food, lets us sleep in his guest room and use his oxcart, and we share with him our best food, guest room and car. The principle is not formal equality but true love and mutual reciprocity.

A sense of oneness with the people creates in us an interest in learning more about them and in sharing in their culture. Our example is Christ, who, because of His love, became incarnate among us in order to bring us God's good news.

THE ORGANIZATION OF SOCIETIES AND CHURCH GROWTH

Another way of looking at social structures is to see how individual societies as wholes are put together. What are the various social groups and institutions within a given society, how do these articulate with one another and how does change occur? Here, again, two or three illustrations can show best the application and usefulness of the concept.

Tribal Societies

In many tribes, social groups play an important role in the life of an individual, more so than they do in our own society with its strong emphasis on individualism and freedom. In a tribe, a person is born and raised within a large kinship group or lineage made up of all the male descendants of some remote ancestor, plus all the families of these males. To get something of a feel for this type of society, imagine living together with all of your relatives who share your last name, on a common farm and sharing responsibilities for one another. All the men one generation older than you would be your "fathers" responsible for disciplining you when you deviate from the family rules and customs. All the women of that generation would be your "mothers" who care for you. All in your lineage of your own age would be "brothers" and "sisters," and all the children of all your "brothers" would be your "sons" and "daughters."

In some tribes, a lineage is made up of all the female descendants of a remote ancestress, together with their families. But, again, the authority of and responsibility to the group remains central in the life of the person.

Strong kinship groups in a tribe provide the individual with a great deal of security. They provide for you when you are sick or without food, support you when you go away to school, contribute to your purchasing a field or acquiring a bride and fight for you when you are attacked. In turn, the group makes many demands on you. Your lands and your time are not strictly your own. You are expected to share them with those in your lineage who need them.

Tribal Societies

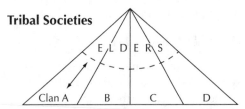

- Stress on kinship as basis for social bonding
- Strong group orientation with mutual responsibility and group decision–making processes
- Minimal social hierarchy
- Vertical communication

Important decisions in these tribes are generally made by the elders—the older men who have had a great deal of experience with life. This is particularly true of one of the most important decisions of life, namely, marriage. Unlike in our society where young people are all too ready to get married when they "fall in love" without carefully testing the other person's social, economic, mental and spiritual qualifications, in most tribes weddings are arranged by the parents. From long experience they know the dangers and pitfalls of marriage. They are less swayed by the passing emotional attachments of the present. The parents make the match only after a long and careful examination of all the prospective partners. Love grows in these marriages as in any marriage by each partner learning to live with and to love the other.

Lineage and tribal decisions are also made by the elders. Family heads have their say,

but they must comply with the decisions of the leaders if they want to remain a part of the tribe.

This type of social organization raises serious questions for Christian evangelism. Take, for example, Lin Barney's experience. Lin was in Borneo when he was invited to present the gospel to a village tribe high in the mountains. After a difficult trek he arrived at the village and was asked to speak to the men assembled in the longhouse. He shared the message of the Jesus Way well into the night and, finally, the elders announced that they would make a decision about this new way. Lineage members gathered in small groups to discuss the matter and then the lineage leaders gathered to make a final decision. In the end they decided to become Christians, all of them. The decision was by general consensus.

What should the missionary do now? Does he send them all back and make them arrive at the decision individually? We must remember that in these societies no one would think of making so important a decision as marriage apart from the elders. Is it realistic, then, to expect them to make an even more important decision regarding their religion on their own?

Should the missionary accept all of them as born again? Afterall some may not have wanted to become Christian and will continue to worship the gods of their past.

Group decisions do not mean that all of the members of the group have converted, but it does mean that the group is open to further Biblical instruction. The task of the missionary is not finished—it has only begun—for he must now teach them the whole of the Scriptures.

Such people movements are not uncommon. In fact, much of the growth of the Church in the past has occurred through them, including many of the first Christian ancestors of most of the readers of this book.

Peasant Societies

The social organization of peasant societies is quite different from that of tribal societies. Here we often have the weakening of extended kinship ties and the rise of social classes and castes. Power is often concentrated in the hands of an elite that is removed from the commoners.

We can turn to India for an illustration of how peasant social structure influences church growth. Villages are divided into a great many *jatis* or castes. Many of these, such as the Priests, Carpenters, Ironsmiths, Barbers, Washermen, Potters and Weavers, are associated with certain job monopolies. Not only does a person inherit the right to perform his caste's occupation, he must marry someone from within his own caste. A rough analogy would be for American high school teachers to marry their children to other children of high school teachers, for preachers to marry their children to other preachers' children and for each other occupation to do the same. One can see, therefore, the need to begin marriage negotiations early.

Peasant Societies

Dominant Ethnic Group or Class

Subordinate Groups or Classes

- Stress on kinship as basis for social bonding
- Strong group orientation with group decision–making processes
- Intergroup hierarchs
- Communication horizontal within groups, vertical between them

Castes are also grouped into the clean castes and the untouchables. The latter are ritually polluting and their touch, in the past, polluted clean-caste folk who had to take a purification bath to restore their purity. Consequently, the untouchables formerly had to live in hamlets apart from the main villages and were forbidden to enter the Hindu temples.

When the gospel came, it tended to move in one group of castes or the other, but not in both. Some of the first converts were from the clean caste, but when many of the untouchables accepted Christ, the clean-caste people objected. They did not want to associate with the folk from the wrong part of town. The missionaries continued to accept all who came and required that they all join the same church. Consequently, many of the clean-caste people reverted back to Hinduism.

The problem here is not simply a theological one. Many of the high-caste converts sincerely believed the gospel, and even today many are secret believers. It is a social problem. The high-caste folk did not want to associate with the untouchables. Before we judge them, let us stop and look at the churches and denominations in America. In how many of them do we find a wide mixture of people from different ethnic groups and social classes? How long has it taken them to break down the last remnants of racial segregation? In how many of them have differences in wealth, social class and political power become unimportant in the fellowship and the operation of the churches?

The dilemma is that theologically the Church should be one, but, in fact, people are socially very diverse, and, they find it hard to associate closely and intermarry with people markedly different from themselves. Can we expect people to change their deep-seated social ways at the moment of their conversion—in other words, should we expect them to join the same church? Or is changing our social customs a part of Christian growth—should we allow them to form different churches with the hope that with further teaching they will become one? The question is similar to one many American churches face—is giving up smoking or drinking alcohol or any other behavior defined as sinful essential to salvation, or is it a part of Christian growth?

There have been some in India who have held that the peoples' salvation is not tied to their joining a single church and they have, therefore, started different churches for the clean castes and the untouchables. They have had a much greater success in winning people from the clean castes, but they have also faced a great deal of criticism from those who argue that this is contrary to the will of God.

The Urban Scene

The recent growth of cities has been phenomenal. In 1800 no city in the world had a population of a million, and fewer than 25 had more than 100,000 inhabitants. By 1950, 46 cities had more than a million residents, with two cities having more than eight million. By the year 2000, there will be 22 cities with more than eight million. Thirty-three cities are expected to exceed the eight million mark by 2015.

This rapid urbanization of the world raises many questions for those concerned with church growth. What is the social structure of a city and how does this structure influence communication and decision making? How do changes take place in the highly mobile and varied city society?

The social processes affecting church growth in tribal and peasant societies are less evident in urban societies. Large people movements in which people come to Christ on the basis of group decisions, or in which the message is shared through caste and kinship ties, seem almost absent. On the other hand, there are new forces at work. City folk are often caught up in rapid change. Their ideas are molded by mass media, educational institutions and voluntary associations. Communication often follows networks of people who are

Urban Individualistic Societies

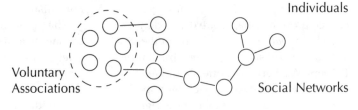

Individuals

Voluntary Associations

Social Networks

- Stress on individualism and personal decision–making
- Organizations on basis of voluntary associations, networks and geographic groupings
- Heterogenents and hierarchs
- Use of mass media in addition to networks

mutually acquainted. In other words, a friend tells a friend, who, in turn, tells another friend.

What methods should missions use in the city? So far no clear-cut strategy has emerged. Mass media, friendship, neighborhood and apartment evangelism, large educational and medical institutions and mass rallies have all been tried, and with mixed success. There is no simple formula that will bring success— there never has been. Building churches is a difficult and long-range task.

Cities also offer tremendous opportunity. They are the centers for world communication and the source from which ideas spread to the countryside. One reason for the rapid spread of early Christianity was its movement through the cities. We desperately need to look more closely at modern urban dynamics in order to understand how change takes place, and then to apply these insights to today's mission planning.

Study Questions

1. Explain the development and function of the "bicultural bridge."

2. Hiebert describes some roles assumed by missionaries that were inappropriate for communication of the gospel. What types of roles *are* appropriate?

3. Explain how the structure of society affects the way messages are communicated within society.

Communication and Social Structure

Eugene A. Nida

Eugene A. Nida, a linguist, anthropologist and biblical scholar, began his association with the American Bible Society in 1943. He was the Translations Research Coordinator for the United Bible Societies from 1970 to1980. He continues his work as a consultant with the Bible Societies as well as ongoing research and lecturing in Europe and Asia. He has written 22 books on translation and missions.

From *Message and Mission*, Revised Edition, by Eugene A. Nida, 1990. Used by permission of William Carey Library, Pasadena, CA.

Communication never takes place in a social vacuum, but always between individuals who are part of a total social context. These participants in the communicative event stand in a definite relationship to each other; for example, as boss to employee, son to father, policeman to offender, and child to baby-sitter. Moreover, in every society there are definite rules about what types of people say what kinds of things to certain classes of persons. On the other hand, what is quite proper for one class to say may be unbecoming for another, and even the same remarks from different persons may be quite differently interpreted. The same behavior interpreted as offensive arrogance in an underling may be considered charming insouciance on the part of the boss, and what is squirming subservience in the lower middle class may be interpreted as lovable modesty in the upper class.[1] Whatever different classes of people say is inevitably influenced by their respective positions in society. For man is more than an individual; he is a member of a very large "family," whether clan, tribe, or nation, and there are always important, though usually unformulated, rules that apply to all interpersonal communication.

This aspect of communication within the social structure is particularly important from the religious point of view. For wherever there are tribal or national gods, these deities inevitably occupy special positions of importance in the social structure, either as mythical ancestors or as guardians of the social patterns and mores of the people. One thing is sure, these deities can usually be depended upon to conserve the status quo and in this way help to regulate the traditional relations between people. For this reason religion is often in opposition to any breach with the past, any breaking away of individuals from the "faith," and any presumed undermining of the prestige of traditional leadership. More often than not, a new convert to Christianity in a predominantly pagan society will feel very much like one Hopi Indian who returned to his own village after having been away at school, where he had been baptized a Christian. The first day of his return, when all the villagers went off to a dance and left him sitting in the shadow of the mission wall, he felt, as he described it later, "like a man without a country."

Unfortunately, some missionary approaches to non-Christians have involved the creation of a Christian caste or subculture. Almost unconsciously some well-meaning missionaries in India, before that nation's independence, felt that new converts, in order to become truly Christian and remain faithful to their new stand, needed full identification with the missionaries and the foreign community. But the result in some instances was the development of a wholly artificial, "hothouse" environment, where Christian converts might be protected, but could never really grow. In a sense they were being taught to be square pegs in round holes.

Well-intentioned missionary work has sometimes failed to communicate the gospel because the source adopted a role completely incompatible with any effective identification with those to be reached. In one mission to Indians in South America the role of the communicators is that of a rich landowner. Such a person can accomplish a good deal on the basis of this prestige. He cannot, however, effectively relate the good news to the people he seeks to reach because the roles of the participants in communication block effective understanding. These missionaries have unselfishly done much for the people, but they have never been able to do anything with the people. Given the roles of landowner and peon, there is never a two-way traffic of meaningful communication about the real issues of life, and without two-way communication there can be no identification.

Types of Social Structures

Social structures, together with the networks of communication they represent, are very diverse. We shall attempt neither a detailed analysis of all the various types of social structures nor a discussion of the many factors that give rise to different patterns of social life. Here we are concerned only with a particular aspect of social structure—namely, that which is significant in terms of interpersonal communication. For this purpose two primary types of distinctions, intersecting on various levels, may be distinguished. First, we must distinguish between the urban (or so-called "metropolitan" society) and the rural (or "face-to-face" society) types of structures. Second, we must analyze these types of structures in terms of their homogeneous or heterogeneous character. The urban society is characteristic of the typical city dweller in large urban centers, whether in New

York, London, or Calcutta, and the rural society is characteristic of the peasant community, whether it is an Indian village near Mexico City or a mountain hamlet in northern Thailand.

By a homogeneous society we mean one in which most or all of the people participate in the common life in more or less the same way. Such groups may have class differences and distinctions of leadership and positions of authority, but the society is nevertheless an integrated whole, sharing much the same system of values; it is not merely an aggregate of subcultures which operate along quite different lines. Sweden, for example, may be regarded as a more or less homogeneous society, in contrast to the United States with its large, heterogeneous population in varying degrees of "assimilation." It may be contrasted also with a country like Peru, which maintains an Ibero-American culture in its cities, but has a distinctly different culture in the villages of the altiplano and the eastern jungle.

Diagrammatic Models of Social Structure

In order to understand more clearly certain of the essential features of social structure, it is convenient to diagram such social patterns, using as a general base an "inverted" diamond jewel shape.

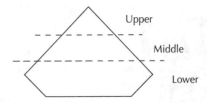

In this generalized and schematic diagram we indicate not only the relative positions and sizes of the different classes—upper, middle, and lower—but also something of the total configuration. This configuration suggests that the upper class tapers off into a relatively limited number of top leaders and that the lower class (which might be called the indigent section of the population) are generally fewer in number at the very bottom than are those somewhat higher in the social structure.

We have arbitrarily chosen to represent social structure in three classes. In some societies, however, one must recognize four, five, six, or even more classes. In such a case it is customary to speak of such distinctions as upper upper, lower upper, upper middle, lower middle, upper lower, and lower lower. Haitian society, for example, can be described as having five principal classes. The elite, who constitute the upper class, are divided into two groups, called "first-class elite" and "second-class elite." The middle class, a relatively small group, is growing rapidly. The lower class is divided into (1) an upper-lower class consisting of the better-to-do tradesmen and farmers who own their own land, and (2) an indigent class who eke out a bare existence as tenant farmers and common laborers.

It would be wrong, however, to leave the impression that all societies differ radically in structural configuration. As a result, it is possible to describe diagrammatically certain of the over-all "impressionistic" features of certain societies in the contrastive manner below.

The forms of these diagrams are not based upon statistical data, for such data are not available in terms of class criteria. They are obviously impressionistic, but very useful.

It should be noted, for example, that in Haitian society the upper class constitutes a very narrow, stratified group, while the society almost bulges at the base. In the diagram of Denmark, the upper class does not tower proportionately so much above the rest of the structure, the middle class is rather large, and the lower tapers off to a very restricted indigent base. Mexico, on the other hand, represents a somewhat more "typical" structure, with a growing middle class, a somewhat attenuated upper class, and the bulk of the society in the lower class, though not with the proportionately heavy concentration at the bottom that characterizes Haiti.

Communication within Social Structures

The significance of social structure for communication can be summarized in two basic principles: (1) people communicate more with people of their own class; that is, interpersonal communication of a reciprocal nature is essentially horizontal; and (2) prestigious communication descends from the upper classes to the lower classes, and this vertical communication is primarily in one direction and tends to be principally between adjacent groups.

1. Interpersonal communication is horizontal

Truly effective communication, however, is not unidirectional. There must be reciprocity in communication (which we may call "social feedback"), or the results may be unsatisfactory. In war, for example, the general must know not only how to give order to the troops; he must also know precisely how the troops are faring, or his orders are likely to result in bungling tragedies, as in the collapse of France in World War II. As a general must know where the men are and the type of resistance they are meeting, so in all types of organizational communication in which there is a centralized source of communication, orders must go out, but information must be fed back continuously. It is interesting that organization and management engineers have discovered that, through the system of communication is usually well developed from headquarters to the front, or from the boss down to the man at the lathe, the reverse system of communication, whether in the military or in business, is often quite lacking, with resultant military fiascoes and bad labor relations.

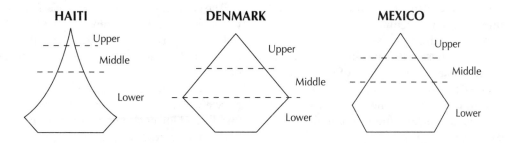

2. *Prestigious communication is vertical and unidirectional*

Both in the ministry and in missionary work it is usual for the religious professional to do most of the talking. Too often the minister or missionary regards himself solely as intermediary of a superior message from God, and hence not aware of or dependent upon the feedback which should come from the congregation. He has gone forth to tell people the truth, not to listen to other people's ideas about the truth. If this attitude is pushed to an extreme, the message inevitably will become irrelevant. Even though it may be true, it does not reach its receptor, for the "master of the household" does not know the conditions under which the servants live and work. And even if he does know, his communication will be immeasurably strengthened, provided those to whom he speaks are convinced of the fact that he knows and understands.

One reason for misjudging the harm done by the downward type of one-way communication is that we do not see its manifest effects. But when, for example, an African insists on wearing a heavy, cumbersome overcoat on a hot day, simply to demonstrate that he has received such a coat from a white official and thereby has gained some measure of local status, it should be evident to the observe that what comes down from the top carries a tremendous amount of prestige. In some instances, however, lower-class individuals have a surprisingly important influence on upper-class persons. This influence operates, however, only when the roles are in a sense reversed. For example, in upper-class homes of some urban societies it often happens that lower-class women are hired to nurse and care for the children. Not infrequently their attachment to the children and the children's dependence on them are such that these women transmit to their charges many basic values of lower-class society, together with a host of concepts accepted primarily by the lower classes, e.g., bogies, ghosts, and magical penalties for disobedience.

Communicative Approach to Urban Society

In communicative approaches to various societies there have been, in the recent past, three main types of orientation. These can be called generally Roman Catholic, Communist, and Protestant, though one must immediately raise a caution against a tendency to identify a "missionary approach" with a particular institutional structure. Nevertheless, these distinctions, as we shall see, reflect in general the manner in which for the most part Roman Catholics, Communists, and Protestants have set out to influence significantly the social structures.

In the Roman Catholic approach to a new society, primary consideration has usually been given to the upper class, though a number of instances can be cited in which a broad segment of the society has been approached. The tendency, however, has been for the Roman Church to identify itself with the leadership of the society and through it to influence the lower classes. In exchange for partnership in controlling the society, the Church always provides the upper class with many benefits, including the best professional religious services and facilities for the education of children. Moreover, the leadership of the Church is generally drawn from the upper class (Pope John XXIII was a notable exception).

The typical Roman Catholic approach may be schematically diagrammed as follows:

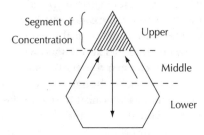

The shaded area indicates the class with which the Church has primarily identified itself, and the arrows indicate both the direction of control (downward) and the pressures of opposition (upward).

The Communist technique in approaching a society is to draw out a segment from the middle and lower classes, usually the lower-middle class and the upper-lower classes. In this segment there is usually a small nucleus of frustrated middle-class intellectuals, who may have been thwarted in their attempts at social climbing or who represent minority group disabilities. These intellectuals then combine with the economically, socially, or politically disenfranchised lower-class elements and by revolution capture the leadership. The former upper class must then be liquidated, either by confiscation to destroy its economic power, or by physical destruction, or by brainwashing. The main features of this development may be diagrammed as follows:

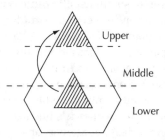

Having taken over leadership, the new upper class of party members and certain technicians then establish a heavy barrier between themselves and the middle classes. Leadership is not recruited from the middle classes (except in so far as certain experts may work for the state); the decisions and the control of communication continue to be exerted by an elite drawing its membership from the lower-middle and upper-lower classes.

Persons who have been selected according to this system, and catapulted by means of party membership from a lower-class status to one of the highest priority, naturally owe all they are to the party, and not primarily to personal achievement or background. They are thus far more obedient to the party than would otherwise be the case; for expulsion from it means not a somewhat horizontal movement, as in our society, but a severe loss of all privileges and status. All this centralized control is made possible in our modern society because of the highly specialized nature of communication and transportation, by means of which a relatively small group of people can control millions. There is no longer any possibility of successful pitchfork rebellions.

The present Protestant approach to society, especially in its missionary aspects, is quite different from the Roman Catholic and Communist orientations. It must be recognized that, in the past, Protestant developments were closely related to broad political and social movements in northern Europe, in which significant changes in church affiliation were considerably influenced by the loyalties of certain princes and rulers. However, it is also possible to read too much significance into the actions of individual kings and to forget that they reflected as well as molded the events that precipitated the break with the Roman Church.

If, however, we are to judge the Protestant approach to society as evidenced both in the mission field and in certain aspects of important Protestant movements in England and America (e.g., the development of Methodism), we may say that Protestants concentrated their efforts on the diagrammatic bulge in society, that is, on the lower-middle and upper-lower classes even as, in a sense, Communists have done. In such areas as Latin America, for example, persons of the lower-middle and upper-lower classes often have little to lose by identifying themselves with the Protestant cause, since they belong largely to a socially "disinherited" group. On the contrary, they often feel that they have much to gain, quite apart from the benefits they believe are derived from a direct personal relationship to God rather than a relationship through some mediating person or institution. These supplementary benefits often involve educational opportunities for their children, medical assistance for themselves and their families, and a new sense of dignity and "belongingness" in a fellowship which is highly interdependent and mutually helpful. The major aspects of this development may be diagrammed as follows (but note that on this diagram the arrow indicates direction of mobility):

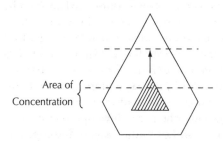

It should be noted that the constituency thus formed tends to have an upward movement. This upward mobility results almost inevitably from a greater sense of personal responsibility, accumulation of capital (for the convert does not spend so much money as formerly on certain forbidden "pleasures"), increased concern for and appreciation of education, a new attitude toward work as virtue (part of the "Protestant ethic"), and opportunities for the expression of leadership within the Protestant fellowship.

The Structure of Face-to-Face Societies

To the structure of urban societies, the rural, peasant, and primitive face-to-face societies present certain striking contrasts. There are, of course, many important differences between, for example, a small rural community in the hills of Kentucky and a village in the northern part of Zaire. Nevertheless, certain significant features are particularly relevant to the problems of communication.

In general, there are two main types of face-to-face societies: (1) folk and (2) primitive. The first is a dependent type of society which looks toward the urban center, derives considerable benefits from it, and also contributes much to it, especially by way of raw materials. The primitive society, on the other hand, is also a strictly face-to-face grouping, whether loosely or tightly organized, but its economy and orientation are almost completely independent of outside influences. Such a group, with its own laws, is quite homogeneous, with little division of labor, except as between sexes. Actually, strictly primitive groups—in this sense of the term—are now few. They consist primarily of small tribelets in Amazonia and New Guinea, as well as certain more isolated parts of Africa. Societies often spoken of as primitive, e.g., Indian tribes in Mexico and the altiplano of South America, are basically "peasant" or dependent societies; and many African tribes south of the Sahara and indigenous groups in India, Southeast Asia and the Islands of the Sea, are rapidly becoming such, though at present they are in a transitional state. The rapid development of transportation and communications and the economic exploitation of so-called primitive areas and peoples have in many instances changed these people from independent to dependent societies.

A typical folk or peasant society is not only economically dependent upon the urban center, whether it looks to the mining area around Lubumbashi in Zaire or sends its produce into a ladino town such as Cuzco in Peru; it also exists in cultural dependency to the prestigeful urban center from which so many cultural influences radiate. In contrast to the large, often heterogeneous and impersonal city society, with its lax morals, softer life, secular attitudes, and aggressive manner, the peasant, folk society is generally small, usually quite homogeneous, and intimate, with a milder, more passive manner, and with emphasis upon strong concepts of traditional morality, capacity for physical endurance, and deep religious sentiments. In such a face-to-face society, everyone knows everyone else, and also knows almost everyone's business, including a good deal about everyone's private life—in fact nothing is hidden from the prying and watchful eyes of neighbors. There is very little formal codification of law, but the customs are generally adhered to with an almost fanatical loyalty. By and large the people are more honest, especially within the in-group (the rural society with which the people identify themselves); but they are also more defensive against outside influences, and hence more likely to suspect ulterior motives and to react with blind stupidity and recalcitrance. In some ways long-established folk societies (though not "transitional societies") are more resistant to change than are strictly primitive groups, to which the outside world is less familiar. Furthermore, the folk society has generally discovered that the only defense against being overwhelmed by the outside world is to resist, passively but stubbornly, any changes sponsored by the out-group (the social grouping of which they are not members). This fact partly explains why Protestant missionaries have generally been more successful in dealing with primitive societies, for example, those in Africa, rather than with such a society as the Andean Indians of South America, whose patterns of resistance have been crystallized in opposition to the threats of domination by the white-sponsored culture of the urban centers.

In contrast to the inverted diamond structure with horizontal class cleavage which is typical of urban cultures, folk societies and, to a considerable extent, primitive societies as well may be diagrammatically described as broad-based, pyramidal forms, with roughly parallel rather than cross-sectional divisions:

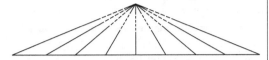

The pyramid in this instance is quite broad-based, for in general the distinctions between those who lead and those who are led are not great. At the same time, there are no simple higher, middle, and lower classes, or elaborations of these distinctions. Rather, the structure of the society breaks down essentially into family groups related by birth or marriage, and consisting of clans, tribelets, phratries, or moieties, depending upon the particular form which any particular social structure may take.

The apex of the diagram indicates the leadership of a small group, the elders of the society, who form an oligarchical control, but who also, as suggested by the dotted lines, individually represent their family affiliations. Such a society has a strong sense of cohesion and presents a more or less uniform front against intrusion. It must be conservative in orientation in order to preserve itself. By and large it makes collective decisions, not by any formal parliamentary techniques but by the kind of informal discussion and interchange of opinions that characterize most types of "family decisions." The effective spread of information in such a society is not describable as along either horizontal or vertical axes (as in our previous diagrams), but rather primarily along family and clan lines. McGavran makes a point of the necessity of using these effective channels of communication as the "bridges of God."[2]

Communicative Approach to a Face-to-Face Society

The methods by which we can best reach people in an urban type of society are quite evident to us, because most of us belong to such a social grouping. But the best type of approach to people living in a face-to-face society is for the same reason strange to most of us, since the social and communicational lines and structures are unfamiliar. However, once we have recognized the fundamental structure of such societies, we can see that the approaches which have proved to be most successful in them are the ones that make optimum use of the natural flow of communication. The basic principles in such an approach are four: (1) effective communication must be based upon personal friendship, (2) the initial approach should be to those who can effectively pass on communication within their family grouping, (3) time must be allowed for the internal diffusion of new ideas, and (4) the challenge for any change of belief or action must be addressed to the persons or groups socially capable of making such decisions.

1. Personal Friendship

In a face-to-face society it is essential to establish a personal basis of friendship and acceptance before communication can become effective. An outstanding early missionary in Peru, John Ritchie, instrumental in establishing more than two hundred congregations among the Indian population, made it an invariable rule never to go into a village except by personal invitation. He went to the home of the villager who had invited him and there remained during his visit of two or three days. In other words, he never went unannounced and unexpected into any Indian community to "evangelize," for he had concluded on the basis of years of experience that this course was simply not to be followed in an Indian community. Indians who were Christians might do so, for they could always establish some "family or clan" connection with the inhabitants, but the missionary, a stranger to the group, always felt that his message could be made acceptable to the people only if he was personally "sponsored" by someone belonging to the village.

2. Effective Communicators

The second and perhaps the most important principle to be followed in approaching such a community is to make the initial approach to those able effectively to pass on the communication. In some instances, the missionary is able to appeal to the chief of the tribe. In the United States, the rural "missionary" may be able to get the backing of the richest farmer in the region where he works. Usually, however, the unqualified support of the "top man" cannot be obtained immediately, for the leaders in a face-to-face society are generally slow to move ahead of their people. In fact, a man's position of leadership in a face-to-face society depends more upon the intimate and knowledgeable support of his followers than is true of a leader in an impersonal, urban society, where "money talks" more successfully. Thus the chief or headman in such a society is likely to be cautious about accepting any new thing; for the society itself is highly conservative and the leader is usually even more traditional in orientation than the majority of the people. In such a society strength lies in conservatism. Accordingly, those successful in reaching people in folk societies have usually approached a key person near the top, but not quite at the top—someone who, though respected within his own family and clan, has not yet assumed responsibility as an elder of the people. This person

is usually a strong personality, well liked by the people. Not infrequently he feels that sponsorship of new ideas may be to his social benefit. However, a word of caution should be added here. It must be recognized that a truly "marginal person" in the cult will not prove satisfactory for this purpose. Such a person's status may mean that he has been ostracized by his own society because of some affront to traditional leadership, or because he has violated the ethical standards of the people. It may mean that he is really an outsider in the face-to-face society, but hangs on in parasitical fashion because he derives economic benefit from exploiting the folk society.

3. Allow time

Allowing sufficient time for the making of decisions is the indispensable third principle in communicating with face-to-face societies. Traditionalists living within the comfortable emotional security of their "extended family" which maintains itself primarily by resistance to ideas from the outside world cannot be pushed into making quick decisions. Such people, confronted by a "crash program,"

will be inclined to reject it at once. Just as a family must be given time to make up its mind, so a face-to-face society must be carefully nursed along until the people are ready to act. At this point, an acute problem arises, for the missionary's tendency is to encourage some especially responsive persons to step out, repudiate the traditions of their tribe, and declare themselves for Christ. Such a procedure often causes the people as a whole to reject the message. For until a people are able to make what seems to them a valid decision, any pulling out of members from the ranks of the closed society immediately raises the fear of loss of solidarity. An instinctive resistance to assault upon the tight-knit social structure follows. By far the most effective work among folk societies has been done by those sensitive to the "timing" of the first converts.

4. Address people socially capable of making decisions

The fourth principle in approaching face-to-face societies is to present the challenge for change of belief to persons socially capable of making valid decisions. We who do not know the meaning of clan life, since we are not ourselves members of such a society, can rarely imagine the pressures upon the individual in such an organization. We take it for granted that anyone can and should make up his own mind about what he believes and what he should do. But this is not true in all cultures. Members of such a society feel an instinctive loyalty to the extended family unit. The individual derives his personal and social security from it, and usually gives it his complete and often unthinking support. Even an adult man may find it impossible to break with such a family unit. It is as though we invited a neighbor child to go to the beach for a day with our family, without consulting his parents. In general, his first response will be, "I'll go ask my mother." In fact, if we handle such an invitation rightly we would ask his mother for him, so that she would recognize the conditions as well as the genuineness of the invitation. Something of the same situation exists in face-to-face cultures, where individuals do not act on their own, but respond as members of families, clans, and tribes.

This group response to the gospel message lies at the core of the so-called "mass movement," called "people's movements" by McGavran. He pleads, and rightly so, for a more intelligent appreciation of the structure of societies in which people normally act as groups. He, therefore, insists that the process of Christianization must be divided between initial "discipling" and later instruction, and that the importance of initial commitment by the people to a new way of life must be fully recognized and built upon. The motives of such a people in mass response should no more be suspect that are the often mixed motives that prompt many individuals in an urban society to declare themselves for Christ, only to find later that they have committed themselves to more than they had earlier thought. In either case the initial commitment of either group or individual provides the basis by which instruction in the faith may be given and through which full maturity of Christian discipleship may be reached.

End Notes
1. David Riesman, *Individualism Reconsidered* (Garden City, N.Y.: Doubleday & Co., Inc., 1954), p. 46.
2. Donald A. McGavran, *The Bridges of God* (London: World Dominion Press, 1955), p. 120.

Study Questions
1. Compare both the patterns of decision-making and the communication approaches needed in urban and face-to-face societies.

2. Nida claims that the average expatriate American "lumps all groups together and proceeds without references to basic differences." What are some possible explanations for this tendency?

The Viable Missionary:
Learner, Trader, Story Teller

Donald N. Larson

Donald N. Larson is Senior Consultant for Cross-Cultural Living and Learning at Link Care Center. He is the Professor of Anthropology and Linguistics at Bethel College, St. Paul, Minnesota. He served the Toronto Institute of Linguistics as director for 25 years.

Reprinted from *Missiology: An International Review*, Arthur F. Glasser, ed., April 1978. Used by permission.

W hen my interest in Christian mission first awakened, I was too old to be acceptable to my denomination as a candidate. But for the past 40 years I have worked behind-the-scenes in mission, helping people deal with the problems of language and culture learning. I have observed missionaries, nationals, some Christians and some not, on all continents and in many countries. From these observations I have concluded that there is often a wide gap in the missionary's conception of his or her role and how it is viewed by those of his or her adopted community. The purpose of this paper is to examine this gap and propose ways and means of closing it.

Typical Encounter Models

When local community members encounter newcoming missionaries, they obviously view them as outsiders. Locals usually view missionaries using one or all of three interpretive backdrops or metaphors: the schoolhouse, the market place and the court room. The missionary may not intend or understand that people are perceiving him or her in these ways. As if he or she were at school, the community member sees the missionary in the role of teacher and himself as student. The purpose of their encounter is to transmit information to be learned. As if he or she were in the market place, he sees the missionary in the role of seller and himself as buyer. The purpose of their encounter is to buy and sell something. As if in the court room, his encounter deals most often with judgment, seeing the missionary in the role of accuser and himself as the accused.

In the schoolhouse the teacher says, "I will teach you something." In the market place the merchant says, "I have something to sell you." In the court room the judge says, "I will measure you by this standard." These three backdrops set the scenery for the local person to discern and decide the value of the missionary and his message. In the schoolhouse he asks himself whether he needs to learn what the teacher has to teach. In the market place he asks himself whether he needs to buy what the merchant has to sell. In the court room he asks himself whether he needs to take the accuser's accusation seriously.

This raises some serious issues. Can an outsider successfully teach or to sell or accuse an insider? Does the community member need what the missionary presents? Is the mis-

Encounter Models: Potential Perceptions of Outsiders

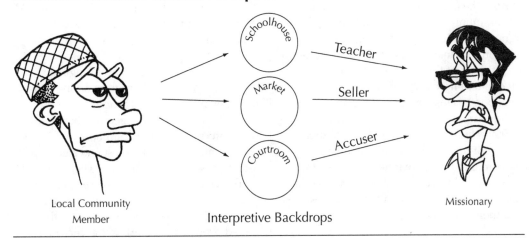

Local Community
Member

Interpretive Backdrops

Missionary

sionary able to communicate the gospel through the roles of seller, teacher or accuser?

To community members, the roles of teacher, seller or accuser may or may not be viable. They may expect the outsider to learn the insider's viewpoint before he can teach effectively about the outside. They may expect him to survive on the level of insiders and depend on the local market before he can sell important goods. They may expect him to measure himself by their own laws before he accuses insiders in terms of an outside standard.

The sequence seems to be important: student before teacher, buyer before seller, accused before accuser. An outsider may have to follow this order before he can be viable in these roles to the insider.

Outsiders cannot live on the edge of a community without coming to the attention of insiders in a negative way. The term "outsider" has negative connotations. So the missionary must become an "insider," at least to some extent, if he hopes to avoid these negative reactions to his presence and become a valuable person in the community.

If the insider is reluctant to learn from an outside teacher or buy from an outside seller or accept the accusations of an outside accuser, the outsider cannot hope to accomplish much until he closes the gap between himself—as outsider—and members of the local community. To close the gap missionaries need to pursue relationships in viable roles. Until missionaries are seen to enter viable role relationships, the gap will remain.

Entry Models: Potential Reception by Insiders

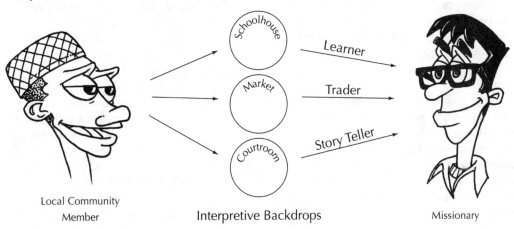

Local Community
Member

Interpretive Backdrops

Missionary

Closing the Gap

Closing the gap between missionary and local community members usually means redesigning old roles and designing new ones. Missionaries may have to learn to be foreigners for the first time in their life. They may have to find new ways to be a friend or a neighbor. To close the gap, typically means that the missionaries will have to measure their *effectiveness* by the standards of their hosts, not their own. Inevitably the missionary comes to realize that he or she must first be *acceptable* by local standards, and to be *acceptable*, local community members must first find them *teachable*.

Three Roles

As I see it, there are three roles that the missionary can develop in order to establish viability and acceptability in the eyes of his host community: *learner*, *trader* and *story teller*. These roles correspond with the three backdrops of schoolhouse, marketplace and courtroom.

If I were entering a new society, I would first become a *learner*. After a couple of months I would add another: *trader*. After a couple of more, I would add a third: *story teller*. Continuing as learner and trader, I would begin to develop other roles specified in my job description. Each new role would represent an important step in closing the gap between me and members of my local community.

Let me elaborate. From his position as an outsider, if he hopes to influence people, the missionary must find a way to be recognized as acceptable within the society. Some roles will help him to make this move. Others will not. His first task is to identify those which are most appropriate and effective. Then he can begin to develop ways and means of communicating his experience through the roles in which he has found acceptance.

Learner

More specifically, as a learner during my first days, my major emphasis is on language, the primary symbol of identification in my host community. I try to get off to a good start. When I make serious efforts to learn it, they know that I mean business—that they are worth something to me because I try to communicate on their terms. I learn a little

each day. I talk to a new person every day. I say something new every day. I gradually reach the point where I understand and am understood a little. I can learn much of the basics in a couple of months.

I spend my mornings with a language helper (in a structured program or one that I design on my own) from whom I elicit the kinds of materials that I need to talk to people in the afternoons. I show him how to drill me on these materials and then spend a good portion of the morning in practice. Then in the afternoon, I go out into public places and make whatever contacts are natural with local residents, talking to them the best I can with my limited proficiency—starting the very first day. I initiate one conversation after another, each of which says both verbally and non-verbally, "I am a learner. Please talk with me and help me." At first these little monologues will take just a few seconds. As I get a little more practice and a little more proficiency they'll take a little longer.

After a few weeks, I have made dozens of new acquaintances and a few friends. With potentially dozens of people, I've reached the point where I can make simple statements, ask and answer simple questions, find my way around, learn the meaning of new words on the spot, and most importantly, experience some measure of "at-homeness" in my adopted community. I cannot learn the "whole language" in a couple of months, but I can learn to initiate conversations, to communicate in a limited way and to learn a little more about the language from people I meet.

Trader

When people know me as a learner, I add a role—that of trader. It is here that the role of "*tentmaker*" may help to legitimize my presence. If I have come with some recognizable commercial purpose, my motives tend to make sense. As I begin to trade experience and insight with people of my adopted community, I present myself more clearly as part of humankind, as a visiting alien from another place. I prepare for this role by living in as many other places as I can, or by residing vicariously, through course work in anthropology and related fields. I have come equipped with photos of my own extended family and country. I can exchange elements of my background with others, as I open discussion about a wide range of ways to be human.

During these "trader months" I concentrate on *fitting in* and *establishing relationships*. I continue to spend mornings with my language helper learning to talk about the photos in my collection. Thus I build on the language proficiency developed in the first couple of months. I practice my description of these pictures and prepare myself the best I can to answer questions about them. Then in the afternoon, I visit casually in the community, using the photos as part of my "show and tell" demonstration. I tell as much as I can about the way others live, how they make their livings, what they do for enjoyment, how they hurt and how they struggle for survival and satisfaction.

At the end of this "trader phase," I have established myself not only as a learner but as one who is interested in other people and seeks to trade one bit of information for another. My language proficiency is still developing. I meet many people. Depending upon the size and complexity of the community, I have established myself as a well-known figure by this time. I have become a bridge between the people of the local community and a larger world—at least symbolically.

Story Teller

When I begin my seventh month, I again add a new role. Now I become a story teller. I spend mornings with my language helper. My focus now is to learn to tell a very simple story to the people whom I meet and respond to their inquiries as best I can. The stories that I tell are based on the wanderings of the people of Israel, the coming of Christ, the formation of God's new people, the movement of the Church into all the world and ultimately into this very community, and finally, my own story of my encounter with Christ and my walk as a Christian. During the mornings I develop these stories and practice them intensively. Then in the afternoon, I go into the community, as I have been doing for months, but now to encounter people as a story teller. I am still a language learner and a trader, but I have added the role of story teller. I share as much of the story with as many people as I can each day.

At the end of this third phase, I have made acquaintances and friends. I have had countless experiences that I will never forget. I have left positive impressions as a learner, trader and story teller. I am ready for then another role, and another and another.

Viability Revisited

Before we take for granted these roles of learner, trader and story teller, let's examine them again from the important viewpoint of viability. Any role that myself, as a missionary, takes on must be viable from four perspectives: (1) the community in which I reside, (2) its other missionary residents, (3) the agency that sends me and (4) myself.

To elaborate, my role must allow me to be myself; to be my own person. It must also be viable in the local missionary community. If the local missionary community doesn't recognize my role and its importance, I won't be able to survive for long. My role must also be viable from the standpoint of the sending agency. I need their support and encouragement. I cannot survive for long if they do not give me an important place in their community. Finally, my role must be viable from the point of view of the local community. I do not want to parade myself around in this community as some kind of a freak, or a misfit, or a spy or useless. This matter of community viability is often overlooked. It should not be. It is important, for I must have positive experiences in order to continue. Local residents must feel good about my presence in their community. My contribution must reinforce and complement the ongoing missionary program. The sending agency must have a solid rationale underlying its programs and the opportunities it provides for me.

What do local residents think of learners, traders and story tellers? From the standpoint of local residents, an outsider who is ready, willing and able to learn, probably has an entree. Furthermore, the average person in these communities probably has a natural curiosity about people in other places. This curiosity can probably be tapped and traded by a sensitive approach. Finally, story telling and the reporting of incidents is common in every community. Everyone does it. Of course, there are rules which must be re-spected. I assume that someone who has already established himself as learner and trader can share stories and experiences of his own with other people. Local residents will probably listen and perhaps even help him to tell others.

Most missionaries find these roles viable. Effective missionaries enjoy learning and know how to go about it. They have a general understanding of different ways that people live and appreciate the possibilities inherent in the trader role. They love to tell stories and enjoy listening to them, especially when the storyteller is deeply involved in them himself.

Viable Role Dimensions

If I were volunteering for missions today and hoped to be productive and happy, I would make certain that I was pursuing viable roles as learner, trader, and story teller.

But from the standpoint of the sending agency and the local missionary community, these roles may be questionable. Of the three, the story teller role is perhaps the easiest one to develop, though one often finds missionaries to be sermonizers, theologizers or lecturers, not story tellers. The viability of the learner role is open to question. A new missionary, expected to be a learner as far as the affairs of his local missionary organization are concerned, is not always given the time or encouraged to get to know local residents intimately. The viability of the trader role is largely untested, though with the current emphasis on tentmaking, it seems that sending agencies and local missionary communities are considering their importance carefully.

Why not exploit the learner role to the fullest? Most people who live as aliens sooner or later realize its importance. Why not get the new missionary off on the right foot—especially if it has increasing payoff in his second and third phases? Furthermore, the learner role symbolizes a number of important things to local residents that are important in the communication of the gospel. The learner's dependence and vulnerability convey in some small way the messages of identification and reconciliation that are explicit in the gospel. Coming to be known as a learner can certainly do the local missionary community no harm. It may be able to do some good.

The viability of the trader role has become generally accepted as "tentmakers" are welcomed to foreign communities as professionals and business people. But as described in the role of trader exchanging ideas and images of what it means to be human in today's world may seem too "secular" for some missionaries. From the community's standpoint, this secular role may be much more natural and acceptable for the alien. Coming as some sort of "sacred specialist," the outsider generates all sorts of questions, objections and barriers. But there is still another consideration. This role reinforces the idea of the gospel as something for all people. Except for anthropologists, demographers and a few other specialists, Christians probably have a wider understanding of human variation than any other group of people, simply because of our multi-ethnic, multi-racial and multi-lingual diversity. The trader role complements the more formal presentation of the gospel through the sharing of essentially "secular knowledge" about peoples of the world.

There are obvious implications here for the selection, orientation and evaluation of missionaries. A discussion of them however is beyond the scope of this paper.

Backing In

We face a challenging situation today. As the colonialism continues to wane, and as the strength of maturing national churches continues to grow, missionaries are becoming more and more frustrated as the viability of their role is questioned. We must take this situation seriously. If the mission movement is to continue, new roles must be added and old ones must be redesigned. The biblical mandate challenges the Christian to identify with those to whom he brings words of life. Furthermore, history shows that this apparent weakness of vulnerability and flexibility has always been part of the most powerful witness to the gospel message.

Some years ago at a language and culture learning workshop in East Africa, a missionary asked me if I knew anything about elephants. When I replied that I did not, she asked more specifically if I knew what happens when a herd of elephants approaches a water hole that is surrounded by another herd. I replied that I did not know what would happen. She then proceeded to explain that the lead elephant of the second group turns around and backs down toward the water hole. As soon as his backside is felt by two of the elephants gathered around the water hole, they step aside and make room for him. This is then the signal to the other elephants that the first herd is ready to make room for them around the hole. When I asked what point she was trying to make, she stated simply, and powerfully, "We didn't back in." The continuing movement of mission in the world today may require missionaries to "back in" to their host communities. The roles of learner, trader and story teller may not be appropriate in a "head first" approach, but they may be necessary in an approach which emphasizes "backing in."

Study Questions

1. Can you suggest other useful roles besides the three that Larson describes?

2. As a "trader," what do you demonstrate as valuable to locals? What additional communication skills are likely to be learned as you function as a trader?

3. Larson suggests that there is an appropriate sequence of beginning as a learner, continuing as a trader, in order to emerge into an effective place as a storyteller. Discuss this idea.

The Difference Bonding Makes

E. Thomas and Elizabeth S. Brewster

Elizabeth S. Brewster and the late E. Thomas Brewster have been a husband-wife team specializing in helping missionaries develop effective techniques for learning any language and adapting to the broader culture of which the language is a part. Tom held a Ph.D. from the University of Arizona and Betty Sue holds a Ph.D. from the University of Texas. Their work has taken them to more than 80 countries and they have helped train over 2,000 missionaries. Their book *Language Acquisition Made Practical* (LAMP) has been widely acclaimed for its innovative approach and pedagogical creativity. Thomas Brewster died in 1985.

Adapted from, *Bonding and the Missionary Task*, Brewster & Brewster. Lingua House. Used by permission.

"And the Word became flesh and dwelt among us" (John 1:14).

We have a new little boy who was born into our home just a few months ago. In preparing for his childbirth we were introduced to the concept of bonding. The psychological and physiological make up of a newborn immediately after birth uniquely prepares the baby to bond with his or her parents.[1] If parents and infant are together at that time, a close bond can result which can withstand subsequent separations. Certainly the excitement and adrenaline levels of both the child and the parents are at a peak. The senses of the infant are being stimulated by a multitude of new sensations. The birth is essentially an entrance into a new culture with new sights, new sounds, new smells, new positions, new environment and new ways of being held. Yet, at that particular time, he or she is equipped with an extraordinary ability to respond to these unusual circumstances and new stimuli.

Pediatricians have observed that a non-drugged newborn is often more alert during the first day than at any time in the following week or two. These alert hours facilitate the formation of the early bonding. When a baby is groggy from medications given to the mother in labor, however, neither the baby nor mother can take advantage of this God-given period. Or when the baby is whisked away to the isolation of a nursery, this time of acute awareness may be lost as well.

The Missionary Analogy

There are important parallels between the infant's arrival into his or her first culture and an adult's entrance into a new, foreign culture. In this situation the adult's senses, too, are bombarded by a multitude of new sensations, sights, sounds and smells. And often he or she is uniquely able to respond to these experiences at every turn—and to even enjoy them. There have been months, even years, of planning and preparation. Excitement, anticipation and adrenaline are at a peak. The just-arrived missionary is in an unusual state of readiness, both physiologically and psychologically, to bond in the new environment. The new missionary is prepared, perhaps more than ever again, to bond—to become a "belonger" with the people to whom he or she is called to share the good news.

Establishing a Sense of Belonging

The timing can be critical because bonding best occurs when the participants are uniquely ready for the experience. If the newly arrived missionary is whisked away to the familiar comforts of a missionary contingency, a crucial window of readiness is lost. If a missionary is to establish a sense of belonging to the people among whom the missionary is called to serve, the way he or she spends the first few weeks can be of critical importance. It's not uncommon for a baby who is kept in the nursery to become bonded with hospital personnel instead of with his or her parents. New missionaries, as well, can fulfill their need for belonging by bonding with the expatriate community.

If a sense of belonging is established with the other foreigners, a new missionary is then more likely to carry out ministry by the "foray" method. The missionary may live in isolation from local people, perhaps in a "missionary compound," but venture out into the local community a few times each week, returning always to the security of the expatriate community. If the missionary does not feel at home in the local cultural context, he or she may not pursue significant relationships in that community as a way of life. This lack of bonding may be reflected in exasperated statements like, "Oh these people! Why do they always do things *this* way?" or "When will these people ever learn?"

Implications of Bonding for the Missionary Task

A missionary is one who goes into the world to give people an opportunity to belong to God's family. The missionary goes because he or she is a belonger in this most meaningful of relationships. His or her life should proclaim: "I belong to Jesus who has given me a new kind of life. By my becoming a belonger here with you, God is inviting you through me to belong to Him."

The missionary's task thus parallels the model established by Jesus who left heaven, where He belonged, and became a belonger with humankind in order to draw people into a belonging relationship with God.

Becoming a Belonger

The missionary who is immediately immersed in the local community has many advantages. If the newcomer lives with a local family, he or she can learn how the insiders organize their lives, how they get their food and do their shopping, and how they get around with public transportation. Much can be learned during the first months about the insiders' attitudes and their feelings about the ways foreigners live. As the newcomer experiences an alternative lifestyle, he or she can evaluate the value of adopting it. On the other hand, the missionary whose first priority is to get settled will only be able to settle in a familiar way. Since nothing else has been experienced, no other options are possible. And once a missionary is comfortably settled in the old life-style, that person is virtually locked into a pattern that is foreign to the local people.

In our first culture, it comes naturally to go about things in a way that works. We know which way to look for traffic as we step off the curb, how to get a bus to stop for us, how to pay a fair price for goods or services, how to get the information we need or where to go for help. But in a new culture, the way to do things seems unpredictable. This results in a disorientation that can lead to culture shock. A new missionary who first establishes a sense of belonging with other missionary expatriates has his or her entry into the new life cushioned by these foreigners. In the past, it was generally thought that this cushioning was important for the adjustment of the newcomer. Often a newcomer's arrival was planned to coincide with a field council pow-wow. We would like to suggest, however, that this "cushion" can be an unfortunate disservice.

Like the first day of an infant's life, the first two or three weeks of a newcomer's stay is of crucial importance. The initial blush of life in the new environment is when developing a sense of belonging is most possible. During this time, a person may be especially able to cope with the unpredictable situations encountered in the new culture, and cushioning is the *last* thing needed.

The individual who hopes to enter another culture in a gradual way faces greater obstacles and, in fact, may never enjoy the experience of belonging to the people. Better to plunge right in and experience life from the insiders' perspective. Live with the people, go shopping with them, use public transportation with them, worship with them as it may be appropriate.

From the very first day, it is important to develop many relationships with local people. The newcomer should early on communicate his or her needs and the desire to be a learner. People help other people who are clearly in need. When potentially stressful situations come up, the new missionary can, as a learner, secure help, receive answers or be given insight from these insiders. In the same situation, the one who is being cushioned receives outsiders' answers to insiders' situations and that person's foreignness and alienation can thereby be perpetuated.

many ways. We supported each other but at times the burdens seemed so big and we didn't have anyone else to talk to or look to for advice. But I suppose that is why we have such good national friends.

Bonding is the factor that makes it possible for the newcomer to belong to "such good national friends." Of course there will be stressful situations, but the bonded newcomer, experiencing the wonder of close relationships, is able to derive support from the network of the local friendships he or she has developed. This in turn facilitates the acquisition of the insiders' ways and gives a sense of feeling at home. The one who feels at home may feel discouraged or even melancholy for a time and some cultural stress is to be expected, but it may not be necessary to experience severe and prolonged culture shock.

> Language acquisition is essentially a social activity, not an academic one. Gaining proficiency in the language is challenging, but normal for a person who is deeply engaged in relationships in a new society.

A couple who has chosen to be isolated from Western people during their first months in a Muslim context wrote us about the victories they have experienced:

> We knew before we left that we would have different types of adjustments. I knew the hardest time for me would be at first and he felt that his hard times would occur after he had been here a while. So it has been. I really had a hard time leaving our family. But after I started getting out with the people here, my homesickness faded. The local community has so warmly received us. At Christmas, 125 of these friends came to our Christmas celebration. And during that season, the closeness of our interpersonal relationships amazed us.
>
> I'm not exactly sure why my husband just recently went through a depression. Christmas for us was different than it has been. Plus he was laid up for a week with the flu. During that time, he yearned for familiar things. And he says he was tired of always trying to be sensitive as to how he is coming across. And yet the Lord has blessed our work here, and two Muslim converts that he is discipling are what is helping him get over this. We really have been alone in

Learning the Language

Living with a family not only facilitates bonding, but it also significantly enhances language learning. Newcomers learn language best when immersed in relationships with local people. It's similar to the way they learned their mother tongue: listening, imitating and actively experimenting with language. Classroom instruction can be helpful, but it can not replace genuine face-to-face conversations in relationship with local people.

Only a minimum of the target language is needed to initiate bonding relationships. "The best thing that happened to me was on the first day when you challenged us to take the little we knew how to say and go talk with fifty people," a missionary wrote us. "I didn't talk with fifty, I only talked with forty-four. But I *did* talk with forty-four." The "text" she was able to say that first day was limited to a greeting and an expression of her desire to learn the language; then she could tell people that she didn't know how to say any more but she would see them again. She closed with a thank you and a leave-taking. The ice was broken on her very first day and, from then on, she was able to begin to feel at home in her new community. From that point, she continued as she had started: she learned a little, but used it a lot.

Language acquisition is essentially a social activity, not an academic one. Gaining proficiency in the language is challenging, but normal for a person who is deeply engaged in relationships in a new society. Language study will often be a burden and frustration for these who maintain their primary relationships with expatriates. It is therefore important to facilitate an opportunity for new missionaries to become bonded with (and hence belongers in) their new community. New missionaries should be challenged with the bonding objective and prepared to respond to the opportunity to become a belonger.

Newcomers need to be encouraged to totally immerse themselves in the life of the new community from day one. If a newcomer is going to successfully establish himself as a belonger, live with a local family and learn from relationships on the streets, a prior decision and commitment to do so is essential. Without such a prior commitment it doesn't usually happen.

We have found that a prior preparation of perspective and expectations is helpful, along with training in how to develop language learning skills. When we counsel people, we recommend that they accept four conditions for their first few weeks:

1) Be willing to live with a local family,
2) Limit personal belongings to 20 kilos,
3) Use only local public transportation, and
4) Expect to carry out language learning in the context of relationships that the learner is responsible to develop and maintain.

A willingness to accept these conditions tells a lot about an individual's attitude and flexibility.

With a prepared mentality, a newcomer is freed to respond creatively to the bonding and learning opportunities that surround him. The new missionary—whether single, married, or even with children—usually can successfully live with a local family immediately upon arrival. In some situations, team members, mission agency personnel or local contacts can find a family. But newcomers have often found their own families by learning to say, "I want to learn your language. I hope to find a family to live with for about three months, and I will pay my expenses. Do you know of a possible family?" It would be unusual to say this to fifty people without getting at least some positive response, at least a mediator to help with the search.

Those who are bonding and carrying out their language learning in the context of relationships in the new community also have the opportunity to pursue the development of their new ministry from the earliest days of language learning. A few years ago the authors supervised the initial language learning time for a team of eleven newcomers in Bolivia.

"...Over 30 people came to know Christ as a result of the involvement ministry that these new language learners were able to develop during those (first) three months. Many of these were either members of families with whom we were living, or were on a route of regular listeners. In both cases, as a result of the personal relationships that they had developed, they were able to follow up and disciple the new believers. Little wonder that this was a fulfilling experience for these new language learners."[2]

The Better Risk of Bonding

There are few times in life with as much stress and danger as birth. And it would be wrong to imply that immediate and total immersion in a new culture is without risk. It is likely, however, that even the stress and risk components are essential to the formation of the unique environment that makes bonding possible. And there is another side to the risk question. If a new missionary doesn't take the initial risk and seek to become comfortable as soon as possible with the new society, he or she may be opting for a longer-term risk. The problem of missionary casualties suggests that there is a heavy price to be paid by those who fail to become belongers—a great many of them do not return for a second term of service. It is not easy to live with a family, make friends with strangers and learn a new language, but neither is it easy to continue as a stranger, living without close friendships with insiders or an understanding of their cultural cues.

Is bonding possible after the first critical months are past? Is it possible for an established missionary to experience a belated bonding? The answer is yes. It is a normal human process to establish belonging relationships. An established missionary who sees the potential of a belonging relationship with the local people can implement this commitment by adopting a learner role and moving in with a local family for a few weeks or months.

The concept of bonding implies a bi-cultural individual with a healthy self-image. Bonding and "going native" are not the same thing. Going native implies the rejection of one's first culture. This reaction is seldom seen in missionaries and may not be possible for normal, emotionally stable adults. Nor is being bi-cultural the same as having a "split personality." A person with a split personality has a broken and fragmented self. A bi-cultural person is developing a new outlet for his or her God-given personality. The person with this new creative outlet can be free to behave at times with child-like disregard for upholding an image. This person is freed to make mistakes and try, try again. For the Christian missionary, the process of becoming bi-cultural begins with the recognition that God in His sovereignty does not make mistakes in creating us within our first culture; yet in His sovereignty He taps some of us on the shoulder and calls us to belong to people of a different culture so that we can be good news to them.

"And the Word became flesh and dwelt among us" (John 1:14).

End Notes

1. *Maternal-Infant Bonding,* Marshall H. Klaus & John H. Kennell, C V Mosby Co., St. Louis, 1976.
2. Brewster & Brewster, "I have never been so fulfilled," *Evangelical Missions Quarterly,* April 1978, p. 103.

Study Questions

1. Why is it important especially for a new missionary to bond with his/her hosts? Is a belated bonding possible and why?

2. If, as the Brewsters say, language learning is "essentially a social activity, not an academic one," is language learning any easier for a missionary who is attempting to immerse themselves in the life of a new community?

3. Why do the Brewsters recommend limiting personal belongings and living with a local family?

Identification in the Missionary Task

William D. Reyburn

William D. Reyburn has served the United Bible Societies as a Translations Consultant in South and Central America, West Africa, Europe and the Middle East. He served as World Translations Coordinator based in London, England from 1968 to 1972. Reyburn retired in 1997 at the age of 75 and lives with his wife, Marie Fetzer Reyburn in north Georgia.

Adapted from *Readings in Missionary Anthropology II*, edited by William A. Smalley, 1978. Used by permission of William Carey Library, Pasadena, CA.

A steady downpour of rain had been falling from late afternoon until long after dark. A small donkey followed by a pair of men slowly made its way down the slippery sides of the muddy descent which wound into the sleepy town of Baños, high in the Ecuadorean Andes. No one appeared to pay any attention as the two dark figures halted their burro before a shabby Indian hostel. The taller of the two men stepped inside the doorway where a group of men sat at a small table drinking *chicha* by candlelight. No sooner had the stranger entered the room than a voice from behind the bar called out, "*Buenas noches, meester.*" The man in the rain-soaked poncho turned quickly to see a fat-faced woman standing half concealed behind the counter. "*Buenas noches, señora,*" he replied, lifting his hat slightly. Following a short exchange of conversation the man and barmaid reappeared outside and led the donkey through a small gate to a mud stable. The two men removed their load and carried it to a stall-like room beside the stable where they were to spend the night.

I sat down on the straw on the floor and began pulling off my wet clothes. I kept hearing the word *meester* which I had come to dislike intensely. Why had that funny little woman there in the semi-darkness of the room addressed me as *meester*? I looked at my clothes. My hat was that of the poorest *cholo* in Ecuador. My pants were nothing more than a mass of patches held together by still more patches. On my dirty mud-stained feet I wore a pair of rubber tire *alpargatas* the same as any Indian or *cholo* wore. My red poncho was not from the high class Otavalo weavers. It was a poor man's poncho made in Salcedo. It had no fancy tassels and in true *cholo* fashion there were bits of straw dangling from its lower edge, showing that I was a man who slept with his burro on the road. But why then did she call me *meester*, a term reserved for Americans and Europeans? At least she could have addressed me as *señor*, but no, it had to be *meester*. I felt as though my carefully devised disguise had been stripped from me with the mention of that word. I kept hashing it over and over in my mind. It wasn't because she detected a foreign accent, because I had not as yet opened my mouth. I turned to my Quechua Indian companion, old Carlos Bawa of Lake Colta. "Carlos, the lady knew I am a *meester*. How do you think she knew, Carlitos?"

My friend sat huddled in the corner of the room with his legs and arms tucked under his two ponchos. "I don't know, *patroncito*." Looking up quickly at Carlos I said, "Carlos, for three days I have been asking you not to call me patroncito. If you call me that people will know I am not a *cholo*." Carlos flicked a finger out from under the collar of his woolen poncho and touching his hat brim submissively replied, "I keep forgetting, *meestercito*."

Disgusted and aching in my rain-soaked skin I felt like the fool I must have appeared. I sat quietly watching the candle flicker as Carlos dozed off to sleep in his corner. I kept seeing the faces of people along the road we had walked for the past three days. Then I would see the face of this woman in Baños who had robbed me of what seemed like a perfect disguise. I wondered then if perhaps I hadn't been taken for a European even earlier. I was hurt, disappointed, disillusioned, and to make things worse I was dreadfully hungry. Reaching into our packsack I pulled out the bag of *machica* flour my wife had prepared for us, poured in some water and stirred the brown sugar and barley mixture with my finger and gulped it down. The rain was letting up now and from a hole in the upper corner of the room I could see the clouds drifting across the sky in the light of the moon. A guitar was strumming softly out in the street and in the stall next to us a half dozen Indians had just returned from the stable and were discussing the events of their day's journey.

Blowing out the candle I leaned up against the rough plank wall and listened to their conversation, then eventually fell asleep. It was some hours later when I was startled awake from the noise of our door creaking open. I got to my feet quickly and jumped behind the opening door, waiting to see what was going to happen. The door quietly closed and I heard old Carlos groan as he settled down onto his mat to sleep. Carlos was returning, having gone out to relieve himself. My companion had been warning me for several days that Indians often rob each other and I should always sleep lightly. It was quiet now, deathly silent. I had no idea what time it may have been, as a watch was not suitable for my *cholo* garb. I lay on the floor thinking about the meaning of identification. I asked myself again and again what it meant to be identified with this old Quechua Indian who was so far removed from the real world in which I lived.

I was traveling the Indian markets of the Ecuadorean Andes in order to know what really lay hidden in the hearts of these Quechua Indians and Spanish-speaking *cholos*. What was the real longing in their hearts that could be touched? I wanted to know what it was that drunkenness seemed to satisfy. Was the Quechua Indian really the sullen withdrawn personality that he appeared to be before his *patrón*? Was he so adjustable to life conditions that his attitude could incorporate most any conflict without upsetting him seriously? Was he really a good Catholic, a pagan, or what kind of a combination? Why underneath was he so opposed to outward change? What was he talking about and worrying over when he settled down at night in the security of his own little group? I was after the roots that lay behind the outward symbols which could respond to the claims of Christ. The answer to questions like these would form the basis for a missionary theology, a relevant communication to these people's lives. I could see no purpose in putting the Christian proposition before a man unless it was made in such a way that it forced him to struggle with it in terms of surrender to the ultimate and most basic demand that could be placed upon him. In order to know what had to be addressed to the depths of his being I had to wade down to it through what I was convinced were only outward displays of a deeper need in his heart.

A major aspect of the missionary task is the search for what in German is called *der Anknüpfungspunkt*, connection or point of contact. The proclamation of the gospel aside from such a contact point is a proclamation which skirts missionary responsibility. This is simply the process in which the one who proclaims the good news must make every effort to get into touch with his listener. Man's heart is not a clean slate that the gospel comes and writes upon for the first time. It is a complex tablet which has been scrawled upon and deeply engraved from birth to death. The making of a believer always begins with an unbeliever. Clearly this is the job of the Holy Spirit. However this does not remove man from his position of responsibility.

It is man in his rational hearing and understanding that is awakened to belief. It is the conquering of man's basic deceit that allows the Holy Spirit to lay claim to him and to make of him a new creature. A man must be aware that he stands in defiance of God's call before he can be apprehended by God's love. Before an enemy can be taken captive he must stand in the position of an enemy.

The Forms of Identification

Missionary identification may take on many different forms. It may be romantic or it may be dull. It may be convincing or it may appear as a sham. The central point is that identification is not an end in itself. It is the road to the task of gospel proclamation. Likewise the heart of the controversial matter of missionary identification is not how far one can go but rather what one does with the fruits of identification. Going native is no special virtue. Many missionaries in the humdrum of their daily routine about a school or hospital have awakened men's hearts to the claim of the gospel.

Some so-called identification is misoriented and tends to create the impression that living in a native village or learning the native tongue is automatically the "open sesame" of the native's heart. It is not the sheer quantity of identification that counts; it is rather the purposeful quality that comprehends man as a responsible being seeking to be in touch with his reality. The limitations for knowing what is this contacted reality are great. The practical obstacles for missionary identification are many. In the pages that follow we shall attempt to outline some of these as we have lived in them and to evaluate the effects of the lack of missionary identification and participation.

Strength of Unconscious Habit

Without doubt the nature of the obstacle to identification is the fact that one has so well learned one's own way of life that one practices it for the most part without conscious reflection. In the case described above the old Quechua Indian Carlos Bawa, the donkey and I had been traveling across the plateau of the Andes spending the days in the markets and the nights cramped into tiny quarters available to itinerant Indians and *cholos* for approximately 10 cents U.S. We had made our way from Riobamba to Baños, a three-day trek by road, and no one except an occasional dog appeared to see that all was not quite normal. It was not until stepping into the candle-lit room of the inn at Baños that I was taken for a foreigner (at least it so appeared). I suspect that it bothered me a great deal because I had created the illusion for a few days that I was finally on the inside of the Indian-*cholo* world looking around and not in the least conspicuous about it. When the innkeeper addressed me as *meester* I had the shock of being rudely dumped outside the little world where I thought I had at last gained a firm entrance.

The following morning I went to the lady innkeeper and sat down at the bar. "Now, tell me, *señora*," I began, "how did you know I was a *meester* and not a local *señor* or a *cholo* from Riobamba?" The fat little lady's eyes sparkled as she laughed an embarrassed giggle. "I don't know for sure," she replied. I insisted she try to give me the answer, for I was thoroughly confused over it all. I went on. "Now suppose you were a detective, *señora*, and you were told to catch a European man dressed like a poor *cholo* merchant. How would you recognize him if he came into your inn?" She scratched her head and leaned forward over the counter. "Walk outside and come back in like you did last night." I picked up my old hat, pulled it low on my head, and made for the door. Before I reached the street she called out, "Wait, *señor*, I know now what it is." I stopped and turned around. "It's the way you walk." She broke into a hearty laugh at this point and said, "I never saw anyone around here who walks like that. You Europeans swing your arms like you never carried a load on your back." I thanked the good lady for her lesson in posture and went out in the street to study how the local people walked. Sure enough the steps were short and choppy, the trunk leaning forward slightly from the hips and the arms scarcely moving under their huge ponchos.

> The central point is that identification is not an end in itself. It is the road to the task of gospel proclamation.

Limits of Identification

Perhaps the most outstanding example in which I was reminded of the limitations of identification occurred while we were living in a mud-and-thatch hut near Tabacundo, Ecuador. We had moved into a small scattered farming settlement near the Pisque river about a kilometer from the United Andean Mission for whom we were making a study. My wife and I had agreed that if we were to accomplish anything at the U.A.M. we would have to settle among the people and somehow get them to accept us or reject us. We were accepted eventually but always with reservations. We wore nothing but Indian clothes and ate nothing but Indian food. We had no furniture except a bed made of century plant stalks covered with a woven mat exactly as in all the Indian houses. In fact, because we had no agricultural equipment, weaving loom, or granary, our one-room house was by far the most empty in the vicinity. In spite of this material reduction to the zero point the men addressed me as *patroncito*. When I objected that I was not a *patrón* because I owned no land they reminded me that I wore leather shoes. I quickly exchanged these for a pair of local made *alpargatas* which have a hemp fiber sole and a woven cotton upper. After a time had passed I noticed that merely changing my footwear had not in the least gotten rid of the appellation of *patroncito*. When I asked again, the men replied that I associated with the Spanish townspeople from Tabacundo. In so doing I was obviously identifying myself with the *patrón* class. I made every effort for a period to avoid the townspeople but the term *patroncito* seemed to be as permanently fixed as it was the day we moved into the community.

The men had been required by the local commissioner to repair an impassable road connecting the community and Tabacundo. I joined in this work with the Indians until it was completed two months later. My hands had become hard and calloused. One day I proudly showed my calloused hands to a group of men while they were finishing the last of a jar of fermented *chica*. "Now, you can't say I don't work with you. Why do you still call me *patroncito*?" This time the truth was near the surface, forced there by uninhibited alcoholic replies. Vicente Cuzco, a leader in the group, stepped up and put his arm around my shoulder and whispered to me. "We call you *patroncito* because you weren't born of an Indian mother." I needed no further explanation.

Ownership of a Gun

Living in an African village caused us to become aware of the effect of other formative attitudes in our backgrounds. One of these in particular is the idea of personal ownership. While living in the south Cameroun village of Aloum among the Bulu in order to learn the language, we had been received from the first day with intense reception and hospitality. We were given Bulu family names; the village danced for several nights and we were loaded with gifts of a goat and all kinds of tropical foods.

We had been invited to live in Aloum and we were not fully prepared psychologically to understand how such an adoption was conceived within Bulu thinking. Slowly we came to learn that our possessions were no longer private property but were to be available for the collective use of the sub-clan where we had been adopted. We were able to adjust to this way of doing because we had about the same material status as the others in the village. Their demands upon our things were not as great as their generous hospitality with which they provided nearly all of our food.

Then one night I caught a new vision of the implication of our relation to the people of Aloum. A stranger had appeared in the village and we learned that Aloum was the home of his mother's brother. It was the case of the nephew in the town of his maternal uncle, a most interesting social relationship in the patrilineal societies in Africa. After dark when the leading men in the village had gathered in the men's club house, I drifted over and sat down among them to listen to their conversations. The fires on the floor threw shadows which appeared to dance up and down on the mud walls.

Finally silence fell over their conversations and the chief of the village arose and began to speak in very hushed tones. Several young men arose from their positions by the fires and moved outside to take up a listening post to make sure that no uninvited persons would overhear the development of these important events. The chief spoke of the welcome of his nephew into his village and guaranteed him a safe sojourn while he was there. After these introductory formalities were finished the chief began to extol his nephew as a great elephant hunter. I was still totally ignorant of how all this affected me.

I listed as he eulogized his nephew's virtue as a skilled hunter. After the chief finished another elder arose and continued to cite cases in the nephew's life in which he had displayed great bravery in the face of the dangers of the jungles. One after another repeated these stories until the chief again stood to his feet. I could see the whites of his eyes which were aimed at me. The fire caused little shadows to run back and forth on his dark face and body. "Obam Nna," he addressed me. A broad smile exposed a gleaming set of teeth. "We are going to present our gun to my nephew now. Go get it."

I hesitated a brief moment but then arose and crossed the moonlit courtyard to our thatch-covered house where Marie and some village women sat talking. I kept hearing in my ears: "We are going to present our gun...our gun..." almost as if it were a broken record stuck on the plural possessive pronoun. It kept repeating in my ears, "...ngale jangan...ngale jangan..." Before I reached the house I had thought of half a dozen very good reasons why I should say no. However I got the gun and some shells and started back to the club house. As I re-entered the room I caught again the sense of the world of Obam Nna. If I were to be Obam Nna I should have to cease to be William Reyburn. In order to be Obam Nna I had to crucify William Reyburn nearly every day. In the world of Obam Nna I no longer owned the gun as in the world of William Reyburn. I handed the

gun to the chief and, although he didn't know it, along with it went the surrender of a very stingy idea of private ownership.

Symbolic Value of Food

Another problem in village participation is the matter of food and water. I had gone into the village of Lolo to carry out some studies relative to the translation of the book of Acts and had taken no European food, determined to find what the effects of an all-Kaka diet would be. I found that the simple mixture of cassava flour and hot water to form a mush was an excellent sustaining diet. On one occasion over a period of six weeks on this diet I lost no weight, had no diarrhea, and suffered no other ill effects. All of this food was prepared by village women and I usually ate on the ground with the men wherever I happened to be when a woman would serve food. On several occasions when I was not in the right place at the right time it meant going to bed with an empty stomach. I carefully avoided asking any woman to prepare food especially for me, as this had a sexual connotation which I did not care to provoke.

Once I had been talking most of the afternoon with a group of Kaka men and boys about foods people eat the world over. One of the young men got his Bulu Bible and read

from the 10th chapter of Acts the vision of Peter who was instructed to kill and eat "all manner of four-footed beasts of the earth, and wild beasts, and creeping things, and fowls of the air." This young Kaka who had been a short while at a mission school said, "The Hausa people don't believe this because they won't eat pigs. Missionaries, we think don't believe this because they don't eat some of our foods either." I quite confidently assured him that a missionary would eat anything he does.

The missionary task is that of sacrifice. Not the sacrifice of leaving friends and comfortable situations at home, but the sacrifice of reexamining one's own cultural assumptions.

That evening I was called to the young man's father's doorway, where the old man sat on the ground in the dirt. In front of him were two clean white enamel pans covered by lids. He looked up at me and motioned for me to sit. His wife brought a gourd of water which she poured as we washed our hands. Then flicking wet fingers in the air to dry them a bit, the old man lifted the lid from the one pan. Steam arose from a neatly rounded mass of cassava mush. Then he lifted the lid from the other pan. I caught a glimpse of its contents. Then my eyes lifted and met the unsmiling stare of the young man who had read about the vision of Peter earlier in the afternoon. The pan was filled with singed caterpillars. I swallowed hard, thinking that now I either swallowed these caterpillars or I swallowed my words and thereby proved again that Europeans have merely adapted Christianity to fit their own selfish way of life. I waited as my host scooped his shovel-like fingers deep into the mush, then with a ball of the stuff he pressed it gently into the caterpillar pan. As he lifted it to his open mouth I saw the burned and fuzzy creatures, some smashed into the mush and others dangling loose, enter between his teeth.

My host had proven the safety of his food by taking the first portion. This was the guarantee that he was not feeding me poison. I plunged my fingers into the mush but my eyes were fixed on the caterpillars. I wondered what the sensation in the mouth was going to be. I quickly scooped up some of the creeping things and plopped the mass into my mouth. As I bit down the soft insides burst open and to my surprise I tasted a salty meat-like flavor which seemed to give the insipid cassava mush the ingredient that was missing.

We sat silently eating. There is no time for conversation at the Kaka "table" for as soon as the owner has had his first bite male hands appear from every direction and the contents are gone. As we sat eating quickly the old man's three wives with their daughters came and stood watching us from their kitchen doorways. They held their hands up and whispered busily back and forth, "White man Kaka is eating caterpillars. He really has a black heart." The pans were emptied. Each one took a mouthful of water, rinsed his mouth and spat the water to one side, belched loudly, said "Thank you, Ndjambie" (God), arose and departed into the rays of the brilliant setting sun. My notes on that night contain this one line: "An emptied pan of caterpillars is more convincing than all the empty metaphors of love which missionaries are prone to expend on the heathen."

Ideological Insulation

There are other obstacles to missionary participation in native life which arise from background as well as local Christian tradition. It does not take a folk or primitive people long to size up the distance which separates themselves from the missionary. In some cases this distance is negligible but in others it is the separation between different worlds. Missionaries with pietistic backgrounds are prepared to suspect that everything the local people do is bad and that therefore, in order to save them, they must pull them out and set up another kind of life opposed to the original one. This process seldom if ever works, and when it does the result is the creation of a society which consists of converted souls, but no converted life. The missionary under these circumstances takes the path of least resistance, keeps himself untouched by the world and of course does not get in touch with the world in order to save it.

Freedom to Witness

The Christian church sealed off from the world becomes unintelligible to the world it attempts to reach. It is like the father who can never remember how to be a child and therefore is looked upon as a foreigner by his children. Missionary participation and identification are not produced by a study of anthropology but by being freed through the Spirit of the Lord to witness to the truth of the gospel in the world.

My caterpillar experience illustrates the importance of identification. But identification is not an end in itself. It is the road to gospel proclamation.

Christianity calls men into a brotherhood in Christ, but at the same time Christians often negate that call by separating mechanisms which run the gamut from food taboos to racial fear. The Christian gospel is foreign enough to the self-centeredness of man's view of the universe. However, before this misconception of the self can be corrected, there is a barrier that must be penetrated. In Christian terminology it is the cross which leads man from his walled-up self out into the freedom for which he was intended.

There is yet another foreignness which must be overcome through sacrifice of one's own way of thinking and doing things. Christianity cannot be committed to one expression of civilization or culture. The missionary task is that of sacrifice. Not the sacrifice of leaving friends and comfortable situations at home, but the sacrifice of reexamining one's own cultural assumptions and becoming intelligible to a world where one must not assume that intelligibility is given.

A missionary theology asks this question: "At what points in this man's heart does the Holy Spirit challenge him to surrender?" The missionary task is to ferret out this point of contact through identification with him. The basis of missionary identification is not to make the "native" feel more at home around a foreigner nor to ease the materialistic conscience of the missionary but to create a *communication* and a *communion* where together they seek out what Saint Paul in 2 Corinthians 10:5 calls the "arguments and obstacles"—"We destroy arguments and every proud obstacle to the knowledge of God, and take every thought captive to obey Christ." This is the basis for a missionary science, the Biblical foundation of a missionary theology and the *raison d'être* of the missionary calling in which one seeks, even in the face of profound limitations, to identify oneself in the creation of new creatures in a regenerate communion.

Study Questions

1. Explain both the necessity and the limits of identification for missionary communication.

2. "An emptied pan of caterpillars is more convincing than all the empty metaphors of love which missionaries are prone to expend on the heathen." Can you suggest other "caterpillar" tests that might confront a missionary in a cross-cultural context?

God's Messenger

Phil Parshall

I t is a great calling and privilege to be a missionary. It is my joy to have rubbed shoulders with hundreds of foreign missionaries over the past decades. By and large, they impress me very positively.

The missionary calling has unique features. The missionary must be reasonably well-educated, cross geographical boundaries, leave loved ones behind, sacrifice financially (though not always), adjust to another language and culture, and work on a closely-knit team. At the same time, missionaries must open themselves to criticism, both from friend and foe. They must be willing to reevaluate sacrosanct methodology.

Dr. Saeed Khan Kurdistani was an outstanding Iranian Christian who died in 1942. In 1960, a man went to the area where Dr. Saeed had lived and ministered. An aged man of the community was asked by the visitor if he had known Dr. Saeed. The elderly man caught his breath and whispered: "Dr. Saeed was Christ himself!" Reverently, it can be said that this is our goal. But as we head into a new millennium we need to take a hard look at such practical matters as missionary finances, housing, intellectual life and ministry with churches.

Finances

There is an overwhelming difference of opinion on this subject. Some feel it is imperative to "go native" and to denounce all who do not meet their standard. Others feel strongly that they must live on a Western standard for the sake of their family's mental and physical health. They defend their position by saying the nationals will understand their needs. Between these two extremes will be found every conceivable view.

Many Third World countries are economically depressed. This fact sets the stage for the conflict between the living standard of the Western missionary and the national. Chaeok Chun, a Korean missionary in Pakistan, comments on this tension. "I think it is significant that today's image of the Christian missionary endeavor from the Asian receptor's point of view is an image of comfort and privilege. Hence, Asians tend to reject the missionary and misunderstand his message." [1]

The Irish monks of the seventh and eighth centuries were well-known for their asceticism. Their entire outfit consisted of a pilgrim's staff, a wallet, a leather water bottle and some relics. When they received money from the wealthy, they quickly gave it away to the needy. [2] Is this

Phil Parshall has served among Muslims in Asia for 37 years and is the author of six books on Christian ministry among Muslims. He has a D.Miss. from Fuller Theological Seminary and fellowships from Harvard and Yale University.

Used by permission from *Evangelical Missions Quarterly*, October 1979, published by EMIS, P.O. Box 794, Wheaton, IL 60189.

a proper model for the contemporary missionary? In this vein, Dr. Donald McGavran suggested that "the missionary from affluent countries lives on a standard far higher than he needs to. What is called for—if we are to meet this problem head on—is an order of missionaries, celibate or married without children, who live in Bangladesh on 300 rupees a month (i.e., ten dollars). *But any such move is at present unthinkable, alas.*" [3]

I would, at the risk of being controversial, like to pull some thoughts together on this very important issue.

1. It *does* matter what nationals think about the financial profile of the missionary community. Generally, they are appalled at the gap between the living standard of themselves and the western missionary. If we turn away from this concern with indifference, we are in danger of being insensitive to Paul's clear teaching about being a stumbling block to others.

2. Singles and couples without children can more easily make the adjustment to a simple lifestyle. This should be encouraged but not legislated.

3. Experimentation should be allowed. One couple with a newborn infant is living in a bamboo hut with a mud floor in a Muslim rural village. They should be supported, but at the same time, not made to feel embarrassment when at any time they feel withdrawal advisable.

4. Each family should be open before the Lord on this subject. They should prayerfully evaluate their own physical and emotional needs. The goal is to live as closely as possible to the style of life of their target people without adverse results to anyone in the family. Balance is a key word.

5. Often the missionary can reside in stark simplicity in a rural area and then take an occasional week-end trip to a nearby city for relaxation and necessary shopping. This accommodation to our cultural backgrounds is not, in my view, an act of hypocrisy. We must be realistic concerning our needs and various levels of capacity to endure deprivation within foreign culture.

6. It is permissible to consider this a moot issue with missionaries, but idle criticism, a judgmental attitude, and self-righteousness must be studiously avoided. Often, missionaries living in extreme poverty or those living in great affluence are the most opinionated and self-defensive. For the sake of unity in the body, it may be wise to avoid entering into heavy discussions with these particular missionaries on this subject.

Housing

The day of the "mission compound" is by no means over. These western enclaves are still found throughout the developing world. They are often misunderstood and, in some cases, despised by the nationals. A convert questioned their existence by asking, "Am I wrong if I say that mission bungalows are often a partition wall between the hearts of the people and the missionaries?" [4]

It is my personal conviction that remaining mission compounds should be dismantled. This would free the missionary to move into the community and share his incarnational testimony among them, rather than being shut off in a large plot of land that has a very negative appraisal in the minds of the people. It is preferable also for the Christians to scatter out among their non-Christian townspeople rather than live in a sealed-off community. Light must be diffused to be of any benefit. Our first five-year term living in a small town in Bangladesh was a great learning and sharing experience. Just outside the bedroom window of our rented home lived a Muslim lady who was separated from her husband. Her two young daughters lived with her. Quickly we became very intimate friends. The girls were always coming over to borrow a spice or an egg. We felt free to do the same. When the youngest daughter had a raging fever, we brought her over and nursed her. From our bedroom window, we learned more about Muslim culture than scores of books could ever have taught us. A mission compound experience would not have made such a life style and involvement in the community possible.

There needs to be some latitude as regards city, town or village life. The main concern is to relate to the group with whom one is working. Student work in a university area would demand facilities quite different from a rural village setting.

Intellectual Life

Missionary work has undergone a radical transformation since the end of the colonial era. New approaches and attitudes have been demanded. Pioneers like Dr. Donald McGavran have popularized the science of missiology. Hundreds of case studies and textbooks are now on the market that can be utilized as resource material. Outstanding graduate schools with mission studies include Fuller, Trinity, Columbia, Dallas, Wheaton and Asbury. Extension study for the missionary on the field is offered through Fuller, Columbia, and Wheaton. Journals like *Evangelical Missions Quarterly* and *Missiology* keep the missionary abreast of fast-breaking concepts and practical outreaches around the world.

One relevant bit of advice to missionaries is that they should "keep an open mind, realizing that times change and one must make adjustments. Tactics of ten years ago will not work and even those of five years ago are outdated."[5] It is always sad to see older missionaries become rutted and inflexible. Their orientation and allegiance to traditional methodology makes it seem to them to be almost a denial of truth to move carefully into new areas of sensitive experimentation. Younger missionaries arriving on the field become frustrated. Their ideas and zeal are often lost in a patronizing "Keep it under your hat for a few years. Experience will mellow you and mature your input." There must develop a fresh and non-threatening relationship between the senior and junior missionary. One adds experience and the other brings the latest in theory and enthusiasm. United, they are almost unbeatable. Divided, they are a catastrophe, not only to the inner team of missionaries, but also to the perceptive onlooking national community.

Our commitment to Jesus Christ means that we want to be the best servant possible for his glory. It means stretching, not only in spirit, but also in intellect. True academic excellence leads to greater effectiveness, not to pride or snobbery. We must beware of vegetating on the mission field. Both our hearts and our minds must stay alive and alert.

Still fresh in my mind are the words Harold Cook, for many years professor of missions of Moody Bible Institute, told his missions class, in 1959: "Students, the single most important area of your life and ministry will be in the realm of attitudes. It is here you will either succeed or fail as a missionary. Attitudes touch every nerve end of life. Your relationship to Christ, fellow missionary, national believer and non-Christian will be deeply affected by proper or improper attitudes."

There are a number of ingredients to a positive attitude toward nationals. One is empathy. Let me illustrate. Each morning at sunrise, a Hindu neighbor in our village would rise up, wash, and go out and stand near his cow. He would then look up at the sun, fold his hands and go through a ceremony which involved worship of both the sun and the cow. I watched our Hindu friend perform this ritual scores of times. One day the cow became ill and died suddenly. Grief struck the Hindu household. It was indeed a tragic loss to them. I personally disagreed with worshiping a cow, but I had somehow entered into the world view of that Hindu. He hurt and I hurt. Quickly I learned a few appropriate phrases (as we were new in the country) and went along to his shop. I stuttered out a few incorrectly pronounced words about being sorry that his cow had died. My Hindu friend was deeply touched. We were worlds apart in culture and religion, yet I cared. I had for a brief moment stepped into his life.

There is an old adage that contains a great deal of truth. "The gift without the giver is bare." Missionaries are giving people. Their job demands that role. They may be engaged in relief, teaching, medical work, or some other ministry that necessitates the act of sharing. But the act of giving is inadequate in itself. What is the force behind the action? Is there love? Is there a deep concern for the other person? Has giving become a professional obligation? Have the poor or the heathen become a product to sell? These are heavy questions.

Ministry

It is time now to consider the ministerial focus of the missionary. When we turn to New Testament missions, we find that Paul's involvement was exceedingly temporary. He came, stayed a few weeks or months, or at most a few years, and left to go into new areas. The churches he planted did not remain in his control. Even if a heretical influence came into the churches, Paul could only exhort the Christians to walk in truth. He had no funds to cut off. The believers were totally free. Certainly the contemporary picture of missions is different from Paul's day.

Leslie Newbegin writes of Paul totally entrusting leadership into local hands. He pungently comments that Paul didn't do what modern missionaries have done, "He does not build a bungalow."[6] George Peters maintains Paul could have rightfully said, "Here is enough work for me to do. This is where I am." Paul resisted the temptation and kept on the move.[7] Roland Allen points out that Paul didn't neglect the churches. He continued to visit and correspond with them. But the basic leadership responsibility was all put in local hands.[8]

The missionary must move on as soon as possible after worshiping groups have been established. Converts must not transfer their dependence onto the missionary and away from the Lord.

Having travailed, given birth, and cared for young churches, the missionaries (whether Tamil or Naga or American or Australian) should turn over authority to indigenous leaders. Travail must not go on too long. It must be followed by weaning and pushing out of the nest. Then the missionary goes on and repeats the process. [9]

The missionary must keep before him constantly the imperative of pressing out to new frontiers.

Conclusion

A beautiful picture of a ship on an ocean in the midst of a storm graces my bedroom door. The inscription reads, "A ship in a harbor is safe, but that is not what ships are built for." The front line of a battle is risky, but no victory has ever been registered in the annals of history as having been won solely by those supportive people who linger far behind the range of enemy gunfire. Our task calls for reflection, decision and engagement.

End Notes

1. Chaeok Chun, "An Exploration of the Community Model for Muslim, Missionary Outreach by Asian Women," an unpublished D. Miss. dissertation. Fuller Theological Seminary, Pasadena, CA 1977.
2. Sister Mary Just, *Digest of Catholic Mission History* (Maryknoll, N.Y.: Maryknoll Publications, 1957), p. 22.
3. Donald McGavran, letter to the author, March, 1979.
4. D. A. Chowdhury, "The Bengal Church and the Convert," *The Moslem World* no. 29 (1939), p. 347.
5. Joseph A. McCoy, *Advice From the Field* (Baltimore: Helicon Press, 1962), p. 144.
6. Lesslie Newbegin, *The Open Secret* (London: SPCK, 1978), p. 144.
7. George W. Peters, "Issues Confronting Evangelical Missions," *Evangelical Missions Tomorrow* (Pasadena, CA: William Carey Library, 1977), p. 162.
8. Roland Allen, *Missionary Methods: St. Paul's or Ours?* (Grand Rapids: Eerdmans, 1962), p. 151.
9. Donald McGavran, *Ethnic Realities and the Church* (Pasadena, CA: William Carey Library, 1979), p. 130.

Study Questions

1. Why is the issue of missionary living standards so emotionally charged?
2. *Should* remaining mission compounds be dismantled? Why or why not?
3. Parshall recommends a significant long-term immersion into the adopted community. Same time he urges missionaries to consider following Paul's example of staying for a few months or years. Explain how these ideas work together in practice.

Do Missionaries Destroy Cultures?

Don Richardson

Don Richardson pioneered work for Regions Beyond Missionary Union (RBMU) among the Sawi tribe of Irian Jaya in 1962. Author of *Peace Child*, *Lords of the Earth*, and *Eternity in Their Hearts*, Richardson is now Minister-at-Large for WORLD TEAM (formerly RBMU). He speaks frequently at missions conferences and Perspectives Study Program classes.

Used by permission of Don Richardson.

James Michener's austere Abner Hale, a missionary in the novel (and movie) *Hawaii*, has become the archetype of an odious bigot. In the book, Hale shouts hellfire sermons against the "vile abominations" of the pagan Hawaiians. He even forbids Hawaiian midwives to help a missionary mother at the birth of "a Christian baby." As a result, the mother dies. Hale forbids Hawaiians to help his wife with housework lest his children learn the "heathen Hawaiian language;" his wife works herself into an early grave. And when Buddhist Chinese settle in the islands, Michener has Hale barging into their temples to smash their idols.

It makes an interesting plot, but, unfortunately, "Abner Hale" came to be synonymous with "missionary" for many North Americans—and missionaries have been carrying him on their backs ever since. Anthropologist Alan Tippett of the Fuller Seminary School of World Mission once researched hundreds of early missionary sermons stored in the Honolulu archives. None of them had the ranting style Michener suggests as typical of that time.

It will serve us all to examine the actual record rather than to circulate distorted stereotypes. There have indeed been occasions when missionaries were responsible for needless destruction of culture. When Fray Diego de Landa, a Catholic missionary accompanying Spanish forces in the New World, discovered extensive Maya libraries, he knew what to do. He burned them all, an event, he said, the Maya "regretted to an amazing degree, and which caused them much affliction." The books, in his opinion, were all of "superstition and lies of the devil." And so, in 1562, the poetry, history, literature, mathematics, and astronomy of an entire civilization went up in smoke. Only three documents survived de Landa's misguided zeal.

Magnificent totem poles once towered in Indian villages along Canada's Pacific coast. By 1900 virtually all such native art had been chopped down, either by missionaries who mistook them for idols, or by converts zealously carrying out the directives of missionaries.

These incidents and many more show that we missionaries have sometimes acted in a culture-destroying manner. Whether through misinterpreting the Great Commission, pride, culture shock, or simple inability to comprehend the values of others, we have needlessly opposed customs we did not understand. Some, had we understood them, might have served as communication keys for the gospel!

Critics seem to suggest that if only missionaries stay home, primitive people will be left undisturbed to live out the myth of Rousseau's "noble savage." In fact, David Livingstone was preceded by Arab slave traders; Amy Carmichael by victimizers who dragged boys and girls to the terrors of child prostitution in the temples. At times, evil forces like these have destroyed entire peoples. In North America, not only California's Yahi but also the Hurons—and possibly 20 other Indian tribes—were pushed into extinction by land-hungry settlers. On one occasion, pioneers sent gifts to a tribe, wagonloads of blankets known to be infected with smallpox.

Only 200,000 Indians remain in Brazil from an original population estimated at four million. More than one tribe per year has disappeared in the past 75 years. People may assume that the missing tribes have been absorbed into society, but this is not the case. Thousands have been brutally poisoned, machine-gunned, or dynamited from low-flying aircraft. Thousands more have succumbed to a slower, more agonizing death—death by *apathy*. Indian men have even been known to cause their wives to miscarry. As encroachment caused their cultures to disintegrate, they have refused to bring children into a world they no longer understand.

Similar tragedies are unfolding throughout the world. Concern is widespread today for endangered animal species, and justly so, but hundreds of our own human species are in even greater danger. It may be a conservative figure to put the loss at five or six linguistically distinct tribes per year.

The "enlightened" policy of "leave them alone" clearly isn't working. What then, can halt the march of tribal cultures toward extinction? Land grants and secular welfare programs may help on a physical level, but the greatest danger to tribal people is one that such programs cannot touch. The greatest danger is the breakdown of the aboriginal's sense of "right" relationship with the supernatural. Every aboriginal culture acknowledges the supernatural and has strict procedures for "staying right" with it. When arrogant outsiders ridicule a tribe's beliefs—or shatter its mechanisms for staying right—severe disorientation sets in. Believing they are cursed for abandoning the old ways, tribespeople become morose and apathetic. Believing they are doomed to die as a people, they act out a self-fulfilling prophecy.

Materialistic social workers and scientists can't help these people. The tribespeople can sense even an unspoken denial of the supernatural, and it causes them to grow further depressed. Who then can best serve such people as spiritual ombudsmen? None other than the ones popular myth has maligned as their number one enemy—the Bible-guided, Christ-honoring missionary.

Two Case Histories

1. According to Robert Bell of the Unevangelized Fields Mission, less than a generation ago Brazil's Wai Wai tribe had been reduced to its last sixty members. This was due largely to foreign diseases and the Wai Wai custom of sacrificing babies to demons in attempts to prevent these diseases. Then a handful of UFM missionaries identified themselves with the tribe, learned their language, gave it an alphabet, translated the Word of God, taught Wai Wai to read, and brought modern medical care.

Far from denying the supernatural world, the missionaries showed the Wai Wai that a God of love reigned supreme over it and had prepared a way for them to "stay right," on a deeper level than they had ever dreamed. The Wai Wai now had a rational, even delightful, basis for *not* sacrificing babies to demons. The tribe began to grow, and today is fast becoming one of Brazil's more stable tribes. Wai Wai Christians are now teaching other dwindling groups of Indians how to cope with the 20th century through faith in Jesus Christ.

2. In 1796, near Stockbridge, in what is now Massachusetts, early American missionary John Sargent and his associates established a community to preserve Indian rights, preparing them for survival among encroaching Europeans. Before ethnocentrism was named a social evil, and before the birth of

anthropology as a science, Sargent and his helpers tilled the soil side by side with their Indian friends. Practicing what anthropologists now call "directed change," they also shared their Christian faith and the Indians received it as their own.

> We risk our lives to get to them first because we believe we are more sympathetic agents of change than profit-hungry commercialists.

That faith, and the love of their spiritual paracletes, sustained the tribe through more than a century of suffering. Greedy settlers soon decided that the land was too good for "mere Indians" and evicted them. After an unsuccessful protest, Sargent obtained guarantees of land further west. A few years later the community was uprooted again by other settlers. And again. Fifteen times they were forced to move. Each time the missionaries moved with them, wresting concessions for new land and holding the community together. At last the community settled in Michigan where it was allowed to rest, and it survives to this day.

In both cases, the missionaries introduced culture change, but it was not arbitrary nor was it imposed by force. The missionaries brought only changes required for New Testament ethics and for the survival of the people. Often the two requirements overlap.

Once an interviewer chided me, perhaps facetiously, for persuading the Sawi tribe in Indonesia to renounce cannibalism. "What's wrong with cannibalism?" he asked. "The Sawi practiced it for thousands of years. Why should they give it up now?"

"Can a people who practice cannibalism survive in the world today?" I asked in reply. "No, they cannot. The Sawi are now citizens of the Republic of Indonesia. The Indonesian Republic does not permit its citizens to eat other people. Therefore, part of my task was to give the Sawi a rational basis for *voluntarily* renouncing cannibalism before the guns of the police decided the issue."

The Sawi are among perhaps 400 black-skinned Melanesian tribes just emerging from the Stone Age in Irian Jaya. Some years ago, the Netherlands ceded Irian Jaya, then called New Guinea, to Indonesia. Now over 100,000 Indonesians have migrated to Irian Jaya. Will the tribal people be prepared to cope with their more enterprising migrant neighbors? Or will they become extinct?

Scattered throughout Irian Jaya, more than 250 evangelical missionaries (all too few) are ministering the gospel to both races. Knowledgeable in Indonesian as well as in many of Irian's 400 tribal languages, they are helping members of clashing cultures to understand each other. With the sympathetic help of the Indonesian government, the missionaries are optimistic that major culture shock may be averted. Already, through faith in Christ, tens of thousands of Irianese have begun a smooth transition into the 20th century. Surely ethnic crises of this magnitude are too sensitive to be left to the dubious mercy of purely commercial interests. Missionaries, whose hearts overflow with the love of Christ, are the key.

Are missionaries cultural imperialists? You decide.

Consider one journalist's charges against missionaries. When Hamish McDonald visited Irian Jaya to cover the effects of a severe earthquake in June 1976, he turned his attention instead to what he thought he observed in the relationship between tribespeople and missionaries. The resulting article appeared in the Washington Post on August 3, 1976:

JAYAPURA, Irian Jaya: Fundamentalist Christian missionaries are provoking hostile and occasionally murderous reactions from primitive tribespeople in mountain areas south of here. In the most savage of recent incidents, about eighteen months ago, 13 local assistants of a mission were killed and eaten as soon as the European missionary went away on leave.

The missionaries are also coming under attack by anthropologists and other observers for attempting the almost total destruction of local cultures in the areas they evangelize. This is seen as the basic cause of recent violent outbreaks, and is contrasted with the more adaptive policies of Roman Catholic and mainstream Protestant missionary groups.

The fundamentalists are working in the remote Jayawijaya mountains where they are now carrying the brunt of relief work following recent severe earthquakes believed to have killed as many as a thousand people.

They belong to five missionary groups: the Christian and Missionary Alliance, the Unevangelized Fields Mission, the Regions Beyond Missionary Union, The Evangelical Alliance Mission, and the Asia-Pacific Christian Mission banded together in an organization called The Missionary Alliance. They are joined by a technical missionary group, the Missionary Aviation Fellowship, an efficient air service with 15 light aircraft and a helicopter essential in a territory where the longest paved road is the 25-mile drive from Jayapura, the provincial capital, to the airport. They are well backed by Congregationalist, Baptist, and nondenominational Bible groups in North America, Europe, and Australia, although most members and funds come from the United States.

Sometimes rejecting the label "fundamentalist," they describe themselves as "orthodox" or "faith" Christians. Their central characteristic is belief in the literal truth of the Bible.

In recent years they have set up several missions in the Jayawijaya mountains, an unmapped and little-known area that had its first outside contact only about twenty years ago. The Melanesian people there learned the use of metal only recently. They live on sweet potatoes, sugar cane, and bananas, supplemented by pork and occasional small marsupials or birds that they hunt with bows and arrows.

Their only domestic animals are their pigs, which they regard as having souls. When I asked an anthropologist there why they ate such close friends, he said: "It doesn't matter. They eat people, too."

The men wear only the *koteka*, a penis gourd, and the women small tufts of grass fore and aft. Divided by rugged terrain and language from even close neighbors, they feud periodically in set-piece confrontations.

Although their culture recognizes personal and family property, they are remarkable for their willingness to share. Tobacco is their only vice, imported from the coast somehow in the forgotten past. Cowrie shells are the only currency resembling money.

Their culture and traditional religion express the most basic human concepts. They and the other nine hundred thousand people in Irian Jaya produce dazzling works of art in traditional carvings and handicrafts.

Typically, a newly arrived missionary builds his house by itself, next to a grass airstrip. One told me: "The first thing is to move in and live with the people. You must prove that you want to help them, by giving them food, medicine and shelter, teaching them, and learning their language. Often it takes two to four years to learn the language. I guess what you are looking for is the cultural key, the key that unlocks the culture and opens the way for the gospel."

But many missionaries appear to regard the gospel as totally incompatible with the traditional culture, in which they see no deep value. One missionary from the Papua New Guinea border region referred to the old men who stayed aloof from his mission as "having no interest in spiritual things." The first action of a missionary who stayed awhile in Valley X recently was to hand out shirts to tribesmen. At

Nalca Mission, women have been persuaded to lengthen their grass skirts to knee length, apparently to satisfy missionary modesty.

Smoking tobacco is condemned and forbidden as sinful. Until recently, the mission air service searched baggage and refused to fly anyone found carrying tobacco or alcohol.

In 1968 two Western missionaries were killed on the south slope of the Jayawijaya range. Three months ago an American missionary was virtually chased out of the Fa-Malinkele Valley because of his manner.

The incident of cannibalism occurred at a mission called Nipsan, where the Dutch missionary had been using local Irianese assistants from the longer evangelized area near Wamena, further west. When the missionary went on leave, the tribespeople turned on 15 assistants, killing and eating 13. Two escaped to the jungle. An Indonesian army unit later entered but dropped the case because of the baffling problems of law involved.

The Dutch missionary subsequently made a fund-raising tour of Europe and North America to buy a helicopter from which he proposed to conduct aerial evangelization through a loudspeaker. But the first time this was tried, a month ago, volleys of arrows reportedly greeted the airborne preacher.

The fundamentalists are compared unfavorably with the Roman Catholic missionaries who operate on the southern side of Irian Jaya under a territorial division initiated by the Dutch and maintained by the Indonesians after the 1963 transfer of administration.

"The difference between them is quite simple," said one source at Jayapura. "The Protestants try to destroy the culture. The Catholics try to preserve it."

At a mission called Jaosakor near the southern coast, the Catholics recently consecrated a church largely designed by the local people and incorporating traditional Asmat carvings around the walls. Bishop Alphonse Sowada, of the Nebraska-centered Crosier Fathers, carried out the ceremony in Episcopal robes accompanied by local leaders in full regalia of paint, tooth necklaces, and nose-bones. The method of dedication was to scatter lime, made from fired seashells, from bamboo containers over walls, floors, and altars in the way the Asmat people inaugurate their own communal buildings.

Nearly all Catholic missionaries in Irian Jaya are required to hold degrees in anthropology before beginning their calling. Many have published articles and writings on the local peoples. "The basis of our approach is that we believe God is already working through the existing culture, which follows from the belief that God created all things and is present in all of them," one priest said.

On September 21, 1976, I sent a letter to the Post. It never appeared in the "letters to the editor" column, nor, to my knowledge, was it used to offer any sort of counterbalance to Hamish McDonald's assertions of what he thought he observed in Irian Jaya. It has, however, been included as a chapter in John H. Bodley's widely-used anthropology textbook, Tribal Peoples and Development Issues: A Global Overview *(Mayfield Publishing, Mountain View, CA, 1988, pp 116-21) Here, slightly condensed, is my open letter:*

Dear Sirs:

A few weeks ago journalist Hamish McDonald arrived in Irian Jaya to report on the earthquake which recently devastated a mountainous region here. At least that's what he told the missionaries whose help he needed to reach the area.

The earthquake was of particular interest because it struck the habitat of a number of the earth's last remaining Stone Age tribes, some of whom still practice cannibalism. Triggering literally thousands of landslides, the upheaval wiped out fifteen tribal villages, killed more than a thousand people, and left fifteen thousand survivors with only fifteen percent of their gardens. The missionaries McDonald approached were busy staging an urgent food airlift. Still, they graciously offered him space on one of their overloaded mercy flights from Jayapura into the interior.

The world might never have known that these tribes exist, nor would relief agencies have been informed of their plight, had not a dozen or more evangelical Protestant missionaries explored their uncharted mountainous habitat during the past fifteen years. At risk to their own lives, the evangelicals succeeded in befriending several thousand of these highly suspicious, unpredictable tribesmen. Meticulously, they learned and analyzed unwritten tribal languages, a task so agonizing that less motivated persons would have had no time for it. They also carved out the four airstrips which now make relief operations possible and, as a sidelight, enabled McDonald to carry out his assignment on location.

The missionary aircraft taxied to a halt on one of these airstrips. McDonald leaped out and began snapping pictures....

There are reasons why the missionaries had to go into isolated areas like Irian Jaya as soon as they could. History has taught them that even the most isolated minority cultures must eventually be overwhelmed by the commercial and political expansion of majority peoples. Naive academics in ivy-covered towers may protest that the world's remaining primitive cultures should be left undisturbed, but farmers, lumbermen, land speculators, miners, hunters, military leaders, road builders, art collectors, tourists, and drug peddlers aren't listening.

They are going in anyway. Often to destroy. Cheat. Exploit. Victimize. Corrupt. Taking, and giving little other than diseases for which primitives have no immunity or medicine.

This is why, since the turn of the century, more than ninety tribes have become extinct in Brazil alone. Many other Latin American, African, and Asian countries show a similar high extinction rate for their primitive minorities. A grim toll of five or six tribes per year is probably a conservative worldwide estimate.

We missionaries don't want the same fate to befall these magnificent tribes in Irian Jaya. We risk our lives to get to them first because we believe we are more sympathetic agents of change than profit-hungry commercialists. Like our predecessor John Sargent, who in 1796 launched a program which saved the Mohican tribe from extinction in North America, and like our colleagues in Brazil who just one generation ago saved the Wai Wai from a similar fate, we believe we know how to precondition tribes in Irian Jaya for survival in the modern world. The question, "Should anyone go in?" is obsolete because obviously someone *will*.

It has been replaced by a more practical question: "Will the most sympathetic persons get there first?" To make the shock of coming out of the Stone Age as easy as possible. To see that tribals gain new ideals to replace those they must lose in order to survive. To teach them the national language so they can defend themselves in disputes with "civilizados." And yet produce literature in their own language so it will not be forgotten. To teach them the value of money, so that unscrupulous traders cannot easily cheat them. And better yet, set some of them up in business so that commerce in their areas will not fall entirely into the hands of outsiders. To care for them when epidemics sweep through or when earthquakes strike. And better yet, train some of them as nurses and doctors to carry on when we are gone. We go as ombudsmen who help clashing cultures understand each other.

We missionaries are advocates not only of spiritual truth, but also of physical survival. And we have enjoyed astonishing success in Irian Jaya and elsewhere. Among the Ekari, Damal, Dani, Ndugwa, and other tribes, more than one hundred thousand Stone Agers welcomed our gospel as the fulfillment of something their respective cultures had anticipated for hundreds of years. The Ekari called it *aji*. To the Damal, it was *hai*. To the Dani, *nabelan-kabelan*, an immortal message which one day would restrain tribal war and ease human suffering.

The result: cultural fulfillment of the deepest possible kind. And it opened the door to faith in Jesus Christ for tens of thousands.

Along with our successes, there have been setbacks. Nearly two years ago one of our colleagues from a European mission, Gerrit Kuijt, left some coastal helpers in charge of a new outpost while he returned to Holland. In his absence, a few of the coastals began to molest the surrounding tribespeople for private reasons. Thirteen coastals were killed in retaliation.

Sympathize. Sometimes it is not easy to find responsible helpers willing to venture with us into these wild areas. At times you have to trust someone; you have no choice.

Earlier, in 1968, two of our buddies, Phil Masters and Stan Dale, died together while probing a new area of the Yali tribe. But then Kusaho, a Yali elder, rebuked the young men who had killed them, saying: "Neither of these men ever harmed any of us, nor did they even resist while you killed them. Surely they came in peace and you have made a terrible mistake. If ever any more of this kind of men come into our valley, we must welcome them."

And so a door of acceptance opened through the wounds of our friends. It was a costly victory. Stan's and Phil's widows were each left with five small children to raise alone. Yet neither widow blamed anyone for the death of her husband, and one of them still serves with us in Irian Jaya today.

Ours is a great work, and a very difficult one. It is not subsidized by any government, and can succeed only as it has sympathetic support from churches, private individuals, and the public in general. That is where correspondent McDonald could have helped.

Instead McDonald now transferred to a Mission Aviation Fellowship helicopter loaded with sweet potatoes contributed by Christians from the Dani tribe and rice from Indonesian government stores. Pilot Jeff Heritage thought McDonald seemed surprisingly uninterested in the many tribal hamlets stranded like islands in the midst of uncrossable landslides, their inhabitants on the edge of starvation. After only a few hours in the interior, he returned to the coast and wrote his report.

Wielding the cliché "fundamentalist" with obvious intent to stigmatize and nettle us, McDonald launched a scathing yet baseless attack which appeared as a major article in the *Washington Post* and was relayed by wire service to hundreds of newspapers around the world. Citing the loss of Gerrit Kuijt's 13 helpers and the murder of Phil and Stan eight years ago, he made the absurd accusation that we are "provoking hostile and occasionally murderous reactions from primitive tribesmen." He continued: "The missionaries are also coming under attack by anthropologists and other observers for attempting the almost total destruction of cultures...."

Who are the anthropologists and other observers? Within our ranks we have a number of men who hold degrees in anthropology,

and they have not warned us of any such attack by members of their discipline. We have cooperated with a number of anthropologists in Irian Jaya over the past 20 years and have had good mutual understanding with them.

Perhaps McDonald is referring to the three remaining members of a German scientific team he met on one of his helicopter stops in the interior. Some of them, reportedly, have been critical toward us, not on the basis of wide knowledge of our work, but because of anti-missionary sentiments they brought with them to Irian Jaya.

Their problem is that they hold to an old school of anthropology, still current in some areas, which favors isolating primitive tribes from all change in zoo-like reserves. A new school, now rising in America, has at last recognized the futility of this approach, and advocates instead that primitive tribes be exposed to survival-related "directed change," in order that they may learn to cope with encroachment, now seen as inevitable.

Directed change is exactly what evangelical missionary John Sargent practiced back in 1796 and what we are practicing now. In fact, missionaries are virtually the only persons who do. Anthropologists don't remain with tribesmen long enough. And humanists aren't sufficiently motivated. But if, indeed, we are under attack, a careful reporter should have asked us for our defense, if any. McDonald did not do this, though he had opportunity. What evidence does he present for his charge that we are "attempting the almost total destruction of local cultures in Irian Jaya?"

He writes: "The first action of a missionary... in Valley X recently was to hand out shirts to the tribesmen." The tribesmen concerned had just lost most of their homes in the earthquake. Indonesian officials had provided shirts to help them stay warm at night in their crude temporary shelters at mile-high elevations. No one wanted a rash of pneumonia cases complicating the relief operation. Johnny Benzel, the missionary, cooperated with the government directive by handing out the shirts.

Nowhere have we ever provided Indonesian or Western-style clothing until demand for it arose among the tribal people themselves. This usually took from seven to fifteen years. Tribal church elders preached in the open or under grass-roofed shelters, wearing their penis gourds, and no one thought anything of it. Even today the vast majority of men still wear gourds and women wear grass skirts.

It is the Indonesian government, not missionaries, which tries to shame tribals into exchanging gourds and grass skirts for shorts and dresses under *Operation Koteka*. But they do it for understandable reasons. They want the tribesmen to become part of Indonesian society as soon as possible, find employment, etc.

At Nalca, McDonald snapped a photo of a native with a ball-point pen stuck through the pierced septum of his nose. This photo appeared in some newspapers with the ludicrous caption: "Ball-point pen replaces nosebone; fundamentalist preachers destroy culture." A native forages a used ball-point pen out of Johnny Benzel's wastepaper basket, sticks it through his nose, and presto! Johnny is accused of destroying culture. Very tricky, McDonald.

McDonald slams Johnny again: "At Nalca mission, women have been persuaded to lengthen their grass skirts to knee-length...." What actually happens is that families of the Dani tribe follow missionaries to places like Nalca, and over a period of years the Nalca women begin to imitate the style of their Dani counterparts, which happens to be the longer skirts.

Do we, then, approve of everything in the local cultures? No, we do not, just as no one in our own Western culture automatically approves of everything in it.

We are out to destroy cannibalism, but so also is the Indonesian government. The difference is, we use moral persuasion, and if we fail, the government will eventually use physical force. Our task is to give the tribals a rational basis for giving it up voluntarily before the guns of the police decide the issue with traumatic effect.

We also want to stop the intertribal warfare that has gone on for centuries. In view of all they have to go through in the next 50 years, it is imperative that the tribes stop killing and wounding each other *now*. Often we are able

to stop the fighting by emphasizing little-used peace-making mechanisms within the cultures themselves. Or we simply provide the third-person presence which enables antagonists to see their problems in a new light.

We are against witchcraft, suspicion of which is a major cause of war. Killing by witchcraft is contrary, not only to Christian concepts of goodness, but also to those of the humanists, isn't it?

We are against sexual promiscuity, and not for religious reasons only. In 1903, Chinese traders seeking bird-of-paradise plumes landed on the south coast of Irian Jaya. They introduced a venereal disease called lymphogranuloma venereum among the one hundred thousand members of the Merind tribes. Since group sex was widely accepted, the disease spread like wildfire. It wiped out 90,000 lives in ten years. Had missionaries introduced a different sexual ethic before the chinese traders arrived, unnumbered lives could have been spared.

McDonald attempts to antagonize us still further by comparing our methods unfavorably with "the more adaptive policies of Roman Catholic and mainstream Protestant groups."

Only one mainstream Protestant mission works in interior Irian Jaya, and they have experienced the same problems McDonald uses as grounds to incriminate us. For example, that mission's director was seriously wounded with three arrows eight years ago, and eight of his carriers were killed while trekking through a wild area. Such incidents are merely an occupational hazard and should not be used to levy blame.

As far as I know, Roman Catholic missionaries have not been wounded or slain by tribals in Irian Jaya. This is due, not to "more adaptive policies," but to the fact that they limit their work mainly to areas already well-controlled by the government. But this is no shame to them as they have counted their martyrs across the border in Papua New Guinea.

If McDonald had taken time to visit Roman Catholic and evangelical Protestant areas of operation and compare them, he would have found the degree of culture change at least as great if not greater in the

Roman Catholic areas. For example, in all Roman Catholic areas primitives are expected to give up their tribal names and take Latin names, like Pius or Constantius, whereas in evangelical Protestant areas they still use their Irianese names, like Isai or Yana. But here again, if it is survival-related directed change, it cannot be faulted on anthropological grounds.

McDonald continues, "Nearly all Roman Catholic missionaries in Irian Jaya are required to hold degrees in anthropology." Actually, the percentage of Roman Catholic and evangelical Protestant missionaries holding degrees in anthropology is approximately equal, and when it comes to prowess in learning tribal dialects, the evangelicals excel by far. The majority of Roman Catholic priests teach in Indonesian even where it is not understood.

McDonald describes the lime-scattering dedication of a new Catholic church at Jaosakor. Surely if this is the limit of their cultural penetration, our Catholic friends must be far from satisfied. Cultural penetration, to be effective, must go far deeper than mere externals like scattering lime. Not until you come to grips with internal concepts in the category of the Ekari tribe's *aji* or the Dani tribe's *nabelan-kabelan* are you getting close to the heart of a people. As one of our members said to McDonald, "What we are looking for is the cultural key...." McDonald quoted his words, yet failed totally to appreciate them.

Another point of McDonald's article calls for refutation: Gerrit Kuijt raised funds for a helicopter for general service to all tribal peoples in Irian Jaya, not for "aerial evangelism." In fact, it was this helicopter which was on hand just in time to help in the earthquake relief operation and which bore McDonald on his reporting mission. Thank you, Gerrit, for your foresight. The rest of us are not unappreciative like McDonald.

McDonald, your article was erroneous, inept, and irresponsible. You have made a perfect nuisance of yourself. You and the *Washington Post* owe us a printed apology.

Sincerely,
Don Richardson

Do missionaries destroy cultures? It's true that we destroy certain things in cultures, just as doctors sometimes must destroy certain things in a human body if a patient is to live. But as we grow in experience and God-given wisdom, we must not—and will not—destroy cultures themselves.

Study Questions

1. What variations on McDonald's criticisms have you read or heard? Do you think these criticisms of missionaries are justified or not? Why?

2. Does Richardson adequately answer McDonald's criticisms? What would you add to or subtract from Richardson's response?

3. Do you see any better policy than that of directed change in tribal societies? Why or why not?

Toward a Cross-Cultural Definition of Sin

T. Wayne Dye

Pete is a missionary to a tribal culture. He has become extremely concerned with the problems of polygamy, betel nut chewing, and smoking. The local people aren't too concerned about Pete's standards of sin. They focus instead on avoiding discord in the village. Disobeying husbands and leaders, refusing hospitality and inter-clan payments, and expressing anger are to them the far more serious sins.

Pete is eager to do the right thing, but he has a hard time communicating this to the local people. They think he is stingy with things they would normally share, and he doesn't seem to understand about their kinship obligations. Frequently, he appears to them to be angry in public (to Pete it's only "frustration") and it disturbs them that he sins so often. Because of this, the local leaders don't really listen to Pete.

Pete is frustrated because, among other things, many of his converts don't seem to have grasped the meaning of living in obedience to God. Several have even fallen into overt sexual sin. As a result, Pete has become convinced that he must be the judge of these converts. He reasons that they don't show enough evidence of real repentance to be trusted. Not knowing the local people well enough to determine their interior motives, he has decided to focus on external matters, single marriages, smoking, and betel nut chewing. Right now, these are the only fruits of repentance he believes he can easily identify.

Pete has a problem, but he doesn't understand that it started long before he arrived on the mission field. Like many missionaries, Pete had something of a prophet's role at home. His leadership was valued among his peers, and in most situations, he found himself able to judge between right and wrong. As a Christian professional, he learned to sense what was wrong for others by noting what was wrong for himself. Intuition tells him that this same approach will work on the field. As the most highly trained, fully dedicated and "spiritual" person in the village, Pete doesn't question his assumptions. He now lives in a place which presumably needs even more of a word from the Lord than his homeland. He is obviously the one to speak on the Lord's behalf.

There's really just one problem. It doesn't seem to be working. The local people just don't "get it." The truth is that no matter how hard he tries to adapt externally, Pete

T. Wayne Dye is an International Missiology Consultant with Wycliffe Bible Translators. He and his wife, Sally Dye, team teach translators and national pastors in 30 countries to more effectively use translated Scripture in Christian ministry. In the past he served extensively in Papua New Guinea.

Reprinted from *Missiology: An International Review*, Arthur F. Glasser, ed., Jan. 1976. Used by permission.

has come into this new culture with a heavy load of internalized cultural baggage. Many of the things which he assumes to be right, sensible and natural are not, in fact, biblical ideals. They are simply part of Pete's own culture. American values like efficiency, punctuality and cleanliness are very important to many American Christians, but hard to document from Scripture. Yet these differences between his own culture and the tribal culture strike Pete most heavily. Of course, the tribal culture, like all cultures under God's judgment, has plenty of true evils to correct. This compounds Pete's shock at being in such a different culture and affects his perceptions so that he finds local values even harder to accept. It soon becomes hard for Pete to remember (if he ever differentiated) which of his own values are simply home country values and which are based on the Bible.

> Prohibitions against lying, stealing, murder and adultery are virtually universal, although what exactly constitutes each sin varies from culture to culture.

Pete spends time preaching against the things that seem worst to him in the local culture. These may not be points which have bothered the consciences of his listeners. The people soon learn what actions he disapproves of, but they don't really understand what he's driving at. They know some things are morally wrong (different things from the ones Pete harps on) and they feel a sense of guilt (again at different things from the ones that bother Pete). So they turn a deaf ear to him or perhaps to be polite they dutifully "confess" things over which they feel no guilt and become Christians without ever repenting of that which truly troubles their consciences.

A Universal Definition of Sin

What in good conscience can a missionary do about the problem of sin in the lives of those to whom he or she is called to minister? In order to answer this, one must first determine how sin is defined for any particular culture. A review of Scripture gives a universal standard from which to start. Romans 3:23 talks about a definite standard and says that falling short of this mark is sin. In Matthew 22:37-40, Jesus makes it clear that the standard is wholehearted love for God, and love for one's neighbor as one's self. In Romans 13:8-10, Paul states explicitly that this kind of love is the supracultural, essence of the Levitical law. He ends by saying, "To love, then, is to obey the whole law."

The universal nature of this law of love is evident in the behavioral ideals of all cultures. Prohibitions against lying, stealing, murder and adultery are virtually universal, although what exactly constitutes each sin varies from culture to culture. This information, however, often does not appear in ethnographies because it is considered irrelevant to many anthropological inquiries. Furthermore, some anthropologists are so focused on actual behavior that they fail to explore cultural ideals and values. One study on polygamy in Mexico seemed peculiar to me at first because the wives usually lived in different villages and were not known to each other. I finally realized that this particular culture did not have polygamy at all. Instead, a high proportion of men were keeping mistresses. The researcher mistakenly equated the way people were observed to behave with the underlying value system of the culture. Apparently, he had never asked if the people approved of their "polygamy" or whether they were, in fact, troubled by guilt over their behavior.

Universal moral principles may seem clear enough on the surface, but the actual realization of them is determined partly by each culture's distinctions. What exactly does the law of love mean when it manifests the attributes of Galatians 5 kindness, humility, peace, self-control and so on? An executive in an industrial country is patient if he waits for ten minutes for his next appointment. A Bahinemo native of Papua New Guinea thinks nothing of waiting two hours for someone. The people of a village in southern Mindanao demonstrated their hospitality by giving visitors gifts equal to one month's wages. In the United States, even the most lavish hospitality to a stranger rarely adds up to a day's wages.

Even standards like the Ten Commandments have fuzzy borders when they are translated between cultures. Is it stealing to pick up a child's toy from a suburban sidewalk? In the United States, yes. In Mexico, no. In ancient Israel, one could pick and eat fruit while passing through another man's orchard. That would be considered theft while trespassing in present day Southern California. Papua New Guineans see a clear violation of the fifth commandment in our culture's practice of leaving the care of the elderly to the state. It seems that while the essence of each commandment is clear, the edges are defined differently by different cultures.

If God's universal standard of love must be realized in different ways by different cultures, what determines a particular action to be sinful? The crucial principle is presented in Romans 2:

> "Their conduct shows that what the Law commands is written in their hearts. Their consciences also show that this is true, since their thoughts sometimes accuse them and sometimes defend them. This, according to the Good News I preach, is how it will be on that day when God, through Jesus Christ, will judge all the secret thoughts in men's hearts" (Rom 2:15-16).

The role of culture in conditioning the conscience is seen in Romans 14. The Roman church was divided over two issues: what could be eaten and what special days should be observed. In the first issue, the vegetarians were probably the formerly idolatrous converts; in the second, those who kept special days were probably the Jewish Christians (perhaps the "missionaries" in the situation). Their different cultural backgrounds resulted in these disagreements about behavior.

In his answer, Paul says that it's not the act itself which is important, but the underlying character of one's relationship to God (vs 17). A person must do what he or she believes will please God (vs 12, 18, 22-23). Different people, however, will do different, even

Allowing the Holy Spirit to Convict and Transform

1. Learn the ethical system of the culture to which you are sent.

2. Compare your findings with your own culture. Then compare both cultures with the Bible. Be sensitive to the strengths and weaknesses in both cultures. This helps overcome blind spots and ethnocentrism.

3. Without going against your own conscience, learn to live a loving life by the cultural standards in which you are serving. For each decision you make, remember in which cultural framework you are thinking: your own culture, your host culture, or the New Testament culture. Make decisions within the appropriate cultural framework.

4. Preach repentance for areas in which the Holy Spirit is already convicting new converts. Teach patiently about God's standards for things which, though cultural, are in conflict with the Bible. Pray that you will be able to accept the aspects of the culture which, although they bother you, are compatible with the Christian faith.

5. Expect the Holy Spirit to steadily enlighten their consciences and eventually to transform their society. Keep getting feedback from others on how He is working in their lives. Learn to trust the insights of new converts.

6. Teach new converts to obey and rely on the Holy Spirit. Teach them how to keep their consciences clear so that the Holy Spirit can use their consciences to teach them new truths. Expose them to the Bible, not just the "pre-digested" form of your lesson plans. Teach them to find principles in the Bible for wise and truly Christian answers.

opposite, things to please God (vs 2-3, 5-6). God not only judges each differently, but actually makes each one succeed in pleasing Him (vs 4). Therefore, it is wrong to be contemptuous of those who follow rules that seem irrelevant; nor should we feel more spiritual than those who don't follow our own ideals of Christian behavior (vs 10). Put another way, each of us is answerable to God. Only the Master knows exactly what He wants each servant to do.

The Role of the Holy Spirit

This does not imply that God is satisfied with any one person's understanding of righteousness. Instead, He is constantly leading each one into greater love and obedience. He is continually teaching new truth, correcting their understanding of sin, of goodness, and of how God deals with people (John 16:8). He brings each one to Christian maturity by, among other things, a long process of enlightening and changing their consciences. A missionary's job is to sense where in a convert's life the Spirit is working, and to assist that work.

As the Holy Spirit teaches individuals, societies also are changed toward greater justice, mercy and moral uprightness. Throughout history, reforms in society have been instigated by responsive Christians.

No existing cultural system is entirely pleasing to God. This fact may seem particularly graphic when a new missionary encounters the standards of morality in a pagan culture. That society may be quite concerned about rituals, yet say nothing about humility or cruelty. It may treat moral issues as civil or even personal matters which do not concern the gods. In such a society, the present state of the people's consciences can be a poor reflection of God's ultimate goal for them. As they respond to God, He will undoubtedly lead them to make changes in their social order.

The fact that some things we now consider wrong were not spoken against in the New Testament shows that God can allow time for converts to realize the cultural implications of being Christians. As practiced by the Roman world, slavery was far more cruel and inhuman than anything missionaries and na-

tional Christians disagree over today. Yet, it was never directly condemned in the Bible. People were taught how to live for Christ within their culture.

The implications for today are clear. One cannot automatically know how God has been teaching another person. Behavior one considers natural may violate another's conscience. Things that violate one's own conscience may not be an issue for someone else. There will be large areas of agreement among individuals within a culturally homogeneous unit. In this context, there is an obligation to share one's own convictions with others. In the context of another culture, however, it is wiser to speak about the biblical principles behind one's actions.

In the opening description of Pete's troubles with the tribal culture, Pete did not understand that God was not speaking to the local converts about behavior which would be, for him, clearly sinful. Instead he preached against "sins" for which the nationals did not feel convicted, and which, in fact, may not have been sins for them at all. At the same time, he ignored other sins that were real problems for them. In effect, Pete unintentionally tried to take on the role of the Holy Spirit instead of asking the Holy Spirit what He was doing and cooperating with His work in the lives of individuals, and in the ongoing story of the entire people group.

In spite of Pete's confusion, converts were won from his preaching. But they faced difficult problems. Because the things they heard from the missionary did not match the things they heard from their consciences, they faced a long struggle in learning what God wanted for them. In cases like this, one result may be a slavish obedience to *everything* the missionary suggests or does including brushing one's teeth and putting flowers on the dinner table. This inability to function independently delays the development of an indigenous church. Converts need to be introduced to the whole range of Scripture. As they are taught how to use the Bible for themselves, they may come to see how different the teaching they have been given is from their own sense of what's right.

An understanding of the complexities of the doctrine of sin presented here requires the missionary to begin as a learner. He or she must take time to learn the values and rules of the culture, then categorize the difficult aspects: a) areas in which the Holy Spirit is already convicting; b) things that are not yet points of conviction although still in conflict with the Bible; c) aspects of the culture that are compatible with the Christian faith although troublesome to the missionary. This kind of categorization requires care to make certain one is after value systems and meanings, to go beneath the surface and uncover the true ideals of a culture. Even then, the answers are only approximations. The real answers will eventually be hammered out by the converts themselves, as they work out their own salvation "with fear and trembling" (Phil 2:12).

Study Questions

1. What does your family or culture value more highly: stewardship of time efficiency or quality of interpersonal relationships?

2. Does God have different standards for different cultures? Or are there diverse pathways by which the Holy Spirit guides a people group toward full obedience?

Cultural Implications of an Indigenous Church

William A. Smalley

William A. Smalley was Professor Emeritus of Linguistics at Bethel College in St. Paul, Minnesota. Smalley worked for 23 years for the United Bible Societies and as a consultant to the Bible societies in his retirement. He was also active in the formation of the Toronto Institute of Linguistics. He was editor of the journal *Practical Anthropology* from 1955 to 1968. Smalley died in 1997.

Adapted from *Readings in Missionary Anthropology II*, edited by William A. Smalley, 1978. Used by permission of William Carey Library, Pasadena, CA.

I t seems to have become axiomatic in much missionary thinking that a church which is "self-governing, self-supporting, and self-propagating" is by definition an "indigenous church." It further seems to follow in the thinking of many people that such an indigenous church (and so defined) is the goal of modern missions. There are some very serious reservations which may be made to this point of view, however, and it is a point of view which may be very misleading as it molds policy for the development of a church, if we look at some of its cultural implications.

It seems to me, first of all, that the criteria of "self-governing, self-supporting, and self-propagating" are not necessarily diagnostic of an indigenous movement. The definition of such a movement has to be sought elsewhere, and though these three "self" elements may be present in such a movement, they are essentially independent variables. The three "selfs" seem to have become catch phrases which can be stamped without any particular understanding on one church or on another. Yet it is evident on an examination of the facts that they are not necessarily relevant at all.

Misinterpretation of Self-government

It may be very easy to have a self-governing church which is not indigenous. Many presently self-governing churches are not. All that is necessary to do is to indoctrinate a few leaders in Western patterns of church government, and let them take over. The result will be a church governed in a slavishly foreign manner (although probably modified at points in the direction of local government patterns), but by no stretch of imagination can it be called an indigenous church.

It is further possible for a genuinely indigenous Christian movement to be "governed" to a degree by foreigners. Even in the large-scale Christward movements which have taken place in the world, movements which have been so extensive that the foreign body has had more difficulty in controlling them than what it has had in most of its mission work, the mission body has often exerted its governing influence upon the upper level of society, at least, where it was related in any way to the movement. This may have been by the direct action of missionaries or by the action of church leaders who were trained in the foreign patterns of government. Although such government may be unfortunate in many cases, it does not in the least detract from the indigenous nature of such a Christward movement on the part of a group of people.

Misapplication of Self-support

It is unlikely that there would be any disagreement with the idea that the Jerusalem church in the first century was an indigenous church. The Jerusalem Christians were so strongly Jewish in their attitudes that they resented the conversion of Gentiles unless they joined the Jewish ritualistic performance of the law. That church, however, in its time of need received gifts from abroad, from Europe—in modern-day terminology, from the West. Paul himself carried some of those gifts to Jerusalem. No one would argue that the receiving of such gifts infringed upon the indigenous nature of the Jewish church.

Neither can one argue, I believe, that the receiving of such gifts by the younger churches today will necessarily infringe upon their indigenous character. This is true in spite of the very real dangers which exist in the subsidy of the younger churches by the mission bodies.

I was in Indo-China as a missionary during some of the years of civil war. Those were days when the whole country was badly upset, when church congregations could be cut off from the mission without more than a few hours notice as the battle line shifted, when groups which had been under mission subsidy could suddenly lose their mission help and be placed in a fearful economic position. Together with most of my colleagues, I felt the tremendous weakness of a missionary program which was based upon the foreign financing of its national workers. In a time of crisis such as that, we worked hard to see to it that the church was placed on a footing of self-support.

Self-support is, wherever possible, really the soundest method of church economics. It is healthy for the church and for the mission, but there certainly are situations in which it is not possible, or where it is not advisable, where self-support can make church growth nearly impossible, and in such situations its presence does not necessarily imply the lack of an indigenous church. It is an independent variable within the pattern of the mission and church. All depends on how the problems are handled, and how the temptation to control church life through the manipulation of funds is resisted by the mission body. If foreign funds are handled in an indigenous way, they may still have their dangers, but they do not preclude an indigenous church.

Examples of areas in which the younger churches can usually not be expected to be self-supporting are publication, Bible translation, education, health and medicine, and many other fields entirely outside the range of their economy. These are not indigenous activities, but they are valuable activities for many churches in the modern world. Whether or not such things enter into the life of a church in an "indigenous manner" is entirely dependent upon the way in which the changes take place, not the source of income.

Misunderstanding of Self-propagation

Of the three "selfs," it seems to me that of self-propagation is the most nearly diagnostic of an indigenous church, but here again the correlation is by no means complete. In a few areas of the world it may be precisely the foreignness of the church which is the source of attraction to unbelievers. There are parts of the world where aspirations of people lead them toward wanting to identify themselves with the strong and powerful West, and where the church provides such an avenue of identification.[1] Self-propagation in such a case may be nothing more than a road to a non-indigenous relationship.

I very strongly suspect that the three "selfs" are really projections of our American value systems into the idealization of the church, that they are in their very nature Western concepts based upon Western ideas of individualism and power. By forcing them on other people, we may at times have been making it impossible for a truly indigenous pattern to develop. We have been Westernizing with all our talk about indigenizing.

The Nature of an Indigenous Church

What, then, is an indigenous church? It is a group of believers who live out their life, including their socialized Christian activity, in the patterns of the local society, and for whom any transformation of that society comes out of their felt needs under the guidance of the Holy Spirit and the Scriptures. There are several basic elements in this tentative formulation. For one thing, the church is a society. As society, it has its patterns of interaction among people. If it is an indigenous society, an indigenous church, those patterns of reaction will be based upon such patterns existing in the local society. This is true simply because people learn to react with each other in their normal process of enculturation, of growing up, and those normal habits are carried over into church structure. If other patterns are forced upon a church by missionaries, consciously or unconsciously, such a church will not be an indigenous one.

The presence of the Holy Spirit, however, is another basic factor in the indigenous church, and the presence of the Holy Spirit implies transformation both of individual lives and of society. But, as I have tried to point out in another article on the nature of culture change,[2] such transformation occurs differently in different societies, depending on the meaning which people attach to their behavior and the needs which they feel in their lives. Missionaries generally approve of and strive for culture change which makes people more like themselves in form (and this is true even though they may overlook the meaning of this form). An indigenous church is precisely one in which the changes which take place under the guidance of the Holy Spirit meet the needs and fulfill the meanings of that society and not of any outside group.

Many have said things like this, and such a statement should and could be elaborated considerably to provide a more adequate description of the nature of an indigenous church. Sometimes in our search for an understanding of the nature of the church, we turn to the New Testament (as we rightly should) and seek for it there. But it is not in the formal structure and operation of the churches in the New Testament that we find our answer. As a matter of fact, the church of Jerusalem was ap-

> An indigenous church is one in which the changes that take place under the guidance of the Holy Spirit meet the needs and fulfill the meanings of that society and not of any outside group.

parently different even in operational matters from the churches in Europe, and it was certainly different in the outlook on the basic cultural issues which were so important to the Jews. In the New Testament we do find the picture of the indigenous church. It is that of a church in which the Holy Spirit has worked its transformation within the society. And where that society differs from another (as the Greek world is different from the Jewish world) the church resulting is different.

Missionaries Do Not Like It

But having said this much, we would now like to stress some of the implications of an "indigenous church," implications which have often not been realized. One is that missionaries often do not like the product. Often a truly indigenous church is a source of concern and embarrassment to the mission bodies in the area.

An example of this is that of the Toba Indians as reported by Dr. William D. Reyburn.[3] The mission was disturbed and unhappy about the indigenous church which spread so rapidly among the Toba people because it assumed a form so different from that of the mission group. It was not until they saw something of the nature of the church in the sense in which we are discussing it here and of the working of the Holy Spirit in societies other than their own, that the missionaries not only became reconciled to the indigenous church's existence, but sought to harmonize their program with it, to the strengthening of that church and to the greater glory of God.

There have been indigenous movements which missionaries have approved of. This approval was sometimes due to the unusual insight and perception of the missionaries who saw beyond the limitations of their own cultural forms and recognized the movement of the Holy Spirit among other people. At other times the general value systems of the new church group so nearly coincided with our own that the result was a church which reflected many of the things that we hold very valuable. Movements in China such as the Jesus Family displayed outstanding personal qualities of frugality, cleanliness, thrift, and other virtues which rate so highly in our own society and which were considered to be the fruits of the Christian movement. These are, however, ideals present in non-Christian Chinese life. A transformed life in such a case resulted in the perfection of such value systems already in existence in the culture. But that was not the case among the Tobas, where the giving away of possessions, the sharing with one's relatives and neighbors, and the joining in of emotional expressions of religion characterized the group because it was in these ways that their values were expressed.

However, as Dr. William D. Reyburn put it some time ago, most of us want to join in the jury as God in making his judgments upon people and cultures, yet we don't even understand the meaning of the trial. We are quick to make our evaluations and quick to decide what course the new church should follow or what course a new Christian individual should take, but we simply are neither competent nor qualified to make such decisions, having little or no real knowledge of the cultural background of the people or individual.

It is our work first of all to see the Bible in its cultural perspective, to see God dealing with men through different cultural situations. It is our responsibility to see God change in dealing with people as the cultural

history of the Jews changes, to recognize that God has always, everywhere dealt with people in terms of their culture. It is next our responsibility to take new Christians to the Bible and to help them see in the Bible God interacting with other people, people whose emotions and problems were very similar to their own so far as their fundamental nature is concerned, but also at times very different from their own in the specific objective or working of their forms of life. It is our responsibility to lead them in prayer to find what God would have them do as they study His Word and seek the interpretation and leadership of the Holy Spirit.

It is the missionary task, if the missionary believes in "the indigenous principle," to preach that God is in Christ Jesus, reconciling the world unto Himself. That message is supercultural. It applies to all cultures and all places. The faith it engenders is supercultural, but the medium of its communication and the outworking of its faith in individual lives is not supercultural—it is bound in with the habits and values of every people. It is to deliver that message—the message that turned the world upside down and continues to do so—that the missionary is called.

It is, furthermore, the missionary's responsibility to be a source of cultural alternatives for people to select if they want and need them. Missionaries with their knowledge of history, their understanding of the

Scriptures, and their knowledge of the church in their own land and in other missionary areas, can often suggest to local groups that there are ways out of their dilemma, that there are ways of a better life in Christ than what they are now living. This is certainly a legitimate missionary function, their role in cultural change. But if genuine change is to take place, the decision, the selection, has to be made by the people themselves, and if the church is to be an indigenous one, we can know that the selection will be made in the light of the needs, problems, values and outlooks of those people.

It is the church which will have to decide whether boiling water, abstinence from alcohol, the wearing of clothes, and monogamy are the proper expressions of a Christian in that society. It is the church under the leadership of the Holy Spirit which will have to determine the best ways of fostering its own growth, spreading its own witness, and supporting its own formal leadership (if it should have any formal leadership at all).

As we have already suggested, the problem of the implications of the indigenous church are as old as the Judaizers of Jerusalem. Those Judaizers saw Greek Christianity through Hebrew eyes. They are like many missionaries in that, if they were content that any Gentile should be converted at all, they saw conversion in the light of filling of a formal mold.

The New Testament, however, clearly repudiated that view and sets up the church as a group of believers within its own society, working a chemical change within the society like salt in a dish, rather than cutting the society to pieces as the Judaizers would. This is not to gainsay the exclusiveness of Christianity. The church is a separate group, but it is separate in spiritual kind, in relationship to God. It is in the indigenous church that the relationship between the Holy Spirit and society comes into being. This is the New Testament church.

The converts of an indigenous movement are not necessarily cleaner than their neighbors, not necessarily more healthy, not necessarily better educated. It is, furthermore, often the moment at which they become cleaner, more healthy and more educated that the barrier begins to grow which makes their indigenous interaction with their neighbors less likely, and the growth of the movement begins to taper off. As Dr. McGavran has pointed out in his tremendously significant book *The Bridges of God*, missions have traditionally poured their funds not into the people's movements but into the station churches, into the huge mission compounds, into the churches which are their satellites, rather than into the grass roots growing development of an embarrassing indigenous church.

Not only do many missionaries not like some of the outstanding examples of indigenous church movements, but to an even greater degree, their supporting home constituencies are likely not to approve of them. Our cultural values as applied to our churches are so strong that we feel that a corporate structure, a profit motive, individualism, and thrift are *ipso facto* the expressions of Christianity. That God should work in any other forms than our own is inconceivable to most of us.

An implication of the indigenous church which I think is very unwelcome to many missionaries is that the missionary can make no cultural decisions for the Christians. By this I do not mean that the missionary does not make value judgments. Individual missionaries cannot help doing so, nor should they wish not to do so. Their value judgments, if they are to be worthwhile, have to be cross-culturally oriented, but they will be there. Neither do I mean by this that missionaries cannot exercise an important measure of guidance, of suggestion, on the younger church as they fulfill their functions of teaching and preaching and, in many respects, advising.

An Indigenous Church Cannot be "Founded"

The next implication which has often not fully penetrated into the thinking of missionaries who discuss indigenous movements is that it is impossible to "found" an indigenous church. The Biblical figure of planting and harvesting is far more realistic than our American figure based on our American values and expressed in the idea of the "establishment" or "founding" of a church.

No, indigenous churches cannot be founded. They can only be planted, and the mission is usually surprised at which seeds grow. Often they have the tendency to consider the seeds which do grow in any proliferation to be weeds, a nuisance, a hindrance in their carefully cultivated foreign mission garden; meanwhile, the carefully cultivated hothouse plants of the mission "founded" church are unable to spread roots and to derive their nurture either from the soil of their own life or from the Word of God in the root-confining pots of the mission organization and culture.

Indigenous Churches Start Apart from Missions

Another implication of the whole idea of an indigenous church is that the great indigenous movements are often not the result of foreign work in any direct way. Sometimes they are the result of the witness of someone who was converted by the efforts of foreign missionaries, but usually it is not the foreign missionary whose witness brings about the establishment or beginning of an indigenous movement. Saint Paul was not a foreigner to the Greek world. He was a bi-cultural individual, one who was as much at home in the Greek world as he was in the Hebrew world, and whose preaching carried to the Greek world the message which came to him from the Christians of the Hebrew world.

Prophet Harris, who wandered along the west coast of Africa preaching about the men who would come with a Book, was not a foreign missionary. The men from whom the Tobas heard the gospel as it came to them in its pentecostal form were not foreigners. True, they were not Tobas, but they were the poorer-class Latin-Americans and mixed Spanish-Indian inhabitants of the areas where the Tobas lived. They were very much a part of the cultural picture in which the Tobas found themselves; they were not foreign missionaries. The people's movements in China were usually the result of the energetic faithful work of a Chinese Christian, not the result of foreign missionary evangelism except as he may have been a convert of missionaries.

The Hmong movement described by G. Linwood Barney was not brought about through the preaching of a missionary, but through the cooperative work of a Hmong shaman who had been converted (under a missionary) and who took another tribesman of the area with whom the Hmong were very familiar from village to village, preaching from town to town. Our distance from most other cultures is so great, the cultural specialization of the West is so extreme, that there are almost no avenues of approach whereby the work which we do can normally result in anything of an indigenous nature. It is an ironical thing that the West, which is most concerned with the spread of Christianity in the world today, and which is financially best able to undertake the task of world wide evangelism, is culturally the least suited for its task because of the way in which it has specialized itself to a point where it is very difficult for it to have an adequate understanding of other peoples.

Conclusion

Until we are willing for the Church to have different manifestations in different cultures—rather than export the denominational patterns rooted in our history and often irrelevant to the rest of the world—we will not have indigenous churches. It does not matter whether they are "self-governing, self-supporting, and self-propagating" or not. It is not until we are willing to let churches grow also that we have learned to entrust the Holy Spirit with society. We are treating the Holy Spirit as a small child with a new toy too complicated and dangerous to handle. Our paternalism is not only a paternalism toward other peoples; it is also a paternalism towards God.

End Notes

1. McGavran, Donald, *The Bridges of God* (London: World Dominion Press, 1955).
2. Smalley, William A., "The Missionary and Culture Change," *Practical Anthropology*, 4, no. 5 (1957), pp. 231-237.
3. Reyburn, William D., *Conflicts and Contradictions in African Christianity*.

Study Questions

1. What constitutes an "indigenous" church, according to Smalley?

2. Why cannot the missionary "found" an indigenous church?

3. Why does Smalley say that missionaries do not like truly indigenous churches? What connection does this have with his conclusion about what missionaries are willing to allow?

The Missionary's Role in Culture Change

Dale W. Kietzman and William A. Smalley

Dale W. Kietzman is President of Latin American Indian Ministries. He became a member of Wycliffe Bible Translators in 1946, working with the Amahuaca Indians of Peru. He was founder of Wycliffe Associates. He also served as President of World Literature Crusade/Every Home for Christ and more recently as Professor of Intercultural Communication at William Carey International University.

William A. Smalley was Professor Emeritus of Linguistics at Bethel College in St. Paul, Minnesota. Smalley worked for 23 years for the United Bible Societies and as a consultant to the Bible societies in his retirement. He was also active in the formation of the Toronto Institute of Linguistics. He was editor of the journal Practical Anthropology from 1955 to 1968. Smalley died in 1997.

From *Readings in Missionary Anthropology II*, edited by William A. Smalley, 1978. Used by permission of William Carey Library, Pasadena, CA.

No informed, thinking person would deny that missionaries have historically been agents of culture change in non-Western societies. However, their role of initiating culture change has often been seriously misunderstood in different ways by missionaries themselves, their supporters and their critics. The basic attitudes of missionaries on this matter, and fundamental missionary policy in an area with respect to it, will inevitably have a profound influence on the successful communication of the gospel and the possible development of an "indigenous" expression of Christianity.

Some critics of the missionary enterprise have grossly exaggerated missionary influence resulting in their condemnation of the "rape" of non-Western cultures with destruction of values, detribalization, apathy or conflict. There certainly have been some direct cases of unnecessary and damaging cultural disturbance in missionary history, but for the most part, the missionary's role has been very minor relative to the impact of Western business, politics and education, not to speak of the often unsavory influences of motion pictures and printed matter. There have also been some outstanding cases where the gospel and resulting culture change have provided an opportunity for the reintegration of a segment of a culture already in rapid change.

Many supporters of Christian missions, on the other hand, have gauged the success of their whole program in terms of some overt, symbolic types of culture change. These may be anything from monogamy to haircuts, from attendance at church to the disappearance of scarification. But missionaries see in them as signs that their ministry is taking effect. Missions and missionaries which declare that they are not going out to introduce Western culture, but only to preach the gospel, are no different in this respect from those with whom they contrast themselves. It is usually institutionalism (hospitalization, education, agricultural mission, etc.) which they are rejecting by such statements, not really their roles as agents of Westernization. They, too, are thrilled when Ay Blah learns to bathe with Ivory soap, brush his teeth with Crest and cut his hair in "civilized" fashion. And if Ta Plooy does not give up his second and third wives or contribute to the church treasury, this is a matter for deep concern, for Ta Plooy obviously is not following the "gospel teaching" which he has been getting.

The Motivation for Culture Change

Culture change comes only as an expression of a need felt by individuals within a society. People do not change their behavior unless they feel a need to do so. The need may be trivial, as for some new excitement or amusement, or it may be profound, as for security in a disintegrating world. Usually it is relatively unconscious. People have not analyzed it or given it a name, but it motivates behavior. The missionary who senses culture change should never forget that the need being satisfied by a change may not be the need casually observed by others.

Among some of the tribal peoples of Laos and Vietnam, for example, the missionary sees the need for clothing. Many missionaries might feel the people need clothing for reasons of modesty (as in cases where women habitually wear nothing above the waist) or for warmth in the chilly season. Another need

> The Church (the Body of believers) is the real agent of the Holy Spirit for cultural change in any society.

is one which is felt by the people themselves to some degree, but it is strongly overshadowed by the other needs which they feel and which will be discussed in a moment. The need for modesty in the use of additional clothing is not felt at all, because people consider themselves adequately dressed from that point of view.

When the missionary barrel arrives and the clothes are given out, or when the missionary gives away an old shirt, or when some individual buys a new piece of clothing, what are the needs which he is meeting? One is the need to look respectable in the sight of outsiders—the need for being accepted by people who have prestige. This is why women will often not wear blouses in the village, but will wear them into town or put them on when the missionary shows up. Thus clothing may be a symbol of acceptance by the missionaries, of status and prestige in relation to them. Another is the desire to look well among one's equals, to wear something

difficult to obtain, something impossible for one's neighbors to buy.

A case in point, is a preacher from one of the tribes of Southeast Asia, after he had been given a topcoat out of the missionary barrel. This was the only topcoat in the lot; he was the only tribesman who possessed a topcoat. It never got so cold in the area that a missionary ever wore a topcoat, although a woolen suit was comfortable in the evening for two or three months of the year. On a trip through rather rugged, mountainous jungle, while people in T-shirts and cotton trousers were perspiring profusely because of the heat, our friend was wearing the topcoat. How else would people see him with a topcoat, unless he wore it?

Then there was the woman who wore nothing above the waist but a substantial pink bra....

A man who starts to wash his clothes after his conversion is probably not doing so because of his love for Christ, even though this seems to the missionary to be vindication of the view that cleanliness is next to godliness. What are the needs being expressed in a change from polygamy to monogamy, in church attendance, in church government, in learning to read, or in sending children to school? We would be the last to say that man's need for God is never involved in some of these, in some places. But even then, as in all human situations, motives are mixed.

Clearly, the typical missionary reaction to culture change is to approve of that which makes other peoples more like themselves, in the outward aspects of behavior, whether the meaning of the behavior is the same or not. It is quite possible to encourage the development of a form which expresses a meaning and fulfills a need, which the missionary would seriously deplore.

The Church's Role in Culture Change

Culture is constantly changing, and what is vital for our purpose, is that it constantly changes from within. While a good bit is said and written about acculturation, seldom has the role of the innovator, the nonconformist, the rebel been described. Yet all societies have them, and they have their place in bringing about the constant change that is characteristic of culture. The important thing for the missionary to note is that change is almost always initiated by someone within the cultural community. Even though the idea may have been sparked by contact with another culture, it still must be introduced from within to be accepted. The alternative to this scheme is change forced upon a people through superior might, whether moral or physical. This is the sort of change for which missions have often been responsible, and resulted in unfortunate reactions.

The Church (the Body of believers) is the real agent of the Holy Spirit for cultural change in any society (*not* necessarily the organized church of any particular denomination). The Church is the salt working through the whole dish. It is that part of the society which has a new relationship to God yet reacts in terms of the attitudes and presuppositions of that society. The Body of Christ understands intuitive, unanalyzed motives and meanings in a way the missionary cannot. The Church must make the decisions.

The Missionary's Part

What, then, can missionaries do about culture change? Are they only to be evangelists preaching a noncultural gospel without making value judgments? This is an impossibility, even if it were desirable. There cannot be preaching except in cultural terms and no human being can or should try to escape value judgments. Missionaries cannot legitimately force or enforce any culture change. Nor do they have an adequate basis for advocating specific changes in a culture unless they have a profound knowledge of that culture.

Missionaries do, however, have an extremely important function in the tactful, thoughtful, serious presentation of alternate forms of cultural behavior to the Christians in a society. On the basis of their knowledge of history, their understanding of the Church elsewhere, and above all, their knowledge of the tremendously varied ways in which God deals with people as recorded in the Scriptures, they can make it clear to them that there are alternative ways of behavior to their own. They can help them in prayer, in study and in experimenting to select those cultural forms which would be the best expression for the Christians' relationship to God in their culture.

The missionary's basic responsibility is to provide the material upon which the native Christian and church can grow. As they grow "in grace and knowledge" they can make reliable and Spirit-directed decisions with regard to their own conduct within the existing culture. This involves a complete freedom of access to the Word of God. With such encouragement, instruction and guidance in its use, the likely result will be a healthy and growing Christian community.

The missionary's role in culture change, then, is that of a catalyst and of a source of new ideas and new information. It is the voice of experience, but an experience based on his own culture for the most part and therefore to be used only with care and understanding. Part of the value of anthropological study, of course, is that it gives at least vicarious experience in more than one cultural setting. By study in this field, missionaries can gain awareness of the much wider choice of alternatives than their own culture allows.

It is the Church which is the legitimate agency in which the missionary should work. It is the people who must make the decisions based on the new ideas which they have received. It is they who must reinterpret old needs and expressions, examined now in the light of their relationship to God and to their fellow men in Christ Jesus.

Study Questions

1. What role in culture change is suggested here for the missionary? For the national church? To what extent should missionaries become engaged in political activities in their host countries?

2. How can the underlying motivation for culture change be discerned?

The Willowbank Report

The Lausanne Committee for World Evangelization

Wherever human beings develop their social organization, art and science, agriculture and technology, their creativity reflects that of their Creator.

"The Willowbank Report," used by permission of the Lausanne Committee for World Evangelization, 1978.

The Willowbank Report *is the product of a January 1978 consultation on "Gospel and Culture," sponsored by the Lausanne Committee for World Evangelization and conducted in Willowbank, Somerset Bridge, Bermuda. Some 33 theologians, anthropologists, linguists, missionaries, and pastors attended. The report reflects the content of 17 written papers circulated in advance, summaries of them and reactions to them made during the consultation, and viewpoints expressed in plenary and group discussions.*

1. The Biblical Basis of Culture

"Because man is God's creature, some of his culture is rich in beauty and goodness. Because he is fallen, all of it is tainted with sin and some of it is demonic." (Lausanne Covenant, para. 10).

God created mankind male and female in his own likeness by endowing them with distinctive human faculties—rational, moral, social, creative and spiritual. He also told them to have children, to fill the earth and to subdue it (Gen 1:26-28). These divine commands are the origin of human culture. For basic to culture are our control of nature (that is, of our environment) and our development of forms of social organization. Insofar as we use our creative powers to obey God's commands, we glorify God, serve others and fulfill an important part of our destiny on earth.

Now, however, we are fallen. All our work is accompanied by sweat and struggle (Gen 3:17-19), and is disfigured by selfishness. So none of our culture is perfect in truth, beauty or goodness. At the heart of every culture—whether we identify this heart as religion or world-view—is an element of self-centeredness, of man's worship of himself. Therefore a culture cannot be brought under the Lordship of Christ without a radical change of allegiance.

For all that, the affirmation that we are made in God's image still stands (Gen 9:6; Jas 3:9), though the divine likeness has been distorted by sin. And still God expects us to exercise stewardship of the earth and of its creatures (Gen 9:1-3, 7), and in his common grace makes all persons inventive, resourceful and fruitful in their endeavors. Thus, although Genesis 3 records the fall of humanity, and Genesis 4 Cain's murder of Abel, it is Cain's descendants who are described as the cultural innovators, building cities, breeding livestock, and making musical instruments and metal tools (Gen 4:17-22).

Many of us evangelical Christians have in the past been too negative towards culture. We do not forget the human fallenness and lostness which call for salvation in Christ. Yet we wish to begin this Report with a positive affirmation of human dignity and human cultural achievement. Wherever human beings develop their social organization, art and science, agriculture and technology, their creativity reflects that of their Creator.

2. A Definition of Culture

Culture is a term which is not easily susceptible of definition. In the broadest sense, it means simply the patterned way in which people do things together. If there is to be any common life and corporate action, there must be agreement, spoken or unspoken, about a great many things. But the term "culture" is not generally used unless the unit concerned is larger than the family—unitary or extended.

Culture implies a measure of homogeneity. But, if the unit is larger than the clan or small tribe, a culture will include within itself a number of subcultures, and subcultures of subcultures, within which a wide variety and diversity is possible. If the variations go beyond a certain limit, a counterculture will have come into being, and this may prove a destructive process.

Culture holds people together over a span of time. It is received from the past, but not by any process of natural inheritance. It has to be learned afresh by each generation. This takes place broadly by a process of absorption from the social environment, especially in the home. In many societies certain elements of the culture are communicated directly in rites of initiation, and by many other forms of deliberate instruction. Action in accordance with the culture is generally at the subconscious level.

This means that an accepted culture covers everything in human life.

At its center is a world-view, that is, a general understanding of the nature of the universe and of one's place in it. This may be "religious" (concerning God, or gods and spirits, and of our relation to them), or it may express a "secular" concept of reality, as in a Marxist society.

From this basic world-view flow both standards of judgment or values (of what is good in the sense of desirable, of what is acceptable as in accordance with the general will of the community, and of the contraries) and standards of conduct (concerning relations between individuals, between the sexes and the generations, with the community and with those outside the community).

Culture is closely bound up with language, and is expressed in proverbs, myths, folk tales, and various art forms, which become part of the mental furniture of all members of the group. It governs actions undertaken in community—acts of worship or of general welfare; laws and the administration of law; social activities such as dances and games; smaller units of action such as clubs and societies, associations for an immense variety of common purposes.

Cultures are never static; there is a continuous process of change. But this should be so gradual as to take place within the accepted norms; otherwise the culture is disrupted. The worst penalty that can be inflicted on the rebel is exclusion from the culturally defined social community.

Men and women need a unified existence. Participation in a culture is one of the factors which provide them with a sense of belonging. It gives a sense of security, of identity, of dignity, of being part of a larger whole, and of sharing both in the life of past generations and in the expectancy of society for its own future.

Biblical clues to the understanding of the human culture are found in the threefold dimension of people, land, and history on which the Old Testament focuses attention. The ethnic, the territorial, and the historical (who, where and whence we are) appear there as the triple source of economic, ecological, social and artistic forms of human life in Israel, of the forms of labor and production, and so of wealth and well-being. This model provides a perspective for interpreting all cultures.

Perhaps we may try to condense these various meanings as follows: Culture is an integrated system of beliefs (about God or reality or ultimate meaning), of values (about what is true, good, beautiful and normative), of customs (how to behave, relate to others, talk, pray, dress, work, play, trade, farm, eat, etc.), and of institutions which express these beliefs, values and customs (government, law courts, temples or churches, family, schools, hospitals, factories, shops, unions, clubs, etc.), which binds a society together and gives it a sense of identity, dignity, security, and continuity.

3. Culture in the Biblical Revelation

God's personal self-disclosure in the Bible was given in terms of the hearers' own culture. So we have asked ourselves what light it throws on our task of cross-cultural communication today.

The biblical writers made critical use of whatever cultural material was available to them for the expression of their message. For example, the Old Testament refers several times to the Babylonian sea monster named "Leviathan," while the form of God's "covenant" with his people resembles the ancient Hittite Suzerain's "treaty" with his vassals. The writers also made incidental use of the conceptual imagery of the "three-tiered" universe, though they did not thereby affirm a pre-Copernican cosmology. We do something similar when we talk about the sun "rising" and "setting."

> There is a broad distinction in form between the work of the prophets, historians and writers of letters. Yet the same Spirit uniquely inspired them all.

Similarly, New Testament language and thought-forms are steeped in both Jewish and Hellenistic cultures, and Paul seems to have drawn from the vocabulary of Greek philosophy. But the process by which the biblical authors borrowed words and images from their cultural milieu, and used them creatively, was controlled by the Holy Spirit so that they purged them of false or evil implications and thus transformed them into vehicles of truth and goodness. These undoubted facts raise a number of questions with which we have wrestled. We mention five:

The nature of biblical inspiration

Is the biblical author's use of the words and ideas of their own culture incompatible with divine inspiration? No. We have taken note of the different literary genres of Scripture, and of the different forms of the process of inspiration which they imply. For instance, there is a broad distinction in form between the work of the prophets, receiving visions and words of the Lord, and historians and writers of letters. Yet the same Spirit uniquely inspired them all. God used the knowledge, experience and cultural background of the authors (though his revelation constantly transcended these), and in each case the result was the same, namely God's word through human words.

Form and meaning

Every communication has both a meaning (what we want to say) and a form (how we say it). The two—form and meaning—always belong together, in the Bible as well as in other books and utterances. How then should a message be translated from one language into another?

A literal translation of the form ("formal correspondence") may conceal or distort the meaning. In such cases, the better way is to find in the other language an expression which makes an equivalent impact on the hearers now as did the original. This may involve changing the form in order to preserve the meaning. This is called "dynamic equivalence. " Consider, for example, the RSV translation of Romans 1:17, which states that in the gospel "the righteousness of God is revealed through faith for faith." This gives a word-for-word rendering of the original Greek, that is, a "formal correspondence" translation. But it leaves the meaning of the Greek words "righteousness" and "from faith to faith" unclear. A translation such as TEV—"the gospel reveals how God puts people right with himself: it is through faith from beginning to end"—abandons the principle of one-to-one correspondence between Greek and English words; but it expresses the meaning of the original sentence more adequately. The attempt to produce such a "dynamic equivalence" translation may well bring the translator to a deeper understanding of Scripture, as well as make the text more meaningful to people of another language.

Some of the biblical forms (words, images, metaphors) should be retained, however, because they are important recurring symbols in Scripture (e.g., cross, lamb, or cup). While retaining the form, the translators will try to bring out the meaning. For example, in the TEV rendering of Mark 14:36—"take this cup of suffering away from me"—the form (i.e., the "cup" image) is retained, but the words "of suffering" are added to clarify the meaning

Writing in Greek, the New Testament authors used words that had a long history in the secular world, but they invested them with Christian meanings as when John referred to Jesus as "the Logos." It was a perilous procedure because "logos" had a wide variety of meanings in Greek literature and philosophy, and non-Christian associations doubtlessly clung to the word. So John set the title within a teaching context, affirming that the Logos was in the beginning, was with God, was God, was the agent of creation, was the light and life of men, and became a human being (John 1:1-14). Similarly some Indian Christians have taken the risk of borrowing the Sanskrit word "avatar" (descent), used in Hinduism for the so-called "incarnations" of Vishnu, and applied it, with careful explanatory safeguards, to the unique incarnation of God in Jesus Christ. But others have refused to do so, on the ground that no safeguards are adequate to prevent misinterpretation.

The normative nature of Scripture

The Lausanne Covenant declares that Scripture is "without error in all that it affirms" (para. 2). This lays upon us the serious exegetical task of discerning exactly what Scripture is affirming. The essential meaning of the biblical message must at all costs be retained. Though some of the original forms in which this meaning was expressed may be changed for the sake of cross-cultural communication, we believe that they too have a certain normative quality. For God himself chose them as wholly appropriate vehicles of his revelation. So each fresh formulation and explanation in every generation and culture must be checked for faithfulness by referring back to the original.

The cultural conditioning of Scripture

We have not been able to devote as much time as we would have liked to the problem of the cultural conditioning of Scripture. We are agreed that some biblical commands (e.g., regarding the veiling of women in public and washing one another's feet) refer to cultural customs now obsolete in many parts of the world. Faced by such texts, we believe the right response is neither a slavishly literal obedience nor an irresponsible disregard, but rather first a critical discernment of the text's inner meaning and then a translation of it into our own culture. For example, the inner meaning of the command to wash each other's feet is that mutual love must express itself in humble service. So in some cultures we may clean each other's shoes instead. We are clear that the purpose of such "cultural transposition" is not to avoid obedience but rather to make it contemporary and authentic.

The controversial question of the status of women was not debated at our Consultation. But we acknowledge the need to search for an understanding which attempts with integrity to do justice to all the biblical teaching, and which sees the relations between men and women as being both rooted in the created order and at the same time wonderfully transformed by the new order which Jesus introduced.

The continuing work of the Holy Spirit

Does our emphasis on the finality and permanent normativeness of Scripture mean that we think the Holy Spirit has now ceased to operate? No, indeed not. But the nature of his teaching ministry has changed. We believe that his work of "inspiration" is done, in the sense that the canon of Scripture is closed, but that his work of "illumination" continues both in every conversion (e.g., 2 Cor 4:6) and in the life of the Christian and the Church. So we need constantly to pray that he will enlighten the eyes of our hearts so that we may know the fulness of God's purpose for us (Eph 1:17ff) and may be not timorous but courageous in making decisions and undertaking fresh tasks today.

We have been made aware that the experience of the Holy Spirit revealing the application of God's truth to personal and church life is often less vivid than it should be: we all need a more sensitive openness at this point.

Questions for discussion

1. The commands of Genesis 1:26-28 are sometimes referred to as "the cultural mandate" which God gave to mankind. How responsibly is it being fulfilled today?

2. In the light of the definition of culture above, what are the main distinctive elements of your own culture?

3. If you know two languages, make up a sentence in one and then try to find a "dynamic equivalence" translation of it into the other.

4. Give other examples of "cultural transposition" which preserve the biblical text's "inner meaning" but transpose it into your own culture.

4. Understanding God's Word Today

The cultural factor is present not only in God's self-revelation in Scripture, but also in our interpretation of it. To this subject we now turn. All Christians are concerned to understand God's Word, but there are different ways of trying to do so.

Traditional approaches

The commonest way is to come straight to the words of the biblical text, and to study them without any awareness that the writer's cultural context differs from the reader's. The reader interprets the text as if it had been written in his own language, culture and time.

We recognize that much Scripture can be read and understood in this way, especially if the translation is good. For God intended his Word for ordinary people; it is not to be regarded as the preserve of scholars; the central truths of salvation are plain for all to see; Scripture is "useful for teaching the truth, rebuking error, correcting faults, and giving instruction for right living" (2 Tim 3:16, TEV); and the Holy Spirit has been given to be our teacher.

The weakness of this "popular" approach, however, is that it does not seek first to understand the text in its original context; and, therefore, it runs the risk of missing the real meaning God intends and of substituting another.

A second approach takes with due seriousness the original historical and cultural context. It seeks also to discover what the text meant in its original language, and how it relates to the rest of Scripture. All this is an essential discipline because God spoke his Word to a particular people in a particular context and time. So our understanding of God's message will grow when we probe deeply into these matters.

The weakness of this "historical" approach, however, is that it fails to consider what Scripture may be saying to the contemporary reader. It stops short at the meaning of the Bible in its own time and culture. It is thus liable to analyze the text without applying it, and to acquire academic knowledge without obedience. The interpreter may also tend to exaggerate the possibility of complete objectivity and ignore his or her own cultural presuppositions.

The contextual approach

A third approach begins by combining the positive elements of both the "popular" and the "historical" approaches. From the "historical" it takes the necessity of studying the original context and language, and from the "popular" the necessity of listening to God's Word and obeying it. But it goes further than this. It takes seriously the cultural context of the contemporary readers as well as of the biblical text, and recognizes that a dialogue must develop between the two.

It is the need for this dynamic interplay between text and interpreters which we wish to emphasize. Today's readers cannot come to the text in a personal vacuum, and should not try to. Instead, they should come with an awareness of concerns stemming from their cultural background, personal situation, and responsibility to others. These concerns will influence the questions which are put to the Scriptures. What is received back, however, will not be answers only, but more questions. As we address Scripture, Scripture addresses us. We find that our culturally conditioned presuppositions are being challenged and our questions corrected. In fact, we are compelled to reformulate our previous questions and to ask fresh ones. So the living interaction proceeds.

In this process of interaction our knowledge of God and our response to his will are continuously being deepened. The more we come to know him, the greater our responsibility becomes to obey him in our own situation, and the more we respond obediently, the more he makes himself known.

It is this continuous growth in knowledge, love and obedience which is the purpose and profit of the "contextual" approach. Out of the context in which his Word was originally given, we hear God speaking to us in our contemporary context, and we find it a transforming experience. This process is a kind of upward spiral in which Scripture remains always central and normative.

The learning community

We wish to emphasize that the task of understanding the Scriptures belongs not just to individuals but to the whole Christian community, seen as both a contemporary and a historical fellowship.

There are many ways in which the local or regional church can come to discern God's will in its own culture today. Christ still appoints pastors and teachers in his church. And in answer to expectant prayer he speaks to his people, especially through the preaching of his Word in the context of worship. In addition, there is a place for "teaching and admonishing one another" (Col 3:16) both in group Bible studies and in consulting sister churches, as well as for the quiet listening to the voice of God in the Scriptures, which is an indispensable element in the believer's Christian life.

The Church is also a historical fellowship and has received from the past a rich inheritance of Christian theology, liturgy and devotion. No group of believers can disregard this heritage without risking spiritual impoverishment. At the same time, this tradition must not be received uncritically, whether it comes in the form of a set of denominational distinctives or in any other way but rather be tested by the Scripture it claims to expound. Nor must it be imposed on any church, but rather be made available to those who can use it as a valuable resource material, as a counterbalance to the spirit of independence, and as a link with the universal Church.

Thus the Holy Spirit instructs his people through a variety of teachers of both the past and the present. We need each other. It is only "with all the saints" that we can begin to comprehend the full dimensions of God's love (Eph 3:18, 19). The Spirit "illumines the minds of God's people in every culture to perceive its (that is, the Scripture's) truth freshly through their own eyes and thus discloses to the whole Church ever more of the many-coloured wisdom of God" (Lausanne Covenant, para. 2, echoing Eph 3:10).

The silences of Scripture

We have also considered the problem of Scripture silences, that is, those areas of doctrine and ethics on which the Bible has nothing explicit to say. Written in the ancient Jewish and Graeco-Roman world, Scripture does not address itself directly, for example, to Hinduism, Buddhism, or Islam today, or to Marxist socio-economic theory, or modern technology. Nevertheless, we believe it is right for the church guided by the Holy Spirit to search the Scriptures for precedents and principles which will enable it to develop the mind of the Lord Christ and so be able to make authentically Christian decisions. This process will go on most fruitfully within the believing community as it worships God and engages in active obedience in the world. We repeat that Christian obedience is as much a prelude to understanding as a consequence of it.

Questions for discussion

1. Can you recall any examples of how either of the two "traditional approaches" to Bible reading had led you astray?

2. Choose a well known text like Matthew 6:24-34 (anxiety and ambition) or Luke 10:25-38 (the Good Samaritan) and use the "contextual approach" in studying it. Let a dialogue develop between you and the text, as you question it and it questions you. Write down the stages of the interaction.

3. Discuss some practical ways of seeking the guidance of the Holy Spirit today.

5. The Content and Communication of the Gospel

Having thought about God's communication of the gospel to us in Scripture, we now come to the very heart of our concern, our responsibility to communicate it to others, that is, to evangelize. But before we consider the communication of the gospel, we have to consider the content of the gospel which is to be communicated. For "to evangelize is to spread the good news…" (Lausanne Covenant, para. 4). Therefore there can be no evangelism without the evangel.

The Bible and the gospel

The gospel is to be found in the Bible. In fact, there is a sense in which the whole Bible is gospel, from Genesis to Revelation. For its overriding purpose throughout is to bear witness to Christ, to proclaim the good news that he is Lifegiver and Lord, and to persuade people to trust in him (e.g., John 5:39, 40; 20:31; 2 Tim 3:15).

The Bible proclaims the gospel story in many forms. The gospel is like a multi-faceted diamond, with different aspects that appeal to different people in different cultures. It has depths we have not fathomed. It defies every attempt to reduce it to a neat formulation.

The heart of the gospel

Nevertheless, it is important to identify what is at the heart of the gospel. We recognize as central the themes of God as Creator, the universality of sin, Jesus Christ as Son of God, Lord of all, and Savior through his atoning death and risen life, the necessity of conversion, the coming of the Holy Spirit and his transforming power, the fellowship and mission of the Christian Church, and the hope of Christ's return.

While these are basic elements of the gospel, it is necessary to add that no theological statement is culture-free. Therefore, all theological formulations must be judged by the Bible itself, which stands above them all. Their value must be judged by their faithfulness to it as well as by the relevance with which they apply its message to their own culture.

In our desire to communicate the gospel effectively, we are often made aware of those elements in it which people dislike. For example, the cross has always been both an offense to the proud and folly to the wise. But Paul did not on that account eliminate it from his message. On the contrary, he continued to proclaim it, with faithfulness and at the risk of persecution, confident that Christ crucified is the wisdom and the power of God. We too, although concerned to contextualize our message and remove from it all unnecessary offense, must resist the temptation to accommodate it to human pride or prejudice. It has been given to us. Our responsibility is not to edit it but to proclaim it.

Cultural barriers to the communication of the gospel

No Christian witness can hope to communicate the gospel if he or she ignores the cultural factor. This is particularly true in the case of missionaries. For they are themselves the product of one culture and go to people who are the products of another. So inevitably they are involved in cross-cultural communication, with all its exciting challenge and exacting demand. Two main problems face them.

Sometimes people resist the gospel not because they think it false but because they perceive it as a threat to their culture, especially the fabric of their society, and their national or tribal solidarity. To some extent this cannot be avoided. Jesus Christ is a disturber as well as a peacemaker. He is Lord, and demands our total allegiance. Thus, some first-century Jews saw the gospel as undermining Judaism and accused Paul of "teaching men everywhere against the people, the law, and this place," i.e., the temple (Acts 21:28). Similarly, some first-century Romans feared for the stability of the state, since in their view the Christian missionaries, by saying that "there is another King, Jesus," were being disloyal to Caesar and advocating customs which were not lawful for Romans to practice (Acts 16:21; 17:7). Still today Jesus challenges many of the cherished beliefs and customs of every culture and society.

At the same time, there are features of every culture which are not incompatible with the lordship of Christ, and which therefore need not be threatened or discarded, but rather preserved and transformed. Messengers of the gospel need to develop a deep understanding of the local culture, and a genuine appreciation of it. Only then will they be able to perceive whether the resistance is to some unavoidable challenge of Jesus Christ or to some threat to the culture which, whether imaginary or real, is not necessary.

The other problem is that the gospel is often presented to people in alien cultural forms. Then the missionaries are resented and their message rejected because their work is seen not as an attempt to evangelize but as an attempt to impose their own customs and way of life. Where missionaries bring with them foreign ways of thinking and behaving, or attitudes of racial superiority, paternalism, or preoccupation with material things, effective communication will be precluded.

Sometimes these two cultural blunders are committed together, and messengers of the gospel are guilty of a cultural imperialism which both undermines the local culture unnecessarily and seeks to impose an alien culture instead. Some of the missionaries who accompanied the Catholic *conquistadores* of Latin America and the Protestant colonizers of Africa and Asia are historical examples of this double mistake. By contrast, the apostle Paul remains the supreme example of one whom Jesus Christ first stripped of pride in his own cultural privileges (Phil 3:4-9) and then taught to adapt to the cultures of others, making himself their slave and becoming "all things to all men" in order by all means to save some (1 Cor 9:19-23).

Cultural sensitivity in communicating the gospel

Sensitive cross-cultural witnesses will not arrive at their sphere of service with a prepackaged gospel. They must have a clear grasp of the "given" truth of the gospel. But they will fail to communicate successfully if they try to impose this on people without reference to their own cultural situation and that of the people to whom they go. It is only by active, loving engagement with the local people, thinking in their thought patterns, understanding their world-view, listening to their questions, and feeling their burdens, that the whole believing community (of which the missionary is a part) will be able to respond to their need. By common prayer, thought and heart-searching, in dependence on the Holy Spirit, expatriate and local believers may learn together how to present Christ and contextualize the gospel with an equal degree of faithfulness and relevance. We are not claiming that it will be easy, although some Third World cultures have a natural affinity to biblical culture. But we believe that fresh creative understandings do emerge when the

Spirit-led believing community is listening and reacting sensitively to both the truth of Scripture and the needs of the world.

Christian witness in the Islamic world

Concern was expressed that insufficient attention had been given at our Consultation to the distinctive problems of the Christian mission in the Islamic world, though there are approximately 600 million Muslims today [*Ed. note: over 1 billion in 1998*]. On the one hand, a resurgence of Islamic faith and mission is taking place in many lands; on the other hand, there is a new openness to the gospel in a number of communities which are weakening their ties to traditional Islamic culture .

There is a need to recognize the distinctive features of Islam which provide a unique opportunity for Christian witness. Although there are in Islam elements which are incompatible with the gospel, there are also elements with a degree of what has been called "convertibility." For instance, our Christian understanding of God, expressed in Luther's great cry related to justification, "Let God be God," might well serve as an inclusive definition of Islam. The Islamic faith in divine unity, the emphasis on man's obligation to render God a right worship, and the utter rejection of idolatry could also be regarded as being in line with God's

Photo courtesy of Caleb Project

purpose for human life as revealed in Jesus Christ. Contemporary Christian witnesses should learn humbly and expectantly to identify, appreciate and illuminate these and other values. They should also wrestle for the transformation—and, where possible, integration—of all that is relevant in Islamic worship, prayer, fasting, art, architecture, and calligraphy.

All this proceeds only within a realistic appreciation of the present situation of the Islamic countries characterized by technological development and secularization. The social liabilities of new wealth and traditional poverty, the tensions of political independence, and the tragic Palestinian dispersion and frustration—all of these afford areas of relevant Christian witness. The last has given birth to much passionate poetry, one note in which is the paradigm of the suffering Jesus. These and other elements call for a new Christian sensitivity and a real awareness of the habits of introversion under which the Church has for so long labored in the Middle East. Elsewhere, not least in sub-Sahara Africa, attitudes are more flexible and possibilities more fluid.

In order to fulfill more adequately the missionary challenge, fresh attempts are needed to develop ways of association of believers and seekers, if need be outside the traditional church forms. The crux of a lively, evangelizing sense of responsibility towards Muslims will always be the quality of Christian personal and corporate discipleship and the constraining love of Christ.

An expectation of results

Messengers of the gospel who have proved in their own experience that it is "the power of God for salvation" (Rom 1:16) rightly expect it to be so in the experience of others also. We confess that sometimes, just as a Gentile centurion's faith put to shame the unbelief of Israel in Jesus' day (Matt 8:10), so today the believing expectancy of Christians in other cultures sometimes shows up the missionary's lack of faith. So we remind ourselves of God's promises through Abraham's posterity to bless all the families of the earth and through the gospel to save those who believe (Gen 12:1-4; 1 Cor 1:21). It is on the basis of these and many other promises that we remind all messengers of the

gospel, including ourselves, to look to God to save people and to build his Church.

At the same time, we do not forget our Lord's warnings of opposition and suffering. Human hearts are hard. People do not always embrace the gospel, even when the communication is blameless in technique and the communicator in character. Our Lord himself was fully at home in the culture in which he preached, yet he and his message were despised and rejected, and his Parable of the Sower seems to warn us that most of the good seed we sow will not bear fruit. There is a mystery here we cannot fathom. "The Spirit blows where he wills" (John 3:8). While seeking to communicate the gospel with care, faithfulness and zeal, we leave the results to God in humility.

Questions for Discussion

1. In the above text, the Report refuses to give a "neat formulation" of the gospel, but identifies its "heart." Would you want to add to these "central themes," or subtract from them, or amplify them?

2. Clarify the "two cultural blunders." Can you think of examples? How can such mistakes be avoided?

3. Think of the cultural situation of the people you are wanting to win for Christ. What would "cultural sensitivity" mean in your case?

6. Wanted: Humble Messengers of the Gospel!

We believe that the principal key to persuasive Christian communication is to be found in the communicators themselves and what kind of people they are. It should go without saying that they need to be people of Christian faith, love, and holiness. That is, they must have a personal and growing experience of the transforming power of the Holy Spirit, so that the image of Jesus Christ is ever more clearly seen in their character and attitudes.

Above all else we desire to see in them, and especially in ourselves, "the meekness and gentleness of Christ" (2 Cor 10:1), in other words, the humble sensitivity of Christ's love. So important do we believe this to be that we are devoting the whole of this section of our Report to it. Moreover, since, we have no wish to point the finger at anybody but ourselves, we shall use the first person plural throughout. First, we give an analysis of Christian humility in a missionary situation, and secondly, we turn to the Incarnation of God in Jesus Christ as the model we desire by his grace to follow.

An analysis of missionary humility

First, there is the humility to acknowledge the problem which culture presents, and not to avoid or over-simplify it. As we have seen, different cultures have strongly influenced the biblical revelation, ourselves, and the people to whom we go. As a result, we have several personal limitations in communicating the gospel. For we are prisoners (consciously or unconsciously) of our own culture, and our grasp of the cultures both of the Bible and of the country in which we serve is very imperfect. It is the interaction between all these cultures which constitutes the problem of communication; it humbles all who wrestle with it.

Secondly, there is the humility to take the trouble to understand and appreciate the culture of those to whom we go. It is this desire which leads naturally into that true dialogue "whose purpose is to listen sensitively in order to understand" (Lausanne Covenant, para. 4). We repent of the ignorance which assumes that we have all the answers and that our only role is to teach. We have very much to learn. We repent also of judgmental attitudes. We know we should never condemn or despise another culture, but rather respect it. We advocate neither the arrogance which imposes our culture on others, nor the syncretism which mixes the gospel with cultural elements incompatible with it, but rather a humble sharing of the good news—made possible by the mutual respect of a genuine friendship.

Thirdly, there is the humility to begin our communication where people actually are and not where we would like them to be. This is what we see Jesus doing, and we desire to follow his example. Too often we have ignored people's fears and frustrations, their pains and preoccupations, and their hunger, poverty, deprivation or oppression, in fact their "felt needs," and have been too slow to rejoice or to weep with them. We acknowl-

edge that these "felt needs" may sometimes be symptoms of deeper needs which are not immediately felt or recognized by the people. A doctor does not necessarily accept a patient's self-diagnosis. Nevertheless, we see the need to begin where people are, but not to stop there. We accept our responsibility to gently and patiently lead them on to see themselves, as we see ourselves, as rebels to whom the gospel directly speaks with a message of pardon and hope. To begin where people are not is to share an irrelevant message; to stay where people are and never lead them on to the fulness of God's good news, is to share a truncated gospel. The humble sensitivity of love will avoid both errors.

Fourthly, there is the humility to recognize that even the most gifted, dedicated and experienced missionary can seldom communicate the gospel in another language or culture as effectively as a trained local Christian. This fact has been acknowledged in recent years by the Bible Societies, whose policy has changed from publishing translations by missionaries (with help from local people) to training mother-tongue specialists to do the translating. Only local Christians can answer the questions, "God, how would you say this in our language?" and "God, what will obedience to you mean in our culture?" Therefore, whether we are translating the Bible or communicating the gospel, local Christians are indispensable. It is they who must assume the responsibility to contextualize the gospel in their own languages and cultures. Would-be cross-cultural witnesses are not on that account necessarily superfluous; but we shall be welcome only if we are humble enough to see good communication as a team enterprise, in which all believers collaborate as partners.

Fifthly, there is the humility to trust in the Holy Spirit of God, who is always the chief communicator, who alone opens the eyes of the blind and brings people to new birth. "Without his witness, ours is futile" (Lausanne Covenant, para. 14).

Incarnation as model for Christian witness

We have met for our Consultation within a few days of Christmas, which might be called the most spectacular instance of cultural identification in the history of mankind, since by his Incarnation the Son became a first-century Galilean Jew.

We have also remembered that Jesus intended his people's mission in the world to be modeled on his own. "As the Father has sent me, even so I send you," he said (John 20:21; cf. 17:18). We have asked ourselves, therefore, about the implications of the Incarnation for all of us. The question is of special concern to cross-cultural witnesses, whatever country they go to, although we have thought particularly of those from the West who serve in the Third World.

Meditating on Philippians 2, we have seen that the self-humbling of Christ began in his mind: "he did not count equality with God a thing to be grasped." So we are commanded to let his mind be in us, and in humility of mind to "count" others better or more important than ourselves. This "mind" or "perspective" of Christ is a recognition of the infinite worth of human beings and of the privilege it is to serve them. Those witnesses who have the mind of Christ will have a profound respect for the people they serve, and for their cultures.

aries are they should not be in control or work alone, but always with—and preferably under—local Christians who can advise and even direct them. And whatever the missionaries' responsibility may be they should express attitudes "not of domination but of service" (Lausanne Covenant, para. 11) .

Next the renunciation of independence. We have looked at Jesus—asking a Samaritan woman for water, living in other people's homes and on other people's money because he had none of his own, being lent a boat, a donkey, an upper room, and even being buried in a borrowed tomb. Similarly, cross-cultural messengers, especially during their first years of service, need to learn dependence on others.

Thirdly, the renunciation of immunity. Jesus exposed himself to temptation, sorrow, limitation, economic need, and pain. So the missionary should expect to become vulnerable to new temptations, dangers and diseases, a strange climate, an unaccustomed loneliness, and possibly death.

Turning from the theme of renunciation to that of identification, we have marvelled afresh at the completeness of our Saviour's identification with us, particularly as this is taught in the Letter to the Hebrews. He shared

> A searching test of identification is how far we feel that we belong to the people, and still more—how far they feel that we belong to them.

Two verbs then indicate the action to which the mind of Christ led him: "he emptied himself...he humbled himself...." The first speaks of sacrifice (what he renounced) and the second of service, even slavery (how he identified himself with us and put himself at our disposal). We have tried to think what these two actions meant for him, and might mean for cross-cultural witnesses.

We began with his renunciation. First, the renunciation of status. "Mild he laid his glory by," we have been singing at Christmas. Because we cannot conceive what his eternal glory was like, it is impossible to grasp the greatness of his self-emptying. But certainly he surrendered the rights, privileges, and powers which he enjoyed as God's Son. "Status" and "status symbols" mean much in the modern world, but are incongruous in missionaries. We believe that wherever mission-

our "flesh and blood," was tempted as we are, learned obedience through his suffering and tasted death for us (Heb 2:14-18; 4:15; 5:8). During his public ministry Jesus befriended the poor and the powerless, healed the sick, fed the hungry, touched untouchables, and risked his reputation by associating with those whom society rejected.

The extent to which we identify ourselves with the people to whom we go is a matter of controversy. Certainly it must include mastering their language, immersing ourselves in their culture, learning to think as they think, feel as they feel, do as they do. At the socio-economic level we do not believe that we should "go native," principally because a foreigner's attempt to do this may not be seen as authentic but as play-acting. But neither do we think there should be a conspicuous disparity between our life style and that of the people around us. In between these extremes, we see the possibility of developing a standard of living which expresses the kind of love which cares and shares, and which finds it natural to exchange hospitality with others on a basis of reciprocity, without embarrassment. A searching test of identification is how far we feel that we belong to the people, and still more—how far they feel that we belong to them. Do we participate naturally in days of national or tribal thanksgiving or sorrow? Do we groan with them in the oppression which they suffer and join them in their quest for justice and freedom? If the country is struck by earthquake or engulfed in civil war, is our instinct to stay and suffer with the people we love, or to fly home?

Although Jesus identified himself completely with us, he did not lose his own identity. He remained himself. "He came down from heaven…and was made man" (Nicene Creed); yet in becoming one of us he did not cease to be God. Just so, "Christ's evangelists must humbly seek to empty themselves of all but their personal authenticity" (Lausanne Covenant, para. 10). The Incarnation teaches identification without loss of identity. We believe that true self-sacrifice leads to true self-discovery. In humble service there is abundant joy.

Questions for Discussion

1. If the main key to communication lies in the communicators, what sort of people should they be?

2. Give your own analysis of the humility which all Christian witnesses should have. Where would you put your emphasis?

3. Since the Incarnation involved both "renunciation" and "identification," it was obviously very costly for Jesus. What would be the cost of "incarnation evangelism" today?

7. Conversion and Culture

We have thought of the relations between conversion and culture in two ways. First, what effect does conversion have on the cultural situation of converts, the ways they think and act, and their attitudes to their so-cial environment? Secondly, what effect has our culture had on our own understanding of conversion? Both questions are important. But we want to say at once that elements in our traditional evangelical view of conversion are more cultural than biblical and need to be challenged. Too often we have thought of conversion as a crisis, instead of as a process as well; or we have viewed conversion as a largely private experience, forgetting its consequent public and social responsibilities.

The radical nature of conversion

We are convinced that the radical nature of conversion to Jesus Christ needs to be reaffirmed in the contemporary church. For we are always in danger of trivializing it, as if it were no more than a surface change, and a self-reformation at that. But the New Testament authors write of it as the outward expression of a regeneration or new birth by God's Spirit, a recreation, and resurrection from spiritual death. The concept of resurrection seems to be particularly important. For the resurrection of Jesus Christ from the dead was the beginning of the new creation of God, and by God's grace through union with Christ we have shared in this resurrection. We have therefore entered the new age and have already tasted its powers and its joys. This is the eschatological dimension of Christian conversion. Conversion is an integral part of the Great Renewal which God has begun, and which will be brought to a triumphant climax when Christ comes in his glory.

Conversion involves as well a break with the past so complete that it is spoken of in terms of death. We have been crucified with Christ. Through his cross we have died to the godless world, its outlook, and its standards. We have also "put off" like a soiled garment the old Adam, our former and fallen humanity. And Jesus warned us that this turning away from the past may involve painful sacrifices, even the loss of family and possessions (e.g., Luke 14:25ff).

It is vital to keep together these negative and positive aspects of conversion, the death and the resurrection, the putting off of the old and the putting on of the new. For we who died are alive again, but alive now with a new life lived in, for, and under Christ.

The lordship of Jesus Christ

We are clear that the fundamental meaning of conversion is a change of allegiance. Other gods and lords—idolatries every one—previously ruled over us. But now Jesus Christ is Lord. The governing principle of the converted life is that it is lived under the lordship of Christ or (for it comes to the same thing) in the Kingdom of God. His authority over us is total. So this new and liberating allegiance leads inevitably to a reappraisal of every aspect of our lives and in particular of our world view, our behavior, and our relationships.

First, our world view. We are agreed that the heart of every culture is a "religion" of some kind, even if it is an irreligious religion like Marxism. "Culture is religion made visible" (J. H. Bavinck). And "religion" is a whole cluster of basic beliefs and values, which is the reason why for our purposes we are using "world view" as an equivalent expression. True conversion to Christ is bound, therefore, to strike at the heart of our cultural inheritance. Jesus Christ insists on dislodging from the center of our world whatever idol previously reigned there, and occupying the throne himself. This is the radical change of allegiance which constitutes conversion, or at least its beginning. Then once Christ has taken his rightful place, everything else starts shifting. The shock waves flow from the center to the circumference. The convert has to rethink his or her fundamental convictions. This is *metanoia*, "repentance" viewed as a change of mind, the replacement of "the mind of the flesh" by "the mind of Christ." Of course, the development of an integrated Christian world view may take a lifetime, but it is there in essence from the start. If it does grow, the explosive consequences cannot be predicted.

Secondly, our behavior. The lordship of Jesus challenges our moral standards and whole ethical life style. Strictly speaking, this is not "repentance" but rather the "fruit that befits repentance" (Matt 3:8), the change of conduct which issues from a change of outlook. Both our minds and our wills must submit to the obedience of Christ (cf. 2 Cor 10:5; Matt 11:29, 30; John 13:13).

Listening to case studies of conversion we have been impressed by the primacy of love in the new convert's experience. Conversion delivers both from the inversion which is too preoccupied with self to bother about other people and from the fatalism which considers it impossible to help them. Conversion is spurious if it does not liberate us to love.

Thirdly, our relationships. Although the convert should do his utmost to avoid a break with nation, tribe and family, sometimes painful conflicts arise. It is clear also that conversion involves a transfer from one community to another, that is, from fallen humanity to God's new humanity. It happened from the very beginning on the Day of Pentecost: "Save yourselves from this crooked generation," Peter appealed. So those who received his message were baptized into the new society, devoted themselves to the new fellowship, and found that the Lord continued to add to their numbers daily (Acts 2:40-47). At the same time, their "transfer" from one group to another meant rather that they were spiritually distinct than that they were socially segregated. They did not abandon the world. On the contrary, they gained a new commitment to it, and went out into it to witness and to serve.

All of us should cherish great expectations of such radical conversions in our day, involving converts in a new mind, a new way of life, a new community, and a new mission, all under the lordship of Christ. Yet now we feel the need to make several qualifications.

The convert and his culture

Conversion should not "de-culturize" a convert. True, as we have seen, the Lord Jesus now holds his or her allegiance, and everything in the cultural context must come under his Lord's scrutiny. This applies to every culture, not just to those of Hindu, Buddhist, Muslim, or animistic cultures but also to the increasingly materialistic culture of the West. The critique may lead to a collision, as elements of the culture come under the judgment of Christ and have to be rejected. At this point, on the rebound, the convert may try to adopt the evangelist's culture instead; the attempt should be firmly but gently resisted.

The convert should be encouraged to see his or her relation to the past as a combination of rupture and continuity. However much new converts feel they need to renounce for the sake of Christ, they are still the same people with the same heritage and the same family. "Conversion does not un-make; it remakes." It is always tragic, though in some situations it is unavoidable, when a person's conversion to Christ is interpreted by others as treachery to his or her own cultural origins. If possible, in spite of the conflicts with their own culture, new converts should seek to identify with their culture's joys, hopes, pains, and struggles.

Case histories show that converts often pass through three stages: (1) "rejection" (when they see themselves as "new persons in Christ" and repudiate everything associated with their past); (2) "accommodation" (when they discover their ethnic and cultural heritage, with the temptation to compromise the new-found Christian faith in relation to their heritage); and (3) "the re-establishment of identity" (when either the rejection of the past or the accommodation to it may increase, or preferably, they may grow into a balanced self-awareness in Christ and in culture).

The power encounter

"Jesus is Lord" means more than that he is Lord of the individual convert's world view, standards and relationships, and more even than that he is Lord of culture. It means that he is Lord of the powers, having been exalted by the Father to universal sovereignty; principalities and powers having been made subject to him (1 Pet 3:22). A number of us, especially those from Asia, Africa, and Latin America, have spoken both of the reality of evil powers and of the necessity to demonstrate the supremacy of Jesus over them. For conversion involves a power encounter. People give their allegiance to Christ when they see that his power is superior to magic and voodoo, the curses and blessings of witch doctors, and the malevolence of evil spirits, and that his salvation is a real liberation from the power of evil and death.

Of course, some are questioning today whether a belief in spirits is compatible with our modern scientific understanding of the universe. We wish to affirm, therefore, against the mechanistic myth on which the typical Western world view rests, the reality of demonic intelligences which are concerned by all means, overt and covert, to discredit Jesus Christ and keep people from coming to him. We think it vital in evangelism in all cultures to teach the reality and hostility of demonic powers, and to proclaim that God has exalted Christ as Lord of all and that Christ, who really does possess all power, however we may fail to acknowledge this, can (as we proclaim him) break through any world-view in any mind to make his lordship known and bring about a radical change of heart and outlook.

We wish to emphasize that the power belongs to Christ. Power in human hands is always dangerous. We have called to mind the recurring theme of Paul's two letters to the Corinthians—that God's power, which is clearly seen in the cross of Christ, operates through human weakness (e.g., 1 Cor 1:18-2:5; 2 Cor 4:7; 12:9, 10). Worldly people worship power; Christians who have it know its perils. It is better to be weak, for then we are strong. We specially honor the Christian martyrs of recent days (e.g., in East Africa) who have renounced the way of power, and followed the way of the cross.

Individual and group conversions

Conversion should not be conceived as being invariably and only an individual experience, although that has been the pattern of Western expectation for many years. On the contrary, the covenant theme of the Old Testament and the household baptisms of the New should lead us to desire, work for, and expect both family and group conversions. Much important research has been undertaken in recent years into "people movements" from both theological and sociological perspectives. Theologically, we recognize the biblical emphasis on the solidarity of each ethnos, i.e., nation or people. Sociologically, we recognize that each society is composed of a variety of subgroups, subcultures or homogeneous units. It is evident that people receive the gospel most readily when it is presented to them in a manner which is appropriate—and not alien—to their culture, and when they can respond to it with and among their own people. Different societies have different procedures for making group decisions, e.g., by consensus, by the head of the family, or by a group of elders. We recognize the validity of the corporate dimension of conversion as part of the total process, as well as the necessity for each member of the group ultimately to share in it personally.

Is conversion sudden or gradual?

Conversion is often more gradual than traditional evangelical teaching has allowed. True, this may be only a dispute about words. Justification and regeneration, the one conveying a new status and the other a new life, are works of God and instantaneous, although we are not necessarily aware when they take place. Conversion, on the other hand, is our own action (moved by God's grace) of turning to God in penitence and faith. Although it may include a conscious crisis, it is often slow and sometimes laborious. Seen against the background of the Hebrew and Greek vocabulary, conversion is in essence a turning to God, which continues as all areas of life are brought in increasingly radical ways under the lordship of Christ. Conversion involves the Christian's complete transformation and total renewal in mind and character according to the likeness of Christ (Rom 12:1,2).

This progress does not always take place, however. We have given some thought to the sad phenomena called "backsliding" (a quiet slipping away from Christ) and "apostasy" (an open repudiation of him). These have a variety of causes. Some people turn away from Christ when they become disenchanted with the Church; others capitulate to the pressures of secularism or of their former culture. These facts challenge us both to proclaim a full gospel and to be more conscientious in nurturing converts in the faith and in training them for service.

One member of our Consultation has described his experience in terms of turning first to Christ (receiving his salvation and acknowledging his lordship), secondly to culture (rediscovering his natural origins and identity), and thirdly to the world (accepting the mission on which Christ sends him). We agree that conversion is often a complex experience, and that the biblical language of "turning" is used in different ways and contexts. At the same time, we all emphasize that personal commitment to Jesus Christ is foundational. In him alone we find salvation, new life, and personal identity. Conversion must also result in new attitudes and relationships, and lead to a responsible involvement in our church, our culture, and our world. Finally, conversion is a journey, a pilgrimage, with ever-new challenges, decisions, and returnings to the Lord as the constant point of reference, until he comes.

Questions for Discussion

1. Distinguish between "regeneration" and "conversion" according to the New Testament.

2. "Jesus is Lord." What does this mean for you in your own culture? What are the elements of your cultural heritage which you feel (a) you must, and (b) you need not, renounce for the sake of Christ?

3. What is sudden and what is (or may be) gradual in Christian conversion?

8. Church and Culture

In the process of church formation, as in the communication and reception of the gospel, the question of culture is vital. If the gospel must be contextualized, so must the church. Indeed, the sub-title of our Consultation has been "the contextualization of Word and Church in a missionary situation."

Older, traditional approaches

During the missionary expansion of the early part of the 19th century, it was generally assumed that churches "on the mission field" would be modeled on churches "at home." The tendency was to produce almost exact replicas. Gothic architecture, prayer book liturgies, clerical dress, musical instruments, hymns and tunes, decision-making processes, synods and committees, superintendents and archdeacons—all were exported and unimaginatively introduced into the new mission-founded churches. It should be added that these patterns were also eagerly adopted by the new Christians, determined not to be at any point behind their Western friends, whose habits and ways of worship they had been attentively watching. But all this was based on the false assumptions that the Bible gave specific instructions about such matters and that the home churches'

pattern of government, worship, ministry, and life were themselves exemplary.

In reaction to this monocultural export system, pioneer missionary thinkers like Henry Venn and Rufus Anderson in the middle of the last century and Roland Allen earlier in this century popularized the concept of "indigenous" churches, which would be "self-governing, self-supporting and self-propagating." They argued their case well. They pointed out that the policy of the apostle Paul was to plant churches, not to found mission stations. They also added pragmatic arguments to biblical ones, namely that indigeneity was indispensable to the church's growth in maturity and mission. Henry Venn confidently looked forward to the day when missions would hand over all responsibility to national churches, and then what he called "the euthanasia of the mission" would take place. These views gained wide acceptance and were immensely influential.

In our day, however, they are being criticized, not because of the ideal itself, but because of the way it has often been applied. Some missions, for example, have accepted the need for indigenous leadership and have then gone on to recruit and train local leaders, indoctrinating them (the word is harsh but not unfair) in Western ways of thought and procedure. These Westernized local leaders have then preserved a very Western-looking church, and the foreign orientation has persisted, only lightly cloaked by the appearance of indigeneity.

Now, therefore, a more radical concept of indigenous church life needs to be developed, by which each church may discover and express its selfhood as the body of Christ within its own culture.

The test of any model for helping churches develop appropriately, is whether it can enable God's people to capture in their hearts and minds the grand design of which their church is to be the local expression.

The dynamic equivalence model

Using the distinctions between "form" and "meaning," and between "formal correspondence" and "dynamic equivalence," which have been developed in translation theory and on which we have commented, it is being suggested that an analogy may be drawn between Bible translation and church formation. "Formal correspondence" speaks of a slavish imitation, whether in translating a word into another language or exporting a church model to another culture. Just as a "dynamic equivalence" translation, however, seeks to convey to contemporary readers meanings equivalent to those conveyed to the original readers, by using appropriate cultural forms, so would a "dynamic equivalence" church. It would look in its culture as a good Bible translation looks in its language. It would preserve the essential meanings and functions which the New Testament predicated of the church, but would seek to express these in forms equivalent to the originals but appropriate to the local culture.

We have all found this model helpful and suggestive, and we strongly affirm the ideals it seeks to express. It rightly rejects foreign imports and imitations, and rigid structures. It rightly looks to the New Testament for the principles of church formation, rather than to either tradition or culture, and it equally rightly looks to the local culture for the appropriate forms in which these principles should be expressed. All of us (even those who see limitations in the model) share the vision which it is trying to describe.

Thus, the New Testament indicates that the church is always a worshipping community, "a holy priesthood to offer spiritual sacrifices to God through Jesus Christ" (1 Pet 2:5), but forms of worship (including the presence or absence of different kinds of liturgy, ceremony, music, color, drama, etc.) will be developed by the church in keeping with indigenous culture. Similarly, the church is always a witnessing and a serving community, but its methods of evangelizm and its program of social involvement will vary. Again, God desires all churches to have pastoral oversight, but forms of government and ministry may differ widely, and the selection, training, ordination, service, dress, payment, and accountability of pastors will be determined by the church to accord with biblical principles and to suit the local culture.

The questions which are being asked about the "dynamic equivalence" model are whether by itself it is large enough and dynamic enough to provide all the guidance which is needed. The analogy between Bible translation and church formation is not exact. In the former the translator controls the work, and when the task is complete it is possible to make a comparison of the two texts. In the latter, however, the original to which an equivalent is being sought is not a detailed text but a series of glimpses of the early church in operation, making the comparison more difficult, and instead of a controlling translator, the whole community of faith must be involved. Further, a translator aims at personal objectivity, but when the local church is seeking to relate itself appropriately to the local culture, it finds objectivity almost impossible. In many situations it is caught in "an encounter between two civilizations" (that of its own society and that of the missionaries). Furthermore, it may have great difficulty in responding to the conflicting voices of the local community. Some clamor for change (in terms of literacy, education, technology, modern medicine, industrialization, etc.) while others insist on the conservation of the old culture and resist the arrival of a new day. It is asked whether the "dynamic equivalence" model is dynamic enough to face this kind of challenge.

The test of this or any other model for helping churches develop appropriately, is whether it can enable God's people to capture in their hearts and minds the grand design of which their church is to be the local expression. Every model presents only a partial picture. Local churches need to rely ultimately on the dynamic pressure of the Living Lord of history. For it is he who will guide his people in every age to develop their church life in such a way as both to obey the instructions he has given in Scripture and to reflect the good elements of their local culture.

The freedom of the church

If each church is to develop creatively in such a way as to find and express itself, it must be free to do so. This is its inalienable right. For each church is God's church. United to Christ, it is a dwelling place of God through his Spirit (Eph 2:22). Some missions and missionaries have been slow to recognize this and to accept its implications in the direction of indigenous forms and an every-member ministry. This is one of the many causes which have led to the formation of Independent Churches, notably in Africa, which are seeking new ways of self-expression in terms of local culture.

Although local church leaders have also sometimes impeded indigenous development, the chief blame lies elsewhere. It would not be fair to generalize. The situation has always been diverse. In earlier generations there were missions which never manifested a spirit of domination. In this century some churches have sprung up which have never been under missionary control, having enjoyed self-government from the start. In other cases missions have entirely surrendered their former power, so that some mission-founded churches are now fully autonomous, and many missions now work in genuine partnership with churches.

Yet this is not the whole picture. Other churches are still almost completely inhibited from developing their own identity and program by policies laid down from afar, by the introduction and continuation of foreign traditions, by the use of expatriate leadership, by alien decision-making processes, and especially by the manipulative use of money. Those who maintain such control may be genuinely unaware of the way in which their actions are regarded and experienced at the other end. They may be felt by the churches concerned to be a tyranny. The fact that this is neither intended nor realized illustrates perfectly how all of us (whether we know it or not) are involved in the culture which has made us what we are. We strongly oppose such "foreignness," wherever it exists, as a serious obstacle to maturity and mission, and a quenching of the Holy Spirit of God.

It was in protest against the continuance of foreign control that a few years ago the call was made to withdraw all missionaries. In this debate some of us want to avoid the word "moratorium" because it has become an emotive term and sometimes betrays a resentment against the very concept of "missionaries." Others of us wish to retain the word in order to emphasize the truth it expresses. To us it means not a rejection of missionary personnel and money in themselves, but only of their misuse in such a way as to suffocate local initiative. We all agree with the statement of the Lausanne Covenant that "a reduction of foreign missionaries and money…may sometimes be necessary to facilitate the national church's growth in self-reliance…" (para. 9).

Power structures and mission

What we have just written is part of a much wider problem, which we have not felt able to ignore. The contemporary world does not consist of isolated atomic societies, but is an interrelated global system of economic, political, technological, and ideological macro-structures, which undoubtedly results in much exploitation and oppression.

What has this got to do with mission? And why do we raise it here? Partly because it is the context within which the gospel must be preached to all nations today. Partly also because nearly all of us either belong to the Third World, or live and work there, or have done so, or have visited some countries in it. So we have seen with our own eyes the poverty of the masses, we feel for them and with them, and we have some understanding that their plight is due in part to an economic system which is controlled mostly by the North Atlantic countries (although others are now also involved). Those of us who are citizens of North American or European countries cannot avoid some feeling of embarrassment and shame, by reason of the oppression in which our countries in various degrees have been involved. Of course, we know that there is oppression in many countries today, and we oppose it everywhere. But now we are talking about ourselves, our own countries, and our responsibility as Christians. Most of the world's missionaries and missionary money come from these countries, often at great personal sacrifice. Yet we have to confess that some missionaries themselves reflect a neo-colonial attitude and even defend it, together with outposts of western power and exploitation such as Southern Africa.

So what should we do? The only honest response is to say that we do not know. Armchair criticism smacks of hypocrisy. We have no ready-made solutions to offer to this worldwide problem. Indeed, we feel victims of the system ourselves. And yet we are also part of it. So we feel able to make only these comments.

First, Jesus himself constantly identified with the poor and weak. We accept the obligation to follow in his footsteps in this matter as in all others. At least by the love which prays and gives we mean to strengthen our solidarity with them.

Jesus did more than identify, however. In his teaching and that of the apostles the corollary of good news to the oppressed was a word of judgment to the oppressor (e.g., Luke 6:24-26; Jas 5:1-6). We confess that in complex economic situations it is not easy to identify oppressors in order to denounce them without resorting to a shrill rhetoric which neither costs nor accomplishes anything. Nevertheless, we accept that there will be occasions when it is our Christian duty to speak out against injustice in the name of the Lord who is the God of justice as well as of justification. We shall seek from him the courage and wisdom to do so.

Thirdly, this Consultation has expressed its concern about syncretism in Third World churches. But we have not forgotten that Western churches fall prey to the same sin. Indeed, perhaps the most insidious form of syncretism in the world today is the attempt to mix a privatized gospel of personal forgiveness with a worldly (even demonic) attitude to wealth and power. We are not guiltless in this matter ourselves. Yet we desire to be integrated Christians for whom Jesus is truly Lord of all. So we who belong to, or come from, the West will examine ourselves and seek to purge ourselves of western-style syncretism. We agree that "the salvation we claim should be transforming us in the totality of our personal and social responsibilities. Faith without works is dead" (Lausanne Covenant, para. 5).

The danger of provincialism

We have emphasized that the Church must be allowed to indigenize itself, and to "celebrate, sing and dance" the gospel in its own cultural medium. At the same time, we wish to be alert to the dangers of this process. Some churches in all six continents go beyond a joyful and thankful discovery of their local cultural heritage, and either become boastful and assertive about it (a form of chauvinism) or even absolutize it (a form of idolatry). More common than either of these extremes, however, is "provincialism," that is, such a retreat into their own culture as cuts them adrift from the rest of the Church and from the wider world. This is a frequent stance in Western churches as well as in the Third World. It denies the God of creation and redemption. It is to proclaim one's freedom, only to enter another bondage. We draw attention to the three major reasons why we think this attitude should be avoided.

First, each church is part of the universal Church. The people of God are by his grace a unique multi-racial, multi-national, multi-cultural community. This community is God's new creation, his new humanity, in which Christ has abolished all barriers (see Eph 2 and 3). There is therefore no room for racism in the Christian society, or for tribalism—whether in its African form, or in the form of European social classes, or of the Indian caste system. Despite the Church's failures, this vision of a supra-ethnic community of love is not a romantic ideal, but a command of the Lord. Therefore, while rejoicing in our cultural inheritance and developing our own indigenous forms, we must always remember that our primary identity as Christians is not in our particular cultures but in the one Lord and his one Body (Eph 4:3-6).

Secondly, each church worships the living God of cultural diversity. If we thank him for our cultural heritage, we should thank him for others' also. Our church should never become so culture-bound that visitors from another culture do not feel welcome. Indeed, we believe it is enriching for Christians, if they have the opportunity, to develop a bi-cultural and even a multi-cultural existence, like the apostle Paul who was both a Hebrew of the Hebrews, a master of the Greek language, and a Roman citizen.

Thirdly, each church should enter into a "partnership...in giving and receiving" (Phil 4:15). No church is, or should try to become, self-sufficient. So churches should develop with each other relationships of prayer, fellowship, interchange of ministry and cooperation. Provided that we share the same central truths (including the supreme lordship of Christ, the authority of Scripture, the necessity of conversion, confidence in the power of the Holy Spirit, and the obligations of holiness and witness), we should be outgoing and not timid in seeking fellowship; and we should share our spiritual gifts and ministries, knowledge, skills, experience, and financial resources. The same principle applies to cultures. A church must be free to reject alien cultural forms and develop its own; it should also feel free to borrow from others. This way lies maturity.

One example of this concerns theology. Cross-cultural witnesses must not attempt to impose a ready-made theological tradition on the church in which they serve, either by personal teaching or by literature or by controlling seminary and Bible college curricula. For every theological tradition both contains elements which are biblically questionable and have been ecclesiastically divisive and omits elements which, while they might be of no great consequence in the country where they originated, may be of immense importance in other contexts. At the same time, although missionaries ought not to impose their own tradition on others, they also ought not to deny them access to it (in the form of books, confessions, catechism, liturgies and hymns), since it doubtless represents a rich heritage of faith. Moreover, although the theological controversies of the older churches should not be exported to the younger churches, yet an understanding of the issues, and of the work of the Holy Spirit in the unfolding history of Christian doctrine, should help to protect them from unprofitable repetition of the same battles.

Thus we should seek with equal care to avoid theological imperialism or theological provincialism. A church's theology should be developed by the community of faith out of the Scripture in interaction with other theologies of the past and present, and with the local culture and its needs.

The danger of syncretism

As the church seeks to express its life in local cultural forms, it soon has to face the problem of cultural elements which either are evil or have evil associations. How should the church react to these? Elements which are intrinsically false or evil clearly cannot be assimilated into Christianity without a lapse into syncretism. This is a danger for all churches in all cultures. If the evil is in the association only, however, we believe it is right to seek to "baptize" it into Christ. It is the principle on which William Booth operated when he set Christian words to popular music, asking why the devil should have all the best tunes. Thus many African churches now use drums to summon people to worship, although previously they were unacceptable, as being associated with war dances and mediumistic rites.

Yet this principle raises problems. In a proper reaction against foreigners, an improper flirtation with the demonic element of local culture sometimes takes place. So the church, being first and foremost a servant of Jesus Christ, must learn to scrutinize all culture, both foreign and local, in the light of his lordship and God's revelation. By what guidelines, therefore, does a church accept or reject culture traits in the process of contextualization? How does it prevent or detect and eliminate heresy (wrong teaching) and syncretism (harmful carry-overs from the old way of life)? How does it protect itself from becoming a "folk church" in which church and society are virtually synonymous?

One particular model we have studied is that of the church in Bali, Indonesia, which is now about 40 years old. Its experience has provided the following guidelines:

The believing community first searched the Scriptures and learned from them many important biblical truths. They then observed that other churches (e.g., round the Mediterranean) used architecture to symbolize Christian truth. This was important because the Balinese are very "visual" people and value visible signs. So it was decided, for example, to express their affirmation of faith in the Trinity in a Balinese-style three-tiered roof for their church buildings.

The symbol was first considered by the council of elders who, after studying both biblical and cultural factors, recommended it to local congregations.

The detection and elimination of heresy followed a similar pattern. When believers suspected an error in life or teaching, they would report it to an elder, who would take it to the council of elders. Having considered the matter, they in their turn passed their recommendations to the local churches who had the final word.

> The church, being first and foremost a servant of Jesus Christ, must learn to scrutinize all culture, both foreign and local, in the light of His lordship and God's revelation.

What was the most important safeguard of the church? To this question the answer was: "we believe that Jesus Christ is Lord and Master of all powers." By preaching his power, "the same yesterday and today and forever," by insisting at all times on the normative nature of the Scriptures, by entrusting elders with the obligation to reflect on Scripture and culture, by breaking down all barriers to fellowship, and by building into structures, catechism, art forms, drama, etc., constant reminders of the exalted position of Jesus Christ, his church has been preserved in truth and holiness.

Sometimes, in different parts of the world, a cultural element may be adopted which deeply disturbs oversensitive consciences, especially those of new converts. This is the problem of the "weaker brother" of whom Paul writes in connection with idol-meats. Since idols were nothing, Paul himself had liberty of conscience to eat these meats. But for the sake of "weaker" Christians with a less well-educated conscience, who would be offended to see him eat, he refrained, at least in specific situations in which such offense might be caused. The principle still applies today. Scripture takes conscience seriously and tells us not to violate it. It needs to be educated in order to become "strong," but while it remains "weak" it must be respected. A strong conscience will give us freedom; but love limits liberty.

The church's influence on culture

We deplore the pessimism which leads some Christians to disapprove of active cultural engagement in the world, and the defeatism which persuades others that they could do no good there anyway and should therefore wait in inactivity for Christ to put things right when he comes. Many historical examples could be given, drawn from different ages and countries, of the powerful influence which—under God—the church has exerted on a prevailing culture, purging, claiming, and beautifying it for Christ. Though all such attempts have had defects, they do not prove the enterprise mistaken.

We prefer, however, to base the Church's cultural responsibility on Scripture rather than on history. We have reminded ourselves that our fellow men and women are made in God's image, and that we are commanded to honor, love, and serve them in every sphere of life. To this argument from God's creation we add another from his kingdom which broke into the world through Jesus Christ. All authority belongs to Christ. He is Lord of both universe and Church. And he has sent us into the world to be its salt and light. As his new community, he expects us to permeate society.

Thus we are to challenge what is evil and affirm what is good; to welcome and seek to promote all that is wholesome and enriching in art, science, technology, agriculture, industry, education, community development and social welfare; to denounce injustice and support the powerless and the oppressed; to spread the good news of Jesus Christ, which is the most liberating and humanizing force in the world; and to actively engage in good works of love. Although, in social and cultural activity as in evangelism, we must leave the results to God, we are confident that he will bless our endeavors and use them to develop in our community a new consciousness of what is "true, noble, right,

pure, lovely, and honorable" (Phil 4:8, TEV). Of course, the Church cannot impose Christian standards on an unwilling society, but it can commend them by both argument and example. All this will bring glory to God and greater opportunities of humanness to our fellow human being whom he made and loves. As the Lausanne Covenant put it, "churches must seek to transform and enrich culture, all for the glory of God" (para. 10).

Nevertheless, naive optimism is as foolish as dark pessimism. In place of both, we seek a sober Christian realism. On the one hand, Jesus Christ reigns. On the other, he has not yet destroyed the forces of evil; they still rampage. So in every culture Christians find themselves in a situation of conflict and often of suffering. We are called to fight against the "cosmic powers of this dark age" (Eph 6:12, TEV). So we need each other. We must put on all God's armor, and especially the mighty weapon of believing prayer. We also remember the warnings of Christ and his apostles that before the end there will be an unprecedented outbreak of wickedness and violence. Some events and developments in our contemporary world indicate that the spirit of the coming Antichrist is already at work not only in the non-Christian world, but both in our own partially Christianized societies and even in the churches themselves. "We therefore reject as a proud, self-confident dream the notion that man can ever build a utopia on earth" (Lausanne Covenant, para. 15), and as a groundless fantasy that society is going to evolve into perfection.

Instead, while energetically laboring on earth, we look forward with joyful anticipation to the return of Christ, and to the new heavens and new earth in which righteousness will dwell. For then not only will culture be transformed, as the nations bring their glory into the New Jerusalem (Rev 21:24-26) but the whole creation will be liberated from its present bondage of futility, decay and pain, so as to share the glorious freedom of God's children (Rom 8:18-25, TEV). Then at last every knee will bow to Christ and every tongue openly proclaim that he is Lord, to the glory of God the Father (Phil 2:9-11).

Questions for Discussion

1. Is your local church "free" to develop its own selfhood? If not, what forces are hindering it?

2. Some hard things have been said in this text about "power-structures." Do you agree? If so, can you do anything about it?

3. "Provincialism" and "syncretism" are both mistakes of a church which is trying to express its identity in local cultural forms. Is your church making either mistake? How can they be avoided without repudiating indigenous culture?

4. Should the church in your country be doing more to "transform and enrich" its national culture? If so, in what way?

9. Culture, Christian Ethics and Life Style

Having considered some of the cultural factors in Christian conversion, we come finally to the relations between culture and Christian ethical behavior. For the new life Christ gives his people is bound to issue a new life style.

Christ-centeredness and Christ-likeness

One of the themes running right through our Consultation has been the supreme Lordship of Jesus Christ. He is Lord of the universe and the Church; he is Lord of the individual believer also. We find ourselves gripped by the love of Christ. It hems us in and leaves us no escape. Because we enjoy newness of life through his death for us, we have no alternative (and desire none) but to live for him who died for us and rose again (2 Cor 5:14, 15). Our first loyalty is to him, to seek to please him, to live a life worthy of him, and to obey him. This necessitates the renunciation of all lesser loyalties. So we are forbidden to conform ourselves to this world's standards, that is, to any prevailing culture which fails to honor God, and are commanded instead to be transformed in our conduct by renewed minds which perceive the will of God.

God's will was perfectly obeyed by Jesus. Therefore, "the most outstanding thing about a Christian should not be his culture, but his Christlikeness." As the mid-second century *Letter to Diognetus* puts it: "Christians are not distinguished from the rest of mankind by country or by speech or by customs…they follow the customs of the land in clothing and food and other matters of daily life, yet the condition of citizenship which they exhibit is wonderful…in a word, what the soul is in the body, that Christians are in the world."

Moral standards and cultural practices

Culture is never static. It varies both from place to place and from time to time. And throughout the long history of the church in different countries, Christianity has, in some measure, destroyed culture, preserved it, and in the end created a new culture in place of the old. So everywhere Christians need to think seriously about just how their new life in Christ should relate to contemporary culture.

In our Consultation's preliminary papers two rather similar models were set before us. One suggested that there are several categories of customs which need to be distinguished. The first includes those practices which the convert will be expected to renounce immediately as being wholly incompatible with the Christian gospel (e.g., idolatry, the possession of slaves, witchcraft and sorcery, head hunting, blood feuds, ritual prostitution, and all personal discriminations based on race, color, class or caste). A second category might comprise institutionalized customs which could be tolerated for a while but would be expected to disappear gradually (e.g., systems of caste, slavery, and polygamy). A third category might relate to marriage traditions, especially questions of consanguinity, on which the churches are divided, while into a fourth category would be put the "matters indifferent" which relate only to customs and not to morals, and therefore may be preserved without any compromise (e.g., eating and bathing customs, forms of public greeting to the opposite sex, hair and dress styles, etc.).

The second model we have considered distinguishes between "direct" and "indirect" encounters between Christ and culture, which correspond approximately to the first and second categories of the other model. Applied to 19th century Fiji in the case-study presented to us, it was assumed that there would be "direct encounter" with such inhuman practices as cannibalism, widow-strangling, infanticide, and patricide, and that converts would be expected to abandon these customs upon conversion. "Indirect" encounter would take place, however, either when the moral issue was not so clear-cut (e.g., some marriage customs, initiation rites, festivals and musical celebrations involving song, dance and instruments) or when it becomes apparent only after the convert has begun to work out his or her new faith in the applied Christian life. Some of these practices will not need to be discarded, but rather to be purged of unclean elements and invested with Christian meaning. Old customs can be given new symbolism, old dances can celebrate new blessings, and old crafts can serve new purposes. To borrow an expression from the Old Testament, swords can be hammered into ploughs and spears into pruning knives.

The Lausanne Covenant said: "The Gospel does not presuppose the superiority of any culture to another, but evaluates all cultures according to its own criteria of truth and righteousness, and insists on moral absolutes in every culture" (para. 10). We wish to endorse this, and to emphasize that even in this present age of relativity moral absolutes remain. Indeed, churches which study the Scriptures should not find it difficult to discern what belongs to the first or "direct encounter" category. Scriptural principles under the guidance of the Holy Spirit will also guide them regarding the category of "indirect encounter." An additional test proposed is to ask whether a practice enhances or diminishes human life.

It will be seen that our studies have focused mainly on situations where younger churches have to take up a moral stance against certain evils. But we have been reminded that the Church needs to confront evil in Western culture too. In the 20th century West, often more sophisticated but no less horrible examples of the evils which were opposed in

19th century Fiji exist. Parallel to cannibalism is social injustice which "eats" the poor; to widow-strangling, the oppression of women; to infanticide, abortion; to patricide, a criminal neglect of senior citizens; to tribal wars, World Wars I and II; and to ritual prostitution, sexual promiscuity. In considering this parallelism, it is necessary to remember both the added guilt adhering to the nominally Christian nations, and also the courageous Christian protest against such evils, and the immense (though incomplete) successes which have been won in mitigating these evils. Evil takes many forms, but it is universal, and wherever it appears Christians must confront and repudiate it.

The process of cultural change

It is not enough for converts to make a personal renunciation of the evils in their culture; the whole church needs to work for their elimination. Hence the importance of asking how cultures change under the influence of the gospel. Of course, the evil and the demonic are deeply entrenched in most cultures, and yet Scripture calls for national repentance and reform, and history records numerous cases of cultural change for the better. In fact, in some cases culture is not as resistant to necessary change as it may appear. Great care is needed, however, when seeking to initiate it.

First, "people change as and when they want to." This seems to be axiomatic. Further, they want to change only when they perceive the positive benefits which change will bring them. These will need to be carefully argued and patiently demonstrated,

whether Christians are advocating in a developing country the benefits of literacy or the value of clean water, or in a Western country the importance of stable marriage and family life.

Secondly, cross-cultural witnesses in the Third World need to have great respect for the in-built mechanisms of social change in general, and for the "correct procedures of innovation" in each particular culture.

Thirdly, it is important to remember that virtually all customs perform important functions within the culture, and that even socially undesirable practices may perform "constructive" functions. That being so, a custom should never be abolished without first discerning its function and then substituting another custom which performs the same function. For example, it may be right to wish to see abolished some of the initiatory rites associated with the circumcision of adolescents and some of the forms of sex education which accompany it. This is not to deny that there is much of value in the processes of initiation; great care must be taken to see that adequate substitutes are provided for the rites and forms of initiation which the Christian conscience would desire to see abolished.

Fourthly, it is essential to recognize that some cultural practices have a theological undergirding. When this is so, the culture will change only when the theology changes. Thus, if widows are killed in order that their husbands may not enter the next world unattended, or if older people are killed before senility overtakes them, in order that in the next world they may be strong enough to fight and hunt, then such killings, because founded on a false

eschatology, will be abandoned only when a better alternative, the Christian hope, is accepted in its place.

Questions for Discussion

1. Can "Christ-likeness" be recognized in every culture? What are its ingredients?

2. In your own culture, what would you expect a new convert to renounce immediately?

3. Take some "institutionalized custom" in your country which Christians hope will "disappear gradually" (e.g., polygamy, the caste system, easy divorce, or some form of oppression). What active steps should Christians be taking to work for change?

Conclusion

Our Consultation has left us in no doubt of the pervasive importance of culture. The writing and the reading of the Bible, the presentation of the gospel, conversion, church and conduct—all these are influenced by culture. It is essential, therefore, that all churches contextualize the gospel in order to share it effectively in their own culture. For this task of evangelization, we all know our urgent need of the ministry of the Holy Spirit. He is the Spirit of truth who can teach each church how to relate to the culture which envelops it. He is also the Spirit of love, and love is "the language—which is understood in every culture of man." So may God fill us with his Spirit! Then, speaking the truth in love, we shall grow up into Christ who is the head of the Body, to the everlasting glory of God (Eph 4:15).

NOTE: Unattributed quotations in this report have been drawn from various papers presented at this Consultation.

THE
STRATEGIC
PERSPECTIVE

Finishing the Task:
The Unreached Peoples Challenge

Ralph D. Winter and Bruce A. Koch

After serving ten years as a missionary among Mayan Indians in the highlands of Guatemala, Winter was called to be a Professor of Missions at the newly established School of World Mission at Fuller Theological Seminary. After ten years there, he and his wife, Roberta, founded a mission society called the Frontier Mission Fellowship (FMF) in Pasadena, California. He is the General Director of the Frontier Mission Fellowship. See the expanded biographical sketch at the end of the book.

Bruce A. Koch earned a B.A. in Cultural Anthropology from the University of Utah before joining the Frontier Mission Fellowship in 1988. As an FMF member, he has served in a wide variety of roles ranging from Personnel Director to software developer. Bruce conducted an ethnographic survey of a large unevangelized city, using both anthropological and missiological perspectives.

"Look at the nations and watch—and be utterly amazed. For I am going to do something in your days that you would not believe, even if you were told." (Habakkuk 1:5)

God's promise to bless all the "families of the earth," first given to Abraham 4,000 years ago, is becoming a reality at a pace "you would not believe." Although some may dispute some of the details, the overall trend is indisputable. Biblical faith is growing and spreading to the ends of the earth as never before in history.

The Amazing Progress of the Gospel

One of every ten people on the planet is of the Bible-reading, Bible-believing stream of Christianity. The number of believers in what used to be "mission fields" now surpasses the number of believers in the countries from which missionaries were originally sent. In fact, more missionaries are now sent from non-Western churches than from the traditional mission-sending bases in the West. The Protestant growth rate in Latin America is well over three times the biological growth rate.

Believers as a Percentage of Total World Population in the 20th Century

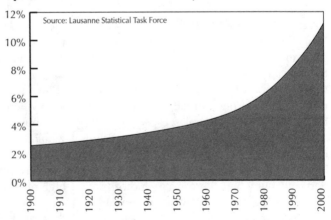

Source: Lausanne Statistical Task Force

It took 18 centuries for dedicated believers to grow from 0% of the world's population to 2.5% in 1900, only 70 years to grow from 2.5% to 5% in 1970, and just the last 30 years to grow from 5% to 11.2% of the world population. Now for the first time in history, there is one believer for every nine people worldwide who aren't believers.

E-Scale

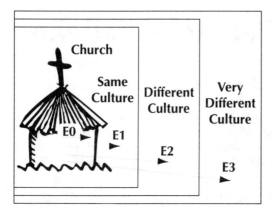

P-Scale

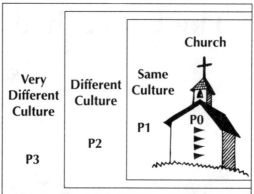

The **E-Scale** helps compare the cultural distances that Christians need to move in order to communicate the gospel with others. E0 refers to evangelism of church-going Christians. E1 extends to the very same culture through one barrier, that of "church culture." E2 evangelism presses into a close, but still different, culture. E3 evangelism pushes to very different cultures.

The **P-Scale** is more than a mirror of the E-Scale. The P-Scale helps compare the different cultural distances that potential converts need to move in order to join the nearest church.

Protestants in China grew from about one million to over 80 million believers in less than 50 years, with most of that growth occurring in just the last few decades. In the 1980s, Nepal was still a staunch Hindu kingdom with only a small persecuted church. Today there are hundreds of thousands of believers and churches have been started within each of the more than 100 distinct people groups.

Tragic Reality:
Two Billion Still Cut Off

While this amazing progress of the gospel gives much cause for rejoicing, it obscures a tragic reality. How could that be? The fact is that the gospel often expands within a community but does not normally "jump" across boundaries between peoples, especially boundaries that are created by hate or prejudice. People can influence their "near neighbors" whose language and culture they understand, but where there is a prejudice boundary, religious faith, which is almost always bound up with many cultural features of the first group, simply does not easily "jump" to the next group, unless that group desires to adopt the other's culture in preference to its own.

So what does this mean? If all the members of every church in the world were to bring every one of their friends and relatives within the same cultural group to obedient faith in Christ, and they in turn were able to bring all their friends and relatives to Christ and so on, no matter how much time you allow, there would still be billions who would never come to faith. They would be held at a distance from the gospel by boundaries of prejudice and culture. The church does not readily grow within peoples where relevant churches do not exist. One third of the individuals in the world live within peoples with no church. They are no more spiritually "lost" than your cousin who has never gone to church, but unlike your cousin, there is no church made up of people like themselves with whom they can fellowship.

Thus, while there are still tens of millions who have never heard the name "Jesus" at all, there are hundreds of millions more who may have heard of Jesus, and may even have high regard for Him, but who cannot see a way to become His disciples. Standing before them are barriers ranging from the relatively trivial to the seemingly insurmountable, many of them beyond the demands of the gospel. Cornelius in Acts 10 would have had to cross the barrier of circumcision as an adult—a painful and actually dangerous price to pay for entrance into fellowship with

Regular Missions and Frontier Missions

E-Scale: Evangelist's Cultural Distance from Potential Convert

				Less ◄	► Greater	
P-Scale	People without a church whose culture is very different from that of the nearest group with a church.	**P3**	Unreached		III. Frontier Mission	
	People without a church whose culture is similar to a people with a church.	**P2**				
	A people whose culture contains a local church.	**P1**	Reached	I. Evangelism	II. Regular Mission	
	People participating in a local culturally relevant church.	**P0**				

P-Scale: People Group's Cultural Distance from Nearest Church

Greater ▲ / Less ▼

	Mono-cultural		Cross-cultural	
	E0	**E1**	**E2**	**E3**

E0: Renewal evangelism of church members.
E1: Evangelism of non-Christians with no contact with the church.
E2: Evangelism of non-Christians in a similar but different culture.
E3: Evangelism in a completely different culture.

E-Scale

I. Evangelism: by a same-culture worker, where the missiological breakthrough of a viable church has already taken place.

II. Regular Missions: cross-cultural evangelism by a different-culture worker, in association with same-culture workers if possible, where a missiological breakthrough has already taken place.

III. Frontier Missions: cross-cultural evangelism is essential, since no missiological breakthrough has yet been made.

Jewish believers. A Muslim Turk similarly faces huge obstacles if he were to become a "Christian." All his life he has been told, "To be a Turk is to be a Muslim." To him, Christianity is the religion of the barbarian "Infidel" Crusaders who brutally ravaged the land and peoples of Turkey, Muslim and Christian alike. To become a Christian is to become a traitor, turning his back on his family, community, and country.

"A Witness to All the Nations"

We shouldn't really be surprised to see the thrilling advances of the gospel all over the world. That is exactly what Jesus said would take place, "And this gospel of the kingdom shall be preached in the whole world for a witness to *all the nations*, and then the end shall come" (Matthew 24:14). A close look at the end of this verse says a lot about what we should watch and work for at the end of the age. Jesus says that as the missionary task is completed, there will be "a witness to all the nations."

By "witness" Jesus was saying that the "gospel of the kingdom" will be established in open view throughout entire human communities. The gospel of the kingdom is Christ prevailing over evil, liberating people so that they can live obediently free under His mastery and blessing. God wants a persuasive display of that kingdom victory exhibited in every people. What better exhibit of God's kingdom than a community of people who are living under Christ's kingship? That's why we should aim at church planting movements within every people. While not the only way to glorify God, nothing puts Christ's lordship on display like a community of people dedicated to follow Him.

By the phrase "all the nations," Jesus was not referring at all to countries or nation-states. The wording he chose (the Greek word *ethne*) instead points to the ethnicities, the languages and the extended families which constitute the peoples of the earth.

Who are these peoples? Jesus did not provide a list of the peoples. He did not define the idea of peoples with precise detail. What matters most is not that the peoples can be *counted*, but that the missionary task will be *completed* within all the peoples of the earth. We'll know we are finished only when a visible testimony to the gospel of the kingdom—a church planting movement—has been established within every people.

FOUR DIFFERENT APPROACHES TO PEOPLE GROUP THINKING

In order to work together strategically, mission leaders have been refining the concept of "people groups" as a rough measure of our progress toward completing the entire task. There are four useful ways of looking at the idea of people groups: *Blocs of peoples, ethnolinguistic peoples, sociopeoples, and unimax peoples.* The first two are especially useful for summarizing the total task and developing strategies and partnerships to approach known peoples. The latter two are more useful for those who are on the field working to establish churches. Each is of significant value and corresponds to a distinct aspect of strategic thinking. Only one allows us to speak of closure of the essential mission task, in the sense that every person has a reasonable opportunity to respond to the gospel.

1) Blocs of peoples for global level perspective and strategies

Blocs of peoples are a limited number of summary categories into which we can place peoples in order to analyze them.

Major Cultural Blocs: We have grouped peoples, particularly "unreached" peoples, along major cultural lines according to the predominant religion within the group. The major cultural blocs of unreached peoples were: Muslim, Hindu, Buddhist, Tribal, Chinese, and Others.[1] This model allows us to summarize the remaining task in relation to the potential mission force.

Affinity Blocs: Patrick Johnstone has suggested another model which combines sets of closely related ethnolinguistic peoples into "people clusters" and further combines people clusters into "affinity blocs" based on language, history, culture, etc. The 12 blocs

that comprise the majority of the least evangelized peoples[2] are: African Sahel, Cushitic, Arab World, Iranian, Turkic, South Asian, Tibetan, East Asian, South East Asian, Malay, and Eurasian. Combining groups along these lines enables mission organizations to begin exploring ways of establishing strategic partnerships to reach related peoples.[3]

2) Ethnolinguistic peoples for mobilization and preparation

An ethnolinguistic people is an ethnic or racial group distinguished by its self-identity with traditions of common descent, history, customs, and language.

The Laz people from the Black Sea region of Turkey, for example, are easily identified by other Turks not only by their distinctive facial features but also by their unique "romantic" pronunciation of Turkish.

Sometimes what appears initially to be a single ethnolinguistic group turns out, in fact, to be many more. Cameron Townsend, the founder of Wycliffe, began his Bible translation work with the Cakchiquel of Guatemala. The translators who followed him discovered that the Cakchiquel could not be reached with one translation but would, in fact, require translations for six distinct dialects. It is likely that if they were producing gospel cassettes rather than written translations, they would have to target even more dialects. Cultural prejudices and differences in pronunciation often make people unwilling to listen to a message spoken by a member of a different group even though the message appears the same on the printed page.

Recent cooperative efforts among mission researchers have produced fairly comprehensive lists of ethnolinguistic peoples. These lists have given a great boost to the cause of frontier mission. Much of the information is being used to make profiles and other relevant information widely available through printed media and the world-wide web.[4]

People blocs and ethnolinguistic lists give us a simple way to identify peoples and make the larger body of Christ aware of their existence and the need to reach them. The ethnolinguistic approach stimulates prayer and initial planning for specific peoples leading to serious strategic efforts to evangelize them.

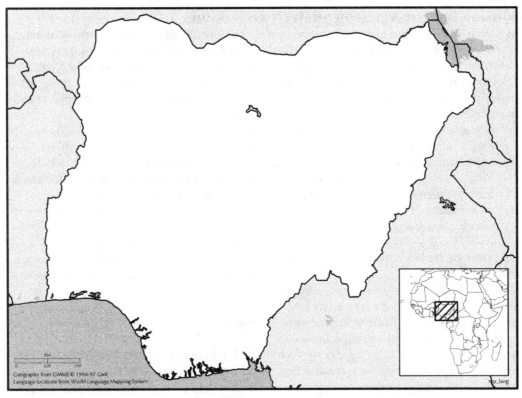

Political Boundaries: Nigeria and Surrounding Countries

Ethnolinguistic Peoples by Language of the Same Area

Mission Leaders Agree on Strategic Definitions

In March 1982 a group of mission leaders came together in Chicago for a meeting sponsored by the Lausanne Strategy Working Group. It was designed to help bring clarity and definition to the remaining missionary task. At no time before or since this meeting has as large or as representative a group gathered for two days to focus specifically upon the necessary definitions for a strategy to reach the unreached peoples. Two basic definitions came from this meeting:

1. **A People Group** is "a significantly large grouping of individuals who perceive themselves to have a common affinity for one another because of their shared language, religion, ethnicity, residence, occupation, class or caste, situation, etc., or combinations of these." *For evangelistic purposes it is "the largest group within which the gospel can spread as a church planting movement without encountering barriers of understanding or acceptance."*

2. **An *Unreached* People Group** is "a people group within which there is no indigenous community of believing Christians able to evangelize this people group."

3) Sociopeoples and preliminary evangelism

A sociopeople is a relatively small association of peers who have an affinity for one another based upon a shared interest, activity, or occupation.

Once we actually send long-term missionaries to a pioneer mission field, they have to learn a great deal just to be able to live, communicate, and better understand the target people. After the initial phase of cultural learning and adaption, the question remains as to how to begin to establish a church within that people.

Quite often we can effectively evangelize individuals by starting a Bible study or a small prayer group within these specialized groups. The group may be women who wash at the river, taxicab drivers, college students living in dorms, or new arrivals in the big city from a particular rural group. There are almost unlimited potential opportunities for this type of group evangelism in our world today. For mission purposes, we can work with sociopeoples for preliminary evangelism as an intermediate bridge to long-range church planting goals.

Thus, approaching a sociopeople can be strategic in giving a focus for ministry among a specific sub-set of the larger society as a first step to full-blown church planting. Some types of groups may prove to be especially helpful when establishing churches, while others may hinder the process. Natural leaders and Bible teachers for churches might be discovered by first reaching businessmen or teachers. Some have even managed to be effective among religious leaders such as Buddhist monks and Muslim mullahs, who are already recognized as spiritual leaders. On the other hand, you could choose the wrong group, such as focusing on children's ministry for initial evangelism within a people, which in nearly every case would be interpreted as a threat to their natural families.

4) Unimax peoples for people movements to Christ

*A unimax people is the **max**imum sized group sufficiently **uni**fied to be the target of a single people movement to Christ, where "unified" refers to the fact that there are no significant barriers of either understanding or acceptance to stop the spread of the gospel.*

In 1982, mission leaders hammered out a useful definition for a "people group."

For evangelistic purposes [a people group] is *"the largest group within which the gospel can spread as a church planting movement without encountering barriers of understanding or acceptance."* (see above)

The term "unreached peoples"[5] is used widely today to refer to ethnolinguistic peoples, which are based on other criteria and would normally be larger in size than groups as defined in the 1982 definition. To avoid confusion and help clarify the missiological task before us, we can use the term *unimax peoples* to distinguish the kind of group intended by the 1982 definitions.

Jungle tribes and other small, geographically remote peoples are almost always single unimax peoples. Discovering unimax realities within larger ethnolinguistic peoples in complex societies is a bit more challenging.

While language is often a primary means by which a person understands his or her cultural identity, in order to reach all peoples we must consider other factors that keep peoples separate. Religion, class distinctions, education, political and ideological convictions, historical enmity between clans or tribes, customs and behaviors, etc., all have potential to develop strong cultural boundaries within ethnolinguistic clusters of unimax peoples. This fact alone helps to explain the differing numbers for the totals of "unreached peoples."

For example, India cannot be approached on an ethnolinguistic basis alone. In addition to over 1600 major languages and dialects, India is further divided by religion, caste and other socio-cultural barriers. A sociological survey in 1991 identified 4,635 peoples in India alone.

Sadly, neighboring groups often hate and fear each other. Thus, in the early stages of evangelism such groups often refuse to become part of the same "people movement" church. Rivalries between major clans among the Muslim Somali people are so severe that they have almost dragged the entire country into ruin. In the early stages of evangelism and church planting, such simmering hostilities will likely mean that such groups can most effectively be approached with the gospel message separately. The bright hope of the gospel is, of course, that new Christ-following movements in such settings of strife will work for the healing of enmities between peoples.

Indeed, history shows that eventually a host of smaller hostile groups, once they become Christian, start to coalesce into larger groups. For example, at the time Christianity first began to be adopted in the Scandinavian area, hundreds of mutually hostile tribes inhabited the region. The Norwegian, Swedish and Danish spheres today are the result of widespread reconciliation and consequent unification resulting from the adoption of Christian faith on the part of many smaller, formerly warring groups.

The first three approaches to people group thinking—as blocs, as ethnolinguistic peoples, and as sociopeoples—are each helpful in understanding and responding to the task to which Christ has commissioned us. Yet they all, in one way or another, point the way toward beginnings. This fourth (unimax) way of looking at peoples has more to do with finishing, not in the sense that there is nothing left to do, but in the sense that the essential first step for the gospel to flourish within a people has been accomplished. The unimax approach to peoples can help us press on toward closure—our corporate *finishing* of what is completable about Christ's mission mandate.

The value of the unimax approach lies in the way it identifies boundaries hindering the flow of the gospel, while at the same time firing the ambitions of dedicated Christians to pursue the evangelization of the peoples beyond those boundaries, leaving no smaller group sealed off within a larger group.

Can They Be Counted?

These often subtle but powerful socio-cultural barriers exist within groups which often appear unified to outside observers. Some have dismissed the usefulness of the unimax concept because socio-cultural prejudice barriers cannot easily be identified or precisely

Four Approaches to People Group Thinking

Types of People	Blocs	Ethnolinguistic Peoples	Unimax Peoples	Sociopeoples
Composition	broad categories	one or more related groups	inter-generational	peers
What Defines Group	religious-cultural spheres	linguistic, ethnic & political boundaries	cultural prejudices	activities or interests
How Identified	available published data	available published data	discovered on site	discovered on site
Strategic Significance	global overview	mobilization and strategy	church planting	small group evangelism
Quantity	8 major cultural blocs	approx. 3,000 "unevangelized"	est. 10,000 "unreached"	number unknown

quantified. But even though intangible "prejudice barriers" cannot be quantified these factors are not irrelevant. What could be more important than identifying and penetrating every barrier which holds people from following Christ?

The unimax peoples definition was never intended to quantify precisely the total task. Instead, it helps us recognize when the unreached peoples task is finished and identify where the that task is not yet begun.

Approaching Peoples Cautiously

Each of these four approaches to various kinds of peoples has a proper and valuable use. *Blocs* help us sum up the task. The *ethnolinguistic* approach helps us mobilize. *Sociopeoples* help us begin evangelizing. But beware of focusing church planting efforts on *sociopeoples* or ethnolinguistic peoples which simply appear on a list. There is often discouragement or, even worse, a deliberate, typically American "people blindness" as workers find that there are many more people groups then they expected to find. The opposite can happen, too. Sometimes the very same people group is listed twice because it is found on both sides of a political boundary. In actuality, it is the same people group. It may only need a single church planting effort bridging the political line. For example, Uzbek groups are reported in 20 countries in addition to those in Uzbekistan.

On the other hand, the country of Uzbekistan reports 56 groups within it that do not speak Uzbek, and only one (very large group—15 million strong) that does! It is almost certainly true that this "one" large group represents a number of different groups that need to be reached separately.

Using political boundaries to distinguish people groups is like dropping cookie cutters down on the geographical distribution of a people group, then calling the pieces within each cutter a different type of dough. Granted in many cases of extended separation groups do become distinct—especially if new migration ceases—but not often antagonistic. In much of the developing world, the concept of political separation is quite artificial since borders are often quite permeable.

Consider the challenge of the Kurds; these fiercely independent people are found in a homeland that spans at least five countries: Turkey, Iran, Iraq, Syria, and Azerbaijan. For the sake of mission strategy, they are certainly not just one people group. They are not even just seven groups. In addition to having four major language subgroups, traditional rivalries keep them fighting one another even when you would think they would unite to fight non-Kurds for the sake of a Kurdish homeland.

Missionaries need to be aware of the possibility, as in the case of the Kurds, that peoples are not necessarily unified even if millions are in one country. Yet, smaller populations of Kurds found in significant numbers in 13 countries outside of the "Kurdistan" homeland are potentially strategic "bridge" populations back to groups in their homeland area. And those who are dislocated from their natural homeland are often more open to the gospel. Once a remote segment of a larger group comes to accept Christ, it may become an effective bridge back to its people in their homeland. Political boundaries do not often limit the spread of the gospel. Of course, all of this "country specific" information can be very useful for planning strategy and forming partnerships for reaching widely scattered members of specific people groups.

THE ESSENTIAL MISSIONARY TASK

What is needed in every people group is for the gospel to begin moving throughout the group with such compelling, life-giving power that the resulting churches can themselves finish spreading the gospel to every person.

Good but lesser goals may delay or distract us. Evangelism among street vendors or students might lead to discipleship groups for personal growth and even evangelism. But why stop short of anything less than a burgeoning movement of Christ-followers characterized by whole families? Why not expect that God is well able and willing to attract to His Son a substantial movement that will spread rapidly, spontaneously and thoroughly within whole peoples?

The essential missionary task is to establish *a viable indigenous church planting movement* that carries the potential to renew whole extended families and transform whole societies. It is *viable* in that it can grow on its own, *indigenous* meaning that it is not seen as foreign, and a *church planting movement* that continues to reproduce intergenerational fellowships that are able to evangelize the rest of the people group. Many refer to this achievement of an indigenous church planting movement as a *missiological breakthrough.*

We have done our basic mission job when individuals within the society (even those outside of the church) acknowledge that the movement belongs to their society. Only when this level of cultural adaptation is achieved will the dynamic, life-changing love of Jesus become available to move freely throughout the people group. Donald McGavran referred to these missiological breakthroughs as "people movements to Christ." We can hold this goal as the minimal achievement within every people in order to give a realistic opportunity for everyone in that people group to say "yes" to Jesus Christ, without adding cultural barriers to the already steep spiritual demands of the gospel. Only in this way will we be able to give everyone in the world a chance to say "yes" to Christ and His Kingdom. Jesus commissioned us to accomplish nothing less. We should settle for nothing less.

Missiological closure—
a breakthrough in every unimax people

The word "closure" refers simply to the idea of finishing. In the 1970s, the Lord began to open the eyes of many to the fact that the irreducibly essential mission task of a breakthrough in every people group was a completable task. At the time, over half of the world's population lived within unreached people groups. Even so, a small group of mission activists had the faith to believe that if a movement could be mobilized to focus attention on the unreached peoples, which for a time were called "hidden peoples," then the essential mission task could be completed within a few decades. In faith, they coined the watchword "A Church for Every People by the Year 2000" to capture the essence of

the completable nature of the mission mandate. While no one ever predicted that it *would* be completed by the end of the year 2000, they were confident that it was possible. The watchword succeeded in igniting the hearts of countless thousands with a passion for seeing Christ honored, worshiped and obeyed within every people. God was at work in similar ways among others in order to birth the now global movement focused on the unreached peoples challenge. Today we are seeing the fulfillment of vision that only a few dared to dream just two decades ago.

It is unreasonable to even talk of evangelizing every person, since day by day hundreds of thousands of children grow into the age of accountability. By contrast, the idea of "A Church for Every People" is one possible and reasonable approximation of what the Great Commission may mean, and it is a completable task. We know of no better interpretation of what it means to fulfill Jesus' mandate to have a "witness" among every people or in other words to "disciple all the nations" (Matt 24:14; 28:19,20).

We can confidently speak of closure to this unreached-peoples mission. There were an estimated 17,000 unreached peoples in 1976. Today there are an estimated 10,000 unreached peoples (unimax peoples), and a dynamic global movement now exists that is committed to establishing "a church for every people."

Reaching unimax peoples:
not measurable, but verifiable

But how measurable is the presence of a "viable indigenous church planting movement"? It might perhaps be better to say "verifiable" than "measurable." We don't normally say a woman is partially pregnant, or that a person is partially infected by AIDS. Rather, in such cases we "verify" the presence or absence of a condition.

In the case of reaching unimax peoples, there can only be three possibilities: 1) definitely reached, 2) definitely unreached, and 3) doubtfully reached. Logically we expect to focus our highest priority energies on those that are in doubt or definitely unreached. Just as in the case of asking, how many unreached peoples are there, we cannot very well evaluate whether a group has truly had a missiological breakthrough from a distance or from sources that are not concerned with such things.

We can make some well informed guesses about presence or absence of a church movement from quantifiable data. But what if an ethnolinguistic people is actually a cluster of unimax peoples and one of them is experiencing a church planting explosion, other groups in the cluster have little or nothing happening? The presence of those unreached unimax groups in the same cluster, may dilute or even vigorously oppose the movement in the group that is ablaze for God. Secondly, the growth of the church in the one may divert missionary attention from the needs of the other.

THE MANDATE IS
MORE THAN CLOSURE

What God will do is always more than what He has given us to do. He has given us a clear and simple thing to finish: to see that Christ is worshiped and followed in every people. This is the essential missionary task. This we must do with utmost focus and passion until it is finished. But there is still more to be done. The missiological breakthrough is just the beginning of all that God intends to do within every people. God will continue to fulfill His promise to undo the works of Satan and bring forth the blessing of Abraham to all peoples.

The Declaring of His Glory by All the Nations

How did Jesus teach His disciples to pray? "Thy Kingdom come, Thy will be done on earth as it is in heaven." Our concept of God's desire to reach all peoples and persons is obviously part of His desire for His Kingdom to come on earth. Other verses say that He looks toward the time when all the nations of the world will declare His glory (Isa 66:19).

Thus, we look confidently forward to the time when "the kingdoms of this world are become the kingdoms of our Lord, and of His Christ, and He shall reign forever and ever" (Rev 11:15). Surely God seeks to vanquish the "rulers of the darkness of this earth" (Eph 6:12).

Fairly soon there may not be a single "kingdom of this world" where His name is not glorified. A spiritual breakthrough into every people is a precursor to making the gospel available to every person on earth. Satan holds whole peoples in bondage. We can't wrestle a single soul out of his hand without challenging his authority in that particular people group. In each group where no real breakthrough has yet occurred, there will be a "power encounter" between the armies of God and the powers of darkness. Conquering the "kingdoms of this world" requires an invasion of God's glory within each people.

The apostle Paul was sent to the non-Jewish peoples specifically "to open their eyes and turn them from darkness to light, and from the power of Satan to God, so that they may receive forgiveness of sins and a place among those who are sanctified by faith in me" (Acts 26:17-18). Is it possible that we have become so tied up with our measurements of evangelism, social reform, and economic growth that we have forgotten that God is primarily in the business of expanding the reign of His Kingdom and conquering Satan?

That this is primarily a spiritual battle, certainly does not mean we can set aside careful planning and training for evangelism and pioneer penetration and just sit back and pray that God will go out and do His thing.

"We fight not against flesh and blood but against principalities, against powers, against the rulers of the darkness of this world, against the spiritual forces of evil in the heavenly realms" (Eph 6:12).

And we know that it is also our fight, not just His, and that we are joining Him in His battle against the Evil One. We know that in every place on earth the key effort is not going to be our wisdom or even our hard work. It will be all of that—plus His sovereign power breaking down the strongholds of His enemies to bring His glory to the ends of the earth.

Jesus gave us a clear mandate by His unique authority to "disciple all the peoples." We can and must go all out to obey Him. Certainly we should take our evangelistic measurements seriously, but not as ultimate parameters of God's plan. We must press forward, knowing that He may evaluate things by measures we cannot fully comprehend. His thoughts are higher than our thoughts.

All of this cannot entirely be brought together into a single human plan; yet it calls upon every planning effort, all creative approaches, and all the sacrifice we can muster. We know that all our measurements—of peoples and persons—are merely objective goals. It is more important that we are with Him and He is with us and we are acting in obedience as He leads us in our heavenly calling.

LOOKING AT THE TASK GRAPHICALLY

Although the world is large and complex there exist helpful methods of quantifying progress toward closure of the essential mission task. Modern researchers are now able to collect, manage and summarize vast amounts of data with the use of computers. We owe a great deal to those who have attempted to trace the hand of God as He continues His pursuit of all peoples.[6] All of our global charts and graphs to date have been dependent on the research of others as well as our own estimates where additional estimates have been needed. However, no database can ever do more than approximate the dynamic reality of the world.

When looking at the charts in this chapter, you need to understand how we are using the predominant religion within a group as a cultural feature to tag the group as a whole. This does not mean that every person in the group is a member of that religion. Thus you can have a Muslim group that is "reached" if there is a church movement within it even though the group is still predominantly Muslim.

All of the charts in this chapter, except those on the "Protestant Mission Force," are derived from the numbers on the "All Humanity in Mission Perspective" chart (page 521).

The Great Imbalance

Looking at "The Globe at a Glance" (p. 520), you can readily see that the bulk of the *individuals* who live within unreached groups (white) are within the Muslim, Tribal, Hindu, and Buddhist blocs. We need to continue to send well trained and insightful missionaries to these challenging peoples. There have been some very encouraging people movements within a limited number of Hindu, Buddhist, and Muslim groups. These three blocs are often seen as the most resistant, but we are learning that when a people seems "resistant" it may only mean our approach has been defective. Half of those living within unreached peoples are in the Muslim bloc which is a bloc that has very favorable attitudes toward Jesus Christ.

Only an estimated 10,000 of the global *foreign* mission force[7] are working within the 10,000 unreached groups, while 41 times that number of foreign missionaries continue to work within people groups already reached. What an imbalance! Even if you include the foreign missionaries working with Christians within the entire major cultural blocs, reached and unreached (see chart below and page 522), it is still a glaring fact that most foreign missionaries work within peoples which are predominantly Christian.

Patrick Johnstone analyzed the data in *Operation World '93* to approximate distribution of the Protestant Mission Force[8] (see page 522). While this is a more positive picture than we have ever seen before, it still shows a great imbalance in that only 26 percent of the

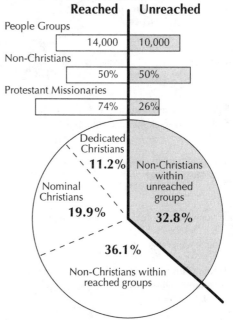

The Great Imbalance

	Reached	Unreached
People Groups	14,000	10,000
Non-Christians	50%	50%
Protestant Missionaries	74%	26%

Dedicated Christians **11.2%**

Nominal Christians **19.9%**

Non-Christians within unreached groups **32.8%**

36.1% Non-Christians within reached groups

Sources: David B. Barrett, Todd M. Johnson,[6] Patrick Johnstone[8]

The Globe at a Glance

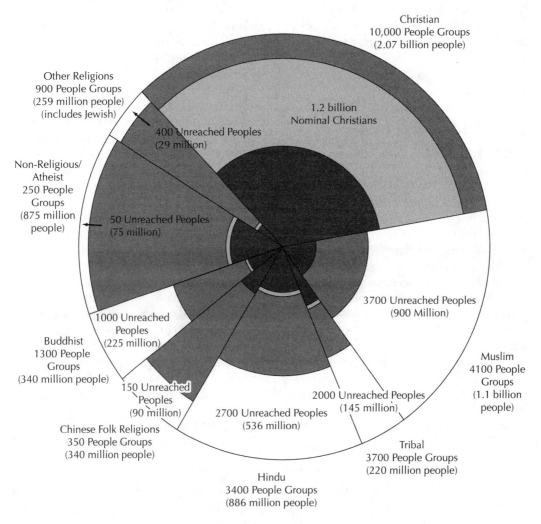

Christian
10,000 People Groups
(2.07 billion people)

Other Religions
900 People Groups
(259 million people)
(includes Jewish)

400 Unreached Peoples
(29 million)

1.2 billion
Nominal Christians

Non-Religious/
Atheist
250 People
Groups
(875 million
people)

50 Unreached Peoples
(75 million)

3700 Unreached Peoples
(900 Million)

1000 Unreached
Peoples
(225 million)

Buddhist
1300 People
Groups
(340 million people)

150 Unreached
Peoples
(90 million)

Muslim
4100 People
Groups
(1.1 billion
people)

2000 Unreached Peoples
(145 million)

2700 Unreached Peoples
(536 million)

Chinese Folk Religions
350 People Groups
(340 million people)

Tribal
3700 People Groups
(220 million people)

Hindu
3400 People Groups
(886 million people)

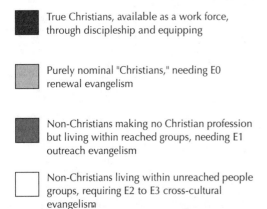

True Christians, available as a work force, through discipleship and equipping

Purely nominal "Christians," needing E0 renewal evangelism

Non-Christians making no Christian profession but living within reached groups, needing E1 outreach evangelism

Non-Christians living within unreached people groups, requiring E2 to E3 cross-cultural evangelism

The chart is divided by the predominant religion within each unimax people.* ("Peoples" = "People Groups") All individuals in the world can be found somewhere on this diagram. Religion is seen as part of the cultural identity of the group as a whole. For instance, when a Buddhist people has a church movement established within it which seeks to evangelize the rest of the members of that people, the group is considered "reached," but still within the Buddhist cultural bloc.

* **Unimax People**: The **MAX**imum sized group sufficiently **UNI**fied to be reached by a single indigenous church planting movement.

Based on Todd M. Johnson's "All Humanity in Mission Perspective" in AD 2000.

All Humanity in Mission Perspective in 2000 AD

				Predominant Religion within Culturally Defined Peoples						
			Frontier Missions				Evangelism and "Domestic" Missions			
	Totals	Christianity	Buddhism	Chinese Folk	Hinduism	Judaism	Islam	Non-Religious	Tribal Religions	Other Religions
Least Evangelized and Unreached Peoples — Individuals (in millions)										
Least Evangelized Ethnolinguistic Peoples	4,400	-	300	50	350	180	2,000	20	1,400	100
Unreached Unimax Peoples	10,000	-	1,000	150	2,700	200	3,700	50	2,000	200
Great Commission Christians (GCC)	3	-	0.3	0.5	0.4	0.01	0.3	0.7	0.5	0.29
Non-Christians (P2): E2 to E3	1,099	-	100	80	465	8	310	74	45	17
Non-Christians (P2.5): E2.5 to E3	824	-	110	10	60	1	580	0.3	60	2.7
Non-Christians (P3): E3	75	-	14.7	0	10.6	0	9.7	0	40	0
Total	2,000	-	225	90	536	9	900	75	145	20
Global Foreign Missionaries	10,000	-	800	800	1,500	100	1,500	1,200	3,700	400
Most Evangelized and Reached Peoples — Individuals (in millions)										
Most Evangelized Ethnolinguistic Peoples	8,720	6,750	150	100	120	50	300	100	1,000	150
Reached Unimax Peoples	14,000	10,000	300	200	700	100	400	200	1,700	400
Great Commission Christians (GCC)	677	489	11	22	45	0.2	30	54	22	4
Nominal-Christians (P0, P.5): E0 to E3	1,218	1,191	1	0.5	10	0.02	1	11	3	1
Non-Christians (P1): E1 to E3	2,196	392	103	227	295	8	169	735	50	217
Total	4,091	2,071	115	250	350	8	200	800	75	222
Global Foreign Missionaries	410,000	384,400	1,000	1,200	3,500	900	1,500	8,000	7,500	2,000
World Totals										
Ethnolinguistic	13,120	6,750	450	150	470	230	2,300	120	2,400	250
Unimax Peoples	24,000	10,000	1,300	350	3,400	300	4,100	250	3,700	600
Total (in millions)	6,091	2,071	340	340	886	17	1,100	875	220	242
All Missionaries	420,000	384,400	1,800	2,000	5,000	1,000	3,000	9,200	11,200	2,400

The table above was generated by Todd M. Johnson using data from the peoples database for the forthcoming *World Christian Encyclopedia* (WCE), 2nd edition, Oxford University Press (Barrett, Kurian, Johnson).

Other Religions includes peoples that are predominantly Confucianist, Mandean, Zoroastrian, Sikh and Spiritist.

Least Evangelized Ethnolinguistic Peoples: Peoples less than 50% evangelized* with relatively few Christians.

Unreached Peoples: Estimate of Unimax peoples (1982 definition) without a viable church planting movement or a viable, indigenous, evangelizing church.

The number of unimax peoples (1982 definition) are estimates. Clues are taken from linguistic and social factors (e.g., language clusters, caste).

Most Evangelized Ethnolinguistic Peoples: Peoples more than 50% evangelized* with a substantial Christian presence, including all peoples predominantly Christian (6,750).

Reached Peoples: Estimate of Unimax peoples (1982 definition) with a viable church. This includes all peoples predominantly Christian.

Great Commission Christians (GCC): Christians of evangelical conviction attempting to obey the Great Commission.

Global Foreign Missionaries includes all kinds of Christians (Roman Catholics, Orthodox, Protestants, Anglicans, Independents and Marginals).

*"Evangelized" is based on David B.Barrett's Index of Evangelization which does not yet have a published definition.

Distribution of Protestant Mission Force within the Major Cultural Blocs

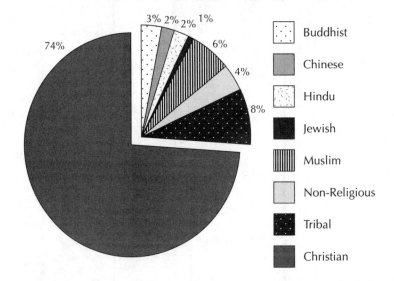

Only one out of every four missionaries is working in a pioneer ministry among non-Chrisitian peoples of the major religious blocs.

These two charts represent an inclusive view of the Protestant Mission Force. They include: foreign missionaries, missionaries working within their own country (both cross-culturally and in near cultures) bi-vocational missionaries, and home staff who are classified as missionaries who support field missionaries. The breakdown was preliminary assessment based on several days of analysis done specifically for this volume.   Source: Patrick Johnstone[8]

Distribution of Protestant Missionary Force Relative to the Size of the Major Cultural Blocs

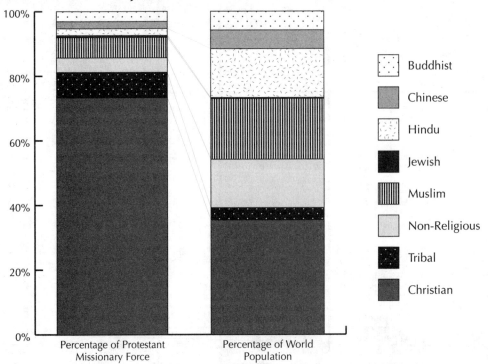

"Protestant" mission effort is going to the two-thirds of the world that is predominantly non-Christian. It will take the best efforts of the best the Church has to offer if we are to reach complete the task of frontier mission any time soon.

After nearly 2000 years, 10,000 unimax peoples encompassing 2 billion people still live beyond the reach of any local church.

Great Momentum

While talking about billions of people might seem overwhelming, astounding progress continues to be made. In 1974, we were stunned by the revelation that three out of four of the non-Christians in the world were beyond the reach of same-culture evangelism. Today, only one out of every two non-Christians is beyond reach! An easy-to-remember new insight which you can easily see in the chart on page 519, is that you can divide the world up into meaningful thirds. One third of the world would at least claim to be Christian; another third are non-Christians that live within reached peoples; the final third are non-Christians within unreached peoples. Again this is significant progress; in 1974 approximately half of the world's population was beyond the reach of the church. In fact, for the first time in history there are fewer non-Christians within unreached groups than there are within reached groups! As missionaries succeed in establishing church movements in more un-reached peoples, that is exactly what you would expect to happen.

We are in the final era of missions. For the first time in history it is possible to see the end of the tunnel when there will be a church movement within the language and social structure of every people group on earth, powerful face to face evangelism taking over in all peoples. God is moving throughout His global body to fulfill His promise to the nations in ways that we could not possibly have imagined 20 years ago. Thousands of new missionary recruits are no longer coming just from the West, but also from Asia, Africa and Latin America—fruits of missionary movements—wholeheartedly embracing the Great Commission. More so than ever before it is a global, cooperative movement. We have to be prepared for new partnerships, new insights, and new approaches by non-Western mission structures. At the same time we need to recognize that the Western missionary story is a reservoir of mission experience that can serve the emerging missions.

The job is large, but relatively small for the enormous body of believers around the world. There are approximately 670 churches in the world for every remaining unreached unimax people group! We need only a small percentage of dedicated believers to be mobilized and equipped. Judging the remaining task by the potential work force makes it quite small and within reach by comparison to the forbidding prospect faced by our forefathers.

Number of Foreign Missionaries per Million in Major Cultural Blocs

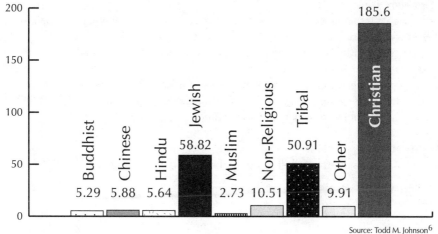

Source: Todd M. Johnson[6]

Notice how much more do-able the mission task seems when we focus on the size of the potential mission force and on penetrating people groups. Instead of talking of evangelizing 2 billion individuals, we can talk of *beginning* in approximately 3000 ethnolinguistic peoples and then *finishing* in maybe as few as 10,000 unimax peoples. Within a very short time all of the 3000 "least evangelized" ethnolinguistic groups will be targeted and engaged by some mission-sending structure in the world. It is already true for more than half of them!

Identifying and penetrating the remaining unreached unimax peoples—the great challenge of "discipling all the nations"—still lies before us. God will reveal the glory of His kingdom among all peoples. We are within range of finishing the task with more momentum than ever before in history. Be a part of it—"Declare His glory among the nations!"

End Notes

1. For the charts in this chapter the Non-Religious and Jewish categories have been added for the sake of using data as categorized in the *World Christian Encyclopedia* although the Jewish category is not always graphed if too small to be seen.
2. "Evangelized" is based David B. Barrett's Index of Evangelization and does not yet have a published definition.
3. To learn more about the usefulness of these groupings see his marvelous book, *The Church is Bigger Than You Think* (Christian Focus Publications/WEC/WCL, 1998).
4. Just search for "unreached people profiles" and you're off and surfing.
5. The AD2000 Movement refers to groups that are less than 2% Evangelical or 5% Christian adherents.
6. In the past, we have relied on a variety of expert sources for our figures and estimates for our "All Humanity in Mission Perspective" chart. We are now using information supplied by Todd M. Johnson of the World Evangelization Research Center. Todd is familiar with the unimax principle and is a caretaker of the data underlying the *World Christian Encyclopedia* (David B. Barrett, Ed.) His table reflects Todd's interpretation of missiologically significant groups within larger ethnolinguistic peoples and gives estimates of the numbers based upon analyzing statistical clues and making adjustments where necessary. No attempt has been made to adjust the estimates to make them more in line with previous estimates. If you were to compare with previous charts, you would notice that some of the numbers for unimax groups within a bloc have gone up instead of down. In fact, the overall number of estimated unimax groups has increased back to our earlier published estimate of 10,000 from several years ago. This is can be attributed to a change in sources and methodology.
   Other changes from previous versions of this chart: 1) the Jews and non-Religious/Atheist categories have been added. 2) because of the inclusion of the non-Religious/ Atheist category, the Chinese bloc was split between the between that category and the Chinese Folk bloc.
7. The global foreign mission force includes all kinds of Christians (Protestants, Anglican, Roman Catholic, Orthodox, etc).
8. The graphs for the Protestant Mission Force were generated from data derived from Appendix 3, Protestant Missionary Force found in the 1993 edition of *Operation World.* The country figures were analyzed based on Patrick Johnstone's extensive knowledge of mission work around the world. The separation of the cross-cultural work force into the different religious blocks was a preliminary analysis done specifically for this volume. Missionaries in church development ministries within non-Christian peoples are not included in the pioneer categories. Our thanks to Patrick Johnstone and his assistant Jason Mandryk for their willing hearts and expedient labor.

Study Questions

1. What is the definition of a unimax people? What is the value of this definition?

2. According to the authors, what is the essential mission task?

Who (Really) Was William Carey?

Vishal and Ruth Mangalwadi

Vishal and Ruth Mangalwadi have served the rural poor in central India, through community development, political empowerment, evangelism, leadership training and writing. Vishal has authored seven books, besides the book on William Carey, which they wrote together. *Christianity Today* described Vishal as "India's Foremost Christian Intellectual." Currently Vishal and Ruth are seeking to make a documentary on the Bible as "The Book Of The Millennium."

From *Carey, Christ and Cultural Transformation*, by Ruth and Vishal Mangalwadi, Copyright 1993. Used by permission of OM Publishing and Crossway Books.

I magine a quiz master at the finals of the All Indian Universities' competition. He asks the best-informed Indian students, **"Who was William Carey?"**

All hands go up simultaneously.

He decides to give everyone a chance to answer. The audience is asked to judge the correct answer.

"William Carey was the botanist," answers a **Science student**, "after whom *Careya herbacea* is named. It is one of the three varieties of Eucalyptus, found only in India."

"Carey brought the English daisy to India and introduced the Linnaean system to gardening. He also published the first books on science and natural history in India such as *Flora Indica*, because he believed the biblical view, 'All Thy Works praise Thee, O Lord.' Carey believed that nature is declared 'good' by its Creator; it is not *maya* (illusion), to be shunned, but a subject worthy of human study. He frequently lectured on science and tried to inject a basic scientific presupposition into the Indian mind that even lowly insects are not souls in bondage, but creatures worthy of our attention."

"William Carey was the first Englishman to introduce the steam engine to India, and the first to make indigenous paper for the publishing industry," pipes up the student of **Mechanical Engineering**. "Carey encouraged Indian blacksmiths to make copies of his engine using local materials and skills."

"William Carey was a missionary," announces an **Economics major**, "who introduced the idea of Savings Banks to India, to fight the all-pervasive social evil of usury. Carey believed that God, being righteous, hated usury, and thought that lending at the interest of 36-72 per cent made investment, industry, commerce and the economic development of India impossible."

"The moral dimensions of Carey's economic efforts," the student continues, "have assumed special importance in India since the trustworthiness of the Savings Banks has become questionable, due to the greed and corruption of the bankers, and the nationalization of the banks, in the name of socialism. The all-pervasive culture of bribery has, in many cases, pushed the interest rates up to as much as 100 per cent, and made credit unavailable to honest entrepreneurs."

"In order to attract European capital to India and the modernize Indian agriculture, economy and industry, Carey also advocated the policy that Europeans should be allowed to own land and property in India. Initially the British Government was against such a policy because of its questionable results in the United States. But by the time of Carey's death, the same Government had acknowledged the far-reaching economic wisdom of his stand. Just as our India Government, after one-half century of destructive xenophobia, has again opened the doors for Western capital and industry."

"William Carey was the first man," asserts a **Medical student,** "who led the campaign for a human treatment for leprosy patients. Until his time they were sometimes buried or burned alive in India because of the belief that a violent end purified the body and ensured transmigration in to a healthy new existence. Natural death by disease was believed to result in four successive births, and a fifth as a leper. Carey believed that Jesus' love touches leprosy patients so they should be cared for."

The student of **Printing Technology** stands up next. "Dr. William Carey is the father of print technology in India. He brought to India the modern science of printing and publishing and then taught and developed it. He built what was then the largest press in India. Most printers had to buy their fonts from his Mission Press at Serampore."

"William Carey," responds a student of **Mass Communications**, "was a Christian missionary who established the first newspaper ever printed in any oriental language because Carey believed that, "Above all forms of truth and faith, Christianity seeks free discussion." His English-language journal, *Friend of India*, was the force that gave birth to the Social Reform Movement in India in the first half of the nineteenth century."

"William Carey was the founder of the Agri-Horticultural Society in the 1820's, thirty years before the Royal Agricultural Society was established in England," says the post-graduate student of **Agriculture**. "Carey did a systematic survey of agriculture in India, wrote for agriculture reform in the journal, *Asiatic Researches*, and exposed the evils of the indigo cultivation system two generations before it collapsed.,"

"Carey did all this," adds the agriculturist, "not because he was hired to do it, but because he was horrified to see that three-fifths of one of the finest countries in the world, full of industrious inhabitants, had been al-

lowed to become an uncultivated jungle abandoned to wild beasts and serpents."

"Carey was the first man to translate and publish great Indian religious classics such as the *Ramayana*, and philosophical treaties such as *Samkhya* in to English," says the student of **Literature**. "Carey transformed Bengali, which was previously considered 'fit only for demons and women' in to the foremost literary language of India. He wrote gospel ballads in Bengali to bring the Hindu love of musical recitations to the service of his Lord. He also wrote the first Sanskrit dictionary for scholars."

"Carey was a British cobbler," joins in the student of **Education**, "who became a professor of Bengali, Sanskrit and Marathi at the Fort William College in Calcutta where civil servants were trained. Carey began dozens of schools for Indians children of all castes and launched the first college in Asia at Serampore, near Calcutta. He wanted to develop the Indian mind and liberate it from the darkness of superstition. For nearly three thousand years, India's religious culture had denied to most Indians free access to knowledge, and the Hindu, Mughal, and British rulers had gone along with this high caste strategy of keeping the masses in the bondage of ignorance. Carey displayed enormous spiritual strength in standing against the priests, who had a vested interest in depriving the masses of the freedom and power that comes from knowledge of truth."

"William Carey introduced the study of Astronomy into the Subcontinent," declares a student of **Mathematics**. He cared deeply about the destructive cultural ramifications of astrology—fatalism, superstitious fear and an inability to organize and manage time.

"Carey wanted to introduce India to the scientific culture of astronomy. He did not believe that the heavenly bodies were 'deities that governed our lives.' He knew that human beings are created to govern nature, and that the sun, moon, and the planets are created to assist us in our task of governing. Carey thought that the heavenly bodies ought to be carefully studied since the Creator had made them to be signs or markers. They help divide the monotony of the universe of space into directions—East, West, North and South—and of time into days, years, and seasons. They make it possible for us to devise calendars; to study geography and history; to plan our lives, our work and our societies. The culture of astronomy sets us free to be rulers, whereas the culture of astrology makes us subjects, our lives determined by our stars."

A post-graduate students of **Library Science** stands up next. "William Carey," she reveals, "pioneered the idea of lending libraries in the Subcontinent."

"While the East India Company was importing shiploads of ammunition and soldiers to subdue India, Carey asked his friends in the Baptist Missionary Society to load educational books and seeds into those same ships. He believed that would facilitate his task of regenerating Indian soil and empowering Indian people to embrace ideas that would generate freedom of the mind. Carey's objective was to create indigenous literature in the vernacular. But until such indigenous literature was available, Indians needed to receive knowledge and wisdom from around the world to catch up quickly with other cultures. He wanted to make worldwide information available to Indians through lending libraries."

"William Carey was an evangelist," maintains the **student from the Indian Forest Institute**. "He thought that 'if the gospel flourishes in India, the wilderness will, in every respect, become a fruitful field.' He became the first man in India to write essays on forestry, almost fifty years before the government made its very fist attempt at forest conservation, in Malabar. Carey both practiced and vigorously advocated the cultivation of timber, giving practical advice on how to plant trees for environmental, agricultural and commercial purposes. His motivation came from the belief that God has made man responsible for the earth. It was in response to Carey's journal, *Friend of India*, that the government first appointed Dr. Brandis of Bonn to care for the forests of Burma and ar-

ranged for the supervision of the forests of South India by Dr. Clegham."

"William Carey," argues a feminist **Social Science scholar**, "was the first man to stand against both the ruthless murders and the widespread oppression of women, virtually synonymous with Hinduism in the eighteenth and nineteenth centuries. The male in India was crushing the female through polygamy, female infanticide, child marriage, widow-burning, euthanasia and forced female illiteracy, all sanctioned by religion. The British Government timidly accepted these social evils as being an irreversible and intrinsic part of India's religious mores. Carey began to conduct systematic sociological and scriptural research. He published his reports in order to raise public opinion and protest both in Bengal and in England. He influenced a whole generation of civil servants, his students at Fort William College, to resist these evils. Carey opened schools for girls. When widows converted to Christianity, he arranged marriages for them. It was Carey's persistent battle against *sati* for twenty-five years which finally led to Lord Bentinck's famous Edict in 1829, banning one of the most abominable of all religious practices in the world: widow-burning."

"William Carey was an English missionary," pronounces a student of **Public Administration**, "who initially was not allowed to enter British India because the East India Company was against proselytizing of Hindus. Therefore, Carey worked in the Danish territory of Serampore. But because the Company could not find a suitable professor Bengali for Fort William College, he was later invited to teach there. During his professorship, lasting thirty years, Carey transformed the ethos of the British administration from indifferent imperial exploitation to 'civil' service."

"William Carey," reflects a student of **Indian Philosophy**, "was a preacher who revived the ancient idea that ethics and morality were inseparable from religion. This had been an important assumption underlying the *Vedic*

> Carey was an evangelist who used every available medium to illuminate every dark facet of Indian life with the light of truth. He is the central character in the story of the modernization of India.

religion. But the *Upanishadic* teachers separated ethics from spirituality. They thought that the human self (*Atman*) was the divine Self (*Brahma*). Therefore, our spirit cannot sin. Our *Atman* only gets deluded and begins to imagine itself as distinct from God. What we require is not deliverance from sin but enlightenment, i.e. a direct experience of our divinity. This denial of human sinfulness and emphasis on the mystical experience of our divinity made it possible for us in India to be intensely 'religious,' yet at the same time unabashedly immoral."

"Carey began to affirm that human beings were sinners and needed both forgiveness for sin and deliverance from its power over them. He taught that it was not ignorance but sin that had separated us from God; therefore, it was impossible to please God without holiness. According to him, true spirituality began only when we repented of our sin. This teaching revolutionized the nineteenth century religious scene in India. For example, after Raja Ram Mohun Roy, one of the greatest Hindu scholars of the nineteenth century, came in contact with Carey and the other missionaries at Serampore, he began to question seriously the spirituality then prevalent in India. He summed up his conclusion thus:

> The consequence of my long and uninterrupted researches into religious truth has been that I have found the doctrine of Christ more conducive to moral principles, and better adapted for the use of rational beings, than any other which has come to my knowledge.

A student of **History** stands up last. "Dr. William Carey is the father of the Indian Renaissance of the nineteenth and twentieth centuries. Hindu India had reached its intellectual, artistic, architectural, and literary zenith by the eleventh century AD. After the Absolute Monism of Adi Shankaracharya began to sweep the India subcontinent in the twelfth century, the creative springs of humanity dried up, and India's great decline began. The material environment, human rationality, and all that enriches human culture became suspect. Asceticism, untouchability, mysticism, the occult, superstition, idolatry, witchcraft, and oppressive beliefs and practices became the hallmark of Indian culture. The invasion, exploitation, and the resulting political dominance of foreign rulers made matter worse."

"Into this chaos Carey came and initiated the process of India's reform. He saw India not as a foreign country to be exploited, but as his heavenly Father's land to be loved and served, a society where truth, not ignorance, needed to rule. Carey's movement culminated in the birth on Indian nationalism and of India's subsequent independence. Carey believed that God's image was in man, not in idols; therefore, it was oppressed humanity that ought to be served. He believed in understanding and controlling nature instead of fearing, appeasing, or worshipping it; in developing one's intellect instead of killing it, as mysticism taught. He emphasized enjoying literature and culture instead of shunning it as *maya*. His this-worldly spirituality, with as strong an emphasis on justice and love for one's fellows, as on love for God, marked the turning-point of Indian culture from a downward to an upward trend. The early Indian leaders of the Hindu Renaissance, such as Raja Ram Mohun Roy, Keshub Chandra Sen and others, drew their inspiration from William Carey and the missionaries associated with him."

So who was William Carey?

Well, he was a pioneer of the modern missionary movement of the West, reaching out to all parts of the world; a pioneer of the Protestant Church in India; and the translator and/or publisher of the Bible in 40 different Indian languages. Carey was an evangelist who used every available medium to illuminate every dark facet of Indian life with the light of truth. He is the central character in the story of the modernization of India.

Study Questions

1. What motivations are shown for Carey's involvement with science and nature?

2. How did Carey's faith affect social and economic structures and practices?

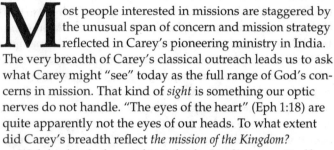

The Mission of the Kingdom

Ralph D. Winter

After serving ten years as a missionary among Mayan Indians in the highlands of Guatemala, Ralph D. Winter was called to be a Professor of Missions at the School of World Mission at Fuller Theological Seminary. Ten years later he and his wife, Roberta, founded a mission society called the Frontier Mission Fellowship (FMF) in Pasadena, California. This in turn spawned the U.S. Center for World Mission and the William Carey International University, both of which serve other missions working at the frontiers of mission. He is the General Director of the Frontier Mission Fellowship. See expanded biographical sketch at the end of the book.

In this brief chapter certain comments derive from the fact that Winter's wife, Roberta, has been diagnosed with an incurable form of cancer, multiple myeloma.

Most people interested in missions are staggered by the unusual span of concern and mission strategy reflected in Carey's pioneering ministry in India. The very breadth of Carey's classical outreach leads us to ask what Carey might "see" today as the full range of God's concerns in mission. That kind of *sight* is something our optic nerves do not handle. "The eyes of the heart" (Eph 1:18) are quite apparently not the eyes of our heads. To what extent did Carey's breadth reflect *the mission of the Kingdom?*

With his kind of special insight the Lord's prayer itself may very well suddenly take on new and unusual meaning: "Thy Kingdom come, Thy will be done on earth as it is in heaven" (Matt 6:10). What does "Thy Kingdom come" mean? Ponder, if you will, how different it seems to be from a conventional evangelistic activity in which people are "invited to accept Christ." Only when we emphasize that He is Savior *and Lord*, do we add an element of authority and governance that draws in the Kingdom concept.

We note that in an instance where Jesus is accused of calling on the powers of Satan's domain, He claims rather the coming of God's Kingdom: "If I cast out demons by the finger of God , then the Kingdom of God has come upon you" (Luke 11:20). Apparently a Kingdom "not of this world" (Jn 18:36) is still a powerful presence that can "*come,*" that can physically banish the powers of Satan.

Later, Jesus said, "This Gospel of *the Kingdom* will be preached in the whole world for a witness to all the Gentiles and then the end shall come" (Matt 24:14). He may have been talking about the *coming* of the Kingdom in the same sense—that is, the coming of the power and presence of God into and "upon" human situations dominated by Satan.

Let us not suppose that our modern cities represent the final form of the kingdom of God. It is righteousness that exalts a nation, not skyscrapers. William Carey's activism in so many directions is more indicative of Carey's sense of God's righteousness and glory than it is of any kind of secular utopia. William Carey cared more about the restoration of justice, the concept of right and wrong, a sense of God's creative good, an expression of His love and the reestablishment of His good name. This is less and more than building a city, a school or a hospital. Medical missions are not primarily a "bait" to attract people to Christianity but a concrete means of portraying more accurately the true nature of a loving God.

Thus, Evangelicals are justly suspicious of assumptions that human efforts can successfully "build the Kingdom of God" on earth. Even Hitler might have claimed to be doing just that. (The Nazis, in fact were the first to detect a link between smoking and cancer and actually do something about it.) To make the world a safe place for either fascism or democracy is not exactly what Jesus meant when he talked about the the fortress of Satan being unable to resist the advance of the church (Matt 16:18). More likely He was talking about Gospel triumph over evil rather than a social/political achievement of earthly prosperity.

John said, "The Son of God appeared for this purpose: that He might destroy *the works of the devil*" (1 Jn 3:8). We don't think much about precisely what are *the works of the devil.*

According to Gregory Boyd (See Chapter 11), one reason is that our Christian tradition imbibed some harmful paganism in Augustine's time, a perspective rendering the salt and light of the Christian mission "strangely passive" in the presence of evil. This syncretistic strand in our tradition may explain how a medieval Mother Superior could leave untouched a worm burrowing into her forehead. One day, when it fell out as she bent over, she returned it because her theology urged her to believe that God is behind all suffering and that suffering calls for *resignation* rather than *resistance.* Protestant ministers once opposed smallpox vaccination on the same grounds— that it would interfere with Divine Providence. Some Hindus (and Americans) will not kill any form of life no matter how evil or destructive to other life. Is the Kingdom of God an active, aggressive, expanding, conquering power that does not merely endure evil but is set to "destroy the works of the devil?"

If so, we must think more clearly about what those "works" actually are. This won't be quick and easy since, it would appear, the Evil One is more successful at working unseen and unnoticed than in withstanding frontal spiritual warfare. William Carey knew nothing about germs, good or evil. He did not live in "a world of largely invisible predators" as someone has said. Can Carey guide us now?

A major hurdle exists partly because our theological tradition emerged before we had become aware of the world of vicious and destructive microbes. Are they the work of Satan? Modern Christians have finally dared to insist that nature reveals "intelligent design." Are we also prepared to recognized "intelligent *evil* design" and risk our lives to kill off— totally eradicate—evil-working parasites that drag millions down in terrible suffering and death? *Is our God misrepresented if we don't?*

Jonathan Edwards died experimenting with smallpox vaccine. Did that kind of vision die with him? Do our missionaries tell people (their actions speaking louder than their words) that God's Kingdom has no power over tiny evil? Or, that we can give people beds to lie on while they die but we cannot fight the *source* of their disease? Would Carey have fought back at the microbial level, had he known what we know?

Until recently I have never thought much about the growth or non-growth of world population and the degree to which Satanically inspired "war and pestilence" has depressed it. In the 2,000 years from Abraham to Christ world population increased from 27 to 200 million—.1% per year. *Horrendous war and pestilence must have held the growth rate down to that!*

Shortly before 2000 A.D. war and pestilence had been greatly reduced—though not banished—such that global population was 1.7%, growing seventeen times as fast as the ancient rate. At that point, in order to slow global growth to the ancient rate, 96 million people would have to die per year—*in addition* to all the people already being killed off by genocide and disease and all other factors. Thus, by AD 2000 "the works of the devil" in the form of war and pestilence had been significantly reduced. But, is the total eradication of evil microbes part of, and essential to, the task of winning souls and reaching unreached peoples? Is *the mission of the Kingdom* that broad? If so, is it not ominous that neither our sermons nor conventional missiology seriously reflect this dimension of the task? Do we know what it means to "destroy the works of the devil?" Is that a mission frontier?

On the Cutting Edge of Mission Strategy

C. Peter Wagner

Mission strategy has taken a sharp new focus today. No longer is it enough to say we are "faithful" missionaries—we must also be "successful" in evangelizing and discipling all nations. This is abundantly clear in the parable of the talents. If evangelism is our highest priority in mission, then we need to understand what the task involves—and that power encounters are a crucial factor in missions today.

Today's cutting edge issues in missions fall under three general headings: (1) mission principles—thinking clearly about our task, (2) mission practices—planning strategically as we move out, and (3) mission power—ministering supernaturally as we encounter the enemy. Much of what we do emerges from what we think. Thus, I have no hesitation in starting with some aspects of missiological theory. I believe that an important starting point is understanding what mission is, what evangelism is, what the task is, and what is actually happening on the field.

The Mission—No Options Here!

The definition of mission has been a topic of constant debate for the past one hundred years. It revolves chiefly around the relationship of what have been called the cultural mandate and the evangelistic mandate.

The cultural mandate, which some refer to as Christian social responsibility, goes as far back as the Garden of Eden. After God created Adam and Eve, He said to them: "Be fruitful and multiply; fill the earth and subdue it; have dominion over the fish of the sea, over the birds of the air, and over every living thing that moves on the earth" (Gen 1:21). As human beings, made in the image of God, we are held accountable for the well-being of God's creation. In the New Testament we are told that we are to love our neighbors as ourselves (Matt 22:39). The concept of neighbor, as the parable of the Good Samaritan teaches, includes not only those of our own race or culture or religious group, but all of humanity. Doing good to others, whether our efforts are directed toward individuals or to society as a whole, is a biblical duty, a God-given cultural mandate.

The evangelistic mandate is also first glimpsed in the Garden of Eden. For a period of time, whenever God went to the Garden, Adam and Eve were waiting for Him and they had fellowship. But sin entered into the picture. The very next time

C. Peter Wager is the Donald A. McGavran Professor of Church Growth at Fuller Theological Seminary School of World Mission. He is the President of the World Prayer Center, the Founding President of Global Harvest Ministries and Coordinator for the United Prayer Track of the AD 2000 Movement. He has authored over 40 volumes on missions and church growth.

that God went to the Garden, Adam and Eve were nowhere to be found. Fellowship had been broken. Humans had been alienated from God. God's nature, in light of the events, was made clear by the first words which came out of His mouth, "Adam, where are you?" (Gen 3:9). He immediately began seeking Adam. The evangelistic mandate involves seeking and finding lost men and women, alienated from God by sin. Romans 10 tells us that whoever calls on the name of the Lord will be saved. But they cannot call if they have not believed and they cannot believe if they have not heard and they cannot hear without a preacher. "How beautiful are the feet of those who preach the gospel of peace" (Rom 10:15). Bearing the gospel which brings people from darkness to light is fulfilling the evangelistic mandate.

Both the cultural mandate and the evangelistic mandate are essential parts of biblical mission, in my opinion. Neither is optional. There is a growing consensus on this point in Evangelical circles.

This consensus is a recent reality. At the Berlin World Congress on Evangelism held in 1966, there was virtually no mention of the cultural mandate. John R. W. Stott even defined mission as including only the evangelistic mandate, and not the cultural mandate, although he did not use that precise terminology. The social consciousness generated by the social upheavals of the 1960's brought the cultural mandate to prominence until it was given a relatively high profile on the platform of the International Congress on World Evangelization at Lausanne in 1974. By then John Stott himself had changed his views, recognizing that mission included both the cultural and the evangelistic mandates. The Lausanne Covenant makes a strong statement on the cultural mandate in Article 5, and on the evangelistic mandate in Article 6.

The current debate involves four positions: (1) those who would prioritize the cultural mandate over the evangelistic, (2) those who would give equal weight to both—even arguing that it is illegitimate to divide them by using such terminology, (3) those who would prioritize the evangelistic mandate, and (4) those who would hold the pre-Lausanne view that mission is the evangelistic mandate, period.

My personal view aligns with that of the Lausanne Covenant. But I spend little time fussing with those who hold that mission should be understood as evangelism and that social ministry should be termed a Christian duty or an outcome of mission rather than part of mission itself. I see either of these positions as contributing more positively to the evangelization of the world than the other options. But I do not accept the prioritization of evangelism solely on pragmatic grounds. I believe it best reflects the New Testament doctrine of mission. Jesus came to seek and to save the lost (Luke 10:10), and we move out in Jesus's Name to do the same. While we must not neglect our Christian social responsibility, in my opinion, it must never get in the way of soul-winning evangelism.

Evangelism—Making Disciples

If evangelism is the highest priority in mission, it is extremely important that we clearly understand what evangelism is.

The three prominent ways of defining evangelism in the Christian world today can be labeled presence, proclamation and persuasion. Presence holds that evangelism is helping people to fulfill their needs. It is giving a cup of cold water in the Name of Jesus. It is lending a helping hand. Proclamation recognizes that presence is necessary, but goes beyond it and says that evangelism is making known the message of Jesus so that people hear it and understand it. But once people are exposed to the gospel message they are evangelized whether they accept it or not according to a strict proclamation definition. Persuasion argues that presence and proclamation are both necessary, but that biblical evangelism goes beyond that and insists on making disciples.

My view of evangelism affirms both presence and proclamation, but neither as adequate definitions of evangelism in themselves. But I believe that a person should not be considered evangelized until he or she has become an ongoing disciple of Jesus Christ.

This is rooted in the Great Commission. While the Great Commission appears in all four Gospels and Acts, the Matthew account is the most complete for understanding it in context. "Go, therefore, and make disciples of all the nations, baptizing them in the name of the Father and of the Son and of the Holy Spirit, teaching them to observe all things that I have commanded you" (Matt 28:19-20). Three of the four action verbs in the Great Commission are participles in the original Greek: "go," "baptize," and "teach." They are helping verbs. The one imperative is "make disciples." If the Great Commission is the key text for evangelism, its goal, exegetically speaking, is to make disciples.

If making disciples is that important, what then is a disciple? Theologically, a disciple is one who has been regenerated by the Holy Spirit, a new creature in Christ Jesus (2 Cor 5:17). Empirically, a disciple is one who is known by the fruit. When true regeneration takes place, visible fruit inevitably follows. Those of us who identify with the Church Growth Movement agree that, while there are many, many legitimate fruits of regeneration, one which is an excellent indicator is responsible church membership. In order to be counted as a disciple, a person should be committed not only to Jesus Christ, but also to the body of Christ.

Field research increasingly indicates that evangelistic efforts based on presence or proclamation alone are considerably less effective in terms of resulting church growth than those seeing evangelism as persuasion.

The Task—
Reaching the 70% Outside

Jesus said that the good shepherd who has a flock of 100 sheep and discovers that one is lost, leaves the 99 who are safe in the fold and searches for the lost sheep until it is found. This is another indicator of where God's priorities lie. We must spend time nurturing existing Christians. We must strive for healthy churches. We must stress quality as well as quantity. But we also must be good shepherds and never rest so long as there are human beings who are lost. Christ died for them and He wants them to be reconciled to the Father. Today we do not have 99 in the fold and one outside. At best, it is more like 30 in the fold and 70 outside.

In the world today over four billion people are outside the fold. Of them, about 2.2 billion can be reached by ordinary evangelism within a given culture. We missiologists call it E-1. That is a massive task in itself, and one for which large amounts of human, financial and

technological resources are being invested. But far overshadowing that task are the 2 billion people who as yet do not have a viable, evangelizing church within their own culture. These 2 billion, comprising 48 percent of those outside the fold, will be reached only through what we ordinarily call missions. Someone will have to leave the comforts of their own culture, learn a new language, learn how to eat new food, live a different lifestyle, love people who may appear to be unlovely, and share the gospel of Christ with them. This is cross-cultural evangelism, E-2 and E-3. Ralph Winter showed in the Lausanne Congress of 1974, it is the highest priority for planning the task of world evangelization.

> **Cross-cultural evangelism is the highest priority for planning the task of world evangelization.**

The Field—Third World Missionaries Go Out

We are in the springtime of Christian missions. The spread of the gospel and the growth of Christian churches around the world far outstrip anything that has been known throughout history. The age of modern missions began roughly in 1800 when William Carey went to India. More people have been won to Christ and more Christian churches have been planted in the 185 years since then than in the total of 1800 years previously. Every day of the year sees an estimated 78,000 new Christians and every week there are 1,600 new Christian churches worldwide.

Time will not permit me to go into detail about church growth in different parts of the world. Flash points of growth include Central America, Korea, the Philippines, Nigeria, Brazil, Ethiopia, China, and many other places. Thirty percent of the Korean population is now Christian and the percentage is rising rapidly. There were one million Chinese believers in 1950 when Marxism took over. With all the persecution, many of us on the outside thought they must have been obliterated. Instead, we now know that they have grown to a conservative 50 million, probably many more. It is believed that most of the growth occurred since 1970, which means that for the rest of the century China may well continue to be the greatest harvest field in the world, evangelistically speaking.

To meet the challenge of reaping the tremendous harvest which God has ripened, He is calling forth large numbers of workers here in the United States and abroad. Not since the decade following World War II has there been such a vital interest in missions among Christian young people.

Churches in Asia, Africa and Latin America are also mobilizing their forces for cross-cultural missions. In 1972, 3,400 Third World missionaries were identified. By 1980 the figure had risen to 13,000 and researchers such as Larry Keyes of O.C. Ministries are estimating that there may be ten times that today. The growth has been so astounding that it's been hard to estimate, but there are probably more non-Western missionaries at work in our day than missionaries from the Western nations.

Thinking clearly about our task is an essential starting point for mission strategy. It gives us a base for sound and effective practice.

Mission Practice—
Planning Strategically

One of the most significant missiological works of our time is *Planning Strategies for World Evangelization* by Edward Dayton and David Fraser. They say, "As Christians, a strategy forces us to seek the mind of God and the will of the Holy Spirit. What does God desire? How can we conform to the future that He desires?" I agree with Dayton and Fraser who argue that setting goals and developing a strategy to reach them is a way of expressing faith. It is putting substance on things hoped for, as Hebrews 11:1 recommends. Since it is impossible to please God without faith according to Hebrews 11:6, I believe that planning strategy according to the will of God is pleasing to Him.

Planning strategy must not be seen as a substitute for the work of the Holy Spirit. Jesus said, "I will build My Church" and we do well to emphasize the "I." He has been building His Church for 2,000 years, and He will continue to build it until He returns— with or without the help of any of us. But He cordially invites each of us to join Him in the worldwide task of building that Church. And if we accept the invitation, we become instruments in Jesus' hands for the accomplishment of His task. All that I am advocating here is that we do whatever is necessary to become the best servants possible as the Master uses us to do His work.

Thus, I see obedience to the Master as a starting point for formulating our attitudes toward mission strategy. The Great Commission is a clear commandment. We are to go into the world, preach the gospel to every creature, and make disciples of all nations—*panta ta ethne*. God is not willing that any should perish (2 Peter 3:9). As servants we need have no doubt as to the will of the Master.

The New Testament directs us to serve God with the faithfulness of wise stewards. In that day, a steward was a servant entrusted to fulfill great responsibilities. And we are told explicitly that we are stewards of the mysteries of God—a parallel expression to the gospel (1 Cor 4:1). What is the gospel for? It is the power of God for salvation (Romans 1:16).

We are also told that stewards are required to be found faithful (1 Cor 4:2). It is important to understand what is meant by "faithful," here. I have heard some say, "God, I thank you that you do not require me to be successful, only faithful." But the central passage on stewardship, the parable of the talents in Matthew 25:14-30, makes no distinction between the two. It tells us that the stewards who did their master's will and turned two talents and five talents into four and ten respectively were regarded as good and faithful servants. Here success and faithfulness go hand in hand. The steward who buried the talent and made no money, not even bank interest, from it was considered unfaithful.

The foundational principle of New Testament stewardship is that the steward takes the resources given by the Master, uses them for the Master's purpose, and returns to give the benefits and the honor to the Master.

This has a direct application to mission strategy. Since we know that the Master's will is to make disciples of all nations, we are responsible, as good stewards, to use what resources He has given us to accomplish that task. To the degree that we are successful, we will be called faithful.

Setting goals for world evangelization and planning strategies to accomplish those goals require a degree of pragmatism. I realize that pragmatism can be carnal, but here I am speaking of consecrated pragmatism. I am not suggesting pragmatism concerning doctrine or ethics. But I am advocating pragmatism as to methodology. If we are investing resources of time, personnel and money in programs which are supposed to make disciples but are not, we need to reconsider them and be willing to change the program if needed. Jesus' parable suggests that if the fig tree does not bear fruit after an appropriate lapse of time, it should be cut down and the ground used for something more productive (Luke 13:6-9).

The Targets For Strategy

If we agree to take a positive attitude toward strategy planning for world missions, the precise targets of our activity then become highly important. Much research is being carried out these days in many parts of the world to help us get a clear picture of exactly what we are aiming for. I will mention but three here: the unreached peoples, the cities, and whole nations.

Unreached Peoples

The concept of unreached peoples as target groups for mission strategy first surfaced prominently in the International Congress on World Evangelization in Lausanne, Switzerland in 1974. Edward Dayton of the MARC division of World Vision distributed the first Unreached Peoples Directory to all the participants. Then Ralph Winter, now director of the U.S. Center for World Mission, highlighted the concept of people groups in a plenary session address.

For several years a spirited discussion was carried on among the leaders of unreached peoples research as to the definition of an unreached people group. A blow by blow account of this is given in Ralph Winter's chapter, "Unreached Peoples: The Development of the Concept," in Harvie Conn's book, *Reaching the Unreached*. By the way, I highly recommend this book for those who wish an introduction to the subject. As Winter points out, the definition now agreed upon by all concerned is:

An unreached people is a people group among which there is no indigenous community of believing Christians with adequate numbers and resources to evangelize this people group without outside (cross-cultural) assistance.

An estimated 48 percent of the world's non-Christians find themselves in unreached people groups. That means that over two billion individuals for whom Christ died will not hear of His love unless someone follows the call of God and leaves their own culture. This is mission, pure and simple. The age of missions is far from over. On the contrary, cross-cultural service for Christ is the most massive and most exciting challenge for Christians today.

It is yet unclear exactly how many unreached people groups exist. For years many of us used the figure 16,750, which was Ralph Winter's somewhat symbolic estimate around 1980. Some say the number may turn out to be 100,000 or more. Time will tell. Whatever the final number, over 5,000 have been identified and listed in the *Unreached Peoples Annuals* so far, even more in the Joshua Project list. Happily, some originally classified as unreached have now become reached over the past few years. But my point is that among missiologists there is a wide agreement that this unit, namely, people groups, is the most useful primary target for planning mission strategy.

Cities

Many people groups find themselves clustered in close proximity to each other in the cities of the world. A major socio-demographic phenomenon of our age, especially post-World War II, is the urban explosion. At the time of World War II only New York and London had over 8 million inhabitants. Now there are nearly twenty such megacities, and the projection for the year 2015 is thirty-three. Mexico City had fewer than three million people during World War II, but it is expected to contain over 30 million by the end of the century, the largest city in the world.

Raymond Bakke, the outstanding urbanologist, has identified over 250 of what he calls "world class cities," and he has visited most of them. A world class city is one which has over one million persons (form or structure), and international influence (function or role). The number of world class cities is expected to rise to 500 by the end of the century.

Bakke explains how the dual targets of unreached peoples and world class cities relate to each other by making the helpful distinction between (1) the geographically distant unreached peoples and (2) the culturally distant unreached peoples. Granted, there is a cultural distance in both cases, but in the first there is also a significant geographical barrier. Traditionally, geographically distant peoples have been the chief target of those we send to the mission field. But in today's cities, culturally distant peoples may be living right next door or a block or two away, but we may be blind to their existence as targets for sharing the gospel. Bakke says, "They will not be reached for Jesus Christ unless existing churches become multicultural by intention or unless user-friendly churches are started by and for them."

Whole Nations

While cities are increasingly important as evangelistic targets, the politically-defined nations of the world continue to maintain the highest profile in the national and international media. They also are extremely prominent in international social psychology. With all the necessary emphasis on people groups and urbanization, our strategy planning for missions must not ignore the geo-political countries of the world. At this point in time, the cutting-edge leader who, I believe, has seen this most clearly and who has taken aggressive action to implement it is James Montgomery. Montgomery left Overseas Crusades in the early 80s to form a new mission agency called DAWN Ministries. DAWN is an acronym for "Discipling a Whole Nation."

The aim of DAWN is to mobilize the entire body of Christ in a given nation for a determined effort to complete the Great Commission by working towards the goal of providing an Evangelical congregation for every village and urban neighborhood in the country. Montgomery believes in the people group concept, but argues that concentration on the people groups located within given countries is the most practical way of reaching all the unreached.

The DAWN program is long term, extending over several years. It begins with an exten-sive research project on the status of evangelism and church growth in the country, with the results published in a book in the national language. Christian leaders are organized into task forces to provide coordination of activities and accountability for results. A major national DAWN congress is held for motivation, inspiration, training and goal setting. This is either preceded or followed by regional DAWN conferences over a period of time.

DAWN is more than just an idea. The pilot project was undertaken in the Philippines where DAWN-type congresses were held in 1974, 1980, and 1985. They recently held their sixth. The results have been amazing. More than 30 DAWN or DAWN-type projects have passed the phase of holding a national congress with a total of close to three million new churches projected.

Mission Power— Ministering in the Spirit

We have looked briefly at the mission principles which help us think more clearly about our task. We have examined cutting-edge mission practices which are enabling us to reach out more efficiently than ever before. Now, finally, I want to consider what I am calling "mission power."

Many of us who come from non-Pentecostal and non-Charismatic backgrounds have not known as much about the workings of the supernatural and the miraculous in the world today as we should have. But one of the cutting edges of contemporary mission strategy has been a relatively new manifestation of the Holy Spirit among more traditionally straight line Evangelicals. I found myself playing an increasingly active role in this during the decade of the 80s. I see what is happening as the "third wave" of the Spirit of God in the 20th century. The first was the Pentecostal movement at the beginning of the century. The second was the Charismatic movement at the mid-point of the century. Both of these continue strong and I see them expanding vigorously throughout the rest of the century.

The third wave involves those of us—and I include myself—who, for one reason or another, do not personally wish to identify with either the Pentecostals or the Charismatics. We love, respect and admire our friends in those movements and we pray God's blessing on them in all their work. We recognize that currently they represent the most rapidly growing segment of the body of Christ worldwide. We have learned a great deal from them and desire to learn more. But our style is slightly different. We minister in very similar ways, but explain what we do in alternate theological terminology. We serve the same Lord and are involved in the same task of world evangelization. I believe that we Evangelicals need a fresh look at supernatural power, a fresh awareness of worldview, and a fresh examination of the theology of the Kingdom.

A Fresh Look At God's Supernatural

Jesus sent his disciples out with "power over unclean spirits, to cast them out, and to heal all kinds of sickness and all kinds of diseases" (Matt 10:1). The Apostle Paul testified that he preached the gospel to the Gentiles from Jerusalem to Illyricum "in mighty signs and wonders, by the power of the Spirit of God" (Rom 15:19). Hebrews records that salvation has come through God's witness "both with signs and wonders, with various miracles, and gifts of the Holy Spirit...." (Heb 2:4).

While we do not deny the validity of the Word of God, many of us have not experienced this kind of New Testament power in our personal ministries. I for one never saw it at all during my 16 years as a missionary to Bolivia. To me the power of God was to save souls and help us live a good Christian life. I now see that as correct, but only a partial view of God's power. It is some consolation for me that all of my colleagues on the Fuller School of Mission faculty look back on their missionary careers with similar observations.

As Timothy Warner of the Trinity School of World Mission and Evangelism says: "The issue of encounter with demonic forces is one which has understandably been avoided by large segments of the church. For most of my life, I was among those who steered clear of such involvement." But, he goes onto say, "We can no longer afford this luxury." Warner believes that power and the power encounter is a crucial factor in today's mission. As he looks out on the unreached peoples he observes that "In many parts of the world...people are much more power-conscious than they are truth-conscious. We may preach a very logical and convincing message by Western standards, but our hearers remain unimpressed. Let them see Christian power displayed in relation to the spirit world in which they live with great fear, however, and they will 'hear' the message more clearly than our words alone could ever make it."

A similar concern is expressed by Richard De Ridder of Calvin Theological Seminary in his book *Discipling the Nations*. De Ridder reflects on his missionary experience in Sri Lanka in these words:

One thing deeply impressed me: how irrelevant so much of traditional Reformed Theology was to these people and their situation, and how seldom this theology spoke to their real needs. The questions that concern Satan, demons, angels, charms, etc., are not of great concern, nor do they receive much attention in the West. These are living issues to the Christians of these areas, surrounded as they were by animism and the continual fear of the spiritual realm. Among the greatest joys that we experienced was to proclaim to men the victory of Christ over the powers and see the shackles of slavery to elemental spirits broken by Christ. When the "Five Points of Calvinism" were preached to these people, they often responded with the question, "What's the issue?" Missionaries and pastors were scratching where they didn't itch.

I receive a large number of letters, both form letters and personal letters, from missionaries around the word. Since this was a personal letter and I do not have permission to cite the writer, I will disguise the identity of the person and the mission agency in my paraphrase of the letter, but suffice it to say that the writer is a traditionally and impeccably Evangelical mission executive:

> As you know, we are committed to planting churches in the Muslim world. We are face to face with a power encounter of gigantic proportions. I am convinced that there is a demonic base to Islam that is much greater than most of us have ever dared admit. Of course, it doesn't make good copy to say these things or write them, and we are all rather embarrassed by our ineptitude in facing Islam today. Why does the Christian church have to lie down and let the Islamic horde sweep over us as so many tanks?

This is an increasing cry. Large numbers of missionaries and international church leaders in our school at Fuller are asking the same questions and we are beginning to provide them with some answers, however elementary at this stage. Two of our students, serving with the Latin America Mission in Costa Rica, wrote of several experiences with supernatural power in a recent newsletter. Among them was this:

> Since our return to Costa Rica in January, we have been operating in a new power we never knew in our previous six years here. We have ministered to a person that had been diagnosed to be epileptic only to be freed by the expulsion of demons. This person had an experience early in life with witchcraft, through contact with a Ouija board. Her mother also had been very much involved in the occult. Now after 46 years of torment, she is totally free.

These missionaries lamented the fact that "Christianity has all too often been presented as a religion of the textbook and the head." They now see how distant this is from the Christianity of the New Testament where "worship was alive and meaningful, prayer was an avid encounter, and signs and wonders drew people to faith."

An O.M.F. missionary to Singapore recently wrote that he witnessed to a man there who said, "No point in becoming a Christian. My brother is a pastor. When my mother got ill, he couldn't do anything to help. We took her to the temple and she was healed." Another woman, a Hindu, said, "The trouble with you Christians is that you have no power!" My friend comments, "How tragic when people get the idea that Christianity is a matter of mere intellectual conviction, a religion of words largely devoid of power."

An increasing number of our Evangelical seminary missions faculties and our Evangelical mission agencies have begun to raise issues of spiritual power. I am convinced that it is an area which requires some fresh study and some discerning implementation if we are to participate fully in contemporary world evangelization.

A Fresh Awareness of Worldview

Due to the pervasive influence of cultural anthropology in our current missiological research, the concept of worldview has gained a great deal of prominence. We are able to talk about worldview and to understand its implications for daily life much more freely and accurately than we used to. One of the more disturbing things we are beginning to discover is that, in more cases than we would care to think, our missionary message in the Third World has been having a secularizing influence.

I first realized this when I read an article by my colleague, Paul G. Hiebert, called "The Flaw of the Excluded Middle" in 1982. He begins the article by citing the question that John the Baptist had his disciples ask Jesus: "Are you the Coming One, or do we look for another?" (Luke 7:20). Hiebert emphasized that Jesus' reply was not a carefully reasoned argument, but rather a demonstration of power in healing the sick and casting out of evil spirits.

"When I read the passage as a missionary in India, and sought to apply it to missions in our day," says Hiebert, "I had a sense of uneasiness. As a Westerner, I was used to presenting Christ on the basis of rational arguments, not by evidence of His power in the lives of people who were sick, possessed and destitute." He goes on to point out that the worldview of most non-Westerners is three-tiered. There is a cosmic tier on top, an everyday life tier on the bottom, and a large middle zone where the two constantly interact. This is a zone largely controlled by spirits, demons, ancestors, goblins, ghosts, magic, fetishes, witches, mediums, sorcerers, and such powers. The common reaction of Western missionaries, whose worldview does not contain such a middle zone, is to attempt to deny the existence of the spirits rather than claim the power of Christ over them. As a result, says Hiebert, "Western Christian missions have been one of the greatest secularizing forces in history."

Most of us are aware that secular humanism has deeply influenced our culture in America. But relatively few of us have understood how profoundly this has permeated even our Christian institutions including churches, colleges and seminaries. The more we realize it, however, and the more we recognize that our secularized worldview is significantly different from those of the Jews and the Greeks in the New Testament context, the more we can become open to what is called a paradigm shift. This paradigm shift is very helpful in bringing missionaries more in touch with the worldview of the men and women to whom they are attempting to communicate the gospel.

A Fresh Examination of the Theology of the Kingdom
In the Lord's prayer we say, "Thy kingdom come, Thy will be done on earth as it is in heaven." I must confess that up until recently those words had very little meaning for my life. I repeated them by rote memory without much spiritual processing taking place as I did. For one thing, my understanding was that the Kingdom was something that was future, so my assumption was that I was praying for the return of the Lord. An accompanying assumption was that, because God is sovereign, His will is in fact being done on earth today and that we can rather passively accept what happens as something which God directly or indirectly approves of.

I now see the theology of the Kingdom in a different light. I now believe that when Jesus came, He introduced the Kingdom of God into the present world.

This was a direct confrontation or invasion of the kingdom of darkness ruled by Satan who is called "the god of this age" (2 Cor 4:4). I take Satan more seriously than I used to, recognizing that some things which occur today do so because of the will of the enemy, not because they are the will of God. The era between the first and second comings of Christ is an era of warfare between the two kingdoms. Two strong powers are occupying the same territory.

Let me say quickly that I still believe in the sovereignty of God who, for His own reasons, has allowed this spiritual warfare to take place for almost 2,000 years now. And there is no doubt as to the outcome. Satan and all his demonic forces were defeated by the blood of Jesus on the cross. His is, at best, a holding action, but a ferocious, destructive and dehumanizing action which God expects us, as His servants, to actively oppose.

What are some things clearly out of God's will which are happening today? In heaven there is not one poor, at war, oppressed, demonized, sick or lost. As Evangelicals we understand the last one best. Even though it is not God's will that any should perish according to 2 Peter 3:9, the world today is full of those who are perishing, as I have previously mentioned. There are three billion of them out there and our task, as instruments of God's hands, is to reach out to them and bring them into the Kingdom through the new birth (John 3:3). This is the great missiological challenge.

We do the best we can to reach the lost for Christ knowing full well ahead of time, on both biblical and experiential grounds, that we are not going to win them all. That knowledge does not discourage us, even though we know the reason why some do not respond. We learn from 2 Corinthians 4:3-4 that it is essentially because Satan has succeeded in blinding their eyes to the light of the gospel. We weep knowing that each year millions of people die and go into a Christless eternity, and we know that it is not God's will that they should perish.

Three billion in the world today are perishing and our task, as instruments of God's hands, is to reach out to them and bring them into the Kingdom through the new birth.

If this is true about the lost, it may well be true about the poor, those at war, the oppressed, the demonized and the sick. So long as Satan is the god of this age, they will all be with us. But meanwhile, as citizens of the Kingdom of God, we must reflect the values of the Kingdom and combat these evils as strenuously as possible. For example, we must heal the sick knowing ahead of time that not all will be healed. I was pleased when this was recognized at a high level Evangelical conference in 1982. At that time the Lausanne Committee sponsored a consultation on the relationship of evangelism to social responsibility in Grand Rapids, and recognized in its report that among the signs of the Kingdom were "making the blind see, the deaf hear, the lame walk, the sick whole, raising the dead, stilling the storm, and multiplying loaves and fishes." The report mentions that "Demon possession is a real and terrible condition. Deliverance is possible only in a power encounter in which the name of Jesus is invoked and prevails." This is what missiologists, such as Timothy Warner, are also saying to us.

I agree with Charles Kraft, who once said in a faculty meeting, "We can no longer afford to send missionaries and national church leaders back to their fields or to send young people to the missions field for the first time without teaching them how to heal the sick and cast out demons." We are still at the beginning stages of this, and we are not yet satisfied with the way we are doing the job, but we are trusting God to continue to teach us so that we can in turn teach others.

I feel that one of the callings that God has given me is to be an encouragement to traditional Evangelical non-Pentecostal and non-Charismatic institutions so that they will begin to take a new look at mission power—ministering supernaturally as we encounter the enemy.

References

Bakke, Raymond J. "Evangelization of the World's Cities," *An Urban World: Churches Face the Future*,.Nashville: Broadman.

Dayton, R. Edward. *Planning Strategies for World Evangelization*. Grand Rapids: Eerdmans, 1980, p. 16.

De Ridder, Richard R. *Discipling The Nations*. Grand Rapids: Baker, 1975, p. 222.

Hiebert, Paul G. "The Flaw of the Excluded Middle," *Missiology: An International Review*, Vol.X, Number 1, Jan. 1982, pp. 35-47.

Hinton, Keith and Linnet. Singapore: May 20, 1985 Newsletter.

Lausanne Committee for World Evangelization and the World Evangelical Fellowship. *Evangelism and Social Responsibility: An Evangelical Commitment*, 1982. p. 31.

Wagner, Doris M. ed. *Missiological Abstracts*. Pasadena, CA. Fuller School of World Mission, 1984.

Warner, Timothy "Power Encounter in Evangelism," *Trinity World Forum*, Winter 1985, pp. 1, 3.

Weinand, George and Gayle. San Jose, Costa Rica. May 1985 Newsletter.

Winter, Ralph D. "Unreached Peoples: The Development of a Concept," *Reaching the Unreached*. Phillipsburg, New Jersey: Presbyterian and Reformed Publishing Company, 1984.

Study Questions

1. Why does Wagner say that good strategy for world evangelization brings together faith and faithfulness?

2. Explain how a reexamination of the theology of the Kingdom of God will affect mission practice of ministering in power.

Covering the Globe

Patrick Johnstone

W e have good reason to be encouraged because of what God is doing in the world, but that must be balanced by the solemn reality that so much remains to be done and that the forces opposed to us are so formidable. The finish of world evangelization is in sight, but there are huge barriers to jump and strongholds to break down before the end when Jesus returns.

Isaiah foretold the massive spiritual harvest with a promise:

For you will spread abroad to the right and to the left, your descendants will possess the peoples[1] and will settle the desolate cities.

Three phrases in this verse point to three major challenges we face if we are to complete the task. These are **geographical**—reaching every inhabited part of the world; and **ethnic**—reaching every people; and **urban**—reaching the cities.

THE GEOGRAPHIC CHALLENGE

The promise is that God's people will spread abroad to the right and the left, or we could equally say, to the north and the south, the east and the west. Every inhabited part of our world must be exposed to the gospel of the Lord Jesus Christ. This is a geographical challenge. There are tough challenges, but for missionaries to reach them:

no valley is too isolated—like the remote unevangelized
Kingdom of Mustang on Nepal's northern border,
no island is too distant—like the yet-unreached Maldive
Islands in the Indian Ocean,
no forest is too dense—like the Congo jungles where the
Pygmy people live,
no mountain is too inaccessible—like the remote and harsh
Tibetan plateau of central Asia,
no city is too fortified—like Mecca where no Christian is
allowed to set foot, and
no desert is too hostile—like the Saharan oases in Algeria
where the Mzab Berber peoples live.
Here are some of the geographical challenges:

The 10/40 Window

Great swathes of the surface area of our globe are still without a significant indigenous Christian witness. The maps which follow give the extent to which the gospel has not spread.

Patrick John-stone is Director of Research at WEC International. While serving many years as a missionary in several countries in Africa, he began to develop well-researched materials designed to help Christians lift-up informed intercession for world evangelization. The result was his well known book, *Operation World*, which is used around the world as a tool for praying for the unreached.

From *The Church is Bigger than you Think*, Chapters 21-22. Copyright 1998, Christian Focus Publications, Great Britian. Used by permission.

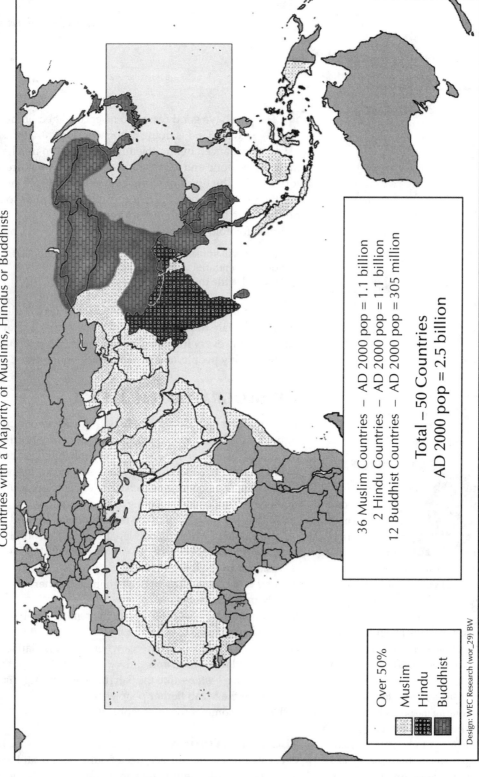

The Resistant Belt and the 10/40 Window
Countries with a Majority of Muslims, Hindus or Buddhists

36 Muslim Countries – AD 2000 pop = 1.1 billion
2 Hindu Countries – AD 2000 pop = 1.1 billion
12 Buddhist Countries – AD 2000 pop = 305 million

Total – 50 Countries
AD 2000 pop = 2.5 billion

Over 50%

Muslim
Hindu
Buddhist

Design: WEC Research (wor_29) BW

This is predominantly in North Africa and Asia where Islam, Hinduism and Buddhism are usually the dominant religions. The map on the previous page highlights this challenging part of the world. This must be the area of major focus for pioneer mission in the next decade or more. However it has been the area of greatest neglect until recently.

For years I called this **the Resistant Belt**. Since 1990 the phrase, **The 10/40 Window**, coined by Luis Bush of the AD2000 Movement,[2] has become widely known. This is the area between the latitudes 10° and 40° north of the equator and between the Atlantic and Pacific Oceans. The concept is good and the publicity impact brilliant—even if this rectangle only approximates to the areas of greatest spiritual challenge.[3] Basically the countries in or near the 10/40 Window that are under-evangelized have only 35% of the world's surface area, but 65% of its population. The map opposite includes both the 10/40 Window concept shown by the rectangle and the Resistant Belt with shading.

The sheer number of people living in the Window area is daunting. Of the 6 billion people in the world in 2000, I reckon that 1.2—1.4 billion have never had the chance to hear the gospel,[4] and over 95% of these individuals reside in the Window area. How can we smugly ignore such a huge number facing a Christless eternity with no opportunity to hear the good news and experience the love of God as revealed in the Lord Jesus? What a challenge to faith, intercession and action—we are obligated to **do** something about it, for the love of Christ constrains us.[5]

To add to the challenge, over 90% of the world's poorest and most deprived, the children that are most abused and most of the world's illiterate live in the Window area. This is where diseases such as AIDS, tuberculosis and malaria rampage largely unchecked and untreated. It is also these areas that are the least accessible for any overt mission endeavor either because of antagonistic political and religious systems, geography or lifestyle. For instance, almost all of the world's nomads live here. We face our biggest challenge yet in world evangelization. The tide of the gospel has risen and flowed over two thirds of the earth, and is lapping at the one third where the final bastions and citadels of Satan's kingdom have yet to be broken down. Let us not minimize the size of the remaining task, but also not be discouraged by its magnitude.

The following diagram shows the number and proportion of Christians, non-Christians with opportunity to hear the gospel and totally unevangelized non-Christians in the 10/40 Window and rest of the world.

World Evangelization & the 10/40 Window

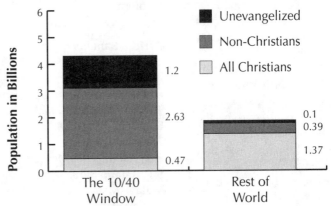

THE PEOPLE CHALLENGE

Jesus clearly stated that we must make disciples of all peoples in the great Matthew 28:19 statement. It is not enough to have a Christian presence in every *place*, but also to have followers of Jesus in every *people*. We have examined the breath-taking progress that has been made in reaching the world's peoples.[6] We not only dream of discipling every people, we could actually see it realized in our lifetime. There are various important ministries that must be strengthened for this discipling to be effective and lasting.

Research

We must know the facts if we are to disciple every people. Research information is therefore vital. There has been research carried on all through this century. The momentum for research on the world's peoples has accelerated over the past 20 years. We need to know who are the unreached peoples, where they live and what is their evangelization status. The Global Consultation on World Evangelization in Pretoria in June 1997 was an opportunity to present a fairly complete overview of unreached peoples at the end of the twentieth century.

For the months prior to that gathering, much work was done on the list of the peoples of the world. It had been decided several years before that for the remaining years of this millennium we needed to make a strategic limitation of the peoples to those over 10,000 population and under 5% Christian or 2% Evangelical, and also to limit our listing to peoples defined by ethnicity or language.[7] The cut-off points were reasonable, but arbitrary. The difficulty in obtaining accurate information on the smaller peoples was a major consideration.[8] This reduced the number from about 3,000 to 1,500 least reached strategic peoples. Further investigation into which mission agencies were committed to specific peoples in this latter list revealed from responses that there were only about 500 peoples in the 1,500 without known outreach activity.[9] From other sources I know that there were a number of these peoples with mission outreach, but for which we had not received questionnaire responses.

We also realized that a long list of 1,500 peoples is a daunting challenge to read, understand and act upon in a meaningful way. We therefore grouped the peoples in two categories:

Affinity Blocs—of which we defined 12. Into these 12 we grouped every one of the 1,500 listed peoples. On the next page is a map of 11 of these.[10] The 12th Bloc is for the Jews[11] who are global and therefore not represented on this map. The 13th grouping is hardly a 'bloc', but a catch-all category for unrelated peoples all over the world which did not fit into the other 12. These 11 regional Blocs are grouped by affinities of language, history, culture, etc. All these 11 are located within or near the 10/40 Window. It is interesting that nearly all the least reached peoples elsewhere in the world are actually migrants from these 11 blocs who now live in Europe, the Americas and Australasia.

People Clusters—Within each of these affinity blocs are other smaller groupings of peoples, often with a common name or identity, but divided by political boundaries, dialect differences, etc. We have identified about 150 of these People Clusters, which include nearly 80% of the 1,500 peoples on the Joshua Project list. Here are 50 better known examples of these less reached People Clusters in the various Affinity Blocs:

African Sahel: *Fula, Mandingo, Wolof, Hausa, Kanuri.*
Cushitic: *Nubian, Somali, Beja.*
Arab World: *Algerian Arab, Kabyle, Riff, Libyan Arab.*
Iranian: *Kurd, Farsi, Tajik, Pathan, Baloch, Luri.*
Turkic: *Turk, Azeri, Kazak, Tatar, Uzbek, Uighur.*
S. Asian: *Bengali, Bihari, Hindi speakers, Urdu, Gond.*
Tibetan: *Lhasa Tibetan, Amdo, Bhutanese, Khampa.*
East Asian: *Hui, Mongolian, Japanese.*
S.E. Asian: *Burmese, Thai, Zhuang, Laotian, Dal.*
Malay: *Minangkabau, Acehnese, Sundanese, Madurese.*
Eurasian: *Chechen, Cherkess, Bosnian, Siberian groups.*

These peoples are categorized in the table below.

Affinity Bloc Name	No. of People Clusters	No. of Peoples in Bloc
African Sahel	19	395
Cushitic	4	37
Arab World	19	271
Iranian	12	181
Turkic	12	256
Indo-Aryan (S. Asia)	30	449
Tibetan	5	197
East Asian	6	70
S.E. Asian	14	93
Malay	18	175
Eurasian	5	44
Jewish	1	56
Totals (approx)[12]	145	2,224

Major Affinity Blocs and the 10/40 Window

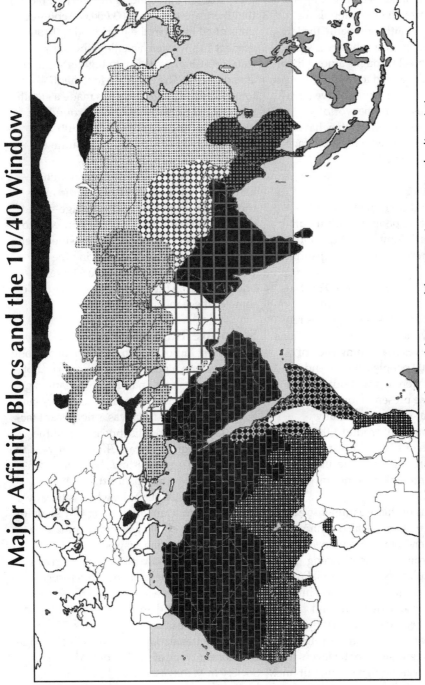

The least evangelized peoples of the world grouped for strategic purposes by linguistic, cultural, economic or political commonalities into eleven Affinity Blocs.

Arab
(280 peoples)

Indo-Aryan
(450 peoples)

Horn of Africa
(40 peoples)

Thai/Dai
(130 peoples)

Sub-Saharan
(400 peoples)

Tibetan
(80 peoples)

Turkic
(260 peoples)

Sinitic
(60 peoples)

Indo-Iranian
(180 peoples)

Malay
(180 peoples)

Eurasian
(100 peoples)

Design: WEC Research (wor_35) Sources: Patrick Johnstone, AD2000 and Beyond Movement, GMI

A book was prepared for the October 1997 Praying Through The Window III[13] initiative containing a short description of, and prayer items for, 128 of these People Clusters. [14] It has been estimated that up to 50 million Christians around the world used these materials for prayer during that month—probably the largest prayer initiative the world has ever seen. God will give the breakthroughs among these peoples that appear so hard to reach!

For the first time in history we have a reasonably complete listing of the world's peoples and the extent to which they have been evangelized. This is why the next stage of church planting is possible.

Church Planting

Can we really see church planting initiatives launched for all peoples within our present generation? Some might question that. In answer I report on what transpired in GCOWE 97.

Luis Bush, the Director of the AD2000 Movement, made a great effort during GCOWE to encourage mission agencies represented and the various national delegations to commit themselves to reaching each of these remaining 500 peoples. By the end of GCOWE only 172 were left without any commitment from those present. However it must be added that we know of many smaller peoples (possibly around 1,000) with populations less than 10,000 who are just as worthy of attention, and part of Jesus' discipling command which are not included in these totals.

The implications of this are immense and exciting. It means that we are also running out of peoples where there is no pioneer work already in progress or in planning. To have reached this point is a very special moment in the history of missions! It also underlines the need for wise networking and partnering with others to ensure that the most effective way to achieve this is pursued.

Planting one congregation of believers in a small tribe of 1,000 can be significant, but one church among the 6 million Tibetans or a few churches among the 200 million Bengalis is less than a drop in the bucket. Our aim should be at minimum a church for every people, but this is only a beginning. This is where the Discipling A Whole Nation vision of Jim Montgomery is so valid. We need to ensure that there is a vital, worshipping group of believers within easy reach of every man, woman and child in the world. I reckon that there are now about 3,000,000 congregations of all kinds in the world today. Montgomery has written a challenging book *7,000,000 Churches to Go!* to highlight the task ahead of us.[15] The DAWN Movement founded by Montgomery has made a significant impact in many countries around the world in setting country-wide, multi-denominational goals for church planting to achieve that vision.

Church planting has been greatly enhanced by many support and media ministries which are people and language-sensitive. Immense efforts are being poured into these ministries, all of which have the potential of almost completely covering the world's population and peoples. Here I briefly describe the possibilities and goals of some of these mega-ministries.

Scripture Translation

It is almost impossible to conceive of a strong church within a people that has no word of the Bible translated into their own language. The lack of the Scriptures for the Berber languages of North Africa was a significant factor in the surprising disappearance of the once-large North African Church between the coming of Islam in 698 and the twelfth century. The same was true for the Nubian peoples of the Upper Nile, who eventually succumbed to Islam after being Christian for 1,500 years; the Bible was never translated into their Nubian languages.

William Carey saw Bible translation as so important that it became the main thrust of his mission work. He wanted to lay the foundations for strong Indian churches through the labors of his missionary successors. The impact of the translation of the Bible is shown by the pioneer work of the London Missionary Society in Madagascar. The LMS made it a high priority to translate the New Testament into Malagasy. Soon after, terrible persecution broke out under Queen Ranavalona. The missionaries were expelled, but in spite of this the church survived and even multiplied.[16]

We can only praise God for the remarkable ministry of the Bible Societies around the world who have multiplied over and over the number of languages that now have Scriptures. More recently God raised up the Wycliffe Bible Translators with the specific vision to provide a New Testament for every language without the Scriptures. WBT is now one of the largest crosscultural mission agencies in the world. Their workers had, by 1997, translated the Scriptures into 420 languages, and have teams working in a further 965. The rate of increase of Bible translations into new languages is shown in this dramatic diagram.

Languages with Scriptures 1600–2000

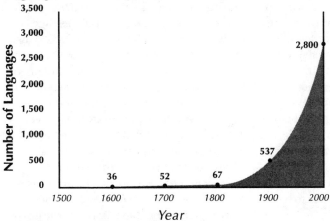

Of the world's 6,703 languages, at least 925 and possibly over 2,000 languages still have a need for New Testament translation work. The majority of these languages are in the African Sahel and Horn of Africa, the Iranic peoples, Central Asia, the Caucasus, China and India. We should be urgently recruiting many more dedicated and talented missionary Bible translators in order to see this task achieved. There is much work to keep an army of translators busy for another generation or more.

Literature

The power of non-Christian literature in corrupting millions is well known, for one only has to think of the pernicious evil that came through Hitler's racist *Mein Kampf*, or Marx's warped theories in *Das Kapital*, and Mao Tse Tung's poisonous diatribes in the *Little Red Book*.

The power of Christian literature should not be underestimated. Some reckon that over half of evangelical Christians attribute their conversion, at least in part, to Christian literature.

Today there is a prodigious volume of Christian literature produced and distributed quite apart from, and complementary to, the work of the Bible Societies—such as The Bible League, Scripture Gift Mission, the Gideons, Pocket Testament League and many others. Here I will only describe what I regard as the most globe-covering literature vision the world has ever seen—that of Every Home for Christ. The vision is very simple, but its outworkings have had extraordinary coverage and impact.

A Forum of Bible Agencies was formed in 1992 linking together the efforts of 17 Bible translation and distribution agencies. The aims are courageous and need to be covered in prayer. In 1993 these were:

1. The whole Bible translated into all languages spoken by five million or more by the end of 1999. There were 33 languages in this category that needed to be translated.
2. The New Testament translated into all languages spoken by over 500,000 people by the end of 1998. This meant a commitment to 77 languages that needed to be translated.
3. Some Scriptures in audio or written form for all languages spoken by more than 250,000 by the end of 1997.
4. Translation begun in all languages spoken by over 100,000 people by the end of 1997.

That vision is to prayerfully distribute a simple, relevant gospel presentation to every home and institution in each country of the world. Every Home for Christ has systematically distributed almost two billion multi-page gospel messages globally, each with a decision card, in languages spoken by 95% of the world's population. Illiterate people are reached with audio messages and the blind are provided messages prepared in braille. Over 19 million of these decision cards have been returned to 80 global offices where each is followed up with a four-part Bible Correspondence Course. The aim is that every contact be introduced to a worshipping group of believers.

Other statistics are equally impressive. In 1997 almost 2,000 full-time nationals were employed in 80 countries, who coordinated as many as 10,000 volunteer distributors in the field during any given week. On average, these workers physically take the gospel to 350,000 new families every seven days, or approximately 50,000 families a day. Based on a global average of 5.2 persons per household, this means that as many as 250,000 persons are provided reasonable access to the message of salvation through EHC activity every day.

In areas of EHC activity where there are no Bible-believing churches of any kind, converts are encouraged to come together for fellowship, Bible study and worship in small groups called "Christ Groups." These sometimes develop into well-established congregations. To date, some 15,000 Christ Groups have been established world-wide with the majority being in such regions as India, Indonesia, Nepal, Africa, the South Pacific, and the former Soviet Union. According to a report received recently from Africa, just one Christ Group near Kinshasa, Congo Republic, has grown to become a well-established church with more than 2,000 members in less than two years. In a city in the Ukraine another Christ Group grew to more than 3,000 in only 18 months.

Since the first EHC was launched in Japan in 1953, systematic every-home distribution has been carried out in more than 166 countries. Seventy-five have had at least one complete nation-wide coverage. Others, like Singapore, Hong Kong and Taiwan have had multiple coverages. Some countries, like India and the Philippines, have had two coverages and are being covered for the third time. The EHC ministry is currently active in 80 countries including many new works in the former Soviet Union, French Africa, Asia, and the Pacific. By 1997 EHC activity world-wide had been responsible for distributing over 1.78 billion pieces of gospel literature in hundreds of languages.

One cannot but be impressed with the breadth of this vision and the above results—even if the magnitude of such figures obscures the disappointments and failures. Yet by this means we have to admit that even in such a large and complex country as India, with the largest concentration of unevangelized individuals in the world, it is likely that nearly all the homes have been visited twice!

Audio Ministries

The story of Joy Ridderhof and Gospel Recordings, the mission she founded, is one of the great missionary sagas of this century.[17] It was a brilliant innovation to devise the means for painstakingly recording simple gospel messages onto records, and later, tapes and CDs even in languages where there were yet no believers or missionaries. The medium also lends itself to being able to fairly quickly produce gospel messages for a multitude of languages and dialects. This linked with simple play-back devices such as the Card-talk for records or manually operated play-back machines for cassettes enabled missionaries to leave an audio message that could be played over and over again. Illiteracy, lack of resident believers or lack of missionaries speaking their languages did not prevent the truth being given to unevangelized peoples. This tool has often been the first means by which totally unevangelized peoples first hear the gospel.

Gospel Recordings has grown into an international network of missions organizations under the title Global Recordings Network with bases in 30 countries. They produce and distribute **audio evangelism materials** in many of the tongues spoken in every country on earth. In 1997 GRN succeeded in preparing a gospel message in their 5,000th language.[18]

One of the advantages of this medium is that the resources and time needed are small enough to enable recordings to be made for the smaller peoples that could not otherwise be served with radio broadcasts or Bible translation for many years to come. A Bible translator would need to think carefully before committing all the effort and the 10-15 years to translating the New Testament into a language spoken by 300 people, but there is far less hesitation for preparing a recording, or series of recordings for a people of 50 speakers.

GRN have a program called *Tail-enders*— those who are the last to get served, if they **ever do** get served. Gospel Recordings/Global Recordings Network is committed to finding and providing for the evangelization of "Tail-enders," who are being ignored and neglected. The ultimate aim is to have a recording for every living language and dialect on earth; possibly a total of around 16,000[19]

There is not the space to tell of many other worthy agencies that specialize in producing audio materials for evangelism and discipleship—Scriptures on tape, teaching, and so on. Here I simply want to show the power of this medium in contributing to the evangelization of the least reached peoples on earth, especially those bypassed by other ministries because of smallness of size or isolation. This further enhances our potential to reach every race, tribe, people and tongue within our lifetime.

The Jesus Film and Videos

The Jesus Film Project is a literal portrayal of the life of Jesus according to the Gospel of Luke. It has become one of the most powerful evangelistic tools of recent times and the most-watched film in history.[20]

The year 2000 vision is that at least all of the world's 300 languages spoken by more than one million people and at most languages spoken by more than 75,000 people, and many of the smaller ones, will have a version of the film available and in use by then. The intermediate goal was 271 translations ready by the end of 1993. By August 1997 this total had reached 417 translated and a further 226 in production.

The effort, planning and resources needed to produce this film in so many languages is staggering. Many thousands of Christian workers in many agencies are working hard in preparing new language versions or extensively showing this film. It has become a significant contributor to world evangelization.

Radio

Christian Radio has had an extraordinary history with some thrilling results in gradually breaking down long-held prejudice against the gospel. It has also made a pivotal contribution to providing teaching to Christians and their leaders especially where no other teaching resources were accessible.

Technology lessens our sole dependence on physical nearness and direct personal contacts, but does not lessen its value.

The most dramatic evangelistic results have been where regular culturally-relevant broadcasts have been beamed into areas closed for most overt mission outreach. Justin Long of the Global Evangelization Movement and working on the World Christian Encyclopedia reckons that there are probably around 3 million people who have come to faith in Christ as a result of radio and television broadcasting, of which possibly 400,000 of these are isolated, often secret believers in areas where no church exists. Such figures are almost impossible to verify, but amazing stories have emerged from Russia, China, India and many parts of the Middle East, of large numbers of churches being planted and nurtured almost entirely by Christian radio. The ministries of HCJB in Ecuador, Trans World Radio, Far East Broadcasting Company & Association, Radio IBRA, and many others have borne fruit beyond all that earlier detractors would have expected.

In recent years many of these large global ministries have come together to form the **World by 2000 International Network**. The aim was the Gospel by Radio to all Peoples. To be more specific, the aim was to provide the gospel by means of radio to every mega-language (this is a language spoken by more than 1,000,000 people) with a daily half-hour broadcast. This means that over 99.5% of the world's population would have the potential to hear the gospel in a language they could understand. The logic behind this is that nearly all of the people who speak a language of less than 1,000,000 would be at least partially bilingual and know sufficient of a more widely spoken language to understand the message. Of course in many areas radio listeners would be few, but in others many. For instance it was reckoned a few years ago that 15% of the population of the southern part of

Muslim Yemen listened to the Christian FEBA station on Seychelles in the Indian Ocean.

At the time the World by 2000 Network made the commitment to broadcast daily for at least 30 minutes to every language of over one million speakers, it was estimated that about 140 of the world's mega-languages had Christian broadcasts. This meant that a further 160 language services needed to be developed.

Since its inception World by 2000 broadcasters have added 75 new languages—and the initiative continues to provide impetus as the year 2000 approaches. There are now approximately 90 remaining languages which are scheduled for development.[21]

It is astonishing to see the progress towards this goal. However, with many of the remaining peoples, the difficulties look almost insurmountable, and will need a large investment of expertise and funds, development of scarce or non-existent follow-up ministries, and a sufficient pool of native- speaker Christians with the maturity in the Lord to make the programs. Just a few examples of the challenge:

- **The 3,000,000 Luri people in Iran** are one of the least reached peoples in the world. There are no known Christians in Iran directly involved in reaching them, and there are few Luri communities in other countries where they are more accessible. How, then, can broadcasts be made when no Christians are available to speak into a radio microphone?
- **The 4,000,000 Kanuri of Niger, Nigeria and Chad** have been evangelized by SUM, SIM and other missions for decades, but after all this effort, the Christians among this Muslim people can be counted on fingers and toes. There are no viable churches and few Christian leaders to recruit for radio ministry, and even if there were, those vital workers would probably have to leave another key ministry to do this. To prepare a daily 30 minute broadcast with the content and necessary appeal is a challenge that needs a team of dedicated workers for broadcasts and the essential follow-up ministries to be maintained.

Satellite Communications

The rapid development of satellite TV broadcasting and the widespread distribution of ever-smaller receiving dishes has radically affected our world—sadly often for the worse with ubiquitous programming that panders to the basest instincts of man. Yet even this medium is proving a remarkable means for proclaiming the gospel in lands hitherto almost inaccessible for the gospel.

For some nations, the advent of satellite technology is a boon for avoiding the need for provision of expensive cables for both national telephone systems and also a network of ground-based television transmitters. This means that even the less-developed countries could leap-frog into twenty-first century technology. Poverty is no longer necessarily a major factor in accessing high technology communications. We can therefore expect that prayerfully launched and wisely managed Christian TV broadcasting could have and is having a significant impact on large numbers of peoples that are otherwise very little exposed to the gospel.

There are a number of Muslim countries that have been very aware of the subversive and corrupting effects to existing morals and religious beliefs by widely accessible programming over which they have no control. Some countries have tried to ban satellite receiver dishes, but to no avail—the dishes get smaller by the year and more easily concealed. It is reckoned that by 1997 about 80% of all homes in Saudi Arabia had satellite dishes, and in Tehran, Iran over 100,000 dishes were being set up every month.

There has been a rapid rise in Christian investment in this medium. In 1997 the Christian broadcasting organizations, **SAT-7** (Cyprus), **The Bible Channel** (UK) and the **Miracle Network** (Norway) were all started using the AMOS satellite with a footprint covering the whole Middle East. By September 1997, 25 million people a week were hearing about the gospel in India by satellite TV, but this will increase to more than 50 million in 11 languages by January 1998. There are big plans for such satellite networks for Latin America and East Asia.

The rapid expansion of "bandwidth" available is enabling more broadcasting with the possibility of interactive discipling programmes, whether by email, sound or TV with computers and satellites. This opens up the way for individual discipling in any language over satellite links. All closed borders become increasingly irrelevant and less of a barrier for any ministry. It is hard for us to imagine in ten years time what might become reality–a missionary based in Germany discipling Mantsi believers in northern Siberia, a Korean intensive TEE course run for Mauritanians in Arabic based in Seoul or a group of refugee Hmong in French Guiana having fellowship with their fellow Hmong believers in Laos! This all opens up the potential for significant mission work to the ends of the earth to be run from a local congregation's own facilities.

We must not be dazzled by the wonders of technology and think that the need for mighty intercessory prayer is obviated, the need for the cross and suffering nullified, or the value of real life acculturation and incarnation of expatriate missionaries within the culture lessened. Technology lessens our sole dependence on physical nearness and direct personal contacts, but does not lessen its value. Every people on earth must be reached with the gospel and discipled for the Kingdom, but the flexibility and variety of tools and possibilities have multiplied. Let us use them where appropriate.

Each medium provides another layer of global coverage. Not every layer will affect every person equally, but the cumulative multiplicity of media layers does give us grounds to give greater expectation that the task can be finished if we mobilize the resources of the Church.

THE URBAN CHALLENGE

The great cities of the world are the key challenge for mission in the twenty-first century. We ignore the cities to our peril. The great cities of our world are the source of most of our wealth and misery, wisdom and depravity, innovations and sin. The engine for societal change is in the cities, but, if used wisely, it could be the dynamo for the growth of the Kingdom.

The twenty-first century will be an urban world, just as the previous 20 centuries of Christianity have been a rural world. The end of the second millennium is also the end of the rural majority with just over 50% of the world's population urbanized.

Two centuries ago the world was rural, with an urbanization of 4% and only one megacity in existence– Beijing with 1,100,000.[22] By 1900 these had increased to 14%, 18 megacities and 2 supercities– London and New York. By 2000 these will have reached 51% urbanized, about 20 supergiants (only one of which is in Europe or North America), 79 supercities and 433 megacities. That trend will continue so that by 2100 the number of rural inhabitants may be only 10% of the world's population. The cities are even more vital for mission strategy than they were in Paul's day.

Pioneer missions in the twentieth century have been characterized by the need to reach unreached peoples; a process within sight of conclusion. The twenty-first century will be characterized by the need for pioneer missions in the great cities of the world– a much more complex and multi-layered kaleidoscope of needs. Mission frontiers in the twentieth century were perceived as rural, but we must switch our thinking to the urban challenge as the frontier of the future.

We have been winning the countryside and losing the cities, and all the time our rural constituency has been draining away to the cities. The glamour and romanticism associated with the jungles, mountains, deserts and remote islands seem like "real" mission work to the home constituency, but living in a concrete jungle, or squalid slum is far less attractive, and undesirable as a place of ministry.

One of the most powerful advocates of the need of the urban poor is Viv Grigg. When I first met him, he was living in a squalid slum in Manila. We walked through the smells and noise of the area where he lived. We had to climb up a ladder, through a trap door to sit with him and drink tea. His meager possessions were scattered round this hot, stuffy little room. I felt he had earned the right to speak with passion as a prophet on behalf of the urban poor. He does not mince his words in speaking about the challenge to missions:

> ...we must thrust out groups similar to the devotional communities of the twelfth century preaching friars, or the wandering Irish monks that converted Northern Europe between the fifth and ninth centuries...In our case we must send communities of men and

women, married couple and singles, with commitments to live as the poor among the poor in order to preach the kingdom and establish the church in these great slum areas...[23]

and

God is offering Western missions the chance to return to a biblical commitment to the poor and to incarnation as the primary mission-ary role model. The need is urgent: several thousand catalysts in the slums of scores of third-world cities who can generate movements in each city. Two billion people cry out.

Our desolate cities are an immense challenge, but I believe a new day for urban ministry is dawning. The Lord promises us that these cities will be populated with his people.

End Notes

1. Nearly all English translations use the word "nation." This miscommunicates today because we think of modern nation-states, whereas Isaiah was speaking of ethnic groups or people rather than political entities. Many English translations use the term *dispossess* rather than *possess*, which unfortunately restricts the application to the Old Testament context of Israel taking the Promised Land; I am convinced the application is wider and also of application to the times in which we live.

2. AD2000 and Beyond Movement publications.

3. Indonesia, Mongolia, the Muslim republics of Central Asia, Sri Lanka, Maldives and Somalia should be included but are outside the Window. Countries in the Window with significant, often nominal, Christian populations such as South Korea, Philippines, Eritrea and many European Mediterranean countries should perhaps be or are omitted.

4. Johnstone 1993:27 (est. 20% unevangelized, 47% non-Christians living where they are likely to be evangelized and 33% professing Christian), Barrett, 1987, *Cosmos, Chaos and the Gospel*. (Birmingham AL: New Hope) p. 85 (est. 17% unevangelized).

5. 2 Corinthians 5:14-15.

6. See Johnstone, Patrick. 1998. *The Church is Bigger Than You Think: Structures and Strategies for the Church in the 21st Century*, Great Britain: Christian Focus Publications/WEC.

7. Further research and field responses indicated that some of the 1,500 peoples were not ethno-linguistic, but ethno-cultural. This came to light at the same time as a plea from Indian Christian leaders that the ethno-linguistic categories did not fit the ethno-cultural realities for church planting among the caste groups of India. We therefore had to draw up a parallel list containing these categories for where it was more relevant in a church planting situation.

8. By the year 2000, we plan to have a full list of all less-reached peoples including those with populations below 10,000.

9. The full list is available in book form from the AD2000 and Beyond Movement office, 2860 S. Circle Dr., Suite 2112, Colorado Springs, CO 80906, USA. Also on the WWW: <http://www.ad2000.org/>.

10. A good colored map of these Affinity Blocs has been published by Global Mapping International. 7899 Lexington Drive, Suite 200A, Colorado Springs CO 80920, Email: <info@gmi.org.> WWW <http://www.gmi.org/>.

11. Fischer, 1997. *Intercessor's Prayer Guide to the Jewish World*. 1997: USA: YWAM Publishing.

12. These figures must be seen as approximations, for further research is showing that some peoples are more reached than realized and therefore omitted and other peoples are added—usually because migrant communities of larger peoples are discovered in other lands.

13. The AD2000 and Beyond Movement sponsored annually from 1982 an annual global prayer emphasis, each focusing on a particular category of the world's population.

14. Hanna 1997. *Praying Through The Window III*.

15. Montgomery 1975, 1989, 1997, *Dawn 2000: 7 Million Churches to Go*. Montgomery's challenge as to the need for church multiplication applies both to areas not yet evangelized and to areas that have been evangelized, but where accessibility to churches is inadequate.

16. Neill 1964, *A History of Christian Missions*, (Hasmondworth, Middlesex: Penguin Books Ltd), pp. 269-70.

17. Barlow, S. M. , 1952, *Mountains Singing; The Story of Gospel Recordings in the Philippines* (Chicago: Moody Press). Thompson, Phyllis, 1978, *Count it all Joy: The Story of Joy Ridderhof*, Gospel Recordings.

18. Gospel Recording Network has an email address at <GloReNet@aol.com> and a web site at <http://ourworld-compuserve.com/homepages/GloReNet>

19. The latest WBT Ethnologue total for known languages of the world is 6,700. However, the Ethnologue also lists known dialects of these languages. This adds almost 10,000 dialects to the language list. The difference between language and dialect is hard to determine, but decided not only on linguistic, but also historical, cultural and social factors. If one group of people dislikes their same-language neighbours, a few words that differ, or shades of pronunciation are all that are needed to make a dialect into another language and another New Testament preferred!

20. Eshleman, Paul 1995, *The Touch of Jesus* (The story of the Jesus Film) Orlando: New Life Publications. This book tells something of the history, struggles, triumphs and fruit of this extraordinary gospel tool.

21. The World By 2000 Network has a web site where more details may be found of languages broadcast, and languages for which broadcasts are needed: <http://www.wb2000.org/>.

22. Barrett defines a megacity as one with 1,000,000 population, super-cities with 4,000,000 and super-giants with 10,000,000. Barrett 1986. Cities and World Evangelization. Birmingham AL, USA: New Hope.

23. Grigg 1992. The Cry of the Urban Poor: Reaching the Slums of Today's Megacities. Monrovia, CA: MARC Publications.

The Challenge of the Cities

Roger S. Greenway

Cities are the new frontier of Christian missions. Because of their size, influence, diversity and needs, cities present enormous challenges. To neglect cities would be a strategic mistake because, as cities go, the world goes.

Cities are the centers of political power, economic activity, communication, scientific research, academic instruction, and moral and religious influence. Whatever happens in cities affects entire nations. When Christ's kingdom advances in cities, the number of people worshiping and serving the true God multiplies.

The 20th Century was the time when the world became an urban world. When the century began, only 13 percent of the world's population lived in cities. By the end of the century, half the world will live in cities.

In 1950, only two cities, New York and London, had more than eight million inhabitants. By the end of the century, there will be 22. By the year 2015, 33 cities are expected to have more than eight million. Nineteen of these will be in Asia.

Migration from rural areas to urban centers explains about half of the growth of cities. The other half is due to internal growth, which is determined by the number of births over deaths. The movement of more than a billion people to the cities over the last two decades is the largest population movement in history.

Causes of Rural-Urban Migration

An underlying cause of migration to the cities is the worldwide increase in population. Generally, people today live longer, infant mortality has decreased, and medicines keep people alive who years ago would have died. With the increase in population comes the need for more jobs. This forces millions to leave their traditional rural homes and move to cities in search of employment.

There are other causes also. Cities offer educational opportunities that are not available in small towns and villages. There are hospitals and health centers in cities for people with special medical needs. Young people, especially, are attracted to the cities because cities offer excitement, entertainment and new opportunities. Often they come to cities dreaming of riches and a better life, only to have their dreams destroyed by the hard realities of urban life.

Roger S. Greenway is Professor of World Missiology at Calvin Theological Seminary in Grand Rapids, Michigan. For 24 years he served in overseas missions, first in Sri Lanka, later in Latin America and eventually as Executive Director of Christian Reformed World Ministries.

Asia (in millions)

Bangladesh
Dhaka 19.0

China
Beijing 19.4
Shanghai 15.1
Tianjin 10.4
Shenyang 9.4

Japan
Tokyo 28.7
Osaka 11.6

Korea
Seoul 13.1

Thailand
Bangkok 13.9

India
Mumbai 27.4
New Delhi 17.6
Calcutta 17.6
Hyderabad 10.4
Madras 8.4

Indonesia
Jakarta 21.2

Pakistan
Karachi 20.6
Lahore 10.6

Philippines
Manila 14.7

Megacities of Tomorrow

Analysts predict these populations (in millions) for some of the world's largest cities in the year 2015.

Keep in mind that every one of these millions of people is a human being made in God's image. Each one has many needs and, above all else, needs Jesus Christ and salvation through Him. What a tremendous missionary challenge awaits us in the cities!

Africa

Nigeria
Lagos 24.4
Zaire
Kinshasa 13.9

Europe and Middle East

Egypt
Cairo 14.5
France
Paris 9.6
Iran
Teheran 14.6
Russia
Moscow 9.2
Turkey
Istanbul 12.3

North America

Mexico
Mexico City 18.8
United States
New York 17.6
Los Angeles 14.3

South America

Argentina
Buenos Aires 12.4
Brazil
Sao Paulo 20.8
Rio de Janeiro 11.6
Peru
Lima 12.1

* Much larger population figures are reported when they include both cities and the wider metropolitan areas around cities. The numbers above include cities only.

Urban Poverty and Suffering

Some of the worst suffering is found among people who have recently arrived in cities. People from rural peasant classes are seldom prepared for the difficulties they encounter. They lack the skills required for the jobs that are available. They cannot afford to buy property or pay high rent. They are forced to live in squatter settlements, in shacks built of discarded wood, tin, and tar paper, usually located on the fringes of the city.

In their early stages, squatter communities lack water, sewage, electricity and regular streets. Because the land does not belong to them, the residents are vulnerable to eviction and the sudden loss of their homes. Those who are fortunate enough to find work must spend exhausting hours each day walking and traveling on public buses. Family life suffers as young and old work seven days a week at whatever jobs they can find.

Life is hard for the poor in cities. Crime is prevalent, and security is low. Nevertheless, large numbers of new people continue to arrive from the villages. They are drawn as though by invisible magnets to the cities. And despite the poverty and suffering, their level of optimism regarding the future is generally high. They firmly believe that if not the parents, certainly the children will enjoy better lives in the city.

Openness to the Gospel

As a general rule, people who are recently dislocated, and are experiencing major changes in their lives, are more open to the gospel than they were before. In my experience, this is true also among people who have recently arrived in cities.

New people in the cities are open to new ideas, including ideas about God and religion. As a result, I have come to believe that God is behind the migration of masses of people to the cities. He is creating new opportunities for spreading the gospel among unreached people coming from remote towns and villages. It is our task to take hold of the opportunity and carry out Christ's missionary command.

During my years in Mexico City, I worked with students in evangelizing and planting churches in squatter communities and other low-income areas. At first we tried other parts of the urban population. But we found that the greatest openness to the gospel was among people who had arrived in the city less than ten years earlier.

Using the simplest and least costly methods, going door-to-door, witnessing personally to families in their homes, praying for the sick and starting Bible studies, we began dozens of "cells" and house churches. Many of them developed into well established congregations. This led me to believe that the massive migration to the cities that is occurring around the world may be, in God's providence, a key to world evangelization. Through urbanization, God is drawing people of every race, tribe and language to places where they can be reached with the gospel.

Practical Issues in Urban Missions

There are five important considerations for inner city ministry.

1. Poverty. In many cities, between 30 and 50 percent of the population is poor, often *desperately* poor. Urban mission work, in most cases, demands that missionaries follow a comprehensive strategy that proclaims the gospel of God's saving love and demonstrates the same Gospel in practical ways. Coping daily with social inequities and economic differences is a very practical issue for urban missionaries.

2. Racial, ethnic and cultural diversity. In most countries, city populations are composed of people from many different backgrounds. They represent different tribes, castes, races and social classes, and they speak different languages. Unavoidably, this affects mission strategy and church development. It also calls for missionaries who enjoy being near many different people.

3. Religious pluralism. In villages, most people follow one particular religion. But city people follow a variety of religious beliefs and practices. Urban missionaries may give major attention to one group, but they must be prepared to witness to others as well. They must also be prepared to respond to people who reject all religion, and others who regard all religions as equally true.

4. Anti-urban attitudes. Traditionally, most mission work was done in rural areas. In the past, that made sense because most people lived in rural communities. But the biggest challenge is now in cities, and there we find a shortage of workers. Many missionaries are so disturbed by the noise and traffic in cities, the pollution, social problems, crime and crowded housing, that they prefer working in rural areas. Unreached villages certainly need to hear the gospel. But in view of the masses of unsaved and unchurched people in cities, more attention must be given to urban centers.

> Through urbanization, God is drawing people of every race, tribe and language to places where they can be reached with the gospel.

5. High cost. A major practical issue for mission agencies is the higher financial costs of urban work. To begin with, housing for missionaries is more expensive in cities. In villages, a piece of land for a church building often costs little or nothing, and local believers can erect their own place of worship. But in cities, property is expensive. There are building codes to follow, labor unions and higher wages to pay. These and other factors tempt missionaries to avoid cities in favor of rural areas.

God's Word for Cities

God's Word must always be our starting point in missions. In order to understand God's will for cities, we need more than scattered verses of the Bible. We need to see God's overall plan from creation and the fall, to redemption and consummation, as it applies to cities. In that light I suggest that the following biblical teachings be considered:

1. All human beings are creatures of God, made in His image and fallen into sin, and the gospel of God's saving grace in Christ applies to everybody. By this I mean that the gospel meets the spiritual needs of people of all races, nationalities, tribes and social classes.

Cities impress us by the fact that they are multi-ethnic, multi-cultural, and multi-religious. But the Bible teaches that there is one gospel, from the one God, through the one Savior, and it is for all the people cities contain. That truth is basic to our understanding of urban mission.

2. While felt needs differ from person to person and place to place, ultimate needs are universal and must be addressed. People in the city have differing perceptions as to what they need. Some will identify their needs as jobs, better housing, medical care and education. These needs are real and legitimate, and a holistic approach to urban mission will address many of them.

However, the temptation is to become so absorbed in helping people meet their felt needs that ultimate needs are neglected. Ultimate needs are those that the Bible declares to be peoples' most urgent and critical needs. They are the universal needs of repentance and conversion, reconciliation with God, and eternal life through faith in Christ.

3. It is God's will that cities be evangelized. In view of the anti-urban bias that we have mentioned, this point must be underscored.

In the Bible, urban mission began with the story of Jonah, the Old Testament prophet whom God called to preach to the wicked in the city of Nineveh. Jonah represented all who, down through the years, tried to avoid the call to the city. But as Jonah discovered, God was serious about bringing His message to the city. God cared about the Ninevites, their children, and even the animals (Jonah 4:11).

Christ's commission to "go and make disciples of all peoples," forbids neglecting cities with their multitudes from all tribes and races. It is significant that the missionary strategy of the apostle Paul was completely urban. Even though hostilities met him in most of the cities in which he worked, Paul knew God wanted cities evangelized.

4. Vital, gospel-preaching churches are the hope of cities, and developing such churches is a key to urban missions. The New Testament treats churches as "new covenant" communities in Christ whose mission is to communicate the gospel and, by their presence and activity, be lighthouses and showcases of Christ's Kingdom. City churches are Christ's agents of transformation in society. Paul's strategy typically began with evangelism and went on to church-planting. By his teaching, writing and example, Paul equipped churches to be light, salt and leaven in their communities. Churches that fail in this are of little good to the city.

5. Cities are battle fields where spiritual warfare between Christ's Kingdom and Satan's is very evident. Saint Augustine wrote that in every city there are *two* cities, the city of God and the city of Satan, and they are in continual conflict with one another. It is undeniable that cities contain strongholds of satanic power that resist the spread of the gospel and promote unrighteousness in society.

Cities are not evil because they are cities. Rather, cities maximize human potential for both good and evil. There is much that is beautiful and good in cities. By their schools, hospitals and productivity, cities enhance the quality of human life. But at the same time, the power of evil is evident. Sin expresses itself not only in the wrongdoing of individuals, but also in institutions whose policies and actions exploit and oppress, as well as in the wrong use of the systems by which cities are managed.

To keep ourselves from both excessive optimism as to what we can accomplish and from depression when setbacks come, urban workers must possess biblical awareness of the spiritual warfare going on.

6. To bring Shalom —God's Kingdom peace—to cities with their varieties of people, cultures, religions and problems requires multi-faceted, holistic ministries. These holistic ministries should be designed to: (a) make disciples of Jesus Christ, (b) multiply churches in every people group, (c) demonstrate compassion and promote justice, (d) care for the environment as God's creation, and (e) pray continually that Satan will be defeated and Christ exalted in every corner of the city.

In cities containing people of many languages and cultures, vigorous church-planting must be carried out in all the different communities so that the gospel can be heard and understood by everyone.

Care for God's creation is a Christian obligation, and Christ's disciples in urban centers ought to be at the forefront of efforts to preserve and protect the earth, air and water. Not only are people hurt, but God Himself is dishonored by polluted air, toxic water and contaminated earth.

Prayer for cities is missionary activity. "Seek the *shalom* of the city," Jeremiah told God's people in Babylon, "and *pray for it!*" Neither Satan nor city problems can withstand the effects of prayer.

7. The eschatological vision of the New Jerusalem inspires Christ's urban workers and shapes the mission agenda. The movement of history throughout the Bible is from the garden of Eden where the fall occurred, to the New Jerusalem, the city that God is preparing for us.

Believe it or not, all God's children will eventually be urbanites! Life in a city lies ahead of us. It will be a city where truth and righteousness are the way of life and Christ's name alone is honored (Rev 21:10-27). That vision should motivate us now, and keep us going despite the obstacles. For like Abraham, our faces are turned toward "the city with foundations, whose architect and builder is God (Heb 11:10).

Steps Toward Engagement in Urban Missions

I plead with all who are concerned about doing God's will and reaching lost people for Christ to consider the challenge of the growing cities of the world. The migration to the cities is so large that it must have a divinely-ordained, redemptive purpose behind it. How shall we respond?

Our response should not depend on whether we prefer to live in cities or not. As it was for Jonah, and no doubt for Paul, the question is whether we will go where workers are needed and where God wants us to go.

For those who are willing to explore what God may have in mind for them, I suggest certain steps:

1. Grow

Most important is your own spiritual development. Ministry in cities requires that you "put on the full armor of God"(Eph 6:11), not just once or occasionally, but daily. There-

Photo courtesy of Caleb Project

fore, stretch your spiritual horizons. Go beyond your individual development into church-related concerns and areas of ministry in which you must pay a price in order to strengthen others.

2. Get Involved

Become involved in some kind of organized urban mission work. It will give you valuable experience and will test your gifts for ministry. Offer yourself as an "apprentice" to an effective urban pastor, evangelist or missionary. Observe carefully how the Lord uses his workers. Learn all you can about presenting the gospel to different kinds of people and meeting a variety of needs.

3. Learn

Read books and journals that deal with mission work in cities and learn all you can about different models of urban ministry. If possible, take a course in urban ministry at a Bible college or seminary. Some schools offer advanced academic programs in urban mission.

4. Explore

Investigate a particular city. Begin by studying a map of the city and identifying its different parts—the commercial areas, industrial zones and residential neighborhoods. Look closely at the areas that are growing in population and the kinds of people and cultures found there. Then choose one neighborhood and study its people—their religions, cultures, languages and social conditions. Inquire about their spiritual, social and material needs. Find out if there are vital churches in every language group. Then think about ways to advance Christ's Kingdom in particular neighborhoods.

5. Pray

Develop and maintain a prayer ministry for cities. Prayer is missionary action. You can begin your urban mission immediately by making a list of certain cities in various parts of the world. Learn all you can about the people and their needs. Then pray regularly that God will build His Kingdom in those cities.

Follow these steps and you will grow in your understanding of what urban mission entails. God will increase the burden of your heart for cities and will show you what role He wants you to play. Consider it a great privilege if He calls you to be his co-worker in building His kingdom in the most strategic places in the world, the cities.

Study Questions

1. Explain why cities are so strategic for missions today.

2. Explain why millions of people are migrating to cities.

3. How should missionaries prepare themselves for mission work in cities?

4. What factors should guide mission agencies in the division of personnel between work in villages and cities?

5. What attracts you to cities, and what makes you want to avoid cities?

From Every Language

Barbara F. Grimes

"After this I looked and there before me was a great crowd that no one could count, from every nation, tribe, people, and language, standing before the throne and in front of the Lamb." Revelation 7:9

We have been commanded to make disciples of all peoples. To do this, every communicator of the gospel—evangelist, teacher, development worker or church planter—makes choices about which language they will use for ministry. Too often the choice of which language to use is made on the basis of what is easiest for the communicator, rather than what communicates best to the hearers.

Conducting ministry in the mother tongue of hearers is obviously more effective. But for ministry that really reaches unreached peoples, mother tongue ministry is not just valuable, it is crucial. The necessity of mother-tongue ministry and the use of mother-tongue Scriptures becomes clear by looking at the kind of disciples and churches that we would like to see.

Making Mother Tongue Disciples

A lot of what a disciple is commanded to do involves language. Being a disciple of Jesus Christ involves getting to know Him personally. That requires adequate comprehension of the good news and of God's Word. Understanding and knowledge are repeatedly emphasized throughout the Scriptures. The Apostle Paul said it was his responsibility to make the message clear (Col 4:4).

But being a disciple involves more than passive comprehension. A disciple is commanded to witness to his faith, encourage other Christians, exhort those who need it, pray, give praise, give thanks, sing, memorize God's Word, teach his own children, older women to teach younger women, instruct one another, meditate; exercise gifts of the Spirit given to him that involve verbal behavior, such as communicating wisdom, passing on knowledge, prophecy, interpretation of tongues, fulfilling the functions of appointed messengers, evangelists, pastors, and teachers. Some persons are to read Scripture publicly, to teach, preach, and interpret any foreign language used in church.

The mother tongue is the language people learn first at their mother's knee; in which they learn to think and talk about the world around them, to interact with people closest to them, to acquire and express their values, the language

Barbara F. Grimes has been a member of Wycliffe Bible Translators since 1951. She worked with her husband Joseph among the Huichol Indians of Mexico, where they and Huichol speakers produced the Huichol New Testament and other literature. She has been the editor of *Ethnologue: Languages of the World* since 1971. Since 1988 she and her husband have been translating Scripture with speakers of Hawaii Pidgin into that language.

Used by permission of the author. Diagram from *Bible Translation Update*, Wycliffe Bible Translators, Vol. 12, Issue 2, 1998.

which becomes part of their personality and identity, and which expresses ethnicity and solidarity with their people. People can handle the verbal skills required for adequate comprehension of the good news and functioning as a disciple in their mother tongue; the question is whether or not they can do those things in their second language.

Planting Churches That Endure

It is possible to plant churches without mother-tongue clarity, but it is almost never desirable. Without Scriptures in the mother tongue, churches are not able to sustain spiritual depth into succeeding generations. They have difficulty answering false teaching, waging spiritual warfare, and avoiding syncretism. Many in or around the church fail to recognize that the Christian God is the universal God to whom all must answer. It's not hard to see why churches without this are not only hindered from reaching out to others in their own community, they often do not get a vision for obeying God's missionary call to go elsewhere.

Two approaches often distract gospel communicators from doing the more difficult and lasting work to make disciples in the local mother tongue: First, in multilingual situations there is a perceived possibility of conveying the good news in a second language, and secondly, there is often a hope that bilingual language brokers will carry the message to others within their community.

Multilingual Populations

Careful study of how different languages are used in multilingual societies has given important insights to sociolinguists in recent decades. Multilingual people use each of their languages in different circumstances, with different people, to talk about different topics, with varying degrees of success in speaking and understanding, and with different psychological connotations. It is important for those who want to communicate the most important message in the world to be aware of these factors, lest both they and their message be misunderstood or rejected.

Because the second language is learned in certain situations, and depends on the amount and kind of contact an individual has

had with it, and his desire and need to learn it, there are differences in fluency across a population. It is not possible to judge the bilingual proficiency of a population by looking at only a small sample of the population. It is necessary to investigate how different age groups, both sexes, people in different regions and with different educational levels use their languages, and to study any other factors which may influence contact with the second language in that culture. The importance of reaching everyone for Christ, including women, older people, the uneducated, and those in remote areas, justifies the time and effort needed to carry out a reliable investigation of these differences.

Working with Bilingual Brokers

Often eager mission efforts look for rapid communication by routing the message through a bilingual person. This approach, used extensively in missions with dubious results, has been called "the language broker model." In this model, a bilingual person hears the message or reads Scripture in his or her second language, and then is expected to transfer the meaning into his mother tongue for the benefit of those who do not understand the other language. Unfortunately, few people are able to do that kind of transferring without extensive training and experience in that skill. Most bilingual speakers of minority languages have learned their second language through direct oral contact outside a classroom, and lack training in language transfer.

The Scriptures are often available to those churches only in a second language. This model avoids having to translate the Scriptures into the first language, but assumes that spontaneous paraphrases of Scripture are adequate. There is no guarantee that such impromptu paraphrases done repeatedly by various speakers in different situations are at all accurate. The language broker model often results in a bilingual elite in the church being the only ones eligible to become leaders. Others to whom God may have given the gifts of teaching, preaching, and other gifts involving using language may be hindered from exercising those gifts by lack of sufficient bilingual proficiency to function in the second language.

From Every Language

Wise good news communicators will work for lasting results. They will do the challenging work of linguistic assessment and Bible translation. They'll do this difficult work with the people in mind, with the outcome in view, so that they will endeavor to bring the gospel to every people in a language that they not only understand, but that the people will use to become mature disciples, build the church, extend the good news, and worship God in meaningful ways for their own people. It's not enough for a few people to understand part of the message. For God to hear His praise spoken by flourishing churches "from every language," His communicators must do the important work of bringing God's word in a way that speaks to their hearts and homes in every language.

Bible Translation: How Many Languages to Go?

In 1951, the *Ethnologue* was created to try to find out where Bible translations were still needed. By 1974, research had progressed so that all known languages in the world were included.

How many languages still need Bible translation in 1999? Language surveys are still needed in nearly 2,800 languages to be able to answer that question. In addition, many surveys are discovering additional languages that were not recognized or counted earlier. Past experience shows that about 5 out of every 6 languages listed as needing survey end up in the Definite Translation Need category.

It is not enough for people to have only one book of Scripture to become mature, growing disciples. With 5,000 or more languages still to receive a Bible or New Testament in a language that speaks clearly to them, there is a big translation job to do.

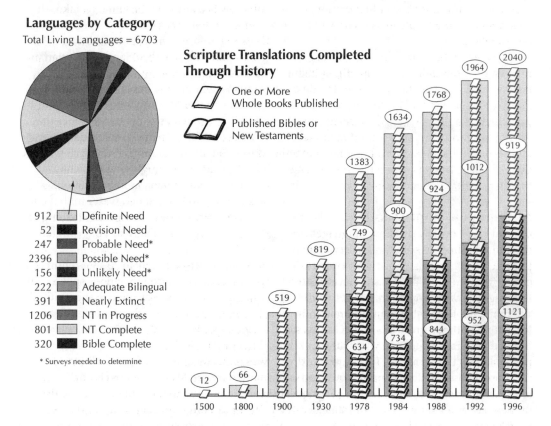

Languages by Category
Total Living Languages = 6703

912	Definite Need
52	Revision Need
247	Probable Need*
2396	Possible Need*
156	Unlikely Need*
222	Adequate Bilingual
391	Nearly Extinct
1206	NT in Progress
801	NT Complete
320	Bible Complete

* Surveys needed to determine

Scripture Translations Completed Through History

One or More Whole Books Published

Published Bibles or New Testaments

Sources: Grimes, Barbara F., ed. 1996. *Ethnologue: Languages of the World, 13th edition.* Dallas: Summer Institute of Linguistics, Inc. <http://www.sil.org/ethnologue/>
Bible Translation Needs Bulletin Vol. 3, 1996. Dallas: Wycliffe Bible Translators, International.
Lupas, Liana, and Erroll F. Rhodes, eds. 1996. *Scriptures of the World.* Reading, England: United Bible Societies.

How Many People Groups are There?

Larry Walker

Larry Walker is the Southwest Regional Director for ACMC (Advancing Churches in Missions Commitment). He has served as a Missions Pastor as well as a missionary in Guatemala.

From *Mission Frontiers Bulletin*, January-February 1994. Used by permission.

Researchers have argued about the definition of a people group. How many are there, and how many are truly unreached? At the time of this writing, The Global Evangelization Database gives the number of ethnolinguistic peoples as 11,874. But within these are various dialects and other sub-groupings which may raise the number to 24,000 or more. Herein lies the confusion between the numbers of unreached peoples given by different researchers.

All the lists of peoples or estimates of the total number of peoples are based on "obtainable" second-hand data. While such lists and estimates are helpful for mobilizing mission resources and planning the initial phases of a people focused strategy, we never truly know just how many distinct peoples a name on a list represents until someone takes the plunge and lives long-term among them.

During the late '70s, my family and I moved into a Tzutujil (Sutuheal) Indian Village called Santiago Atitlan, in the highlands of Guatemala.

I will never forget my first plunge into Tzutujil culture. The first week I was there I went to the shore of the lake to fetch water. As I tried to push a plastic container under the water I lost my balance and fell into the lake. My daughters were screaming, "Are you all right, Daddy?" Tzutujil women were trying their best to hide their laughter at the lanky gringo trying to crawl out of an embarrassing situation.

I learned later that only women fetched water in that culture. That incident symbolizes how awkward I felt trying to navigate my way through a culture that was very different from my own.

My responsibility was to train leaders in 20 some churches located around Lake Atitlan. Those congregations spoke one of three Mayan languages—Cakchiquel, Quiche and Tzutujil. Among the Cakchiquel is where one of the most significant initial events of the modern mission movement took place. It was a Cakchiquel man who asked a young Cameron Townsend who was trying to sell him a Spanish Bible, "If your God is so smart, why can't he speak Cakchiquel?"

That question echoed in Townsend's mind until he finally translated the New Testament into Cakchiquel and eventually started Wycliffe Bible Translators to reach the other Bibleless peoples of the world. But as it turns out, after missionaries had lived among the Cakchiquels for a number of years, they began to realize that Cakchiquel was not just one of the Mayan languages in Guatemala, but it was really a cluster of six different dialects. As a result, Wycliffe is now doing a simultaneous translation of the New Testament so that our God will finally "speak" in all six written dialects of Cakchiquel.

A very similar process occurred among the nearby Tzutujil people with whom I was working. Interestingly, Cameron Townsend was one of the first pioneer missionaries to bring the gospel to the Tzutujil people as well. One of the very first converts in Santiago Atitlan told me he remembers Townsend sleeping on the shore of the lake because the people would not let him sleep in the village. It was common for missionaries to be dragged through the streets by the hair, to be jailed, or have their homes burned, etc., in those early days.

The number of converts were very few at first. But there was a dramatic change in the lifestyle of the new believers. So even though the early believers were ostracized and persecuted, their positive testimony became the fuel that sparked the beginnings of a genuine people movement among the villages around the lake. Still the Tzutujil lacked the Bible in their own language.

In the early sixties, Jim and Judy Butler arrived to translate the New Testament into Tzutujil. They decided to live and do their translation work in San Pedrano de La Laguna because the Pedrano-Tzutujil were more progressive and assertive than Tzutujil in other villages. When we took the plunge into the Tzutujil world in the late 70s, the Butlers had just finished the New Testament.

I was delighted to have the New Testament in the Tzutujil language. But I very soon discovered that the Atitecos-Tzutujil (people of Santiago Atitlan) did not want to use the Tzutujil translation. The only thing that separated the two villages was a volcano. But as I soon learned, the languages of the two groups were quite different.

In time, I came to realize that the problem was not even a problem of one group not understanding the other. The Atitecos could understand 90% of the translation. The problem was that it was from San Pedro de La Laguna and it sounded foreign to them.

I came to understand that one of their core values is a pride in local traditions and a built-in resistance to anything foreign. Americans value progress and "building better mouse traps," but this is totally contrary to the way the Tzutujil think. For example, if a teenage girl decides to wear sandals in public for the first time, she will have to suffer ridicule for at least a week from her peers. Each village has its own distinctive dress for men and women as well as many customs that give them their own separate identity.

I came to the conclusion that a New Testament for the Atiteco-Tzutujil villages would be necessary to maintain an indigenous people movement among these people. I recruited my language helper to begin the translation. After I left the field, Jim Butler continued to supervise the translation into the Atiteco-Tzutujil dialect. The translation was dedicated in September of 1993.

So what originally was thought to be one people group, came to be seen as really two, with two translations needed. The indigenous people movement continues to grow among these villages around the lake. Today, some 25-35% of the people are evangelicals. Translations in the various dialects will play an important role in maintaining that people movement for years to come, giving every individual the ability to hear the gospel and read the Bible in his or her own dialect.

This is just one example of what is going on around the world in hundreds of people groups. Missionaries will never really know how many people groups there are until they "take the plunge" and live among the people.

Study Questions

1. Based on Walker's experience what process is necessary to determine how many people groups are not yet reached?

2. Why is it important for every people group to have the Scriptures in their own language?

Healing the Wounds of the World

John Dawson

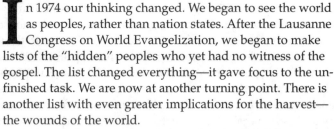

John Dawson is the founder of the International Reconciliation Coalition in Ventura, California. He is a member of the Global Leadership Team of Youth With A Mission. The International Reconciliation Coalition is dedicated to healing wounds between people groups and elements of society. Beginning with Native American and African American issues, the coalition has quickly become a global network, dealing with the wounds of many nations. He has authored *Taking Our Cities for God* and *Healing America's Wounds*.

Used by permission of the author.

I n 1974 our thinking changed. We began to see the world as peoples, rather than nation states. After the Lausanne Congress on World Evangelization, we began to make lists of the "hidden" peoples who yet had no witness of the gospel. The list changed everything—it gave focus to the unfinished task. We are now at another turning point. There is another list with even greater implications for the harvest—the wounds of the world.

Today we live in a wounded world. The Cold War is over. The great transnational ideologies have either failed or proved to be weak. Communism has collapsed, and even the fanatical fervor of Islamic fundamentalism has been unable to bring Islamic regions and peoples together.

Into the sociopolitical vacuum have rushed the much older claims of nationality, language, religious schism and tribal identity. The old hatreds are back with a vengeance. Ancient fault lines that were briefly covered over are once again exposed.

Racial strife among the immigrants of New World cities, people-group wars in the post-colonial states of Africa, and ethno-religious convulsions in east Europe are all symptoms of the foundational conflicts that this generation receives as a legacy of the past.

Racial conflict in particular has dramatically impacted my personal life. I am a white man. I have lived for the past 20 years in an African-American community in the United States. My neighborhood became famous world wide as the place where officers of the Los Angeles police department were caught on video mercilessly beating a black man named Rodney King. Following their acquittal, the city erupted. Fifty-nine people died in the rioting and more than 5,000 buildings were damaged or destroyed. Mr. King was later quoted in banner headlines around the world asking the desperate question, "Can't we all just get along?" Mr. King's question hangs over us still. The answer, of course, is "no."

Business as usual for the human heart is envy, fear and contention, and God will ultimately thwart any attempt to usurp the place of His own kingdom through solutions based in a counterfeit system or philosophy. Nation will rise against nation and people against people, and the false hope generated by false prophets will be shattered in a series of devastating failures that will culminate in the final failure of the Anti-Christ's one world system.

The Ministry of Reconciliation

What an exciting time then to be a believer in Jesus, an intercessor involved in Christ's ministry of reconciliation! We have the answer! (See 2 Cor 5:18.) It is only when we are reconciled to God the Father that the "otherness" of another gender, race or culture becomes an attraction rather than a source of insecurity and division.

This is why Jesus gives the ministry of reconciliation to the redeemed in Christ, the living Church. The pagans will never succeed as peacemakers. There is only one Prince of Peace.

Even now a wave of repentance is spreading through the world's prayer movements, addressing the foundational sins that have hindered the progress of the gospel for centuries. Much has taken place in the decade of the '90s, starting with the issues that have wounded the New Zealand Maoris, American Indians and other indigenous peoples. I personally have witnessed stadiums filled with weeping Christians where people flooded platforms to confess not only their personal sins but also the sins of their group against other groups.

In May 1995, for example, brokenness, repentance and reconciliation swept the almost 4,000 evangelical leaders from 186 nations meeting in Seoul, South Korea. Leaders from Turkey and Armenia reconciled and embraced one another.

Japanese leaders knelt and asked forgiveness from other Southeast Asians. Such deep repentance, I'm convinced, not only demonstrates God's healing love but also robs Satan of ancient strongholds and triggers the harvest.

As the Church of Jesus Christ, our goal, of course, has always been to see people reconciled to God through the gospel. The main hindrance to this end, however, has been us. The world has not been able to "see" Jesus because of the sectarian strife within the Body of Christ.

For centuries, this spirit of religious controversy has made us part of the problem. But now, I believe, we are finally becoming part of the answer. The growing wave of repentance over historic sins is leading believers of differing denominations, cultures and movements to unprecedented affection and respect for one another. Jesus said that when this kind of unity occurred, the world would believe the Father sent Him (see John 17:21). Ultimately, the world will "see" Jesus when a united Church carries the ministry of reconciliation beyond its own walls.

The Wounds of the World

When we study human conflict, we see that Satan's method of getting one group to abuse another is rooted in the hard-headed collision of self-righteous people within each group. Take some truth, polarize the people with different sides of that truth, tempt them to unrighteous judgment and then watch them wound one another with rejection, harsh words, injustice…and so it goes on.

We know that two people can hurt each other through selfish and unjust behavior. It is also possible for a wound to be sustained by a nation or people within a nation. Animosity and bitterness can fester unresolved for generations.

At a Canadian conference in 1995, Christian delegates from over 40 nations identified 14 general categories of deep-rooted, systematic alienation between peoples and elements of a society, 14 areas in which reconciliation ministry must be applied:

1. Indigenous peoples to immigrant peoples (such as the Aboriginal peoples to European-Australians)
2. Residual antagonisms, when there is justice under the law but wounds continue (for example, between black and white Americans because of the legacy of slavery or the hearing and hearing-impaired because of a perception of society's continuing insensitivity)
3. People-group conflicts (such as the Kurds vs. the Turks or the Hutus vs. the Tutsis)
4. Nation-state rivalries (such as the border disputes between Pakistan and India)
5. Independence movements (for example, the Timorese resistance to Javanese Indonesians as a result of colonialism)
6. Civil wars (as in Bosnia)
7. Alienation between generations (such as a generation returned from war dealing with the counter-cultures of their teenage children)
8. Societal conflicts (for example, Leftist vs. Rightist ideologies on the environment or abortion)
9. Gender-based abuses (such as the forced prostitution of Korean, Chinese and Philippine women by the Japanese military during the 1940's)
10. Industry, trade and labor disputes (such as migrant farm workers vs. agribusiness enterprises)

11. Social-class divisions (such as those caused by the Indian caste system, socialist governing elites, land and business dynasties or aristocratic cultures)
12. Interreligious conflicts (as between Christians and Jews)
13. Inter-Christian conflicts (sectarian divisions)
14. Christianity to peoples (when elements of Christian civilization have misrepresented God's character, putting a stumbling block between those peoples and their Creator; an example is the impact of the Conquistadors on Amerindian peoples)

How do we respond to such deep, gaping, sometimes ancient wounds? The simple answer lies in the humility of Jesus expressed through His Body, the Church.

A Model For Reconciliation

Although the Judeo-Christian ethos present in many national cultures gives us some basis for hope that reconciliation can occur through governmental or societal entities, I believe that reconciliation ministry is primarily the responsibility of the living Church. There is, after all, no substitute for the atonement Jesus provided for sin.

During the great seasons of revival in the past, the Church always placed a considerable emphasis on open acknowledgement of sin and called for changed attitudes and just actions. Likewise, today's Christians have the potential to demonstrate a model of reconciliation in the troubled world of the new century.

What is that model? As Christians, we believe in confession, repentance, reconciliation and restitution. In the context of healing the wounds of the world, this means:

Confession: Stating the truth; acknowledging the unjust or hurtful actions of myself or my people-group toward other people or categories of people.

Repentance: Turning from unloving to loving actions.

Reconciliation: Expressing and receiving forgiveness and pursuing intimate fellowship with previous enemies.

Restitution: Attempting to restore that which has been damaged or destroyed and seeking justice wherever we have power to act or to influence those in authority to act.

Sometimes we can begin this process by organizing events and ceremonies in which representatives of offending or offended subcultures have an opportunity to express regret or extend forgiveness.

Of course, in initiating such acts, we recognize that the issues involved are complex. Today's generation has inherited the task of both honoring righteous ancestors and seeking forgiveness for ancestral sins. Honesty dictates that we embrace both the guilt and the grandeur that has attached itself to our various identities.

> The world will "see" Jesus when a united Church carries the ministry of reconciliation beyond its own walls.

It is also true that when we are redeemed, we become part of the transcendent bride of Christ in whom there is neither male nor female, Jew nor Greek (Gal 3:28). But the Bible teaches that we become even more responsible for dealing with the implications of our identity when new life is born in us.

Even though each person stands alone before God and is in no way guilty for the sins of their ancestors or any other group, God is looking for volunteers who will open themselves to experience godly sorrow and confess the sins of the land. This is where reconciliation begins.

God's Momentum

The reconciliation prayer movement seems to have found a God-breathed momentum far beyond human promotion. We are, I believe, in an unusual season of grace, a season of jubilee.

I work with the International Reconciliation Coalition founded in 1990 as a fellowship of Christians attempting to deal with conflict in a Christian way. The IRC has grown rapidly into a worldwide network of like-minded but culturally diverse, praying servants from all streams within God's Church. There are intercessors, prophetic ministries, researchers, strategic planners, training ministries and ambassadors of reconciliation who lead the way in public confession, repentance and reconciliation at "solemn assemblies" and other special events.

A reconciliation initiative is launched when people who trust each other form an alliance around a major reconciliation issue and determine to take action together. The IRC helps like-minded people find each other and learn from other reconcilers in the network.

As I write, I am aware of over 60 major initiatives gaining momentum. One of the most significant is the "Reconciliation Walk," coinciding with the 900th anniversary of the Crusades. European intercessors have walked the routes of the Crusades from west to east, carrying proclamations of repentance to Muslim and Jewish communities for the slaughter done in Christ's name.

The response has been mind-boggling. Identificational repentance is proving to be the key to opening doors that have been closed for centuries. I don't know why we waited 900 years to repent for the Crusades, but I'm glad the breakthrough among Islamic peoples is coming in our lifetime!

In the United States, people are taking prayer journeys where American Indians were oppressed or massacred. In addition, there are prayer journeys to the historical slave ports of West Africa where black and white Americans weep together, learn together and find an intimacy that has eluded less radical believers.

Healing by the Power of the Cross

I have a Welsh friend named Rhiannon Lloyd who holds trauma recovery classes for both Hutu and Tutsi survivors of the Rwanda genocide. If you were in her shoes, what would you say to these devastated people? Many have experienced rape or maiming or witnessed the murder of their family members.

This is what she does: In the shelter of a church house, they meet for three days. Dr. Lloyd first persuades her grieving flock to write down on a piece of paper the worst experience that they had. When the awful facts have been confronted in this way, she has them come together in small groups to tell each other their stories. This is often the first trembling step towards trusting other people again.

Finally, the terrible atrocities are listed on a large sheet of paper for all to see and the group is asked "What does God feel about this?" She then draws a big red cross through the list of hurts, symbolizing the cross of Christ. "This is the only place we can bring our sorrows," she tells them. "This is one of the reasons Jesus came to earth, not only to take upon Himself our sins, but also the sins of those who sinned against us. Stand and tell God of the pain in your heart," she tells them, "What you saw…what it did to you. If you're angry, tell Him. If strong emotion comes, don't hold it back, because God will be weeping with you."

At first there is silence, but sobbing and wailing soon overcomes the cultural reserve of the Rwandans as people pour out their grief, anger and hopelessness before the crucified Christ. A long time later, when quiet returns, they sing softly the old chorus "What a friend we have in Jesus, all our sins and griefs to bear." Eventually Rhiannon brings in a big, rough wooden cross and positions it on the floor with a pile of nails. One at a time, believers begin to slip forward and taking their tear-stained piece of paper with its record of horrors, they kneel and nail it to the cross of Jesus. All afternoon the hammer pounds, echoing the agony of Golgotha, a reminder of Jesus' complete identification with our sufferings.

On the third day, an amazing thing happens. People begin to testify that in the midst of genocide, God was at work in the darkness. They talk of heroes, Christian reconcilers, who were the first to die. Anger at God begins to turn to empathy for God as believers contemplate His heartbreak over the way we humans treat one another.

With grief now resting lighter upon many, talk of forgiveness begins to emerge. Jesus is seen, not only as the innocent and suffering Lamb of God, but also the resurrected and righteous Judge who will uncompromisingly administer justice. Even now His hand of vengeance is stretched out toward the wicked, the very persons haunting the memory of survivors.

"If they repent, is it all right with you if God forgives them?" Rhiannon asks. Each person contemplates this question, weighing their own testimony of cleansing against their grief, many finally concluding that if God forgave them, they must eventually forgive others. Truly this is "beauty for ashes," the promise of God (Isa 61:1-4).

Healing the Land

Finally, Rhiannon tells them a personal story. "I come from a nation where two tribes have hurt each other," she says. "One day I was in a prayer meeting when an English Christian knelt at my feet. 'We have often made the Welsh our servants' she said. 'Please forgive us.' And she proceeded to wash my feet. A deep healing took place in my heart that day because of the humility of one person who chose to identify with the sins of her people against my people."

Rhiannon's simple story contains a key. The key to the ancient gates that isolate peoples and elements of society from one another. She has given a wisdom gift to Hutu and Tutsi as they struggle to live together in the same land.

You see, Jesus didn't tell us to apply the cross to the other person, but to ourselves. This is what gives us power to be reconcilers. It is a mystery revealed in the cross of Christ. Each believer must take up the cross and apply it to their own identity. Even now God is looking for people like Rhiannon's humble English friend. He's looking for those who will express the humility of Christ and bring healing to the nations.

Rhiannon acts upon this truth. She does one more thing. As a white person surrounded by Africans, she takes a position of complete identification with Europeans. She cannot represent Europeans in any official way, let alone confess the sins of others, but she realizes that there are no "generic" Christians. We all come from somewhere and it is obvious to the Africans that she is from one of the European peoples that long held power in Africa.

Rhiannon knows that her very appearance reminds many Africans of rejection and unjust dominance, but instead of disclaiming all association with the colonial past by such statements as, "I'm not from Belgium," or "It was all in a past generation," or "My people have been oppressed too." She volunteers to stand in the gap as an intercessor. The Bible reveals that God is looking for such people. Not just people who will stand in the gap before Him, but people who will repair the breeches in human relationships.

God does not put guilt on the intercessor. We are not individually guilty for what our group did or our parents did, but He is waiting for the "royal priesthood", which is the redeemed in Christ, to openly confess the truth of a matter before Him and before people, just as the ancient Hebrew priests once did over the sins of Israel. You see, it is very difficult to forgive if you have never heard an open acknowledgement of the injustices that wounded you or your people. On the other hand, such grace for forgiveness is released when we are asked for forgiveness by those who identify themselves in some way with the identity of those who contributed to our suffering.

I recently discovered the testimony of a missionary working in the Pacific in the 1830's. In his diary, he describes early attempts to reach the warlike Maori tribes of New Zealand. To my amazement, I found that these young followers of Jesus constantly risked their lives to avert intertribal conflict, often placing their bodies between war parties bent on Utu (revenge killing). It was the ministry of reconciliation which gave credibility to the gospel more than anything else, and within a generation a large percentage of the indigenous population became believers.

What was effective then is even more important in today's missionary endeavors. Intercession is more than prayer, it is living out the mediating, reconciling life of Christ in a wounded, bitter world with no answers for the broken relationships that torment all cultures. This is a day of God's favor: "But you will be called the priests of the Lord; you will be spoken of as ministers of our God" (Isa 61:6).

Study Questions

1. Dawson presents a four-stage process of reconciliation. Is it necessary for a church to be present in a society for this model to work? Why or why not?

2. What can you learn from the example of Dr. Rhiannon Lloyd's ministry to the traumatized?

3. What position did Dr. Rhiannon Lloyd take as an "outsider" in the Hutu/Tutsi conflict? Did her own people play any paricular role in the colonial era among the Hutu or Tutsi?

State of World Need

World Relief Corporation

When the Son of Man comes in his glory, and all the angels with him, he will sit on his throne in heavenly glory. All the nations will be gathered before him, and he will separate the people one from another as a shepherd separates the sheep from the goats. He will put the sheep on his right and the goats on his left.

Then the King will say to those on his right, "Come, you who are blessed by my Father; take your inheritance, the kingdom prepared for you since the creation of the world. For I was hungry and you gave me something to eat, I was thirsty and you gave me something to drink, I was a stranger and you invited me in. I needed clothes and you clothed me, I was sick and you looked after me, I was in prison and you came to visit me."

Then the righteous will answer him, "Lord, when did we see you hungry and feed you, or thirsty and give you something to drink? When did we see you a stranger and invite you in, or needing clothes and clothe you? When did we see you sick or in prison and go to visit you?"

The King will reply, "I tell you the truth, whatever you did for one of the least of these brothers of mine, you did for me." (Matthew 25:31-40)

World Relief Corporation is the international assistance arm of the National Association of Evangelicals. The group works with churches to bring help and hope to nearly one million victims of disaster, poverty and persecution in 24 countries, including 35 U.S. locations, every year.
Updated in 1998.

Jesus and the poor are inseparable. The needy flocked around him everywhere he went—the beggars, the blind, the lame, the destitute with no other place to go, the hungry. And he was touched by their infirmities. Ten times the New Testament records that Jesus was "moved with compassion," each time in the context of Jesus' personal confrontation with suffering people. The bereaved, refugees floundering, the hungry masses, the sick whom he delighted in touching. Jesus is the Son of the God of Isaiah, the God who declared through his prophet Isaiah, "Is not this the kind of fasting I have chosen: to loose the chains of injustice and untie the cords of the yoke, to set the oppressed free and break every yoke? Is it not to share your food with the hungry and to provide the poor wanderer with shelter—when you see the naked, to clothe him? (Isa 58:6,7)

"I was hungry and you gave me something to eat."

For nearly two out of every three people alive today, hunger is not merely an occasional pang felt before lunchtime. It's a lifestyle.

- Three quarters of a billion people are chronically undernourished.
- Malnutrition is the underlying cause of 55% of deaths of children under five. Ten percent of these deaths are di-

rectly caused by severe malnutrition.

- Thirty-four thousand children die every day of hunger and preventable diseases. That's 24 a minute. Real children with names and siblings and dreams—kids who never see adulthood because they struggle with hunger and lose.

Poverty is at the heart of the world's hunger. To understand the diversity of the contributors to poverty, one must analyze a web of problems—unbalanced distribution of wealth, climatic limitations, greed, lack of work ethic, overpopulation, political maneuvering, technological inadequacy, unemployment. No one factor can be effectively treated in isolation. All must be dealt with.

The exasperating truth is that the world produces enough food to feed everybody. It just isn't being distributed equitably. The imbalance in food distribution is the number one reason a hunger problem haunts our world today. Developed countries nearly empty the food basket before passing the scraps to developing nations.

- Industrialized countries include only 20% of world population but consume 80% of the food resources.
- In the United States, we spend between $30 and $50 billion every year on diets and related expenditures to reduce calorie intake. Obesity and cardiovascular disease are rampant. Many North Americans literally eat themselves to death.

Rich industrialized countries compose the front line of liability. But wealthy elites in poor countries also bear part of the responsibility. Too often overall economic growth primarily benefits only the richest citizens of poorer countries. Some progress is made, but it rarely reaches those who need it most desperately.

There are signs of hope. Since 1970 both the percentage and the actual number of hungry people have fallen significantly in the developing countries.

- In 1970, 918 million people, or 35% of the developing world, were chronically undernourished. By 1991, those figures had fallen to 841 million people, which was 20 percent of the people in the developing countries.
- Even though more than two million people have already died in Sudan alone and another 2.6 million there are at risk of starvation, Christians around the globe are responding. Emergency feeding centers try to meet the need for immediate nutrition. Seeds and gardening tools are being distributed. In the summer of 1998, families harvested the first of the food crops these produced.
- Microcredit has emerged as one of the most promising ways to combat severe poverty. Small loans (beginning at approximately $50) enable poor people to establish small businesses like food preparation or handicrafts. The income generated by these businesses allows people to pay off their initial loan and to meet their families' financial needs. Many applicants then apply for a larger loan and expand their business, providing greater financial benefits for themselves and their families as well as offering employment to others in the local community. Money that is repaid can be reloaned over and over again, so that an initial investment is multiplied many times over. Opportunity International and World Relief each will touch a million people with this chance to earn their own way with dignity over the next five years.

"I was thirsty and you gave me drink."

Water is the most precious of all resources, a vital necessity of life. A human being cannot live more than a few days without it. It composes 90 percent of your blood, 80 percent of your brain, 75 percent of your flesh and 25 percent of your bones.

And yet, 1.1 billion people in our world lack access to clean water.

In most developed countries, if you want an abundant, clean water supply, you just turn your faucet on.

In developing countries, people often travel miles on foot to secure a jug of water. It may well take half a day to make the trip. In other countries, even a half day trek won't lead to water. There simply isn't any.

Besides being essential for drinking, water serves a critical role in food production, food preparation, and hygiene. Subtracting water from any of these is like snapping a bicycle chain in half and expecting the bike to work smoothly. It can't. Imagine trying to grow a garden, fix dinner, wash without water, or with water infested with parasites and waste products. You might as well wash with mud.

Two sides of the water supply problem plague developing countries: Quantity and quality.

Water shortages parch countries with arid climates like Africa and India. In the Sahel region of Africa, the desert is creeping southward at a rate of 9 miles each year, scorching everything in its path.

Quality is the other half of the water supply dilemma. Even where water is available, it frequently is useless due to the damaging elements the water contains. Diseases which spread through impure water cripple and kill. Contaminated water is the principle agent in transmitting typhoid, cholera, and bacillary dysentery, prevalent diseases in developing countries. Ignorance of hygienic practices is part of the problem. In many areas of the world the same water is used for washing, drinking, and bathing.

Water pollution is more common in rural areas than urban. The most prevalent contributor to pollution is organic human and livestock waste. Soil erosion and runoff of fertilizer and pesticides in farming areas also reduce fresh water availability.

Ironically, the more industrial and commercial development taking place in a country, the more likely it is that chemical waste will pour into rivers and streams, leading to pollution. Industrialization and development may increase the gross national product of a country, but they may also mean more polluted water for the thirsty poor. Growing populations, industrialization, and food production will all increase the demand for clean water.

"I was a stranger and you invited me in."

In the simplest terms, refugees are persons who have felt compelled (or have been forced) to leave their homes. Unable or unwilling to return, many remain in a homeless limbo. According to the United States Committee for Refugees, they are the "ultimate victims of war and oppression. Too often … the forgotten by-products of ideological disputes, political repression or a foreign policy gone awry."

In most cases they have fled in fear because of war or civil strife. Persecution for reasons of race, religion, national origin or group affiliation may have precipitated the move. Oppression or lack of protection by a new or ineffectual government may prompt a propulsion of people from a country.

Every continent harbors stateless or homeless victims of war, intolerance and social unrest. Because a small percentage each year manage to return home or become viably resettled, and because vast numbers of new refugees continually emerge, the world refugee situation is in a constant state of flux. Statistics on refugees and other uprooted people are often inexact and controversial. One country's refugee is another's illegal alien. Today's internally displaced person may be tomorrow's refugee. The U.S. Committee for Refugees estimates that there were 13.6 million refugees and asylum seekers in need of protection at the end of 1997.

Refugees are often in dire need. The extent and specifics of that need depend on the reasons for dislocation, the understanding that individuals have of the forces acting upon them, the degree of violence and deprivation encountered, and the speed of resettlement. Yet the majority of the world's refugees are confronted with poor health, little food, inadequate shelter and no money. A complex mixture of emotional problems results from culture shock and other frustrations of the situation.

There are signs of hope. Habitat for Humanity will soon be the largest private house builder in the world. They have already built 60,000 houses for the poor around the globe. World Relief Corporation alone has resettled over 125,000 refugees, helping them find not only shelter but productive employment and a new life in a safe environment.

"I was naked and you clothed me."

Imagine that one night as you sat down to dinner, the blasts of gunshots, screams and rumblings invaded your dining room. Looking outside, you discover homes blazing with fire and neighbors bleeding in the street. A band of angry men streams toward your house. The only possible escape is an immediate one. You leave everything you own—

home, car, food, clothing—and run for safety. Episodes like this interrupt the pulse of life in countries around the world when disasters like war disrupt a nation.

In addition to the man-made disasters forcing refugees to flee, other violent events leave thousands of people homeless and in need of assistance in their own countries: the awesome upheavals of the natural world.

More than 90 percent of all loss of life and damage to man and the environment is the result of four main natural hazards: drought, floods, tropical cyclones and earthquakes. Over half of all natural disasters originate with meteorological events including storms, floods, drought and temperature extremes.

In disaster-prone developing countries, these events often serve as enormous barriers to economic growth, sometimes canceling out any hard won increase in gross national product, or actually causing a loss.

In more immediate terms, natural disasters kill thousands of people each year, cause disease and injury for tens of thousands more, and leave hundreds of thousands homeless.

Immediately following a major disaster, food and water supplies may be cut off or contaminated. Electricity and gas supplies are often involved in explosions and fires, and cut off. Medical supplies and facilities may be destroyed. The danger of disease epidemics spread through contaminated water, destroyed sanitation facilities and large number of dead bodies lurks in the aftermath. Economic loss of property, crops and personal possessions is usually in the millions of dollars, if not immeasurable. For developing nations the economic impact can be devastating.

Total recovery from a disaster often requires outside help extending beyond the initial relief response. The minimum goal may be to restore normal pre-disaster conditions. Yet in developing countries "normal conditions" frequently include malnutrition, disease and economic deprivation. True need is often greater than the effects of the disaster alone. Thus, the goals of rehabilitation must aim at higher than pre-disaster levels of living.

"I was sick and you cared for me."

Malaria, tuberculosis, and parasitic infections invade and destroy millions every year. Millions of people die every year from infectious and parasitic diseases we know how to prevent. Diseases now rare in developed countries continue to kill in other countries where immunizations are not available. Even preventable diseases like tetanus and measles often result in death.

One of the most reliable gauges of health status in a country is the measure of life expectancy. The average life expectancy in developing lands is 15 to 25 years less than in developed countries.

Three basic types of diseases dominate developing countries: fecally-related, air-borne and vector-borne.

The most wide-spread diseases are the fecally-related. Transmitted by human feces through unsanitary waste disposal conditions, they include parasitic and diarrheal disease like typhoid and cholera.

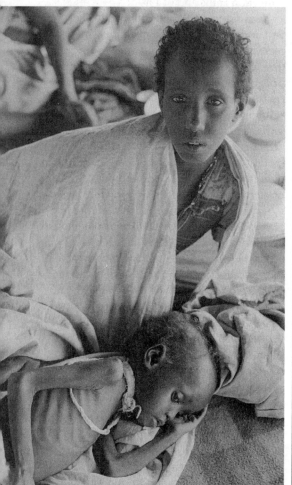

Eric Mooneyham © 1998

Air-borne diseases comprise the next largest group. They spread through persons breathing airborne respiratory secretions of infected persons. Diseases of this kind are tuberculosis, pneumonia, diptheria, bronchitis, whooping cough, meningitis, influenza, measles, smallpox and chicken pox. Although most are preventable in developed countries, they transform into killers in lands where medicine and doctors reside hundreds of miles away.

The third group of diseases are less common, though still a sober and deadly reality in developing countries. Called vector-borne diseases, transmitted by insects, they include malaria, sleeping sickness and river blindness. Another category of preventable diseases are sexually transmitted. The vectors which carry these diseases are other people. The HIV/AIDS epidemic is the most well-known among these diseases. More than 16,000 people a day contract HIV/AIDS, with over 30 million cases at the end of 1997, most of them in sub-Saharan Africa.

Fecally-related, air- and vector-borne diseases share common roots of cause—poverty. Crowded, unsanitary living conditions underlie the origin and spread of these diseases. These conditions include: water teeming with parasites, families of five or ten crammed into tiny tins of refuge, inadequate diets, ignorance of nutrition and hygiene, immunizations or preventive health care. Most of the uneducated in developing countries make no connection between systems of waste disposal and concurrent illnesses.

Even if these roadblocks to health could be flattened, simple health care is a fleeting mirage to more than 80 percent of rural areas and poor urban sections. Efforts to alleviate disease usually concentrate on major urban areas. Large hospitals are frequently built in places where poor rural dwellers cannot reach them. One out of every four people in our world today lacks access to basic health services.

There are signs of hope.

- In 1981 in some areas of Africa 40 percent of all adults lost their sight to river blindness by the age of 40. At that time there was no real hope in sight. The Merck company recently developed a tablet to treat river blindness and the Jimmy Carter Center distributes it. Twenty-two million people were treated with this medical discovery in 1997. They will never go blind.
- Diarrhea used to be the number one killer of children. Efforts over the past decade to train mothers in simple oral rehydration techniques have saved hundreds of thousands of children from this fate.
- In 1980, only 20 percent of the children in developing nations received immunization for typical childhood diseases. In 1998—thanks in part to Bread for the World's advocacy work to set in place a U.S.-funded Child Survival Fund—80 percent do.

"I was in prison and you came to visit me."

Saleema, a teenager, sits in a Pakistan prison. Months ago she shared her Bible with Raheela, a friend of hers from a Muslim background. Raheela came to believe in Christ and, fearing for her life from angry family members, went into hiding. Saleema was then accused of helping Raheela escape. Saleema was imprisoned. She was repeatedly raped and beaten.

Raheela was eventually found by religious authorities. She refused to renounce Christ and was therefore publicly executed. The Islamic authorities have now charged Saleema with murder. Why? They reasoned that, had Saleema not given a Bible to Raheela, Raheela would not have followed Christ and been executed for apostasy from Islam. Saleema will also be executed if found guilty.

Cases like Saleema and Raheela are on the rise. Because prisoners of conscience are often charged with political or criminal crimes, it is almost impossible to assess how extensive the imprisonment of Christians may be.

International Christian Concern reports: "More Christians are persecuted and martyred for their faith in this century than all previous centuries combined. Nearly two thirds of all Christians alive in the world today suffer persecution in varying degrees, including the loss of freedom, discrimination, imprisonment, slavery, and torture."

House church leaders are routinely imprisoned and tortured in China. For example, house church pastor Xu Gou Xing was arrested and placed in a cell block with violent criminal prisoners on the assumption that he would be beaten and abused there by other prisoners. However, the Lord protected him, granting him favor with one of the criminal "leaders" who had a Christian relative. Xu soon began to lead several prisoners to the Lord. Authorities have now placed him in solitary confinement.

What Can We Do?

In a world of desperate need, we ask ourselves what we can do about problems so vast and all-encompassing. The child who recommends sending his leftover dinner to Africa elicits chuckles from wiser generations. But too often we answer our own questions silently. "Nothing. I can do nothing about all the suffering in the world."

As Ron Sider says, "Nobody can do everything, but everybody can do something, and together we can change the world."

We dare not watch a child die for the lack of a cup of powdered milk or a spoonful of rice when we represent the wealth of North America, especially Bible-believing Americans, where even a fraction of that wealth could save millions of children from starvation.

We dare not stand aside and leave people homeless, their eyes staring empty into the hopeless future, when we can put a roof over their heads for a pittance, by North American standards.

We dare not take a spectator's seat watching refugees who huddle just out of gunshot range. They are not just "inevitable victims of war." They are creations of God and He has called us to minister to them.

In other words, what we really believe in, we do. Everything else is just so much religious rhetoric. God never intended for the righteous to sit idle while the restless poor struggle for survival. And we dare not leave at a point where their survival is assured but their eternal destiny is not.

> The words of Jesus knife through the dismal state of the world and through our inaction. "Whatever you did for one of the least of these brothers of mine, you did for me."

It is easy for us to become insulated against action. Lulled into the belief that the problems confronting us lie beyond our realm of control. The needs of the poor—and the rich—transcend the physical and the psychological. They are spiritual as well. The most effective plans meet the needs of the whole person. Such plans do not come easily. And, there are so many individual people suffering from so many different scourges.

The solutions to problems in the world today will not be found in the actions of one or two people. But, collectively, individuals can respond to them in a significant manner. While you or I may not be able to completely solve the problems alone, we need to respond as God has commanded us to. In Jesus' name.

Christians today have a total annual income of over $10 trillion. According to the United Nations, it would cost only $30-$40 billion a year to provide all people in developing countries with basic education, health care, and clean water—the same amount spent on golf every year.

The words of Jesus knife through the dismal state of the world and through our inaction: "Whatever you did for one of the least of these brothers of mine, you did for me."

The problems are worldwide, but individual responses are eternally significant. A loaf of bread. A cup of clean water. A shelter. The Gospel lived out and proclaimed. These actions command immeasurable importance to someone who is hungry, thirsty or homeless.

Study Questions

1. Study Matthew 25:31-46. How does this passage relate to the Great Commission?

2. According to this article, "what we really believe, we do." Can you identify areas of action in your life that are in *conflict* with your stated beliefs? Can you also identify areas that demand action to *match* your stated beliefs?

Evangelism:
The Leading Partner

Samuel Hugh Moffett

he New Testament uses the word *evangelize* in what seems to be a shockingly narrow sense. A whole cluster of verbs, actually, is used to describe evangelism: "preaching the word" (Acts 8:4), "heralding the kingdom" (Luke 9:2), "proclaiming the good news" (Luke 4:18, 8:1). But in essence, what all these words describe is simply the telling of the good news (the gospel) that Jesus the Messiah is the saving King. Evangelism is the announcement of Christ's kingdom. However, it is more than an announcement—it is also an invitation to enter that kingdom, by faith and with repentance.

What Evangelism is Not

Evangelism, therefore, is not the whole of the Christian mission. It is only a part of the mission. Jesus and the disciples did many other things besides announce the kingdom and invite response. Evangelism is not worship or sacraments. "Christ did not send me to baptize but to evangelize," said Paul (1 Cor 1:17).

And it is not church growth or church planting. The planting and growth of the Church are surely goals of evangelism and its hoped-for results. But evangelism does not always produce a church or more members for it.

Neither is evangelism confined to apologetics. Paul says, "We try to persuade" (2 Cor 5:11), but insists that he was sent to tell the good news "without using the language of human wisdom" (1 Cor 1:17, 20).

Finally, evangelism in the New Testament was not confused with Christian service, or Christian action and protest against the world's injustices. A revealing and disturbing incident in the Book of Acts tells how Greek-speaking Jews among the early Christians rose as a minority group to complain of discrimination in the distribution of funds. The reply of the apostles seems almost callously narrow: "We cannot neglect the preaching of God's word to handle finances" (Acts 6:1, 2 *TEV*). Of course, they did immediately proceed to do something about the injustice. But they did not call it evangelism.

In Kingdom Context

In the context of the kingdom, however, the evangelistic proclamation was never so narrow that it became isolated from the immediate pressing needs of the poor, the imprisoned, the blind and the oppressed.

Samuel Hugh Moffett is the Henry Winters Luce Professor of Ecumenics and Mission, Emeritus at Princeton Theological Seminary in Princeton, New Jersey. Previously he served as a missionary to China and Korea and has written numerous articles in missions and theology. Used by permission of the author.

Here I am reminded of Korean evangelism. I asked a pastor in the Philadelphia area why his church was growing so fast. "When Koreans come in," he replied, "first I get them jobs; I teach them some English; I help them when they get in trouble with their supervisors; I invite them to church, and then I preach to them the gospel." That is putting evangelism into context.

> The real good news is not what we, in our benevolence, do for others, but what God has done for us all in Christ.

But if there is anything worse than taking the text out of context, it is taking the context without the text. Just as Christ's salvation is never to be isolated from the immediate, real needs of the people, neither is it to be identified with those present needs. When Jesus quoted the Old Testament about "good news to the poor" and "freedom for the oppressed," he did so on his own terms. His salvation is not Old Testament *shalom*, and his kingdom is not Israel.

There is nothing quite so crippling to both evangelism and social action as to confuse them in definition or to separate them in practice. Our evangelists sometimes seem to be calling us to accept the King without His kingdom; while our prophets, just as narrow in their own way, seem to be trying to build the kingdom without the saving King.

More Than Balance

There was a time when most Christians believed that evangelism was the only priority. They were wrong. Then the Church swung too far the other way. The only Christian priority for some has been social justice through reconstruction. That, too, is an important priority but it is not the only one. And when they made it the only clear mission of the Church, the result was a disaster. In trying to speak to the world, they almost lost the Church.

Others tried to restore the balance by pointing out that "Christ mediates God's new covenant through both salvation and service.... Christians are called to engage in both evangelism and social action." But even that is not enough. What the Church needs for the future in mission is more than balance. It needs mo-

mentum. Not an uneasy truce between faith and works, but a partnership.

Now in most practical, working partnerships, there must be a leading partner, a first among equals, or nothing gets done. Which should be the leading partner in mission: evangelism or social action?

I submit that what makes the Christian mission different from other commendable and sincere attempts to improve the human condition is this: in the Christian mission our vertical relationship to God comes first. Our horizontal relationship to our neighbor is "like unto it," and is just as indispensable, but it is still second. The leading partner is evangelism.

This is not to exalt the proclamation at the expense of Christian action. They belong together. But it does insist that, while without the accompanying deeds the good news is scarcely credible, without the word the news is not even comprehensible! Besides, the real good news is not what we in our benevolence do for others, but what God has done for us all in Christ. Evangelism, as has been said, is one beggar telling another where to find bread.

The supreme task of the Church, then, now and for the future, is evangelism. It was the supreme task for the Church of the New Testament. It is also the supreme challenge facing the Church today.

Half the World Unreached

The determining factor in developing evangelistic strategies, I believe, is that evangelism moves always in the direction of the unreached. "It must focus on those without the gospel." More than one-half of the world's people are still without the simplest knowledge of the good news of God's saving love in Jesus Christ. There is no greater challenge to evangelism in mission than that.

Christians are rightly concerned about the grievous unbalances of wealth and food and freedom in the world. What about the most devastating unbalance of all: the unequal distribution of the light of the knowledge of God in Jesus Christ?

I am not overly addicted to statistics. But what does it say about a "six continent approach to evangelism," for example, to find that most of our church mission funds still go to ourselves on the sixth continent, which is between 70 percent and 80 percent at least nominally Christian? Africa, however, is perhaps 40 percent Christian by the same rough and imprecise standards. And Asia, which holds more than one-half of all the people in the world, is only three percent to four percent even nominally Christian.

In the next ten years, the number of non-Christians which will be added to the population of Asia will be greater than the entire present population of the United States multiplied almost three times (650 million, compared to 220 million). Treating all six continents as equals for strategical purposes is a selfish distortion of the evangelistic realities of the world.

One last thought. There is an unexpected bonus to keeping the definition of evangelism simple. It means that anyone can get into the act. One of the happiest lessons I ever learned about evangelism came not from a professional evangelist, but from a watermelon vendor.

It was in a Korean village, and my wife came up to ask him how much a watermelon cost. He was so surprised at finding a long-nosed foreigner who spoke Korean that at first he was struck dumb. He even forgot to tell her the price. There was something more important he wanted to say. He asked, "Are you a Christian?" And when she replied, "Yes," he smiled all over. "Oh, I'm so glad," he said, "because if you weren't I was going to tell you how much you are missing."

If more of us were so happy about what we have found in the Lord Jesus Christ that we couldn't wait to tell those who have not found him how much they are missing, we would need to worry no longer about the future of evangelism.

Study Questions

1. In what ways does Moffett suggest that evangelism is to be the "leading partner" in Christian ministry among the poor? Do you agree or disagree?

2. What relationship exists between the imbalance of the distribution of wealth and food and the distribution of the light of Jesus? What is the primary reason cited by the author for the imbalance of the distribution of basic needs and the good news?

What is Poverty Anyway?

Bryant Myers

I often express concern over whether we Christians use ideas that are more modern than truly biblical and Christian. Recently, I have been wondering about our use of the word *poverty*. Most of us believe we understand the meaning of the word. And the meaning we give to an abstract noun like *poverty* reflects the way we look at, think about and make sense of our world.

Where Do We Begin?

The common definition of poverty is that it is the condition of those groups of people we abstractly describe as "the poor." But the poor are not abstract. They are human beings with names, made in the image of God, those for whom Jesus died. People who live in poverty are valuable to God—as important to Him, as loved by Him, as those who do not live in poverty.

Why is this reminder important? The world tends to view the poor as a helpless group. The poor become nameless, and this invites us to treat them as objects of our compassion, people toward whom we have the right to act as we believe best.

For a Christian understanding of poverty, we must remember that the poor are people with names, people to whom God has given gifts, and people with whom and among whom God works—before we even know they exist.

Poverty as Deficit

Poverty results from a lack of things. It is obvious that poor people do not have enough to eat, a place to sleep or clean water. Their land is poor, there is no water for irrigation, the roads are poor and there are no schools for their children.

And so we plan to provide the missing things: food aid, low-cost housing and wells.

We also recognize that some poor people lack knowledge and skills. Poor people may not understand nutrition, the need to boil water, the importance of child spacing, how to read the instructions on a packet of improved seeds. They don't know about sustainable agriculture, running small businesses and the importance of saving money. So, we provide programs that feature education, both formal and nonformal. We assume that when the poor have the knowledge they lack, they will no longer be poor.

Bryant Myers is the Vice President for International Programs Strategies at World Vision International. He is also the Executive Director for MARC (Mission Advanced Research and Communications Center). He is a member of Lausanne's Theology and Strategy Working Group and has authored numerous books.

From *MARC Newsletter*, March 1997. Used by permission.

Christians tend to add another dimension to poverty as deficit: the non-Christian poor lack knowledge about God and the good news of Jesus Christ. To understand poverty holistically, Christians add the gospel to the list of other things the poor do not have.

These views of poverty are true, and, as far as they go, they are helpful. People do need things: skills, knowledge and a chance to hear the gospel. However, limiting our understanding of poverty to this framework creates some serious problems.

When we limit our understanding of poverty in this way we see ourselves as providers. The poor are passive recipients, incomplete human beings whom we make whole. This unwitting attitude has two negative consequences.

First, this attitude demeans and devalues the poor. Our view of them, which quickly becomes their view of themselves, is that they are defective and inadequate.

Second, our attitude about ourselves can become messianic. We are tempted to believe that we are the deliverers of the poor and that we make their lives complete.

So if the deficit view of poverty is helpful yet inadequate, what might we add to our view of poverty?

Poverty as Broken Relationships

A careful look at the Bible suggests that understanding the gospel in terms of relationships helps. Too often, we evangelicals limit our reading to a legal or transactional framework that centers on our sin, God's wrath, God's grace in Christ, and our being forgiven. While this transactional framework is both biblical and important, it is not the only framework.

The Bible contains a lot of relational emphases. The consequences of the first sin were all relational—Adam blamed Eve, Cain killed Abel, they left Eden and were separated from an intimate relationship with God. The Ten Commandments frame social relationships. In the gospels, the only two statements that Jesus called commandments were relational—to love God and to love our neighbor as ourselves.

Seeing the world in terms of relationships gives us new insights into poverty. This vantage point allows us insight to trace who is doing what to whom.

Poverty involves being excluded. We make people poor when we label them as the other, the outsider, the outcast. We begin the process of exclusion when we say people are lazy, dirty, uneducated, crazy or unsafe to be around. When we withdraw because some-

one has leprosy or AIDS, is homosexual, has a different skin color or comes from a different culture, we impoverish them and ourselves.

Labels and stereotypes devalue the image of God in people. This kind of poverty is both powerful and debilitating both for those who do this and as for those to whom it is done.

A Han woman once told me, "I can believe that God might let His Son die for a white man. Maybe He might do this for a black man. But God would never allow His Son to die for a bushman."

This woman cannot believe that she is made in the image of God. She has internalized a history of ruthless exploitation and genocide.

Poverty as Misused Power

When those who have power over others use it to benefit themselves, poverty results. Poverty is created when:

- the Brahmin lives out a social system that exploits the *harijan* (untouchables).
- a man uses the culture of *machismo* to legitimize drinking, womanizing and beating his wife.
- a corporation uses its political connections to get a poor section of town condemned so a sports stadium can be built.

People in positions of social privilege are often tempted to use their power for personal advantage, ignoring the consequences of their decisions for those who have less power. Managers can misuse the power they have over their subordinates. Pastors can misuse the power they have over lay people. Even if we desire to be fair and righteous, we continually face temptations to believe that we are due certain privileges because of the positions we hold. This view makes many of us uncomfortable. It means we, too, are part of the causes of poverty.

Working against poverty within a framework of relationships is dangerous in that it demands the counter-cultural gospel of scandal that Paul talks about. It will anger the authorities—religious, political, economic, and even those in your own agency. It will challenge and demand change in culture—both the local culture and your own.

The world cannot and will not transform political, economic, and social power into something that is pro-life, pro-poor and pro-kingdom. Sustainable change will not come through community organizing, political processes or more education.

Challenging the poverty-creating nature of power demands the transformational power of the gospel. It is about personal sin and social sin. Only the good news—all of it—contains the hope that the poor will someday be able to build homes and live in them.

Poverty as Fear

One final way of thinking about poverty: you are poor when you are afraid. This is true especially when you are afraid of those who have influence over your future and well being.

Some fear the spirit world, the unseen world of demons, spirits and ancestors. Others fear those in this world who have power over them: the Brahmin, the priest, the corporation or the professor. This kind of fear, whatever its source, is disabling.

The Gospel of Mark teaches that fear is the opposite of faith. Fear, then, is a spiritual problem. It can be dispelled only by faith in the Son of God, who is more powerful than any source of fear.

Summing Up

Once we move beyond understanding poverty as the absence of things and knowledge, we see that at its heart poverty is a spiritual issue. Relationships that don't work, power that is misused and disabling fear cannot be set aside.

Churches, missions and Christian relief and development agencies must bring the gospel to the poor, not because it is something extra that Christians do, but because it is the only source of truth and power that can address a serious understanding of poverty.

Study Questions

1. Is poverty defined so broadly that everyone should be considered impoverished?

2. How might Myers' ideas help field practitioners?

The Urban Poor:
Who Are We?

Viv Grigg

Viv Grigg is a voice calling workers to the slums of third world cities. As International Director of Urban Leadership Foundation he coordinates the Cities Resource Network of the AD2000 movement, encouraging indigenous city leadership teams that initiate strategic planning to the 1,700 least evangelized cities. He has pioneered teams in Manila and Calcutta, and catalyzed apostolic missions from various countries to the slums. A New Zealand engineer, married to a Brazilian, he is author of *Companion to the Poor, Cry of the Urban Poor* and *Transforming Cities*.

From *Cry of the Urban Poor*, by Viv Grigg, Copyright 1992. Used by permission of Viv Grigg.

What if the size of the Muslim world or of the Hindu population doubled every ten years? Suppose furthermore that these population blocs were found to be among the most responsive to the gospel on the earth? How would this affect our present strategies of Christian mission? Would we take up the challenge?

The Answer is a Dramatic "Yes!"

Yet the number of urban squatters and slum dwellers in the world's major cities constitutes a bloc as large as either the Muslims or the Hindus, it doubles in size every decade, and all indicators show it to be a responsive group. Logically, missions must swing their strategies to make these their priority target.

The majority of migrants to the mega-cities will move into the *slums* (Bangkok), *squatter areas* (Manila), *shanty towns* (South Africa), *bustees* (India), *bidonvilles* (Morocco), *favelas* (Brazil), *casbahs* (Algeria), *ranchitos* (Venezuela), *ciudades perdidas* (Mexico), and *barriadas* or *pueblos jovenes* (Peru). I will describe these in general with the term *squatter areas*.

These tend to be *slums of hope*. Their occupants have come in search of employment, have found some vacant land and gradually have become established. They are building their homes, finding work and developing some communal relationships similar to those of the *barrios* or villages from which they have come. In *slums of hope* social forces and expectations create a high degree of receptivity to the gospel.

Missions today must reach the last tribes and fulfill prior commitments to the rural poor. But new mission strategies must focus on the crucial point of spiritual warfare for the mega-cities. Within this broad objective, mission to the urban poor becomes a central target, as they are the ultimate victims of the oppression and evil of the mega-cities and nation states. They loom large in the heart of God. They are the key to the elite and the heart of the city. Among the most reachable of people groups today are migrants living in community, groups of peasants who have moved to cities and live in squatter areas.

Over the past 30 years, about one billion people have moved from rural areas to cities. In the next ten years, another one billion will board overladen buses and come to the cities. For most of them, the first step is into squatter areas—centers of great darkness and demonic activity.

Between 1950 and 1980, urban growth in Third World mega-cities rose from 275 million to just under one billion. It is expected to double by the year 2000. Wherever land can be found, huts and plywood shacks will go up. Few governments have the capacity to prevent it or to serve the needs of the people arriving. Even the United States may not remain immune as its economy slows down.

An understanding of the breadth of need and the range of potential responses enables us to reflect both on God's responses and on strategic possibilities to implement as we walk with God.

Some of the most destitute of the poor live in mud homes on the streets of modern Dhaka city in Bangladesh, a new city that is now home to five million people, a city that will grow to contain 20 million people by the turn of the century. The 730,000 people in Dhaka's 771 squatter areas will increase, until by the year 2000, they will make up the majority of the city's population. Because of the lack of raw materials and other factors, there is little possibility for the city's industrial growth to keep pace with the migration influx.

Almost all of the world's population growth in the next decades will be in cities. Rural populations will tend to remain at present levels.

There is usually one mega-city per country. It drains resources from the entire country. Its bureaucracy locks up the potential for growth in the smaller cities. The next largest city as a rule is only ten percent the size of this mega-city. Chiang Mai, the second largest city of Thailand, for example, is thirty times smaller than Bangkok.

The Migrant Poor: Who Are We?

One was a big man with a good education speaking English fluently with an English accent. The other was a Nepalese, small in stature but full of big dreams.

"What business would you get into if you were to make it off the street?" asked my friend, a Kiwi businessman.

"We would establish a tea stall," they replied.

Several further discussions led to a conclusion that it was a worthy goal for $100. But to find a piece of unoccupied street took ten days. They only had to pay the police a reasonable two rupees each day for protection, But paying the local mafia cut their profit margin to zero.

A daughter fell sick from a fever. She had been caught in the rain without good blankets in the cold Calcutta winter. This crisis slowly consumed their financial capital.

Unable to pay the mafia, members of the family were beaten up.

City of Joy

Calcutta, oh Calcutta! City where the powers of darkness have so gained control over the political and judicial leadership that only darkness prevails, and a mafia rules the city's people. Poverty and evil triumph and infest the lives of ordinary people until they go crazy with the pain.

Calcutta has more poverty and more grades of poverty than any other city in the world. I walk down the street, and a well-fed wraith-like figure, baby on hip, comes after me pleading, pleading. There are four of them fighting each day for this territory. An amputee shakes his cup on the corner, an old man lies on the path further along, near death.

In 1984, Geoffrey Moorehouse estimated that there were 400,000 men in town without a job.[1] The 1981 census put it at 851,806. Ganguly comments that perhaps no other city has one million educated youth registered with the employment exchanges.[2] There is beggary all over India, but nowhere is there beggary on the scale of Calcutta's.

Beyond the beggars are anywhere from 48,000 to 200,000 people who live permanently on the streets. One survey shows that two-thirds of them have some kind of regular employment, while 20 percent are beggars. Most have some kind of part-time work or have earned money by selling vegetables, paper, firewood and scraps.

More than half of the 3.5 million living within the metro core are slum dwellers. Two-thirds of Calcutta's families earn *350 rupees or less a month* (the poverty level is Rs600 or US$50 per month for a family). Less than 20 percent of its workforce work in an organized industry. Agriculture and small crafts, not major or modern manufacturing, are the principal occupation of the people. In as much as 80 percent of its extended land surface of 1,350 square kilometers, there are 3.15 million *bustee* and slumdwellers.[3]

There is a level of poverty still lower than that experienced by beggar, street-dweller or bustee-dweller—the poverty of those who are approaching death. The dying are faces along the streets. An old man, his eyes fixed. Some passers-by leaving a few coins. A visit with the Brothers of Charity to the street-sleepers under an unfinished overpass. A plaintive plea from a silver-haired mother shivering violently with fever for some coins to buy medicine. Behind her, two pot-bellied little boys displaying their first-degree malnutrition.

Calcutta daily demands that we face not just poverty, not alone inhumanity, but this gray face of approaching death. The burden is increased by the knowledge that the continued overfertility inherent in poverty will force five times this number of people off the land in the next generation (about 20 years). The fact is that there is no more land, no more subdivision of farms possible. Increased agricultural productivity will only add to the migration, for it will increase the number of living children without bettering the quality of rural life.

The constant bickering of Bengali politics is death for these poor, as is the economic dislocation introduced by a theoretically Marxist state government—in reality a continued domination by a rich ruling class. The perpetual bondage of Hindu caste and culture adds to the death.

Some Levels of Urban Poverty

It would be a mistake to consider that the poor are to be found only in slums or squatter areas. Or that the people in the slums are necessarily all poor. Slums and poverty are not to be equated. And even among the poor there is a class structure or ranking. What then are the relationships between squatters and poverty?

Differences between First and Third World Urban Poor

Absolute poverty is a term used to describe poverty when people have an absolute insufficiency to meet their basic needs—food, clothing, housing. Indeed, many who are in absolute poverty starve to death. Within this category there are many levels. For example, we may talk of first, second and third-degree malnutrition.

Relative poverty is found in the developed world and is measured by looking at a person's standard of living relative to others in the community or nation. It is sometimes called secondary poverty. It is a measure of the extent to which people are on the margins of society.

The measure of this relative or secondary poverty is often in terms not of a material or economic level, but of capacity to own and consume goods and services and to have opportunities for development. It is often an ex-

clusion from opportunity and participation, a marginalization from society.

This marginal status is associated with and caused by (or causative of) a low material standard of living in relationship to present social perspectives of how one should live well. To be without a car in a New Zealand city, for example, means one is poor and largely unable to participate in society. This is not true in Lima, Peru. An International Labor Organization study uses a measure of disposable income to establish the standard poverty line, dividing the total available income in the country by the population, thus determining this level relative to others within the nation.

Thus when talking of poverty in Third World squatter areas, we are generally talking of something that occurs at a level not even to be seen among the poor of a Western country. The middle class of Calcutta are poorer than the poor of Los Angeles.

The definition of poverty is also, to a large extent, a historically perceived issue. The poor of Manila are not as poor as the middle class of England even 400 years ago. But they are poor compared with the present-day middle class in any country in the world. Our definition of poverty has changed with the availability of technology that enables us to enjoy a healthier, happier life.

Poverty can also be defined in terms of what man and society could be, in terms of a future vision of a reasonable, or ideal, lifestyle. Biblical scholars have recently clustered their definitions around the theme of *shalom* in the Old Testament—peace that comes out of a just and secure society.

Reachable Communities of Urban Poor

The physical characteristics and culture of each squatter community differ from country to country. Yet the processes that generate them and the resultant evils are universal among the major cities of the Third World countries.

We may talk of three major international categories of urban poor—inner-city slums, squatters, and specialized groups.

Inner-city slums are decaying tenements and houses in what were once good middle and upper-class residences. They may be described as *slums of despair* where those who have lost the will to try and those who cannot cope gravitate. Yet here too are the recent immigrants, living near employment opportunities, and students in their hundreds of thousands, seeking the upward mobility of education.

In Sao Paulo, approximately half of the migrant poor that come to the city find their first residence in *favelas*, or shanty towns. The other half move to the *corticos* (run-down, inner-city housing), then within four years move down into the *favelas*. In Lima these are called *tugurios*.

In inner-city slums of despair there is little social cohesion, or positive hope to facilitate a responsiveness to the gospel. Since they are older poor areas of several generations of sin, they are not responsive, and hence do not constitute a high priority for church planting.

In terms of response it is more strategic to focus on *squatter areas*, which tend to be *slums of hope*. Here people have found a foothold into the city, some vacant land, jobs and some communal relationships similar to the *barrio* back home.

Features of First and Third World Poverty

First World	Third World
Relatively few of society	Significant percentage of population
Objects of discrimination	Originates in lower and middle classes
Upward mobility difficult	Upward mobility from urban and rural roots
Job mobility limited	Flexible and adaptive labor
Hard to find permanent employment	Self-inflationary employment generation
"Secure" poverty/welfare	Daily subsistence search

The Task Ahead

Into this scene Jesus speaks the words, "And this is eternal life, to know You, the only true God, and Jesus Christ whom You have sent." (John 17:3). The confrontation of life with death involves aid, development, organization, politics. But as the brilliant Francis Xavier (a pioneer missionary to Asia) learned early in life, the issues of this world are not determined by politics and force, but by the mysteries of grace and faith. In the preaching of the cross comes the vanquisher of this slow death that grips the city. Eventually it must be movements of the righteous who can turn the flood tide. The question is how to generate movements of disciples among these poor and subsequently among the rich.

Defining poverty, its types, causes and potential responses, is an important step in the process of generating such movements. An understanding of the breadth of need and the range of potential responses enables us to reflect both on theology—that is, God's responses—and on strategic possibilities to implement as we walk with God.

End Notes

1. Moorehouse, Geoffrey, *Calcutta,* Penguin Books, 1984.
2. Ganguly, Tapash, "Pains of an Obese City," *The Week,* Nov 17-23, 1985.
3. Calcutta Metropolitan Planning Organization, A *Report on the Survey of 10,000 Pavement Dwellers in Calcutta: Under the Shadow of the Metropolis—they are citizens too,* Sudhendu Muukherjee, ed., 1973.

Study Questions

1. What distinctives are shown between Third World poor and the poor in the Western world?

2. Explain the difference between a slum of despair and a slum of hope. Why is this distinction important for urban mission?

3. Grigg says that "eventually it must be movements of the righteous" that transform cities. What does this suggest for strategies of church planting?

Transformational Development:

God at Work Changing People and Their Communities

Samuel J. Voorhies

W e drove for hours across Africa. We had left the capital city four hours earlier, but even so, we would arrive at a small town well after dark. We planned to stay the night since we would have to drive another three hours on unpaved, rough "secondary" roads to reach our destination the next day. In the small town we met who we hoped we would find—the project officer for a development project we had come to observe. A small office for the endeavor was located in this small town because it was the nearest place to the remote development project that had telephones or electricity.

The next morning, we met the staff of the development project. They told us about why the project was launched:

They explained that the area had once been a game preserve. It was considered so remote that it had been neglected by the government. There were no basic human services, such as education, health and water. When people were forced to settle in the area, a previous government administration had made promises, but these had never been fulfilled.

While some mission work had been carried out in the area, few NGOs (non-governmental organizations) or Christian aid agencies had come to bring any help. At last this particular agency explored how it might be able to help carry out transformational development in the area. The first step was to go through a process with community leaders and members to identify their community resources. With resources in view, they looked together as to how these resources could be used to solve the community's problems. It wasn't hard to see the problems:

- They lacked a clean source of water.
- There were no health services.
- There were no school facilities.
- The food production was inadequate to provide enough to supply the people until the next growing season.
- There had been no churches in the area.
- The area had been neglected by government and NGOs.

But we were assured that we would find something different after we endured the rough three-hour ride to reach the community. Before we could step from the truck, women, men and children had gathered, singing a song in

Samuel J. Voorhies has for the past 18 years worked in international relief and development in nearly 30 countries. He is also an Adjunct Professor in International Development at Fuller Theological Seminary. Currently, he is focusing on senior leadership development for the World Vision International Partnership.

the local language, "Up with development—we can do it ourselves with God's help and to His glory we will become all that we can be." I was inspired by the enthusiasm and commitment of these people. They had so little, yet, in very difficult circumstances with little help, they were doing so much.

Sitting with the crowd under a big tree for the next hour, we heard progress reports from community representatives—about what the people had done for themselves and what the agency had helped them to do. Then we were invited to walk around the community and see some of the improvements that they had made.

They showed us their former water supply—a pool of dirty water. "This is where we used to get our drinking water. It is the same place the animals drink from," said one of the ladies. We walked a little further and there was a new well. It was covered with a concrete slab, surrounded by a neat fence with a pump for retrieving clean water from deep underground. With a big smile the lady began to pump the water. "It's clean—would you like a drink?" she asked. I tasted the clean fresh water. "When we drank from the pool, our children were always sick with stomach problems and diarrhea. Now they are much healthier," another lady explained.

A little further on we saw a field where some beautiful corn was growing. "I was given a loan of improved seed and trained in planting methods and using organic fertilizers to double the amount of corn I will harvest," said a farmer. He continued, "The amount of corn I will get from this field will not only be enough to feed my family, but I will have enough left over to sell and help pay my children's school fees. I am planning to save some money each year and in three years, I will be able to buy oxen, cultivate more land and grow more crops."

As we walked on to the primary school, a young boy pointed to a fig tree. "This is where we used to sit for our lessons. There was no chalk board or chairs—just the hard ground," he explained. We went inside to the new classroom where desks had been built and a big chalkboard covered the front wall. "Now we are able to learn our lessons much better!" exclaimed another student.

After finishing our walk, we sat together under the tree again. I asked them what had been the most significant achievement of the project so far.

"We are together now and organized to help ourselves. We can meet and talk about our problems and how we can solve them together. Before we were isolated, living apart and not helping each other. We realize that we can do something to help better our lives. We don't have to wait on the government."

"We realize that as women we were loved and valued by God. We can contribute something to the development of this community. Our husbands now treat us with respect and we have more time to spend with our children. The men have stopped drinking."

"We now have clean water and healthier children. We don't have to walk so far for water and that gives us more time with our families."

The chairman boasted, "It has been a dream come true. We never imagined that we could have our own well and have pure, clean drinking water. We praise God for His faithfulness to our prayers through the work of the Christian aid agency."

The results of this project may seem like simple things. The availability of clean water; mothers with healthier children, who do not have to walk so far to get help when sick; children who have a school where they can sit and learn, and who can now hope and plan for the future. People with more confidence in themselves and their ability to work together and help change their future. Yet these technical and social interventions were much more. They were a powerful witness for the gospel. All things have an origin. With the assistance of dedicated local Christian workers people understand that this assistance comes because God loves them and has demonstrated His care for the community through other believers.

The community had pulled together. With some assistance from the agency, they had organized committees in collaboration with the government's and traditional leadership's infrastructure to take responsibility for and lead the development initiatives in the community.

People in the community were working together to bring about changed lives, to support each other in sustained programs, to meet both the physical and spiritual needs. Churches were launched, playing a vital part to demonstrate kingdom values, to offer instruction, and to foment hope by prayers. People recognized that their help ultimately came from God and they sought to know more about Him, giving Him glory in sincere thanks.

Does it sound too good to be true? Are there problems, failures, conflicts and differences? Of course. More needs to be done at the political level to change policies. Issues of gender and the environment need more careful consideration. More training is needed to equip the local pastors and to provide biblical resources. Yet, the truth is that we are seeing simple efforts by ordinary people bring about marvelous changes in their own societies. These people are practicing principles of we have come to call the process of holistic Christian transformational development.

It is "development" because it refers to the intentional process of facilitating change throughout a community or region. The idea of "transformation" speaks of change in the whole of the person—material, social and spiritual—as well as in the community—economics, social and political. It is "Christian" transformation because there is a vision of people throughout whole communities being changed to be like Christ, "being transformed into His likeness" (2 Cor 3:18). Christian transformation looks toward the hope that Christ's likeness will not only be the goal, but that the living Christ will bring about substantial changes for good through the practice of kingdom values.[1]

Different Perspectives of Development

There are four basic approaches to alleviating poverty. The four strategies can be compared by setting two basic methods against two ba-

Method / Focus	Help from without	Help from within
Structure	Strategy I *Economic Growth*	Strategy II *Political Liberation*
Needs	Strategy III *Relief*	Strategy IV *Community Development*

sic foci of action in a simple matrix. Each of these strategies has been referred to as "development." Each has a different focus concerning the nature of the problem and, therefore, the nature of the solution.

The matrix suggests two approaches to development. One focuses on aid brought from outside while the other seeks to facilitate changes from within. Each approach has validity. For the most part, they are interdependent and complementary. Each aspect should be considered as Christians seek to meet basic needs of human communities in the name of Christ.

Strategy I: Economic Growth

External aid usually comes in the form of money or technical assistance. Economic growth is most often determined through increases in macro-economic measurements, such as higher per capita income and/or improvements in the balance of trade. In the recent past, the World Bank and the IMF (International Monetary Fund) have led economic development programs by providing loans on the basis of nations agreeing to "structural adjustment."

In general, structural adjustment involves: a balancing of the nation's budget against its tax base, lowering government expenditure, which usually means laying off government employees and selling government businesses, a liberalization of the currency and economic policies. This involves a lowering of trade barriers and tariffs and, usually, a devaluation of the country's currency to reflect real market value. In the long run, this is intended to lower government debt and increase trade and production to bring in more revenue, benefiting all. In the short run, it usually means many people lose their jobs with no alternative sources of income. Those with some income have less purchasing power because of increased inflation and currency devaluation.

> Simple efforts by ordinary people bring about marvelous changes in their own societies.

While, in the recent past, some countries, such as the "Asian Tigers," have experienced economic growth through such policies, it has yet to be demonstrated that the poorest people will see significant improvements in their incomes and life circumstances. Furthermore, the conditions necessary to replicate the success in Asia have not been demonstrated to exist elsewhere.

Christians have kept such global economic policies in view, but have rarely depended on them to bring the desired changes. Mission efforts particularly have focused instead on bringing about micro-economic development as focus for helping the poor. Time and again it has been demonstrated that when determined people are provided with training and a small amount of capital, they can achieve economic success in their local context.

One woman in Malawi was given a small loan (about $40) to start a small bakery. She baked various "fast food" items, such as rolls and muffins, and sold them in the market each day. From this small investment, she was able to pay back the loan in six months and generate enough surplus income to send her four children to school. She was also able to purchase clothes, soap school supplies and food to supplement what they grew. She and her husband had not had this buying power before. As a result of her business success, she indicated they were able to support their local church with their increased income. She was now earning as much a local primary school teacher. When asked if she had a "dream" or future plans, she quickly explained that she had plans to expand her business and open a restaurant.

Strategy II: Political Advocacy

By contrast with seeking to bolster the existing government, the political advocacy strategy tends to challenge the national government along with systems of international trade and economic policies. The systems are seen as the primary problem. This approach calls for a direct interface with governments, both at local national and international levels. Changes are sought in the areas of unfair and unfavorable government policies as well as international trade agreements. In the most extreme cases, political advocacy can lead to

violent conflict with government, such as what we have seen in Nigeria in recent years. In most cases, it involves local and international lobbying to bring about change that will benefit the majority of people.

Through out history, Christians have been a powerful force in policy matters such as, land reform, refugee's rights, and the abolition of slavery. While it is important that Christians continue to address these kinds of issues, their primary role today must be to support and assist local people to take the lead in calling for internal political change. Nationals must take the leading role in their situation. Western Christians can also act as advocates back home, at points where they see their own governments policies perpetuating injustice for the poor.

Political advocacy has not been seen to bring about lasting positive change without some measure of Strategy IV. Structural and policy changes will only be as effective as the people who are implementing them. Without personal spiritual liberation, development will always be limited to the greed and corruption of individuals. Working to promote justice and peace is a biblical mandate and must be done with great prayer and sensitivity. However, success will be limited if not combined with the spiritual development of the individuals who run governments and implement policies.

Strategy III: Relief

Relief aims to address the emergency needs for victims of war, famine, disaster and often prolonged injustice. Christian organizations have launched massive relief efforts, but these efforts only bring temporary help and must not be confused with development. Relief primarily focuses on what the outsider must do to help the victim, not what the people must do to help themselves. Such relief efforts can be viewed as detrimental if prolonged, because they take away incentive for local production and development.

Some have criticized relief efforts coupled with evangelism for producing "rice Christians"—someone who becomes a Christian to assure himself and/or his family of getting daily food. Relief assistance must never be conditioned on one's beliefs or on having to hear a gospel message. Relief must be given freely in love without condition, just as Jesus gave and loved freely without condition (John 13:34-35). It is this kind of love that identifies us as Christ's disciples to the world. Relief aid stops people from dying and keeps them from "eating their seed-corn" so there can be a restart of long-term growth and life. It is the long-range hope that moves Christians to search for answers to deep-seated problems.

In such disastrous circumstances of war and famine, relief carried out unconditionally by Christians can be a powerful gospel witness. After receiving a day's portion of grain from a Christian aid camp in the height of a drought, one nomadic Muslim man was overheard saying, "If this is the way Christians love those they don't even know, surely this is enough for me to believe in their God."

Strategy IV: Transformational Development

Transformational development addresses poverty with a long view in a local way. In deeply impoverished areas in remote rural areas and, increasingly, in urban slums, the problems are usually quite complex. There may be a lack of infrastructure, such as passable roads or working vehicles, to bring crops to market or supplies to the community. Basic health care is often unavailable. A lack of a steady, clean water supply can devastate entire regions. Fuel is essential, but in very scant supply in some areas. Approaching the complex of difficulties requires long-term local attention at the community level. Local people need to take leadership to bring about sustained changes.

The work of Christian development workers is to facilitate change from within the society for an entire community or area. The core transformation is at the point of values and vision. Concerning vision, people come to see that their community can be made different, that they are not locked in a unchangeable despair. Concerning values, people come to see afresh that they are valuable. Christians who labor at this kind of development have a clear advantage of working toward the values of the kingdom of God.

Principles of Holistic Christian Transformational Development

I see ten fundamental principles and values of holistic transformational development. Each of them has a rich biblical foundation.

1. Recognize the value of people. Respect and value people in the context of their local culture.
2. Understand and respect local culture. Yet discern that while each person is intrinsically valuable, every culture has both positive and negative aspects that may or may not be compatible with biblical teaching.
3. Believe in the person's capacity to contribute and determine his/her future. Help people meet their basic needs with dignity and self-respect. No matter how poor, every community and every individual has something to contribute. Identifying and starting with local resources is a key to people's sense of ownership and self-dignity.[2]
4. Make people, rather than technology, the focal point. When local people are involved in making decisions they ultimately take responsibility for determining their future.
5. Realize that poverty includes both physical, material, spiritual and social dimensions. Involve the whole person—mind, body and spirit, in any development effort. Avoid segregating these and design programs that address the whole problem and the whole person.
6. Approach development in a way that seeks to communicate Christ through word—communicating the gospel of Christ; deed—serving as Christ would, bringing healing and exemplifying righteousness; and sign—working with God's help so that Christ's kingdom life is demonstrated.
7. Realize that all interventions into a group of people (social, technical, economic or educational) carry a message that must be understood and interpreted from the recipient's world view.
8. Recognize that God is already at work in the community. Part of the external facilitator's tasks is to discover what God is doing and support what may already be

happening as a bridge to how God wants to use the external resource and revelation.

9. Believe that transformation in a person comes through a relationship with Christ. There is no substitute for such a living, growing faith.[3]

10. Recognize churches as foundational for sustained and abundant transformation. To strengthen existing churches, or to plant new ones where none exist, forms a powerful community of transformed lives empowered by God with hope and kingdom values.

The Hope of Abundant Life

In Ethiopia, the Ansokia Valley had been ravished by the famine of 1984 when some 20 people were dying every day from starvation. Today, this valley is a garden of hope for its people and those in the surrounding communities. Over 7000 households, some 45,000 people, have gone from the brink of starvation and destitution to abundance, through a transformational development program. New innovations for crops, animal husbandry improvement and reforestation were adopted, resulting in people growing an abundance of food and having a safe, sustainable environment in which to live. Through the lives of Christians working in the community to help carry out these development efforts, it is estimated that some 700 people have come to Christ and now attend the first church to be established in the area.

As one man noted, "I resisted the call of Jesus from the witness of many of the development workers. But as I continued to be involved in development work, their accountability and dedication to the spiritual and physical work touched my heart. I watched them praying and talking about ways we could have a better life. Then last year I received Jesus. Now I share the joy, responsibility and work that the staff shared with us. I now understand why the staff came to share with us and help us improve our living."[4]

I have been to Ansokia, both during the famine and several years later, after the transformational development program was implemented. Where there was death, today there is life—abundant life—where children and families are healthier, happier and have the assurance of eternal life through Jesus Christ our Lord.

End Notes

1. Yamamori, Tetsunao, Serving With the Poor in Africa: Cases in Holistic Ministry, MARC Publications, 1996.

2. Voorhies, Samuel I., *Community Participation and Holistic Development*, pp 123-48, in Yamamori, Tetsunad, *Serving with the Poor in Africa: Cased in Holistic Ministry*, MARC Publications. 1996.

3. Cheyne, John R., Incarnational Agents: A Guide to Developmental Ministry, New Hope 1996.

4. Abebe, Mulugeta, From Relief to Development in Ethiopia, pps 15-27 in Yamamori, Tetsunao, Serving With the Poor in Africa: Cases in Holistic Ministry, MARC Publications, 1996.

Study Questions

1. What would happen if we apply the principles of community participation to the establishment and building of the church as we do for agricultural, health and school projects?

2. How does the idea of building people's capacity to plan and manage their own development relate to the establishment and sustainability of a local church and the believer's spiritual life?

3. Underline the words and/or phrases and each of the ten principles of wholistic Christian transformational development that suggest the distinctive quality of the principle? When and how does evangelism and church planting take place?

Dependency

Glenn Schwartz

The well-intended generosity of Christians often backfires by creating dependency. We can learn valuable lessons from the past failings of misguided kindnesses.

How to Destroy Local Initiative–Step One:

A Navajo Indian believer from the western United States, whose people have suffered much at the hands of the rest of the population, is reported to have shared this remarkable insight. He said, "The missionaries did not teach us to tithe because they thought we were too poor. They did not know that we were poor because we did not tithe." There is a law in the universe that if God gives you something, you're supposed to give some of it back to Him. Now I am not saying that tithing is the answer to all the church's problems, but I am saying that if we assume people cannot give back to God some of what they have been given—if we assume they are too poor to give to God—we deprive them of a blessing that God has in store for them.

How to Destroy Local Initiative–Step Two:

When outsiders construct church buildings for local people, they can inadvertently become thieves of self-respect. Foreign funding for buildings can take away the privilege that local people should have of building their own churches, clinics or schools. Instead of preserving dignity, we can create a dependency that often comes back to haunt us.

During a seminar on this subject, an American missionary in the back of the room raised his hand and said, "I know what you're talking about. Some years ago I took a group of 36 people from North America to South America to build a church building for the local believers. We stayed there several weeks, finished the building, gave it to the local people and then went home. Two years later we got a letter from the people at that church: 'Dear friends, the roof on your church building is leaking. Please come and repair it….'"

On the other hand, some mission societies, from the beginning, insist on the involvement of local people when building their buildings, supporting their evangelists and sending out missionaries. Some of these churches not only build their own buildings, but send out their own missionaries within the first decade of their existence.

Glenn Schwartz is the Founding Executive Director of World Mission Associates in Lancaster, Pennsylvania. In the past he was the Assistant to the Dean at the Fuller School of World Mission. He has also served in Zambia and Zimbabwe.

Chapter 86

If It Is Not Reproducible, Forget It

The structure of the Christian movement introduced to many parts of Central and East Africa is not reproducible. This complex foreign structure was created and built up over decades with an expenditure of millions of dollars, pounds and deutschemarks.

If the visiting foreign personnel during the colonial period could not run the programs without heavy foreign subsidy, how could they expect that believers to do so when the subsidy was removed? The result is that, in Central and East Africa, church after church cannot think of cross-cultural evangelism beyond their borders because of the weight of the structures inherited from the past. Furthermore, since many of these church programs could not be sustained locally, how could they be reproduced elsewhere?

Hence, well-intentioned national church leaders are preoccupied with maintenance rather than dynamic missionary outreach. They have little energy left over to make cross-cultural outreach a reality, let alone a spiritually rewarding adventure. In the end, local leaders are made to appear like poor managers, or even failures, for not being able to keep elaborate church programs going. That is just one of the many regrettable results of creating irreproducible structures.

How to Keep a Church Poor

Perhaps one of the most lamentable aspects of irreproducible church and mission structures is that the enormous flow of outside funding is what actually keeps many churches "poor." Believers through the years found that it was not necessary to put paper money into the church offering. They knew that if they sat back and waited long enough, funds would eventually come from some unseen source. Indeed, those who created the programs could not afford to let them fail. People of "compassion" would find the funding and close the gap, if for no other reason than to save the reputations of those who started the programs in the first place.

Even mainline churches which have experienced the blessing of being organizationally and financially independent find it necessary to continue teaching their people that "it is more blessed to give than to re-

ceive." Sometimes the ease with which other groups receive outside money becomes a strong temptation. It helps to be reminded that if people can be bought with money, perhaps they can be bought. The march of Islam across Africa, fueled by Middle East petrodollars, is a real source of danger to nominal African Christianity.

Another Sad Story

A major Christian organization in East Africa was well on the way toward functioning entirely with local funding. Culturally appropriate structures were in place. Local funds were being raised. Then a donor in Europe offered them a substantial grant. They felt they couldn't refuse it without offending the donor. But something tragic happened in the process. Board members of the institution said, "If overseas money is that easy to get, why do we go through all the work of trying to raise funds locally?" Sadly, the local fund raising plans were scrapped. The soul of the institution was sold in favor of easy money. We should all weep.

And a Happy Story

A pastor in the Cape Province of South Africa has a vision for a ministry with a budget of a hundred million rand. My heart sank when I heard that he was recently on a visit to Europe. Imagine my surprise when I learned that God spoke to him on that trip, telling him that the money should be raised at home, from business people within the Cape Province of South Africa. If this happens, blessing will abound among all the people of the Cape Province, rather than being restricted to a few European donors.

A Story of Hard Work

After securing permission from the local authorities, a pastor bought a field and set about plowing it. A neighboring villager saw what he was doing. He approached the church leader in the field and said, "Reverend, why are you plowing this field?" He replied, "Because church offerings are down and I need to support my family."

The neighbor responded, "You are a man of God, you should be doing God's work. You go do God's work, and I'll plow your field for you." When harvest time came the neighbor offered to help the minister again.

That church leader later made this observation. "When our people see that we as church leaders are willing to work for our own living, then our people will show that they, too, are willing to help. That is how the attitude of our people will change."

Think of it again this way: So long as there is a veiled source of income from some unknown place, local people will not feel the need to support their own ministries. The question is this: Does anyone have the courage to let the system collapse so that what rises up truly belongs to the people?

What Can be Done: Mobilize Local Resources

More than a hundred years ago missiologists discovered the importance of self-support for establishing mission churches. Now, a century later, not only are the lessons of healthy self-support not being applied, but many rationalize that the only reasonable thing to do is to supplement or in some cases replace local giving with global resources. They do not seem to realize that when global resources replace local resources, people are deprived of the joy of giving back to the Lord some of what He has given to them. Even more tragically, somewhere the gospel will not be preached because too much money is being diverted to churches already in existence.

One leader from East Africa told me that he faced a double challenge: "We must do more than successfully raise local funds. That we can do. In addition, we must challenge the Western structures and assumptions which continually pour in funds from the outside." Now is the time to staunch the flow of misguided funding to emerging churches, so that we can see churches move in the blessing of God.

Study Questions

1. In cross-cultural situations, what disincentives are created by outside funding?

2. List two ways that the mobilization of local resources fosters advancement of the kingdom of God.

The Spontaneous Multiplication of Churches

George Patterson

O ur Lord sends us to disciple every "nation" (people group) by training them to obey all His commands (Matt 28:18-20). This means that we disciple a "nation" only when it is permeated by obedient disciples who also disciple other unevangelized peoples. So we don't fulfill the mandate by simply starting one church amidst a people. We, or those we send, must start the kind of church that grows and reproduces spontaneously as churches will, in daughter churches, granddaughter churches, great-granddaughter churches and so on. *Spontaneous* reproduction of churches means the Holy Spirit moves a church to reproduce daughter churches on its own, without outsiders pushing it (Acts 13:1-3).

I began training pastors in Honduras in a traditional theological institution and had the traditional problems for the traditional reasons. I assumed the bright young men I trained were dedicated because they came to our resident Bible school. Our plan was for them to return to their home towns as pastors. But the graduates found the gold lettering on their diplomas did not go well with the white-washed adobe walls back home. It enabled them, however, to earn more in the office of the Dole Banana Co.

My raspy supervisor had the gall to blame us teachers; he told us, "Close the school; start discipling the people."

"No," I argued, "that's too hard."

"Excuses! They're poor, semi-literate, subsistence farmers but you teach as though they were educated, middle class Americans."

I wrote my missionary buddies from language school, now spread all over Latin America, fishing for sympathy. They had the same problem!

"I'm a teacher without a classroom!" I complained.

"So," my supervisor rasped, "teach by extension."

"What's that?"

He handed me a smelly old saddle, explaining, "You're promoted. This is the Chair of Evangelism and Church Planting in your new extension Bible institute."

After a few weeks of blisters on my south side I learned to communicate with the mission mule and announced, "Hey, I can do this TEE stuff. It's great."

My supervisor warned me, "Then your students had better raise up and pastor their own churches or we'll close down this Theological Education by Extension, too."

George Patterson teaches in the Division of Intercultural Studies at Western Seminary in Portland, Oregon. He coaches and trains missionaries to multiply churches in many areas of the world. He worked for 21 years in northern Honduras through a program of Theological Education and Evangelism by Extension.

I took the pastoral studies to family men (Biblical "elder" types) in the poverty-ridden villages, mountains and cities. Unlike their single young sons, they had crops, jobs or family responsibilities that kept them from going off to our resident Bible school. They also lacked the education to absorb its intensive teaching. But these older men, with roots in their villages and barrios, could begin pastoring with the respect of their people easier than the single young men could. By God's mercy I slowly learned to evangelize and disciple these *elders* in a way that enabled them to raise up and pastor their small village churches. As will be the case in many of today's remaining unreached fields, we began to see growth not through any one church growing big or fast, but through the slow, steady reproduction of many small churches.

I could have avoided years of struggle searching for principles of church reproduction had I looked first in the operator's manual. New Testament discipling principles, conscientiously applied, are enabling churches to reproduce in Honduras and many other fields. Field testing of programs based on these principles give consistently good results in Latin America and Asia, including hostile fields where evangelism is illegal.

We must distinguish between these general *principles* and culture-specific *applications*. Biblical principles themselves, if applied with culturally relevant methods, should enable churches to reproduce wherever there is plenty of "good soil." Theologically speaking, good soil for the gospel seed to take root in and multiply is *bad people*, and lots of them (Rom 5:20-21; Matt 13:18:23; Eph 2:1-10).

The simplicity of the principles disappoints some educators. They expect something more sophisticated, at least new or expensive. Missionary or not, one can multiply disciples doing these four simple things:

1. Know and love the people you disciple.
2. Mobilize your disciples to edify immediately those they are discipling.
3. Teach and practice obedience to Jesus' basic commands, in love, before and above all else.
4. Build loving, edifying accountability relationships between disciples and churches in order to reproduce churches.

1. Know And Love the People You Disciple.

We must know and love a people before we can disciple them. When Jesus told His disciples to "Look at the fields," they were finding it hard to love the Samaritans around them; they could not see them receiving God's grace.

Limit Your Area of Responsibility to One People or Community.

We must focus on one people group, the one God has given us. Paul knew his area of responsibility before God (2 Cor 10:12-16; Acts 16:6-10; Gal 2:8). He knew what kind of churches to plant and where. For a *movement of church reproduction* a church planting team needs a clear focus from God. My area was "the Spanish speaking people of the Aguan Valley and surrounding mountains." It helps to be exact.

At home or abroad every discipler needs to ask: "For whom am I responsible?" If a missionary fails to do this, the geographic and ethnic limits of his ministry remain blurred. He will jump from opportunity to opportunity. I asked one of these wandering gold prospectors in Central America what his area of responsibility was. "Oh," he said, "I am winning the country for Christ." He goes from city to city preaching in prisons and army camps; he bombs villages with tracts from his Cessna. It's fun and folks back home eagerly finance it. But he will never plant a reproductive church until he learns to hold the people of a community in his heart.

Choosing your people in a new field needs study and prayer. Confer with other missionaries, nationals and God Himself for guidance.

Knowing a people means touching the heart of individuals. Laughing with those who laugh. Weeping with those who weep. Playing marbles with 2-year old Chimbo and checkers with his grandpa (or whatever they play in the town square). It may help if you let him beat you. This applies to arguing religion, too. It's dangerous always to be "right" when you're the new kid on the block. Learn to appreciate the people and their ways, even the toothless old men. Listen and learn until you have discovered those things in their folk religion or culture that help communicate the gospel.

Once you know your area and people, discern which segment among them is most receptive to you and to Jesus Christ. To penetrate restricted, resistant fields, aim *first* at the working class or an oppressed minority. This contradicts some popular church growth theories. We are not dealing with second generation growth in Pasadena, California, however, but the *initial beachhead* where people get a curved blade in their ribs for witnessing. Jesus did not begin His public ministry among the influential middle class and natural leaders in the political nerve centers of Rome or Jerusalem, but with the working class upriver in Galilee where they spoke Hebrew with a backwoods accent—otherwise He would have been crucified prematurely.

Let the Church Be of the People.

Like most inexperienced church planters I started "preaching points" at first, instead of genuine New Testament churches. Someone went every week to a community where a group gathered to hear their pulpit oratory and sing (well, at least to sing). Converts were not baptized. Local leaders were not trained. The Lord's Supper was neglected. No one knew for sure who were Christians. Obedient, sacrificial discipling gave way to entertaining (a tradition brought by American missionaries). Preaching points develop a personality of their own; they stubbornly refuse to evolve into obedient, giving, reproductive churches. They become sponges soaking up the time and efforts of outside workers and producing nothing—except where God's sheer mercy overrides our routine.

Find what a church's people can do and plan that, before planning its structure, forms and organization. I hope it takes you less time than it took me to learn that formal pulpit preaching is ineffective (often illegal) in many of today's remaining unreached fields. You can preach the Word with power in many other ways, if you know your people. We used dramatic Bible reading, songs with music and lyrics composed by nationals, poems, symbols and story telling. They sang with more enthusiasm when they composed songs in the local style.

Let the new church's self-identity be evident. Know exactly what you are aiming at within the community: a well defined body of obedient disciples of Jesus Christ. Once I made the mistake of allowing more outside helpers to be present than members of the community during the first baptism and celebration of the Lord's Supper. The church died at birth. There must be a majority from the community itself, especially at the first baptism or worship meetings, or the church is not born as a distinct entity within the community. Our converts felt that they had simply been added to some organization of the outsiders. I robbed them of the thrill of looking at each other and saying, "*We* are now the church here!" They must see the new church being born as a part of their community.

List What You Will Do to Reproduce Disciples Among a People.

Let's assume you research well all the factors: race, culture, logistics, urban versus rural backgrounds, language similarities, education and economic levels, etc. You learn the language. Then you go in a crowded bus to your new field, with a team of church planters as similar to the local people as possible in every aspect. Some or all of them may be from another developing country. You are happy because they do not have to make that long cultural leap that delays church planting by years (the less responsive the people are to missionaries, the more crucial this cultural fit). Now you finally arrive, unpack your toothbrush, take a deep breath, pray, step out the door and find fifty thousand people living around you who think Jesus was John Wayne's cousin. Now what?

What you do first often determines the direction of your work, for good or bad, for years to come. Will it lead to reproductive churches? The right steps will vary for each field but will always include teaching the converts first to obey Jesus' basic commands (Matt 28:18-20). Take the shortest route possible to start a real church: a group of believers in Christ dedicated to obey His commands. In a pioneer field let it start small, perhaps with only three or four members. It will grow if you disciple the people as Jesus said.

Avoid institutions if possible at this beachhead stage (community development programs unrelated to church planting, schools, clinics, etc.). It's best to let these come later. In Honduras we developed community development work but it grew out of the churches, not vice versa. We taught obedience to the great commandment of loving our neighbor in a practical way. A poverty program can aid church planting if the two are integrated by the Holy Spirit. But churches dependent on charitable institutions are almost always dominated by the foreign missionary and seldom reproduce.

To start a church that will multiply in the normal way in a *pioneer* field with no experienced pastors nor organized churches, take the following steps (change them where local circumstances require it):

1. Witness first to male heads of households. We often told them Bible stories they could pass on immediately, even before being saved, to their own family and friends. We went with them to show them how. But why *male* heads of families? We worked in a macho culture (right where the word *macho* came from, where men carried sharpened machetes and used them readily). Female leadership, right or wrong, limited the outreach of brand new works. Later, when a church was established with male pastor and elders, women could take a higher profile. Be sensitive to your community's norms, especially in the first impressions you give of the church.

2. Baptize all repentant believers without delay (entire families when possible). At first I acted as though a big buzzard were perched on my shoulder just waiting to pounce on our converts that fell away; I delayed baptism to make sure they were "safe." But I soon saw that the very reason many fell away was my distrust. That's the funny thing about God's grace; He wants us to let it slop over on the unworthy (Rom 5:20-21).

3. Provide a style of worship that new elders-in-training can lead and teach to others. Don't invite the *public* until local leaders can lead the services. Celebrate the Lord's Supper weekly as the center of worship, especially until local men are mature enough to preach in an edifying, humble way.

4. Organize a provisional board of elders as soon as mature men are converted. Show them how to win and pastor their own people right away. Remember, this is for pioneer fields with no experienced pastors nor well organized churches. We, like Paul, must use the best men God gives us as the churches multiply, or the new disciples have no leadership at all (Acts 14:23).

5. Enroll these new elders in pastoral training on the job. Don't remove them from their people for training. Meet with them every two or three weeks (more often if possible) until they are mobilized.

6. Provide a list of activities planned for the congregation, starting with the commands of Christ and His apostles. Let everyone know where he is going and what he needs to learn for each activity. Use this as a check list to monitor the progress of the elders you train, in both their studies and pastoral work, as they mobilize their own people in ministry.

2. Mobilize Your Disciples Immediately to Edify Those They Are Discipling.

To build up the church as a living, reproducing body, Paul instructs pastors and teachers to train the members of the church for the ministry, to edify the Body of Christ (Eph 4:11-12).

Build Edifying Relationships with the Leaders you Disciple.

Like most new missionaries, I took myself too seriously. I worried about what my disciples were up to. It took me years to learn to sit back with my coconut milk, laugh at my own goofs and trust the Holy Spirit to do His work in my students. How can we enable the leaders we train to edify each other and their people through personal, loving relationships?

Paul left his pastoral disciple Timothy behind to work with the elders in newly planted churches with these instructions: "The things you have heard from me...these entrust to faithful men who will be able to teach others also" (2 Tim 2:2). How dynamic and reproductive this loving "Paul-Timothy" relationship between teacher and student! If you have not yet tried to teach the way Jesus and His apostles did, you are in for a blessing. If it frightens you, start with just one or two potential leaders. Train them on the job; take responsibility for their effective ministry. Personal discipling does not mean "one-on-one" (Jesus taught twelve), nor is it just to deal with personal needs (Jesus spent most of His time personally discipling the top level leaders of the Church, the very apostles).

In Honduras I usually taught from one to three students, in a way they could imitate and pass on to others immediately. I helped each one have an effective ministry. I taught and modeled what he would pass on to his own people and his own pastoral trainees in the daughter or granddaughter churches. These taught other elders who taught still others as Paul instructed Timothy. The chain

A Passive, Pastor-centered Church

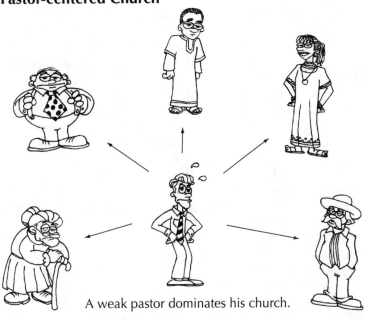

A weak pastor dominates his church.

Interaction in a Dynamic Church

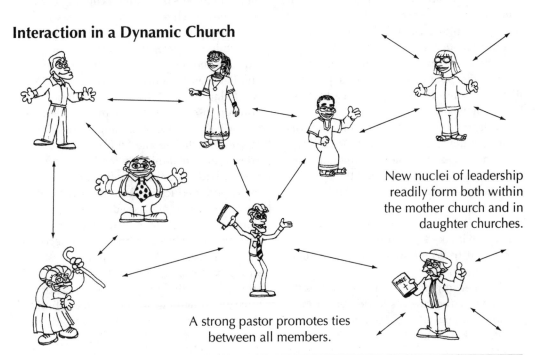

New nuclei of leadership readily form both within the mother church and in daughter churches.

A strong pastor promotes ties between all members.

grew to over a hundred pastors in training, all elders of churches. As soon as a new church was born, the outside worker enrolled a local leader, normally an elder highly respected by his people, and began passing on to him the same doctrine and materials as he was receiving himself. This new "Timothy" taught the rest of the new elders in his young church. It kept multiplying as long as each discipler did *everything* in a way his students could imitate immediately. I stopped teaching and preaching in the professional way in which I was used to (they admired it, but could not imitate it). I stopped using electronic equipment including movies, and anything else that was not available to all our workers. That's hard on a gadget-oriented westerner used to gadgets and conditioned to using the very latest technology for the glory of Christ.

Once we developed loving, Paul-Timothy discipling relationships we seldom had to discuss church planting. The Holy Spirit channeled the Word of God through these relationships to mobilize the Timothies and church reproduction took care of itself. At first I failed to trust the Holy Spirit and pushed the men myself. I dictated rules and prerequisites to keep the doctrine and the church pure and to make sure the men did their job. It stifled the work; one bitter failure followed another. I prayed, "Lord, I don't want a big ministry of my own; just let me help the Hondurans have a good ministry." God answered this prayer. I also learned through disappointments to let the people themselves decide on their own leaders, using 1 Timothy 3:1-7.

We learned not to plant the churches first then train the leaders for them; nor did we train the leaders first then tell them to raise up their churches. We married the two efforts in one ministry. My American culture pushed me at first to compartmentalize our organization, isolating its ministries. But I learned to let the Holy Spirit integrate diverse ministries and gifts in the united body (2 Cor 12:4-26).

I also began with education objectives that focused on educating the leader. But according to Ephesians 4:11-16, our education should seek only to edify the *church* in love. I had to discipline myself to keep my student's people in view as I taught, and not focus only on my student and the teaching content.

Before I learned to imitate the way Christ and His apostles discipled, I was satisfied if my student answered test questions correctly and preached good sermons in the classroom. I neither saw nor cared what he did in his church with what he was learning. I slowly learned to see beyond my student to his ministry with his people. I responded to the needs of his church by listening at the beginning of each session to the reports of my students. Then I often set aside what I had prepared and taught rather what each student's people needed at that time.

It was hard at first to let the developing churches' needs and opportunities dictate the order of a functional curriculum. In time much of my discipling, like the teaching of the Epistles, became *problem solving*. Yes, if we start reproductive churches we will have problems. The apostles did, too. To avoid problems, don't have children and don't have churches.

Encourage Edifying Teaching Relationships Between Leaders and Their Disciples.

The pastor or leading elder sets the example for all the leaders. They in turn enable all the members of an infant congregation to minister to each other in love. A weak pastor dominates his congregation. He tries to do everything, or delegates it in a demanding way. He herds rather than leads (both Jesus and Peter prohibit herding in a demanding way: Matt 20:25-28; 1 Pet 5:1-4). Where do you suppose pastors on the mission field pick up the bad practice of herding others? It's not all cultural; they learned it from us missionaries. I furnished the only model the new pastors had in our pioneer field. Because of my superior education and resources, I made the decisions for my less educated colleagues. At the same time, like most new missionaries, I felt insecure and overprotected the first churches. A strong missionary, like a strong pastor, does not fear to give authority and responsibility to others. He does not force gifted, willing workers into existing slots in his organization, but rather builds ministries around them.

3. Teach and Practice Obedience to Jesus' Commands in Love, Above and Before All Else.

Jesus, after affirming His deity and total authority on earth, commissioned His Church to make disciples who obey all His commands (Matt 28:18-20). So His commands take priority over all other institutional rules (even the hallowed *Church Constitution and Bylaws*). This obedience is always in love. If we obey God for any other reason, it becomes sheer legalism; God hates that.

Start Right Out With Loving Obedience to Jesus' Basic Commands.

To plant churches in a pioneer field, aim for each community to have a group of believers in Christ committed to obey His commands. This definition of a church might get a D minus where you studied theology; but *the more you add to it, the harder it will be for the churches you start to reproduce.* We asked our converts to memorize the following list of Christ's basic commands:

1. Repent and believe: Mark 1:15
2. Be baptized (and continue in the new life it initiates): Matt 28:18-20; Acts 2:38; Rom 6:1-11
3. Love God and neighbor in a practical way: Matt 22:37-40
4. Celebrate the Lord's Supper: Luke 22:17-20
5. Pray: Matt 6:5-15
6. Give: Matt 6:19-21; Luke 6:38
7. Disciple others: Matt 28:18-20

Memorize them; you can neither be nor make obedient disciples unless they are basic to your Christian experience. They are the ABCs of both discipling and church planting.

Define Evangelism and Theological Education Objectives in Terms of Obedience.

Do not simply preach for "decisions;" make obedient disciples. Only disciples produce a church that multiplies itself spontaneously within a culture. Consider the two commands: "Repent and believe" and "Be baptized." In Western culture a man stands alone before his God and "decides" for Christ. But in other cultures sincere conversion needs interaction with family and friends. Faith, repentance and immediate baptism of the entire family or group—no invitation to make a decision—is

the norm (Acts 2:36-41; 8:11; 10:44-48; 16:13-15, 29-34; 18:8). Repentance goes deeper than a decision; it is a permanent change wrought by God's Spirit. We are born all over again. Few purely intellectual decisions in any culture lead to permanent, obedient discipleship.

We found that when we baptized repentant believers reasonably soon, without requiring a long doctrinal course first, the great majority then responded to our training in obedient discipleship. The detailed doctrine came later. Teaching heavy theology *before* one learns loving, childlike obedience is dangerous. It leaves a person assuming that Christianity is having Scripturally correct doctrine and he leaves it at that. He becomes a passive learner of the Word rather than an active disciple.

Orient Your Teaching to Loving Obedience.

We taught our pastors to orient all church activity to New Testament commands. As they taught the Word of God, they accustomed their people to discern three levels of authority for all that they did as a body of disciples:

1. NEW TESTAMENT COMMANDS. These carry all the authority of heaven. They include the commands of Jesus which inspired the apostles in the Epistles. They apply only to baptized, more mature Christians who are already members of a church. We don't vote on them nor argue about doing them. They always take precedent over any human organization's rules.
2. APOSTOLIC PRACTICES (NOT COMMANDED). We cannot enforce these as laws because Christ alone has authority to make laws for His own Church, His Body. Nor can we prohibit their practice because they have apostolic precedent. Examples include: holding possessions in common, laying hands on converts, celebrating the Lord's Supper frequently in homes using one cup, baptizing the same day of conversion, Sunday worship.
3. HUMAN CUSTOMS. Practices not mentioned in the New Testament have only the authority of a group's voluntary agreement. If it involves discipline, the agreement is recognized in heaven (but only for that congregation; we do not judge another congregation by the customs of our own: Matt 18:15-20).

Nearly all church divisions and quarrels originate when a power hungry person seeking followers puts mere apostolic practices or human customs (levels 2 or 3 above) at the top level as law.

We developed a "Congregation Activities Register" listing features of health and the essential ministries of healthy churches. This list was based on the seven general commands of Christ (repent and believe, be baptized, love God and neighbor, celebrate the Lord's Supper, pray, give, and disciple others) and other commands in the Epistles. On this menu of ministries we usually listed: evangelism, prayer, giving, pastoral care, teaching, loving neighbors, building character, counseling, worship, reproducing daughter churches, mission, and more. Under each activity in this chart we listed related studies. It became our pastoral training curriculum guide. We brought in all major areas of Bible, doctrine and church history, precisely where they best aided a church activity. Theological education paralleled church development. Each activity included reading in the relevant areas of Bible, doctrine, church history and pastoral work (all the essential elements of a traditional pastoral training curriculum) as well as questions to verify that the practical work was done. (An example of materials using this functional discipling curriculum is SEAN's *Train and Multiply* program, Casilla 61, Viña DelMar, Chile.)

The sequence in which you select items on the training menu should be based primarily on what you hear. Everything depends on the readiness of the teacher to listen to what the present needs and growth struggles are.

4. Build Loving, Edifying Accountability Relationships Between Disciples and Churches in Order to Reproduce Churches.

Healthy daughter churches need loving, edifying discipling relationships within themselves and with the mother church (Acts 11:19-30; 14:21-28 and 15:1-2, 28-31). If your church, church planting or training organization is already formed, add this personal discipling to it; don't insist on ruthless changes.

Help Each New Church to Reproduce.

Each church should send workers to reproduce daughter churches, as did the Antioch church (Acts 13:1-3). In Ephesians 4:1-12 God has promised to give "apostles" to every church (by apostles let's assume that it means "sent ones" in a general sense). These "apostles" are the ones God places in every church that have itchy feet for carrying the church's DNA to new areas. The longer you wait to mobilize a church for multiplication, the harder it is to reprogram its thinking. Teach your people the joy of sacrificing to separate from their strongest tithers and leaders, in the power of the Holy Spirit as in Antioch, to extend Christ's kingdom. After prayer, perhaps fasting, hold a formal separation service with laying on of hands, as they did. Remember, it is not the individuals that reproduce, but *congregations* that pray and are moved by the Holy Spirit. Let each new church be a link in the chain. The individual extension worker is only an arm of his church.

Ask the new church leaders to chart their own plans. They must take the initiative (don't push your plans on them; simply teach them what the Word says about their task and let them respond). For example, we asked our pastors to draw a large map, with arrows to the villages which they planned for their church to reach directly or through their daughter or granddaughter churches. Their church workers then signed their names by those towns or neighborhoods for which they would pray and plan.

Show Each New Believer How to Witness to Friends and Relatives.

The Holy Spirit flows readily through the bonds that exist between family members and close friends (Acts 10:24, 44). Keep new converts in a loving relationship with them (don't pull them out of their circle to put them in a safe Christian environment, or those very bonds which aid the spread of the gospel become barriers).

We prepared simple gospel studies (mostly Bible stories) that even illiterates could use at once to share their new faith. We accompanied them to show them how to do it, modeling it all in a way they could immediately imitate.

Build Edifying Inter-church Discipling Relationships.

At first I applied church "body life" only to local congregations. Then I learned to build inter-church discipling relationships with accountability. Elders in one church sacrificially discipled less experienced pastors in the daughter or granddaughter churches.

Sometimes travel was difficult for an older elder, and the main worker from the daughter church rode his horse to the mother church every two weeks or so. Where the churches were one or two days' walk apart the teacher and student took turns slogging through the muddy trails.

Beware of the bad strategy of a mother church sending workers to several daughter churches at once, as though she were the only church with God's reproductive power.

The "hub" strategy (shown below) wears out the workers and discourages the mother church. God's power, inherent in all churches in which His Spirit dwells, enables a mother church to start a daughter church and train its new elders to help it develop *and* reproduce in granddaughter churches. Just disciple the disciplers and watch it happen!

The chain was not a hierarchy to control; volunteer teachers with no organizational authority worked with volunteer students. It took sweat and guts to build these loving ties between churches, helping men to know, love and train each other for immediate pastoral ministry. In the process men were shot, put to death by machete, weakened by disease and almost drowned. It was worth it.

The modern Western missionary's most common sin is controlling the national churches. I had to learn to keep out of the way and let the Spirit's power inherent in the churches produce the ministries by which the churches were edified and reproduced. I guided, encouraged, taught the Word and counseled, but I no longer pushed. Then we saw the chain reaction; one of the extension networks produced five generations and over twenty churches. (See final diagram.)

We met occasionally to reaffirm our plans and decide which church would reach certain villages or communities. We divided our entire area of responsibility into nine regions and planned the steps to start a daughter church that would reproduce in each region. The pastoral students of the Honduras Extension Bible Institute have for many years been starting an average of five new churches a year, each of which has from one to three new pastors in training. After turning the leadership of this program over to Hondurans, it has continued to reproduce in spite of other missionaries' pressure to revert to traditional pastoral training methods.

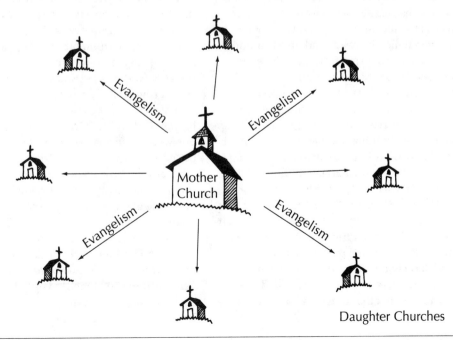

Mother Church

Evangelism

Daughter Churches

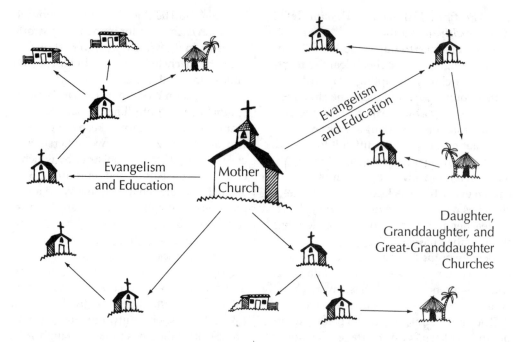

Evangelism and Education

Evangelism and Education

Mother Church

Evangelism and Education

Daughter, Granddaughter, and Great-Granddaughter Churches

When a chain gets too long for good communication, simply reorganize the teaching relationships. Don't assume that doctrine will get watered down the longer the chain. Each Spirit-filled teacher in the chain has the same love for the Word and will rejuvenate the flow. I discovered that the strongest churches were usually one or two links removed from me, the foreign missionary. The key to maintaining the chains is loving communication in both directions. Accurate student reports from each daughter church are essential for his teacher to respond, applying the Word accurately to its life, needs and opportunities.

Pray for protection from traditions that hamper this spontaneous reproduction. We have mentioned teaching that neglects discipleship, and failure to mobilize newly repentant converts to obey beginning with baptism. Another almost universal impediment to reproduction is a missionary subsidy that stifles nationals' own giving and builds a dependent spirit. Don't rob poor believers of the blessing of sacrificial giving! God multiplies their mite by special celestial mathematics that will prosper them now and for eternity. Paying national pastors with outside funds nearly always stifles spontaneous reproduction and eventually leads to deep resentment when the source no longer equals the demand.

Pray for Reproduction Power

Each new church in a chain, like a grain of wheat, has the same potential to start the reproduction all over again. Christ's parables in Matthew 13, Mark 4 and John 15 compare the growth and reproduction of His churches to that of plants. Like all other living creatures God has created, the Church has her own seed in herself to reproduce after her own kind. Every time we eat, we eat the fruit of God's tremendous reproduction power given to plants and animals. Look around out of doors; it's everywhere—grass, trees, birds, bees, babies and flowers. All creation is shouting it! This is the way God works! Reproduction is His *style*. Pray for it! (God in His infinite wisdom acts a bit lazy when we don't ask Him to move; He limits His absolute power to our weak faith!) We ourselves don't make the church grow or reproduce, any more than pulling on a stalk of corn would make it grow. Paul plants, Apollos waters, God gives the growth. We sow, water, weed, fertilize and fence the crop, but rely on the Church's own God-given potential to reproduce. An obedient, Spirit-filled church *has* to reproduce at home or abroad. It's her very nature; she is the Body of the risen, life-giving Son of God.

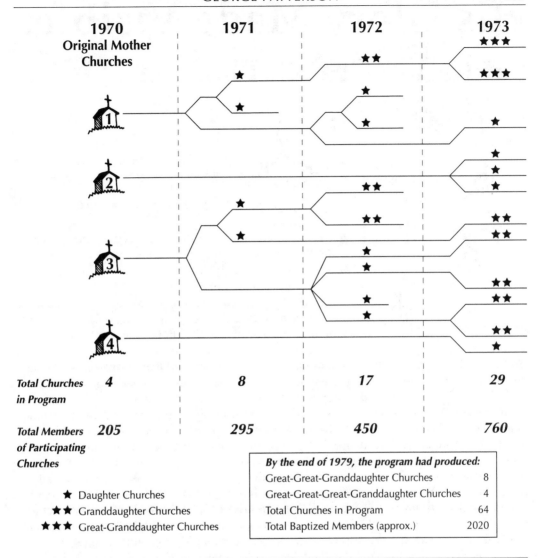

	1970	1971	1972	1973
Total Churches in Program	4	8	17	29
Total Members of Participating Churches	205	295	450	760

★ Daughter Churches
★★ Granddaughter Churches
★★★ Great-Granddaughter Churches

By the end of 1979, the program had produced:	
Great-Great-Granddaughter Churches	8
Great-Great-Great-Granddaughter Churches	4
Total Churches in Program	64
Total Baptized Members (approx.)	2020

Study Questions

1. What are the basic commands of Christ as Patterson summarizes them? Why is it important to make sure your disciples, and those they disciple, seek to obey all of them?

2. Traditional theological objectives focus on educating a student while Biblical education objectives aim to edify the church. Explain the difference between the way a typical theological professor teaches and the way a discipler of pastors works.

3. How is it possible for a church to become a great-grandmother church without any pastors who have been to a residential seminary? Why might it be more likely that there will be great-grand-daughter churches if none of the pastors have been to a residential seminary?

His Glory Made Visible:
Saturation Church Planting

Jim Montgomery

> All that is mine is yours, and that which is yours is mine;
> my glory is made visible in them.
>
> *John 17:10, from a Spanish translation*

S aturation Church Planting (SCP) is the vision of seeing the incarnate Christ present in the midst of every small unit of population in a people group, a region, a city, a country and in the world.

This SCP concept sounds simple and obvious now, but for me it came only after 20 years of agonizing over how to go about making disciples of all nations. The whole story of seeking an optimum strategy for world evangelization is told in the book *DAWN 2000: 7 Million Churches to Go*.[1] One success after another was followed by one huge disappointment after another.

The strategic breakthrough came about as the "Christ the Only Way Movement" came to an encouraging conclusion in the Philippines. In a very responsive land, virtually the whole church was mobilized around the vision of seeing 10,000 evangelistic Bible study groups established, a method of proven value in this essentially Roman Catholic nation. The goal was surpassed, but I was not at all satisfied. Why wasn't I thrilled? It was because out of 35 million Filipinos, there were still almost 35 million that did not have a personal relationship with the Lord.

"Why, Lord," I began to pray over a period of weeks, "did you give us a command that you knew was impossible to obey? Did you deceive us? Did you mean something different than what your Word seems clearly to say?"

"If you truly wanted *nations* to be *discipled*, why didn't you stay here on the earth? You could have gone about every village as you did in Galilee. You could have appeared speaking the language, wearing the dress, intimately knowing the culture, eating the food and having relatives and contacts in every village and neighborhood of every 'nation' in every country in the world."

"You could have gone demonstrating your power, showing your love and compassion and forcefully communicating your great message of the Kingdom. Why did you leave it to us, when you knew it was totally beyond our capabilities?"

"Now that I have your attention," the Lord seemed to say after weeks of praying this prayer, "I want you to know that is exactly how to go about completing the Great Commission.

Jim Montgomery is the founder and President of DAWN Ministries in Colorado Springs, Colorado. He served with OC International for 27 years and has written six books. Among them is *DAWN 2000: 7 Million Churches to Go* which describes the vision and history of the DAWN movement.

This article is excerpted from *Then the End Will Come*, 1997. Used by permission of William Carey Library.

"See to it that I, the Lord, truly become incarnate, as you have been suggesting, in every small group of people on the earth."

In a flash of insight from the Lord it all became very clear. Where does the Lord dwell?

"Christ in you, the hope of glory" (Col 1:27).

"…the one who is in you is greater than the one who is in the world" (1 Jn 4:4).

"Where two or three come together in my name, there am I with them" (Matt 18:20).[2]

It became clear that Christ could be alive and well and present in all his power and glory and compassion while communicating his wonderful message of the Kingdom in a totally contextualized way in every small community of people on Earth if only there were some truly born-again believers exercising the gifts of the Spirit and functioning in each place as the body of Christ.

Shortly after my family and I completed our missionary stint in the Philippines in the mid-1970s, I happened to talk with Dr. David Liao, then a professor of missions at Biola University. I told him about the dream and commitment of the Church in the Philippines to grow from about 5,000 congregations to 50,000 by the year AD 2000.

"Oh, you mean saturation church planting," he said.

I had followed the saturation *evangelism* movements such as Evangelism in Depth in Latin America, but I had never before heard the term saturation *church planting*.

But yes, that described exactly the concept that was developing in the Philippines. I had felt the Lord saying to me in 1974 that to work most directly at completing the Great Commission would mean seeing the risen Christ become incarnate within easy access of every person of every class, kind and condition of man in the world.

This translated into planting a Christ-centered church in the midst of every small group of people in every nation.

Disciple A Whole Nation

Though we may not have had a word for it, the concept of SCP was at the heart of that first DAWN (Discipling A Whole Nation) project in the Philippines. The Church pursued its goal of increasing from about 5,000 churches in 1975 to 50,000 by AD 2000. They made it even more specific by aiming to plant a church in every *barangay* (village). They are well on the way. In 1997 there were over 29,000 by actual count with an additional 5,000 to 10,000 new churches estimated.

What I felt the Lord saying to me about the Philippines in the 1970s I now hear echoed around the world. The DAWN strategy in 1998 is in some phase of development in over 140 nations. About 45 of those countries have reached the stage of conducting a national DAWN Congress. Combined, the active DAWN efforts are aiming at planting close to two million new churches. And there are more DAWN-type projects forming all the time. One ministry in China has recently set an additional goal of one million new churches in that land.

Of the four letters of the acronym DAWN, the emphasis is always on the third: whatever it takes to reach the *Whole* nation. Reaching the whole nation leads to an amplified understanding of the word "Nation" in the DAWN acronym. When we began, we used the word as it referred to the political nation-states or countries of the world. But we also understand the word "nation" in its foundational and biblical sense to refer to tribes, languages and people groups. The DAWN vision calls people to envision what it will take to make disciples throughout an entire nation (country) by specifically considering every one of the "nations" or people groups within it.

We are convinced that God wants far more than a small handful of believers in every people group. God desires that His glory be seen throughout every ethnic community as they may be found in every part of cities and countries. One way of approaching a breakthrough in every people is to aim for a beginning in every place. To be specific, this would call for a cell of believers to be established in every village and city neighborhood, or a church for every 500 to 1,000 people.

Thus, saturation church planting (SCP) became the essence of the strategy we suggest for completing the Great Commission, the strategy for the end of the age.

That is why in establishing DAWN Ministries in 1985 we wrote our purpose statement to say that our calling was "to see saturation church planting become the generally accepted and fervently practiced strategy for completing the task of making disciples of all peoples in our generation."

Seeing SCP in the Bible

I am aware, of course, that the validity of a strategy for world evangelization depends on much more than my testimony and what seems to work. Though my gifting is not as a scholar or theologian, I am encouraged by the fact that over the past 24 years of the existence and spread of the DAWN strategy, I have yet to hear a theologian speak against it. Actually, the reverse has been true. I frequently come across comments of theologians and missiologists that tend to reinforce that which I felt I heard from the Lord or learned from godly mentors.

This is not to imply that I did not find support for the SCP concept from my own Bible study. Take the ministry of the Apostle Paul, for example. While his methods varied and were highly contextualized, the fruit of his ministry was powerfully consistent: there were always strings of multiplying congregations permeating large populated areas left behind him. It could then be said "that all the Jews and Greeks who lived in Asia heard the word of the Lord" (Acts 19:10).

As Peter Wagner wrote in *Spreading the Fire* (his first of three volumes in "The Acts of the Holy Spirit" series), "The most concrete, lasting form of ministry in Acts is church planting. Preaching the gospel, healing the sick, casting out demons, suffering persecution, holding church councils and multiple other activities of the apostles and other Christians that unfold before us have, as their goal, multiplying Christian churches throughout the known world."[3]

In the third volume of this series, Wagner also wrote, "Part of Paul's influence in the new churches was, undoubtedly, to stir them to evangelize the lost in their cities and to plant new house churches in every neighborhood. *No missiological principle is more important than saturation church planting*" (italics mine).[4]

Later, I began to connect this multiplication of churches with an Old Testament vision and prophecy that was repeated in at least four books of the Bible.

Numbers 14:21, for example, records that "all the earth shall be filled with the glory of the Lord" (RSV). Similar prophecies are recorded in Isaiah 11:9 and Habakkuk 2:14.

A few months ago, Luis Bush, International Director of the massive AD2000 and Beyond Movement, pointed out to me the last two

The Shopping Window of God   *Wolfgang Simson*

Jesus commissioned us to go and make disciples of all nations. Many Christians around the world have the growing conviction that discipling the nations will only be achieved by having a church—the shopping window of God—in walking distance of every person on the globe. The church must again become the place where people can literally see the Body of Christ, where his glory is revealed in the most practical of all terms—hands-on, down-to-earth, right next-door, unable to overlook or ignore, living every day among us. Many have told me, often with tears in their eyes, that their nation will not truly change its values and be discipled by anything artificial, by being briefly touched for a fleeting moment by the abbreviated gospel of a shortlived campaign, or even by the type of church that has been there for the last 50 or 500 years. It really matters what kind of churches are planted. Nothing short of the very presence of the living Christ in every neighborhood and village of every corner of the nation will do. He has come to live among us—and stay on. We therefore need to plant and water church planting movements that plant and water other church planting movements—until there is no space left for anyone to misunderstand, ignore or even escape the presence of Jesus in the form that he has chosen to take while on earth—the local church.

Wolfgang Simson functions as a strategy consultant, researcher and journalist within the Dawn International Network, a vision- and friendship-based global strategy network.

verses of Psalm 72. Verse 20 says "This concludes the prayers of David son of Jesse." And what were the last words of the last prayer of David? "May the whole earth be filled with his glory. Amen and Amen" (vs. 19).

Where does the glory of the Lord reside? Certainly "the heavens declare the glory of God; the skies proclaim the work of his hands" (Ps 19:1). But many verses also tell us that Christ—and therefore his glory—resides in us.

I saw this again as I was meditating and praying through the priestly prayer of our Lord recorded in John 17. As I was reading in my Spanish Bible, *"mi gloria se hace visible en ellos,"* suddenly jumped from the page (vs. 10).

"My glory is made visible in them."

There it was again! More than planting churches, more than saving souls, we yearn for the day when it can truly be said that the earth is full of the glory of the Lord. And where is His glory? "My glory is made visible in them." In His people.

Peter Wagner illustrates this in *Spreading the Fire* when he writes that "multitudes of churches in many parts of the world, although imperfectly, do accurately reflect the glory of God through Jesus Christ."[5]

SCP, then, is simply the task of seeing that there is the presence of Christ in every place in the form of a gathered body of believers.

Even so, we work at saturation church planting not only because it is a good strategy for completing the Great Commission. We do it because we want to cooperate with the oft repeated Old Testament prophecy that "the earth will be filled with the knowledge of the glory of the Lord" (Hab 2:14).

We do it to answer the last recorded prayer of David: "may the whole earth be filled with his glory" (Ps 72:19).

We do it so that the glory of the Lord may be made visible in every small community of mankind in the world.

Aiming at Converts or Churches

Every once in a while we come across a church growth plan where the goal is set in terms of a certain number of new converts to be made. On the surface, it makes sense. Jesus died for lost sinners, so why not aim at winning as many as possible, or winning a certain number by a certain date?

Ask the Christian and Missionary Alliance Convention in the Philippines. In the first 75 years of this century, they planted 477 churches. This was good, but certainly not extraordinary growth. After the Church Growth Workshop in 1974 when the DAWN vision was first presented, they set a healthy goal of planting 400 more churches in just four years.

> When we stop thinking about how to increase membership and begin looking at the harvest field, we switch from inside-out thinking to outside-in. This is the vision of saturation church planting.

With tremendous zeal and energy, they mobilized their whole denomination as well as their parent C&MA mission around this vision. You can imagine the great rejoicing when they actually exceeded their goal by starting 416 new churches and more than doubling their membership from 26,830 to 58,543 in this four-year period. This increase represented a very strong Average Annual Growth Rate (AAGR) of 13 percent for church planting and quite a remarkable 21.5 percent AAGR for new members.

With the enthusiasm generated by this great leap forward, they developed a new program called "Target 100,000 '83."

This time, there was great consternation when they fell 20,000 members short of their goal. Analyzing what happened, they realized the mistake they made was in aiming at the number of converts they would win, bringing their total membership to 100,000, instead of in the evangelistic activity—church planting—that would bring in the converts.

In their next project, they reinstated church planting as their primary target and evangelistic activity.

Naturally, our desire is to bring as many as possible to know Christ as personal savior. God is not wanting anyone to perish (2 Pet 3:9). But in developing an actual strategy, we have found it better to set our sights on the activity that will bring the greatest number to the Lord rather than on the number to be won.

SCP and Unreached Peoples

What happens when there are few, if any believers in a people group, when there is persecution of any known Christians, when any churches that do exist are forced to meet in secret? Is it rational even to think of multiplying congregations?

Absolutely! My viewpoint is that if we do not go into a situation with the vision of SCP for a people group, we will perhaps never find the strategy that will result in a host of churches being planted. If we expect that it will take years or even decades to start multiplying churches, then that is how long it will take.

It seems to me that unless missionaries and strategists to the Muslim world are dreaming of planting one million churches—whatever they might look like—for the one billion Muslims, they would be unnecessarily prolonging the discipling of those nations. I'm not saying the task would be easy. I'm not saying there would not be martyrs in the process. I am saying unless there is a vision and a goal of planting one million churches from Muslim converts, the way will never be found to do it.

In another predominantly Islamic setting that we dare not even mention by name, a strategy is being implemented where thousands of "churches" are being planted. They do not look like churches, they are not even called "churches." But they are! And the leaders involved are committed to the SCP vision. They are working out a plan to fill this whole nation with cells of believers in the Lord Jesus Christ.

The late Rev. B.A.G. Prasad, who served as Director of Every Home for Christ in India, had a similar vision and plan for reaching Hindus in India. Years of dynamic ministry saw evangelical literature delivered twice to virtually every household in the country. As a result, over five million Indians filled out a card indicating their decision to accept Jesus Christ. It disturbed Prasad, however, that India was still only 2.6 percent Christian, the same as when the ministry started 28 years before.

This called for a change in strategy. Instead of EHC national missionaries merely leaving literature in as many homes and as many villages as was possible in a day, they now focus on planting churches. When they go to a home, they try to determine if any family member is interested in the gospel. If

there is such a person, they stay as long as necessary to lead him or her to Christ. Then it is around this new convert that a house church is ultimately developed.

In this program, now called "Final Thrust 5000," they report the planting of about 3,500 new churches in 1995! They are aiming for 300,000 house churches by AD 2000!

In a stirring message delivered at the EHC World Congress Banquet some months before his death, Prasad explained that "We call it 'Final' because we believe the Lord is coming soon. We call it '5,000' because we determined that is the number of national missionaries we need for 300,000 new churches."

He explained that India is divided into 400 districts and that it would take 10 missionaries to cover each district. That would call for 4,000 missionaries and perhaps another 1,000 for training and administration. Hence the total of 5,000 missionaries that are needed.

God has blessed this new approach since it was launched in July of 1992. Eighteen months after starting they already had 1,500 missionaries in place, performing hundreds of baptisms in about 500 new churches a month. Most of these were multiplying rapidly as house-type churches, but some had grown as larger congregations of 200 to 300 members. The ministry has been empowered and accelerated by incredible miracles. On three different occasions people have been raised from the dead in Jesus' name.

"We are praying that before Christ comes India will be a Christian nation," Prasad told the conferees. Even with his death in 1994, the movement is moving ahead rapidly.

SCP as 'Outside-In' Thinking

Another strong proponent and excellent teacher of the SCP vision of working toward the goal of filling all nations with dynamic, evangelical congregations is Dwight Smith, former president of United World Mission, now founder and president of SCP International. He refers to SCP as "outside-in" thinking.

Usually, according to Smith, a local or denominational body thinks of growth in just the opposite fashion. It thinks in terms of how big it is and what it must do to get a little bigger. Outside-in thinking turns the process around. It draws a circle around a neighborhood, a city, a province, a people group or a whole country and works back from there. It asks the question, "What would it take to win this whole harvest field for the Lord?"

Perhaps I can best illustrate this concept by relating the testimony of Freddie Gwanzura, a local pastor in Zimbabwe.

In 1976, Gwanzura left his building contractor's business and became a full-time worker with the Apostolic Faith Mission. Soon he was pastoring a congregation of 60 on the outskirts of a town. The church building seated a few hundred, but nothing he tried would increase his attendance.

About this time, Reinhardt Bonkke, the German evangelist, held a crusade in the area. He pitched his tent that held 10,000 people just one kilometer from the church. This gave Freddie immediate hope. He was certain his church would grow dramatically as a result of the crusade! The tent was full every night. People came and repented in the thousands.

After the crusade, his church did the follow up and tried their best to keep the fish in the net, but there were few lasting results. A year later, he reports there was one woman attending whom he thought was won at the crusade. But it was still a church of 60 members.

"The one benefit of the crusade," Freddie Gwanzura told us, "was that we had learned the hard way that we could not project our responsibility to evangelize and see the church grow on a visiting evangelist. So we began to do our own evangelism and follow up, using every kind of method the Lord gave us. Even funeral services became an outreach opportunity."

Gradually, the pews of his church began to fill. They had to move into the church yard as their attendance grew from 60 to about 400. By 1982, they began to realize they would have to plant new churches. The first one was in a nearby town. They spun off some of their people from the main fellowship. They thought this would give them breathing room, but within one week they were full again! So, here and there, they planted still more new churches.

But Freddie says that "By the time the DAWN consultation came to our area, I knew something was still missing. My vision was not complete. DAWN changed all this. I had my eyes opened to the importance of research and good information. I had no idea how big my harvest field was, how many villages or towns were in it. I had not looked to see where there were churches or where there were no churches. DAWN showed me how to look at my province, my section of the harvest field. The Lord caused me to see that the existing churches were a drop in the bucket in terms of what we needed. I realized that our job would not be done until there was a church there for everybody."

Today, Freddie has over 200 churches under his supervision. DAWN thinking is at the heart of his work. The message that he wants his life to communicate to the men under his leadership is: "We must plant churches! This is the vision that possesses me. Planting new congregations in all the villages and growth points in our province is the main thing God wants us to do."

When Gwanzura stopped thinking just about how to increase his membership and began looking at the harvest field of his whole province, he had switched from inside-out to outside-in thinking. He had caught the vision of saturation church planting.

Universal Application

There are outstanding examples of this outside-in thinking all over the world and at every level. Anybody can develop an SCP project, but it will take widespread application to complete the Great Commission in our time. As Leighton Ford has observed, "If our goal is the penetration of the whole world, then we must aim at nothing less than the mobilization of the whole Church."[6]

If every Western and non-Western mission society, every one of 22,000 denominations of the world, every para-church ministry and every local church and every intercessory network caught this vision, there is no question that "filling the earth with the knowledge of the glory of the Lord" (by the presence of a local church for every cluster of people) would be easily within our reach by AD 2010—or before!

End Notes

1. Montgomery, James H., *DAWN 2000: 7 Million Churches to Go* (Pasadena, CA: William Carey Library, 1989).
2. Ibid., pp. 29, 30.
3. Wagner, C. Peter, *Spreading the Fire* (Ventura, CA: Regal Books,1994), p.60.
4. Wagner, C. Peter, *Blazing the Way* (Ventura, CA: Regal Books, 1995), p.48.
5. Wagner, C. Peter , *Spreading the Fire,* p.60.
6. Coleman, Robert E., *The Coming World Revival* (Wheaton, IL: Crossway Books, 1989), p.86.

Study Questions

1. Describe the strategy of Saturation Church Planting. Why is Montgomery convinced that SCP is the key to completing the Great Commission?

2. Describe the difference between SCP and DAWN.

3. Why would the DAWN strategies aim to plant a church in each village or city in a region if hundreds of churches existed in other locations within a given nation?

Evangelization of Whole Families

Chua Wee Hian

Year: 1930
Locality: Northwest China
Case studies:
1. The approach and strategy of two single European women.
2. The approach and strategy of the Little Flock Assembly of Chefoo, Shantung.
Objectives: Identical—to plant local churches and to engage in extensive village evangelism.

Case study 1

Two gifted and dedicated women were sent by their missionary society to northwest China. Their mandate was to evangelize and plant congregations in a cluster of villages. They spoke fluent Chinese; they labored faithfully and fervently. After a decade, a small congregation emerged. However, most of its members were women. Their children attended the Sunday School regularly. The visitor to this small congregation would easily detect the absence of men.

In their reports and newsletters, both missionaries referred to the "hardness of hearts" that was prevalent among the men. References were made also to promising teenagers who were opposed by their parents when they sought permission for baptism.

Case study 2

In 1930 a spiritual awakening swept through the Little Flock Assembly in Shantung. Many members sold their entire possessions in order to send *seventy* families to the Northwest as "instant congregations." Another *thirty* families migrated to the Northeast. By 1944, forty new assemblies had been established, and all these were vitally involved in evangelism.

Now, in terms of dedication and doctrinal orthodoxy, both the Europeans and the Little Flock Assembly shared the same commitment and faith. But why the striking contrasts in results and in their strategies of church-planting?

Consider the case of the two single missionary women. Day by day, the Chinese villagers saw them establishing contacts and building the bridges of friendships with women, usually when their husbands or fathers were out working in the fields or trading in nearby towns. Their foreignness (dubbed "red hair devils") was enough to incite cultural and racial prejudices in the minds of the villagers. But their single status was something that was socially questionable.

Chua Wee Hian is the Senior Pastor of Emmanuel Evangelical Church in Westminster, England. He served at the General Secretary of the International Fellowship of Evangelical Students from 1972 to 1991.

This article first appeared in the book *Let The Earth Hear His Voice*, Copyright 1975, World Wide Publications, Minneapolis, MN, U.S.A. Used by permission of the Lausanne Committee for World Evangelization.

It was a well-known fact in all Chinese society that the family constitutes the basic social unit. These units insure security. In Confucian teaching, three of the five basic relationships have to do with family ties—father and son, older brother and younger brothers, husband and wife. The fact that these women were making contacts with individual women and not having dialogues with the elders would make them appear to be foreign agents seeking to destroy the fabric of the village community. A question that would constantly crop up in the gossip and discussion of the villagers would be the fact of the missionaries' single state. Why aren't they married? Why aren't they visibly related to their parents, brothers and sisters, uncles and aunts and other relatives? So when they persuaded the women or the youth to leave the religion of their forefathers, they were regarded as "family-breakers."

By contrast, the Little Flock Assembly in sending out Chinese Christian families sent out agents that were recognizable socio-cultural entities. Thus the seventy families became an effective missionary task force. It is not difficult to imagine the heads of these families sharing their faith with the elders of the villagers. The grandmothers could informally transmit the joy of following Christ and of their deliverance from demonic powers to the older women in pagan villages. The housewives in the markets could invite their counterparts to attend the services that were held each Sunday by the "instant congregations." No wonder forty new assemblies were established as a result of this approach to church-planting and evangelism!

Evangelizing Families in Other Cultures

The strategy of evangelizing whole families is not only applicable in Chinese communities. It is also effective in other Asian communities, African villages and tribes, as well as in Latin American *barrios* and societies. Writing on the rapid spread of the Christian faith in Korea, Roy Shearer observed: "One most important factor governing how the Church grew is the structure of Korean society. In Korea, we are dealing with a society based on the family, not the tribe. The family is strong

even today. The soundest way for a man to come to Christ is in the setting of his own family."

He went on to relate repeated situations when heads of families returned to their clan villages and were successful in persuading their relatives and kinsmen to "turn from idols to serve the living God." He concluded: "The gospel flowed along the web of family relationships. This web is the transmission line for the current of the Holy Spirit that brought men and women into the church."

In her book *New Patterns for Discipling Hindus*, Miss B.V. Subbamma categorically asserted that the Hindu family might be the only social institution through which the gospel could be transmitted and received. Not all would agree with this assertion, because there are evidences of university students who have professed faith in Christ in the great university centers of India. Some could take this step of faith because they were free from parental pressures. However, as a general rule, Miss Subbamma's observation and deduction are correct.

Evangelizing whole families is the pattern of current missionary outreach in parts of Latin America. There in the Roman Catholic culture of web relationships, family structures are strong. Exploiting this social pattern, the Chilean Pentecostals, like the Little Flock Assembly in Shantung forty years ago, dispatch *families* from among their faithful to be agents and ambassadors of church expansion. Through these evangelizing families, many assemblies and congregations have been planted in different parts of that continent. The phenomenal growth of the Pentecostal movement in Latin America reflects the effectiveness of using families to evangelize families.

At times it is difficult for individualistic Westerners to realize that in many "face-to-face" societies, religious decisions are made corporately. The individual in that particular type of society would be branded as a "traitor" and treated as an outcast if he were to embrace a new religious belief. After the Renaissance, in most Western countries, identity is expressed by the Cartesian dictum *Cogito ergo sum*: I think, therefore I am. Man as a rational individual could think out religious options for himself and is free to choose the faith that he would like to follow. This dictum does not apply in many African tribal communities. For the Africans (and for many others) the unchanging dictum is, *I participate, therefore I am*. Conformity to and participation in traditional religious rites and customs give such people their identity. So if there is to be a radical change in religious allegiance, there must be a corporate or multi-individual decision.

This is particularly true of Muslim families and communities. The one-by-one method of individual evangelism will not work in such a society. A lecturer friend of mine who teaches in the multi-racial university of Singapore once made this significant remark, "I've discovered that for most Malay students (who are nearly all Muslims) Islam consists not of belief in Allah the supreme God—it is *community*." Ambassadors for Christ in Islamic lands should cope not only with theological arguments concerning the unity and nature of God, they should consider the social and cultural associations of Muslims. Where sizable groups of Muslims had been converted, their decisions were multi-individual. An excellent illustration would be that of Indonesia. During the past fifteen years, wise missionaries and national

pastors had been engaging in dialogues and discussions with the elders and leaders of local Muslim communities. When these decision-makers were convinced that Christ is the only way to God and that he alone is the Savior of the world, they returned to their villages and towns, and urged all members to turn to Christ. So it was not surprising to witness whole communities being catechized and baptized together.

Such movements are termed as "people movements." Many years before the Indonesian happening, Ko Tha Byu, a remarkable Burmese evangelist, was instrumental in discipling whole Karen communities and villages. Today the Karen church is one of the strongest Christian communities in Southeast Asia.

The Biblical Data

When we turn to the biblical records, we shall discover that families feature prominently both as the recipients as well as the agents of salvation blessing.

To begin with, the family is regarded as divinely instituted by God (Eph 3:15). In fact, all families owe their descent and composition to their Creator. By redemption, the Church—God's own people—is described as "the household of God" (Eph 2:19) and the "household of faith" (Gal 6:10).

In the Pentateuch, great stress is laid on the sanctity of marriage, the relation between children and parents, masters and slaves. This emphasis is underscored in the New Testament (see Eph 5:22-6:9; Col 3:18-4:1; 1 Pet 2:18-3:7).

It is the family or the household that pledges its allegiance to Yahweh. Joshua as head of his own household could declare, "As for me and my house, we will serve the Lord" (Josh 24:15). Through Joshua's predecessor Moses, Yahweh had taught his people to celebrate His mighty acts by sacred meals and festivals. It is interesting to observe that the feast of the Passover was a family meal (Ex 12:3-4). The head of the family was to recite and reenact the great drama of Israel's deliverance at this family gathering. Through Israel's history, even until New Testament days, family feasts, prayer and worship were regularly held. Thus the Jewish family became both the objects of God's grace and the visual agents of his redemptive actions. Their monotheistic faith expressed in terms of their family solidarity and religion must have created a tremendous impression on the Gentile communi-

ties. One of the results was that large numbers of Gentiles became proselytes, "associate members" of the Jewish synagogues. Jewish families made a sizable contribution to the "missionary" outreach.

The apostolic pattern for teaching was in and through family units (Acts 20:20). The first accession of a Gentile grouping to the Christian church was the family of the Roman centurion Cornelius in Caesarea (Acts 10:7,24). At Philippi, Paul led the families of Lydia and the jailer to faith in Christ and incorporation into his Church (Acts 16:15, 31-34). The "first fruits" of the great missionary apostle in Achaia were the families of Stephanas (1 Cor 16:15), Crispus and Gaius (Acts 18:8; Rom 16:23; 1 Cor 1:14). So it was clear that the early church discipled both Jewish and Gentile communities in families.

It was equally clear that households were used as outposts of evangelism. Aquila and Priscilla used their home in Ephesus and Rome as a center for the proclamation of the Gospel (Rom 16:3,5; 1 Cor 16:19). Congregations met in the homes of Onesiphorus (2 Tim 1:16; 4:19) and Nymphas (Col 4:15).

Study Questions

1. Explain why aiming to win families to Christ may be slower in the short run, but multiply swiftly in the long run.

2. Many single women are willing to serve. How might they best be used in reaching a male dominated face-to-face society? What similar challenges would face single male missionaries?

3. What significance does reaching entire households have for church planting among unreached people groups?

A Church in Every People:
Plain Talk About a Difficult Subject

Donald A. McGavran

Known world-wide as perhaps the foremost missiologist, Donald A. Mc-Gavran was born in India of missionary parents and returned there as a third-generation missionary himself in 1923, serving as a director of religious education and translating the Gospels in the Chhattisgarhi dialect of Hindi. He founded the School of World Mission at Fuller Theological Seminary, and was formerly Dean Emeritus. McGavran died in 1990 at the age of 93. McGavran was the author of several influential books, including *The Bridges of God, How Churches Grow*, and *Understanding Church Growth*.

In the last eight years of the twentieth century, the goal of Christian mission should be to preach the gospel, and by God's grace, to plant in every unchurched segment of mankind—what shall we say—"*a church*" or "*a cluster of growing churches*?" By the phrase "segment of mankind I mean an urbanization, development, caste, tribe, valley, plain or minority population. I shall explain that the steadily maintained long range goal should never be the first; but should always be the second. The goal is not one small sealed-off conglomerate congregation in every people. Rather, the long range goal (to be held constantly in view in the years or decades when it is not yet achieved) should be, "*a cluster of growing congregations in every segment.*"

As we consider the question italicized above, we should remember that it is usually easy to start one single congregation in a new unchurched people group. The missionary arrived. He and his family worship on Sunday. They are the first members of that congregation. He learns the language and preaches the gospel. He lives like a Christian. He tells people about Christ and helps them in their troubles. He sells tracts and gospels or gives them away. Through the years a few individual converts are won from this group and that. Sometimes they come for very sound and spiritual reasons; sometimes from mixed motives. But here and there a woman, a man, a boy, a girl do decide to follow Jesus. A few employees of the mission become Christian. These may be masons hired to erect the buildings, helpers in the home, rescued persons or orphans. The history of mission in Africa is replete with churches started by buying slaves, freeing them and employing those who could not return to their kindred. Such as chose to, could accept the Lord. A hundred and fifty years ago this was a common way of starting a church. With the outlawing of slavery, of course, it ceased to be used.

One single congregation arising in the way just described is almost always a conglomerate church—made up of members of several different segments of society. Some are old, some young, orphans, rescued persons, helpers and ardent seekers. All seekers are carefully screened to make sure they really intend to receive Christ. In due time, a church building is erected, and lo, a church in that people. It is a conglomerate church. It is sealed off from all the people groups of that region. No segment of the population says, "That group of worshipers is us." They are quite right. It is not. It is ethnically quite a different social unit.

This very common way of beginning the process of evangelization is a slow way to disciple the peoples of earth—note the plural: "the peoples of earth." Let us observe closely what really happens as this congregation is gathered. Each convert, as he becomes a Christian, is seen by his kin as one who leaves "us" and joins "them." He leaves our gods to worship their gods. Consequently his own relations force him out. Sometimes he is severely ostracized, thrown out of house and home; his life is threatened. Hundreds of converts have been poisoned or killed. Sometimes, the ostracism is mild and consists merely in severe disapproval. His people consider him a traitor. A church which results from this process looks to the peoples of the region like an assemblage of traitors. It is a conglomerate congregation. It is made up of individuals, who one-by-one have come out of several different societies, castes or tribes.

Now if anyone, in becoming a Christian, is forced out of, or comes out of, a tightly-structured segment of society, the Christian cause wins the individual but loses the family. The family, his people, the neighbors of that tribe are fiercely angry at him or her. They are the very men and women to whom he cannot talk. "You are not of us," they say to him; "You have abandoned us; you like them more than you like us. You now worship their gods not our gods." As a result, conglomerate congregations, made up of converts won in this fashion, *grow very slowly*. Indeed, one might truly affirm that where congregations grow in this fashion, the conversion of the ethnic units (people groups) from which they come is made doubly difficult. "The Christians misled one of our people," the rest of the group will say; "We're going to make quite sure that they do not mislead any more of us."

"One-by-one," is relatively easy to accomplish. Perhaps 90 out of every 100 missionaries who intend church planting, get only conglomerate congregations. I want to emphasize that. Perhaps 90 out of every 100 missionaries who intend church planting, get only conglomerate congregations. Such missionaries preach the gospel, tell of Jesus, sell tracts and gospels and evangelize in many other ways. They welcome inquirers, but whom do they get? They get a man here, a woman there, a boy here, a girl there, who for various reasons is willing to become Christian and patiently endure the mild or severe disapproval of their people.

If we are to understand how churches grow and do not grow on new ground, in untouched and unreached peoples, we must note that the process I have just described seems unreal to most missionaries. "What," they will exclaim, "could be a better way of entry into all the unreached peoples of that region than to win a few individuals from among them? Instead of resulting in the sealed-off church you describe, the process really gives us points of entry into every society from which a convert has come. That seems to us to be the real situation."

Those who reason in this fashion have known church growth in a largely Christian land, where men and women who follow Christ are not ostracized, are not regarded as traitors, but rather as those who have done the right thing. In that kind of a society every convert usually can become a channel through which the Christian faith flows to his relatives and friends. On that point there can be no debate. It was the point I emphasized when I titled my book, *The Bridges of God*.

But in tightly-structured societies, where Christianity is looked on as an invading religion and individuals are excluded for serious fault, *there* to win converts from several different segments of society, far from building bridges to each of these, erects barriers difficult to cross.

Now let us contrast the other way in which God is discipling the peoples of planet Earth. My account is not theory, but a sober recital of easily observable facts. As you look around the world, you see that while most missionaries succeed in planting only conglomerate churches by the "one-by-one out of the social group" method, here and there clusters of growing churches arise by the people movement method. They arise by tribe- or caste-wise movements to Christ. This is in many ways a better system. In order to use it effectively, missionaries should operate on seven principles.

1. Aim for a cluster of growing congregations

They should be clear about the goal. The goal is not one single conglomerate church in a city or a region. They may get only that, *but that must never be their goal.* The goal must be a cluster of growing, indigenous congregations every member of which remains in close contact with his kindred. This cluster grows best if it is in one people, one caste, one tribe or one segment of society. For example, if you were evangelizing the taxi drivers of Taipei, then your goal would not be to win some taxi drivers, some university professors, some farmers and some fishermen, but rather to establish churches made up largely of taxi drivers, their wives and children, and their assistants and mechanics. As you win converts of that particular community, the congregation has a natural, built-in social cohesion. Everybody feels at home. Yes, the goal must be clear.

2. Concentrate on one people

The principle is that the national leader or the missionary and his helpers, should concentrate on one people. If you are going to establish *a cluster of growing congregations* amongst, let us say, the Nair people of Kerala, which is the southwest tip of India, then you would need to place most of your missionaries and their helpers so that they can work among the Nairs. They should proclaim the gospel to Nairs, saying quite openly to them, "We are hoping that within your great caste there soon will be thousands of followers of Jesus Christ who also remain solidly in the Nair community." They will, of course, not worship the old Nair gods, but then plenty of Nairs don't worship their old gods. Plenty of Nairs are Communist and ridicule their old gods.

Nairs whom God calls, who choose to believe in Christ, are going to love their neighbors more than they did before and walk in the light. They will be saved and beautiful people. They will remain Nairs, while at the same time they become Christians. To repeat, concentrate on one people group. If you have three mis-

sionaries, don't have one evangelizing this group, another that, and a third 200 miles away evangelizing still another. That is a sure way to guarantee that any churches started will be small, non-growing, one-by-one churches. The social dynamics of those sections of society will work solidly *against* the eruption of any great growing people movement to Christ.

> The great advances of the Church on new ground out of non-Christian religions have *always* come by people movements, never one-by-one.

3. Encourage converts to remain with their people

The principle is to encourage converts to remain thoroughly one with their own people in most matters. They should continue to eat what their people eat. They should not say, "My people are vegetarians, but now that I have become a Christian, I'm going to eat meat." After they become Christians they should be more rigidly vegetarian than they were before. In the matter of clothing, they should continue to look precisely like their kinsfolk. In the matter of marriage, most peoples are endogamous, insisting that "our people marry only our people." They look with very great disfavor on "our people marrying other people." And yet when Christians come in one-by-one, they cannot marry their own people. None of them have become Christian. Where only a few of a given people become Christians there, when it comes time for them or their children to marry, they have to take husbands or wives from other segments of the population. So their own kin look at them and say, "When you become a Christian you mongrelize your children. You have left us and have joined them."

All converts should be encouraged to bear cheerfully the exclusion, the oppression and the persecution that they are likely to encounter from their people. When anyone becomes a follower of a new way of life, he is likely to meet some disfavor from his loved ones. Maybe it's mild; maybe it's severe. He should bear such disfavor patiently. He should say on all occasions,

> I am a better son than I was before; I am a better father than I was before; I am a better husband than I was before; and I love you more than I used to do. You can hate me, but I will not hate you. You can exclude me, but I will include you. You can force me out of our ancestral house, but I will live on its veranda. Or I will get a house just across the street. I am still one of you; I am more one of you than I ever was before.

Encourage converts to remain thoroughly one with their people in most matters.

Please note that word "most." They cannot remain one with their people in idolatry, or drunkenness or obvious sin. If they belong to a segment of the society that earns its living by stealing, they must "steal no more." But, in most matters (how they talk, how they dress, how they eat, where they go, what kind of houses they live in) they can look very much like their people, and ought to make every effort to do so.

4. Encourage group decisions for Christ

The principle is to try to get group decisions for Christ. If only one person decides to follow Jesus do not baptize him immediately. Say to him, "You and I will work together to lead another five, or ten, or God willing, fifty of your people to accept Jesus Christ as Saviour so that when you are baptized, you will be baptized with them." Ostracism is very effective against one lone person. But ostracism is weak indeed when exercised against a group of a dozen. And when exercised against two hundred it has practically no force at all.

5. Aim for constant stream of new converts

The principle is this: Aim for scores of groups of that people to become Christians in an ever flowing stream across the years. One of the common mistakes made by missionaries, eastern as well as western, all around the world is that when a few become Christians, perhaps 100, 200 or even 1,000, the missionaries spend all their time

teaching them. They want to make them good Christians and they say to themselves, If these people become good Christians, then the gospel will spread." So for years they concentrate on a few congregations. By the time they begin evangelizing outside that group, ten to twenty years, the rest of the people no longer want to become Christians. That has happened again and again. This principle requires that, from the very beginning, the missionary keeps on reaching out to new groups. But, you say, "Is not this a sure way to get poor Christians who don't know the Bible? If we follow that principle we shall soon have a lot of 'raw' Christians. Soon we shall have a community of perhaps five thousand people who are very sketchily Christian."

Yes, that is certainly a danger. At this point, we must lean heavily upon the New Testament, remembering the brief weeks or months of instruction Paul gave to his new churches. We must trust the Holy Spirit, and believe that God has called those people out of darkness into His wonderful light. As between two evils, giving them too little Christian teaching and allowing them to become a sealed-off community that cannot reach its own people, the latter is much the greater danger. *We must not allow new converts to become sealed off.* We must continue to make sure that a constant stream of new converts comes into the ever-growing cluster of congregations.

6. Help converts exemplify the highest hopes of their people

Now the point is this: The converts, whether five or five thousand, ought to say, or at least feel:

> We Christians are the advance guard of our people, of our segment of society. We are showing our relatives and neighbors a better way of life. The way we are pioneering is good for us who have become Christians, and will be very good for you thousands who have yet to believe. Please look on us not as traitors in any sense. We are better sons, brothers and wives, better tribesmen and caste fellows, better members of our labor union, than we ever were before. We are showing ways in which, while remaining thoroughly of our own segment of society,

we all can have a better life. Please look on us as the pioneers of our own people entering a wonderful Promised Land.

7. Emphasize brotherhood

The principle I stress is this: constantly *emphasize brotherhood.* In Christ there is no Jew, no Greek, no bond, no free, no barbarian, no Scythian. We are all one in Christ Jesus. But at the same time let us remember that Paul did not attack all imperfect social institutions. For example, he did not do away with slavery. Paul said to the slave, "Be a better slave." He said to the slave owner, "Be a kindlier master."

Paul also said in that famous passage emphasizing unity, "There is no male or female." Nevertheless Christians in their boarding schools and orphanages continue to sleep boys and girls in separate dormitories!! In Christ, there is no sex distinction. Boys and girls are equally precious in God's sight. Men from this tribe, and men from that are equally precious in God's sight. We are all equally sinners, equally saved by grace. These things are true; but at the same time there are certain social niceties which Christians at this time may observe.

As we continue to stress brotherhood, let us be sure that the most effective way to achieve brotherhood is to lead ever increasing numbers of men and women from every ethnos, every tribe, every segment of society into an obedient relationship to Christ. As we multiply Christians in every segment of society, the possibility of genuine brotherhood, justice, goodness and righteousness will be enormously increased. Indeed, the best way to get justice possibly the only way to get justice is to have very large numbers in every segment of society become committed Christians.

As we work for Christward movements in every people, let us not make the mistake of believing that "one-by-one out of the society into the church" is a bad way. One precious soul willing to endure severe ostracism in order to become a follower of Jesus, one precious soul coming all by himself, is a way that God has blessed and is blessing to the salvation of mankind. But it is a slow way. And it is a way which frequently seals off the converts' own people from any further hearing of the gospel.

Sometimes one-by-one is the only possible method. When it is, let us praise God for it, and live with its limitations. Let us urge all those wonderful Christians who come bearing persecution and oppression, to pray for their own dear ones and to work constantly, that more of their own people may believe and be saved.

One-by-one is one way that God is blessing to the increase of His Church. The people movement is another way. The great advances of the Church on new ground out of non-Christian religions have *always* come by people movements, never one-by-one. It is equally true that "one-by-one-out-of-the-people" is a very common beginning way. In the book, *Bridges of God*, which God used to launch the Church Growth Movement, I have used a simile. I say there that missions start out proclaiming Christ on a desert-like plain. There life is hard; the number of Christians remains small. A large missionary presence is required. But, here and there, the missionaries or the converts find ways to break out of that arid plain and proceed up into the verdant mountains. There, large numbers of people live; there, great churches can be founded; there, the Church grows strong; that is people movement land.

I commend that simile to you. Let us accept what God gives. If it is one-by-one, let us accept that and lead those who believe in Jesus to trust in Him completely. But let us always pray that, after that beginning, we may proceed to higher ground, to more verdant pasture, to more fertile lands where great groups of men and women, *all of the same segment of society*, become Christians and thus open the way for Christward movements in each people on earth. Our goal should be Christward movements within each segment. There the dynamics of social cohesion will advance the gospel and lead multitudes out of darkness into His wonderful life. We are calling people after people from death to life. Let us make sure that we do it by the most effective methods.

Study Questions

1. "Indeed, the best way to get justice, possibly the only way to get justice, is to have very large numbers in every segment of society become committed Christians." Do you agree? Why or why not?

2. Why does McGavran insist that "a cluster of growing churches" rather than "a church" is the proper goal in pioneer church planting?

The Evangelization of Animists

Alan R. Tippett

The title given to me seems to imply the existence of a concrete religious system, called *Animism*—something which might be set over against say, Hinduism or Buddhism, not only for purposes of description and study, but also as a subject requiring a strategy for evangelistic approach. Because the greatest number of currently open doors for the gospel are among animist people, the inclusion of the topic is certainly appropriate in spite of any intellectual problems the title may raise. Therefore to avoid the loss of time in debating semantics in our sessions, the preamble seems desirable.

Animism

Some scholars prefer to subdivide Animism and to deal with the subunits—Shamanism, Fetishism, Ancestor Worship, and so on treating each as a religion in its own right, thus avoiding Animism altogether. This may have some descriptive advantages, until one discovers that the sub-units are not discrete: several may be found interwoven together, and their practitioners may have multi-functional roles. The "religious systems" are thus found to be merely functional distinctions within what certainly looks like a general religious system, with no more diversity than Hinduism or Buddhism; and now we are back again to the notion of Animism.

The term Animism is certainly to be preferred to *Tribal Religion(s)* because Animism is active in great cities like Los Angeles, New Orleans or Sao Paulo, and has many non-tribal aspects. It is preferable also to *Primitive Religion(s)*, as it is neither chronologically nor conceptually primitive; indeed, it is currently much alive, and frequently quite sophisticated. Nevertheless, we should recognize that we are using the word as a term of convenience to provide a frame of reference for our discussions, presupposing that Animism is a discrete enough philosophical "system" among the religious to warrant our consideration of an evangelistic strategy for winning its followers to Christ. This is precisely the same position in which the members of our other groups will find themselves, for Hinduism, Islam and Buddhism may also be manifested in a great diversity of systematic forms.

The popular use of the term Animism comes down to us from E. B. Tylor (1871). He did not give it the technical meaning it acquired from the comparative religionists, of a "kind of religion," but used it to signify "the deep-lying doctrine of spiritual beings, which embodies the very essence of

Alan R. Tippett spent over 20 years as a missionary in the Fiji Islands. His *Solomon Islands Christianity* has been acclaimed as a classic by missiologists and anthropologists alike. Perhaps the world's leading authority on animism, Tippett was Professor Emeritus of Anthropology and Oceanic Studies at Fuller Theological Seminary's School of World Mission before his death in 1988 at the age of 77.

Spiritualistic as opposed to Materialistic philosophy." It was for him a "minimum definition of religion" which saw the animistic way of life as accepting the reality of spiritual force(s) and beings in contrast to the materialist outlook on life. "In its full development," Taylor agreed, it formulated concrete beliefs in such notions as the soul(s), the future state, controlling deities and subordinate spirits, especially when these beliefs result in "some kind of active worship."

I believe this is a realistic approach, because it permits us to talk about animism and biblical religion in the same philosophical or conceptual structure, and to weigh one against the other, and therefore to understand the meaning of commitment when a present-day Animist comes to his "moment of truth" and makes his decision for Christ. Thus the very term "evangelizing Animists" puts us into an identifiable category of communication and response. We are not dealing with secularists or scientific agnostics, whom we would need to approach by means of a different path in order to witness. But Animists and Christians have one thing in common—they accept the spiritual view of life. They do not need to be convinced of the existence of the supernatural. This opens many ways for dialogue; even though, at the same time, it exposes us to many problems and dangers, which we shall examine in a moment.

> Evangelism is not merely the winning of individuals, but also their incorporation into relevant local fellowship groups.

In spite of the wide range of categories, forms and functions that may be identified in the study of animistic communities, and which compel us to admit that perhaps every animist community is different from every other one. I firmly believe that Animism can be examined as a cohesive thing, and that enough universals can be identified to permit us to discuss the evangelization of this kind of community in general terms. I believe we should be able to deal with tribes in the forests of Africa, in the highlands of New Guinea, or in the hogans on the mesas of New Mexico under this head—

and to a large extent also the drug cults of Hollywood. My purpose, therefore, is to generalize as far as I can, and to delineate some common problem areas for discussion, rather than diversify one form of Animism as in contrast to another. But I hope the diversity will be apparent in our discussions.

Whether the evangelist be from an old or a young church, if he is witnessing cross-culturally he will be hoping to leave some kind of an indigenous church behind him. The fellowship group will have to be the Body of Christ ministering the mind, touch and heart of Christ in its cultural and animist world; evangelism is not merely the winning of individuals, but also their incorporation into relevant local fellowship groups. Therefore, before I enumerate my common problem areas, I must examine the biblical data base from which I operate.

The Biblical Theology of Animism

From the biblical point of view there is really no such thing as a taxonomy of religions for comparative study. Not even Hinduism or Buddhism has any biblical standing as a religion. For the people of God there is only one God, and all those who do not serve Him are grouped together in a single category. Although there is sufficient data in the biblical narrative for a whole textbook on Animism, the common practice of classifying religions, with Animism at one end and Christianity at the other, as if in an evolutionary scale of development, is not in tune either with Scripture or with the anthropological data.

Of course, I may turn to the Scriptures and read about the deities with whom the people of God came into contact from time to time on their pilgrimage—of Dagon, of Chemosh, of Molech, of Tammuz, and of Bel. I also learn of their confrontations with fertility cults, of heathen sacrifices and libations of ceremonial inhumanity like infanticide, of making cakes to the Queen of Heaven, and of worshiping the smooth round stones of the valley. We have everything—from individual and domestic ritual acts to national assemblies and the worship of national war gods—rites performed in fields, by the wayside, in groves and high places, and in great temples. We have divination, necromancy, and sorcery, and numerous other ideas covered by the biblical word "idolatry." We could break down the whole animistic system of the biblical word into categories for study, but in the last analysis the Bible disposes of them as a *single category* in the first two commandments (Ex 20:2-6)—anything that would usurp the Lord's place in the life of His people and set itself in God's place is grouped together as "against Him" and idolatrous.

Nevertheless, when we consider the world of biblical times—the first two millennia before Christ and the first Christian century afterwards—we find it very similar to that of our own. The people of God stood against all the forms we meet in Christian mission today, on all the various levels—private individual, domestic, peasant and national. The characteristics of each of these levels recur through history with the kind of lives people live on those respective levels, and do not fit into a chronological evolutionary scale from the simple to the sophisticated. The Bible deals with both tribal and great religions, with both simple and complex, with both oral and written religious traditions—and it treats them all under one rubric both in the Old and New Testaments (Ex 20:2-6; Rom 1:19-25).

In this paper I wish to speak of evangelization in a somewhat wider sense than just bringing individuals to an act of "decision for Christ." It is this, of course—but more. It involves both a step of commitment and an experience of consummation, in which the Spirit witnesses with the convert's spirit that he is now a son of the Father, and if a son, then an heir through Christ (Gal 4:6-7)—that the blessing of Abraham might come to the Gentiles, or heathen, through Christ, receiving the promise of the Spirit through faith (Gal 3:14). This is a process, bringing folk out of heathenism—here defined by Paul as "worshiping not-gods" (Gal 4:8). The picture we have here of conversion from heathenism is that of a *process*—an *on-going experience*.

Adoption into the household of God brings the convert into a *group experience*. Some kind of incorporation into the fellowship group is always part of the evangelization process. This comes out clearly in the opening verses of 1 John 1, where witness (vv. 1-2) leads up to

joining in the fellowship (v. 3), and from that verse on, John is dealing not with an individual in isolation, but with one in context, i.e., in a state of fellowship (vv. 6-7).

Now, as we consider the evangelization of Animists, it should be remembered that we are not dealing with individuals in isolation, but with men brought from death unto life *within a fellowship group*. We cannot escape the truth, that to give a man the gospel of personal salvation demands incorporation into a fellowship group as a concomitant. Evangelization implies the existence of, or planting of, a church.

The Evangelization of Animists

The conversion of animists and their incorporation into fellowship groups involves us in each of the following problems, which I have conceptualized anthropologically because I think that such a treatment best opens up the subject for our discussions. I am reminded of the question of Henri Maurier, "Does not every theology have to be accompanied, in counterpoint, by as concrete an anthropology as possible? It is not enough for the apostle to learn what God has said; he also has to understand the men to whom he is bringing the Word."

1. Pay attention to the problem of encounter

Animists cannot just *drift* into the Christian faith. True, they may attach themselves to the fringe of some congregation as interested spectators, and maybe even become what we sometimes call "sympathizers," and it may well be that by so doing they will fall under the influence of the Spirit of God and be brought to vigorous commitment; but the passage from heathenism to the Christian faith is a definite and clear-cut act, a specific change of life, a "coming out of something" and an "entry into something quite different," a change of loyalty—or in the biblical analogy, a change of citizenship (Eph 2:12-13).

The notion of making a definite act of commitment to the LORD is a biblical concept in both the Old and New Testaments, and was normally accompanied by some kind of ocular demonstration of the commitment. The book of Joshua ends with such an episode (24:15)—"Choose you this day whom you will serve; whether the gods your fathers served in the region beyond the river, or the gods of the Amorites in whose land you dwell; but as for me and my house, we will serve the Lord." Here, there is a definite encounter of religions. There are three options—the ancestral animism, or the current environmental animism of the land, or the LORD God. Then, after the public discussion (for no pressure is brought to bear on them) the decision is made and Joshua then demands a demonstration of that decision. "Then, *put away* the foreign gods and incline your hearts to the Lord" (v. 23). A covenant is made at Shechem, and a stone is set up as a *witness* to the act of commitment (vv. 26-27).

Was it not the same in the days of New Testament Ephesus? The people movement among the workers of magic led to the public burning of their magical literature—and so large a bonfire it was that the value of the books burned was recorded as 50,000 pieces of silver (Acts 19:18-19). Be it noted that this demonstration was both an *act of commitment* and an *act of rejection*, a spiritual encounter. Indeed, the anthropologist, Van Gennep, would have called it a *rite of separation*, because it marked a precise cutoff from an old life and status, before entering into a new one. Was it not to these same Ephesians that Paul so articulated it? Put off the old man (4:22), and put on the new man (4:24)—"put off" and "put on," as one changing clothes.

The biblical evidence of this demand for commitment to Christ in some form of dramatic encounter shows the convert(s) demonstrating that the old way no longer has power over him (them), and henceforth he is "God's man" (the collective, "people of God"). Thus Paul, seeking to encourage the young man Timothy, addresses him, "O man of God," committed now to fight the good fight of faith, and to strive for Christian perfection (1 Tim 6:11; 2 Tim 3:17).

In the animist world today the public demonstration, or *rite of separation*, varies with the cultural climate—fetish-burning, burial of ancestral skulls, casting the sacred paraphernalia into the sea or river, eating the forbidden totem fish or animal, according to the pattern of their animism. These are cultural equivalents of Joshua setting up the stone of witness, and the Ephesian magicians burning their books. This is symbolism, but it's more than symbolism. Psychologically, men are strengthened to keep their covenant by having made a public confession and having done it as a *company of converts*. "Let the redeemed of the Lord say so!" said the Psalmist (107:2).

The symbolic rejection of the old way not only involves a religious encounter, but thereafter it serves as a continual reminder of the act of rejection that alone can save the convert from syncretism or polytheism. It was just at this point that Paul had trouble with the Corinthian Christians, who found it easier to incorporate Christ into their heathen pantheon, than reject that pantheon for Christ. "No way!" says Paul, "Ye cannot drink the cup of the Lord and the cup of devils" (1 Cor 10:21). And it is precisely at this same point that the modern mission among animists becomes really Christian or just another kind of Animism.

2. Pay attention to the problem of motivation

Animists may be interested in Christianity for many and varied reasons—some good, others bad. Many factors may bring a field to ripen unto harvest. Of course, we are interested in all inquirers, but problems are bound to arise if the evangelist accepts all such inquiry at its face value without really evaluating the basic motivation; which may be for as materialistic a reason, for example, as the fact that the power of western armies and navies in war surely makes the religion of these powerful foreigners better to have on your side than against you.

Many supposed converts misunderstand both Christianity itself and the salvation it proclaims. They misunderstand their own needs also. The book of Acts (Ch. 8) supplies us with a good example of the problem. On the surface, the conversion of Simon, the sorcerer, at Samaria was quite genuine when he came to Philip (vv. 9-13) and believed. However, shortly afterwards, when confronted with Peter's ministry and the gift of the Spirit, it is immediately apparent that Simon had a complete misunderstanding of the nature of the gospel due to his wrong motivation: he thought he could buy the gift of God with money (vv. 18-24).

Animists sometimes respond because the Christian mission offers a ministry of healing which seems to be more effective than that of their own shamans and medicine-men. Animist chiefs have even invited missionaries to live in their midst in order to have a trade store in their community—this would mean a regular supply of steel knives, fishhooks, nails and axe-heads, all of which are not only utilitarian, but are also symbols of wealth and status for both this chief among other chiefs, and this tribe among other tribes.

The motivation for accepting Christianity naturally affects their view of Christianity, the character of the gospel, the nature of their Christian ethics, and their concept of Christian responsibility.

Let me give you an example of the problem as I met it repeatedly in Papua, New Guinea. One of the real problems there is that of the Cargo Cult. It even occurs where there have been prolonged pre-baptismal training programs. Indeed, perhaps the unduly long period of training has itself made baptism appear as a goal rather than an entry into an experience of nurture and growth. It gives the impression that converts "have arrived," as it were. They came enthusiastically in the first place, but now they want to "back out" in syncretistic cults which deny much that they have been taught. I met a young New Guinean who put it this way to me, "A few years ago I became a Christian because I wanted to achieve the white man's status and wealth. I wanted a good job, with a good wage and a house like the white men have. I worked hard in mission educational institutions, and I was baptized. But now it is all empty and worth nothing." The young man was thoroughly disillusioned with Christianity because his motivation had been wrong in the first place. His spiritual advisers had not detected this. They had interpreted his industry as a behavior-change due to conversion, and now he is a potential trouble-maker.

I also picked up a report from a missionary who had shared his all with a New Guinea colleague—a national pastor—whom he trusted implicitly. After many years, the pastor, recognizing this missionary's openness, asked, "Now we have shared everything, won't you tell me the secrets Jesus gave you?" The missionary was staggered to discover that even his pastoral colleague had what they call "the cargo mentality," which must have been there in his mind from the very motivation of his first attraction to Christianity. One major cause of Cargo Cults is the wrong expectation converts have had of Christianity.

I do not want to give the impression that all conversions from Animism are like this—that would not be true. There are thousands and thousands of wonderful warm-hearted Christians who really know Jesus as Lord. But, nevertheless, it remains quite true that we have never really faced up to the problem of motivation when the convert first comes for instruction. We ought to be asking the question—what is the role of the pastoral counselor when the would-be convert first moves forward to respond to the gospel?

> Communal societies have a high degree of social responsibility, and often the individualistic foreign evangelist has trouble with group decision-making.

3. Pay attention to the problem of meaning

Paul and Barnabas cured the cripple at Lystra in the name of the gospel after proclaiming the Word, thinking, thereby, that the name of God would be praised. The people took the incident to mean that the two evangelists were the Greek gods, Mercury and Jupiter, anthropomorphized; and they brought forth their approved religious paraphernalia and the sacrifice, to worship them—the very last thing Paul and Barnabas wanted (Acts 14:8-13)—and, indeed, the people could hardly be restrained from this intention (v. 18). Here we are confronted with the problem of meaning. The proclamation, no doubt, was faithfully given, but alas, quite misunderstood.

Anthropology has a number of suggestions to offer the evangelist in this area of communication—at least to indicate why this kind of thing can happen. Let me enumerate a few, for purposes of discussion.

The biblical case I have just cited represented a confusion which arose from the *world view of the listeners.* Seeing the miracle, which was beyond the normal powers of science as they knew it, and, therefore, had to be due to supernatural factors, they interpreted it in terms of their own mythology. Every cross-cultural missionary runs into this problem sooner or later. It is the problem of translation and of Scripture interpretation. Every word selected—the word for God, for the Spirit, for the Son of God, for sin, for love, for prayer, for forgive comes from a non-biblical world view, and is a potential for misunderstood meaning. If it is a problem for the evangelist, who speaks in the language of his listeners, it is doubly so for the evangelist who does not learn the language, but uses a third party to come between him and his audience.

The meaning of the message can be distorted also by *the image of the evangelist* in the eyes of his audience. It was for this reason that western missionaries to China before the Communist days, were often heard as imperialists and capitalists, even though they did not think of themselves in that way. As one scholar put it, they became essential to the revolution, so that Christianity could be rejected. I know the documents of one place where missionaries worked for sixteen years without a convert, living devout, industrious lives, and by their very industry giving the impression that salvation was merely a gospel of hard work and trade—the very last thing they desired to do.

Then again the *evangelist's conceptualization of his message* can condition the meaning ascribed to it. Is he proclaiming a faith prophetically or teaching philosophically? Does the teaching of Scripture come through in a foreign or denominational garment? Is it presented as a moral, legal code, or oriented to the joy of the Lord and the glory of God? Is it directed to the problems of the evangelist, or to the felt needs of the listeners? The animists have come from a world of power encounter and presumably they, therefore, need a God who speaks and demonstrates with power. The preaching of a purely ethical gospel is hardly likely to inspire such a people; but a life transformed by a God of power will lead to a new ethic. Why do the charismatic figures of so many nativistic movements retain the use of the Bible in their cultic practices? Several prophets have spoken on the point. Recognizing the power of the Word, they have pointed out that the missionaries of each denomination interpret the Word in their own way, and asked, "Why cannot we do it in our way?" And this they then do—in terms of their mythology.

Thus there are three points where the message of the Word may be blurred in communication: (i) *at the "advocate end"* (evangelist), (ii) *at the "accepter end"* (convert), and (iii) *in the message itself* (the theological emphasis of the evangelist). We can no longer run the risk of sending out missionaries (westerners or nationals) without some cross-cultural training, and, of course, it follows also that they should be competent interpreters of the Word.

4. Pay attention to the problem of social structure

At first thought we may wonder what social structure has to do with evangelization. This is because many of us are individualists, and we assume that everyone should do things the way we do. But the peoples of the world do not have identical social behavior patterns. This creates problems when evangelization is cross-cultural. The people to whom the evangelist goes may organize their daily life very differently from him, and he should remember that the process of evangelization should lead to the formation of fellowship groups, and that these should be indigenous and not foreign in structure. At least, the evangelist ought to be aware of social structure, and reckon on the Holy Spirit being able to use ways of life different from his own. Let me cite two examples of the importance of social structure for evangelization.

Most animist societies are communally orientated; they tend to operate in homogeneous groups. These groups, of course, do not ignore the individual; he is always an individual within a group context, however groups are multi-individual. Discussions of important issues for decision go on and on until a *consensus* is reached. This may take a long time, but it eliminates the problem created by "majority decision" which denies some of the rights of the minority that is outvoted. These communal societies have a high degree of social responsibility, and often the individualistic foreign evangelist has trouble with group decision-making. Groups exist at different levels of social organization, and authority for decisions may lie at different levels—e.g., decision-making in domestic affairs, agriculture, religion, politics, and war may be the responsibility of household, extended-family, village or clan. It is important for the evangelist to identify these because the manifest behavior of the multi-individual group in turning from heathenism to Christ will have the appearance of *group movements*—households, villages, age-grades, extended families or clans, according to their normal social organization. Unless it is so, it will not be meaningful to the people.

There is nothing strange or unbiblical about this. The apostles found that the rural villages and townships of Palestine often "turned to the Lord" as whole communities, like Sharon and Lydda (Acts 9:35), whereas, in other cases, like that of the centurion at Philippi (Acts 16:30-34) and Crispus, the chief of the synagogue at Corinth (Acts 18:8), the groups became Christian as households. They were acting within the regular operative social mechanisms of daily life.

In the same way those who respond in these group movements have to be formed into fellowship groups or churches; the operating character of these should either reflect or, at least, be compatible with their familiar structures. This applies especially to any leadership patterns introduced. For example, a common blunder in church-planting across cultures has been to appoint a young Christian leader (on the grounds that he can read and has had some education) over a new Christian community in a gerontocratic society, normally led by a council of elders, where the basic values are maturity, experience and gray hairs. In this way the evangelization of these people brings an unfortunate and unnecessary bone of contention.

These two illustrations, at the levels of decision-making and leadership, will serve to make the point that effective evangelization requires a church indigenous from the beginning and the more foreign organizational structures imposed on a church-planting situation the more problems will be created for the subsequent generation which has to find the passage "from mission to church," which can be a painful experience.

5. *Pay attention to the problem of incorporation*

One of the tests of valid biblical evangelism is the provision of a way for incorporating converts into the fellowship of believers. The Bible demonstrates this in several ways. First, there are passages, like the introduction of John's first letter, wherein, the notion of *witness* (vv. 1-2) is associated with that of fellowship (v. 3); the Great Commission itself does not end with "Go and make disciples," but continues "baptize and teach" (Matt 28:19-20). For the purpose of study, we take these texts separately, but in reality they a whole. The analysis must be adjusted by synthesis, or our evangelization is only partial.

Second, the notion of the *fellowship* is crucial in biblical argument. True, we can speak of evangelism as bringing individual men face to face with Christ, but we cannot leave it there because the New Testament did not leave it there. Christ is, of course, the Ultimate, and in that sense we need no more than to be with Him. But for this present point of time in which He has been born, the convert has to be incorporated into some

precise fellowship group, the Church, which is Christ's Body. In the records of the early Church (Acts) and the letters which tell us so much of its inner life, the configuration which holds it all together structurally is the Church—be it theologically the Church universal, or practically the local church. Remove that concept from the New Testament and look for a disembodied collection of isolated people who had met Christ, and you will soon be disillusioned. Christian activity and theology are always spoken of in collective figures—Christians are "fellow citizens," "members of the household of God," a "priesthood," a "nation," a "flock," a "fellowship," "members of the Body," or "the church which is at...."

Fellowship-forming or church-planting is thus part of evangelization. Right at the beginning of Acts (1:13-14), we have a fellowship group in prayer, and immediately a worshiping, witnessing, growing body (Acts 2:46-47), meeting for instruction, fellowship, breaking of bread and prayer (2:42). Thus is the Church His Body, fulfilling His ministry in this world in this day, and if evangelization does not mean that, it is defective.

To pass from this biblical base to the situation in the animist world, where men are being won to Christ in communities completely different in both social life and values perhaps from that to which the evangelist belongs, the latter has to consider what a convert from animism needs to find in the fellowship group into which he is incorporated. How does he get his new experience of Christian *belonging*, so that he becomes a participating, worshiping, witnessing, and serving member of the Body of Christ *in his own kind of world* ? I hope for a profitable discussion of this issue, not only to provide us with some worthwhile directions for ministry in such situations, but also to help cross-cultural evangelists at large to appreciate a problem which many of them have never thought about at all.

6. Pay attention to the problem of the cultural void

Over the last ten years I have been able to visit a great many young churches whose members have come to Christ out of animist backgrounds. Apart from their wide range of cultural differences, there are also manifest spiritual differences. Some of them, though quite strange to me culturally and linguistically, have nevertheless been obviously vibrant with life, creative in their worship, using their own indigenous forms of music and art with enthusiasm, and performing significant service ministries in the animist world about them. On the other hand, others have been the very opposite. They have tried to worship according to patterns more familiar in the West, and sing hymns in Western music and to have many quite obvious accouterments of European denominationalism. These churches have been misfits in their own worlds. They limp along as if almost ready to die; as if trying to be what they really are not. In some cases they are even led entirely by a foreigner, and there is little, if any, congregational participation; and financially their work is possible only with the aid of foreign funds. If they have a national pastor, he is a little replica of the foreign missionary. How is this church ever going to see itself as the Body of Christ, ministering the mind and heart and Word of Christ to the animist world outside? In a hundred years of history it has no more than a hundred members, and is currently static. The truth remains that the Christian programs of evangelization used over the last century of Christian missions produced these two kinds of churches. And I believe that in each case their characters were, more often than not, formed in the early periods when the first fellowship groups were being formulated. I believe that the majority (I did not say all) of our second generation problems have their roots in faulty follow-up of the original religious awakenings. In church growth parlance we say, "The people movement has to be effectively consummated."

> How does the converted animist meet the physical and spiritual needs that spring from the tribal way of life...and how does one discover the will of God for him?

One of the problems of following up a great movement of the Spirit of God in bringing many persons to Christ, is not just to incorporate them into a Christian group, but to be sure that it is an indigenously structured and meaningful group, in which they can participate in their own way. Thus, for example, a New Guinea convert should not have to become American or Australian to be a Christian; linguistically and culturally he should be a *New Guinea* Christian. Likewise the fellowship group should be New Guinean. The members' participation, praying, worship and service ministry should be New Guinean. A gifted New Guinean animist musician, on becoming Christian, should be a *New Guinean* Christian musician—and so on.

If we get into this kind of a situation where evangelists dispose of all cultural values and creative arts on the presupposition that they are all incompatible with Christianity because they have been used previously for heathen purposes (as many evangelists do argue), we find ourselves with creative people who can no longer create, and would-be participators who become non-participants, and before long the cultural voids we have created begin to be felt. Cargo Cults are only partly due to foreign domination; they are also due to cultural voids. Those who believe they are called to evangelism should remember that evangelization does not take place in a vacuum.

The problem of *maintenance* (as the anthropologist, F. E. Williams called the preservation of traditional techniques and values in a situation of changing culture), of course, involves a value judgment—can this or that element be preserved and be made truly Christian? Or will its maintenance involve the church in syncretism? The New Testament warns us that we are bound to meet this problem and that it must be faced squarely. This is why I began

this statement with "Pay attention to the problem of encounter." But, even so, when the basic commitment to Christ has been effectively faced, there will yet remain an indigenous way of life which is also worth winning for Christ. It should be possible for a tribal man from, say, Africa or New Guinea, to be a Christian without having to reject his tribe. It must be so or we could hardly hope for the "great multitude which no man can number of all nations, and kindreds, and peoples and tongues (standing) before the throne and before the Lamb" (Rev 5:9) in that day.

I asked a tribal man whose people had come into Christianity from animism, but whose Christian life was largely innocuous and foreign, making little impact on its surrounding world, "What happened to your tribal skills?" He told me sadly that they had "melted away" and that life was empty because of it. He was feeling the cultural void. Something within him was crying out to be creative. He had discovered another Christian church in his country which utilized the indigenous arts and crafts to the glory of God, and he felt his own tribe had been robbed of something precious. A basic question recurs: what does it mean to a Christian convert from animism to be a Christian in an animist world, and to be a participating member in a fellowship group of converted animists? This applies to more than arts and crafts. How does the converted animist meet the physical and spiritual needs that spring from the tribal way of life—problems of danger, of death, of sickness or of sorcery—and how does one discover the will of God for him?

Evangelization does not end with an offer of the gospel, or with the conversion of an individual, but with the coming into being of an ongoing fellowship, which is the Body of Christ in that kind of world.

Study Questions

1. Explain what Tippett means by "confession…in a company of converts."

2. Which of the six points applies to urban, non-animist situations? Which of them speak to issues of church planting?

3. How can effective church planting avoid the problem of "cultural voids?"

Christian Witness to Hindus

The Lausanne Committee for World Evangelization

Christ, as the
Author and Giver
of peace,
with the promise
of heavenly bliss,
provides ample
incentive for
the Hindu to look
into the Christian
Gospel of peace
with God.

From "Christian Witness to Hindu People," *Lausanne Occasional Paper #14*. Lausanne Committee for World Evangelization, 1980. Used by permission.

HISTORICAL SKETCH AND CONTEMPORARY SITUATION

The Hindu Population

The Aryans from Central Asia entered India in the third century BC and settled on the banks of the river Indus. Their search for God resulted in the writing of the Vedas. Based on the Vedic scriptures, the Aryan religion was born, which evolved into Hinduism. It absorbed everything, covering tribals and Dravidians. Hinduism dominated and built a strong sense of community in the Indian society, stratifying it into different castes. Wherever the Indian was taken, either to serve in plantations or in the British army, Hinduism followed, spreading far and wide.

Generally speaking, a Hindu is born, not made. Except for recent trends of conversion to Hinduism, by and large the growth of Hinduism has been biological. The world population is said to be 6.1 billion of which Hindus make up over 795 million or 13 per cent of the total population. Of that number, 730 million live in India and 65 million have moved to places such as the Middle East, United Kingdom, the United States, South Africa, East Africa, Malaysia, Fiji, Singapore, and Sri Lanka. In India, 72 per cent of the total population are Hindus (730 million), whereas the Christian population in India is only 3 per cent (30 million).[1]

The Hindu Religion

There is no one definition which explains Hinduism in its entirety. In fact, it is a conglomeration of ideas, beliefs, convictions and practices, varying from people to people and from region to region. For example, Aryan Hinduism of northern India is radically different at many points from Dravidian Hinduism of southern India. However, Hinduism can be understood in the following ways:

Philosophic Hinduism

This form of Hinduism is dominated by the authority of the Vedas and Upanishads (scriptures). Concerning the understanding of the Ultimate Reality, there are three popular schools of thought:

Advaita—non-dualism
Dvaita—dualism
Visishtadvaita—modified dualism

They teach from the ancient Vedas that there is a spark of divinity in man, and hence to call a man a sinner is blasphemous; there is, then, no need for a savior.

Religious Hinduism

Adherents to this type believe in the Puranas (epics) and in the Mahabharatha, Ramayana and Bhagavadgita, saying these epics are revelations from God. There is a strong belief in avatars (incarnations of gods). Their theology is syncretistic. Man is at liberty to choose his own god from among a pantheon of 33 *crores* (330 million), and to worship any number of gods. Salvation may be attained in one of three ways:—

Gnanamarga—(way of knowledge)
Bhaktimarga—(way of devotion)
Karmamarga—(way of good deeds)

Popular Hinduism

This form of Hinduism is far removed from philosophy and Brahmanism. The followers of this form are influenced by ancestral tradition, animal worship, temple cults, magic, exorcism, etc. They are indifferent to the authority of the Vedas and are concerned only about a god who protects them blesses them and makes them prosperous. The majority of Hindus adhere to this form.

Mystic Hinduism

Gurus with mysterious personal experiences are drawing many to themselves. The claims of these gurus are sensational, often asserting that they are avatars and that they have supernatural gifts of healing, ability to perform miracles, to read the inner thoughts of people and to prophesy the future. Prominent among the gurus who have a mass following are Satya Sai Baba, Bal Yogeshwar, and Acharya Rajnesh. The Transcendental Meditation of Mahesh Yogi has drawn many disciples from India and other countries.

Tribal Hinduism

This type is very much influenced by animism, spiritism, the occult, necromancy and animal worship. The fear of the unknown exercises its instinctive dread over followers' minds.

Secular Hinduism

Those who belong to this group are generally nominal in their beliefs and indifferent to religious practices. Even the few religious customs that they follow are motivated by materialistic tendencies.

Modern trends in Hinduism

Although the Christian faith is claimed to have been brought to India in the first century AD by the apostle Thomas, resulting in the formation of a Christian church, it remained introverted and did not spread. In the 16th century, Catholic missionaries, such as Francis Xavier and Robert de Nobili, brought the gospel to the Hindus. After them came the Protestants in a floodstream, with various mission societies establishing churches, as people movements spread mostly into the lower category of Hindu community. The emphasis on higher education by Alexander Duff and succeeding missionaries led to a Hindu renaissance giving birth to Hindu reform movements such as Brahma Samaj, Arya Samaj, and Prarthana Samej. The formation of Hindu missionary movements, such as the Rama Krishna Mission, followed.

A concept of mission is not one of the main tenets of Hinduism. But Hindu theologians, such as Vivekananda and Aurobindo, by their interpretation of the main teaching of Hinduism, have added this new missionary dimension. The missionary vision of some Hindus is posing a threat to Christian evangelistic activities. We now hear of cases of nominal Christians, as well as Hindu converts to Christianity, reverting to Hinduism. Further, western converts to Hinduism are being sent as Hindu missionaries to some parts of the world. The Hare Krishna movement has a notable impact in many western countries. This movement has a big appeal to young people. In some western countries it has established centers for the propagation of this movement.

In conclusion, modern trends in Hinduism find expression in the Harijan movement [Harijans, often called "untouchables," were called "children of God" by Mahatma Gandhi] initiated and propagated by Mahatma Gandhi, in the missionary movement designed by Vivekananda, in a secular socialist ideology advocated by Jawaharlal Nehru and in the militant communal sectarian groups such as Rashtriya Swayam Sevak (RSS).

The post-independence Indian society has developed into a secular democracy. The agnostic leadership emphasized industrialization, resulting in rapid secularization, modernization and westernization. The urban population developed popular nominal Hinduism which leaves it open to new influences. The rural Hindu, oppressed by poverty and corruption, sought a liberating gospel. The unrest caused by several philosophies and a weak political structure has softened the Hindus within India to the gospel, even though the above varieties of Hinduism continue to prevail. Overseas Hindus are in a very unsettled, fluid state. In some countries of the world they are undergoing a period of great strain and change, which may influence their receptivity to the gospel.

> We must be aware that the Holy Spirit who has gone before us, is alongside us and guides us, and alone can reveal Jesus Christ.

BIBLICAL FRAMEWORK FOR HINDU EVANGELIZATION

Jesus Christ, the Son of God, became flesh within an Asian context. During the days of His flesh, He lived within a Hebraic cultural framework within this Asian context. He was poor. He walked among the villages and wept over the cities. He accepted social rejects and understood the fluctuating fortunes of leadership within a tangible human society. The Hindu can understand Him.

Before such an understanding can be effected, however, Jesus Christ must be made known to the Hindu. In this effort to communicate Jesus Christ to the Hindu, the Indian Christian faces the tension between being faithful to the content of the Bible and relating this content to the theological, philosophical and religious context of the Hindu.

The resolution of this problem does not lie in interfering with the content of biblical truth, but in the proper use of the context of Hindu categories and needs in the process of communicating that truth.

This is not the first time for such an effort to be attempted because, as early as the 19th century AD, many Christian congregations existed in South India within a culturally Hindu environment. Jesus Christ, the Son of God, is relevant and relates to all human cultures. He can be made known to a Hindu in a traditionally Hindu culture in India, likewise to Hindus living outside of India.

Theological Perspective

The gospel is never proclaimed within a vacuum. India provides a particular context which influences the kind of communication we should pursue. Thus we need to examine the Indian context in the light of the Scriptures and see which aspects warrant our careful consideration in Christian communication. The following are some crucial factors which will influence Hindu evangelism:

Spirituality

Hindus are a very religious people. An aura of holiness characterizes every man who claims to be spiritual. They identify externals to be reflective of holiness. The Bible calls us to live a holy life (1 Pet 1:16; Rom 12:1,2) and to keep our behavior excellent among unbelievers so that they may glorify God (1 Pet 2:12; Matt 5:16). The power of God through a transformed holy life will be a powerful influence on the Hindu.

Community

Human dignity stems from man being made in the image of God (Gen 1:26,27) and is reinforced by Christ's death for all (1 Jn 2:2). Christians are a human community. However, their equality before God is not affirmed within Indian society. Although people like to become Christians without crossing cultural boundaries, we believe that scripture demands spiritual unity of all believers. It is here that the functioning of the community of Jesus Christ in biblically relevant ways can be a formidable witness to the dignity that is restored in Christ. When true community is practiced within the Church it will prove to the world our discipleship (John 13:35). Further, when the Church participates in the lives of people through genuine love, our verbal messages will be validated (Jas 2:24, 26).

Poverty

Perhaps the starkest reality of populous India is her poverty. While we will do everything humanly possible to rectify this situation, in God's eyes a man's worth is not determined by poverty because he is made in the image of God. Christ not only identified with the poor, He was poor (2 Cor 8:9; Phil 2:7). Elsewhere, it is seen that God has a special heart for the poor (Prov 14:31). This message has special relevance to the Hindu within the Indian context.

Theological Blocks

Four particular theological barriers to effective communication with Hindus should be highlighted.

Syncretistic

They believe that all religions lead to God, implying that there is, therefore, no need to change from one religion to another. Indeed, Hindus find the very mention of change of religion by the Christian highly objectionable. Such demands must be presented with clarity and respect.

The concept of sin

The Hindu understanding of the concept of sin varies from group to group and even from individual to individual (e.g., to some, sin is just committing bad deeds; to others, it is disobedience to one's conscience; to still others, it is mere selfishness; and to some, sin is just non-existent. Vivekananda said, "It is sin to call anyone a sinner.").

The doctrine of karma

You reap what you sow. Behavior in the past determines fate in the present, and deeds in the present determine the future. The cycles of rebirths keep recurring till finally "moksha" (salvation) is attained. However, just as karma is a block, it is also a bridge.

The doctrine of salvation

This highlights the difficulty of terminology. Although the concept of salvation exists within Hinduism, its understanding as liberation from the cycle of rebirth is radically different from the Christian viewpoint.

Theological Bridges: Introduction

We must recognize that Hinduism revolves around a different center than does Christianity, asking fundamentally different questions and supplying different answers. The use of any theological bridge, therefore, is fraught with difficulty, particularly if we attempt to use a specific term or concept to demonstrate that Christ is the fulfillment or crown of Hinduism.

No concept of Hinduism can be accepted into Christianity without change. By way of illustration, the following bridges can be grouped into two categories:

Points of Content

Those concepts which require radical change of content are:

The concept of God. In evangelism among Hindus we are speaking into a pantheistic world view, and although clarification and re-definition are required, it is not necessary to defend the existence of God.

Respect for Scripture. The Hindu respect for the sacred writings can be developed in the context of the unique authority of the Bible. Unlike any other religious community, Hindus will listen attentively to an exposition of scripture. The sole authority of the Bible must be stressed without any compromise whatsoever.

The person of Christ. The quality of Christ's relationship with people, His teachings (particularly the Sermon on the Mount), and His unique vicarious self-giving and suffering have a strong appeal to the Hindu. As the Christian communicator fills this respect for Christ with an understanding of the unique and absolute claim to be "the Word made flesh," a significant bridge may be built.

The doctrine of karma. While this doctrine is a barrier in terms of defining moksha (salvation), it also can serve as a bridge while communicating the gospel to the Hindu. The Hindu seeks to get free from the cycle of rebirth which his sin causes. He must be told of the Savior Jesus Christ, who by His vicarious suffering and death on the cross, triumphed over sin and has taken upon Himself the penalty of the sins of mankind.

Points of caution and clarification

Concepts which require a radical conceptual redefinition are:

View of history. Christianity and Hinduism differ radically in their understanding of history. We should use this dissimilarity as a bridge, stressing the purposes of God in time, creation, the historical resurrection, and the coming judgment.

Hindu spirituality. There is a deep desire in the Hindu for spiritual experience (anubhava). This is noticeable, for example, among the Bhakti Margis. The emphasis on meditation, austerity and the willingness to accept physical suffering are commendable aspects of the Hindu way of life. At the same time, however, the Christian communicator must stress the degree of personal freedom that comes in Christian worship, and the Christian understanding that spirituality is not an end in itself, nor is it merely by spiritual exercises that one inherits the Kingdom. Essentially, the value of this bridge lies in the importance of the spiritual qualities of the evangelist or communicator of the gospel in gaining credibility.

Incarnation. Hindu beliefs in the intervention of God in human history through avatars must be radically redefined in Christian communication. Avatars enter the world to destroy sinners, and this requires repeated avatars. The incarnation of Christ is unique, historical, sufficient for all time, and is rooted in the love of God, saving sinners.

HINDRANCES TO EVANGELIZATION OF HINDUS

Western culture has been injected into Indian culture as an acceptable form of Christianity. This alienates non-Christians to a large extent. The following are some of the issues that have alienated Hindus and proved a hindrance to evangelism:

Socio-Cultural Issues

1. Food habits among Christians which are totally contrary to Hindu religious sentiments—i.e., beef eating.

2. The Christian way of worship which is predominantly non-Indian.

3. Excessive social mingling of boys and girls in Christian families and in religious activities.

4. The practice of Christians in forbidding the use of vermillion [a red spot on the forehead].

5. Christianity appears as a foreign religion—i.e., western.

6. Christianity is seen as a threat to Indian culture and identity, because of the prevailing thought that "Indian" means "Hindu."

7. The wrong notion that Christians are not patriotic.

8. The wrong notion that only "untouchables" (Harijans) embrace Christianity.

9. The fact that caste is the Hindu's strongest forte of social security. Conversion to Christianity destroys this, leading to: excommunication from the community, damage to family reputation, termination of marital prospects, and physical assault and persecution.

10. Superstition: Many Hindus live under the constant fear of invoking the wrath of the Kula Devata (family god), if they accept the gods of other religions.

Economic Issues

1. The fear of loss of property upon conversion to Christianity.

2. Loss of privileges and position in society, because of the non-recognition of caste distinction in the Christian faith.

3. The misunderstanding that Christians are a middle-class people. Hence low-caste people hesitate to mingle with Christians even socially.

4. The wrong understanding that the Indian church is quite rich, supported by the influx of foreign money. This notion is partly due to the huge, widely publicized gospel crusades conducted by foreign evangelists in Indian cities.

5. The loss of economic privileges—e.g., withdrawal of financial aid by the government to Harijan students converted to Christianity.

Methodological Issues

1. We should enunciate theology in Indian categories so that the Hindu can understand the gospel.
2. We must develop a truly Christian world view consistent with the Indian context.
3. While presenting the gospel, we must be aware of the fact that the Hindu understands the doctrine of God, man, sin, and salvation in a way entirely different from the biblical doctrine.
4. We need to review our communication approaches. In our presentation of the gospel we must:
    (a) Speak to the context of the listener.
    (b) Be deeply involved in the life of the listener.
    (c) Grapple openly with the problems, questions, and needs of our listener.
    (d) Present our message in such a way that it answers those problems, questions and needs.
    (e) Speak in such a way that we demonstrate love and a deep respect for the listener, and his questions. There is no room in our evangelism for a condescending attitude.
    (f) Recognize that the response of a person to the gospel has both intellectual and emotional elements. Much gospel communication in the past has emphasized a rational response and has failed to appeal to the heart. This statement must not be interpreted as an endorsement of emotional gospel appeals, but a recommendation that our message must speak to the whole person, mind and heart.
    (g) Recognize the fact that our listener lives in a particular social context. The response of an individual is undoubtedly affected by the attitudes of those around him. As we become aware of the specific social environment in which we communicate, principles of evangelism will emerge. Our concern must go beyond the individual response to understand the broader questions related to the acceptance of Christ by the entire society.
    (h) Communicate the gospel through indigenous methods such as bhajans, drama, dialogue, discourse, Indian music, festival processions, etc.
    (i) Be loving and compassionate, and adopt a life-style that is contextualized and communicative.
    (j) Recognize what Hindus consider essential qualities in a spiritual leader (guru) that authenticate a person to be: willing to wait, willing to mortify his body and desires, willing to suffer pain, and willing to fast. Christian leaders with this type of spiritual qualification are a powerful means of communication.

CONCLUSION

The Hindu Quest

The Hindu quest for peace (shanti) and bliss is so overwhelming that he is willing to exert extreme effort in a relentless search to find this. Christ, as the Author and Giver of peace, with the promise of heavenly bliss, provides ample incentive for the Hindu to look into the Christian gospel of peace with God.

Love Dynamic

Principles of love, to become meaningful, must be personalized within a given context. The incarnation is the model for this (John 3:16). The communicator to the Hindu must first feel and know and respond to this intense love of God for the Hindu. The love of God for the Hindu provides the reason for the relentless search to understand the Hindu and identify with him. The communicator's love for Jesus Christ is the rationale for continued obedience to love, even when it seems unreasonable to do so. You cannot question the intentions behind the demands of Calvary love (John 15:12-14).

The reaching of the Hindu is one of the greatest challenges to the people of God in this generation. To this end we call for:

1. Personal and corporate intercession for the evangelization of Hindu people groups all over the world.
2. Personal and corporate sacrificial giving to support this evangelization.
3. The acceptance of Christ's call to personal involvement at every opportunity for such evangelism.
4. The mobilization of the loving concern, intercession, and financial resources from the worldwide body of Christ.

Closing Concern

We have waited on the Lord and have used the best insights among us to produce the preceding statements. They are not in any way exhaustive nor adequate, but they do seek to alert the earnest Christian, seeking to reach unreached Hindu people groups, concerning some points of contact and concern.

Having said that, we know that reaching any "people group" for Christ cannot be merely academic; and we cannot, and must not, place our total confidence in correct words and statements, but upon the living Lord who seeks all Hindus. We must be aware that the Holy Spirit who has gone before us, is alongside us and guides us, and alone can reveal Jesus Christ (1 Cor 12:3). Without Him we cannot succeed (John 15:5).

End Notes

1. Numbers for Hindu and world populations are projections for the year 2000 and were taken from "The Annual Statistical Table on Global Mission" by D. B. Barrett and T.M. Johnson, *International Bulletin of Missionary Research*, Vol. 22 No. 1, 1998 pp. 26-27.

   The figure for the percentage of Christians in India was given by the India Center for Mission based on the campus of the U.S. Center for World Mission.

Study Questions

1. Which characteristics of Hinduism are bridges and which are barriers to communication of the Gospel?

2. How must incarnation be "redefined" if Christians are to bear witness to the Incarnation of Jesus among Hindu peoples?

Christian Witness to the Chinese People

Thomas Wang and Sharon Chan

T he Chinese people constitute more than one-fifth of the human race, with a total population of 1.3 billion. Their unbroken history of more than 5,000 years marks a culture that is durable and resilient. They have survived the ravages of countless internal struggles and foreign invasions, and remain today a distinct and yet complex people. The majority of the people, 93 percent, belong to the Han group. But, there are at least 55 minority groups, mostly located in the border regions on the edge of the nation. These minority groups use 78 languages other than Mandarin Chinese. Even among the Han Chinese there are hundreds of dialects. These dialects are as different as German is from French. However, Mandarin Chinese is the official language of China.

The Christian Movement in China

Throughout China's long history, the Triune God of the Bible has been almost a stranger to them. True, there have been periods in which those who know the true and living God dwelled in their midst, but for a variety of tragic reasons, the great majority of Chinese learned little of Christ's Name and salvation.

Jewish synagogues and Nestorian merchant communities were scattered throughout China during the Tang Dynasty (7th to 9th centuries) when Chinese civilization was more advanced than anything Europe had to offer. Franciscan missionaries struggled to survive on the fringes of that empire during the years of Mongol dominance (13th century), while creative Jesuits followed in the 16th and 17th centuries. Nevertheless these relatively brief periods of Roman Catholic missionary presence produced little lasting spiritual benefit for the common people.

It was only when renewed Catholic missions and Protestant missionaries came to China in force in the 19th and 20th centuries that it could be said that the Christian Church had at long last been planted among China's millions. Even then, this church was more identified with Western cultural influence than with any spontaneous acceptance by the Chinese themselves. By the end of the 19th century the church in China felt pressure from authorities as in the Chinese government who mistakenly associated the church with Western "imperialistic" powers. During the anti-foreign Boxer Uprising in 1900, nearly 200 mission-

Thomas Wang is the President of the Great Commission Center International in Argyle, Texas. He is also the International Chairman for the AD2000 and Beyond Movement and served as International Director for the Lausanne Committee for World Evangelization from 1986-1989.

Sharon Chan is the Vice-President of the Great Commission Center International in Argyle, Texas.

aries and over 2,000 Chinese Christians in North China were martyred. The infant Chinese church tasted trial by fire.

An anti-Christian movement broke out in March 1922 to attack the World Student Christian Federation's International Conference, which was to meet in Qinghua University in April of that year. Christianity was branded as the cultural arm of Western imperialism. Unavoidably, the Chinese church also came under severe attack. In response, many churches separated themselves from foreign missions, and began to establish independent churches. Thus, the Chinese indigenous church movement started. As a result, the Chinese church experienced a great revival during the years 1927-1937 and an able and vigorous Chinese leadership emerged. All these experiences prepared the whole church to meet the forthcoming anguish which occurred after 1949.

Since 1949, the church in China has experienced a series of painful convulsions under revolutionary fervor. It was in God's providence that all Western missionaries were forced to evacuate from China (largely gone by 1951). Still God allowed the church to be severely tested, since the authorities were determined to break the church's ties with the West and make them subservient to the State in the 1950s. The Three Self Patriotic Movement (TSPM) was formed with the encouragement of the government to "liberate the church from the control of Western imperialism." Churches in the same city or area, even with different denominational backgrounds, were ordered to merge. Many Christians suffered for their faith, and some died in prison. During the Cultural Revolution (1966-1976), all churches were closed and Bibles confiscated. However, many Christians continued to have their worship and fellowship at home.

After the death of Chairman Mao Zedong and the arrest of the "Gang of Four" in late 1976, China began to adopt more moderate policies. When Deng Xiaoping emerged as the leader of the country in 1978, the bamboo curtain of China gradually began to be lifted.

From 1949 to 1979, Christians in the outside world did not have much information on the actual situation in China. Had the labor of thousands of foreign missionaries and Chinese workers been in vain? To everyone's surprise, in 1979 when China re-normalized its relationship with the United States and allowed foreigners to visit, there they found a living, growing church, with thousands upon thousands of Christians courageously confessing that Jesus Christ alone is Lord! In fact, the Chinese Christian population had grown from 840,000 in 1949 to an estimate of 35 million in 1982, according to Jonathan Chao of China Ministries International, Inc.

In March 1979 the Chinese Communist Party began to restore its religious policy. TSPM was rejuvenated in August 1979, and churches were allowed to reopen under the direction and supervision of the TSPM, first in large cities and for foreigners only. Gradually, however, Chinese were allowed to attend worship services in these "open churches."

In the 20 years between 1979-1998, the church in China not only existed but prospered in two fairly distinct groups: 1) those churches officially registered with the TSPM and the China Christian Council (CCC), and 2) the diversified house churches. The Three Self churches had registered meeting points and conducted their worship in church buildings which were in existence prior to 1949, or were newly built structures. The house churches usually worship in private homes, although in Wenzhou of the Zejiang province they have their own church buildings, much like those in the West.

The registered churches comply with the government's regulations and are under the political control of the Communist Party and policies set forth by the TSPM. They operate with limitations imposed by the civil authority (such as only government-authorized pastoral staff is allowed to serve in the church, fixed meeting locations and no evangelistic outreach outside of the church, etc.). According to statistics released by the Three Self Church, in 1997 there were more than 12,000 registered churches and 25,000 meeting points, with over 13 million Protestant Chinese Christians.

On the other hand, the house churches claim to have 70 to 80 million believers worshiping regularly in various homes. Apparently, the house churches are the main stream ecclesiastical realities in China. However, they are not recognized by the government and have always been under some form of persecution.

Looking at the world in general, since 1949 there are 57 million so-called "overseas" Chinese (including 21 million in Taiwan) scattered in more than 60 countries around the world. God has seen fit to work among them in different patterns, placing them in positions of leadership in academic, professional and business fields. The Chinese in North America are mostly professionals, while those in Southeast Asia are mainly business people. God has also made them receptive to the Christian message, By 1998 there were at least 8,000 Chinese churches in more than 50 countries of the world. According to a random sampling survey conducted by the *Los Angeles Times* in 1997, 32 percent of the Chinese in Southern California regularly attend church (6 percent of these were Catholics and less than 10 percent were evangelical Christians). Among these evangelical Christians, many felt that they were being prepared for a significant role in God's kingdom in the days ahead, especially the evangelization of the Chinese in their homeland.

Indeed, we cannot but praise God for what He has been doing in the last 50 years among the Chinese, thereby glorifying His Name through the suffering church in China and among other Chinese overseas which in the past decades have planted a diversified church. It is already true to say that the entire Chinese church is a global church which will more and more join forces with Western and other Third World churches for global missions in the years ahead.

Having said this, we at the same time must not ignore the fact that the Chinese churches (both inside and outside of Mainland China) are still occupied with issues and problems which must be objectively analyzed and studied.

Official Religious Policy in China

Because the Chinese government has adopted a policy of legislative control over all religious activities, Christian groups must register with the government, accept the leadership of the TSPM, and operate under the religious guidelines of the government. Only the Three Self churches and their meeting points are considered legal. They consider themselves the sole representatives of Protestants in China. Most experts on Communism agree that the Chinese government's intention of implementing this legislation has been to curb the rapid growth of Christianity.

Thus, the house churches that have chosen not to register with the government and to join the Three Self Movement are considered in some cases to be illegal groups or religious cults, and are subject to suppression by the civil authority. As a result, the house churches, being the main stream of ecclesiastical reality in China, are often considered illegal organizations by the government, and their church activities are punishable by law. Although facing persecution and pressure, the majority of the house churches still refuse to register with the government. Their sole purpose has been to maintain their purity and freedom to choose their own pastoral personnel, conduct local and distant evangelism, and carry out their church affairs according to the teachings of scripture rather than the stipulations of the state.

During the 1990s we saw a great interest in Christianity among some official leaders. Many scholars study Christianity as an academic subject or philosophy. Universities and secular publishers in the preceding decade published many books and research papers on Christianity and its influence on China. In early 1998, a Christianity Research Center was formally established as a branch of the Institute of World Religions under the

> We should prepare for that day when China relaxes all restrictions on religious activities and open its door for missionaries to be received *and* to be sent to the rest of the world!

banner of the Chinese Academy of Social Science. Many Chinese researchers from there (mostly non-Christians) have been sent overseas to study in different seminaries. These non-Christian scholars receive theological training and are familiar with the function and operation of Christian churches overseas. They will be the future leaders of the Religious Affairs Bureau (RAB) and will be working with TSPM, teaching in an official seminary or in Bible schools approved by the state, and pastoring official churches, thereby participating in shaping the religious policies of China.

Current Growth of the Church in China

Since 1989, there has been a noted growth in the number of believers and churchgoers in both the official churches and house churches. After the June 4, 1989 Tiananmen Square incident, Chinese intellectuals were disappointed with the Communist Party and the government. Their dreams for less authoritarian ruling and political reform were broken and their trust and loyalty to the Communist Party shaken. Their disillu-

sion with Communism as a government system urged them to seek other alternatives, especially the ideology of the Western world that is based on Christianity. Therefore, more and more intellectuals started coming to the Church for answers, thereby changing the assumption that churches were only for the elderly and less educated people. It was also encouraging to see Bible study and fellowship groups formed by students and professors in some universities.

In spite of the nationwide pressure for registration with the Religious Affairs Bureau (RAB) and TSPM, house churches continue to grow. It is reported there are "Non-Registered Meeting Points" (as distinguished from the registered meeting points) in practically every village in most of the provinces north of the Yangze River, such as Henan, Hebei, Anhui, Shandong, Jiangsu, Sichuan and the three provinces in the northeast (Heilongjiang, Jilin and Liaoning). Some villages have even become "Christian villages" as believers make up 50 percent to 80 percent of the inhabitants.

After several decades of development and expansion, house churches now are no longer

a loose body. They are organized in terms of large groups much like denominations in the West, with several thousand or several million members, structured by county, prefecture, provincial, and national levels to oversee the operations of hundreds, even thousands of house churches.

At this point, we must point out that in recent years some rural *official* church leaders have become evangelical. They are sympathetic and also friendly to house churches. In some isolated cases, a few house church leaders are in cooperation with official churches to conduct training inside the registered churches.

With great growth comes a great need for all kinds of training, full-time workers and literature. Both official churches and house churches are in dire need of trained pastors. In the 80s and 90s, the Chinese Church Council opened one seminary and 17 Bible schools and training centers throughout China. For the house churches, numerous short or middle term training classes of different levels have been conducted by house church leaders with or without help from Christians outside. Each "house church governing system" has its own network and training programs.

Mission to China

China is an old mission field. Since the Qing Dynasty, Christianity has been portrayed by the Chinese government as a "cultural invasion and enemy to the people." Any mission work to the Chinese must not ignore the historical complexity of the social and ecclesiastical realities of China.

At the present hour there are at least two general categories of mission work, "primary mission" (or "direct mission") is either person-to-person evangelism or equipping the existing local churches and Christians so that they can more effectively reach out to their non-Christian countrymen. "Secondary mission" (or "indirect mission") aims at cultivating a "receptive" atmosphere for Christian presence among non-Christian communities, struggling always with the crucial missiological problem of the official attitude to Christianity.

With these two categories in mind, there are three distinctive approaches for specific ministries to China:

1. The "Incarnational Servanthood" approach

Invasion from the West in past centuries has left Chinese people with deep suspicions about Christianity. Perhaps the greatest missiological problem we face today is how to resolve these unfortunate and deeply rooted misunderstandings. The "incarnational servanthood" approach seeks to work outside church structures by placing mature Christian professionals and business people in China. There these people make significant professional and economical contributions to the country while at the same time rubbing shoulders on a regular basis with their Chinese counterparts, many of whom are government officials. It is hoped that such an incarnational servanthood approach will ultimately affect the attitudes of government leaders resulting in more trust, affirmation and freedom for Christianity.

Such ministry efforts can seek placement in Chinese settings in three ways. First, by *academic* involvement: Christian professionals from overseas can teach in universities and colleges, conduct research, teach foreign languages, and more. Secondly, there is opportunity for *business* investment to develop real estate, establish manufacturing facilities, develop tourism facilities, establish consulting firms, and much more. Thirdly, professionals can do *community development* work among minority groups in remote provinces. In these situations, professionals can endeavor to help develop medical services, bring assistance in education, agriculture and any number of other development challenges faced by China.

2. The "Official Church" approach

Following Deng Xiaoping's reform policy, the Three Self and official churches are encouraged to engage in cross-cultural exchange with Chinese and non-Chinese churches outside of China. Most Western church leaders have taken in this approach as they usually do not have contacts with house churches. Since the return of Hong Kong's sovereignty to China, some evangelical Hong Kong churches have established regular exchange programs with Three Self churches, seminary, and Bible schools. The exchange activities include funding the construction of church buildings, participating in leadership training and evangelism, and in church worship, such as preaching, baptism, choir presentation, etc. These activities are arranged by the official churches and are legal and open. The missiological problem is how to empower a weak church within the legal limits imposed by the religious laws of China. This approach accepts the reality that there are both true and false Christians in the church, especially on the leadership level. But the hope remains that because of the true Christian witnesses from outside, even the false Christians would come to a true faith and confession in Jesus Christ some day. The Three Self and official churches are therefore both partners and "mission fields" to these missionary efforts. To the Chinese government, such exchange activities are controlled, legal, and acceptable. Specific ministries in this approach might include preaching in official churches or teaching in official Bible schools and training centers.

3. The "House Church" approach

In recent years, most mission initiatives have sought to help and work through the house church movements. Overseas Chinese churches particularly have seen this approach as valid since house churches usually have no ties with the government. Numbers alone draw mission efforts to seek out house church involvement: As much as 85 percent of the Christians in China are part of house churches.

It is undeniable that house churches have experienced tremendous persecution in the past and perhaps even at present. We need to remember our brothers and sisters in their suffering and speak out for the silent majority. Most Chinese Christian leaders have the view that this persecution has, under God's providence, resulted in a purified church that remains faithful to the Lord. Ministries to the house churches are usually conducted in a secret and "underground" fashion as the Chinese government views such "missionary" activities as illegal, subversive, threatening and undesirable.

The urgent need in the house churches is not missionary outreach, but Bible teaching designed to help them to grow in sound doctrine and in defense against heresies. Heresies have created a very serious problem among house churches. Various ministries are working to answer the need for trained leadership by carefully and creatively providing practical, biblical training for full-time pastors, lay pastors and itinerant evangelists. Much more needs to be done. With great care, finances can be provided without encouraging a damaging dependence. There is still a great need for Bibles, commentaries, training materials and other reference books.

All the above three approaches are legitimate means to reach China's millions. When one chooses certain means or ways to help the ministries in China, should be aware that there are still other avenues, and should not criticize other groups or build a new ministry at the expense of those who choose other avenues. Whoever is engaged in China ministries should have a servanthood spirit and avoid a paternalistic attitude. They should try to learn from the rich spiritual and ministerial experiences of the Christians in China and, at the same time, share resources with them.

Chinese Scholars Outside of China—A New Mission Field

God has brought many Chinese people to our doorstep. Since 1980 thousands of China scholars have gone overseas for further studies; most are Ph.D. students or post-doctorate researchers. It is estimated that there are over 500,000 China scholars in overseas areas today, including 170,000 in North America, 100,000 in Japan, 100,000 in Europe, 30,000 in Australia and New Zealand, 50,000 in Southeast Asia, etc. We believe God in his providence has brought them to us. We should evangelize these scholars and their families and give them basic Christian training while they are overseas.

A number of Chinese and non-Chinese churches, para-church organizations and Christian groups are working among these China scholars. They make friends with them, help them to adjust to Western culture and introduce them to Christ. Many have already embraced Christianity after coming overseas. In North America, it is estimated that at least 10 percent of the 170,000 China scholars have become Christians. A small portion have dedicated themselves for full-time Christian service. It is our firm belief that these Christian scholars will have a significant impact on the Chinese Church and on China when they return.

China in the 21st Century

China will speed up its economic reform in the years ahead. Well-known forecasters have projected that China's economy will catch up with the United States by AD 2020, and will become a super power by 2030. The crucial question is: how will China affect her neighbors and the world at that time—negatively, or positively? Of course, we hope it will be positive. But for that to happen, it is important to complete the evangelization of China. Even though we celebrate the wonderful explosion of the gospel in China, still only about 7 percent of the people there are Christians.

There are entire villages which are considered Christian villages. Shall we dare to believe that someday China may become a "Christian nation?" If, by the grace of God, the number of Christians in China grows to 50 percent or higher by the year 2030, imagine what she might contribute to the rest of the world!

Present day realities will help us to strategically focus our mission efforts in China. Economic reform up to now has benefited the coastal areas. However, remote areas are still poor, especially among minority peoples in the southwestern regions. They need medical, educational and all kinds of help. Christian professionals are most welcome to join forces to show Christian love to these needy peoples.

It was reported in the mid 1990s, 87 percent of China's population was rural. The government aims to decrease the rural population to 50 percent. We can expect that more and more rural dwellers will migrate to cities. Thus, more and more mega-cities will emerge in the near future. China needs help to solve its urban problems.

Looking ahead, China's economic change may lead to more freedom for the common people and more opportunity for them to contact the outside world. These changes may eventually lead to a day when China can have ideological pluralism and religious freedom. We should prepare for that day when China relaxes all restrictions on religious activities and opens its door for missionaries—both to be received *and* to be sent to the rest of the world!

Hope for China

Christianity has sought to take root in China for hundreds of years. Today is a golden opportunity to unload the baggage of history left behind by the failures of the past. May God grant wisdom to every servant of God to serve with love, patience and humility in China. As we seek out the best approaches and pursue fruitful partnerships, we will work together for the ultimate evangelization of nearly one quarter of humankind.

Study Questions

1. Discuss the complexity of the issue of house churches registering with the Chinese government. Why is this a significant issue?

2. What is the potential for reaching Chinese students while they are studying outside of China?

3. Since the house church movement is growing so rapidly, does this mean that China no longer has unreached peoples?

4. Describe the potential of Chinese missionaries going to other countries. Why has this not yet happened? What can be done now to strengthen these Chinese churches for this kind of future?

Reaching Muslim People with the Gospel

Ishak Ibraham

In any attempt to evangelize Muslims today, we can hardly afford the mistakes of the past. One of our greatest mistakes has been that of not sufficiently taking into account cultural, linguistic, ethnic, and sociological factors in the background of the people. Nor can we afford the luxury of ancient but erroneous prejudices against the Muslim world.

Perhaps the most damaging mistake of all has been our neglect of Muslims. Hiding behind excuses such as "monolithic Islam," and "Muslims are resistant to the gospel," we have invested less than two percent of North American Protestant missionaries in reaching Muslims. There has been little sowing; there has been little reaping.

The Muslim world, however, has been subjected to the secularizing influences of the West. Past Western domination of present-day independent Muslim nations has not helped the Christian mission, but it did transmit Western ideas and values to a whole generation of Muslim elite.

Some observers felt that these secularizing influences, which have eroded the faith of many in the West in Christ, might well erode Islamic beliefs, too. Little did they suspect the opposite reaction, a revival within Islam in reaction to the secularizing influence of the West.

And yet, in the midst of our miscalculations, prejudices and neglect, I believe God has made this the hour for Muslim evangelism. Surprising stories from Muslim countries tell us of unprecedented events in the evangelization of Muslims. They reveal that the Muslim world is not everywhere resistant. They give hope to the Church to redeem her neglect, to erase her prejudices, and to turn back from former mistakes.

The Ideological Struggle In The Muslim World—God's Opportunity

We have observed an increase in Islamic militancy in recent years. In Algeria, Pakistan, Iran, Iraq, Afanistan, Egypt, Libya and Sudan, militant movements are spreading. Ironically, even though most Muslim nations are the signatories of the U.N.'s Declaration on Human Rights, they interpret that declaration in a distinctive way. They reason that since Islam is a total way of life, the people of a given nation are free under Islam, and since God's law is above human laws and declarations, whatever Islam says is right.

In the midst of this kind of struggle and anxiety, the Christian gospel can be very attractive. Militants struggle

Ishak Ibraham was born in Egypt and has travelled extensively throughout the Middle East.

Used by permission.

Chapter 94

against what they perceive to be a virtual crusade of corrupt Western values. Other leaders are looking for stability. We should be watching for stress points in the ideological struggles of the Muslim world. Rather than pulling our people out of such situations, we need to persevere as witnesses. In Iran, for example, a young believer recently led twenty people to Christ in a period of six months! In America, where many Iranians have been stranded by the present government, there are Iranian converts to Christ in almost every major city. Stress produces openness. Restless hearts in search of meaning and peace are finding their rest in Christ.

The Use of the Qur'an as a Bridge

It is of particular relevance to Muslim evangelism to examine the Scriptures and what they show about culturally-sensitive approaches to other people. Jesus' approach is especially suggestive. He did not come to preach Judaism, nor did he come to preach salvation through the Law. Yet he never attacks the Law. Rather he shows the Jews that the Law was in fact pointing to him.

Is there a similar way in which we can use the Qur'an with Muslims? Before I answer, I must make it clear that in no way do I equate the Qur'an with the Old Testament. I am merely making an analogy. The vast majority of Muslims take the Qur'an to be the direct word of God. We should meet them where they are.

The Qur'an contains some magnificent verses about Jesus. So exhilarating and glorifying are these stories that from its pages we see Jesus as the greatest prophet and in a special way close to God. This could not be called the "gospel in the Qur'an," but it nevertheless gives the Christian an excellent opportunity to talk to Muslims about Christ.

I am personally convinced that the prophet Muhammad was confused in his understanding of who Jesus was. On the one hand he denied his deity and crucifixion. On the other hand, Jesus is called *Kalamet Allah*, "the Word of God" (4:171), and *Rouh Allah*, "the Spirit of God" (2:87). Jesus is significantly quoted as saying, "His (God's) blessing is upon me wherever I go" (19:30). A better translation would be "He (God) has made me blessed wherever I may be." Also, in the Qur'an, Jesus is the only prophet who raises the dead. There is also mention of his miracles and healings and his miraculous virgin birth.

I believe the Qur'an can be used to bring Muslims to the feet of Jesus. Virtually all converts from Islam say that the God they knew distantly in the Qur'an they now know more fully in Jesus Christ. As Jesus and his apostles were able to point to the gospel from the Old Testament, so we can point our Muslim friends to Jesus from the Qur'an.

I know someone will say, "But Muslim teachers and leaders do not believe that Jesus is elevated to deity in the Qur'an." This is true. But back in the first century, neither did the Pharisees and other Jewish religious leaders accept Jesus as the fulfillment of the Old Testament prophecies. Yet the gospel nevertheless spread among those who responded

to Christian preaching. Using the Qur'an as a bridge, we can reach Muslims who have been prepared by God to see Jesus as the one he has sent for their redemption.

The Islamic Monolith: Fact or Fancy?

Underlying our concern for culturally-sensitive models is the awareness of the rich diversity within Islam. Muslims are divided into hundreds of "homogeneous units" that differ from each other geographically, ethically, ideologically, culturally, and often theologically. Iran, for example, cannot be called a monolithic society. Ethnic Persians make up only 48 percent of the population. Eight percent of Iran's population is Kurdish, 19 percent Turkish-speaking, 18 percent tribal Gulani, Baluchi, and Luri, and the remaining are divided among many smaller groups. Religiously, Iran's Muslims are divided into Shias, Sunnis, Bahais, Ismailis, Ahl-i-Haqq, Yezidis, communists, secularists, and both progressive and conservative Muslims. This kind of diversity can be observed in dozens of Muslim countries.

Other examples of surprising diversity are the 20,000 Chinese Muslims who have migrated and presently live in Saudi Arabia, 145,000 Kurds living in Kuwait, and 20,000 Circassian Muslims living in Jordan. The one billion Muslims of the world speak at least five hundred different languages and are subdivided into probably 3,500 different homogeneous units.

Differing Kinds of Soils—A Clue

Just as there were different kinds of soil in Jesus' parable, so we are likely to find many different kinds of Muslim peoples. Unfortunately, some people treat the whole Muslim world as if it were a single type of soil and erroneously attempt to use only one method on it. It is not, as many who are currently involved in a ministry to Muslims can testify.

Indonesia, for example, is the largest Muslim country in the world, with 195 million Muslims (over 80 percent of the population). Yet Indonesia is not an Islamic state. The number of Muslims in Indonesia who are responsive to the Christian faith is quite astounding. The Sundanese of Java, for example, long considered resistant to the gospel, are of varying levels in their commitment to Islam. Some areas are highly orthodox and resistant to Christianity. Others are far less Islamicized. House churches have been successfully planted in nonresistant areas.

The point is that we can find responsive people (good soil) even in the world's most populous Muslim nation. This does not mean we should neglect the unresponsive segment of the population. But it does mean that we should invest our greatest efforts on the fruitful ground and encourage our converts, who appreciate the reasons for resistance to the gospel, to evangelize the less responsive areas. And we must simultaneously experiment with new strategies.

Opportunities for Cross-Cultural Workers of All Nationalities

Sometimes we can learn from our Muslim friends. For example, there is a growing effort by Saudi Arabia and other Middle Eastern countries to strengthen the growth of orthodox Islam within Indonesia. Most of the missionaries in that movement are Cairo-trained Arabs sent to Indonesia to teach the Arabic language and Islamic theology.

A suggested strategy, in this case, would be to send Arab Christians as missionaries to these heavily populated Muslim islands of Indonesia. They, too, can teach Arabic, and preach the gospel. They will be very acceptable because it is prestigious to be an Arabic-speaking person.

Korean Christians are having a great impact upon the Muslims in Saudi Arabia. Saudis expect the adherents of the Greek, Coptic, and Syrian orthodox churches along with the Armenians to be Christians. They expect the Americans, Germans and British to be at least nominally Christians. But what is baffling to them is how the Koreans, having no Christian background or history, can be dedicated believers in Christ. What could be more significant than a Korean mission in Saudi Arabia, in the form of technical advisors, laborers, doctors, engineers, etc.?

In the aftermath of the oil boom and the rumble of war, the Arabian Gulf States have been greatly shaken. Cultural, economic, and sociological change should be viewed very seriously by missionary-minded people. The cultural distortion and disorientation is proving to be fertile ground for Christians with sensitive testimony.

The influx of foreigners to the Gulf area, from India, Pakistan, Iran, Egypt, Lebanon, Europe and America, now exceeds the population of the nationals. Among these people are a sizable number of Christians. In Kuwait, for example, it is estimated that five percent of the population is Christian. In Bahrain, about two percent of the population are Christians; in Qatar, over two percent; in Abu Dhabi, about four percent; in Dubai, a little over three percent. Mind you, the vast majority of these Christians are foreigners. There are very few Christian nationals, if any. The largest Christian community by far in the Arabian Gulf area is the Indian Christian community. It is estimated that over 30 percent of all Indians living in the Arabian Gulf are Christians. This can be, in my judgment, one of the greatest opportunities for Indian missionaries.

Conclusion

One billion Muslims cannot be forgotten by the Church. We must not spare any effort to make the gospel relevant to Islam's various ethnic units.

When Jesus was asked "Which is the greatest commandment of the law?" He replied by quoting Deuteronomy 6:5 "You shall love the Lord your God with all your heart, and with all your soul, and with all your might."

But Jesus added a highly significant clause not found in Deuteronomy, "with all your mind." For full Christian missionary commitment, it is necessary not only to dedicate ourselves to evangelism; but also to think through the most effective way in which we can carry out Christ's command.

The apostle Paul planned and thought out the best way to allow the gospel to make its maximum impact. We need to plan Muslim evangelism with the same thoroughness. Let us adopt the appropriate means to produce a rich harvest in the Muslim world in our day.

Study Questions

1. What are some of the most convincing facts that have led Ishak Ibrahim to believe this is God's hour for Muslim evangelism?

2. Which aspects of strategy in this article are unique to Muslim evangelism?

On Turning Muslim Stumbling Blocks into Stepping Stones

Warren Chastain

"Why should I spend my life reaching Muslims when they are so unresponsive?"

Nate floored me with his question. I found myself unable to give a quick answer to a problem I had mentally wrestled with for two decades! Perhaps it was his Thomas-like, honest doubt which prevented me from delivering a glib, off-the-shelf response. Basically, he was facing the issue: he had a lifetime of service for the Lord before him, but he wondered whether it was wise to sacrifice it for a people as unresponsive as the Muslims. I could easily sympathize with him—and he didn't know half the problem!

Our Stumbling Blocks

Psychological block

The first stumbling block to overcome in Muslim work is in our own mind: the psychological block of our own attitude. Are we willing to lay our lives on the altar? A statement by Bishop Hill captures the heart of the problem:

> Look to the heathen without Christ, and you will find an altar…and may God help you to be a sacrifice.

But who wants that kind of an altar? Most of us prefer the kind where we offer up something else—anything but ourselves! Knives are notoriously hard, sharp, and cold—and made for cutting.

I wondered whether Nate would have asked the question if he were really ready to be a sacrifice. Was his attitude correct? But then I felt a bit guilty about questioning his motives; he was really counting the cost, which the Lord would approve. I had fumbled the answer to Nate's probe, and I was glad. It was better that no answer be given than one that would try to sweeten a knifethrust. It is easier to sing about "laying all on the altar" as long as we ourselves do not end up on the altar. In order that we might share the suffering of Christ, God has engineered the fruit-making process so that it always involves sacrifice. But people invariably seek ways to turn the altar into a stage for seeking applause.

Warren Chastain served as a missionary for 22 years with the Overseas Missionary Fellowship in Thailand, Singapore and Indonesia. He coordinated the translation of the New Testament into the Minangkabau language, planted churches in West Java and Kalimantan, and taught in both government and Christian schools. Chastain currently serves on the staff of the Zwemer Institute, in Fort Wayne, Indiana.

So we must face the question: Are we going into the Lord's service in order to compete for success, to show what we can do, to prove ourselves? If that is our attitude, then Muslim work may be daunting and frustrating. We think of success as what we *achieve* for God, but He values more who we *are*, or what He achieves *in* us. Ultimately we have to be willing to serve on God's terms, whether that means He gives the kind of results we like to see or not.

A bottom-line mentality

Another subjective block which may endanger the Church's commitment to Muslim work is our *bottom-line mentality* which suggests that growth is the only significant value. Westerners tend to quantify, to make scientific distinctions based on observation and mathematical calculation. Current church growth theory stresses harvests, countable converts and specific churches formed. Thus, contemporary missiology provides theoretical and biblical underpinnings to seeking success in terms of evident growth. Church growth ideas have been a great boon to missions as a corrective to older mission practices which tended to fear large harvests as dangerous to good order and sound doctrine.

We need to beware of this *bottom-line mentality* which has also developed as a result of the application to missions of (1) modern business managerial practices, and (2) the scientific methods and findings of the social sciences. If strictly applied, the result will be that missions will decline to invest money and personnel where quantifiable results are not available fairly quickly. This mentality can gain a quasi-biblical justification by arguing that we must be ready to "shake the dust off our feet" when the message is rejected. In terms of evident fruit, it must be admitted that in the past the Christian mission to Islam has largely been a failure in most places. One of the reasons for this failure is the role of violence in Islam. Islam permits the use of social and legal pressures, or even physical violence in both the first stage, of *gaining* members, and in the second stage, of *retaining* members. Muslims prefer peaceful means, but there are innumerable cases of pressures and violence being used against people who "apostacize" from Islam.

But any ideology which must use force to maintain its adherents is admitting its inherent weaknesses. Building the Berlin Wall did not prove the attractiveness of Communism. The "Qur'anic Curtain" does not prove the strength of Islam. The current Muslim fanaticism suggests the wall is crumbling.

Our *bottom-line mentality* could mean the death-knell of Muslim missions. What missionary would choose a life-long uphill struggle, when he could work somewhere else and be able to write to the home churches glowing success stories about the numerous, countable converts? The best answer to a false *bottom-line mentality* is to realize that any line man draws is not the bottom line. The real bottom line is the Day of Judgment when we stand before Christ and give account. This does not mean that we cannot draw any lines at all, but, at best, they are merely "tentative lines." So let us be willing to let God draw the bottom line, lest by our own action, we effectively shut out at least one-sixth of the people of the world from an effective preaching of the gospel.

The second answer to overcoming this *bottom-line mentality* is to fill our minds with a "harvest-mentality." No matter how resistant Islam has been in the past to the gospel, each new generation is a new opportunity for a God who is unwilling to let any man perish. A harvest mentality has two crucial components: (1) a *knowledge* that Jesus declared that this age, in which he has defeated Satan and risen from the dead, is an age of harvest: "Look unto the fields, for they are white already to harvest" (Jn 4:35), and (2) *faith* that the gospel really is the power of God to every one who believes. If we are going to call people to faith, we ourselves must exert our faith in God to be faithful to His promise to win to Himself at least a representative segment from every tribe and tongue on earth (Rev 5:9,10). Satan will not ultimately be victorious in shutting out the gospel from any people group in the world. "Success," in biblical terms, requires the *primary expansion* of the gospel to the ends of the earth to all tribes. The *secondary expansion*, within each tribe so that each individual is won, is not a requirement for successful completion of the missionary task.

Jesus' parable of the sower should fortify our determination. As in the parable, today's sower should not fail to sow seed in the entire field. We must not criticize the sower for throwing seed on ground that is rocky, full of thorns, or shallow. The sower is not blind, or inept; rather he has a passion to bring life out of all kinds of ground. He will not write anything off, even in the rockiest ground. He has faith that the good seed can cling to life in the hardest places and bear a specially precious harvest (Matt 13:3-9).

Muslim Stumbling Blocks

Turning now from psychological stumbling blocks *in our minds*, let us look at a few key stumbling blocks *in the Muslim mind*.

The Incarnation

We should be able to sympathize with the Muslim's offense at the great stumbling block of the incarnation. Did God really have to go to all that trouble (as Christianity affirms) to deal with some "foibles" or weaknesses of man (the Muslim estimate of sin)? Can the human state be so bad that God must take on human form and come to earth to correct it? Was Jesus' trip necessary? It is inconceivable to the Muslim that God could be humbled. And to suggest that God must in some way sacrifice Himself is incomprehensible.

Only the Holy Spirit can turn this stumbling block into a stepping stone. But to a thoughtful Muslim the very unthinkability of the incarnation may hint at its truth. Surely no human mind would dream up such a scheme—and then to glory in it and to make it the foundation of salvation is too grand a concept for some religious hucksters to conceive and peddle. We might also suggest that there is no evidence that God loves man at all if the sacrifice of the incarnation is false. This is the kind of love that is worthy of an infinite God. In fact, if God loves at all, it must be a vast infinite love which only the incarnation and its culmination—the Cross—can demonstrate. Another way to encourage the Muslim to believe the incarnation, might be to turn his thinking to a problem which Islam has, one which is similar, if not even harder to accept.

Revelation

The Muslim concept of *revelation* seeks to protect God's Word from any taint of man's influence. Like the goddess Diana of the Eph-

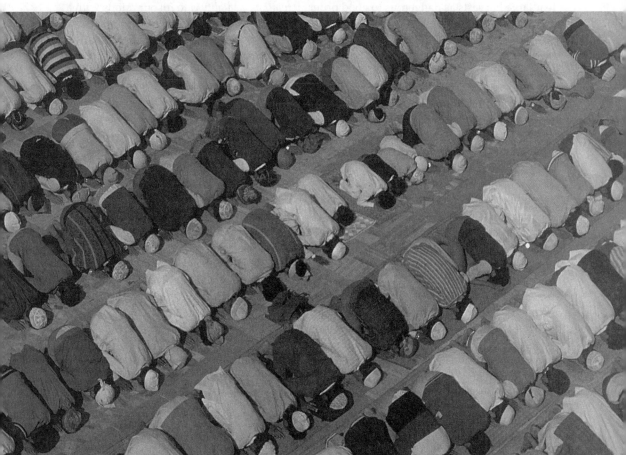

esians, the Qur'an is seen as coming down out of heaven direct to man untouched by human hands. This view seems more honoring to God's revelation, and it makes a more defensible view, avoiding the complexities of the Christian position which has God active within history, and bringing a revelation out of the fire and tribulation of man's experiences.

Many Muslims are unaware of many of the problems inherent within their own theological system. In their zeal to guard the purity and authority of the Word of God, Muslims have conceived of revelation as being a kind of "incarnation" of an attribute of God, that is, God's speech. Since God and his speech must be eternal; the Qur'an must also be eternal. It is ironic that the holy book which denies the incarnation of Christ is itself supposed to be an incarnation of the speech of God. If it is within the power of God to set apart one of his own attributes and send it down to earth in the form of a book, surely it is not impossible for God to reveal His person in the form of a person who comes to earth. It is not a case of a man being made into a god by the Church, but rather God having the power to use the human body which He created in the first place. What we can do to overcome this stumbling block is to shift the focus of discussion to the person of Christ rather than to a battle of books or concepts of revelation.

The Trinity

Another major stumbling block in the mind of the Muslim is his fixation on the concept of the oneness of God. Impatient with the subtleties of the Trinity, the Muslim believes we have some kind of tritheism. It will not do to answer his 1+1+1=3 logic with an evasive 1 x 1 x 1=1. A better answer might use the infinity symbol as in $\infty + \infty + \infty = \infty$, but even this is more philosophical than biblical in flavor. The basic problem with Muslim thought is that it proposes mathematical oneness instead of the organic oneness of life; an abstract oneness instead of the composite oneness of personality; a cold, conceptual solitariness, instead of a vital, friendly, loving Father.

In their zeal to fight polytheism, Muslims have opted for this chilling, impersonal mystery—the "Unknown God." For the Christian to overcome this stumbling block, he must get beyond the mathematics of God to the character of God. We do not worship the number "one" written large; we need to personally know a Father who relates to man. Although the Trinity is unique so that every illustration drawn from nature has shortcomings, we can suggest that in God's creation as one rises from the lower forms of life to the higher we encounter a progression away from simple oneness to a complexity of unity. Each man is one, but he is more complex than a one-celled bacterium. Is it glorifying to God to proclaim Him to have a simple mathematical oneness akin to a germ? If the oneness of man involves spiritual aspects as well as physical, surely the oneness of God is not diminished by seeing complexity within that oneness. The mind of man makes a complex one God a possibility; the heart of man makes it a necessity. The Muslim belief in the Qur'an and the Christian belief in Jesus show they both agree that a bridging of the gap between God and man is necessary. We may suggest that if God is a person, then only a person can reveal a person adequately. If we have only a book then we can know only *about* God, but God himself remains unknown. Even though theological problems like the Trinity and the deity of Christ may be unavoidable, it is better to shift away from those at the beginning to consider a basic issue: how people can be saved.

The Cross

Muslims do not have clearly-defined theology on salvation. A spectrum of answers may be given to the question, "How is a person saved?" The more liberal may say as long as a person believes in one God he can hope for eventual salvation. A traditionalist may demand that a person believe in Muhammad as the preeminent prophet as well as in the one God for salvation. A rigorist may demand godly living in addition to true belief in Allah and his prophet. A fatalist may shrug that no one can ever be sure while another may bring in some kind of purgatory to pay for sins.

The person of Christ is the most attractive means of turning Muslim stumbling blocks into stepping stones. The love of God is revealed in the idea of sacrifice which has been maintained in Islam by a yearly festival where an animal is offered in the Eid sacrifice. We can show from the books of Moses that from the beginning all the prophets acknowledged that sacrifice was the God-ordained way of being reconciled with God. From the days of Adam and Noah, we see God accepting sacrifice. Abraham, by God's direction, was willing to offer up his son, so essential was the sacrifice principle. If the Muslim wishes to assert that it was Ishmael, not Isaac, we may bypass a debate and say whichever one was offered, still it is the principle of sacrifice that is undeniable. This brings together the three ideas of salvation, sacrifice, and Jesus as the focus of our discussion, rather than some theological abstractions. This will bring us to the one stumbling stone—the Cross—which will in some way always retain its character as a stumbling stone, even to the Christian, while at the same time becoming a stepping stone to salvation.

We have considered only a few of the theological booby-traps Satan has planted in Islam. The wise Christian witness will study how to defuse each Muslim weapon so that any criticism can be turned positively to the person of Christ and His salvation. By this tactic we cooperate with the God who delights to turn Satan's instruments of death into instruments that bring life. God's weapons are crosses, empty tombs, and willing witnesses.

But missionaries may deny the Cross in their own way as well. If we preach a message of ultimate sacrifice but deliver it through a lifestyle which denies sacrifice, we make void our own message. If we preach a message of love in an unloving way, our hearers will doubt that we believe it ourselves. We may thus turn a stepping stone back into a stumbling block.

Study Questions

1. How does Chastain suggest we develop a "harvest" mentality?

2. Why does Chastain think the person of Christ is the most attractive means of turning Muslim stumbling blocks into stepping stones?

Going Too Far?

Phil Parshall

Recently I was speaking to a group of young people who are highly motivated about Muslim evangelism. They excitedly told me of a missionary who had shared a "new" *modus operandi* for winning the Sons of Ishmael to Christ. This strategy centers around the Christian evangelist declaring himself to be a Muslim. He then participates in the *salat* or official Islamic prayers within the mosque. The missionary illustrated the concept by mentioning two Asian Christians who have recently undergone legal procedures to officially become Muslims. This was done to become a Muslim to Muslims in order to win Muslims to Christ.

Actually taking on a Muslim identity and praying in the mosque is not a new strategy. But legally becoming a Muslim definitely moves the missionary enterprise into uncharted territory. I address this issue with a sense of deep concern.

Contextualization Continuum

John Travis (a pseudonym) a long-term missionary among Muslims in Asia, has put us in his debt by formulating a simple categorization for stages of contextualization within Islamic outreach. He defines his six C's as "Cross-Cultural Church-Planting Spectrums." (see pages 658-9)

Some years ago, a well-known professor of Islam alluded to my belief that Muslim converts could and should remain in the mosque following conversion. Quickly I corrected him, stating that I have never held that position, either in my speaking or writing. My book *Beyond the Mosque* deals extensively with the issue of why, when and how a convert must disassociate himself or herself from the mosque (though not from Muslim community *per se*).

I do, however, make room for a transitional period wherein the new believer, while maturing in his adopted faith, slowly pulls back from mosque attendance. Too sudden of a departure may spark intense antagonism and subsequent alienation. See 2 Kings 5 for an interesting insight on how Elisha responded to the new convert, Naaman, who brought up the subject of his ongoing presence in the heathen temple of Rimmon.

The diagram on the next page helps place in linear perspective the C1 to C5 categories. I submit that C1 starts at low contextualization and works up incrementally to C4 at the high end. All within this sector is legitimate, provided it is constantly cross-referenced and subordinated to biblical truth.

Phil Parshall has served among Muslims in Asia for 37 years and is the author of six books on Christian ministry among Muslims. He has a D.Miss. from Fuller Theological Seminary and fellowships from Harvard and Yale University.

Used by permission from *Evangelical Missions Quarterly*, 34:3 (October 1998), published by EMIS, P.O. Box 794, Wheaton, IL 60189. Originally titled "DANGER! New Directions in Contextualization."

Low ————————————— High | Low ————————————————— High
     Contextualization   *Syncretism*

The Great Divide

C5 can be placed anywhere along the syncretism spectrum, depending on how each issue is presented to and understood by the Muslim community. Personally, I can only put conversion (or reconversion) to official Islam as high syncretism, regardless of motivation.

When, in 1975, our team of missionaries commenced a C4 strategy (highly contextualized, but believers are no longer seen as Muslims by the Muslim community) in an Asian Muslim country, we faced considerable opposition. One long term Christian worker in an Islamic land told me basically, "You are on a dangerous slide. Next you will be denying the cross." Well, 23 years later, we are still at C4 and still preaching the cross. And the Lord has greatly honored our efforts in that country.

But now I am the one to protest the "slide," not by our team, but by others who are ministering in various parts of the Muslim world. This slide is incremental and can be insidiously deceptive, especially when led by people of highest motivation. Now, it seems to me, we need to bring these issues before our theologians, missiologists, and administrators. Let us critique them before we suddenly find that we have arrived at a point which is indisputably sub-Christian.

A Ministry Experiment

We do have help. In a very limited and remote geographical area in Asia, a C5 experiment ("Messianic Muslims" who follow Isa (Jesus) the Messiah and are accepted by Muslims as Muslims) has been ongoing for many years. This ministry provides us with a pretty solid baseline for evaluation, even though it has experienced significant personnel changes over the years.

Recently, researchers visited Islampur* to examine the C5 movement there. Researchers found that this movement numbers in the thousands.

On one hand, the findings are very encouraging. Nearly all of the key people interviewed indicated a very strong value on reading the New Testament and meeting regularly for Christian worship. Most would say that Allah loves and forgives them because Jesus died for them. They pray to Jesus for forgiveness. Virtually all believe that Jesus is the only Savior, and is able to save people from evil spirits.

On the other hand, nearly all say there are four heavenly books, i.e., Torah, Zabur, Injil, and Qur'an (This is standard Muslim belief, i.e., Law, Prophets, Gospels, and Qur'an) of which the Qur'an is the greatest. Nearly half continue to go to the traditional mosque on Friday where they participate in the standard Islamic prayers which affirm Muhammad as a prophet of God. And nearly half do not affirm the Trinity.

Contextualization or syncretism?

What do we have here? Contextualization or syncretism? Is this a model to follow or avoid? Certainly there is an openness and potential here that is expansive and exciting. But whereas a C5 advocate is happy to keep it all within an Islamic religious environment, I am not.

Can the Mosque be Redeemed?

The mosque is pregnant with Islamic theology. There, Muhammad is affirmed as a prophet of God and the divinity of Christ is consistently denied. Uniquely Muslim prayers *(salat)* are ritually performed as in no other religion. These prayers are as sacramental to Muslims as is partaking of the Lord's Supper for Christians. How would we feel if a Muslim attended (or even joined) our evangelical church and partook of communion… all with a view to becoming an "insider?" This accomplished, he then begins to promote Islam and actually win our parishioners over to his religious persuasion.

Even C4 is open to a Muslim charge of deceit. But I disagree and see it as a proper level of indigenization. We have not become a "fifth column" within the mosque, seeking to undermine its precepts and practices. C5, to me, seems to do just that and open us to the charge of unethical and sub-Christian activity.

In my former country of ministry, our team had an agreement that none of us would go into a mosque and engage in the Islamic prayers. One of our group, however, wanted to secretly "experiment" with saying the *salat*. One Friday he traveled to a remote village and became friendly with the Muslims there. Harry* expressed his desire to learn how to perform the rituals and forms of the prayers.

The Muslim leaders were quite excited to see that a foreigner wanted to learn about Islam. They gave Harry the necessary instruction. At 1 p.m. our missionary was found in the front row of the mosque going through all the bowing and prostrations of the *salat*. No matter that he was silently praying to Jesus. No one knew.

After worship, the Muslim villagers all came up to Harry and congratulated him on becoming a Muslim. Embarrassed, Harry explained that he was a follower of *Isa* (Jesus) and that he just wanted to learn about Islam. Immediately, upon hearing these words, the crowd became very angry.

Harry was accused of destroying the sanctity of the mosque. Someone yelled that he should be killed. A riot was about to break out.

The local imam sought to pacify the crowd by admitting that he had mistakenly taught the foreigner how to do the prayers. He asked forgiveness from his fellow Muslims. it was then decided that Harry should leave that village immediately and never return.

Another experience relates to Bob,* a very intelligent, productive, and spiritually oriented missionary to Muslims. We met to-

gether at a conference and exchanged letters and at least one cassette tape over several years. My great concern was that he openly and dogmatically affirmed Muhammad as a prophet of God. To me, Bob had crossed the line into syncretism. Perhaps his motives were pure, but this progression of identification with Muslims had gone much too far. Today Bob is out of the ministry and is divorced from his wife.

Guidelines

In 1979, I wrote the following guidelines to help us avoid syncretism while engaged in Muslim evangelism. Nineteen years later, I reaffirm (and reemphasize) these principles.

1. We must be acquainted with biblical teaching on the subject of syncretism. New Testament passages on the uniqueness of Christ should be carefully observed.
2. Islam as a religion and culture must be studied in depth.
3. An open approach is desired. Careful experimentation in contextualization need not lead to syncretism as long as one is aware of all the dangers.
4. Contextualization needs constant monitoring and analysis. What are the people really thinking? What does the contextualized communication convey?

What do specific forms trigger in the mind of the new convert? Is there progress in the grasp of biblical truth? Are the people becoming demonstrably more spiritual?

5. Cross-cultural communicators must beware of presenting a gospel which has been syncretized with Western culture. The accretions to Christianity that have built up over the centuries as a result of the West's being the hub of Christianity should be avoided as far as possible.

Conclusion

No, I am not maligning the motivation of godly missionaries who are practicing and promoting C5 as an appropriate strategy to win Muslims to Christ. Several of these Christian workers are my friends. They long to see a breakthrough in Muslim evangelism. Their personal integrity is unquestioned.

But, yes, I am apprehensive. Where does all this lead us? In that earlier mentioned conference, one young Muslim convert came up to me and said he had followed the lead

The C1 to C6 Spectrum   *John Travis**

A Practical Tool for Defining Six Types of "Christ-centered Communities" ("C") found in the Muslim Context

The C1-C6 Spectrum compares and contrasts types of "Christ-centered communities (groups of believers in Christ) found in the Muslim world. The six types in the spectrum are differentiated by language, culture, worship forms, degree of freedom to worship with others, and religious identity. All worship Jesus as Lord and core elements of the gospel are the same from group to group. The spectrum attempts to address the enormous diversity which exists throughout the Muslim world in terms of ethnicity, history, traditions, language, culture, and in some cases, theology.

The diversity means that myriad approaches are needed to successfully share the gospel and plant Christ-centered communities among the world's 1 billion followers of Islam. The purpose of the spectrum is to assist church planters and Muslim background believers to ascertain which type of Christ-centered communities may draw the most people from the target group to Christ and best fit in a given context. All of these six types are presently found in some part of the Muslim world.

C1—Traditional Church Using Outsider** Language

May be Orthodox, Catholic, or Protestant. Some predate Islam. Thousands of C1 churches are found in Muslim lands today. Many reflect Western culture. A huge cultural chasm often exists between the church and the surrounding Muslim community. Some Muslim background believers may be found in C1 churches. C1 believers call themselves "Christians."

C2—Traditional Church Using Insider** Language

Essentially the same as C1 except for language. Though insider language is used, religious vocabulary is probably non-Islamic (distinctively "Christian"). The cultural gap between Muslims and C2 is still large. Often more Muslim background believers are found in C2 than C1. The majority of churches located in the Muslim world today are C1 or C2. C2 believers call themselves "Christians."

C3—Contextualized Christ-centered Communities Using Insider Language and Religiously Neutral Insider Cultural Forms

Religiously neutral forms may include folk music, ethnic dress, artwork, etc. Islamic elements (where present) are "filtered out" so as to use purely "cultural" forms. The aim is to reduce foreignness of the gospel and the church by contextualizing to biblically permissible cultural forms. May meet in a church building or more religiously neutral location. C3 congregations are comprised of a majority of Muslim background believers. C3 believers call themselves "Christians."

of the missionary speaker. He went in the local mosque and told the imam that he is a Muslim and wanted to learn more of Islam. His secret goal was to build a relationship with the imam. I asked Abdul* how he felt about what he did. With a look of pain and sadness, he replied that he felt very badly about it and would not do it again.

Before C5 people broadly propagate this strategy to young, impressionable minds who are excited about the "new" and "untried," I urge them to more fully consider both the Islamic charge of deception as well as the long-term consequences of their actions. I am convinced that C5 missionaries are on very shaky theological and missiological ground.

Let's bring the subject out in the open and dialogue together.

C4—Contextualized Christ-centered Communities Using Insider Language and Biblically Permissible Cultural and Islamic Forms

Similar to C3, however, biblically permissible Islamic forms and practices are also utilized (e.g. praying with raised hands, keeping the fast, avoiding pork, alcohol, and dogs as pets, using Islamic terms, dress, etc.). C1 and C2 forms avoided. Meetings not held in church buildings. C4 communities comprised almost entirely of Muslim background believers. C4 believers, though highly contextualized, are usually not seen as Muslim by the Muslim community. C4 believers identify themselves as "followers of Isa the Messiah" (or something similar).

C5—Christ-centered Communities of "Messianic Muslims" Who Have Accepted Jesus as Lord and Savior

C5 believers remain legally and socially within the community of Islam. Somewhat similar to the Messianic Jewish movement, aspects of Islamic theology which are incompatible with the Bible are rejected, or reinterpreted if possible. Participation in corporate Islamic worship varies from person to person and group to group. C5 believers meet regularly with other C5 believers and share their faith with unsaved Muslims. Unsaved Muslims may see C5 believers as theologically deviant and may eventually expel them from the community of Islam. Where entire villages accept Christ, C5 may result in "Messianic mosques." C5 believers are viewed as Muslims by the Muslim community and refer to themselves as Muslims who follow Isa the Messiah.

C6—Small Christ-centered Communities of Secret/Underground Believers

Similar to persecuted believers suffering under totalitarian regimes. Due to fear, isolation, or threat of extreme governmental/community legal action or retaliation (including capital punishment), C6 believers worship Christ secretly (individually or perhaps infrequently in small clusters). Many come to Christ through dreams, visions, miracles, radio broadcasts, tracts, Christian witness while abroad, or reading the Bible on their own initiative. C6 (as opposed to C5) believers are usually silent about their faith. C6 is not ideal; God desires his people to witness and have regular fellowship (Heb 10:25). Nonetheless C6 believers are part of our family in Christ. Though God may call some to a life of suffering, imprisonment, or martyrdom, He may be pleased to have some worship Him in secret, at least for a time. C6 believers are perceived as Muslims by the Muslim community and identify themselves as Muslims.

*   A pseudonym.
** "Insider" pertains to the local Muslim population; "outsider" pertains to the local non-Muslim population.
John Travis (a pseudonym) has been involved in planting congregations among Muslims in Asia for the past 12 years. He is currently working on a Ph.D. through an American university. Used by permission from "The C1 to C6 Spectrum," *Evangelical Missions Quarterly*, 34:3 (October 1998), published by EMIS, P.O. Box 794, Wheaton, IL 60189.

Must all Muslims Leave "Islam" to Follow Jesus?

John Travis

For the past decade, my family and I have lived in a close-knit Muslim neighborhood in Asia. My daughter, who loves our neighbors dearly, asked one day, "Daddy, can a Muslim go to heaven?" I responded with an Acts 15:11-type "yes": "If a Muslim has accepted Isa (Jesus) the Messiah as Savior and Lord, he or she is saved, just as we are." We affirmed that people are saved by faith in Christ, not by religious affiliation. Muslim followers of Christ (i.e. C5 believers) are our brothers and sisters in the Lord, even though they do not change religions.

Can a Muslim truly accept Jesus as Savior and Lord, thereby rejecting some elements of normal Islamic theology, and yet (for the sake of the lost) remain in his or her family and religious community? Due to the extreme importance Islam places on community, its nearly universal disdain for those who have become "traitors" by joining Christianity, and our desire to see precious Muslims come to Christ, finding the answer to this question is essential. I agree with Dr. Parshall; it is time for missiologists, theologians, and others, especially those who work face-to-face with Muslims, to seriously seek God's will over this C5 issue.

The Islampur case study

The results indicate that nearly all of the leaders of this movement hold firmly to biblical teachings about the identity and work of Christ. Not only is their basic theology solid, they are active in their faith through prayer, scripture reading and listening, and coming together for worship. The fact that over half understand the Trinity well enough to affirm God as Father, Son, and Holy Spirit is actually astounding considering it would be considered apostasy by most Muslims! How many American pastors would be delighted to find the same vitality among their own congregations?

Regarding the retention of some Islamic practice and belief, we should not be surprised that nearly half feel close to God when hearing the Qur'an read. Since they don't understand Arabic, it may be the familiar melodious chanting that touches their hearts. (Some C4 and C5 believers where I work sing a beautiful worship song which sounds a great deal like Muslim chanting.) It is also not surprising that half continue to worship in the mosque in addition to attending weekly C5 gatherings. This practice is reminiscent of the early Jewish followers of Christ meeting both in the temple

John Travis (a pseudonym) has been involved in planting congregations among Muslims in Asia for the past 12 years. He is currently working on a Ph.D. through an American university.

Used by permission from "Must all Muslims leave 'Islam' to follow Jesus?," *Evangelical Missions Quarterly*, 34:3 (October 1998), published by EMIS, P.O. Box 794, Wheaton, IL 60189.

and in homes (with the old community and the new). One village C5 group I know prays at the mosque at noon on Friday, then meets afterwards in a home for Bible study and prayer led by "Achmad" (a pseudonym), a C4 pastor and former Muslim teacher.

In this case these believers actually find mosque gatherings shallow and lifeless, and, for a time, stopped attending. Their absence greatly threatened the mosque leader and he tried to stamp out their Friday afternoon meetings. Achmad suggested they go back to the mosque, meaningless as it was for them. The imam's face was saved and the new believers have continued to meet for over a year. New Muslim inquirers (even two Islamic teachers) have attended.

Concerning the high regard for the Qur'an among Islampur believers, an apologetic response concerning the Qur'an must be developed whereby the truth in it can be affirmed (especially for purposes of a bridge for witness), yet it is not put on equal (or superior!) status to the Injil. Fortunately, until such an apologetic is developed, the Islampur believers are regularly reading the Injil rather than the Qur'an. Returning to the case of my friend Achmad, he holds evening "Holy Book reading sessions" in his home. He often opens by reading a Qur'anic passage in a respectful manner, then proceeds to the heart of the evening reading from the Torah, Zabur, and Injil (the Bible).

Unsaved Muslims are more likely to attend Bible reading sessions when they also contain some Arabic Qur'anic reading. Achmad is careful to read Qur'anic passages which do not conflict with the Bible.

Three final points concerning the Islampur study: First, these C5 Christ-centered communities consist entirely of new believers from a highly resistant people group. They are very much in process, and their struggles are not unlike what many first century congregations faced. We must pray that the same Holy Spirit whom Paul so relied upon to guide and purify those first groups of believers is active as well in these new Islampur groups.

Second, to attain a more accurate perspective, we need to assess the quality of the new believers' lives in Christ and not just their theology. Is the fruit of the Spirit evident and do they now show a deeper love for others?

Scripture is clear that by qualities such as these we will recognize true followers of Christ (Matt. 7:20, John 13:35).

Last, were it not for the C5 approach used in this church-planting ministry, would there be these many thousands of new believers to analyze in the first place?

C5 missionaries (Christians becoming Muslims to reach Muslims)

This perhaps is Dr. Parshall's greatest concern, and overall I agree. Christians becoming Muslims to reach Muslims (i.e. C5 Missionaries) is a step beyond simply urging new believers to remain in the religious community of their birth (i.e. C5 believers) for the sake of their unsaved family and friends. In our current situation I have counseled my own Christian background co-workers, especially the expatriates, to take on a C4 expression of faith, and not enter Islam to reach Muslims. Yet I could imagine that in some instances God may call uniquely gifted, well-prepared individuals, whose ministries are firmly backed by prayer, to C5 outreach and religious identity. These C5 missionaries would be Muslims in the literal Arabic sense of the word (i.e. "one submitted to God") and their theology would, of course, differ from standard Muslim theology at a number of key points. They would have to be ready for persecution, and it would be best if these believers were of Muslim background.

If over time they made their beliefs clear, and the surrounding Muslim community chose to allow them to stay, should we not praise God for the opportunity they have to share the Good News in a place few would dare to tread? It would appear that neither "Abdul," the Muslim convert, nor "Harry," the Western missionary, were called and prepared for this kind of work.

Regarding how Muslims would "feel" about such an approach, I think the question is a bit irrelevant. The majority of Muslims that I have talked to object to any activity they perceive as an attempt to attract Muslims to Christianity. However, the C5 approach, which communicates the message of salvation in Christ without the intent to persuade Muslims to "change their religion," might in fact be the one most appreciated by Muslims. By separating the gospel from the myriad of legal, social, and cultural issues implied in changing religious camps, a more straightforward, less encumbered message can be shared and (we hope) embraced. On the question of how Christians would feel if Muslims entered a church with the purpose of winning converts to Islam, I personally would not be fearful. Indeed, for a variety of reasons, non-Christians often grace the doors of churches, and many in the process come to Christ!

Reinterpreting Muhammad and the Qur'an

Can individuals be a part of the community of Islam and not affirm standard Muslim theology? Yes, so long as they remain silent about their unorthodox beliefs. Indeed, there are millions of "cultural Muslims" who have divergent beliefs or know virtually nothing about Islam, yet who, because of birth and the fact they have not formally left the fold, are seen as a part of the community of Islam. However the goal of C5 believers (unlike C6 believers) is not to remain silent about their faith, but rather to be a witness for Christ. As they share, eventually the issue of the prophethood of Muhammad and the inerrancy of the Qur'an will arise. A follower of Jesus cannot affirm all that is commonly taught about the Qur'an and Muhammad.

Certain aspects of the role of Muhammad and the Qur'an must be reinterpreted. This will perhaps be the most challenging task of C5; to not do so will in time cause these believers to move toward C4 (contextualized, yet not Muslim) or C6 (underground/silent believers). Reinterpretation goes far beyond the scope of this brief article and would require the input of Muslim leaders who have put their faith in Christ. A tremendous starting point toward reinterpretation is found in Accad's excellent book *Building Bridges (1997)*. As an Arab scholar and pastor, he suggests ways that Muhammad, the Qur'an, and Qur'anic verses which seem to deny the crucifixion can be reinterpreted *(pp. 34-46; 138-141)*. He cites, as well, examples of Muslims who have successfully remained in the community of Islam after accepting Christ, some referring to themselves as "Muslims who are truly surrendered to God through the sacrifice of Messiah Isa" *(p. 35)*.

Guidelines for avoiding syncretism in a C5 movement

The idea of Muslim followers of Jesus or messianic mosques has been suggested by a number of key missiologists (see Winter, 1981; Kraft, 1979; Conn, 1979; Woodberry, 1989). We do need guidelines, however, so that a C5 expression of faith does not slip into a harmful syncretism. Those working with new believers should emphasize at least the following in the discipleship process:

1. Jesus is Lord and Savior; there is no salvation outside of him.
2. New believers are baptized, meet regularly with other believers (this may need to be done with great discretion), and take communion.
3. New believers study the Injil (and Torah plus Zabur if available).
4. New believers renounce and are delivered from occultism and harmful folk Islamic practices (i.e. shamanism, prayers to saints, use of charms, curses, incantations, etc.).
5. Muslim practices and traditions (e.g. fasting, alms, circumcision, attending the mosque, wearing the head covering, refraining from pork and alcohol, etc.) are done as expressions of love for God and/or respect for neighbors, rather than as acts necessary to receive forgiveness of sins.
6. The Qur'an, Muhammad, and traditional Muslim theology are examined, judged, and reinterpreted (where necessary) in light of biblical truth. Biblically acceptable Muslim beliefs and practices are maintained, others are modified, some must be rejected.
7. New believers show evidence of the new birth and growth in grace (e.g. the fruit of the Spirit, increased love, etc.) and a desire to reach the lost (e.g. verbal witness and intercession).

We must bear in mind that C5 believers, at some point, may be expelled from the community of Islam. C5 may only be transitional, as Dr. Parshall suggests. Yet, would it not be much better for Muslim followers of Jesus to share the Good News over months or years with fellow Muslims who may eventually expel them, than for these new believers to leave their families and community by their own choice, being seen as traitors by those whom they love?

Conclusion

If perhaps the single greatest hindrance to seeing Muslims come to faith in Christ is not a theological one (i.e. accepting Jesus as Lord) but rather one of culture and religious identity (i.e. having to leave the community of Islam), it seems that for the sake of God's kingdom much of our missiological energy should be devoted to seeking a path whereby Muslims can remain Muslims, yet live as true followers of the Lord Jesus. The issues involved in such an approach are thorny and complex and require consideration from a number of different disciplines (e.g. church history, Islamics, theology, missiology). A consultation comprised primarily of people involved in sharing Christ with Muslims, which would grapple with the implications of C5, would be beneficial. Any type of ministry undertaken in the Muslim world involves great risk. But for the sake of millions of souls bound for a Christless eternity, and for the glory of God, the risks, efforts, and tensions are worth the price.

References

Accad, Fouad Elias. *Building Bridges: Christianity and Islam* (Colorado Springs, CO.: Navpress, 1997).

Conn, Harvey. "The Muslim Convert and His Culture" in *The Gospel and Islam*. Don McCurry, ed. (MARC, 1979), pp. 61-77.

Kraft, Charles It., "Dynamic Equivalence Churches in Muslim Society" in *The Gospel and Islam*. Don McCurry, ed. (Monrovia, Calif.: MARC, 1979), pp. 78-92.

Winter, Ralph and David Frazier. "World Missions Survey" in *Perspectives on the World Christian Movement*. Steve Hawthorne and Ralph Winter, eds. (Pasadena, CA.: William Carey Library, 1981), pp. 198-201. See also Chapter 52 of this book.

Woodberry, J. Dudley. "Contextualization Among Muslims: Reusing Common Pillars" in *The Word Among Us*. Dean S. Gilliland, ed. (Word Publishing: Dallas, Tex., 1989), pp. 282-312.

Study Questions

1. Does "Travis" feel that the greatest hindrance to faith in Christ among Muslims is a theological one or that of cultural identity?

2. What does the author suggest as guidelines for treatment of the Qur'an and of Muhammed for Muslim followers of Jesus?

3. What difference is there between C5 missionary and a C5 movement in terms of credibility with Muslim culture, fidelity to Biblical faith, or viability of church planting?

Context is Critical:

A Response to Phil Parshall's "Going Too Far"

Dean S. Gilliland

Dean S. Gilliland is Professor of Contextual Theology and African Studies at the School of World Mission, Fuller Theological Seminary. Previously he served as a missionary to Nigeria for 21 years.

Used by permission from "Context is critical in 'Islampur' case," *Evangelical Missions Quarterly*, 34:3 (October 1998), published by EMIS, P.O. Box 794, Wheaton, IL 60189.

The "Islampur" study was part of a larger research project designed to compare and test various models for evangelizing Muslims. The particular report Phil Parshall refers to did not endorse or condemn but provided case studies in different situations for whatever light they might shed on approaches to Muslims in various communities.

Phil Parshall's article mentions the "Islampur" case. More needs to be said in fairness to the research. The researcher himself concluded the data presentation with careful words: "Whether in fact a person can be an authentic follower of Jesus and still remain within the fold of Islam raises strong opinions and emotions on many sides…. It is, of course, possible that those who endorse radical contextualization of the gospel within Islam are wrong." He also wrote, however, that after looking at the entire report, "It does seem that there has been a real work of God among the (name withheld) Muslims."

Little is known from Phil's article about the internal problems caused by leaders who took these followers of Jesus in two directions, causing, finally, a near abandonment of the teaching that should have been continuing. In the background are many painful factors which added to the burden of these simple people who say they believe in and follow Jesus. At one point, the names of key believers in the movement were turned over to the government. Despite internal and external problems, these clusters of followers were able to testify honestly and without coaching to what Jesus, the Bible, the power of the gospel, and other Jesus-people mean to them.

While the context and contextualization are what this case is all about, too often conclusions about what is right or wrong are generalized without attention to a particular case. A practicable and fitting approach in one place will probably not be appropriate somewhere else. For example, the case behind Parshall's example does not fit the research's second case, which was done in Nigeria.

Some 45 million Muslims live in Nigeria. The big difference with "Islampur" is that Nigeria also has 45–50 million people who call themselves Christians. There is no way that Muslims who convert to Jesus Christ in Nigeria would ever call themselves Muslims.

In fact, it was a rather well-known esoteric model of evangelizing Muslims in northern Nigeria that attracted the research in the first place. The ministry was not integrated with the churches and was supposedly producing believers who were suffering intensely for their faith. Evangelical churches had come to disown the movement because of the secrecy and clandestine style of the leaders. The movement has now collapsed, even though it had received a lot of private publicity and support outside of Nigeria.

Therefore, the Nigeria situation is *totally different from* the one in "Islampur." In Nigeria the churches are almost apostolic in their boldness before and among Muslims. Form contextualization (except in the far north) is seen as a kind of imitation of the Muslim way and therefore is looked upon as neither necessary nor desirable. Christian-Muslim confrontation saturates the life of Nigerian people—socially, politically, and religiously.

The Parshall article discusses the appropriateness of an approach in a particular Asian context. The size and strength comparison between Muslims and Christians in "Islampur" is like the elephant to the fly, as it were.

Obviously, this little flock that has turned to follow Jesus—with members who pray to Jesus for forgiveness, who believe that Jesus died for them, and who say he is the only Savior—has to be taken very seriously. Even though they call themselves Muslims, they are not like other Muslims.

The words of Jesus are poignant and sobering: I have other sheep that are not of this fold; I must bring them also and they will heed my voice. So there shall be one flock, one shepherd (John 10:16)." I have mentioned the need for the passage of time because, like any other movement, this one is in process. In the meantime, we should never forget that the Holy Spirit does not abandon his Word or his people. While conversations about the dangers of syncretism are well-intended, God goes on doing his work through his Holy Spirit, to bless and honor truth and to remove his blessing from error.

I recall discussions I had with African pastors about the implications of the Apostle Paul baptizing the Philippian jailer and his family immediately, coming as they did straight out of "paganism." It was an emotional and a highly charged situation, with no church except, perhaps, some women of Lydia's household who had also been baptized quickly and privately. Then, after a confrontation with the police, Paul left them for Thessalonica (Acts 16). How much hope would there seem to have been for isolated converts in a place like Philippi? Still, the church developed there.

I am not saying the situation in "Islampur" is the same as in Philippi, but the Holy Spirit is still at work in poorly informed, sometimes misguided believers. Beyond any human comprehension, the Spirit faithfully guides those who seek the truth. The Good Shepherd said, "I know my own and my own know me" (John 10:14). The church has always been a mystery (Eph 3:3,9), but it is God's Church, and in the end God will make the judgment.

Study Questions

1. On what can new gatherings of believers base their trust to avoid syncretism?

2. Can an effective strategy for planting an indigenous church among Muslims be easily transferred to another people group?

Going Far Enough

Taking Some Tips From The Historical Record

Ralph D. Winter

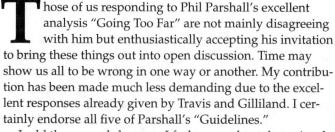

After serving ten years as a missionary among Mayan Indians in the highlands of Guatemala, Ralph D. Winter was called to be a Professor of Missions at the School of World Mission at Fuller Theological Seminary. Ten years later he and his wife, Roberta, founded a mission society called the Frontier Mission Fellowship (FMF) in Pasadena, California. This in turn spawned the U.S. Center for World Mission and the William Carey International University, both of which serve other missions working at the frontiers of mission. He is the General Director of the Frontier Mission Fellowship. See expanded biographical sketch at the end of the book.

Those of us responding to Phil Parshall's excellent analysis "Going Too Far" are not mainly disagreeing with him but enthusiastically accepting his invitation to bring these things out into open discussion. Time may show us all to be wrong in one way or another. My contribution has been made much less demanding due to the excellent responses already given by Travis and Gilliland. I certainly endorse all five of Parshall's "Guidelines."

I add these words because I feel we need to take seriously the wealth of experiences and events during over 1,000 years since Muhammed's death, and we need to realize the most important result of all this may be a better understanding of the New Testament!

In the first place, that 1,000+ year dynamic record involves deep and almost constant heresy within the very Christian tradition of which we are so often proud. I have already described some of the powerful political and cultural factors in the rise of both Christianity and Islam, in Chapter 33 (The Kingdom Strikes Back). There has always been a lot of disturbing debate about the best way to believe. Early Christian theologians have struggled to define at different times Arian, Athanasian, Monophisite, Catholic, Orthodox, and Muslim theologies, etc., as heretical without singling out any one of them as "non-Christian."

What needs to be very clear in the present discussion is the fact that in recent history Christians and Muslims have each developed highly sensitive and extensively prejudicial attitudes toward each other, especially since the Crusades. This especially makes it very hard to peel away layers of prejudice and think objectively.

It is incredible how political configurations can warp our sensitivities. True blue American democracy worked closely with Russian Communist Allies when it was necessary to put down the Nazi juggernaut. Once that threat was removed we returned to American/Soviet conflict again. Conflict and polarization in former Yugoslavia is just as great between Croatian and Serb (both Christian) as it is between either of them and the Bosnian Muslims, and objectivity is virtually impossible.

Thus, my first point is that our attitudes in this discussion must take into account the possible warping of our perspective resulting from historical events. Semi-barbarian Christians from Western Europe committed awful atrocities against both Eastern Christians in Constantinople and Muslims in Jerusalem. Eastern Christians were considered by Western Christians as heretical as Muslims. Today, a simple Bible-church believer might suffer even greater culture shock inside a highly decorated Catholic cathedral than he would in a Muslim mosque.

Indeed, for centuries there have been millions of "Muslims" who believe that Jesus is the Son of God, as well as millions of "Christians" who are very foggy on that point, such as devout, Bible-revering pentecostal "unitarians" in Mexico.

In other words, whether believers in Jesus are called Muslims or Christians does not make a whole lot of difference when it comes to precise doctrinal fidelity to the Word of God. Within the 32 million "African Initiated Churches" you can find almost every sort of heresy, but we tend automatically to be tolerant of their theological understanding and are willing to give them time to understand the Bible better—partly because it is our habit to call them *Christians*. Basically, mission strategists are less concerned to get these 32-million people out of these movements than they are to get the Bible into them.

Could not this be the case with those thousands, and perhaps some day millions of "Muslims" whose main problem is that they are not as familiar with the Bible as they ought to be? Can't we think of the Qur'an as we do the Apocrypha and let it gradually take a back seat to our Bible simply because it is not as edifying intellectually or spiritually? That will happen despite the emotional attachment Muslims may have to its Arabic and its cadences (no better understood than Catholics used to understand the Latin Mass). What a handicap the Qur'an has in comparison to the meaningful flow of drama in the Gospels! And what a handicap if, like the Latin Mass for so many centuries, the Qur'an cannot and must not be translated into any other language! How can it ever compete with the Bible? Maybe the *Torah* and

the *Injil* simply need to be rediscovered within Islam the way the Bible has needed again and again to be rediscovered within Christian and Jewish history.

Then, speaking of tolerance, it is not widely recognized by Christians but it is nonetheless absolutely true that throughout history Muslims have been more tolerant of Christians than the reverse! For thirteen centuries Muslims have been in charge of Jerusalem, and during that time they have preserved four quarters: Muslim, Christian, Armenian, and Jewish. Until modern times only when that city has been under Christians or Jews have all others been dealt with genocidal violence.

Finally, we are forced to restudy the New Testament. The major missiological issue there is precisely *how to go far enough*. Do we feel sure Cornelius was hell-bound before Peter got to his door? Is there such a thing as being "saved" from legalism that corresponds to the Evangelical concept of "a second (or third?) work of grace"—often called filling of the Holy Spirit, deeper life, entire sanctification, baptism of the Spirit? If we are not entirely sure among ourselves whether such a second work of grace is necessary to pull people out of hell into heaven, then let us not hastily judge the level of faith of Muslim seekers. Part of Peter's explanation, in Acts 15:8, was a "God who knows the heart." *That is precisely what we as humans don't know.* Let us not let our theological formulations outrank the Word of God.

Across the centuries of our own history, and the mission fields of the world, movements to Christ have rarely if ever been entirely sound by our present biblical understanding. Today we would not accept Luther's escatology, nor Calvin's willingness to execute heresy. All our backgrounds, in fact, are "sub-Christian" and syncretistic. Should we not be as eager for Muslims to know Christ and His Word as we are grateful that our forefathers were allowed to catch dim rays of light from that same Word centuries ago?

Case Studies

This series of case studies is a representative sample of contemporary church planting among classically defined unreached peoples. Examples appear from the major blocs of unreached peoples: Chinese, Muslim, Hindu, Tribal and Buddhist. An urban population in Latin America is also included. Most are recent. All were initiated within the last generation.

The point of these case studies is to explore the complexity and the feasibility of pioneer church planting in our day. You won't find simplistic formulas for success. You'll see ordinary people prayerfully developing unique approaches for different situations. Some cases are short, reduced to a rough outline of what took place. Each story reveals a great deal about how each movement was initiated and nurtured through embryonic phases.

Compare and contrast the stories. Notice the crucial role of local workers laboring alongside expatriate missionaries. Observe how foreign workers enter culture and develop ways to communicate the gospel. Note how obstacles were faced and overcome, how partnerships were formed and bore fruit, the years required, the perseverance and creativity demanded. You'll see how community development can be integrated with evangelism. You'll notice setbacks, mistakes and disappointments along with dramatic breakthroughs. Take note of how prayer was lifted, suffering was endured and God's hand was extended in order to establish movements of obedient faith in Christ.

The names of some authors, peoples and places have been changed at the author's request.

A Pioneer Team in Zambia, Africa

Phillip Elkins

This church planting case study differs from some in that it describes a team of missionaries who banded together *prior* to entering a field. Most efforts are put together by a sending agency and they bring together several people who may meet for the first time in the field. This team came together in 1967 out of a common concern to reach an unreached or "hidden" people whom God had already prepared to be receptive to His redemptive message.

The team took as its model the "Apostolic Band" of the first century. This multi-talented, multi-gifted group had varying degrees of field experience. Stan Shewmaker had already worked in Zambia, Africa for five years; Frank Alexander in Malawi, Africa for four years; Phillip and Norma Elkins had been involved in visiting and research of missions in 71 countries and two other couples had been on short-term assignments in Africa. Ages of members ranged from 25 to 33. The five men in the group had degrees in Biblical studies and just prior to leaving for the field completed master's degrees in missiology.

Because of this experience and training, the team felt it could function as its own

Phillip Elkins is the President of the Mission Training & Resource Center in Pasadena, California. He is also the Executive Director of the Paraclete Mission Group, which is composed of 24 associates serving as missionaries or partners bringing consultative solutions to strategic issues facing agencies and churches. In the early 70s with a team of five families, he planted churches among the unreached Tonga of Zambia. For many years he worked as a tentmaker missionary in Liberia.

agency in the same sense that the Paul-Timothy-Luke-Silas "band" of the New Testament did. The group was sent by an "Antioch" congregation in San Fernando, California. This church body recognized that the true "sending" agent was the Holy Spirit (Acts 13: 4, "so being sent by the Holy Spirit") and thus did not consider itself the governing or "decision making" organization. Responsibility for field decisions was left to the team, directed by the Holy Spirit, in partnership with the national Christian leadership on the field.

Early Decisions and Convictions

As the team searched for an unreached people (two years), they concluded the Holy Spirit was leading them to a segment of the Tonga tribe (one of the largest in Zambia, numbering over 300,000) called the Toka-Leya. Ninety-five percent of these people were adherents of an ethnic, or localized, folk-religion (some would use the term *animistic*). Within a twelve-mile radius of where the team settled (the primary target area) were 100 villages with four small congregations that had not grown for several years (a total of 75 Christians).

The team spent most of the first two years (1970-71) learning the language and culture, without engaging in overt evangelistic activities. By the end of 1973 there were four times as many churches (16) and six times the membership (450). Beyond this immediate twelve-mile area, completely new movements were started. For example, in the Moomba chieftaincy, 70 miles to the north, newly trained national Christians planted six churches with 240 members within a few months. This was done in 1973 and involved winning the chief, a third of all the village headmen and both court judges.

I mention this early rapid response to show that we were indeed led to a "ripe pocket" in God's mosaic of peoples. We knew that the national church, motivated and trained, had to be the vehicle to gather the harvest. By 1974 we felt most of the American team could pull out. By 1979, the last two "foreign" families felt they could responsibly move on to another new people to begin the process again. Today a national church continues the process of winning and discipling "to the fringes."

"Methods," "approaches," and "strategy" may be "unspiritual" words in some Christians' vocabulary. I feel in the context of this effort there was validity in the strategy and specific methods followed by the team. In addition to what has been described, I think the first two years in which we were involved as in-depth "learners" of the Tonga world view (language, lifestyle, values, politics, social structure, beliefs, educational systems and other aspects of culture) were essential to our efforts as church planters. My wife and I lived in a village of 175 people and followed a lifestyle closely identified with that of other Toka-Leya families. We learned to "hurt" where they hurt and "feel" what they felt. We identified, not so much to be "accepted," though that is important, but to understand and appreciate their culture for its finest and best dimensions. We had to know what parts were already functioning positively within the will and purpose of God. We needed to know what had to be confronted and changed to fit the demands of the kingdom of God.

Perhaps most critical was the need to learn where people had "felt needs" through which God's message of redemption could be accepted as Good News. The message that had been proclaimed as "Gospel" by earlier Christian efforts was in fact perceived as "Bad News." The "Gospel" was perceived as God calling men to have one wife and not to drink beer. Though Christians were saying many other things, this was perceived as the "banner" of the message. Because missionaries showed a major interest in setting up schools for children, the adult population found the message alright for children but almost unthinkable for adults.

Understanding the Tonga World View

During our two years of "incarnational identification," the Tongas' perception of reality (world view) became increasingly clear to us. Graphically, it might be described to a Westerner as follows:

Tonga World-View

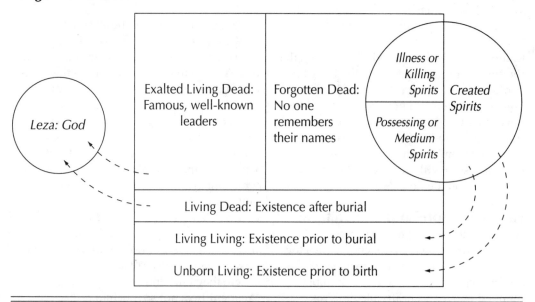

It was to this perception of reality that we had to address our lives and message. Tongas believed that one can affect the *unborn fetus* in another person's body. For example, if a pregnant woman's family had brought death to members of your family, you could enlist the aid of a medicine man to cause the death of the fetus (without having physical contact with the pregnant woman).

The category of *living living* corresponds to our concept of living people with their finite physical limitations. But after physical death this person continues as the *living dead*. The personality, personal enemies, prejudice, taste preferences and so forth, continue intact. Therefore, one can go to the grave of the *living dead* person and request assistance based on a knowledge of that person's personality and the obligations of relationship. Similarly, the *exalted living dead* are to be supplicated on the basis of the status they attained while in the *living living* existence.

The *forgotten dead* are those persons whose names and personalities have passed from living memory. Therefore, no one can now appeal to them, placate them, or appease them. This group represents a dimension of reality which strikes at the heart of the fears, apprehensions and frustrations of the Tonga.

Within this framework of "reality" I will describe how our team of Christians found an opening to speak to felt needs. The Tonga believed that God (*Leza*) created humans and, for a while, lived together with them. But as people became abusive in their relationship with him (in one story a woman strikes God) God left them, and all direct communication became impossible. The only remaining way to speak to God then, is through the living dead or exalted living dead. But the inability to "hear back" from God, to know his personality, to understand whether their needs were adequately communicated, represented an area of *felt need*.

Forgotten ancestors are commonly believed to be the *spirits* which enter people to kill them. A violent illness is associated with such spirits, and unless the person can get this spirit expelled, death will result. Other spirits represent alien forgotten dead (they come from another tribe) which frequently are associated with a long-term, frustrating, but not fatal illness. These spirits also frequently possess the person and use the person as a medium to communicate with the community. The community responds to this possession by special gatherings to dance and sing to the spirit. The purpose of these gatherings is to appease, control and hopefully rid the person of the spirit.

Finally, there are spirits which humans play a role in creating. These particular spirits were the most feared and frustrating for the people with whom I lived. None of the literature I studied on spirits in Africa dealt with this particular spirit, though humanly created spirits do exist in other African tribes.

Our understanding came in this way. A very sick boy was brought to me one day. The child was near death and I felt it was beyond my own limited medical skills to help. I took the parents and child to a hospital, but as I watched the child died. From a Western medical perspective, the child died from complications growing out of malaria and anemia. A year later I attended a village court case where a man was accused of killing this very child. The man finally admitted, after weeks of trial procedures, that he was guilty. The reason was that the man felt he had been wronged by the father of the child and he wanted to create his personal *isaku* spirit. No one during the trial was willing to explain to me what an *isaku* spirit was. People who were normally generous with information would deny knowing anything about these spirits. During this time my wife and I visited a village one evening where none of the women around a fire had their children on their backs. This was very unusual. I asked them why and they explained that it was because there were many *isaku* spirits in their village and they were afraid for the safety of their children. They explained that their children were in huts where they could be watched. When they discovered that I did not know what an *isaku* spirit was they explained only that it was an evil spirit. Since all spirits were considered evil, that was not much help.

As the weeks went by, I finally persuaded a medicine man, who occasionally visited our area, to explain *isaku*. This spirit could be created by people who wanted a being to steal, kill or otherwise serve their own interests. To create an *isaku* one would first have to dig up and decapitate a freshly buried body. The head would be removed in the middle of the night to an isolated area where two paths cross. A fire would be built and certain medicines would be added to it. The ensuing smoke would engulf the head to which portions of certain animals had been attached (snake skin, bird feathers, feet of a rabbit, etc.). This ceremony, if correctly done, would result in a living spirit called *isaku*. The physical part of this spirit was to be kept, fed and hidden. If one properly cared for *isaku*, the person would have his wishes granted. If not properly cared for, *isaku* would kill the person or a member of his family. When a person who owns an *isaku* dies, the relative who inherits the dead person's *name* also inherits their *isaku*. Normally no one would reveal that they had an *isaku*. Thus, if a relative who was asked to receive a name was suspicious that an *isaku* was associated with it, that person might refuse to receive the *name*.

If anyone inherits a *name*, and unknowingly should have received an *isaku*, they learn of the mistake very painfully. They may arrive home one day to learn that a child has died suddenly.

As our knowledge grew of *isaku* spirits, many gaps in our understanding of the Tonga were eliminated. We grew increasingly conscious of how *powerless* the people felt to adequately deal with *isaku* spirits and those who would create them. This, coupled with the realization that the Tonga felt every death was the result of someone's overt effort to cause it, helped us to understand the extent of much of the animosity and anger between individuals and families.

Responding to Felt Needs

From all of the above insights a picture of *felt needs* emerged to which God could speak meaningfully. The first *Good News* from God for the Tonga was that He had given to us a *Holy Spirit*. The Tongas knew nothing of a good spirit, much less a *Holy Spirit* from God Himself as a gift. We shared that we were not afraid, as they were, of *isaku* spirits because we had residing in us continually a *Spirit* that would not tolerate other spirits. The Spirit in us was more powerful than any other spirit. This explained the lack of fear they had seen in our lives, the joy, the confidence and hope.

The second part of our *Good News* was that the God, which they already knew by name, had *not abandoned them*. The Tonga had left God but He was willing to live among them again. He had already proved His willingness by sending a Son who lived as a human and showed humans how to really live. We explained that one can now talk directly to God about their needs and that this *Son* also serves as a person's special advocate before God. We further explained that God's Son was so concerned to remove the sin and guilt for all of the offensive ways that we live that He Himself accepted the punishment on our behalf.

The Tongas began to realize the verification and proof of what we said was the *Holy Spirit* which lived in us. Lest I be misunderstood by a reader of this, I am not talking about a special gift of speaking in tongues. I am speaking of that which every Christian receives at his *new birth.*

We also spoke of the verification that would come from knowing the Bible. This had little immediate impact, as most of the people could not read. However, the Word is not confined to the printed page. The Word was communicated daily by a God who was willing to reveal Himself in their lives. He revealed Himself one day as we went to a village where we were stopped by a drunken woman who forbade us to come into her village. She said they followed Satan and not God. That night she died and the next day hundreds of people came wanting to know more of God's will for their lives.

The major political leader of our area had been leading the people to the graves of their ancestors annually to solicit rain. When he accepted the *Good News,* he demonstrated his faith by leading his people in a new way. When the first drought occurred he called the people together to spend a day calling to God to give them rain. This was a bold move which exceeded the faith of some of the missionaries. But God honored the boldness and before the sun set the earth was drenched in rain.

In the village where we made our home, almost half of the adult population accepted baptism. At their initiative we all spent a night in prayer before going out as a group to share our faith with another village.

As our team of American missionaries saw more and more churches planted, we began to modify our role as leaders in evangelism and church planting. I believe it was a good strategy for us to identify with the Tongas physically and to provide a physical and spiritual model for evangelism. I know this is a concept that is considered "past" in many circles, but I feel it should still be an emphasis in pioneer mission efforts.

To train an indigenous leadership we set up 16 extension centers for training every Christian in the basics of the Christian faith, and instituted a special course for those who emerged as church leaders. This was done with the new Christians bearing the cost of the courses. We followed the practice of not subsidizing the construction of buildings, or providing funding for those who entered the preaching ministry.

Prepared for Battle

I cannot close this story without admitting that we, like the team that Paul worked with, experienced some interpersonal conflict and setbacks in our ministry goals, including betrayals by believers and reversions by some of those we had the greatest hopes for. But we accept that as normal in the battle "against the principalities and powers, against the world rulers of this darkness, the spiritual hosts of wickedness in the heavenly places" (Eph 6:12).

I think it is important for one to know the Bible well enough to be able to know where the battle is. I think we invite defeat when we do not make the effort to learn the local language well enough to teach effectively in it. I think it is essential that we participate in a real way in the lifestyle and struggles of the people we are sent to. When we do not ground our proclamation on an understanding of a people's hurts and felt needs, and when we allow our own cultural understanding of the Christian message to blind us to what God wants said in a radically different setting and culture, we invite failure.

I heartily commend the team approach for pioneer mission efforts. During the five years I was in Zambia one of our original families left, but others came and were incorporated. In addition, from the very beginning, we tried hard to expand the team leadership to include Tonga Christians. This kind of team approach is not the only way to approach the task, but it was part of what made our five years in Zambia a productive and happy experience.

A Work of God Among the Hakka of Taiwan

Ernest Boehr

The ministry in the Tungshih area of central Taiwan is an excellent example of how rapidly the Gospel follows along the web of family relationships. It also shows the wisdom of the missionary in guiding the Christians to make functional substitutes and thus satisfy the people's desire to express in a Hakka way their respect of the departed.

The Transformation of Mrs. Chan

The work of God began with the transformation of Mrs. Chan, who had moved with her husband from Cholan in central Taiwan to Kaohsiung, a southern port city. She had been troubled with demons for some years and they really began to bother her when her son wrote from the off-shore island of Chinmen of his fear from the noise of exploding shells from Communist China.

Mrs. Chan went to a monk in Tainan, 50 miles to the north, who was known for his ability to cast out demons. For $15 Mrs. Chan got the advice to make a straw effigy of herself, put her clothes on it and have it buried. She was covered with a fishing net and taken to a dark corner to hide until the effigy was buried. The action was intended to deceive the demons into thinking that she was dead. "Do you think that drove away the demons?," she will ask in her testimony. "No!," she will shout. "It didn't help one bit."

About that time an elder's wife from the Hsinsheng Presbyterian Church in Kaohsiung began visiting her and inviting her to church. She had all kinds of excuses but was finally enticed to see some slides on the life of Christ. The demon seized her in the meeting and she ran out, but the pastor came later to see her.

He said she would not get rid of the demon without first accepting Christ. He kept on visiting her and teaching her of Christ.

Almost two years later Mrs. Chan woke up early one morning and began breaking the idols on the home altar. Her daughter-in-law thought she was possessed again and called Mr. Chan. He told them to leave Mrs. Chan alone because she was preparing to believe in Jesus. She asked them if they could think of any help the idols had been, in the twenty years they had served them. Since they could think of none, she finished cleaning up the altar and sold to the scrap man what couldn't be burned. She later was baptized and within three years her husband and two sons believed, too.

Mrs. Chan's Family and Friends

Mrs. Chan began praying for her brothers and sisters near Tungshih immediately after she was saved. Over a period of ten years she visited them as often as she could, telling them what the Lord had done for her and encouraging them to trust in Christ. One brother was the village elder and he loved to drink. His liver became diseased from too much liquor, so Mrs. Chan prayed that the Lord would both heal his liver and take the taste for liquor from him. When the Lord answered her prayer, she encouraged her brother to trust in Christ. He said they needed to know more and would welcome a preacher to their home.

Mrs. Chan had not lived near Tungshih for many years, so she prayed as she walked to town that the Lord would lead her to the right person. She arrived at the Norwegian

Ernest Boehr spent 35 years in Taiwan with the The Evangelical Alliance Mission working for 12 years with refugees from mainland China, and then for 23 years among the Hakkanese. Adapted from *Taiwan Church Growth Bulletin*, 1974. Used by permission.

Evangelical Lutheran Free Church at seven o'clock in the morning that May day in 1968. Mrs. Johansen was home and she called Miss Cho to interpret what Mrs. Chan was saying. Mrs. Chan told her story and asked Mrs. Johansen to go with her to Henglung.

Mrs. Johansen suggested that she instead should send Miss Ammon, who at that time was in Tungshih and who spoke Hakka. Mrs. Chan objected, "No, the Holy Spirit led me here. You are the one." Then Mrs. Johansen suggested they wait until her husband came back. Again Mrs. Chan objected, "No, someone needs to go in now and each Sunday night as well as one night during the week." Another fellow missionary was available and she went with Miss Cho and Mrs. Chan for the first meeting that day in the Yeh home in Henglung.

Rev. Johansen and Miss Cho began regular meetings in the Yeh home in mid-May in 1968. He spoke in Mandarin and Miss Cho interpreted into Hakka. They wrote out some choruses and a brief prayer asking the Lord's forgiveness and blessing. The oldest women seemed the most responsive. When someone asked about worshipping their ancestors, Rev. Johansen hesitated. Then the oldest brother's wife said, "In all these years that I have offered food to our ancestors not once have they taken what I offered." There were no more questions on ancestor worship.

In May, 1969, Mrs. Chan came again and told Rev. Johansen, "Pastor, tonight you must speak on baptism." Actually he had spoken on salvation and baptism before, but was not planning to give an invitation that night. He did some quick altering of his message and was ready to give the invitation that night when Mrs. Chan came forward to take over. She held a lively invitational meeting until twenty-six had raised their hands professing faith in Christ. At the baptismal service three weeks later, nineteen followed the Lord in baptism—the entire family of the village elder (six people), five members of the third brother's family, three relatives and five friends. The oldest brother had gotten mad and refused to let his family be baptized. They were baptized at a later date.

A Funeral Takes New Meaning

Old mother Yeh passed away in February, 1970, at 94 years of age. She, too, had responded to the Gospel and loved to hear as much as Miss Cho had time to tell her. Her peaceful passing was a wonderful testimony to all. Mrs. Chan came up from Kaohsiung to make sure the funeral was "Christian." There was no question about keeping idol and ancestor worship out of the ceremony, but a brother-in-law argued hard with Mrs. Chan for reading eulogies to the dead. Rev. Johansen asked if eulogies could be read facing the audience rather than facing the dead. Mrs. Chan agreed to the change.

A group from mother Yeh's side of the family came to express their sorrow by playing Chinese horns, violins and cymbals. Mrs. Chan refused to let them play and the village elder was very chagrined. He explained to Rev. Johansen that the group had come to express their sorrow. Rev. Johansen suggested to Mrs. Chan that the group play at that time and not at the funeral. Mrs. Chan consented and the brother was delighted. He ran up the road to where the group was waiting and told them to come.

The seven-week memorial for old mother Yeh became an excellent opportunity for teaching about life and death and what Christ accomplished in his death and resurrection. Each week for seven weeks, Rev. Johansen went in to Henglung to hold services in the home. This took the place of the heathen rites of having a monk come in each week to report the progress of the soul through hell. It was a very satisfying time for the family. They felt they had done all they could for the departed.

Other Fellowships Begin

During the funeral Mrs. Chan stayed with her youngest sister in Tamap'u, a town nearby. She encouraged her to have meetings in her home. She agreed to the idea. So on Easter Sunday 1970, Rev. Johansen began services there, too. It was not long before the youngest sister and her son believed and were baptized with several older neighbor ladies.

In the meantime, old Mr. Tai, who had been baptized in the Henglung home, asked if they could use the village elder's office in

Chungk'o for services. Mr. Yeh was agreeable and Rev. Johansen started services there about the same time as those in Tamap'u. There have been five more baptized in Chungk'o and the group is now renting a small building for services. In November 1980, a new church building was dedicated in Chungk'o.

Since 1969 there have been 50 baptized in the three places. Twenty-three of them are in the immediate Yeh family and three more are close relatives. The remaining twenty-four are friends and neighbors of the family. The meetings in the three places always have a good number of unsaved in attendance because the natural setting of the home is neither foreign nor unnerving. All the meetings are at night when the people have time on their hands.

In the fall of 1972, the Johansens began studying Hakka. Rev. Johansen preaches now in the Hakka dialect. Mrs. Chan continues her ministry of prayer and encouragement. Since 1974, Mrs. Chan has not been in good health. However, the home fellowships in Henglung and Chungk'o continue and the vigorous group in Chungk'o has seen steady growth.

The Impact of Missionary Radio on Church Planting

William Mial

Historically, the role of radio broadcasting of the gospel by missionary radio stations has varied greatly from country to country. In a geographically remote region, such as a river basin area in Venezuela, radio has provided the first contact of the gospel with the listener, ultimately culminating in a nucleus of listeners in a village accepting Jesus Christ as personal Savior and going on to use the Bible study programs on the radio as the focal point of their weekly worship.

In other areas of the world, which are unreachable by any other means than radio due to political restrictions, we find that gospel missionary radio broadcasting is used by the head of the house to give basic Bible training to his family. In some cases the radio is used as an evangelist to bring his family to a saving knowledge of Jesus Christ.

One significant development in church planting through missionary radio is found in India as a result of the Trans World Radio broadcast from Sri Lanka. The strategy behind this type of ministry is first a presentation of the gospel through various types of radio programs, such as a morning devotional program patterned somewhat after the Hindu morning worship, but with gospel music and scripture reading. This attracts a large number of Hindu morning worshipers, providing them with a familiar atmosphere but bringing to them the message of the only true God and the hope of eternal life found in His only Son, Jesus Christ. Various types of traditional and more innovative programming are broadcast throughout the morning and evening in approximately forty one major Indian languages. A variety of Bible correspondence courses are offered and a certain measure of spiritual awareness is developed through this follow-up method.

A less conventional type of follow-up has also been carried on in several language groups in the form of "Seekers Conferences"—three day extended weekends.

William Mial has served for over 40 years with Trans World Radio. Since his start as a studio operator in Tangier, Morocco, Bill's vision and administrative abilities have allowed him to oversee the development of new transmitters and new programming in Monte Carlo, the Netherland Antilles, Hong Kong, Sri Lanka, Guam and Europe. Bill is presently serving as Assistant to the President and Senior International Director of TWR.

Through a mail offering, true seekers of Christianity have the opportunity to register for these special conferences. As a result, there has been as much as 100 percent response by these men and women to accept Jesus Christ as personal Savior. In other cases, "Radio Rallies" have been held when radio listeners are encouraged to join other in their area in attending a series of meetings held over a period of several nights. Here again we find a high percentage of attendees choose to follow Christ, resulting many times in the spontaneous desire to follow the Lord in believer's baptism. In the such cases, Trans World Radio makes every effort to place these new converts into existing evangelical churches in their particular area. But often there is no church. The response has been so great that special follow-up strategies have been developed which train leaders and help encourage new churches.

In sections of India, primarily in Andhra Pradesh, we find such a strong wave of popular response to the radio broadcast that we utilize a daily 30-minute Bible study transmission. This provides the core for evangelism and Bible study in many homes.

The Founder of Trans World Radio, Dr. Paul Freed reported,

I went into home after home where "house churches" were assembled. People crowd into small houses until there isn't a square foot of standing space left. And this is an everyday occurrence! They work all day, and then begin to arrive for the radio services two hours before the programs even start! In one of the homes I visited, a man had taken a wire and attached it to a speaker outside. When the broadcasts begin in the evening, they can be heard throughout the area surrounding the house.

Hundreds of house groups have been started by the 650 member staff of TWR's sister organization in India, Vishwa Vani. Often, it all begins by the head of a home bringing in his neighbors to listen to the radio transmissions. At the conclusion of the programs in that particular language, the content of the program is discussed. Following this, the new believers begin to give a personal witness to the non-Christians who have come to the house Bible study group. This practice is often carried out on a seven day per week basis.

Church planting of course implies at some point that an adequate number of trained pastors would be available to carry out pastoral responsibilities in these new congregations. Over the years, the spiritual fruit of this outreach has led TWR India to further develop the ministry. Vishwa Vani workers are systematically trained for follow up, leading ultimately to the establishment of churches. In order to accommodate these developments, another arm of this radio outreach has been created called India Believers Fellowship. This organization takes the mature house groups and forms them into congregations where a full church life experience will be provided to the new believers. Recently, such a group was started in the midst of a highly Hindu area in Varanasi (one of the holy cities of Hinduism). Vishwa Vani workers began the work of establishing a new fellowship when 90 were baptized as a result of the radio broadcasts.

In this case and many others, radio provided the foundation for a complete ministry cycle: the preaching of the Gospel, the response of the listeners, the personal follow up with listeners, the preaching of the Word both by radio and also by lay leaders and local workers, and ultimately in the establishment of centers of worship.

Pigs, Ponds and the Gospel

James W. Gustafson

For decades, Christians have talked about integrating evangelism and development in world mission, but there have been obstacles. Perhaps the foremost has been a narrow definition of evangelism, limiting it to the verbal presentation of the gospel. The gospel of Jesus Christ, however, is not simply a spoken word; it is a Living Word. The gospel is Life. It is the incarnation of the Word of God into the cultures and lives of humankind.

The secular definition of development has been a second obstacle for mission-minded Christians. The secular approach to development focuses most often on economic growth. With the goal of increasing profit, this focus becomes individualistic and often pits entrepreneurs against one another. This emphasis on individualism and self-attainment contrasts with the Word of God. The Bible focuses on the good of the group, teaching self-denial and service to others. As Christians, it's important to remember that our definition of development comes from the principles and values of God's Word, not from Wall Street.

A third obstacle to integrating development with evangelism arises when it is attempted by Christians who are not living out the transformation of Christ in their own lifestyles. I am deeply concerned about what I feel is a departure from the gospel of grace in the church today. We are duped by the religious value system of American society which teaches that humans must work at being morally good. It is only as Christians truly understand and believe the gospel of God's grace—living out that grace in every aspect of organizational life and work—that grace results in the ongoing transformation both of the Church and the society around it.

A final obstacle to integrating development with evangelism is that the Church is presented in many settings as a cultural foreigner. This is especially true in Third World countries where local cultures are seen by missionaries explicitly or implicitly, as sinful. Western church forms are held up as pure. The result is that relevant forms of church life are not explored or established. Western Christianity remains foreign to the hearts and minds of non-Western people.

Integrated Holistic Development

As a missionary of the Evangelical Covenant Church—for the past 27 years in Northeast Thailand, an area also known as Issaan—I am part of a ministry that seeks to overcome these obstacles to integrate development, church planting and evangelism. Several North American missionaries and a staff of Northeast Thai (150 as of 1998) are engaged in what we call "integrated holistic development." It is "development" in that it seeks to transform people from what they are into what they are meant to be in Christ. It is "holistic" in that it deals with the whole person, with all areas of life. It is "integrated" in that all aspects of the ministry are tied together and do not function or exist independently. The ministry currently consists of the Thailand Covenant Church, the Issaan Development Foundation (which addresses social, economic and physical needs), and the Institute for Sustainable Development (which conducts research and curriculum development training for the Church).

The ministry has one primary focus, that of enabling Jesus Christ to be born into Northeast Thai culture. Team members gifted in "holy gab" go out into villages to talk about Jesus.

James W. Gustafson is the Executive Director of World Mission for the Evangelical Covenant Church of America. Gustafson grew up with missionary parents in Laos and Vietnam. He spent 27 years in Thailand serving in church planting and community development. Used by permission of the author.

They don't talk about religion. Instead they say, "We're not here to change your religion, because all religions are basically the same; they're all about making people good." Then they talk about knowing the Word, the Living Word who is Jesus Christ, Jesus who is above all religions. Many who have responded positively to this method of sharing the gospel were religious people searching for truth, yet not finding it in Buddhism. They agree that they can't possibly live up to the demands of religion, but by accepting Jesus they can find salvation. These new believers quickly began sharing the Good News with their family members and friends. In this way, the Church continues to expand spontaneously.

Some of our team members focus on training. They develop contextualized theology and study materials to ground new believers in the Word of God. Those who study the materials teach others. Instead of translating English materials into Thai, the team has Thai theologians working with missionaries to write Thai materials for Thai people. To date, the ministry has given birth to over 40 "mother" churches and over 250 "daughter" churches. Our team also has some people who specialize in the arts. It's their job to get the gospel into the cultural forms and expressions of the Thai people. When you visit these churches, you see gospel stories told by means of Thai drama and dance forms. You hear worship songs with Thai tunes accompanied by Thai instruments. Through all these means, we create a way for Jesus to come alive to the Northeast Thai and to be understood by them.

The Northeast is the poverty belt of Thailand. There is a great need for development work, but we believe development must serve, not lead. Our development is always based in the local church. It is not viewed strictly as a means of evangelism. Rather, it is seen as a way for the local church to impact the social, economic and physical lives of the people. The centerpiece is the Udon Patina Farm, a complex of three different eco-system farms which demonstrates sustainable agriculture in the region.

One of the farms involves a system of fish ponds, ducks and pigs. When duck and pig manure is composted with grasses on the surface of the ponds, the fish thrive on the phytoplankton that multiply. Pond water and dead fish provide organic fertilizer for the grasses and trees growing along the pond dikes. Ducks also feed on pig manure. The pigs, fish, and ducks can be used for food or sold for profit to support the church work. These farms are the models for cooperative projects undertaken at the village level.

A Cooperative Project in Action

The village of Nong Hua Koo provides a good look at a cooperative project in action. Kitlow is a typical villager. He is a tenant farmer on someone else's land. Since half of his harvest goes back to the landlord, he was constantly in debt to moneylenders. His children often did not have enough to eat. Wunde is typical as well. Although he owns a small rice field, the climate and the soil of the region are not good for growing rice. He, too, was often forced to borrow from moneylenders to make ends meet until harvest. With interest rates of 120 percent or more, it was impossible to make a decent living. The Issaan Development Foundation approached the Covenant church where Kitlow and Wunde are members. They offered help to start a fish-duck-pig cooperative. The foundation would lend the initial stock of animals, provide training in the business, and donate a grant to buy land. For their part, co-op members would find land for sale, build pig and duck pens, dig a fish pond, and agree to work together. Eventually, they would pay back the loan with their own animals.

Kitlow's and Wunde's families, along with five others, accepted the offer. Now that

> As the local church in every culture is enabled and equipped to reach into its own context with the power of God's grace, evangelism and development will merge to bring about the true transformation of society.

the co-op is established, each family works for it one day a week. From this, they earn enough selling pigs and fish to avoid money-lenders. They don't go hungry because they eat about half the fish they raise. They tithe their profits to the church and also use another 10 percent for village projects like stocking the pond used for fish for the elementary school's lunches. Neighbors notice not only the generosity, but the unusual cooperation as well. They see members filling in for someone who is sick or less able, yet still sharing the profits equally. Village cooperatives like this one improve the economic situations of participating families and provide resources for the church. Most importantly, they provide the opportunity for members to live out their faith—learning to love, serve and forgive each other.

In addition to agricultural projects, the foundation also helps local churches impact their communities with vocational training in skills like sewing or mechanics, with primary health training, and with meeting the basic needs of the rural poor. All the programs focus on the participation of groups of people rather than individuals. In this way, new communities are being established in Northeast Thailand filled with people who are being transformed. The people grow in a new relationship with God, with others, and with nature. In response to God's grace, they develop a dynamic new lifestyle, the result of a change their entire value system.

There are seven basic principles at the heart of this ministry:

1. *Authority.* Central to all of our activities is a firm belief in the authority of the Word of God. The gospel of God's grace, with all its implications, forms the set of beliefs on which all policies and practices of the ministry are based.

2. *Integration.* Every aspect of the ministry is tied together by the grace of God. We manage our organization and our lives by grace. We plan, implement, evaluate and correct problems by referring to the principle of grace as our model and guide, by depending on the power of grace.

3. *Flexibility.* We try to do everything possible to allow God's grace to be communicated to the Northeast Thai. To reach that goal, we are willing to change anything and everything about our organizations if necessary.

4. *Contextualization.* People communicate clearly only if they share a common culture. Effective communication is what is understood, not necessarily what is spoken or meant. Thus, the worship and life of the local church, as well as the structure and management system of the development programs, have grown out of local Northeast Thai culture.

5. *Power encounter.* As the gospel of grace is incarnated into Northeast Thai culture and into every area of our ministry, it is brought to bear on the local cultural value system in a powerful and effective way. The result is transformation at the level of values and mind-sets.

6. *Process/broker approach.* The institute and foundation are in a process/broker relationship with the local church. *Process* means going "down and in." Development starts with people themselves, especially with the poor at the bottom of society. It begins with dialogue that involves them in a participatory approach. The *broker* function involves going "up and out." The foundation can link local churches to outside settings and resources. It can assess markets, research technology and so on.

7. *Local church focus.* The local church as the basic unit of Christian society is the obvious starting point for holistic development. The final goal is that the local church become the local development organization that impacts its own larger community with the transforming power of God's grace.

This ministry has not been without problems. The first was the tendency to grow too much. An increasing number of staff meant that the basic philosophy behind the work became watered down, especially in the lives of those at the periphery. When we reduced the size of the organizations, we were able to reconsecrate ourselves to our basic core values. As we had grown larger, there was also a tendency to have the financial support of the organizations become the highest priority. When we found that we were more focused on support for operational costs than on mission, we knew we must cut down to a more manageable size.

Another problem was a failure to relate honestly and to address wrong values in ourselves and in others. Thai culture, just like Western culture, has a natural tendency to avoid such encounters. In order to grow in power for service, we needed to learn how to talk to each other and to counter each other in love. Other problems in our work could be mentioned, but they all come back to the central point: the more we have learned to deny ourselves, to accept our weaknesses and to depend on God in every detail, the more we have found His wisdom and strength to be sufficient for all our needs.

The role of mission agencies, Christian aid agencies, and local development organizations includes the ongoing integration of evangelism and development at the local church level. Both elements are critical ingredients of the mission of the Church, and this is where the transformation of society begins. As the local church in every culture is enabled and equipped to reach into its own context with the power of God's grace, evangelism and development will merge to bring about the true transformation of society.

South Asia: Vegetables, Fish and Messianic Mosques

Shah Ali with J. Dudley Woodberry

My Muslim father tried to kill me with a sword when I became a follower of Jesus after comparing the Qur'an and the Bible. He interpreted my decision as a rejection not only of my faith, but of my family and culture, as well. Historically Christians were largely converts from the Hindu community and had incorporated Hindu words and western forms into their worship.

In trying to express my faith, I encountered two sets of problems. First, as indicated, Christianity seemed *foreign*. Secondly, attempts by Christians to meet the tremendous human need in the region had frequently led to the attraction of opportunistic, shallow converts and the consequent resentment of the Muslim majority.

Christian Faith in Muslim Dress

I was able to start dealing with the foreignness of Christianity when a missionary hired me to translate the New Testament using Muslim rather than Hindu vocabulary and calling it by its Muslim name, *The Injil Sharif* ("Noble Gospel"). Thousands of *injils* were bought, mostly by Muslims, who now accepted this as the "Gospel" of which the Qur'an spoke. This approach may be supported not only pragmatically by the amazing results but, more importantly, theologically as well. Unlike the Hindu scriptures, the Qur'an shares a lot of material with the Bible. In fact, most Muslim theological terms were borrowed from Jews and Christians.[1]

Shah Ali is the pseudonym of a follower of Christ from a Muslim family in South Asia. His identity is being concealed—currently, there is persecution of Christians in his country. He translated the New Testament into his national language using Muslim terms.

J. Dudley Woodberry is Dean and Professor of Islamic Studies at the School of World Mission, Fuller Theological Seminary. His publications include editing *Muslims and Christians on the Emmaus Road* and co-editing *Missiological Education for the 21st Century*.

"South Asia: Vegetables, Fish, and Messianic Mosques," *Theology, News and Notes* (March 1992), p. 12-13. Used by permission, Fuller Theological Seminary Pasadena, CA 91182.

Subsequently, a graduate of Fuller's School of World Mission asked me to train twenty-five couples to live in villages and do agricultural development. Only one couple was from a Muslim background. All the others had problems: Muslims would exchange visits with them but would not eat their food until they began to shower in the morning, hence were ceremonially clean by Muslim law after sleeping with their spouses.

The Christian couples were called angels because they were so kind, honest, and self-sacrificing, and they prayed to God. However, they were not considered truly religious because they did not perform the Muslim ritual prayer five times a day. Thereafter, we only employed couples who followed Jesus from a Muslim background, and we developed a ritual prayer that retained all the forms and content that Muslims and Christians share but substituted Bible passages for Qur'anic ones. Little adaptation was necessary, because early Islam borrowed so heavily from Jewish and Christian practice in the formulation of the "pillars" of religious observance (the confession of faith, ritual prayer, almsgiving, fasting, and pilgrimage).[2]

Our Muslim neighbors defined "Christianity" as "a foreign religion of infidels;" so we often referred to ourselves as "Muslims" (literally, "submitters to God"). The necessity of submitting to God is certainly Christian (see Jas 4:7), and Jesus' disciples call themselves "Muslims" according to the Qur'an (5:111).[3]

When villages have decided to follow Christ, the people continued to use the mosque for worship of God but now through Christ. Where possible, the former leaders of mosque prayers (imams) are trained to continue their role as spiritual leaders.

Persuasion, Power and People

God used other means as well as contextualization to bring Muslims to faith in Christ. On several occasions I have had public discussions with Muslim teachers (*malvis*) and have been able to show that, contrary to popular belief, the Qur'an does not name Muhammad as an intercessor. Rather, it states that on the judgment day "intercession will not avail, except [that of] him to whom the Merciful will give permission, and of whose speech He approves" (5:109 Egyptian ed./108 Fluegel ed.). But the *Injil* ("Gospel"), which is from God according to the Qur'an (5:47/51), not only states that God approves of Jesus (e.g., Matt 3:17) but that He is the *only* intercessor (1 Tim 2:5).

God has also shown His power through answered prayer—the recovery of a three-year-old girl who, the doctors said, would die in a few hours; the sending of rain and the stopping of flooding; and the appearance of an unknown man to stop a crowd bent on killing an *imam* who followed Christ.

A conscious effort has been made to foster the movement of groups rather than just individuals to Christ. People have only been baptized if the head of the family was baptized. Effort was made to see that leaders understood the message. A Muslim mystic (Sufi) sheikh, upon learning that the veil of the temple had been rent from top to bottom, threw down his Muslim cap, followed Christ, and brought his followers with him.

Since illiteracy is high, the Bible and training materials are recorded on cassettes, and inexpensive cassette players are made available to the villagers.

There has been persecution. Our training center was closed down. A court case was made against me and three fellow workers. Likewise, there has been friction between the leaders and misunderstanding by other Christian groups. But the movement of people to Christ continues. Most new believers remain in independent Messianic mosques, but some contextualized congregations have joined the major denomination, while still other individuals are absorbed into the traditional, Hindu-background church.

Toward Responsible Self-Help

Besides trying to express our faith in meaningful cultural forms, we have been trying to meet the tremendous human need around us. We want to proclaim the Kingdom and demonstrate its values. Trying to do both presents certain problems.

First, there is the problem of using human need for evangelistic purposes—of manipulating people and attracting the insincere. Consequently, we help all the villagers despite their religious affiliation and give no financial help to Jesus mosques or their imams.

Secondly, the former colonizer-colonized dependency easily gets transferred to donor-recipient dependency.

Thirdly, even the distribution of donated food from abroad may only help in the city, because of the difficulty of distribution, while giving little incentive to the peasants to produce more because of the artificially reduced price.

Fourthly, the introduction of technology may only help those with the skills or the finances to make use of it, while the poorest can just watch the gap between the haves and have-nots widen.

To deal with these problems we have followed such common development practices as loaning planting seed to be replaced at harvest time and providing pumps that are paid for from increased productivity. Now, however, we are adapting a program developed in Southeast Asia which should express holistic Christian concern, deal with the problems outlined, and ensure that the indigenous church remains self-supporting.

The program is training national workers in contextualized church planting and an integrated fish and vegetable cultivation system. The workers are, in turn, sent to needy districts where they are responsible for training local farmers in the easily transferable technology so that they can become self-sufficient. Increased population means less land is available for cultivation, and a poor transportation infrastructure means food must be produced near its consumption.

The intensive food production system was developed elsewhere. In that system, fish ponds are dug and the excavated dirt used for raised vegetable plots. Excess stems and leaves from the vegetables are used to feed the fish, and the waste from the fish is used as fertilizer for the vegetables. These food production centers are within walking distance of regional urban centers for daily sales and provide space for training of regional farmers and leaders of the Jesus mosques.

The concept of Messianic mosques and completed Muslims (following the model of Messianic synagogues and completed Jews) still causes considerable misunderstanding among other Christians. The combining of evangelism and humanitarian ministries by the same people also raises concerns among those who feel Christian agencies should only focus on one or the other. Nevertheless, the models we are developing have been used by God in the raising up of many new disciples and expressing His concern for total persons with physical and spiritual needs. Likewise the Messianic Muslim movement has spilled over into a neighboring country through the normal visiting of relatives; when colleagues and I visited a Southeast Asian country recently, a whole Muslim village began to follow Jesus.

End Notes

1. See Arthur Jeffery, *The Foreign Vocabulary of the Qur'an* (Oriental Institute, 1938).
2. For the details of this argument see J. D. Woodberry, "Contextualization Among Muslims: Reusing Common Pillars," *The Word Among Us*, ed. Dean S. Gilliland (Word Publishers, 1989), 282-312.
3. In this context, however, they demonstrated their submission by believing in God and His apostle (apparently Muhammad, who had not yet been born).

Study Questions

1. Why do attempts to use meaningful cultural forms and attempts to meet human needs present such problems?

2. Can missionaries call themselves "Muslims" or express their faith in Islamic cultural fashion? Why or why not?

Reaching the Baranada People of Barunda

Paul Pearlman

Nestled between Maluwa, Batu, and the blue ocean, Barunda is a tropical nation of fifteen million people. There are some twenty-eight million Baranada; they are the second-largest Muslim ethnic group in Africa. About 60 percent of the ethnic Baranada are Muslims; the remainder are animists. Present-day Barunda is the ancestral homeland of the Baranada people, who are distinct from the surrounding animistic tribes. Barunda, which is unusual for its ethnic homogeneity, is 90 percent Muslim with a 10 percent animist population, mostly of ethnic Baranada background. Eighty-five percent of the ethnic Baranada outside of Barunda are animists, the remainder being Muslims.

The vast majority of the Baranada, both Muslim and animist alike, are subsistence grain farmers. The low-lying terrain of Barunda is ideally suited to such agriculture, but it has been subject to severe weather, including both flooding and drought. Population is quite dense in areas where arable land is at a premium.

The countryside is socially divided along patrilineal kinship lines. Kinship, which includes the widest possible range of people "related" by blood or marriage, is reckoned in several complex ways and is ingeniously expandable to include close social relationships. The basic community structure is the village, within which there is considerable interrelationship. Households are divided into "eating groups," which are communally run. This household unit symbolizes its mutual interdependence through the preparation and sharing of common food and living quarters. The concept of "community" is a cultural norm traceable well into the animistic past of the Baranada. A person's family membership and place of residence are thus the focal points for all of his activities in the world.

Islam came to the Baranada during the fourteenth century and experienced a rapid growth under the influence of Sufi sheikhs, whose egalitarianism was very appealing during the period of slave trading. The Baranada are Sunni Muslims, for whom the five pillars of Islam are deeply embedded in daily life. The custom of female seclusion is quite strong. Sufi orders also continue to flourish in the rural areas. There are, however, a number of animistic practices the Baranada maintain, one of which is saint worship, as witnessed by the widespread participation in natu, "commemorative gatherings," at the tombs of their saints.

The Status of Christianity in Barunda

Christians number some thirty thousand—equally divided between Protestants and Catholics—and comprise less than one percent of the population. The Church is derived entirely from Baranada people who have had an animistic background. Despite their common racial background, animists have no dealings with Muslims. The various denominations are almost entirely dependent financially on western Christian assistance. This applies to church budgetary needs as well as to job opportunities in mission institutions and western developmental organizations. As pressures continue to increase for the establishment of shariat, or Islamic sacred law, in Barunda, the Church has been concerned with the growing instances of persecution and social second-class status.

The Church, a small, introspective, and often insecure body of believers, has been growing slowly. Twenty-five Protestant mission societies have some 250 missionaries working throughout Barunda, and Catholics 169. There are twelve denominations in the

Adapted from *Unreached Peoples '80*, edited by Dr. C. Peter Wagner and Edward R. Dayton. Copyright 1980. David C. Cook Publishing Co., Elgin, Illinois. Used by permission.

country. Most missionaries work within the established Church or are attached to mission-operated institutions. There is a definite trend to place more missionaries in full-time evangelistic outreach.

New Efforts to Reach the Baranada in the Mawasa Area

Despite the Baranada's seeming resistance to the Gospel, some recent breakthroughs have occurred among them under the leadership of the Overseas Christian Missionary Fellowship (OCMF). In 1959, the OCMF entered the town of Mawasa, which has a population of eight thousand in a district of two hundred thousand. Between one and three missionary couples have resided in the town up to the present. Until 1975, their efforts proved fruitless; no church was established and almost no one was led to Christ. Mawasa appeared to be barren and resistant. The OCMF field council determined that it would be expedient to withdraw from that area unless a breakthrough occurred in the ensuing twelve months. Then, the miraculous began to unfold. Through the influence of two Muslim converts, Tabbar and Sadig, the OCMF began to adopt Baranada Muslim forms in their work of communicating the Gospel. Presently there are two worshipping groups of believers in the Mawasa area. Each fellowship is made up of fifteen Muslim converts, almost all of whom are male heads of families. Numerous factors have played a part in the new responsiveness. For example, the response of Christian agencies during natural catastrophe has built up an attitude of goodwill. However, the vast majority of converts cite the Baranada-like quality of the message as being the main reason for their conversion. The Baranada have a highly developed culture and sense of historical tradition. Thus, adapting the forms of the message of the Gospel to fit their patterns and to speak to the needs of their society has been the key factor in establishing the fellowships. The following descriptions of these groups illustrate this point.

Description of Converts

The majority of converts are farmers who, on the average, are barely literate; economically they are self-supporting; and they are close enough sociologically to be able to intermarry. Those showing the most rapid spiritual growth were formerly devout Muslims. Almost all converts are reading the Bible (or having it read to them), praying and meeting together informally in their village homes for worship—without the presence of a foreign missionary. Witnessing to their neighbors and extended families began on the day of their conversion and has been the major cause of reproduction. Until now, it has not been the missionary who has won these men to the Lord, with a very few exceptions. His role is basically to give spiritual encouragement and biblical teaching. The believers have shown initiative and vision. After a study of 1 Corinthians 12, one group on their own appointed an evangelist, an administrator, a prayer coordinator and a pastor. A few of the wives and children have accepted Christ, but this area of evangelism still remains an obstacle. There has been an appreciation of the supernatural on a practical level, with visions and dreams of spiritual significance occurring fairly frequently. There is a simple faith that prayer is an instrument of change. Crying out to God and fasting are utilized to effect release from difficulty as well as to bring healing to the afflicted.

> The missionary's role is basically to give spiritual encouragement and biblical teaching. The believers have shown initiative and vision.

Form Adaptations

The apostle Paul in 1 Corinthians 9:19-23 set down some practical theological guidelines for his involvement in the cross-cultural communication of the Gospel. In Barunda, we are seeking to minister within the same liberties and restrictions that Paul experienced. The offense of the nature of God and the atonement of the Cross will and must remain. However, there are innumerable peripheral areas that can be subject to alteration without violation of scriptural command or principle. A list of implemented form adaptations follows:

The missionary

1. Our men wear the clothing of the target group, which is the village farmer. Our women wear the local dress and at times have worn the veil covering, which has been very much appreciated by the Muslim and convert community.
2. Several of our men have full beards, which is part of the appearance of a Muslim religious man.
3. Lifestyles are simple.
4. Eating style corresponds to Muslims. No pork is eaten.
5. Time is regarded as more "event oriented" than the traditional time absolutes of the West. Some have adopted the 8 PM Barunda suppertime and thus have entered into the social visitation pattern of the society, which takes place each evening between 6 and 8 PM.

The national

1. A place for washing before prayer is provided for optional use. It is explained that there is no merit attached to such ceremonial washing.
2. Shoes are removed before entering the worship center.
3. All worshipers sit on the floor.
4. Bibles are placed on folding stands such as are used for the Koran.
5. Occasionally, Greek and Hebrew Bibles are placed in a prominent position in front of the worshipers, thus demonstrating our regard for the "original" Bible, such as Muslims feel toward the Arabic Koran.
6. Hands are lifted up Muslim style during prayer times. Prostration is frequently done in Muslim fashion. Some pray with their eyes open, wearing traditional prayer hats.
7. Muslim tunes with Christian words are utilized. Scripture is chanted, as are personal testimonies.
8. The local Muslim dialect, rather than the animist dialect of the Christian church, is spoken and read in the services.
9. Embracing is done in Muslim fashion.
10. Days and times of worship are pragmatically regulated.
11. Fasting is an area of liberty, but is scripturally explained.

12. A Muslim-convert, homogeneous church has developed rather than one of a heterogeneous character.
13. Informal church organization is promoted, basically along the lines of the mosque.
14. The Muslim names of converts are retained.
15. The word Christian is avoided because of negative connotations. Presently Christians are called "followers of Isa" (Jesus).
16. Bible study, prayer and fasting are emphasized. A higher profile of religious observance is encouraged because Muslims feel Christians are spiritually lazy when they are never seen praying.
17. The converts have chosen their own leadership.
18. The church grows along family and friendship lines.

Financial Considerations

Gifts and employment opportunities from the West have created a horizontal dependence syndrome within the Barunda Christian community. There is little motivation to give sacrificially or to pray about church needs when one is assured budgets will be met with foreign assistance. Christians are given preferential treatment at mission hospitals and schools. A select few are granted theological scholarships abroad. Comparison of lifestyles between nationals and missionaries convinces Barunda Christians that personal sacrifice is not particularly relevant to the "dedicated life." In my view, all of this points to a basic failure on the part of missionaries to live, teach, and administer sound indigenous financial policy in relationship to the national church. The crashing wave of a forced missionary evacuation, which was only barely averted last December, would most likely reduce our practicing Christian community by a minimum of 50 percent. In Mawasa there is a fresh slate. No traditional Christians reside in the area. The emerging Muslim convert church is the only worshipping group present. Our approach has been as follows:

Missionary adjustments

OCMF possesses no compounds or purchased property. This assures mobility as well as a lower financial profile. Missionaries live on as low a lifestyle as emotional and physical health permit. One family presently lives in a small bamboo hut with a mud floor. Others are in simple cement houses rented from Muslim landlords.

Financial relationships with nationals

OCMF aims to preserve the financial autonomy of the convert in relationship to himself, his family and his peers. Existing economic structures should, at all costs, be preserved. The convert is told from the start that Christianity will only be credible among his Muslim friends if he stands without foreign financial assistance. No option for flight from his village is offered. Jobs, scholarships and relief are not part and parcel of the Gospel. New believers must learn to stand on their own resources from the commencement of their pilgrimage of faith. OCMF has not been involved in institution or relief work. We have no national evangelists, although we have used Sadiq Jabbar occasionally as volunteer help. The emphasis is on lay witness and ministry.

The Existing Evangelistic Team

At present six foreign missionaries and the forty national believers from among the converted Muslims comprise the major functioning evangelistic team. Other Muslim converts have and will continue to be involved on an itinerant basis. At present, the Baranada church with its animistic background has been very wary of this Islamic-flavored movement. Those Christians are a potential team to assist with evangelism, as are the missionaries of other societies. However, for the time being they have adopted a wait-and-see attitude and are uninvolved in this work.

God Wanted the Matigsalogs Reached

Jun Balayo

Two hours of Toyota land-cruising over newly constructed roads cut through seemingly endless mountains brought us to an altitude of over one thousand feet. The unfamiliar breeze was now cool, soothingly fresh and chilling. From this mountain top one could view the majestic rain forest spread thick and deep as far as one's eyes could see. This vast frontier is the heartland of Mindanao in the Philippines, the ancestral territory of the Matigsalogs, a highland tribe whose favorite habitats are the banks of swift rivers.

The Matigsalogs are a group of people characterized by their shyness and independent-mindedness. Generally, they are peace-loving but may suddenly turn fierce and violent when their cultural rights are violated.

Considered to be the largest cultural group numbering over 80,000 families, the Matigsalogs attracted national attention during a month-long rebellion in July, 1975. The conflict was resolved only after the Matigsalogs, led by Datu Lorenzo Gawilan, obtained from the government a specific area which is now called the "Matigsalog Ancestral Territory."

The way the General Baptists (G.B.) received a mission to reach the Matigsalogs was a bit sensational. Totally devoid of any prior human plans, it could only be explained as part of God's wonderful ways.

The G.B. work started in 1969 when Angel Digdigan, a rather small, unassuming young family man, could not continue with his last year in the Bible school. Utterly frustrated and discouraged, he wandered adrift like a rudderless *banca* (boat). In spite of his name which suggests celestial assets, Angel was no better than a bird with broken wings!

From Empty Bottles to a Clear Vessel

Not knowing what to do or where to go, Angel could only roam the barrios in search of

Jun Balayo serves with O.C. Ministries in the Philippines. Reprinted by permission of *Global Church Growth Bulletin*. Copyright January-February 1980, Volume XVII, No. 1.

empty bottles to buy and then sell. This he did to make a few centavos to keep himself and his family physically and spiritually intact.

Angel could not explain how the Lord led him to the land of the Matigsalogs in Mindanao's hinterland. It was like the experience of the beloved apostle John who was isolated on the Isle of Patmos by the Holy Spirit. All that Angel can recall was that he received God's definite call the moment he was with the people. There the vision became clear and the burden grew heavy.

Beckie, his understanding wife, had entertained thoughts that Angel might have died since she had not heard from him for three months. When at last he suddenly returned home, it was only to fetch his family so that together they would obey a clear vision, a truly exciting mission to reach precious souls in the heartland of the "land of promise."

Blazing the Trail

It does not always require academic trappings before a man can apply his basic principles in pioneering a church planting work. At times it only takes the yieldedness and the willingness of a man to be usable in God's hand. Angel approached the delicate work within the very world of the Matigsalogs. He lived as one with them in their village. His own native hut was made out of split bamboo and cogon grass. He easily learned their dialect. He ate and played with them. His acceptance with the people stems from the fact that Angel's first friend was Datu Madut Tawas, their influential village chieftain.

Aware of the basic problems of the Matigsalogs, Angel helped to explain government laws of which the people were ignorant. In the very early part of the evenings Angel and Beckie would teach from 80 to 100 adults and children how to read and write. Since farming was still very primitive, Angel shared with them some simple techniques. He maintained a small vegetable garden for purposes of actual demonstration and as a source of income to support their various projects. This includes a small elementary school which was started in 1971.

As the work expanded gradually through the years, more workers were needed. During a church growth workshop conducted by an O.C. Ministries team for the General Baptists in 1976, Angel presented a dramatic appeal by exhibiting four Datus garbed in their exquisitely hand-woven, colorful, Matigsalog costume. The timeliness of a principle in church growth "to direct manpower and logistics to responsive areas" strengthened Angel's call for immediate reinforcement.

The response of the G.B. mission was beyond what Angel expected. Soon an intensified program was decided upon and the General Baptist Tribal Ministry became a major ministry.

Rev. Dean Trivitt, who now resides with his family in Senuda Mission Station among the Matigsalogs, has been designated as missionary in charge. Rev. Robert Carr, a new missionary, directs the Bible School where some Matigsalogs are being trained for the ministry. Mrs. Mary Howard, a missionary nurse, is in charge of a greatly needed paramedic program. Angel Digdigan has been given supervisory responsibility over G.B. pioneering and church planting programs with about 14 national workers.

As of April 1979, encouraging results had already been noted in the G.B. work among the Matigsalogs. Churches increased from four in 1976 to 13. Twenty-two other outstations are being maintained which will eventually be organized into local congregations.

At the height of the rebellion in 1975, Angel was probably the only lowlander who remained with the Matigsalogs when others fled. He may have been the only lowlander who could enter the Matigsalog territory and come out alive when it became a no-man's-land. Angel must have been the only lowlander who dared risk being caught in the crossfire as he passionately interceded and pleaded with the authorities in the cities and the rebels in the mountains to put an end to the senseless shedding of Filipino blood by Filipinos themselves.

It is then no wonder that today the G.B.s enjoy preferential treatment from a grateful people. Such a privilege could only be the fruit of a precious seed of a dedicated life that is totally committed to God's divine call and unreservedly devoted to the people that He seeks to win.

Sarabia: An Indigenous Arab Church

Greg Livingstone

A church lives in Sarabia. It is a truly indigenous church. The believers are baptized, nationals are recognized leaders, whole families are Christian, believers meet regularly over the Word of God. The church assumes responsibility for its own financial affairs, spiritual growth and witness. Long years of faithful labor on the part of both missionaries and nationals resulted in this fellowship. It is one of a precious few gatherings of mature Christians in Sarabia. More are sure to come.

Sarabia's inhabitants include both Arabs and indigenous people of Berber descent. The Berber existed before the Arabs settled, and now consist of both Arabized Berbers and mountain rural Berbers of different kinds. The Muslim government of Sarabia assumes that every Sarabian is a Muslim. Although the government might be described as socialist, it is actually an eclectic mixture of Islam, socialism and the charismatic personalities of the rulers.

Because of the French colonial influence, the educated people speak mostly French, have had their education in French, and in many cases do not even read Arabic well. Although the government has attempted to Arabize the country, it is evident that French will dominate the culture until those born after 1970 are in leadership. The people of the capital city tend to be affected by French culture with its pessimistic existentialism. Consequently, university students with no awareness of the Sermon on the Mount may be quite familiar with Camus and Sarte. The people of Sarabia, particularly those in the capital, are not fanatical Muslims. Only a small percentage perform the daily prayers. Most are caught up eking out an existence, often due to a critical shortage of housing. Many show little motivation to get ahead because most business and commerce is nationalized.

A Missionary Presence

Although Christian missionaries have worked in Sarabia for a hundred years, they have never been present in great numbers. It is probably safe to say that the capital city has never had as many as 25 missionaries at one time. As in most Muslim lands, Christian work in Sarabia ebbs and flows. At one time there were Arab pastors, salaried by the American Methodist Church, but this is no longer the case. Nevertheless, in the past two decades, individual Muslims have responded to Christ. Although there are no full-time Christian workers, there are up to ten expatriate workers in the city. Many of these have been working a full 20 years. It may be that the continuity of this expatriate presence enabled a church to take root.

Each of these missionaries came to Sarabia with a good working knowledge of Arabic and French. At least half were from secular university backgrounds. One American couple seem to have been the major facilitators in starting the church that is now growing. The husband continues as the only foreigner of the seven elders in the church. Together with a former Inter-Varsity worker, this couple befriended students in a university reading room and began an investigative Bible study. About ten years ago, the investigative Bible study led to a believers' Bible study. This led in turn to a worshiping group and finally to an organized church with elders and membership. The church still meets in that same room today. Because it is crowded on Sunday mornings, they have a multiple-meeting system. Sunday School

Greg Livingstone is co-Founder and General Director of Frontiers, near London, England. Greg helped launch Operation Mobilization and previously served as North American President of North African Mission. He is also the author of *Planting Churches in Muslim Cities*.

meets at a different time from worship services or in private homes while the adults meet in the reading room.

There may be as many as 100 known believers in the capital city of Sarabia. Perhaps half of them are members of the church, committed to its purposes. Most believers are between 18 and 40 years old, with the notable exception of a few who, being older, have provided credibility and stability to the group. A high percentage of the converts come out of the university or technical colleges. This has resulted in a congregation that is well educated. The church has been hesitant to appoint young university students to the position of elders before they find wives and marry. But since it is a long process in prayer, searching and family negotiation to find a Christian mate, only four of the current elders are married.

Mid-week prayer meetings are relevant and dynamic times of dealing with real needs among believers. They also provide occasions for salvation of other Muslims who have been invited to attend by the Muslim converts (note 1 Cor 14:14-25). Although the Sarabian elders organize all meetings, the style is similar to the Plymouth Brethren format in that they are participatory services. Expatriates provide deeper Bible study and training for six to eight Sarabians at any one time. These Theological Education by Extension (TEE) classes meet in the homes of the expatriates.

The Testimony of Arab Believers

It has been difficult for Sarabian Christians to understand that commitment to Christ, the Head, also means commitment to Christ's Body. Sarabians do not normally commit themselves to people outside their own families. Many still fear repercussions or find little motivation to identify themselves with the established church. Still, for several years there has been a good body life, supportive relationships, and, for the Muslim world, a reasonably high level of trust — all making the Sarabian congregation an attractive one. As Arabs are able to meet converted Arabs, the credibility of Christ is greatly enhanced. The testimony of an Arab believer is by far the primary means of communicating the gospel.

Most Sarabians have grown up believing that Christianity and the Western lifestyle are synonymous and, therefore, that Christianity is an inferior and "dirty" religion. Because Islam and politics are completely integrated, the Muslim assumes that Western politics and Christianity are integrated as well. Rejection of the one brings rejection of the other. For most Sarabians, it is a totally new consideration that one can be a follower of Christ *and* a good Sarabian. Christian baptism brings about such alienation in this Muslim culture that it is thought best by many converts not to broadcast such realities and let them be discovered slowly. A number of the believers have not told even their families that they are followers of Christ. Even their marriages, although both the bride and groom are believers, are thought to be Muslim.

There has not been any organized opposition to break up the congregation in the capital city or to keep it from meeting. The police frequently "raid" meetings of believers, but they seem interested only in whether the unauthorized group has *political* intentions. The fact of the raids, however, does keep those who fear repercussions from regular attendance. The stronger believers in the congregation have taken a bold stand with the police and the result has been greater courage on the part of the weaker members.

A Call for Expatriate Missionaries

Expatriates enter Sarabia initially as tourists, then move into Arabic study for which they can get a resident visa. This visa can be good for two or three years, allowing enough time to make contacts and secure a job. Job status is required for a long-term visa. These jobs are often limited to six months to a year, however, and leave the expatriate worker looking for a new raison d'etre. Witnessing opportunities abound. Many Sarabians who have heard radio programs from France and enrolled in Bible correspondence courses, want to check out Christianity through personal visits. A number, if not most, of the believers in the church initially were contacted through radio and Bible correspondence courses. Web evangelism, in which believers themselves witness to friends and relatives, may be more common now than it was before.

Missionaries in Sarabia pray and plan carefully with the national believers. They have made plans to start a new house church in at least four other cities, beginning with the one to seven believers that already exist in those cities. One of the leaders of the capital city church has been identified as an evangelist-church planter and helped financially to visit these believers and hold house meetings in these target cities. Nevertheless, both expatriates and Sarabians verbalize a tremendous need for outside missionaries who can pioneer efforts in the country's 15 cities with populations of over 100,000. Except for the capital city, not one of them has an established church.

The church in the capital city emerged in the midst of hardship mostly due to the skill and dedication of pivotal people. Three or four Sarabians and three or four missionaries kept the goal of an indigenous church always before them. The missionaries established the following criteria for an indigenous church: a) baptized Christians, b) recognized national elders, c) Christian families, d) regular meetings for ministry of the Word in a place not provided by foreigners, e) group responsibility for finances, spiritual activity, discipline, administration of ordinances and witness. They taught that it is God's purpose for those who accept Christ's Lordship to also make a commitment to the existence of a church. Per-

haps because of their higher education, the Sarabian believers were not as intimidated by social disapproval and government opposition as some believers in other Muslim countries. Perhaps the missionary presence over 20 years provided a stability and continuity that was crucial to the emerging church.

The church in the capital city provides a model for what could happen in other cities of Sarabia. It has also shown other missionaries what they can do. There are good prospects for church planting when missionaries and willing nationals team up on compatible intellectual and spiritual levels. This will be possible as soon as missionaries who can speak both French and Arabic become available. These missionaries must understand how to set goals and how to motivate and coach national Christians without making them overly dependent. Progress is slow in planting a new church until there is a "critical mass" of believers, enough to make Christianity a viable alternative in the minds of seekers. The church in the capital began as an investigative Bible study. Now Christians from other cities can gain a vision of how they, too, might plant an indigenous church— perhaps beginning, as well, with an investigative Bible study.

An Upper Class People Movement

Clyde W. Taylor

In recent months I have become acquainted with a fascinating movement in Latin America where the Gospel is spreading by a pattern as close to the New Testament pattern as I have ever seen. I'll not name a country, for the leaders do not want any publicity. But what is happening is to the glory of God and represents a quite significant breakthrough.

I learned of it when I was invited to hold a missionary conference in that country a couple

of years ago. I was not prepared for what I encountered. I understood the missionary involved had a small work, but I discovered the Gospel was spreading in a way that Dr. McGavran would call a "people movement."

The unusual aspect of this movement is that its faith is spreading almost exclusively among the upper-middle and the upper classes of the nation. Furthermore, the number of converts involved is relatively high for the size of the segment of society in-

Clyde W. Taylor, a missionary to Latin America, directed the Evangelical Foreign Missions Association (EFMA) and the National Association of Evangelicals (NAE), and served with the World Relief Corporation, the relief and development arm of the NAE. He died in 1988. Reprinted by permission of *Global Church Growth Bulletin.* Copyright March-April 1980, Volume XVII, No. 2.

volved. Since the movement is intentionally not highly structured, it is difficult to get accurate statistics; but my extensive conversation with leaders lead me to conclude that a minimum of 2,000 converts were actively involved. The number could easily be as high as 5,000 or more.

Beginnings

The work of the missionary, whom I'll call "John Swanson," began in the 1950's in somewhat typical fashion as he witnessed and evangelized among the responsive lower classes. After several years of ministry in the capital city, he had some 20 to 25 converts whom he was training in his home. He came to realize that he was really not a pastor and preacher—his skills were in music and teaching and so asked another mission to shepherd his little flock.

In 1962, Swanson moved to the second largest city in the nation where, after studying the methods of Paul in the books of Acts, he changed his approach. He went to the university and started witnessing to students. Within a few months he won 12 of these to Christ whom he then began to train in discipleship. For seven years he led them in their spiritual growth and trained them also in theology, church history, books of the Bible and so on.

While Swanson was writing, translating and mimeographing materials for the daily sessions with his disciples, they were out witnessing to other students. By 1964 they had won and discipled about 300 others. These were all baptized in and some became members of various churches in the city. (At present about a dozen of these early converts are full-time workers in some of these churches.) The movement at this point was focused in small groups meeting in private homes and university lounges.

Churches Grow and Multiply

These early converts, it should be remembered, were all students and therefore single. In time, when some of them graduated and got married, they began thinking in terms of their own church. In 1969, therefore, the first church with five couples was organized in a home and a second church was organized three years later.

In 1977 the first house church, which had grown to 120 members, divided into two separate churches of 60 members each. The second church grew to 160 members and in 1978 divided into two congregations of 80 each. In February of that year another church was formed bringing the total to five house churches with a combined membership of about 500.

This gives a partial picture only of the work, for, in addition to the many who joined existing churches, the leaders of this new movement to Christ estimate that at least 50 percent of their members have scattered to other sections of the country and even to the U.S. In many cases they begin the process of witnessing, training new converts and establishing house churches all over again.

Furthermore, cells of believers have been established in many of the universities of the region. I was told, for instance, of a type of church meeting for 35 medical students, another for 15 in the biology department and another for 12 in the technical institute of one university.

In 1964 one of the original 12 leaders graduated and returned to the capital city. He began a work along the same lines in which he had come to know the Lord and had been trained. Swanson followed him a few years later.

When I visited there in 1979, I was told that there may be as many as 100 Christian cell meetings among the upper classes in the city. These seem to be spreading on their own. The churches (cells) directly identified with Swanson and his workers, however, have grown to 15 with a total membership approaching 1,000. They told me about a number of similar house churches in other cities as well.

An Inside View

One of the unique features of these house churches is that they are made up of members from the upper-middle and the upper classes of people. The churches in the capital city, in particular, are made up primarily of those from the highest circles of society. This is not to say that they are unconcerned about the poor and less educated. They have evangelized among them and gained many converts. They discovered, however, that as soon as people from the lower and middle classes began attending their churches, ingathering from among the upper class ceased.

Taking Paul's statement that he became all things to all men, they concluded that if they were going to win upper class people they were going to have to win them with Christians who were likewise from the upper classes. As soon as they gain enough converts from the lower classes, therefore, they organize separate churches for them. For these leaders, it is not a matter of not wanting to associate with those on lower rungs of society, but a matter of how best to win the most people to Jesus Christ on *all* levels.

> It is not a matter of not wanting to associate with those on lower rungs of society, but a matter of how best to win the most people to Jesus Christ on *all* levels.

The growth of this cluster of congregations looks a lot like that of New Testament congregations. The converts meet in homes where they worship, fellowship, study the Word and are sent out to bring others to Christ. Each convert is not so much "followed up" but receives the Gospel in a very personal context to begin with. For example, the group has printed and distributed millions of tracts, but none of them have a name and address printed on them. Instead, the one passing out the tract gives his own name and address. When someone comes to know the Lord, he is immediately given training in discipleship.

I talked with one girl, for example, who meets with four new converts at 6 AM They pray, have fellowship and study the Word until breakfast at seven. She meets for lunch with three other girls who are older Christians. They pray and discuss problems together.

Each church is completely independent, though they all carry the same name. They do not keep any membership lists, but they do seem to know everyone who belongs. They baptize, serve communion and train and ordain their own pastors whom they call "elders." They are not highly structured, but their high level of caring and training binds them together.

It is an interesting paradox that these converts are wealthy but they can expand indefinitely with almost no funds since they meet in their large homes and ordain their own lay and unpaid elders (pastors). They do give 20 percent of their incomes on the average, however. With these funds they send out missionaries to other parts of Latin America and even Europe. Money is never mentioned until someone is ready to go to the field and needs support. Then it is not uncommon for someone to say, "I'll give $200 a month," and another to say, "I'll give $150," and so on. Support is thereby raised very quickly.

I heard of one missionary lady who is supported by four of her friends, all executive secretaries. They give her full personal support which is equal to what she would earn as an executive secretary in her home country. They also pay her transportation to and from the field and her ministry needs as well. One of the girls gives 80 percent of her salary, another 60 percent, another 50 percent and another 30 percent. Altogether the fellowship of house churches fully supports 16 missionaries.

The exciting thing about this Christward movement is not just that millionaires, government officials and leading businessmen are becoming believers. The Lord loves the poorest beggar and his conversion is no less precious in His sight. It's significant that disciple-making and church planting is now spreading quickly through a segment of society that has been heretofore unreached. If it can happen in one nation of Latin America, it can happen in others. The Lord of the harvest—of all kinds of crops—will be pleased when it does.

Ann Croft and the Fulani

Fatima Mahoumet

Although Ann Croft's father had planted many churches in the U. S. Midwest during her childhood, she wasn't thinking of herself as a missionary when she went to Nigeria. She was simply a teacher of English as a Second Language. She was able to get to know some of her Nigerian students better, joining them for some meals and eventually reading and discussing stories from the Bible. One student expressed an extraordinary interest in the Bible.

Open Doors

As their friendship grew, her student opened doors for her into the labyrinth of extended family life among the Fulani people in her area. He had many sisters who had married into a number of families in the area. When her student visited them, Ann accompanied him and met each family member.

As a teacher, Ann was also respected by the male leaders of the community. At their request, she spent many hours answering their questions about the Bible, helping them to understand more fully the biblical events and characters, including Jesus, whom they had encountered in the Qur'an. In preparation she had done a comparative study of the Qur'an and Bible, noting their uniqueness, differences and similarities. She used their folk tales as bridges for discussing Scripture.

Soon, Ann had access to every part of the Muslim community. As a woman, she was able to meet the women related to all of her male contacts, even those in the strictest *purdah* (seclusion) who would otherwise be well beyond the sphere of married, let alone single, Christian men. One of the women was especially drawn to Ann. She took her to all the special ceremonies, such as naming ceremonies, weddings and funerals. She helped her with the language and provided many needed bridges of communication and explanations as Ann continued to learn about the Muslim way of life. Ann also learned the traditional stories of her new people and grew to deeply love and appreciate the rich fabric of their lives.

She discovered that being a single woman had its advantages too. In response to questions as to why she was not married, Ann referred to 1 Corinthians 7 and a comparable passage in the Qur'an about single women being able to be totally involved in the work of the Lord. She added that the Bible, unlike the Qur'an, allowed her to do so well past her 20th birthday. Besides, she remarked, how could she otherwise teach their children and always be available to them any time they were having trouble, day or night? She wasn't subject to the demands of marriage or the constraints of *purdah*. She was always free to help.

Caring for Cattle

Ann began to focus her efforts among the Fulani people of Northern Nigeria.

The Fulani are a largely nomadic people, whose search for good pasture for their cattle has scattered them throughout sub-Saharan West Africa. Strong clan fidelity and six centuries of Muslim evangelism have made them the most effective champions of Islam in West Africa. Of 6.7 million Fulani, only 400 are known Christians.

As Ann studied more about the people to whom God had sent her, she discovered ways of showing the Fulani cattle-herders that they are very special to God. She found numerous references in the Bible to nomadic cattle-herding peoples who played special roles in biblical history.

Knowing the great importance of cattle to them, Ann began to help upgrade the health of the cattle with veterinary medicine and so helped the Fulani begin to cope with some of the economic problems they faced with the growing pressure of urbanization.

Adapted from *The Zwemer Institute Newsletter*, Spring 1981. Used by permission of the Zwemer Institute, Fort Wayne, IN.

Caring for cattle was the way to the Fulani heart. On one occasion she helped a Fulani elder get tuberculosis medicine for his son and worm medicine for himself. But it was not until she gave him medicine for his cows that he said, "Now I know you *really* love us!"

Ann was able to join forces with another mission agency in a distant city that was planning an evangelistic three-day "conference" especially for Fulani. Fulani people were told that it would be a religious conference studying one of the prophets—Abraham, a super-herdsman who had cows and sheep and donkeys and goats and camels. This was a big event for the Fulani, not accustomed to special events just for their people.

At the end of the evangelistic conference, the chief of the area said to Ann that he wanted his people to become part of the Christian community. He had seen that Christians and their Holy Book cared about the needs of his people. Some of the greatest prophets, after all, like Abraham, were cattle-herders too! He also told her that to get a lot of people interested in the Christian faith, one of the best things she could do would be to continue to show a real, genuine interest in every aspect of their culture.

Gathering new believers into viable fellowships is proving to be a tremendous challenge. It is hard enough for some Fulani youth to settle down for Bible school. A permanent location for a tribe might unravel nomadic life. Perhaps now is the time for the Fulani people, as they move towards a future that is economically, politically and socially uncertain.

Distant Thunder: Mongols Follow the Khan of Khans

Brian Hogan

In the 13th Century the Mongol tribes, united under Genghis Khan, thundered across the steppes of Central Asia and terrorized the known world. In a short time, these fierce horsemen had carved out an empire that dwarfed those of Cyrus and Caesar combined.

The Mongol empire was not to endure for long. The Mongols embraced Tibetan Buddhism and became a backward hinterland ruled by a succession of Chinese dynasties. In 1921, a Communist revolution turned Mongolia into the first "independent" Soviet satellite. All missionaries were expelled before any church had been planted, and the darkness of Communism settled over this "closed" country. Mongolia was one of the very few countries on earth with no church, and no known national believers.

Doors Begin to Open

Finally, in 1990, Communism released its weakening hold. The doors—closed for so long—began to open. Creative strategies sparked the beginnings. A team of Christian Native Americans entered Mongolia as tourists in 1990. Their visit generated a great deal of interest among Mongols and even in the national press. By the end of their second visit in 1991, they had publicly baptized 36 new Mongol believers. The spiritual landscape of Mongolia would never be the same.

A young Swedish couple, Magnus and Maria, came to Mongolia intending to help plant churches. They settled in the capital, Ulaan Baatar, where they befriended some of the growing number of local believers.

Brian Hogan was part of a YWAM (Youth With A Mission) Church Planting team working in Mongolia. Brian is currently a church planting trainer with YWAM–Church Planting Coaches in Arcata, California. Adapted from *Multiplying Churches Among Unreached People Groups: Guiding Principles*, Kevin Sutter, YWAM Arcata, CA.

Eventually Magnus and Maria moved to Erdenet, the third largest city of Mongolia. With them went a nineteen year old Mongolian believer named Bayaraa. The first to respond to their evangelism efforts were a handful of teenage girls. It was not a promising beginning, but after teaching on faith and repentance, several of the girls invited their friends to follow Christ with them. In 1993, Mongolians were baptized in Erdenet for the first time in the city's history. Fourteen were baptized—all of them teenage girls!

The first fourteen converts were quickly organized into three "cell groups." They gathered for prayer, fellowship and teaching in an atmosphere of support and accountability. Together they learned to obey the two greatest commandments: "Love the Lord your God with all your heart and with all your soul and with all your strength and with all your mind " and "Love your neighbor as yourself." (Luke 10:27)

Active, faithful believers were equipped to lead the cells as they multiplied. A monthly "celebration service" formed for all the cells to unite. A year passed: the number of believers grew to 120…still, mostly teenage girls! At this point the embryonic "church" was not multi-generational or family based. It was essentially a rapidly growing youth group.

After a year of language study in Ulaan Baatar, the capital city, my wife Louise, our three daughters and I arrived to join Magnus, Maria, and Bayaraa. We were later joined by others from Russia, America and Sweden.

Breakthrough into the Mainstream

We all realized that teenage girls were not an appropriate foundation for starting a church movement. At that time however, youth were only ones responding anywhere in Mongolia. So we worked with the fruit the Lord had provided and prayed for a breakthrough to begin reaching whole families. We established "provisional elders" (starting with two younger men and Bayaraa) in order to begin the process of allowing a Mongolian style of church leadership to develop and to allow us to work more in the background.

Breakthrough of relevance

There was a great divide between the youthful, urban circle of friends and the family-oriented heart of traditional Mongolian society. Even our early converts had the impressions that the gospel wasn't relevant for "real Mongols." To the Mongol understanding, "real Mongols" are the traditional shepherds and *gher* (traditional round felt tents) dwellers. A visiting short-term team began to pray for the sick in some of the traditional *gher* suburbs on the outskirts of town. God answered prayer dramatically. One lame person, one deaf person, one mute person, and one blind person were all healed. These healings provided a seal of authenticity recognized by the older Mongols. The news spread like wildfire and the fellowship was flooded with growth from every age group and segment of the city. The urbanized youth were especially surprised that "real Mongols" were coming to faith. Soon two older men who were heads of households joined the ranks of our provisional elders.

Breakthrough of understanding

The second factor for the sudden acceptability of the good news by the older traditional Mongols was the decision by our team and the "elders-in-training" to begin using the Mongolian term *"Burhan"* to refer to the God of the Bible. Many centuries before, when the Buddhists arrived in Mongolia, they adopted the term *"burhan,"* the generic Mongolian term for "god," for their purposes. In the early 90's, nearly all the believers in Mongolia used another term for God, *Yertontsiin Ezen*, which was a brand new term composed by a translator in an attempt to avoid any potential confusion or syncretism with the erroneous beliefs of Buddhism. But the new term, which can be translated "Master of the Universe," sounded unfamiliar and unreal to the Mongol's ears. It had no intrinsic meaning and was essentially a foreign word made up of Mongolian elements. Although the Erdenet elders-in-training were used to using the term *Yertontsiin Ezen*, they decided the traditional term *Burhan* would be more appropriate and acceptable and was capable of being filled with biblical meaning.

Developing Indigenous Leadership

During this period of explosive growth our team deliberately stayed in "behind the scenes" roles, giving on-the-job training for the emerging leaders. Care was taken to do everything in imitable fashion—baptisms were in bathtubs, worship songs were not imported, but written by church members, etc.

The team recalled what we had learned from veteran missionary George Patterson before coming to Mongolia. He got to the heart of discipleship saying, "People are saved to obey the Lord Jesus Christ in love." So in the new church, Jesus' basic commands were taught in practical ways. The cells provided the atmosphere of loving support and accountability. Believers helped one another to "be doers of the word, not hearers only."

Yet there were serious problems from our point of view where the cultural norms of Mongolian society conflicted with some of the moral teaching of the scriptures. The elders-in-training were encouraged to search the scriptures to find solutions for sin problems in the emerging church. Cultural blind spots in the areas of sexual purity and courtship were dealt with by defining principles, then teaching and enforcing them. The solutions that these Mongol leaders crafted were both biblical and culturally correct—much better than any we missionaries could have crafted.

The emerging Mongolian church looked far different from any of the team's home churches in Sweden, Russia or America. Dramas and testimonies quickly became prominent features of the large celebration meetings (which went from once to twice a month; and eventually weekly). The "drama team" wrote and produced their own skits, plays, and dramatic dances from Bible stories and everyday Mongolian life. This became a powerful teaching and evangelistic tool. Time was always set aside for testimonies from "real Mongols"—often new believers in their 60s just in off the steppes. These long and, to Western ears, rambling stories of salvation gripped the fellowship in a state of rapt wonder and awe. God was on the move among their people—dressed in the most traditional of Mongolian clothing. Worship rose from their hearts as they sang new songs that had

been written by their own people in their own language and unique musical style. This was no foreign fad or import!

About a year and a half into the church's "life," the Mongol "provisional elders" decided to politely decline further funds from supporting churches abroad. The funds had been used to provide some of the Mongol church worker's salaries for about a year. Their own people were now giving and that would suffice. When the foreign church insisted on sending the funds, they were passed along to the daughter churches for their church workers, with the understanding that this too was only temporary.

The expatriate team concentrated our efforts upon discipling, equipping and releasing Mongols to take the lead in building up the church and reaching the lost. A school of discipleship was formed and by its third class was entirely Mongol led.

With the emphasis upon "learning by doing," new leaders were trained locally in the ministry rather than being sent away. The leadership of the cells had been placed into their hands almost immediately, and soon the local believers also carried the majority of the responsibility for the weekly services.

Overcoming

All of this progress and growth was not overlooked by the Enemy. Beginning in November of 1994, our team and the fledgling church endured two solid months of unrelenting spiritual attacks: three cult groups targeted our city, the church was almost split, leaders fell into sin, some were demonized. Our team came close to despairing and pulling out.

Finally, two sudden and unexplainable deaths rocked the missionary team and the church. My only son, Jedidiah, had been born on November 2nd. On the morning of Christmas Eve our apartment rang with screams when my wife discovered Jedidiah's cold and lifeless body—dead of Sudden Infant Death Syndrome at two months. We buried our boy and a piece of our hearts in the frozen soil on a cold windswept hillside outside of town. The next day a young girl in the church died of no known cause.

In response the believers and our team came together for 24 hours of prayer and fasting in our office apartment. At three in the morning, a breakthrough occured and everyone knew it. The church has never been overwhelmed by an episode of spiritual warfare like that since.

Explosive Growth

One of the beauties of the cell church model was that, where other churches in Mongolia were sorely hindered by government harassment that usually took the form of evictions from Sunday meeting locations, the church being planted in Erdenet was largely unaffected by such moves—since worship mainly took place in living rooms all over town! Growth was constantly taking place in the cells and going months without "celebration services" didn't slow things down. When the cells did gather, united in God's presence, the believers were encouraged, seeing their numbers continue to grow.

By early 1997, the celebration service had grown so that no building in the city could house the 750 people who would attend! So they held two services. Recently appointed Mongol pastor/elders lead their church made up of over 57 cell groups. A healthy multi-generational Mongol church had become a reality.

The Beginnings of a Church Planting Movement

Was this the mission breakthrough we had been looking for? To stop with a single church in a city of 70,000 and a country of 2.6 million would mean we'd have gained almost no ground in the task of discipling the Mongols as a people. Our goal had always been an indigenous movement of multiplying churches that would spread throughout the once spiritually barren land of Mongolia.

From the beginning we made it our aim to help the new leaders catch this vision. We taught them to treat their church as an organism rather than thinking of it as an organization. All healthy, living organisms grow and reproduce. The Mongols saw that their church should become a "mother church" giving birth to daughter churches and that could reproduce granddaughter churches. The local leaders presented the vision before their congregation: "God wants to work through our church to create another new church!"

In 1993, the church sent teams of Mongol deacons to a town 60 kilometers away. They were commissioned to plant a daughter church and, the next year, an elder was sent to lead it. As fellow Mongolians it was easy for them to relate to the people in the new community. God blessed their efforts as they shared the gospel and discipled new believers. A daughter church was born, and soon, two of the new leaders got busy planting granddaughter churches in other places that were even more remote from Erdenet.

The End of The Beginning

The work progressed to such an extent that in 1996, after just three years, our team realized we had reached an important landmark. Actually, we had been anticipating our "phase-out" from the beginning and had kept it in the forefront of all our plans and activities. But that bitter-sweet time had come.

We reported to our supporters: "We were blessed to hand over the authority in the church to the elders we had trained...this was the crowning moment for us." A special service was held on Easter Sunday, 1996. In the midst of worship and prayer the team followed the example of Paul's farewell to the Ephesian elders: "Now I commit you to God and to the word of His grace, which can build you up and give you an inheritance...." Half of the missionary team left Mongolia that very day. The others remained through June as distant advisors while they finished secular teaching contract commitments.

The newly independent Mongol church moved ahead in faith and action as the Holy Spirit led. At Christmas 1996, 101 new believers were baptized! On Easter 1997, the first anniversary of the "passing of the baton," 120 more were baptized.

The church is finding ways to bring blessing in Jesus' name to their city. One ongoing effort was initiated and is carried out by Mongol believers: Every day many of the city's cast-off street kids are offered food and clothing (not a small matter in frigid Mongolia). A prison ministry is also flourishing, as is a cell group among the garbage dump dwellers!

The movement continues. At last count, the mother church had given birth to 13 daughter churches in towns scattered across the province. The church they planted in Darhan, the second largest city in Mongolia, has over 100 in 11 cell groups and is quite unique in Mongolia because it has mostly families and older people as members. This young body has reproduced two grand-daughter churches. A very satisfying report considering we started five years earlier with only teenage girls!

This movement has also begun to work cross-culturally, having planted a church among Erdenet's Russian population. Teams of Mongols have recently been sent to cultur-ally distinct peoples in two other countries, to an unrelated animistic forest tribal people, as well as to several remote Mongolian prov-inces. A missionary training school has opened in Erdenet to train the church's emerging mission force. Some of the expatri-ate church planters have returned to lead the school, but exercise no authority in the indig-enous church.

God seems to have made the spiritual soil of Mongolia especially fertile for church planting. The gospel continues to do its life giving and community-changing work. Churches continue to grow and reproduce. A conservative estimate states that the number of believers has grown from two in 1990 to over 10,000 believers in 1998. Given the zeal of the believers, Mongolia will eventually shift from a mission field to being a powerful mission force. As in a previous age, Mongols will again thunder off to the nations beyond their barren hills—this time under the leader-ship of the "Khan of Khans"—King Jesus!

A Movement of Christ Worshipers in India

Dean Hubbard

Before 1991 the gospel had managed to attract very few converts in a particu-lar district in Central India. Seven years later hundreds of newly baptized be-lievers from at least 24 different people groups are learning to follow Jesus. They are gathering regularly in village level churches under the name, "Krista Bhakta Mandali"— "The Gathering of Christ Worshipers." How did so many people suddenly turn to hope in Christ from centuries of practicing animistic spiritism blended with Hinduism?

A Key Leader

Bhimrao was a local, third generation Chris-tian who had been a social and political activ-ist for impoverished farmers, serving, suffer-ing and going to jail with them over a several year period. Believing God wanted him to address the deeper spiritual needs of the ru-ral peoples among whom he had grown up,

he cooperated with an Indian mission organi-zation to open avenues for the gospel among the Kowadi people. As an agrarian peasant group, the Kowadis have largely adapted their animistic traditions to the religious practices of the surrounding rural Hindu cul-ture. They had resisted previous mission ef-forts, viewing Christianity as a religion for peoples of lower social standing than them-selves. To present the gospel to the Kowadis in a way that they could understand and value, Bhimrao first confronted the failure of the two sources of power in which they had placed their hopes for social and economic upliftment: the government and their tradi-tional gods. His message to them focused on Jesus: Since Jesus had created the Kowadis, Jesus has always been their rightful Lord and God. He loves them and is concerned about every dimension of their lives-social, eco-nomic and spiritual. Yet they had never

Dean Hubbard (a pseudonym) has served with Youth With A Mission in the Pacific and Asia region for over 20 years. For the last eight years he has lived in India with his family, serving an indigenous ministry among the poor, helping develop church leadership. Names of persons and people groups have been changed.

known his blessing because they had placed their hope in others. He had made the way for them to again come under his Lordship and know his blessing, but only if they would put their hope in him.

Bhimrao spent three months explaining this message in 150 Kowadi villages. Finally, a large three-day gathering summoned the Kowadis from these villages. The days were filled with Kowadi songs, dances and presentations of Jesus' teaching in their language. At the end, 41 Kowadi affirmed Jesus as "Their Lord and Lord of the Kowadi" by taking baptism. Several of them were village leaders who were now convinced that Jesus was the true answer for their people.

Opposition Tests Faith and Attests to Credibility

Hindu religious zealots immediately disrupted the intended plans for follow-up and establishment of churches. The Kowadi people, known for their timidity, appeared to withdraw from further contact with the missionaries working with Bhimrao. Bhimrao had to leave the area temporarily for the birth of his first child. When he returned three months later he discovered that the other Indian missionaries themselves had withdrawn, discouraged and uncertain how to proceed. Upon further investigation, Bhimrao, realized that there had been some confusion following the persecution, but no lack of resolve. The converts still wanted to follow Jesus. With few resources and little support, Bhimrao had to form a new organization to facilitate the larger intent of serving the spiritual, church formation and socio-economic development needs of the Kowadi. He called it, "Din Sevak — Servant to the Poor." Bhimrao was joined by a non-Indian, Dean, and Bhimrao's brother, Kishor, and their wives. Still, limited resources and personnel required that from the start the new believers would do most of the ministry in the villages. As a result of the witness of village locals to their own friends and family, and partly helped by the publicity brought about by the initial persecution, many approached Bhimrao for an explanation.

Bhimrao's earlier social activist work had earned him great credibility in their eyes. The false accusations of the Hindu nationalist me-dia was doubted because of the known character and longstanding service that Bhimrao had performed throughout the region. Members of other people groups seemed to be asking, "If this is good for the Kowadi who are so similar to us socially and economically, then will it not also be good for us?" For decades the Indian government had sought to remove caste segregation with minimal success. Now it appeared that the gospel was leaping over traditional caste boundaries by virtue of a broader identity based on socio-economic condition. Even some of those opposed to conversion in principle opened up to the gospel along with those who were more readily responsive. As a result, doorways of opportunity began to open into a variety of people groups and their villages.

"Why Should We Follow Small Gods?"

With the intention of initiating a movement of self-reproducing churches filled with worshipers of Jesus and not merely a scattering of baptized believers, a group of potential leaders were soon identified and gathered for a week of teaching. Although limited in scope, it proved a watershed experience—not so much for the new believers as for Bhimrao and Dean. A visiting foreign Christian researcher conducted one of the sessions. He simply shared stories of people groups in other countries that were embracing Christ as well. At the end of the week, participants indicated that that session had been the most significant for them. "We can see now that this Jesus is greater than all other gods. All the gods we have ever known have been gods only of a village, a tribe, a region, or of the nation of India. But this Jesus, he has followers from all over the world. Why should we follow small gods, when we can follow the greatest God of all?"

God Sends "Angels"

This insight was further reinforced when short-term teams with foreigners would come to help. One such team had located in a village populated entirely by Poharis. The Poharis are highly transient hunters who engage in animistic rituals while honoring Hindu brahminical priestcraft. They had asked for someone to come and teach them also about Christ. But the only ones available were a short-term team of young Scandinavian women who could not have been further removed from them in almost every way.

While discussing Christ with these young women with pale skin, bright blond hair and blue eyes, the Poharis began telling about a particular priest in their village. Five years prior he had passed through a period when most of the people thought he was crazy. He often seemed tormented by spirits. They brought him repeatedly before various gods & goddesses for healing. All the while he kept saying, "People who look like angels will come from around the world to our village. They will tell us about the real God. We should follow him." So the team asked him what he saw in his vision. He said, "I saw people like you, white kind of people—they were angels. They will come and tell about God." When they asked, "Do you think that we are those people?" he responded, "I don't know yet." But after four days of listening he trusted the Lord Jesus Christ and received him as his savior. In the end, most of those residing in that particular village were baptized.

In spite of promising beginnings, the general timidity of the Kowadi and the remote location of many of their villages continually inhibited healthy church formation. The transient hunting activities and almost universal illiteracy of the Poharis severely undermined effective church leadership development. But the bold, settled situation of the Bansaris proved a different story.

The Bansari number in the millions and also observe a mixture of folk religion and Hindu practices. Continued hostility toward conversions from the local press had acted like free publicity resulting in a young, educated Bansari man coming to Bhimrao seeking help. Experiencing severe depression and contemplating suicide, he finally found deliverance in Christ. Returning to his home in a distant area of the district he soon led 14 friends to trust Christ. Of these, the roles of three proved especially effective for the extension of the gospel. One was the leader of the Bansaris in his village. Another was a leader in a family that extended into many villages throughout that area. The third was a tailor near the central bus stand where people come from all the surrounding vil-

lages. All three began aggressively evangelizing within their respective networks of relationship. As people responded, they began visiting their villages.

> **Seekers were called to follow Christ, not to become members of the Christian community, which has generally come to be perceived simply as a caste in contrast to other castes.**

By this time "Servant to the Poor" had initiated a weekly time of fasting, prayer and teaching. These men were invited to join with men and women from other people groups who gathered weekly to learn how to better serve the needs of the churches that were forming in their villages. Very soon there were too many villages with new believers for them to care for. In the earliest stages they were required to identify potential church leaders. These also participated in the training and soon groups were meeting for regular worship in villages that were led by converts of the converts of the first convert.

Following Christ Without Betraying Family

The earlier experiences with other people groups, both successes and failures, resulted in critical lessons that shaped the approach taken with the emerging Bansari Krista Bhakta Mandalis. Seekers were called to follow Christ, not to become members of the Christian community, which has generally come to be perceived simply as a caste in contrast to other castes. To worship Christ was not to betray, but rather to fulfill their people group's highest destiny. This destiny was for their entire group, not just a few individuals. New seekers from different communities are routinely welcomed into these fellowships, but are encouraged to focus their witness among people of their own family and caste.

One reason that the Krista Bhakta Mandali has not been perceived as a new Christian caste is that the small gatherings of worship and teaching have been primarily people-group specific. Occasional celebrations are held in which Christ worshipers from diverse castes come together to worship and partake of what is referred to as "the Lord's Meal." For some it is the first time in their lives that they have shared bread with people from any other caste community in their lives. The joy of sharing Christ together affirms all the finest of what they now have in common without requiring them to abandon the identity with their community. Leadership for potential churches was identified early and allowed to carry significant responsibility for the discipling of others. Those potential elders were identified primarily on the basis of initiative, faithfulness and effectiveness in imparting the gospel. Then they were brought into the weekly training process that focused on learning foundations of a Biblical worldview and simple obedience to Christ. Practical help would be given on how to break from old behavior patterns and to cope with the struggles of living for Jesus in an environment that was often diametrically opposed to his values and teachings. All the while they would be active in witness and bearing responsibility for the welfare of new believers—not because they had been told to do so, but because they believed Jesus wanted them to do so. They were held accountable to their own declared commitment through regular reporting and coaching visits to their area of work. The role of the "Din Sevak" team members was not primarily to direct, but to encourage, support and coach the village leaders. The support was given in several ways. Regular and special training opportunities were arranged. Both Indian and multi-national teams were channeled to help them minister in their villages. Language and culture specific tools were made available; and if none existed, they were created, including scripture translation, and the publication and promotion of appropriate worship forms. Seed loans for farmers and income generation skills training for women were also implemented to limited degrees.

Persecution: Purging Then Multiplying

Unfortunately, hard lessons had preceded the later successes. A self-sustaining church has yet to develop among the Poharis. It is clear that even supernatural, prophetic preparation does not supersede the need for ongoing discipling and development. Opposition eventually took its toll on Kowadi leaders. The Bansari leaders have until now stood firm in the face of persecution, and they seem to be demonstrating the greatest potential for an actual movement of self-reproducing churches. Perhaps it is for this reason that they are now experiencing some of the greatest persecution, not so much from within their own group, but from the more traditional Hindus that surround them. Religious nationalism is gaining ground in India's places of power. What were formerly verbal threats from local groups have given way to physical violence against some KBM village groups.

Yet, perhaps one of the most important lessons from seven years of ministry has been that opposition has invariably resulted in a "purging then multiplying" effect on the overall movement, especially when the leaders stood firm. What is intended to destroy this young movement may in the end make its spontaneous multiplication unstoppable. May it be so!

What it Means to Be a World Christian

David Bryant

In 1979, David Bryant published a book titled "In the Gap" which revived the concept of living as a World Christian. The book has recently been revised and abbreviated under the title, "Stand in the Gap." In the full-length book, Bryant uses the imagery of "the Gap" to describe the unfulfilled global purpose of God. "The widest end of the Gap" describes situations in which Christ is known and followed the least. Christ is seen as the sole mediator in "the Gap." This excerpt of the original book remains one of the clearest statements of what it means to be a World Christian.

What, then, shall we call this discovery that can change us so radically and yet make us so healthy? And, what shall we call those who have experienced it?

By now it should be obvious that *all* Christians are born again *into* the Gap between God's world-wide purpose and the fulfillment of it. But there's more than one kind of *response* to that Gap.

Some are asleep, some are on retreat, and some are determined to stand in the Gap, particularly at its widest end where billions await the opportunity to hear of Christ for the first time. Some are heading into the "sunrise of missions" while others huddle in the shadows. Many move along at a sluggish pace, changing little in the Gap because of their own internal gap-of-unbelief. Others run the race before them setting no limits on how, where, or among whom God will use them.

Some are trapped in boxes of pea-sized Christianity, full of myths about missions that rob them of incentive to care about the unreached. Others have broken though into cause-Christianity, ready to reach out with God's love to the ends of the earth. They are determined to make Christ's global cause the unifying focus—the context—for all they are and do in the Gap. Yielded to the mediator, they are willing to be broken and remolded to fit in the Gap wherever they can make the most strategic impact. In turn, they're growing to know Christ, obey Him, and glorify Him as the mediator.

So, what shall we call the discovery that redirects Christians toward the needs of the Gap? And how shall we distinguish those who have made it?

Some Christians in the Gap are stunted by selfishness and petty preoccupations or by a cautious obedience and love reserved for the closest and easiest to care about. How shall

David Bryant is founder and Director of Concerts of Prayer International, and Chairman of America's National Prayer Committee. Formerly he was a pastor and later missions specialist with InterVarsity Christian Fellowship. He has developed a broad spectrum of practical training materials on united prayer, spiritual renewal and world missions. His latest trilogy on revival includes: *The Hope at Hand, Stand in the Gap* and *Messengers of Hope.*

we distinguish the others in the Gap whose growth in discipleship is unmistakable, with a vitality that comes only to those who help bring lost sinners from many nations home?

What shall we call this distinct group of Christians who have taken a stand that says:

> We want to accept personal responsibility for reaching some of earth's unreached, especially from among the billions at the widest end of the Gap who can only be reached through major new efforts by God's people. Among every people group where there is no vital, evangelizing Christian community there should be one, there must be one, there shall be one. Together we want to help make this happen.

For a moment, let's call them WORLD CHRISTIANS. Of course, any new term might be misunderstood. For example, some might think I said "worldly" Christians, not World Christians. By now we know, however, if you are one, you can't be the other. If you are one you don't *want* to be the other!

No, the term is not in your Bible concordance. Don't worry. It isn't another cliche like the words of the bumper sticker that read "Honk-if-the-Rapture-starts." Nor is it an attempt to label some new spiritual elite who have a corner on a super-secret blessing. Rather, the term describes what all of us are meant to be and what some of us have started to become.

The term "World Christian" may have been coined first by Daniel Fleming in a 1920 YMCA book entitled *Marks of a World Christian*. More recently the term has appeared in publications of such groups as the World Team missions, Conservation Baptist Foreign Missionary Society, United Presbyterian Center for Mission Studies, the Mission Renewal Teams, Inc., and the Fellowship of World Christians, as well as Campus Crusade for Christ and Inter-Varsity Christian Fellowship.

A World Christian isn't better than other Christians. But by God's grace, he has made a discovery so important that life can never be the same again. He has discovered the truth about the Gap, the fact that he is already in it, and the call of Christ to believe, think, plan,

and act accordingly. By faith, he has chosen to *stand* in the Gap as a result.

Some World Christians are missionaries who stand in the Gap by physically crossing major human barriers (cultural, political, etc.) to bring the gospel to those who can hear no other way. But every Christian is meant to be a World Christian, whether you physically "go," or "stay at home" to provide the sacrificial love, prayers, training, money, and quality of corporate life that backs the witness of those who "go."

World Christians are day-to-day disciples for whom Christ's global cause has become the integrating, overriding priority for all that He is for them. Like disciples should, they actively investigate all that their Master's Great Commission means. Then they act on what they learn.

World Christians are Christians whose life-directions have been solidly transformed by a world vision. This is not a term for frustrated Christians who feel trapped into the world missionary movement and sporadically push a few buttons to say they've done their part. Having caught a vision, World Christians want to keep that vision and obey it unhesitatingly.

World Christians are (in Corrie Ten Boom's phrase) tramps for the Lord who have left their hiding places to roam the Gap with the Savior. They are heaven's expatriates, camping where the Kingdom is best served. They are earth's dispossessed, who've journeyed forth to give a dying world not only the gospel but their own souls as well. They are members of God's global dispersion down through history and out through the nations, reaching the unreached and blessing the families of earth.

By taking three steps we become World Christians. First, World Christians *catch* a world vision. They see the cause the way God sees it. They see the full scope of the Gap. Next, World Christians *keep* that world vision. They put the cause at the heart of their life in Christ. They put their life at the heart of the Gap. Then World Christians *obey* their world vision. Together they develop a strategy that makes a lasting impact on the cause, particularly at the widest end of the Gap.

Many years ago a World Christian named John R. Mott, leader of the Student Volunteer Movement that sent out 20,000 new missionaries, outlined similar steps:

An enterprise which aims at the evangelization of the whole world in a generation, and contemplates the ultimate establishment of the Kingdom of Christ, requires that its leaders be Christian statesmen with far-seeing views, with comprehensive plans, with power of initiative, and with victorious faith.

Catch! Keep! Obey!—these are the three steps to becoming a World Christian. Let's examine them a little more closely in outline form:

Step One: Catch a World Vision
- See God's world-wide *purpose* in Christ
- See a world full of *possibilities* through Christ
- See a world full of *people* without Christ
- See my world-sized *part* with Christ

Step Two: Keep a World Vision
- *Be* a World Christian
- *Join* with other World Christians
- *Plan* to obey the vision

Step Three: Obey a World Vision
- Obey as you regularly *build* your vision
- Obey as you *reach out* directly in love
- Obey as you *give* your vision to other Christians
- Obey as you *pray* your vision back to God.

How can someone know if they've taken these three basic steps toward becoming a World Christian? Here are some important clues:

STEP ONE: Have I caught a world vision?
PURPOSE: Do I see the big picture of Christ's global cause from God's point of view?
POSSIBILITIES: Do I see the Church's potential in our generation for closing the Gap between God's world-wide purpose and its fulfillment?
PEOPLE: Do I see the great scope of the earth's unreached peoples, espe-

cially the billions at the widest end of the Gap who have yet to clearly hear the gospel?
PART: Do I believe that I, along with other Christians, can have a strategic impact on Christ's global cause right now?

STEP TWO: Have I kept a world vision?
BE: Am I willing to stand in the Gap with Christ, to unite my whole relationship with Him around His global cause?
JOIN: Am I willing to team-up with other World Christians to stand in the Gap together?
PLAN: Am I willing to design specific ways to obey my world vision and help close the Gap?

STEP THREE: Do I obey a world vision?
BUILD: Do I take time to study the cause? Am I letting my world vision grow?
REACH OUT: Do I personally get involved in the cause? Am I helping to reach unreached peoples, especially at the widest end of the Gap?
GIVE: Do I transfer my vision to other Christians? Am I seeking more World Christians to stand in the Gap and serve the cause?
PRAY: In solidarity with the promises of God, am I interceding for those who cannot (yet) intercede for themselves? Even more strategically, am I seeking God for a spiritual awakening to Christ throughout the Church, which alone can mobilize and empower a fresh, vital missionary movement among the nations?

Ultimately, however, becoming a World Christian goes beyond "steps" that we take. It is the gracious work of Christ Himself! Our faith must always be in Him, not in any simple three-step process. It is Christ who opens us up to catch His world vision. He alone anchors us to that vision and then empowers us to effectively obey it. With the hymn writer all World Christians appeal to Christ: "Be Thou my Vision, Oh Lord of my Heart."

Reconsecration to a Wartime, Not a Peacetime, Lifestyle

Ralph D. Winter

After serving ten years as a missionary among Mayan Indians in the highlands of Guatemala, Ralph D. Winter was called to be a Professor of Missions at the School of World Mission at Fuller Theological Seminary. Ten years later he and his wife, Roberta, founded a mission society called the Frontier Mission Fellowship (FMF) in Pasadena, California. This in turn spawned the U.S. Center for World Mission and the William Carey International University, both of which serve other missions working at the frontiers of mission. He is the General Director of the Frontier Mission Fellowship. See expanded biographical sketch at the end of the book.

The Queen Mary, lying in repose in the harbor at Long Beach, California, is a fascinating museum of the past. Used both as a luxury liner in peacetime and a troop transport during the Second World War, its present status as a museum the length of three football fields affords a stunning contrast between the lifestyles appropriate in peace and war. On one side of a partition you see the dining room reconstructed to depict the peacetime table setting that was appropriate to the wealthy patrons of high culture for whom a dazzling array of knives and forks and spoons held no mysteries. On the other side of the partition the evidences of wartime austerities are in sharp contrast. One metal tray with indentations replaces fifteen plates and saucers. Bunks, not just double but eight tiers high, explain why the peace-time complement of 3000 gave way to 15,000 people on board in wartime. How repugnant to the peacetime masters this transformation must have been! To do it took a national emergency, of course. The survival of a nation depended upon it. The essence of the Great Commission today is that the survival of many millions of people depends on its fulfillment.

But obedience to the Great Commission has more consistently been poisoned by affluence than by anything else. The antidote for affluence is reconsecration. Consecration is by definition the "setting apart of things for a holy use." Affluence did not keep Borden of Yale from giving his life in Egypt. Affluence didn't stop Francis of Assisi from moving against the tide of his time.

Curiously enough, while the Protestant tradition has no significant counterpart to the Catholic orders within its U.S. base (unless we think of the more recent campus evangelistic organizations such as Inter-Varsity, Campus Crusade, and Navigators), nevertheless the entire Protestant missionary tradition has always stressed a practical measure of austerity and simplicity as well as a parity of level of consumption within its missionary ranks. Widespread reconsecration leading to a reformed lifestyle with wartime priorities is not likely to be successful (even in an age of increasing awareness of the lifestyle issue itself) unless Protestantism can develop patterns of consecration among the people back home that are comparable to what has characterized the Protestant missionary movement for nearly two hundred years.

There will only be a way if there is a will. But we will find there is no will:

- so long as the Great Commission is thought impossible to fulfill;
- so long as anyone thinks that the problems of the world are hopeless or that, conversely, they can be solved merely by politics or technology;
- so long as our home problems loom larger to us than anyone else's;
- so long as people enamored of Eastern culture do not understand that Chinese and Muslims can and must as easily become evangelical Christians without abandoning their cultural systems as did the Greeks in Paul's day;
- so long as modern believers, like the ancient Hebrews, get to thinking that God's sole concern is the blessing of our nation;
- so long as well paid evangelicals, both pastors and people, consider their money a gift from God to spend however they wish on themselves rather than a responsibility from God to help others in spiritual and economic need;
- so long as we do not understand that he who would seek to save his life shall lose it.

America today is a "save yourself" society if there ever was one. But does it really work? The underdeveloped societies suffer from one set of diseases: tuberculosis, malnutrition, pneumonia, parasites, typhoid, cholera, typhus, etc. Affluent America has virtually invented a whole new set of diseases: obesity, arteriosclerosis, heart disease, strokes, lung cancer, venereal disease, cirrhosis of the liver, drug addiction, alcoholism, divorce, battered children, suicide, murder. Take your choice. Labor-saving machines have turned out to be body-killing devices. Our affluence has allowed both mobility and isolation of the nuclear family and, as a result, our divorce courts, our prisons and our mental institutions are flooded. In saving ourselves we have nearly lost ourselves.

How hard have we tried to save others? Consider the fact that the U.S. evangelical slogan "Pray, give or go" allows people merely to pray, if that is their choice! By contrast the Friends Missionary Prayer Band of South India numbers 8,000 people in their prayer bands and supports 80 full-time missionaries in North India. If my denomination (with its unbelievably greater wealth per person) were to do that well, we would not be sending 500 missionaries, but 26,000. In spite of their true poverty, those poor people in South India are sending 50 times as many cross-cultural missionaries as we are! This fact reminds me of the title of a book, *The Poor Pay More.* They may very well pay more for the things they buy, but they are apparently willing to pay more for the things they believe. No wonder the lukewarm non-sacrificing believer is a stench in the nostrils of God. Luis Palau (1977) coined the phrase "studied mediocrity" in reference to America today. When will we recognize the fact that the wrath of God spoken of in the Bible is far less directed at those who sit in darkness than it is against those who refuse to share what they have?

How hard have we tried to save others? The nearly two billion dollars American evangelicals give per year to mission agencies is one fourth of what they spend on weight-loss programs. A person must overeat by at least two dollars worth of food per month to maintain one excess pound of flesh. Yet two dollars per month is more than what 90% of all Christians in America give to missions. If the average mission supporter is only five pounds overweight, it means he spends (to his own hurt) at least five times as much as he gives for missions. If he were to choose simple food (as well as not overeat) he could give ten times as much as he does to mission and not modify his standard of living in any other way!

Where does this line of reasoning lead? It means that the overall lifestyle to which Americans have acquiesced has led us to a place where we are hardening our hearts and our arteries simultaneously. Is our nation not described by Isaiah?

> My people are like the dead branches of a tree...a foolish nation, a witless, stupid people...The only language they can understand is punishment. So God will send against them foreigners who speak strange gibberish! Only then will they listen to Him! They could have rest in their own land if they would obey Him, if they were kind and good (Isa 27:11; 28:11,12 *TLB*).

Or, hear Ezekiel:

> They come as though they are sincere and sit before you listening. But they have no intention of doing what I tell them to; they talk very sweetly about loving the Lord, but with their hearts they are loving their money...

> My sheep wandered through the mountains and hills and over the face of the earth, and there was no one to search for them or care about them..."As I live," says the Lord God..."you were no real shepherds at all, for you didn't search for them (my flock). You fed yourselves and let them starve..." Therefore, the Lord God says: "I will surely judge between these fat shepherds and their scrawny sheep...and I will notice which is plump and which is thin, and why!" (Ezek 34:8,20,22 *TLB*).

We must learn that Jesus meant it when He said, "Unto whomsoever much is given, of him shall much be required" (Luke 12:48). I believe that *God cannot expect less from us as our Christian duty to save other nations than our own nation in wartime conventionally requires of us in order to save our own nation.* This means that we must be willing to adopt a wartime lifestyle if we are to play fair with the clear intent of scripture that the poor of this earth, the people who sit in darkness, shall see a great light (Isa 9:2).

The essential tactic to adopt a wartime lifestyle is to build on pioneer mission perspective and to do so by a very simple and dramatic method. Those who are awakened from the grogginess and stupor of our times can, of course, go as missionaries. But they can also *stay home and deliberately and decisively adopt a missionary support level as their standard of living and their basis of lifestyle, regardless of their income.* This will free up an unbelievable amount of money—so much, in fact, that if a million average Presbyterian households were to live within the average Presbyterian minister's salary, it would create at least two billion dollars a year. Yet that happens to be only one-seventh of the amount Americans spend on tobacco. But what a mighty gift to the nations if carefully spent on developmental missions!

In order to help families shift to a wartime lifestyle, two organizations are proposing a six-step plan. With both education and coaching this plan will lead gradually to the adoption of the salary provisions of an existing mission agency. The remainder of their income, at their own discretion at every point would be dedicated to what they believe to be the highest mission priority. The United Presbyterian Order for World Evangelization is a denominational sister of the general Order for World Evangelization. The twofold purpose of each of these organizations is 1) to imbue individuals and families with a concern for reaching the unreached peoples and 2) to assist them in practical ways to live successfully within the maximum limits of expenditure as defined by an agreed upon existing mission structure.

Even missionary families need help in staying within their income limitations, but ironically, no more so than people with twice their income. These organizations believe that families can be healthier and happier by identifying themselves with the same discipline with which missionary families are coping. For two hundred years it has been the undeviating pattern of all Protestant missionary agencies to establish a single standard for all their overseas personnel, adjusted of course to known costs of living and for various kinds of special circumstances. Some boards extend this system to their home office staff. No agency (until now) has gone the one logical step further— namely, to offer to the donors themselves this unique and long tested system. In view of the widespread concern of our time for a simple lifestyle, it would seem that this is an idea whose time has come.

We have Weight Watcher Clinics all over the country. We have Total Woman Clinics. Why not mission-focused Family Lifestyle Clinics? How much more significant these clinics will be with ends as noble as the Great Commission!

To reconsecrate ourselves to a wartime lifestyle will involve a mammoth upheaval for a significant minority. It will not go uncontested—any more than did the stern warnings of Isaiah and Ezekiel. But we do not need to defend our campaign. It is not ours.

Senders

Steven C. Hawthorne

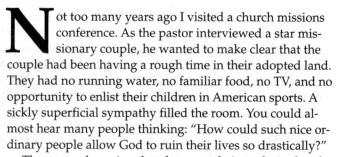

Not too many years ago I visited a church missions conference. As the pastor interviewed a star missionary couple, he wanted to make clear that the couple had been having a rough time in their adopted land. They had no running water, no familiar food, no TV, and no opportunity to enlist their children in American sports. A sickly superficial sympathy filled the room. You could almost hear many people thinking: "How could such nice ordinary people allow God to ruin their lives so drastically?"

The pastor, knowing that they were being admired and pitied all at once, found words to express the mixed mood of the crowd by saying, "Three years ago they were normal people—like you. But now look at them!" And everyone did look at them for a long moment. They were dressed in the pale baggy robes of their adopted land, quite a bizarre costume from an American view. One of the missionaries, sensing the moment, took the microphone in hand and reported what another pastor of the church had told her while saying farewell at the airport three years earlier: "I'm glad you are going, that means I don't have to." While the entire room broke out in nervous laughter, my mind reeled and finally settled on what had been bothering me about the whole scene: It was almost as if the missionaries were heroes for hire, the few and the true who were willing to do whatever God wanted, so that the rest of the church could slide by doing whatever they wanted. Offering plates would be passed and money would be raised. But the offering may have been helping people to buy their way out of missions more than it helped them to buy their way in. On that morning, that particular church seemed more *mercenary* than it was *missionary*.

I'm convinced that God intends better for us. God wants each believer and every church to live in the joy of fulfilling His global purposes. God never intended a few heroes to carry all of the joy and the labor. He gives us all a part.

THE ROLE OF SENDERS

We mistakenly used to classify someone as a missionary because they worked for God in some faraway place. No longer. Now we understand missionaries as people who cross cultural distances to advance the gospel rather than merely crossing geographical distances. Alongside frontline missionaries, others work as full-time missionaries in direct

Steven C. Hawthorne is the Founder and Director of WayMakers in Austin, Texas. After co-editing the course and book called *Perspectives on the World Christian Movement* in 1981, he launched a series of research expeditions among unreached peoples in world class cities called "Joshua Project." He co-authored (with Graham Kendrick) *Prayerwalking: Praying On Site with Insight,* and has written numerous articles.

support capacities such as training, facilitating, and day-to-day administrative tasks. All of these are missionaries. And yet, not one of them can do their work without another class of volunteer co-workers. We use the term "senders" to describe people who volunteer their labor in supportive ways for specific missionaries and for the overall task of world evangelization. For every fruitful missionary we invariably find a dozen or more people undergirding their efforts.

Recognizing missionaries as well as the senders who co-labor behind them in the cause is a powerful distinction with biblical ground. Paul asks, "How can they preach unless they are sent?" (Rom 10:15). The Apostle John made the same distinction. Of missionaries he says, "They went out for the sake of the Name." The next sentence describes senders: "Therefore we ought to support such men, that we may be fellow workers with the truth" (3 John 1:7-8).

Sending on Two Levels

Senders operate on two levels. Some senders focus on supporting specific missionaries. Others mobilize for the missionary cause in general ways, boosting efforts for the entire global cause, very often by enabling mission agencies or facilitating training and mobilization.

Specific Sending:
Supporting Missionaries

Every sender should look for God to give them ways to support specific missionaries. Neil Pirolo wrote a fine book, *Serving as Senders*, which frames the task of sending around the life and labor cycle of missionaries: anticipation of approval, departure for the field, "honeymoon" period in adopted culture, early culture stress, years of labor, and the return home with all the reverse culture stress that can take place.

Prayerfully consider serving as a sender in any one or more of six areas of support:

- Moral Support—just "being there"
- Logistics Support—all the bits and pieces
- Financial Support—money, money, money
- Prayer Support—spiritual warfare at its best

- Communication Support—letters, tapes and more
- Re-entry Support—more than applauding the safe landing of the jumbo jet

Each area has its unique responsibilities; each is best served by specific gifts within the Body of Christ. Allow His Spirit to speak to your heart about your possible involvement in one of these phases of support.[1]

General Sending:
Advancing the Global Cause

Bob Sjogren and Bill and Amy Stearns put together an excellent book called *Run With The Vision*. They see God "raising up a whole new army of home-front believers whose lives are saturated with a passion for His global cause." They list five ways that "sender-specialists" can go beyond supporting specific missionaries in ways that serve the Body of Christ at large. Such sending activity is more generalized, but altogether strategic.

Consider the possibilities of serving as a

- Missionary trainer
- Missionary pastor/counselor
- Administrative worker
- Researcher
- Mobilizer [2]

Mobilizers are Senders

The sender-specialist role of a mobilizer bears special mention because every sender can play a part in the work of mobilization. Sjogren and Stearns offer this definition of mobilization:

When a country goes to war, it isn't just the frontline soldiers whose lives are affected. An entire line of support personnel must stand behind them, supplying whatever the combat troops need to do battle. And back on the home front, massive mobilization is required to keep people aware of their part in the war. Posters and radio programs, small-town parades and publicity campaigns urge people to pray for their troops, to write to them to keep up their battle-fatigued morale, to sacrifice luxuries for the sake of the war effort, to give up the use of items that are more desperately needed on the front lines, to volunteer for support positions from medical assistants to trainers, to put their personal money into special accounts such as "war bonds" so the proceeds can be used for the war effort, to go to work at new jobs in order to produce materials needed in the conflict.

Think back over the items of this analogy and ask how you might motivate, train, and activate people in your culture to such vital responses to a national crisis. Those ideas are probably exactly how you can motivate, train, and activate believers to their part in the global spiritual warfare against Satan's false kingdom of darkness. To mobilize is to get them moving. [3]

Senders Usually Counter-Cultural

In some ways missionaries may have it easier than senders. Missionaries are at least immersed in their work. Their role is clear. Their task is before them constantly. But what about living as one who sends? It may be easier for you to "go" in some ways than to "stay."

If you go as a missionary ... at least you can introduce yourself with a one-word title: missionary. But if you dare stay and order your life around sending others as missionaries, you will not be readily understood. Missionary work is *cross*-cultural, but active sending can be *counter*-cultural.

Senders will probably lead what appear to many to be fairly normal lives. Most will hold jobs and have families. They will be noted for their zeal to make disciples wherever they are. But they will be caught up in a war that many of their friends and relatives do not or will not acknowledge. Their hearts yearn for people they have never seen. They discipline themselves to doggedly love friends that they see once every four or five years. They give away up to half or more of what they earn. Their lives are simple. A glad soberness attends their lives. They speak often of distant peoples. They relish extended times of prayer. Theirs is a joyous detachment and yet an earnest involvement in the affairs of the world. [4]

THE LIFE AND WORK OF SENDERS

God is summoning millions of believers to serve as senders with the same zeal and conse-

cration of life purpose as frontline missionaries. These senders serve with a single-hearted joy — the joy of laying down their lives so that others' obedience will be abundant.

> **Paul's greatest joy, as well as the Philippian church, was to pour out their lives so that other people's faith had full opportunity to burst into flame.**

Paul urged his friends to pour out their lives in order that others' faithfulness would be lived out. He used the imagery of a libation, or "drink offering" of wine or oil. Such offerings were sometimes poured on sacrificial offerings in order to ignite them to full flame.

Even if I am being poured out as a drink offering upon the sacrifice and service of your faith, I rejoice and share my joy with you all. And you too, I urge you, rejoice in the same way and share your joy with me (Phil 2:18).

Paul's greatest joy, as well as that of the Philippian church, was to pour out their lives so that other people's faith had full opportunity to burst into flame. In our day, dedicated senders need this same passion so that sending becomes an integrated joy instead of a seasonal distraction or a perfunctory part in a few missions programs.

Partnership

Paul delights in their "participation in the gospel from the first day until now" (Phil 1:5). The word behind "participation" is a Greek word *koinonia*. It's a fantastic word, often translated as "partnership" or "fellowship." It blends the ideas of a sturdy friendship and task-oriented camaraderie. It's the kind of purposeful friendship that people have always been hungry for: close community with the significance of a clearly-defined mission.

Paul identifies two aspects of *koinonia*: first, a partnership in the gospel, linking them in the purpose of evangelization; and second, a sharing in grace, a Spirit-given endowment of power in order to fulfill a specific assignment together.

Vision-Driven Partnership

First, the *koinonia* that Paul and the Philippians enjoyed was a partnership "in the gospel." Paul often used the word "gospel" in the same way that we use the English word "evangelization." For Paul the gospel was more than a message; it was the mission itself.

- He says, "my circumstances have turned out for the greater progress of the gospel" (Phil 1:12). For the gospel to make progress, Paul is referring to the cause, or the mission of the gospel.
- To live "worthy of the gospel of Christ" is far more than merely believing in Jesus, it is living to see that the gospel is believed, even though doing so will almost certainly bring on opposition and suffering (1:27-30).
- Paul had friends who shared (the *koinonia* word again) in his "struggle in the cause of the gospel" (4:3).

Apparently from the first day he knew them, his Philippian comrades were eagerly involved in advancing the gospel, sharing it themselves, and laboring to see others do even more. Such passion is not reserved for a few elite apostolic leaders. Paul invited every believer to make world evangelization the center point of their lives in the statement: "I do all things for the sake of the gospel, that I may become a fellow partaker of it" (1 Cor 9:23).

God-Given Partnership

Paul declares that he is linked in heart with them, "I have you in my heart," because they shared in the same enabling grace that he enjoyed, "... in the defense and confirmation of the gospel, you all are partakers of grace with me" (Phil 1:7). Paul is referring to enabling grace, a supernatural endowment bestowed on every believer enabling them to play a valuable part in fulfilling His global purposes. God's grace bestows vision, spiritual gifts, relationships, power, authority, opportunities and more. [5]

In this case, Paul says that God had entrusted the very same assignment to both the missionary and the senders as a shared grace. By God's design, neither would be successful without the other. Paul's sending friends weren't tagging along out of duty

or guilt. They knew that God had bestowed on them a rare gift to join with Paul as coworkers to defend, advance and confirm the gospel.

Becoming a Sender

How does one become a sender? By entering the two realities of partnership mentioned above, both receiving *grace* from God and living in the larger *gospel* purpose for God.

First, receive what God is giving.

Make sure that you are living in all the grace God is giving to you. Paul says that God had "graced" (the Greek word is the verbal form of "grace") the Philippians "for Christ's sake, not only to believe in Him, but also to suffer for His sake" (Phil 1:29). Has God "graced" you with something more than merely believing in Him? Anything of lasting substance will start with God's grace. What does God, in His kindness, intend to release to you as an integrating life purpose? You can live with power and joy for all that is truly God-given. Work with other mentors in your church to help you understand what God has given you as an individual. Pray and explore with several others of your church family, including your pastor, to understand what God may be assigning your church, or communities within your church.

Second, give yourself to God.

Sending is best done as a total life purpose. It's perfectly legitimate to volunteer some of your time now and then, or to occasionally give extra when you have surplus cash. But before you find a convenient way to merely help out a little, consider the joy of throwing yourself entirely into Christ's global purpose. It's a privilege that God intends for many, but few receive. You can be one of them. Paul mentions that many believers were seeking "after their own interests, not those of Christ Jesus" (Phil 2:21). In contrast, the Philippians had vigorously given themselves to Christ and "for the work of Christ" (2:30) from the earliest point of becoming believers (1:5). This attitude of consecration freed them to share in Paul's "struggle in the cause of the gospel" (4:3).

Growing as a Sender

Three core activities which need to be a routine part of every sender's life: serving, giving and praying.

Acting as Personal Servants

The Philippian church found ways to serve Paul when it was not at all convenient to do so. They initiated the sending of Epaphroditus to help Paul. He traveled long distances at considerable risk and cost. When he arrived, the prison visitation environment was less than the best. He caught some kind of deadly disease that he wouldn't have had if he had stayed home. Paul said Epaphroditus had been "risking his life" to complete all that could possibly be done for Paul (2:30). What did Epaphroditus actually do? We aren't given details, but from the way that Paul described him you can imagine that he was performing errands of every kind. Nothing was beneath him: "my brother and fellow worker and fellow soldier, who is also your messenger and minister to my need" (2:25).

To grow as a servant, be creative in ways to support field missionaries. Short-term visits to where missionaries labor can be planned so that missionaries are encouraged more than they are interrupted. You may be able to get more done for a missionary family by mobilizing the right people to come alongside them with needed resource or encouragement.

Giving for Provision and Devotion

The Philippians gave money out of a concern and a profound sense of partnership. They actually gave at a time when it was not possible for them to know of his actual need. That means that they had not been giving minimally toward his need. They had given abundantly, and Paul implies that if they had enjoyed the opportunity, they would have given regularly (4:10). How right Paul was to accept their gift as an act of devotion to God Himself (4:18).

To grow as a giver, begin right away by regularly supporting a field missionary. It doesn't matter how large or small the regular gifts may be. The point is to be involved with "the matter of giving and receiving" (4:15). The next step may be to strategically support a mobilization or support ministry. Adjust your lifestyle so that you will have freedom to give abundantly. Generosity flows from simplicity, not abundance.

Praying with Urgency and Hope

Paul said that his life was depending on their prayers: "I know that this shall turn out for my deliverance through your prayers and the provision of the Spirit of Jesus Christ" (Phil 1:19). The Philippians were not merely praying *for* Paul, they were praying *with* Paul. No doubt they were making requests *for* Paul's release from prison. But they were praying along *with* Paul's hopes and ambitions. He was counting on them to pray for God to pour out upon him a provision of the Spirit of God so that he would fulfill his calling, "according to my earnest expectation and hope, that I shall not be put to shame in anything, but that with all boldness, Christ shall even now, as always, be exalted in my body" (1:20).

> Senders adjust their lifestyle in order to be free to give, serve and pray. Generosity flows from simplicity, not abundance.

To grow as a sender who prays with steady passion and hope, try praying like the Philippians did for Paul. Pray first with them, according to their vision and biblical hopes for the fruit of their efforts. Let missionaries know how you are praying. Pray huge, kingdom-sized prayers (such as Christ being glorified throughout a city), along with specific prayer requests (such as generators operating smoothly for a Jesus film showing). Learn to pray daily, using prayers that at least mention the names of missionaries. Learn to pray for the advance of the gospel in a particular people or place even if you do not know any specific missionaries.

End Notes

1. From the book called *Serving as Senders* by Neil Pirolo, published in 1991, page 21, published by Emmaus Road, International, 7150 Tanner Court, San Diego, CA, 92111. Pirolo's book is a comprehensive handbook for missionary supporters.

2. Bob Sjogren and Bill and Amy Stearns, *Run With the Vision* (Minneapolis: Bethany House Publishers, 1995), p. 162.

3. Sjogren, Stearns, 1995, p 206-207.

4. From an article called "Serving as Senders" by Steven C. Hawthorne, first published in 1981 in the first edition of *Perspectives on the World Christian Movement*, edited by Ralph D. Winter and Steven C. Hawthorne.

5. The original language term for "grace" is a word related to the idea of giving. When God gives grace, He is doing something far more than being kind or loving. He is influencing people by the magnificent way He has of giving of Himself to people. Without manipulation or coercion, people are enabled to become more than they are. That's why the Bible declares that people are saved by grace. God influences people without coercing them. In much the same way, we are enabled by grace to serve Him in specific ways to fulfill the Great Commission. This grace is marvelous, not to be ignored or assumed. It wouldn't have to be this way. God might have just left us to do the best with our aptitudes or skills. As much as half of Paul's uses of the word "grace" in the New Testament have to do with God's bestowing of power to co-labor with Him to advance His purposes. Some examples: Rom 1:5, 15:15, 1 Cor 15:10, Gal 2:9, Eph 3:2-8, 4:7, Phil 1:7, 1:29, 1 Tim 1:14, 2 Tim 1:8-9.

Study Questions

1. Describe how missionaries can be admired and pitied at the same time they are being supported. What kind of relationship and ownership is better?

2. Explain how the phrase "fellowship in the gospel" can be understood as a vision-driven partnership.

3. Compare the difficulties of laboring *cross*-culturally to the difficulty of living *counter*-culturally?

4. What is the difference between praying *for* a missionary and praying *with* a missionary?

Charting Your Journey to the Nations:

Ten Steps to Help Get You There

Steve Hoke and Bill Taylor

Steve Hoke is Vice-President of Staff Development and Training with Church Resource Ministries. Raised by missionary parents in Japan, Steve has followed and helped many others in God's journey to the nations. He has spent over 26 years as a pastor, professor, short-term missionary, training director, missions executive and mentor.

Bill Taylor is the Director of Missions Commission, World Evangelical Fellowship. Having served in Latin America for 30 years, he now travels widely as a consultant to churches, missions and training schools throughout the world.

The key reason for developing "perspective" as a World Christian is to see the world as God sees it. But a razor-sharp biblical perspective is not a static thing you possess. You really cannot just stand at this high vantage point as a spectator, watching what God is doing around the world. To see what God sees, and to value what God values is no small thing. This kind of vision is so compelling and inviting, perhaps the most dangerous response is to do nothing. Such a vision of God's mission virtually thrusts you into the middle of all that He is doing throughout the world and all through history.

Some of you will be "goers," seeking to move out as soon as you can into a more active role in global mission. And some of you will be "growers," men and women committed to serving and supporting others who move to the frontiers. But, whatever role God opens for you, there are some action steps to consider.

The following ten steps are arranged in a logical, but not necessarily fixed sequence intended to help you chart your journey to active engagement with the peoples of the world. It's a pathway primarily for those who will be "goers." Of what use is the following list for those who are gifted to serve instead as a "grower?" Understand this process all the more! You will be called upon for the rest of your life to help launch many others who will serve as front-line missionaries.

Within each major phase are several smaller steps. The exact sequence of the steps is not the critical issue. Pursue them in any order, but be sure you keep them all before you. You'll notice that some of them are not steps that you accomplish and then stop doing. They are really courses of growth and obedience that you will want to continue pursuing throughout your life. The point is to step into a path of obedience as if it were a prolonged journey. You've no doubt already begun. Don't hesitate to act boldly to fulfill the vision God is giving you. Take purposeful steps from this day forward!

PHASE ONE: Getting Ready—Stretching

1. Personal Spiritual Formation:

Who you are—your character and spiritual formation as a disciple of Jesus Christ—are essential to the role you will play in missions. Clarifying your basic commitment, your spiritual gifts, your call, and making sure your spiritual foundation is solid are necessary first steps to ensure an effective journey. Finding a personal mentor early on in this journey is foundational to your long-term effectiveness.

2. Body Boost—Getting On-the-Job Experience in Your Home Church:

Understanding your church's unique vision, how the church functions for missions, and finding your place and gifted role in it is critical to your ultimate effectiveness in extending the church into other cultures. Making disciples in your home culture will hone your ministry skills and help sharpen your spiritual giftedness before serving in a cross-cultural setting. Investing in the supporting of missionaries will better equip you for the day when you may be on support. Again, seeking out and submitting yourself to fruitful senior saints in your local church as mentors or "spiritual directors" will encourage you along the ministry path. Ask God to give you such a relationship with older and wiser people.

3. Exposure to Other Cultures:

Growing up in only one culture limits our ability to understand others, appreciate diversity, and learn other languages. Frankly, being mono-cultural is really boring for today's global citizen in a pluralistic society. So gaining some early cross-cultural exposure, either locally or globally, stretches our mental, physical and spiritual muscles, and helps us to understand and accept people in other cultures. Hundreds of churches and agencies offer one or two-week exposure trips, up to three-six month short-term ministry experiences. Be choosy. The best short terms are not a substitute for the critical need for long-term missionaries. Study in another country is another useful way to earn academic credit while broadening your world view. It's also an invaluable crucible for testing your gifts, your passions, your dreams, and your capacity to go longer term.

4. Basic Education:

Academic preparation for a short or long-term ministry needs to be customized to your experience, skills and gifts. What steps can you take at this point that will broaden your worldview and enrich your basic educational background? Not everyone has to have university degrees to be used by God, but don't cut your formal schooling short just because you suspect God is running out of time! Check out the possibility of studying abroad, especially in restricted access areas, where the only visiting students or language learners are granted visas. This way, schooling doesn't interrupt education but actually completes it. Pursue a mentoring relationship with those who have gone ahead of you.

PHASE TWO: Getting There—Linking

5. Church or Agency Contact and Candidacy:

What sending group or "team" is the best "fit" for you as the vehicle for service? Your best work is not a solo effort. It's not really about a career choice for your fulfillment as it is about bearing much fruit. Get grafted into a living, fruitbearing organism of church life, be it a church or a church supporting your efforts in league with a mission agency. What kind of team do you need to make you most effective and to help you grow the most? What kind of team leadership do you need to keep you focused and effective? Many of the strongest teams are intergenerational and international.

What are the options? There are thousands of strong churches and over 700 mission sending agencies with a wide span of cross-cultural ministry interests. They range in size from those with thousands of missionaries to those with just a handful. Begin with input from your home church. Continue with the agency you know best. Check out their theology, model of ministry, vision and leadership. Talk with several until you find a few with whom you are compatible on the major issues.

Some agencies are deeply involved in church planting, while others serve the existing church. Some target specific peoples groups, such as Muslims or Native American peoples. Many have broad, holistic ministries-from relief and development to theological education. Check out the key source of agency information—the most recent edition of *The MARC Mission Handbook-North American Protestant Ministries Overseas*.

The initiative lies with you. Remember, God has a distinctive purpose for your life which involves providing His guidance to take you exactly where He wants you to be. That place is worth seeking in faith.

6. Assignment Search:

Related to the question of the mission sending groups is the question of location, people group, and specific role on a church planting team that God is asking you to fulfill in reaching others with the Gospel. Who are they? Where are they? How can your gifts be used to reach them or to build up the national church?

A word of caution here about searching and exploring. Searching does not mean "picking out what I'd like to do." In fact, some of the best assignments are often those given by mature and discerning senior leaders. Initial or early assignments are usually the times in which one proves out who they really are and can move onward from there to subsequent phases of ministry of the highest significance. The reality is that almost all of us have been divinely deflected from our intended career path. Those who are most fruitful can speak of taking on an assignment that they did not search for and decide for themselves, but submitted to and found that they became so much more for it. On the other hand, the best lived lives are sometimes the ones that were devoted to one people or place through all the different twists and turns.

What is critical is an initial exploration of what God is doing, seeking to discover your place in God's overall game plan. When God's gifting and assignment become clear, you are ready and willing to step out in obedience as a committed team player.

7. Hands-On Missionary Training:

Let's assume you've completed your basic academic training. Let's also assume you've had serious on-the-job ministry training within a local church. By now you have probably spent at least one brief period of time in another culture, and perhaps as long as two years in a ministry-focused cross-cultural experience. You've been stretched, and you've grown stronger as a result.

Now it's time to figure out what kind of practical missionary training and/or ad-vanced training you're going to need. The kind of missionary role you will fill, and the particular continent, country or people groups among whom God wants you to minister will greatly focus the specific requirements. It will require time and actual ministry experience to develop competencies in three important dimensions—character and spiritual qualities, ministry skills, and knowledge.

The most relevant preparation for church planting in another culture is participation in and significant responsibility on a church planting team at home. Starting evangelistic Bible studies, creating cell groups, raising up leaders from the harvest and discipling new believers to the second and third generation are critical church-planting skills. You can develop in your own congregation, especially when done in partnership with a potential sending agency.

Language and culture learning are part of a missionary's "Basic Training." A brief introduction to language learning in your own country can help orient you to becoming an active language learner on the field.

PHASE THREE:
Getting Established—Bonding

8. Apprenticeships and Internships:

Effective missionaries don't just emerge fully formed from their educational experience. On-the-job ministry either at home or on the field tests what you've learned, provides models in ministry, and helps you develop your own approaches for ministry. Once on the field, a structured internship is the best way for new missionaries to learn the ropes and the rules of the game in another culture. Experienced missionaries or national pastors are the best on-the-job mentors to aid your effective acculturation. Don't try to go it alone. Apprentice yourself to a master craftsman or woman for maximum ministry learning.

9. Life-Long Learning: On-the-Job, On-the-Field

When missionaries stop learning, they die. Establishing a life-long learning pattern early in your career is essential to finishing well. Setting yearly reading, self-study and personal development goals in the areas of spiritual formation, ministry formation, and strategic formation will be life-changing. Being accountable to peers and to mentors is one of the best ways to insure that you are growing for all you're worth! Many will profit through ongoing degree-granting programs that will upgrade skills and ministry viability.

10. Finishing Strong:

God's pilgrimage is rich and vast. Understanding the keys to life-long development and knowing how to intentionalize your spiritual development will help you grow stronger through cross-cultural service. And we don't assume that mission service is necessarily a life-long thing for you in the same place.

Throughout scripture and church history the sad fact is that "few leaders finish well." Part of the idea of "finishing well" is to become the kind of person who helps others to "start well." Becoming an example and a mentor to others may set them on a course to surpass your wildest dreams.

CONCLUSION:

God is at work around the world completing the Big Picture. So "charting your journey" is not so much about planning a vacation cruise to the Caribbean as it is becoming intentional in joining God's foreign policy. It's taking time to pray and plan how you are going to get actively involved. It's about taking intentional steps forward rather than being shoved around sideways by peer and career pressure. It's about moving from the grandstand to the playing field, whether as a grower or a goer. It's all about becoming "glory spreaders."

Your own journey will be unique. And charting your journey will be a life-changing process. These ten steps will help you transform your newly gained 'perspective' into a powerful vision for spiritual change.

The full interactive workbook from which this summary is taken, *Charting Your Journey to the Nations*, is designed for two kinds of people: Those who have a deep desire to serve God cross-culturally (goers), and those who want to help them (growers). It is designed to work through the process of charting a course or journey from where you are to where God would have you. It describes the path to cross-cultural service in ten steps, from initial commitment to field placement and beyond.

Each step presents an explanation of the importance of that phase of the process, and includes a place for you to keep notes, reflect, journal and gather information as you collect, plan and pray. A selected resource section in the back of the workbook will give you further information about education, missionary training and contacting mission agencies.

Remember: Your own journey will be unique. Charting your journey will be a life-changing process.

You and the nations await each other.

Study Questions

1. Which of Hoke and Taylor's steps would require a person to be in a regular relationship with others who have experience in ministry?

2. Why is mentoring a key component?

Join the World Christian Movement

Ralph D. Winter

After serving ten years as a missionary among Mayan Indians in the highlands of Guatemala, Ralph D. Winter was called to be a Professor of Missions at the School of World Mission at Fuller Theological Seminary. Ten years later he and his wife, Roberta, founded a mission society called the Frontier Mission Fellowship (FMF) in Pasadena, California. This in turn spawned the U.S. Center for World Mission and the William Carey International University, both of which serve other missions working at the frontiers of mission. He is the General Director of the Frontier Mission Fellowship. See expanded biographical sketch at the end of the book.

When you decided to sign up for the Perspectives class you may not have realized what you were getting into—that it is not so much a *class* as it an introduction to a *movement*. Perhaps you just didn't catch the full significance of the word *movement* in the title of the course—Perspectives on the World Christian *Movement*. Now you know. Now you understand you are being seriously invited to join that movement—the World Christian *Movement*!

But what are the next steps beyond spectator status? It may not be clear to you yet just what God has in mind for you. You don't want to make a false start. What can you do for sure? What do you need to learn next? How is the calling to mobilization different from, but as important as, that of being a front-line missionary?

Most people think of the cause of missions as a bunch of missionaries out there in a tropical forest working with their bare hands. Well, for that matter, some people think wars consist of boys out there on the front lines popping away with guns. But wars are usually a "war effort" encompassing many more people than those right at the front. So, missions is a "mission effort" involving, necessarily, far more people in the support structure than those right at the front.

To be more specific, suppose you grew up with a great interest in the drilling of oil wells. You saw a video as a young person of the "wildcatters" who sometimes strike oil in unexpected places. You decided you would like to become a well-driller.

But, as you studied the subject you discovered the "oil industry." You learned all about oil refineries, oil diplomats who dicker with foreign governments, geophysisists who make precise measurements of feedback from deep under the earth, etc. So, whoopee, you decided you would rather be a geophysicist! But you wouldn't have known such a possibility existed if all you knew about were organizations apparently recruiting only well-drillers.

In the same way, the World Christian Movement has become a highly developed international enterprise. At the core of this historic global movement are professionals and hundreds of dedicated, seasoned organizations. It's proper to look upon this core of the World Christian Movement as the "mission industry." In the USA alone it's a two to three billion dollar per year activity—and its influence is far beyond what that money would do in any commercial venture.

To find your way into this incredibly influential enterprise, it is helpful to distinguish the roles of front-line teams who labor cross-culturally, let's call them *missionaries*, and those who marshal support for them, let's call them *mobilizers*. Whatever your role may be, as a missionary or as a mobilizer, you need a working relationship with others in the mission industry. William Carey wasn't a loner.

Next to doing nothing, the most certain way to squander your life's work would be to maintain an ignorant detachment from this astounding movement of dedicated mission professionals. Most of the important mistakes have been made. Most of the crucial matters of missiological wisdom have been explored. If we ignore this seasoned wisdom, the tempered courage, the proven ideas, and the heartfelt prayers of the generations before us, we are simply consigning ourselves to beating the air for quite a while. This may apply even if all you do is join an organization that has not been around for some time.

Never concede to doing something so small that it could be accomplished entirely in your lifetime. Be a part of something that began before you were born, and will continue onward toward the fulfillment of all that God has purposed to accomplish. God has uniquely formed you to be part of this significant movement. You cannot participate in what you do not know. Becoming a student of the mission industry is the best way to become a valuable part of the World Christian Movement.

Mission Agencies

As soon as possible begin to get acquainted with the astounding array of different mission agencies.

"Service missions" serve other agencies. Some are purely technical, like Mission Aviation Fellowship, with work ranging from jungle air strips to a marvelous internet service open to all agencies. Others are literature missions, tape-recording experts, or Bible translators, or radio experts. Missionary radio today outranks all secular radio systems for blanketing the earth with the greatest sophistication and highest-powered transmitters in use anywhere.

"Standard missions" concern themselves with every aspect of human need, ranging from medical, educational, church planting, etc.

Place great value on these incredible organizations. No one need start from scratch. Since agencies are designed for teamwork, they are not only able to sustain efforts over many generations, veteran workers are able to pass on to newcomers the cumulative know-how and field knowledge of generations of earlier workers.

Training Institutions

Springing from, but feeding the mission agencies, are mission training institutions, seminaries and Bible colleges which have long offered programs in many disciplines (such as theology, linguistics, anthropology, history, and many more) which together undergird the grand discipline of missiology. Those offering formal degrees in a residential setting are most visible, but it is getting more common for training to take place away from campuses. "Distance education" brings the instruction not only to where the trainees live and work, it often brings to learners the material that they most need and the optimal moment for them to take it in.

Pressing the extension idea further are fully accredited BA and MA degree-granting programs offering training by way of mentoring. Internet connections are fascinating and helpful, but the most effective training resource will continue to be local, face-to-face mentoring.[1]

Associations and Societies

All of the people in these various missions and schools are intentionally networked by organizational associations and professional societies. Be a student of the mission industry. No missionary or mobilizer can be fully effective without an awareness of the IFMA (Interdenominational Foreign Mission Association) and the EFMA (Evangelical Fellowship of Mission Agencies). Avail yourself of their meetings and publications, which are the cutting edge of missiology. Jointly they publish the *Evangelical Missions Quarterly*.[2] You may never become a professor of missions at a graduate institution, but you will likely mentor many others in your lifetime in crucial matters of missiology. What you will do as a missionary or a mobilizer is so important that it is foolhardy not to gain professional skills in your pursuit of this high calling. Why not become an eager participant in the mission industry by joining a professional mission society? The ISFM (International Society for Frontier Missiology) might be the place to start.[3]

Mission Frontiers talks about the cutting edge of missions in the form of a 60-page newsprint bulletin that goes to 100,000 people all over the world. Produced by the U.S. Center for World Mission on a donation basis, it comes out every two months.[4]

Local Churches

Churches obviously play a crucial role in the missionary enterprise. Many churches offer components of training beyond normal catechism. Some ambitious churches have attempted to send their own mission teams. To succeed, of necessity they form new mission structures. Such overachieving vision is commendable, but is usually best expressed in alignment with existing mission structures. The entire complex tapestry of the mission industry is affected by the vision and knowledge of the sending churches.

The good news is that, more than any other force, the cause of missions unites an enormous variety of otherwise separate church traditions. It is truly amazing what unity and understanding has *flowed back from the field* to the disparate church traditions at home. It turns out that all our home church traditions shine best on the mission field. Seemingly dead traditions often have marvelously devout and competent missionaries on the field. Surprising to many people is the fact that missionaries on the field from many traditions cooperate very readily in all kinds of joint projects. Over 225 mission agencies are involved in 36 regional partnerships with another 25 in the process of formation. Phil Butler of Interdev (a specialized mission that coordinates all this!) calls these "Strategic Partnerships."

Church people back home don't know all this. You don't very often find congregations holding joint picnics—like Presbyterians with Nazarenes. Yet their missionaries cooperate on the field with no trouble at all.

The bad news is that congregations usually need to be extensively educated and mobilized to remain effective in the World Christian Movement. The cultural momentum of church traditions, when imposed elsewhere—on the

mission field—is where the World Christian Movement has often been impeded. It is illusory for any group anywhere to come up with some new emphasis and make it seem so important that all the other traditions are considered wrong or inadequate. Read the story of the last two thousand years in the most balanced account ever written—Kenneth Scott Latourette's *A History of Christianity*. You will see that every age has been marked by all kinds of spurting out in many different directions as godly people have struggled and groped for better light. We can look back and "improve" on practically everything that we see, but meanwhile our own form of Christianity may be bogged down by all kinds of cultural baggage!

For example, missions itself is a "new" emphasis in the Protestant tradition. Why didn't the Reformation leaders, who so highly prized the Bible, find the Great Commission in the Bible? It took William Carey, a kid in a poverty-stricken backward gulch in rural England, to come up with clear-eyed questions as to what the Bible plainly said about God's concern for all of the peoples of the earth. Sure, his elders had all the "right theology" but failed Bible 101 in regard to the main theme of the Bible.

Why do the widely-respected Westminster Confession of Faith, the Lutheran's Non-altered Augsburg Confession, and even the Nicene Creed (to which we all pledge allegiance) say nothing whatsoever about the Great Commission? It is a wonder that missions ever came up at all. In few Christian traditions around the world is the call of missions anything like a major or even minor concern for the vast majority of their adherents. How strange!

Why Mission Mobilizers?

This strange situation brings us to the very reason mission mobilizers are so crucial for the advance of the World Christian Movement. It is evident that the World Christian Movement has moved forward by a dedicated few calling the church to its central mission. Over the centuries the Church has occasionally exhibited powerful passion for Christ's global cause, and then, within a few years, sunk into a self-absorbed morass of disobedience.

Congregations which have set their heart on other things need a heart transplant! How would you like to have a heart transplant done by an untrained person? Unthinkable! Transplanting a heart is too important to leave to an untrained person. But, *the task of reaching the nations is the most important task which God has assigned to His Church*. And this requires transplanting a heart of vision and understanding in order to do it right. A mission mobilizer owes it to the church and the nations to acquire the skill and knowledge necessary to help do an effective heart transplant of vision and understanding.

This is equally true of the role of a field missionary. The mobilizer who stays home may need to learn about more parts of the world, but the missionary needs different tools. Missionary skills are different. Mobilizers and missionaries have two very different kinds of jobs, both of them essential—equally essential—to the World Christian Movement. Many people unthinkingly equate "missions" with missionaries. But there would be few missionaries unless there were also intensely committed and skilled mobilizers.

The famous "Cambridge Seven" stayed home long enough—a whole year—to visit the universities of England before they went out to China. Who knows, perhaps 500 missionaries went out because of their pre-field work as mobilizers! We have already read about one of those students. C. T. Studd's older brother never did go as a missionary. But he went from campus to campus in the United States and, among other things, persuaded John R. Mott to go to the Mt. Hermon meeting. What if that had not happened? Or, *what if Mott had decided to be a missionary rather than a mobilizer*? Probably no two people in history are traceably responsible for more missionaries going to the field than Mott and another SVM student, Robert E. Speer, who also stayed home to be a full-time mobilizer.

But were they qualified to do that without field experience? Oh, they eventually traveled all over the world. In fact, they gained a more comprehensive view of global needs than was possible for any one missionary. Mott could plan and lead the 1910 meeting at Edinburgh in a way no missionary was qualified to do.

But they had signed the pledge to go. That meant that they were qualified to stay—if only because they were willing to go! Note, however, if they had not been willing to go they would not have been spiritually qualified to stay. Why? Because those who are not willing to stay, if that is God's will, are not—and cannot—be qualified to go!

Yes, being a mobilizer is just as much a spiritual calling as being a missionary. After all, missions is a cause, not just a career. In the end, as we shall see, a mobilizer needs to know a whole lot of things a missionary does not usually know. And vice versa.

But, beware! Just as missionaries face special problems in their cross-cultural work, so do mobilizers. In some ways it is much more difficult to be a mobilizer. Most churches will not readily support mobilizers. Or, worse still, they can "survive" missionary letters but it is too much to have to cope with resident, local mobilizers, constantly reminding them of their global obligations!

Look again at these two different types of work within the World Christian Movement: *the mobilizer and the missionary*.

Mobilizer and Missionary

Which one is for you? God obviously does not want everyone overseas. In the days of the massive Student Volunteer Movement four out of five who volunteered to go to the ends of the earth ended up staying home. That's right: 20,000 out of 100,000 volunteers were able to make it to the field *only because four out of five were willing to continue to believe and work for the cause of missions back home*. Stirring up the church and keeping it envisioned is a much larger task than the frontline work itself.

I can't believe that God is content with mobilizers that are not the Bible students and prayer warriors missionaries have to be. I can't believe that a person doesn't need to be as committed to the Lord if he stays home to mobilize. Mobilization, either as a full or part-time task, requires intense prayer, vision and commitment. By contrast the missionary task is a relatively well-accepted "calling," while mobilization is not! All pastors are mobilizers of many good things and can be superb mission mobilizers. They are certainly worthy of support. We think ministers of music and youth workers are worthy of support. Why not mission mobilizers?

Mobilizing Yourself

More basic than anything else: you cannot be a mobilizer if you are not yourself mobilized! But how do you become mobilized?

Feed yourself. Get to conferences, subscribe to periodicals, buy the key books, study the issues for yourself or you will never be all God wants you to be as a mobilizer.[5] You yourself must be caught up in the drama of the global countdown of the kingdom of God. It is not enough to be caught up in local church goals for next year.

Support missions yourself. "Where your treasure is there will your heart be also" (Matt 6:21).

Use the **Global Prayer Digest** *daily* in a family setting. Pray for specific missionaries. *Nothing that does not occur daily will ever dominate your life.* Being a World Christian is of little value, really, unless you are a *daily* World Christian! The *Global Prayer Digest* can change your life more in one month than many "drive by" experiences that gradually fade away.[4] Everything grows slowly. How can you keep growing without daily renewal of vision?

Write missionaries. Be aware of their problems and needs. They may want you to buy something for them and bundle it up and send it to them. Take them in overnight as they pass through your area. Go on picnics with them and their children. Debrief them. Share with them from your studies. Compare notes from one field to another.

Of course, don't wait to begin mobilizing in your local congregation. Also, be ready to visit other local congregations. Become active in denominational policies and mission strategies as well as interdenominational mission events.

How About You?

And, are *you* thinking clearly about yourself? *You* need to ask God on your knees where *you* fit in. Maybe the place God has for *you* is teaching a Sunday School class with a relentlessly international perspective. Maybe God wants *you* to be one more globally-minded pastor—that kind of pastor is worth more than quite a few missionaries. God will likely ask you to do the hardest thing you are capable of!

The key thing is to realize that the development of your own *career* must not be your main concern, but rather the development of the mission *cause. The question of career vs. cause will be an issue in your heart of hearts again and again.* Jesus, today, might have put it, "Seek first the Kingdom of God and your career will take care of itself." We have already said a lot about preparations, especially those which can be pursued right on the job. But if you are willing to prepare and work, simultaneously, for the rest of your life, God may indeed reward you with a startling career—*but you will probably not know the details in advance.*

Someone has said, "God reserves the best for those who leave the choice with Him." Another (the founder of the Navigators, Dawson Trotman) said, "Don't ever do something that others can do or will do if there are things to be done that others can't do or won't do." See, getting what we want—by going after it—is not in the cards for Christians. Jesus turned it completely around the other way: "He that seeks to save himself will lose his life; he that will lose his life for my sake will find it" (Luke 9:24). God's will for us is not mere *advice.* We can't "take it or leave it;" we must "accept it or reject it." His will is His command.

Make no mistake. God honors those who seek His work above their worries. One of our staff members once said, "Now I think I understand what faith is; it is not the confidence that God will do what we want Him to do *for us*, but the conviction that we can do what He wants done *for Him* and let Him take care of the consequences."

Is your problem that you can't see very far into the future? As Trotman said, "If you can't see very far ahead, go ahead as far as you can see."

Lots of people would be glad to follow God if He would only tell them in advance exactly all the wonderful things He would do for them and what high-sounding job titles they might one day hold. But, remember Genesis 12:1? *It is characteristic of the Christian life that God asks us to go without telling us where!* This is not to be considered unfair or capricious on His part. The fact is that when we walk in the little light we have, and keep going on and on taking steps in faith, the ways in which He leads us are almost always, as we look back, something we could have never been told in advance!

Untold marvels lie *beyond* each step of faith. You don't really have to know what is beyond the next step, and you can't find out without taking the next step. Again, it is characteristic of the Christian life that we do not know very far in advance. In fact, if you think you've got the next few years lined up you may well be mistaken, or you may still be trying to make your plans for God to bless.

Wouldn't His will inevitably focus on your doing "your utmost for His highest?" It is not a question of how much of our own desires we can get away with. Some young people make the final, dramatic decision "to be a missionary" and immediately begin thinking where the climate would be nicest. You can't be any kind of a solid Christian if you are unwilling to do anything He asks. What does he ask? Nothing more than all we are and possess. That's all. He doesn't ask us to do the easiest job we can think of but the hardest we are able to handle. He does not ask us to do what we cannot do, although He often enables us to do what we could not do without His special grace. He is not a tyrant who doesn't care about our welfare in the task. It is amazingly true that when we are willing to do the most difficult thing, we find that we are better off because of it. Oh, sure, missionaries have their share of disease and pain, but some of the most diseased and pained are people who stayed home in order to avoid all that!

Jesus said, "Are you burdened and weary? Take my yoke upon you and learn of me; you will find me gentle and kindly, and you will find rest for your souls. My yoke fits perfectly and my burden is light." Jesus Himself "endured the cross and ignored the shame for the joy that was set before Him."

But we sometimes seem more geared to do our "utmost," than we are to seek out patiently, deliberately, and painstaking that role which will make the maximum contribution to "His highest"—the coming of His kingdom and power and glory to all the peoples of the earth. Again, beware of how easy it is to make that difficult choice to live for Him rather than for ourselves, throwing away our secular aspirations, and then turning aggressively to try to find out the most pleasing assignment within the new arena of life. It is not to please ourselves that we give our lives to Christ. Yet, we may find that His will involves greater pleasure and fulfillment than anything we ourselves could have chosen!

A famous missionary wrote back to fellow students and pled with them: "Give up your small ambitions and come East to proclaim the glorious gospel of Christ." For me to give "My utmost for His highest" is no guarantee of health, wealth, or happiness—which, incidentally, is true of any choice one can make—but that kind of crucial choice is, in the experience of thousands who have tried it, the most exhilarating and demanding path of all callings. You don't lose if you go with God. But you have to be willing to lose or you can't stick close to God.

End Notes

1. The *World Christian Foundations* program allows you to achieve a fully accredited M.A. or B.A. degree while you continue in work or ministry anywhere in the world. Instruction is centered on weekly mentoring sessions which allow both work and study. Contact World Christian Foundations, 1539 E. Howard Street, Pasadena, CA 91104, phone (626) 398-2106.

2. The IFMA and the EFMA are each comprised of about 100 mission agencies. The IFMA has Canadian members as contrasted to the EFMA, which represents only the National Association of Evangelicals of the USA. The largest mission agency not affiliated with either the IFMA or the EFMA is the Wycliffe Bible Translators. To subscribe to *Evangelical Missions Quarterly* send $21.95 to Box 794, Wheaton, IL 60189. Another large mission not in either the IFMA or the EFMA is Baptist Mid-Missions, which is the main group within a smaller association—the Fellowship of Missions (FOM). More recently AIMS (Association of International Missions/Services) has arisen within the general sphere of the charismatic tradition. The Association of Professors of Mission (APM) consists of seminary and college professors. The American Society of Missiology was founded from its beginning to intentionally include anyone seriously interested in missiology without regard to his/her denominational orientation. The ASM publishes the journal *Missiology, An International Review*. When you join the society you are automatically a subscriber to the journal. Send $21 ($17 students) to 616 Walnut Ave., Scottdale, PA 15683. The Evangelical Missiological Society (EMS) evolved from the Association of Evangelical Professors of Missions in order to welcome into its membership mission executives as well as professors from fields other than missions. It has a newsletter but no journal; instead it gives members a free book (or two) per year from its new EMS monograph series.

3. The International Society for Frontier Missiology (ISFM) has chosen to focus upon the remaining task in the world today still requiring the earlier type of "pioneer" work—for example, the initial-breakthrough type of mission activity. Its annual dues, $15, include a subscription to the *International Journal of Frontier Missions*. Send that amount to: IJFM, 1605 Elizabeth St., Pasadena, CA 91104.

4. Subscribe to the *Global Prayer Digest* for $9.00 per year, Global Prayer Digest, 1605 Elizabeth, Pasadena, CA 91104. Write *Mission Frontiers* at the same address. No charge.

5. For resources and encouragement in mobilizing, visit www.perspectives.org and watch for future updates.

The Power of Integrated Vision

Bill and Amy Stearns

Bill and Amy Stearns are a mission resource and mobilization team. As a couple they speak often in churches and training schools throughout the world on the "big picture" of God's work and how churches can be more strategically involved in the Great Commission.

W e are all familiar with Acts 1:8: "But you will receive power when the Holy Spirit comes on you; and you will be my witnesses in Jerusalem, and in all Judea and Samaria, and to the ends of the earth." This verse is often misquoted, changing its meaning. The first misquote goes something like this: "You will be my witnesses *either* in Jerusalem, or Judea, or Samaria, or to the ends of the earth." Thinking that the text reads that way, many say, "I think I'll choose to witness in Jerusalem. Yep. Sounds good to me. Okay, God, use me here."

A second misquote goes something like this: "...and you will be my witnesses *first* in Jerusalem, then Judea, then Samaria, *then* to the ends of the earth." Thinking of Jesus' command as a progression allows many people to think that they have to become proficient at sharing their faith in their "Jerusalem" first; then, having mastered that, they can move on to the Judeas, Samarias, and finally the ends of the earth. Few ever make it beyond their "Jerusalem."

The idea behind this text isn't "either/or" or "first/then" but "both/and," as in "...you will be my witnesses *both* in Jerusalem, and Judea, and Samaria, and to the ends of the earth."

That helps us to clarify the impact our lives are to make here on this earth. What our Heavenly Father wants us to realize is that no matter what we do individually or corporately as a church, our impact is to be both local (where you are) and international (to the nations). It's not an either/or option or a progressive one. It's simultaneous.

Put another way, whatever ministry God wants you to focus on—again, individually or as a church—whether reaching unwed mothers in downtown Singapore, or being a Christian mechanic witnessing in an auto shop, or being a full-time mom, your ministry isn't an end in itself. It is instead to be a means toward God's goal of reaching the nations!

Too often, those who have caught a vision for the global world are ineffective (or even blinded) in reaching out to the world in their own backyards, often damaging their day-to-day ministry effectiveness because they lack balance in their overall life perspective.

So, too, becoming a healthy World Christian is a process. Your vision must be on the global world, while being effective and passionate for those in your local world—not becoming so globally minded that you're of no local good.

The biblical theme of God blessing His people to bless every people provides an inspired structure for our overall mission as the Church. Understanding and acting on this principle results in an integrated personal and corporate ministry, and encompasses reaching the unreached nations of the earth.

The psalmist wrote:

> May God be gracious to us and bless us
> And cause His face to shine upon us
> That Your way may be known on the earth,
> Your salvation among all nations.
> …God blesses us, that all the ends of the
> earth may fear him (Ps 67:1-2, 7).

God blesses His people with His relationship and health and talents and finances and spiritual gifts and skills. And, in the biblical pattern of "blessed is the nation [the people group] whose God is the Lord," we can joyfully receive God's blessings. It's part of what He has promised to do in His plan to demonstrate His character to all the peoples of the world.

How does this twofold program—being blessed to be a blessing—form a structure for integrating ministries? Consider the following illustration as descriptive of the overall mission of a church. This illustration is inherently limited, but for now consider the parallels: The local church is like a four-stage rocket!

Each of the four dynamics illustrated is present in a healthy, growing local church. Consider each as part of an integrated whole:

The First Dynamic:
God blesses His people
to strengthen the Church.

If the Church is to be a channel of God's blessing to every people, the Church itself must first be strengthened. Children need nurture in the admonition of the Lord, families need encouragement and equipping in everything from communication skills to financial management, couples must be counseled, youth discipled, offerings collected, prayers offered in behalf of the fellowship, bodies exercised, sermons preached, walls painted, fellowship enjoyed, and buildings built. All the gifts, skills and ministries that go on within the Church itself can be affirmed and encouraged because the Church needs to be strong for its world-level purpose. This is the power dynamic, the "booster stage" of the rocket.

The Second Dynamic:
The church is to bless every people
group—including its own.

Here's where the church begins impacting the world outside its walls while at the same time praying for the nations. Going to every people includes going to our own! The easiest people group to offer God's blessing is, of course, that fellowship's own people group. As part of its overall mission to the world, the local church becomes salt and light to its own community:

The Integrated, Overall Mission of the Church

Psalm 67; Acts 1:8

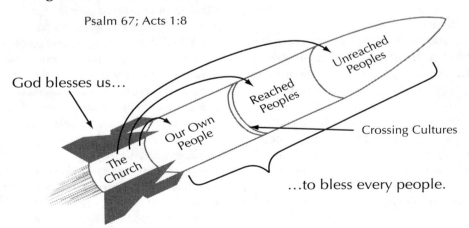

God blesses us… The Church / Our Own People / Reached Peoples / Unreached Peoples / Crossing Cultures / …to bless every people.

- *In evangelism*. As a church movement is established in a people group, it is that church's obligation to evangelize its own culture. Mass and personal evangelism aren't just compartments of a local church's ministry; sharing the Good News with neighbors is crucial to the global scope of the Great Commission. This is because the goal is not merely to reach out and save those who are lost, but to see those who are brought into the Kingdom blessed by God to become tomorrow's laborers for the nations.

- *In ministering to community needs*. Ministering goodness within a fellowship's own culture isn't just being nice. Caring for the homeless, visiting the sick, ministering to those in prison, tending suicide hot-lines, giving to the poor, sponsoring an unwed mothers' home, cleaning up trash on the highway, offering free baby-sitting for mothers' days off, raising money for medical research, or singing Christmas carols in the mall for the enjoyment of shoppers are all ways of blessing one's own culture by simply "going about doing good" (see Acts 10:38).

- *In standing up for righteousness in one's own people group*. A church must often bless its culture the hard way, by standing for God's character on social issues. When Christians fight pornography, battle drug abuse, child abuse, crime, corruption and injustice, they help bless their own culture.

The Third Dynamic: The church is to bless every people group—including reached peoples.

Here the church begins to cross cultural barriers into "reached peoples," those distinct ethnic groups with a viable church movement capable of evangelizing its own culture. About half of the world's people groups are in this category.

A fellowship's ministries in this third stage bridge language, social, or other cultural barriers. Blessing other reached peoples entails:

- serving their churches
- empowering them to bless their own culture (their own Stage Two) and to

equip other reached peoples (their own Stage Three)

- partnering with them to offer Christ's redemption to unreached peoples.

When a church crosses language, social, or other cultural barriers and comes alongside the local churches in a reached culture, it should come not to take over, but to serve. The result of this partnering can be a strengthened local church, better able to fulfill its role in Gods global purpose: to bless its own people through evangelism, doing good, and standing up for righteousness in its society.

The Fourth Dynamic: The church is to bless every people group, including the remaining unreached peoples of the world.

This dynamic of a church is to see that the blessing of redemption is offered to every remaining unreached people group. This has been God's goal from the beginning of Genesis, and it needs to be the end goal of all we do as a church. It is an essential element of an integrated church's structure.

This is the realm of frontier, pioneer missions, where the believers worldwide can join together as partners to focus their resources. What happens in this stage of the "rocket" of the church?

- *Pre-Evangelism*. Relief efforts, Christians winning favor in political, educational or business realms, medical work, etc. This prepares the way, establishing the reputation of the character of God in Christ among an unreached people.

- *Church-Planting*. Unbelievers come to faith in Christ and churches are planted. Those newborn congregations must be discipled to be strengthened, reaching out into their own people and crossing cultural barriers in their own history of being blessed to be a blessing to every people.

An Integrated Vision

The whole church, with its varying parts, functions, giftings and ministries working in unity, goes about the Father's business. We're not just a Family—we're a Family Business. God pours His blessings upon us in order to make us a blessing to the world. We're working toward the fulfillment of God's purpose—that those from "every tribe and tongue and people and nation" would be blessed and believe so as to worship Him and give Him His due.

It's essential that the different portions of your life-mission, and the mission of your church be integrated. An integrated vision is:

- *Specific.* Rather than just a vague, open-ended hope of things going well, it is a measurable, thoughtful approach to reaching the goal. It can consist of a step-by-step plan to build on the resources and strengths of the Body, with specific targets in mind.
- *Noncompetitive.* Those whose interests and ministries emphasize the spearhead of bringing the gospel to the unreached do not allow that spearhead to become a wedge that divides the body. Instead, the true mission visionary thinks through how the various home-front ministries fit into the overall mission of the church, and seeks to encourage and promote those other ministries toward the fulfilling of God's purpose.
- *Liberating.* An integrated, single vision in a local church frees up the resources of a congregation. As a fellowship identifies its assets in manpower, prayer power, finances, and talents, it will also recognize its limitations, and respond accordingly. For example, when those zealous for unreached peoples see that their local church is not ready to sustain a concerted thrust toward the unreached, energy can still be applied to foster and encourage what the church is capable of sustaining. This might consist of regular prayer for the unreached, information gathering, strengthening of the other ministries of the fellowship, etc. Reliance on God's faithfulness to accomplish His purposes will bring freedom from anxiety.

Malfunctions in the Mission

How can this desire to be used by God among the nations backfire? It can be divisive. Among all the competing interest groups in a church, the little "unreached peoples club" can whine for more bulletin space, more budget allotments, more volunteers. These frontier mission fanatics can point long, bony fingers in judgment at other believers in the fellowship and announce that if a Christian doesn't have a personal involvement in reaching an unreached people, he or she isn't in the will of God.

This "us-them" mentality can do more to destroy unity in the church than anything else. In fact, focusing on an unreached people and touting oneself as one of those rare, noble disciples called World Christians can be one of the most obnoxious steps mission-minded believers can take in a local fellowship. They are rarely appreciated and hence are given little time or resources.

The image of the rocket representing the mission of the church can, of course, be faulty for various reasons. But the image may help identify two of the main malfunctions of mission zeal in the church:

- Focusing on Stage One, while ignoring Stages Three and Four

A church that concentrates only on Stage One is like the powerful booster stage of a rocket with no place to go. The first stage blasts into action and careens in every direction like a deflating balloon. A church with no clear direction but lots of activity diffuses its resources; the people tire of activity and suffer burnout. Ministry activity—virtually all of it taking place within the fellowship—can proceed at a furious pace, but the fruit of ministry is sparse.

- Focusing on Stage Four, while ignoring Stages One and Two

Another malfunction of our single-vision mission is neglect of Stage One. A fellowship might concentrate on blessing an unreached people but neglect strengthening its base. That congregation might be like a needle-nosed rocket nose cone drifting through space with no thrust.

Often, mission activist groups feel a clear sense of purpose and direction but are frustrated by lack of prayer power, financial power, and people power. In frustration, these folks point fingers at the lack of vision of the pastor or elders, or at the rest of the congregation for their obvious selfishness.

If your overriding problem as a mission task force or mission mobilizer is the lack of resources, slow down somehow: You need to reconnect in new ways with the booster stage—with a strengthened church. You need to affirm and encourage the various ministries of the church, to work at integrating a vision of frontier mission within every God-given ministry in the church.

A church with a vision of its mission to reach the uttermost parts of the earth must have a strong Stage Two. Fulfilling your obligation to bless your own culture gives the credibility that missionary enterprises too often lack in offering God's blessing to an unreached people.

The Church With a Unifying Vision

What happens when a church catches a vision of God's heart for every people, and works to integrate that direction into its overall mission?

"I've never seen such ownership of a project by our congregation," says senior pastor Ron Mahurin of Cedar Crest Bible Fellowship Church in Allentown, Pennsylvania. "We started in 1987 with a vision of reaching one people group. Since then we have had many families prepared and sent out, our missions and building giving doubled, then tripled. Our congregation has grown, and our people have a heart for God's heart for all peoples!"

It all began when the church teamed up with AIM (formerly Africa Inland Mission) to focus on the Sandawe people of Tanzania. Later a three-way partnership was created between the church, AIM, and the Tanzanian national church. Cliff Boone, the church's youth pastor, together with his wife, soon went to work as part of a team serving among the Sandawe.

The integration of the church's total mission was evident in the Wednesday night prayer meetings. Cliff Boone and his wife, Becky, still rave about their home church prayer meetings: "With all the many serious prayer concerns of that large church body, the people never fail to mention the Sandawe. There they are, old and young, from all walks of life, bowed before the Father, pleading on behalf of the Sandawe people whom they have never seen but whom they committed themselves to reaching with the gospel."

The people have learned that their prayers really matter. One hot Thursday morning in Kwamtoro, Tanzania—just a few hours after the Allentown church Wednesday night prayer-warriors had risen from their knees, a middle-aged Sandawe man called to the Boones from outside their shack. He pulled out three tattered Swahili tracts that the Boones had given him months before.

"I have stayed with these little books for two months," he said. "I have read them and read them. I have talked with my wife about them. Now I have come here to be saved."

After serving refreshments, Cliff opened his Bible and carefully explained the gospel message. After a long discussion and lots of questions, the man said, "This is what I want. I want to believe in Jesus."

Every Wednesday night prayer meeting doesn't produce this kind of report, but with this kind of solid ownership by the home church, the Boones can say, "We have seen God do more than we could have imagined." Recently Cliff reported 20 believers among the nearly 40,000 Sandawe. Furthermore, the Africa Inland Church, mostly Swahili-speaking nationals from the majority tribe, had trained and sent their first missionary couple to the Sandawe!

But what has happened to the home church with this focus on an unreached people? Has the missionary zeal drained local ministry? According to Pastor Ron, since 1987:

- Two major church building projects have been undertaken
- Missions giving has grown from $40,000 in 1987 to over $125,000 in 1992
- The congregation has nearly doubled from about 275 members to its present size of 500 members

The original concentration on one people group has expanded to a mission vision that seems to encompass all peoples, and has served to spearhead the entire mission program of the church. It also led to partnering between eight different churches in three states who have worked together in reaching the Sandawe.

What is your part in the overall mission of the Body of Christ? And how can you help others find their niche in God's plan? Consider the dynamic of an integrated vision for the work of God in the church, at home and across cultural barriers, as we walk in His blessing to be a blessing to every people.

The Awesome Potential for Mission Found in Local Churches

George Miley

God is releasing the potential of His Church into mission as never before. Now more than ever, He is summoning forth the awesome beauty and capacity that He has deposited among His people worldwide.

The responsibility for world evangelization has for too long fallen on the shoulders of too few. Seeing Jesus proclaimed, trusted and worshiped among all the earth's peoples is a complex undertaking. It is a process which calls forth the full diversity of spiritual gifts and practical expertise resident among God's people. It beckons the participation of every believer.

The greatest resource of the local church is her people. We are God's treasure, placed together in the community of the redeemed. And the unique, God-given potential within each one of us becomes even more effective when it is blended together and expressed in harmony with the unique, God-given potential of our brothers and sisters.

Local churches contain the broadest spectrum of spiritual gifts and life experience found among God's people. Gifts of administration order and facilitate the energies of the visionary. Gifts of discernment protect against unwise investment of strength and resources. Ability to shepherd and heal frees people for productive ministry. Entrepreneurs, when their skills are focused on kingdom ends, create enterprises which are channels for kingdom extension. In fact, the whole range of vocational expertise is a vast kingdom resource when designing entry strategies among unreached peoples.

Some churches make significant contributions to missions, either by pooling their finances as a denominational family of churches or by applying portions of their budget to support individual missionaries. They have members who faithfully pray for these missionaries and encourage them in any way possible. This is wonderful. It's exactly right for many churches.

But other communities of believers (churches) yearn to do more. The facts of the world inspire great dreams. When it becomes clear that world evangelization will be completed only when new efforts are born to plant churches among unreached peoples; and when it is known that there are specific peoples which are still without a church, some-

George Miley is the President of Antioch Network and helps local churches activate church planting initiatives among unreached peoples. Previously, he was a missionary with Operation Mobilization for 20 years: 5 years in India and 15 years as general director of the OM Ships LOGOS and DOULOS.

thing fires the imagination of people hungry for more hands-on and active missions participation. They find themselves wondering if they can do anything to help bring about the yet non-existent churches. As they turn themselves to pray for God to do what only He can do, they find that their thoughts are locked on what *they* might be able to do. They yearn to express who they are in the process of fulfilling God's mission.

Quite often this apostolic zeal is expressed in the traditional ways. But sometimes churches as a whole come to recognize that God is entrusting them with a specific part of the task. A focus emerges toward a particular people group: to do whatever it takes to bring about a church planting movement among that particular group. This strategic mind-set can permeate a congregation, calling forth a sense of corporate, church-wide embracing of a task.

When something forms with a God-given hope, it becomes a matter of shared ownership by the whole church. Ownership triggers investment. Instead of finding a few more donors, we see churches full of co-owners of the mission. They can see the end result and savor its value. God summons all the innovation and time-tempered wisdom of scores of people, from all walks of life.

I've seen local churches take on an assignment from God for a people, for a place, a city, a language or a tribe. The distinctive is that the church carries more than just an ambition for the fruitful work of a missionary. The body of believers carries a sense of holy trust from God, that God has given them a holy task that they are to pursue to completion.

Years ago a church in the northern suburbs of Atlanta sensed God's call to the Muslims of Bosnia. They had been in an extensive process of seeking Him about their missions involvement. They were committed to playing a strategic part in the completion of world evangelization. They were also focused on the multiplication of churches, both at home and among the unreached. In addition to starting churches in Atlanta, they aspired to play an active role in starting churches in Bosnia. To do so just seemed to be expressing who God had really made them to be.

They sought counsel from their denominational mission leaders, from other mission agencies, and from a few national church leaders in the region. In front of their church building they installed a marker which cemented the fact that, as a fellowship of believers, they were "On the Road to Sarajevo." When civil war broke out in 1992, they saw it as an open door from the Lord. They began sending teams of their people to live and minister in a refugee camp filled with refugees fleeing their target city. From these teams of short-termers has emerged godly, competent leadership and a growing long-term team of church planters, working in fellowship with and submission to the emerging Bosnian church. The national leadership testifies that workers from this church are some of the most effective and respected in the country.

Pursuing a people-group focused mission is a complex process. Every church is different. Each people group requires a unique approach. There is no standard formula for how a church is to pursue this effort. There are scores of ways that it can be done well. But it can also be done poorly.

People Group Focus Pursued Poorly

Even with the best of intentions, a church might go about this poorly. Here are some of the factors church should be careful to guard against:

1. An independent attitude. Churches contain awesome potential as springboards for launching kingdom initiatives. But a motivation to show what we can do all by ourselves, or that we don't need anybody else, is unworthy of the gospel. God is not in the business of blessing an independent spirit, which can be rooted in pride and selfish ambition. Where God is at work in power, there is humility, an esteeming of the other as better than ourselves and unity.

2. A failure to count the cost. Any commitment to kingdom advance among an unreached people will be contested by Satan every step of the way. This is not a casual activity, not something to be entered into lightly or unadvisedly. Are we prepared to pay the price that our dreams may cost us?

If a church is going to commit itself to church planting among the unreached, especially if it is going to send some of its own people to do this (and thereby place them in a spiritually, emotionally and physically vulnerable place), the permanent leadership of the church should be as committed to the initiative as those who are sent forth.

3. A short-term mentality. Short-term mission trips, done well, can yield wonderful results. They can give people a much deeper understanding of the task remaining among unreached peoples. They can fire vision, quicken prayer and catalyze commitment to more permanent engagement. But any short-term activity finds its greatest value when it exists, not for its own benefit, but as an integral part of a long-term process. This allows the fruits of the short-term mission to be evaluated, and the good to be preserved and channeled. The mission effort of a local church inevitably fails when they set out thinking that a people group can be reached in a year or two.

4. A lack of training. A local church can be a wonderful environment for informal mentoring in evangelism, discipling, serving and character formation that is so crucial in church-planting. Jesus trained His disciples in the context of real life, where principles of walking with God could be observed and passed on through intimate life contact between teacher and pupil. Still, no local church has all the resources and experience needed for the mission field. The Body of Christ is bigger than any one of us. Churches must seek the best blend of formal, informal and non-formal mission training for their workers, and this pursuit will ultimately lead them into relationship with other members of the great commission community.

> We see people-group focused mission efforts from local churches emerging all over the world. It's a thrilling hour. We all have so much to learn from each other.

5. A lack of proper care. Healthy local churches are richly endowed with the potential to care for their people. Throughout the fellowship there are those who are motivated to shepherd, protect, care and heal. But this need must be recognized from the start, and plans laid as to how long-term care will be provided. We cannot afford to be casual or naive in this area.

People Group Focus Done Well

I've seen churches do this well. Here are some outstanding features found in such churches:

1. Learning to pray. Churches that have been successful in missions have learned to wait on the Lord. They have learned to be still until they have heard what God has to say and have tested His guidance. These churches schedule prolonged times of intercession, praying not only for the missionaries they support, but intentionally for the people group they are trying to reach.

2. Committing for the long-haul. Churches that do well in missions often plan for decades of service. There is a commitment to remain with a mission project until a flourishing church movement has been planted or Jesus returns—whichever comes first. This long-range planning allows time to do things well. It provides time to plant dreams for the future in the minds of the children and new directions for retirement in the hearts of middle-aged couples. It gives time to form steady partnerships with other churches and mission agencies.

3. Taking ownership. When everyone in a church takes ownership of a mission project, there is a prolonged investment on the part of both church leaders and members. Short-term mission efforts no longer stand alone. When church members travel on a prayer journey visiting their people group, or spend time encouraging their missionary workers, they know they are investing in the future of both their own church and their mission work. Their vision is refueled and the entire congregation is renewed.

4. Utilizing Structures. Churches who push on toward fruitful church planting do one of two things regarding structure. They form a new mission organizational structure, rooted in and springing forth from the shared life of the body of believers. Such structures are bonded to the church relationally, and serve as easy avenues for the expression of the spiritual gifts and vocational expertise of the members. Or, a church develops a vital partnership with an experienced mission agency. In either case, some organizational entity serves as a conduit for the release of the group's vision, energy and capacity.

Mission to unreached peoples requires apostolic structures. Local churches are primarily pastoral structures. The local church is designed to nurture its members. Its focus is on protection, continuity, avoiding risks and bringing its members to spiritual maturity. This type of structure is called a "modality." An apostolic structure is designed to carry out the mission of extending the Kingdom. It focuses on initiation, plans on taking risks and perseveres against great odds. This type of structure is often called a "sodality." Modalities can forge vital partnerships with sodalities. They can also give birth to new sodalities.

A church in Indiana prepared a team for church planting among a Muslim people group in Central Asia. In order to carry out their mission, they formed a separate apostolic structure. They created a 501(c)(3) corporation. The senior pastor and other church leaders were on the board, which was chaired by a business person who was a member of the congregation. They also invited other mission experienced people to serve on the board who were not members of their church.

This organization has served them well. It has provided the basis for engaging this people group as medical and educational professionals. It has allowed the church to access resources beyond their own fellowship, and it has provided them access to counsel beyond themselves.

A growing number of local churches and established mission agencies are forging effective partnerships. Mission agencies are approaching churches where vision is alive and asking how they can serve the church's direction. Churches are identifying areas where they need help and are enlisting the experience of the agencies. Written partnerships are being crafted in the context of careful communication and planning, identifying the areas of responsibility the church will carry and the areas where it will rely on the agency. When done well, everybody wins through this kind of beautiful humility and submission to one another in love, especially the unreached peoples. And Christ is honored as His people serve, submitting to one another in love.

We see people-group focused mission efforts from local churches emerging all over the world. Indian churches are sending their own to other parts of India. Central American churches are launching teams to North Africa. Churches in Minneapolis are sending their own to Central Asia. It's a thrilling hour.

We have so much to learn from each other. Churches can learn so much from other churches, and from mission agencies who have labored cross-culturally in some cases for generations. And, yes, these same agencies can be profoundly enriched by working together with churches. Mission agencies who embrace a high view of the local church will see their own efforts strengthened and their influence expanded for the glory of our Lord and the advance of His kingdom throughout the earth.

Study Questions

1. Miley says that mission to unreached peoples requires "apostolic structures," which are not naturally found within local churches. How then does Miley see the potential of local churches being expressed?

2. Miley says that "people-group focused mission" is not for every local church. Why is this important?

3. Evaluate Miley's idea that a sense of ownership results from sharing in a God-given hope for a people group.

Tentmakers Needed for World Evangelization

Ruth E. Siemens

As we enter the 21st century, astonishing events have radically altered the world's landscape of nations, multiplying both the opportunities and the need for tentmakers. To finish world evangelization, thousands of Christians must support themselves abroad with their trades and professions and make Him known to people around them.

Today's global job market, which began during the decolonization period after World War II, has now been vastly expanded by the crumbling of the Soviet Union, the last of the European colonial powers. Its collapse resulted in 15 new ex-Soviet republics, in the liberation of seven satellite nations and a score of client states on every continent. Bereft of Soviet subsidies, they struggle to meet tough new demands for international aid. Most are trying to implement free market economics, multiparty politics and improved human rights. Russia's continuing instability portends that some of its remaining 100+ people groups will also gain the independence they seek. Yugoslavia has broken into separate states. Wars between countries have given way to a rash of civil wars. Along with this worldwide trend toward disassociation, are cross-currents of association, like the reunited Yemens, Vietnams, China and Hong Kong, and regional economic blocs as varied as the European Union and OPEC. Arab countries exhibit new vitality. All these factors are reshaping the world job market to provide more openings than ever before.

But before I list reasons for tentmaking, I must define this term lest someone ask, as one woman did—why China needs to have so many tents!

What are Tentmakers?

Historically, tentmakers are missions-committed Christians who, like Paul, support themselves in secular work, as they engage in cross-cultural evangelism on the job and in free time. But over a dozen experience-based definitions have recently come into use, making it difficult to communicate on the subject. We must have a single, biblically based definition. Paul used his craft to earn his living as an essential part of his unique approach to missionary finance and practice. So tentmaking becomes a missiological term to designate his whole strategy. The main part of this paper is a study of his strategy, to learn how we can use our trades and professions strategically to win our post-modern world for Christ, as

Ruth E. Siemens served for 21 years in Peru, Brazil, Portugal and Spain, pioneering campus fellowships for the International Fellowship of Evangelical Students (IFES). During the first six years she supported herself in secular binational schools, where she integrated work and witness. In 1976, on missions staff of IVCF, she founded Global Opportunities (GO) to provide counseling, training and job referral, to help Christians serve abroad as tentmakers. She continues on the board of GO and promotes tentmaking through speaking and writing.

Used by permission of the author.

Paul used his craft to win the ancient Roman world. The study confirms the historic definition, so note some of the characteristics of Paul-type tentmakers.

1. Tentmakers use their trades or professions to support themselves abroad. In contrast, regular missionaries receive church or donor support, and are perceived by local people as religious workers even if they do medicine, agriculture or education. Between these two ministry models is a continuum of combinations—all of them valid and good. Missionaries are still viewed as religious workers even if they take part-time employment for increased support or better contact with seekers. Professionals are still tentmakers even if they supplement low pay with modest donor gifts, providing they spend significant time at genuine secular employment.

2. Tentmakers do cross-cultural ministry. So most of the several hundred thousand evangelical expatriates with jobs abroad are not tentmakers. Most have little or no missions-commitment and little or no ministry with locals. Probably not more than one percent are tentmakers, evangelizing the people of their new host country.

3. Tentmakers do full-time ministry—even in the context of a full-time job. People regularly ask me, "Wasn't it frustrating to spend so many hours in your secular school and to have so little time left over for God?" But I believed all my time was God's. He helped me do low-key evangelism with teachers, students and parents at work and other ministries in my free time. A job is no inconvenience to tolerate in exchange for a residence visa. Rather, it is the God-given context for living out the gospel full-time, while under the full-time scrutiny of non-believers—and for sharing it in an attractive, wholesome, non-judgmental way.

4. Tentmakers do workplace evangelism. Must tentmakers evangelize at work and maybe risk dismissal or even expulsion from the country? The many hours on the job make them spiritually responsible for people around them. If they evangelize elsewhere but not at work, sooner or later they lose credibility. But we will examine the low-key kind of evangelism Paul teaches his converts, which is appropriate for the workplace and for hostile environments.

5. Tentmakers also do free-time ministries. In both Peru and Brazil, God helped me serve churches and to pioneer IVCF-IFES university fellowships, in addition to discrete evangelism in the schools where I earned my living....A linguistics professor translated the New Testament for six million Muslims while he did university teaching and his wife taught English to the wife of a sheik.... A young high school science teacher evangelized his students in rural Kenya, and preached every third Sunday in the local church....A young symphony violinist in Singapore had Bible studies with fellow musicians and worked in a Chinese church.... A faculty person and an engineer set up a Christian bookstore in an Arab Gulf city.... A theology graduate doing "study abroad" in India, also did campus evangelism and taught part-time in a seminary. Tentmakers do varied ministries as God leads and enables.

6. Tentmakers are not second rate witnesses. (as often implied because they are unfairly lumped with other expatriates), but often have full theological and missiological training, even though they serve as lay people. But in this cosmic, spiritual war for control of the world, not everyone needs officer's training. Foot soldiers are needed to develop quality friendships with seekers. But all must know how to use "the sword of the Spirit"—good personal and group Bible study skills—and how to do spiritual warfare with evangelism and prayer. All need a course on missions, and cultural orientation for their target country.

7. Tentmakers are not "lone rangers." They work together in fellowship and accountability groups. They seek prayer support from their home churches and friends, and in their new host country they work with a tentmaker team, a national church, or with a mission agency—if it will allow them to retain their tentmaker distinctives. An expatriate church can be helpful if it does not distract them from the host country culture and people.

Practical Reasons for Tentmaking

1. Tentmakers can gain entry into restricted-access countries. About 80% of the world's people live under governments that deny entry to missionaries but welcome professionals with needed expertise. Some recently opened doors into Marxist countries have been newly restricted, because the driving force behind anti-communism is not democratic principles, but nationalism. Local people are hostile to all but their own historic religion. Orthodoxy, Judaism, Islam, Hinduism and Buddhism have all become more aggressive. But economic need will keep doors open for educators, engineers and technicians, computer experts, health care personnel, business people, agriculturists, athletes and artists, etc. (Even missionaries can also enter, if they can go as tentmakers.)

2. Tentmakers can serve in needy open countries. After a century of missions, Japan is less than one percent evangelical. European Mediterranean countries have a lower percentage of evangelicals than India or China, and France has more Muslims than Christians. Educated people worldwide listen more readily to professional people, suspecting that religious workers say religious things mainly because they must do it to earn their living. Younger generations in the once Christian West have little knowledge of Jesus. Dr. Lesslie Newbigin, after years in India, said we should give high priority to Western youth because of their powerful negative worldwide influence. The Church is not an end in itself. It demonstrates God's kingdom. But its mandate is also to engage culture and to challenge unbiblical world views, especially in this new post-modern age. This must be done by Christian professionals in the marketplace, at home and abroad.

3. Tentmakers can alleviate the cost of missions, working for years at little or no expense to the church, as mission overheads and cost-of-living indices rise. The average couple needs two and a half years to raise donor support. One church reports sixty members training for missions and a budget that will accommodate only five. A church can multiply its ministry abroad with tentmakers, reserving limited funds for those missionaries requiring full support.

4. Tentmakers can solve our problem of personnel. Missionary recruitment has slowed, even though former receiving countries now send workers. We will need many more. Even though most unreached peoples have now been adopted, it may take years before they can evangelize their own people. And our mandate is not finished when these groups are reached.

Many countries inside and outside the 10/40 Window are still unevangelized.

Although missionary recruits have tapered off, lay people are the church's great untapped resource. They move naturally in their professional circles, in the worlds of finance, commerce, industry, science, education, health care, etc., understanding the mentality, the jargon and the hangups of colleagues. Missionaries provide excellent role models abroad for religious workers, but only professionals can provide role models for the other 99% of the church. Tentmakers can be an almost cost-free, parallel force to complement and assist the work of regular missionaries, and to pioneer where they cannot go.

5. Tentmakers can reduce the missionary attrition rate. Thirty percent of missionaries do not stay for a second term, after a first term learning the language and culture at donor expense. The expatriate failure rate reported by secular firms is similar. Some recruiters now seek applicants who have served with the Peace Corps. Mission agencies should recruit tried and proven tentmakers who have learned the language, culture and ministry skills at their own expense, and now commit themselves to a life they already understand. We should use the training potential of study abroad, modestly paid internships and expense-paid voluntary service.

6. Tentmakers are ideal for new sending countries. Many new sending countries cannot follow our Western model of donor-support—if their currency is low in relation to their target country, or their government limits currency export. But it may not be wise for Western churches to finance their operations. Some national ministries refuse foreign funds because they stifle local responsibility, enthusiasm and dependence upon God. But tentmaking provides them with an almost cost-free option. Every country has access to the global market in different ways. Labor is the invisible export—the main source of income for many countries.

7. Today's international job market itself is a powerful argument for tent-making. It is no accident, but is designed by God to help us finish world evangelization. Like many rulers, our King of Kings has a repopulation program. He transfers millions of hard-to-reach people into freer countries—Turks to Germany, Kurds to Austria, everyone to America—and sends Christian professionals into restricted regions, so all may hear the good news.

The U.K. had a long tradition of tentmaking in its far-flung empire, but there were few jobs for Americans until after World War II. Then war-ravaged countries and 100+ newly independent European ex-colonies all needed development help. Now add to them all the ex-Soviet bloc countries. An estimated four million Americans work abroad, and millions more from other countries. But Muslims, Mormons and other cults make much better use of overseas jobs than Christians.

Only tentmakers can reach that 80% of the world which is largely closed to regular missionaries.

For almost 20 years, our Global Opportunities staff laboriously researched overseas jobs, turning up about 3000 a month. But today 60,000 or 70,000 jobs can be accessed on the Internet in a day! Thousands of employers (about 40 kinds) hire people in every career field for positions in cities everywhere, as well as some rural and tribal locations. Most contracts require degrees in a needed field, and work experience, because governments protect less skilled jobs for their own people. But mineral-rich, sparsely populated countries also import unskilled labor, mainly from the poorer Asian countries. Westerners would not work for their wages and would be suspect if they did. But these men and women earn much more abroad than at home. In an affluent Arab city, Pakistani street sweepers joyfully share the good news.

Most initial contracts are for one to three years, and renewable. Serious tentmakers commit themselves to a region as long as God keeps opening doors. Salaries range from modest but adequate, to high, with generous benefits, and include round trip travel for employees and their families. This is true if they are hired while in their home country. If they go abroad to seek employment, they are usually considered local hires, with local pay and no benefits. Many Christians do not qualify for the contract positions. Many do not wish for full-time jobs because they do not understand workplace evangelism, and they consider secular work a waste of time instead of vital ministry.

Some tentmakers begin their own businesses—construction, manufacturing, tourism, computer software applications, import-export, business consulting, language institutes, elementary schools, and so on. A chemical engineer in the Middle East started twenty businesses—including a restaurant, a job placement service and miniature golf course. But experience and capital are required, and your own business usually demands more time and effort than a salaried position. And phantom businesses are an abomination to governments and to the Lord.

Tentmaking is for all ages because the Great Commission has no age clause. Young people can choose from hundreds of "study abroad" options and join campus ministry teams. Modestly paid internships and voluntary service are good tentmaker contexts, and in a more limited way, so are unglamorous summer jobs. Retirees are in demand. Never before have there been so many healthy, educated and affluent senior citizens as in our Western (and other) countries today. They may take full-time or part-time employment abroad, like a teaching couple Bill and Fern, both in their seventies, who still bicycle around a Chinese city, teach English and win their students to the Lord!

Although there are compelling practical reasons for tentmaking, the biblical reasons are more important, and a biblical basis is essential and urgent for the whole tentmaking movement.

Biblical Reasons for Tentmaking

Several Old Testament believers supported themselves while making God known in foreign countries. But it is Paul, maker and repairer of tents, who explained, demonstrated and strongly defended this ministry model for us. He also reminds us there are two basic approaches to missionary work, his *self-support* model and Peter's *donor support* model.

Remember that Jesus had called Peter to leave his fishing business forever in order to trust God's people for his livelihood (Luke

5:1-11). When he returned to his business after the resurrection, Jesus met him on the lakeshore and asked him to renew his earlier commitment—three times (John 21). Years later Paul writes approvingly that Peter and his wife still make their missionary journeys on church support (1 Cor 9). This was not a problem for the Jewish people with whom they worked, but Paul knew it would put off his ever suspicious Gentile friends.

But in that same chapter, Paul lists strong arguments in favor of church support. This passage and three others are often used to prove that Paul mainly received church support and made tents only in financial emergencies. But these are proof-texts—taken out of context. An inductive study and careful correlation of all the relevant passages show that self-support was Paul's deliberate policy, part of his well-designed strategy.

We will consider these proof texts, as we seek to answer six basic questions: 1) How much did Paul work? 2) How much did he receive in donor gifts? 3) Why did he work at all when he did not have to? 4) What did he teach converts about lay ministry? 5) What was the result of his unique strategy? 6) How can a study of Paul help us today?

How Much Did Paul Work?

Paul's three journeys took about ten years, but he had already evangelized for more than ten years in Arabia (the puppet kingdom of Nabataea), in his home province of Cilicia and in Syria, including Antioch. But let's look at the three journeys.

The first journey. Paul and Barnabas took the gospel through the island of Cyprus and the Galatian-Phrygian region. In 1 Corinthians 9:6 Paul suggests they already supported themselves at that time and continued that financial practice when they formed two separate teams.

The second journey. Paul's team did church planting in the Roman provinces of Macedonia and Achaia. In both of Paul's brief letters to the Thessalonians he said he worked "night and day"—that is, morning and late afternoon shifts. In Corinth, Paul's job and house hunting had resulted in employment and lodging with Aquila and Priscilla, Jewish refugees from Rome, because they had the same trade (Acts 18:3).

"Tentmakers" were not weavers, but artisans who made animal skin products, including tents. Verse five records the arrival of Silas and Timothy who had stayed on in Macedonia after Paul had to flee. It is usually assumed that they brought money, and that Paul immediately desisted from his manual labor. The men probably did bring money. But the Greek text suggests no change in Paul's activity—only his colleagues' surprise at the intensity of his preaching and the amount of ministry he had already done.

The third journey. They spent three years in the Roman province of Asia, which was already the most economically important region in the empire, and the center for the worship of Artemis, or Diana, whose temple was one of the seven wonders of the ancient world. In Acts 20, in Paul's farewell instructions to the Ephesian elders, he says, "I coveted no man's silver or gold or apparel. You yourselves know that these hands have ministered to my necessities, and to those who were with me. In all things I have shown you that by so toiling you must also help the weak…" (Acts 20:33-35). Even pastor-elders were to continue their self-support, not just to give to the poor, but to provide a model for easily tempted converts from unsavory backgrounds.

Paul taught converts "from house to house"—house churches. He preached in the Hall of Tyrannus, probably during the long noon hours when the teacher did not need it himself. (F. F. Bruce considered the Early Western Text to be accurate in this detail.) Paul's listeners borrowed his apron and his handkerchief (the sweat rag around his brow), to heal the sick—a poignant glimpse of Paul in work clothes, teaching an audience similarly dressed (Acts 19:11,12).

But near the end of Paul's ministry in Ephesus, a crisis in Corinth gives us our best information about his tentmaking. Judaizers came to Corinth to discredit his apostleship. They criticized his simple preaching style, and deemed his message superficial, because he refused to make Gentiles adopt Jewish rituals in order to become Christians. But mainly they attacked his manual labor, saying it proved he could not get church support, because he was not an apostle. He was an imposter! Why didn't Paul quickly defuse the whole controversy, saying he made tents only when church support was low? Why didn't the Corinthian converts say he quit tentmaking when money came from Macedonia? Because it wasn't true.

Instead, Paul wrote 1 Corinthians, with an impassioned defense of his manual labor in chapter nine. First he gives evidences for his apostleship. Then he gives that long list of arguments in favor of church support—to prove his own right to receive it. But then, immediately he says three times—for emphasis—that he has never made use of this right! Never. This triple affirmation must cover all three journeys, and his prior ministry as well. Then he adds his reasons for self-support.

He sent the letter to Corinth with Timothy. But neither Timothy nor the letter convinced the now disillusioned Corinthians. Alarmed, Paul made an emergency visit to Corinth—his "painful visit," because he was rebuffed. Then, back in Ephesus, he sent his "severe letter" with Titus, his senior coworker (it no longer exists). Meanwhile, Demetrius the silversmith incited the riot against Paul, who once again had to flee for his life. Too anxious to await Titus' return at Troas, Paul proceeded to Philippi, and intercepted him there. Titus reported that most of the Corinthians were repentant. But there may have been a holdout or two, because Paul then wrote 2 Corinthians, with more arguments for his self-support. He said that on his imminent third visit to Corinth, he would do manual labor as before, and as he was then doing in Philippi (2 Cor 11:12ff).

That Paul insisted on his self-support, even at the risk of his apostolic authority, suggests that this was a non-negotiable part of his pioneering. Before we examine his reasons, we must consider the extent of his church support.

What Financial Contributions Did Paul Receive?

In 2 Corinthians 11:8-9 he says he even "robbed churches" to serve the Corinthians. The Macedonians had sent a gift to Corinth. But "robbery?" Paul uses hyperbole to shame the Christians in Corinth. But the crucial passage is Philippians 4:15-16 which he wrote more than a decade later. Paul was in Nero's palace prison, and totally dependent on friends for his needs. The Philippians sent a gift—the first in years. In his thank you letter, Paul reminds them that they were the only church that ever gave toward his ministry (Antioch was not a donor church). How often had these Philippians given—a time or two? When Paul's enemies hinted that he was only pretending self-support and probably getting contributions on the sly, he strongly denied it (2 Cor 12:16-18). He said he received no funding at all. He even paid his hosts for food and lodging (2 Thess 3:6-16). Why was this so important to him?

Why Did Paul Work At All When He Did Not Have To?

We will consider three of the most important of his reasons.

Credibility. Paul says twice (1 Cor 9:12; 2 Cor 6:3ff) that he works in order not to put an "obstacle" in the way of the gospel. He gives Gentiles no reason to distrust his message or motivation. He is not a "peddler of God's Word," "not a people-pleaser," saying things to gain fatter profits. He does not want to be classed with unscrupulous orators who roamed the empire, exploiting audiences. He is "free from all men"—owes no favors, is not beholden to any wealthy patron who could influence his message, nor any donor church or Corinthian faction. He gets no financial gain out of his preaching. Instead, it costs him dearly in every way.

Identification. Paul says he adapts culturally to people, in order to win them—to the Jews as a Jew and to the Greeks as a Greek—as an educated Gentile. But he also adapts to the "weak"—the lower classes. A skilled artisan was somewhere in the lower middle (1 Cor 9:19ff). As a highly educated upper class person, Paul quickly attracted the interest of the philosophers in Athens, affluent men and women in Corinth, and the Asiarchs in Ephesus. But he had to immerse himself in the marketplace to gain the trust of artisans and laborers. Why did he focus on them? Because most of the people in the empire were at the bottom—70 to 90 percent were slaves. His identification was not phony—he genuinely earned his living (1 Cor 4:11-12). Paul says his costly, incarnational service did not originate with him. He was imitating Jesus, whose identification with us cost him everything (Phil 2:5-11).

Modeling. Paul demonstrated Christian living because no one in the region had ever seen a Christian. He lived a holy life in the same immoral, idolatrous, cesspool society where he expected converts to live holy lives. Paul also modeled a Christian work ethic in this culture where indolence and thievery were the norm. In 1 Thess 3:8 he says, "With toil and labor, we worked night and day that we might not burden any of you, and to give you an example to follow." Work was not optional for believers. Paul turned newly converted thieves, idlers and drunkards into good providers for their families and generous givers to the need (1 Cor 6:10-11; Eph 4:28; 1 Tim 5:8). Paul says much in his brief letters about work, because without a strong work ethic, there could not be godly converts, healthy families, independent churches—nor productive societies. And God wants his people to be a blessing to the countries in which they live and work (Jer 29:7).

More important, Paul established a pattern for lay ministry. All converts were to be full-time, unpaid evangelists in their workplaces, as well as in their extended households and communities. They were to answer the questions of all who asked about their changed lives and new hope. Each convert represented a beachhead into enemy territory, so Paul told them not to move or change jobs too quickly—unless slaves could get their freedom (1 Cor 7:17-24). Nothing matures new believers like evangelism. The churches multiplied.

What Did Paul Teach About Tentmaker Ministry?

He modeled and taught workplace evangelism because most people spent most of their time at work. Also, evangelism in the marketplace was the best way to infiltrate all of society, because it was where people of every social level rubbed shoulders. But how were the converts to evangelize? Colossians 4:5-6 describes Paul's basic approach. "Conduct yourselves wisely toward outsiders...." "Making the most of the time...." The Greek word for time here is *kairos*—special opportunity. So Paul does not mean incessant talking about God to avoid waste of time, but less talking and

more listening for special moments to make brief, fitting comments. Too much religious talk creates an awkward situation—so colleagues avoid you. "Let your speech always be gracious...." Good evangelism is always kind and courteous. "Seasoned with salt, so that you may know how you ought to answer every one." Salty comments are thought-provoking, thirst-creating, and question-inducing. Our character, conduct and conversation should cause people to ask us questions about God.

This low-key approach is selective evangelism, not indiscriminate. It is fishing, not hunting. You "fish out" seekers from among the indifferent and antagonistic people around you, and talk where you won't arouse hostility in others. This is sensitive evangelism because you are building on what the Holy Spirit is already doing in the seekers. You do not run ahead of him. You let their questions pace the conversations, as they are ready. This is contextualized evangelism because their questions show you what to say—revealing what truths they already know, their misconceptions, felt needs, hurts, hangups and obstacles to faith. You answer from your personal experience and from scripture. It is easier for us than for Paul because we can pull out a New Testament and do a one-on-one mini-study with the seeker. Soon you have the seeker in an evangelistic Bible study group, and you can take more initiative in the conversations.

But Paul is also specific about what constitutes a godly workplace lifestyle. Note four essentials: personal integrity, quality work, caring relationships and brief, fitting comments about God. In Colossians 3:22-24 and Eph 6:5-8, Paul tells Christians to serve their employer as though he were Jesus Christ. That attitude turns all labor into worship. The New Testament seems to have few instructions for evangelism, but actually it is filled with them. But the focus is not on techniques, but on lifestyle. So all Paul's ethical teaching told converts how to live in the workplace, their extended households, their neighborhoods and social circles. His doctrinal teaching helped them answer seekers' questions.

What Were the Results of Paul's Strategy?

On Paul's third visit to Corinth, he wrote Roman believers of his intended visit. But in Romans 15:19-24 he makes an astounding claim. "From Jerusalem and as far round as Illyricum (today's Yugoslavia) I have fully preached the gospel of Christ.... I no longer have room for work in these regions." In just over 20 years Paul had finished establishing the church in six Roman provinces—the whole eastern, Greek-speaking half of the Mediterranean.

He accomplished this with only a handful of foreign workers and virtually no foreign funds. How did he do it? First, he had a strategy—he did not work haphazardly. He says, "Like a skilled master builder I laid a foundation.... Let each man take care how he builds upon it" (1 Cor 3:10). The foundation was theological and methodological, and self-support was an essential part of it.

Personnel and funding. To fulfill his commission to the Gentile world, Paul needed several hundred times more workers than he had on his little team. He acquired them, not by bringing in more foreigners, but by multiplying himself hundreds of times over in his converts. His ministry model turned them into unpaid evangelists. So he had all the personnel he needed, and they required no foreign salaries. He needed no building funds. Paul aimed at householders, many of whom are named. Family solidarity meant that a father's conversion committed his whole extended family and his servants to his new faith ("you shall be saved and your house"). To win a householder was to gain a leader, a new congregation and a meeting place. This might be a city workshop with living quarters upstairs or behind, or a country villa. Paul won clan heads by transforming their lying, pilfering slaves into trustworthy servants—like Philemon's Onesimus.

Paul's churches. His ministry model guaranteed indigenous, independent churches that were self-supporting—everyone worked—and self-governing. He never allowed them to become dependent on foreign funds or foreign leadership.

He quickly appointed lay leaders for the house churches. Some were converted householders, the natural leaders. He taught house church elders "the whole counsel of God" so they could teach others (Acts 20:26-28). They were not paid (Acts 20:33-35). By the time regional heads were needed, it was clear which house church leaders were the most spiritual and most respected by the local Christians and non-Christians. Work experience was required (1 Tim 3:7). Otherwise, how could they "equip" converts for the marketplace? (Eph 4:10)

By the time regional elders were needed, local funds were available for their support. Paul, the maker of tents, was also an apostle, preacher and teacher. He was never against clergy or paid ministry (1 Cor 9). He wrote the maturing Galatian churches to pay their pastors (Gal 6:6), and at a later date recommended pay for the leading Ephesian elders (1 Tim 5:17-18). But Paul wanted no paid ministry in the pioneer stage, until the pattern of unpaid evangelists was well established. If you start with paid ministry it can be almost impossible to produce lay movements.

Paul's churches were self-reproducing. Although his evangelists were mainly from unsavory, uneducated, pagan backgrounds, with neither anthropological nor missiological training, most received the gospel at enormous risk, and they risked their lives to win others. In the marketplace, Paul's converts were strategically placed at all levels of society. The gospel spread like a forest fire.

But we see Paul working only in major cities. What about the hinterlands? He tells the Romans (1:14-16) that he is debtor also to the barbarians. These were not savages, but most of the people who were not native Greek speakers (Acts 14 recounts a near disaster in Lystra because trilingual Paul did not understand Lycaonian). The Roman empire was never more than a chain of city colonies and military outposts, each with its own customs, local laws and deities, which were usually respected by the Roman authorities. Neither the Greeks nor the Romans had ever tried to integrate or to educate the rural and tribal peoples. Many became day laborers or slaves in the cities. Captives from beyond the empire were sold in the slave markets. Many languages could be heard on city streets.

By focusing his evangelism on these multilingual laborers Paul guaranteed the evangelization of the hinterlands—without months of language lessons for his team. Converts ran to share the gospel in their home towns, and village people came to locate friends in the city. Converts took the gospel home, clothed in their own language and culture. This automatic contextualization of the gospel fueled its rapid spread.

Paul's regional lay movements. After only a few months in Philippi, there were Macedonian churches. In Paul's first follow-up letter to the Thessalonians he said the gospel had already sounded out from them through the whole region! Corinth spread the gospel through Achaia. But Ephesus was even more remarkable. Paul stayed three years, but Luke writes in Acts 19:8-10 that after a little over two years, "all the residents of Asia heard the word of the Lord, both Jews and Greeks." The whole Roman province of Asia. Did Luke exaggerate? Not likely. Acts 19:23-27 records even stronger testimony from a hostile witness. Demetrius, the silversmith (and crafter of gods made with hands), shouts to the rioting craftsmen, "Not only in Ephesus, but almost throughout all Asia this Paul has persuaded and turned away a considerable company of people, saying that gods made with hands are not gods!" The public bonfire of magic books in Ephesus had probably been repeated in many locations. The penetration of the gospel was so thorough that the silver and copper crafts were in distress, and the worship of Artemis was threatened with extinction!

The penetration of the gospel was also fast. Speed matters in hostile cultures. Hundreds of converts joined the lay evangelists so quickly, that by the time the opposition had geared up for action, it was too late to put out the fire.

The role of self-supporting lay ministry. To attribute Paul's phenomenal success to his making of tents would claim too much for "tentmaking." In various passages, Paul credits his success to the power of the Holy Spirit,

his Christ-centered message, his holy life, his suffering, his love for the people, his constant prayers, and his healings and signs and wonders. But Paul also considered his self-support model as essential to his total strategy. It was a non-negotiable policy. He would not have expended so much energy on manual labor if donor-paid ministry could have accomplished his goal. Only his workplace evangelism could produce the missionary lay movement that was his only hope of winning the Gentile world, and fulfilling his Damascus Road commission from Jesus.

How Does a Study of Paul Help Us?

An inductive, correlated study of all the passages relating to Paul's ministry gives us a very different picture from that usually deduced from a few proof texts. A study of Paul gives us a definition of genuine tentmaking: *Tentmakers are missions-committed Christians who support themselves abroad in secular work, as they engage in cross-cultural evangelism, on the job and in their free time.* The essential criteria are self-support and cross-cultural workplace evangelism. It may be more, but it should not be less. Beyond a definition, Paul provides a manual for marketplace evangelism—a liberating, selective, lifestyle, fishing approach that is ideal for the workplace and is essential for hostile environments.

In conclusion, the Peter model and the Paul model are both biblical and needed. But only tentmakers can reach that 80% of the world which is largely closed to regular missionaries. To finish world evangelization thousands of Christians with solid trades and professions must do Paul-style workplace evangelism as they support themselves in unevangelized countries. With many more tentmakers in today's global job market and more missionaries, working together under our Commander-in-Chief, we can "fill the earth with the knowledge of the Lord as the waters cover the sea" (Isa 11:9)!

Study Questions

1. List the characteristics of tentmakers which distinguish them from Christians who simply work overseas.

2. What reasons does the author give for Paul's strategy of tentmaking?

The World at Your Door

Tom Phillips and Bob Norsworthy

Tom Phillips is the President and CEO of International Students, Inc., in Colorado Springs, Colorado, a ministry reaching out to the 554,000 international students in America. Previously he was Senior Crusade Director and Director of Counseling and Follow-Up with the Billy Graham Evangelistic Association.

Bob Norsworthy is First Vice-President of International Ministries for International Students, Inc., overseeing ministry to international students on nearly 300 campuses as well as the development of ISI's international overseas ventures. A graduate of Multnomah School of the Bible, Bob served as a pastor and businessman before his thirteen years of service with ISI.

From *The World at Your Door*, by Tom Phillips and Bob Norsworthy with W. Terry Whalin, Copyright 1997, Bethany House Publishers, Minneapolis, Minnesota. Used by permission.

While it has always been God's plan for the Church to go to distant parts of the world, this strategy is only half of God's equation for reaching the people who don't know Christ. Over the centuries, the Church has missed or nearly missed an equally significant part of God's plan—reaching the world that God brings to the Church. The New Testament book of Acts records in its early pages how men and women were gathered together from around the world. In Jerusalem, these people heard the gospel of Jesus Christ, accepted it, and returned to their countries as ambassadors for God.

Today history repeats itself in the U.S., where over 550,000 of the world's best, brightest, and/or privileged students from every nation are within minutes of a local church. Such a representative gathering is unparalleled in human history. These students are attending America's institutions of higher learning. Their present quest is not for land or gold but for the prestige of an American education or a grasp of new Western technologies. These future leaders will return to their societies with the competitive skills for the geo-economic race into the future.

Each year over 120,000 new international students and scholars begin a four-year sojourn in American universities and other institutions of higher learning. While these students come to America with specific goals and plans, most of them are unaware of a personal divine plan from God. As caring and committed Christians come across their paths and offer friendship in Him, they can learn about the greatest friend of all Jesus Christ.

Immersed in a new culture and away from family and friends, these international students are often lonely. They often feel out of place, lost, and anxious about understanding new people and a new situation. Simple tasks can be bewildering for the international student—as they would be to us if we were overseas for a period of time—such as how to locate housing or banking, or the difference between a grocery store, drugstore, specialty shops, and a department store. When these internationals face these challenges alone, daily life can become extremely discouraging to them.

The course of history might have been different during the 1940s if the lonely student Matsuoki had been befriended by loving Christians 20 years earlier. Mistreated as a student in the United States, he returned home and helped plan the attack on Pearl Harbor. Later in his memoirs, Matsuoki attributed his anger toward America to his experience during his short sojourn in the United States.

Mengistu Mariam, from Ethiopia, arrived at Aberdeen, Maryland, in the 1950s for military training. He soon became embittered and resentful as a result of the way he was treated by Americans. Over time, he too rose to a position of power, and in 1974 was a key figure in the coup against King Haile Selassie. Mariam established a Marxist government and began a relentless campaign to root out what he called "alien religion" in Ethiopia, even though Christianity originated in the Middle East. In an address to the nation, Mariam called missionaries the number one source of imperialist infiltration in the past. Shortly after the speech, he expelled all missionaries and made it impossible for anyone who attempted to evangelize to continue their work. He also confiscated a $15 million missionary radio station and began to broadcast Marxist propaganda. Churches were closed, and believers in Jesus Christ fell under intense religious persecution, including frequent imprisonment. The key leader in this effort was one international student who had a bad experience in the "land of the free."

In stark contrast is the experience of Bakht Singh, a Sikh man who came from northern India to study engineering in Canada. This young Indian began his studies like any other foreign student, but a Christian couple reached out to Bakht in friendship and love. They gave him a Bible and encouraged him to meet other Christians. Through their friendship, Bakht accepted Christ. The couple also taught him the Scriptures. Later he returned to India not only as an engineer but as a preacher and evangelist. As a result of his faithful work for Christ, over 700 churches have been established in India, Pakistan, Sri Lanka, and Nepal.

Time magazine attests to the exploding opportunities to shape future leaders at American universities. In an April 13, 1992 article, Jim Smolowe says, "American universities and colleges are the envy of the world. For all their abiding troubles, this country's 3,500 institutions were flooded with 407,530 foreign students (a number up nearly 150,000 in six years with enrollment at 554,000 in 1997) from 193 different countries last year. Asia led the way with 40,000 from the Peoples Republic of China, and 36,610 from Japan, followed by India and Canada." In fact, international students are capturing a large proportionate share of the Ph.D.s awarded annually in the United States.

Beverly Watkins, in the *Chronicle of Higher Education*, stated, "The U.S. educates more foreign students than any other country in the world. Nearly one-third of all students worldwide who study abroad enroll at U.S. institutions." Nearly 75 percent of these students and scholars use funds from family or other non-U.S. resources for their primary means of financial support during their studies, says Richard Krasno with the Institute of International Education. This fact points out that these students come from the upper levels of their society. Traditional missionaries would rarely meet or impact these people, but near our homes, we can meet, interact with, and serve these future leaders. These young people are incredibly sensitive, kind, and appreciative. They don't know that they are future leaders. Dressed in running shoes, jeans, and open-collar shirts, they are respectful, yet personally searching for a friend—away from their traditional peer pressure, family pressure, political pressure, and religious pressure. In the midst of their pilgrimage is a search for truth, and we have the honor of loving each one of them for Christ's sake.

Developing a friendship with internationals isn't complicated. Every day kindness is all you need to entertain them in your home. It's not hard to develop a friendship. As relationships form you can find sensitive ways to respectfully present the claims of Christ and help them grow in his or her Christian faith. We're learning some of the ways that international students can be helped as they return to their homelands.

Study Questions

1. What kind of simple tasks could be done with an international student which could be a significant act of caring?

2. What factors make international students more receptive to truth when studying in the West?

A Global Harvest Force

Larry Keyes

Moises Vega is a cross cultural worker. Born in Panama, he committed his life to the lordship of Christ in 1984 while working as an engineer in a remote area of the Sudan. One day in 1986, while praying and seeking God's direction, he was touched by the words "As I blessed you, go and bless my work." He knew God spoke to him so, along with his wife and family, he began to witness to the Dinka and Shilluk tribes located 250 miles south of Khartoum. It was an exciting challenge being both an engineer and cross cultural worker. God blessed his efforts and many found the Savior.

In 1991, the Lord encouraged him to return back to Panama and enter the ministry as a full-time worker in order to strengthen the church and receive further missionary training. From 1994 until the present, he participated in various kinds of training programs including the chance to attend GCOWE (the Global Consultation for World Evangelization) in Seoul, Korea. As a result, God led him to understand his obligation to plant churches in Egypt, Sudan and other similar places. So, Moises, together with his wife and five children, is returning to the Sudan applying his background and training toward church multiplication in north Africa.

The story of Moises can be multiplied many times over! In a vast variety of settings and situations, God has raised up thousands of new workers. An army is being mobilized from many tongues and nations to every tongue and nation, committed to reaching the unreached and planting the church among them.

An Army of Workers...

In the beginning, (from the perspective of the West), missionary outreach from Africa, Asia, Latin America and Oceania (together called here the two-thirds world) began in the 1820s when workers like Ini Kopuria and Josua Mateinaniu moved from one island to another in the Pacific. Dozens of preachers like them planted churches and fueled the launching of many missionary societies in Oceania. One of the reasons islands throughout the Pacific are largely Christian today is because of such organizations like the Melanesian Brotherhood which sent workers to many unreached areas almost two centuries ago.

In Asia, one of the most famous of India's over one hundred societies is the Indian Missionary Society, founded in 1909 to evangelize other cultures within the country. In 1925

Larry Keyes is the President of OC International, Inc. and has served as President of the EFMA (Evangelical Fellowship of Mission Agencies). He was a missionary in Brazil for 11 years.

the Dipti Mission unique for its focus on tribal evangelism was formed in the sub-continent. In 1939, the Apostles Revelation Society was formed in Ghana to reach Ghanaians and eventually Togoans. For over 170 years, non-Western Christians have been active in cross-cultural evangelistic endeavors. Yet only in the last forty years have Western churches become fully aware of this phenomenally growing movement.

God is allocating this growing number of missionaries in diverse ways. They are sent in every conceivable way: Some are working cross-culturally within their own country. Others are working as "tentmakers" in distant lands. Some are focused on people of their own language and culture in other countries. Some are sent for short periods of time, others leave home never to return. A few short years ago we were able to measure the total numbers with some confidence that our estimates were close.[1] But now, because of the diversity of sending styles and structures, and because of the sheer increase in numbers, it is increasingly difficult to offer precise summary figures for the total global movement as we have in the past.

This much is clear: During the last three decades, two-thirds world missionary growth has increased almost five times faster than the missionary gain in the West. In fact, the projection is that by AD 2000 there will be 164,000 non-Western or two-thirds world missionaries working cross-culturally around the world compared to an estimated 132,000 Western workers. Is it any wonder that many are expecting that the bulwark of mission leadership and resource in the years ahead will come from the two-thirds world?

...Growing Globally...

A few examples of this growth should encourage any Christian looking for the fulfillment of the Great Commission. From Korea at least 4402 missionaries now serve in 138 countries around the world. This is a 116% increase from 1972 to 1996 (1972 being the first year a global survey of two-thirds world missionaries and agencies was completed). During that 25 year period, the number of countries to which Korea sent missionaries increased over five-fold. The largest contin-

gent of Korean missionaries is serving in the former Soviet Union, followed by the Philippines, Japan, China and Taiwan.

From the Philippines, an estimated 600 "units" (singles and couples) serve outside the country and another 2,000 Filipino missionary units operate in a cross-cultural environment within their nation. This is a significant 23% increase over the number of estimated missionaries in 1972, and as Eric Smith, a veteran missionary in the Philippines states, "the ranks of Filipino missionaries are swelling."

From Singapore, there were 400 workers serving as career missionaries in 1994, all outside the island-nation in a cross-cultural context. While 55% were in their first term; the other 45% were in their second term or beyond. This number is 40% larger than the estimated number in 1972.

According to research just completed in Latin America, 1997 saw at least 3,921 cross-cultural missionaries on the field working through 284 mission agencies in 86 nations of the world. In addition, there were 932 other workers in administration or in roles assisting these missionaries. Overall, this represents a 7% increase in the number of workers since 1972 and a 5% increase in the number of mission agencies. Ted Limpic, veteran missionary in Brazil writes that each missionary sent out by the church represents a major victory for the Lord. Together these Latins are a significant phenomenon, as well as a reason for which to give God glory.

...Involved in Missions Like the West...

All around the world God is adding rapidly to His army of witnesses. These cross-cultural workers believe it takes "people messages," not just "word messages" to see His Kingdom grow and mature. Many are involved in holistic ministries, caring for social along with spiritual need. Quite a few become tentmakers developing, like the apostle Paul, a means to earn additional support to maintain themselves and their families while sharing God's truth.

Many of these laborers are seasoned intercessors and quickly see the potential for God to be glorified by dramatic answers to prayer. Such was the case when Hong Kong-based missionary Lun Poobuanak and his newly-planted church prayed for rain in the Kalasin province of Thailand. During an extreme drought, a village leader told Lun, "If you ask your God to give us rain this month, all households in our clan will worship your God and become Christians." On the fourth day, after fasting and prayer, a storm came that filled the rice fields and saved their crops. Soon after, 134 families became Christians.

Like those in the West, this new army of workers is also involved in short-term efforts. Recently, the Christians in southern Sudan welcomed a short-term team from Capetown, South Africa, with singing, dancing and a lavish feast. This was the first group of outsiders to visit the Mundri district in years. The missionaries were "literally mobbed" by eager Morus when they began passing out Bibles and other devotional literature. As a result, this host Sudanese church was encour-

aged to continue its own mission efforts to other groups and tribes.

Two-thirds world mission endeavors also include training schools, clusters of mission-minded churches and country-based mission associations. There are annual mission conferences and special congresses where information and friendships are gained. To assist in the rapid growth, local publications on evangelistic strategies have originated with more to come. Many organizations have established goals and are working toward their accomplishment. Most are very aware of the locations of unreached people groups and have focused energy and resource toward those needs.

As elsewhere, faithful two-thirds world servants also face persecution, terror and loss. In Chechnya, a former Soviet Union Republic, missionary Vasili Luppof from Moscow established the First Chechnyan Christian Church of the Full Gospel. Thirty converts from several nationalities, most from Muslim backgrounds, became the initial congregation. During his witness he received numerous threats. Vasili labored on. Eventually, he was taken from his home, not to be seen again!

...and Desirous for Partnership!

There are a number of reasons why many two-thirds world mission leaders desire increased partnership with other like-minded workers. One is a recognition of the need for stronger missionary member care and international support. They also acknowledge the task of missions has become increasingly complex with government bureaucracies, specialized training, and intricate funding sources and channels. Help is needed to understand best how to deal with all these and other critical issues. Most importantly, when they read Scripture about the interdependence of Christ's body, many wish for more formal alliances with others of identical vision and similar theology. It's like the African story of a little child who wandered off into the tall jungle grass and could not be found. The tribal members all held hands and walked through the grass together, enabling them to find the child. It is not enough to share a common goal. We must work together to accomplish it without hesitation.

Throughout the two-thirds world there is much interest in partnership arrangements. Most of the cooperative activity, however, relate to joint-ventures among groups from similar national or ethnic backgrounds in the sending nation. Much of the partnering, as well, is focused among churches within the same denomination or association. Yet, as linkages develop between Western mission groups and two-thirds world churches and agencies, the increased prospect for the development of equitable partnership is very exciting! And truly, partnership is a necessity if we are ever to complete the Great Commission as our Lord commanded!

God's Purpose: Harvest with Joy

There are two primary values to answering God's invitation to co-laboring as partners at this crucial hour. First, there is a strategic value. Mission endeavor is likened in the Bible to farming. Jesus describes God as a farmer (Matt 13:3-23). Christ assured us that God was more than a subsistence farmer, but the "Lord of the harvest" with plans so vast that it would require many laborers to complete the Great Commission. Jesus invited His followers to gaze on the harvest in a way that they would see how huge it really was, and be persuaded that they could never do it alone. Thus they would also ask the Master to launch more laborers into the harvest (Matt 9:38).

The prayers and efforts of some of God's finest laborers of earlier generations are now being answered. God is answering on a huge global scale. Because of this growing, competent and committed army of witnesses, Christ's body can press on with hope to complete the task of world evangelization sooner and better than ever before. The job has always been far too great for Western missions alone. The counsel, assistance and strength of the brothers and sisters from Africa, Asia, Latin America and Oceania are indispensable. God has called all to be part of this significant and global harvest. He is asking everyone to join hands with those from all nations to support each other in one of the greatest spiritual armies in history. It's becoming clear that we cannot be fully commited to Him without growing in our willingness to cooperate with the others that He sends.

But there is more than just a strategic value in co-laboring with comrades from non-Western churches. There is a great joy. At one point in His ministry Jesus said of this harvest, "others have labored, and you have entered into their labor." One result of this partnership was so "that he who sows and he who reaps may rejoice together." (John 4:36-38). There is a profound joy that we can experience only when we enter the labor of others as true partners. We will not only rejoice in the harvest, we will rejoice that God enabled us to do it "together." If such joy can be ours by serving, learning, giving, and praying together, then God is now opening to us an incredible moment. It may seem to be slower, or in some ways more costly, but if the Lord of the Harvest is sending us together, let's not too easily forfeit the profound blessing of partnership. Co-laboring will be our finest joy and result in His greatest glory.

End Notes

1. Lawrence E. Keyes, *The Last Age of Missions*, William Carey Library, 1983, and Larry D. Pate, *From Every People*, MARC, 1989.

Study Questions

1. What issues need to be addressed when forming multi-cultural partnerships?

2. Does the growth in the two-thirds world mission agencies mean that Western missions efforts are not needed?

Lessons of Partnership

Bill Taylor

I want that holy and transfixing moment forever engraved on my heart. At the front of that gigantic tent, Michael Maileau, spiritual leader of the Solomon Islands, called to his brothers and sisters from his nation and from Papua New Guinea (PNG). More than 100 came forward, stood and faced the audience. Then Michael invited people from Australia and New Zealand to the front, to kneel before them.

As they knelt, Michael's passionate praying voice spoke, "We thank God that he used the white people to bring us the gospel, for through them we came to a knowledge of the true and living God through his Son, Jesus. We are responsible for the advance of the gospel. So now, we from Papua New Guinea and the Solomon Islands, want to share the torch of the missionary gospel with you. Take the baton with us, may we partner, let us run together, we need each other."

As Michael spoke, the Micronesian believers blessed those kneeling, laying hands on them, praying for them, exhorting them to bold faith, encouraging them to sail with them anew in the "Deep Sea Canoe Missionary Movement" that had become their new rallying banner to reevangelize the islands and then overflow to the rest of the world. I saw believers of different races, languages, histories, cultures, and education united in partnership for the gospel, each bringing strengths to the missionary movement.

The setting was the Fifth South Pacific Prayer Assembly (February, 1995), a six-day gathering of 250 people from eight island nations. I saw a number of expressions of partnership, starting with the common passion of the leaders to celebrate worship and prayer. The diversity of this partnership was striking. It included Maori New Zealanders, along with their white colleagues; dark skinned PNG and Solomon Islanders, along with Western missionaries who had obviously won their trust and affection: and the Fijians and Tongans.

The New Zealand assembly beautifully showed different facets of partnerships. Here I offer some suggestions from my own experience to help your own mission partnerships take shape and function effectively.

Lesson One

I serve with the World Evangelical Fellowship Missions Commission, an international networking and partnering team that shares ideas, information, and resources. Our commission

Bill Taylor is the Director of Missions Commission, World Evangelical Fellowship. Having served in Latin America for 30 years, he now travels widely as a consultant to churches, missions and training schools throughout the world.

Adapted by permission from "Lessons of partnership," *Evangelical Missions Quarterly*, 31:4, (October 1995), published by EMIS, P.O. Box 794, Wheaton, IL 60189.

aims to empower the global missions movement to train and send long-term missionaries. As such, I work with about 60 leaders and some 30 movements, affirming their own vision and plans.

Let me describe two partnerships that grew out of years of listening to national leaders. First, based on our colleagues' requests, the commission has invested in missionary training (consultations, seminars, and publications), with a primary focus on needs in the non-Western world. We have co-sponsored consultations on missionary training and partnered with national or regional mission associations, with Latin America as our initial arena.

We made some mistakes when we unilaterally moved ahead of our national or regional partners. We spun our wheels and spent funds in the wrong projects. I regret some of the decisions I enthusiastically made and wish I could rewind the video machine of history.

The lesson: Listen before entering a partnership, and be willing to learn from mistakes and try again.

Lesson Two

International missions leaders have asked me in recent years: "Bill, why are we losing so many good career missionaries? We sent them with such high hopes, and now they have returned home never to go back. Why is this happening? Is it only in our country? Can WEF help us?"

That launched our second major partnership venture, a research project, which was then coordinated by Guatemalan Rudy Giron, president of COMIBAM International. Our partners are the leaders of mission movements in Nigeria, Ghana, Costa Rica, Brazil, Philippines, Singapore, India, Korea, Australia, Germany, Denmark, United Kingdom, and the United States. We want to keep gifted men and women serving with a sense of Christian challenge and satisfaction in long-term, cross-cultural service.

One of the delights in this partnership is the number of non-Western mission leaders who so believe in the partnership that they are willing to cover their own part of the budget for the research project.

The lesson: Partnerships work best when there is shared ownership of the project, including finances.

Lesson Three

Sometimes people say, "History has changed, and along with it the role of the historic (colonial) missionary. Yes, we thank God for the Western missionaries, though they made many mistakes. But the job can best be done with national missionaries. We plead with you to invest your funds in the most cost-effective manner supporting our national workers."

This is a sensitive issue in some circles. Many missions-minded people and churches are questioning the high cost of recruiting, producing, placing, and sustaining Western missionaries, particularly in high-cost cities. Admittedly, it is hard to defend investing $70,000 per year for an American missionary family to work in Japan, or $50,000 in some European countries. Why not redirect our giving to support 7,000 national workers? This seems to be good stewardship of limited resources.

Because I move among the non-Western missionary movement and try to be sensitive to its needs, I have struggled with these issues. But let me quote an Indian missions leader who told me some years ago:

"If Americans want to send funds to non-Western missionaries, that may be fine in some cases. But do not rob us of the joy and responsibility to support our own people. And I fear that if Americans send now only their dollars and not their sons and daughters, the next step will be to send neither their dollars nor their sons and daughters. There is a non-biblical extreme to be wary of. Biblical partnership means sending and supporting your own flesh and blood." His statement is wise. It is not a matter of either-or, but both-and.

Another Asian missions leader told me: "A lot of Asians are raising funds in the U.S. Please tell your colleagues there to check with respected nationals in our countries who can vouch for the integrity of these ministries. Tell Americans to be careful."

I profoundly respect agencies such as the Friends Missionary Prayer Band of India that refuse foreign money. They want their Indian supporters to sense complete ownership for the mission. In some circumstances, FMPB will accept financial investment for other projects, but they are very careful.

Other non-Western agencies accept funds only for capital investments (property, buildings, equipment, scholarships for advanced study), but not to support their missionaries. Significantly, most of these agencies are growing and having a powerful impact. We won't need to learn some lessons the hard way if we look to the long view in two ways: What will bring about the fullest effort by every part of the partnership in the long run? Consider the downside: What paths of partnership may appear to bring immediate help but engender debilitating dependencies?

The lesson: Be balanced. Don't get sucked in by hard sells based solely on comparisons of cost-effectiveness. Take time to check out potential partners before signing up.

Lesson Four

What about church-to-church partnerships, which offer a growing menu of possibilities? These can be excellent, but we need some values and attitude checks. Who is putting the partnership together? What is expected of each partner? Is it really a partnership, or simply a "mother (U.S., of course) -daughter (Third World, of course)" relationship designed to channel funds, or to mobilize missions in the "mother" church?

In counseling local churches getting into these agreements, I ask them their motives, their expectations, their short-range and long range objectives. I ask them what they hope to contribute, and I probe what they hope to learn from their "sister" church. A surprising amount of American naivete, or simply cultural insensitivity, exists in many well-meaning churches.

The lesson: Church-to-church partnerships have real potential, but must be entered with wisdom, humility, and a teachable spirit.

Lesson Five

What about the church that says, "We can do everything alone to have a successful missions enterprise: screen, train, send, support, etc."? I hear this not only across the U.S. but in many other countries as well—Korea, Singapore, Guatemala, and El Salvador, to mention a few.

Most of them operate alone; others are developing networks of like minded congregations.

First, these churches sense profound ownership of the missionary task. They may have gifted leaders (with vision, management, and technology skills), and they want to be major players on the global scene with a primary (though not exclusive) target on unreached peoples. Second, some are reacting against what they perceive to be mission agency "control." In a few cases, they have had a bad experience. Others are unaware of the agencies.

The Holy Spirit is brooding over his church and creating new ways not only of "being the church," but also new forms of "being the church in missions." I doubt that most of the historic agencies will pass away, although some need to reexamine their reason for existence. Meanwhile, hundreds of new agencies are popping up, some of them solo or "mom and pop" operations. Others are driven by a broader vision that galvanizes creative people.

However, I do worry about these ventures and potential partnerships. Yes, a church can screen, partially train, send, and support missionaries. But there is more that must be done to be fruitful. Remember the "etc." in the above paragraph? This little term is critical, for in it I cluster additional components that must exist for a healthy missionary movement: pastoral care, supervision, strategizing, teamwork, leadership.

It is one thing for the church to serve as a sending agency, but it is very much another matter for the church to serve as an adequate deploying and pastoring agency. Rare is the church that can provide the on-field infrastructure needed to sustain a strong venture over the years. Nor can any church I know of provide the complete training that is desirable and available today.

Nevertheless, some of them persistently argue the opposite. Why? Frankly, they fear losing their keen people to recruiters of other groups during their years in schooling. They also sense (rightly, in many cases) that most Bible colleges and seminaries offer mind-oriented, theoretical learning based on the formal schooling model. They do not see the schools committed to spiritual formation.

They find schools divorced from local church values. They want to provide hands-on, evaluated, experience-driven training that only the local context can provide. But can they offer the complete biblical-theological-missiological training package? No. Then what can be done?

I propose two levels of partnership, training, and member care. For training, why not form strategic alliances with schools? Churches can talk with schools, express their concerns, and negotiate a type of partnership. Perhaps the church will focus on summer school and winter term courses. A number of Bible colleges and seminaries are packaging excellent missions courses during these periods.

Churches can also form alliances with mission agencies for field-based member care, leadership, and ongoing, hands-on training. Churches, after all, pay many of the bills (something schools and agencies should remember), and are seeking ways to give more than money. When partnerships are pursued, churches can retain ultimate responsibility for the well-being of their missionaries. The agencies contribute their considerable field-based experience.

The lesson: Wise churches recognize what they cannot do, and partner with those who can assist them in their long-range goals.

A Maturing Movement

For some, partnership is like the Holy Grail. Everybody is talking about it but nobody has seen it! Perhaps the good term "partnership" risks losing its value through overuse. Nevertheless, God is bringing his people and organizations together. I thank God that I have seen vital and viable partnerships at work. Motives are moving beyond mere partnership pragmatism—of getting more "bang for our buck"—with efficient management mechanisms.

I sense a maturing attitude toward and commitment to sensitive and significant partnership covenants in the globalized body of Christ. Some churches and organizations are developing serious partnerships for the first time.

Many older mission agencies have been forming viable partnerships for years. They are expanding them as rapidly as possible. For example, Trans World Radio has joined with Peter Deyneka Russian Ministries to launch the Moscow Media Center. President Thomas Lowell of TWR explains, "As we studied our common goals and needs as organizations, we realized there would be tremendous synergy from our working together more closely."

Why Some Work

We have noted some lessons we can learn from partnerships. What seems to make some work? Why do others fail? I've asked a number of my colleagues. Here is a summary of their answers.

1. Initiative with relationship. They work when they come into existence after sustained trust and relationship-building, not simply because someone has a passion and rushes into the organizational marriage to get the job done. But, they will fail when someone rushes into the partnership, even if it is presented as a gift that will immeasurably benefit the ministry. They will fail if trust is lost, or if personal conflicts and ego drives sap its energies. Americans in general are known as pragmatic, let's-get-it-done, we've-got-the-funds-and-the-technology people with great programs and managerial skills. These potential strengths can become weaknesses when Americans plunge ahead without building an adequate relational foundation.

2. Cross-cultural wisdom. They tend to work when there is understanding of diverse cultures. Unfortunately, some church and missions leaders still operate from their monocultural framework of values and behavior. They impose themselves on the partner, subconsciously perhaps regarded as the junior, or secondary, player. Westerners do not have a monopoly on this attitude. Ignoring culture makes an easy recipe for failure.

For example, many languages do not have simple equivalents for the English words "partnership" or "accountability." Therefore, if partnerships are to work, the covenants must have the dynamic equivalent terms that partners can share and support. Spell it out. Make it clear.

3. Common Goals. They tend to work when there is a commitment to a common objective, and the recognition that the partners truly need each other. They fail when goals and expectations are fuzzy, or when one partner wants to impose objectives not supported by the other.

4. Understanding of accountability. They tend to work when there is a clear understanding of how each partner functions. They fail when the agreed-upon roles are ignored, or when a partner tries to change midstream without dialogue. The concept of "accountability" is critical, because the word has different meanings in different cultures. Is accountability possible without control? Yes, but it's not easy.

5. Ongoing care and evaluation. They tend to work when the partnerships are carefully cultivated and strengthened. Amazingly, some partners assume everything is fine because the strategic alliance has been inaugurated, but they fail to care for it adequately. If the partners don't treat the venture like a living organism, it will die. Constant monitoring of ventures for effectiveness also helps indicate when the project has been completed, should be changed, or simply needs to be ended. Vigilant care will help us to cut losses before losing friendships.

Conclusion

Now is the time. Surely there is some relationship between partnership in mission and the prayer of our Lord in John 17:11, 21-23. Four times our Lord prayed that ultimately God would enable us to demonstrate a marvelous unity that will make Christ Himself visible to the world. His prayer is now being answered as never before. The global body of Christ is learning about partnerships in every language and culture. Let us continue to grow, to expand, to please the heart of God without creating artificial structures. Let us now be true partners in the gospel.

How do we do this? Here's one example of powerful partnership: Francisco Velas-quez* is a Latin American who serves as a broker for partnerships in the Arabic-speaking world. He works for a Western agency, but his training, gifts, and Latin American personality enable him to serve with unique skill in the Arab world. Some North Americans are mystified at his ability to understand the Arab mind, as well as the ministry needs in the area.

His agency is involved in several strategic partnerships in this difficult area. It's not easy to attain clear accountability without heavy-handed control and at the same time maintain a stringent "need-to-know" security in this sensitive area. Francisco is able to speak lovingly and frankly with his Arab and Berber colleagues, and some wonder how he does this so well. Francisco has been cultivating these trust relationships over years, and he has earned the right to speak. He has spent long hours drinking tea, talking, visiting some of the hottest spots in the region. He encourages, listens, learns, shares his life, and teaches in an indirect way. And he speaks the difficult language of audited financial statements that show how funds were spent. He has served as an intermediary, guarding local initiatives from being over-exposed or over-supplied with resources that might cripple instead of strengthen them.

The best news I hear from Francisco is that people are coming to Christ through these partnerships. There is more fruit than can be openly reported at this time. The micro-minority churches in that sensitive area are being strengthened, proven leaders are being affirmed, and a fresh crop of leaders and ministries are emerging. I'm so glad to have Francisco as my friend, example, and instructor in partnership.

Study Questions

1. Does the author see partnership working best with Western planning and finances, paired with nationals' cultural insights?

2. Is cost-effectiveness a primary motivation for Western and Third-World partnerships? What additional advantages can be found?

*pseudoynm

The Power of Partnership

Phillip Butler

I f we are trying to effectively witness for Christ, which makes more sense—God's people working *together* to share Christ's love, or God's people going their separate ways, each doing their own thing? The Scriptures, international business experience, a growing worldwide trend toward collaboration, and ordinary common sense all point in the same direction: partnership.

Fifteen years ago, there were virtually no registered strategic alliances between North American and Asian businesses. Today, there are over 300 registered alliances and new ones are constantly being born.

Whether in a Western city or in a remote Islamic community where there is no church at all, there are powerful benefits as God's people work together in partnership to share Christ and serve in His name.

Partnership—There is no other option

Once-sworn competitors are rapidly becoming collaborators. Cost and risks are too great and the challenge of entering new regions is too complex to go it alone.

In the world of evangelism and missions, two factors powerfully influence how we work. First, with the radical changes in the world's socio-political structures in the last decade, the open doors of opportunity to share Christ with unreached people are unprecedented. We now have access to nearly a billion people with whom ten years ago we couldn't even share a cup of coffee. Second, in dozens of countries around the world, the number of missionaries and availability of other kingdom resources are exploding. As we begin the 21st Century, more missionaries and church planters will come from the Third World than from the West.

For nearly 200 years, the church in the West has prayed and invested in missions to see the birth of the church in Asia, Africa, and Latin America. Now, that Third World church is taking its place alongside the Western church so that, *together,* they can reach the final segment of the world—the nearly 2 billion who have never heard of Jesus' love.

Working in partnership has been talked of for a long time, but today we have no other option!

Phillip Butler is the President of Interdev in Seattle, Washington. He is an internationally acknowledged expert in partnerships and strategic alliances. He has led development of strategic alliances and inter-organizational partnerships in more that 20 countries.

Adapted from *The Power of Partnership*, Copyright 1998, Interdev. Used by permission.

An idea whose time has come

Imagine that you decided to build a house. Depending on where you live, you might get your friends to help you build it, or you might hire builders. Either way, think what would happen if each builder didn't know what the others were doing or there was no architectural plan.

What if the person planning the size and shape of the house never talked to the one ordering building materials? What if the one cutting materials didn't coordinate with the one putting the pieces in place? What if each worker didn't know when others were coming to build or how his work fit anyone else's?

In some ways, that's what our mission efforts have been like. A radio ministry broadcasts one message about the Lamb of God and sacrifice. Printed materials from another ministry present Christ from a different perspective, perhaps as the King of Kings. Personal evangelists then share films and preaching from the perspective of a "fallen nature," our sin, and the need for forgiveness. Can you see where this might cause some misunderstanding? In addition, all of these ministries train workers separately and may schedule outreaches with little thought about coordinating with others who work in the area.

The non-Christian approached by disorganized ministries is like someone looking at the house where none of the builders worked together. It looks like a strange and uninviting house. The one listening to these ministries hears disjointed messages from different Christian outreaches.

Why Partnership is Valuable

Many times, two or more different ministries will broadcast radio programs, print literature, or send missionaries to one people group, while people from another nearby language group never hear anything of Christ. There is a better way. We are learning to work together. Consider the recent story of a man named Ahmed.

Ahmed, seeking for life's answers, began listening to a Christian radio broadcast in his Muslim homeland. He wrote for a Bible correspondence course, which eventually led to a meeting in person with a Christian worker, who led him to the Lord.

Despite responsibilities of running a shop and caring for his aged mother, Ahmed commuted overnight once a month for an all day Bible course in another town, and became part of a growing church fellowship.

Five different ministry agencies deliberately coordinated their efforts over a period of several years, sharing the good news of Christ with Ahmed until he was part of a growing national church.

It wasn't mere coincidence that Ahmed received a correspondence course, or that someone was in place to talk to him when he was ready. The broadcasters gave Ahmed's name to the correspondence people. The correspondence worker referred him to a missionary in the area, who passed Ahmed on to Bible teachers and national church leaders.

These agencies planned ahead of time how to contact, follow up, bring to Christ, and disciple people into a local church. They agreed to "share" their ministry to Ahmed, each contributing what they did best, whether broadcasting, literature distribution, having local personal workers visit him, or networking with local national Christians.

1. Partnership is biblical

Scripture calls for believers to work together in unity. While Christians generally agree with this, organizational pride, egos, finances, and independent agendas often keep Christians from working with others outside of their own church or organization. In addition, concepts of unity without a scriptural basis in Christ have made some believers suspicious.

Consider John 17:20-23, where twice in four verses Jesus prays that His followers may be one, in order that the world may believe and know that God the Father sent Jesus. Except for the Great Commission itself, this *is one of the strongest comments Jesus made on missions.* He hinged the credibility of our mission message on our oneness in Him.

John 13:35, John 17:11, 1 Corinthians 12:4-17, Ephesians 4:1-16, and Philippians 1:27 all describe facets of our unity in Christ.

The Bible is more than theological theory about unity. 1 Corinthians 12 says that coordination between believers should be as "down-to-earth" and practical as coordination between the parts of a human body.

Why partner together to reach the un-reached? It is biblical.

2. Partnerships model the power of community witness

In the West, most people live at a high level of individual isolation compared to people from traditional societies, who live their lives as an integral part of an extended family and community. Westerners, especially, often don't comprehend the united power that family and community hold over the individual in traditionally- oriented cultures.

The millions of people in unreached language groups and unreached cities are nearly all from traditional cultures. Family, community, and relationships are critically important to them.

Imagine how our missionary efforts look to people within these traditional communities.

Missionaries are usually outsiders, not connected to the local traditional world. And, what seems amazing to traditional people is that the Christian outsiders are not even connected to one another!

Separate, individualistic ministries rob Christianity of believability.

In the John 17:20-23 passage already mentioned, Jesus seems to have anticipated this obstacle. He indicated that the way to be believable is to have believable unity.

To establish viable national churches within the 10/40 Window, missionaries must offer a Christian community at least as strong and relational as the one from which converts come.

Partnerships model these relationships to more effectively equip indigenous leader.

3. Partnerships are the most effective way to develop a church

The ultimate goal of evangelism is always a functioning body of believers. Medical work alone doesn't establish a church. Neither does literature, teaching, or Bible translation. An evangelist or church planter may start a church, but the task of establishing and sustaining a church is vastly easier if there are some contacts and some sowing beforehand with literature and teaching help.

Combining these efforts, so that each specialty contributes its best toward the goal of a viable national church, is the essence of a Strategic Evangelism/ Church-Planting Partnership.

Such a partnership is integrated, including many specialties and contributors. In an integrated partnership, ministries specializing in relief, professional services, translation, radio, literature, evangelism, discipleship, and a multitude of other services can voluntarily coordinate their efforts in one overall ministry goal of establishing believers in a strong national church.

To use the house analogy again, it takes integrated materials to build a house. Wood alone isn't a house. Neither is glass, cement, or stone. Workers who know how to build with these items contribute their part and work together to produce the goal of a new house.

4. Partnerships are needed because of volatile world conditions

The world is a radically different place today than even yesterday. It is estimated that we now have access to countries and people groups representing over a billion people that we couldn't reach ten years ago.

Thus, the greatest mission opportunities of recent history beckon…today.

At the same time, risk and hostility threaten many of these new opportunities.

Sudden, unstable changes in politics and borders cry out for sharing risks and opportunities in a partnership—flexible enough to seize these openings and broad enough to adjust to setbacks.

In these circumstances, no one agency can go it alone—particularly in a holistic Evangelism/ Church Planting strategy for a nation, a great city, or a people group. The linked resources of multiple ministries can provide the diversity, flexibility, funding, prayer support, and speed necessary for a timely, appropriate response.

World conditions call for planning strategically, anticipating change, and preparing responses in coordinated ways.

5. Partnerships maximize over-stretched resources

Our scarce and overworked resources of people, money and equipment cry out for coordination of effort. The Church has the resources to fulfill the Great Commission, but not enough to waste in duplicate efforts and conflicting agendas. Worse than the waste and garbled message that come from duplication, is that some people of the world are left out completely.

Since 1986, Strategic Evangelism/Church-Planting Partnerships have demonstrated that for every pound, dollar, mark, yen, rand, and rouble invested in partnership development, people and financial resources are invested more efficiently many times over in the total evangelism initiative.

The Church has the people, money, prayer resources, and technology to fulfill the Great Commission in our age. But it will not be fulfilled by chance. It can only be fulfilled through godly unity and cooperation.

These partnerships, whether they have a formal, written constitution or merely a general agreement of mutual Kingdom goals, allow the needs of field ministries and indigenous churches to drive the decisions.

The Shape of Partnership

What does a strategic evangelism/ church-planting partnership look like... organizationally?

Partnership is an active step beyond networking. The primary focus of a network is to share information. The focus of a partnership is to take joint action—to do something, and to do it better by working together. Partners need not give up their organizational identity to work together.

In previous case histories, mission agencies worked in partnership. Specifically, they worked together in what Interdev calls a Strategic Evangelism / Church-Planting Partnership.

Strategic because it is an overall plan to reach a whole people group. It includes all the possible ways to reach a people: linking media, medical projects, evangelism, follow-up, discipleship, etc. together.

Strategic Evangelism/Church-Planting because the clear goal is to bring people to ma-

turity in Christ and establish them in their own national churches.

Strategic Evangelism/Church-Planting Partnership because the different parts of the body of Christ work together, each church, donor, and agency contributing resources and expertise to the overall whole.

Strategic Evangelism/Church-Planting Partnerships bring together radio, literature, relief, scripture translators, national evangelists, church planters, and others into a coordinated strategy.

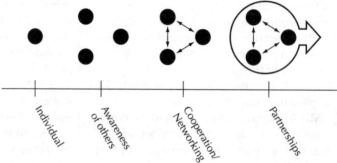

The progress from left to right on the line above shows increasing integration of ministry agencies. It starts with an individual agency working alone, then becoming aware of others, networking with others, and then working together in a partnership. Most partnerships work together on specific, limited projects, as partner agencies continue to retain their individual identities.

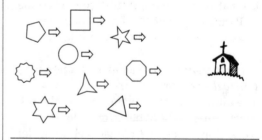

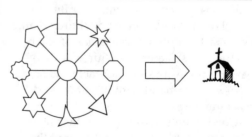

The middle diagram (see previous page) illustrates the old paradigm of ministries working independently. The bottom diagram shows the same agencies retaining their own identities but working together in a Strategic Evangelistic/Church-Planting Partnership.

What does a strategic evangelism/ church-planting partnership look like... to one being evangelized?

From the perspective of someone on the receiving end, a partnership approach looks whole. Message and messengers are connected and work together.

For a horseman in Central Asia, the message he hears on his radio ties in with the literature he got from an Asian evangelist passing through his village. That message fits what he saw in the Jesus film and heard from Christians afterward.

When local Christians meet the horseman and take him to their new church meetings, he finds a seamless continuity in the message and messengers. He doesn't have to puzzle through disconnected groups and information. Relationships—something he implicitly looks for in people—are appropriately modeled. The horseman is able to focus on Christ, without distraction from confusing or contradictory variations of the message, and disorganized or discordant messengers.

What does a strategic evangelism/ church-planting partnership look like... to Christian field workers?

In an effective partnership, Christian workers know they are not alone. They know they can count on many others with more specialties, and in more locations, than their own agency serves. They know they can trust these friends to handle contacts or converts that they pass on to them.

Workers can use each other's materials, and they can work together to improve them. Because more people use the resource, sharing the cost of a project among partners also lowers the expense for each agency.

New believers with whom agencies work will have a larger circle of Christian fellowship. In cultures resistant to Christianity, believers often feel isolated, so there is a tremendous advantage in the wider circle of friends that can come through partnership.

What does a strategic evangelism/ church-planting partnership look like... to the emerging church?

Contacts among believers help build the sense of a national Christian body. In the early stages of evangelism, believers may be few and widely scattered. A partnership between different ministries facilitates contact and fellowship between new Christians.

What does a strategic evangelism/ church-planting partnership look like... to the non-Western church?

The missionary growth rate in the West is presently something over 3% per year. However, in non-Western countries that same growth rate figure is over 13%! Estimates are that by the year 2000, the majority of Protestant missionaries will be from non-Western countries. While effective east-west, north-south ministry relationships have always been a challenging priority, this remarkable growth rate of kingdom resources from non-Western countries makes new, effective forms of ministry mandatory.

Strategic Evangelism/Church-Planting Partnerships demonstrate the practical potential for non-Western and Western personnel to work side by side. They can pray, plan, and then cooperatively implement strategies that call on the best resources that each has to offer.

Frequently, the power and intimidation associated with Western mission agencies' larger budgets and administrative structures have made it difficult for non-Western leadership to have a sense of equity in participation and ownership of cooperative efforts.

What does a strategic evangelism/ church-planting partnership look like... to sending churches and donors?

To a donor, a partnership translates into more results for our missions giving.

We would all like to see our resources have the greatest impact possible for the Kingdom. No one wants to see his or her donation diluted through inefficiency or duplication.

Partnerships maximize the use of resources. For example, giving to one of the 40 mission agencies in a Central Asia partnership assures a donor that the resources of 39 other mission agencies in the region are coordinated for maximum effectiveness with no wasteful duplication.

If a donor gives to a medical worker, he knows that radio broadcasts, literature, evangelists, and national pastors are all working with the medical project. They supply contacts who are interested, help in outreach, and place converts into functioning local churches.

What does a partnership in missions look like? It looks like a body whose parts work together.

What do Partnerships look like...to God?

Imagine Christ's delight as He works amidst His people laboring together. He makes the whole greater than the sum of its parts. Consider these examples of His power in partnership:

Mongolian Breakthrough

When the Mongolia Partnership had its first exploration meeting in Hong Kong in early 1991, only two or three ministries were working in the country and you could count all known believers on two hands. Today, over 35 ministries from over 10 nations are active in the country; the New Testament has been published, revised, and sold out three times and the Old Testament is nearing completion; the Jesus film has been completed and shown to tens of thousands; there are daily Christian Mongolian radio programs on the air; a Christian television station has just been launched in the capital; 10-12,000 Mongolians are worshiping in over 30 churches in the country and many believe the baptized believers now exceed 5,000. Remember, it was less than 100 years ago that nearly 50 Christian missionaries were martyred within 60 days as they sought to take the good news to Mongolia!

Partnership in Pakistan

"Along With Life" is the name of the highly listened to daily Urdu/Punjabi radio program that has anchored the Partnership in Pakistan.

The Partnership draws together Western mission agencies, Pakistani churches, literature, Bible production, broadcasting and Bible correspondence course ministries. Since the Partnership began, several thousand Muslims have made inquiries and continue to do so at a rate of 300-400 per month.

All-Indian Partnership

In the central/southern Indian state of Karnataka, Lingyat Hindus have long been viewed as a breakaway, "reformed" stream of Hinduism. Proud, highly intellectual, and dominant in banking and politics, Lingyats became the focus of a Strategic Evangelism Partnership five years ago. Made up of all Indian agencies, the Partnership has jointly produced evangelistic literature specifically tailored to the Lingyat worldview, held training conferences for member partner agencies on practical "how to's" of evangelism among Lingyats, jointly produced the first-ever Lingyat radio broadcast with a coordinated follow-up effort, and have seen many Lingyats coming into the Kingdom.

Hope for the Islamic World

In a long-neglected Islamic area with a population of over 60 million, the Strategic Partnership began nearly ten years ago with only eight ministries. Their common effort focused on one, single project. Today, that Partnership consists of nearly 80 ministries; a series of working groups, made up of the partner agencies, are addressing a wide range of projects related to evangelism, discipleship and leadership development. It is estimated that Kingdom resources now focused in this region are 20-30 times what they were ten years ago! And, in one of the countries where modern missionary witness was launched in the late 1800s by faithful missionaries, a special task force out of the larger Partnership has seen nearly 8,000 Muslims follow Christ in the last five years.

Study Questions

1. What does partnership *exemplify* which also enhances the *message* it was formed to convey?

2. Give an example of how agencies in a partnership can better function to disciple new believers.

The Lausanne Covenant

The Lausanne Congress on World Evangelization in Lausanne, Switzerland (July 16-25, 1974), brought together 4,000+ participants, including evangelists, missionaries, mission leaders, theologians, pastors and national church leaders from over 150 nations. A drafting committee headed by Dr. John R. W. Stott incorporated the ideas of main speakers and submissions from hundreds of participants. On the final day, Dr. Billy Graham and the leaders and participants signed the document in a moving public ceremony. From Lausanne, the freshly printed document spread quickly around the world. Evangelists shared it with new converts. Missionaries shared it in newly planted churches. Denominations studied its themes and challenges. By the mid-70s many other churches and agencies had already adopted it as their statement of faith. By the 1980's virtually every major evangelical mission agency in North America, and many in other countries, had endorsed the Covenant to replace or supplement their statement of faith. In this way, the fifteen tightly packed sections of the Covenant quickly spread the essence of Lausanne's emphasis on biblical world evangelization, and helped spark what became known as "the Lausanne Movement." An Asian theologian has written: "History may show this Covenant to be the most significant ecumenical confession on evangelism that the church has ever produced."

Introduction

We, members of the Church of Jesus Christ, from more than 150 nations, participants in the International Congress on World Evangelization at Lausanne, praise God for his great salvation and rejoice in the fellowship he has given us with himself and with each other. We are deeply stirred by what God is doing in our day, moved to penitence by our failures and challenged by the unfinished task of evangelization. We believe the gospel is God's good news for the whole world, and we are determined by his grace to obey Christ's commission to proclaim it to every person and to make disciples of every nation. We desire, therefore, to affirm our faith and our resolve, and to make public our covenant.

1. The Purpose of God

We affirm our belief in the one eternal God, Creator and Lord of the world, Father, Son and Holy Spirit, who governs all things according to the purpose of his will. He has been calling out from the world a people for himself, and sending his people back into the world to be his servants and his witnesses, for the extension of his kingdom, the building up of Christ's body, and the glory of his name. We confess with shame that we have often denied our calling and failed in our mission, by becoming conformed to the world or by withdrawing from it. Yet we rejoice that even when borne by earthen vessels the gospel is still a precious treasure. To the task of making that treasure known in the power of the Holy Spirit we desire to dedicate ourselves anew.

(Isa 40:28; Matt 28:19; Eph 1:11; Acts 15:14; John 17:6,18; Eph 4:12; Rom 12.2; 1 Cor 5:10; 2 Cor 4: 72)

2. The Authority and Power of the Bible

We affirm the divine inspiration, truthfulness and authority of both Old and New Testament Scriptures in their entirety as the only written Word of God, without error in all that it affirms, and the only infallible rule of faith and practice. We also affirm the power of God's word to accomplish his purpose of salvation. The message of the Bible is addressed to all men and women. For God's revelation in Christ and in Scripture is unchangeable. Through it the Holy Spirit still speaks today. He illumines the minds of God's people in every culture to perceive its truth freshly through their own eyes and thus discloses to the whole Church ever more of the many-colored wisdom of God.

(2 Tim 3:16; 2 Pet 1:21; Isa 55:11; Rom 1:16; 1 Cor 1:21; John 10:35; Matt 5:17,18; Jude 3; Eph 1:17,18)

3. The Uniqueness and Universality of Christ

We affirm that there is only one Savior and only one gospel, although there is a wide diversity of evangelistic approaches. We recognize that everyone has some knowledge of God through his general revelation in nature. But we deny that this can save, for people suppress the truth by their unrighteousness. We also reject as derogatory to Christ and the gospel every kind of syncretism and dialog which implies that Christ speaks equally through all religions and ideologies. Jesus Christ, being himself the only God-man, who gave himself as the only ransom for sinners, is the only mediator between God and people. There is no other name by which we must be saved. All men and women are perishing because of sin, but God loves everyone, not wishing that any should perish but that all should repent. Yet those who reject Christ repudiate the joy of salvation and condemn themselves to eternal separation from God. To proclaim Jesus as "the Savior of the world" is not to affirm that all people are either automatically or ultimately saved, still less to affirm that all religions offer salvation in Christ. Rather it is to proclaim God's love for a world of sinners and to invite everyone to respond to him as Savior and Lord in the wholehearted personal commitment of repentance and faith. Jesus Christ has been exalted above every other name; we long for the day when every knee shall bow to him and every tongue shall confess him Lord.

(Gal 1: 6-9; Rom 1:18-32; 1 Tim 2:5,6; Acts 4:12; John 3:16-19; 2 Pet 3:9; 2 Th 1:7-9; John 4:42; Matt 11:28; Eph 1:20,21; Phil 2:9-11)

4. The Nature of Evangelism

To evangelize is to spread the good news that Jesus Christ died for our sins and was raised from the dead according to the Scriptures, and that as the reigning Lord he now offers the forgiveness of sins and the liberating gift of the Spirit to all who repent and believe.

Our Christian presence in the world is indispensable to evangelism, and so is that kind of dialog whose purpose is to listen sensitively in order to understand. But evangelism itself is the proclamation of the historical, biblical Christ as Savior and Lord, with a view to persuading people to come to him personally and so be reconciled to God. In issuing the gospel invitation we have no liberty to conceal the cost of discipleship. Jesus still calls all who would follow him to deny themselves, take up their cross, and identify themselves with his new community. The results of evangelism include obedience to Christ, incorporation into his Church and responsible service in the world.

(1 Cor 15:3,4; Acts 2:32-39; John 20:21; 1 Cor 1:23; 2 Cor 4:5; 2 Cor 5:11,20; Luke 14:25-33; Mark 8:34; Acts 2:40,47; Mark 10:43-45)

5. Christian Social Responsibility

We affirm that God is both the Creator and the Judge of all. We therefore should share his concern for justice and reconciliation throughout human society and for the liberation of men and women from every kind of oppression. Because men and women are made in the image of God, every person, regardless of race, religion, color, culture, class, sex or age, has an intrinsic dignity because of which he or she should be respected and served, not exploited. Here too we express penitence both for our neglect and for having sometimes regarded evangelism and social concern as mutually exclusive. Although reconciliation with other people is not reconciliation with God, nor is social action evangelism, nor is political liberation salvation, nevertheless we affirm that evangelism and socio-political involvement are both part of our Christian duty. For both are necessary expressions of our doctrines of God and man, our love for our neighbor and our obedience to Jesus Christ. The message of salvation implies also a message of judgment upon every form of alienation, oppression and discrimination, and we should not be afraid to denounce evil and injustice wherever they exist. When people receive Christ they are born again, into his kingdom and must seek not only to exhibit but also to spread its righteousness in the midst of an unrighteous world. The salvation we claim should be transforming us in the totality of our personal and social responsibilities. Faith without works is dead.

(Acts 17:26, 31; Gen 18:25; Ps 45:7; Isa 1:17; Gen 1:26,27; Lev 19:18; Luke 6:27,35; Jas 3:9; John 3:3,5; Matt 5:20; Matt 6:33; 2 Cor 3:18; Jas 2:14-26)

6. The Church and Evangelism

We affirm that Christ sends his redeemed people into the world as the Father sent him, and that this calls for a similar deep and costly penetration of the world. We need to break out of our ecclesiastical ghettos and permeate non-Christian society. In the Church's mission of sacrificial service, evangelism is primary. World evangelization requires the whole Church to take the whole gospel to the whole world. The Church is at the very center of God's cosmic purpose and is his appointed means of spreading the gospel. But a church which preaches the cross must itself be marked by the cross. It becomes a stumbling block to evangelism when it betrays the gospel or lacks a living faith in God, a genuine love for people, or scrupulous honesty in all things including promotion and finance. The church is the community of God's people rather than an institution, and must not be identified with any particular culture, social or political system, or human ideology.

(John 17:18; 20:21; Matt 28:19,20; Acts 1:8; 20:27; Eph 1:9,10; 3:9-11; Gal 6:14, 17; 2 Cor 6:3,4; 2 Tim 2:19-21; Phil 1:27)

7. Cooperation in Evangelism

We affirm that the Church's visible unity in truth is God's purpose. Evangelism also summons us to unity, because our oneness strengthens our witness, just as our disunity undermines our gospel of reconciliation. We recognize, however, that organizational unity may take many forms and does not necessarily forward evangelism. Yet we who share the same biblical faith should be closely united in fellowship, work and witness. We confess that our testimony has sometimes been marred by sinful individualism and needless duplication. We pledge ourselves to seek a deeper unity in truth, worship, holiness and

mission. We urge the development of regional and functional cooperation for the furtherance of the Church's mission, for strategic planning, for mutual encouragement, and for the sharing of resources and experience.

(Eph 4:3, 4; John 17:21,23; 13:35; Phil 1:27)

8. Churches in Evangelistic Partnership

We rejoice that a new missionary era has dawned. The dominant role of Western missions is fast disappearing. God is raising up from the younger churches a great new resource for world evangelization, and is thus demonstrating that the responsibility to evangelize belongs to the whole body of Christ. All churches should therefore be asking God and themselves what they should be doing both to reach their own area and to send missionaries to other parts of the world. A reevaluation of our missionary responsibility and role should be continuous. Thus a growing partnership of churches will develop and the universal character of Christ's Church will be more clearly exhibited. We also thank God for agencies which labor in Bible translation, theological education, the mass media, Christian literature, evangelism, missions, church renewal and other specialist fields. They too should engage in constant self-examination to evaluate their effectiveness as part of the Church's mission.

(Rom 1:8; Phil 1:5; 4:15; Acts 13:1-3; 1 Th 1:6-8)

9. The Urgency of the Evangelistic Task

More than 2,700 million people, which is more than two-thirds of all humanity, have yet to be evangelized. We are ashamed that so many have been neglected; it is a standing rebuke to us and to the whole Church. There is now, however, in many parts of the world an unprecedented receptivity to the Lord Jesus Christ. We are convinced that this is the time for churches and para-church agencies to pray earnestly for the salvation of the unreached and to launch new efforts to achieve world evangelization. A reduction of foreign missionaries and money in an evangelized country may sometimes be necessary to facilitate the national church's growth in self-reliance and to release resources for unevangelized areas. Missionaries should flow ever more freely from and to all six continents in a spirit of humble service. The goal should be, by all available means and at the earliest possible time, that every person will have the opportunity to hear, understand, and receive the good news. We cannot hope to attain this goal without sacrifice. All of us are shocked by the poverty of millions and disturbed by the injustices which cause it. Those of us who live in affluent circumstances accept our duty to develop a simple life-style in order to contribute more generously to both relief and evangelism.

(Mark 16:15; John 9:4; Matt 9:35-38; Isa 58:6,7; Jas 2:1-9; 1 Cor 9:19-23; Jas 1:27; Matt 25:31-46; Acts 2:44,45; 4:34,35)

10. Evangelism and Culture

The development of strategies for world evangelization calls for imaginative pioneering methods. Under God, the result will be the rise of churches deeply rooted in Christ and closely related to their culture. Culture must always be tested and judged by Scripture. Because men and women are God's creatures, some of their culture is rich in beauty and goodness. Because they are fallen, all of it is tainted with sin and some of it is demonic. The gospel does not presuppose the superiority of any culture to another, but evaluates all cultures according to its own criteria of truth and righteousness, and insists on moral absolutes in every culture. Missions have all too frequently exported with the gospel an alien culture and churches have sometimes been in bondage to culture rather than to Scripture. Christ's evangelists must humbly seek to empty themselves of all but their personal authenticity in order to become the servants of others, and churches must seek to transform and enrich culture, all for the glory of God.

(Mark 7:8,9,13; Gen 4:21,22; 1 Cor 9:19-23; Phil 2:5-7; 2 Cor 4:5)

11. Education and Leadership

We confess that we have sometimes pursued church growth at the expense of church depth, and divorced evangelism from Christian nurture. We also acknowledge that some of our missions have been too slow to equip and encourage national leaders to assume their rightful responsibilities. Yet we are committed to indigenous principles, and long that every church will have national leaders who manifest a Christian style of leadership in terms not of domination but of service. We recognize that there is a great need to improve theological education, especially for church leaders. In every nation and culture there should be an effective training program for pastors and laity in doctrine, discipleship, evangelism, nurture and service. Such training programs should not rely on any stereotyped methodology but should be developed by creative local initiatives according to biblical standards.

(Col 1:27,28; Acts 14:23; Titus 1:5,9; Mark 10:42-45; Eph 4:11,12)

12. Spiritual Conflict

We believe that we are engaged in constant spiritual warfare with the principalities and powers of evil, who are seeking to overthrow the Church and frustrate its task of world evangelization. We know our need to equip ourselves with God's armor and to fight this battle with the spiritual weapons of truth and prayer. For we detect the activity of our enemy, not only in false ideologies outside the Church, but also inside it in false gospels which twist Scripture and put people in the place of God.

We need both watchfulness and discernment to safeguard the biblical gospel. We acknowledge that we ourselves are not immune to worldliness of thought and action, that is, to a surrender to secularism. For example, although careful studies of church growth, both numerical and spiritual, are right and valuable, we have sometimes neglected them. At other times, desirous to ensure a response to the gospel, we have compromised our message, manipulated our hearers through pressure techniques, and become unduly preoccupied with statistics or even dishonest in our use of them. All this is worldly. The Church must be in the world; the world must not be in the Church.

(Eph 6:12; 2 Cor 4:3,4; Eph 6:11, 13-18; 2 Cor 10:3-5; 1 Jn 2:18-26; 4:1-3; Gal 1:6-9; 2 Cor 2:17; 4:2; John 17:15)

13. Freedom and Persecution

It is the God-appointed duty of every government to secure conditions of peace, justice and liberty in which the Church may obey God, serve the Lord Christ, and preach the gospel without interference. We therefore pray for the leaders of the nations and call upon them to guarantee freedom of thought and conscience, and freedom to practice and propagate religion in accordance with the will of God and as set forth in The Universal Declaration of Human Rights. We also express our deep concern for all who have been unjustly imprisoned, and especially for those who are suffering for their testimony to the Lord Jesus. We promise to pray and work for their freedom. At the same time we refuse to be intimidated by their fate. God helping us, we too will seek to stand against injustice and to remain faithful to the gospel, whatever the cost. We do not forget the warnings of Jesus that persecution is inevitable.

(1 Tim 2:1-4; Col 3.24; Acts 4:19; 5:29; Heb 13:1-3; Luke 4:18; Gal 5:11; 6:12; Matt 5:10-12; John 15:18-21)

14. The Power of the Holy Spirit

We believe in the power of the Holy Spirit. The Father sent his Spirit to bear witness to his Son; without his witness ours is futile. Conviction of sin, faith in Christ, new birth and Christian growth are all his work. Further, the Holy Spirit is a missionary spirit; thus evangelism should arise spontaneously from a Spirit-filled church. A church that is not a missionary church is contradicting itself and quenching the Spirit. Worldwide evangelization will become a realistic possibility only when the Spirit renews the Church in truth and wisdom, faith, holiness, love and power. We therefore call upon all Christians to pray for such a visitation of the sovereign Spirit of God that all his fruit may appear in all his people and that all his gifts may enrich the body of Christ. Only then will the whole Church become a fit instrument in his hands, that the whole earth may hear his voice.

(Acts 1:8; 1 Cor 2:4; John 15:26,27; John 16:8-11; 1 Cor 12:3; John 3: 6-8; 2 Cor 3:18; John 7:37-39; 1 Th 5:19; Ps 85: 4-7; Gal 5:22,23; Rom 12:3-8; 1 Cor 12:4-31; Ps 67:1-3)

15. The Return of Christ

We believe that Jesus Christ will return personally and visibly, in power and glory, to consummate his salvation and his judgment. This promise of his coming is a further spur to our evangelism, for we remember his words that the gospel must first be preached to all nations. We believe that the interim period between Christ's ascension and return is to be filled with the mission of the people of God, who have no liberty to stop before the end. We also remember his warning that false Christs and false prophets will arise as precursors of the final Antichrist. We therefore reject as a proud, self-confident dream the notion that people can ever build a utopia on earth. Our Christian confidence is that God will perfect his kingdom, and we look forward with eager anticipation to that day, and to the new heaven and earth in which righteousness will dwell and God will reign forever. Meanwhile, we rededicate ourselves to the service of Christ and of people in joyful submission to his authority over the whole of our lives.

(Mark 14:62; Heb 9:28; Mark 13:10; Matt 28:20; Acts 1:8-11; Mark 13:21-23; 1 John 2:18; 4:1-3; Luke 12:32; Rev 21:1-5; 2 Pet 3:13; Matt 28:18)

Conclusion

Therefore, in the light of this our faith and out resolve, we enter into a solemn covenant with God and with each other, to pray, to plan and to work together for the evangelization of the whole world. We call upon others to join us. May God help us by his grace and for his glory to be faithful to this our covenant! Amen, Alleluia!

Scripture Index

Genesis
1-11	10, 27, 196
1:3	62
1:21	531
1:26-28	483, 634, 761
2:17	18
3:9	532
3:14,15	10, 12, 19
3:17-19	483
3:24	18
4-11	4
4:17-22	483, 762
6	11
6-7	58
9:1-3	483
9:1-17	126
9:6	4, 483
9:27	12
10	27
11	217
12	4
12:1	722
12:1-3	38, 47, 115, 197, 254
12:1-4	3, 21, 491
12:2	9
12:3	9, 11, 110, 115, 117, 189
12:7-8	37
12:10-20	37
14	10, 37
14:18-20	38
14:21-24	38
15:16	40
18:18	115, 117
18:25	160, 761
20:11	37
22	38
22:12	38
26:3,24	112
41:38	197
49:9,10	20

Exodus
1:7	5
2:24	6
3-4	58
4:22	13
7-12	408
7:10-12	189
8:1,20	38
9:13-16	38, 39
12:3-4	616
12:12	39
15:3,7	39
18	10, 244
18:1	39
18:11	39
19	14
19:3	28
19:3-6	6, 11, 13, 254
19:5-6	13, 140, 197
20	28
20:1	13
20:2-6	625
25:8	41
32:1-14	41
33:19	48
34:6	32

Leviticus
19:18	761
20:24,26	117
25	381

Numbers
13:17	40
14:15-16	41
14:17-21	41
14:21	608
23-24	11

Deuteronomy
2:25	117
4:15-24	40
6:5	649
7:14	28
7:6-7	40
9:26	28

9:5	40
10:16,30	197
12:2-14	41
28	146
28:10	254

Joshua 616, 625
1:5	112
4:24	117
7:14	115
24:15	616

Judges
1:7	40
4	197
6:6	146

Ruth 197, 273

1 Samuel
8:20	117

2 Samuel
7:12-16	20

1 Kings
3:8	5
8:41-43	41
8:60	42
9:25	42
11:1-8	42
11:38	112
17	97
18	408

2 Kings
5	655
5:1-14	97
17	197

1 Chronicles
16:27	36

2 Chronicles
5:13-14	48
6:18	41
6:19-21	48
6:33	254
7:20	117
11:17,36	65
12:1	65

Ezra 394
4:5 65
8:1 65
Nehemiah 179, 180
1:8-9 180
6:16 117
9:9-10 39
9:17 32
12:22 65
Esther
3:8 117
4:16 180
Psalms 94, 119
2:8 22
9:17 52
10:16 17
16:11 51, 173
19:1 609
19:1-4 397, 400
19:5,6 400
22:27 189
37:4 51, 54
45:7 761
66:1-4 43
67 11, 197, 254
67:1-2 725
67:1-3 763
67:3-4 45, 49, 51, 54
69:32 51
70:4 51
72:19 609
76:10 18
85:4-7 763
86:9 35
86:9-15 48
86:15 32
96 41, 254
96:3 49, 52
96:7-9 36, 37
97:1 49, 51
103:19 17
104:34 49
105 254
117:1 50
138:4-5 43
Proverbs
1:7, 9 42
14:31 635
24:11,12 305
Ecclesiates
3:11 400

Song of Solomon
2:10-13 190
Isaiah 35, 50, 51, 83, 84, 86, 159
1:11-15 43
1:17 761
2 30
2:1-4 28
2:2-4 126
2:2 117
2:4 64, 86
9:2 707
11:3 15
11:6 64
11:9 608, 741
12:4 35, 52
14:12-14 17
14:14 18
25:6-9 28
26:9 189
27:11 706
28:21 9
30:18 50
40-55 59
40:5 254
40:28 759
41:18 191
42:1-4 6
42:4 29
42:6 22, 59
42:8 172
42:18-20 59
42,49 16
46:1-4 51
49:6 29, 59, 189, 197
53:7 20
55:8,9 57, 303
56:7 44, 116
58:6,7 569, 762
60 28
61 106
61:1-4 568
61:6 568
63:11-14 39
64:4 50
65 30
66:19 518
Jeremiah
3:17 28, 117
9 200
9:24-26 197

10:5 51
12:14-17 254
29:7 739
31:27-34 190
31:34 190
33:22 6
49:34 65
Ezekiel 28, 96, 707
2:3 96
16:60-63 190
20:5-22 43
20:43,44 190
28:12-17 17
34:8,20 707
36:22-23 43
Daniel 28, 43, 60, 66, 96
2:31-35 66
2:37 65
3:2,7 117
7:1-29 28
7:13-14 96, 110, 189
8:23 65
9:15 43
9:16-19 43
12:10 190
Hosea 6
1:10 6
6:1,2 190
6:3 189
10:12 191
Joel 188, 189, 192
2:17 191
2:23 189
2:28,29 188, 192
2:30,31 189
2:32 190
4:2, 11 117
Amos 28, 30, 56, 120
3:7 56
5:21-24 43
9:9-10 28
9:11-15 190
9:12 20, 117
Jonah 30, 33, 557
3:9-4 48
4:1-2 30
4:11 556
Micah
4 30
4:1-4 28
6:6-8 43

Habakkuk
1:5	509
1:13	174
2:5	117
2:14	43, 608, 609

Zephaniah
3:9-10	43

Haggai
1:8	43
1:13	112
2:7	117

Zechariah
2:11	254
7:14	117
8:20	28
8:20-22	191
9:9-10	99
10:1	189, 191
14:9	20

Malachi 94, 95
1:10	95
1:11	43, 189, 254
3:1-3	95
3:2	94
3:17	13
4:5	95

Matthew 532
1:1	20
2	61
3:2	67, 95
3:7	95
3:9	7, 95
3:11	67
3:17	681
3:8	495
4:8	97
4:15	110
4:16	212
4:17	64, 70
4:23-25	110
5:10-12	763
5:16	634
5:17,18	760
5:20	62, 64, 761
5:43-44	388
5:44-45	62
6:5-15	601
6:9-10	52
6:10	65, 66
6:19-21	601
6:21	722
6:24-34	488

6:32	117
6:33	92, 306
7:13-14	157
7:14	62
7:15-20	189
7:20	661
7:28-29	171
8:5	61
8:5-13	104
8:7-12	105
8:8,10	98
8:10	491
8:11	22
8:20	96
8:28	110
8:28-34	98
9:6	96
9:35-38	46, 762
9:36	101
9:37-38	62
9:38	747
10:1	537
10:5-6	97, 111
10:6	62
10:6,15	22
10:16	62
10:17	87
10:26-39	172, 183
11:6	67
11:7	67
11:12	147
11:13-15	95
11:28	760
11:28-30	51, 495
12:8	96
12:27-29	25
12:28	64, 86
12:29	19, 183
12:38-42	33, 410
13	604
13:3-9	652
13:3-23	747
13:10-16	159
13:11	62, 65
13:18	596
13:32	102
13:35	141
13:38	62
14:23	143
14:33	112
15:21-28	105
15:24	98

16:18	102, 135
16:19	62
17:1-8	112
17:12-13	95
17:17	105
17:26	62
18:11-12	309
18:15-20	601
18:20	607
18:23-27	62
19:21	62
19:23	52
20:25-28	425, 600
21:21	145
21:43	99, 117
22:37-40	470, 601
22:39	531
23:1-39	101
23:15	130, 197
24	189
24:3	69, 77
24:4-14	99
24:7	113
24:9	114
24:13	76
24:14	22, 69, 92, 110, 116, 133, 190, 213, 511, 517
24:24,29	189
24:34	99
24:35	171
24:36	99
25:21,23	50
25:31,34	65
25:31-46	762
25:32	114
26:36-45	143
26:41	62
26:42	56
28	31
28:7	112
28:16	102, 112
28:17	112
28:18-20	22, 31, 62, 69, 72, 77, 85, 103, 104, 107, 113, 114, 116, 127, 171, 189, 412, 517, 533, 543, 595, 597, 601, 629, 759, 763

Mark 82, 83, 88, 89, 112
1:14 92
1:15 82, 601
1:25 83
1:32-34 83
1:35 143
1:38 110
2:8-11 172
2:10 171
2:23-26 89
3:10 81, 87
3:22 80
3:24 80, 86
3:27 80, 147
4 604
4:21-25 159
5:34 81
5:6-10 88
6:5 88
7:26-30 105
7:8,9 762
8:34 760
9:1-9 112
9:9,14 112
9:25 81
9:29 87
9:37 52
10:28 62
10:34 87
10:42-45 760, 762
10:45 51
10:47 87
11:17 61, 99, 114, 116
12:44 312
13:8 117
13:10 763
13:26 96
13:30 99
14:36 486
14:50-52 122
14:62 763
15:39 183
16:15 189, 762, 216
16:15-18 412
16:19-20 112, 126, 153
Luke 61, 81, 83, 98, 106, 114, 121, 122, 131, 174, 344, 741
1:45-55 6

2:31-32 61
2:32 117
2:49 100
3:8 7
3:21 143
3:21,22 412
4:1-13 83
4:5-6 80
4:7-8 80
4:16-30 106
4:18 92, 575, 763
4:18-19 83, 139
4:22 106
4:24-30 97
4:31 409
4:33-35 410
4:38-39 83
5 409
5:1-11 736
5:16 143
5:27-28 409
6:12 143
6:24-26 500
6:27,35 761
6:38 601
7:4-5 104
7:20 414, 539
7:21 81, 87
8:10 92
8:11 127
8:30 89
9:1-6 408, 409, 410
9:2 575
9:24 722
9:28-36 112
9:51-56 106
10:1 98, 111
10:8-16 159
10:9 93
10:10 532
10:17-18 81, 87, 183
10:25-38 488
10:27 695
11:2 82
11:14 81
11:15 80
11:20-22 25, 80, 82
11:29-32 33
11:31-32 403
12:30 114
12:32 62, 763
12:36,37 190

12:47-48 159, 254, 707
13:6-9 535
13:11-16 80, 81
13:18,19 102
13:24 62
13:28,29 7, 105
13:29 22
14:16 310
14:25 494
14:25-33 760
16:2-4 141
16:19-31 157
17:11-19 410
17:12-19 98
18:1-8 142, 143, 144
18:8 218
18:32 87
19:11-12 65
19:17-20 85
21:4 312
21:10 117
21:16,18 76
21:24 114
21:32 99
22:17-20 601
22:22-30 65
22:59 122
23:34 180
24:11 177
24:13-35 121
24:13-49 107
24:33 122
24:38-40 102
24:44-45 103
24:45-47 116, 124
24:48,49 103, 122, 412
John 20, 176, 178, 184, 400, 409, 625, 709
1 625
1:1-14 444, 448, 486
1:7-8 709
1:9 397, 400
1:11 134, 197, 312
1:12 175
1:14 24
1:14,18 170
1:29 20, 177
1:45,46 153
2:2 174
2:18 763
3:3 539

John (continued)

3:3,5	761
3:6-8	763
3:8	491
3:16	62, 158, 175, 189, 638, 790
3:18	158
3:19-20	182
4	347
4:1-3	166
4:5-42	98
4:14	172
4:22	61
4:23	44, 119
4:34	56
4:36-38	747
4:42	100, 760
5:17-19	56, 172
5:19	25
5:21	172
5:22-23	172
5:27	172
5:39,40	489
5:44	35
6:35	176
7	22
7:20	86
7:37-39	189, 763
7:46	171
8:12	172
8:32	173
8:33-40	7
8:34	83
8:44	101
9:1-5	87
9:4	322, 762
10	176
10:1-16	62
10:10	176
10:11	172
10:11-15	177
10:11-16	178
10:12-13	176
10:14	665
10:16	176, 665, 177
10:33	172
10:35	760
10:37-38	172
11:52	116, 134, 177
12:20	61
12:20-21	110
12:23	98

12:24-32	44
12:27-32	184
12:31	19
12:31	80
12:31-33	183
12:32	98, 106
13:13	495
13:33	174
13:34-35	590
13:35	635, 661, 754
14	158, 174
14-16	412
14:6	174, 175
14:6-7	170
14:9	410
14:10	56, 57, 171
14:12	85
14:27	172
15	88, 604
15:5	638
15:11	50, 172
15:12-14	638
15:18-21	763
15:26-27	763
16:8	472
16:8-11	763
16:33	76
17	609
17:3	585, 176
17:4,6	44
17:6-8	57
17:6,18	759
17:10	606
17:11,21	752
17:15	762
17:18-20	761
17:20	102
17:20-23	754, 755
17:21	132, 565
17:21-26	182
17:21,23	102, 761
17:24	141
17:26	45
18:8-9	122
19:1	87
20:19	122
20:21	58, 102, 189, 312, 493, 760
20:23	62
21	177, 737
21:15	62
21:15,16	102

21:19	184
22	178
Acts	70, 126, 136, 154, 163, 165, 453, 454, 532, 575, 742
1-12	118
1:8	62, 103, 107, 126, 152, 153, 189, 342, 724
1:9-12	112
1:12-14	127
1:14	191
2	163
2-12	127
2-13	129
2:4	127
2:5	60, 113, 114, 117, 118, 189
2:16,17	188
2:17	76, 192
2:19-20	189
2:21	190
2:36	177
2:36-41	601
2:38	135, 601
2:39	189
2:42	154, 229
3:25	115, 253
4:12	156, 158
5:28	153
6:1,2	575
6:13-14	119
7:60	180
8:1	128, 288
8:4	575
8:12	70
9	128
9:15	117
10	159, 384, 389, 510
10:2	119
10:24	602
10:28	119
10:34	62, 119
10:38	726
10:45	119
11:2-3	120
11:18	120
11:19	119
11:19-30	602
11:20,21	119

11:26	101	1:5,16	200	16:25-26	66
13	166	1:5	22, 53	**1 Corinthians**	738
13-14	384	1:8	761	1:14	616
13:1-3	129, 595, 602	1:16	25, 97, 130,	1:17	575
13:2	221		491, 760	1:17-31	184
13:4	669	1:18-21	160	1:18-20	496
13:13-43	405	1:18-32	760	1:20	575
13:19	114	1:19-25	625	1:21	491
13:46,47	130	1:20	400	1:22	410
13:48	114	2:14,15	160, 400	2:1-5	25
14	740	2:15-16	471	2:9	37
14:8-18	405	2:29	197	3:8-15	48
14:16	114, 400	3:23	164	3:9	62
14:21-23	76, 130, 598	3:29	117	3:10	740
14:27	120, 130	4	7	3:21-23	7
15	384, 389	4:9-13	7	4:1,2	534
15:1	120, 385	4:25	174	4:9	183
15:2	384	5:1	175	4:11-12	738
15:5	120	5:20-21	596, 598	5:10	759
15:8	120, 667	6:1-11	601	6:10-11	739
15:10	120	6:6	72	7:17-24	739
15:12	120	6:23	70	9	737, 740
15:14	111	8:18-25	503	9:6	737
15:17	114	8:19-21	138	9:12	738
15:19	120	8:29	411	9:19-23	133, 275, 384,
15:20	126	8:35-39	54		490, 738, 762
15:21	221	9:4,5	130	10:21	626
16	665	9:6-7	7	12	139, 754
16:6-10	596	9:25-26	6	12:2	114
17:16-34	170	10	532	12:3	638
17:31	177	10:13	190	12:3-31	763
18:3	737	10:13-15	158	12:4-11	190
18:26	269	10:15	532, 709	12:4-17	754
19:8-10	741	10:17	158	12:5	131
19:9	153	11:11,14	130	12:7	131, 132
19:10	131, 153, 608	11:13-24	197	12:27	178
19:11,12	737	11:24-26	190	13:12	387
19:11-20	153	12:1,2	497, 759, 634	14:14-25	689
19:23-27	741	12:3-8	131, 139, 178,	15:3,4	760
20	737		190, 763	15:6	102
20-21	187	15	185	15:10	62, 713
20:26-28	740	15:6	45	15:11	22
20:33-35	737, 740	15:11	116	15:20-22	177
22:3	128	15:15-17	45	15:24	20
26:17-18	128, 155, 518	15:16-17	186	15:24-26	70, 72
28:23,28	70	15:19	48, 132, 537	15:35-54	89
28:31	120	15:19-21	127	16:15	616
Romans		15:20	45, 48	16:19	616
1:1,5	127	15:20-21	313	**2 Corinthians**	738
1:5	45, 52, 111,	15:25-27	132	2:14	63
	114, 124	16:3,5	616	2:17	762
1:5,15	713	16:23	616		

2 Corinthians (continued)
3:18	184, 588, 761, 763
4	25
4:1-2	22
4:3,4	80, 155, 196, 411, 539, 540
4:5	760, 762
4:6	486
4:7	496, 759
5:11	575
5:14-15	504, 552
5:17	533
5:17-21	85
5:18	565
5:18-19	85
5:18-21	131
5:19	63, 174
6:3	738
7:1	190
8:4	131
8:9	635
10:1	491
10:3-5	150, 762
10:4	146
10:5	495
10:12-16	596
11:8-9	738
11:12	738
11:13-14	87
11:14	71
12:4-26	600
12:7	80
12:9-10	25
12:16-18	738

Galatians 201, 351
1:6-8	22
1:6-9	760, 762
1:13	128
1:14	128
1:16	128
2:8	596
2:9,14	117, 713
3	8
3:5	189
3:6-8	115
3:6-16	20
3:8	12, 23, 114, 253
3:14	625
3:28	139, 566
3:29	12, 115

4:4	19
4:6-8	625
4:27-28	214
5	470
5:11	763
5:22,23	131, 763
6:6	740
6:7	175
6:10	131, 615
6:14,17	761

Ephesians 137, 141, 184
1:4	141
1:7	174
1:9,10	761
1:10	137, 138
1:11	759
1:17	486
1:17,18	760
1:20,21	760
1:22-23	178
2:1-10	596
2:2	80, 87
2:12-13	625
2:16	63
2:19	615
2:22	499
2,3	501
3:2	141
3:2-8	713
3:3,9	665
3:6	7, 62, 164
3:7-15	190
3:9-12	167
3:10	138, 184, 488
3:15	615
3:18,19	488
4:1-12	602
4:1-16	754
4:3-6	501, 761
4:8,12	131
4:10	740
4:11-16	598, 600, 762
4:12	759
4:15	506
4:28	739
5:22	616
5:27	190
6:5-8	739
6:7-8	53
6:11-13	69, 147, 412, 419, 503, 518, 557, 672, 762

6:10-18	134

Philippians
1:5	710
1:5	761
1:7	711, 713
1:12	711
1:19	712
1:20	184
1:27	754, 761
1:29	711
2	493
2:5-7	762
2:5-11	738
2:6-11	63
2:7	635
2:9	63
2:9-11	503, 760
2:10-11	52
2:12	473
2:12-13	62
2:13	58
2:18	710
2:21	711
3:3	35
3:4-9	490
3:8	52
3:12	128
4:8	503
4:15-16	738
4:15	501

Colossians 163, 165
1:18	178
1:19-20	90
1:20	138
1:24	134, 312
1:25	141
1:27	607
1:27,28	762
2:8-15	133
2:14-15	84, 183
2:15	25, 412
3:16	488
3:18-40	616
3:24	763
4:4	559
4:15	616

1 Thessalonians
2:18	133
5:19	763
5:26	381

2 Thessalonians
1:7-9	760

2:1-3	189	11:6	534	3:8	82, 83
2:9,10	189	11:8-16	6	4:1-3	189
1 Timothy		11:10	557	4:4	412, 607
1:4	141	11:13	9	5:12	176
1:14	713	11:36	87	5:19	80, 196, 411
2:1-4	763	12:6	87	**3 John**	
2:1-6	154	12:28	91	6-7	53
2:5	4, 681	13:1-3	763	**Jude**	295
2:5,6	760	**James**	106, 112, 409	3	391, 760
2:6	155	1:27	762	6, 8-10	87
2:7	132	2:1-9	762	**Revelation**	
3:1-7	600	2:2	229	1:6	13, 58
3:6	87	2:14-26	761	1:9	76
3:7	740	2:24,26	635	3:20	395
3:16	63	3:9	483, 761	5:1-14	109
5:8	739	4:7	681	5:9	113, 116, 117, 631
5:17-18	740	5:1-6	500		
5:22	129	5:7	189, 190	5:9-10	27, 651
6:11	626	5:7,8	191	5:10	89
6:20	22	12	122	5:12	20
2 Timothy		**1 Peter**	63	6-17	189
1:8-9	713	1:13-16	190	6:12,13	189
1:10	71, 72	1:16	634	7:1-9	190
1:12-14	22	1:20	141	7:9	190, 352, 559
1:16	616	2:5	498	11:1-19	183
2:2	394, 598	2:9	13, 14, 63, 74, 92, 140	11:6	189
2:15	394			11:15	518
2:19-21	761	2:12	63, 634	12:4-7	17
3:1	76	2:15	63	12:9	18
3:12	189	2:18-30	616	12:9-11	183
3:15	489	2:21	190	15:3-4	54
3:16	487, 760	2:24	174	15:4	189
3:17	626	3:15	63	16:7	160
4:17	114, 117	3:18	174	19:7-9	190
Titus	344, 738	3:22	496	20:2	19
1:5,9	762	4:10	131, 139, 190	20:8,21	89
Hebrews	397, 537	5:1-4	600	20:14	71
1:1	23	5:2	139	21:1-5	763
1:2	76	5:8	71	21:3	45
2:4	537	**2 Peter**		21:9	139
2:10	190	1:4	182	21:10-27	557
2:14	70, 72, 82	1:21	23, 760	21:22-26	45
2:14-15	71, 183	2:4	87	21:24-26	503
2:14-18	493	3:9	155, 191, 534, 539, 760	22:1-5	45
4:3	7, 141			22:2	18
6:12	9	3:12	77		
6:18-19	91	3:13	89, 763		
9:22	174	**1 John**			
9:26	72, 134	2:2	634		
9:28	763	2:18-26	762		
10:25	659	3:2,3	190		
11:1	534	3:6	196		

Index

A

Abraham 3–9, 19–20, 21–23, 37, 253, 694
  seed of 7, 8, 12, 19–20, 22, 115
Abrahamic covenant 107
Absolute truth 169–171
Accommodation 243–244, 246, 251, 496
AD 2000 218, 355, 530
Adaptation 243
Affinity Blocs 544–546
Affluence 705–707
African Americans in World Missions
    287–291
African-Initiated Churches 367, 370, 499
Agency 224, 254, 442, 715–717, 734
Agriculture 223, 241–242, 265, 525–526,
    578, 734
AIDS 580
Allegiance 17–20, 408–413, 483
Allen, Roland 251
Alliances 327, 751, 753–758
American Society of Missiology
    (ASM) 723
An Enquiry 293
Anabaptists 226
Ancestor worship 623, 674
Anderson, Rufus 227, 231, 248
Angels 17–20, 74, 79–85, 122, 149, 150,
    177, 183, 187, 699–700
Animism 364, 366, 420, 623–631, 633
Anthropology 466, 468, 627
Apocalyptic 25, 28, 69, 79–82, 96
Apostolic
  bands 129–132, 221–224, 668
  calling 128, 186
  office 234
  passion 185–187
Augustine 223
Authority 17, 22, 65, 72, 79–85, 97, 102,
    105, 109, 112, 117, 171–172, 336,
    459, 600–601, 601, 679, 759
  of the Word of God 285
Awakenings 191, 215
Aylward, Gladys 272

B

Baptism 67–68, 95, 111, 242, 334, 338,
    597–598, 627, 676
Baptized 334, 597, 673–675, 694–698
Behavior 338, 385–387, 423, 470–473
Beliefs
  patterns of 324, 374–376, 375–377, 632
Benedictine 223, 225, 238, 262
Bible
  authority of 21
  story of the 4, 34, 37–43, 73–74
Biblical inspiration 485
Bicultural 422–423, 448
Bilingual 560
Blessing 3–9, 11–16, 20, 21, 37–38, 47,
    107, 115, 116, 253–254, 268,
    592–594, 725
Blocs 512, 515, 516 See also Affinity Blocs
Body of Christ 93, 131, 139–140, 140, 181,
    598, 709, 731
Bonding 444
Boniface 241, 263
Brainerd, David 244, 298–299
Bride of Christ 139–140, 190, 566
Bridges of God 323, 618–622
Brotherhood 319, 621
Buddhism 169, 175, 243, 318, 365, 522,
    543, 678, 694–695
Byzantine 241

C

C1-C6 Spectrum 658, 660–663
Calvin 223
Cannibalism 462–464, 505
Carey, Lott 288, 292
Carey, William 75, 227, 229, 232–235,
    246–247, 254, 257, 260, 265,
    293–299, 360, 525–528, 529–530, 720
Cargo cults 627, 631
Carmichael, Amy 272
Carolingian Renaissance 263
Caste 147, 323, 326, 351, 361, 427, 504,
    566, 619, 636, 699–700

Celtic 224–225, 263
 monks 223
Centrifugal mission 60, 61, 254
Centripetal mission 28, 60, 61, 254
Charlemagne 263
Children 327, 329–330, 335, 554, 669–671
China 318, 320, 334, 336, 358–360, 534, 607, 613–616, 639, 673–675, 743
China Inland Mission 228, 238, 257–258, 259, 279, 303–304, 305
Chinese 319, 334, 360, 522, 550, 613–616, 639, 674–675, 694
Christ *See also* Jesus, Lordship of Christ
 blood of 8, 22, 37, 138, 174
 cross of 8, 25, 85, 322, 496, 567–568
 death of 25, 94–97, 98–99, 119, 157, 173–174, 176–178, 183, 214, 634
 lordship of 173, 332, 495
 name of 179–180
 resurrection of 173
 return of 69, 73
 suffering for 181–184
  See also Suffering
Christ-centered communities 658
Christward movements 333, 335–336, 622
Church 22, 62–63, 69, 72, 84–85, 90–91, 93, 102, 113, 123, 136, 137–141, 138, 140, 147, 155, 157, 162, 166–167, 174, 177, 180, 224, 232, 318–322, 323, 328–338, 575–576, 593, 597–598, 622, 683, 688–690, 696–697, 725–726, 735, 742, 753, 761 *See also* House: churches, Indigenous: church
 as an organism 127
 as community 136, 140
 government 234–236, 249
 growth 166, 217, 260, 330, 332, 334–338, 422–428, 533, 596, 696–697
 mandate 135
 self-governing 136 *See also* Three-Self Patriotic Movement
 self-propogating 136 *See also* Three-Self Patriotic Movement
 self-supporting 136 *See also* Three-Self Patriotic Movement
 structure of 220, 232
 visible 216
Church planting 111, 123, 129–133, 135, 150, 186, 216, 218, 248–249, 260, 516–517, 546, 575, 595–604, 606–612, 608, 668–672, 675, 677–680, 687, 692, 715–717,

730–732, 737, 755
  See also Saturation church planting (SCP)
 clusters 563, 613
 clusters of growing 617–622
 mandate 132, 135
Churches
 house 359, 611, 640–645, 676, 691, 737
 reproduction of 330, 595–596, 600
Circumcision 5, 7, 62, 120, 124, 131, 221, 343
Cistercians 263
Clare 270
Closure 517
Cognitive domain 48, 379–380
Colley, William W. 289
Colonialism 242–243, 249, 500, 593
Comity 250–251
Communication 46, 122–123, 125, 341, 344, 374–377, 380–383, 392, 405–407, 422–428, 429–437, 450, 560, 628, 684–685, 732
 of the gospel 373, 489, 489–490
Communism 253, 354, 564, 641–642, 694
Confession 148, 165, 566
Congregations 329, 332–335, 347–349, 562, 607–608, 614–616, 618–622, 656, 676, 687, 691–692
 conglomerate 617–622
Conscience 573
Consecration 705–707
Contextualization 23, 166, 381–382, 384, 389–390, 490, 497, 607–608, 655–659, 664–665, 679, 681–682, 739
Contributions 738 *See also* Financial help
Conversion 32, 125, 166, 250, 324, 494–497, 496
Converts 323–337, 347, 382, 427, 472, 494–495, 563, 597–598, 620–622, 625, 651, 655–659, 662, 665, 676, 680–682, 684, 690–692, 698–700, 739–741
Cost 322, 749, 762
Counterfeit 564
 kingdom 17–20, 72
Covenant 5–9, 19–20, 21, 28–32, 96, 214, 576, 759
Creator, the 4, 29, 32, 131, 158, 165, 175, 178, 525
Cross-cultural 125, 392–396, 469, 684–685, 715, 717
 evangelism 24, 340, 346–348, 489–491, 593, 733–734, 745

Crusades, the 241–242, 357, 511, 567
Cultural
  blocs 512
  imperialism 24, 351, 364, 490
  mandate 47, 487, 531–540
  misunderstanding 378
  revolution 359, 640
Culture 24, 118, 125, 163–164,
     369–370, 374–376, 384–391, 392,
     397, 422–428, 444–448, 455,
     460–468, 469–473, 480, 483–485,
     525–528, 562, 596, 598, 600–601, 606
  change 462, 466, 580
  definition of 374–379, 385, 392, 484
  shock 222, 373–374

D

Darkness 69, 318
  See also Spiritual: darkness
Daughter churches 595–604, 696–697
David 6
DAWN (Discipling A Whole Nation)
     536, 546, 607–612
Day of the Lord 94–95, 189, 192
de las Casas, Bartholome 242
Demons 71, 79–85, 134, 146–147,
     417, 540, 673
Denominational 730
Dependency 364, 434, 592–594, 598, 682
Developing countries 569
Development
  community 266, 597–598, 643
  need for 569–574, 578–580
  transformational 249, 586–591
Directed change 462, 466
Disciple-making 110, 608
Disciples 67, 69, 83, 90, 98, 102, 104–107,
     127, 130, 152–153, 532, 559–561,
     595, 600–601, 606–608, 618–622,
     703, 714, 759
Diseases 571–572
Dominicans 262
Doxological 30, 46, 47
Dreams 149
Dynamic equivalence 222, 485, 498–499

E

E-Scale (E1-E3) 125, 341–344, 510, 533
  See also P-Scale
Education 245–246, 249–250, 265–266,
     272, 318, 325–326, 330–331,
     335–336, 556, 578, 580, 596, 600,

     689, 715, 734–735, 743, 762
  Theological 595–604, 602, 761, 762
Edwards, Jonathan 191, 233
Elders 329, 502, 598, 615, 692,
     695–697, 737
Election 4, 14, 28, 59
Eliot, John 244–245, 264, 298–299
Elliot, Elizabeth 273
Eternal life 158, 176
Ethno-linguistic peoples 217, 219, 512,
     515, 516, 521
Ethnocentrism 31, 378, 461, 471
Evangelical Fellowship of Mission Agencies
     (EFMA) 719, 723
Evangelism 101, 103, 127, 144, 146,
     154, 244–245, 248, 249–250, 260,
     339–353, 404–406, 531–540, 548,
     575, 595–596, 607, 623, 634, 676,
     677–680, 693, 726, 760
Evangelization 365
Evangelize 319–320, 340–353, 596, 760
Evil 39, 68, 72, 76, 79, 143, 146–147, 182,
     192, 196, 318, 320, 325, 415, 505, 671
  problem of 84–85
  spirits 146
  victory over 25, 72, 530
Expatriate 499, 689–690, 696–697

F

Face-to-face societies 434–437
Faith 5–9, 21, 23, 62, 81, 105, 111, 120,
     124, 145–146, 156, 170, 226, 311,
     317, 319, 323–325, 330–332, 335–
     336, 662, 672, 680–681, 722
  and culture 163–164
Fall of man 11, 137, 294
Families 4, 6–8, 12, 21, 37, 97, 111,
     115–116, 221, 226, 254, 323–324,
     331–333, 425–426, 548, 598, 613,
     669–670, 695, 736, 745
Fear 564, 580
  of the Lord 16, 42, 155
Feelings 375–377
Felt needs 669–672, 739
Finances 456–457, 729
Financial help 682
  See also Giving: for missions
Forgiveness 174, 180
Form and meaning 485
Francis of Assisi 176, 242
Franciscan 242, 262, 270
French, Thomas Valpy 313

G

GCOWE *See* Global Consultation On
    World Evangelization (GCOWE)
Generosity 712
Gentile people
  mission to 97–99, 119, 129
George, Eliza Davis 273
Gifts 131 *See also* Holy Spirit
Gilmour, James 312
Giving
  for missions 133, 299, 302, 534
Global
  Christians 380 *See also* World Christians
  people 380
Global Consultation On World
    Evangelization (GCOWE) 259, 546
Glory 34–47, 57, 65, 600, 606
  of Christ 24
  of God 30, 49, 50, 51, 53, 136,
      172, 180, 184, 303, 762
  of Jesus 120
  of the Messiah 122
God
  at War 30, 72, 78, 529–530
  faithfulness of 6
  household of 179
  judgment of 4–7, 579
  kingdom of 55, 58, 143
  love of 28, 34, 36–37, 45, 53, 55,
      100, 158
  name of 11, 13, 22, 34–47, 52–53, 55,
      58, 95, 111, 123, 143, 186–187, 189,
      400–403
  of mercy 9
  Spirit of 92
  the Creator 4
  the Father 172
  will of 3, 18, 57–58, 136, 137, 143, 722
gods 28, 38, 146, 624, 633, 698–699
    See also Idolatry
  of the nations 51
Goforth, Rosalind 272
Going native 448, 451
Gospel 12, 16, 21, 32, 68–71, 91,
      101–102, 119–120, 122, 125, 129,
      153, 157, 171, 173, 176, 179, 183,
      319–320, 323, 380–383, 397–398,
      402–403, 489–490, 511, 543, 556,
      575–577, 596, 617–622, 651,
      675–676, 698–699, 708, 759
  and culture 381
  redemptive 128

social 284
Grace 19, 25, 32, 45, 51, 105, 118, 120,
      133, 139, 159, 175, 596, 598, 711, 723
  of Christ 677–680
  of God 62, 68, 71
Graham, Billy 192
Great Awakening 191, 265, 280
Great Century 227, 246–248, 265,
      326–328, 331, 335
Great Commission 11, 21, 31, 54, 62,
      69, 90, 102, 104–107, 116, 121,
      152–154, 160, 167, 190, 216–217,
      229, 253–254, 294–295, 306, 310,
      319, 339, 533, 606–607, 705–707
Group decisions 325–326, 426, 496–497,
      620–622, 629
    See also People movements

H

Harvest 15, 46, 68, 150, 188, 190, 214,
      215, 366, 534, 747
Haystack Prayer Meeting 259, 265, 280,
      282
Healing 81, 82–85, 98, 105, 172, 176,
      327, 415, 695
Heiling, Peter 277
Hell 9, 17, 46, 163, 183, 190
Herrnhut 274
Hindu 146, 243, 325, 333, 361–362, 458,
      526, 614, 632–638, 675–676, 680
Hinduism 147, 175, 318, 522, 543,
      632–638, 698–699
History
  meaning of 73–77
Holistic 264, 272, 556, 588–591, 682,
      715, 745
  theology 420, 677
Holy Spirit 22, 67, 111, 118–119, 127,
      135, 154, 188–189, 251, 285, 320,
      332, 337, 379, 390–391, 455,
      476–478, 486, 536–537, 595, 598,
      600–601, 608, 661–663, 665,
      669–672, 759, 762 *See also* Spirit
  role of 472
Homogeneous people groups 260
Hope 42, 45, 63, 64, 78, 91, 93, 116, 122,
      143, 146, 156, 160, 162, 188, 286,
      302, 318, 712
House of prayer 44, 99, 116
Households 115, 137, 140, 548, 616, 625
Humility 148, 492, 568, 730, 750
Hunger 570

I

Identification 24, 425, 430, 449, 493, 738
Identificational repentance 148, 567
Idolatry 40, 130, 146, 294, 318, 501, 528, 625
Illiteracy 335, 527, 543, 700
Imperialism 3, 31, 249
Incarnation 24, 55, 71–73, 85, 170, 358, 493–494, 636, 652–653
Incorporation 625, 629
Independent Churches 640
Indigenous 217, 222, 261, 336, 338, 394, 459, 472, 563, 631, 762
    church 47, 136, 251, 474–479, 624, 688, 740 See also Church
    forms 381
Individualism 475
Infanticide 265, 272, 505, 527
Injil 656, 661–662, 680–681
Injustice 569
Inspiration 23, 759
Inter-Varsity 279, 285, 703
Intercession 191, 216, 321, 551, 568, 638, 731
Interdenominational Foreign Mission Association (IFMA) 719, 723
International Society for Frontier Missiology (ISFM) 720, 723
International students 742–743
Irish peregrini 223
ISFM 723
Islam 318, 490–491, 543, 593, 650–654, 651–654, 655, 655–659, 660, 664–665, 680–682, 683–686, 688–690, 693
Islamic fundamentalism 564

J

Jesuits 225, 243, 244, 262, 639
Jesus See Christ
Jesus Film 355, 549
Jewish 106, 115, 128, 321, 369, 522
    community 118, 119
    congregations 127, 639
    culture 222
    nation 97
    people, mission to 97, 118
John the Baptist 7, 67, 95, 101
Johnathan Edwards 530
Jonah 11, 30
Jones, E. Stanley 170, 178
Joshua Project 218

Joy 49, 52, 54, 91, 173, 183, 708
Judgment 27, 67, 94–97, 158–159, 174, 190, 192
Judson, Adoniram 281, 314, 332
Judson, Ann 272
Justice 29, 131, 142, 144, 146, 151, 160, 175, 494, 566–567, 576, 589, 621, 760
Justification 5, 7–8, 20, 23, 174, 226, 497

K

Karma 635
Kingdom
    gospel of the 68–71, 150, 529–530
    mission of 529–530
    of God 17–20, 23, 30, 56, 64, 82–85, 91–92, 109, 122, 134, 136, 144, 159, 166, 216, 249, 262, 317, 321, 495, 539, 576
    of Satan 72, 76, 80–85
    See also Satan's counterfeit kingdom
Kuhn, Isabel 273

L

Land 79, 329, 333–334, 568
    of Israel 5–9
    of promise 37
Language 658
Latourette, Kenneth Scott 227, 280, 720
Lausanne 21
    Covenant 22, 24
Lausanne Congress 192, 259
Lausanne Covenant 759–763
Leadership 102, 129, 266, 317, 325, 331–332, 336, 381, 424, 429, 436, 459, 469, 598, 715, 762
Learner 438, 446
Liberation 82, 760
Liele, George 288
Life style 302, 456–457, 494, 569–574, 705–707
Literature 246, 250, 610, 754–755, 761
Livingstone, David 279, 312, 315
Local church 678–680, 715, 729–732, 742
Love 53, 182, 322, 327, 470, 596, 600–601, 638, 703
    for God 53
    of Christ 190
    of God 18, 58, 244
Lull, Ramon 242, 312
Luther, Martin 226

M

Malaria 266, 326, 335, 671
Malnutrition 569–574
Marshman, Joshua 293
Martyn, Henry 312
Martyrdom 76, 102, 181–184, 187,
    242–243, 277
Mather, Cotton 244
McGavran, Donald 260, 323–338, 617–622
Medical 272
Medicine 249–250, 268, 326, 415,
    670–671, 693–694, 734
Melchizedek 10
Member care 751
Mentors 711, 715–716
Messiah 7, 16, 20, 43, 67, 70, 94–96, 99,
    109, 111, 119, 121, 128, 177, 190
Messianic 579, 680
Micro-economic development 589
Microcredit 570
Migration 217, 324, 554
Millennium 71, 188
Mills, Samuel 265, 280
Miracles 80, 84, 92, 172
Missio Dei 59
Missiological breakthrough 217, 517
Mission
    agencies 136, 227–228, 255, 260–261,
        362, 544, 719, 730–732, 735, 745,
        751, 756–758
    agencies, need for 303–304
    frontier 511
    regular 511
Mission industry 718–719
Mission-station approach 327–328,
    332–336
Missionary force 522
Missionary mandate 13, 21–22, 92, 112,
    121, 132, 189, 254, 342, 589, 595,
    735
Missionary societies 231, 299
Mobilization 218, 271, 273, 551, 594, 596,
    598, 600, 612, 704, 708–712
Mobilizer 719–721
Modality 224–229, 732
Monasteries 222–223, 239, 241
Monasticism 225, 262–263
Money 321, 331, 499, 578, 593–594, 703,
    712, 749, 755–756, 761
Monks 223, 241, 262
Montgomery, Helen Barret 271
Moody, D.L. 270, 279

Moon, Lottie 273
Moravians 244, 246, 255, 265, 277, 278, 298
Mosque 357, 680
Mother-tongue
    disciples 492, 559–560
Motivation 186, 275, 626–627, 738
Mott, John R. 281–283, 317–322, 721
Multi-individual decision 615
    See also Group decisions
Multiplication 330, 336, 596, 598, 608,
    621–622, 730, 735
    See also Spontaneous: multiplication
of churches 132
Muslim 180, 242, 333–334, 336, 357–358,
    366, 457, 522, 610, 650, 655–659,
    658, 660, 664–665, 680–682,
    683–686, 688–690, 693, 693–694
Mystery of the Kingdom 66, 68

N

Name 158 See also Christ: name of
    fame name 35
    of Christ 179–180
    of Jesus 52, 63, 122 See also Jesus
Nationalism 9, 363, 528, 701
Nations 511–524
Native American 364
Nestorians 262–263, 639
Networking 546, 748, 754
Nevius, John L. 249
New age 169, 175
New humanity 85, 139, 176–177, 501
New Testament church 220–222
Non-Religious 522
Non-western 745–747, 749–750, 757–758
    churches 220

O

Obedience 45, 90, 121, 123–124, 126,
    150, 160, 165, 319–320, 596, 598,
    601, 702, 714
Occult 146, 528, 633
Orthodox 262–263

P

P-Scale 125, 510, 511 See also E-Scale
panta ta ethne 112, 113–117
Partner 328, 575
Partnership 148, 256, 576, 710–711, 716,
    746–747, 748, 753
    strategic 720
    with God 58

Passion 37, 51–53, 90, 93, 179–180, 185, 312, 710–711
   See also Apostolic: passion
  for Christ 275
  for God 49–50
Paternalism 9, 249
Patrick 263
Pentecost 7, 15, 118, 126, 135, 140, 160, 166, 188–189, 215
People blindness 346
People groups 114, 197, 208, 260, 514, 563, 606–607, 610, 617–618, 702–704, 716, 754–756
   See also Peoples
  clusters 544
  focused mission 730, 732
People movements 323–338, 426, 517, 563, 618–622, 633, 690
   See also Group decisions
Peoples 28, 31, 35–36, 38–43, 41, 45, 49–50, 55, 94, 98, 107, 109–111, 113, 116–117, 120, 124, 131, 135, 138, 192, 196–198, 214, 217, 253–254, 318, 323–328, 336–337, 341, 511–524, 535, 541–551, 562–563, 564–568, 595, 729
   See also People groups
  unreached 150, 257, 259, 260–261, 355, 357, 360, 364–365, 514, 519, 535, 537, 544, 562, 610, 618, 729–732, 735, 744, 746, 751, 753, 755
Pierson, A. T. 282
Pietist 226–227, 264
Pluralism 21, 169, 170, 173, 178
Plutschau 264
Polygamy 368, 470, 527
Poor 135, 146, 181, 232, 264, 278, 554, 575, 578–580, 589, 635, 726
Poverty 84, 146–147, 176, 554–555, 569, 573, 578, 582–584, 596, 598, 634, 762
Power 38, 50, 65–67, 71, 75, 80, 83, 111, 147, 152, 154, 160, 189, 320, 330, 336, 338, 421, 500, 531–540, 556, 567, 580, 597, 681, 762
  encounters 153, 408–413, 496, 531–540, 679–680
  for evangelization 25
  of God 21, 57
  of Satan 25
  of the gospel 25
Pray Through The Window 150

Prayer 32, 44, 52, 66, 111, 133, 142–144, 145, 154–155, 172, 179–180, 181, 186, 191, 278, 300, 303, 306, 308, 321, 338, 565–567, 596, 706, 709–710, 727–728, 734, 755
  groups 271
  journeys 150
  prayerwalking 150
  strategic 145, 152, 154
  united 148, 232–233, 354
Presence evangelism 29, 136, 532
Priesthood 13–16, 29, 63, 140, 568
Primary health care 679
Proclamation 145, 450–451, 532, 575, 672, 760
Proclamation evangelism 136, 532
Promise 62, 114
  of God 3–9, 21–22, 28, 31, 46, 107, 124, 188, 214, 268
Promised land 114
Proselytes 98, 124, 130, 221, 616
Proselytizers 220–221
Publishing 247
Puritans 215, 244–245, 264

Q
Qur'an 653, 656, 661–662, 693

R
Radio 355, 360, 549, 675, 689, 719, 755
Reconciliation 55, 63, 131, 137–141, 148, 174, 180, 564, 760
Reformation 215, 222, 226–227, 263, 270, 336, 720
Registered churches 640
Relativism 169, 379–380
Relief 326, 580, 589, 686, 715, 755, 762
Religion 325, 327, 338, 418
Religions 69, 143, 162, 165, 169, 173, 175, 246, 318–319, 327, 329, 543, 596, 678
Repentance 31, 96, 97, 124, 165, 244, 469–473, 565–566
Revelation 21, 23, 35, 55, 67, 125, 157, 160, 169–171, 397–398, 760
Revival 188–189, 215, 227, 233, 336
Ricci, Matteo 243
Ridderhof, Joy 272
Rites of initiation 484
Role 335, 423–424, 430, 438–443, 469, 480, 714
Roseveare, Helen 273
Rural 324, 326, 335, 430, 553, 734

S

Saint, Rachel 273
Salvation 9, 36, 38, 46, 60–61, 69, 100, 102, 115, 124, 128, 135, 138, 146, 154, 156–158, 160, 163–164, 175–176, 184, 319, 321, 324, 327–328, 333, 576, 635, 653–654, 661, 674–675
Satan 25, 68–71, 78–85, 128, 133, 146, 155, 182–183, 187, 539, 556
Satan's counterfeit kingdom 17–20, 72, 81–85, 529–530
Saturation church planting (SCP) 606–612 *See also* Church planting
Science 265, 417, 734–735
Scripture 23, 397–398, 472, 486–487, 559–560, 635, 759
  inspiration of 23
Secularization 634
Sending 299, 708, 730, 747
Serampore Trio 247, 293
Sergeant, John 245
Servant 97, 214, 332
  of the Lord 7, 16, 20, 29, 59
Shalom 149, 576
Short-term mission 731
Siemens, Ruth 272
Signs of the Kingdom 92
Simeon, Charles 278–279
Simpson, A.B. 270
Sin 32, 68–71, 100, 138, 157, 173–174, 182, 318–319, 469, 620, 762
Slavery 146, 264, 290, 505, 565
Slessor, Mary 272
Slums 364
Social action 145–146, 151
Social Structure 422, 429–437, 628
Societies 239, 318, 323, 379, 425–427, 431, 560 *See also* Missionary Societies
Sociopeoples 512–516
Sodality 130, 224–229, 239, 732
Solomon 5, 41
Son of Man 28, 51, 96–98, 109, 172
Sovereignty 17, 65–67, 72, 82, 144
Speer, Robert E. 281–282, 314, 721
Spener, Philip Jacob 264
Spirit 102, 149, 320, 322, 330, 333, 336–337, 455, 670–671 *See also* Holy Spirit
Spiritual
  darkness 4, 25, 146, 148, 182–184

Spontaneous
  multiplication 595, 701 *See also* Multiplication
Standard of living 326–327, 338
Story teller
  role of 441–442
Storytelling 404–407
Strategic partnerships 720
Strategic prayer *See* Prayer
Strongholds 146–147, 150, 556, 565
Studd, Charles Thomas 280, 721
Student Foreign Mission Fellowship 259
Student Foreign Missions Fellowship 285
Student Volunteer Movement 64, 258, 259, 260, 281–284, 317, 721
Subcultures 385, 566
Suffering 52, 134, 181, 186, 190, 567
  strategy of 133
Synagogues 220–222
Syncretism 365, 390–391, 492, 500, 502–503, 560, 626, 635, 656, 662, 695, 760

T

Taylor, J. Hudson 228, 257, 260, 270, 274, 279, 300–304, 305–308
Technology 392, 500
Temple 32, 139
Ten/Forty (10/40) window 541–551, 755
Tentmakers 275, 440, 733, 745
Three-culture model of missionary communication 394
Three-Self formula 248
Three-Self Patriotic Movement 640–642 *See also* Church: self
Tithe 592
Tower of Babel 10, 28, 98
Townsend, Wm. Cameron 260, 309
Training 245, 330, 336, 447, 560, 595, 598, 600, 681–682, 691–692, 695–697, 703, 708–712, 716–717, 731, 734–735, 744, 749, 751–752, 762
  theological 642
Transformation 145–151, 166, 247, 262, 368, 475, 525, 673–675, 677–680
Translation 246, 250, 269, 310, 332, 485, 498, 546, 561, 563, 628, 701, 755, 761
Tribal societies 363–364
Truth encounters 409–413
Two-thirds world missionaries 744–747

U

Ulfilas 263
Unimax 512, 514–515, 520, 521
Unity 149, 350, 634, 730, 754–756, 761
  of churches 46–47
Universalism 28, 157
Unreached peoples *See* Peoples: unreached
Urban 331, 430, 535, 553–558
  mission 46
  societies 428, 581
Urbana Mission Convention 255, 277,
    285–286, 782
Urbanization 428, 555

V

Values 24, 375–377, 430, 470–473, 563
Venn, Henry 227, 248, 255
Victory 76, 102, 147, 183, 215
  of Christ 70–73, 84–85, 91
  of the Church 102
  over Satan 183, 294, 529–530
Vision 46, 50–51, 54, 92, 100,
    106, 121, 186, 216, 317, 320,
    547, 687, 703–704,
    714–715, 724

W

Waldo, Peter 226
Ward, William 293
Warfare 30, 134, 195–196, 529–530,
    560, 762
  motif 78–85
  spiritual 148, 150
Wesley, Charles 278

Wesley, John 232, 265, 278
Wesleyan/Evangelical Revival 265
Widow burning 247, 527
Wilberforce 265, 275
Wilder, Robert C. 281–282, 311
Window, 10/40
    See Ten/Forty (10/40) window
Witness 29, 40, 59–60, 73, 122–123, 180,
    183–184, 320, 333, 337, 408, 511,
    598, 632, 639, 662, 676, 755
Women
  in mission 269–273
  missionaries 268
  single 255, 267, 693
  status of 486
Word of God 21
Works 322
World Christians 702, 714, 724
    See also Global: Christians
World Missionary Conference Edinburgh
    1910 258
World view 78, 106, 375–377, 384,
    415–421, 484, 538
Worship 29, 34–47, 49–50, 54, 57, 95, 98,
    112, 116, 119, 125, 127–128, 131,
    186–187, 278, 333, 338, 381,
    597–598, 696–697, 700–701
Wycliffe Bible Translators 260, 309–310

Z

Ziegenbalg, Bartholomew 246, 264
Zinzendorf, Count Nicolaus Ludwig von
    246, 274, 277
Zwemer, Samuel 282, 311–315

About the Editors

Ralph D. Winter

There probably is a connection between Ralph Winter's deep conviction that Christian organizations can accomplish their best by working closely together and the fact that his father, over a 37 year period, supervised the development of the Greater Los Angeles Freeway System—because this latter achievement was less an engineering achievement than it was a matter of getting 82 cities to agree to a mutually helpful master plan. This also accounts for Ralph Winter's willingness to move from a degree in Civil Engineering at Caltech into an M.A. in teaching English as a Second Language at Columbia University in New York and then a Ph.D. at Cornell University in Structural Linguistics, with a minor cultural anthropology and mathematical statistics.

As he grew up his father was involved in civic and spiritual leadership as well as technical matters. His two brothers also learned from that—one becoming a widely sought structural engineer and the other the longest-serving president of Westmont College.

He was married to Roberta Helm midway during his first year of study for his Ph.D. at Cornell University. Although working as a registered nurse, Roberta also aided him greatly in research and in editing his doctoral dissertation. Although he had been in the first class at Fuller Seminary in 1947 (along with Bill Bright), after graduating from Cornell, he finished his seminary studies at Princeton due to denominational attitudes toward Fuller at that time. While at seminary, he pastored for three years a rural New Jersey church. He was ordained in 1956 and in that same year the two of them and their two children joined what was then called the Presbyterian Board of Foreign Missions.

Their assignment took them to the highlands of Guatemala to work for ten years with a Native American tribal group of the Mayan family of peoples. Their broad interests flowed into the work with the existing national church and included the development of small business skills for mountain bi-vocational pastoral students. In the process, Winter began to see the need to develop local leaders through formal ministerial studies without their needing to go away for seminary training. Jim Emery, a fellow missionary (also a former engineer) had pointed out that the best congregational leaders were being filtered out by the logistics of residential seminary training. Emery, Winter and Ross Kinsler, and others such as C. Peter Wagner and Ralph Covell helped to birth a global movement toward theological education by extension.

Partly on the basis of the latter, Donald McGavran at the School of World Mission at Fuller Theological Seminary invited Dr. Winter to become part of the new school in its second year. Between 1966 and 1976 the Winters learned a great deal from over 1,000 missionaries in and out of class. During this period—partly to help publish some of the wealth of materials being produced by those missionaries—the Winters founded the William Carey Library, a specialized publisher and distributor of mission materials. Dr. Winter also cofounded the American Society of Missiology, assisted in the founding of the Advancing Churches in Mission Commitment (ACMC), and before leaving the Fuller faculty in 1976 inaugurated the Perspectives Study Program then called Institute of International Studies (IIS). He was later helped by a number of younger coworkers, Jay and Olgy Gary, and Steve and Barbara Hawthorne in particular.

Over the years teaching at Fuller, however, it had became more and more clear that someone would have to do something special to recall the mission movement to a focus on the frontiers of gospel outreach distinctly beyond the existing mission field successes. In 1974 he presented a paper at Lausanne, Switzerland to the large (3,000) International Congress on World Evangelization underscoring the special need of such frontiers. A focused mission fellowship was born in 1976 for facilitating that goal, the founding members being mostly alumni of the *Perspectives* course. First the U.S. Center for World Mission (www.uscwm.org) and a few months later the William Carey International University (www.wciu.edu) were founded. In the next 22 years, a community of workers has grown, ready and willing to tackle any problem impeding the mission movement.

Winter served as the CEO of the Center from 1976 until 1990, the University until 1997, and from that time has been the General Director of the Frontier Mission Fellowship (the legal name for the original mission fellowship). He is the Vice President of the Southwest Region of the Evangelical Missiological Society, as well as being active in the International Society for Frontier Missions, which he helped to initiate.

The Winters have four daughters, who, with their families are all involved in full-time mission service.

Steven C. Hawthorne

Steven C. Hawthorne had to sneak his way into Urbana '76, InterVarsity's triennial Missions Conference. At the time, Steve was not at all interested in missions. He simply wanted to hear the biblical exposition of John Stott, one of the plenary speakers. Steve discovered after arriving at Urbana that the conference was sold out. He decided to sleep on a dormitory floor, eat out of vending machines and pay his registration fee by way of the offering in order to take in the conference. The opening address of John Stott forever changed his life. It was called "The Living God is a Missionary God." That address is now Chapter One of this book. The next day Hawthorne met Dr. Ralph Winter, who introduced him to the biblical certainty and the strategic possibility of completing world evangelization. Steve signed up then for a correspondence course called *Understanding World Evangelization* which eventually became the *Perspectives* course.

While completing a Master's degree in Cross-Cultural Studies at the School of World Mission at Fuller Theological Seminary, Steve helped as a class assistant for the Institute of International Studies at the U.S. Center for World Mission. In 1981, along with the community of mission mobilizers at the USCWM, he co-edited the *Perspectives* material with Dr. Ralph Winter.

Steve now directs WayMakers, a mission mobilization ministry focused on activating hope for Christ's greater glory in a prayed-for world. Steve helps churches and mission agencies cultivate maturity in intercession, research, and church planting among unreached peoples and in cities throughout the USA. Before founding WayMakers in 1994, Hawthorne served with the Antioch Network as an advisor to local churches endeavoring to send church planting teams among unreached peoples. Earlier, he served as vice president of Caleb Project, a ministry aiming to mobilize students with vision to complete world evangelism. Before that he worked as executive editor of World Christian Magazine. While working to portray unreached people groups in World Christian Magazine, he conceived and launched the research and mobilization effort called "Joshua Project," a series of field-based research efforts among unreached people groups. For years, Steve recruited, trained and labored with teams who carried out relationally-based field research identifying unreached peoples in world-class cities in Asia and the Middle East.

He has become a spokesperson for a growing global movement of on-site intercession known as prayerwalking. He co-authored with Graham Kendrick the book *Prayerwalking: Praying On-Site with Insight*. He also edited the widely used handbook to short-term mission service called *Stepping Out: A Guide to Short Term Missions*. He says of his writing and speaking, "I like to commit arson of the heart."

Now living in Austin, Texas, Steve and his wife, Barbara, experience the joys of parenting three daughters, Sarah, Emily and Sophia.